The Laudon & Laudon Web site includes technology updates, interactive Web exercises and study guide, a virtual tour of electronic commerce sites, and new case studies.

www.prenhall.com/laudon

Available as a stand-alone item or in a PH Value Pack, this interactive student CD-ROM includes "bullet" text to assist students in their understanding of the material in the text, audio and video tours, and links to the student's Web site exercises and study guide so users can continually check their progress in mastering the material.

Management
Information
Systems

Organization and Technology in the Networked Enterprise

Sixth Edition

Kenneth C. Laudon

New York University

Jane P. Laudon

Azimuth Information Systems

PRENTICE HALL

Upper Saddle River, New Jersey 07458

Library of Congress Cataloging-in-Publication Data
Laudon, Kenneth C. . 1944-
    Management information systems : organization and technology in
  the networked enterprise / Kenneth C. Laudon, Jane P. Laudon. — 6th ed.
        p.   cm.
    Includes bibliographical references and index.
    ISBN 0–13–011732–3
    1. Management information systems.   I. Laudon, Jane Price.
  II. Title.
  T58.6.L376   2000
  658.4′038—dc21   99-16968
                                                                   CIP

Acquisitions Editor: David Alexander
Editor-in-Chief: Mickey Cox
Managing Editor: Lucinda Gatch
Assistant Editor: Lori Cardillo
Editorial Assistant: Keith Kryszczun
Director Strategic Marketing: Nancy Evans
Senior Production Editor: Anne Graydon
Associate Managing Editor/Production: Sondra Greenfield
Manufacturing Buyer: Lisa DiMaulo
Senior Manufacturing Supervisor: Paul Smolenski
Senior Manager, Manufacturing and Prepress: Vincent Scelta
Design Director: Pat Smythe
Design Assistant: Michael Fruhbeis
Interior Design: Jill Little
Cover Designer: Cheryl Asherman
Cover Illustrator: Ralph Mercer Photography
Production and Composition: Carlisle Communications, Inc.
Photo Research: Shirley Webster
Photo Permissions Editor: Charles Morris
Photo Permissions Supervisor: Kay Dellosa
Photo credits appear following the indexes.

Microsoft and Windows are registered trademarks of the Microsoft Corporation in the
U.S.A. and other countries. Microsoft screen shots and icons reprinted with permission from
the Microsoft Corporation. This book is not sponsored or endorsed by or affiliated with the
Microsoft Corporation.

Printed in the United States of America
10   9   8   7   6   5   4   3   2

Prentice-Hall International (UK) Limited, *London*
Prentice-Hall of Australia Pty. Limited, *Sydney*
Prentice-Hall Canada, Inc., *Toronto*
Prentice-Hall Hispanoamericana, S. A., *Mexico*
Prentice-Hall of India Private Limited, *New Delhi*
Prentice-Hall of Japan, Inc., *Tokyo*
Prentice-Hall (Singapore) Pte. Ltd.
Editora Prentice-Hall do Brasil, Ltda., *Rio de Janeiro*

For

Erica and Elisabeth

About the Authors

Kenneth C. Laudon is a Professor of Information Systems at New York University's Stern School of Business. He holds a B.A. in Economics from Stanford and a Ph.D. from Columbia University. He has authored eleven books dealing with information systems, organizations, and society. Professor Laudon has also written over forty articles concerned with the social, organizational, and management impacts of information systems, privacy, ethics, and multimedia technology.

Professor Laudon's current research is on the planning and management of large-scale information systems and multimedia information technology. He has received grants from the National Science Foundation to study the evolution of national information systems at the Social Security Administration, the IRS, and the FBI. A part of this research is concerned with computer-related organizational and occupational changes in large organizations, changes in management ideology, changes in public policy, and understanding productivity change in the knowledge sector.

Ken Laudon has testified as an expert before the United States Congress. He has been a researcher and consultant to the Office of Technology Assessment (United States Congress) and to the Office of the President, several executive branch agencies, and Congressional Committees. Professor Laudon also acts as an in-house educator for several consulting firms and as a consultant on systems planning and strategy to several Fortune 500 firms. Ken works with the Concours Group to provide advice to firms developing enterprise systems.

Ken Laudon's hobby is sailing.

Jane Price Laudon is a management consultant in the information systems area and the author of seven books. Her special interests include systems analysis, data management, MIS auditing, software evaluation, and teaching business professionals how to design and use information systems.

Jane received her Ph.D. from Columbia University, her M.A. from Harvard University, and her B.A. from Barnard College. She has taught at Columbia University and the New York University Graduate School of Business. She maintains a lifelong interest in Oriental languages and civilizations.

The Laudons have two daughters, Erica and Elisabeth.

Management Information Systems: Organization and Technology in the Networked Enterprise reflects a deep understanding of MIS research and teaching as well as practical experience designing and building real world systems.

Brief
Contents

Table of Contents

Preface

Management Information Systems: Organization and Technology in the Networked Enterprise (Sixth Edition) is based on the premise that it is difficult, if not impossible, to manage a modern organization without at least some knowledge of information systems—what they are, how they affect the organization and its employees, and how they can make businesses more competitive and efficient. Information systems have become essential for creating competitive firms, managing global corporations, and providing useful products and services to customers. This book provides an introduction to management information systems that undergraduate and MBA students will find vital to their professional success.

The Information Revolution in Business and Management: The New Role of Information Systems

Globalization of trade, the emergence of information economies, and the growth of the Internet and other global communications networks have recast the role of information systems in business and management. The Internet is becoming the foundation for new business models, new business processes, and new ways of distributing knowledge. Companies can use the Internet and networking technology to conduct more of their work electronically, seamlessly linking factories, offices, and sales forces around the globe. Companies such as Coca-Cola, Dell Computer, and Safeway UK are extending these networks to suppliers, customers, and other groups outside the organization so they can react instantly to customer demands and market shifts. When Coca-Cola corporate managers use information systems to examine their daily operations, they will be able to find out exactly which bottling plant and which channel were used to sell Coca-Cola in a 500 milliliter bottle in any supermarket throughout the world. This digital integration within the firm and without, from the warehouse to the executive suite, is starting to become a reality. Accordingly, we have changed the subtitle of this text to *Organization and Technology in the Networked Enterprise.*

New to the Sixth Edition

The Internet has created a universal platform for buying and selling goods. Its technology also provides powerful capabilities for driving important business processes inside the company and for linking such processes electronically to those of other organizations. This edition more fully explores the electronic business uses of the Internet for the management of the firm as well as the Internet's growing role in electronic commerce. It includes detailed treatment of enterprise resource planning (ERP) systems and related technology for creating extended enterprises that electronically link the firm to suppliers and other industry partners. The text provides a complete set of tools for integrating the Internet and multimedia technology into the MIS course. The following features and content reflect this new direction:

Detailed Coverage of Enterprise Resource Planning (ERP) and Extended Enterprises

We introduce enterprise resource planning (ERP) in Chapter 1 and provide descriptions, discussions, and case studies of ERP systems throughout the text. We have added an entirely new chapter (Chapter 18) with detailed treatment of the management, organization, and technology issues surrounding the implementation of ERP systems and the use of these systems, the Internet, and other technologies to link with other organizations in industry-wide networks and global supply chains.

New Tools for Interactive Learning

A **Tools for Interactive Learning** section concluding each chapter shows students how they can extend their knowledge of each chapter with projects and exercises on the Laudon Web site and the optional CD-ROM multimedia edition.

Students and instructors can see at a glance exactly how the Web can be used to enhance student learning for each chapter. Students can also see immediately how the chapter can be used in conjunction with the optional CD-ROM.

Tools for Interactive Learning

○ **Internet**

The Internet Connection for this chapter will take you to a Web site where you can view an interactive demonstration of an intranet. You can complete an exercise to evaluate how companies can use intranets to reduce agency costs and make the management process more efficient. You can also use the Interactive Study Guide to test your knowledge of the topics in this chapter and get instant feedback when you need more practice.

○ **CD-ROM**

If you purchase and use the Multimedia Edition CD-ROM with this chapter, you will find an interactive exercise which asks you to apply the correct model of organizational decision making to solve a set of problems. You can also find an audio overview of the major themes of this chapter and bullet text summarizing the key points of the chapter.

Focus on Electronic Commerce and Electronic Business

The Internet, electronic commerce, and electronic business are introduced in Chapter 1 and integrated throughout the text and the entire learning package. A full chapter, entitled The Internet: Electronic Commerce and Electronic Business (Chapter 10), describes the underlying technology, capabilities, and benefits of the Internet, with expanded treatment of electronic commerce, Internet business models, and the use of intranets for the internal management of the firm.

Internet, Electronic Commerce, and Electronic Business Integrated into Every Chapter

Every chapter contains a Window On box, case study, or in-text discussion of electronic commerce, electronic business, or the use of the Internet in changing a particular aspect of information systems.

Enhanced Laudon & Laudon Web Site for Management Problem Solving and Interactive Learning

The Laudon & Laudon Web site has been enhanced to provide a wide array of capabilities for interactive learning and management problem solving that have been carefully prepared for use with the text. They include:

Student responses to questions are automatically graded and can be e-mailed to the instructor.

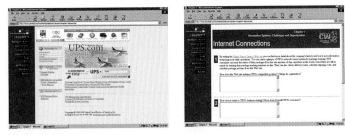

Students are presented with a problem to develop a budget for annual shipping costs. To obtain the information required by the solution, they can input data on-line and use the interactive software at this Web site to perform the required calculations or analysis.

For each chapter of the text, the Web site features an Interactive Study Guide and Internet Connection exercise.

○ The on-line Interactive Study Guide helps students review and test their mastery of chapter concepts with a series of multiple-choice, true-false, and essay questions.

○ Internet Connections noted by marginal icons in the chapter direct students to exercises and projects on the Laudon Web site related to organizations and concepts in that chapter. Included are Web-based exercises and interactive Electronic Commerce exercises that apply chapter concepts to using the Web for management problem solving.

A Virtual Tour of Electronic Commerce Sites

Students can take a tour of electronic commerce sites on the Web, where they can explore the various Internet business models and electronic commerce capabilities discussed in the text. Students can use what they have learned on the tour to complete a comprehensive electronic commerce project.

Additional Case Studies

The Web site contains additional case studies with hyperlinks to the Web sites of the organizations they discuss.

Technology Updates

The Web site provides technology updates to keep instructors and students abreast of leading-edge technology changes.

International Web Sites

Students visit a series of Web sites illustrating different business uses of the Internet and then apply what they have learned to designing an Internet business strategy for a new company.

Links to Web sites of non-U.S. countries are provided for users interested in more international material.

Unique Features of This Text

Management Information Systems: Organization and Technology in the Networked Enterprise (Sixth Edition) has many unique features designed to create an active, dynamic learning environment.

Technology Integrated with Content

Students can reinforce and extend their knowledge of chapter concepts with interactive exercises on the CD-ROM.

An interactive CD-ROM multimedia version of the text can be purchased as an optional item. In addition to the full text and bullet text summaries by chapter, the CD-ROM features interactive exercises, simulations, audio/video overviews explaining key concepts, on-line quizzes, hyperlinks to the exercises on the Laudon Web site, technology updates, and more. Students can use the CD-ROM as an interactive supplement or as an alternative to the traditional text.

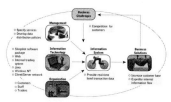

Integrated Framework for Describing and Analyzing Information Systems

An integrated framework portrays information systems as being composed of management, organization, and technology elements. This framework is used throughout the text to describe and analyze information systems and information system problems.

A special diagram accompanying each chapter-opening vignette graphically illustrates how management, organization, and technology elements work together to create an information system solution to the business challenges discussed in the vignette.

Real-World Examples

Real-world examples drawn from business and public organizations are used throughout to illustrate text concepts. More than 100 companies in the United States and 100 organizations in Canada, Europe, Australia, Asia, and Africa are discussed.

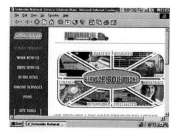

Each chapter contains three Window On boxes (Window on Management, Window on Organizations, Window on Technology) that present real-world examples illustrating the management, organization, and technology issues in the chapter. Each Window On box concludes with a section called *To Think About* containing questions for students to apply chapter concepts to management problem solving. The themes for each box are:

Each chapter opens with a vignette illustrating the themes of the chapter by showing how a real-world organization meets a business challenge using information systems.

Window on Management

Management problems raised by systems and their solution; management strategies and plans; careers and experiences of managers using systems.

Window on Technology

Hardware, software, telecommunications, data storage, standards, and systems-building methodologies.

Window on Organizations

Activities of private and public organizations using information systems; experiences of people working with systems.

Management Wrap-Up Overviews of Key Issues

Management Wrap-Up sections at the end of each chapter summarize key issues using the authors' management, organization, and technology framework for analyzing information systems.

A Truly International Perspective

In addition to a full chapter on managing international information systems (Chapter 17), all chapters of the text are illustrated with real-world examples from one hundred corporations in Canada, Europe, Asia, Latin America, Africa, Australia, and the Middle East. Each chapter contains at least one Window On box, case study, or opening vignette drawn from a non-U.S. firm and often more. The text concludes with five major international case studies contributed by leading MIS experts in Canada, Europe, Singapore, and Australia—Len Fertuck, University of Toronto (Canada); Helmut Krcmar, Stephan Wilczek, and Gerhard Schwabe, University of

Management Wrap-Up

Management

Information technology provides tools for managers to carry out both their traditional and newer roles, allowing them to monitor, plan, and forecast with more precision and speed than ever before and to respond more rapidly to the changing business environment. However, some managerial roles cannot be easily supported by information systems, and managers will need to overcome psychosocial biases and resistance to change to find meaningful ways to use the Internet and other technologies to transform the management process.

Organization

It's clear that there are new ways of organizing work, which are enabled in part by new technology. The central organizational issue is whether traditional organizations can change their internal structures—their business processes—to permit new ways of organizing and managing to emerge.

Technology

Each of the three schools of management can draw on information technology to enhance managerial effectiveness. Networks and communication and collaboration tools are especially useful for supporting managerial work in the "new" organization where more work is distributed among small groups and task forces and more responsibility is given to employees.

For Discussion

1. How would each of the three schools of management use information systems to make managers and organizations more effective?
2. Identify and describe a decision you had to make, such as selecting a college or a major. Use Simon's model of decision-making stages and suggest how an information system might have helped you make the decision.

Management Wrap-Up provides a quick overview of the key issues in each chapter, reinforcing the author's management, organization, and technology framework.

Hohenheim (Germany); Donald Marchand, Thomas Vollmann, and Kimberly Bechler, International Institute for Management Development (Switzerland); Boon Siong Neo and Christina Soh, Nanyang Technological University (Singapore); and Peter Weill and J. B. Barolsky, University of Melbourne, (Australia).

Attention to Small Businesses and Entrepreneurs

A diamond-shaped symbol identifies in-text discussions and specially designated chapter-opening vignettes, Window On boxes, and ending case studies that highlight the experiences and challenges of small businesses and entrepreneurs using information systems.

Pedagogy to Promote Active Learning and Management Problem Solving

Management Information Systems: Organization and Technology in the Networked Enterprise (Sixth Edition) contains many features that encourage students to learn actively and to engage in management problem solving.

Group Projects

At the end of each chapter is a group project that encourages students to develop teamwork and oral and written presentation skills. The group projects have been enhanced in this edition to make even better use of the Internet. For instance, students might be asked to work in small groups to evaluate the Web sites of two competing businesses or to develop a corporate ethics code on privacy that considers e-mail privacy and the monitoring of employees using networks.

Management Challenges Section

Each chapter begins with several challenges relating to the chapter topic that managers are likely to encounter. These challenges are multifaceted and sometimes pose dilemmas. They make excellent springboards for class discussion. Some of these Management Challenges are: finding the right Internet business model; overcoming the organizational obstacles to building a database environment; and agreeing on quality standards for information systems.

Case Studies

Each chapter concludes with a case study based on a real-world organization. These cases help students synthesize chapter concepts and apply this new knowledge to concrete problems and scenarios. Major part-ending case studies, international case studies, and electronic case studies at the Laudon & Laudon Web site provide additional opportunities for management problem solving.

Book Overview

Part One is concerned with the organizational foundations of systems and their emerging strategic role. It provides an extensive introduction to real-world systems, focusing on their relationship to organizations, management, and important ethical and social issues.

Part Two provides the technical foundation for understanding information systems, describing hardware, software, storage, and telecommunications technologies. Part Two concludes by describing how all of the information technologies work together through the Internet to support electronic commerce and electronic business.

Part Three focuses on the process of redesigning organizations using information systems, including reengineering of critical business processes. We see systems analysis and design as an exercise in organizational design, one that requires great sensitivity to the right tools and techniques, quality assurance, and change management.

Part Four describes the role of information systems in capturing and distributing organizational knowledge and in enhancing management decision making. It shows how knowledge management, work group collaboration, and individual and group decision making can be supported by the use of knowledge work, group collaboration, artificial intelligence, decision support, and executive support systems.

Part Five concludes the text by examining the special management challenges and opportunities created by the pervasiveness and power of contemporary information systems and the global connectivity of the Internet: ensuring security, control, developing global systems, and building enterprisewide systems and industrial networks. Throughout the text emphasis is placed on using information technology to redesign the organization's products, services, procedures, jobs, and management structures; numerous examples are drawn from multinational systems and global business environments.

Chapter Outline

Each chapter contains the following:

- ○ A detailed outline at the beginning to provide an overview
- ○ An opening vignette describing a real-world organization to establish the theme and importance of the chapter
- ○ A diagram analyzing the opening vignette in terms of the management, organization, and technology model used throughout the text
- ○ A list of learning objectives
- ○ Management Challenges related to the chapter theme
- ○ Marginal glosses of key terms in the text
- ○ An Internet Connection icon directing students to related material on the Internet
- ○ A Management Wrap-Up tying together the key management, organization, and technology issues for the chapter, with questions for discussion
- ○ A chapter summary keyed to the learning objectives
- ○ A list of key terms that the student can use to review concepts
- ○ Review questions for students to test their comprehension of chapter material
- ○ A group project to develop teamwork and presentation skills
- ○ A Tools for Interactive Learning section showing specifically how the chapter can be integrated with the Laudon Web site and optional CD-ROM edition of the text
- ○ A chapter-ending case study that illustrates important themes

Instructor's Resource CD-ROM (013-040202-8)

Most of the support material described below is now conveniently provided for adopters on the Instructor's Resource CD-ROM. The CD includes the Instructor's Resource Manual, Test Item File, Windows PH Test Manager, Transparency Masters, PowerPoint Slides, and the helpful lecture tool "Image Library."

Image Library

The Image Library is a wonderful resource to help instructors create vibrant lecture presentations. Just about every figure and photo found in the text is provided and organized by chapter for your convenience. Lecture notes are supplied for each image and are housed within each chapter folder. Along with the lecture notes, a complete listing of the images and their copyright information are also provided. These images and lecture notes can be easily imported into Microsoft PowerPoint to create new presentations or to add to existing sets.

Instructor's Manual (013-040201-X)

The Instructor's Manual, written by Dr. Glenn Bottoms of Gardner-Webb University, features not only answers to review, discussion, case-study, and group-project questions, but also an in-depth lecture outline, teaching objectives, key terms, teaching suggestions, and Internet resources. This supplement can be downloaded from the secure faculty section of the Laudon/Laudon Web site and is also available on the Instructor's Resource CD-ROM.

Test Item File (013-040204-4)

The Test Item File is a comprehensive collection of true/false, multiple-choice, fill-in-the-blank, and essay questions, written by Dr. Lisa Miller of Central Oklahoma University. The questions are rated by difficulty level and the answers are referenced by section. An electronic version of the Test Item File is available as the **Windows PH Test Manager,** also found on the Instructor's Resource CD-ROM.

PowerPoint Slides (on Web and Instructor's CD-ROM)

Over one-hundred electronic color slides created by Dr. Edward Fisher of Central Michigan University are available in Microsoft PowerPoint, Version 97. The slides illuminate and build on key concepts in the text. In addition, they contain hyperlinks to the Laudon Web site within each chapter. The PowerPoints can be downloaded from the Web site and are available on the Instructor's Resource CD-ROM within Image Library.

Color Transparencies (013-040207-9)

One-hundred full-color transparency acetates are available to adopters. These transparencies, taken from figures in the text, provide additional visual support to class lectures. The transparency masters are also available as Acrobat files on the Web site and on the Instructor's Resource CD-ROM.

Video (013-040208-7)

Video clips are provided to adopters to enhance class discussion and projects. These clips highlight real-world corporations and organizations and illustrate key concepts found in the text.

Web Site

The Laudon/Laudon text is once again supported by an excellent Web site at **http://www.prenhall.com/laudon** that truly reinforces and enhances text material with Electronic Commerce Projects, Internet Exercises, an Interactive Study Guide, and International Resources. The Web site also features a secure, password-protected faculty area, from which instructors can download the Instructor's Manual, PowerPoint Slides, and Transparency Masters. Please see its complete description found earlier in this preface.

Tutorial Software

For instructors looking for Application Software support to use with this text, Prentice Hall is pleased to offer CBT CD-ROMs for Microsoft Office 97 and, soon, for Office 2000. These exciting tutorial CDs are fully certified up to the expert level of the Microsoft Office User Specialist (MOUS) Certification Program. They are not available as stand-alone items but can be packaged with the Laudon/Laudon text at an additional charge. Please contact your local Prentice Hall representative for more details.

Software Cases

A series of optional management software cases called *Solve it! Management Problem Solving with PC Software* has been developed to support the text. *Solve it!* consists of 10 spreadsheet cases, 10 database cases, and 6 Internet projects drawn from real-world businesses, plus a data disk with the files required by the cases. The cases are graduated in difficulty. The case book contains complete tutorial documentation showing how to use spreadsheet, database, and Web browser software to solve the problems. A new version of *Solve it!* with all-new cases is published every year. *Solve it!* must be adopted for an entire class. It can be purchased directly from the supplier, Azimuth Corporation, 124 Penfield Ave., Croton-on-Hudson, New York 10520 (telephone: 914-271-6321).

Acknowledgments

The production of any book involves many valuable contributions from a number of persons. We would like to thank all of our editors for encouragement, insight, and strong support for many years. Our editor, David Alexander, did an outstanding job in guiding the development of this edition, and we feel very fortunate to work with him. We remain grateful to PJ Boardman, Jim Boyd, and Sandy Steiner for their support of this project. We thank Nancy Evans, Director of Strategic Marketing, for her superb marketing work and her continuing contributions to our texts. Thanks go as well to CIS Senior Marketing Manager Kris King and to CIS Sales Directors Matt Denham, Sharon Koch, Iain Macdonald, and Dana Simmons for their suggestions for improving this edition. We commend Lori Cerreto for directing the preparation of ancillary materials and Anne Graydon and Michael Jennings for overseeing production of this text under an extraordinarily ambitious schedule. We thank Shirley Webster for her energetic photo research work and Katherine Evancie for her careful copy editing.

We remain deeply indebted to Marshall R. Kaplan for his invaluable assistance in the preparation of the text and to James Doughty for his help with this edition. Special thanks to Dr. Glenn Bottoms of Gardner-Webb University, Dr. Edward Fisher of Central Michigan University, and Dr. Lisa Miller of the University of Central Oklahoma for their work on supporting materials.

The Stern School of Business at New York University and the Information Systems Department provided a very special learning environment, one in which we and others could rethink the MIS field. Special thanks to Professors Edward Stohr, Jon Turner, Vasant Dhar, and Roy Radner for providing critical feedback and support where deserved. Professor William H. Starbuck of the Management Department at NYU provided valuable comments and insights in our joint graduate seminar on organization theory.

The Concours Group has provided stimulation, insight, and new research on enterprise systems and industrial networks. We remain especially grateful to Dr. Edward Roche for his contributions and to Jim Ware, Walt Dulaney, Vaughn Merlyn and Peter Boggis of the Concours Group for ideas and feedback.

Professor Gordon Everest of the University of Minnesota, Professors Al Croker and Michael Palley of Baruch College and NYU, Professor Sassan Rahmatian of California State University, Fresno, Professor Lisa Friedrichsen of the Keller Graduate School of Management, and Professor Kenneth Marr provided additional suggestions for improvement. We continue to remember the late Professor James Clifford of the Stern School as a wonderful friend and colleague who also made valuable recommendations for improving our discussion of files and databases.

One of our goals was to write a book that was authoritative, synthesized diverse views in the MIS literature, and helped define a common academic field. A large number of leading scholars in the field were contacted and assisted us in this effort. Reviewers and consultants for *Management Information Systems: Organization and Technology in the Networked Enterprise* are listed in the back endpapers of the book. We thank them for their contributions. Consultants for this new edition include: John Anderson, Northeastern State University; Laurie Eakins, East Carolina University; David Fickbohm, Golden Gate University; Graham Peace, Duquesne University; and Sasan Rahmatian, California State University–Fresno. It is our hope that this group endeavor contributes to a shared vision and understanding of the MIS field.

—*K.C.L.*
—*J.P.L.*

Chapter 1

The Information Systems Revolution:

Transforming Business and Management

Revolution:

Learning Objectives

After completing this chapter, you will be able to:

1. Define an information system.

2. Distinguish between computer literacy and information systems literacy.

3. Explain why information systems are so important today and how they are transforming organizations and management.

4. Compare electronic commerce and electronic business and analyze their relationship to the Internet and digital technology.

5. Identify the major management challenges to building and using information systems in organizations.

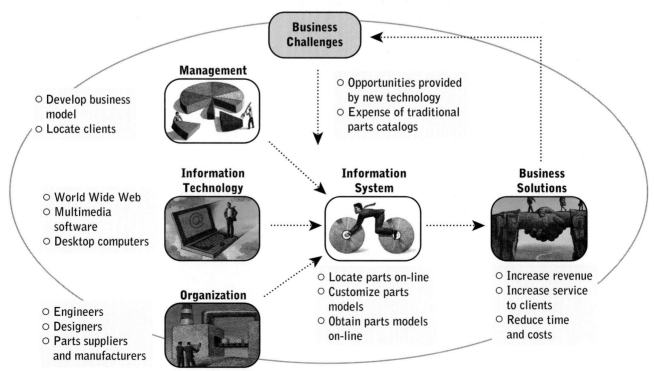

Business Challenges

Management
- Develop business model
- Locate clients

- Opportunities provided by new technology
- Expense of traditional parts catalogs

Information Technology
- World Wide Web
- Multimedia software
- Desktop computers

Information System
- Locate parts on-line
- Customize parts models
- Obtain parts models on-line

Business Solutions
- Increase revenue
- Increase service to clients
- Reduce time and costs

Organization
- Engineers
- Designers
- Parts suppliers and manufacturers

InPart Delivers
Digital Parts on the Internet

Stacey Lawson, who grew up in the lumber mill town of Port Angeles, Washington, had always wanted to do something that would make a difference. While studying for her M.B.A. at Harvard, she was asked to write a mock business plan. She remembered an idea she had picked up from John Major, a former colleague at IBM where she had worked earlier. Major supervised engineers designing 3-D computer models of machines that made disk drives, and he noticed that they spent hours poring through thick paper catalogs from parts suppliers trying to locate the right motors, bearings, and valves for their work. (As much as 70 percent of major product designs consist of such standard components.) Then they would redraw these parts in 3-D form before incorporating them into their design models. As much as 25 percent of engineers' and designers' time might be spent searching for and redrawing standard parts. Major felt that engineers and designers could save lots of time if they could find their parts already rendered in 3-D from a single computerized catalog. Parts manufacturers and suppliers could also benefit because parts catalogs are very costly to print, distribute, and update.

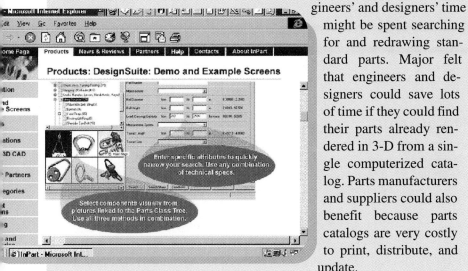

Lawson's business plan took the idea one step further, calling for a business that put this computerized parts catalog on the Internet, where it could be easily accessed and updated. Her proposed business would make money by charging both parts suppliers and users for the service. After she received her M.B.A. in 1996, Lawson teamed up with Major and launched a company called InPart that would do just that.

InPart was launched in March 1998. Its first product, DesignSuite, allows designers to use the Internet to search for and specify standard mechanical components, including gears, actuators, hoses, clamps, tooling fixtures, motors, controls, connectors, pumps, fittings, and bearings, from multiple manufacturers. Parts suppliers pay the company $20,000 annually to be listed on the Web site and corporate customers pay $1000 per computer to use the service.

DesignSuite contains over 200,000 computerized parts models and is adding tens of thousands of models monthly. The Web site provides catalog data such as materials, performance specifications, and installation requirements along with 3-D models of the relevant component and links to the manufacturer's Web

chapter outline

site. Designers and engineers can locate the parts they need by looking through thumbnail pictures of components or by searching by type of component, manufacturer's name, or part number, and they can view each part in 3-D form before selecting it. InPart then delivers users the part models they need over the Internet to their own desktop computers and even customizes their company's design standards into the geometry.

Sources: Bernard Condon, "Bootstrap," *Forbes,* January 25, 1999; David Cohn, "Digital Parts," *Computer Graphics World,* July 1998; and Bruno Valdes, "DesignSuite Delivers Parts Library Data," *Analysis Solutions,* Fall 1998.

InPart's innovative use of the Internet illustrates just one of the many new business opportunities that have been created with this technology. Both small and large companies can use information systems and networks to conduct more of their business electronically to make them more efficient and competitive. In today's global business environment, information systems, the Internet, and other global networks are creating new opportunities for organizational coordination and innovation. Information systems can help companies extend their reach to faraway locations, offer new products and services, reshape jobs and work flows, and perhaps profoundly change the way they conduct business. This chapter starts our investigation of information systems and organizations by describing information systems from both technical and behavioral perspectives and by surveying the changes they are bringing to organizations and management.

1.1 Why Information Systems?

Until recently, information itself was not considered an important asset for a firm. The management process was considered a face-to-face, personal art and not a far-flung, global coordination process. Today it is widely recognized that understanding information systems is essential for managers because most organizations need information systems to survive and prosper.

The Competitive Business Environment

Three powerful worldwide changes have altered the environment of business. The first change is the emergence and strengthening of the global economy. The second change is the transformation of industrial economies and societies into knowledge- and information-based service economies. The third is the transformation of the business enterprise. These changes in the business environment and climate, summarized in Table 1.1, pose a number of new challenges to business firms and their management.

Emergence of the Global Economy

A growing percentage of the American economy—and other advanced industrial economies in Europe and Asia—depends on imports and exports. Foreign trade, both exports and imports, accounts for a little over 25 percent of the goods and services produced in the United States, and even more in countries like Japan and Germany. The success of firms today and in the future depends on their ability to operate globally.

Globalization of the world's industrial economies greatly enhances the value of information to the firm and offers new opportunities to businesses. Today, information systems provide the communication and analytic power that firms need for conducting trade and managing businesses on a global scale. Controlling the far-flung global corporation—communicating with distributors and suppliers, operating 24 hours a day in different national environments, servicing local and international reporting needs—is a major business challenge that requires powerful information system responses.

Table 1.1	The Changing Contemporary Business Environment

Globalization

Management and control in a global marketplace

Competition in world markets

Global work groups

Global delivery systems

Transformation of Industrial Economies

Knowledge- and information-based economies

Productivity

New products and services

Knowledge: a central productive and strategic asset

Time-based competition

Shorter product life

Turbulent environment

Limited employee knowledge base

Transformation of the Enterprise

Flattening

Decentralization

Flexibility

Location independence

Low transaction and coordination costs

Empowerment

Collaborative work and teamwork

Globalization and information technology also bring new threats to domestic business firms: Because of global communication and management systems, customers now can shop in a worldwide marketplace, obtaining price and quality information reliably, 24 hours a day. This phenomenon heightens competition and forces firms to play in open, unprotected worldwide markets. To become effective and profitable participants in international markets, firms need powerful information and communication systems.

Transformation of Industrial Economies

The United States, Japan, Germany, and other major industrial powers are being transformed from industrial economies to knowledge- and information-based service economies, while manufacturing has been moving to low-wage countries. In a knowledge- and information-based economy, knowledge and information are key ingredients in creating wealth.

The knowledge and information revolution began at the turn of the twentieth century and has gradually accelerated. By 1976 the number of white-collar workers employed in offices surpassed the number of farm workers, service workers, and blue-collar workers employed in manufacturing (see Figure 1-1). Today, most people no longer work on farms or in factories but instead are found in sales, education, healthcare, banks, insurance firms, and law firms; they also provide business services like copying, computer programming, or making deliveries. These jobs primarily involve working with, distributing, or creating new knowledge and information. In fact, knowledge and information work now account for a significant 60 percent of the American gross national product and nearly 55 percent of the labor force.

Knowledge and information are becoming the foundation for many new services and products. **Knowledge- and information-intense products** such as computer games require a

knowledge- and information-intense products Products that require a great deal of learning and knowledge to produce.

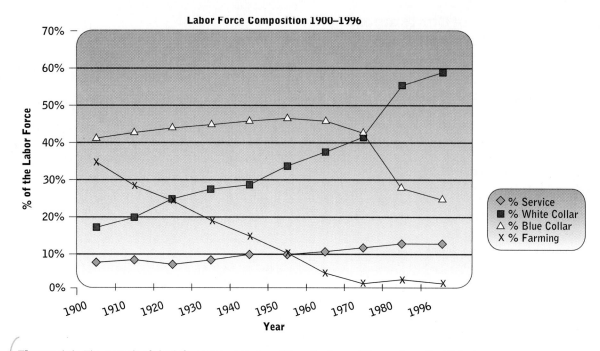

Figure 1-1 The growth of the information economy. Since the turn of the century, the United States has experienced a steady decline in the number of farm workers and blue-collar workers who are employed in factories. At the same time, the country is experiencing a rise in the number of white-collar workers who produce economic value using knowledge and information. **Sources:** U.S. Department of Commerce, Bureau of the Census, Statistical Abstract of the United States, 1997, Table 645: 1900–1970 and Historical Statistics of the United States, Colonial Times to 1970, Vol. 1, Series D 182–232.

great deal of learning and knowledge to produce. Entire new information-based services have sprung up, such as Lexis, Dow Jones News Service, and America Online. These fields are employing millions of people.

Intensification of knowledge utilization in the production of traditional products has increased as well. This trend is readily seen throughout the automobile industry where both design and production now rely heavily on knowledge-intensive information technology. During the past decade, the automobile producers have sharply increased their hiring of computer specialists, engineers, and designers while reducing the number of blue-collar production workers.

New kinds of knowledge- and information-intense organizations have emerged that are devoted entirely to the production, processing, and distribution of information. For instance, environmental engineering firms, which specialize in preparing environmental impact statements for municipalities and private contractors, simply did not exist 30 years ago.

In a knowledge- and information-based economy, information technology and systems take on great importance. Knowledge-based products and services of great economic value, such as credit cards, overnight package delivery, and worldwide reservation systems, are based on new information technologies. Information technology constitutes more than 70 percent of the invested capital in service industries like finance, insurance, and real estate.

Across all industries, information and the technology that delivers it have become critical, strategic assets for business firms and their managers (Leonard-Barton, 1995). Information systems are needed to optimize the flow of information and knowledge within the organization and to help management maximize the firm's knowledge resources. Because the productivity of employees will depend on the quality of the systems serving them, management decisions about information technology are critically important to the prosperity and survival of a firm.

Transformation of the Business Enterprise

The third major change in the business environment is the very nature of organization and management. There has been a transformation in the possibilities for organizing and managing. Some firms have begun to take advantage of these new possibilities.

The traditional business firm was—and still is—a hierarchical, centralized, structured arrangement of specialists that typically relies on a fixed set of standard operating procedures to deliver a mass-produced product (or service). The new style of business firm is a flattened (less hierarchical), decentralized, flexible arrangement of generalists who rely on nearly instant information to deliver mass-customized products and services uniquely suited to specific markets or customers. This new style of organization is not yet firmly entrenched; it is still evolving. Nevertheless, the direction is clear, and this new direction would be unthinkable without information technology.

The traditional management group relied—and still does—on formal plans, a rigid division of labor, formal rules, and appeals to loyalty to ensure the proper operation of a firm. The new manager relies on informal commitments and networks to establish goals (rather than formal planning), a flexible arrangement of teams and individuals working in task forces, a customer orientation to achieve coordination among employees, and appeals to professionalism and knowledge to ensure proper operation of the firm. Once again, information technology makes this style of management possible.

Information technology is bringing about changes in organization that make the firm even more dependent than in the past on the knowledge, learning, and decision making of individual employees. Throughout this book, we describe the role that information technology is now playing in the transformation of the business enterprise form.

What Is an Information System?

An **information system** can be defined technically as a set of interrelated components that collect (or retrieve), process, store, and distribute information to support decision making and control in an organization. In addition to supporting decision making, coordination, and control, information systems may also help managers and workers analyze problems, visualize complex subjects, and create new products.

Information systems contain information about significant people, places, and things within the organization or in the environment surrounding it (see Figure 1-2). By **information** we mean data that have been shaped into a form that is meaningful and useful to human beings. **Data,** in contrast, are streams of raw facts representing events occurring in organizations or the physical environment before they have been organized and arranged into a form that people can understand and use.

information system Interrelated components working together to collect, process, store, and disseminate information to support decision making, coordination, control, analysis, and visualization in an organization.

information Data that have been shaped into a form that is meaningful and useful to human beings.

data Streams of raw facts representing events occurring in organizations or the physical environment before they have been organized and arranged into a form that people can understand and use.

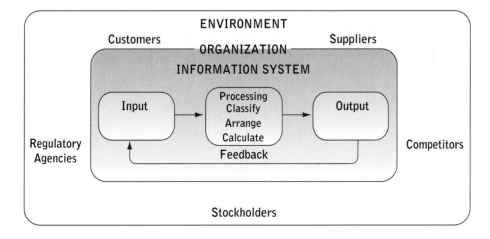

Figure 1-2 Functions of an information system. An information system contains information about an organization and its surrounding environment. Three basic activities—input, processing, and output—produce the information organizations need. Feedback is output returned to appropriate people or activities in the organization to evaluate and refine the input.

Three activities in an information system produce the information that organizations need for making decisions, controlling operations, analyzing problems, and creating new products or services. These activities are input, processing, and output. **Input** captures or collects raw data from within the organization or from its external environment. **Processing** converts this raw input into a more meaningful form. **Output** transfers the processed information to the people who will use it or to the activities for which it will be used. Information systems also require **feedback,** which is output that is returned to appropriate members of the organization to help them evaluate or correct the input stage.

In the information system used by InPart for obtaining parts, the raw input from designers and engineers consists of the type of component, manufacturer's name, part number, part size, or company's standard computerized design format specifications. The computer processes these data by locating components that match these criteria from a massive computerized repository of parts data. Lists of components matching input criteria, three-dimensional representations of parts, online displays of pages from manufacturers' catalogs, and customized computerized parts models become the output. The system thus provides meaningful information such as the right part model for a design, its dimensions and performance specifications, sources for the part models, part availability, and installation requirements.

Our interest in this book is in formal, organizational **computer-based information systems (CBIS)** like those designed and used by InPart and its customers. **Formal systems** rest on accepted and fixed definitions of data and procedures for collecting, storing, processing, disseminating, and using these data. The formal systems we describe in this text are structured; that is, they operate in conformity with predefined rules that are relatively fixed and not easily changed. For instance, InPart's system requires that orders for parts include the manufacturer's name, and a unique number for identifying each part.

Informal information systems (such as office gossip networks) rely, by contrast, on unstated rules of behavior. There is no agreement on what is information, or on how it will be stored and processed. Such systems are essential for the life of an organization, but an analysis of their qualities is beyond the scope of this text.

Formal information systems can be either computer-based or manual. Manual systems use paper-and-pencil technology. These manual systems serve important needs, but they too are not the subject of this text. Computer-based information systems, in contrast, rely on computer hardware and software technology to process and disseminate information. From this point on, when we use the term *information systems,* we will be referring to computer-based information systems—formal organizational systems that rely on computer technology. The Window on Technology describes some of the typical technologies used in computer-based information systems today.

Although computer-based information systems use computer technology to process raw data into meaningful information, there is a sharp distinction between a computer and a computer program on the one hand, and an information system on the other. Electronic computers and related software programs are the technical foundation, the tools and materials, of modern information systems. Computers provide the equipment for storing and processing information. Computer programs, or software, are sets of operating instructions that direct and control computer processing. Knowing how computers and computer programs work is important in designing solutions to organizational problems, but computers are only part of an information system. Housing provides an appropriate analogy. Houses are built with hammers, nails, and wood, but these do not make a house. The architecture, design, setting, landscaping, and all of the decisions that lead to the creation of these features are part of the house and are crucial for finding a solution to the problem of putting a roof over one's head. Computers and programs are the hammer, nails, and lumber of CBIS, but alone they cannot produce the information a particular organization needs. To understand information systems, one must understand the problems they are designed to solve, their architectural and design elements, and the organizational processes that lead to these solutions.

UPS Competes Globally with Information Technology

United Parcel Service, the world's largest air and ground package-distribution company, started out in 1907 in a closet-size basement office. Jim Casey and Claude Ryan—two teenagers from Seattle with two bicycles and one phone—promised the "best service and lowest rates." UPS has used this formula successfully for over 90 years.

UPS still lives up to that promise today, delivering more than 3 billion parcels and documents each year to the United States and to more than 200 other countries and territories. Critical to the firm's success has been its investment in advanced information technology. Technology has helped UPS boost customer service while keeping costs low and streamlining its overall operations.

Using a handheld computer called a Delivery Information Acquisition Device (DIAD), UPS drivers automatically capture customers' signatures along with pickup, delivery, and time-card information. The drivers then place the DIAD into their truck's vehicle adapter, an information-transmitting device that is connected to the cellular telephone network. Package tracking information is then transmitted to UPS's computer network for storage and processing in UPS's main computer in Mahwah, New Jersey. From there, the information can be accessed worldwide to provide proof of delivery to the customer. The system can also generate a printed response to queries by the customer.

Through its automated package tracking system, UPS can monitor packages throughout the delivery process. At various points along the route from sender to receiver, a bar code device scans shipping information on the package label; the information is then fed into the central computer. Customer service representatives can check the status of any package from desktop computers linked to the central computer and are able to respond immediately to inquiries from customers. UPS customers can also access this information directly from their own computers, using either the World Wide Web of the Internet or special package tracking software supplied by UPS.

Anyone with a package to ship can access the UPS Web site to check delivery routes, calculate shipping rates, and schedule a pickup. Eventually people will be able to use the Web to pay for their shipments using a credit card or business account that tracks on-line purchase orders for large regular customers. The data collected at the UPS Web site are transmitted to the UPS central computer and then back to the customer after processing. UPS recently started a new service called UPS Document Exchange to deliver business documents electronically using the Internet. The service provides a high level of security for these important documents as well as document tracking.

UPS's Inventory Express, launched in 1991, warehouses customers' products and ships them overnight to any destination the customer requests. Customers using this service can transmit electronic shipping orders to UPS by 1:00 A.M. and expect delivery by 10:30 that same morning. UPS is enhancing its information system capabilities so that it can guarantee that a particular package, or group of packages, will arrive at the destination at a specified time. If requested by the customer, UPS will be able to intercept a package prior to delivery and have it returned or rerouted.

To Think About: What are the inputs, processing, and outputs of UPS's package tracking system? What technologies are used? How are these technologies related to UPS's business strategy? What would happen if these technologies were not available?

Sources: "When Is Package Tracking Really Tracking?" UPS Public Relations, February 9, 1999; Barb Cole-Gomolski, "Need to Send Secure Documents via the Internet? See UPS," Computerworld, March 8, 1998; and "UPS Launches New Delivery and Information Options," UPS Public Relations, January 2, 1997.

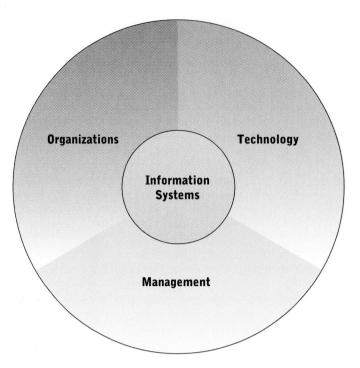

Figure 1-3 Information systems are more than computers. Using information systems effectively requires an understanding of the organization, management, and information technology shaping the systems. All information systems can be described as organizational and management solutions to challenges posed by the environment.

A Business Perspective on Information Systems

From a business perspective, an information system is an organizational and management solution, based on information technology, to a challenge posed by the environment. Examine this definition closely because it emphasizes the organizational and management nature of information systems: To understand information systems—to be information systems literate as opposed to computer literate—a manager must understand the broader organization, management, and information technology dimensions of systems (see Figure 1-3) and their power to provide solutions to challenges and problems in the business environment.

Review the diagram at the beginning of the chapter, which reflects this expanded definition of an information system. The diagram shows how InPart's information system provides a solution to the business challenges of trying to overcome the high expenses of searching for and providing parts for engineers with paper catalogs and of trying to take advantage of opportunities created by new technology—in this case, the Internet. The diagram also illustrates how management, technology, and organization elements work together to create the system. We begin each chapter of the text with a diagram like this one to help you analyze the opening case. You can use this diagram as a starting point for analyzing any information system or information system problem you encounter.

Organizations

Information systems are a part of organizations. Indeed, for some companies, such as credit reporting firms, without the system there would be no business. The key elements of an organization are its people, structure and operating procedures, politics, and culture. We introduce these components of organizations here and describe them in greater detail in Chapter 3. Formal organizations are composed of different levels and specialties. Their structures reveal a clear-cut division of labor. Experts are employed and trained for different functions, including sales and marketing, manufacturing, finance, accounting, and human resources. Table 1.2 describes these functions.

An organization coordinates work through a structured hierarchy and formal, standard operating procedures. The hierarchy arranges people in a pyramidal structure of rising authority and responsibility. The upper levels of the hierarchy consist of managerial, professional, and technical employees, whereas the lower levels consist of operational personnel.

Table 1.2 **Major Organizational Functions**

Function	Purpose
Sales and marketing	Selling the organization's products and services
Manufacturing	Producing products and services
Finance	Managing the organization's financial assets (cash, stocks, bonds, etc.)
Accounting	Maintaining the organization's financial records (receipts, disbursements, paychecks, etc.); accounting for the flow of funds
Human resources	Attracting, developing, and maintaining the organization's labor force; maintaining employee records

Standard operating procedures (SOPs) are formal rules that have been developed over a long time for accomplishing tasks; these rules guide employees in a variety of procedures, from writing an invoice to responding to complaining customers. Most procedures are formalized and written down, but others are informal work practices. Many of a firm's SOPs are incorporated into information systems, such as how to pay a supplier or how to correct an erroneous bill.

Organizations require many different kinds of skills and people. In addition to managers, **knowledge workers** (such as engineers, architects, or scientists) design products or services and create new knowledge, and **data workers** (such as secretaries, bookkeepers, or clerks) process the organization's paperwork. **Production or service workers** (such as machinists, assemblers, or packers) actually produce the products or services of the organization.

Each organization has a unique *culture,* or fundamental set of assumptions, values, and ways of doing things, that has been accepted by most of its members. Parts of an organization's culture can always be found embedded in its information systems. For instance, the concern with putting service to the customer first is an aspect of the organizational culture of United Parcel Service that can be found in the company's package tracking systems.

Different levels and specialties in an organization create different interests and points of view. These views often conflict. Conflict is the basis for organizational politics. Information systems come out of this cauldron of differing perspectives, conflicts, compromises, and agreements that are a natural part of all organizations. In Chapter 3 we will examine these features of organizations in greater detail.

Management

Managers perceive business challenges in the environment; they set the organizational strategy for responding; and they allocate the human and financial resources to achieve the strategy and coordinate the work. Throughout, they must exercise responsible leadership. Management's job is to "make sense" out of the many situations faced by organizations and formulate action plans to solve organizational problems. The business information systems described in this book reflect the hopes, dreams, and realities of real-world managers.

But less understood is the fact that managers must do more than manage what already exists. They must also create new products and services and even re-create the organization from time to time. A substantial part of management is creative work driven by new knowledge and information. Information technology can play a powerful role in redirecting and redesigning the organization. Chapter 4 describes the activities of managers and management decision making in detail.

It is important to note that managerial roles and decisions vary at different levels of the organization. **Senior managers** make long-range strategic decisions about products and services to produce. **Middle managers** carry out the programs and plans of senior management.

standard operating procedures (SOPs) Formal rules for accomplishing tasks that have been developed to cope with expected situations.

knowledge workers People such as engineers or architects who design products or services and create knowledge for the organization.

data workers People such as secretaries or bookkeepers who process the organization's paperwork.

production or service workers People who actually produce the products or services of the organization.

senior managers People occupying the topmost hierarchy in an organization who are responsible for making long-range decisions.

middle managers People in the middle of the organizational hierarchy who are responsible for carrying out the plans and goals of senior management.

Operational managers are responsible for monitoring the firm's daily activities. All levels of management are expected to be creative, to develop novel solutions to a broad range of problems. Each level of management has different information needs and information system requirements.

Technology

Information technology is one of many tools available to managers for coping with change. **Computer hardware** is the physical equipment used for input, processing, and output activities in an information system. It consists of the following: the computer processing unit; various input, output, and storage devices; and physical media to link these devices together. Chapter 6 describes computer hardware in greater detail.

Computer software consists of the detailed preprogrammed instructions that control and coordinate the computer hardware components in an information system. Chapter 7 explains the importance of computer software in information systems.

Storage technology includes both the physical media for storing data, such as magnetic or optical disk or tape, and the software governing the organization of data on these physical media. More detail on physical storage media can be found in Chapter 6, whereas Chapter 8 treats data organization and access methods.

Communications technology, consisting of both physical devices and software, links the various pieces of hardware and transfers data from one physical location to another. Computers and communications equipment can be connected in networks for sharing voice, data, images, sound, or even video. A **network** links two or more computers to share data or resources such as a printer. Chapters 9 and 10 provide more details on communications and networking technology and issues.

Let us return to UPS's package tracking system in the Window on Technology and identify the organization, management, and technology elements. The organization element anchors the package tracking system in UPS's sales and production functions (the main product of UPS is a service—package delivery). It specifies the required procedures for identifying packages with both sender and recipient information, taking inventory, tracking the packages en route, and providing package status reports for UPS customers and customer service representatives. The system must also provide information to satisfy the needs of managers and workers. UPS drivers need to be trained in both package pickup and delivery procedures and in how to use the package tracking system so that they can work efficiently and effectively. UPS customers may need some training to use UPS in-house package tracking software or the UPS World Wide Web site. UPS's management is responsible for monitoring service levels and costs and for promoting the company's strategy of combining low cost and superior service. Management decided to use automation to increase the ease of sending a package via UPS and of checking its delivery status, thereby reducing delivery costs and increasing sales revenues. The technology supporting this system consists of handheld computers, bar code scanners, wired and wireless communications networks, desktop computers, UPS's central computer, storage technology for the package delivery data, UPS in-house package tracking software, and software to access the World Wide Web. The result is an information system solution to a business challenge.

1.2 Contemporary Approaches to Information Systems

Multiple perspectives on information systems show that the study of information systems is a multidisciplinary field; no single theory or perspective dominates. Figure 1-4 illustrates the major disciplines that contribute problems, issues, and solutions in the study of information systems. In general, the field can be divided into technical and behavioral approaches. Information systems are sociotechnical systems. Though they are composed of machines, devices, and "hard" physical technology, they require substantial social, organizational, and intellectual investments to make them work properly.

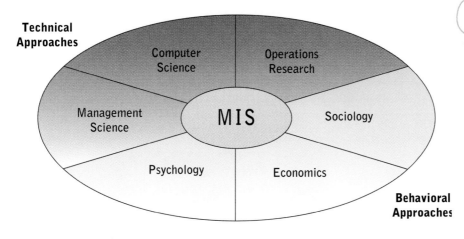

Technical Approach

The technical approach to information systems emphasizes mathematically based, normative models to study information systems, as well as the physical technology and formal capabilities of these systems. The disciplines that contribute to the technical approach are computer science, management science, and operations research. Computer science is concerned with establishing theories of computability, methods of computation, and methods of efficient data storage and access. Management science emphasizes the development of models for decision-making and management practices. Operations research focuses on mathematical techniques for optimizing selected parameters of organizations such as transportation, inventory control, and transaction costs.

Behavioral Approach

An important part of the information systems field is concerned with behavioral issues that arise in the development and long-term maintenance of information systems. Issues such as strategic business integration, design, implementation, utilization, and management cannot be explored usefully with the models used in the technical approach. Other behavioral disciplines contribute important concepts and methods. For instance, sociologists study information systems with an eye toward how groups and organizations shape the development of systems and also how systems affect individuals, groups, and organizations. Psychologists study information systems with an interest in how formal information is perceived and used by human decision makers. Economists study information systems with an interest in what impact systems have on control and cost structures within the firm and within markets.

The behavioral approach does not ignore technology. Indeed, information systems technology is often the stimulus for a behavioral problem or issue. But the focus of this approach is generally not on technical solutions; it concentrates rather on changes in attitudes, management and organizational policy, and behavior (Kling and Dutton, 1982).

Approach of This Text: Sociotechnical Systems

The study of management information systems (MIS) arose in the 1970s to focus on computer-based information systems aimed at managers (Davis and Olson, 1985). MIS combines the theoretical work of computer science, management science, and operations research with a practical orientation toward building systems and applications. It also pays attention to behavioral issues raised by sociology, economics, and psychology.

Our experience as academics and practitioners leads us to believe that no single perspective effectively captures the reality of information systems. Problems with systems—and their solutions—are rarely all technical or all behavioral. Our best advice to students is to understand the perspectives of all disciplines. Indeed, the challenge and excitement of the information systems field is that it requires an appreciation and tolerance of many different approaches.

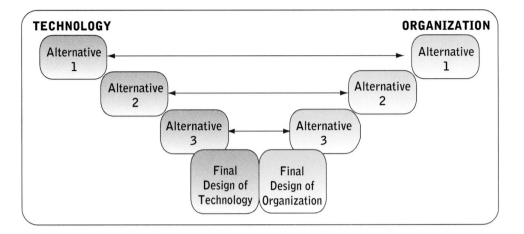

Figure I-5 A sociotechnical perspective on information systems. In a sociotechnical perspective, the performance of a system is optimized when both the technology and the organization mutually adjust to one another until a satisfactory fit is obtained.

A sociotechnical systems perspective helps to avoid a purely technological approach to information systems. For instance, the fact that information technology is rapidly declining in cost and growing in power does not necessarily or easily translate into productivity enhancement or bottom-line profits.

In this book, we stress the need to optimize the performance of the system as a whole. Both the technical and behavioral components need attention. This means that technology must be changed and designed in such a way as to fit organizational and individual needs. At times, the technology may have to be "de-optimized" to accomplish this fit. Organizations and individuals must also be changed through training, learning, and planned organizational change in order to allow the technology to operate and prosper (see, for example, Liker et al., 1987). People and organizations change to take advantage of new information technology. Figure 1-5 illustrates this process of mutual adjustment in a sociotechnical system.

1.3 The New Role of Information Systems in Organizations

Information systems cannot be ignored by managers because they play such a critical role in contemporary organizations. Digital technology is transforming business organizations. The entire cash flow of most Fortune 500 companies is linked to information systems. Today's systems directly affect how managers decide, how senior managers plan, and in many cases what products and services are produced (and how). They play a strategic role in the life of the firm. Responsibility for information systems cannot be delegated to technical decision makers.

The Widening Scope of Information Systems

Figure 1-6 illustrates the new relationship between organizations and information systems. There is a growing interdependence between business strategy, rules, and procedures on the one hand, and information systems software, hardware, databases, and telecommunications on the other. A change in any of these components often requires changes in other components. This relationship becomes critical when management plans for the future. What a business would like to do in five years is often dependent on what its systems will be able to do. Increasing market share, becoming the high-quality or low-cost producer, developing new products, and increasing employee productivity depend more and more on the kinds and quality of information systems in the organization.

A second change in the relationship of information systems and organizations results from the growing complexity and scope of system projects and applications. Building systems today involves a much larger part of the organization than it did in the past

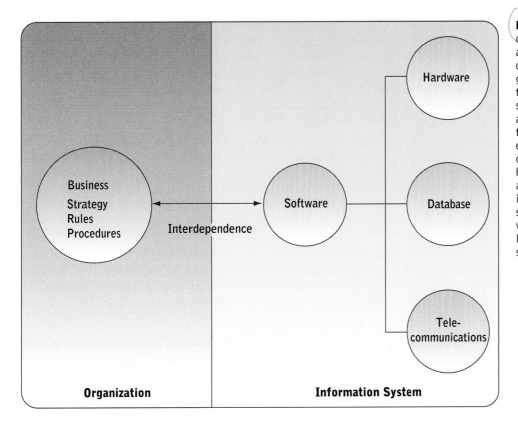

Figure 1-6 The interdependence between organizations and information systems. In contemporary systems there is a growing interdependence between organizational business strategy, rules, and procedures and the organization's information systems. Changes in strategy, rules, and procedures increasingly require changes in hardware, software, databases, and telecommunications. Existing systems can act as a constraint on organizations. Often, what the organization would like to do depends on what its systems will permit it to do.

(see Figure 1-7). Whereas early systems produced largely technical changes that affected few people, contemporary systems bring about managerial changes (who has what information about whom, when, and how often) and institutional "core" changes (what products and services are produced, under what conditions, and by whom).

In the 1950s, employees in the treasurer's office, a few part-time programmers, a single program, a single machine, and a few clerks might have used a computerized payroll system. The change from a manual to a computer system was largely technical: The computer system simply automated a clerical procedure such as check processing. In contrast, today's integrated human resources system (which includes payroll processing) may involve all major corporate divisions, the human resources department, dozens of full-time programmers, a flock of external consultants, multiple machines (or remote computers linked by telecommunications networks), and perhaps hundreds of end users in the organization who use

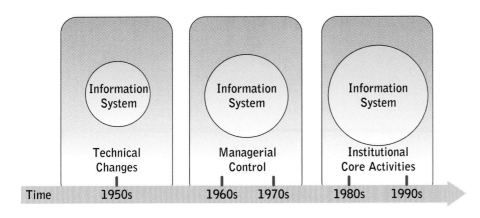

Figure 1-7 The widening scope of information systems. Over time, information systems have come to play a larger role in the life of organizations. Early systems brought about largely technical changes that were relatively easy to accomplish. Later systems affected managerial control and behavior; ultimately systems influenced "core" institutional activities concerning products, markets, suppliers, and customers.

payroll data to make calculations about benefits and pensions and to answer a host of other questions. The data, instead of being located in and controlled by the treasurer's office, are now available to hundreds of employees via desktop computers, each of which is as powerful as the large computers of the mid-1980s. This contemporary system embodies both managerial and institutional changes.

The Network Revolution and the Internet

One reason information systems play such a large role in organizations and affect so many people is the soaring power and declining cost of computer technology. Computing power, which has been doubling every 18 months, has improved the performance of microprocessors 25,000 times since their invention more than 25 years ago. With powerful, easy-to-use software, the computer can crunch numbers, analyze vast pools of data, or simulate complex physical and logical processes with animated drawings, sounds, and even tactile feedback.

The soaring power of computer technology has spawned powerful communication networks that organizations can use to access vast storehouses of information from around the world and to coordinate activities across space and time. These networks are transforming the shape and form of business enterprises and even our society.

The world's largest and most widely used network is the **Internet.** The Internet is an international network of networks that are both commercial and publicly owned. The Internet connects hundreds of thousands of different networks from over 200 countries around the world. More than 150 million people working in science, education, government, and business use the Internet to exchange information or perform business transactions with other organizations around the globe. The number of Internet users is expected to surpass 300 million by the year 2000.

The Internet is extremely elastic. If networks are added or removed or failures occur in parts of the system, the rest of the Internet continues to operate. Through special communication and technology standards, any computer can communicate with virtually any other computer linked to the Internet using ordinary telephone lines. Companies and private individuals can use the Internet to exchange business transactions, text messages, graphic images, and even video and sound, whether they are located next door or on the other side of the globe. Table 1.3 describes some of the Internet's capabilities.

Internet International network of networks that is a collection of hundreds of thousands of private and public networks.

Internet computing. This global network of networks provides a highly flexible platform for information-sharing. Digital information can be distributed at almost no cost to millions of people throughout the world.

Table 1.3 What You Can Do on the Internet

	Function	Description
	Communicate and collaborate	Send electronic mail messages; transmit documents and data; participate in electronic conferences
	Access information	Search for documents, databases, and library card catalogs; read electronic brochures, manuals, books, and advertisements
	Participate in discussions	Join interactive discussion groups; conduct primitive voice transmission
	Supply information	Transfer computer files of text, computer programs, graphics, animations, or videos
	Find entertainment	Play interactive video games; view short video clips; listen to sound and music clips; read illustrated and even animated magazines and books
	Exchange business transactions	Advertise, sell, and purchase goods and services

The Internet is creating a new "universal" technology platform on which to build all sorts of new products, services, strategies, and organizations. It is reshaping the way information systems are being used in business and daily life. By eliminating many technical, geographic, and cost barriers obstructing the global flow of information, the Internet is accelerating the information revolution, inspiring new uses of information systems and new business models. The Window on Management provides some examples.

Of special interest to organizations and managers is the Internet capability known as the World Wide Web because it offers so many new possibilities for doing business. The **World Wide Web** is a system with universally accepted standards for storing, retrieving, formatting, and displaying information in a networked environment. Information is stored and displayed as electronic "pages" that can contain text, graphics, animations, sound, and video. These Web pages can be linked electronically to other Web pages, regardless of where they are located, and viewed by any type of computer. By clicking on highlighted words or buttons on a Web page, one can link to related pages to find additional information, software programs, or still more links to other points on the Web. The Web can serve as the foundation for new kinds of information systems.

All of the Web pages maintained by an organization or individual are called a **Web site.** (The chapter opening vignette illustrates a page from InPart's Web site.) Businesses are creating Web sites with stylish typography, colorful graphics, push-button interactivity, and often sound and video to disseminate product information widely, to "broadcast" advertising and messages to customers, to collect electronic orders and customer data, and increasingly to coordinate far-flung sales forces and organizations on a global scale.

World Wide Web A system with universally accepted standards for storing, retrieving, formatting, and displaying information in a networked environment.

Web site All of the World Wide Web pages maintained by an organization or an individual.

Asian Netrepreneurs Thrive on the Internet

The Internet is creating a new breed of entrepreneurs who are rapidly setting up businesses on the Internet. Wang Zhidong and Sarah Benecke are two examples of "netrepreneurs," who launched new Internet-based businesses for Asia.

In China, free-market enterprise is still very young, and only 1 in 1000 residents use the Internet. Wang was trained as an electrical engineer but set up a software company in Beijing called Stone Rich Sight (SRS) that received $6.5 million in U.S. venture capital in 1997 from Walden International Group and Robertson Stephens. More than one million pages on SRS's Web site were viewed each day, making it one of the most popular Chinese language sites in the world.

In November 1998, SRS merged with Sinanet.com, based in Cupertino, California, which was the most popular portal for "global," or nonmainland, Chinese. (A portal is a Web site or other service offering a broad array of resources or services such as e-mail, on-line shopping, discussion forums, and tools for locating information.) The combined sites are now known as Sina and have become the most heavily trafficked Web sites in the Chinese language market. To avoid clashes over content restrictions with the Chinese government, Sina currently maintains separate portals for mainland Chinese, Taiwanese, Hong Kong, and U.S. markets.

The company is planning locally oriented, full-service, Chinese language portals that combine content, services, and capabilities for searching for information on the Web. For example, Sina's U.S. portal provides news, Dow Jones stock quotes, advertising, shopping, electronic mail (e-mail), links to other Chinese language sites, and tools for searching for information. To provide content for the China site, Wang is negotiating with mainland newspapers, magazines, television stations, and other media. The bulk of Sina's revenue currently comes from advertising, primarily from U.S. and Taiwanese operations. But Sina hopes eventually to charge subscription fees for access and to add electronic commerce and Internet telephone capabilities to its Web sites.

Benecke is the CEO of Asia Sources Media (ASM), a Hong Kong company that offers services via the Internet for companies participating in global trade. ASM began as an Asian trade magazine back in 1970, when U.S. and European trade with Asia was tiny and networking barely existed. In 1991 ASM installed software that automated price quotes and trade documentation for both purchaser and vendor and that included accounting reports. Next ASM offered an interactive catalog of products and factories on a CD-ROM, but it quickly converted its catalog to a Web site.

ASM's Web site, Asian Sources Online, now hosts more than 7200 supplier sites with 37,000 products and receives more than 10,000 inquiries each week. Users can view the products and then contact sellers via e-mail when they are interested. ASM is a matchmaker, helping buyers and sellers to find each other easily and bringing them together quickly without costly travel or telephone calls. For example, one Asian producer of sunglasses received an order for 6,000 pairs after exchanging only three e-mail messages with the buyer. ASM is enhancing the Web site so that money can change hands on-line.

Other services offered by the site include a trade show calendar and a product-alert capability that notifies users by e-mail when products of interest are available. A special section on the site is designed for factories to sell excess stock at discount prices. For example, an importer was able to purchase 11,000 chocolate fondue sets for U.S. $2.30 each.

Some on-line marketplace sites charge a percentage of sales to pay their costs and make their profits, but ASM never considered that. Instead, to earn revenue, ASM gets paid only for listings by sellers (and soon by buyers) and by accepting ads to be displayed on its Web site. With lower infrastructure expenditures and growing business, the company should prove to be quite profitable.

To Think About: How essential is the Internet in the strategy and operations of these businesses?

Sources: James Ryan, "China.com," **The Industry Standard,** January 15, 1999; and Art Jahnke, "Netrepreneurs, The Orient Express," **CIO WebBusiness Magazine,** March 1, 1998.

In Chapter 10 we describe the Web and other Internet capabilities in greater detail. We also discuss relevant features of the Internet throughout the text because the Internet affects so many aspects of information systems in organizations.

New Options for Organizational Design: The Networked Enterprise

The explosive growth in computing power and networks, including the Internet, is turning organizations into networked enterprises, allowing information to be instantly distributed within and beyond the organization. This capability can be used to redesign and reshape organizations, transforming their structure, scope of operations, reporting and control mecha-

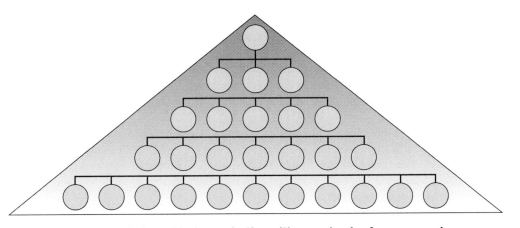

A traditional hierarchical organization with many levels of management

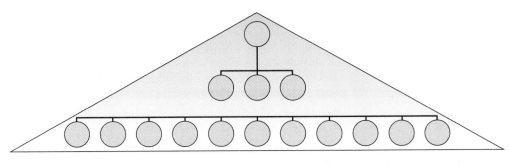

An organization that has been "flattened" by removing layers of management

Figure 1-8 Flattening organizations. Information systems can reduce the number of levels in an organization by providing managers with information to supervise larger numbers of workers and by giving lower level employees more decision-making authority.

nisms, work practices, work flows, products, and services. New ways of conducting business electronically have emerged.

Flattening Organizations

Large, bureaucratic organizations, which primarily developed before the computer age, are often inefficient, slow to change, and less competitive. Some of these organizations have downsized, reducing the number of employees and the number of levels in their organizational hierarchies. For example, by 1994 heavy equipment manufacturer Caterpillar, Inc., was producing the same level of output as it did 15 years earlier, but with 40,000 fewer employees.

Flatter organizations have fewer levels of management, with lower level employees being given greater decision-making authority (see Figure 1-8). Those employees are empowered to make more decisions than in the past, they no longer work standard 9-to-5 hours, and they no longer necessarily work in an office. Moreover, such employees may be scattered geographically, sometimes working half a world away from the manager.

Contemporary information technology has made such changes possible. It can make more information available to line workers so they can make decisions that previously had been made by managers. Networked computers have made it possible for employees to work together as a team, another feature of flatter organizations. With the emergence of global networks such as the Internet, team members can collaborate closely even from distant locations. These changes mean that the management span of control has also been broadened, allowing high-level managers to manage and control more workers spread over greater distances. Many companies have eliminated thousands of middle managers as a result of these changes. AT&T, IBM, and General Motors are just a few of the organizations that have eliminated more than 30,000 middle managers in one fell swoop.

Separating Work from Location

It is now possible to organize globally while working locally: Information technologies such as e-mail, the Internet, and video conferencing to the desktop permit tight coordination of geographically dispersed workers across time zones and cultures. Entire parts of organizations can disappear: Inventory, and the warehouses to store it, can be eliminated as suppliers tie into the firm's computer systems and deliver just what is needed and just in time.

Communications technology has eliminated distance as a factor for many types of work in many situations. Salespersons can spend more time in the field with customers and have more up-to-date information with them while carrying much less paper. Many employees can work remotely from their homes or cars, and companies can reserve space at smaller central offices for meeting clients or other employees.

Collaborative teamwork across thousands of miles has become a reality as designers work on a new product together even if they are located on different continents. Ford Motor Co. has adopted a cross-continent collaborative model to design its automobiles. Supported by high-capacity communications networks and computer-aided design (CAD) software, Ford designers launched the Mustang design in Dunton, England. The design was worked on simultaneously by designers at Dearborn, Michigan, and Dunton, with some input from designers in Japan and Australia. Once the design was completed, Ford engineers in Turin, Italy, used it to produce a full-size physical model. Ford now designs other models this way and is starting to use Web technology for global collaboration (see Chapter 14).

Companies are not limited to physical locations or their own organizational boundaries for providing products and services. Networked information systems are allowing companies to coordinate their geographically distributed capabilities and even coordinate with other organizations as virtual corporations (or **virtual organizations**), sometimes called *networked organizations*. Virtual organizations use networks to link people, assets, and ideas, allying with suppliers and customers, and sometimes even competitors, to create and distribute new products and services without being limited by traditional organizational boundaries or physical location. One company can take advantage of the capabilities of another company without actually physically linking to that company. Each company contributes its core competencies, the capabilities that it does the best. For example, one company might be responsible for product design, another for assembly and manufacturing, and another for administration and sales. These virtual organizations last as long as the opportunity remains profitable. Figure 1-9 illustrates the concept of a virtual corporation.

Calyx and Corolla, which has its headquarters in San Francisco, created a networked virtual organization to sell fresh flowers directly to customers, bypassing the traditional flower shop. The company takes orders via a toll-free telephone number and enters them into a central computer, which transmits them directly to grower farms. Farmers pick the flowers and place them in waiting Federal Express refrigerated vans. Calyx and Corolla flowers are delivered within a day or two to their final destination. They are weeks fresher than flowers provided by traditional florists.

While most organizations will not become fully virtual organizations, some of their key business activities may have "virtual" features, such as using networks and the Internet to source products and components, to leverage knowledge and expertise located inside and outside the firm, and to help customers experience products and services remotely (as illustrated by InPart in the chapter opening vignette) (Venkatraman and Henderson, 1998).

Reorganizing Work Flows

Information systems have been progressively replacing manual work procedures with automated work procedures, work flows, and work processes. Electronic work flows have reduced the cost of operations in many companies by displacing paper and the manual routines that accompany it. Improved work-flow management has enabled many corporations not only to cut costs significantly but also to improve customer service at the same time. For instance, in-

virtual organization Organization using networks linking people, assets, and ideas to create and distribute products and services without being limited by traditional organizational boundaries or physical location.

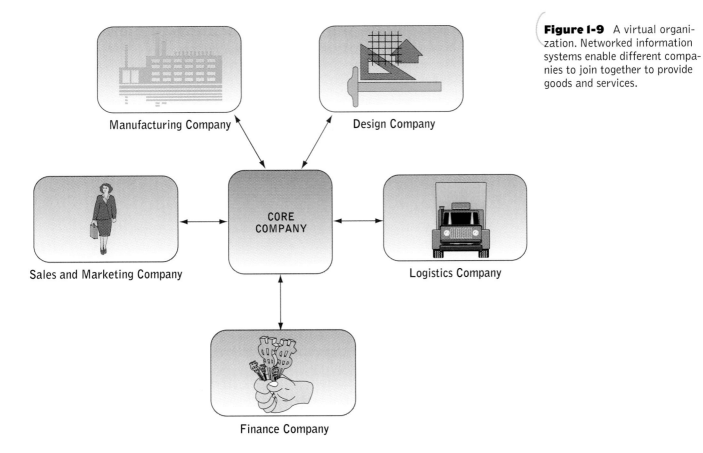

Figure I-9 A virtual organization. Networked information systems enable different companies to join together to provide goods and services.

surance companies can reduce processing of applications for new insurance from weeks to days (see Figure 1-10).

Redesigned work flows can have a profound impact on organizational efficiency and can even lead to new organizational structures, products, and services. We discuss the impact of restructured work flows on organizational design in greater detail in Chapters 3 and 11.

Increasing Flexibility of Organizations

Companies can use communications technology to organize in more flexible ways, increasing their ability to respond to changes in the marketplace and to take advantage of new opportunities. Information systems can give both large and small organizations additional flexibility to overcome

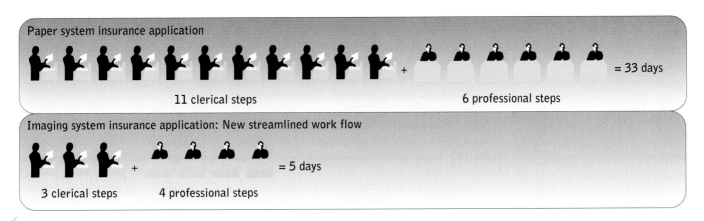

Figure I-10 Redesigned work flow for insurance underwriting. An application requiring 33 days in a paper system would only take 5 days using computers, networks, and a streamlined work flow.

Table 1.4	**How Information Technology Increases Organizational Flexibility**

Small Companies

Desktop machines, inexpensive computer-aided design (CAD) software, and computer-controlled machine tools provide the precision, speed, and quality of giant manufacturers.

Information immediately accessed by telephone and communications links eliminates the need for research staff and business libraries.

Managers can easily obtain the information they need to manage large numbers of employees in widely scattered locations.

Large Companies

Custom manufacturing systems allow large factories to offer customized products in small quantities.

Massive databases of customer purchasing records can be analyzed so that large companies can know their customers' needs and preferences as easily as local merchants.

Information can be easily distributed down the ranks of the organization to empower lower level employees and work groups to solve problems.

some of the limitations posed by their size. Table 1.4 describes some of the ways in which information technology can help small companies act "big" and help big companies act "small." Small organizations can use information systems to acquire some of the muscle and reach of larger organizations. They can perform coordinating activities, such as processing bids or keeping track of inventory, and many manufacturing tasks with very few managers, clerks, or production workers. For example, Beamscope Canada, a Toronto distributor of electronic and computer parts, competes effectively against global giants such as Ingram Micro Inc. and Merisel Inc. Its Beamscope Online system offers customers on-line service and 24-hour ordering capabilities (Engler, 1999).

Large organizations can use information technology to achieve some of the agility and responsiveness of small organizations. One aspect of this phenomenon is **mass customization,** where software and computer networks are used to link the plant floor tightly with orders, design, and purchasing and to finely control production machines. The result is a dynamically responsive environment in which products can be turned out in greater variety and easily customized with no added cost for small production runs. For example, Levi Strauss has equipped its stores with an option called Personal Pair, which allows customers to design jeans to their own specifications, rather than picking them off the rack. Customers enter their measurements into a personal computer, which then transmits the customer's specifications over a network to Levi's plants. The company is able to produce the custom jeans on the same lines that manufacture its standard items. There are almost no extra production costs because the process does not require additional warehousing, production overruns, and inventories. A related trend is micromarketing, in which information systems can help companies pinpoint tiny target markets for these finely customized products and services—as small as individualized "markets of one." We discuss micromarketing in more detail in Chapter 2.

The Changing Management Process

Information technology is recasting the process of management, providing powerful new capabilities to help managers plan, organize, lead, and control. For instance, it is now possible for managers to obtain information on organizational performance down to the level of specific transactions from just about anywhere in the organization at any time. Product managers at Frito-Lay Corporation, the world's largest manufacturer of salty snack foods, can know within hours precisely how many bags of Fritos have sold on any street in America at its customers' stores, how much they sold for, and what the competition's sales volumes and prices are.

Many companies now use information technology for enterprise resource planning. **Enterprise resource planning (ERP)** is a business management system that integrates all facets of the business, including planning, manufacturing, sales, and finance so that they can become more

mass customization Use of software and computer networks to finely control production so that products can be easily customized with no added cost for small production runs.

enterprise resource planning (ERP) A business management system that integrates all facets of the business, including planning, manufacturing, sales, and finance, so that they can become more coordinated by sharing information with each other.

closely coordinated by sharing information. ERP software models and automates many basic processes, such as filling an order or scheduling a shipment, with the goal of integrating information across the company and eliminating complex, expensive links between computer systems in different areas of the business. For instance, when a sales representative in Brussels enters a customer order, the data flows automatically to others in the company who need to see it. The factory in Hong Kong receives the order and begins production. The warehouse checks its progress online and schedules the shipment date. The warehouse can check its stock of parts and replenish whatever the factory has depleted. Updated sales and production data automatically flow to the accounting department. Corporate headquarters in London can view up-to-the-minute data on sales, inventory, and production at every step of the process. Chapter 18 provides an extensive discussion of ERP and its new role in the business enterprise. This new intensity of information makes possible far more precise planning, forecasting, and monitoring than ever before.

Redefining Organizational Boundaries

Networked information systems can enable transactions such as payments and purchase orders to be exchanged electronically among different companies, thereby reducing the cost of obtaining products and services from outside the firm. Organizations can also share business data, catalogues, or mail messages through such systems. These networked information systems can create new efficiencies and new relationships between an organization, its customers, and suppliers, redefining their organizational boundaries. For example, the Chrysler Corporation is networked to suppliers, such as the Budd Company of Rochester, Michigan. Through this electronic link, the Budd Company monitors Chrysler production and ships sheet metal parts exactly when needed, preceded by an electronic shipping notice. Chrysler and its suppliers have thus become linked business partners with mutually shared responsibilities.

The information system linking Chrysler and its suppliers is called an interorganizational information system. Systems linking a company to its customers, distributors, or suppliers are termed **interorganizational systems** because they automate the flow of information across organizational boundaries (Barrett, 1986–1987; Johnston and Vitale, 1988). Such systems allow information or processing capabilities of one organization to improve the performance of another or to improve relationships among organizations.

interorganizational systems Information systems that automate the flow of information across organizational boundaries and link a company to its customers, distributors, or suppliers.

Electronic Commerce and Electronic Business

The changes we have just described are creating new ways of conducting business electronically both inside and outside the firm. Increasingly, the Internet is providing the underlying technology for these changes. The Internet can link thousands of organizations into a single network, creating the foundation for a vast electronic marketplace. An **electronic market** is an information system that links together many buyers and sellers to exchange information, products, services, and payments. Through computers and networks, these systems function like electronic middlemen, with lowered costs for typical marketplace transactions such as selecting suppliers, establishing prices, ordering goods, and paying bills (Malone, Yates, and Benjamin, 1987). Buyers and sellers can complete purchase and sale transactions digitally, regardless of their location.

electronic market A marketplace that is created by computer and communication technologies that link many buyers and sellers.

A vast array of goods and services are being advertised, bought, and exchanged worldwide using the Internet as a global marketplace. Companies are furiously creating eye-catching electronic brochures, advertisements, product manuals, and order forms on the World Wide Web. All kinds of products and services are available on the Web, including fresh flowers, books, real estate, musical recordings, electronics, and steaks.

Many retailers maintain their own site on the Web, such as Virtual Vineyards, an on-line source of wine and food items. Others offer their products through electronic shopping malls, such as the Internet Shopping Network. Customers can locate products on this mall either by manufacturer, if they know what they want, or by product type, and then order them directly. Even electronic financial trading has arrived on the Web, offering electronic trading in stocks, bonds, mutual funds, and other financial instruments (see the Window on Organizations).

The Web is being increasingly used for business-to-business transactions as well. For example, airlines can use the Boeing Corporation's Web site to order parts electronically and check the status of their orders.

Internet Trading Heats Up

When people wanted to trade stocks, they used to call a traditional full-service broker and pay a hefty commission for placing the trade. Today, thanks to the Internet, they are buying and selling stocks, bonds, and mutual funds directly from their desktops using one of a new crop of on-line discount trading services.

These discount Internet trading services offer low-cost trades because they do not have to pay for large research departments, retail offices, or personnel to make the trades. People who actively trade stocks have flocked to these discount brokers because they make their own decisions and only need a broker to enter trades. Using their networked computer, they can bypass brokers and enter their trades electronically on their own. And they pay much less for making those trades. Internet brokerage firms such as E*Trade and Ameritrade charge commissions between $8 and $15 for most trades of any size. In comparison, full-service brokers such as Merrill Lynch, who provide stock selection advice, might charge over $100 for trades of 200 stock shares. Recognizing the Web's convenience and popularity, Merrill Lynch, Paine Webber, and other full-service companies are starting to offer on-line trading capabilities for their clients.

The Web sites maintained by Internet brokerage companies allow customers to access their account data over the Internet. They are open 24 hours a day, so customers can enter their trades any time of the day or night and any day of the year. Internet brokerage sites offer links to other sites at which the investor can obtain stock quotes, charts, investment news, historical data, and all kinds of advice on-line. Some even offer free up-to-the-minute stock quotes and stock graphs, with capabilities to make users' home computers look like the same flashy terminals used by high-powered Wall Street traders.

Internet trading is growing rapidly, with on-line firms signing up 15,000 new accounts each day. Over 5 million investors are using Internet trading tools in the United States alone and this number is expected to quadruple by 2002. Although there are many Internet brokerage companies, Charles Schwab, E*Trade, Ameritrade, and Toronto Dominion Bank are emerging as the leaders.

Charles Schwab & Co., Inc., has been the number 1 discount brokerage firm in the United States for 2 years, with more than 30 percent of the market share of on-line trading. In 1998 Schwab claimed over 2 million on-line accounts containing about $145 billion. Its main domestic competitor, in the minds of many, is E*Trade, a young entrepreneurial company that was a pioneer in Internet-based, on-line trading. However, Schwab's most serious opposition may come from a very large and venerated bank, Toronto Dominion Bank, which is the fifth-largest bank in Canada.

Toronto Dominion has several obvious advantages. First, it has available all the large resources one would expect from a bank. Second, Toronto Dominion is a rare North American bank with real stock brokerage experience—it is not a newcomer to the field. U.S. banks were forbidden to participate in stock brokerage until recently; however, Canadian banks were given permission years earlier. Toronto Dominion ventured into on-line trading in 1992 when it established a dial-up trading system. In 1996 Toronto Dominion acquired Waterhouse Securities, Inc., a U.S. stock brokerage firm, which is now the third largest in the country in on-line trading.

Toronto Dominion's Waterhouse has already achieved virtually the same foreign brokerage expansion as has Schwab. Both, for example, are in the United Kingdom and Hong Kong, two of the largest financial markets in the world. Toronto Dominion's strategy is opening physical offices in other parts of the world using a discount brokerage named GreenLine Investor Services. Combining GreenLine and Waterhouse offices abroad, Toronto Dominion seems to be well ahead of Schwab.

In contrast, E*Trade, the vigorous entrepreneurial company, is not moving to open new offices abroad. Instead, it has 32 licensing agreements to give on-line access to E*Trade through local trading firms in foreign countries. Which approach will win out? Only time will tell, but more and more people are moving to Internet trading every day.

To Think About: How has the Internet changed the brokerage business? In what ways can using electronic marketplaces on the Internet affect other organizations?

Sources: Kimberly Weisul and Kevin Jones, "Online Trading Heats Up Abroad: Move Over, Charles Schwab," Inter@ctive Week, January 6, 1999; Leah Nathans Spiro with Edward C. Baig, "Who Needs a Broker?" Business Week, February 22, 1999; and "Industry Spotlight: Online Trading," The Industry Standard, February 15, 1999.

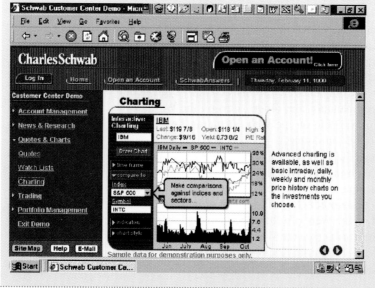

At the Travelocity Web site, visitors can obtain information on airlines, hotels, vacation packages, and other travel and leisure topics, and they can make airline and hotel reservations on-line. The World Wide Web is fueling the growth of electronic commerce.

The global availability of the Internet for the exchange of transactions between buyers and sellers is fueling the growth of electronic commerce. **Electronic commerce** is the process of buying and selling goods and services electronically with computerized business transactions using the Internet, networks, and other digital technologies. It also encompasses activities supporting those market transactions, such as advertising, marketing, customer support, delivery, and payment. By replacing manual and paper-based procedures with electronic alternatives, and by using information flows in new and dynamic ways, electronic commerce can accelerate ordering, delivery, and payment for goods and services while reducing companies' operating and inventory costs.

The Internet is emerging as the primary technology platform for electronic commerce. Equally important, Internet technology is being increasingly applied to facilitate the management of the rest of the business—publishing employee personnel policies, reviewing account balances and production plans, scheduling plant repairs and maintenance, and revising design documents. Companies are taking advantage of the connectivity and ease of use of Internet technology to create internal corporate networks called **intranets** that are based on Internet technology. Use of these private intranets for organizational communication, collaboration, and coordination is soaring. In this text, we use the term **electronic business** to distinguish these uses of Internet and digital technology for the management and coordination of other business processes from electronic commerce.

By distributing information through electronic networks, electronic business extends the reach of existing management. Managers can use e-mail, Web documents, and work-group software to effectively communicate frequently with thousands of employees, and even to manage far-flung task forces and teams. These tasks would be impossible in face-to-face traditional organizations. Table 1.5 lists some examples of electronic commerce and electronic business.

Figure 1-11 illustrates an enterprise making intensive use of Internet and digital technology for electronic commerce and electronic business. Information can flow seamlessly among different parts of the company and between the company and external entities—its customers, suppliers, and business partners. Organizations will move toward this vision as they increasingly use the Internet and networks to manage their internal processes and their relationships with customers, suppliers, and other external entities.

Both electronic commerce and electronic business can fundamentally change the way business is conducted. To use the Internet and other digital technologies successfully for electronic commerce and electronic business, organizations may have to redefine their business models, reinvent business processes, change corporate cultures, and create much closer relationships with customers and suppliers. We discuss these issues in greater detail in following chapters.

electronic commerce The process of buying and selling goods and services electronically involving transactions using the Internet, networks, and other digital technologies.

intranet An internal network based on Internet and World Wide Web technology and standards.

electronic business The use of the Internet and other digital technology for organizational communication and coordination and the management of the firm.

Table 1.5 Examples of Electronic Commerce and Electronic Business

Electronic Commerce

Amazon.com operates a virtual storefront on the Internet offering more than 3 million book titles for sale. Customers can input their orders via Amazon.com's Web site and have the books shipped to them.

Travelocity provides a Web site that can be used by consumers for travel and vacation planning. Visitors can find out information on airlines, hotels, vacation packages, and other travel and leisure topics, and they can make airline and hotel reservations on-line through the Web site.

Mobil Corporation created a private network based on Internet technology that allows its 300 lubricant distributors to submit purchase orders on-line.

Electronic Business

Roche Bioscience scientists worldwide use an intranet to share research results and discuss findings. The intranet also provides a company telephone directory and newsletter.

University of Texas Medical Branch at Galveston publishes nursing staff policies and procedures on an intranet. The intranet reduces paperwork and enhances the quality of nursing services by providing immediate notification of policy changes.

Dream Works SKG uses an intranet to check the daily status of projects, including animation objects, and to coordinate movie scenes.

Figure 1-11 Electronic commerce and electronic business in the networked enterprise. Electronic commerce uses Internet and digital technology to conduct transactions with customers and suppliers, whereas electronic business uses these technologies for the management of the rest of the business.

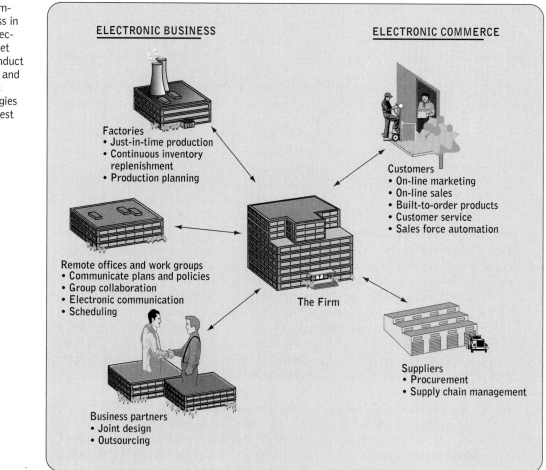

1.4 Learning to Use Information Systems: New Opportunities with Technology

Information systems today are creating many exciting opportunities for both businesses and individuals. They are also a source of new problems, issues, and challenges for managers. In this course, you will learn about both the challenges and opportunities posed by information systems, and you will be able to use information technology to enrich your learning experience.

The Challenge of Information Systems: Key Management Issues

Although information technology is advancing at a blinding pace, there is nothing easy or mechanical about building and using information systems. There are five key challenges confronting managers:

1. **The Strategic Business Challenge: How can businesses use information technology to design organizations that are competitive and effective?** Investment in information technology amounts to more than half of the annual capital expenditures of most large service-sector firms. Yet despite these heavy investments, many organizations are not obtaining significant business benefits. The power of computer hardware and software has grown much more rapidly than the ability of organizations to apply and use this technology. To stay competitive or realize genuine productivity benefits from information technology, many organizations actually need to be redesigned. They will have to make fundamental changes in organizational behavior, develop new business models, and eliminate the inefficiencies of outmoded organizational structures. If organizations merely automate what they are doing today, they are largely missing the potential of information technology. To fully benefit from information technology, including the opportunities provided by the Internet, organizations need to rethink and redesign the way they design, produce, deliver, and maintain goods and services.

2. **The Globalization Challenge: How can firms understand the business and system requirements of a global economic environment?** The rapid growth in international trade and the emergence of a global economy call for information systems that can support both producing and selling goods in many different countries. In the past, each regional office of a multinational corporation focused on solving its own unique information problems. Given language, cultural, and political differences among countries, this focus frequently resulted in chaos and the failure of central management controls. To develop integrated, multinational information systems, businesses must develop global hardware, software, and communications standards and create cross-cultural accounting and reporting structures (Roche, 1992).

3. **The Information Architecture Challenge: How can organizations develop an information architecture and information technology infrastructure that supports their business goals?** Creating a new system now means much more than installing a new machine in the basement. Today, this process typically places thousands of terminals or personal computers on the desks of employees who have little experience with them, connecting the devices to powerful communications networks, rearranging social relations in the office and work locations, changing reporting patterns, and redefining business goals. Briefly, new systems today often require redesigning the organization and developing a new information architecture.

    Information architecture is the particular form that information technology takes in an organization to achieve selected goals or functions. It is a design for the business application systems that serve each functional specialty and level of the organization and the specific way that they are used by each organization. Figure 1-12 illustrates the major elements of information architecture that managers will need to develop. Because managers and employees directly interact with these systems, it is critical for the success of the organization that its information architecture meet business requirements now and in the future.

information architecture
The particular design that information technology takes in a specific organization to achieve selected goals or functions.

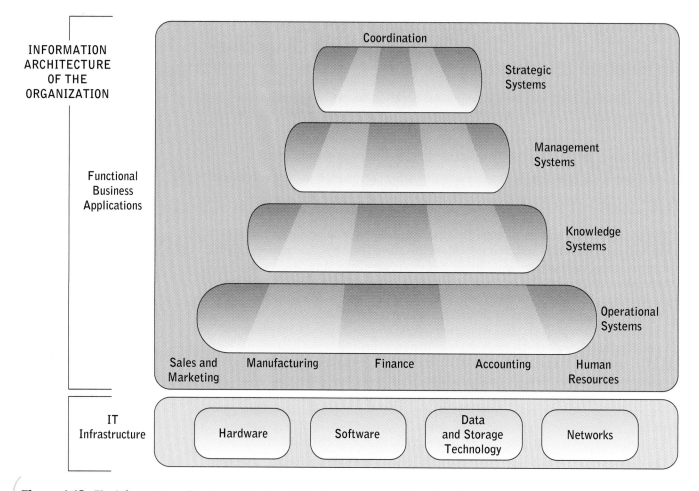

INFORMATION ARCHITECTURE OF THE ORGANIZATION

Functional Business Applications

IT Infrastructure

Figure 1-12 The information architecture of the firm. Today's managers must know how to arrange and coordinate the various computer technologies and business system applications to meet the information needs of each level of their organization, and the needs of the organization as a whole.

information technology (IT) infrastructure Computer hardware, software, data and storage technology, and networks providing a platform of shared information technology resources for the organization.

The technology platform for this architecture is called the **information technology (IT) infrastructure** and consists of computer hardware, software, data and storage technology, networks, and human resources required to operate the equipment. These technologies constitute the *shared* IT resources of the firm and are available to all of its applications. Although this technology platform is typically operated by technical personnel, general management must decide how to allocate the resources it has assigned to hardware, software, data storage, and telecommunications networks to make sound information technology investments (Weill and Broadbent, 1997 and 1998).

Here are typical questions regarding information architecture and IT infrastructure facing today's managers: Should the corporate sales data and function be distributed to each corporate remote site, or should they be centralized at headquarters? Should the organization purchase stand-alone personal computers or build a more powerful, centralized mainframe environment within an integrated telecommunications network? Should the organization build systems to connect the entire enterprise or separate islands of applications? There is no one right answer to these questions (see Allen and Boynton, 1991). Moreover, business needs are constantly changing, which requires the IT architecture to be reassessed continually (Feeny and Willcocks, 1998).

Even under the best of circumstances, combining knowledge of systems and the organization is itself a demanding task. For many organizations, the task is even more formidable because they are crippled by fragmented and incompatible computer hardware, software, telecommunications networks, and information systems. Although Internet standards have solved some of these connectivity problems, integration of diverse computing platforms is rarely as seamless as promised. Many organizations are still struggling to integrate islands of information and technology into a coherent architecture. Chapter 18 includes a more detailed discussion of information architecture and IT infrastructure issues.

4. **The Information Systems Investment Challenge: How can organizations determine the business value of information systems?** A major problem raised by the development of powerful, inexpensive computers involves not technology but management and organizations. It's one thing to use information technology to design, produce, deliver, and maintain new products. It's another thing to make money doing it. How can organizations obtain a sizable payoff from their investment in information systems?

Engineering massive organizational and system changes in the hope of positioning a firm strategically is complicated and expensive. Is this an investment that pays off? How can you tell? Senior management can be expected to ask these questions: Are we receiving the kind of return on investment from our systems that we should be? Do our competitors get more? Understanding the costs and benefits of building a single system is difficult enough; it is daunting to consider whether the entire systems effort is "worth it." Imagine, then, how a senior executive must think when presented with a major transformation in information architecture—a bold venture in organizational change costing tens of millions of dollars and taking many years.

5. **The Responsibility and Control Challenge: How can organizations design systems that people can control and understand?** How can organizations ensure that their information systems are used in an ethically and socially responsible manner? Information systems are so essential to business, government, and daily life that organizations must take special steps to ensure that they are accurate, reliable, and secure. Automated or semiautomated systems that malfunction or are poorly operated can have extremely harmful consequences. A firm invites disaster if it uses systems that don't work as intended, that don't deliver information in a form that people can interpret correctly and use, or that have control rooms where controls don't work or where instruments give false signals. The potential for massive fraud, error, abuse, and destruction is enormous.

Information systems must be designed so that they function as intended and so that humans can control the process. When building and using information systems, organizations should consider health, safety, job security, and social well being as carefully as they do their business goals. Managers will need to ask: Can we apply high quality assurance standards to our information systems, as well as to our products and services? Can we build information systems that respect people's rights of privacy while still pursuing our organization's goals? Should information systems monitor employees? What do we do when an information system designed to increase efficiency and productivity eliminates people's jobs?

This text is designed to provide future managers with the knowledge and understanding required to deal with these challenges. To further this objective, each succeeding chapter begins with a Management Challenges box that outlines the key issues of which managers should be aware.

Integrating Text with Technology: New Opportunities for Learning

In addition to the changes in business and management that we have just described, we believe that information technology creates new opportunities for learning that can make the MIS course more meaningful and exciting. We have provided a Web site and an interactive multimedia CD-ROM for integrating the text with leading-edge technology.

As you read each chapter of the text, you can visit the Prentice Hall Laudon Web site and use the Internet for interactive learning and management problem-solving. The Internet Connection icon in the chapter directs you to Web sites for which we have provided additional exercises and projects related to the concepts and organizations described in that chapter. For selected chapters, you will also find interactive Electronic Commerce projects, tours of Electronic Commerce sites, and a comprehensive Electronic Commerce project. A graded on-line interactive Study Guide contains questions to help you review what you have learned and test your mastery of chapter concepts. You can also use the Laudon Web site to find links to additional on-line case studies, international resources, technology updates, and on-line tutorials on how to use Web browsers and other Internet tools.

An interactive CD-ROM multimedia version of the text can be purchased as an optional item. The Multimedia Edition CD-ROM features interactive exercises, simulations, audio/video overviews explaining key concepts, on-line quizzes, hyperlinks to the exercises on the Laudon Web site, technology updates, and more. You can use the CD-ROM as an interactive study guide or as an alternative to the traditional text.

You will find a Tools for Interactive Learning section with this icon concluding every chapter to show how you can use the Web and interactive multimedia to enrich your learning experience.

Management Wrap-Up

Management

Managers are problem-solvers who are responsible for analyzing the many challenges confronting organizations and for developing strategies and action plans. Information systems are one of their tools, delivering the information required for solutions. Information systems both reflect management decisions and serve as instruments for changing the management process.

Organization

Information systems are rooted in organizations, an outcome of organizational structure, culture, politics, work flows, and standard operating procedures. They are instruments for organizational change, making it possible to recast these organizational elements into new business models and redraw organizational boundaries. Advances in information systems are accelerating the trend toward globalized, knowledge-driven economies and flattened, flexible, decentralized organizations.

Technology

A network revolution is under way. Information systems technology is no longer limited to computers but consists of an array of technologies that enable computers to be networked together to exchange information across great distances and organizational boundaries. The Internet provides global connectivity and a flexible platform for information-sharing, creating new uses for information systems and revolutionizing the role of information systems in organizations.

For Discussion

1. Information systems are too important to be left to computer specialists. Do you agree? Why or why not?

2. As computers become faster and cheaper and the Internet becomes more widely used, most of the problems we have with information systems will disappear. Do you agree? Why or why not?

Summary

1. **Define an information system.** The purpose of a CBIS is to collect, store, and disseminate information from an organization's environment and internal operations to support organizational functions and decision making, communication, coordination, control, analysis, and visualization. Information systems transform raw data into useful information through three basic activities: input, processing, and output.

2. **Distinguish between computer literacy and information systems literacy.** Information systems literacy requires an understanding of the organizational and management dimensions of information systems as well as the technical dimensions addressed by computer literacy. Information systems literacy draws on both technical and behavioral approaches to studying information systems. Both perspectives can be combined into a sociotechnical approach to systems.

3. **Explain why information systems are so important today and how they are transforming organizations and management.** The kinds of systems built today are very important for the overall performance of the organization, especially in today's highly globalized and information-based economy. Information systems are driving both daily operations and organizational strategy. Powerful computers, software, and networks, including the Internet, have helped organizations become more flexible, eliminate layers of management, separate work from location, and restructure work flows, giving new powers to both line workers and management. Information technology allows managers to execute enterprise resource planning for more precise planning, forecasting, and monitoring of the major processes of the business. To maximize the advantages of information technology,

there is a much greater need to plan for the overall informa-tion architecture of the organization.

4. Compare electronic commerce and electronic business and analyze their relationship to the Internet and digital technology. The Internet and other networks have made it possible for businesses to replace manual and paper-based processes with the electronic flow of information. In elec-tronic commerce, businesses can exchange electronic pur-chase and sale transactions with each other and with individ-ual customers. Electronic business uses the Internet and digital technology to expedite the exchange of information that can facilitate communication and coordination both in-side the organization and between the organization and its business partners.

5. Identify the major management challenges to building and using information systems in organizations. There are five key management challenges in building and using informa-tion systems: (1) designing systems that are competitive and ef-ficient; (2) understanding the system requirements of a global business environment; (3) creating an information architecture that supports the organization's goals; (4) determining the busi-ness value of information systems; and (5) designing systems that people can control, understand, and use in a socially and ethically responsible manner.

Key Terms

Communications technology, 12	Enterprise resource planning (ERP), 22	Interorganizational systems, 23	Production or service workers, 11
Computer-based information systems (CBIS), 8	Feedback, 8	Intranet, 25	Senior managers, 11
Computer hardware, 12	Formal system, 8	Knowledge- and information-intense products, 5	Standard operating procedures (SOPs), 11
Computer software, 12	Information, 7	Knowledge workers, 11	Storage technology, 12
Data, 7	Information architecture, 27	Mass customization, 22	Virtual organization, 20
Data workers, 11	Information system, 7	Middle managers, 11	Web site, 16
Electronic business, 25	Information technology (IT) infrastructure, 28	Network, 12	World Wide Web, 16
Electronic commerce, 25	Input, 8	Operational managers, 12	
Electronic market, 23	Internet, 16	Output, 8	
		Processing, 8	

Review Questions

1. Distinguish between a computer, a computer program, and an information system. What is the difference between data and information?

2. What activities convert raw data to usable information in information systems? What is their relationship to feedback?

3. What is information systems literacy?

4. What are the organization, management, and technology dimensions of information systems?

5. Distinguish between a behavioral and a technical approach to information systems in terms of the questions asked and the answers provided.

6. What major disciplines contribute to an understanding of information systems?

7. Why should managers study information systems?

8. What is the relationship between an organization and its information systems? How is this relationship changing over time?

9. What are the Internet and the World Wide Web? How have they changed the role played by information systems in organizations?

10. Describe some of the major changes that information systems are bringing to organizations.

11. How are information systems changing the management process?

12. What is the relationship between the network revolution, electronic commerce, and electronic business?

13. What do we mean by the information architecture of the organization?

14. What are the key management challenges involved in building, operating, and maintaining information systems today?

Group Project

In a group with three or four classmates, find a description in a com-puter or business magazine of an information system used by an or-ganization. Look for information about the company on the Web to gain further insight into the company and prepare a brief descrip-tion of the business. Describe the system you have selected in terms of its inputs, processes, and outputs, and in terms of its organiza-tion, management, and technology features and the importance of the system to the company. Present your analysis to the class.

Tools for Interactive Learning

○ **Internet**

The Internet Connection for this chapter will take you to the United Parcel Service Web site, where you can complete an exercise to evaluate how UPS uses the Web and other information technology in its daily operations. You can use the interactive software at this Web site in an Electronic Commerce project to help a company calculate and budget for its shipping costs. You can also use the Interactive Study Guide to test your knowledge of the topics in this chapter, and get instant feedback where you need more practice.

○ **CD-ROM**

If you purchase and use the Multimedia Edition CD-ROM with this chapter, you will find a simulation showing you how the Internet works, a video clip illustrating UPS's package tracking system, interactive exercises, an audio overview of the major themes of this chapter, and bullet text summarizing the key points of the chapter.

Case Study — Battling Information Overload: A New Business Is Born

Do a search on the Web and all too often you will get back thousands of references, leaving you overwhelmed and almost helpless. Too much information—information overload—has developed into a gigantic problem, and the battle to solve it is moving at a snail's pace. Information overload is the collecting of more information than one can read, absorb, or use. It is a byproduct of computerization and telecommunications. The amount of potentially valuable data has exploded, and computers and the Internet can now be used to obtain, store, search, and communicate that data. We can follow the development of the problem and watch as it has begun to be addressed by following the career of Ron Bienvenu, the founder and CEO of SageMaker Inc.

Bienvenu's career in supplying information began in 1988 when, as a young man, he became an employee of SNL Securities, of Hoboken, New Jersey. This was the time of the savings and loan crisis, a crisis that cost United States taxpayers hundreds of billions of dollars. Although information on the crisis and on the specific banks involved was indispensable to many, it was very difficult for them to obtain. Bienvenu became the editor of SNL's **ThriftWatch** newsletter which was filled with data on Securities and Exchange Commission filings relevant to the banking industry. Its audience was analysts, investors and executives of the banking industry. Bienvenu points out that "We weren't adding value to the information—

we were just repackaging it." In other words, SNL just collected the data and passed it on, making no effort to make it relevant to individual customers. Thus customers received mounds of data, most of which they could not use. Furthermore, because the data were distributed on paper, they could not be searched, reorganized, or combined.

For two years, beginning in 1989, Bienvenu cofounded and published the **Energy Alert** newsletter. Its concept was similar to that of **ThriftWatch**, but it was directed at analysts and executives of the energy industry rather than the banking industry. It followed a similar strategy: collecting and passing on to customers all data that might possibly be relevant in the hope that individual subscribers would turn some of it into useful information. The data came mainly from SEC filings and were faxed daily to subscribers. Bienvenu neither examined the value of the data nor looked at the data needs of individual subscribers. Because he printed everything that looked like it might be relevant, he also made some major blunders. For example, for months he passed on detailed financial data on Oil-Dri due to its name. Only after months did a subscriber inform him that the company was not in energy but rather manufactured kitty litter. The newsletter was not a success.

In 1991 Bienvenu became an employee of John S. Herold Inc., a petroleum industry research and consulting firm. There he was assigned to automate as much as possible the data collection for an existing oil indus-

try newsletter. To prepare the newsletter the staff used a very repetitive method of manually collecting digitized data. The same data would then be collected again manually the next month or quarter, a slow, expensive, and error-prone process. In addition, the data were then published in paper form. Again, no effort was made to customize the data for each subscriber.

While in this job, Bienvenu came to understand that the customers did not want all available information on the industry. They wanted only those data that were relevant to them. Moreover, the Internet was already having an effect on obtaining and providing information. Many subscribers no longer wanted just raw data when they could collect that themselves. Also many customers were now objecting to data on paper such as in journals or faxes. So, in 1993 Bienvenu left his job and founded SageMaker of Fairfield, Connecticut.

SageMaker developed software that automatically locates and collects energy-related information from industry publications via computers for individual customers based on criteria those customers define for themselves. The data come from several thousand sources. Once Bienvenu established his company, a number of publishers, such as McGraw-Hill, came to SageMaker and asked it to make digitized versions of their publications available to SageMaker customers. They paid SageMaker for this privilege.

Because these publications came from different types of computer systems and were in different digital formats, SageMaker had to create five different front-end products in order to make all the publications available to its customers. SageMaker customers quickly let Bienvenu know that obtaining the required information was too difficult because of the need to learn five different interfaces. Bienvenu concluded that instead of easing information overload, he was just adding to it again. Bienvenu moved quickly to change SageMaker into a software system that presented data to the customers in a single format. The system collects data from many different sources in the same way, but customers use only one interface, and the system now is easy to use. Subscribers can access the system over the Internet using the same standard software they would use for accessing information from the Web.

According to the SageMaker Web site, "SageMaker combines, classifies and organizes in-house and on-line content into a single enterprise platform." The software enables users to combine internal and external information sources. To help in this process, the company indexes and organizes the documents so they can be searched. A sample description helps to understand the value of this system. A user might do a search on a country, such as Indonesia, and the system would search all sources of data and produce a wide range of information including, but certainly not limited to: the inquiring company's own fields under production in that country; their and all other current explorations in that country; Indonesia's currency performance correlated to the company's capital investment; the latest analysis of the political stability of Indonesia's government; and an analysis of the position and activities of competitors.

Source documents, such as newsletters, remain available in their original form (that is, users can read the full articles from newsletters).

Bienvenu faced one more problem—competition. "Information aggregation is becoming a commoditized business," he observes, "since providers like Dow Jones and Reuters have roughly the same 4,000 sources in the oil industry." Moreover, companies such as InfoMation Publishing Corp. provide filtering and aggregation tools for this data. So, he asked himself, what could SageMaker do to gain a strategic advantage? The solution is an auditing module known as Information Management Program (IMP). IMP tracks the number of people who are reading and using the data from each publication. This module enables customers to determine which publications they should renew and which to drop. They can, therefore, measure cost against usage, enabling companies to reduce costs by eliminating sources not used enough. J. Stephen Putnam, president of Robert Thomas Securities, explains that "Getting a handle on our return on information, that's something we've been frustrated at not being able to get at for years." Bienvenu himself points out his typical customers are Fortune 100 companies that spend $160 million a year on information. SageMaker can potentially save them 20 percent by distributing it and auditing it. On the other side, publishers can verify that corporations are not over-using their subscriptions. According to Phil Lynch, vice-president of sales for Reuters America Inc., SageMaker's audit function "distinguishes them from anybody else."

SageMaker revenue is growing to an estimated $5.8 million in 1999. One revenue

source is that publishers pay SageMaker subscription royalties of 7 to 15 percent. On the other side, the company has sold its service to about 150 corporate customers with a total of 60,000 users. Its customers include such energy giants as Amoco Inc., ARCO, Conoco, and Royal Dutch Shell. For the energy industry, SageMaker uses over 4,000 business information sources, including magazines, newsletters, financial and industry databases.

Battling information overload appears to offer SageMaker a bright future. Bienvenu plans to expand by offering similar industry-specific software for other industries. He raised $3 million in capital in 1998 for this expansion. He is looking at the financial industry next, and then he is eyeing the pharmaceuticals, health care and telecommunications industries.

Sources: Joshua Macht, "Confessions of an Information Sinner," Inc. Magazine, January, 1999; Kevin Jones, "Fueling Energy Data Management," Inter@active Week Online, December 7, 1998; Jeff Moad, "In Search of Knowledge," PC Week Online, December 7, 1998; and www.sagemaker.com/.

CASE STUDY QUESTIONS:

1. How is SageMaker using the Internet for electronic commerce?

2. What management, organization, and technology challenges did Bienvenu have to address as he tried to create a successful information business?

3. What are some of the problems SageMaker faces that technology cannot address?

4. Observers have commented that the Internet has drastically changed what it means to be a good information provider. Explain.

Chapter 2

The Strategic Role of Information Systems

After completing this chapter, you will be able to:

1. Analyze the role played by the six major types of information systems in organizations.

2. Describe the relationship between the various types of information systems.

3. Distinguish a strategic information system.

4. Describe how information systems can be used to support three levels of strategy used in business.

5. Explain why strategic information systems are difficult to build and sustain.

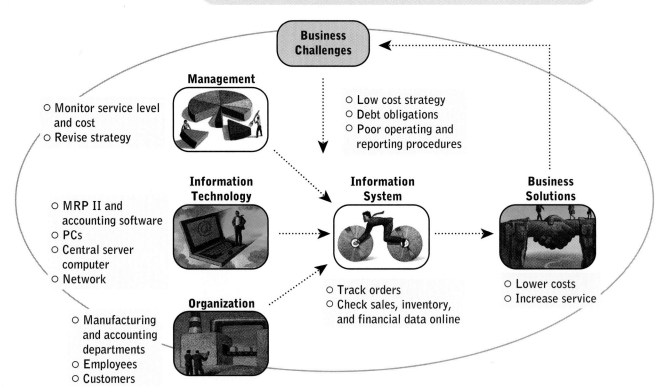

Business Challenges

Management
- Monitor service level and cost
- Revise strategy

- Low cost strategy
- Debt obligations
- Poor operating and reporting procedures

Information Technology
- MRP II and accounting software
- PCs
- Central server computer
- Network

Organization
- Manufacturing and accounting departments
- Employees
- Customers

Information System
- Track orders
- Check sales, inventory, and financial data online

Business Solutions
- Lower costs
- Increase service

Orchids Paper Products

Moves Back on Course

Orchids Paper Products Co. had been a low-cost manufacturer of napkins, tissues, paper towels, and bathroom paper for 50 years, but by the mid-1990s, the company appeared to be losing its way. To capitalize on the booming economy of the late 1980s, management began pursuing the growing market for private-label paper products in California, where the company at that time was headquartered. Unfortunately, the high cost of that strategy combined with debt from a leveraged buyout brought Orchids close to closing down. At one point, its costs for raw materials and processing surpassed what it could charge customers. Orchids was forced to file for bankruptcy in 1992 and again in 1995.

Orchids' new management team, led by General Manager Mike Sage and

Chief Financial Officer Jim Swagerty, decided to refocus the company on its core market of value-seeking customers. They moved the company's converting equipment from California to Pryor, Oklahoma, where utility costs are low (paper production is very energy-intensive) and where there is a strong market for the company's recycled paper. They adopted a "lowest-cost" strategy that would maximize productivity while emphasizing on-time deliveries and keeping customers closely informed about the status of their orders. Orchids' target market spans an area from Oklahoma to the Atlantic.

Before its reorganization, Orchids had a reputation for poor service and missed deliveries. The company had poor operating and reporting practices, and the accounting department was held responsible for the lack of accurate and timely information.

Orchids installed a new manufacturing resources planning (MRP II) system and an accounting system from Macola Software Inc. of Marion, Ohio, that monitors and coordinates sales, inventory, and financial data and provides management with a complete picture of the company's operations on a daily basis. Employees in manufacturing and other departments can directly access production and order information using 25 personal computers networked to a central server computer that stores this information. Accounting staff can use the system to provide timely and accurate information about billing, shipping, and product availability and to answer other customer questions. The accounting staff thus maintains greater control over financial functions and customer service. Operating costs can be kept low because Orchids' staff have instant access to the in-

chapter outline

formation they need to ensure prompt and accurate delivery of orders. The system also helps Orchids operate without a top-heavy management structure using a sharply reduced workforce.

Orchids has returned to profitability, and its organizational and technology changes have helped it carve a place in an industry that traditionally has been dominated by much larger companies.

Sources: Gary Abramson, "From the Ashes," *CIO Magazine,* January 1, 1999; Macola Software, "Customer Success Stories: Orchids Paper Products," *http://www.macola.com/success;* and *http://www.orchidspaper.com.*

Management Challenges

Orchids Paper Products used information systems to gain a temporary market advantage over its competitors by offering its products at low cost while providing a high level of service. But something more than a single technological leap is required to sustain this competitive edge. Managers need to discover ways of maintaining a competitive edge over many years. Specifically, managers need to address the following challenges:

1. **Integration.** Although it is necessary to design different systems serving different levels and functions in the firm, more and more firms are finding advantages in integrating systems; many are pursuing enterprise resource planning (ERP). However, integrating systems for different organizational levels and functions to freely exchange information can be technologically difficult and costly. Managers need to determine what level of system integration is required and how much it is worth in dollars.

2. **Sustainability of competitive advantage.** The competitive advantages conferred by strategic systems do not necessarily last long enough to ensure long-term profits. Competitors can retaliate and copy strategic systems. Competitive advantage isn't always sustainable. Market conditions change. The business and economic environment changes. The Internet can make competitive advantage for some companies disappear very quickly (Yoffie and Cusumano, 1999). Technology and customers' expectations change. The classic strategic information systems—American Airlines' SABRE computerized reservation system, Citibank's ATM system, and Federal Express' package tracking system—benefited by being the first in their respective industries. But then rival systems emerged. Information systems alone cannot provide an enduring business advantage (Mata et al., 1995; Kettinger et al., 1994; Hopper, 1990). Systems originally intended to be strategic frequently become tools for survival, something every firm has in order to stay in business, or they may even inhibit organizations from making the strategic changes required for future success (Eardley, Avison, and Powell, 1997).

The experience of Orchids Paper Products illustrates how critical information systems have become for supporting organizational goals and for enabling firms to stay ahead of the competition. In this chapter, we show the role played by the various types of information systems in organizations. We then look at the problems firms face from competition and the ways in which information systems can provide competitive advantage at three different levels of the business.

2.1 Key System Applications in the Organization

Because there are different interests, specialties, and levels in an organization, there are different kinds of systems. No single system can provide all the information an organization needs. Figure 2-1 illustrates one way to depict the kinds of systems found in an organization. In the illustration, the organization is divided into strategic, management, knowledge, and operational levels and then is further divided into functional areas such as sales and marketing, manufacturing, finance, accounting, and human resources. Systems are built to serve these different organizational interests (Anthony, 1965).

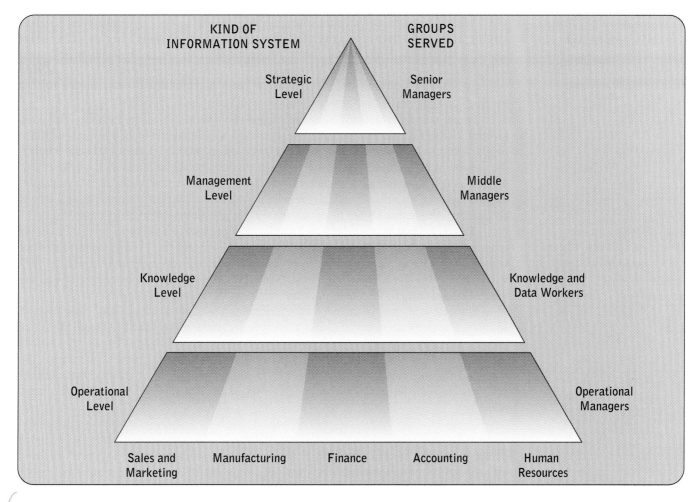

Figure 2-1 Types of information systems. Organizations and information systems can be divided into strategic, management, knowledge, and operational levels. They can be divided further into five functional areas: sales and marketing, manufacturing, finance, accounting, and human resources. Information systems serve each of these levels and functions. Strategic-level systems help senior managers with long-term planning. Management-level systems help middle managers monitor and control. Knowledge-level systems help knowledge and data workers design products, distribute information, and cope with paperwork. Operational-level systems help operational managers keep track of the firm's day-to-day activities.

Different Kinds of Systems

operational-level systems
Information systems that monitor the elementary activities and transactions of the organization.

Four main types of information systems serve different organizational levels: operational-level systems, knowledge-level systems, management-level systems, and strategic-level systems. **Operational-level systems** support operational managers by keeping track of the elementary activities and transactions of the organization, such as sales, receipts, cash deposits, payroll, credit decisions, and the flow of materials in a factory. The principal purpose of systems at this level is to answer routine questions and to track the flow of transactions through the organization. How many parts are in inventory? What happened to Mr. Williams' payment? To answer these kinds of questions, information generally must be easily available, current, and accurate. Examples of operational-level systems include a system to record bank deposits from automatic teller machines or one that tracks the number of hours worked each day by employees on a factory floor.

knowledge-level systems
Information systems that support knowledge and data workers in an organization.

Knowledge-level systems support knowledge and data workers in an organization. The purpose of knowledge-level systems is to help the business firm discover, organize, and integrate new knowledge into the business and to help the organization control the flow of paperwork. Knowledge-level systems, especially in the form of collaboration tools, workstations, and office systems, are the fastest-growing applications in business today.

management-level systems
Information systems that support the monitoring, controlling, decision-making, and administrative activities of middle managers.

Management-level systems are designed to serve the monitoring, controlling, decision-making, and administrative activities of middle managers. The principal question addressed by such systems is: Are things working well? Management-level systems typically provide periodic reports rather than instant information on operations. An example is a relocation control system that reports on the total moving, house-hunting, and home financing costs for employees in all company divisions, noting wherever actual costs exceed budgets.

Some management-level systems support nonroutine decision making (Keen and Morton, 1978). They tend to focus on less structured decisions for which information requirements are not always clear. These systems often answer "what-if" questions: What would be the impact on production schedules if we were to double sales in the month of December? What would happen to our return on investment if a factory schedule delayed for six months? Answers to these questions frequently require new data from outside the organization, as well as data from inside that cannot be drawn from existing operational-level systems.

strategic-level systems
Information systems that support the long-range planning activities of senior management.

Strategic-level systems help senior management tackle and address strategic issues and long-term trends, both in the firm and in the external environment. Their principal concern is matching changes in the external environment with existing organizational capability. What will employment levels be in five years? What are the long-term industry cost trends, and where does our firm fit in? What products should we be making in five years?

Information systems may also be differentiated by functional specialty. Major organizational functions, such as sales and marketing, manufacturing, finance, accounting, and human resources, are each served by their own information systems. In large organizations, subfunctions of each of these major functions also have their own information systems. For example, the manufacturing function might have systems for inventory management, process control, plant maintenance, computer-aided engineering, and material requirements planning.

A typical organization has operational-, management-, knowledge-, and strategic-level systems for each functional area. For example, the sales function generally has a sales system on the operational level to record daily sales figures and to process orders. A knowledge-level system designs promotional displays for the firm's products. A management-level system tracks monthly sales figures by sales territory and reports on territories where sales exceed or fall below anticipated levels. A system to forecast sales trends over a five-year period serves the strategic level.

Finally, different organizations have different information systems for the same functional areas. Because no two organizations have exactly the same objectives, structures, or interests, information systems must be custom-made to fit the unique characteristics of each. There is no such thing as a universal information system that can fit all organizations. Every organization does the job somewhat differently.

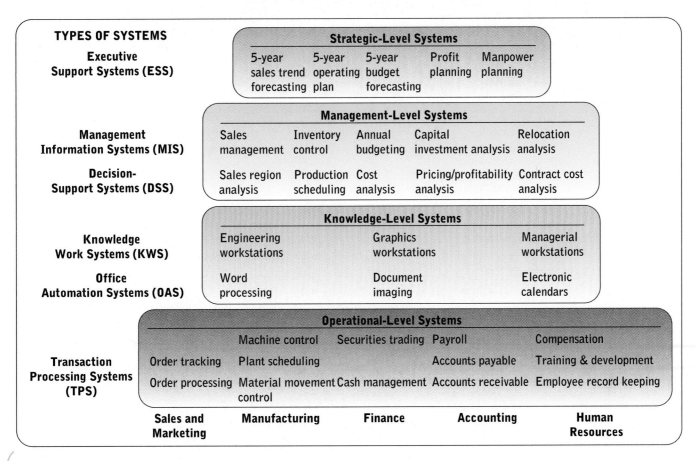

Figure 2-2 The six major types of information systems needed for the four levels of an organization. Information systems are built to serve each of the four levels of an organization. Transaction processing systems (TPS) serve the operational level of an organization. Knowledge work systems (KWS) and office automation systems (OAS) serve the knowledge level of an organization. Decision-support systems (DSS) and management information systems (MIS) serve the management level of the organization. Executive support system (ESS) serves the strategic level of an organization.

Information systems can thus be classified by functional specialty or by the organizational level they serve. Throughout this text are examples of systems supporting the various functional areas—sales systems, manufacturing systems, human resources systems, and finance and accounting systems. For professors and students requiring deeper analysis of information systems from a functional perspective, we have included additional material on the Laudon and Laudon Web site. This chapter analyzes the key applications of the organization primarily in terms of the organizational level and types of decisions they support.

Six Major Types of Systems

In this section we describe the specific categories of systems serving each organizational level and their value to the organization. Figure 2-2 shows the specific types of information systems that correspond to each organizational level. The organization has executive support systems (ESS) at the strategic level; management information systems (MIS) and decision-support systems (DSS) at the management level; knowledge work systems (KWS) and office automation systems (OAS) at the knowledge level; and transaction processing systems (TPS) at the operational level. Systems at each level in turn are specialized to serve each of the major functional areas. Thus, the typical systems found in organizations are designed to assist workers or managers at each level and in the functions of sales and marketing, manufacturing, finance, accounting, and human resources.

Table 2.1 Characteristics of Information Processing Systems

Type of System	Information Inputs	Processing	Information Outputs	Users
ESS	Aggregate data; external, internal	Graphics; simulations; interactive	Projections; responses to queries	Senior managers
DSS	Low-volume data or massive databases optimized for data analysis; analytic models and data analysis tools	Interactive; simulations, analysis	Special reports; decision analyses; responses to queries	Professionals; staff managers
MIS	Summary transaction data; high-volume data; simple models	Routine reports; simple models; low-level analysis	Summary and exception reports	Middle managers
KWS	Design specifications; knowledge base	Modeling; simulations	Models; graphics	Professionals; technical staff
OAS	Documents; schedules	Document management; scheduling; communication	Documents; schedules; mail	Clerical workers
TPS	Transactions; events	Sorting; listing; merging; updating	Detailed reports; lists; summaries	Operations personnel; supervisors

Table 2.1 summarizes the features of the six types of information systems. It should be noted that each of the different kinds of systems may have components that are used by organizational levels and groups other than their main constituencies. A secretary may find information on an MIS, or a middle manager may need to extract data from a TPS.

Transaction Processing Systems

transaction processing system (TPS) Computerized system that performs and records the daily routine transactions necessary to conduct the business; these systems serve the operational level of the organization.

Transaction processing systems (TPS) are the basic business systems that serve the operational level of the organization. A transaction processing system is a computerized system that performs and records the daily, routine transactions necessary to conduct the business. Examples are sales order entry, hotel reservation systems, payroll, employee record keeping, and shipping.

At the operational level, tasks, resources, and goals are predefined and highly structured. The decision to grant credit to a customer, for instance, is made by a lower level supervisor according to predefined criteria. All that must be determined is whether the customer meets the criteria.

Figure 2-3 depicts a payroll TPS, which is a typical accounting transaction processing system found in most firms. A payroll system keeps track of the money paid to employees. The master file is composed of discrete pieces of information (such as a name, address, or employee number) called data elements. Data are keyed into the system, updating the data elements. The elements on the master file are combined in different ways to make up reports of interest to management and government agencies or to generate paychecks sent to employees. These TPS can generate other report combinations of existing data elements.

Other typical TPS applications are identified in Figure 2-4. The figure shows the five functional categories of TPS: sales/marketing, manufacturing/production, finance/accounting, human resources, and other types of TPS that are unique to a particular industry. The UPS package tracking system described in Chapter 1 is an example of a manufacturing TPS. UPS sells package delivery services; the system keeps track of all its package shipment transactions.

All organizations have these five kinds of TPS (even if the systems are manual). Transaction processing systems are often so central to a business that a TPS failure for a few hours can spell the demise of a firm and perhaps other firms linked to it. Imagine what would happen to UPS if its package tracking system was not working! What would the airlines do without their computerized reservation systems?

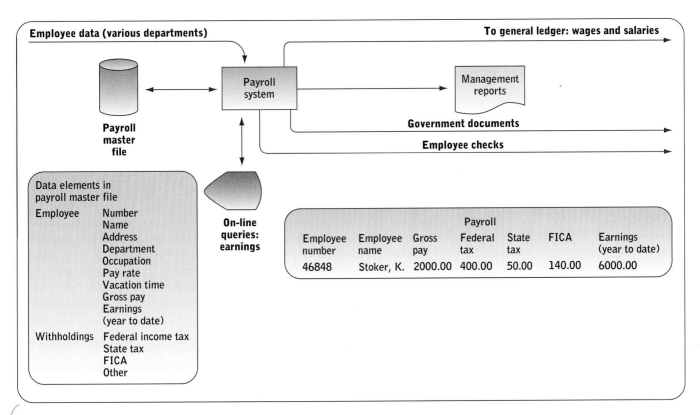

Figure 2-3 A symbolic representation for a payroll TPS.

TYPE OF TPS SYSTEM				
Sales/marketing systems	Manufacturing/production systems	Finance/accounting systems	Human resources systems	Other types (e.g., university)

	Sales/marketing systems	Manufacturing/production systems	Finance/accounting systems	Human resources systems	Other types (e.g., university)
Major functions of system	Sales management	Scheduling	Budgeting	Personnel records	Admissions
	Market research	Purchasing	General ledger	Benefits	Grade records
	Promotion	Shipping/receiving	Billing	Compensation	Course records
	Pricing	Engineering	Cost accounting	Labor relations	Alumni
	New products	Operations		Training	
Major application systems	Sales order information system	Materials resource planning systems	General ledger	Payroll	Registration system
	Market research system	Purchase order control systems	Accounts receivable/payable	Employee records	Student transcript system
	Pricing system	Engineering systems	Budgeting	Benefit systems	Curriculum class control systems
		Quality control systems	Funds management systems	Career path systems	Alumni benefactor system

Figure 2-4 Typical applications of TPS. There are five functional categories of TPS: sales/marketing, manufacturing/production, finance/accounting, human resources, and other types of systems specific to a particular industry. TPS support most business functions in most organizations. Within each of these major functions are subfunctions. For each of these subfunctions (e.g., sales management) there is a major application system.

Managers need TPS to monitor the status of internal operations and the firm's relations with the external environment. Transaction processing systems are also major producers of information for the other types of systems. (For example, the payroll system illustrated in Figure 2-3 along with other accounting TPS supply data to the company's general ledger system, which is responsible for maintaining records of the firm's income and expenses and for producing reports such as income statements and balance sheets.)

Knowledge Work and Office Automation Systems

Both **knowledge work systems (KWS)** and **office automation systems (OAS)** serve the information needs at the knowledge level of the organization. Knowledge work systems aid knowledge workers, whereas office automation systems primarily aid data workers (although they are also used extensively by knowledge workers).

In general, *knowledge workers* are people who hold formal university degrees and who are often members of a recognized profession, such as engineers, doctors, lawyers, and scientists. Their jobs consist primarily of creating new information and knowledge. A knowledge work system (KWS), such as a scientific or engineering design workstation, promotes the creation of new knowledge and ensures that new knowledge and technical expertise are properly integrated into the business. One example of a KWS is the system used by the Sable Offshore Energy Project described in the Window on Technology.

Data workers typically have less formal, advanced educational degrees and tend to process rather than create information. They consist primarily of secretaries, accountants, filing clerks, or managers whose jobs are principally to use, manipulate, or disseminate information. An office automation system (OAS) is an information technology application designed to increase the productivity of data workers in the office by supporting the coordinating and communicating activities of the typical office. Office automation systems coordinate diverse information workers, geographic units, and functional areas: The systems communicate with customers, suppliers, and other organizations outside the firm and serve as a clearinghouse for information and knowledge flows.

Typical office automation systems handle and manage documents (through word processing, desktop publishing, and digital filing), scheduling (through electronic calendars), and communication (through electronic mail, voice mail, or videoconferencing). **Word processing** refers to the software and hardware that creates, edits, formats, stores, and prints documents (see Chapter 7). Word processing systems represent the single most common application of information technology to office work, in part because producing documents is what offices are all about. **Desktop publishing** produces professional publishing-quality documents by combining output from word processing software with design elements, graphics, and special layout features.

Document imaging systems are another widely used knowledge application. **Document imaging systems** convert documents and images into digital form so that they can be stored and accessed by the computer. Figure 2-5 illustrates the imaging system used by the United Services Automobile Association, the fifth-largest provider of auto insurance and the fourth-largest provider of homeowner insurance in the United States. USAA receives more than 100,000 letters and mails more than 250,000 items daily. USAA has developed the largest imaging system in the world, storing 1.5 billion pages. All incoming mail received each day by the policy department is scanned and stored on optical disk. The original documents are thrown away. USAA's major regional offices across the country are hooked up to its imaging network. The network consists of image scanners, optical storage units, a mainframe computer, workstations, and a local area network (LAN) to link service representatives' workstations and the scanner workstations located in the firm's mailroom. Service representatives can retrieve a client's file on-line and view documents from desktop computers. About 10,000 people use the network. Users believe that the imaging system reduces the amount of time their work would take with a paper-based system by one-third, saving paper and storage costs. Customer service has improved because electronic documents can be accessed more rapidly (Korzeniowski, 1997; Lasher, Ives, and Jarvenpaa, 1991).

knowledge work system (KWS) Information system that aids knowledge workers in the creation and integration of new knowledge in the organization.

office automation system (OAS) Computer system, such as word processing, electronic mail system, and scheduling system, that is designed to increase the productivity of data workers in the office.

word processing Office automation technology that facilitates the creation of documents through computerized text editing, formatting, storing, and printing.

desktop publishing Technology that produces professional-quality documents combining output from word processors with design, graphics, and special layout features.

document imaging systems Systems that convert documents and images into digital form so that they can be stored and accessed by the computer.

Canadian Oil Companies Make Data Flow

As more of the world's natural gas and oil energy reserves have been discovered and exploited, it has become increasingly expensive and risky to find new sources of energy. Even the biggest oil companies are reluctant to explore for oil and gas alone. So industry giants are teaming up on natural resource exploration projects as a way of sharing the risks and expenses.

The Sable Offshore Energy Project in the North Atlantic off the coast of Nova Scotia is a leading example. Four major oil companies—Mobil Oil Canada Properties Ltd., Imperial Oil Resources Ltd., Nova Scotia Resources Ltd., and Shell Canada Ltd.—are working together to develop six reserves with an estimated 18 trillion cubic feet of recoverable natural gas. The companies formed a joint technical team to manage the overall exploration program. By working together these energy companies can maximize joint effectiveness and reduce exploration risks.

The project will take several years to produce results. In addition to the four main partners, dozens of subcontractors such as drilling companies and platform fabrication companies will be involved, and engineering project management companies will be enlisted. To keep the entire project on track, the activities of all these companies must be closely coordinated, and information such as engineering, production, and cost data or 3-D geological drawings must flow between them.

Three-dimensional seismic surveys of the Scotian shelf began in the summer of 1998 and will cost approximately $15 million Canadian for that year alone. Data for these surveys are generated when ships bounce sound signals off underground formations and computers translate the responses. Geologists can use the results to determine the location of rock, sand, water, and oil.

The data for the project are scattered in different computer systems in London, England; Calgary, Alberta; and Halifax, Nova Scotia and maintained by the various partners. To make the data available anytime anywhere in the project, regardless of what type of computer they are stored on, the project is using Web technology. A designated computer serves as a central warehouse for data generated by the project partners' computer systems and translates these data into a form that can be accessed using standard off-the-shelf software for obtaining information on the Web. About 200 people use the system.

There are many benefits to linking partners' data through the Web. Before turning to Web technology, the engineering management companies for the Sable project stored their data in separate computers. Maintaining the data this way could be very costly, requiring many people to support each computer system. (A similar project for the four oil companies a few years earlier required 47 information systems specialists to support a separate computer system.) Data that could provide a complete picture of a prospective natural gas site might also be difficult to assemble if it were stored in many different computer systems. Productivity has risen because all information is immediately available to everyone on the project.

To Think About: How does using Web technology benefit these businesses?

Sources: Julia King, "To Find Fuel, First Make Data Flow," *Computerworld,* January 4, 1999; and Shell Canada Ltd., "Shell, Mobil and Imperial Oil Sign Exploration Agreement on Scotian Shelf," May 13, 1998.

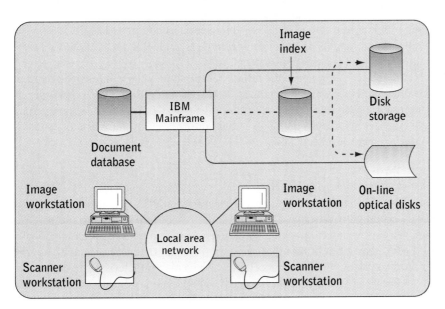

Figure 2-5 United Services Automobile Association's (USAA) imaging network. Scanners enter mail received by USAA's policy department into the imaging system, which stores and distributes the digitally processed image of the document electronically. Service representatives have immediate on-line access to clients' data.

Computer-aided design (CAD) systems eliminate many manual steps in design and production by performing much of the design work on the computer.

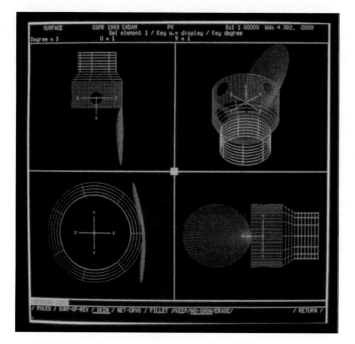

Management Information Systems

Management information systems (MIS) serve the management level of the organization, providing managers with reports and, in some cases, with on-line access to the organization's current performance and historical records. Typically, these systems are oriented almost exclusively to internal, not environmental or external, events. MIS primarily serve the functions of planning, controlling, and decision making at the management level. Generally, these systems are dependent on underlying transaction processing systems for their data.

MIS summarize and report on the basic operations of the company. The basic transaction data from TPS are compressed and are usually presented in long reports that are produced on a regular schedule. Figure 2-6 shows how a typical MIS transforms transaction-level data from inventory, production, and accounting into MIS files that are used to provide managers with reports. Figure 2-7 shows a sample report from this system.

MIS usually serve managers interested in weekly, monthly, and yearly results—not day-to-day activities—and generally address structured questions that are known well in advance. These systems are generally not flexible and have little analytical capability. Most of these systems use simple routines such as summaries and comparisons, as opposed to sophisticated mathematical models or statistical techniques. Table 2.2 describes the characteristics of typical management information systems.

Some researchers use the term *MIS* to include all the information systems that support the functional areas of the organization (Davis and Olson, 1985). However, in this book we prefer to use *computer-based information system (CBIS)* as the umbrella *term* for all information systems and to consider management information systems as those specifically dedicated to management-level functions.

Decision-Support Systems

Decision-support systems (DSS) also serve the management level of the organization. DSS help managers make decisions that are semi-structured, unique, or rapidly changing, and not easily specified in advance. DSS have to be responsive enough to run several times a day in order to correspond to changing conditions. Although DSS use internal information from TPS and MIS, they often bring in information from external sources, such as current stock prices or product prices of competitors. Table 2.3 reveals characteristics of contemporary DSS.

Clearly, by design, DSS have more analytical power than other systems; they are built explicitly with a variety of models to analyze data or they condense large amounts of data into a form in which they can be analyzed by decision-makers. DSS are designed so that users can

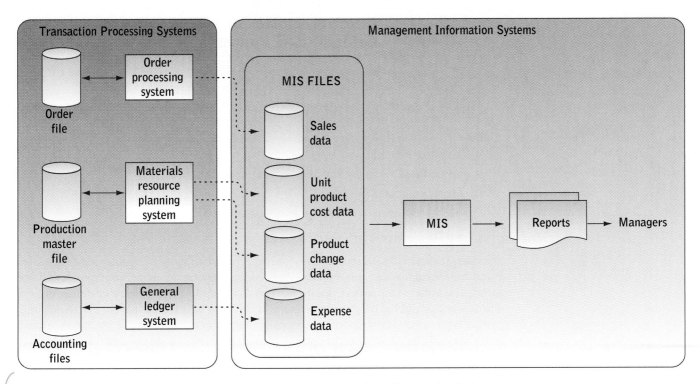

Figure 2-6 How management information systems obtain their data from the organization's TPS. In the system illustrated by this diagram, three TPS supply summarized transaction data at the end of the time period to the MIS reporting system. Managers gain access to the organizational data through the MIS, which provides them with the appropriate reports.

work with them directly; these systems explicitly include user-friendly software. DSS are interactive; the user can change assumptions, ask new questions, and include new data.

An interesting, small, but powerful DSS is the voyage-estimating system of a subsidiary of a large American metals company that exists primarily to carry bulk cargoes of coal, oil, ores, and finished products for its parent company. The firm owns some vessels, charters others, and bids for shipping contracts in the open market to carry general cargo. A voyage-estimating system calculates financial and technical voyage details. Financial calculations include ship/time costs (fuel, labor, capital), freight rates for various types of cargo, and port

Figure 2-7 A sample report that might be produced by the MIS in Figure 2-6.

Consolidated Consumer Products Corporation
Sales by Product and Sales Region: 1999

PRODUCT CODE	PRODUCT DESCRIPTION	SALES REGION	ACTUAL SALES	PLANNED	ACTUAL VS. PLANNED
4469	Carpet Cleaner	Northeast	4,066,700	4,800,000	0.85
		South	3,778,112	3,750,000	1.01
		Midwest	4,867,001	4,600,000	1.06
		West	4,003,440	4,400,000	0.91
	TOTAL		16,715,253	17,550,000	0.95
5674	Room Freshener	Northeast	3,676,700	3,900,000	0.94
		South	5,608,112	4,700,000	1.19
		Midwest	4,711,001	4,200,000	1.12
		West	4,563,440	4,900,000	0.93
	TOTAL		18,559,253	17,700,000	1.05

Table 2.2 Characteristics of Management Information Systems

1. MIS support structured decisions at the operational and management control levels. However, they are also useful for planning purposes of senior management staff.

2. MIS are generally reporting and control oriented. They are designed to report on existing operations and therefore to help provide day-to-day control of operations.

3. MIS rely on existing corporate data and data flows.

4. MIS have little analytical capability.

5. MIS generally aid in decision making using past and present data.

6. MIS are relatively inflexible.

7. MIS have an internal rather than an external orientation.

expenses. Technical details include a myriad of factors such as ship cargo capacity, speed, port distances, fuel and water consumption, and loading patterns (location of cargo for different ports). The system can answer questions such as the following: Given a customer delivery schedule and an offered freight rate, which vessel should be assigned at what rate to maximize profits? What is the ideal speed at which a particular vessel can optimize its profit and still meet its delivery schedule? What is the optimal loading pattern for a ship bound for the U.S. West Coast from Malaysia? Figure 2-8 illustrates the DSS built for this company. The system operates on a powerful desktop PC, providing a system of menus that makes it easy for users to enter data or obtain information. We will describe other types of DSS in Chapter 15.

Executive Support Systems

executive support system (ESS) Information system at the strategic level of an organization designed to address unstructured decision making through advanced graphics and communications.

Senior managers use a category of information systems called **executive support systems (ESS)** to make decisions. ESS serve the strategic level of the organization. ESS address unstructured decisions and create a generalized computing and communications environment rather than providing any fixed application or specific capability. ESS are designed to incorporate data about external events such as new tax laws or competitors, but they also draw summarized information from internal MIS and DSS. These systems filter, compress, and track critical data, emphasizing the reduction of time and effort required to obtain information useful to executives. ESS employ the most advanced graphics software and can deliver graphs and data from many sources immediately to a senior executive's office or to a boardroom.

Unlike the other types of information systems, ESS are not designed primarily to solve specific problems. Instead, ESS provide a generalized computing and communications capacity that can be applied to a changing array of problems. Whereas, DSS are designed to be highly analytical, ESS tend to make less use of analytical models.

Questions that an ESS can assist in answering include the following: What business should we be in? What are the competitors doing? What new acquisitions would protect us from cyclical business swings? Which units should we sell to raise cash for acquisitions (Rockart and Treacy, 1982)? Figure 2-9 illustrates a model of an ESS. It consists of workstations with menus, interactive graphics, and communications capabilities that can access historical and competitive data from internal corporate systems and external databases such as

Table 2.3 Characteristics of Decision-Support Systems

1. DSS offer users flexibility, adaptability, and a quick response.

2. DSS operate with little or no assistance from professional programmers.

3. DSS provide support for decisions and problems whose solutions cannot be specified in advance.

4. DSS use sophisticated data analysis and modeling tools.

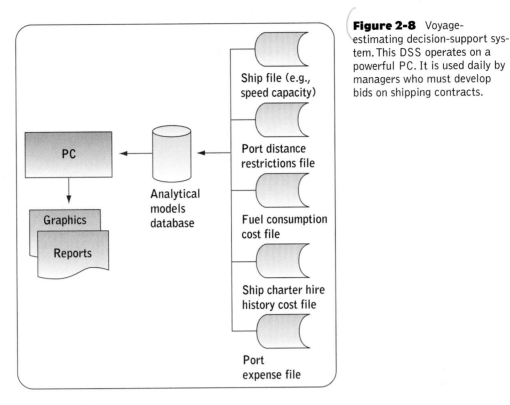

Figure 2-8 Voyage-estimating decision-support system. This DSS operates on a powerful PC. It is used daily by managers who must develop bids on shipping contracts.

Dow Jones News/Retrieval or the Gallup Poll. Because ESS are designed to be used by senior managers who often have little, if any, direct contact or experience with computer-based information systems, they incorporate easy-to-use graphic interfaces. More details on leading-edge applications of both DSS and ESS can be found in Chapter 15.

Relationship of Systems to One Another: Integration

Figure 2-10 illustrates how the various types of systems in the organization are related to one another. A TPS is typically a major source of data for other systems, whereas the ESS is primarily a recipient of data from lower level systems. The other types of systems may exchange data among one another as well. Data may also be exchanged among systems serving different

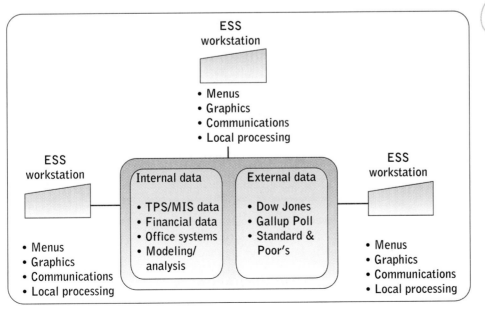

Figure 2-9 Model of a typical executive support system. This system pools data from diverse internal and external sources and makes them available to executives in an easy-to-use form.

Figure 2-10

Interrelationships among systems. The various types of systems in the organization have interdependencies. TPS are a major producer of information that is required by the other systems which, in turn, produce information for other systems. These different types of systems are only loosely coupled in most organizations.

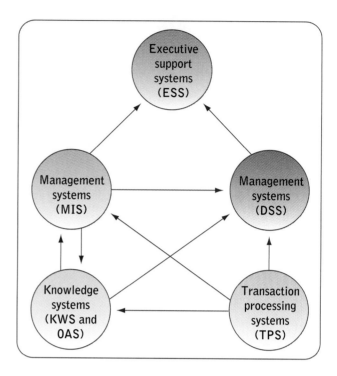

functional areas. For example, an order captured by a sales system may be transmitted to a manufacturing system as a transaction for producing or delivering the product specified in the order.

But how much can or should these systems be integrated? This is a difficult question to answer. It is definitely advantageous to have some measure of integration so that information can flow easily among different parts of the organization. But integration costs money, and integrating many different systems is extremely time consuming and complex. Each organization must weigh its needs for integrating systems against the difficulties of mounting a large-scale systems integration effort. There is no one "right level" of integration or centralization (Allen and Boynton, 1991; King, 1984). Chapter 18 treats this issue in greater detail.

2.2 Information Systems and Business Strategy

Each of the major types of information systems described previously is valuable for helping organizations solve an important problem. In the past few decades, some of these systems have become especially critical to firms' long-term prosperity and survival. Such systems, which are powerful tools for staying ahead of the competition, are called *strategic information systems*.

What Is a Strategic Information System?

strategic information systems Computer systems at any level of an organization that change the goals, processes, products, services, or environmental relationships to help the organization gain a competitive advantage.

Strategic information systems change the goals, operations, products, services, or environmental relationships of organizations to help them gain an edge over competitors. Systems that have these effects may even change the business of organizations. For instance, State Street Bank and Trust Co. of Boston transformed its core business from traditional banking services, such as customer checking and savings accounts and loans, to electronic record keeping and financial information services, providing data processing services for securities and mutual funds, and services for pension funds to monitor their money managers (Rebello, 1995).

Strategic information systems should be distinguished from strategic-level systems for senior managers that focus on long-term, decision-making problems. Strategic information systems can be used at all levels of the organization and are more far-reaching and deep-rooted than the other kinds of systems we have described. Strategic information systems profoundly alter the way a firm conducts its business or the very business of the firm itself. As we will see, organizations may need to change their internal operations and relationships with customers and suppliers in order to take advantage of new information systems technology.

	Strategies	Models	IT Techniques
Table 2.4	**Strategy Levels and IT**		

	Strategies	**Models**	**IT Techniques**
Industry	Cooperation vs. competition	Competitive forces model	Electronic transactions
	Licensing	Network economics	Communication networks
	Standards		Interorganizational systems
			Information partnerships
Firm	Synergy	Core competency	Knowledge systems
	Core competencies		Organization-wide systems
Business	Low cost	Value chain analysis	Datamining
	Differentiation		IT-based products/services
	Scope		Interorganizational systems
			Supply chain management
			Efficient customer response

There is generally no single all-encompassing strategic system, but instead there are a number of systems operating at different levels of strategy—the business, the firm, and the industry level (see Table 2.4). For each level of business strategy, there are strategic uses of systems. And for each level of business strategy, there is an appropriate model used for analysis.

Business-Level Strategy and the Value Chain Model

At the business level of strategy, the key question is "How can we compete effectively in this particular market?" The market might be lightbulbs, utility vehicles, or cable television. The most common generic strategies at this level are (1) to become the low-cost producer, (2) to differentiate your product or service, and/or (3) to change the scope of competition by either enlarging the market to include global markets or narrowing the market by focusing on small niches not well served by your competitors. Moving toward global markets, the firm can generate economies of scale. Moving toward niche markets, the firm can generate high-margin products and services available nowhere else.

Leveraging Technology in the Value Chain

At the business level the most common analytic tool is value chain analysis. The **value chain model** highlights specific activities in the business where competitive strategies can be best applied (Porter, 1985) and where information systems are most likely to have a strategic impact. The value chain model identifies specific, critical leverage points where a firm can use information technology most effectively to enhance its competitive position. Exactly where can it obtain the greatest benefit from strategic information systems—what specific activities can be used to create new products and services, enhance market penetration, lock in customers and suppliers, and lower operational costs? This model views the firm as a series or "chain" of basic activities that add a margin of value to a firm's products or services. These activities can be categorized as either primary activities or support activities.

Primary activities are most directly related to the production and distribution of the firm's products and services that create value for the customer. Primary activities include inbound logistics, operations, outbound logistics, sales and marketing, and service. Inbound logistics include receiving and storing materials for distribution to production. Operations transforms inputs into finished products. Outbound logistics entail storing and distributing products. Marketing and sales includes promoting and selling the firm's products. The service activity includes maintenance and repair of the firm's goods and services. **Support activities** make the delivery of the primary activities possible and consist of organization infrastructure (administration and management), human resources (employee recruiting, hiring, and training), technology (improving products and the production process), and procurement (purchasing input).

value chain model Model that highlights the primary or support activities that add a margin of value to a firm's products or services where information systems can best be applied to achieve a competitive advantage.

primary activities Activities most directly related to the production and distribution of a firm's products or services.

support activities Activities that make the delivery of the primary activities of a firm possible; consist of the organization's infrastructure, human resources, technology, and procurement.

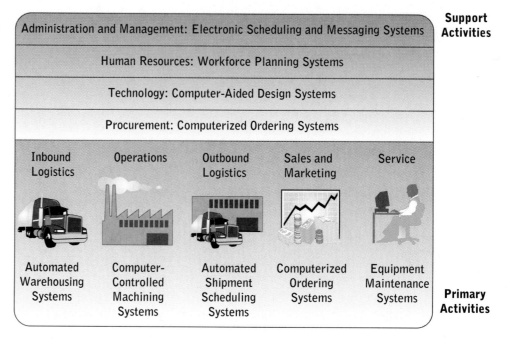

Figure 2-11 Activities of the value chain. Various examples of strategic information systems for the primary and support activities of a firm that would add a margin of value to a firm's products or services.

Organizations have competitive advantage when they provide more value to their customers or when they provide the same value to customers at a lower price. An information system could have a strategic impact if it helped the firm provide products or services at a lower cost than competitors or if it provided products and services at the same cost as competitors but with greater value. Orchids Paper Products' system, described earlier, creates value by both lowering operational costs and providing higher quality service to customers. The value activities that add the most value to products and services depend on the features of each particular firm. Businesses should try to develop strategic information systems for the value activities that add the most value to their particular firm. Wal-Mart, for example, found it could achieve competitive advantage by focusing on logistics. Figure 2-11 illustrates the activities of the value chain, showing examples of strategic information systems that could be developed to make each of the value activities more cost effective.

For instance, a firm could save money in the inbound logistics activity if suppliers made daily deliveries of goods to the factory, thereby lowering the costs of warehousing and inventory. A computer-aided design system might support the technology activity, helping a firm to reduce costs and perhaps to design more high-quality products than the competition produces. Such systems would be more likely to have strategic impact in a manufacturing firm, whereas an electronic scheduling and messaging system or office automation technology would more likely have strategic value in a law firm or consulting firm.

A strategic analysis might identify the sales and marketing activity as an area where information systems would provide the greatest productivity boost. The analysis might recommend a system similar to those used by banks or consumer goods manufacturers for bringing together and analyzing data (as described in this chapter's Window on Organizations and Window on Management) to reduce marketing costs by targeting marketing campaigns more efficiently. The system might also provide information that lets the firm develop products more finely attuned to its target market. Many different projects, or a series of linked systems, may be required to create a strategic advantage.

The role of information technology at the business level is to help the firm reduce costs, differentiate product, and serve new markets. Here are some leading examples of how firms use IT to lower costs, differentiate, and change the scope of competition.

Table 2.5	New Products and Services Based on Information Technology

New Product or Service*	Underlying Technology
On-line banking	Private communication networks; Internet
Cash management accounts	Corporate-wide customer account systems
Derivative investments (options, futures, complex variations)	Management and trader workstations; mainframe transaction systems
Global and national airline, hotel, and auto reservation systems	Worldwide telecommunication–based reservation systems
FedEx and other overnight package delivery	Global package tracking systems
Mail-order retailing	Corporate customer databases
Voice mail systems (call services)	Company- and network-wide digital communication systems
Automatic teller machines	Customer account systems
Microcustomized clothing	Computer-aided design and manufacturing (CAD/CAM) systems

*Many products and services that we take for granted are based on information technology and, of course, the creative insight of managers who dreamed up these products and services.

Information System Products and Services

Firms can use information systems to create unique new products and services that can be easily distinguished from those of competitors. Strategic information systems for **product differentiation** can prevent the competition from responding in kind so that firms with these differentiated products and services no longer have to compete on the basis of cost. Table 2.5 lists some of the new products and services that have been created with information technology.

Many of these information technology–based products and services have been created by financial institutions. Citibank developed automatic teller machines (ATMs) and bank debit cards in 1977. Seeking to tap the largest retail depository market in the United States, Citibank installed its ATMs throughout the New York metropolitan area, everywhere a depositor might find the time to use them to deposit or withdraw money. As a leader in this area, Citibank became at one time the largest bank in the United States. Citibank ATMs were so successful that Citibank's competitors were forced to counterstrike with their own ATM systems.

Citibank, Wells Fargo Bank, and others have continued to innovate by providing on-line electronic banking services so that customers can do most of their banking transactions with home computers linked to proprietary networks. Recently they have offered customers the option of managing their accounts using the World Wide Web. Madrid-based Banco Santander offers a similar service called Banca Supernet. Clients accessing the bank's Web site are presented with a list of their existing accounts and the current balance of each. They can trace the activities in each of these accounts during the past 12 months. Some companies such as Security First Network Bank in Atlanta have used the Web to set up "virtual banks" offering a full array of banking services without any physical branches. (Customers mail in their deposits.)

In the retail world, manufacturers are starting to use information systems to create products and services that are custom-tailored to fit the precise specifications of individual customers. Dell Computer Corporation sells directly to customers using build-to-order manufacturing. Individuals, businesses, and government agencies can buy computers directly from Dell customized with exactly the features and components they need. They can place their orders directly using a toll-free telephone number or Dell's Web site. Once Dell receives the order at the factory the computer is assembled based on the configuration specified by the customer.

product differentiation
Competitive strategy for creating brand loyalty by developing new and unique products and services that are not easily duplicated by competitors.

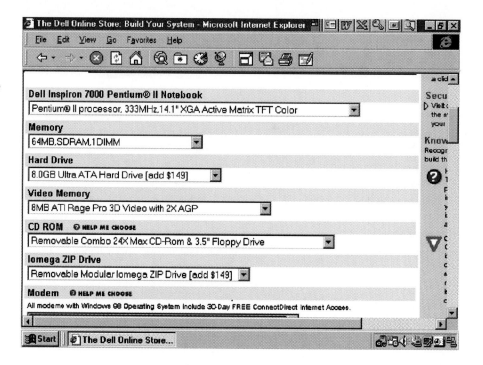

At Dell Computer Corporation's Web site, customers can select the options they want and order their computer custom-built to these specifications. Dell's build-to-order system is a major source of competitive advantage.

Chapter 1 describes other instances in which information technology is creating customized products and services while retaining the cost efficiencies of mass-production techniques.

Systems to Focus on Market Niche

Businesses can create new market niches by identifying a specific target for a product or service that it can serve in a superior manner. Through **focused differentiation,** the firm can provide a specialized product or service for this narrow target market better than competitors.

An information system can give companies a competitive advantage by producing data for finely tuned sales and marketing techniques. Such systems treat existing information as a resource that can be "mined" by the organization to increase profitability and market penetration. Information systems enable companies to finely analyze customer buying patterns, tastes, and preferences so that they efficiently pitch advertising and marketing campaigns to smaller and smaller target markets.

Sophisticated **datamining** software tools find patterns in large pools of data and infer rules from them. These patterns and rules can be used to guide decision making and forecast the effect of those decisions. For example, mining data about purchases at supermarkets might reveal that when potato chips are purchased, soda is also purchased 65 percent of the time. When there is a promotion, soda is purchased 85 percent of the time people purchase potato chips. This information could help firms design better sales promotions or product displays. Table 2.6 describes the various marketing techniques that can be supported by datamining. More detail on datamining can be found in Chapter 15.

Datamining can also be used to locate individual customers with specific interests or determine the interests of a specific group of customers. For example, American Express continually mines a gigantic pool of computerized data on its 30 million credit card holders to create highly personalized marketing campaigns. If, for example, a customer purchases a dress at Saks Fifth Avenue department store, American Express might include in her next bill an offer of a discount on a pair of shoes purchased at the same store and charged on her American Express card. The two goals are to increase the customer's use of the American Express card and to expand the presence of American Express at Saks. A cardholder residing in London, England, who recently took a British Airways flight to Paris might find an offer in a newsletter for a special discounted "getaway" weekend to New York.

focused differentiation
Competitive strategy for developing new market niches for specialized products or services where a business can compete in the target area better than its competitors.

datamining Analysis of large pools of data to find patterns and rules that can be used to guide decision making and predict future behavior.

Table 2.6 **Applications of Datamining**

Identifying individuals or organizations most likely to respond to a direct mailing.

Determining which products or services are commonly purchased together, such as beer and cigarettes.

Predicting which customers are likely to switch to competitors.

Identifying which transactions are likely to be fraudulent.

Identifying common characteristics of customers who purchase the same product.

Predicting what each visitor to a Web site is most interested in seeing.

This approach, which uses personal or individualized messages based on likely individual preferences, is known as one-to-one marketing. It contrasts with earlier reliance on mass marketing in which the same message is directed at virtually everyone. American Express's one-to-one marketing system is capable of supporting hundreds of millions of different promotions.

The data come from a range of sources—credit card transactions, demographic data, and purchase data from checkout counter scanners at supermarkets and retail stores. Some firms are starting to extract and analyze information provided when people access and interact with World Wide Web sites. For example, Stein Roe Investors, a mutual fund company, has a Web site describing its funds and services, which includes software and hardware that capture and analyze data generated when people visit the site. They can use these data to create and manage profiles of Web site visitors and to target individuals and common interest groups with content, advertising, and incentives. Chapter 10 provides more detail on how the Web can be used for this purpose. Companies collect some of these data internally and purchase some from other organizations. By carefully analyzing people's past purchasing patterns, companies can develop a more precise picture of their purchasing interests, form relationships with those customers, and provide them with more personalized products and services. The level of fine-grained customization provided by these datamining systems parallels that for custom manufacturing described in Chapter 1.

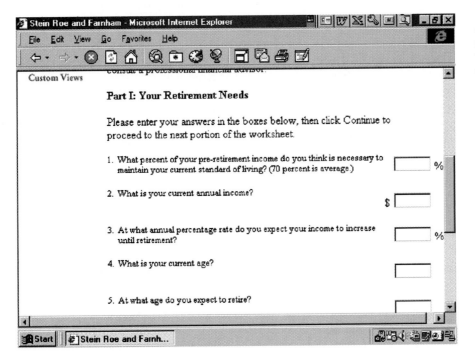

Stein Roe Investors uses data generated by visitors to its Web site to develop profiles that can target advertising more precisely to potential customers. People who express interest in retirement planning might be sent messages about Stein Roe retirement accounts.

Mining for Profitable Customers

Although companies today are vying to provide superior customer service, many can no longer afford to treat all customers as equals. Not all customers are profitable, and the principle that 20 percent of a company's customers tend to generate 80 percent of its profit is often invoked. The ratio varies by industry. For instance, the top 6 percent of cola drinkers in the United Kingdom consume 60 percent of all colas sold there. In the car rental industry, the top 0.5 percent of customers rent 25 percent of cars. According to Market Line Associates, an Atlanta bank consulting firm, the top 20 percent of bank customers can generate up to 150 percent of overall profit, while the bottom 20 percent can cause banks to lose 50 percent of their bottom line.

For banks, the typical "bad" customer keeps less than $1000 in his or her account, visits branches frequently, and calls often to inquire about account balances. The most profitable customers keep at least several thousand dollars in their accounts, use bank tellers less than once a month, and rarely call. Each profitable customer produces more than $1000 in annual revenue for the bank, whereas the worst customers can cost the bank up to $500 each year.

To find out who their most profitable customers are, banks and other industries are using powerful computer systems that mine their vast customer databases. These systems can examine the transactions of each customer and determine that customer's profitability, which helps companies target their best customers for pampering. For example, First Union Corporation uses an application called Einstein that ranks customers based on account balance, account activity, number of visits to branches, and other variables. First Union estimates that the system will produce at least $100 million in additional revenue each year, half of which will come from extra fees for services charged to unprofitable customers. The other half will come from retaining profitable customers who receive special pampering. Along with First Union, half of all large banks with over $1 billion in deposits are using the results of their customer data analyses to make customer decisions.

Canadian Imperial Bank of Commerce (CIBC) recently started using a new customer profitability system to help determine the profitability of individual customers and the needs and behaviors of customers who generated most of its revenue. The system can produce a monthly profit-and-loss statement for each of CIBC's 6 million customers. The bank uses this information to segment its customers and offer sales and services appropriate for each segment and to determine how to maximize its investment in scarce marketing resources.

To Think About: How can datamining change the way organizations conduct their business. What benefits does datamining provide? What problems might it create?

Sources: Rick Brooks, "Alienating Customers Isn't Always a Bad Idea, Many Firms Discover," The Wall Street Journal, January 7, 1999; John Dykeman, "Do You Know Who Your Best Customers Are?" Beyond Computing, March 1999; and Don Peppers and Martha Rogers, "Handshake: Customer Value," CIO Magazine, September 15, 1998.

The cost of acquiring a new customer has been estimated to be five times that of retaining an existing customer. By carefully examining transactions of customer purchases and activities, firms can identify profitable customers and win more of their business. Likewise, companies can use these data to identify nonprofitable customers (Clemons and Weber, 1994). The Window on Organizations shows how banks and other companies are using datamining for this purpose.

Datamining is both a powerful and profitable tool, but it poses challenges to the protection of individual privacy. Datamining technology can combine information from many diverse sources to create a detailed "data image" about each of us—our income, a record of our purchases, our driving habits, our hobbies, our families, and our political interests. Many critics wonder whether companies should be allowed to collect such detailed information about individuals. We explore the privacy dimensions of datamining further in Chapter 5.

Supply Chain Management and Efficient Customer Response Systems

Inventory is just dead weight on a firm. When goods sit in warehouses, or when staff members are underutilized, the firm must pay financial costs without receiving any revenues. Therefore, many firms attempt to use IT to eliminate or greatly reduce inventory.

By keeping prices low and shelves well stocked, Wal-Mart has become the leading retail business in the United States. Wal-Mart uses a legendary inventory replenishment system triggered by point-of-sale purchases that is considered the best in the industry. The "continuous replenishment system" sends orders for new merchandise directly to suppliers as soon as consumers pay for their purchases at the cash register. Point-of-sale terminals

Wal-Mart's continuous inventory replenishment system uses sales data captured at the checkout counter to transmit orders to restock merchandise directly to its suppliers. The system enables Wal-Mart to keep costs low while fine-tuning its merchandise to meet customer demands.

record the bar code of each item passing the checkout counter and send a purchase transaction directly to a central computer at Wal-Mart headquarters. The computer collects the orders from all Wal-Mart stores and transmits them to suppliers. Suppliers can also access Wal-Mart's sales and inventory data using Web technology. Because the system can replenish inventory with lightning speed, Wal-Mart does not need to spend much money on maintaining large inventories of goods in its own warehouses. The system also allows Wal-Mart to adjust purchases of store items to meet customer demands. Competitors such as Sears spend nearly 30 percent of each dollar in sales to pay for overhead (that is, expenses for salaries, advertising, warehousing, and building upkeep). Kmart spends 21 percent of sales on overhead. But by using systems to keep operating costs low, Wal-Mart pays only 15 percent of sales revenue for overhead.

Wal-Mart's continuous replenishment system is an example of efficient supply chain management. **Supply chain management** integrates the supplier, distributor, and customer logistics requirements into one cohesive process. The **supply chain** is a collection of physical entities such as manufacturing plants, distribution centers, conveyances, retail outlets, people, and information, which are linked through processes such as procurement or logistics, to supply goods or services from source through consumption. Goods or services start out as raw materials and move through the company's logistics and production system until they reach customers. To manage the supply chain, a company tries to eliminate delays and cut the amount of resources tied up along the way. This can be accomplished by streamlining the company's internal operations or by reducing inventory costs by asking suppliers to put off delivery of goods—and their payments—until the moment they are needed. Information systems make efficient supply chain management possible by integrating demand planning, forecasting, materials requisition, order processing, inventory allocation, order fulfillment, transportation services, receiving, invoicing, and payment. Enterprise resource planning systems, which have focused on internal business processes, can be extended outside the firm to increase coordination with supply chain partners. Supply chain management systems can not only lower inventory costs, but they can also deliver the product or service more rapidly to the customer.

Supply chain management can be used to create efficient customer response systems that respond to customer demands more efficiently. The convenience and ease of using these information systems raise **switching costs** (the cost of switching from one product to a competing product) which discourages customers from going to competitors.

supply chain management Integration of supplier, distributor, and customer logistics requirements into one cohesive process.

supply chain A collection of physical entities, such as manufacturing plants, distribution centers, conveyances, retail outlets, people, and information, which are linked together into processes supplying goods or services from source through consumption.

switching costs The expense a customer or company incurs in lost time and expenditure of resources when changing from one supplier or system to a competing supplier or system.

Baxter Healthcare International's "stockless inventory" and ordering system uses supply chain management to create an efficient customer response system. Participating hospitals become unwilling to switch to another supplier because of the system's convenience and low cost. Baxter supplies nearly two-thirds of all products used by U.S. hospitals. It uses an information system originally developed by American Hospital Supply Corporation (which Baxter acquired in 1985) to become a full-line supplier for hospitals—a one-stop source for all hospital needs. This effort requires an inventory of more than 120,000 items. Maintaining a huge inventory is very costly. However, it is also costly *not* to have items in stock, because hospitals switch to competitors.

Terminals tied to Baxter's own computers are installed in hospitals. When hospitals want to place an order, they do not need to call a salesperson or send a purchase order—they simply use a Baxter computer terminal on-site to order from the full Baxter supply catalog. The system generates shipping, billing, invoicing, and inventory information, and the hospital terminals provide customers with an estimated delivery date. With more than 80 distribution centers in the United States, Baxter can make daily deliveries of its products, often within hours of receiving an order.

This system is similar to the just-in-time delivery systems developed in Japan and now being used in the American automobile industry. In these systems, automobile manufacturers such as GM or Chrysler enter the quantity and delivery schedules of specific automobile components into their own information systems. Then these requirements are automatically entered into a supplier's order entry information system. The supplier must respond with an agreement to deliver the materials at the time specified. Thus, automobile companies can reduce the cost of inventory, the space required for warehousing components or raw materials, and construction time.

Baxter has even gone one step further. Delivery personnel no longer drop off their cartons at a loading dock to be placed in a hospital storeroom. Instead, they deliver orders directly to the hospital corridors, dropping them at nursing stations, operating rooms, and supply closets. This has created in effect a "stockless inventory," with Baxter serving as the hospitals' warehouse. Stockless inventory substantially reduces the need for hospital storage space and personnel and lowers holding and handling costs (Caldwell, 1991). New Textron Automotive Interiors plants in Columbia, Missouri, and the Netherlands, which build instrument panels for Fords, use a similar stockless inventory system. Textron's suppliers deliver parts directly to its assembly lines.

Figure 2-12 compares stockless inventory with the just-in-time supply method and traditional inventory practices. Whereas just-in-time inventory allows customers to reduce their inventories, stockless inventory allows them to eliminate their inventories entirely. All inventory responsibilities shift to the distributor, who manages the supply flow. The stockless inventory is a powerful instrument for "locking in" customers, thus giving the supplier a decided competitive advantage.

Strategic systems aimed at suppliers, such as Wal-Mart's continuous replenishment system, are designed to maximize the firm's purchasing power (and minimize costs) by having suppliers interact with its information system to satisfy the firm's precise business needs. If suppliers are unwilling to go along with this system, they may lose business to other suppliers who can meet these demands.

These information systems also provide benefits for suppliers. Suppliers can continually monitor product requirements, factory scheduling, and commitments of their customers against their own schedule to ensure that enough inventory will be available. The manufacturers and retailers are their customers. Once these systems are in place and working smoothly, their efficiency and convenience may help discourage the vendors' customers from switching to competitors. Figure 2-13 illustrates the relationships among the various business-level strategies.

Firm-Level Strategy and Information Technology

A business firm is typically a collection of businesses. Often, the firm is organized financially as a collection of strategic business units, and the returns to the firm are directly tied to strategic business unit performance. The questions are, "How can the overall performance of these business units be achieved?" and "How can information technology contribute?"

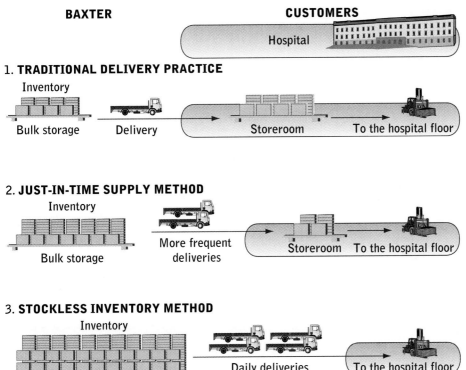

BAXTER

CUSTOMERS

Hospital

1. TRADITIONAL DELIVERY PRACTICE

Inventory

Bulk storage — Delivery — Storeroom → To the hospital floor

2. JUST-IN-TIME SUPPLY METHOD

Inventory

Bulk storage — More frequent deliveries — Storeroom → To the hospital floor

3. STOCKLESS INVENTORY METHOD

Inventory

Bulk storage — Daily deliveries — To the hospital floor

Figure 2-12 Stockless inventory compared to traditional and just-in-time supply methods. The just-in-time supply method reduces inventory requirements of the customer while stockless inventory allows the customer to eliminate inventories entirely. Deliveries are made daily, sometimes directly to the departments that need supplies.

There are two answers in the literature to these questions. One answer involves the concept of synergies: When outputs of some units can be used as inputs to other units, or two organizations can pool markets and expertise, these relationships can lower costs and generate profits. Recent bank and financial firm mergers, such as the merger of Chemical Bank and Chase Manhattan Corp., Wells Fargo and Norwest Corp., Deutsche Bank and Bankers Trust, and Morgan Stanley and Dean Witter Reynolds occurred precisely for this purpose.

How can IT be used strategically here? One use of information technology in these synergy situations is to tie together the operations of disparate business units so that they can act as a whole. Such systems would lower retailing costs, increase customer access to new financial products, and speed up the process of marketing new instruments. The Part 5 Case Study provides more detail on this topic.

Enhancing Core Competencies

A second concept for firm-level strategy involves the notion of "core competency." The argument is that the performance of all business units can increase insofar as these business units develop, or create, a central core of competencies. A core competency is an activity at which a firm is a world-class leader. Core competencies may involve being the world's best fiber-optic manufacturer, the best miniature parts designer, the best package delivery service, or the best thin film manufacturer. In general, a core competency relies on knowledge that is gained over many years of experience (embedded knowledge) and a first-class research organization or just key people who follow the literature and stay abreast of new external knowledge (tacit knowledge).

How can IT be used to advance or create core competencies? Any system that encourages the sharing of knowledge across business units enhances competency. Such systems might encourage or enhance existing competencies and help employees become aware of new external knowledge; such systems might also help a business leverage existing competencies

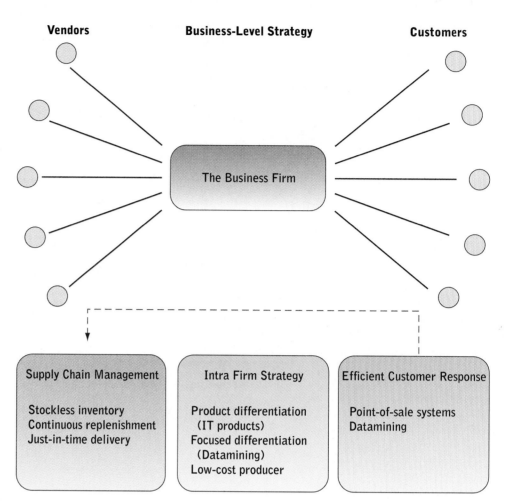

Figure 2-13 Business-level strategy. Efficient customer response and supply chain management systems are often interrelated, helping firms "lock in" customers and suppliers while lowering operational costs. Other types of systems can be used to support product differentiation, focused differentiation strategies, and low-cost producer strategies.

Vendors **Business-Level Strategy** **Customers**

The Business Firm

Supply Chain Management

Stockless inventory
Continuous replenishment
Just-in-time delivery

Intra Firm Strategy

Product differentiation
(IT products)
Focused differentiation
(Datamining)
Low-cost producer

Efficient Customer Response

Point-of-sale systems
Datamining

to related markets. Datamining can be seen as a knowledge generator—it helps a firm know its customers in a unique way. Datamining is therefore a competence enhancer at the firm level as well as at the business level.

Industry-Level Strategy and Information Systems: Competitive Forces and Network Economics

Firms together comprise industries, such as the automotive industry, telephone, television broadcasting, and forest products industries, to name a few. The key strategic question at this level of analysis is "How and when should we compete as opposed to cooperate with others in the industry?" Whereas most strategic analyses emphasize competition, a great deal of money can be made by cooperating with other firms in your industry or firms in related industries. For instance, firms can cooperate to develop industry standards in a number of areas; they can cooperate by working together to build customer awareness, and to work collectively with suppliers to lower costs (Shapiro and Varian, 1999).

information partnership

Cooperative alliance formed between two corporations for the purpose of sharing information to gain strategic advantage.

Information Partnerships

Firms can form information partnerships, and even link their information systems to achieve unique synergies. In an **information partnership,** both companies can join forces, without actually merging, by sharing information (Konsynski and McFarlan, 1990). American Airlines has an arrangement with Citibank to award one mile in its frequent flier program for every dollar spent

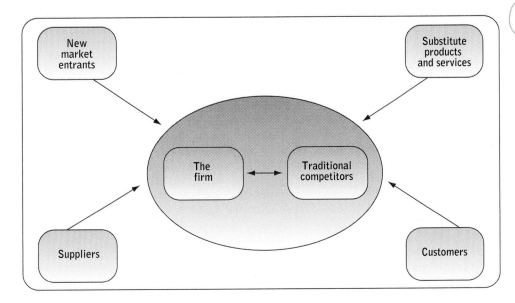

Figure 2-14 The competitive forces model. There are various forces that affect an organization's ability to compete and therefore greatly influence a firm's business strategy. There are threats from new market entrants and from substitute products and services. Customers and suppliers wield bargaining power. Traditional competitors constantly adapt their strategies to maintain their market positioning.

using Citibank credit cards. American benefits from increased customer loyalty, and Citibank gains new credit card subscribers and a highly creditworthy customer base for cross-marketing. Northwest Airlines has a similar arrangement with U.S. Bank. American and Northwest have also allied with MCI, awarding frequent flier miles for each dollar of long-distance billing.

Such partnerships help firms gain access to new customers, creating new opportunities for cross-selling and targeting products. They can share investments in computer hardware and software. Sometimes traditional competitors can benefit from some of these partnerships. Baxter Healthcare International offers its customers medical supplies from competitors and office supplies through its electronic ordering channel. Even companies that were traditional competitors have found such alliances to be mutually advantageous.

At the industry level, two analytic models are used: the competitive forces model and network economics.

The Competitive Forces Model

In the **competitive forces model,** which is illustrated in Figure 2-14, a firm faces a number of external threats and opportunities: the threat of new entrants into its market, the pressure from substitute products or services, the bargaining power of customers, the bargaining power of suppliers, and the positioning of traditional industry competitors.

competitive forces model
Model used to describe the interaction of external influences, specifically threats and opportunities, that affect an organization's strategy and ability to compete.

Competitive advantage can be achieved by enhancing the firm's ability to deal with customers, suppliers, substitute products and services, and new entrants to its market, which in turn may change the balance of power between a firm and other competitors in the industry in the firm's favor.

How can information systems be used to achieve strategic advantage at the industry level? By working with other firms, industry participants can use information technology to develop industry-wide standards for exchanging information or business transactions electronically (see Chapters 9 and 10), which force all market participants to subscribe to similar standards. This increases industry efficiency—making substitute products less possible and perhaps raising entry costs—thus discouraging new entrants. Customers may be better served, and incur switching costs by using products of other industries. Also, industry members can build industry-wide, IT-supported consorti, symposia, and communications networks to coordinate activities vis-à-vis government agencies, foreign competition, and competing industries.

For instance, the OASIS system uses the Web to help member electrical utility companies sell surplus electrical power. The Jigsaw Consortium system for sharing U.K. consumer information that is described in the Window on Management is another example.

Window on Management

British Consumer Companies Pool Their Data

It used to be easy for British consumer goods manufacturers to reach their customers. With only five television channels, they could merely run an advertisement on the daytime soap operas on U.K. television and be assured they were reaching a large percentage of British housewives. Now more than 200 channels plus PCs and the Internet compete for viewers, and many more women are working outside the home, making consumers very difficult to locate.

Unilever, the parent company of Lever Brothers, Birds Eye, T. J. Lipton, and other food and consumer goods companies with dual headquarters in London and Rotterdam, wanted to make sure that its marketing budget of £3.6 billion (approximately U.S. $6 billion) was not being squandered in hit or miss campaigns. After highly publicized product failures such as Persil Power, a laundry detergent that was so powerful it ate right through some fabrics, the company wanted to avoid losing touch with its customers.

In January 1997 Unilever's management decided to share customer data with Kimberly-Clark, Cadbury-Schweppes, and Bass Brewers, three noncompeting consumer goods companies. These companies realized that they probably had a similar set of customers and could benefit by grouping their products together in joint promotions. They formed the Consumer Needs Consortium, which was subsequently renamed the Jigsaw Consortium, and started testing the feasibility of creating a national consumer database.

Major retailers, such as supermarket chains, have data on purchase transactions that they collect at checkout counters, but their wide range of stock makes it difficult to track and analyze customer data with the level of specificity required for targeted marketing campaigns. Before forming the consortium, each member company had collected its own data from promotions, calls to customer service centers, and paper-based surveys. Unilever had a database of 1.5 million U.K. households; Kimberly-Clark had collected data on new mothers for marketing its Huggies diapers; and Bass had begun to build a regional database of beer drinkers. Cadbury did not yet have a database but was eager to collaborate. All of

these companies realized they could benefit by sharing their customer data and by cooperating on the acquisition and analysis of consumer data for the United Kingdom.

The consortium members pooled their data on customers in one region of England and started testing different types of coupon mailings to see if multibrand offers would be more effective than single-brand offers. The results of the pilot confirmed that large households with children tend to consume disproportionate amounts of detergent, chocolate, soap, and diapers. This knowledge of what kinds of households are the most likely to purchase their products helped the consortium members target their direct mail campaigns. Test mailings targeted to specific households showed a coupon redemption rate that was up to 10 times better than random mailings, providing further proof that pooling customer data would provide a favorable return on investment.

Puzzling findings also emerged. The consortium learned that empty nesters are exceptionally heavy consumers of tea, soup, chocolate, and ice cream and that 18- to 24-year-old men did not purchase much of the other consortium members' brands. Bass dropped out of the consortium as a result but continued cross-marketing with the consortium on its Web site for Carling beer.

Consodata, based in Paris, built the final database, which consolidated data from consortium members and supplied additional data gathered from surveys. The new system can provide fine-grained analyses such as how many Huggies are used by families that have two children, a pet, read the **Times,** and have annual incomes of £40,000. Then it can cross-tabulate the information to determine what other products this set of consumers might want. Armed with more precise information, consortium members can develop more efficient marketing promotions.

To Think About: What are the management benefits of forming a consortium to share customer data with other companies? Are there any drawbacks?

Sources: Alice Dragoon, "Looking for Mr. Candybar," **CIO Enterprise Magazine,** January 15, 1999; and Deborah Orr, "A Giant Reawakens," **Forbes Magazine,** January 25, 1999.

Network Economics

network economics Model based on the concept of a network where adding another participant entails zero marginal costs but can create much larger marginal gain. Used as a model for strategic systems at the industry level.

A second strategic concept useful at the industry level is **network economics.** In a network, the marginal costs of adding another participant are about zero, whereas the marginal gain is much larger. The larger the number of subscribers in a telephone system, or the Internet, the greater the value to all participants. Networks may not experience diminishing returns in the short run. It's no more expensive to operate a television station with 1000 subscribers than with 10 million subscribers. And the value of a community of people grows with size, whereas the cost of adding new members is inconsequential.

From this network economics perspective, information technology can be strategically useful. Internet sites can be used by firms to build "communities of users"—like-minded customers who want to share their experiences. This can build customer loyalty and enjoyment, and build unique ties to customers. Microsoft Corporation—the world's dominant PC software manufacturer—uses information technology to build communities of software developers

Table 2.7 Strategic Uses of the Internet

Level of Strategy	Internet Application
Business	Security First Network Bank allows customers to view account statements, pay bills, check account balances, and obtain 24-hour customer service through the World Wide Web.
	Federal Express and UPS maintain World Wide Web sites where customers can track the status of their packages any time of the day by entering their package tracking numbers.
	Hyatt Hotels can track the activities of visitors to its TravelWeb site, which provides electronic information on participating hotels. It can analyze these usage patterns to tailor hospitality-related products more closely to customer preferences.
	J. B. Hunt Transport Services manages the transportation logistics for J.C. Penney. Penney employees can access Hunt's Web site to check the status of any shipment.
Firm	Allegany County (Maryland) Human Resources Development Commission provides client tracking and communications across various county agencies through file sharing and e-mail.
Industry	OASIS Web sites allow consortiums of electric utilities companies to sell their surplus power to wholesalers and locate the transmission facilities for moving it between the power source and the customer.

around the world. Using the Microsoft Developer's Network, these small software development firms work closely with Microsoft to debug its operating system software, provide new applications ideas and extensions, supply customers with tips and new software applications, and in general participate in a powerful and useful network. Table 2.7 shows how the Internet can be used to support different levels of business strategy.

2.3 Using Systems for Competitive Advantage: Management Issues

Strategic information systems often change the organization as well as its products, services, and operating procedures, driving the organization into new behavior patterns. Using technology effectively for strategic benefit requires careful planning and management.

Managing Strategic Transitions

Adopting the kinds of strategic systems described in this chapter generally requires changes in business goals, relationships with customers and suppliers, internal operations, and information architecture. These sociotechnical changes, affecting both social and technical elements of the organization, can be considered **strategic transitions**—a movement between levels of sociotechnical systems.

How much sociotechnical change occurs depends on the specific circumstances. Clearly, however, there is a connection between the strategy of an organization and its internal structure. As companies move to make information systems part of the overall corporate strategy, their internal structure must also change to reflect these new developments. Managers struggling to boost competitiveness will need to redesign various organizational processes to make effective use of leading-edge information systems technology.

Such changes often entail blurring of organizational boundaries, both external and internal. This is especially true of telecommunications-based strategic systems (Cash and Konsynski, 1985; Keen, 1986). Suppliers and customers must become intimately linked and may share each other's responsibilities. For instance, in Baxter International's stockless inventory system, Baxter has assumed responsibility for managing its customers' inventories (Johnston and Vitale, 1988). With the help of information systems, the supplier actually makes the inventory replenishment decisions,

strategic transitions A movement from one level of sociotechnical system to another. Often required when adopting strategic systems that demand changes in the social and technical elements of an organization.

vendor-managed inventory

Approach to inventory management that assigns the supplier the responsibility to make inventory replenishment decisions based on order, point-of-sale data, or warehouse data supplied by the customer.

based on orders, point-of-sale data, or warehouse data supplied by the customer. This approach to inventory management, called **vendor-managed inventory,** is based on the theory that suppliers are the product or "category" experts and thus can do the best job of making sure that supply meets demand. Managers will need to devise new mechanisms for coordinating their firms' activities with those of customers, suppliers, and other organizations (Kambil and Short, 1994).

Firms with successful strategic information systems have broken down organizational barriers that block the sharing of data across functions. Design, sales, and manufacturing departments must work together closely. Federal Express' package tracking system shares information among operations, customer service, and accounting functions. Companies such as Dell Computer and Baxter have redesigned their work processes numerous times to continually improve their overall service level and business relationship with customers (Rangan and Bell, 1998; Short and Venkatraman, 1992).

Other organizational changes may be required as well. Standard operating procedures may need to be redesigned. As companies examine their value chains for strategic opportunities, looking for the activities that add the most value, they are finding many wasted steps or procedures that could be eliminated.

In some cases, reshaping an organization to remain competitive may necessitate an entirely new organizational structure. To produce the Saturn, a new low-cost car competitive with Japanese models, General Motors created an entirely new automotive division with a new factory, a new sales force, and a new design team to utilize the new technologies. Not all strategic information systems require such massive change, but clearly, many do. The organizational change requirements surrounding new information systems are so important that they merit attention throughout this text. Chapters 3, 11, and 13 examine organizational change issues in great detail.

What Managers Can Do

Information systems are too important to be left entirely to a small technical group in the corporation. Managers must take the initiative to identify the types of systems that would provide a strategic advantage to the firm. Although some industries are far ahead of others in their use of information technology, some of those that are far behind may be so for a good reason: The technology may not be appropriate. Other industries have simply failed to keep up with the times and thus offer considerable opportunities for vast and rapid changes. Some of the important questions managers should ask themselves are as follows:

- What are some of the forces at work in the industry? What strategies are being used by industry leaders?

- How is the industry currently using information and communication technology? Which organizations are the industry leaders in the application of information systems technology?

- What are the direction and nature of change within the industry? From where are the momentum and change coming?

- Are significant strategic opportunities to be gained by introducing information systems technology into the industry?

- What kinds of systems are applicable to the industry? Does it require systems to create new products and services, supplier systems, and/or sales and marketing systems?

Once the nature of information systems technology in the industry is understood, managers should turn to their organization and ask other important questions:

- Is the organization behind or ahead of the industry in its application of information systems?

- What is the current business strategic plan, and how does that plan mesh with the current strategy for information services?

- Does the firm have sufficient technology and capital to develop a strategic information systems initiative? (Kettinger et al. 1994.)

- Where would new information systems provide the greatest value to the firm?

Once these issues have been considered, managers can gain a keen insight into whether their firms are ready for strategic information systems.

Studies of successful strategic systems have found that they are rarely planned but instead evolve slowly over a long time, and they almost always originate with practical operational problems. For instance, SABRE, the American Airlines computerized reservation system that is often cited as a classic "strategic system," originated as a straightforward inventory control and order entry system (Copeland and McKenney, 1988; Hopper, 1990). Rather than sprouting from some magical methodology, strategic systems, like most new products, come from closely observing real-world business situations. This finding may provide a clue about how to look for powerful strategic impact systems.

Management Wrap-Up

The key to strategic success with information technology is, of course, managers. Managers need to identify the right technology for the appropriate level of strategy (business, firm, and industry). Managers must identify the business process to be improved, the core competencies to be enhanced, and the relationships with others in the industry. Last, managers have to implement changes in business process and technology throughout the organization.

Management

There are many types of information systems in an organization that serve different purposes, from transaction processing to knowledge management and decision making. Each of these systems can contribute a strategic edge. Increasingly, organizations are recognizing that information is a strategic asset that can be leveraged into long-term market advantage, but meaningful strategic systems generally require sociotechnical change.

Organization

Information technology is used at the business, firm, and industry level of strategy to achieve competitive edge. Technology can be used to differentiate existing products, create new products and services, and nurture core competencies over the long haul. Perhaps the most important contribution of the technology per se is its potential for reducing management costs within the firm and transaction costs among firms.

Technology

For Discussion

1. Several information systems experts have claimed that there is no such thing as a sustainable strategic advantage. Do you agree? Why or why not?

2. Companies are furiously adopting just-in-time delivery systems which minimize inventory by requiring suppliers to deliver just enough materials to meet the day or week's production schedule. Does this practice provide a competitive advantage? Why or why not?

Summary

1. Analyze the role played by the six major types of information systems in organizations. There are six major types of information systems in contemporary organizations that are designed for different purposes and different audiences. Operational-level systems are transaction processing systems (TPS), such as payroll or order processing, that track the flow of the daily routine transactions necessary to conduct business. Knowledge-level systems support clerical, managerial, and professional workers. They consist of office automation systems (OAS) for increasing the productivity of data workers and knowledge work systems (KWS) for enhancing the productivity of knowledge workers.

Management-level systems (MIS and DSS) provide the management control level with reports and access to the organization's current performance and historical records. Most MIS reports condense information from a TPS and are not highly analytical. Decision-support systems (DSS) support management decisions when these decisions are unique, rapidly changing, and not specified easily in advance. These systems have more advanced analytical models and data analysis capabilities than MIS and often draw on information from external as well as internal sources. Executive support systems (ESS) support the strategic level by providing a generalized computing and communications environment to assist senior management's decision making. An ESS has limited analytical capabilities but can draw on sophisticated graphics software and many sources of internal and external information.

2. Describe the relationship between the various types of information systems. The various types of systems in the organization exchange data with one another. Transaction processing systems are a major source of data for other systems, especially MIS and DSS. Executive support systems are primarily recipients of data from lower level systems. However, the different systems in an organization are only loosely integrated. The information needs of the various functional areas and organizational levels are too specialized to be served by a single system.

3. Distinguish a strategic information system. A strategic information system changes the goals, operations, products, services, or environmental relationships of organizations to help them gain an edge over competitors. Today information systems can so dramatically boost a firm's productivity and efficiency that businesses view information as a weapon against competition and a strategic resource. In the past, information used to be considered a bureaucratic nuisance.

4. Describe how information systems can be used to support three levels of strategy used in business. Information systems can be used to support strategy at the business, firm, and industry level. At the business level of strategy, information systems can be used to help firms become the low-cost producer, differentiate products, or serve new markets. Information systems can also be used to "lock in" customers and suppliers using efficient customer response and supply chain management applications. Value chain analysis is useful at the business level to highlight specific activities in the business where information systems are most likely to have a strategic impact.

At the firm level, information systems can be used to achieve new efficiencies or to enhance services by tying together the operations of disparate business units so that they can function as a whole or promote the sharing of knowledge across business units. At the industry level, systems can promote competitive advantage by facilitating cooperation with other firms in the industry, creating consortiums or communities for sharing information, exchanging transactions, or coordinating activities. The competitive forces model and network economics are useful concepts for identifying strategic opportunities for systems at the industry level.

5. Explain why strategic information systems are difficult to build and sustain. Not all strategic systems make a profit; they can be expensive and risky to build. Many strategic information systems are easily copied by other firms, so that strategic advantage is not always sustainable. Implementing strategic systems often requires extensive organizational change and a transition from one sociotechnical level to another. Such changes are called *strategic transitions* and are often difficult and painful to achieve.

Key Terms

Competitive forces model, 59	Knowledge-level systems, 38	Operational-level systems, 38	Supply chain management, 55
Datamining, 52	Knowledge work systems (KWS), 42	Primary activities, 49	Support activities, 49
Decision-support systems (DSS), 44	Management information systems (MIS), 44	Product differentiation, 51	Switching costs, 55
Desktop publishing, 42	Management-level systems, 38	Strategic information systems, 48	Transaction processing systems (TPS), 40
Document imaging systems, 42	Network economics, 60	Strategic-level systems, 38	Value chain model, 49
Executive support systems (ESS), 46	Office automation systems (OAS), 42	Strategic transitions, 61	Vendor-managed inventory, 62
Focused differentiation, 52		Supply chain, 55	Word processing, 42
Information partnership, 58			

Review Questions

1. Identify and describe the four levels of the organizational hierarchy. What types of information systems serve each level?

2. List and briefly describe the major types of systems in organizations. How are they related to one another?

3. What are the five types of TPS in business organizations? What functions do they perform? Give examples of each.

4. Describe the functions performed by knowledge work and office automation systems and some typical applications of each.

5. What are the characteristics of MIS? How do MIS differ from TPS? From DSS?

6. What are the characteristics of DSS? How do they differ from those of an ESS?

7. What is a strategic information system? What is the difference between a strategic information system and a strategic-level system?

8. Describe appropriate models for analyzing strategy at the business level and the types of strategies that can be used to compete at this level.

9. Describe the various ways that information systems can be used to support business-level strategies.

10. Describe the role of information systems in supporting strategy at the firm level.

11. How can the competitive forces model and network economics be used to identify strategies at the industry level?

12. How can industry-level strategies be supported by information systems?

13. Why are strategic information systems difficult to build?

14. How can managers find strategic applications in their firms?

Group Project

Form a group with two or three classmates. Research a business using annual reports or business publications such as *Fortune, Business Week,* and *The Wall Street Journal.* Visit the company Web site to gain further insights into the company. Analyze the business and identify what level or levels of strategy the firm is pursuing (business, firm, or industry). Analyze how the company is using information systems to pursue its strategy or strategies. Suggest additional strategic information systems for that particular business including those using the Internet, if appropriate. Present your findings to the class.

Tools for Interactive Learning

○ Internet

The Internet Connection for this chapter will take you to the Security First Network Bank (SFNB) Web site, where you can see how one company used the Internet to create an entirely new type of business. You can complete an exercise for analyzing the capabilities of this Web site and its strategic benefits. You can also use the Interactive Study Guide to test your knowledge of the topics in this chapter and get instant feedback where you need more practice.

○ CD-ROM

If you purchase and use the Multimedia Edition CD-ROM with this chapter, you can complete two interactive exercises. The first asks you to match various types of information systems described in the chapter to user information needs. The second asks you to perform a value chain analysis for a business. You can also find a video clip illustrating the strategic use of Alamo Rent-a-Car's reservation and rental system, interactive exercises, an audio overview of the major themes of this chapter, and bullet text summarizing the key points of the chapter.

Case Study   Can Sears Reinvent Itself?

Sears, Roebuck used to be the largest retailer in the United States, with sales representing 1 to 2 percent of the U.S. gross national product for almost 40 years after World War II. Its legendary catalog was considered the primary (and sometimes the only) source for everything from wrenches to bathtubs to underwear. During the 1980s, Sears moved into other businesses, hoping to provide middle-class consumers with almost every type of banking, investment, and real estate service in addition to selling appliances, hardware, clothes, and other goods.

This diversification tore Sears away from its core business, which was retail

sales. Sears has steadily lost ground in retailing, moving from the number one position to number three behind discounters Wal-Mart Stores, Inc. and Kmart Corporation. Sears had been slow to remodel stores, trim costs, and keep pace with current trends in selling and merchandising. It could not keep up with the discounters and with specialty retailers such as Toys Я Us, Home Depot, Inc., and Circuit City Stores, Inc. that focus on a wide selection of low-price merchandise in a single category. Nor could Sears compete with trend-setting department stores.

Yet Sears has been heavily computerized. At one time it spent more on informa-

tion technology and networking than all other noncomputer firms in the United States except the Boeing Corporation. Its extensive customer databases of 60 million past and present Sears credit card holders were used to target groups such as appliance buyers, tool buyers, gardening enthusiasts, and mothers-to-be with special promotions. For example, Sears would mail customers who purchased a washer and dryer a maintenance contract and follow up with annual contract renewal forms.

Why hasn't this translated into competitive advantage? One big problem is Sears' high cost of operations. Nearly 30 percent of each dollar in sales is required to cover overhead (e.g., expenses for salaries, maintenance, and advertising) compared to 15 percent for Wal-Mart and about 21 percent for Kmart.

In 1991, retail operations contributed 38 percent of the corporate bottom line. The rest of the merchandising group's profits came from the lucrative Sears credit card. Strategies that worked well for competitors fizzled at Sears. J. C. Penney successfully refocused its business to emphasize moderately priced apparel. Everyday low pricing, the pricing strategy used by Wal-Mart and other retailers, bombed at Sears because the firm's cost structure, one of the highest in the industry, did not allow for rock-bottom prices. Everyday low pricing has become "everyday fair pricing" supplemented by frequent sales.

Sears' catalog sales also stagnated. Although the Sears catalog, founded in 1887, had the largest revenues of any mail-order business, sales had not been profitable for 20 years, and the catalog had lost ground to specialty catalogs such as those of L. L. Bean and Lands' End. On January 25, 1993, Sears stopped issuing its famous "big book" catalogs, closed 113 of its stores, and eliminated 50,000 jobs. In order to return to its core business and recapture its leadership in retailing, the company also disposed of its Dean Witter securities, Discover credit card, Coldwell Banker real estate, and Allstate insurance subsidiaries.

To help turn Sears around and refocus on retailing, CEO Edward A. Brennan hired executive Arthur C. Martinez away from Saks Fifth Avenue in September 1992 and named Martinez his successor as Sears chairman and chief executive officer 2 years later. Martinez ordered the company to combine its half-dozen disparate customer databases to find out who was really shopping at Sears. It turned out that Sears' biggest shoppers were not men looking for Craftsmen tool belts but women aged 25 to 55 with yearly average family incomes of $40,000 who were in the market for everything from skirts to appliances.

Under Martinez, Sears stopped trying to sell everything and started focusing on six core types of merchandise—men's, women's, and children's clothing; home furnishings; home improvement; automotive services and supplies; appliances; and consumer electronics. The company is rearranging its merchandise displays to resemble those of more upscale department stores and is focusing on selling women's apparel, which is considered the most profitable segment of Sears' merchandising. Sears is stocking more upscale women's clothing and cosmetics, using advertising campaigns inviting women to see "the softer side of Sears." It is also offering special merchandise in each store geared to its local customer base. And it is relieving managers and clerks of some reporting and administrative tasks so they have more time to actually sell. Beginning in 1996 every employee's compensation included a measurement for customer service. Sears realized that it could not compete with discounters such as Wal-Mart Corporation on price alone and focused on building a competitive edge through superior service.

Sears embarked on a $4 billion five-year store renovation program to make Sears stores more efficient, attractive, and convenient by bringing all transactions closer to the sales floor and centralizing every store's general offices, cashiers, customer services, and credit functions. New point-of-sale (POS) terminals allow sales staff to issue new charge cards, accept charge card payments, issue gift certificates, and report account information to cardholders. The POS devices provide information such as the status of orders and availability of products and allow associates to order out-of-stock goods directly from the sales floor.

Some stores have installed ATM machines to give customers cash advances against their Sears Discover credit cards. Telephone kiosks have been installed throughout the Sears retail network. Customers can use them to inquire about service, parts, and credit; check the status of their car in the tire and auto center; or call the manager.

Customer service desks have been largely eliminated. Sales personnel are authorized to handle refunds and returns, which eliminates the need for two separate staffs. If a customer forgets his or her charge card, the customer can obtain immediate credit by telling the cashier his or her name and address and presenting identification. Streamlining of patterns of work in back rooms and loading docks has also trimmed staff and created savings. These changes have increased the ratio of selling space to nonselling space at Sears so that an additional 6 million square feet could be used to generate revenues.

Another way Sears improved productivity was by streamlining its extensive logistics process: 600,000 truckload shipments a year from 160 warehouses and distribution centers to 800 stores, plus about 4 million home deliveries annually. When Martinez arrived at Sears, he found multiple channels of distribution operating under a variety of authorities with little coordination or effort to achieve savings or speed. Martinez put William G. "Gus" Pagonis, a retired three-star army general who had been the U.S. military's chief of logistics during the Gulf War, in charge of Sears' logistics. Pagonis cut overall logistics costs by $45 million a year. Merchandise now moves from suppliers to stores in half the time it used to take, reducing inventories and inventory costs.

Sears has been moving its suppliers to an electronic ordering system similar to that described for Baxter Healthcare. By linking its computerized ordering system directly to that of each supplier, Sears plans to eliminate paper throughout the order process and hopes to expedite the flow of goods into its stores.

Sears further tightened its grip on the business by building an even larger database for its Sears Credit and Home Service businesses. It consolidates information on 90 million households, 31 million Sears card users, transaction records, credit status, and related data. Sears hopes to use this information to provide even more finely targeted database marketing. The database houses Sears' Strategic Performance Reporting System (SPRS) and helps the company manage pricing and merchandising for its 1950 North American stores.

Until a few years ago, Sears merchandise buyers lacked reliable information on precisely what customers were buying at each store. They could not view anything more specific than each division's daily performance. Management relied on 18 separate systems that often contained conflicting and redundant pricing information. Today, any authorized Sears employee can use SPRS to look up any sales figure by store, by area, or by item, right down to the size and color of a sweater. Sales can be analyzed by item or product category, by individual store, or company wide. Sales of items advertised in newspapers for a specific day can be tallied so that Sears' 1000 buyers and managers can know what hotselling merchandise to replenish right away.

Buyers can compare current performance of merchandise with that of the previous week or the previous year. The data can be displayed in a number of different ways, including pie charts or graphs.

Sears' Home Service business, which offers merchandise repair services and additional services such as pest control, brings in $3 billion in annual revenues and is the largest house-call service in the United States. It is considered highly profitable and an area that management wants to promote further. Sears' 14,000 technicians conduct about 17 million home visits annually to make repairs. Before 1993, customers scheduled service calls by calling 1 of 650 local repair centers. Representatives at each location would look up the service information on paper and schedule visits. Sears installed a 24-hour toll-free number and consolidated service representatives in five central locations, which pass calls on to 92 regional offices. The calls are routed to technicians, who use wireless handheld computers to respond to service call changes and emergencies and to exchange information on a product's repair and purchase history with the Sears customer database.

Sears has also set up a Web site to promote sales and to allow customers to purchase certain categories of goods electronically. Sears is working on using Internet technology to create a system that will let suppliers check the status of their invoices. Sears wants to give vendors access to SPRS so that they can check the sales of their products and provide just-in-time inventory service.

The Sears charge card, with more than 32 million accounts, is the fourth-largest credit card operation in the United States, serving nearly half the households in the United States. Sears' credit card business generates almost half of corporate profits. About 56 percent of all purchases made in Sears stores are made with the Sears credit card, and this percentage has been growing. In 1993 Sears aggressively began courting new credit card customers, and it has doubled the rate at which it issues new credit cards to more than 6 million per year. Although Martinez claims that Sears did not reduce its standards for determining creditworthy customers, the company attracted too many high-risk

customers, and many of its new credit card holders defaulted on paying their bills. Steve Goldstein, who took charge of Sears credit in 1996, invested in technology to bring Sears' risk-management systems up to the level of leading-edge credit card issuers such as Citicorp.

Troubles mounted in early 1997. Some cardholders in Massachusetts sued Sears over the intimidating methods it used to persuade bankrupt customers to pay their credit card balance. Sears wound up paying $475 million to settle lawsuits in all 50 states. Later that year, bad-debt charge-offs for uncollectible credit card accounts skyrocketed to more than 8 percent of Sears receivables, twice the level of 2 years earlier. Goldstein's group could not properly analyze the delinquent accounts, with systems underreporting early stage delinquencies. Many accounts went past the credit card industry standard of 90 days before they were classified as delinquent. Although teams of people worked day and night, Sears' computer systems weren't state of the art and analysis that should have taken a few hours took weeks. Goldstein resigned in December 1997.

Sears has adopted more conservative accounting procedures which will classify accounts as delinquent much sooner and has tightened credit standards. But holding back on credit has hurt retail sales, just as loosening credit policies boosted store sales in the past, but led to higher loan losses.

Can Sears retail sales grow without easy credit? Will all of Sears' efforts make customers happier? Since Martinez arrived, earnings have rebounded from their dismally low levels of 1992. Sears has had a measure of success in lowering its margins and increasing same-store sales. The question is whether Sears can sustain this momentum. Its operating expenses are still high compared with industry leaders. Market research indicates that Sears continues to be the destination of choice for purchasers of lawn mowers, wrenches, washing machines, and other "hard" goods—and its tools and appliance businesses are posting large sales gains. But Sears has not yet secured itself as a place for fashionable women's clothing. Some critics believe that future earnings growth will lag once the company completes its remodeling program and that Sears remains

vulnerable to aggressive discounters. Can Sears' reinvention keep the company competitive now and in the future?

Sources: Joseph B. Cahill, "Sears Is Tightening Accounting Methods in Credit-Card Unit, Lifting Loan Losses," **The Wall Street Journal,** January 29, 1999; Gene Koprowski, "The Harder Side of Sears," **Software Magazine,** January 15, 1998; Patricia Sellers, "Sears' Big Turnaround Runs into Big Trouble," **Fortune,** February 16, 1998; Jennifer Steinhauer, "Time to Call a Sears Repairman," **The New York Times,** January 15, 1998; Daniel Gross, "Remodeling Sears," **CIO Magazine,** December 1, 1996; Robert Berner, "Retired General Speeds Deliveries, Cuts Costs, Helps Sears Rebound," **The Wall Street Journal,** July 16, 1996; "Yes, He's Revived Sears. But Can He Reinvent It?" **The New York Times,** January 7, 1996; John Foley, "Sears' Data Store Grows," **Information Week,** June 24, 1996; Susan Chandler, "Sears' Turnaround Is for Real—For Now," **Business Week,** August 15, 1994; Stephanie Strom, "Sears Eliminating Its Catalogues and 50,000 Jobs," **The New York Times,** January 26, 1993; Barnaby J. Feder, "Sears Will Return to Retailing Focus," **The New York Times,** September 30, 1992; and Bruce Caldwell, "Sears Shops for Competitive Edge," **Information Week,** January 13, 1992.

CASE STUDY QUESTIONS

1. Evaluate Sears using the competitive forces and value chain models.

2. What management, organization, and technology factors were responsible for Sears' poor performance?

3. Evaluate Sears' new business strategy under Martinez. What level of strategy is Sears pursuing? What management, organization, and technology issues are addressed by this strategy?

4. How successful is Sears' new strategy? What role do information systems play in that strategy?

5. To what extent have information systems provided competitive advantage for Sears? Explain.

6. Visit a Sears store and observe sales patterns. What image or market message is being conveyed in the store? How is it implemented? How might it be improved? (You might make a comparison stop at J. C. Penney's or Wal-Mart or Kmart.)

Chapter 3

Information Systems, Organizations, and Business Processes

After completing this chapter, you will be able to:

1. Identify the salient characteristics of organizations.

2. Assess the changing role of information systems within organizations.

3. Compare models for describing the origins of systems in organizations.

4. Compare the major theories about organizations that help us understand their relationship with information systems.

5. Analyze the impact of information systems on organizational structure, culture, political processes, and management.

6. Describe the organizational implications for the design and implementation of systems.

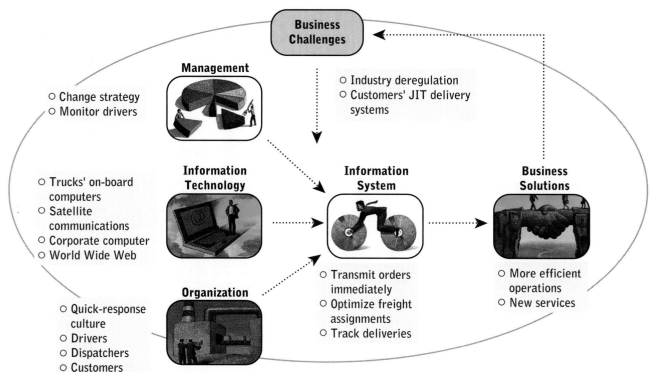

Business Challenges

Management
○ Change strategy
○ Monitor drivers

○ Industry deregulation
○ Customers' JIT delivery systems

Information Technology
○ Trucks' on-board computers
○ Satellite communications
○ Corporate computer
○ World Wide Web

Information System
○ Transmit orders immediately
○ Optimize freight assignments
○ Track deliveries

Business Solutions
○ More efficient operations
○ New services

Organization
○ Quick-response culture
○ Drivers
○ Dispatchers
○ Customers

Schneider Responds to the New Rules
of the Trucking Game

Deregulation revolutionized the business environment for the trucking industry overnight. Competition for customers heated up. Interstate trucking firms no longer had to follow the rules of a regulatory bureaucracy about what kinds of freight to carry and where to take it. Before deregulation these same rules had also made it difficult for customers to change carriers because only certain trucking firms could meet these regulations. Large retailers and manufacturers were installing just-in-time delivery systems. They wanted to use trucking firms that could transport their shipments right away.

Schneider National, based in Green Bay, Wisconsin, one of North America's largest trucking, transportation, and logistics companies, re-

sponded to these demands with a multipronged strategy. First, it tried to make sweeping changes in its corporate culture. Schneider sought to replace its regulated-utility mentality with quick reflexes and an urgency to get things done. CEO Don Schneider democratized the organization by calling all employees "associates" and by removing status symbols like reserved parking places. He encouraged everyone, from drivers on up, to speak out on ways to improve operations. He also instituted an extra bonus paycheck based solely on performance.

Second, the firm deployed new information systems to support these changes. It equipped each truck with a computer and a rotating antenna. A satellite tracks every rig making sure it adheres to its schedule. When an order comes into headquarters, dispatchers know exactly which truck to assign to the job. The dispatchers send an order directly by satellite to the driver's on-board terminal complete with directions to the destination, instructions on what gate to use, and what papers to collect with the merchandise. Within 15 to 30 minutes of sending an order to Schneider's computer, customers know which trucks to expect and when.

Schneider has started using its information systems to provide the logistics management function for other companies, setting up a separate division, Schneider Logistics, Inc., for this purpose. One of its clients is General Motors Corporation. Schneider manages all shipments of GM service parts, amounting to 435,000 outbound "order lines" daily to more than 9000 GM dealers, warehouse distributors, and mass merchandisers. Whereas other providers use only their own trucks, planes, and trains, Schneider uses its information systems to provide solutions that use the best medium for moving freight, even if that isn't its own trucks.

To make shipment information accessible to clients, Schneider Logistics created a Web site with electronic commerce capabilities. Designated customers can use the Web site to "paperlessly" send new load requests directly to Schneider Logistics. Clients can also use the Web site to track the status of their shipments, accessing the information they need in Schneider's information system, such as which freight carrier is transporting a shipment, where the shipment is, and when it is scheduled to reach its destination. The system consolidates information about all modes of transportation, including truck, rail, and small loads grouped together on one truck. Schneider's customers can query the system to locate parts for their just-in-time production systems, while approved carriers can find available loads on-line.

Information systems now play such a powerful role in Schneider's operations that the firm has been described as "an information system masquerading as a trucking line." Don Schneider himself has observed that "people get the mistaken impression that our business is running trucks." Several other competitors responded to deregulation by merely lowering rates. They went bankrupt.

Sources: Verne G. Kopytoff, "18 Wheels, G.P.S. and Radar," *The New York Times,* March 4, 1999; Patrick Dryden, "Keep on Trackin—Using the 'Net," *Computerworld,* July 13, 1998; "Secure Website Goes Live for Schneider Brokerage," *Schneider National, Inc.,* June 17, 1998; and Clinton Wilder, "Tracked on the Web," *Information Week,* September 21, 1998.

Management Challenges

The experience of Schneider National illustrates the interdependence of business environments, organizational culture, management strategy, and the development of information systems. Schneider National developed new information systems in response to changes in competitive pressures from its surrounding environment, but it needed to change its organizational culture before it could use the new systems successfully. The information systems, in turn, changed the way Schneider ran its business. Schneider's story raises the following management challenges:

1. **The difficulties of managing change.** Bringing about change through the development of information technology and information systems is slowed considerably by the natural inertia of organizations. Of course, organizations do change, and powerful leaders are often required to bring about these changes. Nevertheless, the process, as leaders eventually discover, is more complicated and much slower than is typically anticipated.

2. **Fitting technology to the organization (or vice-versa).** On the one hand, it is important to align information technology to the business plan, to senior management's strategic business plans, and to standard operating procedures (SOPs) in the business. Information technology is, after all, supposed to be the servant of the organization. On the other hand, these business plans, senior managers, and SOPs all may be very outdated or incompatible with the envisioned technology. In such instances, managers will need to change the organization to fit the technology or to adjust both the organization and the technology to achieve an optimal "fit."

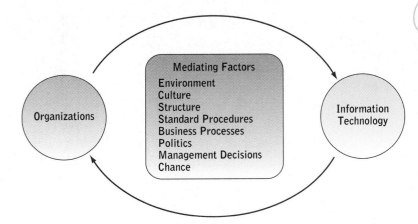

Figure 3-1 The two-way relationship between organizations and information technology. This complex two-way relationship is mediated by many factors, not the least of which are the decisions made—or not made—by managers. Other factors mediating the relationship are the organizational culture, bureaucracy, politics, business fashion, and pure chance.

This chapter explores the complex relationship between organizations and information systems. We introduce the features of organizations that you will need to understand when you design, build, and operate information systems. We examine precisely how information systems affect organizations, and how organizations affect information systems. The chapter concludes by describing why organizations are difficult to change, with or without technology, and the challenges this poses for businesses and management.

3.1 The Relationship Between Organizations and Information Systems

Can information systems "flatten" organizations by reducing their number of levels? Will information systems allow organizations to operate with fewer middle managers and clerical workers? Can they be used to "reengineer" organizations so they become lean, efficient, and hard hitting? Can organizations use information technology to decentralize power down to lower level workers thereby unleashing the creative talents of millions of employees? Can organizations use systems to rebuild their business processes? Can the Internet and World Wide Web substitute for organization?

No one can deny that information systems have contributed to organizational efficiency and effectiveness, but the exact nature of their relationship is a source of vigorous debate. Exactly what can information systems do for organizations? Our goal is to present an overview of the relationship and a discussion of contemporary research so that you can understand the issues.

The Two-Way Relationship

Information systems and organizations have a mutual influence on each other (see Figure 3-1). On the one hand, information systems must be aligned with the organization to provide information needed by important groups within the organization. On the other hand, the organization must be aware of and must open itself to the influences of information systems to benefit from new technologies. Information systems affect organizations, and organizations necessarily affect the design of systems.

The relationship between information systems and organizations is very complex. Figure 3-1 shows a great many mediating factors that influence the interaction between information technology and organizations. These include the organization's structure, standard operating procedures, politics, culture, surrounding environment, and management decisions (Orlikowski and Robey, 1991; Orlikowski, 1992). Managers, after all, decide what systems will be built, what the systems will do, how they will be implemented, and so forth. To a large extent, managers and organizations choose the "computer impacts" they want (or at least receive the impacts they deserve) (Laudon, 1986; Laudon and Marr, 1994; Laudon and Marr, 1995). Sometimes, however, the outcomes are the result of pure chance and of both good and bad luck.

Figure 3-2 The technical microeconomic definition of the organization (A). In the microeconomic definition of organizations, capital and labor (the primary production factors provided by the environment) are transformed by the firm through the production process into products and services (outputs to the environment). The products and services are consumed by the environment, which supplies additional capital and labor as inputs in the feedback loop. (B) The microeconomic view is a technical model of the firm in which the firm combines capital and labor in a production function to produce a single product of the amount Q. The firm can freely substitute the capital for labor anywhere along the curve Q. In this view, the production process is unexamined, largely a black box.

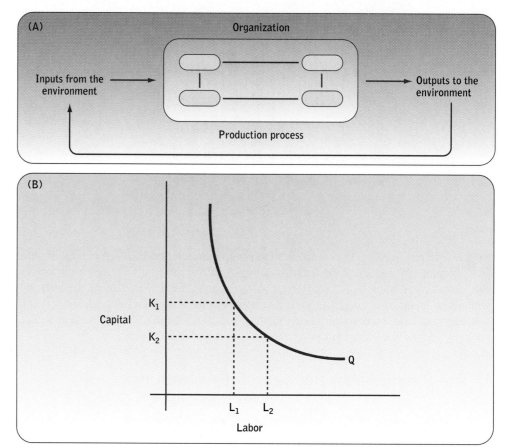

What Is an Organization?

organization (technical definition) A stable, formal social structure that takes resources from the environment and processes them to produce outputs.

An **organization** is a stable, formal social structure that takes resources from the environment and processes them to produce outputs. This technical definition focuses on three elements of an organization (see Figure 3-2). Capital and labor are primary production factors provided by the environment. The organization (the firm) transforms these inputs into products and services in a production function—a process that transforms capital and labor into a product.[1] The products and services are consumed by environments in return for supply inputs.

An organization is more stable than an informal group in terms of longevity and routineness. Organizations are formal because they are legal entities and must abide by laws. They have internal rules and procedures. Organizations are social structures because they are a collection of social elements, much as a machine has a structure—a particular arrangement of valves, cams, shafts, and other parts.

This definition of organizations is powerful and simple, but it is not very descriptive or even predictive of the real-world organizations to which most of us belong. A more realistic, behavioral definition of an **organization** is that it is a collection of rights, privileges, obligations, and responsibilities that are delicately balanced over time through conflict and conflict resolution (see Figure 3-3).

organization (behavioral definition) A collection of rights, privileges, obligations, and responsibilities that are delicately balanced over time through conflict and conflict resolution.

In this behavioral view of the firm, people who work in organizations develop customary ways of working; they gain attachments to existing relationships; and they make arrangements with subordinates and superiors about how work will be done, how much work will be

---

[1] A typical production function is given by Q = A* (K,L), where Q is the quantity of output produced by a firm; K and L are factors of production, capital, and labor. A represents a parameter greater than 0 reflecting the productivity of available technology—factors such as education, knowledge, and changes in technique and technology—which can alter the output Q independent of capital and labor. See any microeconomics textbook for further background. An excellent reference is Robert S. Pindyck and Daniel L. Rubinfield, *Microeconomics* (Upper Saddle River, NJ: Prentice-Hall, 1997). This text has several interesting chapters on information asymmetries, although like most microeconomics texts it is limited in its coverage of technology.

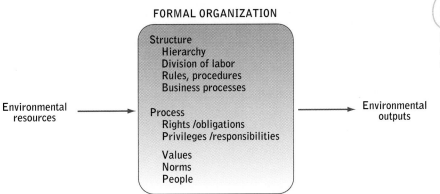

FORMAL ORGANIZATION

Structure
  Hierarchy
  Division of labor
  Rules, procedures
  Business processes

Process
  Rights /obligations
  Privileges /responsibilities

Values
Norms
People

Environmental resources → Environmental outputs

Figure 3-3 The behavioral view of organizations. The behavioral view of organizations emphasizes group relationships, values, and structures.

done, and under what conditions. Most of these arrangements and feelings are not discussed in any formal rule book.

How do these definitions of organizations relate to information system technology? A technical microeconomic view of organizations encourages us to think that introducing new technology changes the way inputs are combined into outputs, like changing the spark plugs on an engine. The firm is seen as infinitely malleable, with capital and labor substituting for one another quite easily.

But the more realistic behavioral definition of an organization suggests that building new information systems or rebuilding old ones involves much more than a technical rearrangement of machines or workers. Instead, technological change requires changes in who owns and controls information, who has the right to access and update that information, and who makes decisions about whom, when, and how. For instance, Schneider's information systems provide central managers with more information to monitor truck drivers. The more complex view forces us to look at the way work is designed and the procedures used to achieve outputs.

The technical and behavioral definitions of organizations are not contradictory. Indeed, they complement one another: The technical definition tells us how thousands of firms in competitive markets combine capital, labor, and information technology, whereas the behavioral model takes us inside the individual firm to see how, in fact, specific firms use capital and labor to produce outputs. Section 3.4 describes how theories based on each of these definitions of organizations can help explain the relationship between information systems and organizations.

Information systems can markedly alter life in the organization. Some information systems change the organizational balance of rights, privileges, obligations, responsibilities, and feelings that has been established over a long time. What this means is that managers cannot design new systems or understand existing systems without understanding organizations.

3.2 Salient Features of Organizations

In this section, we introduce and discuss the major features of organizations of which managers should be aware when building information systems. These organizational features are mediating factors (review Figure 3-1) that influence the relationship between organizations and information technology.

Some features of organizations are common to all organizations; others distinguish one organization from another. Let us look first at the features common to all organizations.

Why Organizations Are So Much Alike: Common Features

You might not think that Apple Computer, United Airlines, and the Aspen Colorado Police Department have much in common, but they do. In some respects, all modern organizations are alike because they share the characteristics that are listed in Table 3.1. A German sociologist, Max Weber, was the first to describe these "ideal-typical" characteristics of organizations in 1911. He called organizations **bureaucracies** that have certain "structural" features (see Table 3.1).

According to Weber, all modern bureaucracies have a clear-cut division of labor and specialization. Organizations employ or train individuals who possess specific talents or skills.

bureaucracy Formal organization with a clear-cut division of labor, abstract rules and procedures, and impartial decision making that uses technical qualifications and professionalism as a basis for promoting employees.

Table 3.1	Structural Characteristics of All Organizations

Clear division of labor

Hierarchy

Explicit rules and procedures

Impartial judgments

Technical qualifications for positions

Maximum organizational efficiency

Organizations arrange specialists in a hierarchy of authority in which everyone is accountable to someone and authority is limited to specific actions. Authority and action are further limited by abstract rules or procedures (standard operating procedures or SOPs) that are interpreted and applied to specific cases. These rules create a system of impartial and universalistic decision making; everyone is treated equally. Organizations try to hire and promote employees on the basis of technical qualifications and professionalism (not personal connections). The organization itself is devoted to the principle of efficiency: maximizing output using limited inputs.

Bureaucracies are so prevalent, according to Weber, because they are the most efficient form of organization. They are much more stable and powerful than mercurial, charismatic groups or formal aristocracies held together by the right of birth. Other scholars supplemented Weber, identifying additional features of organizations. All organizations develop standard operating procedures, politics, and a culture.

Standard Operating Procedures

All organizations, over time, stabilize to produce a given number of products and services. Over long periods of time, the organizations that survive become very efficient, producing a limited number of products and services by following standard routines. In this period of time, employees develop reasonably precise rules, procedures, and practices called **standard operating procedures (SOPs)** to cope with virtually all expected situations. Some of these rules and procedures are written down as formal procedures, but most are rules of thumb to be followed in selected situations.

A great deal of the efficiency that modern organizations attain has little to do with computers but a great deal to do with the development of standard operating procedures. For instance, in the assembly of a car, thousands of motions and procedures must be planned and executed in a precise fashion to permit the finished product to roll off the line. If workers had to decide how each vehicle was to be built, or if managers had to decide how each day's product was to be built, efficiency would drop dramatically. Instead, managers and workers develop a complex set of standard procedures to handle most situations. Any change in SOPs requires an enormous organizational effort. Indeed, the organization may need to halt the entire production process, or create a new and expensive parallel system, which must then be tested exhaustively before the old SOPs can be retired. For example, difficulty in changing standard operating procedures is one reason Detroit auto makers have been slow to adopt Japanese mass-production methods. Until recently, U.S. auto makers followed Henry Ford's mass-production principles. Ford believed that the cheapest way to build cars was to churn out the largest number of autos by having workers repeatedly perform a simple task. By contrast, Japanese auto makers have emphasized "lean production" methods where a smaller number of workers each performing several tasks can produce cars with less inventory, less investment, and fewer mistakes. Workers have multiple jobs and responsibilities and are encouraged to note every glitch and, if necessary, stop production to correct a problem.

Organizational Politics

Organizations are arranged so that people occupy different positions. Because these individuals have different concerns and specialties, they naturally have differences in viewpoint, perspective, and opinion about how resources, rewards, and punishments should be distrib-

standard operating procedures (SOPs) Precise, defined rules, procedures, and practices developed by organizations to cope with virtually all expected situations.

uted. Because of these differences, political struggle, competition, and conflict occur in every organization. Sometimes political struggles occur when individuals or interest groups seek to exercise leadership and to gain advantages. Other times, entire groups compete, leading to clashes on a large scale. In either case, politics is a normal part of organizational life.

One difficulty of bringing about change in organizations—especially concerning the development of new information systems—is the political resistance that any important organizational change seems to bring forth. "Important" changes are those that directly affect who does what to whom, where, when, and how. Virtually all information systems that bring about significant changes in goals, procedures, productivity, and personnel are politically charged.

Organizational Culture

All organizations have bedrock, unassailable, unquestioned (by the members) assumptions that define the goals and products of the organization. **Organizational culture** is the set of fundamental assumptions about what the organization should produce, what business processes should be used and how they should be defined, how it should produce its products, where, and for whom. Generally, these cultural assumptions are taken totally for granted and rarely are publicly announced or discussed. They are simply assumptions that few people, if anyone (in their right mind), would question (Schein, 1985).

> **organizational culture** The set of fundamental assumptions about what products the organization should produce, how and where it should produce them, and for whom they should be produced.

Everything else—technology, values, norms, public announcements, and so on—follows from these assumptions. You can see organizational culture at work by looking around your university or college. Some bedrock assumptions of university life are that professors know more than students, the reason students attend college is to learn, the primary purpose of the university is to create new knowledge and communicate knowledge to students, classes follow a regular schedule, and libraries are repositories of knowledge in the form of books and journals. Sometimes these cultural assumptions are true. Organizational culture is a powerful unifying force, which restrains political conflict and promotes common understanding, agreement on procedures, and common practices. If we all share the same basic cultural assumptions, then agreement on other matters is more likely.

At the same time, organizational culture is a powerful restraint on change, especially technological change. Any technological change that threatens commonly held cultural assumptions will meet with a great deal of resistance. One reason U.S. auto makers were slow to switch to "lean production" methods is because of long-standing assumptions that management should be authoritarian and does not need to listen to the opinions of workers. Not only did U.S. companies change the business processes and standard operating procedures on their assembly lines, but they also had to find ways to involve auto workers in improving factories. These deep-seated changes were difficult given the hierarchical and authoritarian culture of U.S. auto companies.

However, there are times when the only sensible way to employ a new technology is directly opposed to an existing organizational culture. When this occurs, the technology is often stalled or delayed while the culture slowly adjusts (Klotz, 1966).

Why Organizations Are So Different: Unique Features

Although all organizations have some common characteristics, no two organizations are identical. Organizations have different structures, goals, constituencies, leadership styles, tasks, and surrounding environments.

Different Organizational Types

One important way in which organizations differ is in their structure or shape. The differences among organizational structures are characterized in many ways. Mintzberg's classification described in Table 3.2 is especially useful and simple, for it identifies five basic kinds of organizations.

Organizations and Environments

Organizations reside in environments from which they draw resources and to which they supply goods and services. Organizations and environments have a two-way reciprocal relationship. On the one hand, organizations are open to, and dependent on, the social and physical environment that surrounds them. Organizations need financial resources and political legitimacy (a set of laws

Table 3.2 Organizational Structures

Organizational Type	Description	Example
Entrepreneurial structure	Young, small firm in a fast-changing environment. It has a simple structure and is managed by an entrepreneur serving as its single chief executive officer.	Small start-up business
Machine bureaucracy	Large bureaucracy existing in a slowly changing environment, producing standard products. It is dominated by a centralized management team and centralized decision making.	Midsized manufacturing firm
Divisionalized bureaucracy	Combination of multiple machine bureaucracies, each producing a different product or service, all topped by one central headquarters.	Fortune 500 firms such as General Motors
Professional bureaucracy	Knowledge-based organization where goods and services depend on the expertise and knowledge of professionals. Dominated by department heads with weak centralized authority.	Law firms, school systems, hospitals
Adhocracy	"Task force" organization that must respond to rapidly changing environments. Consists of large groups of specialists organized into short-lived multidisciplinary teams and has weak central management.	Consulting firms such as the Rand Corporation

by which to operate) provided by outside institutions and governments. Customers are significant members of the environment. And knowledge and technology are also a part of the environment: They are produced by other actors in the environment and purchased by the organization as educated labor or as pure knowledge assets (such as databases or other information flows).

On the other hand, organizations can influence their environments. Organizations form alliances with others to influence the political process, often altering the tax environment to suit their needs, and they advertise to influence customer acceptance of their products. Organizations also choose to participate in certain environments: General Motors chooses every day to stay in the automobile business.

Information technology, specifically business systems, plays a significant role in helping organizations perceive changes in their environments, and also in helping organizations act on their environments (see Figure 3-4). Information systems are key tools for *environmental scanning*, helping managers identify external changes that might require an organizational response.

Environments generally change much faster than organizations. Organizational environments change for all the reasons described in Chapter 1: changing knowledge and technol-

Figure 3-4 Environments and organizations have a reciprocal relationship. Environments shape what organizations can do, but organizations can influence their environments and decide to change environments altogether. Information technology plays a critical role in helping organizations perceive environmental change, and in helping organizations act on their environment. Information systems act as a filter between organizations and their environments. They do not necessarily reflect reality but, instead, refract environmental change through a number of built-in biases.

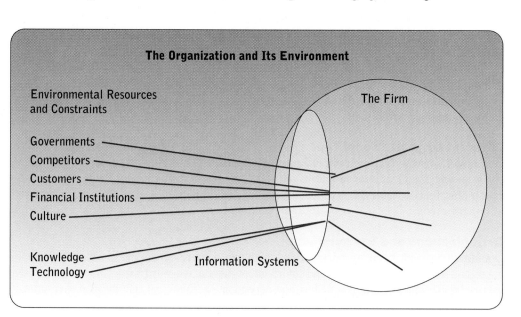

ogy, new values, new markets, and changes in the global distribution of wealth. Environmental change is a main cause of organizational failure. As environments change, they pose new problems for managers of organizations. New knowledge, for instance, can invalidate the existing knowledge of an entire industry. Consider the fate of the coal industry, the vacuum tube industry, and the horse carriage industry. When environments become turbulent, complex, and resource constrained, the knowledge and skills that organizations once possessed can become useless, and even a hindrance to change.

Some organizations fail to perceive, or rather misperceive, changes in their environments. Even if correctly perceived, organizations react to environmental changes in a variety of ways. Some organizations "learn" how to survive in new and changing environments by adopting new information technologies, by changing their products and services and their production process, by reallocating assets of all kinds, and by altering their cultures—explanations of what they are doing. These organizations rapidly acquire new knowledge and technology, and employ these assets in production quickly.

Other organizations, perhaps most, are more resistant to change and they become dysfunctional and fail. These organizations learn by insulating themselves from their environments; they survive by relying on slack resources and savings and by developing rigid standard operating procedures. They become efficient at what they always did, such as learning how to run a traditional steel mill more efficiently. Eventually these coping and learning mechanisms are overwhelmed and the organizations fail.

Most people do not realize how fragile and short-lived formal organizations really are. Consider that less than 10 percent of Fortune 500 companies in 1918 survived more than 50 years; less than 4 percent of all federal government organizations ever created are still in existence; 50 percent of new private organizations are out of business within 5 years (Laudon, 1989).

The main reasons for organizational failure are an inability to adapt to a rapidly changing environment and the lack of resources—particularly among young firms—to sustain even short periods of troubled times (Freeman et al., 1983). New technologies, new products, and changing public tastes and values (many of which result in new government regulations) put strains on any organization's culture, politics, and people. In general, most organizations do not cope well with large environmental shifts.

From an organizational standpoint, technology is a major environmental factor that continually threatens existing arrangements. At times, technological changes occur so radically as to constitute a "technological discontinuity," a sharp break in industry practice that either enhances or destroys the competence of firms in an industry (Tushman and Anderson, 1986). Fast-changing technologies, such as information technology, pose very heavy demands on organizations (Mendelson and Pillai, 1998). For instance, Wang Laboratories, a leading manufacturer of minicomputers and word processors, was a dominant force in the computer industry during the 1970s and early 1980s. But when powerful desktop PCs reduced the need for minicomputers, Wang nearly went out of business because it failed to adapt its products to the new technology.

Other Differences among Organizations

There are many reasons organizations have different shapes or structures. Organizations differ in their ultimate goals and the types of power used to achieve the goals. Some organizations have coercive goals (e.g., prisons); others have utilitarian goals (e.g., businesses). Still others have normative goals (universities, religious groups). The kinds of power and incentives differ accordingly, as does the overall shape of the organization: A coercive organization will be very hierarchical whereas a normative organization will be less hierarchical.

The nature of leadership differs greatly from one organization to another, even in similar organizations devoted to the same goal. Some of the major leadership styles are democratic, authoritarian (even totalitarian), laissez-faire (leadership is absent), technocratic (according to technical criteria, formal models), or bureaucratic (strictly according to formal rules).

Still another way organizations differ is by the tasks they perform and the technology they use. In some cases, organizations use routine tasks that could be programmed; that is, tasks may be reduced to formal rules that require little judgment (e.g., inventory reordering). Organizations that primarily perform routine tasks are typically hierarchical and run

Keying data from tax returns into the Internal Revenue Service computer system is an important activity in the tax collection process. Business processes coordinate work, information, and knowledge.

according to standard procedures. In other cases, organizations work with highly judgmental, nonroutine tasks (e.g., a consulting company that creates strategic plans for other companies).

Business Processes

business processes The unique ways in which organizations coordinate and organize work activities, information, and knowledge to produce a valuable product or service.

Business processes refer to the manner in which work is organized, coordinated, and focused to produce a valuable product or service. On the one hand, business processes are concrete work flows of material, information, and knowledge—sets of activities. But, on the other hand, business processes also refer to the unique ways in which organizations coordinate work, information, and knowledge, and the ways in which management chooses to coordinate work.

The contemporary interest with business processes comes from the recognition that strategic success ultimately depends on how well firms execute their primary mission of delivering the lowest cost, highest quality goods and services to customers. Examples of processes are new-product development, which turns an idea into a manufacturable prototype; or order fulfillment, which begins with the receipt of an order and ends when the customer has received and paid for the product.

Business processes, by nature, are generally cross-functional, transcending the boundaries between sales, marketing, manufacturing, and research and development; processes cut across the traditional organizational structure, grouping employees from different functional specialties to complete a piece of work. For example, the order fulfillment process at many companies requires cooperation among the sales function (receiving the order, entering the order), the accounting function (credit checking and billing for the order), and the manufacturing function (assembling and shipping the order).

The objectives for processes are more external and linked to meeting customer and market demands than are those for the traditional functional approach. Instead of evaluating how well each functional area is performing as a discrete business function, management would evaluate how well a group executes a process. For instance, instead of measuring the manufacturing department independently on how well it reduces the cost to produce each unit and

Mail returns	Sort	Check for mistakes	Key in computer	Check calculations	File paper in cabinet	Send bills, refunds, and error letters
1	2	3	4	5	6	7

Figure 3-5 The Internal Revenue Service tax collection process. Collecting federal income taxes is a multistep process with many activities to coordinate.

the shipping department independently on how quickly it ships out each unit, management might look at the entire logistics process from receipt of raw material to receipt by the customer.

Figure 3-5 depicts the traditional income tax collection process at the U.S. Internal Revenue Service (IRS). Taxpayers mail their income tax returns (and payment checks) to the IRS (Step 1), where they are first sorted by type of return, whether checks are enclosed, and other criteria (Step 2). IRS examiners look over the paper returns for mistakes, making sure all schedules are attached (Step 3). Thousands of people key only the most important pieces of information from each return into the IRS computer system (Step 4). The computers check the calculations and data on the returns, and generate a report of returns with errors (Step 5). The paper returns are filed in cabinets (Step 6). The IRS sends out refunds, bills for additional payments, and letters to taxpayers informing them of errors on their returns (Step 7).

Information systems can help organizations achieve great efficiencies by automating parts of these processes or by helping organizations rethink and streamline these processes through the development of work-flow software. For example, experts have pointed out that the traditional IRS tax collection process could be made more efficient—with taxpayer information more easily accessible—by eliminating some of the manual and paper-based activities. Instead of entering limited pieces of data from paper returns into the computer system, the entire tax return could be scanned into the computer, making instantly available all of its information. The computer could perform all of the returns examination and error checking instead of having people make preliminary examinations of the returns (Johnston, 1998). Chapter 11 treats this subject in greater detail because it is fundamental to systems analysis and design.

Automating business processes requires careful analysis and planning. When systems are used to strengthen the wrong business model or business processes, the business can become more efficient at doing what it should not do. And as a result, the strategic position of the firm suffers, and it becomes vulnerable to competitors who may have discovered the right business model. Therefore, one of the most important strategic decisions that a firm can make is not deciding how to use computers to improve business processes, but instead to first understand what business processes need improvement (Keen, 1997). The choice of which business process to improve is critical.

Levels of Analysis

Within organizations, there are different levels, occupations, divisions, and groups. All organizations have levels, but each organization is quite different from others in terms of what the levels are, who occupies them, and what tasks are assigned to different levels. The impact of information systems will probably be different for different levels and groups within an organization.

Each organizational level has different concerns and a different framework of analysis. This can be seen in Figure 3-6, which describes the various organizational levels and the principal activities at each level, providing examples of information systems that are appropriate for each level.

At the individual and small-group levels of organization, information systems apply to a particular job, task, or project. At the department and division levels, information systems deal with a particular business function, product, or service. At the organization, interorganizational, and organizational network levels, information systems support multiple products, services, and goals and facilitate alliances and coordination between two different organizations or groups of organizations.

Organizational Level		Activity	Example Support System
Individual		Job, task	PC application; personal client database; decision-support systems
Team		Project	Product scheduling; access to mainframe data; access to external data sources; dynamic information requirements; group DSS; groupware
Department		Major function	Accounts payable; warehouse; payroll; human resources; marketing; stable information requirements; MIS; major transaction systems
Division		Major product or service	Systems to support production, marketing, administration, and human resources; access to organizational financial and planning data; MIS; major transaction systems; on-line interactive systems
Organization		Multiple products, services, and goals	Integrated financial and planning systems; MIS; on-line interactive systems; ESS
Interorganization		Alliance Competition Exchange Contact	Communication systems; intelligence, observation, and monitoring systems
Organizational network		Sector of economy: related products, services; interdependencies	Informal communication systems; industry and sector-level formal reporting systems

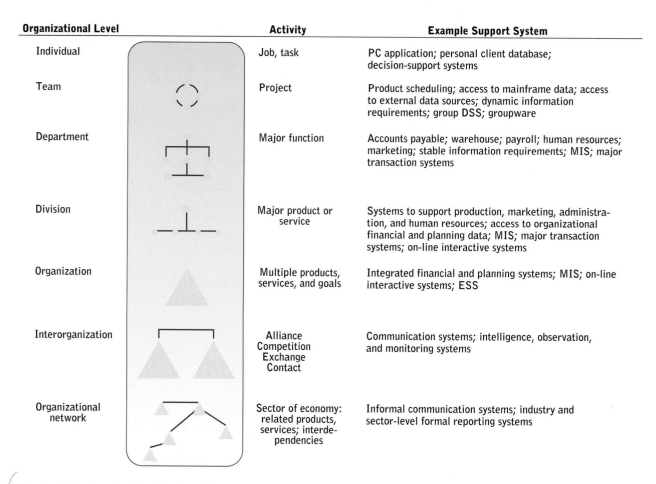

Figure 3-6 Organizational levels and support systems. Systems are designed to support various levels of the organization.

Much of the work of an organization is done by informal task forces, interdepartmental committees, project teams, and committees. Table 3.3 presents the most important work groups and shows how systems can support them. These work groups generally have rapidly changing information needs, peak-load work schedules associated with project deadlines, and high communication requirements. Group collaboration systems are one of the most recently developed system tools directed at work groups (see Chapter 14).

We have developed a rather long list of salient features you should know about when considering information systems in organizations. As you can see in Table 3.4, the list of unique features of organizations is longer than the common features list. What this should suggest to you is that most organizations are quite unique. The impacts of systems will differ from one organization to another, and only by close analysis of a specific organization can a manager design and manage information systems.

3.3 How Organizations Affect Information Systems

We now can look more closely at the two-way relationship between information systems and organizations. We first need to explain how organizations affect technology and systems. There are four important questions to consider in studying this issue.

○ How have organizations actually used information systems?

○ How has the organizational role of information systems changed?

Table 3.3   Work Groups, Problems, and Systems Support

Type of Work Group Support	Description	Problems	Systems
Hierarchical	Formal working relationship between manager and staff	Frequent meetings; dispersed work environments	Video conferencing; electronic mail (one to many)
Interdepartmental committees	Sequential activities; "expediters," "fixers"	Need occasional direct communication	Electronic messaging (one to one)
Project teams	Formally defined groups; close day-to-day interaction	Meeting schedules	Scheduling and communication software; meeting support tools; document interchange; intranet
Committees	Formally defined groups; occasional interaction	High peak load; communications; intermittent meetings	Electronic bulletin boards; video conferencing; electronic mail; computer conferencing
Task forces	Formally defined single-purpose groups	Rapid communication; access to internal and external data	Graphics display; information utility; document interchange; meeting support tools
Peer groups/social networks	Informal groups of similar-status individuals	Intense personal communication	Telephone; electronic mail

Problems of all work groups

Making arrangements

Attending meetings

Long agendas

Cost of meetings

Between-meeting activities

Table 3.4   A Summary of Salient Features of Organizations

Common Features	Unique Features
Formal structure	Organizational type
Standard operating procedures (SOPs)	Environments
Politics	Goals
Culture	Power
	Constituencies
	Function
	Leadership
	Tasks
	Technology
	Business processes
	Levels

Much of the organization's work is accomplished by task forces and project teams using their combined skills.

○ Who operates information systems?

○ Why do organizations adopt information systems in the first place?

Decisions about the Role of Information Systems

Organizations have a direct impact on information technology by making decisions about how the technology will be used and what role it will play in the organization. Chapters 1 and 2 described the ever-widening role of information systems in organizations. Supporting this changing role have been changes in the technical and organizational configuration of systems that have brought computing power and data much closer to the ultimate end users (see Figure 3-7).

Isolated "electronic accounting machines" with limited functions in the 1950s gave way to large, centralized mainframe computers that served corporate headquarters and a few remote sites in the 1960s. In the 1970s, midsize minicomputers located in individual departments or divisions of the organization were networked to large centralized computers. Desktop PCs first were used independently and then were linked to minicomputers and large computers in the 1980s.

In the 1990s, the architecture for a fully networked organization emerged. In this new enterprise-wide architecture, computers coordinate information flowing among desktops and large computers and perhaps among hundreds of smaller local networks. These networks can be connected into a network that connects the entire enterprise or is linked to external networks, including the Internet. Information systems have become integral, on-line interactive tools deeply involved in the minute-to-minute operations and decision making of large organizations.

Information Technology Services

A second way in which organizations affect information technology is through decisions about who will design, build, and operate the technology within the organization. These decisions determine how technology services will be delivered.

The information systems function in the organization is composed of three distinct entities (see Figure 3-8). The first is a formal organizational unit or function called an **information systems department.** The second consists of information systems specialists such as programmers, systems analysts, project leaders, and information systems managers. Also, external specialists such as hardware vendors and manufacturers, software firms, and consultants frequently participate in the day-to-day operations and long-term planning of information systems. A third element of the information systems package is the technology itself, both hardware and software.

information systems department The formal organizational unit that is responsible for the information systems function in the organization.

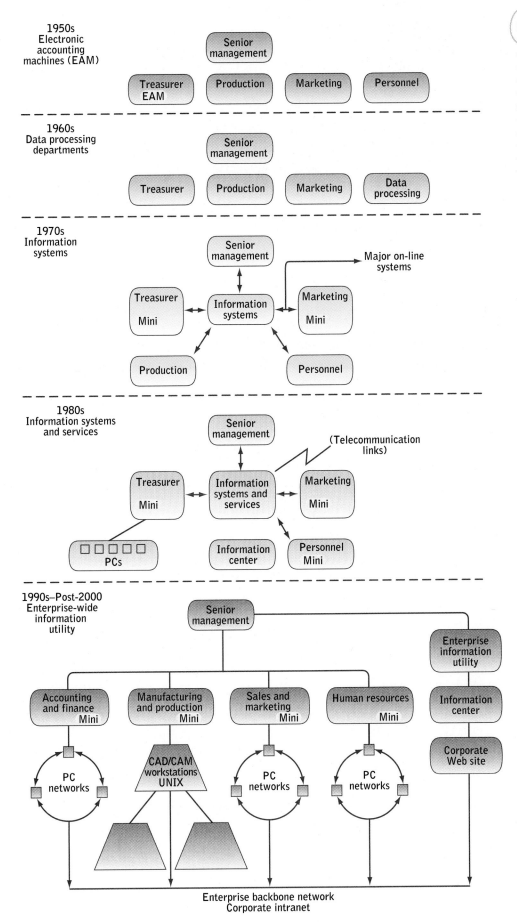

Figure 3-7 The development of information architecture of organizations. The last five decades have seen dramatic changes in the technical and organizational configurations of systems. During the 1950s organizations were dependent on computers for a few critical functions. The 1960s witnessed the development of large centralized machines. By the late 1970s and into the 1980s information architecture became complex and information systems included telecommunications links to distribute information. During the 1990s information architecture has been an enterprise-wide information utility, which in turn is connected to vendors and customers through the World Wide Web.

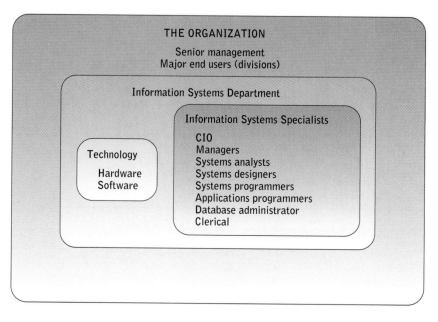

Figure 3-8 The information systems function. Many groups, individuals, and organizations are involved in the design and management of information systems.

THE ORGANIZATION
Senior management
Major end users (divisions)

Information Systems Department

Information Systems Specialists

CIO
Managers
Systems analysts
Systems designers
Systems programmers
Applications programmers
Database administrator
Clerical

Technology

Hardware
Software

Today the information systems group often acts as a powerful change agent in the organization, suggesting new business strategies and new information-based products and coordinating both the development of technology and the planned changes in the organization.

The size of the information systems department can vary greatly, depending on the role of information systems in the organization and on the organization's size. The size of the information systems group and the total expenditures on computers and information systems are largest in service organizations (especially those that sell information products such as Dow Jones News), where information systems can consume more than 40 percent of gross revenues.

In the early years of the computer, when the role of information systems was limited, the information systems group was composed mostly of **programmers,** highly trained technical specialists who wrote the software instructions for the computer. Today, in most information systems groups, a growing proportion of staff members are systems analysts. **Systems analysts** constitute the principal liaison between the information systems group and the rest of the organization. It is the system analyst's job to translate business problems and requirements into information requirements and systems.

Information systems managers are leaders of teams of programmers and analysts; project managers; physical facility managers; telecommunications managers; heads of office automation groups; and, finally, managers of computer operations and data entry staff.

End users are representatives of departments outside the information systems group for whom applications are developed. These users are playing an increasingly large role in the design and development of information systems. In many organizations the information systems department is headed by a **chief information officer (CIO).** The CIO is a senior management position to oversee the use of information technology in the firm.

The last element of the information systems function is the technology itself—the hardware and software instructions. Chapters 6 and 7 provide detailed discussions of these topics.

Why Organizations Build Information Systems

Systems today are, of course, built to increase efficiency and save money but they have become vitally important simply for staying in business and may even be a source of competitive advantage. However, this may not be the only, or even the primary reason for adapting systems.

Some organizations build systems because they are simply more innovative than others. They have values that encourage any kind of innovation, regardless of its direct economic benefit to the company. In other cases, information systems are built because of the ambitions of various groups within an organization. And in some cases, such as Schneider National described in the

programmers Highly trained technical specialists who write computer software instructions.

systems analysts Specialists who translate business problems and requirements into information requirements and systems, acting as liaison between the information systems department and the rest of the organization.

information systems managers Leaders of the various specialists in the information systems department.

end users Representatives of departments outside the information systems group for whom information systems applications are developed.

chief information officer (CIO) Senior manager in charge of the information systems function in the firm.

Window on Organizations

On January 1, 1999, 11 European nations merged their currencies to create a single currency called the euro. The euro replaces such venerable old currencies as the French franc and the German deutsche mark (DM). For 3 1/2 years thereafter, people will be free to use either the euro or the currencies of the 11 eligible European countries. On July 1, 2002, those 11 national currencies will cease to be legal tender, and everyone will have no choice but to use the euro.

Organizations around the globe must convert their information systems to handle the new European monetary unit. Software productivity expert T. Capers Jones estimates that 12 million information system applications are affected. Currency trading firms must adjust their software to handle the euro, but this is just the proverbial tip of the iceberg. Tax software, software for banks, credit cards, and international trades of securities and goods must be modified. Automated teller machines must be upgraded. Ultimately, any business that relates to European currencies must make changes—even telephone booths and corner newspaper machines.

Because the euro will not replace the 11 currencies in 1 day, the problem is exceptionally complex. During the transition period, the national currencies and the euro will exist side by side. Anyone using the money of the 11 countries will be free to choose either the traditional national currency or the euro. Organizations must have systems that can handle transactions in both the local money and the euro.

Currently the value of each of the 11 national currencies is set by the marketplace, and those relationships are very complex. One deutsche mark may be worth 3.352 francs and 987.00 lira. Conversion values almost always have had to be cited in decimals, up to as many as six decimal places in some cases. Traditionally, to convert from one currency to another, you needed to multiply (or divide) the one currency by a given number. However, during the transition period, each national currency first will have to be converted to euros and then converted into the other currency. For example, to convert deutsche marks into francs, the deutsche marks first must be converted into euros, and then the euros will be converted into francs. The European Monetary Union will set the value of the euro against each of the national currencies of the participating countries during the transition period.

One example of the difficulties organizations will face with the interim currency conversion is the rounding problem. Conversion ratios already stretch into seven, eight, ten, or more decimal places, making rounding a necessity. In the new situation, rounding will have to occur on each of the conversion steps between two European currencies. Rounding twice makes the process unpredictable, causing one side to gain unexpectedly while the other one loses. If the amount being converted is very large, the windfall for one side can be quite substantial, as will the unplanned losses for the other.

Bond-trading systems face additional hurdles. By January 1, 1999, for instance, a DM 10 million-denominated bond would become a 19.5xx,xxx.xxx euro-denominated bond. Most current systems can only deal with the issued value of a bond in whole numbers. They would have to be changed to handle numbers after the decimal point.

Most programming had to be completed months before January 1, 1999, to give organizations adequate time to test their newly programmed software. The costs are high. European corporations with worldwide operations may spend from $150 billion to $400 billion to upgrade their systems.

To Think About: How are organizations and information systems affected by the adoption of the euro?

Sources: Thomas Kamm, "Emergence of Euro Embodies Challenge and Hope for Europe," *The Wall Street Journal,* January 4, 1999; Adam Cox, "Cashing in on the Euro," *Sm@art Reseller,* January 1, 1999; Adam Cox, "Specter of Costly Euro Mistake," Reuters, January 1, 1999; and Andrew Ross Sorkin, "A Year before the Millennium Bug, There's the Euro Problem," *The New York Times,* March 3, 1998.

chapter opening vignette, and organizations converting to the new euro currency as described in the Window on Organizations, changes in an organization's environment—including changes in government regulations, competitors' actions, and costs—demand a computer system response.

Figure 3-9 illustrates a model of the systems development process that includes many factors other than economic considerations. This model divides the explanations for why organizations adopt systems into two groups: external environmental factors and internal institutional factors (Laudon, 1985; King et al., 1994).

Environmental factors are factors that are external to the organization that influence the adoption and design of information systems. Some external environmental factors are rising costs of labor or other resources, the competitive actions of other organizations, and changes in government regulations. The environment also provides organizations with opportunities—new technologies, new sources of capital, the development of new production processes, the demise of a competitor, or a new government program that increases the demand for certain products.

environmental factors
Factors external to the organization that influence the adoption and design of information systems.

Figure 3-9 The systems development process. External environmental factors and internal institutional factors influence the types of information systems the organizations select, develop, and use.

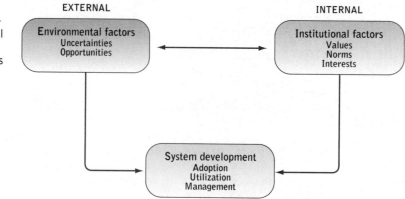

institutional factors Factors internal to the organization that influence the adoption and design of information systems.

Institutional factors are factors internal to the organization that influence the adoption and design of information systems. They include values, norms, and vital interests that govern matters of strategic importance to the organization. For instance, the top management of a corporation can decide that it needs to exercise much stronger control over the inventory process and therefore decides to develop an inventory information system. The resulting system is adopted, developed, and operated for purely internal, institutional reasons (for a similar model, see Kraemer et al., 1989).

3.4 How Information Systems Affect Organizations

We shall now look at another question: How do information systems affect organizations? To find some answers, we need to summarize a large body of research and theory based on economic and behavioral approaches.

Economic Theories

From an economic standpoint, information system technology can be viewed as a factor of production that can be freely substituted for capital and labor. As the cost of information system technology falls, it is substituted for labor, which historically has been a rising cost. Hence, in the **microeconomic model** of the firm, information technology should result in a decline in the number of middle managers and clerical workers as information technology substitutes for their labor.

microeconomic model Model of the firm that views information technology as a factor of production that can be freely substituted for capital and labor.

Information technology also helps firms contract in size because it can reduce transaction costs—the costs incurred when a firm buys on the marketplace what it cannot make itself. According to **transaction cost theory,** firms and individuals seek to economize on transaction costs, much as they do on production costs. Using markets is expensive (Williamson, 1985) because of coordination costs such as locating and communicating with distant suppliers, monitoring contract compliance, buying insurance, obtaining information on products, and so forth. Traditionally, firms have tried to reduce transaction costs by getting bigger, hiring more employees or buying their own suppliers and distributors, as General Motors used to do.

transaction cost theory Economic theory that states that firms exist because they can conduct marketplace transactions internally more cheaply than they can with external firms in the marketplace.

Information technology, especially the use of networks, can help firms lower the cost of market participation (transaction costs), making it worthwhile for firms to contract with external suppliers instead of using internal sources. For example, by using computer links to external suppliers, the Chrysler Corporation can achieve economies by obtaining more than 70 percent of its parts from the outside. Figure 3-10 shows that as transaction costs decrease, firm size (the number of employees) should shrink because it becomes easier and cheaper for the firm to contract the purchase of goods and services in the marketplace rather than to make the product or service itself. Firm size can stay constant or contract even if the company increases its revenues. (For example, General Electric reduced its workforce from about 400,000 people in the early 1980s to about 230,000 while increasing revenues 150 percent.)

Information technology also can reduce internal management costs. According to **agency theory,** the firm is viewed as a "nexus of contracts" among self-interested individuals rather than as a unified, profit-maximizing entity (Jensen and Meckling, 1976). A principal

agency theory Economic theory that views the firm as a nexus of contracts among self-interested individuals rather than a unified, profit-maximizing entity.

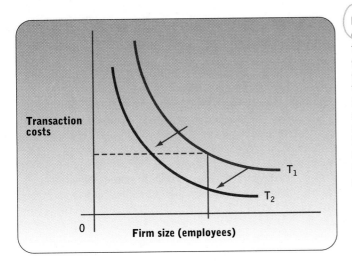

Figure 3-10 The transaction cost theory of the impact of information technology on the organization. Firms traditionally grew in size in order to reduce transaction costs. IT potentially reduces the costs for a given size, shifting the transaction cost curve inward, opening up the possibility of revenue growth without increasing size, or even revenue growth accompanied by shrinking size.

(owner) employs "agents" (employees) to perform work on his or her behalf. However, agents need constant supervision and management, otherwise they will tend to pursue their own interests rather than those of the owners. As firms grow in size and scope, agency costs or coordination costs rise because owners must expend more and more effort supervising and managing employees.

Information technology, by reducing the costs of acquiring and analyzing information, permits organizations to reduce agency costs because it becomes easier for managers to oversee a greater number of employees. Figure 3-11 shows that by reducing overall management costs, information technology allows firms to increase revenues while shrinking the numbers of middle management and clerical workers. We have seen examples in earlier chapters where information technology expanded the power and scope of small organizations by allowing them to perform coordinating activities such as processing orders or keeping track of inventory with very few clerks and managers.

The Window on Technology describes how companies in the oil industry have used information technology to reduce transaction and agency costs.

Behavioral Theories

While economic theories try to explain how large numbers of firms act in the marketplace, behavioral theories from sociology, psychology, and political science are more useful for describing the behavior of individual firms. Behavioral research has found little evidence that information systems automatically transform organizations, although the systems may be

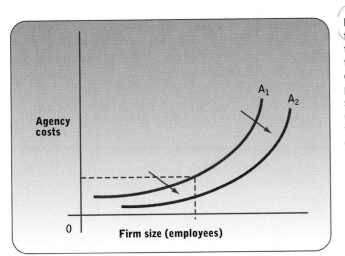

Figure 3-11 The agency cost theory of the impact of information technology on the organization. As firms grow in size and complexity, traditionally they experience rising agency costs. IT shifts the agency cost curve down and to the right, allowing firms to increase size while lowering agency costs.

Window on Technology

Oil Companies Go Virtual

As a source of oil, the Gulf of Mexico has long been considered a "mature" area where the big fields have all been found. Production has been declining for years, and the big companies have moved on to new drilling sites. But these previously worked fields have proved lucrative for smaller companies who use computer technology to find small pockets of oil that the larger firms have overlooked.

One company that has thrived in the Gulf of Mexico is Zilkha Energy Company of Houston, Texas. Zilkha is a virtual organization for oil exploration. Zilkha owns no oil rigs, employs no drillers, and maintains no structure of corporate executives. Management can outsource any of these services when it needs them. The company occupies a single floor in a building in downtown Houston. Zilkha specializes in two areas only—analyzing data in order to find retrievable oil reserves and finding the financing to drill once those areas have been identified. The company does not generate the data it uses, and it does not drill for the oil itself. Because the organization and methods have been so successful, in January 1998, Sonat Energy, one of the largest energy companies in the United States, paid $1 billion to purchase Zilkha.

Those who search for oil no longer rely on educated guesses made by trained geologists. Rather, after doing preliminary surveys, companies now mark out territory they believe has potential, and they buy up leases. Then they generate data on the territory before deciding whether to drill, and if so, where. Zilkha was dealing with an area that had all been leased before and had been explored. Therefore, it was able to reorder the standard process. Rather than surveying and buying leases first, the company began with the data. They purchased huge quantities of existing 3-D seismographic data from other companies for most of the con-

tinental shelf extending about 150 miles from the shore in the Gulf of Mexico. (Such data are generated when ships bounce sound signals off underground formations and computers translate the responses.) Zilkha would then perform its own analysis of the data to find the best drilling prospects.

Zilkha brought in the most advanced computer tools available, spending more than $1 million for its main computer alone. Management hired only top quality geologists to do the analysis for them. Their goal was to find the most likely spots for new drilling. Once those spots had been identified, they bought the leases giving them the right to drill. Of 79 wells they have drilled, they have been successful 66 percent of the time, more than twice the success rate of the industry. What they are finding with improved computer analysis techniques and more modern drilling methods is oil and gas that either could not have been found years ago or could not have been retrieved economically with older drilling technology. Other companies are now doing the same thing in a number of areas around the world, and their discoveries have resulted in a Europe and a North America that are far less dependent on Middle East oil than in the past.

To Think About: How did information systems transform the oil exploration business? How can transaction cost theory and agency theory explain Zilkha's success as a virtual corporation?

Sources: Allen R. Myerson, "A Wildcatter on the Tame Side," **The New York Times,** March 20, 1998; and Susan Warren, "Crude Oil Price Falls, But Firms Still Profit and Sink New Wells," **The Wall Street Journal,** March 17, 1998.

instrumental in accomplishing this goal once senior management decides to pursue this end. Instead, researchers have observed an intricately choreographed relationship in which organizations and information technology mutually influence each other.

Behavioral researchers have theorized that information technology could change the hierarchy of decision making in organizations by lowering the costs of information acquisition and broadening the distribution of information (Malone, 1997). Information technology could bring information directly from operating units to senior managers, thereby eliminating middle managers and their clerical support workers. Information technology could permit senior managers to contact lower level operating units directly through the use of networked telecommunications and computers, eliminating middle management intermediaries (Leavitt and Whisler, 1958). Alternatively, information technology could distribute information directly to lower level workers, who could then make their own decisions based on their own knowledge and information without any management intervention. Some research even suggests that computerization increases the information given to middle managers, empowering them to make more important decisions than in the past, thus reducing the need for large numbers of lower level workers (Shore, 1983). Figure 3-12 illustrates some of these changes in organizational structure.

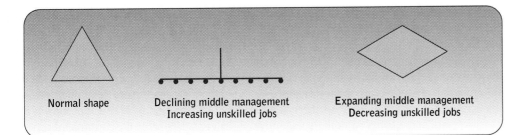

| Normal shape | Declining middle management Increasing unskilled jobs | Expanding middle management Decreasing unskilled jobs |

Figure 3-12 The impact of information systems on organizational structure. There are several hypotheses on how systems can change the structure of an organization. Three outcomes are represented here: Systems can have no effect; they may reduce the number of middle managers, creating an inverted **T** effect; or they may expand the capabilities and numbers of middle managers, producing the diamond effect.

In postindustrial societies, authority increasingly relies on knowledge and competence, and not on mere formal position. Hence, the shape of organizations should "flatten" because professional workers tend to be self-managing; and decision making should become more decentralized as knowledge and information become more widespread throughout (Drucker, 1988). Information technology may encourage "task force" networked organizations in which groups of professionals come together—face-to-face or electronically—for short periods of time to accomplish a specific task (e.g., designing a new automobile); once the task is accomplished, the individuals join other task forces. More firms may operate as virtual organizations, where work no longer is tied to geographic location.

Who makes sure that self-managed teams do not head off in the wrong direction? Who decides which person works on what team and for how long? How can managers judge the performance of someone who is constantly rotating from team to team? How do people know where their careers are headed? New approaches for evaluating, organizing, and informing workers are required; and not all companies can make virtual work effective (Davenport and Pearlson, 1998).

In virtual offices, employees do not work from a permanent location. Here, work spaces are temporary with employees moving from desk to desk as vacancies open.

No one knows the answers to these questions, and it is not clear that all modern organizations will undergo this transformation. General Motors, for example, may have many self-managed knowledge workers in certain divisions, but it still will have a manufacturing division structured as a large, traditional bureaucracy. In general, the shape of organizations historically changes with the business cycle and with the latest management fashions. When times are good and profits are high, firms hire large numbers of supervisory personnel; when times are tough, they let go many of these same people (Mintzberg, 1979). It is not known if the shrinkage of some firms' middle management in the early 1990s resulted from hard times or from computerization.

Organizational Politics and Resistance to Change

Another behavioral approach views information systems as the outcome of political competition between organizational subgroups for influence over the policies, procedures, and resources of the organization (Laudon, 1974; Keen, 1981; Kling, 1980; Laudon, 1986). Information systems inevitably become bound up in the politics of organizations because they influence access to a key resource—namely, information. Information systems can affect who does what to whom, when, where, and how in an organization. For instance, a major study of the efforts of the FBI to develop a national computerized criminal history system (a single national listing of the criminal histories, arrests, and convictions of more than 36 million individuals in the United States) found that the state governments strongly resisted the FBI's efforts. This information would give the federal government, and the FBI in particular, the ability to monitor how states use criminal histories. The states resisted the development of this national system quite successfully (Laudon, 1986).

Because information systems potentially change an organization's structure, culture, politics, and work, there is often considerable resistance to them when they are introduced (see the Window on Management). There are several ways to visualize organizational resistance. Leavitt (1965) used a diamond shape to illustrate the interrelated and mutually adjusting character of technology and organization (see Figure 3-13). Here, changes in technology are absorbed, deflected, and defeated by organizational task arrangements, structures, and people. In this model, the only way to bring about change is to change the technology, tasks, structure, and people simultaneously. Other authors have spoken about the need to "unfreeze" organizations before introducing an innovation, quickly implement the change, and "refreeze" or institutionalize it (Kolb, 1970; Alter and Ginzberg, 1978).

The Internet and Organizations

The Internet, especially the World Wide Web, is beginning to have an important impact on the relationships between firms and external entities, and even on the organization of business processes inside a firm. The Internet increases the accessibility, storage, and distribution of information and knowledge for organizations. In essence, the Internet is capable of dramatically lowering the transaction and agency costs facing most organizations. For instance, brokerage

Figure 3-13 Organizational resistance and the mutually adjusting relationship between technology and the organization. Implementing information systems has consequences for task arrangements, structures, and people. According to this model, in order to implement change, all four components must be changed simultaneously. **Source:** Leavitt, 1965.

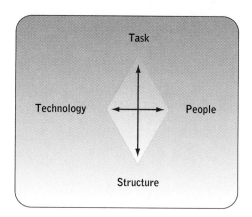

Learning to Share Knowledge

Collaboration and shared knowledge are often necessary for creating better business processes, but it is not necessarily easy to get employees to work together cooperatively. Monsanto, a giant agricultural chemical and pharmaceuticals company, faced this challenge when dealing with its Protiva division, a small (150-person) dairy company in St. Louis, Missouri, that produces Posilac, a dairy enhancer. Protiva's workers were fiercely independent and not at all interested in collaboration. Management had to find ways to completely change Protiva's culture.

Michael Plummer, a consultant to Protiva, characterized the interaction between co-workers as "dysfunctional." He said observers at presentation meetings to review someone's work would notice that those present were more interested in showing off their own knowledge than in serious inquiry. The problem stemmed from a system that rewarded people for specialized knowledge. Employees tended to think that "I get my power and value through expertise; therefore, I want to hold on to it." The problem was made more difficult at Protiva because the multiple downsizings and reorganizations the current employees had experienced resulted in a pervasive mistrust of management.

To address the mistrust, management established ongoing lines of communication with employees, making clear how each individual contributed to the overall mission of the company. Management also listened, giving the employees a greater voice in decision making. The meetings also were used to improve everyone's communications skills.

Information technology staff also participated in this process, and they were required to work on their own communications skills. The team felt this was necessary if IT was to better understand the needs of the users. Ultimately, this changed the way IT developed software because the process became more interactive with users playing a larger role.

After many discussions, a number of employees made clear to management that they were inundated with electronic information and needed an on-line place to store and organize it. In response, IT built a system called Integrated Workspace. The system is meant to provide one-stop access to all the information that employees need to do their jobs and could potentially encourage employees with common interests and expertise to share more freely. The results have been encouraging. About 60 percent of Protiva's workforce are using Integrated Workspace and the atmosphere seems to be changing.

Lotus Development Corporation faced similar issues, even though it had created Lotus Notes, a leading commercial software tool for group collaboration. Its employees were not regularly participating in the company's on-line discussion groups or sharing what they had learned. A 25 member executive team was assigned to this problem. The team started with the customer support help desk, where staff logged telephone calls but did not always enter what they had learned from customers into a common database. Lotus wanted to collect information on recurring problems with software and to identify problems early so they could develop efficient solutions and quick response times. The company's information systems department created a small application to facilitate data capture for customer support personnel. Procedures were changed so no call to the support desk is considered complete until staff have entered the data into the system (and the completion rate is one factor in employee performance reviews).

To Think About: What features of organizations explain employees' resistance to collaboration at both companies? What role was played by management in the solution to the problem?

Sources: Perry Glasser, "Changing the Culture," **CIO Magazine**, January 1, 1999; and Julekha Dash, "Cultivating Collaboration," **Software Magazine**, March 1998.

---

firms and banks in New York can now "deliver" their internal-operations procedures manuals to their employees at distant locations by posting them on their corporate Web site, saving millions of dollars in distribution costs. A global sales force can receive nearly instant price/product information updates via the Web or instructions from management via e-mail. Vendors of some large retailers can access retailers' internal Web sites directly for up-to-the-minute sales information and initiate replenishment orders instantly.

Businesses are slowly rebuilding some of their key business processes based on the new Internet technology. If prior networking is any guide, one result will be simpler business processes, fewer employees, and much flatter organizations than in the past.

Implications for the Design and Understanding of Information Systems

What is the importance of these theories of organizations? The primary significance of this section is to show that you cannot take a narrow view of organizations and their relationship to information systems. Experienced systems observers and managers approach systems change very cautiously. In order to reap the benefits of technology, organizational innovations—changes in the culture, values, norms, and interest-group alignments—must be managed with as much planning and effort as technology changes.

You should develop a checklist of factors to consider in your systems plans. In our experience, the central organizational factors are these:

○ The environment in which the organization must function.

○ The structure of the organization: hierarchy, specialization, standard operating procedures.

○ The culture and politics of the organization.

○ The type of organization.

○ The nature and style of leadership.

○ The extent of support and understanding of top management.

○ The level of organization at which the system resides.

○ The principal interest groups affected by the system.

○ The kinds of tasks, decisions, and business processes that the information system is designed to assist.

○ The sentiments and attitudes of workers in the organization who will be using the information system.

○ The history of the organization: past investments in information technology, existing skills, important programs, and human resources.

Management Wrap-Up

Management

A major contribution of information technology in the past decade has been the focus on organizational and business processes, on how to get things done. Managers are responsible for making the decisions on how to use information technology in these processes. Few textbooks tell managers how to manage organizations that are critically reliant on information technology.

Organization

Each organization has a unique constellation of information systems that result from its interaction with information technology. Contemporary information technology can lead to major organizational changes—and efficiencies—by reducing transaction and agency costs, but its application in each organization will be a result of that organization's unique set of environmental and institutional factors.

Technology

Information technology changes far more rapidly than organizations, and for this reason, it is often a destroyer of organization competence. However, information technology offers managers new ways of organizing work that can promote organizational survival and prosperity. Managers have to keep a keen eye on changes in information technology in order to avoid losing organizational competencies and in order to exploit the opportunities provided by new technology.

For Discussion

1. It has been said that when we design an information system, we are redesigning the organization. As an example, discuss some of the challenges that might arise in developing a corporate Internet application that allowed customers to order products directly instead of going through the sales force or the retailers who traditionally carried the firm's products.

2. You are an information systems designer assigned to build a new accounts receivable system for one of your organization's divisions. What organizational factors should you consider?

Summary

1. Identify the salient characteristics of organizations. All modern organizations are hierarchical, specialized, and impartial. They use explicit standard operating procedures to maximize efficiency. All organizations have their own culture and politics arising from differences in interest groups. Organizations differ in goals, groups served, social roles, leadership styles, incentives, surrounding environments, types of tasks performed, and in their arrangement of business processes for accomplishing their work. These differences create varying types of organizational structures. Mintzberg classified organizations into five structures: the simple entrepreneurial structure, machine bureaucracy, divisionalized bureaucracy, professional bureaucracy, and adhocracy.

2. Assess the changing role of information systems within organizations. Computerized information systems are supported in organizations by a formal organizational unit or information systems department, information specialists, and computer technology. The roles of information systems and the computer package in the organization have become increasingly critical to both daily operations and strategic decision making.

3. Compare models for describing the origins of systems in organizations. Organizations adopt information systems for both external environmental reasons, such as to respond to competition or to promote changes in government regulations, and for internal institutional reasons, such as to promote the values or interests of top management.

4. Compare the major theories about organizations that help us understand their relationship with information systems. Theories that describe the relationship between information systems and organizations can be classified as based on either economic or behavioral models of the firm. Theories based on economic models of the firm include the microeconomic model, the transaction cost theory, and agency theory. Theories based on behavioral models of the firm focus on whether information systems change the hierarchy of decision making in organizations and organizational structure.

5. Analyze the impact of information systems on organizational structure, culture, political processes, and management. The impact of information systems on organizations is not unidirectional. Information systems and the organizations in which they are used interact with and influence each other. The introduction of a new information system will affect the organizational structure, goals, work design, values, competition between interest groups, decision making, and day-to-day behavior. At the same time, information systems must be designed to serve the needs of important organizational groups and will be shaped by the structure, tasks, goals, culture, politics, and management of the organization. The power of information systems to transform organizations radically by flattening organizational hierarchies has not yet been demonstrated for all types of organizations. The World Wide Web has a potentially large impact on organizational business processes and structure because it can dramatically reduce transaction and agency costs.

6. Describe the organizational implications for the design and implementation of systems. Salient features of organizations that must be addressed by information systems include organizational levels, organizational structures, types of tasks and decisions, the nature of management support, and the sentiments and attitudes of workers who will be using the system. The organization's history and external environment must be considered as well.

Implementation of a new information system is often more difficult than anticipated because of organizational change requirements. Because information systems potentially change important organizational dimensions, including the structure, culture, power relationships, and work activities, there is often considerable resistance to new systems.

Key Terms

Agency theory, 86	Environmental factors, 85	Microeconomic model, 86	Programmers, 84
Bureaucracy, 73	Information systems	Organization (behavioral	Standard operating
Business processes, 78	department, 82	definition), 72	procedures (SOPs), 74
Chief information officer	Information systems	Organization (technical	Systems analysts, 84
(CIO), 84	managers, 84	definition), 72	Transaction cost theory, 86
End users, 84	Institutional factors, 86	Organizational culture, 75	

Review Questions

1. What is an organization? How do organizations use information?
2. Compare the technical definition of organizations with the behavioral definition.
3. What features do all organizations have in common?
4. In what ways can organizations diverge?
5. What is meant by a business process? Give two views and two examples.
6. Name the levels of analysis for organizational behavior.

7. Name the changing applications of organizational information systems that existed from the 1950s to the 1990s. How has the role of information systems in the organization changed over this time period?

8. Name the three elements in the information systems function. How has the role of each element in the organization changed over time?

9. Describe the two factors that explain why organizations adopt information systems.

10. Describe the economic theories that help explain how information systems affect organizations.

11. Describe the behavioral theories that help explain how information systems affect organizations.

12. Why should the Internet change organizational structure or process?

13. What is the relationship between information systems and organizational culture?

14. What is the relationship between information systems and organizational politics?

15. Why is there considerable organizational resistance to the introduction of information systems?

16. What aspects of organizations addressed by various theories of organizations must be considered when designing an information system?

Group Project

With a group of three or four students, select a company described in *The Wall Street Journal, Forbes,* or another business publication. Visit the Web site of that company to find out additional information about that company and to see how the firm is using the Web. On the basis of this information, describe some of the features of this organization, such as important business processes, culture, structure, and environment. Assess the impact of this Web site on the organization. Is the Web site helping the company reduce transaction costs? What impact is it having, if any, on the firm's business processes? Present your findings to the class.

Tools for Interactive Learning

○ Internet

The Internet Connection for this chapter will take you to a series of Web sites for virtual organizations where you can complete an exercise to analyze their capabilities and business processes. You can also use the Interactive Study Guide to test your knowledge of the topics in this chapter and get instant feedback when you need more practice.

○ CD-ROM

If you purchase and use the Multimedia Edition CD-ROM with this chapter, you will find an interactive exercise which asks you to analyze the work groups for dealing with several organizational problems. You can also find a video clip illustrating the role of information systems in Schneider National's organization, an audio overview of the major themes of this chapter, and bullet text summarizing the key points of the chapter.

Case Study   Utilities Deregulation Sparks Big Business Changes

The utilities industry used to be very unexciting. Its traditional job was to build, operate, and maintain power plants and power lines, using this infrastructure to supply power to thousands of nearly anonymous customers. Utility companies were state-regulated monopolies that had no need for marketing or sales functions because their customers had no choice as to who would supply their power. Prices changed rarely, and when they did, it was usually only after approval by a regulatory agency.

Deregulation is changing all that. Under deregulation, rates are no longer set by the states, power suppliers will no longer have captive customers, and power consumers will be free to choose their power suppliers, including companies with foreign owners. Many business changes are in order.

Deregulation forces the separation of power generation from power retail sales. Some companies will continue to do both; others will generate power but sell it only to

wholesale buyers; and still other companies will generate no power, but only retail suppliers. Suddenly the need to compete will dominate the culture of these companies as they strive to acquire, satisfy, and keep customers. To hold on to current customers, these companies will have to emphasize service and price. Marketing and sales will become critical—strategic—functions. Information about customers and potential customers will be central to success. Because companies delivering power to retail customers will often purchase their power elsewhere, knowledge of the wholesale power supply market becomes critical. These companies will have no physical end-product to point to, making them service companies.

How will these different power company cultures affect the look, role, and importance of information systems? In a traditional power company, information systems are used primarily to bill and collect from customers, to restore power when outages occur, and to maintain capital assets. Information systems comprise only a tiny percentage of its assets, with capital goods accounting for the overwhelming majority. Senior management seldom, if ever, concerns itself with the information systems of such companies.

However, information systems are strategic for companies operating in a highly competitive market. Employees in companies operating in a deregulated power supply market need to obtain, store, and access up-to-date, detailed information on customers and potential customers. Large databases to collect and store information from various sources become essential. Company computer systems are needed to enter customer information, and networks are necessary for gathering data about potential customers. Marketing and sales systems are needed to support those functions. Rapid repair of outages and downed lines become critical because quality service is essential in a competitive environment. Thus computer systems that locate and analyze power distribution problems become vital. To compete with low prices, these companies must control costs, which means automating many functions and establishing quality controls over those functions. In addition, locating and purchasing the cheapest power to sell is an essential function, and information systems using the Internet and electronic commerce networks are central to these functions.

A number of Web sites and Web-based businesses have been launched for both wholesale and retail selling of electricity and natural gas. The World Wide Retail Energy Exchange [www.wwrex.com] lets gas and utility companies place competing bids for the energy requirements posed by businesses and energy aggregators on-line. Green Mountain Energy Resources (GMER), located in South Burlington, Vermont, is a retail marketer of electric services.

Doug Hyde, GMER's CEO, spent many years managing a traditional $150 million

power company called the Green Mountain Power Company (GMP). His main responsibilities were to keep costs down and to satisfy regulators. The atmosphere in this hierarchical company was very traditional: To speak to him his subordinates had to call his secretary and make a formal appointment. Dress was "suits and ties." In this job, he seldom used computers and knew very little about them.

All of this changed in 1997. GMP established GMER as a new company that would be competitive in the coming deregulated market, and Hyde became its CEO. Technology is the heart and soul of the company. The company owns no generation or distribution facilities, but its start-up costs included nearly $50 million for information technology. The company maintains a relatively flat organization in which anybody can walk into anyone else's office at any time. The dress, not surprisingly, is very relaxed.

Although it is located in Vermont, the company had to be ready to win its first customers in California when deregulation came into being there. Hyde and his associates knew they would have to compete on price, but they decided to differentiate their product in another way so that many customers would prefer to buy from them. GMER offers a customized product that is marketed to environmentally conscious consumers in the hope that they will pay a small premium for "green goods" and will develop a loyalty to GMER electricity. The company buys its electricity from organizations that generate it from water, wind, solar, and geothermal sources. GMER individualizes its product so that, for example, a customer can request 60 percent solar energy and 40 percent wind energy. Because some states require monthly bills that tell consumers how much of their power comes from each energy source, such as nuclear, coal-fired, or gas-powered generators, GMER stands to benefit from consumers who select the companies that pollute the least.

To identify potential customers, the company built a powerful data-gathering information system. Potential clients enroll with GMER by filling out an on-line form on the Web or by phoning a high-tech call center; they provide their name, address, meter number, type of home and energy-consuming appliances, and personal energy use. Using secured Internet connections, the meter number is transmitted electronically to the cus-

tomer's former utility company, which returns a profile of the customer's 12-month energy use. GMER uses that information for customer analysis and also for a supply-forecasting program that guides purchases of electricity. GMER places orders with an electricity wholesaler. The process of supplying electricity requires about 40 electronic "conversations" per customer between GMER and its suppliers.

Additional information on customers is provided by 23 outside contractors and is used for direct mailing and market research. GMER is also banking on high-tech methods of billing and customer support. For example, GMER will bill and accept payment via the Internet according to customer preference. Kevin Hartley, GMER's vice president of marketing, believes that GMER's product is not like anybody else's.

Sources: De'Ann Weimer, "Utilities Prognosis 1999," Business Week, January 11, 1999; Emily Esterson, "A Shock to the System," Inc. Technology, No. 1, March 1998; and Clinton Wilder, "Power Brokers Get on the Web," Information Week, November 3, 1997.

CASE STUDY QUESTIONS

1. What theories about the relationship of information systems and organizations can be used to explain the rise of companies such as GMER?

2. To what extent is GMER a virtual organization? What is the role played by information systems in the way this company conducts its business?

3. How does GMER use the Internet for electronic commerce and electronic business?

4. What management, organization, and technology issues do you think a traditional power company would have to address to convert to a competitive company in the deregulated environment? How well do you think some of these companies will succeed in making the transition? Explain your answers.

5. How might GMER have succeeded without its large investment in information systems? Are there benefits to not relying so completely on computer systems, and if so, what are they?

6. What are some of the problems that GMER will face that technology cannot address?

Chapter 4

Information, Management, and Decision Making

Learning Objectives

After completing this chapter, you will be able to:

1. Evaluate the three main schools of management thinking.

2. Describe the levels, types, and stages of decision making.

3. Compare models for describing individual and organizational decision making.

4. Assess how information technology has changed the management process.

5. Explain how information systems can assist managers and improve managerial decision making.

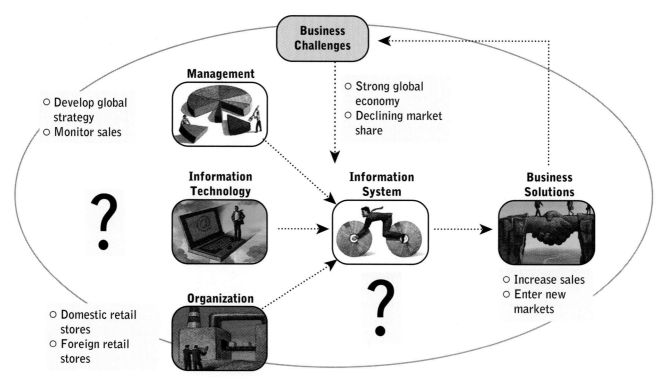

Business Challenges

○ Develop global strategy
○ Monitor sales

Management

○ Strong global economy
○ Declining market share

?

Information Technology

Information System

Business Solutions

○ Increase sales
○ Enter new markets

○ Domestic retail stores
○ Foreign retail stores

Organization

?

Can Marks & Spencer
Spark a Comeback?

In Great Britain, Marks & Spencer is almost as much a part of daily life as the BBC or the monarchy. Affectionately nicknamed Marks & Sparks, the company sells one in four men's suits in the country and is seeking to become a global retailer. Fulfilling this mission will not be easy.

Just as Marks & Spencer added 3 million square feet of selling space to its nearly 700 existing stores, and opened new sites, sales—and profits—started dropping. The initial sales slump was attributed to mistakes in inventory control, pricing, and merchandising. The company rolled out a dull clothing line that didn't tempt buyers, then failed to cut back quickly enough on inventory. Sales continued to slide as economic growth faltered in other parts of the world.

Shares of M&S stock underperformed those of other British retailers by 25 percent and its market share was declining. Analysts believe that Marks & Spencer did not react as quickly to a tough environment as its rivals or introduce new ideas to keep it competitive.

Since 85 percent of sales and 94 percent of profits come from Britain, Marks & Spencer would like to reduce its dependence on the domestic market by diversifying overseas. Yet Marks & Spencer has had to slow down its foreign expansion plans to cut costs. Instead of opening 60 stores on the European continent by 2000, it will open only 44. Management is carefully reviewing growth plans of its North American stores, including the Brooks Brothers chain and King Super Markets Inc., and slowing expansion in Asia. Should Marks & Spencer change its overall strategy? The future of the company—and of its chief executive, Sir Richard Greenbury—is uncertain.

Sources: Julia Flynn, "Marks & Sparks Isn't Throwing Off Any," *Business Week*, November 16, 1998; and Alan Cowell, "Old Guard Repels Challenge at Staid Marks & Spencer," *The New York Times*, November 27, 1998.

The challenges and decisions facing Marks & Spencer's managers are typical of those facing many senior executives. In companies both large and small, managers are asking such questions as "Where is our industry headed? Should we change our business model? How can we enlarge market share? What should our strategy be? How can we design a strategy?" There are no easy answers to these questions. In some instances, managers find solutions using information systems; in other situations, computers may be of little or no use. Applying information systems to the management process raises the following management challenges:

1. **Unstructured nature of important decisions.** Many important decisions, especially in the areas of strategic planning and knowledge, are not structured and require judgment and examination of many complex factors. Solutions cannot be provided by computerized information systems alone. System builders need to determine exactly what aspects, if any, of a solution can be computerized, and exactly how systems can support the process of arriving at a decision.

2. **Diversity of managerial roles.** Up to now, information systems have supported only a few of the roles managers play in organizations. System builders need to determine whether new technologies such as the Internet can create information systems to help managers in their interpersonal and decisional roles that previously were not backed up by formal systems. In addition to helping managers plan, organize, and coordinate, it is vital that systems help managers get things done through interpersonal communication, by implementing personal agendas, and by establishing networks throughout the organization. Such systems require a different vision of information systems that are less formal, offer more communications capabilities, are adjustable to managers' unique situations, and utilize diverse sources of information inside and outside the firm.

The remainder of this text examines how information systems can be designed to support managers. In this chapter we scrutinize the role of a manager and try to identify areas where information systems can contribute to managerial effectiveness. Then we examine the types of decisions managers make and the process of decision making by individuals and organizations.

4.1 What Managers Do

The responsibilities of managers range from making decisions about new products and services, to arranging birthday parties, to writing reports, to attending meetings and giving inspirational speeches to employees.

Putting Management and Information Systems in Context

Although the practice of management is ancient, the effort to systematically observe and theorize about management and organization did not begin until the last half of the nineteenth century. The formal study of management began in the 1880s as an offshoot of engineering. The very first articles on how to manage a modern business appeared in *Engineering Magazine* and

| Table 4.1 | The Three Main Schools in Management Theory* |

School Name	Main Emphasis
Technical–Rational	Emphasizes the precision with which a task can be done, the organization of tasks into jobs, and jobs into production systems.
Behavioral	Emphasizes how well the organization can adapt to its external and internal environment.
Cognitive	Emphasizes how well the organization learns and applies know-how and knowledge, and how well managers provide meaning to new situations.

*Most of the literature on management and organizational theory can be divided into three schools of thought: technical–rational, behavioral, and cognitive.

publications of the American Society for Mechanical Engineers (ASME). "Management" as a discipline began to emerge as industrial organizations grew in size from 100 or so workers, to thousands of workers at a single site. In Europe similar forces produced the first literature on administration and bureaucracy, which in essence is the study of large organizations both public and private. Since then, three schools of management have emerged, each with a distinct literature, a unique theme and viewpoint about how managers should behave to ensure the success of the organization.

After 100 years of writing about management, it comes down to the fact that organizational success has something to do with technical competence, organizational adaptability to environments, and finally with know-how and intimate knowledge of the product and production process. Theoretical schools and literatures have organized around these three observations. The literature that describes the role of technical competence we call the "technical–rational" school; the literature that emphasizes organizational adaptability to internal and external environments is usually called the "behavioral" school; and the literature that emphasizes the role of knowledge and managerial sense-making we will call the "cognitive" school. See Table 4.1.

Each of these theories are in use today as rationales for why information systems should be built and how managers should use information technology. These three schools are not contradictory but rather complement each other. You can think of each of these schools as representing an important dimension of both management and organizations.

Three Schools of Management

Figure 4-1 is a theory map that takes the three dimensions of management theory and places them on an historical time line. Figure 4-1 also places contemporary management movements and slogans into their respective theoretical camps (in italics).

The classical period begins in 1880, when the first widely circulated technical engineering journals appeared and began the systematic theorizing about what made factories, managers, and organizations efficient. During this time period, the technical–rational perspective was ascendant. The contemporary period begins in the late 1920s, spurred on by the growing disciplines of psychology and sociology and new ideas about human motivation and the nature of organizations. During the contemporary period, the behavioral perspective dominated. The postmodern period begins in the early 1960s, when a book entitled *The Production and Distribution of the Knowledge in the United States* began a period of intense speculation about the contribution of knowledge and know-how to organizational success, thus ushering in the cognitive perspective.

The influence of all those theories continues to reverberate throughout the literature and culture in different forms. Each theory describes an important element of being—or becoming—an efficient and effective organization. For instance, the concerns of the technical–rational school for understanding how workers perform tasks, the reduction in variance of output (the emphasis

Figure 4-1 The Evolution of
Management Theory. The history of management theory can be broken into three main historical periods. The classical period (1880–1927) is dominated by the technical–rational view, often held by engineers and "rationalistic" thinkers in scientific management; the contemporary period (1930–1962) is dominated by social psychologists, sociologists, and organizational behavior experts who emphasize individual and collective behavior; the postmodern period (1965–present) is dominated by economists, sociologists, management theorists, and others who emphasize the knowledge basis of organizations. How to read this figure: Time line from the center outward (Classical, Contemporary, Postmodern); Major perspectives in bold (Technical–Rational, Behavioral, Cognitive); Variants and subschool in regular type; Contemporary applications in consulting and information technology in italics

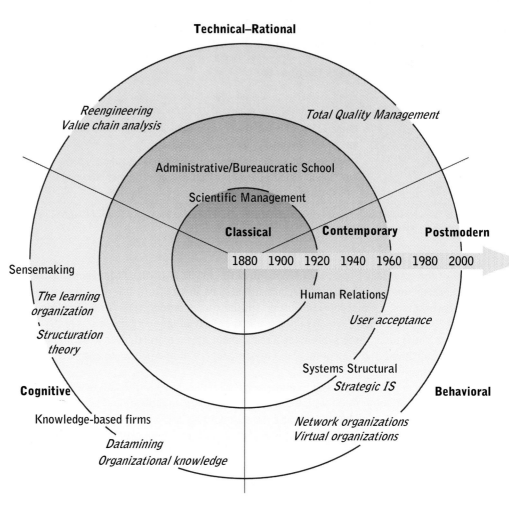

on standards and standard measurable outputs), and the way tasks are properly organized into jobs do not end in the 1920s but instead live on today as "reengineering" and "total quality management."

The Technical–Rational Perspective

technical–rational "classical" perspective

Descriptions of management and organizations that focus on the mechanistic aspects of organization and the formal management functions of planning, organizing, coordinating, deciding, and controlling.

In the **technical–rational** or **classical perspective,** the organization is seen as a closed, mechanical system—much like a watch or an engine. Like an engine, the efficiency and effectiveness of the organization depend on the precision with which the parts are designed, and the cleverness of the designer in integrating the parts. The role of the manager is to design a more perfect mechanism by closely studying the parts (jobs, tasks, people, and machinery), redesigning the parts, and building an effective administration that can closely monitor the entire operation. There are two variations of the technical–rational perspective: the scientific management school and the administrative–bureaucratic school. The first focuses on factory settings and the second on white-collar administrative organizations.

Henri Fayol and other early writers first described the five functions of managers as planning, organizing, coordinating, deciding, and controlling (see Table 4.2). This description of formal management activities dominated management thought for a long time, and still is popular today.

The belief that the organization is a watchlike mechanism whose internal processes and operations can be continuously improved by management is reflected in the information systems field in such popular programs as reengineering, value chain analysis, business process design, and total quality management. Each of these programs argues that managers should use information technology to improve the mechanism of production.

Table 4.2	**The Technical–Rational or Classical Model of Management Functions**

Planning

Organizing

Coordinating

Deciding

Controlling

But as a description of what managers actually do, these five terms are unsatisfactory. The terms do not address what managers do when they plan. How do they actually decide things? How do managers control the work of others? What is needed in a description is a more fine-grained understanding of how managers actually behave.

The Behavioral Perspective

The **behavioral perspective** on management developed in reaction to the limitations of the technical school: its failure to consider the people who worked in organizations as human beings (rather than automaton-like machines); its failure to consider the role of small groups, group norms, and other sociological phenomena; and the failure of the technical school to consider the external environment in which the organization operated. The behavioral perspective in management theory began in the late 1920s and early 1930s, spurred on by the development of large-scale, mass production of consumer goods for a national market, huge multilevel firms, social strife associated with the emergence of powerful labor unions, and the growing acceptance and influence of the social sciences such as sociology and psychology.

In the behavioral perspective the organization is seen as an open, biological organism much like a cell, or animal. Like a biological cell, the efficiency and effectiveness of the organization depend on its ability to adapt to its environment and its ability to arrange itself internally so that all its constituent parts are supported and sustained. The role of the manager is to assist the organization in its quest for survival by continually redesigning the organization so it can "fit" or adapt to its environment, and to ensure that the organization's employees are satisfied and functioning well. There are two major schools within the behavioral perspective: the human relations school, which focuses on the psychological and social–psychological needs of employees; and the systems structural school, which focuses on the structure of the organization and the needs of the organization to adapt to an ever-changing external environment.

The behavioral perspective on management has had a powerful impact on the information systems field: the literature on "user acceptance" of information systems, which emphasizes the sociological and psychological aspects of system success; the "strategic IS" literature, which emphasizes the ability of the organization to respond to and potentially dominate its environment; and the contemporary "network organization" and "virtual organization" literature, which emphasize organizing labor forces without traditional hierarchies. This perspective also sheds light on aspects of the management process that are not addressed by most formal systems.

Contemporary behavioral scientists have discovered from observation that managers do not behave as the classical model of management led us to believe. Kotter (1982), for example, describes the morning activities of the president of an investment management firm.

> 7:35 A.M. Richardson arrives at work, unpacks his briefcase, gets some coffee, and begins making a list of activities for the day.
>
> 7:45 A.M. Bradshaw (a subordinate) and Richardson converse about a number of topics and exchange pictures recently taken on summer vacations.
>
> 8:00 A.M. They talk about a schedule of priorities for the day.

behavioral perspective Descriptions of management based on behavioral scientists' observations of how organizations actually behave and what managers actually do in their jobs.

Table 4.3	The Behavioral Model of Management Activities

High-volume, high-speed work

Variety, fragmentation, brevity

Issue preference: current, ad hoc, specific

Complex web of interactions, contacts

Strong preference for verbal media

Control of the agenda

8:20 A.M. Wilson (a subordinate) and Richardson talk about some personnel problems, cracking jokes in the process.

8:45 A.M. Richardson's secretary arrives, and they discuss her new apartment and arrangements for a meeting later in the morning.

8:55 A.M. Richardson goes to a morning meeting run by one of his subordinates. Thirty people are there, and Richardson reads during the meeting.

11:05 A.M. Richardson and his subordinates return to the office and discuss a difficult problem. They try to define the problem and outline possible alternatives. He lets the discussion roam away from and back to the topic again and again. Finally, they agree on a next step.

In the behavioral perspective, the actual behavior of managers appears to be less systematic, more informal, less reflective, more reactive, less well organized, and much more frivolous than students of information systems and decision making generally expect. In our example, it is difficult to determine which activities constitute Richardson's planning, coordinating, and decision making.

A widely noted study of actual managerial behavior conducted by Mintzberg (1971) indicates that actual managerial behavior often contrasts with the classical description (see Table 4.3):

First, modern researchers have found that the manager performs a great deal of work at an unrelenting pace and works at a high level of intensity. Some studies have found that managers engage in more than 600 different activities each day, with no break in their pace. Managers seem to have little free time.

Second, managerial activities are fragmented and brief. Managers simply lack the time to get deeply involved in a wide range of issues. They shift their attention rapidly from one issue to another, with very little pattern. When a problem occurs, all other matters must be dropped until the issue is solved. Mintzberg found that most activities of general managers lasted for less than nine minutes, and only 10 percent of the activities exceeded one hour in duration.

Third, managers prefer speculation, hearsay, gossip—in brief, they enjoy current, up-to-date, although uncertain, information. They pay less attention to historical, routine information. Managers want to work on issues that are current, specific, and ad hoc.

Fourth, managers maintain a diverse and complex web of contacts that acts as an informal information system. Managers converse with clients, associates, peers, secretaries, outside government officials, and so forth.

Fifth, managers prefer verbal forms of communication to written forms because verbal media provide greater flexibility, require less effort, and bring a faster response.

Despite the flood of work, the press of deadlines, and the random order of crises, Mintzberg found that successful managers appear to be able to control their own affairs. By developing their own long-term commitments, their own information channels, and their own

Table 4.4 — Managerial Roles and Supporting Information Systems

Role	Behavior	Support Systems
Interpersonal Roles		
Figurehead		None exist
Leader	Interpersonal	None exist
Liaison		Electronic communication systems
Informational Roles		
Nerve center		Management information systems
Disseminator	Information processing	Mail, office systems
Spokesperson		Office and professional systems, workstations
Decisional Roles		
Entrepreneur		None exist
Disturbance handler	Decision making	None exist
Resource allocator		DSS systems
Negotiator		None exist

Source: Kenneth C. Laudon and Jane P. Laudon; and Mintzberg, 1971.

networks, senior managers can control their personal agendas. Less successful managers tend to be overwhelmed by problems brought to them by subordinates.

Managerial Roles: Mintzberg

Managerial roles are expectations of the activities that managers should perform in an organization. Mintzberg classified managerial activities into 10 roles that fall into three categories: interpersonal, informational, and decisional. Information systems, if built properly, can support these diverse managerial roles in a number of ways (see Table 4.4).

Interpersonal roles. Managers act as figureheads for the organization when they represent their companies to the outside world and perform symbolic duties such as giving out employee awards. Managers act as leaders, attempting to motivate, counsel, and support subordinates. Lastly, managers act as a liaison between various levels of the organization; within each of these levels, they serve as a liaison among the members of the management team. Managers provide time, information, and favors, which they expect to be returned.

Informational roles. Managers act as the nerve centers of their organization, receiving the most concrete, up-to-date information and redistributing it to those who need to be aware of it. Managers are therefore disseminators and spokespersons for their organization.

Decisional roles. Managers make decisions. They act as entrepreneurs by initiating new kinds of activities; they handle disturbances arising in the organization; they allocate resources to staff members who need them; and they negotiate conflicts and mediate between conflicting groups in the organization.

Table 4.4 enables us to see where systems can help managers and where they cannot. The table shows that information systems do not as of yet contribute a great deal to many areas of management life. These areas will undoubtedly provide great opportunities for future systems and system designers. The Window on Technology shows how Internet technology can support some of those managerial roles.

managerial roles Expectations of the activities that managers should perform in an organization.

interpersonal roles Mintzberg's classification for managerial roles where managers act as figureheads and leaders for the organization.

informational roles Mintzberg's classification for managerial roles where managers act as the nerve centers of their organizations, receiving and disseminating critical information.

decisional roles Mintzberg's classification for managerial roles where managers initiate activities, handle disturbances, allocate resources, and negotiate conflicts.

Schwab's Managers Turn to the Internet

Although giant discount broker Charles Schwab and Co. had many capabilities for providing electronic services and instant financial information to customers, it was much slower in providing essential information to its managers. Schwab once had a general ledger system that ran only at corporate headquarters in San Francisco and was very difficult to learn and use. Managers at regional centers could only obtain financial reports on paper through interoffice mail. Schwab found a way to provide this information more rapidly by using Internet technology to create a general ledger reporting system called FinWeb. Managers at any Schwab office now can access and print reports at any time in easy-to-digest form. In addition to providing managers with better information, FinWeb cut down Schwab's training and printing expenses.

Schwab then created a Web-based reporting and analysis application called SMART, which provides managers with a comprehensive view of Schwab activities. SMART, which stands for Schwab Metric and Analysis Reporting Tool, includes a risk-evaluation template that helps managers assess nine categories of risk. These risk categories include customer satisfaction and the value of proprietary assets at risk, such as market, credit, and operating risks. Access to all of this information will help managers in Schwab's Integrated Consulting and Audit Department become more productive and expert in their ability to perform risk analysis for the company. Another area of the SMART Web site called Virtual Training provides departmental news and information and introduces new employees to company policies and procedures. To help its mutual fund managers, Schwab has installed software that lets it detect real-time data on trades using Web technology. Managers can see how purchases, sales, and exchanges are driving prices and other information that affects their financial decisions.

Schwab now lets managers and other employees use The Sabre Group's Internet-based Travel Planner to book their travel reservations themselves. Travel Planner incorporates Schwab's travel rules and special business rates it has negotiated with airlines and hotels. Schwab employees make reservations and order tickets on-line. They charge expenses using Diners Club cards, and they can download expense information automatically into an electronic expense form. They then fill out the form, typing in items for which they have paid cash. Managers can review and approve these expense reports on-line, and the company electronically reimburses the credit card company and the employees. The system provides summary reports to help managers analyze companywide travel activity. Employees save time by doing all their travel booking themselves.

The application's summary reports help Schwab monitor its travel expenses and negotiate better deals with vendors. Schwab also achieves better discounts on travel by using the electronic ticketing capabilities of this system.

Unlike consumer-oriented Internet travel sites such as Microsoft's Expedia or Sabre's Travelocity, Internet systems for corporate travel allow companies to enforce their travel policies, such as preferred airlines or hotels with which they have negotiated discounted rates.

By using the Internet for travel planning, Schwab has reduced travel-related telephone inquiries from 350 five-minute calls per day to 224 calls and has reduced its internal Travel Division staff from 17 to 11 employees. Savings from Travel Planner amounted to $1.6 million in 1997. Before implementing electronic travel management, Schwab paid almost 40 cents per travel mile. Now Schwab pays 20 to 21 cents per mile. Other companies in the San Francisco area, where Schwab is headquartered, pay an average of 32 to 34 cents per mile.

To Think About: How has the Internet helped Schwab's managers manage? What managerial roles do the systems described here support?

Sources: Beth Davis, "Business Intelligence Goes Internet," **Information Week**, January 18, 1999; Carol Sliwa, "Schwab Saves with 'Net Travel Planning,'" **Computerworld**, April 13, 1998; and Laura DiDio, "Schwab Gets SMART with Reporting App," **Computerworld**, January 26, 1998.

In the area of interpersonal roles, information systems are extremely limited and currently can make only indirect contributions. The systems act largely as a communications aid with some of the newer office automation and communication-oriented applications. These systems contribute more to the field of informational roles: A manager's presentation of information is significantly improved with large-scale MIS systems, office systems, and professional workstations. In the area of decision making, DSS and PC-based systems make important contributions (see Chapters 9 and 15).

How Managers Get Things Done: Kotter

Kotter (1982) uses the behavioral approach to modern management to describe how managers work. Building on the work of Mintzberg, Kotter argues that effective managers are involved

A corporate chief executive learns how to use a computer. Many senior managers lack computer knowledge or experience and require systems that are extremely easy to use.

in three critical activities. First, general managers spend significant time establishing personal agendas and goals, both short and long term.

Second—but perhaps most important—effective managers spend much time building an interpersonal network composed of people at virtually all levels of the organization, from warehouse staff to clerical support personnel to other managers and senior management. These networks, like their personal agendas, are generally consistent with the formal plans and networks of an organization, but they are different and apart. General managers build these networks using a variety of face-to-face, interactive tools, both formal and informal.

Third, Kotter found that managers use their networks to execute personal agendas. In his findings, general managers called on peers, corporate staff, subordinates three or four levels below them, and even competitors to help accomplish goals. There was no category of people that was never used.

What Managers Decide: Wrapp

In the technical–rational model of management, one might expect that managers make important decisions and that the more senior the manager, the more important and profound the decisions will be. Yet in a frequently cited article about general managers, H. Edward Wrapp (1984) found that good managers do not make sweeping policy decisions but instead give the organization a general sense of direction and become skilled in developing opportunities.

Wrapp found that good managers seldom make forthright statements of policy and rarely try to push through total solutions or programs for particular problems. Wrapp was able to show that, contrary to popular belief, successful managers spend much time and energy getting involved in operational decisions and problems to stay well informed. These managers focus time and energy on a small subset of organizational problems that they can directly affect successfully; they are sensitive to the power structure of the organization because any major proposal requires the support of several organizational units and actors; and they appear imprecise in setting overall organizational goals but nevertheless provide a sense of direction. In this way, managers maintain visibility but avoid being placed in a policy straitjacket. The manager seeks to implement plans one part at a time, without drawing attention to an explicit, comprehensive design.

The Cognitive Perspective and Postmodern Era

cognitive perspective Descriptions of management and organization that emphasize the role of knowledge, core competency, and perceptual filters.

In the **cognitive perspective,** the organization is a knowing, sentient organism. Like a human being, organizations seek to make sense out of their environments, and can "learn" as well as "know" things. The efficiency and effectiveness of the organization depend on the correctness, or the appropriateness, of its sense-making judgments, as well as its ability to gather, create, store, disseminate, and use information and knowledge. The role of the manager in this perspective is to use his or her sense-making ability to properly define the situation of the organization so it can act (perceive problems and define solutions) and to build the information- and knowledge-processing infrastructure of the organization. Although the cognitive school has historical precedents, it is largely a child of the post-1960s computer age.

There are two schools within the cognitive perspective. The managerial sense-making school emphasizes the key role of the manager in correctly perceiving and interpreting environmental events, understanding and conceptualizing the problems faced by an organization, defining the solution set, and making the solution decision. Managers create mental models that can serve as the basis for the organization's action plans. The second cognitive school is the knowledge-based view of the firm, which emphasizes the collection, storage, dissemination, and use of knowledge and information.

The cognitive perspective has had a large impact on contemporary thinking about information technology and the firm. There is a growing focus in the information systems field on the role of information technology in helping the organization learn about its environment, in responding to the environment more efficiently, and in storing and disseminating knowledge using the Internet and interactive multimedia software, which are far more effective in communicating knowledge. Finally, there is a small but important body of IS literature that illustrates how organizations use information technology to impose order on and make sense of their environments (Orlikowski, 1992).

Managerial Sense-making

The "managers as sense-makers" school is the collective work of sociologists, cognitive psychologists, information systems experts, computer scientists, and economists. The basic premise of the managerial sense-making school is that managers define the situation for both the employees and the firm. Managers increase firm value, effectiveness, and efficiency, insofar as they are correct in their sense-making. If they are incorrect, the organization loses effectiveness, efficiency, and ultimately fails. Some other premises include the following:

○ Managers create knowledge structures—or mental maps—that transform the chaotic, ambiguous stream of events in the environment into tractable "problems," and become the foundation for organizational programs and policies for coping and survival. Managers do this by applying various filters to information from the environment (Starbuck and Milliken, 1988). The information filters and knowledge structures developed by managers are often wrong as much as they are right (Mintzberg, 1973).

○ Managers are problem solvers and decision makers. Managers must make myriad number of high-speed, correct decisions, and in the process solve problems faced by the organization. Managers define problems for the organization. The success of any organization is largely the result of how well its managers solve problems and make decisions.

○ Managers are information processors. The primary role of management is to process information from the external and internal environments of the firm. This information processing is increasingly aided by information technology tools and systems.

○ Managers create information-processing structures, programs, and routines, which scan external and internal environments in accordance with the managers' knowledge structures. Information does not simply land on the manager's desk in a random stream but instead is produced by the manager on the basis of his or her definition of the situation (Schwenk, 1984).

Figure 4-2 illustrates the managerial sense-making school.

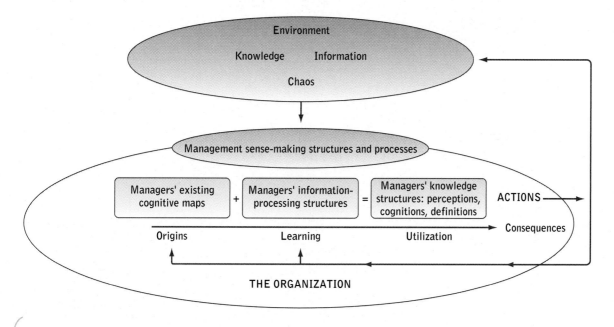

Figure 4-2 The Cognitive View: Management Sense-Making: Managers are problem-solvers who interpret environmental events, define the problems, and develop solutions for the organization.

The Knowledge-Based View of the Firm

The knowledge-based view of the firm focuses less on the manager than on the organization as a whole, reflecting the work of sociologists, information systems and computer scientists, and strategic planners. The basic premise of this school is that the success of the organization—survival and efficiency—depends on the organization's ability to gather, produce, maintain, and disseminate knowledge, which is used to produce products and services. The key premises of this school include the following:

○ Knowledge is the central productive and strategic asset of the firm (Arrow, 1972; Badaracco, 1991; Quinn, 1992).

○ Knowledge is a complex concept and includes information, social relations, personal know-how, and skills. Knowledge is an attribute of both individuals and organizations. Personal knowledge can be appropriated and encoded by the organization in the form of manuals, software, and operating procedures.

○ Knowledge can be explicit or tacit. Explicit knowledge is codified in books, manuals, pictures, and videos. Tacit knowledge is implicit know-how, or a social relationship needed to complete a task, built over years of experience. Tacit knowledge includes craftsmanship, teams that work together well, values, culture and attitudes that support learning, and decision-making patterns based on knowledge. Tacit knowledge is embedded in individuals and organizations (Jensen and Meckling, 1992).

○ Organizations and people can learn in the sense that they can change their behavior on the basis of new information or knowledge (Huber, 1991).

○ All physical capital is an instance of knowledge. Knowledge can be embedded in machines (Machlup, 1962; Boulding, 1966).

○ The function of the firm is to create value—to survive and be efficient—through the integration of specialized knowledge.

○ The strategy of the firm is to develop specialized expertise "core competencies," which other firms cannot copy easily and which cannot be marketed (Prahalad and Hamel, 1990).

Figure 4-3 illustrates the knowledge-based view of the firm.

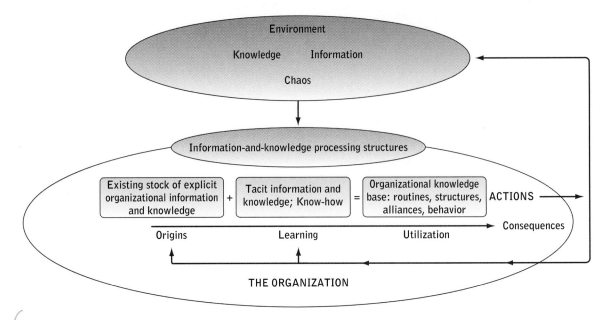

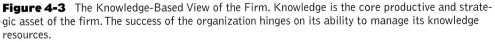

Figure 4-3 The Knowledge-Based View of the Firm. Knowledge is the core productive and strategic asset of the firm. The success of the organization hinges on its ability to manage its knowledge resources.

The knowledge-based view of the firm has important consequences for how organizations are managed and how they use information technology. If intellectual and knowledge-based activities are the very heart of an organization, then a manager's role should be focused more on how to manage knowledge workers; how to gather, acquire, store, and disseminate information and knowledge; and how to build new knowledge into the organization. Information technology applications should focus on knowledge workers and the management of knowledge. Teams and groups become more important in this view simply because problem solving often requires the input of many people who work in the problem area. And if intellectual and knowledge-based activities are central, then the long-term strategy of the firm should be to focus on strengthening its "core" knowledge competencies and building the knowledge base.

Travel Guide Software provides on-line software for travel expense reporting as well as reservation access to all airline, auto rental, and hotel companies. Such tools can help managers monitor and control expenses for the organization.

Each of the three main schools of management thinking—technical–rational, behavioral, and cognitive—has important implications for managing and organizing information technology in today's contemporary organization. Next we take a closer look at how information technology shapes the decision-making process.

4.2 Introduction to Decision Making

Decision making remains one of the more challenging roles of a manager. Information systems have helped managers communicate and distribute information; however, they have provided only limited assistance for management decision making. Because decision making is an area that system designers have sought most of all to affect (with mixed success), we now turn our attention to this issue. In this section we introduce the process; in the next two sections we examine models of individual and organizational decision making.

Levels of Decision Making

Differences in decision making can be classified by organizational level, corresponding to the strategic, management, knowledge, and operational levels of the organization introduced in Chapter 2.

Strategic decision making determines the objectives, resources, and policies of the organization. A major problem at this level of decision making is predicting the future of the organization and its environment and matching the characteristics of the organization to the environment. This process generally involves a small group of high-level managers who deal with complex, nonroutine problems (see the Window on Management).

Decision making for **management control** is principally concerned with how efficiently and effectively resources are utilized and how well operational units are performing. Management control requires close interaction with those who are carrying out the tasks of the organization; it takes place within the context of broad policies and objectives set out by strategic decision making; and, as the behaviorists have described, it requires an intimate knowledge of operational decision making and task completion.

Knowledge-level decision making deals with evaluating new ideas for products and services; ways to communicate new knowledge; and ways to distribute information throughout the organization.

Decision making for **operational control** determines how to carry out the specific tasks set forth by strategic and middle management decision makers. Determining which units in the organization will carry out the task, establishing criteria for completion and resource utilization, and evaluating outputs all require decisions about operational control.

Types of Decisions: Structured versus Unstructured

Within each of these levels of decision making, Simon (1960) classified decisions as being either programmed or nonprogrammed. Other researchers refer to these types of decisions as structured and unstructured, as we do in this book. **Unstructured decisions** are those in which the decision maker must provide judgment, evaluation, and insights into the problem definition. These decisions are novel, important, and nonroutine, and there is no well-understood or agreed-upon procedure for making them (Gorry and Scott-Morton, 1971). **Structured decisions,** by contrast, are repetitive, routine, and involve a definite procedure for handling so that they do not have to be treated each time as if they were new. Some decisions are **semistructured decisions;** in such cases, only part of the problem has a clear-cut answer provided by an accepted procedure.

Types of Decisions and Types of Systems

Combining these two views of decision making produces the grid shown in Figure 4-4. In general, operational control personnel face fairly well-structured problems. In contrast, strategic planners tackle highly unstructured problems. Many problems encountered by knowledge workers are fairly unstructured as well. Nevertheless, each level of the organization contains both structured and unstructured problems.

strategic decision making Determining the long-term objectives, resources, and policies of an organization.

management control Monitoring how efficiently or effectively resources are utilized and how well operational units are performing.

knowledge-level decision making Evaluating new ideas for products, services, ways to communicate new knowledge, and ways to distribute information throughout the organization.

operational control Deciding how to carry out specific tasks specified by upper and middle management and establishing criteria for completion and resource allocation.

unstructured decisions Nonroutine decisions in which the decision maker must provide judgment, evaluation, and insights into the problem definition; there is no agreed-upon procedure for making such decisions.

structured decisions Decisions that are repetitive, routine, and have a definite procedure for handling them.

semistructured decisions Decisions where only part of the problem has a clear-cut answer provided by an accepted procedure.

Managers Look to the Future

Top-level managers need information to help them plan for the future and define their companies' long-term business goals. There are many different ways they can use information and information systems to reach those goals.

Some companies focus on assembling numerical information concerning important metrics for business performance. GE Capital is having 25 executives pilot Gentia's Renaissance Balanced Scorecard system. Balanced scorecard systems allow managers to define the indicators they want to use to measure finances, customer relations, operational efficiency, and employee performance. The software then uses these indicators so that they can be compared with strategic goals, such as increasing market share by 25 percent.

For example, an executive might pull up a scorecard with an icon representing return on equity, with categories for earnings growth, decreased spending, and balanced risk. If the return on equity icon is green, indicating all is well, but the earnings growth icon is red, indicating trouble, the executive might see that market share has dropped because the firm hasn't been gathering new market and customer data. The executive can then look at specific marketing initiatives and take quick corrective action.

Other companies base their planning on information that is nonquantitative. Duncan Highsmith, CEO of Highsmith, Inc., believes that one must take a very broad approach to the future. Every week he pores through piles of articles on topics ranging from dragonfly anatomy to juvenile delinquency, trying to identify emerging trends that should be addressed by his firm.

Highsmith, Inc. is the leading mail-order supplier of equipment such as audio-visual tools, book displays, and educational software for schools and libraries in the United States. Its sales slipped during the early 1990s due to sharp declines in school funding. In retrospect, Duncan Highsmith realized he could have anticipated this development if he had paid attention to reports of tax revolts in local communities that had been occurring since the 1970s. From that point on, Highsmith decided he should spend less time looking at his company's own spreadsheets and sales reports and shift his attention to identifying external information on factors that would shape the fortunes of his business three years or more into the future. He calls this pursuit Life, the Universe, and Everything.

Highsmith works closely with Lisa Guedea Carreno, the company's chief librarian, scanning magazines, books, ads, and Web sites as well as television and radio programs. They meet weekly to share their impressions and ideas about future trends. Guedea Carreno and her team of librarians also help other employees seeking information about topics such as the effect of wellness initiatives on healthcare costs, best practices for trade show exhibits, and competitive activity. They then customize the information they find for each recipient based on their learning styles—whether they are visual, textual, or aural—and the type of information being delivered. For instance, John Kiley, director of marketing, prefers a verbal summary, while other employees prefer bulleted points, charts, and sometimes full text.

To Think About: What kinds of decisions are illustrated here? How useful are information systems in supporting strategic decision making?

Sources: Leigh Buchanan, "The Smartest Little Company in America," Inc, January 1999; and Beth David, "Powered Planning," Information Week, January 18, 1999.

In the past, most success in modern information systems came in dealing with structured, operational, and management control decisions. But now most of the exciting applications are occurring in the management, knowledge, and strategic planning areas, where problems are either semistructured or totally unstructured. Examples include general DSS, PC-based decision-making systems including spreadsheets and other packages, professional design workstations, and general planning and simulation systems (discussed in later chapters).

Stages of Decision Making

Making decisions consists of several different activities that take place at different times. The decision maker has to perceive and understand problems. Once perceived, solutions must be designed; once solutions are designed, choices have to be made about a particular solution; finally, the solution has to be implemented. Simon (1960) described four different stages in decision making (see Table 4.5): intelligence, design, choice, and implementation.

Intelligence consists of identifying the problems occurring in the organization. Intelligence indicates why, where, and with what effects a situation occurs. This broad set of information-gathering activities is required to inform managers how well the organization is

Intelligence The first of Simon's four stages of decision making, when the individual collects information to identify problems occurring in the organization.

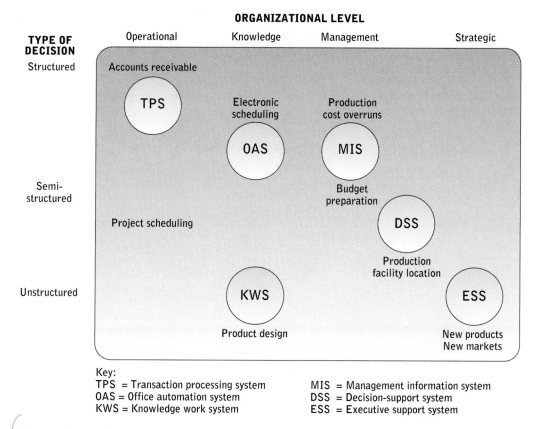

ORGANIZATIONAL LEVEL

Key:
TPS = Transaction processing system
OAS = Office automation system
KWS = Knowledge work system
MIS = Management information system
DSS = Decision-support system
ESS = Executive support system

Figure 4-4 Different kinds of information systems at the various organizational levels support different types of decisions.
Source: G. Anthony Gorry and Michael Scott Morton, "A Framework for Management Information Systems," **Sloan Management Review** 13, no 1. Used by permission.

performing and to let them know where problems exist. Traditional MIS that deliver a wide variety of detailed information can help identify problems, especially if the systems report exceptions.

During **design,** the second stage of decision making, the individual designs possible solutions to the problems. This activity may require more intelligence so that the manager can decide if a particular solution is appropriate. Smaller DSS are ideal in this stage of decision making because they operate on simple models, can be developed quickly, and can be operated with limited data.

design Simon's second stage of decision making, when the individual conceives of possible alternative solutions to a problem.

Table 4.5	**Stages in Decision Making, Information Requirement, and Supporting Information Systems**		
Stage of Decision Making	**Information Requirement**	**Example System**	
Intelligence	Exception reporting	MIS	
Design	Simulation prototype	DSS, KWS	
Choice	"What-if" simulation	DSS; large models	
Implementation	Graphics, charts	PC and mainframe decision aids	

Source: Kenneth C. Laudon and Jane P. Laudon; and Scott-Morton, 1971.

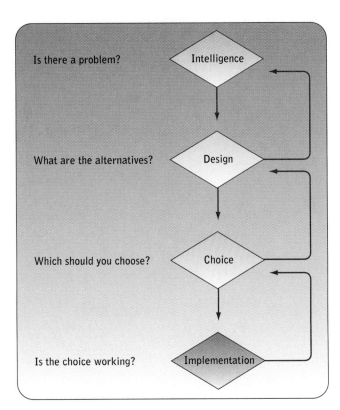

Figure 4-5 The Decision-making Process. Decisions are often arrived at after a series of iterations and evaluations at each stage in the process. The decision-maker often must loop back through one or more of the stages before completing the process.

Is there a problem? — Intelligence

What are the alternatives? — Design

Which should you choose? — Choice

Is the choice working? — Implementation

---

choice Simon's third stage of decision making, when the individual selects among the various solution alternatives.

implementation Simon's final stage of decision making, when the individual puts the decision into effect and reports on the progress of the solution.

rational model Model of human behavior based on the belief that people, organizations, and nations engage in basically consistent, value-maximizing calculations or adaptations within certain constraints.

Choice, the third stage of decision making, consists of choosing among alternatives. Here a manager can use information tools that can calculate and keep track of the consequences, costs, and opportunities provided by each alternative designed in the second stage. The decision maker might need a larger DSS to develop more extensive data on a variety of alternatives and to use complex analytic models needed to account for all the consequences.

The last stage in decision making is **implementation.** Here, managers can use a reporting system that delivers routine reports on the progress of a specific solution. The system will also report some of the difficulties that arise, will indicate resource constraints, and will suggest possible ameliorative actions. Support systems can range from full-blown MIS to much smaller systems as well as project-planning software operating on personal computers.

Table 4.5 lists the stages in decision making, the general type of information required, and specific examples of information systems corresponding to each stage.

In general, the stages of decision making do not necessarily follow a linear path from intelligence to design, choice, and implementation. At any point in the decision-making process, you may have to loop back to a previous stage (see Figure 4-5). For instance, one can often create several designs but may not be certain about whether a specific design meets the requirements for the particular problem. This situation requires additional intelligence work. Alternatively, one can be in the process of implementing a decision, only to discover that it is not working. In such a case, one is forced to repeat the design or choice stage.

4.3 Individual Models of Decision Making

A number of models attempt to describe how individuals make decisions (see Table 4.6). The basic assumption behind all these models is that human beings are in some sense rational.

The Rational Model

The **rational model** of human behavior is built on the idea that people, organizations, and nations engage in basically consistent, value-maximizing calculations or adaptations within certain constraints. The rational model works as follows: An individual has goals or objectives

Table 4.6 Models of Individual Decision Making

Name	Basic Concept	Inference Patterns
Rational model	Comprehensive rationality	Establish goals, examine all alternatives, and choose the best alternative.
Satisficing model	Bounded rationality	Establish goals, examine a few alternatives, and choose the first alternative that promotes the goals.
Muddling through	Successive comparison	Examine alternatives to establish a mix of goals and consequences; choose policies that are marginally different from those of the past.
Psychological	Cognitive types	All decision-makers choose goals, but they differ in terms of gathering and evaluating information. Systematic thinkers impose order on perceptions and evaluations; intuitive thinkers are more open to unexpected information and use multiple models and perspectives when evaluating information. Neither is more rational than the other.

and has a payoff, utility, or preference function that permits that person to rank all possible alternative actions by the action's contribution to the desired goals. The actor is presented with and understands alternative courses of action. Each alternative has a set of consequences. The actor chooses the alternative and consequences that rank highest in terms of the payoff functions, that is, that contribute most to the ultimate goal. In a rigorous model of rational action, the actor has comprehensive rationality, can accurately rank all alternatives and consequences, and can perceive all alternatives and consequences.

There are three criticisms of the rational model. First, people cannot specify all of the alternatives that exist. Second, most individuals do not have singular goals and a consciously used payoff function, and they are not able to rank all alternatives and consequences. Third, in real life the idea of a finite number of all alternatives and consequences makes no sense. In a maze constructed for a rat or in a game of tic-tac-toe, all alternatives and consequences can be meaningful and precise. In the real world of humans, specifying all of the alternatives and consequences is impossible.

Despite these criticisms, the rational model remains a powerful and attractive model of human decision making. It is rigorous, simple, and instructive.

Bounded Rationality and Satisficing

March and Simon (1958) and Simon (1960) proposed a number of adjustments to the rigorous rational model. Rather than optimizing, which presumes comprehensive rationality, Simon argues that people partake in **satisficing**—that is, choosing the first available alternative that moves them toward their ultimate goal. Instead of searching for all the alternatives and consequences (unlimited rationality), Simon proposes **bounded rationality,** that people limit the search process to sequentially ordered alternatives (alternatives not radically different from the current policy). When possible, people avoid new, uncertain alternatives and rely instead on tried-and-true rules, standard operating procedures, and programs. In this way, rationality is bounded.

satisficing Choosing the first available alternative to move closer toward the ultimate goal instead of searching for all alternatives and consequences.

bounded rationality Idea that people will avoid new, uncertain alternatives and stick with tried-and-true rules and procedures.

"Muddling Through"

In an article on the "science of **muddling through,**" Lindblom (1959) proposed the most radical departure from the rational model. He described this method of decision making as one of "successive limited comparisons." First, individuals and organizations have conflicting goals—they want both freedom and security, rapid economic growth and minimal pollution, faster transportation and minimal disruption due to highway construction, and so forth. People have to choose among policies that contain various mixes of conflicting goals. The values themselves cannot be discussed in the abstract; they become clear only when specific policies are considered.

muddling through Method of decision making involving successive limited comparisons where the test of a good decision is whether people agree on it.

Because there is no easy means–end analysis, and because people cannot agree on values, the only test of a "good" choice is whether people agree on it. Policies cannot be judged by how much of X they provide, but rather by the agreement of the people making the policies. Labor and management can rarely agree on values, but they can agree on specific policies.

Because of the limits on human rationality, Lindblom proposes **incremental decision making,** or choosing policies most like the previous policy. Finally, choices are not "made." Instead, decision making is a continuous process in which final decisions are always being modified to accommodate changing objectives, environments, value preferences, and policy alternatives provided by decision makers.

Psychological Types and Frames of Reference

Modern psychology has provided a number of qualifications to the rational model. Psychologists find that humans differ in *how they maximize their values* and in the *frames of reference* they use to interpret information and make choices.

Cognitive style describes underlying personality dispositions toward the treatment of information, the selection of alternatives, and the evaluation of consequences. McKenney and Keen (1974) described two cognitive styles that have direct relevance to information systems: systematic versus intuitive types. **Systematic decision makers** approach a problem by structuring it in terms of some formal method. They evaluate and gather information in terms of their structured method. **Intuitive decision makers** approach a problem with multiple methods, using trial and error to find a solution, and tend to not structure information gathering or evaluation. Neither type is superior to the other, but some types of thinking are more appropriate for certain tasks and roles in the organization.

The existence of different cognitive styles does not challenge the rational model of decision making. It simply says that there are different ways of being rational.

More recent psychological research poses strong challenges to the rational model by showing that humans have built-in biases that can distort decision making. Worse, people can be manipulated into choosing alternatives that they might otherwise reject simply by changing the *frame of reference.*

Tversky and Kahneman (1981), summarizing a decade of work on the psychology of decision making, found that humans have a deep-seated tendency to avoid risks when seeking gains but to accept risks to avoid losses. In other words, people are more sensitive to negative outcomes than to positive ones. College students refuse to bet $10, for instance, on a coin flip unless they stand to win at least $30. Other biases are listed in Table 4.7.

---

incremental decision making Choosing policies most like the previous policy.

cognitive style Underlying personality disposition toward the treatment of information, selection of alternatives, and evaluation of consequences.

systematic decision makers Cognitive style that describes people who approach a problem by structuring it in terms of some formal method.

Intuitive decision makers Cognitive style that describes people who approach a problem with multiple methods in an unstructured manner, using trial and error to find a solution.

Table 4.7 Psychosocial Biases in Decision Making

1. People have no sensible model for dealing with improbable events and either ignore them or overestimate their likelihood; for example, one-in-a-million lotteries are popular, and people have an exaggerated fear of shark attacks.

2. People are more willing to accept a negative outcome if it is presented as a cost rather than a loss; for example, a man will continue playing tennis at an expensive club, despite a painful tennis elbow, by accepting the pain as a cost of the game rather than quit and accept the loss of an annual membership fee.

3. People given the same information will prefer alternatives with certain gains rather than alternatives with certain losses; people will gamble to avoid certain losses. For example, students and professional health workers were given the choice between alternative programs to fight a new disease that was expected to kill 600 people. When described in terms of lives saved, a large majority preferred a program that was certain to save 200 people over a program that had a possibility—but no certainty—of saving all 600. On the other hand, when presented in terms of lives lost, a large majority rejected a program that was guaranteed to lose 400 lives and preferred to gamble, against the odds, on a program that might save everyone but probably would lose everyone.

Source: A. Tversky and D. Kahneman, "The Framing of Decisions and the Psychology of Choice," *Science,* 211, January, 1981.

4.4 Organizational Models of Decision Making

Decision making often is not performed by a single individual but by entire groups or organizations. **Organizational models of decision making** take into account the structural and political characteristics of an organization. While organizations might be visualized as having singular goals pursued by rational decision makers who can weigh alternatives and consequences, other forces are at work. Bureaucratic, political, and even "garbage can" models have been proposed to describe how decision making takes place in organizations. Table 4.8 compares the main features of these models.

organizational model of decision making Model of decision making that takes into account the structural and political characteristics of an organization.

bureaucratic model of decision making Model of decision making where decisions are shaped by the organization's standard operating procedures (SOPs).

Bureaucratic Models

The dominant idea of a **bureaucratic model of decision making** is that whatever organizations do is the result of standard operating procedures honed over years of active use. The particular actions chosen by an organization are an output of one or several organizational subunits (e.g., marketing, production, finance, human resources). The problems facing any organization are too massive and too complex to be attended by the organization as a whole. Problems are instead divided into their components and are parceled out to specialized groups. Competing with low-priced, high-quality Asian cars, for instance, is a complex problem. There are many aspects: production, labor relations, technology, marketing, finance, and even government regulation.

Each organizational subunit has a number of standard operating procedures (SOPs)—tried and proven techniques—that it invokes to solve a problem. Organizations rarely change these SOPs, because they may have to change personnel and incur risks. (Who knows if the new techniques work better than the old ones?)

SOPs are woven into the programs and repertoires of each subunit. Taken together, these repertoires constitute the range of effective actions that leaders of organizations can take. These repertoires are what the organization can do in the short term. As a U.S. president discovered in a moment of national crisis, his actions were largely constrained not by his imagination but by what his "pawns, bishops, and knights" were trained to do (see the Window on Organizations).

Although senior management and leaders are hired to coordinate and lead the organization, they are effectively trapped by parochial subunits that feed information upward and that provide standard solutions. Senior management cannot decide to act in ways that the major subunits cannot support.

Some organizations do, of course, change; they learn new ways of behaving; and they can be led. But these changes require a long time. In general, organizations do not "choose" or "decide" in a rational sense; instead, they choose from among a very limited set of repertoires. The goals of organizations are multiple, not singular, and the most important goal is the preservation

Table 4.8 Models of Organizational Decision Making

Name	Basic Concept	Inference Pattern
Rational actor	Comprehensive rationality	Organizations select goals, examine all alternatives and consequences, and then choose a policy that maximizes the goal or preference function.
Bureaucratic	Organizational output Standard operating procedures	Goals are determined by resource constraints and existing human and capital resources; SOPs are combined into programs, and programs into repertoires; these determine what policies will be chosen. The primary purpose of the organization is to survive; uncertainty reduction is the principal goal. Policies are chosen that are incrementally different from the past.
Political	Political outcome	Organizational decisions result from political competition; key players are involved in a game of influence, bargaining, and power. Organizational outcomes are determined by the beliefs and goals of players, their skills in playing the game, the resources they bring to bear, and the limits on their attention and power.
Garbage can	Nonadaptive organizational programs	Most organizations are nonadaptive, temporary, and disappear over time. Organizational decisions result from interactions among streams of problems, potential actions, participants, and chance.

Window on Organizations

Blockade by the Book

In the evening of October 23, 1962, the Executive Committee of the President (EXCOM), a high-level working group of senior advisors to President John F. Kennedy, decided to impose a naval quarantine or blockade on Cuba to force the Soviet Union to remove its intermediate-range ballistic missiles from the island, located 90 miles south of Miami.

The naval blockade was chosen only after the Air Force reported that it could not conduct what the politicians in EXCOM called a "surgical air strike" to remove the missiles. Instead, the Air Force recommended a massive strategic air campaign against a number of ground, air, and naval Cuban targets. This was considered extreme by EXCOM, and the only other alternative seemed to be a blockade that would give Chairman Khrushchev plenty of time to think and develop several face-saving alternatives.

But EXCOM was worried that the Navy might blunder when implementing the blockade and cause an incident, which in turn could lead to World War III. Secretary of Defense Robert McNamara visited the Navy's chief of naval operations to make the point that the blockade was not in-tended to shoot Russians but rather to send a political message.

McNamara wanted to know the following: Which ship would make the first interception? Were Russian-speaking officers on board? In what way would submarines be handled? Would Russian ships be given the opportunity to turn back? What would the Navy do if Russian captains refused to answer questions about their cargo?

At that point, the chief of naval operations picked up the **Manual of Naval Regulations**, waved it at McNamara, and said "It's all in there." McNamara responded, "I don't give a damn what John Paul Jones would have done. I want to know what you are going to do tomorrow!"

The visit ended with the navy officer inviting the Secretary of Defense to go back to his office and let the Navy run the blockade.

To Think About: What does this story tell you about decision making at a time of national crisis? Is such decision making rational?

Source: Graham T. Allison, **Essence of Decision**, 1971.

---

of the organization itself (e.g., the maintenance of budget, manpower, and territory). The reduction of uncertainty is another major goal. Policy tends to be incremental, only marginally different from the past, because radical policy departures involve too much uncertainty.

Political Models of Organizational Choice

Power in organizations is shared; even the lowest level workers have some power. At the top, power is concentrated in the hands of a few. For many reasons, leaders differ in their opinions about what the organization should do. The differences matter, causing competition for leadership to ensue.

political model of decision making Model of decision making where decisions result from competition and bargaining among the organization's interest groups and key leaders.

In a **political model of decision making,** what an organization does is a result of political bargains struck among key leaders and interest groups. Actions are not necessarily rational, except in a political sense, and the outcome is not what any individual necessarily wanted. Instead, policy–organizational action is a compromise, a mixture of conflicting tendencies. Organizations do not invent "solutions" that are "chosen" to solve some "problem." They develop compromises that reflect the conflicts, the major stakeholders, the diverse interests, the unequal power, and the confusion that constitutes politics.

"Garbage Can" Model

garbage can model Model of decision making that states that organizations are not rational and that decisions are solutions that become attached to problems for accidental reasons.

In Chapter 3 we pointed out that many organizations do not survive. There are surprisingly few theories that explicitly address the fact that organizations are quite short lived. One such theory of decision making, called the **"garbage can" model,** states that organizations are not rational. Decision making is largely accidental and is the product of a stream of solutions, problems, and situations that are randomly associated. That is, solutions become attached to problems for accidental reasons: Organizations are filled with solutions looking for problems and decision makers looking for work.

If this model is correct, it should not be surprising that the wrong solutions are applied to the wrong problems in an organization, or that, over time, a large number of organizations make critical mistakes that lead to their demise. The Exxon Corporation's delayed response to the 1989 Alaska oil spill is an example. Within an hour after the Exxon tanker *Valdez* ran aground in Alaska's Prince William Sound on March 29, 1989, workers were preparing emergency equipment; however, the aid was not dispatched. Instead of sending out emergency crews, the Alyeska Pipeline Service Company (which was responsible for initially responding to oil spill emergencies) sent the crews home. The first full emergency crew did not arrive at the spill site until at least 14 hours after the shipwreck. By the time the vessel was finally surrounded by floating oil containment booms, the oil had spread beyond effective control. Yet enough equipment and personnel had been available to respond effectively. Much of the 10 million gallons of oil fouling the Alaska shoreline in the worst tanker spill in American history could have been confined had Alyeska acted more decisively (Malcolm, 1989).

4.5 How Information Technology Has Changed the Management Process

There is a vast difference between how traditional managers fulfilled the management functions we have just described and how contemporary managers act. And there is a corresponding vast difference between how managers solved problems in the past and how they increasingly do it today (Kanter, 1989).

Traditional and Contemporary Management

Many organizations today believe that the key assets of the organization are knowledge and core competencies from which all products and services derive. Without these, the financial and physical assets of the firm would be worthless. Contemporary views rely much more on the involvement, enabling, and empowering of lower-level managers and workers. The assumption here is that employees and managers know what to do, want to work hard and succeed, and believe in the goals of the firm. The job of management—especially senior management—is to make it possible for the employees to achieve their goals and the company's goals. A very important part of organizational success in the contemporary view is developing a proper understanding of the environment, opening the organization to outside influences, and in general adjusting the organization to contemporary social and ethical currents.

These contemporary views of management and organizations are often directly at odds with the old style of management and organizations. In these more traditional views, workers must be told what to do, do not want to work hard, and either do not know or do not care about the goals of the firm. In these circumstances, management must be micromanagement, involve extensive and costly control systems, and result in centralized organizations where senior management plays critical operational roles.

In older and larger organizations, traditional management styles are pervasive. In younger, entrepreneurial, and smaller organizations, more contemporary management styles are common although not universal. Many Fortune 500 firms are seeking to adopt contemporary management styles as their products, services, and employees change.

Information technology has played a role in the changing process of management by providing powerful tools for managers to carry out both their traditional and newer roles. Contemporary information systems permit managers rapidly to obtain, analyze, and comprehend vast quantities of data. Middle and senior managers can use management information systems (MIS) and executive support systems (ESS) to monitor day-to-day operations at any level of detail needed, from the most general down to the specific transaction, employee, or customer. Decision-support systems (DSS) and ESS do not necessarily guarantee more accurate and predictive forecasting—that also depends on many other factors such as the skill of the planner. But they do enable a more comprehensive examination of both the data and the issues (see Chapter 15). Additionally, they enable managers to respond more quickly to the rapidly changing business environment. Managers monitor, plan, and forecast with more precision and speed than ever before.

Managers can also use information systems to give employees more responsibility and decision-making power in the "new" organization. Employees are working more and more in electronic environments (as opposed to face-to-face environments). Electronic mail and other network-based forms of communication enable managers to broaden their span of control and manage workers and organizations wherever they are located. With new group communication and coordination technologies, including the Internet, managers can establish and manage

WebEx is a Web-based service where companies can share documents, presentations, and applications to conduct on-line meetings. Such tools can help managers broaden their span of control.

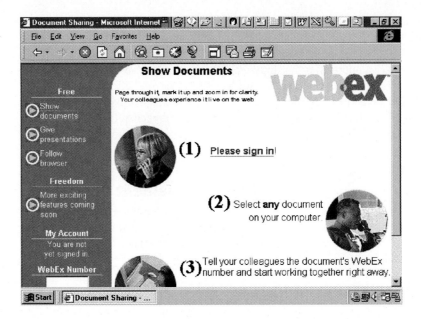

flexible work groups and short-term task forces from around the world that bring together just the right mix of skills for the task at hand. Information can be rapidly distributed to workers so that they can act independently.

Table 4.9 lists some of the differences between contemporary and traditional management and the role played by information technology. Although information technology supports new ways of managing and organizing, it is not the only reason these changes are taking place. General cultural and economic changes in attitudes and the nature of work are important factors.

Implications for System Design

The research on management decision making has a number of implications for information systems design and understanding. First, managers use formal information systems to plan, organize, and coordinate. However, they also use them for a variety of other less obvious (but vital) tasks such as interpersonal communication, setting and carrying out personal agendas, and establishing a network throughout the organization. This should remind information system designers that there are multiple uses for their products and that the way systems are actually used may not, in fact, reflect the original intention of the designers.

Another implication of contemporary investigations of managers is that formal information systems may have limited impact on managers. Ad hoc (less formal) information systems that can be built quickly, use more current and up-to-date information, and can be adjusted to the unique situations of a specific group of managers are highly valued by the modern manager. Systems designers and builders should appreciate the importance of creating systems that can process information at the most general level; communicate with other sources of information, both inside and outside the organization; and provide an effective means of communication among managers and employees within the organization.

Research also shows that decision making is not a simple process, even in the rigorous rational model. The research on organizational decision making should alert students of information systems to the fact that decision making in a business is a group and organizational process. Systems must be built to support group and organizational decision making.

As a general rule, research on management decision making indicates that information systems designers should design systems that have the following characteristics:

○ They are flexible, with many options for handling data, evaluating information, and accommodating changes in individual and organizational learning and growth.

○ They are capable of supporting a variety of styles, skills, and knowledge, and both individual and organizational processes of decision making. *(cont.)*

Table 4.9 **Traditional and Contemporary Management**

Management Schools	Traditional	Contemporary	Role of Information Technology
Technical–Rational School			
Analysis of work	Time/motion studies to increase efficiency of individual workers	Analyze groups of workers and entire business processes	Use IT to "reengineer" business processes, seeking quick but drastic increases in productivity
Administration	Develop intricate, hierarchical reporting structures	Analyze the flow of information	Use IT as "work-flow" software making the movement of documents more efficient for information-intense service sector organizations
Behavioral School			
Planning	Top-down centralized planning by senior management	Decentralized, involving all units and employees with management support	Use IT such as the Internet to involve more people in the planning process
Organizing	Management defines a stable division of labor	Enable employees to self-organize project teams	Use networks to facilitate self-organizing teams
Leading	Management inspires or threatens employees to perform	Enable employees to do their jobs as well as they can and know how; build and activate networks; all employees lead	Use networks to maintain contact with subordinates and to supervise their work
Controlling	Develop precise micromanagement control systems	Push controls down to project teams; use peer group controls; focus on overall results with computer-based systems	Use IT to develop real-time organizational controls
Innovating	Centralized, specialized product research and design units	Innovations come from customers, employees, and managers at all levels	Use electronic conferencing and other techniques to generate new ideas for business; groupware and group decision-support tools helpful
Environments	Hostile and competitive, requires strong boundaries and defensive posture	Competitive but potential for alliances, resources, and coalitions; requires proactive adjustment, proper understanding to succeed	Use IT to continuously monitor key environmental changes; encourage use of nonroutine sources of information to overcome organizational biases
Cognitive School			
Sense-making	Individual managers impose "sense" on the situation of the firm	Formal and informal information systems affect group sense-making activities	Build information systems as reality checkers with much information that cannot be filtered out by biased individuals and groups
Organizational learning	Organizational knowledge is captured by the routines, procedures, and business processes of the firm	Organizational knowledge is captured by the information systems—formal and informal—which operate the organization	Use information technology explicitly to create, store, and disseminate organizational knowledge using datamining, multimedia, and the Internet
Knowledge base	Financial and physical assets are the foundation of the firm	Core competencies, knowledge, and knowledge workers are key assets	Use information technology to capture core competency in software where possible; use IT to coordinate and manage the work of knowledge workers to enhance their productivity

○ They are powerful in the sense of having multiple analytical and intuitive models for the evaluation of data and the ability to keep track of many alternatives and consequences.

○ They reflect the bureaucratic and political requirements of systems, with features to accommodate diverse interests.

○ They reflect an appreciation of the limits of organizational change in policy and in procedure and an awareness of what information systems can and cannot do.

Management Wrap-Up

Management

Information technology provides tools for managers to carry out both their traditional and newer roles, allowing them to monitor, plan, and forecast with more precision and speed than ever before and to respond more rapidly to the changing business environment. However, some managerial roles cannot be easily supported by information systems, and managers will need to overcome psychosocial biases and resistance to change to find meaningful ways to use the Internet and other technologies to transform the management process.

Organization

It's clear that there are new ways of organizing work, which are enabled in part by new technology. The central organizational issue is whether traditional organizations can change their internal structures—their business processes—to permit new ways of organizing and managing to emerge.

Technology

Each of the three schools of management can draw on information technology to enhance managerial effectiveness. Networks and communication and collaboration tools are especially useful for supporting managerial work in the "new" organization where more work is distributed among small groups and task forces and more responsibility is given to employees.

For Discussion

1. How would each of the three schools of management use information systems to make managers and organizations more effective?

2. Identify and describe a decision you had to make, such as selecting a college or a major. Use Simon's model of decision-making stages and suggest how an information system might have helped you make the decision.

Summary

1. Evaluate the three main schools of management thinking. The three main schools of management thinking are technical–rational, behavioral, and cognitive. Each of these schools provides a different perspective on the process of management. Early technical–rational (or classical) models of management stressed the design of job tasks and management functions of planning, organizing, coordinating, deciding, and controlling. Research from the behavioral school has examined the actual behavior of managers to show how managers get things done. Mintzberg found that managers' real activities are highly fragmented, variegated, and brief in duration, with managers moving rapidly and intensely from one issue to another. Other behavioral research has found that managers spend considerable time pursuing personal agendas and goals and that contemporary managers shy away

from making grand, sweeping policy decisions. The behavioral school also emphasizes employee relations and organizational adaptation to its environment. The cognitive school emphasizes the role of knowledge in organizational effectiveness and managers as information processors and problem solvers.

2. Describe the levels, types, and stages of decision making. Decision making in an organization can be classified by organizational level: strategic, management control, knowledge, and operational control.

Decisions can be either structured, semistructured, or unstructured, with structured decisions clustering at the operational level of the organization and unstructured decisions at the strategic planning level. The nature and level of decision making are important factors in building information systems for managers.

Decision making itself is a complex activity at both the individual and the organizational level. Simon described four different stages in decision making: intelligence, design, choice, and implementation.

3. Compare models for describing individual and organizational decision making. Rational models of decision making assume that human beings can accurately choose alternatives and consequences based on the priority of their objectives and goals. The rigorous rational model of individual decision making has been modified by behavioral research that suggests that rationality is limited. People "satisfice," "muddle through" decisions incrementally, or select alternatives biased by their cognitive style and frame of reference.

Organizational models of decision making illustrate that real decision making in organizations takes place in arenas where many psychological, political, and bureaucratic forces are at work. Thus, organizational decision making may not necessarily be rational. The design of information systems must accommodate these realities, recognizing that decision making is never a simple process.

4. Assess how information technology has changed the management process. Information technology has changed all three dimensions of management. IT has made possible the realization of many dreams of the technical–rational school including rational design of business processes, fine-grained monitoring of organizational activities, and real-time management response to environmental changes. IT has changed the behavioral dimension of management by enabling decentralization, empowerment, self-organization, and the sharing of responsibility. At the same time, the cognitive dimension of management has received new importance by the emergence of technologies, which can greatly expand the knowledge base of a firm.

5. Explain how information systems can assist managers and improve managerial decision making. If information systems are built properly, they can support individual and organizational decision making. Up to now, information systems have been most helpful to managers for performing informational and decisional roles; the same systems have been of very limited value for managers' interpersonal roles. Information systems that are less formal and highly flexible will be more useful than large, formal systems at higher levels of the organization.

The design of information systems must accommodate these realities. Designers must recognize that decision making is never a simple process. Information systems can best support managers and decision making if such systems are flexible, with multiple analytical and intuitive models for evaluating data and the capability of supporting a variety of styles, skills, and knowledge.

Key Terms

Behavioral perspective, 101	Implementation, 112	Managerial roles, 103	Strategic decision making, 109
Bounded rationality, 113	Incremental decision making, 114	Muddling through, 113	Structured decisions, 109
Bureaucratic model of decision making, 115	Informational roles, 103	Operational control, 109	Systematic decision makers, 114
Choice, 112	Intelligence, 110	Organizational model of decision making, 115	Technical–rational "classical" perspective, 100
Cognitive perspective, 106	Interpersonal roles, 103	Political model of decision making, 116	Unstructured decisions, 109
Cognitive style, 114	Intuitive decision makers, 114	Rational model, 112	
Decisional roles, 103	Knowledge-level decision making, 109	Satisficing, 113	
Design, 111	Management control, 109	Semistructured decisions, 109	
Garbage can model, 116			

Review Questions

1. Describe the key ideas in the technical–rational (classical) school of management. What are the five functions of managers described in the classical model?

2. Describe the key ideas in the behavioral perspective of management. What characteristics of modern managers does the behavioral school emphasize?

3. What specific managerial roles can information systems support? Where are information systems particularly strong in supporting managers, and where are they weak?

4. What did Wrapp and Kotter discover about the way managers make decisions and get things done? How do these findings compare with those of the classical model?

5. Describe the key ideas of the cognitive perspective on management.

6. Define structured and unstructured decisions. Give three examples of each.

7. What are the four kinds of computer-based information systems that support decisions?

8. What are the four stages of decision making as described by Simon?

9. Describe each of the four individual models of decision making. What is the name, basic concept, and dominant inference pattern of each? How would the design of information systems be affected by the model of decision making employed?

10. Describe each of the organizational choice models. How would the design of systems be affected by the choice of model employed?

11. How has the management process changed? What is the role played by information technology?

Group Project

Form a group with three to four of your classmates. Observe a manager for one hour. Classify the observed behavior in two ways, using the classical model and then the behavioral model.

Compare the results and discuss the difficulties of coding the behavior. Present your findings to the class.

Tools for Interactive Learning

○ Internet

The Internet Connection for this chapter will take you to a Web site where you can view an interactive demonstration of an intranet. You can complete an exercise to evaluate how companies can use intranets to reduce agency costs and make the management process more efficient. You can also use the Interactive Study Guide to test your knowledge of the topics in this chapter and get instant feedback when you need more practice.

○ CD-ROM

If you purchase and use the Multimedia Edition CD-ROM with this chapter, you will find an interactive exercise which asks you to apply the correct model of organizational decision making to solve a set of problems. You can also find an audio overview of the major themes of this chapter and bullet text summarizing the key points of the chapter.

Case Study — A Tale of Two Cities' Information Systems

For the past few years, media headlines have trumpeted the financial problems of Washington, D.C., some of which stemmed from the city government's information systems. School administrators maintained two information systems, one for the public and Congress and a private set of books that enables the administration to pay tens of millions of dollars to school officials whom the City Council ordered be laid off. System errors caused the city to overpay hospitals by $35 million. Because the city's Medicaid and welfare computers are not linked, the city has mistakenly paid an extra $34 million to 20,000 people. The city's Information Systems department

returns new computer systems to manufacturers to have free, installed software removed, and then they accept bids to purchase the same software. Its information systems are antiquated, with some mission-critical systems running on ancient 286-based PCs, which are housed in condemned buildings. The city's 80 data networks are not connected with each other. Forty percent of all telephones are rotary phones, and there is no government-wide phone directory. Procurement red tape is so bad that software for one critical system arrived two years before the hardware did. Redundant computer centers are running at 40 percent of capacity. The city's

mayor at that time, Marion Barry Jr., admitted that senior officials overspend their budgets by millions of dollars by routinely overriding information systems controls.

As bad as Washington sounds, however, it appears to be no worse off than Philadelphia in 1992. At that time Philadelphia was running a budget deficit of $200 million per year and was rapidly heading into bankruptcy. **City and State** magazine designated Philadelphia as the city that "set the standard for municipal distress in the 1990s." Many city departments had their own computer systems or no automation at all. What systems existed were old, poorly supported, and stifled by layers of bureaucracy.

Turnaround came from the newly elected mayor, Edward Rendell. He balanced the city budget starting in 1993 and focused on improving information systems. By 1996 **Fortune** magazine ranked Philadelphia third in its annual list of "Best Cities for Family and Work."

Rendell appointed a 41-member task force composed of members from the private sector to provide advice on management and productivity issues. One of its first recommendations was to establish a Chief Information Officer (CIO) position and a new centralized Mayor's Office of Information Systems. Federal, state, and local governments are increasingly turning to CIOs to improve governance and oversight of their information systems and to help them make more efficient use of technology.

Antiquated systems were replaced, and a high-capacity, wide-area fiber-optic network was installed. The city outsourced much of its information systems work to private contractors, saving the city $450 million in just two years. Philadelphia's Chief Information Officer, John Carrow, focused zealously on cost-effective customer service. Staff was cut while services were maintained or improved. Carrow appointed senior nontechnical managers as portfolio managers to coordinate the Information Systems Department, users in government, and the public. Carrow enforced his new management by meeting with his staff every Friday morning to review information system performance that week.

Philadelphia's Information Systems Department replaced traditional performance measures such as numbers of transactions processed with results-based performance measures such as the percentage of help desk requests resolved by telephone or the number of users trained at the computer training center. Within four years, the number of computer users in the city government increased from 3000 to 12,000. The number of city workers receiving computer training rose from 811 in 1994 to 9317 in 1996. All of these workers are now connected by a new, high-powered wide-area network. By centralizing software purchases, the city saves millions of dollars through volume discounts.

Washington too is now beginning to address its problems, and its people are looking to Philadelphia for inspiration. City management consultants recently recommended 342 management reform projects for the city, 30 to 40 of which are for information systems. The city hired a new Chief Technology Officer (CTO), Michael T. Hernon. He is concerned about the "skill-impaired" workforce but says he may not even try to improve their skills. Instead, like Philadelphia, he is looking to outsource much of the work both to save the city money and to improve services. He has obtained financing to centralize and standardize IS, modernize computer and communication systems, and eliminate redundant facilities.

Washington reformers face special problems Philadelphia did not. For example, Washington does not have full power to govern itself. Instead, the city is governed by the U.S. Congress which does interfere with government activities. Congress scrutinizes reform projects, not always acting in a nonpartisan manner. In addition, Washington does not have county and state governments with which to share its burdens as do Philadelphia and other cities.

Representative Charles H. Taylor from North Carolina, chairman of the House Appropriations Subcommittee, tried unsuccessfully to block a $28 million contract award for a new financial management system (FMS). Taylor claimed that the problems with Washington's existing financial system were primarily "people problems," including insufficient discipline and internal controls, poor management practices, and weak computer and accounting skills.

Calling city government a "management wasteland," Marion Barry noted that senior public officials routinely overrode system controls in order to overspend their budgets. The city's financial control board found in 1995 that millions of dollars were not entered into the financial management system until months and even years after they were paid. Washington pays six times more per capita on information systems than does Philadelphia, with much less payback.

Washington's inspector general stated that the city had not sufficiently analyzed its information or alternatives to justify spending $28 million, and consultants added that the cost of a new FMS could run much higher than originally planned. Nevertheless, the FMS was approved and work on it continued.

Sources: Gary H. Anthes, "A Tale of Two Cities," **Computerworld**, January 12, 1998; and Peter Fabris, "Odd Ducks No More," **CIO** Magazine, November 15, 1998.

CASE STUDY QUESTIONS

1. How much of a role did management play in the conditions of Washington's and Philadelphia's information systems? What other factors were involved?

2. How did the conditions of information systems in Washington and Philadelphia affect managers' ability to make decisions? What kinds of decisions were affected?

3. Do you think Washington, D.C. will be as successful as Philadelphia in turning around its information systems and city government? Why or why not? Explain your answer.

Chapter 5

Ethical and Social Impact of Information Systems

After completing this chapter, you will be able to:

1. Analyze the relationship among ethical, social, and political issues raised by information systems.

2. Identify the main moral dimensions of an information society and apply them to specific situations.

3. Apply an ethical analysis to difficult situations.

4. Examine specific ethical principles for conduct.

5. Design corporate policies for ethical conduct.

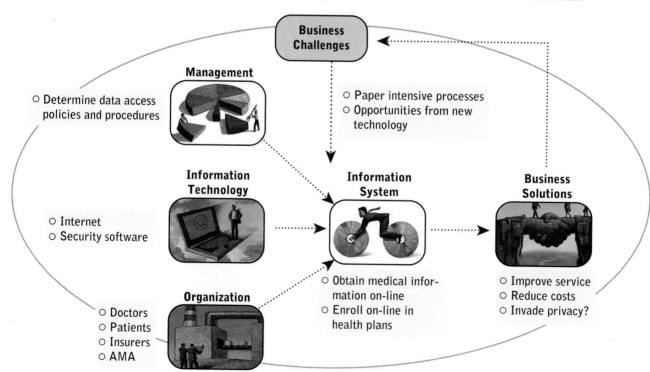

Business Challenges

Management
- Determine data access policies and procedures

- Paper intensive processes
- Opportunities from new technology

Information Technology
- Internet
- Security software

Information System
- Obtain medical information on-line
- Enroll on-line in health plans

Business Solutions
- Improve service
- Reduce costs
- Invade privacy?

Organization
- Doctors
- Patients
- Insurers
- AMA

Health Files on the Internet:
What Price for Convenience?

Many people use the Internet to find information about healthcare, medicine, and treatments. Now, growing numbers of physicians and insurers are using the Net to provide colleagues and patients with medical information such as lab results, plan coverage, and prescriptions.

Aetna U.S. Healthcare hopes to place a large percentage of information for consumers on the Internet, including procedures for obtaining approval for referrals to specialists. Harvard Pilgrim Health Care, based in Massachusetts, is working on a secure Web site that will enable members to obtain information on lab results, doctors' appointments, and prescription drug renewals. A few plans, such as Blue Shield of California and Minnesota-based Health Partners, allow employees and insurance agents to enroll members over the Internet. Employees can select their type of coverage and physicians over a protected Internet line.

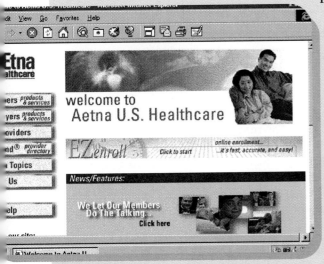

The ease and convenience of making medical records a mouse click away could deliver huge benefits to individuals, physicians, and insurance companies, who are often swamped with paperwork. But providing personal medical information on-line also raises serious questions about the protection of personal privacy. A person might not want his employer to learn he has AIDS, a serious illness, or a mental health problem. According to Dr. Donald J. Palmisano, a trustee of the American Medical Association, the AMA is concerned that if hackers can break into a CIA Web site, they could also break into one for health plans. A determined hacker could probably find a way to access protected records, although he or she probably would not be very interested in medical insurance claims. The AMA believes that patients have a basic right to privacy of their medical data that should be honored.

Insurance companies say they have devised security systems to protect clients' privacy, sometimes more effectively than paper records. For instance, Oxford Health Plan and Kaiser Permanente safeguard personal information by having patients use a personal identification number to access their laboratory results and other information over the Internet.

But security does not guarantee confidentiality. Privacy experts wonder how many people have access to a person's laboratory test results besides the patient in question. Information about a patient's prescription drugs is continually bought, sold, and analyzed without his or her knowledge. They fear that the Internet, which attracts millions of users every day, could be a breeding ground for this type of activity.

Sources: Milt Freudenheim, "Medicine at the Click of a Mouse," *The New York Times,* August 12, 1998; and Art Jahnke, "A Doctor in Every House," *CIO Web Business Magazine,* February 1, 1999.

Management Challenges

Technology can be a double-edged sword. It can be the source of many benefits. One great achievement of contemporary computer systems is the ease with which digital information can be transmitted and shared among many people. But at the same time, this powerful capability creates new opportunities for breaking the law or taking benefits away from others. Balancing the convenience and privacy implications of providing personal data on-line is one of the compelling ethical issues raised by contemporary information systems. As you read this chapter, you should be aware of the following management challenges:

1. **Understanding the moral risks of new technology.** Rapid technological change means that the choices facing individuals also rapidly change, and the balance of risk and reward and the probabilities of apprehension for wrongful acts change as well. Protecting individual privacy has become a serious ethical issue precisely for this reason, in addition to other issues described in this chapter. In this environment it will be important for management to conduct an ethical and social impact analysis of new technologies. One might take each of the moral dimensions described in this chapter and briefly speculate on how a new technology will impact each dimension. There may not always be right answers for how to behave but there should be considered management judgment on the moral risks of new technology.

2. **Establishing corporate ethics policies that include information systems issues.** As managers you will be responsible for developing corporate ethics policies and for enforcing them and explaining them to employees. Historically the information systems area is the last to be consulted, and much more attention has been paid to financial integrity and personnel policies. But from what you will know after reading this chapter, it is clear your corporation should have an ethics policy in the information systems area covering such issues as privacy, property, accountability, system quality, and quality of life. The challenge will be in educating non-IS managers to the need for these policies, as well as educating your workforce.

Protecting personal privacy on the Internet and establishing information rights represent one of the new ethical issues raised by the widespread use of information systems. Others include protecting intellectual property rights; establishing accountability for the consequences of information systems; setting standards to safeguard system quality that protect the safety of the individual and society; and preserving values and institutions considered essential to the quality of life in an information society. This chapter describes these issues and suggests guidelines for dealing with these questions.

5.1 Understanding Ethical and Social Issues Related to Systems

Ethics refers to the principles of right and wrong that can be used by individuals acting as free moral agents to make choices to guide their behavior. Information technology and information systems raise new ethical questions for both individuals and societies because they create opportunities for intense social change, and thus threaten existing distributions of power, money, rights, and obligations. Like other technologies, such as steam engines, electricity, telephone, and radio, information technology can be used to achieve social progress, but it can also be used to commit crimes and threaten cherished social values. The development of information technology will produce benefits for many, and costs for others. In this situation, what is the ethical and socially responsible course of action?

A Model for Thinking about Ethical, Social, and Political Issues

Ethical, social, and political issues are of course tightly coupled together. The ethical dilemma you may face as a manager of information systems typically is reflected in social and political debate. One way to think about these relationships is given in Figure 5-1. Imagine society as a more or less calm pond on a summer day, a delicate ecosystem in partial equilibrium with individuals and with social and political institutions. Individuals know how to act in this pond because social institutions (family, education, organizations) have developed well-honed rules of behavior, and these are backed by laws developed in the political sector that prescribe behavior and promise sanctions for violations. Now toss a rock into the center of the pond. But imagine instead of a rock that the disturbing force is a powerful shock of new information technology and systems hitting a society more or less at rest. What happens? Ripples, of course.

Suddenly individual actors are confronted with new situations often not covered by the old rules. Social institutions cannot respond overnight to these ripples—it may take years to develop etiquette, expectations, social responsibility, "politically correct" attitudes, or approved rules. Political institutions also require time before developing new laws and often require the demonstration of real harm before they act. In the meantime, you may have to act. You may be forced to act in a legal "gray area."

We can use this model as a first approximation of the dynamics that connect ethical, social, and political issues. This model is also useful for identifying the main moral dimensions of the "information society," which cut across various levels of action—individual, social, and political.

Five Moral Dimensions of the Information Age

A review of the literature on ethical, social, and political issues surrounding systems identifies five moral dimensions of the information age that we introduce here and explore in greater detail in Section 5.3. The five moral dimensions are as follows:

○ *Information rights and obligations:* What **information rights** do individuals and organizations possess with respect to information about themselves? What can they protect? What obligations do individuals and organizations have concerning this information?

○ *Property rights:* How will traditional intellectual property rights be protected in a digital society in which tracing and accounting for ownership is difficult, and ignoring such property rights is so easy?

○ *Accountability and control:* Who can and will be held accountable and liable for the harm done to individual and collective information and property rights?

○ *System quality:* What standards of data and system quality should we demand to protect individual rights and the safety of society?

○ *Quality of life:* What values should be preserved in an information- and knowledge-based society? What institutions should we protect from violation? What cultural values and practices are supported by the new information technology?

Before we analyze these dimensions let us briefly review the major technology and system trends that have heightened concern about these issues.

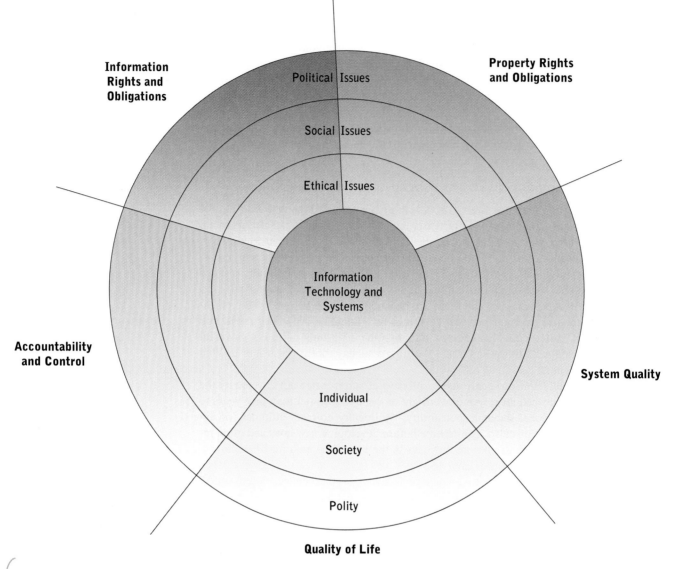

Information Rights and Obligations

Property Rights and Obligations

Political Issues

Social Issues

Ethical Issues

Information Technology and Systems

Individual

Society

Polity

Accountability and Control

System Quality

Quality of Life

Figure 5-1 The relationship between ethical, social, and political issues in an information society. The introduction of new information technology has a ripple effect, raising new ethical, social, and political issues that must be dealt with on the individual, social, and political levels. These issues have five moral dimensions: information rights and obligations, property rights and obligations, system quality, quality of life, and accountability and control.

Key Technology Trends That Raise Ethical Issues

These ethical issues long preceded information technology—they are the abiding concerns of free societies everywhere. Nevertheless, information technology has heightened ethical concerns, put stress on existing social arrangements, and made existing laws obsolete or severely crippled. There are four key technological trends responsible for these ethical stresses.

The doubling of computing power every 18 months has made it possible for most organizations to utilize information systems for their core production processes. As a result, our dependence on systems and our vulnerability to system errors and poor data quality have increased. Occasional system failures heighten public concern over our growing dependence on

Credit card purchases can make personal information available to market researchers, telephone marketers, and direct mail companies. Advances in information technology facilitate the invasion of privacy.

some critical systems. Social rules and laws have not yet adjusted to this dependence. Standards for ensuring the accuracy and reliability of information systems (see Chapter 16) are not universally accepted or enforced.

Advances in data storage techniques and rapidly declining storage costs have been responsible for the multiplying databases on individuals—employees, customers, and potential customers—maintained by private and public organizations. These advances in data storage have made the routine violation of individual privacy both cheap and effective. For example, IBM has developed a wafer-sized disk that can hold the equivalent of more than 500 large novels (Markoff, 1998). Already massive data storage systems are cheap enough for regional and even local retailing firms to use in identifying customers.

Advances in datamining techniques for large databases are a third technological trend that heightens ethical concerns, because they enable companies to find out much detailed personal information about individuals. With contemporary information systems technology, companies can assemble and combine the myriad pieces of information stored on you by computers much more easily than in the past. Think of all the ways you generate computer information about yourself—credit-card purchases, telephone calls, magazine subscriptions, video rentals, mail-order purchases, banking records, and local, state, and federal government records (including court and police records). Put together and mined properly, this information could reveal not only your credit information but also your driving habits, your tastes, your associations, and your political interests.

Companies with products to sell purchase relevant information from these sources to help them more finely target their marketing campaigns. For example, if you buy "upscale" merchandise from one catalog, the catalog company might sell your name to another catalog mail-order company. Chapter 2 describes how companies can use datamining on very large pools of data from multiple sources to rapidly identify buying patterns of customers and suggest individual responses.

Last, *advances in networking,* including the Internet, promise to reduce greatly the costs of moving and accessing large quantities of data, and open the possibility of mining large pools of data remotely using small desktop machines, permitting an invasion of privacy on a scale and precision heretofore unimaginable.

The development of global digital-superhighway communication networks widely available to individuals and businesses poses many ethical and social concerns. Who will account for the flow of information over these networks? Will you be able to trace information collected about you? What will these networks do to the traditional relationships between family, work, and leisure? How will traditional job designs be altered when millions of "employees" become subcontractors using mobile offices that they themselves must pay for?

In the next section we will consider some ethical principles and analytical techniques for dealing with these kinds of ethical and social concerns.

5.2 Ethics in an Information Society

Ethics is a concern of humans who have freedom of choice. Ethics is about individual choice: When faced with alternative courses of action, what is the correct moral choice? What are the main features of "ethical choice"?

Basic Concepts: Responsibility, Accountability, and Liability

Ethical choices are decisions made by individuals who are responsible for the consequences of their actions. Responsibility is a feature of individuals and is a key element of ethical action. **Responsibility** means that you accept the potential costs, duties, and obligations for the decisions you make. **Accountability** is a feature of systems and social institutions: It means that mechanisms are in place to determine who took responsible action, who is responsible. Systems and institutions in which it is impossible to find out who took what action are inherently incapable of ethical analysis or ethical action. Liability extends the concept of responsibility further to the area of laws. **Liability** is a feature of political systems in which a body of law is in place that permits individuals to recover the damages done to them by other actors, systems, or organizations. **Due process** is a related feature of law-governed societies and is a process in which laws are known and understood and there is an ability to appeal to higher authorities to ensure that the laws were applied correctly.

These basic concepts form the underpinning of an ethical analysis of information systems and those who manage them. First, as discussed in Chapter 3, information technologies are filtered through social institutions, organizations, and individuals. Systems do not have "impacts" by themselves. Whatever information system impacts exist are products of institutional, organizational, and individual actions and behaviors. Second, responsibility for the consequences of technology falls clearly on the institutions, organizations, and individual managers who choose to use the technology. Using information technology in a "socially responsible" manner means that you can and will be held accountable for the consequences of your actions. Third, in an ethical political society, individuals and others can recover damages done them through a set of laws characterized by due process.

Ethical Analysis

When confronted with a situation that seems to present ethical issues, how should you analyze and reason about the situation? Following is a five-step process that should help:

○ **Identify and describe clearly the facts.** Find out who did what to whom, and where, when, and how. You will be surprised in many instances at the errors in the initially reported facts, and often you will find that simply getting the facts straight helps define the solution. It also helps to get the opposing parties involved in an ethical dilemma to agree on the facts.

○ **Define the conflict or dilemma and identify the higher-order values involved.** Ethical, social, and political issues always reference higher values. The parties to a dispute all claim to be pursuing higher values (e.g., freedom, privacy, protection of property, and the free enterprise system).

responsibility Accepting the potential costs, duties, and obligations for the decisions one makes.

accountability The mechanisms for assessing responsibility for decisions made and actions taken.

liability The existence of laws that permit individuals to recover the damages done to them by other actors, systems, or organizations.

due process A process in which laws are well-known and understood and there is an ability to appeal to higher authorities to ensure that laws are applied correctly.

Typically, an ethical issue involves a dilemma: two diametrically opposed courses of action that support worthwhile values. For example, the Window on Technology in this chapter illustrates two competing values: the need for companies to use marketing to become more efficient and the need to protect individual privacy.

○ **Identify the stakeholders.** Every ethical, social, and political issue has stakeholders: players in the game who have an interest in the outcome, who have invested in the situation, and usually who have vocal opinions. Find out the identity of these groups and what they want. This will be useful later when designing a solution.

○ **Identify the options that you can reasonably take.** You may find that none of the options satisfy all the interests involved, but that some options do a better job than others. Sometimes arriving at a "good" or ethical solution may not always be a "balancing" of consequences to stakeholders.

○ **Identify the potential consequences of your options.** Some options may be ethically correct, but disastrous from other points of view. Other options may work in this one instance, but not be generalizable to other similar instances. Always ask yourself, "What if I choose this option consistently over time?"

Once your analysis is complete, what ethical principles or rules should you use to make a decision? What higher-order values should inform your judgment?

Candidate Ethical Principles

Although you are the only one who can decide which among many ethical principles you will follow, and how you will prioritize them, it is helpful to consider some ethical principles with deep roots in many cultures that have survived throughout recorded history.

1. Do unto others as you would have them do unto you (the Golden Rule). Putting yourself into the situation of others, and thinking of yourself as the object of the decision, can help you think about "fairness" in decision making.

2. If an action is not right for everyone to take, then it is not right for anyone (**Immanuel Kant's Categorical Imperative**). Ask yourself, "If everyone did this, could the organization, or society, survive?"

3. If an action cannot be taken repeatedly, then it is not right to be taken at any time (**Descartes' rule of change**). This is the slippery-slope rule: An action may bring about a small change now that is acceptable, but if repeated would bring unacceptable changes in the long run. In the vernacular, it might be stated as "once started down a slippery path you may not be able to stop."

4. Take the action that achieves the higher or greater value (the **Utilitarian Principle**). This rule assumes you can prioritize values in a rank order and understand the consequences of various courses of action.

5. Take the action that produces the least harm, or the least potential cost (**Risk Aversion Principle**). Some actions have extremely high failure costs of very low probability (e.g., building a nuclear generating facility in an urban area) or extremely high failure costs of moderate probability (speeding and automobile accidents). Avoid these high failure cost actions, with greater attention obviously to high failure cost potential of moderate to high probability.

6. Assume that virtually all tangible and intangible objects are owned by someone else unless there is a specific declaration otherwise. (This is the **ethical "no free lunch" rule.**) If something created by someone else is useful to you, it has value and you should assume the creator wants compensation for this work.

Unfortunately, these ethical rules have too many logical and substantive exceptions to be absolute guides to action. Nevertheless, actions that do not easily pass these rules deserve some very close attention and a great deal of caution if only because the appearance of unethical behavior may do as much harm to you and your company as actual unethical behavior.

Immanuel Kant's Categorical Imperative A principle that states that if an action is not right for everyone to take it is not right for anyone.

Descartes' rule of change A principle that states that if an action cannot be taken repeatedly, then it is not right to be taken at any time.

Utilitarian Principle Principle that assumes one can put values in rank order and understand the consequences of various courses of action.

Risk Aversion Principle Principle that one should take the action that produces the least harm or incurs the least cost.

ethical "no free lunch" rule Assumption that all tangible and intangible objects are owned by someone else unless there is a specific declaration otherwise and that the creator wants compensation for this work.

Are the Cookies Eating Your Privacy?

When you surf the Net, you are being observed. The only questions are by whom and for what purposes? Tools to monitor your visits to the World Wide Web have been developed for commercial reasons—to help organizations determine how to better target their offerings, and to determine who is visiting their Web sites. For example, many commercial sites log the number of visitors and which site pages they visit to collect marketing information about user interests and behaviors. One key issue arises from this data collection—do they know who you are? If so, then what do they do with such data, and are these uses appropriate, legal, and ethical? In other words, is your privacy being improperly invaded?

Do they know who you are? The answer is—maybe! Of course you are known if you register at a site to purchase a product or service. This situation is the same as using a credit card to purchase any product or service. In addition some sites offer you a free service, such as information, in exchange for your agreeing to register, and when you register they have you identified. This is probably no different from your signing up for a supermarket's frequent shopper or discount card—you voluntarily give up some of your privacy in exchange for something you want. In both cases, the company collects the information to use in its own marketing research and to target specific offers to you. They also might sell it to other companies or organizations, raising the privacy issues discussed elsewhere in this chapter. A March 1998 survey conducted by the U.S. Federal Trade Commission concluded that U.S. companies with Web sites have fallen short of what is needed to protect consumers. For instance 97 percent of financial sites collected data from their visitors, but only 16 percent stated how that information would be used.

But what if you do not volunteer personal information at a site? Can they gather it anyway, without your consent and without your knowledge? The answer seems to be yes, with the help of Internet technology. Using click-stream tracking, a Web site owner can audit the files tracking usage of the Web site to see the path that users take through the site. For example, a merchant could use click-stream tracking to see which icons on the site attract people to click and which are bypassed. Marketers are especially interested in finding out which site the visitor came from before visiting that particular Web site. If a Web site is getting a lot of traffic from another Web site, it might pay to concentrate more advertising efforts there.

Cookies are tiny data files that are deposited on your computer by interested Web sites when you visit those sites. They identify your Web browser software and track your visits to the Web site. When you return to a site that has stored a cookie, it will search your computer, find the cookie, and "know" what you have done in the past. It may also update

Professional Codes of Conduct

When groups of people claim to be professionals, they take on special rights and obligations because of their special claims to knowledge, wisdom, and respect. Professional codes of conduct are promulgated by associations of professionals such as the American Medical Association (AMA), the American Bar Association (ABA), the Data Processing Management Association (DPMA), and the Association of Computing Machinery (ACM). These professional groups take responsibility for the partial regulation of their professions by determining entrance qualifications and competence. Codes of ethics are promises by the profession to regulate themselves in the general interest of society. For example, avoiding harm to others, honoring property rights (including intellectual property), and respecting privacy are among the General Moral Imperatives of the ACM's Code of Ethics and Professional Conduct (ACM, 1993).

Extensions to these moral imperatives state that ACM professionals should consider the health, privacy, and general welfare of the public in the performance of their work and that professionals should express their professional opinion to their employer regarding any adverse consequences to the public (see Oz, 1994).

Some Real-World Ethical Dilemmas

The recent ethical problems described in this section illustrate a wide range of issues. Some of these issues are obvious, ethical dilemmas, in which one set of interests is pitted against another. Others represent some type of breach of ethics. In either instance, there are rarely any easy solutions.

Continental Can: Based in Norwalk, Connecticut, Continental Can Company developed a human resources database with files on all of its employees. Besides the typical employee data, the system included the capability to "red flag" employees nearing retirement or ap-

"Cookies" are tiny files deposited on a computer hard drive when a user visits certain Web sites. Cookies provide information that helps companies track the activities and interests of their Web site visitors. Although it can provide valuable marketing information, the practice of collecting Web-site visitor data raises worries about protecting individual privacy.

the cookie, depending on your activity this visit. In this way, the site can customize its contents for your interests (assuming your past activities indicate your current interest). If you are a regular Web user, search your hard drive for files named

"cookie.txt" and you are likely to find some. The site may use the data from its cookies for itself, or it too may sell that data to others.

You are also monitored as you use Usenet newsgroups. Deja News publicly catalogues thousands of Usenet groups and monitors their visitors. Visit its site (http://dejanews.com) and you can view a profile of your own (or other person's) use of Usenet groups—how many times you posted messages and in which newsgroups. You may not want this information released. For example, you may be part of a political newsgroup that you want kept confidential. That information is available for others to see and may even be sold to interested parties.

To Think About: How would you balance the rights of individuals to privacy against the desire of companies to use this technology to improve their marketing and to better target their products to the interests of individuals?

Sources: Sharon Machlis, "U.S. Firms Gird for Privacy Rules," Computerworld, January 11, 1999; Rivka Tadjer, "Much Ado About Privacy," Internet Computing, March, 1998; and Matthew Hahn, "Easy Now to Keep Tabs on Users' Internet Postings," The New York Times, January 6, 1997.

proaching the age at which a pension would be vested in the individual. Throughout the 1980s, when the red flag went up, management would fire the person even after decades of loyal service. In 1991 a federal district court in Newark, New Jersey, awarded ex-employees $445 million for wrongful dismissal (McPartlin, 1992).

Downsizing with Technology at the Telephone Company: Many of the large telephone companies in the United States are using information technology to reduce the size of their workforce. For example, AT&T is using voice recognition software to reduce the need for human operators by allowing computers to recognize a customer's responses to a series of computerized questions. New algorithms called "word spotting" allow the computer to recognize speech that is halting, stuttering, paused, or ungrammatical. AT&T expects that the new technology will eliminate 3000 to 6000 operator jobs nationwide, 200 to 400 management positions, and 31 offices in 21 states.

GTE Corporation reengineered its customer-service function to reduce the number of repair technicians. Customer-service workers who in the past had passed customer complaints on to repair technicians have been authorized to resolve the problems themselves by performing remote tests on customers' lines. The company also merged 12 operations centers into a single center to monitor the company's entire nationwide network. These and other changes have relied on technology to eliminate 17,000 jobs (Andrews, 1994; Levinson, 1994).

E-mail privacy at Epson: In March 1990, e-mail administrator Alana Shoars filed a suit in Los Angeles Superior Court alleging wrongful termination, defamation, and invasion of privacy by her former employer, Epson America Inc. of Torrance, California. She sought $1 million in damages. In July 1990, Shoars filed a class-action suit seeking $75 million for 700 Epson employees and approximately 1800 outsiders whose e-mail may have been monitored. Shoars contends that she was fired because she questioned the company's policy of monitoring and printing employee's e-mail messages. Epson claims that Shoars was fired because she opened an MCI:Mail account without permission. Many firms claim that they have every right to monitor the electronic mail of their employees because they own the facilities, intend their use to be for business purposes only, and create the facility for a business purpose (Bjerklie, 1994; Rifkin, 1991).

In each instance, you can find competing values at work, with groups lined on either side of a debate. A company may argue, for example, that it has a right to use information systems to increase productivity and reduce the size of its workforce to keep down costs and stay in business. Employees displaced by information systems may argue that employers have some responsibility for their welfare. A close analysis of the facts can sometimes produce compromised solutions that give each side "half a loaf." Try to apply some of the described principles of ethical analysis to each of these cases. What is the right thing to do?

5.3 The Moral Dimensions of Information Systems

In this section, we take a closer look at the five moral dimensions of information systems first described in Figure 5-1. In each dimension we identify the ethical, social, and political levels of analysis and illustrate with real-world examples the values involved, the stakeholders, and the options chosen.

Information Rights: Privacy and Freedom in an Information Society

privacy The claim of individuals to be left alone, free from surveillance or interference from other individuals, organizations, or the state.

Privacy is the claim of individuals to be left alone, free from surveillance or interference from other individuals or organizations including the state. Claims to privacy are also involved at the workplace: Millions of employees are subject to electronic and other forms of high-tech surveillance. Information technology and systems threaten individual claims to privacy by making the invasion of privacy cheap, profitable, and effective.

The claim to privacy is protected in the U.S., Canadian, and German constitutions in a variety of different ways, and in other countries through various statutes. In the United States, the claim to privacy is protected primarily by the First Amendment guarantees of freedom of speech and association and the Fourth Amendment protections against unreasonable search and seizure of one's personal documents or home, and the guarantee of due process.

Due process has become a key concept in defining privacy. Due process requires that a set of rules or laws exist that clearly define how information about individuals will be treated, and what appeal mechanisms are available. Perhaps the best statement of due process in record keeping is given by the Fair Information Practices Doctrine developed in the early 1970s.

Fair Information Practices (FIP) A set of principles originally set forth in 1973 that governs the collection and use of information about individuals and forms the basis of most U.S. and European privacy laws.

Most American and European privacy law is based on a regime called Fair Information Practices (FIP) first set forth in a report written in 1973 by a federal government advisory committee (U.S. Department of Health, Education, and Welfare, 1973). **Fair Information**

> **Table 5.1** **Fair Information Practices Principles**
>
> 1. There should be no personal record systems whose existence is secret.
> 2. Individuals have rights of access, inspection, review, and amendment to systems that contain information about them.
> 3. There must be no use of personal information for purposes other than those for which it was gathered without prior consent.
> 4. Managers of systems are responsible and can be held accountable and liable for the damage done by systems for their reliability and security.
> 5. Governments have the right to intervene in the information relationships among private parties.

Practices (FIP) is a set of principles governing the collection and use of information about individuals. The five Fair Information Practices principles are shown in Table 5.1.

FIP principles are based on the notion of a "mutuality of interest" among the record holder and the individual. The individual has an interest in engaging in a transaction, and the record keeper—usually a business or government agency—requires information about the individual to support the transaction. Once gathered, the individual maintains an interest in the record, and the record may not be used to support other activities without the individual's consent.

Fair Information Practices form the basis of 13 federal statutes listed in Table 5.2 that set forth the conditions for handling information about individuals in such areas as credit reporting, education, financial records, newspaper records, cable communications, electronic communications, and even video rentals. The Privacy Act of 1974 is the most important of these laws, regulating the federal government's collection, use, and disclosure of information. Most federal privacy laws apply only to the federal government. Only credit, banking, cable, and video rental industries have been regulated by federal privacy law.

In the United States, privacy law is enforced by individuals who must sue agencies or companies in court to recover damages. European countries and Canada define *privacy* in a similar manner to that in the United States, but they have chosen to enforce their privacy laws by creating privacy commissions or data protection agencies to pursue complaints brought by citizens.

The European Directive on Data Protection

In Europe, privacy protection is much more stringent than in the United States. On October 25, 1998, the European Directive on Data Protection came into effect, broadening privacy protection in the European Union (EU) nations. The Directive requires companies to inform people when they collect information about them and disclose how it will be stored and used. Customers must provide their informed consent before any company can legally use data about them, and they have the right to access that information, correct it, and request that no further data be collected. EU member nations must translate these principles into their own laws and cannot transfer personal data to countries such as the United States that don't have similar privacy protection regulations (see Chapter 17).

Table 5.2 **Federal Privacy Laws in the United States**

1. General Federal Privacy Laws

Freedom of Information Act, 1968 as Amended (5 USC 552)

Privacy Act of 1974 as Amended (5 USC 552a)

Electronic Communications Privacy Act of 1986

Computer Matching and Privacy Protection Act of 1988

Computer Security Act of 1987

Federal Managers Financial Integrity Act of 1982

2. Privacy Laws Affecting Private Institutions

Fair Credit Reporting Act of 1970

Family Educational Rights and Privacy Act of 1978

Right to Financial Privacy Act of 1978

Privacy Protection Act of 1980

Cable Communications Policy Act of 1984

Electronic Communications Privacy Act of 1986

Video Privacy Protection Act of 1988

Internet Challenges to Privacy

The Internet introduces technology that poses new challenges to the protection of individual privacy which existing Fair Information Practices principles are inadequate to address. Information sent over this vast network of networks may pass through many different computer systems before it reaches its final destination. Each of these systems is capable of monitoring, capturing, and storing communications that pass through it.

It is possible to record many on-line activities, including which on-line newsgroups or files a person has accessed and which Web sites he or she has visited. This information can be collected by both a subscriber's own Internet service provider and the system operators of remote sites that a subscriber visits. E-mail addresses can be collected for the purpose of sending out unsolicited e-mail and electronic messages. This practice is called **spamming,** and it is growing because it only costs a few cents to send thousands of messages advertising one's wares to Internet users. The Window on Technology described some of the challenges to individual privacy posed by Internet technology.

At present, Web site visitors can't easily find out how the information collected about them from their visits to Web sites is being used. Most Web sites do not post their privacy policies (Reagle and Cranor, 1999). To encourage self-regulation in the Internet industry, the U.S. Department of Commerce has issued guidelines for Fair Information Practices in on-line business. Industry groups such as the Online Privacy Alliance (OPA), consisting of over 60 global corporations and associations, have also issued guidelines for self-regulation. Privacy-enhancing technologies for protecting user privacy during interactions with Web sites are being developed (Reiter and Rubin, 1999; Goldschlag, Reed, and Syverson, 1999; Gabber, Gibbons, Kristol, Matias, and Mayer, 1999). Additional legislation and government oversight may be required to make sure that privacy in the Internet age is properly safeguarded.

Ethical Issues

The ethical privacy issue in this information age is as follows: Under what conditions should I (you) invade the privacy of others? What legitimates intruding into others' lives through unobtrusive surveillance, through market research, or by whatever means? Do we have to inform people that we are eavesdropping? Do we have to inform people that we are using credit history information for employment screening purposes?

Social Issues

The social issue of privacy concerns the development of "expectations of privacy" or privacy norms, as well as public attitudes. In what areas of life should we as a society encourage people to think they are in "private territory" as opposed to public view? For instance, should we as a society encourage people to develop expectations of privacy when using electronic mail, cellular telephones, bulletin boards, the postal system, the workplace, the street? Should expectations of privacy be extended to criminal conspirators?

Political Issues

The political issue of privacy concerns the development of statutes that govern the relations between record keepers and individuals. Should we permit the FBI to prevent the commercial development of encrypted telephone transmissions so they can eavesdrop at will (Denning et al., 1993)? Should a law be passed to require direct-marketing firms to obtain the consent of individuals before using their names in mass marketing (a consensus database)? Should e-mail privacy—regardless of who owns the equipment—be protected by law? In general, large organizations of all kinds—public and private—are reluctant to remit the advantages that come from the unfettered flow of information on individuals. Civil libertarians and other private groups have been the strongest voices supporting restraints on large organizations' information-gathering activities.

Property Rights: Intellectual Property

Contemporary information systems have severely challenged existing law and social practices that protect private intellectual property. **Intellectual property** is considered to be intangible property created by individuals or corporations. Information technology has made it difficult

spamming The practice of sending unsolicited e-mail and other electronic communication.

intellectual property Intangible property created by individuals or corporations that is subject to protections under trade secret, copyright, and patent law.

Window on Management

Wall Street spends more than $6.5 billion each year to make its computer terminals deliver a constant stream of up-to-the-second bond and equity prices along with complex analytical tools that combine years of historical data to predict future trends. Reuters Holdings, PLC, the world's largest and oldest financial information service, had more than a century's head start when Michael Bloomberg founded Bloomberg L.P. in 1981. But Bloomberg developed new analytic tools that enabled traders to aggressively analyze purchases and sales of investments, and Reuters started losing market share to this new information service competitor. Reuters spent more than seven years and $100 million developing historical data and analytics capabilities to match Bloomberg's, creating a special subsidiary, Reuters Analytics, to produce competing technology.

Bloomberg routinely monitors the usage levels of its customers to make sure they receive timely service. In 1997, Bloomberg staff noticed that one of its subscribers, Cyberspace Research, was downloading unusually large amounts of data and notified the FBI. The U.S. attorney's office in New York launched an investigation. Prosecutors started examining whether Reuters enlisted Cyberspace Research as a consultant to breach its subscription agreement and improperly transmit Bloomberg data about stocks and bonds and whether Reuters used that information to copy Bloomberg's analytics, incorporating that content into Reuters' new Securities 3000 analytics system.

If these allegations are true, Reuters could be prosecuted under mail or wire fraud laws or under the Economic Espionage Act of 1996, which makes the theft of trade secrets a federal felony. Although Bloomberg data are available to all of its subscribers and its formulas are considered

the standard convention for securities analysis, the information is still proprietary. It could be considered a trade secret because the company took considerable effort to develop the information and protect its use by competitors. Bloomberg develops its databases using public information but puts extensive work into compiling them. For example, creating a database with 10 years of data about the price of an Italian bond for 10 years requires not only the historical data but also fact-checking and "massaging" the data. One cannot look up Bloomberg's formulas in a textbook. Even hiring a consultant to violate the Bloomberg subscription agreement by providing information to Reuters could also be a crime.

On the other hand, conducting market intelligence is not illegal, and Bloomberg customers often print out the Bloomberg screens. Peter Job, Reuters' chief executive officer, wondered whether a subscription agreement unreasonably keeps competitors from studying another company's product. He observed that Reuters tries to compare the performance of its products and services to those of the competition and that the company does not view such assessments to be illegal or improper.

To Think About: Do you think Reuters should be prosecuted for stealing Bloomberg's data and analytical formulas? To what extent was Reuters management responsible? Explain.

Sources: Kurt Eichenwald, "Memos Said to Detail Reuters Effort to Obtain Bloomberg Data," **The New York Times,** February 2, 1998; "Reuters Denies Unit Is Focus of Break-in Probe," **The Wall Street Journal,** February 5, 1998; and Ivy Schmerken, "Did Reuters Cross the Line?" **Wall Street and Technology,** April, 1998.

---

to protect intellectual property because computerized information can be so easily copied or distributed on networks. Intellectual property is subject to a variety of protections under three different legal traditions: trade secret, copyright, and patent law (Graham, 1984).

Trade Secrets

Any intellectual work product—a formula, device, pattern, or compilation of data—used for a business purpose can be classified as a **trade secret,** provided it is not based on information in the public domain. (See the Window on Management.) Trade secrets have their basis in state law, not federal law, and protections vary from state to state. In general, trade secret laws grant a monopoly on the ideas behind a work product, but it can be a very tenuous monopoly.

Software that contains novel or unique elements, procedures, or compilations can be included as a trade secret. Trade secret law protects the actual ideas in a work product, not only their manifestation. To make this claim, the creator or owner must take care to bind employees and customers with nondisclosure agreements and to prevent the secret from falling into the public domain.

trade secret Any intellectual work or product used for a business purpose that can be classified as belonging to that business, provided it is not based on information in the public domain.

The limitation of trade secret protection is that although virtually all software programs of any complexity contain unique elements of some sort, it is difficult to prevent the ideas in the work from falling into the public domain when the software is widely distributed.

Copyright

copyright A statutory grant that protects creators of intellectual property against copying by others for any purpose for a period of 28 years.

Copyright is a statutory grant that protects creators of intellectual property against copying by others for any purpose for a period of 28 years. Since the first Federal Copyright Act of 1790, and the creation of the Copyright Office to register copyrights and enforce copyright law, Congress has extended copyright protection to books, periodicals, lectures, dramas, musical compositions, maps, drawings, artwork of any kind, and motion pictures. The congressional intent behind copyright laws has been to encourage creativity and authorship by ensuring that creative people receive the financial and other benefits of their work. Most industrial nations have their own copyright laws, and there are several international conventions and bilateral agreements through which nations coordinate and enforce their laws.

In the mid-1960s the Copyright Office began registering software programs, and in 1980 Congress passed the Computer Software Copyright Act, which clearly provides protection for source and object code and for copies of the original sold in commerce, and sets forth the rights of the purchaser to use the software while the creator retains legal title.

Copyright protection is explicit and clear-cut: It protects against copying of entire programs or their parts. Damages and relief are readily obtained for infringement. The drawback to copyright protection is that the underlying ideas behind a work are not protected, only their manifestation in a work. A competitor can use your software, understand how it works, and build new software that follows the same concepts without infringing on a copyright.

"Look and feel" copyright infringement lawsuits are precisely about the distinction between an idea and its expression. For instance, in the early 1990s Apple Computer sued Microsoft Corporation and Hewlett-Packard Inc. for infringement of the expression of Apple's Macintosh interface. Among other claims, Apple claimed that the defendants copied the expression of overlapping windows. The defendants counterclaimed that the idea of overlapping windows can only be expressed in a single way and, therefore, was not protectable under the "merger" doctrine of copyright law. When ideas and their expression merge, the expression cannot be copyrighted. In general, courts appear to be following the reasoning of a 1989 case— *Brown Bag Software* vs. *Symantec Corp.*—in which the court dissected the elements of software alleged to be infringing. The court found that neither similar concept, function, general functional features (e.g., drop-down menus), nor colors are protectable by copyright law (*Brown Bag* vs. *Symantec Corp.,* 1992).

Patents

patent A legal document that grants the owner an exclusive monopoly on the ideas behind an invention for 17 years; designed to ensure that inventors of new machines or methods are rewarded for their labor while making widespread use of their inventions.

A **patent** grants the owner an exclusive monopoly on the ideas behind an invention for 17 years. The congressional intent behind patent law was to ensure that inventors of new machines, devices, or methods receive the full financial and other rewards of their labor and yet still make widespread use of the invention possible by providing detailed diagrams for those wishing to use the idea under license from the owner of the patent. The granting of a patent is determined by the Patent Office and relies on court rulings.

The key concepts in patent law are originality, novelty, and invention. The Patent Office did not accept applications for software patents routinely until a 1981 Supreme Court decision that held that computer programs could be a part of a patentable process. Since that time hundreds of patents have been granted and thousands await consideration.

The strength of patent protection is that it grants a monopoly on the underlying concepts and ideas of software. The difficulty is passing stringent criteria of nonobviousness (e.g., the work must reflect some special understanding and contribution), originality, and novelty, as well as years of waiting to receive protection.

Challenges to Intellectual Property Rights

Contemporary information technologies, especially software, pose a severe challenge to existing intellectual property regimes and, therefore, create significant ethical, social, and political issues. Digital media differ from books, periodicals, and other media in terms of ease of replication; ease of transmission; ease of alteration; difficulty classifying a software work as a program, book, or even music; compactness—making theft easy; and difficulties in establishing uniqueness.

The proliferation of electronic networks, including the Internet, has made it even more difficult to protect intellectual property. Before widespread use of networks, copies of software, books, magazine articles, or films had to be stored on physical media, such as paper, computer disks, or videotape, creating some hurdles to distribution. Using networks, information can be more widely reproduced and distributed (Johnson, 1997). With the World Wide Web in particular, one can easily copy and distribute virtually anything to thousands and even millions of people around the world, even if they are using different types of computer systems. Information can be illicitly copied from one place and distributed through other systems and networks even though these parties do not willingly participate in the infringement (Carazos, 1996). The Internet was designed to transmit information freely around the world, including copyrighted information. Intellectual property that can be easily copied is likely to be copied (Chabrow, 1996).

The manner in which information is obtained and presented on the Web further challenges intellectual property protections (Okerson, 1996). Web pages can be constructed from bits of text, graphics, sound, or video that may come from many different sources. Each item may belong to a different entity, creating complicated issues of ownership and compensation (see Figure 5-2). Web sites can also use a capability called "framing" to let one site construct an on-screen border around content obtained by linking to another Web site. The first

Figure 5-2 Who Owns the Pieces? Anatomy of a Web page. Web pages are often constructed with elements from many different sources, clouding issues of ownership and intellectual property protection. Source: © The San Francisco Chronicle. Reprinted with permission.

site's border and logo stay on screen, making the content of the new Web site appear to be "offered" by the previous Web site. For example, TotalNews, Inc., based in Phoenix, maintains a Web site linked to the Web sites of more than 1100 news organizations and frames virtually all of them.

Mechanisms are being developed to sell and distribute books, articles, and other intellectual property on the Internet, but publishers continue to worry about copyright violations because intellectual property can now be copied so easily.

Ethical Issues

The central ethical issue posed to individuals concerns copying software: Should I (you) copy for my own use a piece of software protected by trade secret, copyright, and/or patent law? In the information age, it is so easy to obtain perfect, functional copies of software, that the software companies themselves have abandoned software protection schemes to increase market penetration, and enforcement of the law is so rare. However, if everyone copied software, very little new software would be produced because creators could not benefit from the results of their work.

Social Issues

There are several property-related social issues raised by new information technology. Most experts agree that the current intellectual property laws are breaking down in the information age. The vast majority of Americans report in surveys that they routinely violate some minor laws—everything from speeding to taking paper clips from work to copying software. The ease with which software can be copied contributes to making us a society of lawbreakers. These routine thefts threaten significantly to reduce the speed with which new information technologies can and will be introduced and, thereby, threaten further advances in productivity and social well-being.

Political Issues

The main property-related political issue concerns the creation of new property protection measures to protect investments made by creators of new software. Apple, Microsoft, and 900 other hardware and software firms formed the Software Publishers Association (SPA) to lobby for new protection laws and enforce existing laws. The SPA has established a toll-free anti-piracy hotline for employees to report on their corporations, staged numerous surprise audits or raids, sent hundreds of cease and desist letters, and filed more than 100 lawsuits since its inception (80 percent against corporations; 20 percent against bulletin board operators, training facilities, schools, and universities). The SPA has developed model Employee Guidelines for Using Software, described in the Window on Organizations.

Allied against SPA are a host of groups and millions of individuals who resist efforts to strengthen anti-piracy laws, and instead encourage situations in which software can be copied. These groups believe that software should be free, that anti-piracy laws cannot in any event be enforced in the digital age, or that software should be paid for on a voluntary basis (shareware software). According to these groups, the greater social benefit results from the free distribution of software.

Accountability, Liability, and Control

Along with privacy and property laws, new information technologies are challenging existing liability law and social practices for holding individuals and institutions accountable. If a person is injured by a machine controlled, in part, by software, who should be held accountable and therefore held liable? Should a public bulletin board or an electronic service such as Prodigy or America Online permit the transmission of pornographic or offensive material (as broadcasters), or should they be held harmless against any liability for what users transmit (as is true of common carriers such as the telephone system)? What about the Internet? If you outsource your information processing, can you hold the external vendor liable for injuries done to your customers? Try some real-world examples.

Employee Guidelines for Using Software

PURPOSE

All users will use software only in accordance with its license agreement. Unless otherwise provided in the license, any duplication of copyrighted software, except for backup and archival purposes, is a violation of copyright law. In addition to violating copyright law, unauthorized duplication of software is contrary to [organization's] standards of conduct. The following points are to be followed to comply with software license agreements:

1. We will use all software in accordance with its license agreements.
2. Legitimate software will promptly be provided to all users who need it. No [organization] user will make any unauthorized copies of any software under any circumstances. Anyone found copying software other than for backup purposes is subject to termination.
3. We will not tolerate the use of any unauthorized copies of software in our organization. Any person illegally reproducing software can be subject to civil and criminal penalties including fines and imprisonment. We do not condone illegal copying of software under any circumstances, and anyone who makes, uses, or otherwise acquires unauthorized software will be appropriately disciplined.
4. No user will give software to any outsiders including clients, customers, and others.

5. Any user who determines that there may be a misuse of software within the organization will notify the software manager, department manager, or legal counsel.
6. All software used by the organization on organization-owned computers will be purchased through appropriate procedures.

I have read [organization's] software code of ethics. I am fully aware of our software compliance policies and agree to abide by those policies. I understand that violation of any above policies may result in my termination.

_____

User signature

_____

Date

To Think About: Try to find out your university's policy regarding software. Is there a software code of ethics on campus? If an employee finds routine copying of software in a firm, should the person (a) call the firm's legal counsel or (b) call the SPA on the anti-piracy hotline? Are there any circumstances in which software copying should be allowed?

Source: Published by the Software Publishers Association.

Some Recent Liability Problems

On March 13, 1993, a blizzard hit the East Coast of the United States, knocking out an Electronic Data Systems Inc. (EDS) computer center in Clifton, New Jersey. The center operated 5200 ATM machines in 12 different networks across the country involving more than 1 million card holders. In the two weeks required to recover operations, EDS informed its customers to use alternative ATM networks operated by other banks or computer centers, and offered to cover more than $50 million in cash withdrawals. Because the alternative networks did not have access to the actual customer account balances, EDS was at substantial risk of fraud. Cash withdrawals were limited to $100 per day per customer to reduce the exposure. Most service was restored by March 26. Although EDS had a disaster-recovery plan, it did not have a dedicated backup facility. Who is liable for any economic harm caused individuals or businesses who could not access their full account balances in this period (Joes, 1993)?

In April 1990, a computer system at Shell Pipeline Corporation failed to detect a human operator error. As a result, 93,000 barrels of crude oil were shipped to the wrong trader. The error cost $2 million because the trader sold oil that should not have been delivered to him. A court ruled later that Shell Pipeline was liable for the loss of the oil because the error was due to a human operator who entered erroneous information into the system. Shell was held liable for not developing a system that would prevent the possibility of misdeliveries (King, 1992). Whom would you have held liable—Shell Pipeline? The trader for not being more careful about deliveries? The human operator who made the error?

These cases point out the difficulties faced by information systems executives who ultimately are responsible for the harm done by systems developed by their staffs. In general, insofar as computer software is part of a machine, and the machine injures someone physically or economically, the producer of the software and the operator can be held liable for damages. Insofar as the software acts more like a book, storing and displaying information, courts have been reluctant to hold authors, publishers, and booksellers liable for contents (the exception being instances of fraud or defamation), and hence courts have been wary of holding software authors liable for "booklike" software.

In general, it is very difficult (if not impossible) to hold software producers liable for their software products when those products are considered like books, regardless of the physical or economic harm that results. Historically, print publishers, books, and periodicals have not been held liable because of fears that liability claims would interfere with First Amendment rights guaranteeing freedom of expression.

What about "software as service"? ATM machines are a service provided to bank customers. Should this service fail, customers will be inconvenienced and perhaps harmed economically if they cannot access their funds in a timely manner. Should liability protections be extended to software publishers and operators of defective financial, accounting, simulation, or marketing systems?

Software is very different from books. Software users may develop expectations of infallibility about software; software is less easily inspected than a book, and more difficult to compare with other software products for quality; software claims actually to perform a task rather than describe a task like a book; and people come to depend on services essentially based on software. Given the centrality of software to everyday life, the chances are excellent that liability law will extend its reach to include software even when it merely provides an information service.

Telephone systems have not been held liable for the messages transmitted because they are regulated "common carriers." In return for their right to provide telephone service, they must provide access to all, at reasonable rates, and achieve acceptable reliability. But broadcasters and cable television systems are subject to a wide variety of federal and local constraints on content and facilities. Organizations can be held liable for offensive content on their Web sites; and online services such as Prodigy or America Online might be held liable for postings by their users.

Ethical Issues

The central liability-related ethical issue raised by new information technologies is whether individuals and organizations who create, produce, and sell systems (both hardware and software) are morally responsible for the consequences of their use (see Johnson and Mulvey, 1995). If so, under what conditions? What liabilities (and responsibilities) should the user assume, and what should the provider assume?

Social Issues

The central liability-related social issue concerns the expectations that society should allow to develop around service-providing information systems. Should individuals (and organizations) be encouraged to develop their own backup devices to cover likely or easily anticipated system failures, or should organizations be held strictly liable for system services they provide? If organizations are held strictly liable, what impact will this have on the development of new system services? Can society permit networks and bulletin boards to post libelous, inaccurate, and misleading information that will harm many persons? Or should information service companies become self-regulating, self-censoring?

Political Issues

The leading liability-related political issue is the debate between information providers of all kinds (from software developers to network service providers), who want to be relieved of liability insofar as possible (thereby maximizing their profits), and service users—individuals, organizations, communities—who want organizations to be held responsible for providing high-quality system services (thereby maximizing the quality of service). Service providers argue they will withdraw from the marketplace if they are held liable, whereas service users argue that only by holding providers liable can we guarantee a high level of service and compensate injured parties. Should legislation impose liability or restrict liability on service providers? This fundamental cleavage is at the heart of numerous political and judicial conflicts.

System Quality: Data Quality and System Errors

The debate over liability and accountability for unintentional consequences of system use raises a related but independent moral dimension: What is an acceptable, technologically feasible level of system quality (see Chapter 16)? At what point should system managers say, "Stop testing, we've done all we can to perfect this software. Ship it!" Individuals and organizations may be held responsible for avoidable and foreseeable consequences, which they have a duty to perceive and correct. And the gray area is that some system errors are foreseeable and correctable only at very great expense, an expense so great that pursuing this level of perfection is not feasible economically—no one could afford the product. For example, although software companies try to debug their products before releasing them to the marketplace, they knowingly ship buggy products because the time and cost of fixing all minor errors would prevent these products from ever being released (Rigdon, 1995). What if the product was not offered on the marketplace, would social welfare as a whole not advance and perhaps even decline? Carrying this further, just what is the responsibility of a producer of computer services—should they withdraw the product that can never be perfect, warn the user, or forget about the risk (let the buyer beware)?

Three principal sources of poor system performance are software bugs and errors, hardware or facility failures due to natural or other causes, and poor input data quality. Chapter 16 shows why zero defects in software code of any complexity cannot be achieved and the seriousness of remaining bugs cannot be estimated. Hence, there is a technological barrier to perfect software, and users must be aware of the potential for catastrophic failure. The software industry has not yet arrived at testing standards for producing software of acceptable but not perfect performance (Collins et al., 1994).

Although software bugs and facility catastrophe are likely to be widely reported in the press, by far the most common source of business system failure is data quality. Few companies routinely measure the quality of their data but studies of individual organizations report data error rates ranging from 0.5 to 30 percent (Redman, 1998). Table 5.3 describes some of these data quality problems.

Ethical Issues

The central quality-related ethical issue raised by information systems is at what point should I (or you) release software or services for consumption by others? At what point can you conclude that your software or service achieves an economically and technologically adequate

---

Table 5.3 **Illustrative Reported Data Quality Problems**

An airline inadvertently corrupted its database of passenger reservations while installing new software and for months planes took off with half-loads.

A manufacturer attempted to reorganize its customer files by customer number only to discover the sales staff had been entering a new customer number for each sale because of special incentives for opening new accounts. One customer was entered 7000 times. The company scrapped the software project after spending $1 million.

A manufacturing company nearly scrapped a $12 million data warehouse project because of inconsistently defined product data.

J. P. Morgan, a New York bank, discovered that 40 percent of the data in its credit-risk management database was incomplete, necessitating double-checking by users.

Several studies have established that 5 to 12 percent of bar code sales at retail grocery and merchandise chains are erroneous and that the ratio of overcharges to undercharges runs as high as 5:1, with 4:1 as a norm. The problem tends to be human error in keeping shelf prices accurate and corporate policy that fails to allocate sufficient resources to price checking, auditing, and development of error-free policies.

Source: Catherine Yang and Willy Stern, "Maybe They Should Call Them Scammers," *Business Week,* January 16, 1995; William Bulkeley, "Databases Plagued by a Reign of Error," *Wall Street Journal,* May 26, 1992; and Doug Bartholomew, "The Price Is Wrong," *Information Week,* September 14, 1992.

level of quality? What are you obliged to know about the quality of your software, its procedures for testing, and its operational characteristics?

Social Issues

The leading quality-related social issue once again deals with expectations: Do we want as a society to encourage people to believe that systems are infallible, that data errors are impossible? Do we instead want a society where people are openly skeptical and questioning of the output of machines, where people are at least informed of the risk? By heightening awareness of system failure, do we inhibit the development of all systems, which in the end contribute to social well-being?

Political Issues

The leading quality-related political issue concerns the laws of responsibility and accountability. Should Congress establish or direct the National Institute of Science and Technology (NIST) to develop quality standards (software, hardware, data quality) and impose those standards on industry? Or should industry associations be encouraged to develop industry-wide standards of quality? Or should Congress wait for the marketplace to punish poor system quality, recognizing that in some instances this will not work (e.g., if all retail grocers maintain poor quality systems, then customers have no alternatives)?

Quality of Life: Equity, Access, Boundaries

The negative social costs of introducing information technologies and systems are beginning to mount along with the power of the technology. Many of these negative social consequences are not violations of individual rights, nor are they property crimes. Nevertheless, these negative consequences can be extremely harmful to individuals, societies, and political institutions. Computers and information technologies potentially can destroy valuable elements of our culture and society even while they bring us benefits. If there is a balance of good and bad consequences to the use of information systems, who do we hold responsible for the bad consequences? Next, we briefly examine *some* of the negative social consequences of systems, considering individual, social, and political responses.

Balancing Power: Center versus Periphery

An early fear of the computer age was that huge, centralized mainframe computers would centralize power at corporate headquarters and in the nation's capital, resulting in a Big Brother society suggested in George Orwell's novel, *1984.* The shift toward highly decentralized computing, coupled with an ideology of "empowerment" of thousands of workers, and the decentralization of decision making to lower organizational levels, have reduced fears of power centralization in institutions. Yet much of the "empowerment" described in popular business magazines is trivial. Lower level employees may be empowered to make minor decisions, but the key policy decisions may be as centralized as in the past.

Rapidity of Change: Reduced Response Time to Competition

Information systems have helped to create much more efficient national and international markets. The now-more-efficient global marketplace has reduced the normal social buffers that permitted businesses many years to adjust to competition. "Time-based competition" has an ugly side: The business you work for may not have enough time to respond to global competitors and may be wiped out in a year, along with your job. We stand the risk of developing a "just-in-time society" with "just-in-time jobs" and "just-in-time" workplaces, families, and vacations.

Maintaining Boundaries: Family, Work, Leisure

Parts of this book were produced on trains, planes, as well as on family "vacations" and what otherwise might have been "family" time. The danger to ubiquitous computing, telecommuting, nomad computing, and the "do anything anywhere" computing environment is that it might actually come true. If so, the traditional boundaries that separate work from family and just plain leisure will be weakened. Although authors have traditionally worked just about anywhere (typewriters have been portable for nearly a century), the advent of information systems,

While some people may enjoy the convenience of working at home, the "do anything anywhere" computing environment can blur the traditional boundaries between work and family time.

coupled with the growth of knowledge-work occupations, means that more and more people will be working when traditionally they would have been playing or communicating with family and friends. The "work umbrella" now extends far beyond the eight-hour day.

Weakening these institutions poses clear-cut risks. Family and friends historically have provided powerful support mechanisms for individuals, and they act as balance points in a society by preserving "private life," providing a place for one to collect one's thoughts, think in ways contrary to one's employer, and dream.

Dependence and Vulnerability

Our businesses, governments, schools, and private associations such as churches are incredibly dependent now on information systems and are therefore highly vulnerable if these systems should fail. With systems now as ubiquitous as the telephone system, it is startling to remember that there are no regulatory or standard-setting forces in place similar to telephone, electrical, radio, television, or other public-utility technologies. The absence of standards and the criticality of some system applications will probably call forth demands for national standards and perhaps regulatory oversight.

Computer Crime and Abuse

Many new technologies in the industrial era have created new opportunities for committing crime. Technologies including computers create new valuable items to steal, new ways to steal them, and new ways to harm others. **Computer crime** can be defined as the commission of illegal acts through the use of a computer or against a computer system. Computers or computer systems can be the object of the crime (destroying a company's computer center or a company's computer files), as well as the instrument of a crime (stealing computer lists by illegally gaining access to a computer system using a home computer). Simply accessing a computer system without authorization, or intent to do harm, even by accident, is now a federal crime. **Computer abuse** is the commission of acts involving a computer that may not be illegal but are considered unethical.

No one knows the magnitude of the computer crime problem—how many systems are invaded, how many people engage in the practice, or what is the total economic damage? Many companies are reluctant to report computer crimes because they may involve employees. The most economically damaging kinds of computer crime are introducing viruses, theft of services, disruption of computer systems, and theft of telecommunications services. Computer crime has been estimated to cost more than $1 billion in the United States, and an additional $1 billion if corporate and cellular phone theft is included. "Hackers" is the pejorative term for

computer crime The commission of illegal acts through the use of a computer or against a computer system.

computer abuse The commission of acts involving a computer that may not be illegal but are considered unethical.

Nomad Mobile Research Centre - Files - BestWeb Internet Explorer

File   Edit   View   Go   Favorites   Help

Help NMRC

This is a small collection of files. If you have trouble downloading any link, try shift-clicking on the link or contact files@nmrc.org. There are divided into two categories, Insecurity and Security. The Insecurity Files are "Black Hat" utilities, and the Security Files are "White Hat" utilities.

Insecurity Files   **Security Files**

MS-DOS Files   **MS-DOS Files**

Netware Files   **Netware Files**

NT Files   **NT Files**

Unix Files   **Unix Files**

Start   Nomad Mobile Resea...   phot4.5a.bmp - Paint

persons who use computers in illegal ways. Hacker attacks are on the rise, posing new threats to organizations linked to the Internet (see Chapter 16).

Computer viruses (see Chapter 16) have grown exponentially during the past decade. Thousands of viruses have been documented. The average corporate loss for a bad virus outbreak is $250,000, and the probability of a large corporation experiencing a significant computer virus infection in a single year is 50 percent according to some experts. Although many firms now use anti-virus software, the proliferation of computer networks will surely increase the probability of infections.

Following are some illustrative computer crimes:

○ On May 29, 1996, the Federal Trade Commission announced it had obtained a temporary restraining order to freeze the assets of Fortuna Alliance of Bellingham, Washington. Fortuna had allegedly taken in more than $6 million from thousands of people in an illegal investors' pyramid scheme advertised on the Internet. Fortuna placed ads at several Web sites inviting thousands of customers on the Web to invest $250 to $1750 with the promise of earning at least $5000 per month if they could persuade others to invest. The FTC called Fortuna its largest fraud case to date on the Internet (Wilder, 1996).

○ Timothy Lloyd, a former chief computer network administrator at Omega Engineering Inc. in Bridgeport, New Jersey, was charged with planting a "logic bomb" that deleted all of the firm's software programs on July 30, 1996. A "logic bomb" is a malicious program that is set to trigger at a specified time. The company suffered $10 million in damages. Lloyd had been recently dismissed from his job. Federal prosecutors also charged Lloyd with stealing about $50,000 of computer equipment, which included a backup tape that could have allowed Omega to recover its lost files (Chen, 1998).

○ In July 1992, a federal grand jury indicted a national network of 1000 hackers calling themselves MOD—Masters of Deception. Theirs was one of the largest thefts of computer information and services in history. The hackers were charged with computer tampering, computer fraud, wire fraud, illegal wiretapping, and conspiracy. The group broke into over 25 of the largest corporate computer systems in the United States, including Equifax, Inc. (a credit reporting firm with 170 million records), Southwestern Bell Corporation, New York Telephone, and Pacific Bell. The group stole and resold

Table 5.4 Internet Crime and Abuse

Problem	Description
Hacking	Hackers exploit weaknesses in Web site security to obtain access to proprietary data such as customer information and passwords. They may use "Trojan horses" posing as legitimate software to obtain information from the host computer.
Jamming	Jammers use software routines to tie up the computer hosting a Web site so that legitimate visitors can't access the site.
Malicious software	Cyber vandals use data flowing through the Internet to transmit computer viruses, which can disable computers that they "infect" (see Chapter 16).
Sniffing	Sniffing is a form of electronic eavesdropping by placing a piece of software to intercept information passing from a user to the computer hosting a Web site. This information can include credit card numbers and other confidential data.
Spoofing	Spoofers fraudulently misrepresent themselves as other organizations, setting up false Web sites where they can collect confidential information from unsuspecting visitors to the site.

credit reports, credit card numbers, and other personal information. The hackers—all of whom were under 22 years of age—pleaded guilty. Their convicted leader, Mark Abene, spent 10 months in prison (Gabriel, 1995; Tabor, 1992).

In general, it is employees—insiders—who have inflicted the most injurious computer crimes because they have the knowledge, access, and frequently a job-related motive to commit such crimes.

Congress responded to the threat of computer crime in 1986 with the Computer Fraud and Abuse Act. This act makes it illegal to access a computer system without authorization. Most states have similar laws, and nations in Europe have similar legislation. Other existing legislation covering wiretapping, fraud, and conspiracy by any means, regardless of technology employed, is adequate to cover computer crimes committed thus far.

The Internet's ease of use and accessibility have created new opportunities for computer crime and abuse. Table 5.4 describes some of the most common areas where the Internet has been used for illegal or malicious purposes.

Employment: Trickle-Down Technology and Reengineering Job Loss

Reengineering work (see Chapter 11) is typically hailed in the information systems community as a major benefit of new information technology. It is much less frequently noted that redesigning business processes could potentially cause millions of middle-level managers and clerical workers to lose their jobs. Worse, if reengineering actually worked as claimed, these workers could not find similar employment in the society because of an actual decline in demand for their skills. One economist has raised the possibility that we will create a society run by a small "high tech elite of corporate professionals . . . in a nation of the permanently unemployed" (Rifkin, 1993). Some have estimated that if reengineering were seriously undertaken by the Fortune 1000 companies, about 25 percent of the U.S. labor force could be displaced. Reengineering has been seriously used at only 15 percent of American service and manufacturing companies.

Economists are much more sanguine about the potential job losses. They believe relieving bright, educated workers from reengineered jobs will result in these workers moving to better jobs in fast-growth industries. Left out of this equation are blue-collar workers, and older, less well-educated middle managers. It is not clear that these groups can be retrained easily for high-quality (high-paying) jobs. Careful planning and sensitivity to employee needs can help companies redesign work to minimize job losses.

Equity and Access: Increasing Racial and Social Class Cleavages

Does everyone have an equal opportunity to participate in the digital age? Will the social, economic, and cultural gaps that exist in America and other societies be reduced by information systems technology? Or will the cleavages be increased, permitting the "better off" to become even better off relative to others? When and if computing becomes ubiquitous, does this include the poor as well as the rich?

The answers to these questions are clearly not known; the impact of systems technology on various groups in society is not well studied. What is known is that information and knowledge, and access to these resources through educational institutions and public libraries, are inequitably distributed. Access to computers is distributed inequitably along racial and social class lines, as are many other information resources. Left uncorrected, we could end up creating a society of information haves, computer literate and skilled, versus a large group of information have-nots, computer illiterate and unskilled.

The Clinton administration and public interest groups want to narrow this "digital divide" by making digital information services—including the Internet—available to "virtually everyone" just as basic telephone service is now. An amendment to the Telecommunications Act of 1996, which widened telecommunications deregulation, stipulates subsidies for schools and libraries so that people of all backgrounds have access to the tools of information technology (Lohr, 1996). This is only a partial solution to the problem.

Health Risks: RSI, CVS, and Technostress

repetitive stress injury (RSI)
Occupational disease that occurs when muscle groups are forced through repetitive actions with high-impact loads or thousands of repetitions with low-impact loads.

carpal tunnel syndrome (CTS) Type of RSI in which pressure on the median nerve through the wrist's bony carpal tunnel structure produces pain.

The most important occupational disease today is **repetitive stress injury (RSI).** RSI occurs when muscle groups are forced through repetitive actions often with high-impact loads (such as tennis) or tens of thousands of repetitions under low-impact loads (such as working at a computer keyboard).

The single largest source of RSI is computer keyboards. Forty-six million Americans use computers at work, and 185,000 cases of RSI are reported each year, according to the National Center for Health Statistics. The most common kind of computer-related RSI is **carpal tunnel syndrome (CTS),** in which pressure on the median nerve through the wrist's bony structure called a "carpal tunnel" produces pain. The pressure is caused by constant repetition of keystrokes: In a single shift, a word processor may perform 23,000 keystrokes. Symptoms of carpal tunnel syndrome include numbness, shooting pain, inability to grasp objects, and tingling. So far, about 2 million workers have been diagnosed with carpal tunnel syndrome.

RSI is avoidable. Designing workstations for a neutral wrist position (using a wrist rest to support the wrist), proper monitor stands, and footrests all contribute to proper posture and reduced RSI. New, ergonomically correct keyboards are also an option, although their efficacy has yet to be clearly established. These measures should be backed by frequent rest breaks, rotation of employees to different jobs, and moving toward voice or scanner data entry.

RSI is not the only occupational illness caused by computers; back and neck pain, leg stress, and foot pain also result from poor ergonomic designs of workstations (see Table 5.5).

Table 5.5 Computer-Related Diseases

Disease/Risk	Incidence
RSI	185,000 new cases a year
Other joint diseases	Unknown
CVS	10 million cases a year
Technostress	5 to 10 million cases
VDT Radiation	Unknown impacts

Computer vision syndrome (CVS) refers to any eye strain condition related to computer display screen use. Its symptoms are headaches, blurred vision, and dry and irritated eyes. The symptoms are usually temporary (Furger, 1993).

The newest computer-related malady is **technostress,** defined as stress induced by computer use and whose symptoms are aggravation, hostility toward humans, impatience, and enervation. The problem according to experts is that humans working continuously with computers come to expect other humans and human institutions to behave like computers, providing instant response, attentiveness, and with an absence of emotion. Computer-intense workers are aggravated when put on hold during a phone call, become incensed or alarmed when their PCs take a few seconds longer to perform a task, lack empathy for humans, and seek out friends who mirror the characteristics of their machines. Technostress is thought to be related to high levels of job turnover in the computer industry, high levels of early retirement from computer-intense occupations, and elevated levels of drug and alcohol abuse.

The incidence of technostress is not known but is thought to be in the millions in the United States and growing rapidly. Although frequently denied as a problem by management, computer-related jobs now top the list of stressful occupations based on health statistics in several industrialized countries. The costs worldwide of stress are put at $200 billion.

To date the role of radiation from computer display screens in occupational disease has not been proved. Video display terminals (VDTs) emit nonionizing electric and magnetic fields at low frequencies. These rays enter the body and have unknown effects on enzymes, molecules, chromosomes, and cell membranes. Long-term studies are investigating low-level electromagnetic fields and birth defects, stress, low birth weight, and other diseases. All manufacturers have reduced display screen emissions since the early 1980s, and European countries such as Sweden have adopted stiff radiation emission standards.

The computer has become a part of our lives—personally as well as socially, culturally, and politically. It is unlikely the issues and our choices will become easier as information technology continues to transform our world. The growth of the Internet and the information economy suggests that all the ethical and social issues we have described will be heightened further as we move into the first digital century.

computer vision syndrome (CVS) Eye strain condition related to computer display screen use, with symptoms including headaches, blurred vision, and dry, irritated eyes.

technostress Stress induced by computer use whose symptoms include aggravation, hostility toward humans, impatience, and enervation.

Management Actions: A Corporate Code of Ethics

Some corporations have developed far-reaching corporate IS codes of ethics—Federal Express, IBM, American Express, and Merck and Co. Most firms, however, have not developed these codes of ethics, which leaves them at the mercy of fate, and leaves their employees in the dark about expected correct behavior. There is some dispute concerning a general code of ethics versus a specific information systems code of ethics. As managers, you should strive to develop an IS-specific set of ethical standards for each of the five moral dimensions:

○ *Information rights and obligations.* A code should cover topics such as employee e-mail privacy, workplace monitoring, treatment of corporate information, and policies on customer information.

○ *Property rights and obligations.* A code should cover topics such as software licenses, ownership of firm data and facilities, ownership of software created by employees on company hardware, and software copyrights. Specific guidelines for contractual relationships with third parties should be covered as well.

○ *Accountability and control.* The code should specify a single individual responsible for all information systems, and underneath this individual others who are responsible for individual rights, the protection of property rights, system quality, and quality of life (e.g., job design, ergonomics, employee satisfaction). Responsibilities for control of systems, audits, and management should be clearly defined. The potential liabilities of systems officers and the corporation should be detailed in a separate document.

○ *System quality.* The code should describe the general levels of data quality and system error that can be tolerated with detailed specifications left to specific projects. The code should require that all systems attempt to estimate data quality and system error probabilities.

○ *Quality of life.* The code should state that the purpose of systems is to improve the quality of life for customers and for employees by achieving high levels of product quality, customer service, and employee satisfaction and human dignity through proper ergonomics, job and work-flow design, and human resource development.

Management Wrap-Up

Management

Managers are ethical rule makers for their organizations (Green, 1994). They are charged with creating the policies and procedures to establish ethical conduct, including the ethical use of information systems. Managers are also responsible for identifying, analyzing, and resolving the ethical dilemmas that invariably crop up as they balance conflicting needs and interests.

Organization

Rapid changes fueled by information technology are creating new situations where existing laws or rules of conduct may not be relevant. New "gray areas" are emerging in which ethical standards have not yet been codified into law. A new system of ethics for the information age is required to guide individual and organizational choices and actions.

Technology

Information technology is introducing changes that create new ethical issues for societies to debate and resolve. Increasing computing power, storage, and networking capabilities—including the Internet—can expand the reach of individual and organizational actions and magnify their impact. The ease and anonymity with which information can be communicated, copied, and manipulated in on-line environments are challenging traditional rules of right and wrong behavior.

For Discussion

1. Should producers of software-based services such as ATMs be held liable for economic injuries suffered when their systems fail?

2. Should companies be responsible for unemployment caused by their information systems? Why or why not?

Summary

1. **Analyze the relationship among ethical, social, and political issues raised by information systems.** Ethical, social, and political issues are closely related in an information society. Ethical issues confront individuals who must choose a course of action, often in a situation in which two or more ethical principles are in conflict (a dilemma). Social issues spring from ethical issues. Societies must develop expectations in individuals about the correct course of action, and social issues then are debates about the kinds of situations and expectations that societies should develop so that individuals behave correctly. Political issues spring from social conflict and have to do largely with laws that prescribe behavior and seek to use the law to create situations in which individuals behave correctly.

2. **Identify the main moral dimensions of an information society and apply them to specific situations.** There are five main moral dimensions that tie together ethical, social, and political issues in an information society. These moral dimensions are information rights and obligations, property rights, accountability and control, system quality, and quality of life.

3. **Apply an ethical analysis to difficult situations.** An ethical analysis is a five-step methodology for analyzing a situation. The method involves identifying the facts, values, stakeholders, options, and consequences of actions. Once completed, you can begin to consider what ethical principle you should apply to a situation to arrive at a judgment.

4. **Examine specific ethical principles for conduct.** Six ethical principles are available to judge your own conduct (and that of others). These principles are derived independently from several cultural, religious, and intellectual traditions. They are not hard-and-fast rules and may not apply in all situations. The principles are the Golden Rule, Immanuel Kant's Categorical Imperative, Descartes' rule of change, the Utilitarian Principle, the Risk Aversion Principle, and the ethical "no free lunch" rule.

5. **Design corporate policies for ethical conduct.** For each of the five moral dimensions, corporations should develop an ethics policy statement to assist individuals and to encourage the correct decisions. The policy areas are as follows. Individual information rights: Spell out corporate privacy and due process policies. Property rights: Clarify how the corporation will treat property rights of software owners. Accountability and control: Clarify who is responsible and accountable for information. System quality: Identify methodologies and quality standards to be achieved. Quality of life: Identify corporate policies on family, computer crime, decision making, vulnerability, job loss, and health risks.

Key Terms

Accountability, 130	Descartes' rule of change, 131	Information rights, 127	Risk Aversion Principle, 131
Carpal tunnel syndrome (CTS), 148	Due process, 130	Intellectual property, 136	Spamming, 136
Computer abuse, 145	Ethical "no free lunch" rule, 131	Liability, 130	Technostress, 149
Computer crime, 145	Ethics, 127	Patent, 138	Trade secret, 137
Computer vision syndrome (CVS), 149	Fair Information Practices (FIP), 134	Privacy, 134	Utilitarian Principle, 131
Copyright, 138	Immanuel Kant's Categorical Imperative, 131	Repetitive stress injury (RSI), 148	
		Responsibility, 130	

Review Questions

1. In what ways are ethical, social, and political issues connected? Give some examples.
2. What are the key technological trends that heighten ethical concerns?
3. What are the differences between responsibility, accountability, and liability?
4. What are the five steps in an ethical analysis?
5. Identify six ethical principles.
6. What is a professional code of conduct?
7. What are meant by "privacy" and "fair information practices"? How is the Internet challenging the protection of individual privacy?
8. What are the three different regimes that protect intellectual property rights? What challenges to intellectual property rights are posed by the Internet?
9. Why is it so difficult to hold software services liable for failure or injury?
10. What is the most common cause of system quality problems?
11. Name and describe four "quality of life" impacts of computers and information systems.
12. What is technostress, and how would you identify it?
13. Name three management actions that could reduce RSI injuries.

Group Project

With three or four of your classmates, develop a corporate ethics code on privacy that addresses both employee privacy and the privacy of customers and users of the corporate Web site. Be sure to consider e-mail privacy and employer monitoring of worksites, as well as corporate use of information about employees concerning their off-job behavior (e.g., lifestyle, marital arrangements, and so forth). Present your ethics code to the class.

Tools for Interactive Learning

○ Internet

The Internet Connection for this chapter will direct you to a series of Web sites where you can learn more about the privacy issues raised by the use of the Internet and the Web. You can complete an exercise to analyze the privacy implications of existing technologies for tracking Web site visitors. You can also use the Interactive Study Guide to test your knowledge of the topics in this chapter, and get instant feedback where you need more practice.

○ CD-ROM

If you purchase and use the Multimedia Edition CD-ROM with this chapter, you can complete an interactive exercise asking you to perform an ethical analysis of problems encountered by a business. You can also find a video clip on software piracy and the activities of the Software Publishers Association (SPA), an audio overview of the major themes of this chapter, and bullet text summarizing the key points of the chapter.

Case Study ⟩ Profiling YOU!

Digital data about each of us are multiplying fast. Every time you do many things, including charge something on your credit card, buy something on time, fill out and send in a warranty card, buy a plane ticket, make a telephone call from your home or work, receive a traffic ticket, buy or sell stocks, or visit your doctor, someone is recording that action electronically. This list could go on and on. Recording these actions is absolutely not an invasion of privacy. After all, companies need records to bill you, to reserve your plane seat, or to report your purchases and sales for tax purposes. Your doctor must keep records on your health and the government must know when a ticket is issued, to whom it was issued, and when it was paid. Invasion of privacy does arise when these data are used for purposes other than the reasons for which they were collected. Even worse, someone may put several pieces of this data to-

gether and draw conclusions from it to your detriment.

How might others use these data about you? Assume, for example, that your credit card company analyzes your credit card transaction and finds that your expenditures on prescription drugs have risen, you have made several charges to a resume service, you are charging visits to a psychological counselor, and you are also buying gasoline more frequently but in smaller quantities than in the past. Your credit card issuer could easily conclude that you are having trouble (the counselor and prescription charges) and are possibly without a job (resume service and smaller gasoline purchases). The credit card issuer might logically conclude that you have lost your job and so are a bad credit risk. The result could easily be that you would find your credit limited or your credit account closed altogether.

The newest wrinkle in this privacy invasion is software for electronic profiling. Such software collects data about people, often from various sources, and uses aggressive datamining and artificial intelligence techniques to help an organization evaluate the risk you might present. One such system, Computer-Assisted Passenger Screening (CAPS), was adopted by the Federal Aviation Administration (FAA) and required to be used by all airlines in the United States by the end of 1998. The system was developed on the recommendation of the White House Commission on Terrorism after the July 1996 explosion of TWA Flight 800. CAPS creates a profile on all purchasers of airline tickets. Its goal is to identify potential terrorists.

The specific data and the criteria CAPS uses are secret, although early uses have given observers some insights. Hassan Abbass, a Syrian-born U.S. citizen residing in Cleveland, recently sued US Airways, alleging discrimination because he and his family had been subjected to such actions as "humiliating" luggage searches. Abbass and his wife obviously were targeted because of their frequent visits to Syria, a country that the U.S. State Department has designated a source of terrorism. However, the Abbasses claim their frequent trips are only to visit family, that they are not terrorists, and that they are being unfairly harassed. Greg Nojeim, an American Civil Liberties Union (ACLU) lawyer, claims that this type of targeting singles out people of Middle Eastern descent for special scrutiny and so is discriminatory. "A profile that targets as potential terrorists people who travel frequently to a country on the State Department's terrorist list would have a disparate impact on people who trace their national origin to that country," Nojeim insists. Abbass has settled his lawsuit against US Air but the ACLU predicts many more such suits. The ACLU established a special complaint form on the Web to collect information on incidents of discrimination. Nojeim claims that the ACLU has received "scores of complaints" from passengers, most of them claiming racial discrimination, whereas the U.S. Department of Transportation has investigated 46 complaints. All of these complaints were lodged in only the first few months the system was operating, and while it was being used by only a handful of airlines.

The fact that both the data used and the profile criteria are a secret is a major source of CAPS's problems. An FAA spokesperson refused to state what criteria are used in the profile that selects potential terrorists, because, she claims, if the criteria were made public, actual terrorists would learn how to avoid being pinpointed. She does deny that race, religion, or ethnicity are included, because to use them would violate federal law.

Many acknowledge that electronic-profiling systems do produce benefits, helping corporations save money and reduce various types of risks. Sears, Roebuck and Co. began using electronic-profiling software after the company amassed losses of $688 million in credit card fraud and uncollectable debt in one quarter in 1997. Early reports on the use of the system indicate that it can prevent 20 percent of the purchases by deadbeats and by fraudulent credit card users, for a savings of nearly $550 million per year.

With savings like that, no wonder banks and other retailers are beginning to use similar systems to manage their credit risks. Several vendors of fraud-detection software offer products designed to check credit cards as they are being used for online purchases over the Internet. Companies engaged in electronic commerce have complained of swindles where shoppers place their orders, receive the merchandise, and then dispute the sale, claiming that their credit card numbers were used fraudulently. The seller must give these "shoppers" refunds. IVS Fraud Screen, a detection service from CyberSource Corporation in San Jose, California, uses artificial intelligence to assess the likelihood that a proposed online transaction is fraudulent. The software examines the amount of the sale, the time of the day, and the source of the transaction, along with traditional data, and compares such data with a data pool of known fraudulent transactions to produce a fraud score. It flags suspect sales for further study.

The value of these systems is not being questioned. The ethics of these systems is. Profiling systems can invade people's privacy, resulting in discriminatory treatment; therefore, they raise fears among the general public. The Chicago Police Department developed a profiling system that was meant to locate police officers who might be likely to engage in police brutality. Selection criteria included, for example, officers who had been recently divorced. The system never came into use because of strong opposition from the police union.

Some computer ethics specialists believe that these systems can be used responsibly. One problem, they explain, is that people have too much faith in anything that comes from the computer. Ethicists usually advocate not allowing profiling systems to automatically trigger any action against anyone. Instead, action must be taken only after intervention by a responsible human being. In addition, they urge proper training of system users so the users will understand the sensitive legal and personal issues involved with profiling.

Sources: "Proposed FAA Regulations on Security Profiling," **Federal Register** 64, no. 74 (April 19, 1999); Kim S. Nash, "Electronic Profiling," **Computerworld**, February 9, 1998; and John M. Broder, "Making America Safe for Electronic Commerce," **The New York Times**, June 22, 1997.

CASE STUDY QUESTIONS

1. Name the technologies that have enabled the emergence of electronic-profiling systems, and explain how each has contributed to their development.

2. Which ethical principles apply here? Explain your answer.

3. We have described five moral dimensions of the information age. Pick one of these dimensions and describe the ethical, social, and political aspects of electronic profiling.

4. Airline terrorism presents a special problem because of the number of deaths that could result from one overlooked terrorist. If you were a member of the White House Commission on Terrorism charged with combating terrorism on airlines, what would your arguments be for the adoption of the CAPS system? Then, change yourself into a lawyer arguing for the Abbass family and explain your arguments against the CAPS system. Finally, having considered both sides, explain your personal position on this issue.

DaimlerChrysler and GM: Organization Technology and Business Processes in the U.S. Auto Industry

This case illustrates how two giant automobile corporations, DaimlerChrysler and General Motors, have tried to use information technology to combat foreign and domestic competitors. The case explores the relationship between each firm's management strategy, organizational characteristics, business processes, and information systems. It poses the following question: How has information technology addressed the problems confronting the U.S. automobile industry?

On October 26, 1992 Robert C. Stempel resigned as chairman and CEO of the General Motors Corporation because he had not moved quickly enough to make the changes required to ensure the automotive giant's survival. To counter massive financial losses and plummeting market share, Stempel had announced 10 months earlier that GM would have to close 21 of its North American plants and cut 74,000 of its 370,000 employees over three years. Stempel was replaced by a more youthful and determined management team headed by Jack Smith.

GM's plight reflected the depths of the decline of the once vigorous American automobile industry in the late 1980s. Year after year, as Americans came to view American-made cars as low in quality or not stylish, car buyers purchased fewer and fewer American cars, replacing them mostly with Japanese models.

Ironically, at about the same time, the Chrysler Corporation announced strong earnings and looked forward to a new period of strength and prosperity. During the 1980s, Chrysler had struggled with rising costs and declining sales of mass-market cars. However, demand was strong for its minivans and the hot Jeep Grand Cherokee. A stringent cost-cutting crusade eliminated $4 billion in operating costs in only three years.

Ten years before, Chrysler had been battling bankruptcy and GM was flush with cash. Had Chrysler finally turned itself around? Was this the beginning of the end for the world's largest automobile maker? What is the role of information systems in this tale of two auto makers and in the future of the U.S. automobile industry?

GENERAL MOTORS

General Motors is still the world's largest auto maker, with employees in 35 countries. In the early 1990s, GM's U.S. auto business accounted for about 1.5 percent of the U.S. economy, down from 5 percent in the 1950s. Its sheer size has proved to be one of GM's greatest burdens. For 70 years, GM operated along the lines laid down by CEO Alfred Sloan, who rescued the firm from bankruptcy in the 1920s. Sloan separated the firm into five separate operating groups and divisions (Chevrolet, Pontiac, Oldsmobile, Buick, and Cadillac). Each division functioned as a semiautonomous company with its own marketing operations. GM's management was a welter of bureaucracies.

GM covered the market with low-end Chevys and high-end Caddies. At the outset, this amalgam of top-down control and decentralized execution enabled GM to build cars at lower cost than its rivals; but it could also charge more for the quality and popularity of its models. By the 1960s, GM started having trouble building smaller cars to compete with imports and started eliminating differences among divisions. By the mid-1980s, GM had reduced differences among the divisions to the point that customers could not tell a Cadillac from a Chevrolet; the engines in low-end Chevys were also found in high-end Oldsmobiles. Its own brands started to compete with each other. Under Roger Smith, CEO from 1981 to 1990, GM moved boldly, but often in the wrong direction. GM remained a far-flung vertically integrated corporation that at one time manufactured up to 70 percent of its own parts. Its costs were much higher than either its U.S. or Japanese competitors. Like many large manufacturing firms, its organizational culture resisted change. GM has made steady improvements in car quality, but its selection and styling have lagged behind its U.S. and Japanese rivals. GM's market share plunged from a peak of 52 percent in the early 1960s to just 33 percent today. In 1979, GM's market share was 46 percent.

GM created an entirely new Saturn automobile with a totally new division, labor force, and production system based on the Japanese "lean production" model. Saturn workers and managers share information, authority, and decision making. The Saturn car was a market triumph. But Saturn took seven years to roll out the first model and drained $5 billion from other car projects. GM had been selling Saturn at a loss to build up market share.

In 1992, GM's labor costs were $2358 per car, compared with $1872 for Chrysler and $1563 for Ford. That made GM 40 percent less productive than Ford. These figures do not begin to approach those of the Japanese, whose automotive productivity surpasses all U.S. corporations.

CHRYSLER

In auto industry downturns, Chrysler was always the weakest of Detroit's Big Three auto makers (GM, Ford, and Chrysler). Founded in the 1930s by Walter P. Chrysler through a series of mergers with smaller companies such as Dodge and DeSoto, Chrysler prided itself on superior engineering, especially in engines and suspensions. In the 1940s and 1950s, Chrysler grew into a small, highly centralized firm with very little vertical integration. Unlike Ford and GM, Chrysler relied on external suppliers for 70 percent of its major components and subassemblies, becoming more an auto assembler than a huge vertically integrated manufacturer such as GM. Although Chrysler did not develop a global market for its cars to cushion domestic downturns, its centralized and smaller firm could potentially move faster and be more innovative than its larger competitors.

During the late 1980s, Chrysler lost several hundred thousand units of sales annually because it did not make improvements in engine development and in its mass-market cars—the small subcompacts and large rear-wheel drive vehicles. There was no new family of mid-priced, mid-sized cars to rival Ford's Taurus or Honda's Accord. Customers could not distinguish Chrysler's key car models and brands from each other, and thus migrated to other brands. By the early 1990s, fierce price cutting had upped Chrysler's breakeven point (the number of cars the firm had to sell to start making a profit) to 1.9 million units, up from 1.4 million.

GM's Information Systems Strategy

Despite heavy investment in information technology, GM's information systems were virtually archaic. It had more than 100 mainframes and 34 computer centers but had no centralized system to link computer operations or to coordinate operations from one department to another. Each division and group had its own hardware and software so that the design group could not interact with production engineers via computer. GM adopted a "shotgun" approach, pursuing several high-technology paths simultaneously in the hope that one or all of them would pay off. GM also believed it could overwhelm competitors by outspending them. GM also tried to use information technology to totally overhaul the way it ran its business.

Recognizing the continuing power of the divisions and the vast differences among them, Roger Smith, CEO of GM from 1981 to 1990, sought to integrate the manufacturing and administrative information systems by purchasing Electronic Data Systems (EDS) of Dallas for $2.5 billion. EDS has supplied GM's data processing and communications services. EDS and its talented system designers were charged with conquering the administrative chaos in the divisions: more than 16 different electronic mail systems, 28 different word processing systems, and a jumble of factory floor systems that could not communicate with management. Even worse, most of these systems were running on completely incompatible equipment.

EDS consolidated its 5 computing centers and GM's 34 computing centers into 21 uniform information-processing centers for GM and EDS work. EDS replaced the hundred different networks that served GM with the world's largest private digital telecommunications network. In 1993, EDS launched the Consistent Office Environment project to replace its hodgepodge of desktop models, network operating systems, and application development tools with standard hardware and software for its office technology.

GM started to replace 30 different materials and scheduling systems with one integrated system to handle inventory, manufacturing, and financial data. Factory managers can receive orders from the car divisions for the number and type of vehicles to build and then can create an estimated 20-week manufacturing schedule for GM and its suppliers. The system also sends suppliers schedules each morning on what materials need to be delivered to what docks at what hour during that manufacturing day.

Smith earmarked $40 billion for new plants and automation, but not all investments were fruitful. He spent heavily on robots to paint cars and install windshields, hoping to reduce GM's unionized work force. At first, however, the robots accidentally painted themselves and dropped windshields onto the front seats. Although a number of these problems were corrected, some robots stand unused today. The highly automated equipment never did what was promised because GM did not train workers properly to use it and did not design its car models for easy robot assembly. Instead of reducing its work force, GM had workers stay on the line because of frequent robotic breakdowns.

Chrysler's Information Systems Strategy

In 1980, with $2.8 billion in debt, Chrysler seemed headed for bankruptcy. Its financial crisis galvanized its management to find new ways to cut costs, increase inventory turnover, and improve quality. Its new management team led by Lee Iacocca instituted an aggressive policy to bring its computer-based systems under management control. Chrysler didn't have the money to invest in several high-technology paths at once. It adopted a "rifle" approach to systems: Build what was absolutely essential, and build what would produce the biggest returns. Chrysler focused on building common systems—systems that would work in 6000 dealer showrooms, 25 zone offices, 22 parts depots, and all of its manufacturing plants.

Chrysler built integrated systems. When an order is captured electronically at the dealer, the same order is tied to production, schedules, invoices, parts forecasts, projections, parts and inventory management, and so forth. Chrysler's low degree of vertical integration put the company in a better position to concentrate on only a few technologies. Because it was more of an auto assembler and distributor than a manufacturer, it had less need for expensive manufacturing technologies such as vision systems, programmable controllers, and robotics, all of which are far more important to GM and Ford.

Chrysler directed most of its information systems budget to corporate-wide communications systems and just-in-time inventory management. Just-in-time (JIT) inventory management is obviously critical to a company that has 70 percent of its parts made by outside suppliers. (JIT supplies needed parts to the production line on a last-minute basis. This keeps factory inventory levels as low as possible and holds down production costs.) During the 1980s, Chrysler achieved a 9 percent reduction in inventory and an increase in average quarterly inventory turnover from 6.38 times to 13.9 times. A single corporation-wide network connects Chrysler's large and mid-sized computers from various vendors and gives engineering workstations access to the large computers. This makes it easier to move data from one system, stage of production, or plant to another and facilitates just-in-time inventory management.

Chrysler had decided it needed a centralized pool of computerized CAD specifications that was accessible to all stages of production. In 1981, it installed a system to provide managers in all work areas and in all nine Chrysler plants with the same current design specifications. Tooling and design can access these data concurrently, so that a last-minute change in design can be immediately conveyed to tooling and manufacturing engineers. Chrysler created centralized business files for inventory, shipping, marketing, and a host of other related activities.

All this centralized management information makes scheduling and inventory control much easier to coordinate. Chrysler's cars and trucks share many of the same parts. Chrysler set up electronic links between its computers and those of its suppliers, such as the Budd Company of Rochester, Michigan, which supplies U.S. auto companies with sheet metal parts, wheel products, and frames. Budd can extract manufacturing releases electronically through terminals installed in all work areas and can deliver the parts exactly when Chrysler needs them. A new enhancement verifies the accuracy of advanced shipping notices electronically transmitted by suppliers and helps Chrysler track inventory levels and payment schedules more closely.

Learning from the Japanese

In the mid-1980s, MIT researchers found that the Toyota Motor Corporation's production system represented a sharp departure from Henry Ford's mass-production techniques. In "lean manufacturing," Japanese auto makers focused on minimizing waste and inventory and utilizing workers' ideas. The emphasis is on maximizing reliability and quality, and minimizing waste. The ideal "lean" factory has parts built just as they are needed and has a level of quality so high that inspection is virtually redundant. After studying Honda Motor Company, Chrysler started to cut $1 billion a year in operating costs and began to rethink virtually everything it did, from designing engines to reporting financial results. Chrysler overhauled its top-down autocratic management structure. It replaced its traditional rigid departments, such as the engine division, with nimble Honda-like "cross-functional platform teams." The teams combined experts from diverse areas such as design, manufacturing, marketing, and purchasing together in one location and were given the power to make basic decisions ranging from styling to choice of suppliers.

The platform teams work with suppliers early in the design process and give them more responsibilities. More than 300 resident engineers from supplier firms work side by side with Chrysler employees. A single supplier is held accountable for the design prototypes and production of a specific system or part, including responsibility for cost, quality, and on-time delivery. In the past, Chrysler chose suppliers on the basis of competitive bids. Development time was stretched because suppliers were not chosen until after designs were finalized. Chrysler spent 12 to 18 months sending out bids for quotations, analyzing bids, and negotiating contracts with suppliers before suppliers were selected. Additional time would be wasted correcting problems with the suppliers' parts or systems that were discovered during manufacturing. Under this new collaborative relationship, Chrysler has reduced the number of suppliers by over 50 percent and shortened the production cycle.

Chrysler has asked suppliers to suggest operational changes that it could make to reduce its own costs as well as those of suppliers. Suppliers can use an on-line system to submit suggestions for making improvements. Chrysler and its suppliers can communicate using a common e-mail system. Nearly all suppliers have purchased Catia, Chrysler's preferred CAD/CAM software, to further coordinate their work. Chrysler now has five separate platform teams to design its large cars, small cars, jeeps, minivans, and trucks. Hourly workers provide input to help Chrysler eliminate wasted steps in the assembly process. Toyota cut waste by diagramming every step of its assembly process. It moved tools closer to the workers and eliminated unnecessary motions. Chrysler is now redesigning its assembly lines to be more like those of Toyota. Ten years ago, it took 6000 workers to build 1000 cars a day. Now Chrysler can achieve the same output with half that many workers.

Involving suppliers early in the design process, along with the platform team approach, has cut product development time by 20 to 40 percent while increasing quality. For example, Chrysler was able to develop its Durango utility vehicle in only 24 months. The Dodge Viper sports car was designed in only 36 months, a process that traditionally had taken Chrysler 4.5 years. Consequently, Chrysler's profit per vehicle leaped from an average of $250 in the 1980s to $2110 in 1994.

To support its new approach to product development, Chrysler built a new 3.5-million-square-foot Chrysler Technology Center (CTC) 30 miles north of Detroit in Auburn Hills, Michigan. Chrysler leaders expect the CTC to further enhance productivity by providing the technology that will enable Chrysler to engineer things only once and not repeat them. For instance, a failed crash test in the past might have left engineers scratching their heads. Now they can compare crash data from a test with theoretical predictions, moving closer to a solution with each successive prediction cycle. Only when they need to test a solution would they actually have to crash another car. Because hand-built prototypes cost $250,000 to $400,000, avoiding a few crash tests has a large payoff. Using this approach, engineers designed the LH car so that it passed its crash test the first time out.

Every room in the CTC has eight-inch raised floors covering a total of 10,000 fiber-optic cables that can transmit massive volumes of data at high speed. These cables link CTC's buildings to its main data center. The CTC itself is scheduled to house 10 mainframe computers, 2 supercomputers, and control systems for all the center's data and computer networks. A total of 7000 people work there.

GM similarly revamped its approach to production and product development. The company is moving away from traditional assembly lines into smaller working units called cells, in which workers have more opportunity to design their own processes and improve output. To combat GM's old culture of fiefdoms and interdivisional fighting that stifled innovation, Jack Smith replaced the old committee system with a single strategy board on which GM's top executives from manufacturing, engineering, sales and marketing, finance, human resources, logistics, purchasing, and communications work together on common goals. Every new GM car or truck must be explicitly targeted to 1 of 26 precisely defined market segments, such as small sporty cars or full-size pickup trucks. No two vehicles are allowed to overlap. A new launch center at GM's engineering headquarters north of Detroit acts as a filter for all design ideas. Teams of engineers, designers, and marketers evaluate car and truck proposals for cost, marketability, and compatibility with other GM products. But unlike Chrysler and Japanese auto makers, GM's teams are not empowered to make the important product development decisions. The power of the functional departments such as engineering and purchasing is still maintained.

Jack Smith has put even more emphasis than his predecessors on standardizing GM's business processes and parts, along with its information systems. He called for reducing the number of basic car platforms from 12 to 5. In the past, GM cars were built in plants dedicated to a single model; they seldom ran at full capacity. By reducing the potential variations of each model, GM can now build several models in the same plant; with fewer parts per car, the cars are much easier to assemble. With fewer platforms, GM can operate with fewer engineers, simpler more flexible factories, smaller inventories, more common parts, and greater economies of scale. The company is also adopting a standard software that integrates computer-aided design and manufacturing processes.

Before Stempel stepped down, he initiated efforts to make GM's high parts costs more competitive. GM consolidated 27 worldwide purchasing operations into one at Detroit. GM required its company-owned suppliers to bid against outside suppliers, while pressuring outside suppliers for price reductions of up to 50 percent. In 1992, about 40 percent of GM parts were coming from outside suppliers versus 70 percent of the parts in Chrysler and 50 percent at Ford.

All these efforts have translated into more efficient and quality-driven production and lower costs. From 1991 until the beginning of 1994, GM removed $2800 in costs, before taxes, for every vehicle it manufactured. Assembly time for the Chevrolet Cavalier and the Pontiac Sunfire takes 40 percent less than the models they replaced. The number of parts for these vehicles has been cut by 29 percent.

Under Jack Smith, GM's earnings have continued to improve. The company has benefited from strong and diverse overseas operations and gradual reductions in labor and manufacturing costs in North America. More significantly, GM earned an average of $1000 for each car and light truck sold in North America, up from $500 per vehicle a year earlier. It sold relatively more high-profit vehicles.

Yet GM is still less efficient than its competitors. It still takes GM longer to make a Cavalier than it does Ford to make cars at its most efficient plants. It takes 46.5 hours to produce a GM vehicle, compared with 34.7 hours at Ford and 27.6 hours at Nissan. Production costs remain high because GM still buys a smaller proportion of its parts from outside suppliers than its competitors. (Ford earns $500 more per vehicle and Chrysler $900 more per vehicle than GM for this reason.) Even after strengthening its brand images, it still has too many models and too few the public actually wants, and an infrastructure of poorly located dealerships and underutilized outdated factories. However, engineering problems and parts shortages have crimped production. Implementing new programs and flexible manufacturing, combined with stringent cost cutting, has proved extremely difficult. GM has yet to show that it can once again become an auto-making star.

From near collapse, Chrysler has emerged as a highly profitable cash machine. It continues to dominate the minivan market, and has launched successful new models such as the Jeep Grand Cherokee, the Chrysler Neon, the Chrysler Concorde, and Eagle Vision. One in six vehicles sold in the United States comes from Chrysler, up from one in seven in 1995.

Chrysler still needs to work on quality and productivity. Although its cars and trucks are more reliable than they were a decade ago, they still do not match the competition. While Detroit appears to have stopped losing ground to Japanese autos, Japanese car makers are continuing to improve plant efficiency and reduce their product development time. Nissan and Mazda introduced assembly lines that can make half a dozen different vehicles, whereas most Big Three plants only make one or two different cars.

Approaching the Twenty-First Century: Mergers and the Internet

On May 8, 1998, Chrysler and Daimler-Benz announced a merger of the two automobile companies, a merger that was completed during the autumn of that year. Together the two companies recorded $131 billion in sales in 1997. The new company, DaimlerChrysler AG, will maintain two headquarters, one in Michigan, and one in Stutgart, Germany. The two companies have complementary strengths, making the rationale for the merger rather clear. Chrysler's presence in the United States is strong but in Europe is very limited, whereas Daimler's sales are focused heavily in Europe. By combining, both will have access to established, successful marketing organizations in the two largest automobile markets in the world. Moreover, the two companies offer very different, complementary lines of automobiles. Chrysler focuses on automobiles priced from $11,000 to $40,000.

The merger of Chrysler with Daimler-Benz to create DaimlerChrysler creates a global powerhouse to exploit world markets and withstand new competitive pressures.

GM BuyPower - Netscape

File Edit View Go Communicator Help

BuyPower HOME HELP

Click here to search dealer inventory for this vehicle

Specification Comparisons

1999 Cavalier Coupe
MSRP: $15,476

Here are competitive comparisons of vehicles within the same class, provided by Automotive Information Center (AIC).

Click below to view

Price/Feature Comparisons

Features	1999 Chevrolet Cavalier Coupe	1998 Honda Civic DX Coupe	1998 Mitsubishi Mirage LS Coupe	1998 Ford Escort ZX2 Cool Coupe
Engine				
Type	2.2L I4	1.6L I4	1.8L I4	2.0L I4
Horsepower	115	106	113	130
Torque (lb.-ft.)	135	103	116	127
Dimensions				
Length (in.)	180.7	175.1	168.1	175.2

Document: Done

Start | GM BuyPower - Nets... | General Motors - Netscape

Located at www.gmbuypower.com this Website gives users instant access to details about every GM make and model, independent third party comparisons, unprecedented access to all participating dealer new inventory, the ability to apply on-line for GMAC financing, and the ability to send electronic messages to the participating dealer of their choice to get the best purchase price on the exact vehicle they want.

Daimler's luxury automobiles are much higher priced, starting about $30,000 and ranging up to $135,000. The merger also gives both greater access to each other's manufacturing facilities in various parts of the world, increasing their flexibility to move production to the best location depending upon cost and other key factors. Chrysler's ability to design and bring new automobiles to market rapidly should also be a great help to the Daimler portion of the new company.

Observers believe the biggest challenge in the merger is the culture clash. Germans and Americans tend to view business differently, and those differences will have to be overcome. For example, one company thinks in terms of luxury cars, the other in terms of mass sales—Daimler sold 726,000 vehicles in 1997 whereas Chrysler sold 2.3 million. Information systems problems seem to be limited. Years of integration effort have been avoided by the serendipitous fact that both companies use the same computer-aided design (CAD) system, and both also use SAP AG financial applications. The immediate challenges seem to be the need to build an integrated, robust communications infrastructure that will serve to unite the two

organizations and to include suppliers and dealers. The newly formed company is also looking to cut $1.4 billion in IS costs during the first year and $3 billion more over the following three to five years. Most of the savings will come from personnel reductions and from canceling previously planned application development.

As Detroit's auto makers approach the twenty-first century, they face major changes in economic conditions and in the way cars are bought and sold. Today, at least one-fourth of all new car buyers use the Internet to research car purchases and shop for the best price, and that number is expected to reach 50 percent in a few years. A growing percentage are turning to on-line auto buying services where they can select a car and even take delivery at home without ever setting foot in a dealership. To compete with the on-line car buying services, DaimlerChrysler, GM, and Ford all have established Web sites where shoppers can select options and obtain price quotes, but they must still purchase through the auto companies' dealer networks. GM further enhanced its site to offer proprietary information such as special incentives on cars and dealers' actual inventory and to provide offers from other

GM services such as home mortgages. The car buying sites are fighting back by offering financing and insurance on-line and by providing additional services to their users, such as e-mail notification of service reminders or manufacturers' recall announcements. Chrysler, GM, and Ford have also had to lower their prices while adding new features because Asian competitors have lowered prices during their economic downturn. All of these changes bring new challenges to U.S. auto companies as they look toward the future.

Sources: Fara Warner, "Car Race in Cyberspace," The Wall Street Journal, February 18, 1999; Kathleen Kerwin with Joann Muller, "Reviving GM," Business Week, February 1, 1999; Gregory White, Fara Warner, and Joseph B. White, "Competition Rises, Car Prices Drop: A New Golden Age?" The Wall Street Journal, January 8, 1999; Karen Lowry Miller with Joann Muller, "The Auto Baron," Business Week, November 16, 1998; Kathleen Kerwin, Bob Wallace, "Now It's Cost-Cutting Time," Computerworld, November 23, 1998; "GM: It's Time to Face the Future," Business Week, July 27, 1998; Steven Lipin, "Chrysler Approves Deal with Daimler-Benz: Bit Questions Remain," The Wall Street Journal, May 7, 1998; Gregory L. White, "General Motors to Take Nationwide Test Drive on the Web," The Wall Street

Journal, September 28, 1998; Robert L. Simison, "GM Turns to Computers to Cut Development Costs," **The Wall Street Journal,** October 12, 1998; Jerry Flint, "Company of the Year: Chrysler," **Forbes,** January 13, 1997; Jeffrey H. Dyer, "How Chrysler Created an American Keiretsu," **Harvard Business Review,** July–August 1996; Keith Bradsher, "What's New at GM? Cars, for a Change," **The New York Times,** September 8, 1996; David Woodruff et al., "Target Chrysler," **Business Week,** April 24, 1995; Alex Taylor III, "GM's $11,000,000,000 Turnaround," **Fortune,** October 12, 1994, and "Can GM Remodel Itself?" **Fortune,** January 13, 1992; Steve Lohr with James Bennet, "Lessons in Rebounds from GM and IBM," **New York Times,** October 24, 1994; Kathleen Kerwin, "GM's Aurora," **Business Week,** March 21, 1994; John Greenwald, "What Went Wrong?" **Time Magazine,** November 9, 1992;

Maryann Keller, **Rude Awakening: The Rise, Fall, and Struggle for Recovery of General Motors,** New York: Harper Collins Publishers, 1990; David Woodruff with Elizabeth Lesly, "Surge at Chrysler," **Business Week,** November 9, 1992; and Edward Cone, "Chrysler," **InformationWeek,** September 7, 1992.

CASE STUDY QUESTIONS

1. Compare the roles played by information systems at Chrysler and GM. How did they affect the structure of the automobile industry itself?

2. How much did information systems contribute to GM's and Chrysler's success or failure?

3. What management, organization, and technology issues explain the differences in the way Chrysler and GM used information systems?

4. What management, organization, and technology factors were responsible for Chrysler's and GM's problems?

5. How did GM and Chrysler redesign their business processes to compete more effectively?

6. How important are information systems in solving the problems of the American automobile industry? What are some of the problems that technology cannot address?

Chapter 6

Computers and Information Processing

After completing this chapter, you will be able to:

1. Identify the hardware components in a typical computer system.

2. Describe how information is represented and processed in a computer system.

3. Contrast the capabilities of mainframes, minicomputers, PCs, workstations, and supercomputers.

4. Compare different arrangements of computer processing, including the use of client/server computing and network computers.

5. Describe the principal media for storing data and programs in a computer system.

6. Compare the major input and output devices and approaches to input and processing.

7. Describe multimedia and future information technology trends.

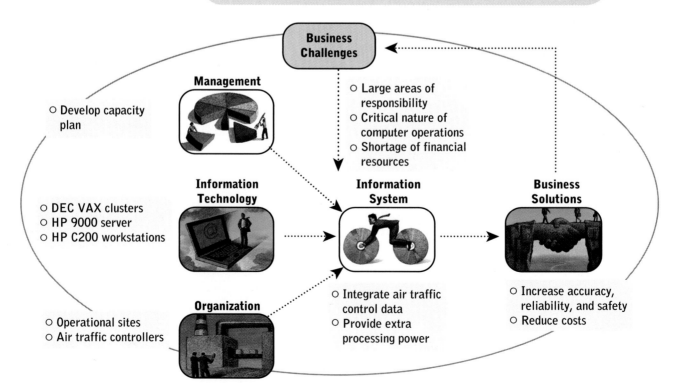

Business Challenges

Management
○ Develop capacity plan

○ Large areas of responsibility
○ Critical nature of computer operations
○ Shortage of financial resources

Information Technology
○ DEC VAX clusters
○ HP 9000 server
○ HP C200 workstations

Information System
○ Integrate air traffic control data
○ Provide extra processing power

Business Solutions
○ Increase accuracy, reliability, and safety
○ Reduce costs

Organization
○ Operational sites
○ Air traffic controllers

Navigation Canada Takes Flight
with New Computers

The area that Canada's air traffic control system monitors is vast—more than 15 million square miles of airspace. Before privatization in November 1996, this responsibility was handled with outdated Digital Equipment Corporation VAX cluster computers that required air traffic controllers to hunt for information on six different systems. The air navigation system was funded by an Air Transportation Tax levied by the government, which did not provide sufficient funds for computer upgrades.

Then a new private, nonprofit company called Navigation Canada took over. Navigation Canada, because it could charge the airline industry fees for its services, was able to raise $600 million to upgrade the computers required

to make the air traffic control system safer and more secure. The upgrade, called the Canadian Air Traffic Control System (CATTS), started in the summer of 1998 and will take three years to complete. Navigation Canada replaced the VAX clusters with HP 9000 server computers and HP C200 UNIX-based workstations. Each of Navigation Canada's 23 operational sites is being outfitted with three servers—a primary server, a backup server, and a third server for training purposes. The built-in redundancy is deliberate. If one of the servers fails, another can take over. Air navigation systems can't afford to be down even for five minutes. Software has been added to ensure that flight data are transmitted and received without modification or corruption.

CATTS gives air traffic controllers radar data, flight path information, computer-based conflict prediction, weather updates, and navigational aid data on a single system. CATTS also automatically routes flight plans to the appropriate people, reducing the chance of human error or loss of critical information. With these new capabilities, Navigation Canada can reduce flight delays and inefficiencies created by airplanes contending for the same runway. Air traffic controllers can support routes that are more direct and fuel-efficient. In addition to making the Canadian skies safer for flyers, Navigation Canada expects the efficiencies created by CATTS to cut annual operating costs by $135 million.

Sources: "Nav Canada Announces Real Time Y2K Testing," *Nav Canada*, January 12, 1999; and Laura DiDio, "$600M Net Upgrade Takes Flight," *Computerworld*, February 16, 1998.

By shifting from old VAX cluster computers to HP servers and workstations, Navigation Canada was able to provide more computing power for its air traffic control operations and to integrate all of the information used by air traffic controllers. To make this decision, Navigation Canada's management needed to understand how much computer processing capacity was required by its business processes and how to evaluate the price and performance of various types of computers. It had to know why HP 9000 server computers and HP C200 workstations were appropriate for its processing needs, and it had to plan for future processing requirements. Management also had to understand how the computer worked with related storage, input/output, and communications technology. Selecting appropriate computer hardware raises the following management challenges:

1. **The centralization vs. decentralization debate.** A longstanding issue among information system managers and CEOs has been the question of how much to centralize or distribute computing resources. Should processing power and data be distributed to departments and divisions, or should they be concentrated at a single location using a large central computer? Client/server computing facilitates decentralization, but network computers and mainframes support a centralized model. Which is the best for the organization? Each organization will have a different answer based on its own needs. Managers need to make sure that the computing model they select is compatible with organizational goals.

2. **Making wise technology purchasing decisions.** Soon after having made an investment in information technology, managers find the completed system is obsolete and too expensive, given the power and lower cost of new technology. In this environment it is very difficult to keep one's own systems up-to-date. A considerable amount of time must be spent anticipating and planning for technological change.

I n this chapter we describe the typical hardware configuration of a computer system, explaining how a computer works and how computer processing power and storage capacity are measured. We then compare the capabilities of various types of computers and related input, output, and storage devices.

6.1 What Is a Computer System?

A contemporary computer system consists of a central processing unit, primary storage, secondary storage, input devices, output devices, and communications devices (see Figure 6-1). The central processing unit manipulates raw data into a more useful form and controls the other parts of the computer system. Primary storage temporarily stores data and program instructions during processing, whereas secondary storage devices (magnetic and optical disks, magnetic tape) store data and programs when they are not being used in processing. Input devices, such as a keyboard or mouse, convert data and instructions into electronic form for input into the computer. Output devices, such as printers and video display terminals, convert electronic data produced by the computer system and display them in a form that people can understand. Communications devices provide connections between the computer and communications networks. Buses are paths for transmitting data and signals among the parts of the computer system.

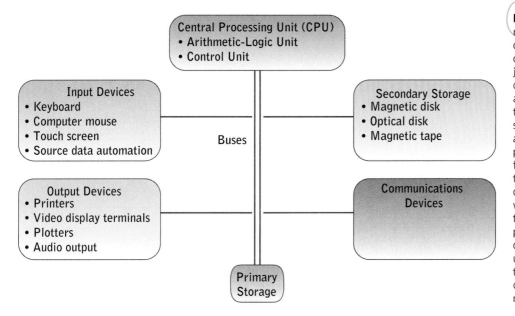

Figure 6-1 Hardware components of a computer system. A contemporary computer system can be categorized into six major components. The central processing unit manipulates data and controls the other parts of the computer system; primary storage temporarily stores data and program instructions during processing; secondary storage feeds data and instructions into the central processor and stores data for future use; input devices convert data and instructions for processing in the computer; output devices present data in a form that people can understand; and communications devices control the passing of information to and from communications networks.

How Computers Represent Data

In order for information to flow through a computer system and be in a form suitable for processing, all symbols, pictures, or words must be reduced to a string of binary digits. A binary digit is called a **bit** and represents either a 0 or a 1. In the computer, the presence of an electronic or magnetic signal means one, and its absence signifies zero. Digital computers operate directly with binary digits, either singly or strung together to form bytes. A string of eight bits that the computer stores as a unit is called a **byte.** Each byte can be used to store a decimal number, a symbol, a character, or part of a picture (see Figure 6-2).

Figure 6-3 shows how decimal numbers are represented using true binary digits. Each position in a decimal number has a certain value. Any number in the decimal system (base 10) can be reduced to a binary number. The binary number system (base 2) can express any number as a power of the number 2. The table at the bottom of the figure shows how the translation from binary to decimal works. By using a binary number system a computer can express all numbers as groups of zeroes and ones. True binary cannot be used by a computer because,

bit A binary digit representing the smallest unit of data in a computer system. It can only have one of two states, representing 0 or 1.

byte A string of bits, usually eight, used to store one number or character in a computer system.

---

0 or 1   One bit

Characters are represented by one byte for each letter.

0 1 0 0 0 0 0 1   One byte for character A

The computer representation in ASCII for the name Alice is

A 0 1 0 0 0 0 0 1

L 0 1 0 0 1 1 0 0

I 0 1 0 0 1 0 0 1

C 0 1 0 0 0 0 1 1

E 0 1 0 0 0 1 0 1

Figure 6-2 Bits and bytes. Bits are represented by either a 0 or 1. A string of eight bits constitutes a byte, which represents a character. The computer's representation for the word "ALICE" is a series of five bytes, where each byte represents one character (or letter) in the name.

Figure 6-3 True binary digits. Each decimal number has a certain value that can be expressed as a binary number. The binary number system can express any number as a power of the number 2.

$$
\begin{array}{l}
10100, \text{ which is equal to:} \quad 0 \times 2^0 = 0 \\
\qquad\qquad\qquad\qquad\qquad\quad 0 \times 2^1 = 0 \\
\qquad\qquad\qquad\qquad\qquad\quad 1 \times 2^2 = 4 \\
\qquad\qquad\qquad\qquad\qquad\quad 0 \times 2^3 = 0 \\
\qquad\qquad\qquad\qquad\qquad\quad 1 \times 2^4 = \underline{16} \\
\qquad\qquad\qquad\qquad\qquad\qquad\qquad\quad 20
\end{array}
$$

Place	5	4	3	2	1
Power of 2	2^4	2^3	2^2	2^1	2^0
Decimal value	16	8	4	2	1

EBCDIC (Extended Binary Coded Decimal Interchange Code) Binary code representing every number, alphabetic character, or special character with eight bits, used primarily in IBM and other mainframe computers.

ASCII (American Standard Code for Information Interchange) A seven- or eight-bit binary code used in data transmission, PCs, and some large computers.

pixel The smallest unit of data for defining an image in the computer. The computer reduces a picture to a grid of pixels. The term pixel comes from picture element.

microsecond One-millionth of a second.

in addition to representing numbers, a computer must represent alphabetic characters and many other symbols used in natural language, such as $ and &. This requirement led manufacturers of computer hardware to develop standard binary codes.

Two common codes are EBCDIC and ASCII. The **Extended Binary Coded Decimal Interchange Code** (**EBCDIC**—pronounced ib-si-dick) was developed by IBM in the 1950s, and it represents every number, alphabetic character, or special character with eight bits. **ASCII,** which stands for the **American Standard Code for Information Interchange,** was developed by the American National Standards Institute (ANSI) to provide a standard code that could be used by many different manufacturers in order to make machinery compatible. ASCII was originally designed as a seven-bit code, but most computers use eight-bit versions. EBCDIC is used in IBM and other mainframe computers, whereas ASCII is used in data transmission, PCs, and some larger computers. Table 6.1 shows how some letters and numbers would be represented using EBCDIC and ASCII. Other coding systems are being developed to represent a wider array of foreign languages.

How can a computer represent a picture? The computer stores a picture by creating a grid overlay of the picture. In this grid or matrix, the computer measures the light or color in each box or cell, called a **pixel** (picture element). The computer then stores this information on each pixel. A high-resolution computer terminal has a 1024×768 SVGA (super video graphics array) standard grid, creating more than 700,000 pixels. Whether pictures or text are stored, it is through this process of reduction that a modern computer is able to operate in a complex environment.

Time and Size in the Computer World

Table 6.2 presents some key levels of time and size that are useful in describing the speed and capacity of modern computer systems.

Very slow, old computers or hardware devices measure machine cycle times in milliseconds (thousandths of a second). More powerful machines use measures of **microseconds**

Table 6.1   Examples of ASCII and EBCDIC Codes

Character or Number	ASCII-8 Binary	EBCDIC Binary
A	01000001	11000001
E	01000101	11000101
Z	01011010	11101001
0	00110000	11110000
1	00110001	11110001
5	00110101	11110101

Table 6.2 Time and Size in the Computer World

Time

Millisecond	1/1000 second
Microsecond	1/1,000,000 second
Nanosecond	1/1,000,000,000 second
Picosecond	1/1,000,000,000,000 second

Storage Capacity

Byte	String of eight bits
Kilobyte	1000 bytes[a]
Megabyte	1,000,000 bytes
Gigabyte	1,000,000,000 bytes
Terabyte	1,000,000,000,000 bytes

[a]*Actually 1024 storage positions*

(millionths of a second) or **nanoseconds** (billionths of a second). Very powerful computers measure machine cycles in picoseconds (trillionths of a second). A very large computer with multiple processors has a machine cycle time of less than one nanosecond. Such computers can execute several billion instructions per second, with each processor executing more than 200 MIPS. MIPS, or millions of instructions per second, is a common benchmark for measuring the speed of larger computers.

Computer storage capacity is measured in bytes. One thousand bytes (actually 1024 storage positions) is called a **kilobyte.** Small PCs used to have internal primary memories of 640 kilobytes. A large PC today can store 128 megabytes of information in primary memory. Each **megabyte** is approximately one million bytes. Large computers have gigabyte storage capacities. A **gigabyte** is approximately one billion bytes. External computer storage devices can store trillions of bytes of data. A **terabyte** is approximately one trillion bytes.

Computer Generations

There have been four major stages, or computer generations, in the evolution of computer hardware, each distinguished by a different technology for the components that do the computer's processing work. Each generation has dramatically expanded computer processing power and storage capabilities while simultaneously lowering costs. For instance, the cost of performing 100,000 calculations plunged from several dollars in the 1950s to less than $0.025 in the 1980s and approximately $.00004 in 1995. These generational changes in computer hardware have been accompanied by generational changes in computer software (see Chapter 7) that have made computers increasingly more powerful, inexpensive, and easy to use.

First Generation: Vacuum Tube Technology, 1946–1956

The first generation of computers relied on vacuum tubes to store and process information. These tubes were colossal in size, consumed a great deal of power, were short-lived, and generated a great deal of heat. First-generation computers had extremely limited memory and processing capability and were used for very limited scientific and engineering work. The maximum main memory size was approximately 2000 bytes (2 kilobytes), with a speed of 10 kiloinstructions per second. Rotating magnetic drums were used for internal storage and punched cards for external storage. Jobs such as running programs or printing output had to be coordinated manually.

nanosecond One-billionth of a second.

kilobyte One thousand bytes (actually 1024 storage positions). Used as a measure of PC storage capacity.

megabyte Approximately one million bytes. Unit of computer storage capacity.

gigabyte Approximately one billion bytes. Unit of computer storage capacity.

terabyte Approximately one trillion bytes. Unit of computer storage capacity.

Second Generation: Transistors, 1957–1963

In the second computer generation, transistors replaced vacuum tubes as the devices for storing and processing information. Transistors were smaller and more reliable than vacuum tubes, they generated less heat, and they consumed less power. Magnetic core memory was the primary storage technology. It was composed of small magnetic doughnuts (about 1 millimeter in diameter), which could be polarized in one of two directions to represent a bit of data. Wires were strung along and through these cores to both write and read data. Second-generation computers had up to 32 kilobytes of RAM, and speeds reached 200,000 to 300,000 instructions per second. Second-generation computers had enough memory and processing power to be used more widely for scientific work and for business tasks such as automating payroll and billing.

Third Generation: Integrated Circuits, 1964–1979

Third-generation computers relied on integrated circuits, which were made by printing hundreds and later thousands of tiny transistors on small silicon chips. These devices were called semiconductors. Computer memories expanded to 2 megabytes of RAM memory, and speeds accelerated to 5 million instructions per second. Third-generation computer technology introduced software that could be used by people without extensive technical training thereby increasing the role of computers in business.

Fourth Generation: Very Large-Scale Integrated Circuits, 1980–Present

The fourth generation extends from 1980 to the present. Computers in this period use very large-scale integrated circuits (VLSIC), which are packed with hundreds of thousands and often millions of circuits per chip. With VLSIC technology, the computer's memory, logic, and control can be integrated on a single chip; hence the name **microprocessor,** or computer on a chip. Microprocessor technology has put the power of a computer that once took up a large room on a small desktop or laptop computer, making computers inexpensive and widely available for use in business and everyday life. Computer memory sizes have mushroomed to the gigabyte range in large commercial machines; processing speeds have exceeded one billion instructions per second. In Section 6.6, we discuss the next generation of hardware trends.

6.2 The CPU and Primary Storage

The **central processing unit (CPU)** is the part of the computer system where the manipulation of symbols, numbers, and letters occurs, and it controls the other parts of the computer system. The CPU consists of a control unit and an arithmetic-logic unit (see Figure 6-4). Located near the CPU is **primary storage** (sometimes called primary memory or main memory), where data and program instructions are stored temporarily during processing. Three kinds of buses link the CPU, primary storage, and the other devices in the computer system. The data bus moves data to and from primary storage. The address bus transmits signals for locating a given address in primary storage. The control bus transmits signals specifying whether to read or write data to or from a given primary storage address, input device, or output device. The characteristics of the CPU and primary storage are very important in determining the speed and capabilities of a computer.

Primary Storage

Primary storage has three functions. It stores all or part of the program that is being executed. Primary storage also stores the operating system programs that manage the operation of the computer. (These programs are discussed in Chapter 7.) Finally, the primary storage area holds data that are being used by the program. Data and programs are placed in primary storage before processing, between processing steps, and after processing has ended, prior to being returned to secondary storage or released as output.

How is it possible for an electronic device such as primary storage to actually store information? How is it possible to retrieve this information from a known location in memory? Figure 6-5 illustrates primary storage in an electronic digital computer. Internal primary storage is often called **RAM,** or **random access memory.** It is called RAM because it can directly access any randomly chosen location in the same amount of time.

Figure 6-5 shows that primary memory is divided into storage locations called bytes. Each location contains a set of eight binary switches or devices, each of which can store

microprocessor Very large-scale integrated circuit technology that integrates the computer's memory, logic, and control on a single chip.

central processing unit (CPU) Area of the computer system that manipulates symbols, numbers, and letters, and controls the other parts of the computer system.

primary storage Part of the computer that temporarily stores program instructions and data being used by the instructions.

RAM (random access memory) Primary storage of data or program instructions that can directly access any randomly chosen location in the same amount of time.

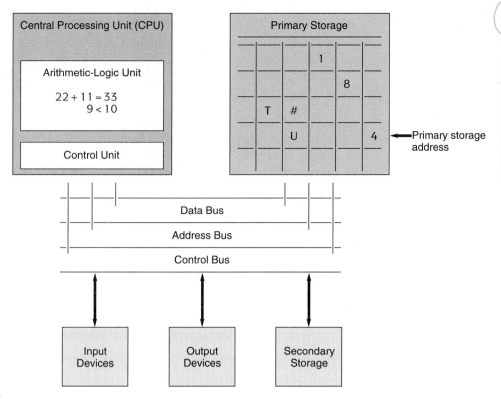

Figure 6-4 The CPU and primary storage. The CPU contains an arithmetic-logic unit and a control unit. Data and instructions are stored in unique addresses in primary storage that the CPU can access during processing. The data bus, address bus, and control bus transmit signals between the central processing unit, primary storage, and other devices in the computer system.

one bit of information. The set of eight bits found in each storage location is sufficient to store one letter, one digit, or one special symbol (such as $) using either EBCDIC or ASCII. Each byte has a unique address, similar to a mailbox, indicating where it is located in RAM. The computer can remember where the data in all of the bytes are located simply by keeping track of these addresses. Most of the information used by a computer application is stored on secondary storage devices, such as disks and tapes, located outside of the primary storage area. In order for the computer to work on information, information must be transferred into primary memory for processing. Therefore, data are continually being read into and written out of the primary storage area during the execution of a program.

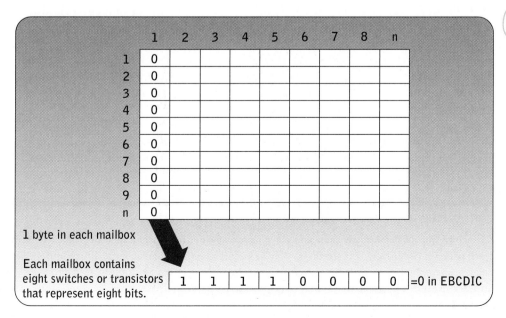

Figure 6-5 Primary storage in the computer. Primary storage can be visualized as a matrix. Each byte represents a mailbox with a unique address. In this example, mailbox [n,1] contains eight bits representing the number 0 (as coded in EBCDIC).

Types of Semiconductor Memory

Primary storage is composed of semiconductors. A **semiconductor** is an integrated circuit made by printing thousands and even millions of tiny transistors on a small silicon chip. There are several different kinds of semiconductor memory used in primary storage. RAM is used for short-term storage of data or program instructions. RAM is volatile: Its contents will be lost when the computer's electric supply is disrupted by a power outage or when the computer is turned off. **ROM, or read-only memory,** can only be read from; it cannot be written to. ROM chips come from the manufacturer with programs already burned in, or stored. ROM is used in general-purpose computers to store important or frequently used programs, such as computing routines for calculating the square roots of numbers.

There are two other subclasses of ROM chips: **PROM, or programmable read-only memory,** and **EPROM, or erasable programmable read-only memory.** PROM chips are used by manufacturers as control devices in their products. They can be programmed once. In this way, manufacturers avoid the expense of having a specialized chip manufactured for the control of small motors, for instance; instead, they can program into a PROM chip the specific program for their product. PROM chips, therefore, can be made universally for many manufacturers in large production runs. EPROM chips are used for device control, such as in robots, where the program may have to be changed on a routine basis. With EPROM chips, the program can be erased and reprogrammed.

The Arithmetic-Logic Unit and Control Unit

The **arithmetic-logic unit (ALU)** performs the principal logical and arithmetic operations of the computer. It adds, subtracts, multiplies, and divides, determining whether a number is positive, negative, or zero. In addition to performing arithmetic functions, an ALU must be able to determine when one quantity is greater than or less than another and when two quantities are equal. The ALU can perform logic operations on the binary codes for letters as well as numbers.

The **control unit** coordinates and controls the other parts of the computer system. It reads a stored program, one instruction at a time, and directs other components of the computer system to perform the tasks required by the program. The series of operations required to process a single machine instruction is called the **machine cycle.** As illustrated in Figure 6-6, the machine cycle has two parts: an instruction cycle and an execution cycle.

During the instruction cycle, the control unit retrieves one program instruction from primary storage and decodes it. It places the part of the instruction telling the ALU what to do next in a special instruction register and places the part specifying the address of the data to be used in the operation into an address register. (A **register** is a special temporary storage location in the ALU or control unit that acts like a high-speed staging area for program instructions or data being transferred from primary storage to the CPU for processing.)

During the execution cycle, the control unit locates the required data in primary storage, places it in a storage register, instructs the ALU to perform the desired operation, temporarily stores the result of the operation in an accumulator, and finally places the result in primary memory. As each instruction is completed, the control unit advances to and reads the next instruction of the program.

6.3 Computers and Computer Processing

Computers represent and process data the same way, but there are different classifications. We can use size and processing speed to categorize contemporary computers as mainframes, minicomputers, PCs, workstations, and supercomputers.

Categories of Computers

A **mainframe** is the largest computer, a powerhouse with massive memory and extremely rapid processing power. It is used for very large business, scientific, or military applications where a computer must handle massive amounts of data or many complicated processes. A **minicomputer** is a mid-range computer, about the size of an office desk, often used in universities, factories, or research laboratories. A **personal computer (PC),** which is sometimes

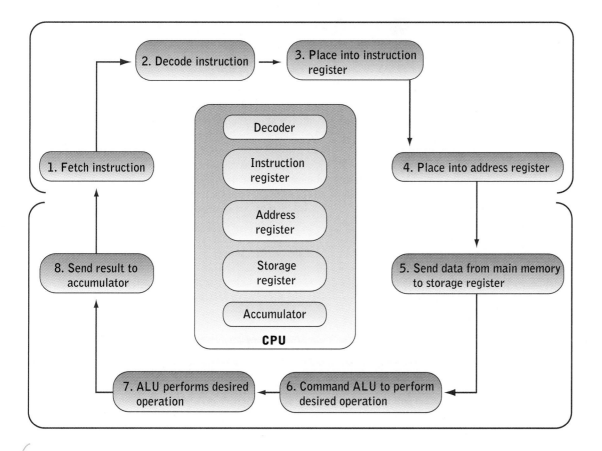

Figure 6-6 The various steps in the machine cycle. The machine cycle has two main stages of operation: the instruction cycle (I-cycle) and the execution cycle (E-cycle). There are several steps within each cycle required to process a single machine instruction in the CPU.

referred to as a microcomputer, is one that can be placed on a desktop or carried from room to room. Smaller laptop PCs are often used as portable desktops on the road. PCs are used as personal machines as well as in business. A **workstation** also fits on a desktop but has more powerful mathematical and graphics-processing capability than a PC and can perform more complicated tasks than a PC in the same amount of time. Workstations are used for scientific, engineering, and design work that requires powerful graphics or computational capabilities. A **supercomputer** is a highly sophisticated and powerful machine that is used for tasks requiring extremely rapid and complex calculations with hundreds of thousands of variable factors. Supercomputers traditionally have been used in scientific and military work, but they are starting to be used in business as well.

The problem with this classification scheme is that the capacity of the machines changes so rapidly. Powerful PCs have sophisticated graphics and processing capabilities similar to workstations. PCs still cannot perform as many tasks at once as mainframes, minicomputers, or workstations (see the discussion of operating systems in Chapter 7); nor can they be used by as many people simultaneously as these larger machines. Even these distinctions will become less pronounced in the future. The most powerful workstations have some of the capabilities of earlier mainframes and supercomputers (Thomborson, 1993).

Any of these categories of computers can be designed to support a computer network, enabling users to share files, software, peripheral devices, such as printers, or other network resources. **Server computers** are specifically optimized for network use, with large memory and disk-storage capacity, high-speed communications capabilities, and powerful CPUs. Powerful workstations are being further customized as Web servers for maintaining and managing Web sites. The Window on Technology explores how larger computers and mainframes can be used for this purpose.

workstation Desktop computer with powerful graphics and mathematical capabilities and the ability to perform several complicated tasks at once.

supercomputer Highly sophisticated and powerful computer that can perform very complex computations extremely rapidly.

server computer Computer specifically optimized to provide software and other resources to other computers over a network.

Window on Technology

Mainframes Learn to Serve the Web

At one time, it looked like powerful inexpensive computers, workstations, and networked computing might make large expensive mainframes a technological dinosaur. Instead, mainframes are flourishing. Many companies are continuing to use mainframes for critical applications with large numbers of transactions because these computers offer unmatched processing power and reliability. Mainframes are also finding new uses supporting electronic commerce on the Web.

Some companies are actually using mainframes as Web servers, arguing that their need for extra processing horsepower justifies the extra cost for a large computer. Merrill Lynch & Co., the giant Wall Street firm, uses a mainframe to support its stock market Web site. Customers use the site to obtain stock quotes, track other market measures, follow their own portfolios, and obtain information about traded companies. For Merrill Lynch, the decision was relatively easy—it was cheaper and easier to use the mainframe as their Web server. "The data were already on the mainframe," explains Merrill Lynch Vice President Jeff Savit. Placing the Web site anywhere else would have meant new hardware, installation costs, staff to support that hardware, and ongoing costs of moving the data from the mainframe to a smaller Web server. Instead, all Merrill Lynch had to do was to put the new Web site application on the existing computer. By linking continuously updated market information to the Web server, the company can easily pump it to internal users, clients, and external Web users.

For SpeedServe of La Vergne, Tennessee, the decision was much more difficult. SpeedServe sells books, videos, and games over the Web. They ran their site on a Windows NT server until the site started averaging 100,000 hits per day. At that point, their NT server no longer could handle the volume of traffic. The company anticipated one million transactions per day by 1998, and adding a second or even a third NT server would not have solved their problem. So they looked to the future and brought in an IBM S/390 mainframe instead. For SpeedServe the short-run costs are greater, but they calculated that by going to a mainframe, their labor and support costs will be lower long-range, and they have no worries about room to grow, speed, reliability, or the other issues they would face by adding smaller computers. SpeedServe is using only three of their mainframe's 10 CPUs, so it has plenty of room for growth in its transaction volume.

Other companies are using smaller computers for Web servers but they are relying on mainframes to deliver the data users need. More than 70 percent of corporate data worldwide still resides on mainframes. Firms are finding that they can utilize the data stored on existing systems in their electronic commerce applications by creating special front-end software that provides a Web interface. The software accesses the requested data from the mainframe and presents them to users in the form of a Web page. Diversified Investment Advisors Inc. in Purchase, New York, a financial investment firm specializing in corporate retirement accounts, realized savings by using this arrangement. Clients can use its Web site to access key information about their accounts and perform transactions such as shifting fund allocations with standard Web software, eliminating the need for expensive new systems and software.

To Think About: Suggest other situations where a company might prefer a mainframe to a network of smaller computers, and explain why the mainframe would be the better choice for management. What management, organization, and technology issues should be considered?

Sources: Elisabeth Horwitt, "Webifying the Mainframe," *Computerworld*, January 25, 1999; Eva Freeman, "Mainframes in the 21st Century," *Datamation*, January, 1999; and Jaikumar Vijayan and Tim Ouellette, "Big Iron Gets a Case of Web Fever," *Computerworld*, January 26, 1998.

Supercomputers and Parallel Processing

A supercomputer is an especially sophisticated and powerful type of computer that is used primarily for extremely rapid and complex computations with hundreds or thousands of variable factors. Supercomputers traditionally have been used for classified weapons research, weather forecasting, and petroleum and engineering applications, all of which use complex mathematical models and simulations. Although extremely expensive, supercomputers are beginning to be employed in business for datamining and the manipulation of vast quantities of data.

Supercomputers can perform complex and massive computations almost instantaneously because they can perform hundreds of billions of calculations per second—many times faster than the largest mainframes. Supercomputers do not process one instruction at a time but instead rely on **parallel processing.** As illustrated in Figure 6-7, multiple processing units (CPUs) break down a problem into smaller parts and work on it simultaneously. Some supercomputers use many thousands of processors. Getting a group of processors to attack the same problem at once requires both rethinking the problems and special software that can divide problems among different processors in the most efficient way possible, providing the needed data, and reassembling the many subtasks to reach an appropriate solution.

parallel processing Type of processing in which more than one instruction can be processed at a time by breaking down a problem into smaller parts and processing them simultaneously with multiple processors.

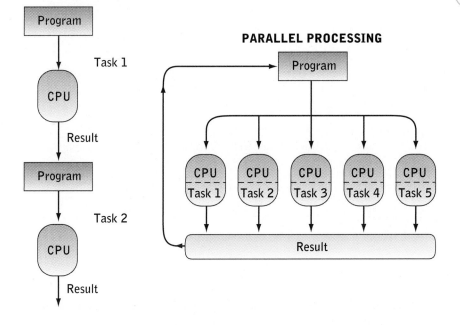

SEQUENTIAL PROCESSING

Program
↓ Task 1
CPU
↓ Result
Program
↓ Task 2
CPU
↓ Result

PARALLEL PROCESSING

Program

CPU Task 1 | CPU Task 2 | CPU Task 3 | CPU Task 4 | CPU Task 5

Result

Figure 6-7 Sequential and parallel processing. During sequential processing, each task is assigned to one CPU that processes one instruction at a time. In parallel processing, multiple tasks are assigned to multiple processing units to expedite the result.

Some supercomputers can now perform more than a trillion mathematical calculations each second—a teraflop. The term *teraflop* comes from the Greek *teras,* which for mathematicians means one trillion, and *flop,* an acronym for floating point operations per second. (A floating point operation is a basic computer arithmetic operation, such as addition, on numbers that include a decimal point.) Work is under way to build supercomputers capable of 10 teraflops.

Microprocessors and Processing Power

Computers' processing power depends in part on the speed and performance of their microprocessors. Some popular microprocessors are listed in Table 6.3. You may see chips labeled as 8-bit, 16-bit, or 32-bit devices. These labels refer to the **word length,** or the number of bits that can be processed at one time by the machine. An 8-bit chip can process 8 bits, or 1 byte,

word length The number of bits that can be processed at one time by a computer. The larger the word length, the greater the speed of the computer.

Table 6.3 Examples of Microprocessors

Name	Microprocessor Manufacturer	Word Length	Data Bus Width	Clock Speed (MHz)	Used In
Pentium	Intel	32	64	75–200	IBM and other PCs
Pentium (MMX)	Intel	32	64	166–233	Multimedia PCs and workstations
Pentium II	Intel	32	64	233–450	High-end PCs and workstations
Pentium III	Intel	32	64	450–500	High-end business PCs, servers, and workstations
PowerPC	Motorola, IBM, Apple	32 or 64	64	100–400	High-end PCs and workstations
Alpha	DEC/ Compaq	64	64	600+	Compaq and DEC workstations

The Pentium III microprocessor contains more than nine million transistors and provides mainframe and supercomputer-like processing capabilities.

megahertz A measure of cycle speed, or the pacing of events in a computer; one megahertz equals one million cycles per second.

data bus width The number of bits that can be moved at one time between the CPU, primary storage, and the other devices of a computer.

reduced instruction set computing (RISC) Technology used to enhance the speed of microprocessors by embedding only the most frequently used instructions on a chip.

MMX Pentium microprocessor modified to improve processing of multimedia applications. Stands for MultiMedia eXtension.

of information in a single machine cycle. A 32-bit chip can process 32 bits or 4 bytes in a single cycle. The larger the word length, the greater the speed of the computer.

A second factor affecting chip speed is cycle speed. Every event in a computer must be sequenced so that one step logically follows another. The control unit sets a beat to the chip. This beat is established by an internal clock and is measured in **megahertz** (abbreviated MHz, which stands for millions of cycles per second). The Intel 8088 chip, for instance, originally had a clock speed of 4.47 megahertz, whereas the Intel Pentium III chip has a clock speed that ranges from 450 to 500 megahertz.

A third factor affecting speed is the **data bus width.** The data bus acts as a highway between the CPU, primary storage, and other devices, determining how much data can be moved at one time. The 8088 chip used in the original IBM personal computer, for example, had a 16-bit word length but only an 8-bit data bus width. This meant that data were processed within the CPU chip itself in 16-bit chunks but could only be moved 8 bits at a time between the CPU, primary storage, and external devices. On the other hand, the Alpha chip has both a 64-bit word length and a 64-bit data bus width. To have a computer execute more instructions per second and work through programs or handle users expeditiously, it is necessary to increase the word length of the processor, the data bus width, or the cycle speed—or all three.

Microprocessors can be made faster by using **reduced instruction set computing (RISC)** in their design. Some instructions that a computer uses to process data are actually embedded in the chip circuitry. Conventional chips, based on complex instruction set computing, have several hundred or more instructions hard-wired into their circuitry, and they may take several clock cycles to execute a single instruction. In many instances, only 20 percent of these instructions are needed for 80 percent of the computer's tasks. If the little-used instructions are eliminated, the remaining instructions can execute much faster.

RISC computers have only the most frequently used instructions embedded in them. A RISC CPU can execute most instructions in a single machine cycle and sometimes multiple instructions at the same time. RISC is most appropriate for scientific and workstation computing, where there are repetitive arithmetic and logical operations on data or applications calling for three-dimensional image rendering.

On the other hand, software written for conventional processors cannot be automatically transferred to RISC machines; new software is required. Many RISC suppliers are adding more instructions to appeal to a greater number of customers, and designers of conventional microprocessors are streamlining their chips to execute instructions more rapidly.

Microprocessors optimized for multimedia and graphics have been developed to improve processing of visually intensive applications. Intel's **MMX (MultiMedia eXtension)** microprocessor is a Pentium chip that has been modified with additional instructions to increase performance in many applications featuring graphics and sound. Multimedia applications such as games and video will be able to run more smoothly, with more colors, and be

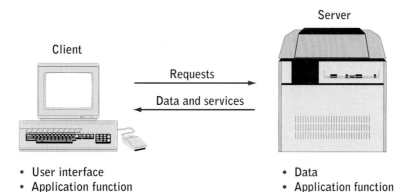

Figure 6-8 Client/server computing. In client/server computing, computer processing is split between client machines and server machines linked by a network. Users interface with the client machines.

Client

Requests

Data and services

Server

- User interface
- Application function

- Data
- Application function
- Network resources

able to perform more tasks simultaneously. For example, multiple channels of audio, high-quality video or animation, and Internet communication could all be running in the same application. Advanced Micro Devices' AMD-K6 microprocessor is compatible with the Pentium and also supports the MMX instruction set. Intel's Pentium III chip also has special capabilities for speech recognition, imaging, video and Internet work.

Computer Networks and Client/Server Computing

Today, stand-alone computers have been replaced by computers in networks for most processing tasks. The use of multiple computers linked by a communications network for processing is called **distributed processing.** In contrast with **centralized processing,** in which all processing is accomplished by one large central computer, distributed processing distributes the processing work among PCs, minicomputers, and mainframes linked together.

One widely used form of distributed processing is **client/server computing.** Client/server computing splits processing between "clients" and "servers." Both are on the network, but each machine is assigned functions it is best suited to perform. The **client** is the user point-of-entry for the required function and is normally a desktop computer, workstation, or laptop computer. The user generally interacts directly only with the client portion of the application, often to input data or retrieve data for further analysis. The **server** provides the client with services and might be anything from a supercomputer or mainframe to another desktop computer. Servers store and process shared data and also perform back-end functions not visible to users, such as managing network activities. Figure 6-8 illustrates the client/server computing concept. Computing on the Internet uses the client/server model (see Chapter 10).

Figure 6-9 illustrates five different ways that the components of an application could be partitioned between the client and the server. The *interface* component is essentially the application interface—how the application appears visually to the user. The *application logic* component consists of the processing logic, which is shaped by the organization's business rules. (An example might be that a salaried employee is only to be paid monthly.) The *data management* component consists of the storage and management of the data used by the application.

The exact division of tasks depends on the requirements of each application, including its processing needs, the number of users, and the available resources. For example, client tasks for a large corporate payroll might include inputting data (such as enrolling new employees and recording hours worked), submitting data queries to the server, analyzing the retrieved data, and displaying results on the screen or on a printer. The server portion will fetch the entered data and process the payroll. It also will control access so that only authorized users can view or update the data.

In some firms client/server networks with PCs have actually replaced mainframes and minicomputers. The process of transferring applications from large computers to smaller ones is called **downsizing.** Downsizing has many advantages. Memory and processing power on a PC cost a fraction of their equivalent on a mainframe. The decision to downsize involves many factors in addition to the cost of computer hardware, including the need for new software, training, and perhaps new organizational procedures.

distributed processing The distribution of computer processing work among multiple computers linked by a communications network.

centralized processing Processing that is accomplished by one large central computer.

client/server computing A model for computing that splits processing between "clients" and "servers" on a network, assigning functions to the machine most able to perform the function.

client The user point-of-entry for the required function in client/server computing. Normally a desktop computer, workstation, or laptop computer.

server In client/server computing, the component that satisfies some or all of the user's request for data and/or functionality and that performs back-end functions not visible to users, such as managing network activities.

downsizing The process of transferring applications from large computers to smaller ones.

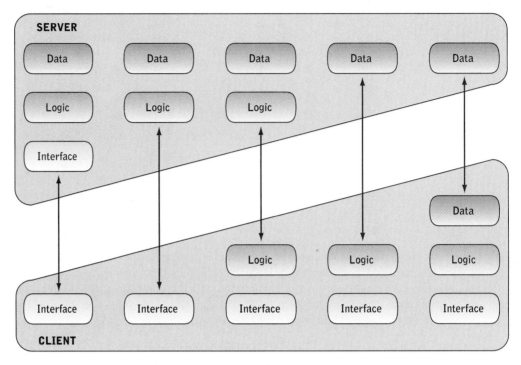

Figure 6-9 Types of client/server computing. There are various ways in which an application's interface, logic, and data management components can be divided among the clients and servers in a network.

Network Computers and Total Cost of Ownership

In one form of client/server computing, the client is so small that the bulk of computer processing occurs on the server. The term *thin client* is sometimes used to refer to the client in this arrangement or to refer to network computers. **Network computers (NCs)** are smaller, simpler, and cheaper versions of the traditional personal computer with minimal storage and processing capabilities. The most simplified network computers do not store software programs or data permanently. Instead, users download whatever software or data they need from a central computer over the Internet or an organization's internal network. The central computer also saves information for the user and makes it available for later retrieval, effectively eliminating the need for secondary storage devices such as hard disks, floppy disks, CD-ROMs, and their drives. A network computer may consist of little more than a stripped-down PC, a monitor, a keyboard, and a network connection.

If managed properly, both network computers and client/server computing can reduce the total cost of ownership of information technology resources. **Total cost of ownership (TCO)** is a popular term to designate how much it costs to own technology resources, including the original cost of the computer and software, hardware and software upgrades, maintenance, technical support, and training.

Network computers have minimal local processing and storage capabilities because they download the software and data users need from a network.

Proponents of network computers believe NCs can reduce TCO because they are less expensive to purchase than PCs with local processing and storage, and because they can be administered and updated from a central network server. (Network computers can cost between $500 and $1000 per unit.) Software programs and applications would not have to be purchased, installed, and upgraded for each user because software would be delivered and maintained from one central point. So much data and information are being delivered through the Web that computers do not necessarily need to store their own content. Network computers thus could increase management control over the organization's computing function.

Not everyone agrees that network computers will bring benefits. Some researchers believe that centralizing control over computing would stifle worker initiative and creativity. Several studies of the cost of owning PCs question whether the savings promised by network computers will actually be realized. PC prices have fallen so that units can be purchased for $1000 or even less. Very little software has yet been designed for the network computing model. If a network failure occurs, hundreds or thousands of employees would not be able to use their computers, whereas people could keep on working if they had full-function PCs. A poorly supervised network computer system could prove to be just as inefficient as PCs sometimes are. Full-function PCs are more appropriate for situations where end users have varied application needs that require local processing. Companies should closely examine how network computers would fit into their information technology infrastructure. These issues are explored in the Window on Management.

The Window on Organizations explores other TCO issues related to the purchase and use of laptop computers in the business.

6.4 Secondary Storage

In addition to primary storage, where information and programs are stored for immediate processing, modern computer systems use other types of storage in order to accomplish their tasks. Information systems need to store information outside of the computer in a nonvolatile state (not requiring electrical power) and to store volumes of data too large to fit into a computer of any size today (such as a large payroll or the U.S. census). The relatively long-term storage of data outside the CPU and primary storage is called **secondary storage.**

Primary storage is where the fastest, most expensive technology is used. Access to information stored in primary memory is electronic and occurs almost at the speed of light. Secondary storage is nonvolatile and retains data even when the computer is turned off. There are many kinds of secondary storage; the most common are magnetic disk, optical disk, and magnetic tape. These media can transfer large bodies of data rapidly to the CPU. However, secondary storage requires mechanical movement to gain access to the data, so in contrast to primary storage, it is relatively slow.

Magnetic Disk

The most widely used secondary-storage medium today is **magnetic disk.** There are two kinds of magnetic disks: floppy disks (used in PCs) and **hard disks** (used on commercial disk drives and PCs). Hard disks are thin steel platters with an iron oxide coating. In larger systems, multiple hard disks are mounted together on a vertical shaft. Figure 6-10 illustrates a commercial hard disk pack for a large system. It has 11 disks, each with two surfaces, top and bottom. However, although there are 11 disks, no information is recorded on the top or bottom surfaces; thus, there are only 20 recording surfaces on the disk pack. On each surface, data are stored on tracks.

Read/write heads move horizontally over the spinning disks to any of 200 positions, called cylinders. At any one of these cylinders, the read/write heads can read or write information to any of 20 different concentric circles on the disk surface areas called **tracks.** (Each track contains several records.) The **cylinder** represents the circular tracks on the same vertical line within the disk pack. Read/write heads are directed to a specific record using an address consisting of the cylinder number, the recording surface number, and the data record number.

The entire disk pack is housed in a disk drive or disk unit. Large mainframe or minicomputer systems have multiple disk drives because they require immense disk storage capacity.

secondary storage Relatively long-term, nonvolatile storage of data outside the CPU and primary storage.

magnetic disk A secondary storage medium in which data are stored by means of magnetized spots on a hard or floppy disk.

hard disk Magnetic disk resembling a thin steel platter with an iron oxide coating; used in large computer systems and in most PCs.

track Concentric circle on the surface area of a disk on which data are stored as magnetized spots; each track can store thousands of bytes.

cylinder Represents circular tracks on the same vertical line within a disk pack.

Window on Management

Network Computers: A New Management Option

Are network computers the next phase in corporate computing? Some companies think so. Companies that have made the switch point to low purchase and maintenance costs as their rationale for switching to NCs.

General Accident Fire & Life Corporation decided on a wide-scale rollout of network computers in early 1998, installing 2200 IBM Network Station NCs in various locations. The British insurer had upgraded its text-based mainframe core processing system for tracking claims, underwriting, and other daily activities with one that displayed output on computer screens in color. With NCs, users can easily access this legacy system, as well as Web-like applications on the company's private intranet. PCs were rejected because they were considered too costly to be used primarily to access a centralized mainframe system. General Accident hasn't computed the cost savings from network computers because it would have to compare the cost of both purchasing and supporting NCs versus local PCs over a full year. The company selected NCs because management wanted more control over what applications run over users' machines and because the NCs worked with its back-end mainframe system.

The Evangelical Lutheran Good Samaritan Society, a nonprofit organization operating 235 nursing homes, long-term care facilities, and low-income housing for senior citizens, turned to network computers because they require less technical support and maintenance than stand-alone PCs. Facility directors and nurses at each of its sites had been supporting PC applications themselves, taking their time and concentration away from their primary responsibility of serving patients. The Society will be running its core financial, human resources, and other applications on a central server at company headquarters in Sioux Falls, South Dakota. Nursing homes and other sites will access the applications using Web browser software running on 1000 to 1500 IBM network computers.

TravelPlus, Inc., the third-largest travel agency in Canada, selected network computers for similar reasons. This Saskatoon, Saskatchewan-based company has rolled out 500 IBM Network Station network computers in its 218 offices throughout the country. TravelPlus believes that using NCs for centralized management of desktops will result in dramatic operating efficiencies and cost savings. The company estimates its NCs will cost $1200 per year to maintain, compared with an estimated $6000 per stand-alone PC.

So far, most companies have not rushed to adopt network computers. Some managers have decided against NCs because of the unreliability of both internal networks and the Internet. Dayna Aronson, information systems manager at Norpac Food Sales, the Lake Oswego, Oregon, division of Norpac Foods, Inc., worries about hundreds of users twiddling their thumbs if the network goes down. Having local processing power and data "provides a level of autonomy and redundancy worth far more than saving $1000."

After months of testing different thin-client machines, Federal Express Corporation decided against network computers as replacements for up to 30,000 aging terminals linked to its mainframe. FedEx management stated that it had not found any NC product that met the company's computing needs. PC prices had fallen to the point where they were competitive with network computers while offering more functionality and flexibility.

Network computers are also not very useful for work such as CAD (computer-aided design) that requires powerful local processing capabilities or environments where every user has a different suite of personal applications. Finance, security, and insurance industries, as well as retail and distribution, appear to be more receptive to network computers because they have applications that connect to the Internet.

To Think About: If you were a manager, what people, organization, and technology factors would you consider in deciding whether to use network computers in your organization?

Sources: Stacy Collett and Stewart Deck, "Where Are the Thin Clients?" **Computerworld**, February 15, 1999; Kristi Essick, "Insurer Picks NCs for Central Management," **Computerworld**, February 2, 1998; David Bank and Don Clark, "Network Computers Fall Short in Contest Against Cheap PCs," **The Wall Street Journal**, April 3, 1998; and Randy Weston, "Health Care Organization Heals IS Wound with NCs," **Computerworld**, January 19, 1998.

RAID (Redundant Array of Inexpensive Disks) Disk storage technology to boost disk performance by packaging more than 100 smaller disk drives with a controller chip and specialized software in a single large unit to deliver data over multiple paths simultaneously.

floppy disk Removable magnetic disk storage primarily used with PCs.

Disk drive performance can be further enhanced by using a disk technology called **RAID (Redundant Array of Inexpensive Disks).** RAID devices package more than a hundred 6.25-inch disk drives, a controller chip, and specialized software into a single large unit. Traditional disk drives deliver data from the disk drive along a single path, but RAID delivers data over multiple paths simultaneously, accelerating disk access time. Small RAID systems provide 10 to 20 gigabytes of storage capacity, whereas larger systems provide more than 10 terabytes. RAID is potentially more reliable than standard disk drives because other drives are available to deliver data if one drive fails.

PCs usually contain hard disks, which can store more than 10 gigabytes, although 4–6 gigabytes is the most common size range. PCs also use **floppy disks,** which are flat, 3.5-inch disks of polyester film with a magnetic coating (5.25-inch floppy disks are obsolete). These disks

Window on Organizations

have a storage capacity ranging from 360 K to 2.8 megabytes and a much slower access rate than hard disks. Floppy disks and cartridges and packs of multiple disks use a **sector** method of storing data. As illustrated in Figure 6-11, the disk surface is divided into pie-shaped pieces. Each sector is assigned a unique number. Data can be located using an address consisting of the sector number and an individual data record number.

Magnetic disks on both large and small computers permit direct access to individual records. Each record can be given a precise physical address in terms of cylinders and tracks or sectors, and the read/write head can be directed to go directly to that address and access the information. This means that the computer system does not have to search the entire file, as in a sequential tape file, in order to find the record. Disk storage is often referred to as a **direct access storage device (DASD).**

For on-line systems requiring direct access, disk technology provides the only practical means of storage today. DASD is, however, more expensive than magnetic tape. Updating information stored on a disk destroys the old information because the old data on the disk are written over if changes are made. The disk drives themselves are susceptible to environmental

sector Method of storing data on a floppy disk in which the disk is divided into pie-shaped pieces or sectors. Each sector is assigned a unique number so that data can be located using the sector number.

direct access storage device (DASD) Refers to magnetic disk technology that permits the CPU to locate a record directly.

Figure 6-10 Disk pack storage. Large systems often rely on disk packs, which provide reliable storage for large amounts of data with quick access and retrieval. A typical removable disk-pack system contains 11 two-sided disks.

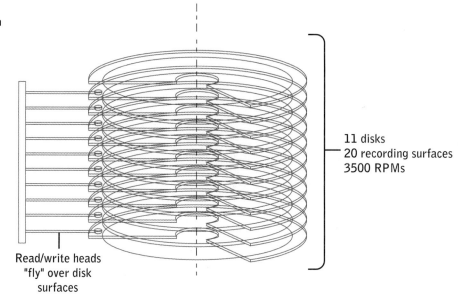

11 disks
20 recording surfaces
3500 RPMs

Read/write heads
"fly" over disk
surfaces

disturbances. Even smoke particles can disrupt the movement of read/write heads over the disk surface, which is why disk drives are sealed from the environment.

Optical Disks

Optical disks, also called compact disks or laser optical disks, store data at densities many times greater than those of magnetic disks and are available for both PCs and large computers. Data are recorded on optical disks when a laser device burns microscopic pits in the reflective layer of a spiral track. Binary information is encoded by the length of these pits and the space between them. Optical disks can store massive quantities of data, including not only text but also pictures, sound, and full-motion video, in a highly compact form. The optical disk is read by having a low-power laser beam from an optical head scan the disk.

The most common optical disk system used with PCs is called **CD-ROM (compact disk read-only memory).** A 4.75-inch compact disk for PCs can store up to 660 megabytes, nearly 300 times more than a high-density floppy disk. Optical disks are most appropriate for applications where enormous quantities of unchanging data must be stored compactly for easy retrieval, or for storing graphic images and sound. CD-ROM is also less vulnerable than floppy disks to magnetism, dirt, or rough handling.

CD-ROM (compact disk read-only memory) Read-only optical disk storage used for imaging, reference, and database applications with massive amounts of unchanging data and for multimedia.

Figure 6-11 The sector method of storing data. Each track of a disk can be divided into sectors. Disk storage location can be identified by sector and data record number.

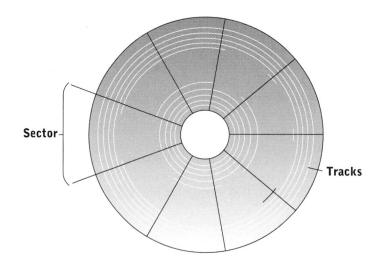

Sector

Tracks

CD-ROM is read-only storage. No new data can be written to it; it can only be read. CD-ROM has been most widely used for reference materials with massive amounts of data, such as encyclopedias and directories, and for storing multimedia applications that combine text, sound, and images (see Section 6.6). For example, U.S. census demographic data and financial databases from Dow Jones or Dun and Bradstreet are available on CD-ROM.

WORM (write once/read many) and **CD-R (compact disk-recordable)** optical disk systems allow users to record data only once on an optical disk. Once written, the data cannot be erased, but can be read indefinitely. CD-R technology allows individuals and organizations to create their own CD-ROMs at low cost using a special CD-R recording device. New *CD-RW (CD-ReWritable)* technology has been developed to allow users to create rewritable optical disks. (Magneto-optical technology was developed earlier for this purpose.) Rewritable optical disk drives are not yet competitive with magnetic disk storage for most applications. Their access speed is slower than that of magnetic disks and they are more expensive than magnetic media. Rewritable optical disks are useful primarily for applications requiring large volumes of storage where the information is only occasionally updated.

CD-ROM storage is likely to become more popular and more powerful in years to come, and access speeds will improve. **Digital video disks (DVDs),** also called digital versatile disks, are optical disks the same size as CD-ROMs but of even higher capacity. They can hold a minimum of 4.7 gigabytes of data, enough to store a full-length, high-quality motion picture. DVDs are initially being used to store movies and multimedia applications using large amounts of video and graphics, but they may replace CD-ROMs because they can store large amounts of digitized text, graphics, audio, and video data.

Magnetic Tape

Magnetic tape is an older storage technology that still is employed for secondary storage of large volumes of information. It is still used in mainframe batch applications and for archiving data. (PCs and some minicomputers use small tape cartridges resembling home audiocassettes to store information.) However, more and more organizations are moving

WORM (write once/read many) Optical disk system that allows users to record data only once; data cannot be erased but can be read indefinitely.

CD-R (compact disk-recordable) Optical disk system that allows individuals and organizations to record their own CD-ROMs.

digital video disk (DVD) High-capacity optical storage medium that can store full-length videos and large amounts of data.

magnetic tape Inexpensive, older secondary-storage medium in which large volumes of information are stored sequentially by means of magnetized and nonmagnetized spots on tape.

away from using the old reel-to-reel magnetic tapes and instead are using mass storage tape cartridges that hold far more data (up to 35 gigabytes) than the old magnetic tapes. Moreover, today, these cartridges are part of automated systems that store hundreds of such cartridges and select and mount them automatically using sophisticated robotics technology. Contemporary magnetic tape systems are used for archiving data and for storing data that are needed rapidly but not instantly. These systems, dubbed *near-line,* can locate and access a record stored somewhere within a bank of cartridges in about 20 seconds or less. Such inexpensive speed is useful in many industries and is used extensively in such fields as banking, broadcasting (replacing videotapes), and healthcare (for example, to store X rays and other medical images).

The principal advantages of magnetic tape are that it is very inexpensive, it is relatively stable, and it can store very large quantities of information. Magnetic tape also can be reused many times.

The principal disadvantages of magnetic tape are that it stores data sequentially and is relatively slow compared to the speed of other secondary storage media. In order to find an individual record stored on magnetic tape, such as your employment record, the tape must be read from the beginning up to the location of the desired record. Tape can also age over time and is labor intensive to mount and dismount. Although magnetic tape is not good for data that need to be accessed in a second or less, it can be very useful if a few extra seconds are not a problem.

6.5 Input and Output Devices

Human beings interact with computer systems largely through input and output devices. Advances in information systems rely not only on the speed and capacity of the CPU but also on the speed, capacity, and design of the input and output devices. Input/output devices are often called *peripheral devices.*

Input Devices

Keyboards remain the principal method of data entry for entering text and numerical data into a computer. However, pointing devices, such as the computer mouse and touch screens, are becoming popular for issuing commands and making selections in today's highly graphic computing environment.

Pointing Devices

The point-and-click actions of the **computer mouse** have made it an increasingly popular alternative to keyboard and text-based commands. A mouse is a handheld device that is usually connected to the computer by a cable. The computer user moves the mouse around on a desktop to control the position of the cursor on a computer display screen. Once the cursor is in the desired position, the user can push a button on the mouse to select a command. The mouse also can be used to "draw" images on the screen. *Trackballs* and *touch pads* often are used in place of the mouse as pointing devices on laptop PCs.

Touch screens are easy to use and appeal to people who can't use traditional keyboards. Users can enter limited amounts of data by touching the surface of a sensitized video display monitor with a finger or a pointer. With colorful graphics, sound, and simple menus, touch screens often are found in information kiosks in retail stores, restaurants, and shopping malls.

Source Data Automation

Source data automation captures data in computer-readable form at the time and place they are created. Point-of-sale systems, optical bar code scanners used in supermarkets, and other optical character recognition devices are examples of source data automation. One of the advantages of source data automation is that the many errors that occur when people use keyboards to enter data are almost eliminated. Bar code scanners make fewer than 1 error in

computer mouse Handheld input device whose movement on the desktop controls the position of the cursor on the computer display screen.

touch screen Input device technology that permits the entering or selecting of commands and data by touching the surface of a sensitized video display monitor with a finger or a pointer.

source data automation Input technology that captures data in computer-readable form at the time and place the data are created.

10,000 transactions, whereas skilled keypunchers make about 1 error for every 1000 keystrokes. The principal source data automation technologies are optical character recognition, magnetic ink character recognition, pen-based input, digital scanners, voice input, and sensors.

Optical character recognition (OCR) devices translate specially designed marks, characters, and codes into digital form. The most widely used optical code is the **bar code,** which is used in point-of-sale systems in supermarkets and retail stores. Bar codes also are used in hospitals, libraries, military operations, and transportation facilities. The codes can include time, date, and location data in addition to identification data. The information makes them useful for analyzing the movement of items and determining what has happened to them during production or other processes. (The discussion of the United Parcel Service in Chapter 1 shows how valuable bar codes can be for this purpose.)

Magnetic ink character recognition (MICR) technology is used primarily in check processing for the banking industry. The bottom portion of a typical check contains characters identifying the bank, checking account, and check number that are preprinted using a special magnetic ink. An MICR reader translates these characters into digital form for the computer.

Handwriting-recognition devices such as pen-based tablets, notebooks, and notepads are promising new input technologies, especially for people working in the sales or service areas or for those who have traditionally shunned computer keyboards. These **pen-based input** devices usually consist of a flat-screen display tablet and a pen-like stylus.

With pen-based input, users print directly onto the tablet-size screen. The screen is fitted with a transparent grid of fine wires that detect the presence of the special stylus, which emits a faint signal from its tip. As users write letters and numbers on the tablet, they are translated into digital form, where they can be stored or processed and analyzed. For instance, the United Parcel Service replaced its drivers' familiar clipboard with a battery-powered Delivery Information Acquisition Device (DIAD) to capture signatures (see the Chapter 1 Window on Technology) along with other information required for pickup and delivery. This technology requires special pattern-recognition software to accept pen-based

optical character recognition (OCR) Form of source data automation in which optical scanning devices read specially designed data off source documents and translate the data into digital form for the computer.

bar code Form of OCR technology widely used in supermarkets and retail stores in which identification data are coded into a series of bars.

magnetic ink character recognition (MICR) Input technology that translates characters written in magnetic ink into digital codes for processing.

pen-based input Input devices such as tablets, notebooks, and notepads consisting of a flat-screen display tablet and a pen-like stylus that digitizes handwriting.

input instead of keyboard input. Most pen-based systems still cannot recognize freehand writing very well.

Digital scanners translate images such as pictures or documents into digital form and are an essential component of image-processing systems. **Voice input devices** convert spoken words into digital form for processing by the computer. Voice recognition devices allow people to enter data into the computer without using their hands, making them useful for inspecting and sorting items in manufacturing and shipping and for dictation. (Documents can be created by speaking words into a computer rather than keying them in.) We describe advances in voice technology in the following section.

Sensors are devices that collect data directly from the environment for input into a computer system. For instance, today's farmers can use sensors on their tractors to monitor speed and adjust the amount of fertilizer or pesticide sprayed on soil. Sensor-equipped combines can monitor, calculate, and record each field's yield as the combines harvest crops (Feder, 1998).

Batch and On-Line Input and Processing

The manner in which data are input into the computer affects how the data can be processed. Information systems collect and process information in one of two ways: through batch or through on-line processing. In **batch processing,** transactions such as orders or payroll time cards are accumulated and stored in a group or batch until the time when, because of some reporting cycle, it is efficient or necessary to process them. This was the only method of processing until the early 1960s, and it is still used today in older systems or some systems with massive volumes of transactions. In **on-line processing,** which is now very common, the user enters transactions into a device that is directly connected to the computer system. The transactions usually are processed immediately.

The demands of the business determine the type of processing. If the user needs periodic or occasional reports or output, as in payroll or end-of-the-year reports, batch processing is most efficient. If the user needs immediate information and processing, as in an airline or hotel reservation system, then the system should use on-line processing.

Figure 6-12 compares batch and on-line processing. Batch systems often use tape as a storage medium, whereas on-line processing systems use disk storage, which permits immediate access to specific items. In batch systems, transactions are accumulated in a **transaction file,** which contains all the transactions for a particular time period. Periodically this file is used to update a **master file,** which contains permanent information on entities. (An example is a payroll master file with employee earnings and deduction data. It is updated with weekly time-card transactions.) Adding the transaction data to the existing master file creates a new master file. In on-line processing, transactions are entered into the system immediately using a keyboard, pointing device, or source data automation, and the system usually responds immediately. The master file is updated continually. In on-line processing, there is a direct connection to the computer for input and output.

Output Devices

The major data output devices are cathode ray tube terminals, sometimes called video display terminals or VDTs, and printers.

The **cathode ray tube (CRT)** is probably the most popular form of information output in modern computer systems. It works much like a television picture tube, with an electronic gun shooting a beam of electrons to illuminate the pixels on the screen. The more pixels per screen, the higher the resolution. CRT display devices for graphics often utilize bit mapping. **Bit mapping** allows each pixel on the screen to be addressed and manipulated by the computer (as opposed to blocks of pixels in character addressable displays). This requires more computer memory but permits finer detail and the ability to produce any kind of image on the display screen. Special-purpose graphics terminals used in CAD/CAM (computer-aided design/computer-aided manufacturing) and commercial art have very

---

digital scanners Input devices that translate images such as pictures or documents into digital form for processing.

voice input devices Technology that converts the spoken word into digital form for processing.

sensors Devices that collect data directly from the environment for input into a computer system.

batch processing A method of collecting and processing data in which transactions are accumulated and stored until a specified time when it is convenient or necessary to process them as a group.

on-line processing A method of collecting and processing data in which transactions are entered directly into the computer system and processed immediately.

transaction file In batch systems, a file in which all transactions are accumulated to await processing.

master file A file that contains all permanent information and is updated during processing by transaction data.

cathode ray tube (CRT) A screen, also referred to as a video display terminal (VDT). Provides a visual image of both user input and computer output.

bit mapping The technology that allows each pixel on the screen to be addressed and manipulated by the computer.

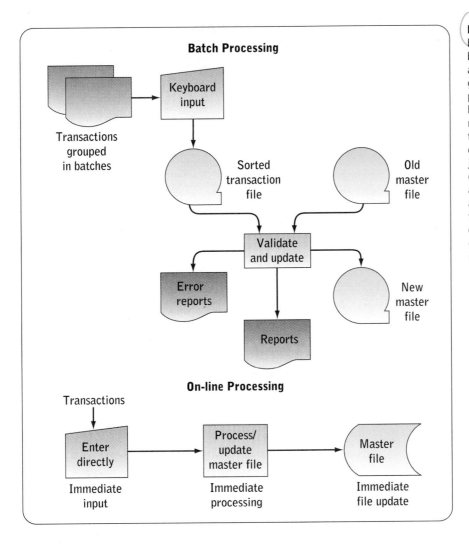

Figure 6-12 A comparison of batch and on-line processing. In batch processing, transactions are accumulated and stored in a group. Because batches are processed on a regular interval basis, such as daily, weekly, or monthly, information in the system will not always be up to date. A typical batch-processing job is payroll preparation. In on-line processing, transactions are input immediately and usually processed immediately. Information in the system is generally up to date. A typical on-line application is an airline reservation system.

high-resolution capabilities (1280 × 1024 pixels). Laptop computers use flat panel displays instead of CRT technology.

Printers and Plotters

Printers produce a printed hard copy of information output. They include impact printers (a standard typewriter or a dot matrix) and nonimpact printers (laser, inkjet, and thermal transfer printers). Most printers print one character at a time, but some commercial printers print an entire line or page at a time. In general, impact printers are slower than nonimpact printers.

High-quality graphics documents can be created using **plotters** with multicolored pens to draw (rather than print) computer output. Plotters are much slower than printers, but are useful for outputting large-size charts, maps, or drawings.

Other Output Devices

A **voice output device** converts digital output data back into intelligible speech. For instance, when you call for information on the telephone, you may hear a computerized voice respond with the telephone number you requested.

Audio output such as music and other sounds can be delivered by speakers connected to the computer. In addition to audio output, multimedia applications, including those on the Web, also can produce graphics or video as visual output. Microfilm and microfiche have been used to store large quantities of output as microscopic filmed documents, but they are being replaced by optical disk technology.

printer A computer output device that provides paper hard-copy output in the form of text or graphics.

plotter Output device using multicolored pens to draw high-quality graphic documents.

voice output device A converter of digital output data into spoken words.

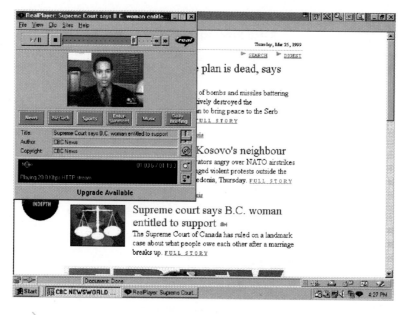

Newsworld Online is a multimedia Web site providing news from Canada, including live video, 24 hours a day. Web sites can incorporate multimedia elements such as graphics, sound, animation, and full-motion video.

6.6 Information Technology Trends

During the past 30 years, each decade has seen computing costs drop by a factor of 10 and capacity increase by a factor of at least 100. Today's microprocessors can put a mainframe on a desktop, a briefcase, and eventually into a shirt pocket. As computers become progressively smaller, more powerful, and easier to use, computer intelligence will be incorporated into more aspects of daily life. Computers and related information technologies will increasingly blend data, images, and sound, sending them coursing through vast networks that can process all of them with equal ease. We can see how this is possible through the use of interactive multimedia, superchips, microminiaturization, and social interfaces.

Interactive Multimedia

multimedia Technologies that facilitate the integration of two or more types of media such as text, graphics, sound, voice, full-motion video, or animation into a computer-based application.

Multimedia is defined as the technologies that facilitate the integration of two or more types of media, such as text, graphics, sound, voice, full-motion video, still video, or animation, into a computer-based application. Multimedia is becoming the foundation of new consumer products and services, such as electronic books and newspapers, electronic classroom-presentation technologies, full-motion video conferencing, imaging, graphics design tools, and video and voice mail. Many Web sites use multimedia.

A simple multimedia system consists of a personal computer with a 32-bit microprocessor, a high-resolution color monitor, a high-capacity hard disk drive, and a CD-ROM disk drive. (A 5-inch optical disk holding more than 600 megabytes of information can store an hour of music, several thousand full-color pictures, several minutes of video or animation, and millions of words.) Stereo speakers are useful for amplifying audio output.

The most difficult element to incorporate into multimedia information systems has been full-motion video, because so much data must be brought under the digital control of the computer. The massive amounts of data in each video image must be digitally encoded, stored, and manipulated electronically, using techniques that compress the digital data. Special adapter cards are used to digitize sound and video.

The possibilities of this technology are endless, but multimedia seems especially well-suited for training and presentations. For training, multimedia is appealing because it is interactive and permits two-way communication. People can use multimedia training sessions any time of the day, at their own pace (Hardaway and Will, 1997). Instructors can easily integrate words, sounds, pictures, and both live and animated video to produce lessons that capture students' imaginations. For example, Duracell, the $2.6 billion battery manufacturer, used an interactive multimedia program to teach new employees at its Chinese manufacturing facility how to use

Table 6.4　Examples of Multimedia Web Sites

Web Site	Description
TerraQuest	Provides interactive tours of exotic destinations including maps, film clips, photos, and on-line discussions.
FedNet	Tracks congressional activities with live and archived floor debates and proceedings.
Newsworld Online	Provides news from Canada, including live video, 24 hours a day.
Moviefone	Provides sneak previews of movies in several formats and the ability to order tickets on-line.

battery-making machinery. Workers can use computer simulations to "stop," "start," and control equipment (Kay, 1997).

Interactive Web pages replete with graphics, sound, animations, and full-motion video have made multimedia popular on the Internet. For example, visitors to the CNN Interactive Web site can access news stories from CNN, photos, on-air transcripts, video clips, and audio clips. The video and audio clips are made available using **streaming technology,** which allows audio and video data to be processed as a steady and continuous stream as they are downloaded from the Web. (RealAudio and RealVideo are widely used streaming technology products on the Web.) Table 6.4 lists examples of other multimedia Web sites. If Internet transmission capacity and streaming technology continue to improve, Web sites could provide broadcast functions that compete with television along with new two-way interactivity.

Multimedia Web sites are also being used to sell digital products, such as digitized music clips. A compression standard known as **MP3,** also called MPEG3, which stands for Motion Picture Experts Group, audio layer 3, can compress audio files down to one-tenth or one-twelfth of their original size with virtually no loss in quality. Visitors to Web sites such as GoodNoise (www.goodnoise.com) can purchase and then download MP3 music clips over the Internet and play them on their own computers.

streaming technology　Technology for transferring data so that they can be processed as a steady and continuous stream.

MP3 (MPEG3)　Compression standard that can compress audio files for transfer over the Internet with virtually no loss in quality.

Superchips and Fifth-Generation Computers

In addition to improving their design, microprocessors have been made to perform faster by shrinking the distance between transistors. This process gives the electrical current less distance to travel. The narrower the lines forming transistors, the larger the number of transistors that can be squeezed onto a single chip, and the faster these circuits will operate. The Pentium III microprocessor, for example, squeezes more than 9 million transistors on a postage-stamp-size silicon pad. Intel is now working on a 64-bit microprocessor known as the IA64 or the Merced, which contains more than 10 million transistors. It will have a clock speed exceeding 800 megahertz.

Researchers already have created semiconductors with circuits as small as .08 microns. Figure 6-13 shows the number of transistors on some prominent microprocessors and memory chips. Both the number of transistors that can fit economically onto a single silicon chip and the speed of microprocessors are doubling every 18 months. One hundred million transistors could soon conceivably be squeezed onto a single microprocessor. There are physical limits to this approach that soon may be reached, but researchers are experimenting with new materials to increase microprocessor speed.

These advances in microprocessor and hardware technology are leading to evermore powerful and sophisticated computers. Conventional computers are based on the Von Neumann architecture, which processes information serially, one instruction at a time. In the future, more computers will use parallel processing and massively parallel processing to blend voice, images, and huge pools of data from diverse sources, using artificial intelligence and intricate mathematical models.

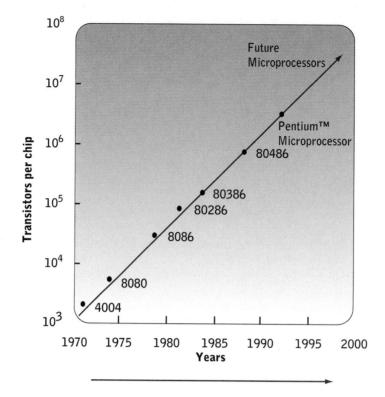

Figure 6-13 The shrinking size and growth in number of transistors.

Massively parallel computers have huge networks of hundreds or even thousands of processor chips interwoven in complex and flexible ways to attack large computing problems. As opposed to parallel processing, where small numbers of powerful but expensive specialized chips are linked together, massively parallel machines chain hundreds or even thousands of inexpensive, commonly used chips to break problems into many small pieces and solve them. For instance, Wal-Mart Stores uses a massively parallel machine to sift through an inventory and sales trend database with 24 trillion bytes of data.

Intel's Merced microprocessor introduces a new style of processing, known as explicitly parallel instruction computing (EPIC), to high-performance computing. An EPIC processor can execute many different instructions at once inside a single processor, using software to sort instructions and decide which ones could be run simultaneously. The Merced is designed to push parallel computing into the mainstream.

New advances in computer memory, input, output, and storage technology will be required to keep pace with these gains in computer processing performance (Messina et al., 1998).

Smart Cards and Microminiaturization

Microprocessor technology has fueled a growing movement toward microminiaturization—the proliferation of computers that are so small, fast, and cheap that they have become ubiquitous. For instance, many of the intelligent features that have made automobiles, stereos, toys, watches, cameras, and other equipment easier to use are based on microprocessors. The future will see even more intelligence built into everyday devices, with mainframe and perhaps even supercomputer-like computing power packed in a pocket- or notebook-size computer. Pen, notebook, and palmtop computers will be as pervasive as handheld calculators.

Microminiaturization is making possible the use of smart cards for many everyday transactions. A **smart card** is a plastic card the size of a credit card that contains a small amount of storage and a tiny microprocessor instead of a magnetic strip. The embedded chip can carry information, such as one's health records, identification data, or telephone numbers, and the cards can serve as "electronic purses" in place of cash. For example, New York City Transit Authority smart cards can be used as alternatives to subway and bus tokens and for paying tolls on highways and bridges. Although smart cards are not as popular in the United States as in Europe, they are very versatile and their uses are growing.

Social Interfaces

Potentially, computer technology could become so powerful and integrated into daily experiences that it would appear essentially invisible to the user (Weiser, 1993). More information and knowledge will be represented visually through graphics (Lieberman, 1996). Social interfaces are being developed that model the interaction between people and computers using familiar human behavior. People increasingly will interact with the computer in more intuitive and effortless ways—through writing, speech, touch, eye movement, and other gestures (Selker, 1996).

Voice-recognition technology is moving closer to natural speech. Until recently, voice recognition only could be used for accepting simple commands. Voice-recognition devices had small vocabularies and could identify individual words. Now continuous-speech voice recognition is possible, using a type of artificial intelligence called natural language processing to identify phrases and sentences. Commercial continuous-speech voice-recognition products have vocabularies large enough for general business use. Continuous-speech recognition with a familiar voice on powerful PCs can be as much as 98 percent accurate today. Within a few years, that level of speech recognition will be available in pocket-size devices (Bulkeley, 1998). Computers increasingly are able to understand what is said to them and to talk back.

Management Wrap-Up

Selection of computer hardware technology for the organization is a key business decision, and it should not be left to technical specialists alone. General managers should understand the capabilities of various computer processing, input, output, and storage options, as well as price/performance relationships. They should be involved in hardware-capacity planning and decisions to distribute computing, downsize, or use network computers.

Management

Computer hardware technology can either enhance or impede organization performance. Selection of appropriate computer hardware technology should consider how well the technology meshes with the culture and structure of the organization, as well as its information-processing requirements.

Organization

Information technology today is not limited to computers but must be viewed as an array of digital devices networked together. Organizations have many computer processing options to choose from, including mainframes, workstations, PCs, and network computers and many different ways of configuring hardware components to create systems.

Technology

For Discussion

1. What factors would you consider in deciding whether to switch from centralized processing on a mainframe to client/server processing?

2. A firm would like to introduce computers into its order entry process but feels that it should wait for a new generation of machines to be developed. After all, any machine bought now will be quickly out of date and less expensive a few years from now. Do you agree? Why or why not?

Summary

1. Identify the hardware components in a typical computer system. The modern computer system has six major components: a central processing unit (CPU), primary storage, input devices, output devices, secondary storage, and communications devices.

2. Describe how information is represented and processed in a computer system. Digital computers store and process information in the form of binary digits called bits. A string of eight bits is called a byte. There are several coding schemes for arranging binary digits into characters. The most common are EBCDIC and ASCII. The CPU is the center of the computer, where the manipulation of symbols, numbers, and letters occurs. The CPU has two components: an arithmetic-logic unit and a control unit. The arithmetic-logic unit performs arithmetic and logical operations on data, while the control unit controls and coordinates the other components of the computer.

The CPU is closely tied to primary memory, or primary storage, which stores data and program instructions temporarily before and after processing. Several different kinds of semiconductor memory chips are used with primary storage: RAM (random access memory) is used for short-term storage of data and program instructions; whereas ROM (read-only memory) permanently stores important program instructions. Other memory devices include PROM (programmable read-only memory) and EPROM (erasable programmable read-only memory).

3. Contrast the capabilities of mainframes, minicomputers, PCs, workstations, and supercomputers. Depending on their size and processing power, computers are categorized as mainframes, minicomputers, PCs, workstations, or supercomputers. Mainframes are the largest computers; minicomputers are mid-range machines; PCs are desktop or laptop machines; workstations are desktop machines with powerful mathematical and graphic capabilities; and supercomputers are sophisticated, powerful computers that can perform massive and complex computations because they use parallel processing. The capabilities of microprocessors used in these computers can be gauged by their word length, data bus width, and cycle speed. Because of continuing advances in microprocessor technology, the distinctions between these types of computers are constantly changing. PCs are now powerful enough to perform much of the work that was formerly limited to mainframes and minicomputers.

4. Compare different arrangements of computer processing, including the use of client/server computing and network computers. Computers can be networked together to distribute processing among different machines. In the client/server model of computing, computer processing is split between "clients" and "servers" connected via a network. Each function of an application is assigned to the machine best suited to perform that function. The exact division of tasks between client and server depends on the application.

Network computers are pared-down desktop machines with minimal or no local storage and processing capacity. They obtain most or all of their software and data from a central network server. Network computers help organizations maintain central control over computing. If managed properly, both network computers and client/server computing can reduce the total cost of ownership (TCO) of information technology resources.

5. Describe the principal media for storing data and programs in a computer system. The principal forms of secondary storage are magnetic tape, magnetic disk, and optical disk. Tape stores records in sequence and only can be used in batch processing. Disk permits direct access to specific records and is much faster than tape. Disk technology is used in on-line processing. Optical disks can store vast amounts of data compactly. CD-ROM disk systems can only be read from, but rewritable optical disk systems are becoming available.

6. Compare the major input and output devices and approaches to input and processing. The principal input devices are keyboards, computer mice, touch screens, magnetic ink and optical character recognition, pen-based instruments, digital scanners, sensors, and voice input. The principal output devices are video display terminals, printers, plotters, voice output devices, and microfilm and microfiche. In batch processing, transactions are accumulated and stored in a group until the time when it is efficient or necessary to process them. In on-line processing, the user enters transactions into a device that is directly connected to the computer system. The transactions are usually processed immediately.

7. Describe multimedia and future information technology trends. Multimedia integrates two or more types of media, such as text, graphics, sound, voice, full-motion video, still video, and/or animation into a computer-based application. The future will see faster chips that can package large amounts of computing power in very small spaces. Microminiaturization will embed intelligence in more everyday devices, including smart cards. Computers using massively parallel processing will be utilized more widely, and computers and related information technologies will be able to blend data, images, and sound. Social interfaces will make using computers more intuitive and natural.

Key Terms

Arithmetic-logic unit (ALU), 168

ASCII (American Standard Code for Information Interchange), 164

Bar code, 181

Batch processing, 182

Bit, 163

Bit mapping, 182

Byte, 163

Cathode ray tube (CRT), 182

CD-R (compact disk-recordable), 179

CD-ROM (compact disk read-only memory), 178

Central processing unit (CPU), 166

Centralized processing, 173

Client, 173

Client/server computing, 173

Computer mouse, 180

Control unit, 168

Cylinder, 175

Data bus width, 172

Digital scanner, 182

Digital video disk (DVD), 179

Direct access storage device (DASD), 177

Distributed processing, 173

Downsizing, 173

EBCDIC (Extended Binary Coded Decimal Interchange Code), 164

EPROM (erasable programmable read-only memory), 168

Floppy disk, 176

Gigabyte, 165

Hard disk, 175

Kilobyte, 165

Machine cycle, 168

Magnetic disk, 175

Magnetic ink character recognition (MICR), 181

Magnetic tape, 179

Mainframe, 168

Massively parallel computers, 186

Master file, 182

Megabyte, 165

Megahertz, 172

Microprocessor, 166

Microsecond, 164

Minicomputer, 168

MMX, 172

MP3, 185

Multimedia, 184

Nanosecond, 165

Network computer (NC), 174

On-line processing, 182

Optical character recognition (OCR), 181

Parallel processing, 170

Pen-based input, 181

Personal computer (PC), 168

Pixel, 164

Primary storage, 166

Printer, 183

Plotter, 183

PROM (programmable read-only memory), 168

RAM (random access memory), 166

RAID (Redundant Array of Inexpensive Disks), 176

Reduced instruction set computing (RISC), 172

Register, 168

ROM (read-only memory), 168

Secondary storage, 175

Sector, 177

Semiconductor, 168

Sensors, 182

Server, 173

Server computer, 169

Smart card, 186

Source data automation, 180

Streaming technology, 185

Supercomputer, 169

Terabyte, 165

Total cost of ownership (TCO), 174

Touch screen, 180

Track, 175

Transaction file, 182

Voice input device, 182

Voice output device, 183

Word length, 171

Workstation, 169

WORM (write once/read many), 179

Review Questions

1. What are the components of a contemporary computer system?

2. Distinguish between a bit and a byte.

3. What are ASCII and EBCDIC, and why are they used?

4. Name and define the principal measures of computer time and storage capacity.

5. Describe the major generations of computers and the characteristics of each.

6. Name the major components of the CPU and the function of each.

7. Describe how information is stored in primary memory.

8. What are the four different types of semiconductor memory, and when are they used?

9. What is the difference between a mainframe, a minicomputer, and a PC? Between a PC and a workstation?

10. Name and describe the factors affecting the speed and performance of a microprocessor.

11. What are downsizing and client/server processing?

12. What is a network computer? How does it differ from a conventional PC?

13. List the most important secondary storage media. What are the strengths and limitations of each?

14. List and describe the major input devices.

15. What is the difference between batch and on-line processing? Diagram the difference.

16. List and describe the major output devices.

17. What is multimedia? What technologies are involved?

18. Distinguish between serial, parallel, and massively parallel processing.

Group Project

It has been predicted that notebook computers will become available that have 10 times the power of a current personal computer, with a touch-sensitive color screen that one can write on or draw on with a stylus or type on when a program displays a keyboard. Each will have a small, compact, rewritable, removable CD-ROM disk that can store the equivalent of a set of encyclopedias. In addition, the computers will have voice-recognition capabilities, including the ability to record sound and give voice responses to questions. The computers will be able to carry on a dialogue by voice, graphics, typed words, and displayed video graphics. Thus, affordable computers will be about the size of a thick pad of letter paper and just as portable and convenient, but with the intelligence of a computer and the multimedia capabilities of a television set.

Form a group with three or four of your classmates and develop an analysis of the impacts such developments would have on one of these areas: university education, corporate sales and marketing, manufacturing, or management consulting. Explain why you think the impact will or will not occur.

Tools for Interactive Learning

○ Internet

The Internet Connection for this chapter will direct you to a series of Web sites where you can complete an exercise to survey the products and services of major computer hardware vendors and the use of Web sites in the computer hardware industry. You can also use the Interactive Study Guide to test your knowledge of the topics in this chapter and get instant feedback where you need more practice.

○ CD-ROM

If you purchase and use the Multimedia Edition CD-ROM with this chapter, you can complete an interactive exercise testing your knowledge of the machine cycle and view a simulation of a program executing on a computer. You can also find a video clip by Intel showing the evolution of computer hardware, an audio overview of the major themes of this chapter, and bullet text summarizing the key points of the chapter.

Case Study   CheckFree Looks at the Total Cost of Ownership

CheckFree, based in Norcross, Georgia, is a leading provider of electronic commerce services, institutional portfolio management services, and financial application software for 2.4 million consumer subscribers, 1000 businesses, and 850 financial institutions, including the 500 largest banks in the United States. CheckFree processes 70 percent of all electronic consumer bill payments. Although the company is a leader in electronic bill payment, growing at an annual rate of 40 percent, it has competitors in all of its major markets.

In 1996 and early 1997, CheckFree made a series of acquisitions designed to expand its range of convenient, reliable, and cost-effective electronic commerce and financial services. One acquisition was Servantis Systems Holdings, an experienced provider of financial applications software and services to financial institutions. Another was Security APL, a vendor of portfolio management and software services to institutional investment managers and consumers. The third acquisition was Intuit Services, a vendor of home banking and bill payment services and Quicken personal finance and small business software.

The integration of these acquisitions left CheckFree with three computer centers in Columbus, Ohio; Aurora, Illinois; and Austin, Texas, to manage. Each company had different hardware and software platforms, business processes, and operational infrastructures. Ravi Ganesan, CheckFree's chief technology officer, was assigned to consolidate the three data centers. He had to design a new computing architecture that could expand to support a potential market of 50 million consumers who might one day use CheckFree's banking and bill paying service.

The project to consolidate the computer centers was called the Genesis Systems Integration Project. CheckFree's original plan called for a multitiered client/server architecture with distributed servers. But by examining the total cost of ownership (TCO), Ganesan found that this distributed architecture would have cost twice as much over time as the company's current centralized mainframe environment.

To calculate CheckFree's TCO, Ganesan looked at the cost of acquisition, lifetime support costs, and the cost of downtime. The acquisition of new computer hardware only represents 20 percent of TCO, whereas labor costs now account for more than 70 percent. Ten or fifteen years ago, most of the total cost of ownership was computer hardware costs.

When calculating TCO, Ganesan looked carefully at the question of value. He didn't just want to minimize costs but to determine the TCO for a particular level of quality of service from information systems. Ganesan was concerned with service because he was expected to provide electronic bill payment services that had the same high level of quality as other service industry firms. Computer downtime, when the system was not operational, of more than 7 minutes per 1 million minutes was unacceptable. Creating a client/server system with the UNIX operating system (see Chapter 7) that could provide this level of reliability would escalate costs. Ganesan estimated that a distributed computing environment would have cost 100 percent more in extra support and downtime than a centralized architecture.

According to the Gartner Group, the Stamford, Connecticut, consulting firm, a large portion of the total cost of ownership comes from "hidden" costs. For example, one of Gartner's clients spent $6 million per year for hardware and software, $3 million per year for information technology management, $3 million per year for support, and several million dollars per year for infrastructure development and communications. The firm also spent an additional $9 million in hidden "end-user" costs, as users wasted time trying to figure out how to solve their desktop computer problems without consulting the company technical support staff. Another $5.5 million in productivity was lost due to system downtime.

Ganesan opted instead to build a leading-edge centralized mainframe computer center called Ecenter in Norcross because he felt it would provide CheckFree with a lower TCO and higher rate of availability than a distributed architecture. Ecenter uses three IBM CMOS mainframes connected to 12 HP UNIX servers and 50 low-end Sun Microsystems UNIX workstations linked by a high-capacity network. Data storage uses EMC's Intelligent Storage Architecture.

About 500 Hewlett Packard Pentium PCs link into this computer center. All the PCs have a standard configuration, which cannot be changed by users, in order to save time and resources required to support desktop systems. If desktop PCs experience problems, they can be fixed within 20 minutes.

In addition to consolidating computer centers, Ganesan is achieving economies by making efficient use of processor and storage capacity, removing unnecessary copies of software, data, and tools. The company has automated many system administration, storage, and operational tasks and has replaced its old bill payment application with more state-of-the-art, efficient software.

CheckFree poured millions of dollars into the Genesis project ($18 million in fiscal 1998 alone) and did not expect to see any returns on its investment before fiscal 1999. While Ganesan would not divulge the exact cost, he acknowledged that CheckFree's costs were much higher than 10 percent of revenue, which is standard in the financial services industry. As of September 1998, the project was on schedule and within budget.

According to CheckFree's public financial statements, its costs of processing, service, and support dropped from 58.2 percent of total revenue to 55.6 percent of total revenue between June 1997 and June 1998 (compared to 66.8 percent of revenue in the third quarter of 1996). The company attributes its continuing improvement in operating efficiency to economies of scale and to an increase in electronic transaction processing over paper processing. (In June 1998 the company processed 55 percent of payments electronically in its core processing business, compared to 45 percent a year earlier.) CheckFree's upgraded systems helped make this possible.

Although TCO analysis appears to have helped CheckFree, some experts believe it is a flawed metric. Companies that focus only on cost cutting may fail to realize how information technology expenditures can add value, adding to the firm's revenue. (Ganesan at CheckFree did measure costs against the level of service his systems provided.) Moreover, calculating costs per user to compare against benchmarks for a particular industry or system architecture can be misleading because each organization has unique problems and system needs.

Sources: Martha Brannigan, "Bill Payments Via the Internet Get a Big Boost," **The Wall Street Journal,** January 28, 1999; Debra O'Donnell, "TCO," **Software Magazine,** August, 1998; Lauren Gibbons Paul, "What Price Ownership?" **Datamation,** December/January, 1998; and CheckFree Holdings Corporation, "Form 10-K" **Annual Report for the Year Ended June 30, 1998.**

CASE STUDY QUESTIONS

1. How was CheckFree's use of computer hardware related to its business strategy?

2. How compatible was the company's choice of hardware with its business strategy?

3. Was total cost of ownership (TCO) a good method for CheckFree to use for evaluating its computer hardware resources? Why or why not?

4. What management, organization, and technology issues should be considered when selecting computer hardware?

Information Systems Software

After completing this chapter, you will be able to:

1. Describe the major types of software.

2. Examine the functions of system software and compare leading PC operating systems.

3. Explain how software has evolved and how it will continue to develop.

4. Analyze the strengths and limitations of the major application programming languages and software tools.

5. Describe new approaches to software development.

6. Identify important issues in the management of organizational software assets.

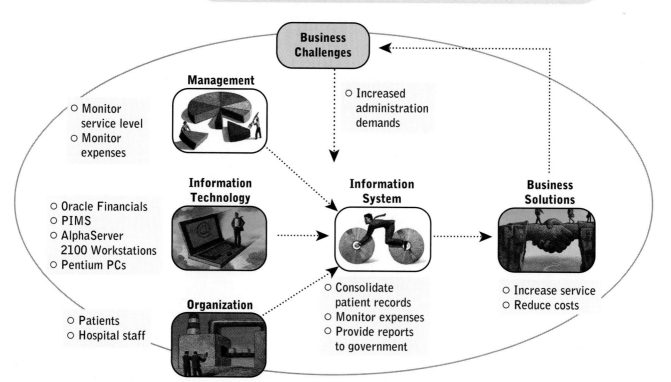

Business Challenges

Management
- Monitor service level
- Monitor expenses

○ Increased administration demands

Information Technology
- Oracle Financials
- PIMS
- AlphaServer 2100 Workstations
- Pentium PCs

Information System
- Consolidate patient records
- Monitor expenses
- Provide reports to government

Business Solutions
- Increase service
- Reduce costs

Organization
- Patients
- Hospital staff

Software Helps Norway's National Hospital Deliver Better Care

Rikshospitalet in Oslo, Norway, is the national hospital and a leading research and teaching institution, but it is also responsible for providing patient care to the local population and to people from other areas requiring specialized care. In 1995, Rikshospitalet merged with two smaller hospitals, leaving it with multiple information systems to coordinate along with a new 600-bed facility. The hospital found it needed new software applications to meet its new hospital administration demands.

Instead of writing most of the software on its own, the hospital opted to purchase commercial off-the-shelf software packages whenever appropriate. It selected Oracle Financials and the Patient Information Management

System (PIMS) from the Oracle Corporation. The system runs on Digital AlphaServer 2100 workstations linked to Pentium PCs.

The new PIMS system creates a hospital-wide repository of patient information to replace various sets of patient records that were kept by each hospital department. It contains 95 percent of the hospital's patient administration data and can be accessed by up to 300 users with PCs around the hospital at the same time. In the old system, there was no comprehensive source of patient information. A patient could be treated in several departments, and each department would have no way of knowing that there were records on that patient maintained by other departments. The practice of maintaining medical records in fragmented files scattered in many different locations is commonplace in hospitals throughout the world; Rikshospitalet was no exception.

Some of the data in the PIMS is used by the Oracle Financials software, which provides complete accounting, budgeting, purchasing, and reporting functions. Rikshospitalet staff can use this software to carefully monitor expenses and meet the Norwegian government's cash-based reporting requirements.

Sources: Cabell Breckinridge, "Rikshospitalet: Norway's National Hospital Delivers Healthy System," *Oracle Magazine*, March/April 1998; and "Quintiles Seeks Mother Lode in Health 'Data Mining,'" *The Wall Street Journal*, March 2, 1999.

chapter outline

Rikshospitalet's software was inadequate to meet its new hospital administration demands. To find the software it needed, the hospital had to know the capabilities of various types of software, and it had to select software that could consolidate patient information and improve financial management. Selecting and developing the right software can improve organizational performance, but it raises the following management challenges:

1. **Increasing complexity and software errors.** Although some software for desktop systems and for some Internet applications can be rapidly generated, a great deal of what software will be asked to do remains far-reaching and sophisticated, requiring programs that are large and complex. Citibank's automatic teller machine application required 780,000 lines of program code, written by hundreds of people, each working on small portions of the program. Large and complex systems tend to be error-prone, with software errors or "bugs" that may not be revealed for years until after exhaustive testing and actual use. Researchers do not know if the number of bugs grows exponentially or proportionately to the number of lines of code, nor can they tell for certain whether all segments of a complex piece of software will always work in total harmony. The process of designing and testing software that is reliable and "bug-free" is a serious quality control and management problem (see Chapter 16).

2. **The application backlog.** Advances in computer software have not kept pace with the breathtaking productivity gains in computer hardware. Developing software has become a major preoccupation for organizations. A great deal of software must be intricately crafted. Moreover, the software itself is only one component of a complete information system that must be carefully designed and coordinated with other people, as well as with organizational and hardware components. Managerial, procedural, and policy issues must be carefully researched and evaluated apart from the actual coding. The "software crisis" is actually part of a larger systems analysis, design, and implementation issue, which will be treated in detail later. Despite the gains from fourth-generation languages, personal desktop software tools, object-oriented programming, and software tools for the World Wide Web, many businesses continue to face a backlog of two to three years in developing the information systems they need, or they will not be able to develop them at all.

The usefulness of computer hardware depends a great deal on available software and the ability of management to evaluate, monitor, and control the utilization of software in the organization. This chapter shows how software turns computer hardware into useful information systems, describes major software types, and presents new approaches to software development. It also introduces some key issues for managing software as an organizational asset.

7.1 What Is Software?

Software is the detailed instructions that control the operation of a computer system. Without software, computer hardware could not perform the tasks we associate with computers. The functions of software are to (1) manage the computer resources of the organization, (2) provide tools for human beings to take advantage of these resources, and (3) act as an

software The detailed instructions that control the operation of a computer system.

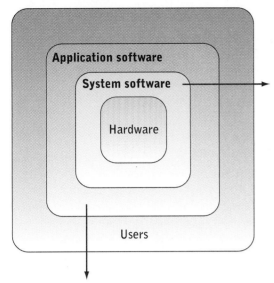

SYSTEM SOFTWARE

Operating System

Schedules computer events
Allocates computer resources
Monitors events

Language Translators

Interpreters
Compilers

Utility Programs

Routine operations (e.g., sort, list, print)
Manage data (e.g., create files, merge files)

APPLICATION SOFTWARE
Programming languages
Assembly language
FORTRAN
COBOL
BASIC
PASCAL
C
"Fourth-generation" languages and PC software tools

Figure 7-1 The major types of software. The relationship between the system software, application software, and users can be illustrated by a series of nested boxes. System software—consisting of operating systems, language translators, and utility programs—controls access to the hardware. Application software, such as the programming languages and "fourth-generation" languages, must work through the system software to operate. The user interacts primarily with the application software.

intermediary between organizations and stored information. Selecting appropriate software for the organization is a key management decision.

Software Programs

A software **program** is a of statements or instructions to the computer. The process of writing or coding programs is termed *programming,* and individuals who specialize in this task are called *programmers.*

The **stored program concept** means that a program must be stored in the computer's primary storage along with the required data in order to execute, or have its instructions performed by the computer. Once a program has finished executing, the computer hardware can be used for another task when a new program is loaded into memory.

Major Types of Software

There are two major types of software: system software and application software. Each kind performs a different function. **System software** is a set of generalized programs that manage the resources of the computer, such as the central processor, communications links, and peripheral devices. Programmers who write system software are called *system programmers.*

Application software describes the programs that are written for or by users to apply the computer to a specific task. Software for processing an order or generating a mailing list is application software. Programmers who write application software are called *application programmers.*

The types of software are interrelated and can be thought of as a set of nested boxes, each of which must interact closely with the other boxes surrounding it. Figure 7-1 illustrates this relationship. The system software surrounds and controls access to the hardware. Application software must work through the system software in order to operate. End users work primarily with application software. Each type of software must be specially designed to a specific machine to ensure its compatibility.

program A series of statements or instructions to the computer.

stored program concept The idea that a program cannot be executed unless it is stored in a computer's primary storage along with required data.

system software Generalized programs that manage the resources of the computer, such as the central processor, communications links, and peripheral devices.

application software Programs written for a specific application to perform functions specified by end users.

7.2 System Software

System software coordinates the various parts of the computer system and mediates between application software and computer hardware. The system software that manages and controls the activities of the computer is called the **operating system.** Other system software consists of computer language translation programs that convert programming languages into machine language and utility programs that perform common processing tasks.

Functions of the Operating System

One way to look at the operating system is as the system's chief manager. Operating system software decides which computer resources will be used, which programs will be run, and the order in which activities will take place.

An operating system performs three functions. It allocates and assigns system resources; it schedules the use of computer resources and computer jobs; and it monitors computer system activities.

Allocation and Assignment

The operating system allocates resources to the application jobs in the execution queue. It provides locations in primary memory for data and programs and controls the input and output devices such as printers, terminals, and telecommunication links.

Scheduling

Thousands of pieces of work can be going on in a computer simultaneously. The operating system decides when to schedule the jobs that have been submitted and when to coordinate the scheduling in various areas of the computer so that different parts of different jobs can be worked on at the same time. For instance, while a program is executing, the operating system is scheduling the use of input and output devices. Not all jobs are performed in the order they are submitted; the operating system must schedule these jobs according to organizational priorities. On-line order processing may have priority over a job to generate mailing lists and labels.

Monitoring

The operating system monitors the activities of the computer system. It keeps track of each computer job and may also keep track of who is using the system, of what programs have been run, and of any unauthorized attempts to access the system. Information system security is discussed in detail in Chapter 16.

Multiprogramming, Virtual Storage, Time Sharing, and Multiprocessing

How is it possible for 1000 or more users sitting at remote terminals to use a computer information system simultaneously if, as we stated in the previous chapter, most computers can execute only one instruction from one program at a time? How can computers run thousands of programs? The answer is that the computer has a series of specialized operating system capabilities.

Multiprogramming

The most important operating system capability for sharing computer resources is **multiprogramming.** Multiprogramming permits multiple programs to share a computer system's resources at any one time through concurrent use of a CPU. By concurrent use, we mean that only one program is actually using the CPU at any given moment but that the input/output needs of other programs can be serviced at the same time. Two or more programs are active at the same time, but they do not use the same computer resources simultaneously. With multiprogramming, a group of programs takes turns using the processor.

Figure 7-2 shows how three programs in a multiprogramming environment can be stored in primary storage. The first program executes until an input/output event is read in the pro-

operating system The system software that manages and controls the activities of the computer.

multiprogramming A method of executing two or more programs concurrently using the same computer. The CPU executes only one program but can service the input/output needs of others at the same time.

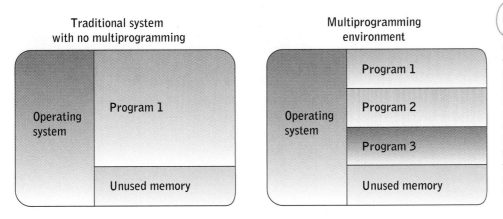

Traditional system with no multiprogramming

| Operating system | Program 1 |
| | Unused memory |

Multiprogramming environment

Operating system	Program 1
	Program 2
	Program 3
	Unused memory

Figure 7-2 Single-program execution versus multiprogramming. In multiprogramming, the computer can be used much more efficiently because a number of programs can be executing concurrently. Several complete programs are loaded into memory. This memory management aspect of the operating system greatly increases throughput by better management of high-speed memory and input/output devices.

gram. The operating system then directs a channel (a small processor limited to input and output functions) to read the input and move the output to an output device. The CPU moves to the second program until an input/output statement occurs. At this point, the CPU switches to the execution of the third program, and so forth, until eventually all three programs have been executed. In this manner, many different programs can be executing at the same time, although different resources within the CPU are actually being utilized.

The first operating systems executed only one program at a time. Before multiprogramming, when a program read data off a tape or disk or wrote data to a printer, the entire CPU came to a stop. This was a very inefficient way to use the computer. With multiprogramming, the CPU utilization rate is much higher.

Multitasking

Multitasking refers to multiprogramming on single-user operating systems such as those in older personal computers. One person can run two or more programs or program tasks concurrently on a single computer. For example, a sales representative could write a letter to prospective clients with a word processing program while simultaneously using a database program to search for all sales contracts in a particular city or geographic area. Instead of terminating the session with the word processing program, returning to the operating system, and then initiating a session with the database program, multitasking allows the sales representative to display both programs on the computer screen and work with them at the same time.

multitasking The multiprogramming capability of primarily single-user operating systems, such as those for older PCs.

Virtual Storage

Virtual storage handles programs more efficiently because the computer divides the programs into small fixed- or variable-length portions, storing only a small portion of the program in primary memory at one time. If only two or three large programs can be read into memory, a certain part of main memory generally remains underutilized because the programs add up to less than the total amount of primary storage space available. Given the limited size of primary memory, only a small number of programs can reside in primary storage at any given time.

Only a few statements of a program actually execute at any given moment. Virtual storage breaks a program into a number of fixed-length portions called **pages** or into variable-length portions called *segments*. Each of these portions is relatively small (a page is approximately 2 to 4 kilobytes). This permits a very large number of programs to reside in primary memory, inasmuch as only one page of each program is actually located there (see Figure 7-3).

All other program pages are stored on a peripheral disk unit until they are ready for execution. Virtual storage provides a number of advantages. First, the central processor is utilized more fully. Many more programs can be in primary storage because only one page of each program actually resides there. Second, programmers no longer have to worry about the size of the primary storage area. With virtual storage, programs can be of infinite length and small machines can execute a program of any size (admittedly, small machines will take longer than big machines to execute a large program).

virtual storage A way of handling programs more efficiently by the computer by dividing the programs into small fixed- or variable-length portions with only a small portion stored in primary memory at one time.

page A small fixed-length section of a program, which can be easily stored in primary storage and quickly accessed from secondary storage.

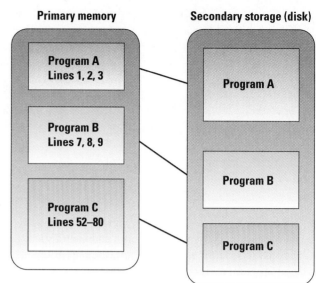

Figure 7-3 Virtual storage. Virtual storage is based on the fact that, in general, only a few statements in a program can actually be utilized at any given moment. In virtual storage, programs are broken down into small sections called pages. Individual program pages are read into memory only when needed. The rest of the program is stored on disk until it is required. In this way, very large programs can be executed by small machines, or a large number of programs can be executed concurrently by a single machine.

Time Sharing

Time sharing is an operating system capability that allows many users to share computer processing resources simultaneously. It differs from multiprogramming in that the CPU spends a fixed amount of time on one program before moving on to another. In a time-sharing environment, thousands of users are each allocated a tiny slice of computer time (2 milliseconds). In this time slot, each user is free to perform any required operations; at the end of this period, another user is given a 2-millisecond time slice of the CPU. This arrangement permits many users to be connected to a CPU simultaneously, with each receiving only a tiny amount of CPU time. But because the CPU is operating at the nanosecond level, a CPU can accomplish a great deal of work in 2 milliseconds.

Multiprocessing

Multiprocessing is an operating system capability that links together two or more CPUs to work in parallel in a single computer system. The operating system can assign multiple CPUs to execute different instructions from the same program or from different programs simultaneously, dividing the work between the CPUs. Whereas multiprogramming uses concurrent processing with one CPU, multiprocessing uses simultaneous processing with multiple CPUs.

Language Translation and Utility Software

When computers execute programs written in languages such as COBOL, FORTRAN, or C, the computer must convert these human-readable instructions into a form it can understand. System software includes special language translator programs that translate high-level language programs written in programming languages such as BASIC, COBOL, and FORTRAN into machine language that the computer can execute. This type of system software is called a *compiler* or *interpreter.* The program in the high-level language before translation into machine language is called **source code.** A **compiler** translates source code into machine code called **object code.** Just before execution by the computer, the object code modules are joined with other object code modules in a process called *linkage editing.* The resulting load module is what is actually executed by the computer. Figure 7-4 illustrates the language translation process.

Some programming languages such as BASIC do not use a compiler but an **interpreter,** which translates each source code statement one at a time into machine code and executes it. Interpreter languages such as BASIC provide immediate feedback to the programmer if a mistake is made, but they are very slow to execute because they are translated one statement at a time.

---

time sharing The sharing of computer resources by many users simultaneously by having the CPU spend a fixed amount of time on each user's program before proceeding to the next.

multiprocessing An operating system feature for executing two or more instructions simultaneously in a single computer system by using multiple central processing units.

source code Program instructions written in a high-level language that must be translated into machine language to be executed by the computer.

compiler Special system software that translates a high-level language into machine language for execution by the computer.

object code Program instructions that have been translated into machine language so that they can be executed by the computer.

interpreter A special translator of source code into machine code that translates each source code statement into machine code and executes them, one at a time.

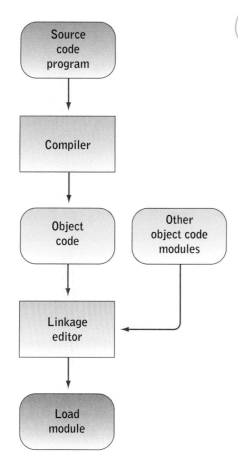

Figure 7-4 The language translation process. The source code, the program in a high-level language, is translated by the compiler into object code so that the instructions can be "understood" by the machine. These are grouped into modules. Prior to execution, the object code modules are joined together by the linkage editor to create the load module. It is the load module that is actually executed by the computer.

An assembler is similar to a compiler, but it is used to translate only assembly language (see Section 7.3) into machine code.

System software includes **utility programs** for routine, repetitive tasks, such as copying, clearing primary storage, computing a square root, or sorting. If you have worked on a computer and have performed such functions as setting up new files, deleting old files, or formatting diskettes, you have worked with utility programs. Utility programs are prewritten programs that are stored so that they can be shared by all users of a computer system and can be used rapidly in many different information system applications when requested.

utility program System software consisting of programs for routine, repetitive tasks, which can be shared by many users.

Graphical User Interfaces

When users interact with a computer, even a PC, the interaction is controlled by an operating system. The user interface is the part of an information system that users interact with. Users communicate with an operating system through the user interface of that operating system. Early PC operating systems were command-driven, but the **graphical user interface,** often called a **GUI,** makes extensive use of icons, buttons, bars, and boxes to perform the same task. It has become the dominant model for the user interface of PC operating systems and for many types of application software.

Older PC operating systems such as DOS, described in the following section, are command-driven, requiring the user to type in text-based commands using a keyboard. For example, to perform a task such as deleting a file named DATAFILE, the user must type in a command such as *DELETE C:\DATAFILE.* Users need to remember these commands and their syntax to work with the computer effectively. An operating system with a graphical user interface uses graphic symbols called *icons* to depict programs, files, and activities. Commands can be activated by rolling a mouse to move a cursor about the screen and clicking a button on the mouse to make selections. Icons are symbolic pictures and they are also used in GUIs to represent programs and files. For example, a file could be deleted by moving the cursor to a

graphical user interface (GUI) The part of an operating system users interact with that uses graphic icons and the computer mouse to issue commands and make selections.

Microsoft's Windows 98 is a powerful operating system with a graphical user interface and capabilities to integrate the user's desktop with the information resources of the Internet.

trash icon. Many graphical user interfaces use a system of pull-down menus to help users select commands and pop-up boxes to help users select among command options. Windowing features allow users to create, stack, size, and move around boxes of information.

Proponents of graphical user interfaces claim that they save learning time because computing novices do not have to learn different arcane commands for each application. Common functions such as getting help, saving files, or printing output are performed the same way. A complex series of commands can be issued simply by linking icons. On the other hand, GUIs may not always simplify complex tasks if the user has to spend too much time first pointing to icons and then selecting operations to perform on those icons (Morse and Reynolds, 1993). Graphic symbols themselves are not always easy to understand unless the GUI is well designed. Existing GUIs are modeled after an office desktop, with files, documents, and actions based on typical office behavior, making them less useful for nonoffice applications in control rooms or processing plants (Mandelkern, 1993). Users may be more productive if the interface is less generic and more customized to specific tasks (Satzinger and Olfman, 1998).

PC Operating Systems

Like any other software, PC software is based on specific operating systems and computer hardware. A software package written for one PC operating system generally cannot run on another. Table 7.1 compares the leading PC operating systems: Windows 98 and Windows 95, Windows NT, Windows CE, OS/2, UNIX, Linux, the Macintosh operating system, and DOS.

DOS was the most popular operating system for 16-bit PCs. It is used today with older PCs based on the IBM PC standard because so much available application software was written for systems using DOS. (PC-DOS is used exclusively with IBM PCs. MS-DOS, developed by Microsoft, is used with other 16-bit PCs that function like the IBM PC.) DOS itself does not support multitasking and limits the size of a program in memory to 640 K.

DOS is command-driven, but it can present a graphical user interface by using Microsoft **Windows,** a highly popular graphical user interface shell that runs in conjunction with the DOS operating system. Windows supports limited forms of multitasking and networking but shares the memory limitations of DOS. Early versions of Windows had some problems with application crashes when multiple programs competed for the same memory space.

Microsoft's **Windows 98** and **Windows 95** are genuine 32-bit operating systems. A 32-bit operating system can run faster than DOS, which could only address data in 16-bit chunks, because it can address data in 32-bit chunks. Both Windows 98 and Windows 95 provide a streamlined graphical user interface that arranges icons to provide instant access

DOS Operating system for 16-bit PCs based on the IBM personal computer standard.

Windows A graphical user interface shell that runs in conjunction with the DOS PC operating system. Supports multitasking and some forms of networking.

Windows 98 Version of the Windows operating system that is more closely integrated with the Internet and that supports hardware technologies such as MMX, digital video disk, videoconferencing cameras, scanners, TV tuner-adapter cards, and joysticks.

Windows 95 A 32-bit operating system with a streamlined graphical user interface and multitasking, multithreading, and networking capabilities.

Table 7.1 Leading PC Operating Systems

Operating System	Features
Windows 98 and Windows 95	32-bit operating system with a streamlined graphical user interface. Has multitasking and powerful networking capabilities and can be integrated with the information resources of the Web.
Windows NT (Windows 2000)	32-bit operating system for PCs, workstations, and network servers not limited to Intel microprocessors. Supports multitasking, multiprocessing, intensive networking.
Windows CE	Pared-down version of the Windows operating system for handheld computers and wireless communication devices.
OS/2	Operating system for IBM PCs that can take advantage of the 32-bit microprocessor. Supports multitasking and networking.
UNIX	Used for powerful PCs, workstations, and minicomputers. Supports multitasking, multi-user processing, and networking. Is portable to different models of computer hardware.
Linux	Free, reliable alternative to UNIX and Windows NT that runs on many different types of computer hardware and provides source code that can be modified by software developers.
Mac OS	Operating system for the Macintosh computer. Supports networking and multitasking and has powerful multimedia capabilities. Supports connecting to and publishing on the Internet.
DOS	Operating system for IBM (PC-DOS) and IBM-compatible (MS-DOS) PCs. Limits program use of memory to 640 K.

to common tasks. They can support software written for DOS but can also run programs that take up more than 640 K of memory. Windows 98 and 95 feature multitasking, multithreading (the ability to manage multiple independent tasks simultaneously), and powerful networking capabilities, including the capability to integrate fax, e-mail, and scheduling programs.

Windows 98 is faster and more integrated with the Internet than Windows 95; it includes support for new hardware technologies such as MMX, digital video disk (DVD—see Chapter 6), videoconferencing cameras, scanners, TV tuner-adapter cards, and joysticks. It provides capabilities for optimizing hardware performance and file management on the hard disk and enhanced 3-D graphics. The most visible feature of Windows 98 is the integration of the operating system with Web browser software. Users will be able to work with the traditional Windows interface or use the Web browser interface to display information. The user's hard disk can be viewed as an extension of the World Wide Web so that a document residing on the hard disk or on the Web can be accessed the same way. Small applet programs (see the discussion of Java in Section 7.4) on the Windows desktop can automatically retrieve information from specific Web sites whenever the user logs onto the Internet. These applets can automatically update the desktop with the latest news, stock quotes, or weather. Windows 98 also includes a group collaboration tool called NetMeeting (see Section 7.3) and Front Page Express, a tool for creating and storing Web pages.

Windows NT (for New Technology) is another 32-bit operating system developed by Microsoft with features that make it appropriate for applications in large networked organizations. It is used as an operating system for high-performance workstations and network servers. Windows NT shares the same graphical user interface as the other Windows operating systems, but it has more powerful networking, multitasking, and memory-management capabilities. Windows NT can support existing software written for DOS and Windows, and it can provide mainframe-like computing power for new applications with massive memory and file requirements. It can even support multiprocessing with multiple CPUs. Windows NT is not tied to computer hardware based on Intel microprocessors.

There are two versions of Windows NT—a Workstation version for users of standalone or client desktop computers and a Server version designed to run on network servers and provide network management functions. Windows NT Server includes tools for creating and operating Web sites. Microsoft renamed its recent release of Windows NT **Windows 2000.**

Windows NT Powerful operating system developed by Microsoft for use with 32-bit PCs and workstations based on Intel and other microprocessors. Supports networking, multitasking, and multiprocessing.

Windows 2000 Recent release of Windows NT for corporate computing.

Windows CE has some of the capabilities of Windows, including its graphical user interface, but it is designed to run on small handheld computers, personal digital assistants, or wireless communication devices such as pagers and cellular phones. It is a portable and compact operating system requiring very little memory. Non-PC and consumer devices can use this operating system to share information with Windows-based PCs and to connect to the Internet.

OS/2 is a robust 32-bit operating system for powerful IBM or IBM-compatible PCs with Intel microprocessors. OS/2 is used for complex, memory-intensive applications or those that require networking, multitasking, or large programs. OS/2 provides powerful desktop computers with mainframe-operating-system capabilities, such as multitasking and supporting multiple users in networks, and it supports networked multimedia and pen computing applications.

OS/2 supports applications that run under Windows and DOS and has its own graphical user interface. There are now two versions of OS/2. OS/2 Warp is for personal use. It can accept voice-input commands and run Java applications without a Web browser (see Sections 7.3 and 7.4). OS/2 Warp Server has capabilities similar to Windows NT for supporting networking, systems management, and Internet access.

UNIX is an interactive, multi-user, multitasking operating system developed by Bell Laboratories in 1969 to help scientific researchers share data. Many people can use UNIX simultaneously to perform the same kind of task, or one user can run many tasks on UNIX concurrently. UNIX was developed to connect various machines together and is highly supportive of communications and networking. UNIX was designed for minicomputers but now has versions for PCs, workstations, and mainframes. It is often used on workstations and server computers. UNIX can run on many different kinds of computers and can be easily customized. Application programs that run under UNIX can be ported from one computer to run on a different computer with little modification. UNIX also can store and manage a large number of files.

UNIX is considered powerful but very complex, with a legion of commands. Graphical user interfaces have been developed for UNIX. UNIX cannot respond well to problems caused by the overuse of system resources such as jobs or disk space. UNIX also poses some security problems because multiple jobs and users can access the same file simultaneously. Vendors have developed different versions of UNIX that are incompatible, thereby limiting software portability.

Linux is a UNIX-like operating system that runs on Intel, Motorola, Digital Alpha, SPARC, and Mips processors. Linux can be downloaded from the Internet free of charge or purchased for a small fee from companies that provide additional tools for the software. Because it is free, reliable, compactly designed, and capable of running on many different hardware platforms, it has become popular during the past few years among sophisticated computer users and businesses as an alternative to UNIX and Windows NT. Major application software vendors are starting to provide versions that can run on Linux. The source code for Linux is available along with the operating system software, so that it can be modified by software developers to fit their particular needs.

Linux is an example of **open-source software,** which provides all computer users with free access to its source code so that they can modify the code to fix errors or to make improvements. Open-source software such as Linux is not owned by any company or individual. A global network of programmers and users manages and modifies the software, usually without being paid to do so. The Window on Organizations describes how organizations are starting to benefit from this new operating system.

Mac OS, the operating system for the Macintosh computer, features multitasking, powerful multimedia and networking capabilities, and a mouse-driven graphical user interface. New features of this operating system allow users to connect to, explore, and publish on the Internet and World Wide Web; use Java software (see Section 7.4); and load Chinese, Japanese, Korean, Indian, Hebrew, and Arabic fonts for use in Web browser software (see Section 7.3). A new search capability called Sherlock provides a standard interface for efficiently searching for files on the Internet as well as on the user's own hard drive.

Should Businesses Switch to Linux?

Burlington Coat Factory, the $1.8 billion clothing discounter based in Burlington, New Jersey, decided to take the plunge with Linux and is installing this new operating system on 1150 computers in its 250 stores. Why would such a large company opt for a new shareware operating system that can be downloaded free from the Internet?

According to Mike Prince, Burlington's CIO, Linux was attractive both for its price and its performance. It's free and "runs like the wind." Prince also believes Linux is more stable than Windows NT, and will be less costly to support. Burlington is known as a company that has been comfortable embracing new technology, including network computers and Java as well as Linux. The company also has used UNIX for many years and was using Linux on development workstations for about a year before installing it in its stores.

Burlington's previous in-store systems were based on aging technology—Sun Microsystems' SPARC workstations running the SunOS 4.1 operating system. Its client computers for back-office and inventory applications were either radio-frequency handheld scanners or dumb terminals. Burlington's point-of-sale system, which will not change, uses old PCs running MS-DOS. Prince is replacing the dumb terminals with Pentium PCs but hasn't made up his mind about whether to scrap the SPARC workstations entirely or install Linux on them. When Burlington completes its upgrade, the new hardware should cost between $1.15 million and $1.8 million, but the cost of Linux will only be a few hundred dollars. Burlington expects to save thousands of dollars in each store by not buying a commercial operating system.

The low cost, fast performance, and reliability of Linux also made it attractive to Jay Jacobs, Inc., another retailer based in Seattle, which is installing Linux servers in all of its 120 stores. The Linux servers will be tracking purchases by customer as well as by item. Bill Lawrence, the firm's Chief Financial Officer, thinks that Linux will provide fast, UNIX-like performance for less cost than the slower Windows NT environment. By using Linux instead of another operating system, the company is saving $666 per store, amounting to $80,000.

On the other hand, both Burlington and Jay Jacobs are not relying solely on Linux. Jay Jacobs is using the more established UNIX and Windows NT operating systems at its corporate headquarters. Burlington is keeping Windows NT for desktop productivity applications such as Microsoft Excel and Word that aren't available on Linux. Burlington is sticking with UNIX servers from Sequent Computer Systems to house and manipulate its corporate data. Other retailers have primarily selected Windows NT when upgrading the operating systems for their stores.

Until more kinds of applications are developed for Linux, this operating system is being used primarily on specialized departmental servers providing Web, e-mail, or printing services or to run custom applications that only require a simple interface. Retailers such as Burlington, which run very few third-party applications, are in a stronger position to select more obscure software platforms. Businesses are also waiting for computer hardware vendors to provide more services and software so that Linux can run easily on their machines.

Burlington is using Red Hat Software's version of Linux, an inexpensive commercial version available on CD-ROMs that offers technical support. Red Hat's version is the market leader but it represents only one of a number of different versions of Linux that are currently in use. Since Linux has no single owner, the software is updated by a large group of programmers around the globe. Unlike Windows, which is controlled by Microsoft, anyone can find errors and make changes to Linux code, raising the danger that Linux could splinter into many slightly different versions as did UNIX. The Linux Standards Base is working on rules to keep different Linux versions compatible. Different versions of Linux would discourage its widespread adoption in business.

To Think About: Should a company select Linux as its operating system for its major business applications? What management, organization, and technology factors would have to be addressed when making that decision?

Sources: David Orenstein, "Burlington Commits to Linux in 250 Stores," **Computerworld**, February 15, 1999 and "Retailer Bets Big on Linux," **Computerworld**, February 8, 1999; and Alex Lash, "Standardizing Linux," **The Industry Standard**, March 8, 1999.

7.3 Application Software

Application software is primarily concerned with accomplishing the tasks of end users. Many different languages can be used to develop application software. Each has different strengths and drawbacks.

Generations of Programming Languages

To communicate with the first generation of computers, specialized programmers wrote programs in **machine language**—the 0s and 1s of binary code. Programming in 0s and 1s (reducing all statements such as add, subtract, and divide into a series of 0s and 1s) made early programming a slow, labor-intensive process.

machine language A programming language consisting of the 1s and 0s of binary code.

Figure 7-5 Generations of programming languages. As the capabilities of hardware increased, programming languages developed from the first generation of machine and second generation of assembly languages of the 1950s to 1960s, through the third-generation, high-level languages such as FORTRAN and COBOL developed in the 1960s and 1970s, to today's fourth-generation languages and tools.

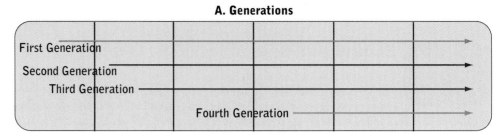

A. Generations

First Generation
Second Generation
Third Generation
Fourth Generation

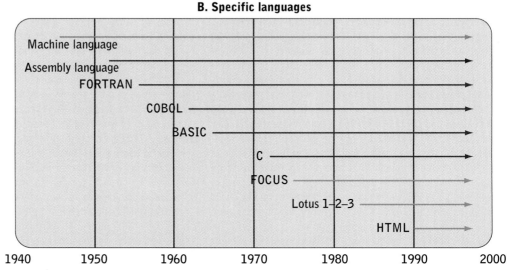

B. Specific languages

Machine language
Assembly language
FORTRAN
COBOL
BASIC
C
FOCUS
Lotus 1–2–3
HTML

1940   1950   1960   1970   1980   1990   2000

As computer hardware improved and processing speed and memory size increased, computer languages changed from machine language to languages that were easier for humans to understand. Generations of programming languages developed to correspond with the generations of computer hardware. Figure 7-5 shows the development of programming languages during the past 50 years as the capabilities of hardware have increased. The major trend is to increase the ease with which users can interact with hardware and software.

Machine language was the first-generation programming language. The second generation of programming languages occurred in the early 1950s with the development of assembly language. Instead of using 0s and 1s, programmers could substitute language-like acronyms and words such as *add, sub* (subtract), and *load* in programming statements. A language translator called a *compiler* converted the English-like statements into machine language.

From the mid-1950s to the mid-1970s, the third generation of programming languages emerged. These languages, such as FORTRAN, COBOL, and BASIC, allowed programs to be written with regular words using sentence-like statements. These languages are called **high-level languages** because each statement generates multiple statements when it is translated into machine language. Programs became easier to create and became more widely used for scientific and business problems.

Beginning in the late 1970s, fourth-generation languages and tools were created. These languages dramatically reduced programming time and made software tasks so easy that many could be performed by nontechnical computer users without the help of professional programmers. Software such as word processing, spreadsheets, data management, and Web browsers became popular productivity tools for end users.

Popular Programming Languages

Most managers need not be expert programmers, but they should understand how to evaluate software applications and be able to select programming languages that are appropriate for their organization's objectives. We will now briefly describe the more popular high-level languages.

high-level language Programming languages in which each source code statement generates multiple statements at the machine-language level.

AR 5, 3

Figure 7-6 Assembly language. This sample assembly language command adds the contents of register 3 to register 5 and stores the result in register 5.

READ (5,100) ID, QUANT, PRICE
TOTAL = QUANT * PRICE

Figure 7-7 FORTRAN. This sample FORTRAN program code is part of a program to compute sales figures for a particular item.

MULTIPLY QUANT-SOLD BY UNIT-PRICE GIVING SALES-TOTAL.

Figure 7-8 COBOL. This sample COBOL program code is part of a routine to compute total sales figures for a particular item.

Assembly Language

Like machine language, **assembly language** (Figure 7-6) is designed for a specific machine and specific microprocessors. Each operation in assembly corresponds to a machine operation. Assembly language makes use of certain mnemonics (e.g., *load, sum*) and assigns addresses and storage locations automatically. Although assembly language gives programmers great control, it is costly in terms of programmer time; it is also difficult to read, debug, and learn. Assembly language is used primarily today in system software.

assembly language A programming language developed in the 1950s that resembles machine language but substitutes mnemonics for numeric codes.

FORTRAN

FORTRAN (FORmula TRANslator) (Figure 7-7) was developed in 1956 to provide an easier way of writing scientific and engineering applications. FORTRAN is especially useful in processing numeric data. Many kinds of business applications can be written in FORTRAN, and contemporary versions provide sophisticated structures for controlling program logic. FORTRAN is not very good at providing input/output efficiency or in printing and working with lists. The syntax is very strict and keying errors are common, making the programs difficult to debug.

FORTRAN (FORmula TRANslator) A programming language developed in 1956 for scientific and mathematical applications.

COBOL

COBOL (COmmon Business Oriented Language) (Figure 7-8) came into use in the early 1960s. It was developed by a committee representing both government and industry. Rear Admiral Grace M. Hopper was a key committee member who played a major role in COBOL development. COBOL was designed with business administration in mind, for processing large data files with alphanumeric characters (mixed alphabetic and numeric data), and for performing repetitive tasks such as payroll. It is poor at complex mathematical calculations. Also, there are many versions of COBOL, and not all are compatible with each other.

COBOL (COmmon Business Oriented Language) Major programming language for business applications because it can process large data files with alphanumeric characters.

BASIC

BASIC (Beginners All-purpose Symbolic Instruction Code) was developed in 1964 by John Kemeny and Thomas Kurtz to teach students at Dartmouth College how to use computers. Today it is a popular programming language on college campuses and for PCs. BASIC can do

BASIC (Beginners All-purpose Symbolic Instruction Code) A general-purpose programming language used with PCs and for teaching programming.

almost all computer processing tasks from inventory to mathematical calculations. It is easy to use, demonstrates computer capabilities well, and requires only a small interpreter. The weakness of BASIC is that it does few tasks well even though it does them all. It has no sophisticated program logic control or data structures, which makes it difficult to use in teaching good programming practices. Different versions of BASIC exist.

Pascal

Named after Blaise Pascal, the seventeenth-century mathematician and philosopher, **Pascal** was developed by the Swiss computer science professor Niklaus Wirth of Zurich in the late 1960s. Pascal programs can be compiled using minimal computer memory, so they can be used on PCs. With sophisticated structures to control program logic and a simple, powerful set of commands, Pascal is used primarily in computer science courses to teach sound programming practices. The language is weak at file handling and input/output and is not easy for beginners to use.

C and C++

C is a powerful and efficient language developed at AT&T's Bell Labs in the early 1970s. It combines machine portability with tight control and efficient use of computer resources, and it can work on a variety of different computers. It is used primarily by professional programmers to create operating system and application software, especially for PCs.

C++ is a newer version of C that is object-oriented (see Section 7.4). It has all the capabilities of C plus additional features for working with software objects. C++ is used for developing application software.

Other Programming Languages

Other important programming languages include Ada, LISP, Prolog, and PL/1.

○ **Ada** was developed in 1980 by the U.S. Defense Department to serve as a standard for all of its applications. Named after Ada, Countess of Lovelace, a nineteenth-century mathematician, it was designed to be executed in diverse hardware environments. Ada is used for both military and nonmilitary applications because it can operate on different brands of computer hardware.

○ **LISP** (designating LISt Processor) and **Prolog** (designating PROgramming LOGic) are used for artificial-intelligence applications. LISP, created in the late 1950s, is oriented toward putting symbols such as operations, variables, and data values into meaningful lists. Prolog was introduced about 1970 and also is well-suited to manipulating symbols. It can run on a wider variety of computers than LISP.

○ **PL/1 (Programming Language 1)** is a powerful general-purpose programming language developed by IBM in 1964. It can comfortably handle both mathematical and business problems, but it has not replaced COBOL or FORTRAN because organizations have already invested so heavily in COBOL and FORTRAN systems.

Fourth-Generation Languages and PC Software Tools

Fourth-generation languages consist of a variety of software tools that enable end users to develop software applications with minimal or no technical assistance or that enhance the productivity of professional programmers. Fourth-generation languages tend to be nonprocedural or less procedural than conventional programming languages. Procedural languages require specification of the sequence of steps, or procedures, that tell the computer what to do and how to do it. Nonprocedural languages need only specify what has to be accomplished rather than provide details about how to carry out the task. Thus, a nonprocedural language can accomplish the same task with fewer steps and lines of program code than a procedural language.

Pascal A programming language used on PCs and used to teach sound programming practices in computer science courses.

C A powerful programming language with tight control and efficiency of execution; is portable across different microprocessors and is used primarily with PCs.

C++ Object-oriented version of the C programming language.

Ada A programming language that is portable across different brands of hardware; is used for both military and nonmilitary applications.

LISP Programming language used for artificial-intelligence applications. Stands for LISt Processor.

Prolog Programming language for artificial-intelligence applications.

PL/1 (Programming Language I) A programming language developed by IBM for both business and scientific applications.

fourth-generation language A programming language that can be employed directly by end users or less-skilled programmers to develop computer applications more rapidly than conventional programming languages.

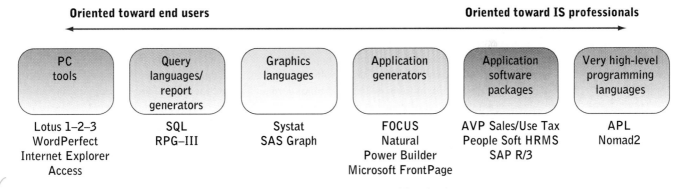

Figure 7-9 Fourth-generation languages. The spectrum of major categories of fourth-generation languages; commercially available products in each category are illustrated. Tools range from those that are simple and designated primarily for end users to complex tools designed for information systems professionals.

There are seven categories of fourth-generation languages: query languages, report generators, graphics languages, application generators, very high-level programming languages, application software packages, and PC tools. Figure 7-9 illustrates the spectrum of these tools and some commercially available products in each category.

Query Languages

Query languages are high-level languages for retrieving data stored in databases or files. They are usually interactive, on-line, and capable of supporting requests for information that are not predefined. They are often tied to database management systems (see Chapter 8) or some of the PC software tools described later in this section. For instance, the query

SELECT ALL WHERE age >40 AND name = "Wilson"

requests all records where the name is "Wilson" and the age is more than 40. Chapter 8 provides more detail on Structured Query Language (SQL), which has become a standard query language.

Available query tools have different kinds of syntax and structure, some being closer to natural language than others (Vassiliou, 1984–85). **Natural language** software allows users to communicate with the computer using conversational commands that resemble human speech. Natural language development is one of the concerns of artificial intelligence (see Chapter 14). Some consider the movement toward natural language as the next generation in software development.

Report Generators

Report generators are facilities for creating customized reports. They extract data from files or databases and create reports in many formats. Report generators generally provide more control over the way data are formatted, organized, and displayed than query languages. The more powerful report generators can manipulate data with complex calculations and logic before they are output. Some report generators are extensions of database or query languages.

Graphics Languages

Graphics languages retrieve data from files or databases and display them in graphic format. Users can ask for data and specify how they are to be charted. Some graphics software can perform arithmetic or logical operations on data as well. SAS and Systat are examples of powerful analytical graphics software.

query language A high-level computer language used to retrieve specific information from databases or files.

natural language Programming language that is very close to human language.

report generator Software that creates customized reports in a wide range of formats that are not routinely produced by an information system.

graphics language A computer language that displays data from files or databases in graphic format.

Application Generators

Application generators contain preprogrammed modules that can generate entire applications, greatly speeding development. A user can specify what needs to be done, and the application generator will create the appropriate code for input, validation, update, processing, and reporting. Most full-function application generators consist of a comprehensive, integrated set of development tools: a database management system, data dictionary, query language, screen painter, graphics generator, report generator, decision support/modeling tools, security facilities, and a high-level programming language. Application generators now include tools for developing full-function Web sites.

Very High-Level Programming Languages

Very high-level programming languages are designed to generate program code with fewer instructions than conventional languages such as COBOL or FORTRAN. Programs and applications based on these languages can be developed in much shorter periods of time. Simple features of these languages can be employed by end users. However, these languages are designed primarily as productivity tools for professional programmers. APL and Nomad2 are examples of these languages.

Application Software Packages

A **software package** is a prewritten, precoded, commercially available set of programs that eliminates the need for individuals or organizations to write their own software programs for certain functions. There are software packages for system software, but the vast majority of package software is application software.

Application software packages consist of prewritten application software that is marketed commercially. These packages are available for major business applications on mainframes, minicomputers, and PCs. Although application packages for large complex systems must be installed by technical specialists, many application packages, especially those for PCs, are marketed directly to end users. Systems development based on application packages is discussed in Chapter 12.

PC Software Tools

Some of the most popular and productivity-promoting software tools are the general-purpose application packages that have been developed for PCs, especially word processing, spreadsheet, data management, presentation graphics, integrated software packages, e-mail, Web browsers, and groupware.

Word processing software. **Word processing software** stores text data electronically as a computer file rather than on paper. The word processing software allows the user to make changes in the document electronically in memory. This eliminates the need to retype an entire page to incorporate corrections. The software has formatting options to make changes in line spacing, margins, character size, and column width. Microsoft Word and WordPerfect are popular word processing packages. Figure 7-10 illustrates a Microsoft Word screen displaying text, spelling and grammar checking, and major menu options.

Most word processing software has advanced features that automate other writing tasks: spelling checkers, style checkers (to analyze grammar and punctuation), thesaurus programs, and mail merge programs, which link letters or other text documents with names and addresses in a mailing list. The newest versions of this software can create and access Web pages.

Spreadsheets. Electronic **spreadsheet** software provides computerized versions of traditional financial modeling tools such as the accountant's columnar pad, pencil, and calculator. An electronic spreadsheet is organized into a grid of columns and rows. The power of the electronic spreadsheet is evident when one changes a value or values because all other related values on the spreadsheet will be automatically recomputed.

Spreadsheets are valuable for applications in which numerous calculations with pieces of data must be related to each other. Spreadsheets also are useful for applications that require

---

application generator Software that can generate entire information system applications; the user needs only to specify what needs to be done, and the application generator creates the appropriate program code.

very high-level programming language A programming language that uses fewer instructions than conventional languages. Used primarily as a professional programmer productivity tool.

software package A prewritten, precoded, commercially available set of programs that eliminates the need to write software programs for certain functions.

word processing software Software that handles electronic storage, editing, formatting, and printing of documents.

spreadsheet Software displaying data in a grid of columns and rows, with the capability of easily recalculating numerical data.

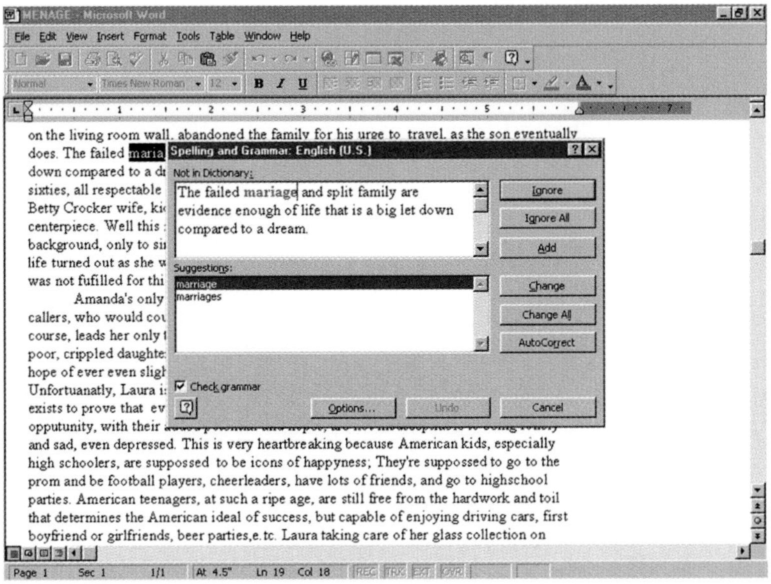

Figure 7-10 Text and the spell-checking option in Microsoft Word. Word processing software provides many easy-to-use options to create and output a text document to meet a user's specifications. **Source:** Courtesy of Microsoft.

modeling and what-if analysis. After the user has constructed a set of mathematical relationships, the spreadsheet can be recalculated instantaneously using a different set of assumptions. A number of alternatives can easily be evaluated by changing one or two pieces of data without having to rekey in the rest of the worksheet. Many spreadsheet packages include graphics functions that can present data in the form of line graphs, bar graphs, or pie charts. The most popular spreadsheet packages are Microsoft Excel and Lotus 1-2-3. The newest versions of this software can read and write Web files.

Figure 7-11 illustrates the output from a spreadsheet for a breakeven analysis and its accompanying graph.

Data management software. Although spreadsheet programs are powerful tools for manipulating quantitative data, **data management software** is more suitable for creating and manipulating lists and for combining information from different files. PC database management packages have programming features and easy-to-learn menus that enable nonspecialists to build small information systems.

Data management software typically has facilities for creating files and databases and for storing, modifying, and manipulating data for reports and queries. A detailed treatment of data management software and database management systems can be found in Chapter 8. Popular database management software for the personal computer includes Microsoft Access, which has been enhanced to publish data on the Web. Figure 7-12 shows a screen from Microsoft Access illustrating some of its capabilities.

Presentation graphics. Presentation graphics software allows users to create professional-quality graphics presentations. This software can convert numeric data into charts and other types of graphics and can include multimedia displays of sound, animation, photos, and video clips. The leading presentation graphics packages include capabilities for computer-generated slide shows and translating content for the Web. Microsoft PowerPoint, Lotus Freelance Graphics, and Aldus Persuasion are popular presentation graphics packages.

Integrated software packages and software suites. Integrated software packages combine the functions of the most important PC software packages, such as word processing, spreadsheets, presentation graphics, and data management. This integration provides a more general-purpose software tool and eliminates redundant data entry and data maintenance. For example, the breakeven analysis spreadsheet illustrated in Figure 7-11 could

data management software Software used for creating and manipulating lists, creating files and databases to store data, and combining information for reports.

presentation graphics Software to create professional-quality graphics presentations that can incorporate charts, sound, animation, photos, and video clips.

integrated software package A software package that provides two or more applications, such as word processing and spreadsheets, providing for easy transfer of data between them.

Figure 7-11 Spreadsheet software. Spreadsheet software organizes data into columns and rows for analysis and manipulation. Contemporary spreadsheet software provides graphing abilities for clear visual representation of the data in the spreadsheets. This sample breakeven analysis is represented as numbers in a spreadsheet as well as a line graph for easy interpretation.

Total fixed cost	19,000.00
Variable cost per unit	3.00
Average sales price	17.00
Contribution margin	14.00
Breakeven point	1,357

Custom Neckties Pro Forma Income Statement

Units sold	0.00	679	1,357	2,036	2,714
Revenue	0	11,536	23,071	34,607	46,143
Fixed cost	19,000	19,000	19,000	19,000	19,000
Variable cost	0	2,036	4,071	6,107	8,143
Total cost	19,000	21,036	23,071	25,107	27,143
Profit/Loss	(19,000)	(9,500)	0	9,500	19,000

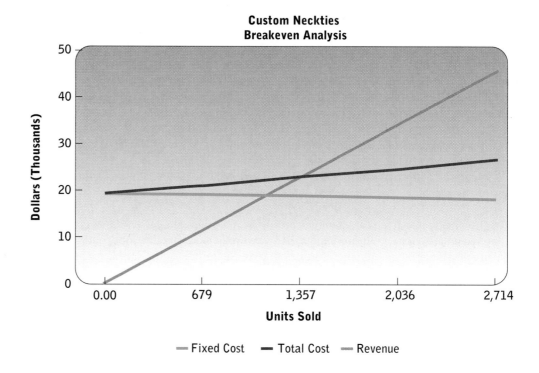

be reformatted into a polished report with word processing software without separately keying the data into both programs. Integrated packages are a compromise. Although they can do many things well, they generally do not have the same power and depth as single-purpose packages.

Integrated software packages should be distinguished from software suites, which are collections of applications software sold as a unit. Microsoft Office is an example. This software suite contains Word word processing software, Excel spreadsheet software, Access database software, PowerPoint presentation graphics software, and Outlook, a set of tools for e-mail, scheduling, and contact management. Office 2000 contains additional capabilities to support collaborative work on the Web, including in-line discussions about documents and the ability to automatically notify others about changes to documents. Documents created with Office tools can be viewed with a Web browser and published on a Web server. Software suites have some features of integrated packages, such as the ability to

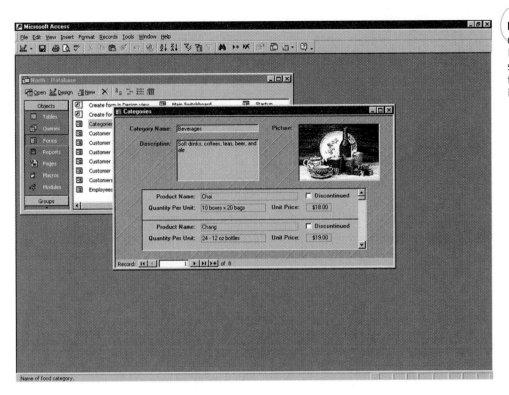

Figure 7-12 Data management software. This screen from Microsoft Access illustrates some of its powerful capabilities for managing and organizing information.

share data among different applications, but they consist of full-featured versions of each type of software.

E-mail software. **Electronic mail (e-mail)** is used for the computer-to-computer exchange of messages and is an important tool for communication and collaborative work. A person can use a networked computer to send notes or lengthier documents to a recipient on the same network or a different network. Many organizations operate their own electronic-mail systems, but communications companies such as MCI and AT&T offer these services, along with commercial on-line information services such as America Online and Prodigy and public networks on the Internet.

electronic mail (e-mail) The computer-to-computer exchange of messages.

Web browsers and the PC software suites have e-mail capabilities, but specialized e-mail software packages such as Eudora are also available for use on the Internet. In addition to providing electronic messaging, many e-mail software packages have capabilities for routing messages to multiple recipients, message forwarding, and attaching text documents or multimedia to messages.

Web browsers. **Web browsers** are easy-to-use software tools for displaying Web pages and for accessing the Web and other Internet resources. Web browser software features a point-and-click graphical user interface that can be employed throughout the Internet to access and display information stored on computers at other Internet sites. Browsers can display or present graphics, audio, and video information as well as traditional text, and they allow you to click on-screen buttons or highlighted words to link to related Web sites. Web browsers have become the primary interface for accessing the Internet or for using networked systems based on Internet technology. You can see examples of Web browser software by looking at the illustrations of Web pages in each chapter of this text.

Web browser An easy-to-use software tool for accessing the World Wide Web and the Internet.

The two leading commercial Web browsers are Microsoft's Internet Explorer and Netscape Navigator, which is also available as part of the Netscape Communicator software suite. They include capabilities for using e-mail, file transfer, on-line discussion groups and bulletin boards, along with other Internet services. Newer versions of these browsers contain support for Web publishing and workgroup computing. (See the following discussion of groupware.)

Groupware facilitates collaboration by enabling members of a group to share documents, schedule meetings, and discuss activities, events, and issues. Illustrated here are capabilities for following a threaded discussion.

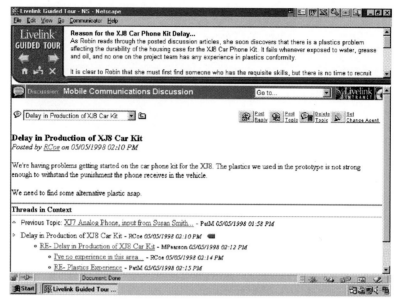

Groupware. **Groupware** provides functions and services to support the collaborative activities of work groups. Groupware includes software for information-sharing, electronic meetings, scheduling, and e-mail and a network to connect the members of the group as they work on their own desktop computers, often in widely scattered locations. Table 7.2 describes the capabilities of groupware.

Groupware enhances collaboration by allowing the exchange of ideas electronically. All the messages on a topic can be saved in a group, stamped with the date, time, and author. All of these messages can be followed in a **thread** to see how a discussion has evolved. (A thread is a series of messages in an on-line discussion that have been posted as replies to each other.) Any group member can review the ideas of others at any time and add to them, or individuals can post a document for others to comment on or edit. Members can post requests for help, allowing others to respond. Finally, if a group so chooses, members can store their work notes on the groupware so that all others in the group can see what progress is being made, what problems occur, and what activities are planned.

The leading commercial groupware product has been Lotus Notes from the Lotus Development Corporation. The Internet is rich in capabilities to support collaborative work. Recent versions of Microsoft Internet Explorer and Netscape Communicator include groupware functions, such as e-mail, electronic scheduling and calendaring, audio and data conferencing, and electronic discussion groups and databases (see Chapters 10 and 14). Microsoft's Office 2000 software suite includes groupware features using Web technology. Powerful Web-based groupware features can also be found in products such as Opentext's Livelink.

Table 7.2	Groupware Capabilities

Group writing and commenting

Electronic mail distribution

Scheduling meetings and appointments

Shared files and databases

Shared time lines and plans

Electronic meetings and conferences

7.4 New Software Tools and Approaches

A growing backlog of software projects and the need for businesses to fashion systems that are flexible or that can run over the Internet have stimulated new approaches to software development with object-oriented programming tools and new programming languages such as Java, hypertext markup language (HTML), and Extensible Markup Language (XML).

Object-Oriented Programming

Traditional software development methods have treated data and procedures as independent components. A separate programming procedure must be written every time someone wants to take an action on a particular piece of data. The procedures act on data that the program passes to them.

What Makes Object-Oriented Programming Different?

Object-oriented programming combines data and the specific procedures that operate on those data into one *object*. The object combines data and program code. Instead of passing data to procedures, programs send a message for an object to perform a procedure that is already embedded into it. (Procedures are termed *methods* in object-oriented languages.) The same message may be sent to many different objects, but each will implement that message differently.

For example, an object-oriented financial application might have Customer objects sending debit and credit messages to Account objects. The Account objects in turn might maintain Cash-on-Hand, Accounts-Payable, and Accounts-Receivable objects.

An object's data are hidden from other parts of the program and can only be manipulated from inside the object. The method for manipulating the object's data can be changed internally without affecting other parts of the program. Programmers can focus on what they want an object to do, and the object decides how to do it.

An object's data are encapsulated from other parts of the system, so each object is an independent software building block that can be used in many different systems without changing the program code. Thus, object-oriented programming is expected to reduce the time and cost of writing software by producing reusable program code or software *chips* that can be reused in other related systems. Future software work can draw on a library of reusable objects, and productivity gains from object-oriented technology could be magnified if objects were stored in reusable software libraries and explicitly designed for reuse (Fayad and Cline, 1996). However, such benefits are unlikely to be realized unless organizations develop appropriate standards and procedures for reuse (Kim and Stohr, 1998).

object-oriented programming An approach to software development that combines data and procedures into a single object.

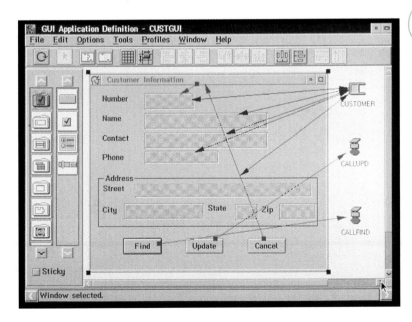

With visual programming tools such as IBM's Visual Age Generator, working software programs can be created by drawing, pointing, and clicking instead of writing program code.

Object-oriented programming has spawned a new programming technology known as **visual programming.** With visual programming, programmers do not write code. Rather, they use a mouse to select and move around programming objects, copying an object from a library into a specific location in a program, or drawing a line to connect two or more objects. Visual Basic is a widely used visual programming tool for creating applications that run under Microsoft Windows.

Object-Oriented Programming Concepts

Object-oriented programming is based on the concepts of class and inheritance. Program code is not written separately for every object but for classes, or general categories, of similar objects. Objects belonging to a certain class have the features of that class. Classes of objects in turn can inherit all the structure and behaviors of a more general class and then add variables and behaviors unique to each object. New classes of objects are created by choosing an existing class and specifying how the new class differs from the existing class, instead of starting from scratch each time.

Classes are organized hierarchically into superclasses and subclasses. For example, a *car* class might have a *vehicle* class for a superclass, so that it would inherit all the methods and data previously defined for *vehicle.* The design of the *car* class would only need to describe how cars differ from vehicles. A banking application could define a Savings-Account object that is very much like a Bank-Account object with a few minor differences. Savings-Account inherits all the Bank-Account's state and methods and then adds a few extras.

We can see how class and **inheritance** work in Figure 7-13, which illustrates a tree of classes concerning employees and how they are paid. Employee is the common ancestor of the other four classes. Nonsalaried and Salaried are subclasses of Employee, whereas Tem-

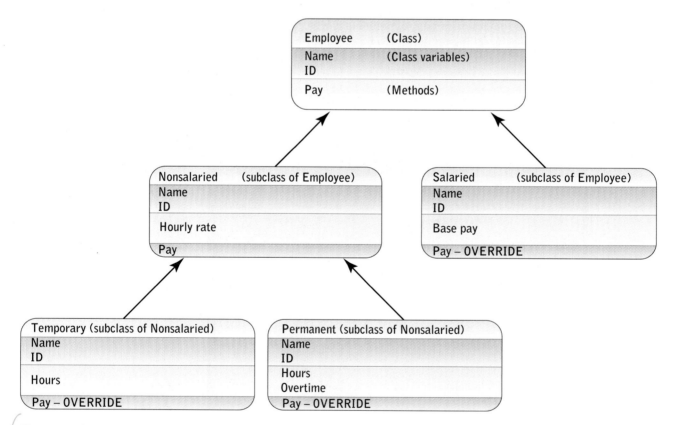

Figure 7-13 Class, subclasses, inheritance, and overriding. This figure illustrates how a message's method can come from the class itself or an ancestor class. Class variables and methods are shaded when they are inherited from above.

porary and Permanent are subclasses of Nonsalaried. The variables for the class are in the top half of the box, and the methods are in the bottom half. Darker items in each box are inherited from some ancestor class. (For example, by following the tree upward, we can see that Name and ID in the Nonsalaried, Salaried, Temporary, and Permanent subclasses are inherited from the Employee superclass [ancestor class].) Lighter methods, or class variables, are unique to a specific class and they override, or redefine, existing methods. When a subclass overrides an inherited method, its object still responds to the same message, but it executes its definition of the method rather than its ancestor's. Whereas Pay is a method inherited from some superclass, the method Pay-OVERRIDE is specific to the Temporary, Permanent, and Salaried classes.

Object-oriented software can be custom-programmed or it can be developed with rapid-application development tools, which can potentially cost 30 percent to 50 percent less than traditional program development methods. Some of these tools provide visual programming environments in which developers can create ready-to-use program code by "snapping" together prebuilt objects. Other tools generate program code that can be compiled to run on a variety of computing platforms. The Window on Technology explores some of the benefits of object-oriented software creation.

Java

Java is a programming language named after the many cups of coffee its Sun Microsystems developers drank along the way. It is an object-oriented language, combining data with the functions for processing the data, and it is platform-independent. Java software is designed to run on any computer or computing device, regardless of the specific microprocessor or operating system it uses. A Macintosh Apple, an IBM personal computer running Windows, a DEC computer running UNIX, and even a smart cellular phone or personal digital assistant can share the same Java application.

Java can be used to create miniature programs called "applets" designed to reside on centralized network servers. The network delivers only the applets required for a specific function. With Java applets residing on a network, a user can download only the software functions and data that he or she needs to perform a particular task, such as analyzing the revenue from one sales territory. The user does not need to maintain large software programs or data files on his or her desktop machine. When the user is finished with processing, the data can be saved through the network. Java can be used with network computers because it enables all processing software and data to be stored on a network server, downloaded via a network as needed, and then placed back on the network server.

Java is also a very robust language that can handle text, data, graphics, sound, and video, all within one program if needed. Java applets often are used to provide interactive capabilities for Web pages. For example, Java applets can be used to create animated cartoons or real-time news tickers for a Web site, or to add a capability to a Web page to calculate a loan payment schedule on-line in response to financial data input by the user. (Microsoft's **ActiveX** sometimes is used as an alternative to Java for creating interactivity on a Web page. ActiveX is a set of controls that enables programs or other objects such as charts, tables, or animations to be embedded within a Web page. However, ActiveX lacks Java's machine independence and was designed for a Windows environment.)

Java also can be used to create more extensive applications that can run over the Internet or over a company's private network (see the Window on Management). Java can let PC users manipulate data on networked systems using Web browsers, reducing the need to write specialized software. For example, Sprint PCS, the mobile-phone partnership, is using Java for an application that allows its employees to use Web browsers to analyze business data and send reports to colleagues via e-mail on an internal network. The system it replaced required specialized desktop software to accomplish these tasks and restricted these reports to a smaller number of employees (Clark, 1998).

To run Java software, a computer needs an operating system containing a Java Virtual Machine (JVM). (A JVM is incorporated into Web browser software such as Netscape

Java Programming language that can deliver only the software functionality needed for a particular task as a small applet downloaded from a network; can run on any computer and operating system.

ActiveX A set of controls for the Windows software environment that enables programs or other objects such as charts, tables, or animations to be embedded within a Web page.

Banque Generale Luxembourg Competes with Object Technology

The formation of the European Union (EU) provides many benefits by creating a unified European economic community, but it has also created new challenges for businesses in that area. One is the Banque Generale Luxembourg, with $25 billion in assets, which faces new competition from other parts of Europe. The bank is active in Zurich, Frankfort, the Netherlands, and Germany and maintains a network of domestic branches in Luxembourg itself. The bank has decided to respond by personalizing and streamlining customer service. One way to do this is by making information affecting customers immediately available to service representatives so that questions can be answered in one keystroke.

According to Yves Stein, who heads the bank's marketing function, clients want their bank adviser to know their needs and be able to see their entire financial profile. Speedy responses are essential because customers don't like to be told that their customer service advisers won't be able to get back to them with the information the customers requested for several days. Banque Generale Luxembourg wants to assemble all of the information about a specific customer—his or her checking and savings accounts and investments—in one place so bank advisers do not have to make multiple and lengthy queries to several different information systems. Much of this customer information was organized along traditional product lines in a number of different systems and was difficult to assemble to provide a complete picture of a customer's interaction with the bank. The bank's information systems management recommended using object-oriented software to make this possible.

Information systems specialists created an object-oriented application architecture that lets bank customer service advisers access information from their desktops no matter where the information is stored. Data can be combined from disparate sources to provide a single view of a customer. The object-oriented software reduces the amount of programming required for new applications, leaving application developers to focus on creating the business logic. The business logic applications will use the J Application Server by Gemstone Systems, Inc., which allows thousands of users to access shared software objects simultaneously. That way users don't have to wait for a specific software object to be available. The Common Object Request Broker Architecture (CORBA) will transfer data between end users' client computers and 20-year-old COBOL applications residing on the bank's mainframe. (CORBA is a technology specification that outlines how objects can share capabilities to form applications and is used to solve compatibility problems among objects written in different languages that run on different machines.) The client computers, which are located in the bank's main office and 40 branch offices, use Windows NT.

Because software developers can store and reuse objects they have already built, object technology is expected to save staff time and help them respond more quickly to new business information requirements.

Besides helping the bank attract and retain existing customers for traditional banking services, it hopes the technology will help it move into new markets. To sell stock information and securities, they will need to know what their customers are doing and what they want to do.

To Think About: How was the selection of object-oriented software technology related to Banque Generale Luxembourg's business strategy?

Sources: Sharon Gaudin, "Bank System Turns into Service Edge," *Computerworld*, March 16, 1998; and Gemstone Systems Inc., "Gemstone Systems Signs Major Deal with Banque Generale in Luxembourg," March 31, 1998.

Navigator or Microsoft Internet Explorer.) The Java Virtual Machine is a compact program that enables the computer to run Java applications. The JVM lets the computer simulate an ideal standardized Java computer, complete with its own representation of a CPU and its own instruction set. The Virtual Machine executes Java programs by interpreting their commands one by one and commanding the underlying computer to perform all the tasks specified by each command.

Management and Organizational Benefits of Java

Companies are starting to develop more applications in Java because such applications can potentially run in Windows, UNIX, IBM mainframe, Macintosh, and other environments without having to be rewritten for each computing platform. Sun Microsystems terms this phenomenon "write once, run anywhere." Java also could allow more software to be distributed and used through networks. Functionality could be stored with data on the network and downloaded only as needed. Companies might not need to purchase thousands of copies of commercial software to run on individual computers; instead users could download applets over a network and use network computers.

Java is similar to C++ but considered easier to use. Java program code can be written more quickly than with other languages. Sun claims that no Java program can penetrate the user's computer, making it safe from viruses and other types of damage that might occur when downloading more conventional programs off a network.

Despite these benefits, Java has not yet fulfilled its early promise to revolutionize software development and use. Programs written in current versions of Java tend to run slower than "native" programs, which are written for a particular operating system, because they must be interpreted by the Java Virtual Machine. Vendors such as Microsoft are supporting alternative versions of Java that include subtle differences in their Virtual Machines that affect Java's performance in different pieces of hardware and operating systems. Without a standard version of Java, true platform independence cannot be achieved. The Window on Management explores the management issues posed by Java as companies consider whether to use this programming language.

Hypertext Markup Language (HTML) and XML

Hypertext markup language (HTML) is a page description language for creating hypertext or hypermedia documents such as Web pages. (See the discussions of hypermedia in Chapter 8 and of Web pages in Chapter 10.) HTML uses instructions called *tags* (see Figure 7-14) to specify how text, graphics, video, and sound are placed on a document and to create dynamic links to other documents and objects stored in the same or remote computers. Using these links, a user need only point at a highlighted key word or graphic, click on it, and immediately be transported to another document.

HTML programs can be custom-written, but they also can be created by using the HTML authoring capabilities of Web browsers or of popular word processing, spreadsheet, data management, and presentation graphics software packages. HTML editors such as Claris Home Page and Adobe PageMill are more powerful HTML authoring tool programs for creating Web pages.

An extension to HTML called *Dynamic HTML* enables Web pages to react to user input without having to send additional requests to the Web server. Web pages using Dynamic HTML appear less static and more like active and alive applications.

XML, which stands for **eXtensible Markup Language,** is a new specification designed to improve delivery of Web documents. It is actually a general-purpose language for creating other markup languages, so that it can be used to create structured documents that can be exchanged and easily understood by properly written applications. Whereas HTML describes the display format of a document, XML describes the structure of a document and supports links to multiple documents (while HTML links can only reference one destination per link). XML users can tag document contents for meaning so that the data in a document can be manipulated, whereas HTML affects only the appearance of a document. XML is expected to become a serious technology for Web-based applications and non-Web applications such as document management or the movement of data from one system to another.

7.5 Managing Software Assets

Software costs are one of the largest information technology expenditures in most firms—amounting to more than double the expenditures for computer hardware—and thus software represents a major asset. At many points in their careers, managers will be required to make important decisions concerning the selection, purchase, and utilization of their organization's software assets. Here are some important software issues they should be aware of.

Software Trends

A number of key software trends are of special interest to managers. As computer hardware costs drop, concern with machine efficiency is being replaced with efforts to create software that provides more natural, seamless relationships between people and information systems—through graphical interfaces, natural language, voice recognition, touch, or other gestures (see Section 6.6 of Chapter 6). Technology expenditures will increasingly focus on ways to use

Adding Java to the Programming Mix

For several years, Java has been the hot new language to enliven Web site programming, but there are other reasons to utilize the new language. Corporate managements are finding that using Java can cut programming time and costs compared with such languages as C++. In addition, Java is a genuine cross-platform language—the same code can be moved from computing platform to platform and still work—saving the organization programming time and expenses.

Atlanta-based Home Depot, with nearly 700 stores on its computer network, is using Java for many of its new applications. Its fundamental business requirement is to use network computers so a technician does not "have a hard drive to deal with every time I turn around," according to Curtis Chambers, the designer of the company's distributed applications. He explains that, with no hard drives, the hardware cost-per-unit is lower, and management has better control over which applications each store is using. Michael Anderson, Home Depot's director of information systems, adds that Java is an easier language to use and so speeds up development time. Perhaps most important in terms of reducing long-range cost, Anderson believes that by programming in Java, "We'll cut our support by 75 percent."

The company already has built a number of systems using Java. One application enables district managers to download sales and inventory information to their local PCs. No longer does each district have to create its own reports. Instead, the reports are automatically waiting for them when they log on to the company network. Java also is being used in the employment area. When a potential employee submits an application to one of the stores, one Java application automatically sends the application to all of Home Depot's 700 stores, making it more likely the company will find a good fit for the applicant while also saving job seekers considerable effort and time. In addition, the company is building an employment-tracking system. Management expects this system ultimately will become a paperless benefits system.

Daiwa Securities America, Inc. of New York is another convert to Java. The company wants to develop a system that will give it straight-through processing, which will move trade data from their entry when a trade is placed and completed through to all systems where that data are needed. Such a system would eliminate the cost of duplicate data entry. All financial trading companies have front-office (trading) systems and back-office (record keeping and accounting) systems. What is missing is a middle-office system that connects the two. Daiwa is using Java for several reasons. First, Java gives the applications platform independence—the Daiwa staff can develop each application only once and then run it on any platform, saving Daiwa a great deal in development and maintenance costs. In addition the company likes Java because it will be running many of its applications on internal and external networks, the kind of environment for which Java was created.

Datek Online Brokerage Services sees other benefits from Java for financial services because it can create applications that can handle increased capacity as electronic trading grows. For example, Java for presenting stock quotes on the company's Web site will reduce the load on Datek's servers because only 20 bytes of data will be transferred each time a quote is updated.

On the other hand, Bethesda Healthcare System, a healthcare provider in Boynton Beach, Florida, has no plans to switch from C++ to Java for its software development. Different versions of Java used by various software vendors include subtle differences in their Java Virtual Machines, which can cause errors in how applications behave. Glitches in how information is displayed by Web browsers could create life-or-death issues because physicians rely on such data to make treatment decisions. Bethesda transmits images such as X rays to clinics and doctor's offices, which expect the images to be absolutely accurate. Bethesda Healthcare has no control over what hardware is used by the health care providers with whom it shares its data, so true cross-platform compatibility would be essential.

To Think About: What are the management benefits of using Java to develop software? What management organization and technology issues should be addressed when deciding whether to use Java?

Sources: Gregory Dalton with Jennifer Mateyaschuk, "Well Equipped," Information Week, January 25, 1999; Sharon Gaudin, "Users Praise Business Benefits of Java," Computerworld, January 19, 1998; and Ann Mallory, "Java Journeys," Computerworld, March 23, 1998.

software to cut down on "people" costs as opposed to computer hardware costs by increasing the ease with which users can interact with the hardware and software. Use of software packages, fourth-generation languages, and object-oriented tools is growing because such software further reduces "people" costs by cutting down the need for custom-crafted software written by skilled computer programmers.

Increased use of Java and the Internet will find more software tools integrated and available through networks. Instead of using stand-alone PCs storing separate word processing or communication programs, for example, users will find software services (such as voice-to-text

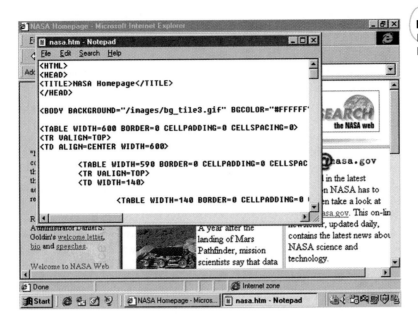

Figure 7-14 Sample of the HTML code used to create the NASA Web page displayed here.

transcription or bill paying and accounting) available on the Internet. Software components or objects which can be assembled into complete systems may also be available through networks as well. These network-based software services should lead to further software economies for firms.

Another major software trend is the development of integrated programs such as enterprise resource planning systems (ERP) that support organizational needs for communication and control. Such systems require the development of very large, sophisticated programs to manage data for the organization as a whole, to prepare data for end users, to integrate parts of the organization, and to permit precise control and coordination of organizational decision making. These very large systems integrate what once were separate systems (e.g., accounts receivable and order processing) operated by separate departments (e.g., accounting and sales). Chapter 18 provides more detail on the technical and organizational issues that must be addressed when implementing ERP software.

Most firms cannot jettison all of their existing systems and create such systems from scratch. Many legacy mainframe applications are essential to daily operations and very risky to change, but they can be made more useful if their information and business logic can be integrated with other applications (Noffsinger, Niedbalski, Blanks, and Emmart, 1998). One way to integrate various legacy applications is to use special software called **middleware** to create an interface or bridge between two different systems. Middleware is software that connects two otherwise separate applications to pass data between them and may consist of custom software written in-house or a software package. Middleware is used to link client and server machines in client/server computing and increasingly to link a Web server to data stored on another computer. This allows users to request data from the computer in which they are stored using forms displayed on a Web browser, and it enables the Web server to return dynamic Web pages based on information requested by the user. The use of middleware to integrate applications is becoming another important software trend.

middleware Software that allows two different applications to exchange data.

Software Maintenance and the Year 2000 Problem

After software has been created for the organization, it usually has to be modified over time to incorporate new information requirements. Because of the way software is currently designed, this process of maintenance is very costly, time-consuming, and challenging to manage. In most information systems departments more than 50 percent of staff time is spent maintaining the software for existing systems. As the end of the millennium approaches, an even larger maintenance problem called the *Year 2000 Problem* has emerged. The **Year 2000 Problem,** sometimes referred to as the *millennium bug* or the **Y2K** problem, is the inability of software programs to handle any dates other than those of the twentieth century—years that begin with "19." Date fields in many older computer programs (and even some recent PC programs) store the dates as six digits, two digits each for the day, month, and year (MM–DD–YY). Programs were written this way for decades because it saved data entry time and storage space if the century number "19" did not have to be entered.

Human beings know that the year 1999 is followed immediately by the year 2000, and we even know that the year 2000 is also a new century and a new millennium. But "ask" any computer and a great many of them will give a strange answer—1999 is followed by the year 1900. This is an enormous problem, especially for any software that is time-sensitive.

Imagine that you were born in 1940 and are a citizen of the United States. You expect that when you turn 65 in the year 2005, you will collect Social Security benefits. But, if the computer calculates the year to be 1905, you will receive no payments because you will not be eligible. In fact, you won't even have been born yet. Assume that you are in charge of maintenance for one of your company's large plants. Your computer runs a maintenance system that schedules plant equipment maintenance, and for that maintenance also schedules the purchase of supplies and allocates the staff time. You have scheduled maintenance in 1995, 1998, and 2001. If your computer jumps to 1900 and so never reaches the year 2000, your plant and your whole operation will be in chaos. Inability to recognize the right date could seriously affect airline operations, distribution of electrical power, billing records, and many other critical activities of everyday life. The Year 2000 Problem affects organizations of all sizes—business, nonprofit, and government alike—and we have devoted the Case Study concluding this chapter to this topic.

To solve the problem before 2000 arrives, organizations need to comb through their programs to locate all coding in which dates are used. They then must determine whether each of those places is a problem. Many companies have computer programs amounting to many millions of lines of code, making this a daunting task. Because many organizations have distributed computing environments, desktop systems and servers must be examined for Y2K problems as well as large mainframe applications (Gowan, Jesse, and Mathieu, 1999). Where problems are found, they must be corrected. It has been estimated that organizations can expect to spend $400 billion to $600 billion worldwide to fix this problem.

Many types of solutions are possible, but most require massive expenditures and software projects. Organizations may opt to keep their legacy software and either fix each date field by increasing the year field to four digits and inserting the century number or change the program code to compensate for the problem. Some organizations are using the Year 2000 Problem as an opportunity to create completely new systems that are Year 2000 compliant using software packages or outsourcing the entire system to external vendors. Chapter 12 provides more detail on these various system-building alternatives.

Selecting Software for the Organization

Although managers need not become programming specialists, they should be able to use clear criteria in selecting application and system software for the organization. The most important criteria are as follows.

Appropriateness

Some languages are general-purpose languages that can be used on a variety of problems, whereas others are special-purpose languages suitable for only limited tasks. Special-purpose graphics programs, for example, may be poor at routine processing of transactions. COBOL is excellent for business data processing but poor at mathematical calculations. Language selection involves identifying the organizational use for the software and the users. Application software should also be easy to maintain and change, and flexible enough so that it can grow with the organization. These organizational considerations have direct long-term cost implications.

Efficiency

Although less important than in the past, the efficiency with which a language compiles and executes remains a consideration when purchasing software. Some programming languages are more efficient in the use of machine time than others and there are instances where such considerations outweigh personnel costs. Languages with slow compilers or interpreters like BASIC or Java or fourth-generation languages may prove too slow and expensive in terms of machine time for high-speed transaction systems, which must handle thousands of transactions per second (see Chapter 12).

Compatibility

Application software must be able to run on the firm's hardware and operating system platform. Likewise, the firm's operating system software must be compatible with the software required by the firm's mainstream business applications. Mission-critical applications typically have large volumes of transactions to process and require robust operating systems that can handle large complex software programs and massive files.

Support

In order to be effective, a programming language must be easily learned by the firm's programming staff, and the staff should have sufficient knowledge of that software so that they can provide ongoing support for all of the systems based on that software. It is also important to purchase package software that has widespread use in other organizations and is supported by many consulting firms and services. Another kind of support is the availability of software editing, debugging, and development aids.

Management Wrap-Up

Management should be aware of the strengths and weaknesses of software tools, the tasks for which they are best suited, and whether these tools fit into the firm's long-term strategy and information architecture. Tradeoffs between efficiency, ease of use, and flexibility should be carefully analyzed. These organizational considerations have long-term cost implications.

Management

Software can either enhance or impede organizational performance, depending on the software tools selected and how they are used. Organizational needs should drive software selection. The software tool selected should be easy for the firm's IS staff to learn and maintain and be flexible enough so that it can grow with the organization. Software for non-IS specialists should have easy-to-use interfaces and be compatible with the firm's other software tools.

Organization

A range of system and application software technologies is available to organizations. Key technology decisions include the appropriateness of the software tool for the problem to be addressed, compatibility with the firm's hardware, the efficiency of the software for performing specific tasks, vendor support of software packages, and other support capabilities for debugging, documentation, and reuse.

Technology

For Discussion

1. Why is selecting both system and application software for the organization an important management decision?

2. Should organizations develop all of their systems with "fourth-generation" tools? Why or why not?

Summary

1. Describe the major types of software. The major types of software are system software and application software. Each serves a different purpose. System software manages the computer resources and mediates between application software and computer hardware. Application software is used by application programmers and some end users to develop specific business applications. Application software works through system software, which controls access to computer hardware.

2. Examine the functions of system software and compare leading PC operating systems. System software coordinates the various parts of the computer system and mediates between application software and computer hardware. The system software that manages and controls the activities of the computer is called the operating system. Other system software includes computer-language translation programs that convert programming languages into machine language and utility programs that perform common processing tasks.

The operating system acts as the chief manager of the information system, allocating, assigning, and scheduling system resources and monitoring the use of the computer. Multiprogramming, multitasking, virtual storage, time sharing, and multiprocessing enable system resources to be used more efficiently so that the computer can attack many problems at the same time.

Multiprogramming (multitasking in PC environments) allows multiple programs to use the computer's resources concurrently. Virtual storage splits up programs into small portions so that the main memory can be utilized more efficiently. Time sharing enables many users to share computer resources simultaneously by allocating each user a tiny slice of computing time. Multiprocessing is the use of two or more CPUs linked together working in tandem to perform a task.

In order to be executed by the computer, a software program must be translated into machine language via special language-translation software—a compiler, an assembler, or an interpreter.

PC operating systems have developed sophisticated capabilities such as multitasking and support for multiple users on networks. Leading PC operating systems include Windows 98 and 95, Windows CE, Windows NT (Windows 2000), OS/2, UNIX, Linux, Mac OS, and DOS. PC operating systems with graphical user interfaces have gained popularity over command-driven operating systems.

3. Explain how software has evolved and how it will continue to develop. Software has evolved along with hardware. The general trend is toward user-friendly, high-level languages that both increase professional programmer productivity and make it possible for amateurs to use information systems. There have been four generations of software development: (1) machine language; (2) symbolic languages such as assembly language; (3) high-level languages such as FORTRAN and COBOL; and (4) fourth-generation languages, which are less procedural and closer to natural language than earlier generations of software. Software is starting to incorporate both sound and graphics and to support multimedia applications.

4. Analyze the strengths and limitations of the major application programming languages and software tools. The most popular conventional programming languages are assembly language, FORTRAN, COBOL, BASIC, Pascal, and C. Conventional programming languages make more efficient use of computer resources than fourth-generation languages and each is designed to solve specific types of problems.

Fourth-generation languages include query languages, report generators, graphics languages, application generators, very high-level programming languages, application software packages, and PC software tools. They are less procedural than conventional programming languages and enable end users to perform many software tasks that previously required technical specialists. Popular PC software tools include word processing, spreadsheet, data management, presentation graphics, and e-mail software along with Web browsers and groupware.

5. Describe new approaches to software development. Object-oriented programming combines data and procedures into one *object,* which can act as an independent software building block. Each object can be used in many different systems without changing program code.

Java is an object-oriented programming language designed to operate on the Internet. It can deliver precisely the software functionality needed for a particular task as a small applet that is downloaded from a network. Java can run on any computer and operating system. HTML is a page description language for creating Web pages. XML is a language for creating structured documents in which data can be manipulated.

6. Identify important issues in the management of organizational software assets. Software represents a major organizational asset which should be carefully managed. The growing use of more "people-friendly" software, software on networks, middleware, and large complex programs integrating many different organizational functions and processes are important trends that managers should follow closely. Maintenance can account for over 50 percent of information system costs, and that figure is even higher right now as organizations rewrite outdated software to handle the year 2000 and future dates. Criteria such as efficiency, compatibility with the organization's technology platform, support, and whether the software language or tool is appropriate for the problems and tasks of the organization should govern software selection.

Key Terms

ActiveX, 215

Ada, 206

Application generator, 208

Application software, 195

Assembly language, 205

BASIC (Beginners All-purpose Symbolic Instruction Code), 205

C, 206

C++, 206

Class, 214

COBOL (COmmon Business Oriented Language), 205

Compiler, 198

Data management software, 209

DOS, 200

Electronic mail (e-mail), 211

FORTRAN (FORmula TRANslator), 205

Fourth-generation language, 206

Graphical user interface (GUI), 199

Graphics language, 207

Groupware, 212

High-level language, 204

Hypertext markup language (HTML), 217

Inheritance, 214

Integrated software package, 209

Interpreter, 198

Java, 215

Linux, 202

LISP, 206

Machine language, 203

Mac OS, 202

Middleware, 219

Multiprocessing, 198

Multiprogramming, 196

Multitasking, 197

Natural language, 207

Object code, 198

Object-oriented programming, 213

Open-source software, 202

Operating system, 196

OS/2, 202

Page, 197

Pascal, 206

PL/1 (Programming Language 1), 206

Presentation graphics, 209

Program, 195

Prolog, 206

Query language, 207

Report generator, 207

Software, 194

Software package, 208

Source code, 198

Spreadsheet, 208

Stored program concept, 195

System software, 195

Thread, 212

Time sharing, 198

UNIX, 202

Utility program, 199

Very high-level programming language, 208

Virtual storage, 197

Visual programming, 214

Web browser, 211

Windows, 200

Windows CE, 202

Windows 95, 200

Windows 98, 200

Windows NT, 201

Windows 2000, 201

Word processing software, 208

XML (eXtensible Markup Language), 217

Year 2000 Problem (Y2K), 220

Review Questions

1. What are the major types of software? How do they differ in terms of users and uses?

2. What is the operating system of a computer? What does it do?

3. Describe multiprogramming, virtual storage, time sharing, and multiprocessing. Why are they important for the operation of an information system?

4. What is the difference between an assembler, a compiler, and an interpreter?

5. Define and describe graphical user interfaces.

6. Compare the major PC operating systems.

7. What are the major generations of software, and approximately when were they developed?

8. What is a high-level language? Name three high-level languages. Describe their strengths and weaknesses.

9. Define fourth-generation languages and list the seven categories of fourth-generation tools.

10. What is the difference between fourth-generation languages and conventional programming languages?

11. What is the difference between an application generator and an application software package? Between a report generator and a query language?

12. Name and describe the most important PC software tools.

13. What is object-oriented programming? How does it differ from conventional software development?

14. What is Java? How could it change the way software is created and used?

15. What are HTML and XML? Why are they becoming important?

16. Name and describe three software trends that managers should be aware of.

17. What is the Year 2000 (Y2K) Problem? Why is it a serious problem for organizations?

18. What criteria should be used when selecting software for the organization?

Group Project

Which is the better Internet software tool, Internet Explorer or Netscape Communicator? Your instructor will divide the class into two groups to research this question. Each group will present their findings to the class. To prepare your analysis, use articles from computer magazines and the Web and examine the software.

Tools for Interactive Learning

○ Internet

The Internet Connection for this chapter will direct you to a series of Web sites of various computer software vendors where you can complete an exercise to analyze the capabilities of various types of computer software. You can visit a Web site with interactive software to complete an Electronic Commerce project for logistics planning. You can also use the Interactive Study Guide to test your knowledge of the topics in this chapter and get instant feedback where you need more practice.

○ CD-ROM

If you purchase and use the Multimedia Edition CD-ROM with this chapter, you can complete an interactive exercise asking you to select the appropriate programming language or application software for a series of business problems. You can also find a video clip illustrating the capabilities of geographic information system (GIS) software, an audio overview of the key themes of this chapter, and bullet text summarizing the key points of the chapter.

Case Study   The Year 2000 Problem

Is the Year 2000 Problem "the biggest business problem in human history?" Some experts think so, believing 10 to 15 million software applications are affected. The Gartner Group, a Stamford, Connecticut, consulting firm, estimates that the worldwide cost for fixing the Y2K problem will run between $1 to $2 trillion, representing as much as $300 for every person on this planet. As the millennium approaches, businesses can expect to spend 40 percent of their information technology budget—and more—fixing date problems. The total Y2K bill for companies such as Sears or Chase Manhattan will amount to hundreds of millions of dollars. And even if these companies have made all of their systems fully Year 2000 compliant, they still could face serious problems if the organizations with which they exchange data have not readied their systems.

In addition to software programs in computers, Year 2000 bugs may be lurking in programmed computer chips that have been built into electronic equipment, such as industrial machinery, traffic lights, elevators, security alarms, automobiles, and microwave ovens. Billions of these embedded systems are everywhere, in factories, nuclear power plants, hospitals, offices, and homes. Millions of these embedded systems are vulnerable, making it likely that some of us will experience problems with our electrical power, telephones, or transportation systems at the start of the next millennium.

The Year 2000 Problem affects all organizations—business, nonprofit, and government alike. Let us look at how one United States government agency, the Department of Defense, is faring.

The Department of Defense (DOD) has more than 7000 computer systems with perhaps 360 million lines of code. These systems do everything from managing inventories to controlling weaponry; 2965 of these

systems are considered mission-critical, more than any U.S. government agency. Failure to address the Year 2000 Problem could easily result in chaos. Transportation and other logistics systems, maintenance systems, accounting, and many other systems are very date dependent. Many weapons systems are also date dependent. The failure of these systems in a time of military crisis could easily be catastrophic. As explained by Bryce Ragland, the head of a Year 2000 task force team at the Air Force Software Support Center, "There's a real risk that some wacko in another country might decide to launch an attack against the U.S. a few seconds after midnight just to see if our defenses can handle it."

One common approach to addressing the problem is first to review each system, placing each program into one of three groups. Group 1 applications are already Year 2000 compliant (probably because they were developed within the past few years when people already were aware of the problem). Group 2 applications are those that are mission-critical, technically sound, and not going to be replaced, but not yet Year 2000 compliant. These must be addressed. Group 3 applications are those not being kept (the DOD, like many organizations, sees the Year 2000 Problem also as an opportunity to eliminate a lot of dead wood). Next, the necessary changes for Group 2 systems must be made. Finally, all changes must be thoroughly tested, a massive job which will take up at least half the total Year 2000 effort. All programs must be tested not only for how they handle the change from 1999 to 2000, but also for the years before and after 2000. In addition, all links to other programs must be tested so that programmers are certain that wrong data are neither sent to nor received from other programs and systems.

Changing programs or stored data presents a massive problem to the DOD because, like most of industry, it has had poor development practices over the years. The DOD used obscure, specialty programming languages, such as Jovial, for which few analytical and debugging tools are available to aid in solving the Year 2000 Problems. Quality documentation does not exist for most systems, documentation that would have enabled the staff to review the programs quickly or that would have enabled programmers to quickly make changes. Moreover, like most organizations, the DOD has had few programming standards, so that date calculations were written differently by different programmers, adding confusion to the problem.

The costs of scanning more than 7000 computer systems and identifying and fixing the trouble spots are enormous. The problem is so massive that, according to an April 1996 survey conducted by the House of Representatives, the DOD hadn't yet finished inventorying its roughly 358 million lines of program code. The DOD has an annual IT budget of $3 billion, but this is surely too little for such an enormous task. Congress, which is well aware of the Year 2000 Problem, has budgeted $2.3 billion to address the problem for the whole federal government. But a study of 24 federal agencies by Federal Sources Inc. estimates that it will cost about $5.6 billion for the federal government to rewrite all of its code to be Year 2000 compliant. Without Congress allocating a major increase in funds, the DOD will have to focus on identifying the problems and making the changes, ignoring testing, or testing superficially at best. That means many systems will have to be put back in production with many hidden problems in them. Nor can the deadline for the changes be extended—the year 2000 will arrive on schedule, no matter what.

In early 1999 a report issued by the House Subcommittee on Government, Management, Information, and Technology stated that only 72 percent of the DOD's critical systems were Year 2000 compliant. Nonetheless, with so many systems remaining, the task the department faces is gargantuan to say the least. Another report issued by the DOD itself several months earlier showed that the DOD was falling further behind in its Y2K efforts. When intelligence community systems were included in the assessment, the number of mission-critical systems that fell at least two months behind the DOD's own internal remediation schedule increased from 51 to 65 systems. Experts estimate that the DOD will not be able to fix all of its systems until 2001.

Attached to the DOD's report was a letter from Art Money, the DOD's senior civilian official, stating that the "massive coordination" effort required for an enterprise the size of DOD along with "interfaces across agency or governmental boundaries" presented "leading obstacles" to resolving the DOD's Year 2000 Problems. Money suggested a possible moratorium on all other DOD information technology initiatives until at least January 1, 2001.

Sources: Bob Violino, "Feds Gain on Y2K Fix," **Information Week**, March 1, 1999; Peter de Jager, "Y2K: So Many Bugs . . . So Little Time," **Scientific American**, January 1999; Orlando DeBruce, "Y2K: 4 Agencies Critical," **Federal Computer Week**, November 23, 1998; Marcia Stepanek, "Y2K Is Worse Than Anyone Thought," **Business Week**, December 14, 1998; Matt Hamblen, "Y2K Shortcoming May Shutter Some Banks," **Computerworld**, February 16, 1998; and Robert L. Scheier, Gary H. Anthes, and Allan E. Alter, "Year 2000 May Ambush U.S. Military," **Computerworld**, February 24, 1997.

CASE STUDY QUESTIONS

1. Why is the Year 2000 Problem a serious management issue?

2. What management, organization, and technology factors were responsible for causing the Year 2000 Problem at the Defense Department?

3. How well is the Department of Defense handling the Year 2000 Problem?

4. What management, organizational, and technical issues must be considered when planning to address the Year 2000 Problem?

5. It has been said that if information systems were all thoroughly object oriented, the Year 2000 Problem would probably be a minor annoyance. Do you agree or disagree?

Chapter 8

Managing Data Resources

After completing this chapter, you will be able to:

1. Compare traditional file organization and management techniques.

2. Explain the problems of the traditional file environment.

3. Describe how a database management system organizes information.

4. Identify the three principal database models and some principles of database design.

5. Discuss new database trends.

6. Analyze the managerial and organizational requirements for creating a database environment.

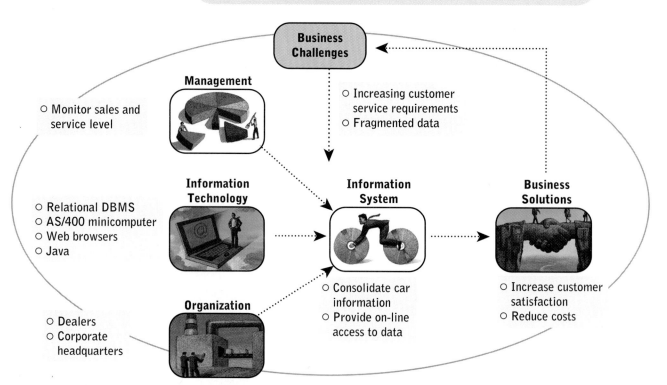

Business Challenges

Management
○ Monitor sales and service level

○ Increasing customer service requirements
○ Fragmented data

Information Technology
○ Relational DBMS
○ AS/400 minicomputer
○ Web browsers
○ Java

Information System
○ Consolidate car information
○ Provide on-line access to data

Business Solutions
○ Increase customer satisfaction
○ Reduce costs

Organization
○ Dealers
○ Corporate headquarters

Saab Centralizes
Customer Data

Saab Cars USA wants its dealers to be able to have all the information they need to keep their customers happy—including the ability to track each car they sell, from assembly line to the junkyard. Until recently, this was an impossible task, because all of Saab's data concerning a specific car are not in one place. Records about service, ownership, warranties, and parts are scattered among three different systems. Some of the data are maintained on an AS/400 minicomputer at Saab's U.S. headquarters in Norcross, Georgia. Other pieces of data are on an IBM Systems 390 mainframe at Saab's parts distributor, and still other pieces are in dealer management systems at Saab's dealerships.

Several Saab dealers teamed up with Saab Cars USA representatives to solve this problem. They worked with IBM Global Services in White Plains, New York, to develop IRIS (Intranet Retail Information System). The system extracts data from Saab's corporate and dealer systems, as well as from the parts-distributor's mainframe, and stores these data in an IBM DB/400 relational database installed on Saab's AS/400 computer. The database acts

as a central repository for customer information. Dealers can use their Web browser to access the data over an internal network based on Internet technology. A Java applet pulls the data from the DB/400 relational database and delivers them to the dealers' Web browsers.

Saab USA's managers and dealers believe the system will pay off by improving customer satisfaction. All of the information about a car, including ownership, service history, and warranty, is instantly available, so customer questions can be answered on the spot. By integrating this information and making it accessible via Web browsers, Saab is also increasing dealer productivity and lowering costs.

Sources: Jaikumar Vijayan, "Server Readies Saab Data for Web," *Computerworld,* July 13, 1998; and Justin Hibbard, "Saab's Driving Force," *Information Week,* January 26, 1998.

Saab's IRIS system illustrates how much the effective use of information depends on how data are stored, organized, and accessed. Proper delivery of information not only depends on the capabilities of computer hardware and software but also on the organization's ability to manage data as an important resource. It has been very difficult for organizations to manage their data effectively. Two challenges stand out.

1. Organizational obstacles to a database environment. Implementing a database requires widespread organizational change in the role of information (and information managers), the allocation of power at senior levels, the ownership and sharing of information, and patterns of organizational agreement. A database management system (DBMS) challenges the existing power arrangements in an organization and for that reason often generates political resistance. In a traditional file environment, each department constructed files and programs to fulfill its specific needs. Now, with a database, files and programs must be built that take into account the full organization's interest in data. Although the organization has spent the money on hardware and software for a database environment, it may not reap the benefits it should because it is unwilling to make the requisite organizational changes.

2. Cost/benefit considerations. The costs of moving to a database environment are tangible, up front, and large in the short term (three years). Most firms buy a commercial DBMS package and related hardware. The software alone can cost $0.5 million for a full-function package with all options. New hardware may cost an additional $1 million to $2 million annually. It soon becomes apparent to senior management that a database system is a huge investment.

Unfortunately, the benefits of the DBMS are often intangible, back loaded, and long term (five years). Several million dollars have been spent over the years designing and maintaining existing systems. People in the organization understand the existing system after long periods of training and socialization. For these reasons, and despite the clear advantages of the DBMS, the short-term costs of developing a DBMS often appear to be as great as the benefits. When the short-term political costs are added to the equation, it is convenient for senior management to defer the database investment. The obvious long-term benefits of the DBMS tend to be severely discounted by managers, especially those unfamiliar with (and perhaps unfriendly to) systems. Moreover, it may not be cost effective to build organization-wide databases that integrate all the organization's data (Goodhue et al., September 1992).

T his chapter examines the managerial and organizational requirements as well as the technologies for managing data as a resource. First we describe the traditional file management technologies that have been used for arranging and accessing data on physical storage media and the problems they have created for organizations. Then we describe the technology of database management systems, which can overcome many of the drawbacks of traditional file management. We end the chapter with a discussion of the managerial and organizational requirements for successful implementation of database management systems.

8.1 Organizing Data in a Traditional File Environment

An effective information system provides users with timely, accurate, and relevant information. This information is stored in computer files. When the files are properly arranged and maintained, users can easily access and retrieve the information they need.

You can appreciate the importance of file management if you have ever written a term paper using 3 × 5 index cards. No matter how efficient your storage device (a metal box or a rubber band), if you organize the cards randomly your term paper will have little or no organization. Given enough time, you could put the cards in order, but your system would be more efficient if you set up your organizational scheme early on. If your scheme is flexible enough and well documented, you can extend it to account for any changes in your viewpoint as you write your paper.

The same need for file organization applies to firms. Well-managed, carefully arranged files make it easy to obtain data for business decisions, whereas poorly managed files lead to chaos in information processing, high costs, poor performance, and little, if any, flexibility. Despite the use of excellent hardware and software, many organizations have inefficient information systems because of poor file management. In this section we describe the traditional methods that organizations have used to arrange data in computer files. We also discuss the problems with these methods.

File Organization Terms and Concepts

A computer system organizes data in a hierarchy that starts with bits and bytes and progresses to fields, records, files, and databases (see Figure 8-1). A *bit* represents the smallest unit of data a computer can handle. A group of bits, called a *byte*, represents a single character, which can

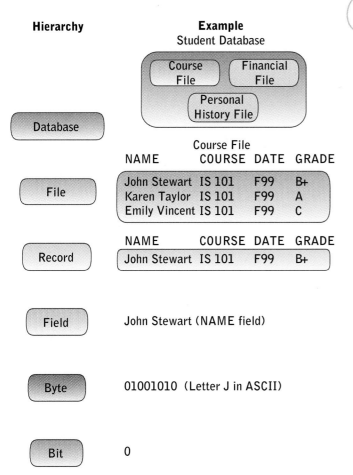

Hierarchy

Example
Student Database

Course File   Financial File

Personal History File

Database

Course File

NAME	COURSE	DATE	GRADE
John Stewart	IS 101	F99	B+
Karen Taylor	IS 101	F99	A
Emily Vincent	IS 101	F99	C

File

NAME	COURSE	DATE	GRADE
John Stewart	IS 101	F99	B+

Record

Field   John Stewart (NAME field)

Byte   01001010 (Letter J in ASCII)

Bit   0

Figure 8-1 The data hierarchy. A computer system organizes data in a hierarchy that starts with the bit, which represents either a 0 or a 1. Bits can be grouped to form a byte to represent one character, number, or symbol. Bytes can be grouped to form a field, and related fields can be grouped to form a record. Related records can be collected to form a file, and related files can be organized into a database.

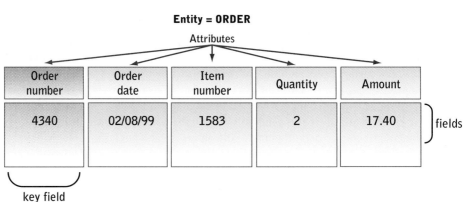

Figure 8-2 Entities and attributes. This record describes the entity called ORDER and its attributes. The specific values for order number, order date, item number, quantity, and amount for this particular order are the fields for this record. Order number is the key field because each order is assigned a unique identification number.

Entity = ORDER

Attributes

Order number	Order date	Item number	Quantity	Amount
4340	02/08/99	1583	2	17.40

fields

key field

field A grouping of characters into a word, a group of words, or a complete number, such as a person's name or age.

record A group of related fields.

file A group of records of the same type.

entity A person, place, thing, or event about which information must be kept.

attribute A piece of information describing a particular entity.

key field A field in a record that uniquely identifies instances of that record so that it can be retrieved, updated, or sorted.

sequential file organization A method of storing data records in which the records must be retrieved in the same physical sequence in which they are stored.

direct or random file organization A method of storing data records in a file so that they can be accessed in any sequence without regard to their actual physical order on the storage media.

indexed sequential access method (ISAM) A file access method to directly access records organized sequentially using an index of key fields.

be a letter, a number, or another symbol. A grouping of characters into a word, a group of words, or a complete number (such as a person's name or age), is called a **field.** A group of related fields, such as the student's name, the course taken, the date, and the grade, comprises a **record;** a group of records of the same type is called a **file.** For instance, the student records in Figure 8-1 could constitute a course file. A group of related files makes up a database. The student course file illustrated in Figure 8-1 could be grouped with files on students' personal histories and financial backgrounds to create a student database.

A record describes an entity. An **entity** is a person, place, thing, or event on which we maintain information. An order is a typical entity in a sales order file, which maintains information on a firm's sales orders. Each characteristic or quality describing a particular entity is called an **attribute.** For example, order number, order date, order amount, item number, and item quantity would each be an attribute of the entity order. The specific values that these attributes can have can be found in the fields of the record describing the entity *order* (see Figure 8-2).

Every record in a file should contain at least one field that uniquely identifies that record so that the record can be retrieved, updated, or sorted. This identifier field is called a **key field.** An example of a key field is the order number for the order record illustrated in Figure 8-2 or an employee number or social security number for a personnel record (containing employee data such as the employee's name, age, address, job title, and so forth).

Accessing Records from Computer Files

Computer systems store files on secondary storage devices. Records can be arranged in several ways on storage media, and the arrangement determines the manner in which individual records can be accessed or retrieved. One way to organize records is sequentially. In **sequential file organization,** data records must be retrieved in the same physical sequence in which they are stored. In contrast, **direct** or **random file organization** allows users to access records in any sequence they desire, without regard to actual physical order on the storage media.

Sequential file organization is the only file organization method that can be used on magnetic tape. This file organization method is no longer popular, but some organizations still use it for batch processing applications in which they access and process each record sequentially. A typical application using sequential files is payroll, in which all employees in a firm must be paid one by one and issued a check. Direct or random file organization is utilized with magnetic disk technology (although records can be stored sequentially on disk if desired). Most computer applications today utilize some method of direct file organization.

The Indexed Sequential Access Method

Although records may be stored sequentially on direct access storage devices, individual records can be accessed directly using the **indexed sequential access method (ISAM).**

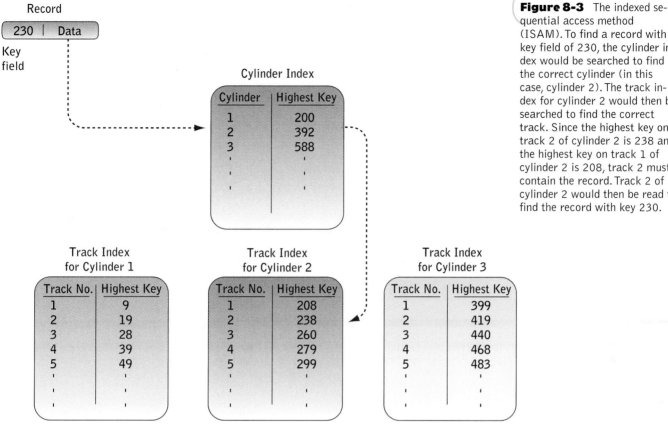

Record

| 230 | Data |

Key field

Cylinder Index

Cylinder	Highest Key
1	200
2	392
3	588
¦	¦
¦	¦
¦	¦

Track Index for Cylinder 1

Track No.	Highest Key
1	9
2	19
3	28
4	39
5	49
¦	¦
¦	¦
¦	¦

Track Index for Cylinder 2

Track No.	Highest Key
1	208
2	238
3	260
4	279
5	299
¦	¦
¦	¦
¦	¦

Track Index for Cylinder 3

Track No.	Highest Key
1	399
2	419
3	440
4	468
5	483
¦	¦
¦	¦

Figure 8-3 The indexed sequential access method (ISAM). To find a record with a key field of 230, the cylinder index would be searched to find the correct cylinder (in this case, cylinder 2). The track index for cylinder 2 would then be searched to find the correct track. Since the highest key on track 2 of cylinder 2 is 238 and the highest key on track 1 of cylinder 2 is 208, track 2 must contain the record. Track 2 of cylinder 2 would then be read to find the record with key 230.

This access method relies on an index of key fields to locate individual records. An **index** to a file is similar to the index of a book, as it lists the key field of each record and where that record is physically located in storage to expedite location of that record. Figure 8-3 shows how a series of indexes identifies the location of a specific record. Records are stored on disk in their key sequence. A cylinder index shows the highest value of the key field that can be found on a specific cylinder. A track index shows the highest value of the key field that can be found on a specific track. To locate a specific record, the cylinder index and then the track index are searched to locate the cylinder and track containing the record. The track itself is then sequentially read to find the record. If a file is very large, the cylinder index might be broken down into parts and a master index created to help locate each part of the cylinder index. ISAM is used in applications that require sequential processing of large numbers of records but that occasionally require direct access of individual records.

index A table or list that relates record keys to physical locations on direct access files.

Direct File Access Method

The **direct file access method** is used with direct file organization. This method uses a key field to locate the physical address of a record. However, the process is accomplished using a mathematical formula called a **transform algorithm** to translate the key field directly into the record's physical storage location on disk. The algorithm performs some mathematical computation on the record key, and the result of that calculation is the record's physical address. This process is illustrated in Figure 8-4.

This access method is most appropriate for applications in which individual records must be located directly and rapidly for immediate processing only. A few records in the file need to be retrieved at one time, and the required records are found in no particular sequence. An example might be an on-line hotel reservation system.

direct file access method A method of accessing records by mathematically transforming the key fields into the specific addresses for the records.

transform algorithm A mathematical formula used to translate a record's key field directly into the record's physical storage location.

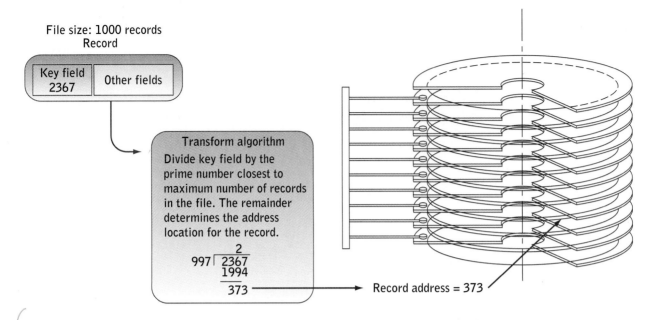

File size: 1000 records
Record

| Key field 2367 | Other fields |

Transform algorithm
Divide key field by the prime number closest to maximum number of records in the file. The remainder determines the address location for the record.

$$997\overline{\smash{\big)}\,2367}$$
$$\,2$$
$$1994$$
$$\overline{373}$$

Record address = 373

Figure 8-4 The direct file access method. Records are not stored sequentially on the disk but are arranged according to the results of some mathematical computation. Here, the transform algorithm divides the value in the key field by the prime number closest to the maximum number of records in the file (in this case, the prime number is 997). The remainder designates the storage location for that particular record.

Problems with the Traditional File Environment

Most organizations began information processing on a small scale, automating one application at a time. Systems tended to grow independently, and not according to some grand plan. Each functional area tended to develop systems in isolation from other functional areas. Accounting, finance, manufacturing, human resources, and marketing all developed their own systems and data files. Figure 8-5 illustrates the traditional approach to information processing.

Each application, of course, required its own files and its own computer program to operate. For example, the human resources functional area might have a personnel master file, a payroll file, a medical insurance file, a pension file, a mailing list file, and so forth until tens, perhaps hundreds, of files and programs existed. In the company as a whole, this process led to multiple master files created, maintained, and operated by separate divisions or departments.

There are names for this situation: the **traditional file environment;** the *flat file organization* (because most of the data are organized in flat files); and the *data file approach* (because the data and business logic are tied to specific files and related programs). By any name, the situation results in growing inefficiency and complexity.

As this process goes on for five or ten years, the organization is saddled with hundreds of programs and applications, with no one who knows what they do, what data they use, and who is using the data. The organization is collecting the same information in far too many files. The resulting problems are data redundancy, program-data dependence, inflexibility, poor data security, and inability to share data among applications.

Data Redundancy and Confusion

Data redundancy is the presence of duplicate data in multiple data files. Data redundancy occurs when different divisions, functional areas, and groups in an organization independently collect the same piece of information. For instance, within the commercial loans division of a bank, the marketing and credit information functions might collect the same customer infor-

traditional file environment
A way of collecting and maintaining data in an organization that leads to each functional area or division creating and maintaining its own data files and programs.

data redundancy The presence of duplicate data in multiple data files.

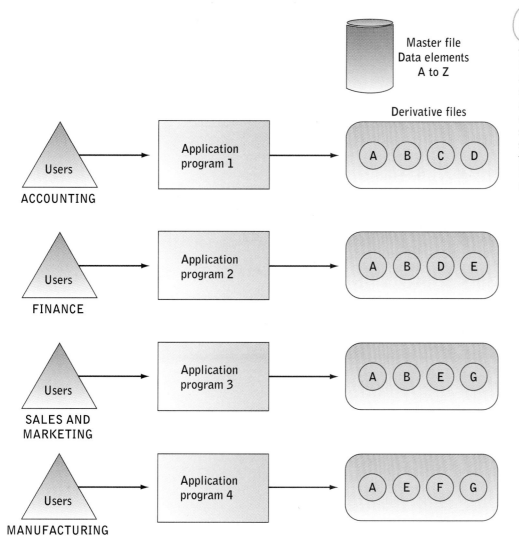

Master file
Data elements
A to Z

Derivative files

Application program 1 → A B C D

Users
ACCOUNTING

Application program 2 → A B D E

Users
FINANCE

Application program 3 → A B E G

Users
SALES AND MARKETING

Application program 4 → A E F G

Users
MANUFACTURING

Figure 8-5 Traditional file processing. The use of a traditional approach to file processing encourages each functional area in a corporation to develop specialized applications. Each application requires a unique data file that is likely to be a subset of the master file. These subsets of the master file lead to data redundancy, processing inflexibility, and wasted storage resources.

mation. Because it is collected and maintained in so many different places, the same data item may have different meanings in different parts of the organization. Simple data items such as the fiscal year, employee identification, and product code can take on different meanings as programmers and analysts work in isolation on different applications.

Program-Data Dependence
Program-data dependence is the tight relationship between data stored in files and the specific programs required to update and maintain those files. Every computer program has to describe the location and nature of the data with which it works. In a traditional file environment, any change in data requires a change in all programs that access the data. Changes, for instance, in tax rates or ZIP-code length require changes in programs. Such programming changes may cost millions of dollars to implement in programs that require the revised data.

program-data dependence
The close relationship between data stored in files and the software programs that update and maintain those files. Any change in data organization or format requires a change in all the programs associated with those files.

Lack of Flexibility
A traditional file system can deliver routine scheduled reports after extensive programming efforts, but it cannot deliver ad hoc reports or respond to unanticipated information requirements in a timely fashion. The information required by ad hoc requests is somewhere in the system but too expensive to retrieve. Several programmers would have to work for weeks to put together the required data items in a new file.

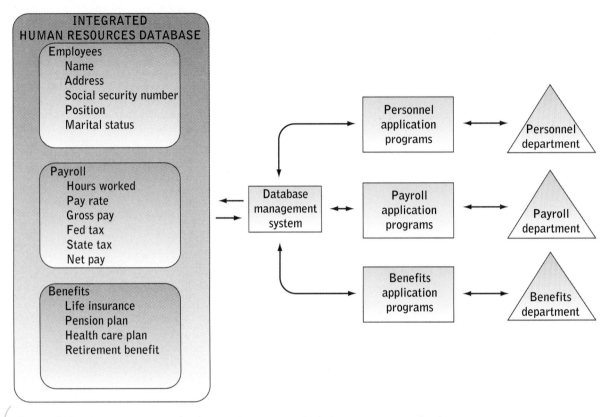

Figure 8-6 The contemporary database environment. A single human resources database serves multiple applications and also allows a corporation to easily draw together all the information for various applications. The database management system acts as the interface between the application programs and the data.

Poor Security
Because there is little control or management of data, access to and dissemination of information are virtually out of control. What limits on access exist tend to be the result of habit and tradition, as well as of the sheer difficulty of finding information.

Lack of Data-Sharing and Availability
The lack of control over access to data in this confused environment does not make it easy for people to obtain information. Because pieces of information in different files and different parts of the organization cannot be related to one another, it is virtually impossible for information to be shared or accessed in a timely manner.

8.2 The Database Environment

Database technology can cut through many of the problems created by traditional file organization. A more rigorous definition of a **database** is a collection of data organized to serve many applications efficiently by centralizing the data and minimizing redundant data. Rather than storing data in separate files for each application, data are stored physically to appear to users as being stored in only one location. A single database services multiple applications. For example, instead of a corporation storing employee data in separate information systems and separate files for personnel, payroll, and benefits, the corporation could create a single common human resources database. Figure 8-6 illustrates the database concept.

database A collection of data organized to service many applications at the same time by storing and managing data so that they appear to be in one location.

Database Management Systems

A **database management system (DBMS)** is simply the software that permits an organization to centralize data, manage them efficiently, and provide access to the stored data by application programs. The DBMS acts as an interface between application programs and the physical data files. When the application program calls for a data item such as gross pay, the DBMS finds this item in the database and presents it to the application program. Using traditional data files the programmer would have to define the data and then tell the computer where they were. A DBMS eliminates most of the data definition statements found in traditional programs.

A database management system has three components:

- A data definition language
- A data manipulation language
- A data dictionary

The **data definition language** is the formal language used by programmers to specify the content and structure of the database. The data definition language defines each data element as it appears in the database before that data element is translated into the forms required by application programs.

Most DBMS have a specialized language called a **data manipulation language** that is used in conjunction with some conventional third- or fourth-generation programming languages to manipulate the data in the database. This language contains commands that permit end users and programming specialists to extract data from the database to satisfy information requests and develop applications. The most prominent data manipulation language today is **Structured Query Language,** or **SQL.** Complex programming tasks cannot be performed efficiently with typical data manipulation languages. However, most mainframe DBMS are compatible with COBOL, FORTRAN, and other third-generation programming languages, permitting greater processing efficiency and flexibility.

The third element of a DBMS is a **data dictionary.** This is an automated or manual file that stores definitions of data elements and data characteristics such as usage, physical representation, ownership (who in the organization is responsible for maintaining the data), authorization, and security. Many data dictionaries can produce lists and reports of data utilization, groupings, program locations, and so on. Figure 8-7 illustrates a sample data dictionary report that shows the size, format, meaning, and uses of a data element in a human resources database. A **data element** represents a field. In addition to listing the standard name (AMT-PAY-BASE), the dictionary lists the names that reference this element in specific systems and identifies the individuals, business functions, programs, and reports that use this data element.

By creating an inventory of data contained in the database, the data dictionary serves as an important data management tool. For instance, business users could consult the dictionary to find out exactly what pieces of data are maintained for the sales or marketing function or even to determine all the information maintained by the entire enterprise. The dictionary could supply business users with the name, format, and specifications required to access data for reports. Technical staff could use the dictionary to determine what data elements and files must be changed if a program is changed.

Most data dictionaries are entirely passive; they simply report. More advanced types are active; changes in the dictionary can be automatically utilized by related programs. For instance, to change ZIP codes from five to nine digits, one could simply enter the change in the dictionary without having to modify and recompile all application programs using ZIP codes.

In an ideal database environment, the data in the database are defined only once and used for all applications whose data reside in the database, thereby eliminating data redundancy and inconsistency. Application programs, which are written using a combination of the data manipulation language of the DBMS and a conventional programming

database management system (DBMS) Special software to create and maintain a database and enable individual business applications to extract the data they need without having to create separate files or data definitions in their computer programs.

data definition language The component of a database management system that defines each data element as it appears in the database.

data manipulation language A language associated with a database management system that is employed by end users and programmers to manipulate data in the database.

Structured Query Language (SQL) The standard data manipulation language for relational database management systems.

data dictionary An automated or manual tool for storing and organizing information about the data maintained in a database.

data element A field.

```
NAME: AMT-PAY-BASE
FOCUS NAME: BASEPAY
PC NAME:      SALARY

DESCRIPTION: EMPLOYEE'S ANNUAL SALARY

SIZE: 9 BYTES
TYPE: N         (NUMERIC)
DATE CHANGED: 01/01/85
OWNERSHIP: COMPENSATION
UPDATE SECURITY: SITE PERSONNEL
ACCESS SECURITY: MANAGER, COMPENSATION PLANNING AND RESEARCH
                 MANAGER, JOB EVALUATION SYSTEMS
                 MANAGER, HUMAN RESOURCES PLANNING
                 MANAGER, SITE EQUAL OPPORTUNITY AFFAIRS
                 MANAGER, SITE BENEFITS
                 MANAGER, CLAIMS PAYING SYSTEMS
                 MANAGER, QUALIFIED PLANS
                 MANAGER, SITE EMPLOYMENT/EEO
BUSINESS FUNCTIONS USED BY: COMPENSATION
                            HR PLANNING
                            EMPLOYMENT
                            INSURANCE
                            PENSION
                            ISP


PROGRAMS USING:  PI01000
                 PI02000
                 PI03000
                 PI04000
                 PI05000


REPORTS USING:  REPORT 124 (SALARY INCREASE TRACKING REPORT)
                REPORT 448 (GROUP INSURANCE AUDIT REPORT)
                REPORT 452 (SALARY REVIEW LISTING)
                PENSION REFERENCE LISTING
```

language, request data elements from the database. Data elements called for by the application programs are found and delivered by the DBMS. The programmer does not have to specify in detail how or where the data are to be found.

Use of a DBMS can reduce program-data dependence along with program development and maintenance costs. Access and availability of information can be increased because users and programmers can perform ad hoc queries of data in the database. The DBMS allows the organization to centrally manage data, utilization, and security.

Logical and Physical Views of Data

Perhaps the greatest difference between a DBMS and traditional file organization is that the DBMS separates the logical and physical views of the data, relieving the programmer or end user from the task of understanding where and how the data are actually stored.

The database concept distinguishes between logical and physical views of data. The **logical view** presents data as they would be perceived by end users or business specialists, whereas the **physical view** shows how data are actually organized and structured on physical storage media.

Suppose, for example, that a professor of information systems wanted to know at the beginning of the semester how students performed in the prerequisite computer literacy course

logical view A representation of data as they would appear to an application programmer or end user.

physical view The representation of data as they would be actually organized on physical storage media.

Student Name	ID No.	Major	Grade in Computer Literacy 101
Lind	468	Finance	A-
Pinckus	332	Marketing	B+
Williams	097	Economics	C+
Laughlin	765	Finance	A
Orlando	324	Statistics	B

Figure 8-8 The report required by the professor. The report requires data elements that may come from different files but can easily be pulled together with a database management system if the data are organized into a database.

(Computer Literacy 101) and the students' current majors. Using a database supported by the registrar, the professor would need something similar to the report shown in Figure 8-8.

Ideally, for such a simple report, the professor could sit at an office terminal connected to the registrar's database and write a small application program using the data manipulation language to create this report. The professor first would develop the desired logical view of the data (Figure 8-8) for the application program. The DBMS would then assemble the requested data elements, which might reside in several different files and disk locations. For instance, the student major information might be located in a file called *Student,* whereas the grade data might be located in a file called *Course.* Wherever they were located, the DBMS would pull these pieces of information together and present them to the professor according to the logical view requested.

The query using the data manipulation language constructed by the professor might resemble that shown in Figure 8-9. DBMS working on both mainframes and PCs permit this kind of interactive report creation.

8.3 Designing Databases

There are alternative ways of organizing data and representing relationships among data in a database. Conventional DBMS use one of three principal logical database models for keeping track of entities, attributes, and relationships. The three principal logical database models are hierarchical, network, and relational. Each logical model has certain processing advantages and certain business advantages.

Hierarchical Data Model

The earliest DBMSs were hierarchical. The **hierarchical data model** presents data to users in a treelike structure. The most common hierarchical DBMS is IBM's IMS (Information Management System). Within each record, data elements are organized into pieces of records called *segments.* To the user, each record looks like an organization chart with one top-level segment called the *root.* An upper segment is connected logically to a lower segment in a parent–child relationship. A parent segment can have more than one child, but a child can have only one parent.

hierarchical data model One type of logical database model that organizes data in a treelike structure. A record is subdivided into segments that are connected to each other in one-to-many parent–child relationships.

```
SELECT Stud_name, Stud.stud_id, Major, Grade
FROM Student, Course
WHERE Stud.stud_id = Course.stud_id
AND Course_id = "CL101"
```

Figure 8-9 The query used by the professor. This example shows how Structured Query Language (SQL) commands could be used to deliver the data required by the professor. These commands join two files, the student file (Student) and the course file (Course), and extract the specified pieces of information on each student from the combined file.

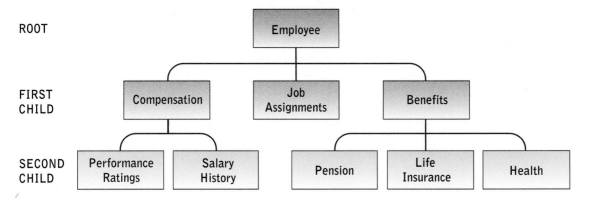

ROOT

FIRST
CHILD

SECOND
CHILD

Figure 8-10 A hierarchical database for a human resources system. The hierarchical database model looks like an organizational chart or a family tree. It has a single root segment (Employee) connected to lower level segments (Compensation, Job Assignments, and Benefits). Each subordinate segment, in turn, may connect to other subordinate segments. Here, Compensation connects to Performance Ratings and Salary History. Benefits connects to Pension, Life Insurance, and Health Care. Each subordinate segment is the child of the segment directly above it.

pointer A special type of data element attached to a record that shows the absolute or relative address of another record.

network data model A logical database model that is useful for depicting many-to-many relationships.

Figure 8-10 shows a hierarchical structure that might be used for a human resources database. The root segment is Employee, which contains basic employee information such as name, address, and identification number. Immediately below it are three child segments: Compensation (containing salary and promotion data), Job Assignments (containing data about job positions and departments), and Benefits (containing data about beneficiaries and benefit options). The Compensation segment has two children below it: Performance Ratings (containing data about employees' job performance evaluations) and Salary History (containing historical data about employees' past salaries). Below the Benefits segment are child segments for Pension, Life Insurance, and Health, containing data about these benefit plans.

Behind the logical view of data are a number of physical links and devices to tie the information together into a logical whole. In a hierarchical DBMS the data are physically linked to one another by a series of **pointers** that form chains of related data segments. Pointers are data elements attached to the ends of record segments on the disk directing the system to related records. In our example, the end of the Employee segment would contain a series of pointers to all Compensation, Job Assignments, and Benefits segments. In turn, at the end of the Compensation and Benefits segments are pointers to their respective child segments.

Network Data Model

The **network data model** is a variation of the hierarchical data model. Indeed, databases can be translated from hierarchical to network and vice versa to optimize processing speed and convenience. Whereas hierarchical structures depict one-to-many relationships, network structures depict data logically as many-to-many relationships. In other words, parents can have multiple children, and a child can have more than one parent.

A typical many-to-many relationship in which a network DBMS excels in performance is the student–course relationship (see Figure 8-11). There are many courses in a university and many students. A student takes many courses and a course has many students. The data in Figure 8-11 could be structured hierarchically. But this could result in considerable redundancy and a slowed response to certain types of information queries; the same student would be listed on the disk for each class he or she was taking instead of only once. Network structures reduce redundancy and, in certain situations (when many-to-many relationships are involved), respond more quickly. However, there is a price for this reduction in redundancy and increased speed: The number of pointers in network structures rapidly increases, making maintenance and operation potentially more complicated.

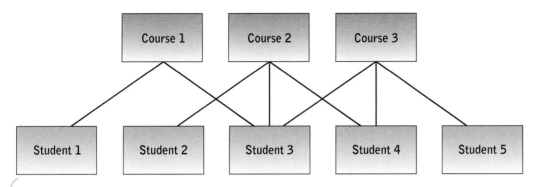

Figure 8-11 The network data model. This illustration of a network data model showing the relationship the students in a university have to the courses they take represents an example of logical many-to-many relationships. The network model reduces the redundancy of data representation through the increased use of pointers.

Relational Data Model

The **relational data model,** the most recent of these three database models, overcomes some of the limitations of the other two models. The relational model represents all data in the database as simple two-dimensional tables called *relations*. The tables appear similar to flat files, but the information in more than one file can be easily extracted and combined. Sometimes the tables are referred to as files.

Figure 8-12 shows a supplier table, a part table, and an order table. In each table the rows are unique records and the columns are fields. Another term for a row or record in a relation is a **tuple.** Often a user needs information from a number of relations to produce a report. Here is the strength of the relational model: It can relate data in any one file or table to data in another file or table *as long as both tables share a common data element.*

To demonstrate, suppose we wanted to find in the relational database in Figure 8-12 the names and addresses of suppliers who could provide us with part number 137 or part number 152. We would need information from two tables: the supplier table and the part table. Note that these two files have a shared data element: SUPPLIER-NUMBER.

In a relational database, three basic operations are used to develop useful sets of data: select, project, and join. The *select* operation creates a subset consisting of all records in the file that meet stated criteria. *Select* creates, in other words, a subset of rows that meet certain criteria. In our example, we want to select records (rows) from the part table where the part number equals 137 or 152. The *join* operation combines relational tables to provide the user with more information than is available in individual tables. In our example we want to join the now shortened part table (only parts numbered 137 or 152 will be presented) and the supplier table into a single new result table.

The *project* operation creates a subset consisting of columns in a table, permitting the user to create new tables that contain only the information required. In our example, we want to extract from the new result table only the following columns: PART-NUMBER, SUPPLIER-NUMBER, SUPPLIER-NAME, and SUPPLIER-ADDRESS.

Leading mainframe relational database management systems include IBM's DB2 and Oracle from the Oracle Corporation. Microsoft Access is a PC relational database management system.

Advantages and Disadvantages of the Three Database Models

The principal advantage of the hierarchical and network database models is processing efficiency. For instance, a hierarchical model is appropriate for airline reservation transaction-processing systems, which must handle millions of structured routine requests each day for reservation information.

Hierarchical and network structures have several disadvantages. All the access paths, directories, and indices must be specified in advance. Once specified, they are not easily changed

relational data model A type of logical database model that treats data as if they were stored in two-dimensional tables. It can relate data stored in one table to data in another as long as the two tables share a common data element.

tuple A row or record in a relational database.

Table (Relation)

Columns (Fields)

ORDER

ORDER-NUMBER	ORDER-DATE	DELIVERY-DATE	PART-NUMBER	PART-AMOUNT	ORDER-TOTAL
1634	02/02/99	02/22/99	152	2	144.50
1635	02/12/99	02/29/99	137	3	79.70
1636	02/13/99	03/01/99	145	1	24.30

Rows (Records, Tuples)

PART

PART-NUMBER	PART-DESCRIPTION	UNIT-PRICE	SUPPLIER-NUMBER
137	Door latch	26.25	4058
145	Door handle	22.50	2038
152	Compressor	70.00	1125

SUPPLIER

SUPPLIER-NUMBER	SUPPLIER-NAME	SUPPLIER-ADDRESS
1125	CBM Inc.	44 Winslow, Gary IN 44950
2038	Ace Inc.	Rte. 101, Essex NJ 07763
4058	Bryant Corp.	51 Elm, Rochester NY 11349

Figure 8-12 The relational data model. Each table is a relation and each row or record is a tuple. Each column corresponds to a field. These relations can easily be combined and extracted to access data and produce reports, provided that any two share a common data element. In this example, the ORDER file shares the data element "PART-NUMBER" with the PART file. The PART and SUPPLIER files share the data element "SUPPLIER-NUMBER."

without a major programming effort. Therefore, these designs have low flexibility. For instance, if you queried the human resources database illustrated in Figure 8-10 to find out the names of the employees with the job title of administrative assistant, you would discover that there is no way that the system can find the answer in a reasonable amount of time. This path through the data was not specified in advance.

Both hierarchical and network systems are programming intensive, time consuming, difficult to install, and difficult to remedy if design errors occur. They do not support ad hoc, English language-like inquiries for information.

The strengths of relational DBMS are great flexibility in regard to ad hoc queries, power to combine information from different sources, simplicity of design and maintenance, and the ability to add new data and records without disturbing existing programs and applications. However, these systems are somewhat slower because they typically require many accesses to the data stored on disk to carry out the select, join, and project commands. Selecting one part number from among millions, one record at a time, can take a long time. Of course the database can be indexed and tuned to speed up prespecified queries. Relational systems do not have the large number of pointers carried by hierarchical systems.

Large relational databases may be designed to have some data redundancy to make retrieval of data more efficient. The same data element may be stored in multiple tables. Updating redundant data elements is not automatic in many relational DBMS. For example, changing the employee status field in one table will not automatically change it in all tables. Special arrangements are required to ensure that all copies of the same data element are updated together.

Table 8.1	Comparison of Database Alternatives			
Type of Database	Processing Efficiency	Flexibility	End-User Friendliness	Programming Complexity
Hierarchical	High	Low	Low	High
Network	Medium–high	Low–medium	Low–moderate	High
Relational	Lower but improving	High	High	Low

Hierarchical databases remain the workhorse for intensive high-volume transaction processing. Banks, insurance companies, and other high-volume users continue to use reliable hierarchical databases such as IBM's IMS, developed in 1969. Many organizations have converted to DB2, IBM's relational DBMS for new applications, while retaining IMS for traditional transaction processing. For example, Dallas-based Texas Instruments depends on IMS for its heavy processing requirements, including inventory, accounting, and manufacturing. As relational products acquire more muscle, firms will shift away completely from hierarchical DBMS, but this will happen over a long period of time. Table 8.1 compares the characteristics of the different database models.

Creating a Database

To create a database, one must go through two design exercises: a conceptual design and a physical design. The conceptual or logical design of a database is an abstract model of the database from a business perspective, whereas the physical design shows how the database is actually arranged on direct access storage devices. Physical database design is performed by database specialists, whereas logical design requires a detailed description of the business information needs of actual end users of the database. Ideally, database design will be part of an overall organizational data planning effort (see Chapter 11).

The conceptual database design describes how the data elements in the database are to be grouped. The design process identifies relationships among data elements and the most efficient way of grouping data elements together to meet information requirements. The process also identifies redundant data elements and the groupings of data elements required for specific application programs. Groups of data are organized, refined, and streamlined until an overall logical view of the relationships among all the data elements in the database emerges.

Database designers document the conceptual data model with an **entity-relationship diagram,** illustrated in Figure 8-13. The boxes represent entities and the diamonds represent relationships. The *1* or *M* on either side of the diamond represents the relationship among entities as either one-to-one, one-to-many, or many-to-many. Figure 8-13 shows that the entity ORDER can have only one PART and a PART can only have one SUPPLIER. Many parts can be provided by the same supplier. The attributes for each entity are listed next to the entity and the key field is underlined.

To use a relational database model effectively, complex groupings of data must be streamlined to eliminate redundant data elements and awkward many-to-many relationships. The process of creating small, stable data structures from complex groups of data is called **normalization.** Figures 8-14 and 8-15 illustrate this process. In the particular business modeled here, an order can have more than one part but each part is provided by only one supplier. If we built a relation called ORDER with all the fields included here, we would have to repeat the name, description, and price of each part on the order and the name and address of each part vendor. This relation contains what are called *repeating groups* because there can be many parts and suppliers for each order, and it actually describes multiple

entity-relationship diagram A methodology for documenting databases illustrating the relationship between various entities in the database.

normalization The process of creating small stable data structures from complex groups of data when designing a relational database.

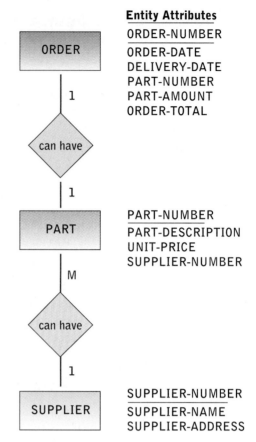

Figure 8-13 An entity-relationship diagram. This diagram shows the relationships between the entities ORDER, PART, and SUPPLIER that were used to develop the relational database illustrated in Figure 8-12.

Entity Attributes

ORDER

ORDER-NUMBER
ORDER-DATE
DELIVERY-DATE
PART-NUMBER
PART-AMOUNT
ORDER-TOTAL

PART

PART-NUMBER
PART-DESCRIPTION
UNIT-PRICE
SUPPLIER-NUMBER

SUPPLIER

SUPPLIER-NUMBER
SUPPLIER-NAME
SUPPLIER-ADDRESS

entities—parts and suppliers as well as orders. A more efficient way to arrange the data is to break down ORDER into smaller relations, each of which describes a single entity. If we go step by step and normalize the relation ORDER, we emerge with the relations illustrated in Figure 8-15.

If a database has been carefully considered, with a clear understanding of business information needs and usage, the database model will most likely be in some normalized form. Many real-world databases are not fully normalized because this may not be the most sensible way to meet business information requirements. Note that the relational database illustrated in Figure 8-12 is not fully normalized because there could be more than one part for each order. The designers chose to not use the four relations described in Figure 8-15 because this particular business has a business rule specifying that a separate order must be placed for each part. The designers might have felt that there was no business need for maintaining four different tables.

8.4 Database Trends

Recent database trends include the growth of distributed databases and the emergence of object-oriented and hypermedia databases.

ORDER

ORDER-NUMBER	PART-AMOUNT	PART-NUMBER	PART-DESCRIPTION	UNIT-PRICE	SUPPLIER-NUMBER	SUPPLIER-NAME	SUPPLIER-ADDRESS	ORDER-DATE	DELIVERY-DATE	ORDER-TOTAL

Figure 8-14 An unnormalized relation for ORDER. In an unnormalized relation there are repeating groups. For example, there can be many parts and suppliers for each order. There is only a one-to-one correspondence between ORDER-NUMBER and ORDER-DATE, ORDER-TOTAL, and DELIVERY-DATE.

ORDER

ORDER-NUMBER	ORDER-DATE	DELIVERY-DATE	ORDER-TOTAL

`Key`

ORDERED-PARTS

ORDER-NUMBER	PART-NUMBER	PART-AMOUNT

`Key`

SUPPLIER

SUPPLIER-NUMBER	SUPPLIER-NAME	SUPPLIER-ADDRESS

`Key`

PART

PART-NUMBER	PART-DESCRIPTION	UNIT-PRICE	SUPPLIER-NUMBER

`Key`

Figure 8-15 A normalized relation for ORDER. After normalization, the original relation ORDER has been broken down into four smaller relations. The relation ORDER is left with only three attributes and the relation ORDERED-PARTS has a combined, or concatenated, key consisting of ORDER-NUMBER and PART-NUMBER.

Distributed Databases

The growth of distributed processing and networking has been accompanied by a movement toward distributed databases. A **distributed database** is one that is stored in more than one physical location. Parts of the database are stored physically in one location, and other parts are stored and maintained in other locations. There are two main ways of distributing a database (see Figure 8-16). The central database (see Figure 8-16a) can be partitioned so that each remote processor has the necessary data to serve its local area. Changes in local files can be justified with the central database on a batch basis, often at night. Another strategy is to

distributed database A database that is stored in more than one physical location. Parts or copies of the database are physically stored in one location, and other parts or copies are stored and maintained in other locations.

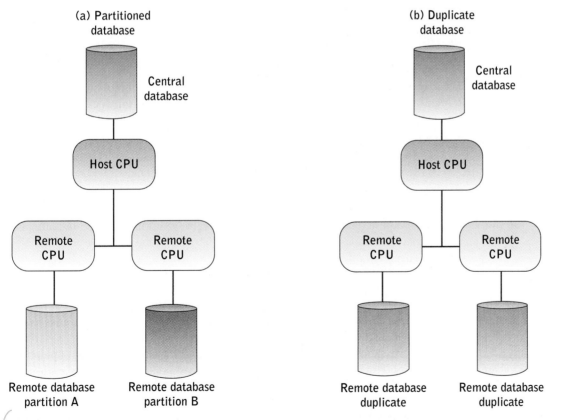

Figure 8-16 Distributed databases. There are alternative ways of distributing a database. The central database can be partitioned (a) so that each remote processor has the necessary data to serve its own local needs. The central database also can be duplicated (b) at all remote locations.

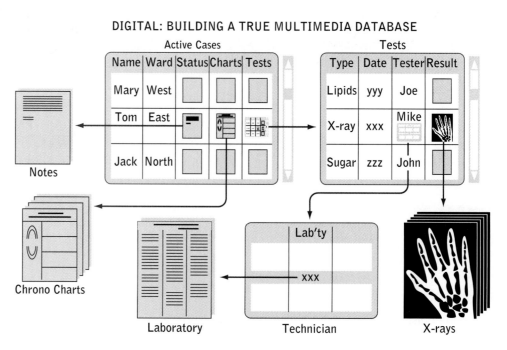

Figure 8-17 An object-oriented multimedia database. Medical data on patients in a hospital might likely be stored in a multimedia database such as this. Doctors could access patient files including vital medical images to generate the reports and derive the information they need to deliver quality health care quickly. Reprinted by permission of Digital Equipment Corporation, Maynard, MA.

replicate the central database (Figure 8-16b) at all remote locations. For example, Lufthansa Airlines replaced its centralized mainframe database with a replicated database to make information more immediately available to flight dispatchers. Any change made to Lufthansa's Frankfort DBMS is automatically replicated in New York and Hong Kong. This strategy also requires updating of the central database on off hours.

Both distributed processing and distributed databases have benefits and drawbacks. Distributed systems reduce the vulnerability of a single, massive central site. They permit increases in systems' power by purchasing smaller, less expensive computers. Finally, they increase service and responsiveness to local users. Distributed systems, however, are dependent on high-quality telecommunications lines, which themselves are vulnerable. Moreover, local databases can sometimes depart from central data standards and definitions, and they pose security problems by widely distributing access to sensitive data. The economies of distribution can be lost when remote sites buy more computing power than they need. Despite these drawbacks, distributed processing is growing rapidly.

Object-Oriented and Hypermedia Databases

Conventional database management systems were designed for homogeneous data that can be easily structured into predefined data fields and records. But many applications today and in the future will require databases that can store and retrieve not only structured numbers and characters but also drawings, images, photographs, voice, and full-motion video (see Figure 8-17). Conventional DBMS are not well suited to handling graphics-based or multimedia applications. For instance, design data in a CAD database consist of complex relationships among many types of data. Manipulating these kinds of data in a relational system requires extensive programming to translate these complex data structures into tables and rows. An **object-oriented database,** on the other hand, stores the data and procedures as objects that can be automatically retrieved and shared.

Object-oriented database management systems (OODBMS) are becoming popular because they can be used to manage the various multimedia components or Java applets used in Web applications, which typically integrate pieces of information from a variety of sources. OODBMS also are useful for storing data types such as recursive data. (An example would be parts within parts as found in manufacturing applications.) Finance and trading applications often use OODBMS because they require data models that must be easy to change to

object-oriented database

An approach to data management that stores both data and the procedures acting on the data as objects that can be automatically retrieved and shared; the objects can contain multimedia.

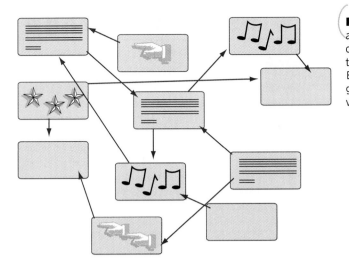

Figure 8-18 Hypermedia. In a hypermedia database, the user can choose his or her own path to move from node to node. Each node can contain text, graphics, sound, full-motion video, or executable programs.

respond to new economic conditions. Motorola Corporation is using the Objectivity OODBMS to store complex celestial information required for its IRIDIUM satellite network because the object model allows navigation directly from data element to data element. A relational DBMS for this application would require extensive joining of separate tables to recombine their data (Watterson, 1998).

The **hypermedia database** approach to information management transcends some of the limitations of traditional database methods by storing chunks of information in the form of nodes connected by links established by the user (see Figure 8-18). The nodes can contain text, graphics, sound, full-motion video, or executable computer programs. Searching for information does not have to follow a predetermined organization scheme. Instead, one can branch instantly to related information in any kind of relationship established by the author. The relationship between records is less structured than in a traditional DBMS. In most systems each node can be displayed on a screen. The screen also displays the links between the node depicted and other nodes in the database. Web sites use a hypermedia database approach to store information as interconnected pages containing text, sound, video, and graphics.

Although object-oriented and hypermedia databases can store more complex types of information than relational DBMS, they are relatively slow compared with relational DBMS for processing large numbers of transactions. *Hybrid* object-relational systems are now available to provide capabilities of both object-oriented and relational DBMS. A hybrid approach can be accomplished in three different ways: by using tools that offer object-oriented access to relational DBMS, by using object-oriented extensions to existing relational DBMS, or by using a hybrid object-relational database management system. The Window on Technology describes some of the benefits of using a hybrid object-relational DBMS.

Multidimensional Data Analysis

Sometimes managers need to analyze data in ways that cannot be represented by traditional database models. For example, a company selling four different products—nuts, bolts, washers, and screws—in the East, West, and Central regions, might want to know actual sales by product for each region and might also want to compare them with projected sales. This analysis requires a multidimensional view of data.

To provide this type of information, organizations can use either a specialized multidimensional database or a tool that creates multidimensional views of data in relational databases. Multidimensional analysis enables users to view the same data in different ways using multiple dimensions. Each aspect of information—product, pricing, cost, region, or time period—represents a different dimension. So a product manager could use a multidimensional

hypermedia database An approach to data management that organizes data as a network of nodes linked in any pattern established by the user; the nodes can contain text, graphics, sound, full-motion video, or executable programs.

La Scala's Multimedia Database

Founded in 1776, La Scala is one of the world's oldest and most famous opera houses, with a repertory spanning both unfamiliar works and popular favorites. To restore and preserve La Scala's heritage and make it more widely available to musicians, scholars, and the general public, the Laboratorio di Informatica Musicale (LIM) of the Information Science Department at the University of Milan has undertaken a project to digitize the theater's recordings, scores, and scenography materials dating back to 1951.

The archives include digital audio recordings of operas and excerpts, graphic representations of opera scores, including conductors' notations, photos of conductors, videos of opera performances, documentary videos, and reproductions of historical scenery and costumes. Conductors and musical scholars will be able to use these data to trace the evolution of performances of a particular opera over the past 50 years. They will be able to see how other conductors performed a particular opera and the changes made to the score.

The archive is based on an Oracle8 object-relational database and can run on UNIX, Microsoft Windows NT, Windows 95, and Macintosh platforms in a client/server architecture. Professor Goffredo Haus, LIM's director, said that Oracle8 was chosen specifically because it could support a distributed database, multiple platforms, and because it could cope with the management of information in many different formats, including audio, graphics, and video. Brief captions and descriptions can be stored in a relational format, whereas sounds, videos, and images require object-oriented organization and management. Internal users can access the database using a client/server interface, but the project is also creating an Internet browser interface for wider distribution.

Eventually over 1.2 million pages of musical scores will be available through a graphical display associated with the sound so that users can view scores or excerpts while listening to them. The system is organized around La Scala "nights," each of which encompasses the score, audio elements, and other graphical and video items related to a performance. Users will be able to sing a few bars into a microphone attached to the computer and initiate a search to bring up all similar pieces of music stored within the system. They can also view the graphical music scores or excerpts from them and simultaneously play the music by pointing a mouse at specified parts of the score.

The first database developed consisted of digitized recordings and took up five terabytes. The second database, designed to hold graphical information, will be much larger. Each operatic score, which is usually about 500 pages long, is expected to generate approximately 13 gigabytes of audio data and 7 gigabytes of graphical data. The La Scala archives are planned to be fully on-line by the end of 1999.

To Think About: Why was an object-relational DBMS appropriate for the La Scala archives? What management, organization, and technology issues had to be addressed by this project?

Sources: Sara Record, "Brava, La Scala!" Oracle Magazine, May/June 1998; and Martin J. Garvey, "Multimedia Venture to Link Oracle8, Inx-Goal Is to Provide Advanced Video," Information Week, July 27, 1998.

---

on-line analytical processing (OLAP) Capability for manipulating and analyzing large volumes of data from multiple perspectives.

data analysis tool to learn how many washers were sold in the East in June, how that compares with the previous month and the previous June, and how it compares with the sales forecast. Another term for multidimensional data analysis is **on-line analytical processing (OLAP).**

Figure 8-19 shows a multidimensional model that could be created to represent products, regions, actual sales, and projected sales. A matrix of actual sales can be stacked on top of a matrix of projected sales to form a cube with six faces. If you rotate the cube 90 degrees one way, the face showing will be product versus actual and projected sales. If you rotate the cube 90 degrees again, you can see region versus actual and projected sales. If you rotate 180 degrees from the original view, you can see projected sales and product versus region. Cubes can be nested within cubes to build complex views of data.

Data Warehouses

Decision makers need concise, reliable information about current operations, trends, and changes. What has been immediately available at most firms is current data only (historical data were available through special IS reports that took a long time to produce). Data often are fragmented in separate operational systems such as sales or payroll so that different managers make decisions from incomplete knowledge bases. Users and information system specialists may have to spend inordinate amounts of time locating and gathering data (Watson and Haley, 1998). Data warehousing addresses this problem by integrating

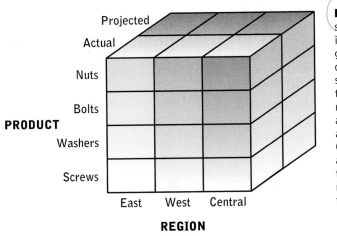

PRODUCT
Projected
Actual
Nuts
Bolts
Washers
Screws

East   West   Central

REGION

Figure 8-19 Multidimensional data model. The view that is showing is product versus region. If you rotate the cube 90 degrees, the face that will be showing is product versus actual and projected sales. If you rotate the cube 90 degrees again, you can see region versus actual and projected sales. Other views are possible. The ability to rotate the data cube is the main technique for multidimensional reporting. It is sometimes called "slice and dice."

key operational data from around the company in a form that is consistent, reliable, and easily available for reporting.

What Is a Data Warehouse?

A **data warehouse** is a database, with tools, that stores current and historical data of potential interest to managers throughout the company. The data originate in many core operational systems and external sources and are copied into the data warehouse database as often as needed—hourly, daily, weekly, monthly. The data are standardized and consolidated so that they can be used across the enterprise for management analysis and decision making. The data are available for anyone to access as needed but cannot be altered. A data warehouse system includes a range of ad hoc and standardized query tools, analytical tools, and graphical reporting facilities. These systems can perform high-level analyses of patterns or trends, but they can also drill into more detail where needed. Figure 8-20 illustrates the data warehouse concept.

Companies can build enterprise-wide data warehouses where a central data warehouse serves the entire organization, or they can create smaller, decentralized warehouses called data marts. A **data mart** is a subset of a data warehouse in which a summarized or highly focused portion of the organization's data is placed in a separate database for a specific population of users. For example, a company might develop marketing and sales data marts to deal with customer information. A data mart typically focuses on a single subject area or line of business, so it usually can be constructed more rapidly and at lower cost than an enterprise-wide data warehouse. On the other hand, complexity, costs, and management problems will rise if an organization creates too many data marts (Francett, 1997). The Window on Management describes some of the management issues raised by construction of data marts for the organization.

data warehouse A database, with reporting and query tools, that stores current and historical data extracted from various operational systems and consolidated for management reporting and analysis.

data mart A small data warehouse containing only a portion of the organization's data for a specified function or population of users.

Benefits of a Data Warehouse

Data warehouses not only offer improved information, but they make it easy for decision makers to obtain it. They even include the ability to model and remodel the data. These systems also enable decision makers to access data as often as they need without affecting the performance of the underlying operational systems.

Through the use of on-line analytical processing (OLAP) and data marts, Office Depot was able to "refocus the business." Merchandisers, salespeople, and executives reviewed the retailer's PC business by generating detailed analyses of gross-margin return on investments by store and product type. They found that the company was carrying too much fringe stock in the wrong stores. Office Depot narrowed its inventory of PCs from 22 to 12 products. Profits rose by eliminating unnecessary inventory and avoiding markdowns on equipment that wasn't selling (Hoffman, 1998).

Victoria's Secret Stores was spending too much time trying to locate information and not enough time analyzing it. Through data warehousing, the lingerie chain learned that its system

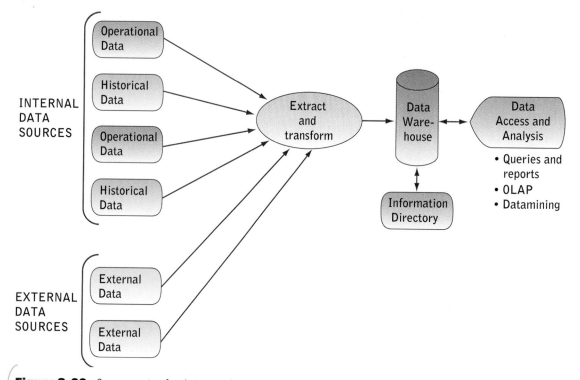

Figure 8-20 Components of a data warehouse. A data warehouse extracts current and historical data from operational systems inside the organization. These data are combined with data from external sources and reorganized into a central database designed for management reporting and analysis. The information directory provides users with information about the data available in the warehouse.

Hyperion Essbase OLAP Server allows users to perform ad hoc multidimensional data analysis on organizational databases through a Web interface. Users can work with OLAP applications such as planning, budgeting, and forecasting over corporate intranets or the Internet.

Top 3 Southern States By Product Report - Microsoft Internet E

File Edit View Go Favorites Help

Launch Spreadsheet

		Actual	Retail	Bottles	Sales
		Jan	**Feb**	**Mar**	**Qtr1**
Kool Cola	**Texas**	$5,344.00	$2,015.00	$2,386.00	$9,745.00
	Tennessee	$2,374.00	$896.00	$1,060.00	$4,330.00
	Oklahoma	$2,295.00	$864.00	$1,025.00	$4,184.00
Caffeine Free Cola	**Texas**	$5,140.00	$1,937.00	$2,296.00	$9,373.00
	Tennessee	$2,843.00	$1,073.00	$1,271.00	$5,187.00
	Louisiana	$1,855.00	$699.00	$826.00	$3,380.00
Diet Cola	**Texas**	$3,915.00	$1,473.00	$1,744.00	$7,132.00
	Tennessee	$1,846.00	$693.00	$823.00	$3,362.00
	Louisiana	$1,543.00	$583.00	$686.00	$2,812.00
Old Fashioned	**Texas**	$5,987.00	$2,262.00	$2,674.00	$10,923.00
	Louisiana	$2,532.00	$954.00	$1,129.00	$4,615.00
	Arizona	$2,301.00	$899.00	$1,064.00	$4,354.00

Start

Canned Data Marts to the Rescue

Storing, protecting, and accessing data was a major management problem for Quaker Chemical. Quaker, a $250 million chemical company from Conshohocken, Pennsylvania, sells products for more than a dozen industries, from pulp and paper to aerospace. Moreover, they operate on six continents. Controller Irving Tyler's problem was how to collect the data from Quaker's far-flung sites and then make this information available to those who need it.

In the past, financial managers who needed to analyze data and report on sales and other key indicators would first have to go to many different financial systems to get the data. Then they would enter the data into their own spreadsheets and perform their analyses and prepare their reports. The process was very expensive, not only because it was time-consuming, but also because reentering data is highly error-prone. To Tyler, the obvious solution was a small data warehouse, known as a data mart. Such a system, Tyler said, would "pull in data from all these systems, cleanse it, and make it comparable."

Tyler realized that building one's own data mart can be costly and complicated. An organization has to extract the data from the relevant systems, "cleanse" the data, and put the data into a form for easier reporting and analysis. Various tools for data transfer, data loading, and datamart management need to work together. The organization also needs to create the data model and business rules. For instance, GTE Airfone in Oak Brook, Illinois, built its own data mart to target customers and improve service using credit card data gathered when customers place calls. The company wanted to combine these data with third-party credit card user profiles purchased from external sources. By combining this information, GTE can pinpoint the average income and age of travelers using the system and tailor special promo-

tions, such as telephone use offers to frequent flyers. But because some of the data in the data mart came from external sources, GTE had to "cleanse" the data and make them compatible with the data it had captured internally.

Quaker needed a versatile system, one that could meet the range of reporting requirements of such a diverse company. It had to extract data from around the world in multiple industries, cleanse and normalize that data, and then store the information. Managers then needed to be able to access the data from a system that would handle Quaker's own financial rules and reporting requirements. Tyler concluded that his company should not be creating such a complex system itself. As he searched the market, he found a new type of software called canned data marts.

The system Tyler purchased is CFO Vision from SAS Institute. The system includes the tools to extract, cleanse, and transform the data. It also includes the tools necessary for managing and tuning the data mart, including tools for transferring and loading the data. The canned data mart was not a turnkey solution that could be loaded and run on day one—information systems specialists and users still had to spend time populating and building the data mart. But CFO Vision also provided preconfigured analytical applications. With all of this in a single package, Quaker's financial managers are now able to prepare their reports more quickly, at a lower cost, and with more confidence in the validity of the data.

To Think About: What are the management benefits of using a canned data mart? Are there any disadvantages?

Sources: Alan Radding, "It's in the Can," **Datamation**, January 1999; and Randy Wilson, "Data Mart Improves GTE Airfone's Marketing," **Computerworld**, June 1, 1998.

---

of allocating merchandise to its 678 shops, based on a mathematical store average, was wrong. For example, an average store sells equal pieces of black and ivory lingerie, but Miami-area consumers buy ivory designs by a margin of 10 to 1. Geographic demand patterns also showed that some stores did not need to discount merchandise. Data warehousing gave this firm a more precise understanding of customer behavior (Goldberg and Vijayan, 1996).

Linking Databases to the Web

It has been estimated that 70 percent of the world's business information resides on mainframe databases, many of which are for older legacy systems. Many of these legacy systems use hierarchical DBMS or even traditional flat files where information is difficult for users to access. A new series of software products has been developed to help users gain access to this mountain of legacy data through the Web.

There are a number of advantages to using the Web to access an organization's internal databases. Web browser software is extremely easy to use, requiring much less training than even user-friendly database query tools. The Web interface requires no changes to the legacy

The Environmental Protection Agency (EPA) created a Web site where employees and the general public can access its Envirofacts data warehouse. More and more organizations are using the World Wide Web to provide an interface to internal databases.

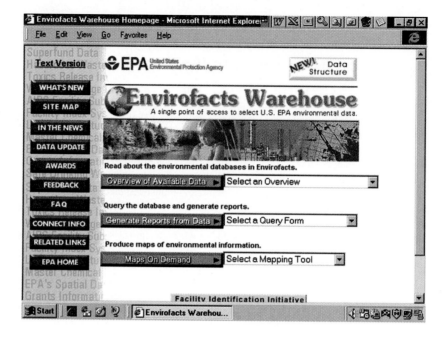

database. Companies leverage their investments in older systems because it costs much less to add a Web interface in front of a legacy system than to redesign and rebuild the system to improve user access.

Accessing corporate databases through the Web is creating new efficiencies and opportunities, in some cases even changing the way business is being done. For example, the Dreyfus Corporation, a New York mutual funds company, created a Web application that allows brokers to use Netscape Navigator Web browser software to access its mainframe database to obtain on-line prospectuses and fund histories (Garvey, 1997). The chapter-ending Case Study describes some of the benefits of providing the public with Web access to government databases.

8.5 Management Requirements for Database Systems

Much more is required for the development of database systems than simply selecting a logical database model. Indeed, this selection may be among the last decisions. The database is an organizational discipline, a method, rather than a tool or technology. It requires organizational and conceptual change.

Without management support and understanding, database efforts fail. The critical elements in a database environment are (1) data administration, (2) data planning and modeling methodology, (3) database technology and management, and (4) users. This environment is depicted in Figure 8-21 and now will be described.

Data Administration

Database systems require that the organization recognize the strategic role of information and begin actively to manage and plan for information as a corporate resource. This means that the organization must develop a **data administration** function with the power to define information requirements for the entire company and with direct access to senior management. The chief information officer (CIO) or vice president of information becomes the primary advocate in the organization for database systems.

Data administration is responsible for the specific policies and procedures through which data can be managed as an organizational resource. These responsibilities include developing information policy, planning for data, overseeing logical database design and data

data administration A special organizational function for managing the organization's data resources, concerned with information policy, data planning, maintenance of data dictionaries, and data quality standards.

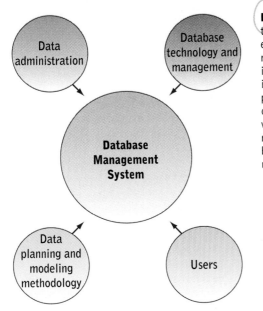

Figure 8-21 Key organizational elements in the database environment. For a database management system to flourish in any organization, data administration functions and data planning and modeling methodologies must be coordinated with database technology and management. Resources must be devoted to train end users to use databases properly.

dictionary development, and monitoring the usage of data by information system specialists and end-user groups.

The fundamental principle of data administration is that all data are the property of the organization as a whole. Data cannot belong exclusively to any one business area or organizational unit. All data are to be made available to any group that requires them to fulfill its mission. An organization needs to formulate an **information policy** that specifies its rules for sharing, disseminating, acquiring, standardizing, classifying, and inventorying information throughout the organization. Information policy lays out specific procedures and accountabilities, specifying which organizational units share information, where information can be distributed, and who has responsibility for updating and maintaining the information. Although data administration is a very important organizational function, it has proved very challenging to implement.

information policy Formal rules governing the maintenance, distribution, and use of information in an organization.

Data Planning and Modeling Methodology

The organizational interests served by the DBMS are much broader than those in the traditional file environment; therefore, the organization requires enterprise-wide planning for data. Enterprise analysis, which addresses the information requirements of the entire organization (as opposed to the requirements of individual applications), is needed to develop databases. The purpose of enterprise analysis is to identify the key entities, attributes, and relationships that constitute the organization's data. These techniques are described in greater detail in Chapter 11.

Database Technology, Management, and Users

Databases require new software and a new staff specially trained in DBMS techniques, as well as new management structures. Most corporations develop a database design and management group within the corporate information system division that is responsible for the more technical and operational aspects of managing data. The functions it performs are called **database administration.** This group does the following:

database administration Refers to the more technical and operational aspects of managing data, including physical database design and maintenance.

○ Defines and organizes database structure and content

○ Develops security procedures to safeguard the database

○ Develops database documentation

○ Maintains the database management software

DNA Databases: Crime Fighters or Threats to Privacy?

DNA evidence has become a potent crime-fighting tool, allowing a criminal to be fingered by his or her own genes. Computer analysis can discover the identity of a killer or rapist by matching DNA from blood, saliva, or other body fluids left at a crime scene with a DNA profile in a database. DNA evidence is especially useful for solving violent crimes, where the people care deeply about identifying the perpetrators and getting them off the street.

Until recently DNA "hits" have been sporadic because databases of DNA profiles were small and localized. The development of a national DNA database could change that. The Federal Bureau of Investigation and state laboratories have established new technical standards for testing DNA strands to support a national system of quick, cheap testing. In December 1997, eight states started to use FBI software to pool their data on-line, enabling them to identify criminals across their borders. Within minutes they scored their first hit, linking a convicted sex offender in Illinois to a 1989 offense and attempted murder in Wisconsin. According to the U.S. Department of Justice, an experiment in 17 states over a three-year period matched 193 convicted criminals with DNA taken from crime scenes. In October 1998 a national 50-state DNA database was activated.

If DNA is such a powerful tool for identifying criminals, why wasn't a national DNA database established earlier, such as the one in Britain, which has scored thousands of hits? One obstacle is money—it is very costly to add the required equipment, gather hundreds of thousands of DNA samples, enter and analyze the data, and convert existing databases to the new technology.

Another obstacle is the fear that the creation of a national DNA database would pose threats to individual privacy. In February 1998 a Massachusetts judge halted the collection of blood samples for DNA profiling from thousands of prison inmates, probationers, and parolees. Several had sued the state, arguing that it was an illegal search and seizure conducted without proper safeguards. In other states, questions have arisen about exactly who must submit to DNA testing and who can have access to the data. The O.J. Simpson trial called attention to concerns about whether police and laboratory workers are properly trained to handle such powerful evidence.

Civil libertarians contend that the existence of a national DNA database represents more of a Big Brother invasion of privacy than a national computerized network of fingerprints. Taking blood is much more invasive than taking fingerprints, and DNA carries information that could be abused by insurance companies or even geneticists seeking a gene for something like pedophilia. Benjamin Keehn, a Boston public defender who represented some of the inmates who challenged DNA collection, believes it is dangerous to round up thousands of convicts, probationers, and parolees, as Massachusetts did, on the assumption that they are more likely to commit a crime. If poor people are more likely to commit a crime, why not have their DNA on file, or even take samples at birth? he counters.

In South Dakota, DNA samples are taken routinely on arrest, like fingerprints. Virginia now gathers samples from all convicted felons and some juveniles and has created the most comprehensive DNA database in the nation with 160,000 samples. Dr. Paul Ferrera of Virginia's Division of Forensic Sciences notes that more than half of his "hits" from the crime scenes of rapes and murders came from felons who had previously been convicted only of breaking and entering or burglary.

Dr. George Rowe, a forensic sciences professor at Georgetown University, believes that a national DNA database could have enormous impact. Studies have shown that most violent crimes are committed by a very small number of individuals, many of whom are repeat offenders. "If we're able to identify these guys and send them away . . . think about the impact that will have on the safety of citizens."

DNA analysis also can benefit prisoners. The Innocence Project at Yeshiva University's School of Law already has exonerated 53 convicts after DNA testing was applied to the evidence in their cases. Project head Barry Scheck, who helped defend O. J. Simpson, believes that abuses can be avoided if states develop DNA database laws that carefully stipulate that the data can be used by law enforcement agencies for identification purposes only.

To Think About: Should we allow national DNA databases to be created? Why or why not? What management, organization, and technology issues should be addressed if such databases are created?

Sources: David Rohde, "Quietly, DNA Testing Transforms Sleuth's Job," **The New York Times**, March 9, 1999; Carey Goldberg, "DNA Databanks Giving Police a Powerful Weapon, and Critics," **The New York Times**, February 19, 1998; and Richard Willing, "FBI Activates 50-State DNA Database Today," **USA Today**, October 12, 1998.

In close cooperation with users, the design group establishes the physical database, the logical relations among elements, and the access rules and procedures.

A database serves a wider community of users than traditional systems. Relational systems with fourth-generation query languages permit employees who are not computer specialists to access large databases. In addition, users include trained computer specialists. To optimize access for nonspecialists, more resources must be devoted to training end users. Professional systems workers must be retrained in the DBMS language, DBMS application development procedures, and new software practices.

Database technology has provided many organizational benefits, but it allows firms to maintain large databases with detailed personal information that pose a threat to individual privacy. The Window on Organizations describes the privacy issues surrounding the creation of a national DNA database.

Management Wrap-Up

Selecting an appropriate data model and data management technology for the organization is a key management decision. Managers will need to evaluate the costs and benefits of implementing a database environment and the capabilities of various DBMS or file management technologies. Management should ascertain that organizational databases are designed to meet management information objectives and the organization's business needs.

Management

The organization's data model should reflect its key business processes and decision-making requirements. Data planning may need to be performed to make sure that the organization's data model delivers information efficiently for its business processes and enhances organizational performance. Designing a database is an organizational endeavor.

Organization

Many database and file management options are available for organizing and storing information. Key technology decisions should consider the efficiency of accessing information, flexibility in organizing information, the type of information to be stored and arranged, compatibility with the organization's data model, and compatibility with the organization's hardware and operating systems.

Technology

For Discussion

1. It has been said that you do not need database management software to create a database environment. Discuss.

2. To what extent should end users be involved in the selection of a database management system and database design?

Summary

1. Compare traditional file organization and management techniques. In a traditional file environment, data records are organized using either a sequential file organization or a direct or random file organization. Records in a sequential file can be accessed sequentially or they can be accessed directly if the sequential file is on disk and uses an indexed sequential access method. Records on a file with direct file organization can be accessed directly without an index.

2. Explain the problems of the traditional file environment. By allowing different functional areas and groups in the organization to maintain their own files independently, the traditional file environment creates problems such as data redundancy and inconsistency, program-data dependence, inflexibility, poor security, and lack of data-sharing and availability.

3. Describe how a database management system organizes information. A database management system (DBMS) is the software that permits centralization of data and data management. A DBMS includes a data definition language, a data manipulation language, and a data dictionary capability. The most important feature of the DBMS is its ability to separate the logical and physical views of data. The user works with a logical view of data. The DBMS software translates user queries into queries that can be applied to the physical view of the data. The DBMS retrieves information so that the user does not have to be concerned with its physical location. This feature separates programs from data and from the management of data.

4. Identify the three principal database models and some principles of database design. There are three principal logical database models: hierarchical, network, and relational. Each has unique advantages and disadvantages. Hierarchical systems, which support one-to-many relationships, are low in flexibility but high in processing speed and efficiency. Network systems support many-to-many relationships. Relational systems are relatively slow but are very flexible for supporting ad hoc requests for information and for combining information from different sources. The choice depends on the business requirements. Designing a database requires both a logical design and a physical design. The process of creating small, stable data structures from complex groups of data when designing a relational database is termed *normalization.*

5. Discuss new database trends. It is no longer necessary for data to be centralized in a single, massive database. A complete database or portions of the database can be distributed to more than one location to increase responsiveness and reduce vulnerability and costs. There are two major types of distributed databases: *replicated databases* and *partitioned databases.* Object-oriented, hypermedia, and multidimen-sional databases may be alternatives to traditional database structures for certain types of applications. Object-oriented and hypermedia databases can store graphics and other types of data in addition to conventional text data to support multi-media applications. Hypermedia databases allow data to be stored in nodes linked together in any pattern established by the user. A multidimensional view of data represents relation-ships among data as a multidimensional structure, which can be visualized as cubes of data and cubes within cubes of data, allowing for more sophisticated data analysis. Data can be more conveniently analyzed across the enterprise by using a data warehouse, in which current and historical data are ex-tracted from many different operational systems and consoli-dated for management decision making. Databases can be linked to the Web or to Web browser software to facilitate user access to the data.

6. Analyze the managerial and organizational requirements for creating a database environment. Development of a data-base environment requires much more than selection of technol-ogy. It requires a change in the corporation's attitude toward in-formation. The organization must develop a data administration function and a data planning methodology. There is political re-sistance in organizations to many key database concepts, espe-cially to sharing of information that has been controlled exclu-sively by one organizational group. There are difficult cost/benefit questions in database management. Often, to avoid raising diffi-cult questions, database use begins and ends as a small effort iso-lated in the information systems department.

Key Terms

Review Questions

1. Why is file management important for overall system performance?

2. Describe how indexes and key fields enable a program to access specific records in a file.

3. Define and describe the indexed sequential access method and the direct file access method.

4. List and describe some of the problems of the traditional file environment.

5. Define a database and a database management system.

6. Name and briefly describe the three components of a DBMS.

7. What is the difference between a logical and a physical view of data?

8. List some benefits of a DBMS.

9. Describe the three principal database models and the advantages and disadvantages of each.

10. What is normalization? How is it related to the features of a well-designed relational database?

11. What is a distributed database, and what are the two main ways of distributing data?

12. What are object-oriented and hypermedia databases? How do they differ from a traditional database?

13. Describe the capabilities of on-line analytical processing (OLAP) and multidimensional data analysis.

14. What is a data warehouse? How can it benefit organizations?

15. What are the four key elements of a database environment? Describe each briefly.

16. Describe and briefly comment on the major management challenges in building a database environment.

Group Project

Review Figure 8-6, which provides an overview of a human resources database. Some additional information that might be maintained in such a database are an employee's date of hire, date of termination, number of children, date of birth, educational level, sex code, Social Security tax, Medicare tax, year-to-date gross pay and net pay, amount of life insurance coverage, health care plan payroll-deduction amount, life insurance plan payroll-deduction amount, and pension plan payroll-deduction amount.

Form a group with three or four of your classmates. Prepare two sample reports using the data in the database that might be of interest to either the employer or the employee. What pieces of information should be included on each report? In addition, prepare a data dictionary entry for one of the data elements in the database similar to the entry illustrated in Figure 8-7.

Your group's analysis should determine what business functions use this data element, which function has the primary responsibility for maintaining the data element, and which positions in the organization can access that data element. Present your findings to the class.

Tools for Interactive Learning

○ Internet

The Internet Connection for this chapter will direct you to a series of Web sites where you can complete an exercise to evaluate various commercial database management system products. You can also use the Interactive Study Guide to test your knowledge of the topics in this chapter and get instant feedback where you need more practice.

○ CD-ROM

If you purchase and use the Multimedia Edition CD-ROM with this chapter, you can complete an interactive exercise asking you to select the appropriate database management system for a series of business problems. You can also find a video clip illustrating the THOR satellite tracking application based on a relational database management system, an audio overview of the major themes of this chapter, and bullet text summarizing the key points of the chapter.

The Environmental Protection Agency (EPA) is charged with monitoring and cleaning up the environment, overseeing over 700,000 sites, including local businesses. It had had a longstanding mess of its own that needed cleaning up. The EPA consists of divisions devoted to enforcing various pieces of environmental legislation. Over the years the EPA had built a series of databases in response to laws passed by Congress. Separate databases were established to support each pollution law: the Clean Air Act, permits for waste water discharge, the Superfund Authorization Bill for cleaning up hazardous waste sites, the classification of more than 300 chemicals as toxic that have been or could be released into the environment, the issuing of more than 450,000 site permits for hazardous cleanup activities, record keeping on the more than 675,000 facilities regulated or monitored by the EPA, and an index of the chemical data in the various databases. These databases were so isolated from each other that they used five different database management systems, including Oracle and IBM's DB2.

These data were difficult to obtain. Only registered users, representing a small fraction of EPA employees, had access to the data. And those with access sometimes had trouble making sense of the data because the various databases were supported by different technologies. If a citizen requested information on the sources of pollution in his or her community, EPA staff had to run reports from multiple databases to assemble this information. The data might be presented in an unnatural way that could not be easily understood. For instance, there was no way to pinpoint the location of polluters, so the EPA provided special insight and training in order to interpret the numerical data and provide citizens with answers they could comprehend.

Many thousands of people, such as EPA employees, chemical industry employees, environmental organization employees, and residents of specific local areas, wanted some part of the information that is stored in those databases. However, because the data are not integrated, they have been extremely difficult to access. Those who wanted access, including most EPA employees, had to call an EPA information systems specialist who then had to retrieve the data for them, a very slow,

time-consuming, and expensive operation.

Management has found a better way, relying on more advanced information technology, including the Internet. The first issue, the need to integrate the data, was addressed through a data warehouse known as Envirofacts. Although the independent databases remain, an integrated data warehouse database was completed in 1995. It combines data from five of the EPA databases with additional databases to be added soon. The Envirofacts warehouse can map the 700,000 sites that handle potentially dangerous chemicals and identify their harmful substances. The data stored in Envirofacts are automatically updated monthly from the five isolated databases. EPA employees gain access through a proprietary EPA interface called Gateway. Using Gateway and Envirofacts, EPA employees are able to quickly access most of the data they need. The Gateway interface was installed on many of the EPA's 24,000 desktop PCs. They access Envirofacts through an EPA network. Nonemployees were also able to access the data directly through a dial-up line. The new system not only made it quicker for many people to procure the data they needed, but it also greatly reduced the workload for the EPA's information systems staff, freeing them for more productive work than simply retrieving data.

Nonetheless, problems remained. Support of Gateway, installed on thousands of machines, required a great deal of information systems staff time. Moreover, for those who were not EPA employees, access through a dial-up line was slow, difficult, and costly. So management turned to the Internet to allow access to anyone. The Internet offers several advantages. First, no special interface, such as Gateway, is needed. Instead, all anyone needs is Web browser software that many people use for all their Internet access. Moreover, the public no longer needs to gain access through an EPA dial-up line. Instead, they use their own Internet access providers. EPA employees have also been given access in this manner. Eventually, the EPA is going to phase out the use of Gateway. However, this will be done slowly so employees who prefer to access that way can continue to do so. Ultimately Gateway will be retired totally and all access will be

achieved through the Internet.

Envirofacts uses a UNIX-based Digital Equipment Corporation (DEC) Alpha server for the warehouse platform and an IBM ES/9000 mainframe using fourth-generation software tools such as Natural, Focus, and Platinum Technology's Reporting Facility to extract the data from the various legacy EPA databases. An Oracle 7.3 Web server provides Web-based access to the database. A Netscape Enterprise server is used as the host for the EPA and Envirofacts Web sites.

Here are some examples of how Envirofacts is being used:

○ An environmental lawyer can access Envirofacts to keep track of clients or potential clients. For instance, she could look up a metal fabricating plant and find out what kinds of solvents it uses and the compliance issues it faces.

○ A newspaper reporter can use Envirofacts to research an article about the level of carcinogenic chemical emissions in his community.

○ EPA personnel from the various divisions can share data more easily. In the 1990s the EPA started to take a more holistic view of pollution in geographic areas requiring the integration of data from various sources. The agency now tracks pollution from all sources that affect a specific region. Water specialists, for example, might use a Web browser to analyze how a municipal dump contributed to the pollution of a nearby river. In the past, specialists had to obtain paper reports from the mainframe that could take days to deliver.

The Envirofacts warehouse project cost about $24 million over a five-year period. The system receives more than 300,000 hits per month and fulfills 500 map requests each week. By providing a common interface for previously unconnected database systems, Envirofacts has produced internal cost savings, increased productivity, and facilitated its service to the public. By providing the means for citizens to obtain EPA data themselves, the agency has reduced the number of requests its staff must service under the Freedom of Information Act by about 20 percent. More than $9 million in annual labor costs over five years are saved this way. An additional $30 to $40 million per year are saved by providing a low-cost architecture to link disparate systems. But numbers alone can't explain the full value of Envirofacts. The agency also believes that increased public awareness will lead to more efforts to clean up pollution.

In addition to adding more databases to Envirofacts, the EPA has launched another project to enhance access to the data people need. The agency will be adding to its Web site hot links to other government agencies and universities that make environmental data available to the public. In that way, both the EPA and other organizations of all kinds will have quick and easy access to the data they need to help clean up and protect our environment.

Sources: Peter Fabris, "A Civilian EPA Action," CIO Magazine, February 1, 1998; and Richard Adhikari, "Saved by the Web," Information Week, March 17, 1997.

CASE STUDY QUESTIONS

1. What problems did the EPA face? What management, organization, and technology factors were responsible for those problems?

2. Evaluate the Envirofacts warehouse as a solution to these problems.

3. What management, organization, and technology issues had to be addressed in building the Envirofacts warehouse?

4. To what extent is building a data warehouse a technical decision and to what extent is it a business decision? Explain.

Chapter 9

Telecommunications and Networks

After completing this chapter, you will be able to:

1. Describe the basic components of a telecommunications system.

2. Calculate the capacity of telecommunications channels and evaluate transmission media.

3. Compare the various types of telecommunications networks and network services.

4. Describe important connectivity standards for enterprise networking.

5. Identify principal telecommunications applications for supporting electronic commerce and electronic business.

6. Analyze the management problems raised by enterprise networking and suggest solutions.

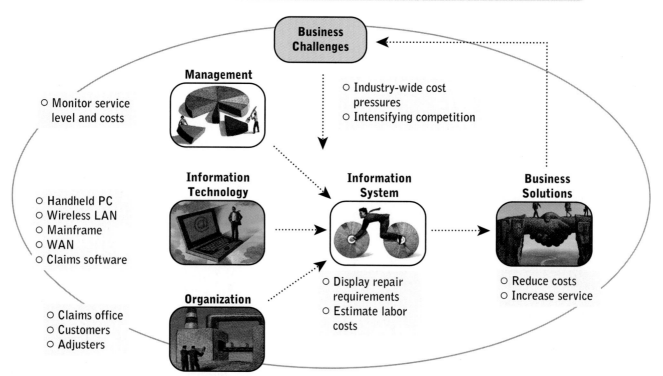

Business Challenges

Management
- Monitor service level and costs
- Industry-wide cost pressures
- Intensifying competition

Information Technology
- Handheld PC
- Wireless LAN
- Mainframe
- WAN
- Claims software

Information System
- Display repair requirements
- Estimate labor costs

Business Solutions
- Reduce costs
- Increase service

Organization
- Claims office
- Customers
- Adjusters

Manitoba Insurance

Goes Wireless

Manitoba Public Insurance, which insures all cars in the Canadian province, turned to pen-based PCs with wireless links to improve customer service and efficiency. It created a drive-through claims center where claimants could instantly view their data and estimates for damage via a pen-based tablet PC linked to a wireless network.

Manitoba Public Insurance operates 19 claims offices throughout the province, servicing 800,000 vehicle owners. Each claims office processes about 100 claims per day. In the past, claimants for auto accidents waited alone while the insurance adjuster went to a back office to calculate the estimate after inspecting the vehicle and gathering information. Now, as claimants drive

into a bay at a claims center, an adjuster will enter the vehicle's license number onto the handheld PC. The data are transmitted via a wireless local area network (LAN) to a server at the claims center, which communicates with the company's central mainframe. The system downloads information on the driver and the car that has been maintained in the system and transmits it to the adjuster's PC. After the adjuster appraises the damage from the accident, the PC screen displays a list of parts, prices, and the labor required for the repairs. Appraisers can complete estimates on the spot without leaving the customer.

The software used by the system can spot ways to save money by using overlap logic to deduct labor time on common operations or performing calculations to estimate painting time. It was supplied by Mitchell International Inc., a San Diego reseller, and runs on a Fujitsu Stylistic 1000 tablet. This handheld PC measures 11 by 7.3 by 1.6 inches, has an 8-inch color screen and a 340-megabyte hard drive, and weighs only 3.4 pounds.

The system with the first "drive-through" insurance claims processing in North America has reduced customer waiting time while improving service. Pen-based computer systems with wireless links are proving so useful that other auto insurers are adopting them as well.

Sources: Tom Davey, "A Touch of Data," *Information Week,* January 26, 1998; and "Fujitsu Pen Tablets Used in First North American 'Drive Through' Insurance Claims Facility" *www.tpsi.fujitsu.com/news.*

Manitoba Public Insurance, like many companies all over the world, is finding ways to benefit from telecommunications technology to coordinate its internal activities and to communicate more efficiently with customers, suppliers, and other external organizations. Uses of networks and communications technology for electronic commerce and electronic business are multiplying, but they raise several management challenges:

1. **Managing LANs.** Although local area networks appear to be flexible and inexpensive ways of delivering computing power to new areas of the organization, they must be carefully administered and monitored. LANs are especially vulnerable to network disruption, loss of essential data, access by unauthorized users, and infection from computer viruses (see Chapter 16). Dealing with these problems requires special technical expertise that is not normally available in end-user departments and is in very short supply.

2. **Selecting a telecommunications platform for enterprise networking.** Internet technology can only provide limited connectivity. There are still major application areas where disparate hardware, software, and network components must be coordinated. Networks based on one standard may not be able to be linked to those based on another without additional equipment, expense, and management overhead. Networks that meet today's requirements may lack the connectivity for domestic or global expansion in the future. Managers may have trouble choosing the right telecommunications platform for the firm's information architecture.

Most of the information systems we use today require networks and communications technology. Companies, large and small from all over the world, are using networked systems and the Internet to locate suppliers and buyers, to negotiate contracts with them, and to service their trades. Uses of networks are multiplying for research, organizational coordination, and control. Networked systems are fundamental to electronic commerce and electronic business.

Today's computing tasks are so closely tied to networks that some believe "the network is the computer." This chapter describes the components of telecommunications systems, showing how they can be arranged to create various types of networks and network-based applications that can increase the efficiency and competitiveness of an organization. It also describes the management challenges introduced by the growth of vast enterprise-wide networks and suggests solutions so organizations can maximize the benefits of communications technology.

9.1 The Telecommunications Revolution

telecommunications The communication of information by electronic means, usually over some distance.

Telecommunications can be defined as the communication of information by electronic means, usually over some distance. Previously, telecommunications meant voice transmission over telephone lines. Today, a great deal of telecommunications transmission is digital data transmission, using computers to transmit data from one location to another. We are currently in the middle of a telecommunications revolution that is spreading communications technology and telecommunications services throughout the globe.

The Marriage of Computers and Communications

Telecommunications used to be a monopoly of either the state or a regulated private firm. In the United States, American Telephone and Telegraph (AT&T) provided virtually all telecommunications services. Telecommunications in Europe and in the rest of the world traditionally has been administered primarily by a state post, telephone, and telegraph authority (PTT). The United States monopoly ended in 1984 when the Justice Department forced AT&T to give up its monopoly and allow competing firms to sell telecommunications services and equipment. The 1996 Telecommunications Deregulation and Reform Act widened deregulation by freeing telephone companies, broadcasters, and cable companies to enter each other's markets. Other areas of the world are starting to open up their telecommunications services to competition as well.

Thousands of companies have sprung up to provide telecommunications products and services, including local and long-distance telephone services, cellular phones and wireless communication services, data networks, cable TV, communications satellites, and Internet services. Managers will be continually faced with decisions on how to incorporate these services and technologies into their information systems and business processes.

The Information Superhighway

Deregulation and the marriage of computers and communications also has made it possible for the telephone companies to expand from traditional voice communications into new information services, such as those providing transmission of news reports, stock reports, television programs, and movies. These efforts are laying the foundation for the **information superhighway,** a vast web of high-speed digital telecommunications networks delivering information, education, and entertainment services to offices and homes. The networks comprising the highway are national or worldwide in scope and accessible by the general public rather than restricted to use by members of a specific organization or set of organizations such as corporations. Some analysts believe the information superhighway will have as profound an impact on economic and social life in the twenty-first century as railroads and interstate highways did in the past.

information superhighway
High-speed digital telecommunications networks that are national or worldwide in scope and accessible by the general public rather than restricted to specific organizations.

The information superhighway concept is broad and rich, providing new ways for organizations and individuals to obtain and distribute information that virtually eliminate the barriers of time and place. Uses of this new superhighway for electronic commerce and electronic business are quickly emerging. The most well known and easily the largest implementation of the information superhighway is the Internet.

Another aspect of the information superhighway is the national computing network proposed by the U.S. federal government. The Clinton administration envisions this network linking universities, research centers, libraries, hospitals, and other institutions that need to exchange vast amounts of information while being accessible in homes and schools.

9.2 Components and Functions of a Telecommunications System

A **telecommunications system** is a collection of compatible hardware and software arranged to communicate information from one location to another. Figure 9-1 illustrates the components of a typical telecommunications system. Telecommunications systems can transmit text, graphic images, voice, or video information. This section describes the major components of telecommunications systems. Subsequent sections describe how the components can be arranged into various types of networks.

telecommunications system
A collection of compatible hardware and software arranged to communicate information from one location to another.

Telecommunications System Components

The following are essential components of a telecommunications system:

1. Computers to process information
2. Terminals or any input/output devices that send or receive data

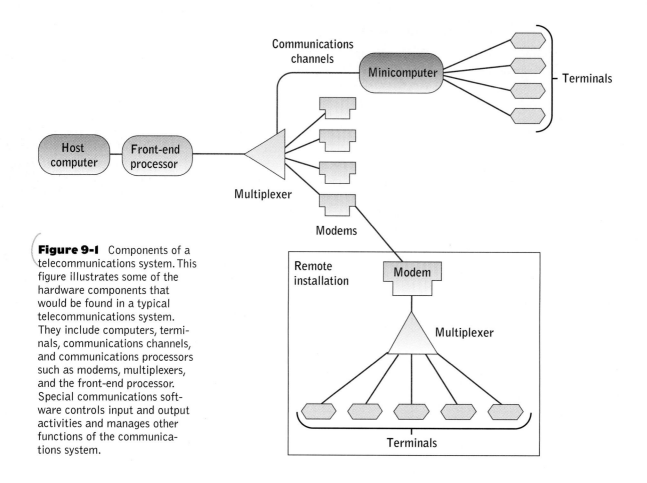

Communications
channels

Minicomputer

Terminals

Host
computer

Front-end
processor

Multiplexer

Modems

Remote
installation

Modem

Multiplexer

Terminals

Figure 9-1 Components of a telecommunications system. This figure illustrates some of the hardware components that would be found in a typical telecommunications system. They include computers, terminals, communications channels, and communications processors such as modems, multiplexers, and the front-end processor. Special communications software controls input and output activities and manages other functions of the communications system.

3. Communications channels, the links by which data or voice are transmitted between sending and receiving devices in a network. Communications channels use various communications media, such as telephone lines, fiber-optic cables, coaxial cables, and wireless transmission

4. Communications processors, such as modems, multiplexers, controllers, and front-end processors, which provide support functions for data transmission and reception

5. Communications software, which controls input and output activities and manages other functions of the communications network

Functions of Telecommunications Systems

In order to send and receive information from one place to another, a telecommunications system must perform a number of separate functions. The system transmits information, establishes the interface between the sender and the receiver, routes messages along the most efficient paths, performs elementary processing of the information to ensure that the right message gets to the right receiver, performs editorial tasks on the data (such as checking for transmission errors and rearranging the format), and converts messages from one speed (say, the speed of a computer) into the speed of a communications line or from one format to another. Finally, the telecommunications system controls the flow of information. Many of these tasks are accomplished by computer.

A telecommunications network typically contains diverse hardware and software components that need to work together to transmit information. Different components in a network can communicate by adhering to a common set of rules that enable them to talk to each other. This set of rules and procedures governing transmission between two points in a network is called a **protocol.** Each device in a network must be able to interpret the other device's protocol. The principal functions of protocols in a telecommunications network are to identify each

protocol A set of rules and procedures that govern transmission between the components in a network.

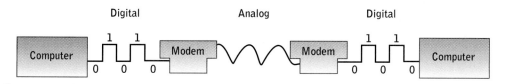

Digital　　　　　**Analog**　　　　　**Digital**

Figure 9-2 Functions of the modem. A modem is a device that translates digital signals from a computer into analog form so that they can be transmitted over analog telephone lines. The modem also is used to translate analog signals back into digital form for the receiving computer.

device in the communication path, to secure the attention of the other device, to verify correct receipt of the transmitted message, to verify that a message requires retransmission because it cannot be correctly interpreted, and to perform recovery when errors occur.

Types of Signals: Analog and Digital

Information travels through a telecommunications system in the form of electromagnetic signals. Signals are represented in two ways: analog and digital signals. An **analog signal** is represented by a continuous waveform that passes through a communications medium. Analog signals are used to handle voice communications and to reflect variations in pitch.

A **digital signal** is a discrete, rather than a continuous, waveform. It transmits data coded into two discrete states: 1-bits and 0-bits, which are represented as on–off electrical pulses. Most computers communicate with digital signals, as do many local telephone companies and some larger networks. However, if a traditional telephone network is set up to process analog signals, a digital signal cannot be processed without some alterations. All digital signals must be translated into analog signals before they can be transmitted in an analog system. The device that performs this translation is called a **modem.** (Modem is an abbreviation for MOdulation/DEModulation.) A modem translates the digital signals of a computer into analog form for transmission over ordinary telephone lines, or it translates analog signals back into digital form for reception by a computer (see Figure 9-2).

Communications Channels

Communications **channels** are the means by which data are transmitted from one device in a network to another. A channel can utilize different kinds of telecommunications transmission media: twisted wire, coaxial cable, fiber optics, terrestrial microwave, satellite, and other wireless transmission. Each has advantages and limitations. High-speed transmission media are more expensive in general, but they can handle higher volumes, which reduces the cost per bit. For instance, the cost per bit of data can be lower via satellite link than via leased telephone line if a firm uses the satellite link 100 percent of the time. There is also a wide range of speeds possible for any given medium depending on the software and hardware configuration.

Twisted Wire

Twisted wire consists of strands of copper wire twisted in pairs and is the oldest transmission medium. Most of the telephone systems in a building rely on twisted wires installed for analog communication, but they can be used for digital communication as well. Although it is low in cost and already is in place, twisted wire is relatively slow for transmitting data, and high-speed transmission causes interference called *crosstalk*. However, new software and hardware have raised the twisted-wire transmission capacity to make it useful for local- and wide-area computer networks as well as telephone systems.

Coaxial Cable

Coaxial cable, like that used for cable television, consists of thickly insulated copper wire, which can transmit a larger volume of data than twisted wire. It often is used in place of twisted wire for important links in a telecommunications network because it is a faster, more interference-free

analog signal A continuous waveform that passes through a communications medium; used for voice communications.

digital signal A discrete waveform that transmits data coded into two discrete states as 1-bits and 0-bits, which are represented as on–off electrical pulses; used for data communications.

modem A device for translating digital signals into analog signals and vice versa.

channels The links by which data or voice are transmitted between sending and receiving devices in a network.

twisted wire A transmission medium consisting of pairs of twisted copper wires; used to transmit analog phone conversations but can be used for data transmission.

coaxial cable A transmission medium consisting of thickly insulated copper wire; can transmit large volumes of data quickly.

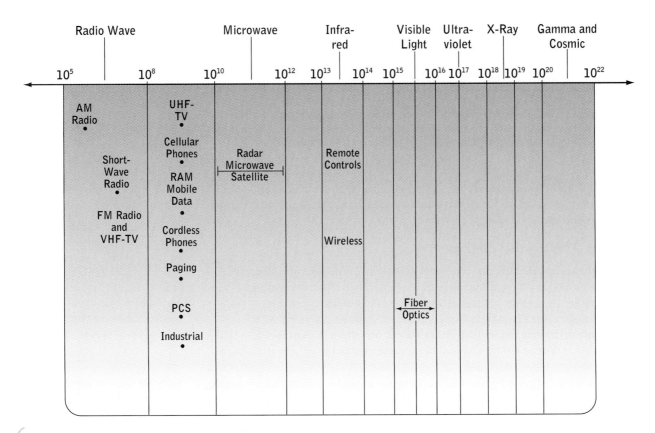

Figure 9-3 Frequency ranges for communications media and devices. Each telecommunications transmission medium or device occupies a different frequency range, measured in megahertz, on the electromagnetic spectrum.

transmission medium, with speeds of up to 200 megabits per second. However, coaxial cable is thick, is hard to wire in many buildings, and cannot support analog phone conversations. It must be moved when computers and other devices are moved.

Fiber Optics

Fiber-optic cable consists of thousands of strands of clear glass fiber, each the thickness of a human hair, which are bound into cables. Data are transformed into pulses of light, which are sent through the fiber-optic cable by a laser device at a rate from 500 kilobits to several billion bits per second. Fiber-optic cable is considerably faster, lighter, and more durable than wire media and is well suited to systems requiring transfers of large volumes of data. However, fiber-optic cable is more difficult to work with, more expensive, and harder to install. In most networks, fiber-optic cable is used as the high-speed **backbone,** while twisted wire and coaxial cable are used to connect the backbone to individual devices. A backbone is the part of a network that handles the major traffic. It acts as the primary path for traffic flowing to or from other networks.

Wireless Transmission

Wireless transmission that sends signals through air or space without any physical tether has emerged as an important alternative to tethered transmission channels such as twisted wire, coaxial cable, and fiber optics. Today, common uses of wireless data transmission include pagers, cellular telephones, microwave transmissions, communication satellites, mobile data networks, personal communications services, personal digital assistants, and smart phones.

The wireless transmission medium is the electromagnetic spectrum, illustrated in Figure 9-3. Some types of wireless transmission, such as microwave or infrared, by nature occupy specific spectrum frequency ranges (measured in megahertz). Other types of wireless trans-

fiber-optic cable A fast, light, and durable transmission medium consisting of thin strands of clear glass fiber bound into cables. Data are transmitted as light pulses.

backbone Part of a network handling the major traffic and providing the primary path for traffic flowing to or from other networks.

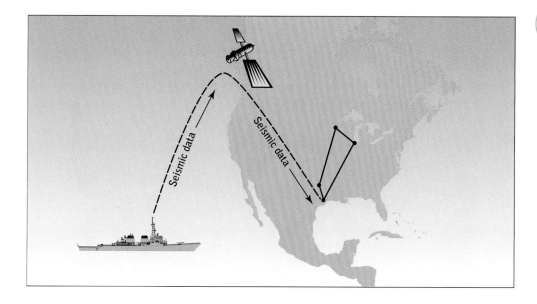

Figure 9-4 Amoco's satellite transmission system. Satellites help Amoco transfer seismic data between oil exploration ships and research centers in the United States.

missions are actually functional uses, such as cellular telephones and paging devices, that have been assigned a specific range of frequencies by national regulatory agencies and international agreements. Each frequency range has its own strengths and limitations, and these have helped determine the specific function or data communications niche assigned to it.

Microwave systems, both terrestrial and celestial, transmit high-frequency radio signals through the atmosphere and are widely used for high-volume, long-distance, point-to-point communication. Microwave signals follow a straight line and do not bend with the curvature of the earth; therefore, long-distance terrestrial transmission systems require that transmission stations be positioned 25 to 30 miles apart, adding to the expense of microwave.

This problem can be solved by bouncing microwave signals off **satellites,** enabling them to serve as relay stations for microwave signals transmitted from terrestrial stations. Communication satellites are cost effective for transmitting large quantities of data over very long distances. Satellites are typically used for communications in large, geographically dispersed organizations that would be difficult to tie together through cabling media or terrestrial microwave. For instance, Amoco uses satellites for real-time data transfer of oil field exploration data gathered from searches of the ocean floor. Exploration ships transfer these data using geosynchronous satellites to central computing centers in the United States for use by researchers in Houston, Tulsa, and suburban Chicago. Figure 9-4 illustrates how this system works.

Conventional communication satellites move in stationary orbits approximately 22,000 miles above the earth. A newer satellite medium, the low-orbit satellite, is beginning to be deployed. These satellites travel much closer to the earth and are able to pick up signals from weak transmitters. They also consume less power and cost less to launch than conventional satellites. With such wireless networks, businesspeople will be able to travel virtually anywhere in the world and have access to full communication capabilities.

Other wireless transmission technologies recently have been developed and are being used in situations requiring mobile computing power. **Paging systems** have been in common use for several decades, originally just beeping when the user received a message and requiring the user to telephone an office to learn about the message. Today, paging devices can send and receive short alphanumeric messages that the user reads on the pager's screen. Paging is useful for communicating with mobile workers such as repair crews; one-way paging also can provide an inexpensive way of communicating with workers in offices. For example, Ethos Corporation in Boulder, Colorado, markets mortgage-processing software that uses a paging system that can deliver daily changes in mortgage rates to thousands of real estate brokers. The data transmitted through the paging network can be downloaded and manipulated, saving brokers approximately one and a half hours of work each week.

microwave A high-volume, long-distance, point-to-point transmission in which high-frequency radio signals are transmitted through the atmosphere from one terrestrial transmission station to another.

satellite The transmission of data using orbiting satellites to serve as relay stations for transmitting microwave signals over very long distances.

paging system A wireless transmission technology in which the pager beeps when the user receives a message; used to transmit short alphanumeric messages.

Motorola's Pagewriter™ 2000X two-way pager allows users to send and receive e-mail, faxes, or messages and to download information from the Internet. Pagers are often used for wireless transmission of brief messages.

cellular telephone A device that transmits voice or data, using radio waves to communicate with radio antennas placed within adjacent geographic areas called cells.

mobile data networks Wireless networks that enable two-way transmission of data files cheaply and efficiently.

personal communication services (PCS) A wireless cellular technology that uses lower power, higher frequency radio waves than does cellular technology and so can be used with smaller size telephones.

personal digital assistants (PDA) Small, pen-based, handheld computers with built-in wireless telecommunications capable of entirely digital communications transmission.

Cellular telephones (sometimes called mobile telephones) work by using radio waves to communicate with radio antennas (towers) placed within adjacent geographic areas called cells. A telephone message is transmitted to the local cell by the cellular telephone and then is handed off from antenna to antenna—cell to cell—until it reaches the cell of its destination, where it is transmitted to the receiving telephone. As a cellular signal travels from one cell into another, a computer that monitors signals from the cells switches the conversation to a radio channel assigned to the next cell. The radio antenna cells normally cover eight-mile hexagonal cells, although their radius is smaller in densely populated localities. The cellular telephone infrastructure was developed for voice transmission, but it is being enhanced for two-way digital data transmission.

Wireless networks explicitly designed for two-way transmission of data files are called **mobile data networks.** These radio-based networks transmit data to and from handheld computers. The wireless network used by Manitoba Insurance in the chapter opening vignette is an example. Another type of mobile data network is based on a series of radio towers constructed specifically to transmit text and data. Ardis (jointly owned by IBM and Motorola) is a publicly available network that uses such media for national two-way data transmission. Otis Elevators uses the Ardis network to dispatch repair technicians around the country from a single office in Connecticut and to receive their reports.

Personal communication services (PCS) is a wireless cellular technology for voice and data that uses lower power, higher frequency radio waves than does cellular technology. PCS cells are much smaller and more closely spaced. The higher frequency signals enable PCS devices to be used in many places where cellular telephones are not effective, such as in tunnels and inside office buildings. Moreover, because PCS telephones need less power, they can be much smaller (shirt-pocket size) and less expensive than cellular telephones. They also operate at higher, less crowded frequencies than cellular telephones (see Figure 9-3), so they will have the bandwidth to offer video and multimedia communication.

Personal digital assistants (PDA) are small, pen-based, handheld computers capable of entirely digital communications transmission. They have built-in wireless telecommunications capabilities as well as work-organization software. A well-known example is the 5.7-ounce PalmPilot by 3COM. It can display and compose e-mail messages (transmission requires additional software and an external modem) and can provide Internet access. The hand-held device includes applications such as an electronic scheduler, address

Table 9.1 Typical Speeds and Costs of Telecommunications Transmission Media

Medium	Speed	Cost
Twisted wire	300 BPS–10 MBPS	Low
Microwave	256 KBPS–100 MBPS	
Satellite	256 KBPS–100 MBPS	
Coaxial cable	56 KBPS–200 MBPS	
Fiber-optic cable	500 KBPS–10 GBPS	High

BPS = bits per second
KBPS = kilobits per second
MBPS = megabits per second
GBPS = gigabits per second

book, and expense tracker and can accept data entered with a special stylus through an on-screen writing pad.

Smart phones combine the functions of pagers, cellular telephones, and personal digital assistants into a small single device. A smart phone is a wireless phone with text and Internet capabilities. It can handle wireless telephone calls, voice mail, e-mail, and faxes, save addresses, and access information from the Internet.

Wireless networks can be more expensive, slower, and more error prone than wired networks. Bandwidth and energy supply in wireless devices require careful management from both hardware and software standpoints (Imielinski and Badrinath, 1994). Security and privacy will be more difficult to maintain because wireless transmission can be easily intercepted (see Chapter 16). Data cannot be transmitted seamlessly between different wireless networks if they use incompatible standards.

smart phone Wireless phone with voice, text, and Internet capabilities.

Transmission Speed

The total amount of information that can be transmitted through any telecommunications channel is measured in bits per second (BPS). Sometimes this is referred to as the *baud rate*. A **baud** is a binary event representing a signal change from positive to negative or vice versa. The baud rate is not always the same as the bit rate. At higher speeds a single signal change can transmit more than one bit at a time, so the bit rate generally will surpass the baud rate.

One signal change, or cycle, is required to transmit one or several bits per second; therefore, the transmission capacity of each type of telecommunications medium is a function of its frequency. The number of cycles per second that can be sent through that medium is measured in *hertz* (see Chapter 6). The range of frequencies that can be accommodated on a particular telecommunications channel is called its **bandwidth.** The bandwidth is the difference between the highest and lowest frequencies that can be accommodated on a single channel. The greater the range of frequencies, the greater the bandwidth and the greater the channel's transmission capacity. Table 9.1 compares the transmission speed and relative costs of the major types of transmissions media.

baud A change in signal from positive to negative or vice versa that is used as a measure of transmission speed.

bandwidth The capacity of a communications channel as measured by the difference between the highest and lowest frequencies that can be transmitted by that channel.

Communications Processors and Software

Communications processors, such as front-end processors, concentrators, controllers, multiplexers, and modems, support data transmission and reception in a telecommunications network. In a large computer system, the **front-end processor** is a small computer dedicated to communications management and is attached to the main, or host, computer. The front-end processor performs communications processing such as error control, formatting, editing, controlling, routing, and speed and signal conversion.

A **concentrator** is a programmable telecommunications computer that collects and temporarily stores messages from terminals until enough messages are ready to be sent economically. The concentrator bursts signals to the host computer.

front-end processor A small computer managing communications for the host computer in a network.

concentrator Telecommunications computer that collects and temporarily stores messages from terminals for batch transmission to the host computer.

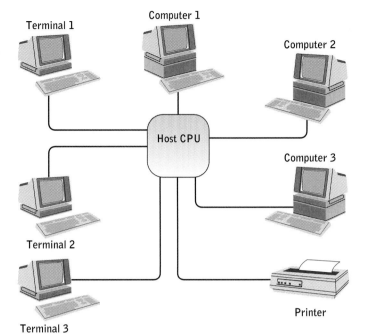

Figure 9-5 A star network topology. In a star network configuration a central host computer acts as a traffic controller for all other components of the network. All communication between the smaller computers, terminals, and printers must first pass through the central computer.

Terminal 1

Computer 1

Computer 2

Host CPU

Computer 3

Terminal 2

Computer 3

Terminal 3

Printer

---

controller A specialized computer that supervises communications traffic between the CPU and the peripheral devices in a telecommunications system.

multiplexer A device that enables a single communications channel to carry data transmissions from multiple sources simultaneously.

topology The shape or configuration of a network.

star network A network topology in which all computers and other devices are connected to a central host computer. All communications between network devices must pass through the host computer.

A **controller** is a specialized computer that supervises communications traffic between the CPU and peripheral devices such as terminals and printers. The controller manages messages from these devices and communicates them to the CPU. It also routes output from the CPU to the appropriate peripheral device.

A **multiplexer** is a device that enables a single communications channel to carry data transmissions from multiple sources simultaneously. The multiplexer divides the communications channel so that it can be shared by multiple transmission devices. The multiplexer may divide a high-speed channel into multiple channels of slower speed or may assign each transmission source a very small slice of time for using the high-speed channel.

Special telecommunications software residing in the host computer, front-end processor, and other processors in the network is required to control and support network activities. This software is responsible for functions such as network control, access control, transmission control, error detection/correction, and security. More detail on security software can be found in Chapter 16.

9.3 Communications Networks

A number of different ways exist to organize telecommunications components to form a network and hence provide multiple ways of classifying networks. Networks can be classified by their shape, or **topology.** Networks also can be classified by their geographic scope and the type of services provided. This section will describe the ways of looking at networks and the management and technical requirements of creating networks linking entire enterprises.

Network Topologies

One way of describing networks is by their shape, or topology. As illustrated in Figures 9-5 to 9-7, the three most common topologies are the star, bus, and ring.

The Star Network

The **star network** (see Figure 9-5) consists of a central host computer connected to a number of smaller computers or terminals. This topology is useful for applications where some processing must be centralized and some can be performed locally. One problem with the star network is its vulnerability. All communication between points in the network must pass through the central computer. Because the central computer is the traffic controller for the other com-

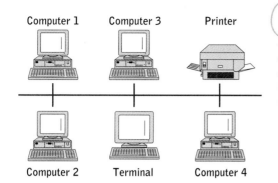

Computer 1   Computer 3   Printer

Computer 2   Terminal   Computer 4

Figure 9-6 A bus network topology. This topology allows for all messages to be broadcast to the entire network through a single circuit. There is no central host, and messages can travel in both directions along the cable.

puters and terminals in the network, communication in the network will come to a standstill if the host computer stops functioning.

The Bus Network

The **bus network** (see Figure 9-6) links a number of computers by a single circuit made of twisted wire, coaxial cable, or fiber-optic cable. All of the signals are broadcast in both directions to the entire network, with special software to identify which components receive each message (there is no central host computer to control the network). If one of the computers in the network fails, none of the other components in the network are affected. However, the channel in a bus network can handle only one message at a time, so performance can degrade if there is a high volume of network traffic. When two computers transmit messages simultaneously, a "collision" occurs, and the messages must be re-sent.

bus network Network topology linking a number of computers by a single circuit with all messages broadcast to the entire network.

The Ring Network

Like the bus network, the **ring network** (see Figure 9-7) does not rely on a central host computer and will not necessarily break down if one of the component computers malfunctions.

ring network A network topology in which all computers are linked by a closed loop in a manner that passes data in one direction from one computer to another.

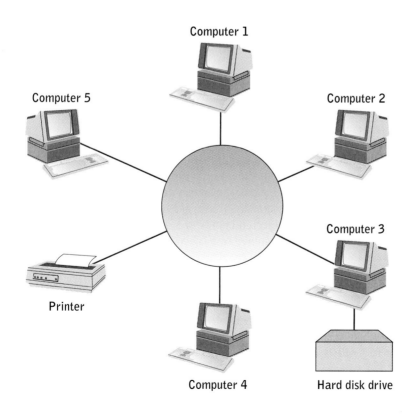

Computer 1

Computer 5

Computer 2

Printer

Computer 3

Computer 4   Hard disk drive

Figure 9-7 A ring network topology. In a ring network configuration, messages are transmitted from computer to computer, flowing in a single direction through a closed loop. Each computer operates independently so that if one fails, communication through the network is not interrupted.

Each computer in the network can communicate directly with any other computer, and each processes its own applications independently. However, in ring topology, the connecting wire, cable, or optical fiber forms a closed loop. Data are passed along the ring from one computer to another and always flow in one direction. Both ring and bus topologies are used in local area networks (LANs), which are discussed in the next section.

Private Branch Exchanges and Local Area Networks (LANs)

Networks may be classified by geographic scope into local networks and wide area networks. Wide area networks encompass a relatively wide geographic area, from several miles to thousands of miles, whereas local networks link local resources such as computers and terminals in the same department or building of a firm. Local networks consist of private branch exchanges and local area networks.

Private Branch Exchanges

A **private branch exchange (PBX)** is a special-purpose computer designed for handling and switching office telephone calls at a company site. Today's PBXs can carry voice and data to create local networks. PBXs can store, transfer, hold, and redial telephone calls, and they also can be used to switch digital information among computers and office devices. Using a PBX, you can write a letter on a PC in your office, send it to the printer, then dial up the local copying machine and have multiple copies of your letter created.

The advantage of digital PBXs over other local networking options is that they do not require special wiring. A PC connected to a network by telephone can be plugged or unplugged anywhere in a building, utilizing the existing telephone lines. PBXs also are supported by commercial vendors, so the organization does not need special expertise to manage them.

The geographic scope of PBXs is limited, usually to several hundred feet, although the PBX can be connected to other PBX networks or to packet switched networks (see the discussion of value-added networks in this section) to encompass a larger geographic area. The primary disadvantages of PBXs are that they are limited to telephone lines and they cannot easily handle very large volumes of data.

Local Area Networks

A **local area network (LAN)** encompasses a limited distance, usually one building or several buildings in close proximity. Most LANs connect devices located within a 2000-foot radius, and they have been widely used to link PCs. LANs require their own communications channels.

LANs generally have higher transmission capacities than PBXs, using bus or ring topologies and a high bandwidth. They are recommended for applications transmitting high volumes of data and other functions requiring high transmission speeds, including video transmissions and graphics. LANs often are used to connect PCs in an office to shared printers and other resources or to link computers and computer-controlled machines in factories.

LANs are more expensive to install than PBXs and are more inflexible, requiring new wiring each time a LAN is moved. One way to solve this problem is to create a *wireless LAN*, such as that used by Manitoba Public Insurance described in the chapter opening vignette. LANs are usually controlled, maintained, and operated by end users. This means that the user must know a great deal about telecommunications applications and networking.

Figure 9-8 illustrates one model of a LAN. The *server* acts as a librarian, storing programs and data files for network users. The server determines who gets access to what and in what sequence. Servers may be powerful PCs with large hard-disk capacity, workstations, minicomputers, or mainframes, although specialized computers are available for this purpose.

The network gateway connects the LAN to public networks, such as the telephone network, or to other corporate networks so that the LAN can exchange information with networks external to it. A **gateway** is generally a communications processor that can connect dissimilar networks by translating from one set of protocols to another. A **router** is used to route packets of data through several connected LANs or to a wide area network.

LAN technology consists of cabling (twisted wire, coaxial, or fiber-optic cable) or wireless technology that links individual computer devices, network interface cards (which are spe-

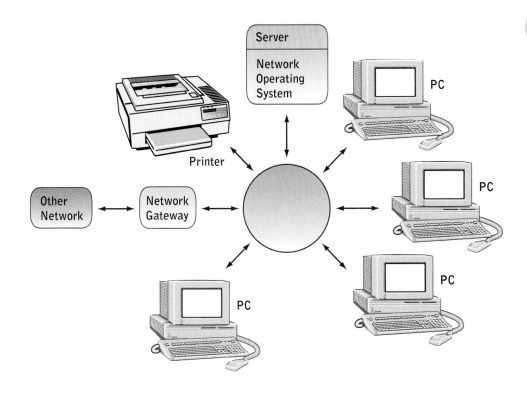

Figure 9-8 A local area network (LAN). A typical local area network connects computers and peripheral devices that are located close to each other, often in the same building.

cial adapters serving as interfaces to the cable), and software to control LAN activities. The LAN network interface card specifies the data transmission rate, the size of message units, the addressing information attached to each message, and network topology (Ethernet utilizes a bus topology, for example).

LAN capabilities also are defined by the **network operating system (NOS).** The network operating system can reside on every computer in the network, or it can reside on a single designated server for all the applications on the network. The NOS routes and manages communications on the network and coordinates network resources. Novell NetWare, Microsoft Windows NT Server (Windows 2000 Server and Windows 2000 Enterprise Server), and IBM's OS/2 Warp Server are popular network operating systems.

LANs may take the form of client/server networks, in which the server provides data and application programs to "client" computers on the network (see the Chapter 6 discussion of client/server computing) or they may use a peer-to-peer architecture. A **peer-to-peer** network treats all processors equally and is used primarily in small networks. Each computer on the network has direct access to each other's workstations and shared peripheral devices.

Wide Area Networks (WANs), Value-Added Networks (VANs), and Network Services

Wide area networks (WANs) span broad geographical distances, ranging from several miles to entire continents. WANs may consist of a combination of switched and dedicated lines, microwave, and satellite communications. **Switched lines** are telephone lines that a person can access from his or her terminal to transmit data to another computer, the call being routed or switched through paths to the designated destination. **Dedicated lines,** or nonswitched lines, are continuously available for transmission, and the lessee typically pays a flat rate for total access to the line. The lines can be leased or purchased from common carriers or private communications media vendors. Most existing WANs are switched. Amoco's network for transmitting seismic data illustrated in Figure 9-4 is a WAN.

Individual business firms may maintain their own wide area networks. The firm is responsible for telecommunications content and management. However, private wide area networks are expensive to maintain, or firms may not have the resources to manage their own wide area networks. In such instances, companies may choose to use commercial network services to communicate over vast distances.

network operating system (NOS) Special software that routes and manages communications on the network and coordinates network resources.

peer-to-peer Network architecture that gives equal power to all computers on the network; used primarily in small networks.

wide area network (WAN) Telecommunications network that spans a large geographical distance. May consist of a variety of cable, satellite, and microwave technologies.

switched lines Telephone lines that a person can access from a terminal to transmit data to another computer, the call being routed or switched through paths to the designated destination.

dedicated lines Telephone lines that are continuously available for transmission by a lessee. Typically conditioned to transmit data at high speeds for high-volume applications.

Value-Added Networks (VANs)

Value-added networks are an alternative to firms designing and managing their own networks. **Value-added networks (VANs)** are private, multipath, data-only, third-party-managed networks that can provide economies in the cost of service and in network management because they are used by multiple organizations. The value-added network is set up by a firm that is in charge of managing the network. That firm sells subscriptions to other firms wishing to use the network. Subscribers pay only for the amount of data they transmit plus a subscription fee. The network may utilize twisted-pair lines, satellite links, and other communications channels leased by the value-added carrier.

The term *value added* refers to the extra value added to communications by the telecommunications and computing services these networks provide to clients. Customers do not have to invest in network equipment and software or perform their own error checking, editing, routing, and protocol conversion. Subscribers may achieve savings in line charges and transmission costs because the costs of using the network are shared among many users. The resulting costs may be lower than if the clients had leased their own lines or satellite services.

The leading international value-added networks provide casual or intermittent users international services on a dial-up basis and can provide a private network using dedicated circuits for customers requiring a full-time network. (Maintaining a private network may be most cost-effective for organizations with a high communications volume.)

International VANs have representatives with language skills and knowledge of various countries' telecommunications administrations. The VANs already have leased lines from foreign telecommunications authorities or can arrange access to local networks and equipment abroad.

Network Services

Packet switching is a basic switching technique that can be used to achieve economies and higher speeds in WANs. **Packet switching** breaks up a lengthy block of text into small, fixed bundles of data called packets (see Figure 9-9). (The X.25 packet switching standard uses packets of 128 bytes each.) The packets include information for directing the packet to the right address and for checking transmission errors along with the data. Data are gathered from many users, divided into small packets, and transmitted via various communications channels. Each packet travels independently through the network. Packets of data originating at one source can be routed through different paths in the network before being reassembled into the original message when they reach their destination.

Frame relay is a shared network service that is faster and less expensive than packet switching and can achieve transmission speeds up to 1.544 megabits per second. Frame relay packages data into frames that are similar to packets, but it does not perform error correction. It works well on reliable lines that do not require frequent retransmissions because of error.

Most corporations today use separate networks for voice, private-line services, and data, each of which is supported by a different technology. A service called **asynchronous transfer mode (ATM)** may overcome some of these problems because it can seamlessly and

Figure 9-9 Packet switched networks and packet communications. Data are grouped into small packets, framed by identifying information, which are transmitted independently via various communication channels to maximize the potential of the paths in a network.

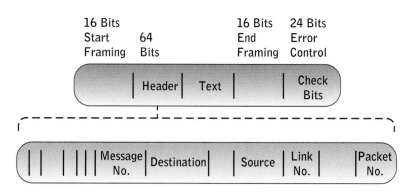

dynamically switch voice, data, images, and video between users. ATM also promises to tie LANs and wide area networks together more easily. (LANs generally are based on lower speed protocols, whereas WANs operate at higher speeds.) ATM technology parcels information into uniform cells, each with 53 groups of 8 bytes, eliminating the need for protocol conversion. It can pass data between computers from different vendors and permits data to be transmitted at any speed the network handles. ATM can transmit up to 2.5 GBPS.

Integrated Services Digital Network (ISDN) is an international standard for dial-up network access that integrates voice, data, image, and video services in a single link. There are two levels of ISDN service: Basic Rate ISDN and Primary Rate ISDN. Each uses a group of B (bearer) channels to carry voice or data along with a D (delta) channel for signaling and control information. Basic Rate ISDN can transmit data at a rate of 128 kilobits per second on an existing local telephone line. Organizations and individuals requiring high-bandwidth transmission or the ability to provide simultaneous voice or data transmission over one physical line might choose this service. Primary Rate ISDN offers transmission capacities in the megabit range and is designed for large users of telecommunications services.

Other high-capacity services include digital subscriber line (DSL) technologies, cable modems, and T1 lines. Like ISDN, **digital subscriber line (DSL)** technologies also operate over existing copper telephone lines to carry voice, data, and video, but they have higher transmission capacities than ISDN. There are several categories of DSL. Asymmetric digital subscriber line (ADSL) supports a transmission rate of 1.5–9 MBPS when receiving data and up to 640 KBPS when sending data. Symmetric digital subscriber line (SDSL) supports the same transmission rate for sending and receiving data of up to 3 MBPS. **Cable modems** are modems designed to operate over cable TV lines. They can provide high-speed access to the Web or corporate intranets of up to 10 MBPS. Most cable networks only let users receive data, so the usefulness of this technology will be limited until the cable companies upgrade their networks for two-way transmission. A **T1 line** is a dedicated telephone connection comprising 24 channels that can support a data transmission rate of 1.544 megabits per second. Each of these 64-kilobit-per-second channels can be configured to carry voice or data traffic. These services often are used for high-capacity Internet connections. Table 9.2 summarizes these network services.

Integrated Services Digital Network (ISDN) International standard for transmitting voice, video, image, and data to support a wide range of service over the public telephone lines.

digital subscriber line (DSL) A group of technologies providing high-capacity transmission over existing copper telephone lines.

cable modem Modem designed to operate over cable TV lines to provide high-speed access to the Web or corporate intranets.

T1 line A dedicated telephone connection comprising 24 channels that can support a data transmission rate of 1.544 megabits per second. Each channel can be configured to carry voice or data traffic.

Table 9.2 **Network Services**

Service	Description	Bandwidth
X.25	Packet switching standard that parcels data into packets of 128 bytes	Up to 1.544 MBPS
Frame Relay	Packages data into frames for high-speed transmission over reliable lines but does not use error-correction routines	Up to 1.544 MBPS
ATM (Asynchronous Transfer Mode)	Parcels data into uniform cells to allow high-capacity transmission of voice, data, images, and video between different types of computers	25 MBPS–2.5 GBPS
ISDN	Digital dial-up network access standard that can integrate voice, data, and video services	Basic Rate ISDN: 128 KBPS Primary Rate ISDN: 1.5 MBPS
DSL (Digital Subscriber Line)	Series of technologies for high-capacity transmission over copper wires	ADSL—up to 9 MBPS for receiving and up to 640 KBPS for sending data SDSL—up to 3 MBPS for both sending and receiving
T1	Dedicated telephone connection with 24 channels for high-capacity transmission	1.544 MBPS
Cable Modem	Service for high-speed transmission of data over cable TV lines that is primarily one way	Up to 10 MBPS

Banco do Brasil Competes with a Multiservice WAN

Banco do Brasil is the largest bank in Brazil, with over 4300 branches in 2700 locations in Brazil and 30 countries abroad. The bank handles more than 35 million transactions each day and services more than 15 million checking accounts. Competition in the Brazilian banking industry is fierce and banks face high telecommunication costs. For example, a leased line in an urban area such as Sao Paulo with a well-developed infrastructure can cost U.S. $6000 per month, and a single data-only telephone line between Latin American cities can cost up to U.S. $50,000 monthly. Banks are the heaviest users of Brazilian telecommunication services.

Leased lines in Brazil frequently experience trunk failures. Banco do Brasil created redundant infrastructures to ensure 24-hour availability of its transaction processing applications. Consequently, voice and data telecommunications costs were its single largest expense.

To remain competitive, Banco do Brasil started looking for ways to deliver innovative banking services and increase customer satisfaction while reducing costs. The bank set a goal of reducing customers' waiting time in bank branches by 65 percent as a means of both increasing customer satisfaction and reducing banking transaction costs. Each customer transaction completed at a bank branch teller's counter costs about U.S. $1.50. The bank also wanted to create a comprehensive set of electronic home banking, Internet banking, and call-center services and deliver new financial products with the shortest time-to-market in its industry. It needed a fast multiservice network infrastructure to meet these objectives.

The bank selected Cisco System's IGX 8400 services wide-area switch with Voice Network Switching (VNS) to provide the speed and intelligence to integrate voice, data,

and video. The WAN uses 53 Cisco IGX 8400 switches connected using E3 ATM trunks to link three data centers in Brazil. Approximately 40 Cisco Catalyst 5500 series multilayer switches are also deployed at the bank's headquarters and 3000 Cisco routers are installed in the bank's branches. Transactions and other network traffic are transported using Frame Relay over the IGX 8400 network backbone. With this multiservice network, Banco do Brasil can leverage its data network to provide voice services to every location without expenditures for additional voice channels between cities, significantly reducing telephone costs.

The bank's new Internet, home banking, and call-center services have changed the way it conducts its business. Today, 60 percent of its branches manage transactions electronically, compared to 20 percent in the past. The electronic services have reduced the number of customers waiting in line in branches and have slashed customer service costs from U.S. $1.50 to $.10 per transaction. The network has reduced transaction processing time while enhancing reliability.

By the year 2000, Banco do Brasil expects to have 30,000 automatic teller (ATM) machines processing six times today's transaction volume. Its new multiservice WAN will allow it to deliver new data, voice, and video applications with a high level of performance.

To Think About: What were the organizational benefits of Banco do Brasil's new WAN? What management, organization, and technology issues should be addressed when deciding whether to use a multiservice network?

Sources: Heliomar Lima, "Multiservice WAN Extends Banking Services to Every Corner of Brazil—and Beyond," **Packet Magazine** 11, no. 1 (First Quarter, 1999); and Amy K. Larsen, "Voice with Data," **Information Week**, February 1, 1999.

Network Convergence

Most companies maintain separate networks for voice, data, and video, but products are now available to create networks which can deliver voice, data, and video in a single network infrastructure. These multiservice networks can potentially reduce networking costs by eliminating the need to provide support services and personnel for each different type of network. Multiservice networks can be attractive solutions for companies running multimedia applications such as video collaboration, voice-data call centers, distance learning, or unified messaging or for firms with high costs for voice services. The Window on Organizations shows how one organization used a multiservice network solution to enhance its competitive position.

Enterprise Networking and Standards

enterprise networking An arrangement of the organization's hardware, software, telecommunications, and data resources to put more computing power on the desktop and create a companywide network linking many smaller networks.

Organizations can link their LANs and WANs to create networks that link entire enterprises. In **enterprise networking,** the organization's hardware, software, telecommunications, and data resources are arranged to put more computing power on the desktop and to create a companywide network linking many smaller networks. These enterprise networks also may be linked to the networks of other organizations outside the firm or to the Internet.

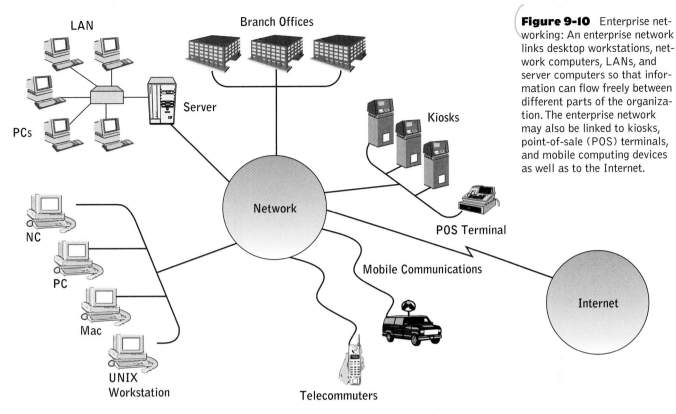

Figure 9-10 Enterprise networking: An enterprise network links desktop workstations, network computers, LANs, and server computers so that information can flow freely between different parts of the organization. The enterprise network may also be linked to kiosks, point-of-sale (POS) terminals, and mobile computing devices as well as to the Internet.

Figure 9-10 illustrates how enterprise networking might look in many organizations today. For example, at the main offices of the National Basketball Association (NBA) in Manhattan and Secaucus, New Jersey, computers are linked in local area networks (LANs). An enterprise-wide network links the main offices with regional and international offices, NBA teams, and sports arenas in one large network. Operating on these networks are a range of hardware, including IBM server computers, desktop Pentium Pro PCs running Windows NT, a Digital Equipment Corporation (DEC) VAX computer used as a gateway, and various routers and switching hubs. These networked systems run applications such as a player–contract management system and information kiosks for fans with full-motion video based on Lotus Notes groupware.

Another example of enterprise networking is at Vienna University in Austria. The university's network consists of 3500 computers, including an IBM Enterprise System/9000 mainframe, UNIX workstations, and thousands of PCs. A backbone network uses Cisco routers to connect various university departments to the university's Computer Center, where traffic is routed to other universities in Vienna, to the Austrian Academic Network (ACOnet), Austria's national research network, and to the public Internet.

In this enterprise architecture, organizations use a mixture of computer hardware supplied by different vendors. Large, complex databases that need central storage are found on mainframes, minis, or specialized servers, whereas smaller databases and parts of large databases are loaded on PCs and workstations. Client/server computing often is used to distribute more processing power to the desktop.

The system is a network. In fact, for all but the smallest organizations the system is composed of multiple networks. A high-capacity backbone network connects many local area networks and devices. The backbone may be connected to external networks like the Internet. The linking of separate networks, each of which retains its own identity, into an interconnected network, is called **internetworking.**

internetworking The linking of separate networks, each of which retains its own identity, into an interconnected network.

Connectivity and Standards

Enterprise networking is most likely to increase productivity and competitive advantage when digitized information can move seamlessly through the organization's web of electronic networks, connecting different kinds of machines, people, sensors, databases, functional divisions, departments, and work groups. This ability of computers and computer-based devices

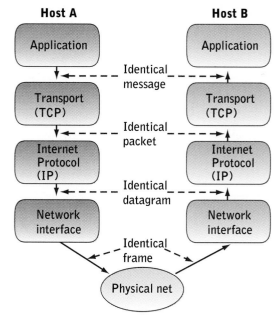

Figure 9-11 The Transmission Control Protocol/Internet Protocol (TCP/IP) reference model. This figure illustrates the five layers of the TCP/IP reference model for communications.

to communicate with one another and "share" information in a meaningful way without human intervention is called **connectivity.** Internet technology and Java software provide some of this connectivity, but the Internet cannot be used as a foundation for all of the organization's information systems. Most organizations still will require their own proprietary networks. They will need to develop their own connectivity solutions to make different kinds of hardware, software, and communications systems work together.

Achieving connectivity requires standards for networking, operating systems, and user interfaces. Open systems promote connectivity because they enable disparate equipment and services to work together. **Open systems** are built on public, nonproprietary operating systems, user interfaces, application standards, and networking protocols. In open systems, software can operate on different hardware platforms and in that sense can be "portable." Java software, described in Chapter 7, can create an open system environment. The UNIX operating system supports open systems because it can operate on many different kinds of computer hardware. However, there are different versions of UNIX, and no one version has been accepted as an open systems standard. Linux also supports open systems.

Models of Connectivity for Networks

There are different models for achieving connectivity in telecommunications networks. The **Transmission Control Protocol/Internet Protocol (TCP/IP)** model was developed by the U.S. Department of Defense in 1972 and is used in the Internet. Its purpose was to help scientists link disparate computers. Figure 9-11 shows that TCP/IP has a five-layer reference model.

1. *Application:* Provides end-user functionality by translating the messages into the user/host software for screen presentation.

2. *Transmission Control Protocol (TCP):* Performs transport, breaking application data from the end user down into TCP packets called datagrams. Each packet consists of a header with the address of the sending host computer, information for putting the data back together, and information for making sure the packets do not become corrupted.

3. *Internet Protocol (IP):* The Internet Protocol receives datagrams from TCP and breaks the packets down further. An IP packet contains a header with address information and carries TCP information and data. IP routes the individual datagrams from the sender to the recipient. IP packets are not very reliable, but the TCP level can keep resending them until the correct IP packets get through.

4. *Network interface:* Handles addressing issues, usually in the operating system, as well as the interface between the initiating computer and the network.

5. *Physical net:* Defines basic electrical-transmission characteristic for sending the actual signal along communications networks.

Two computers using TCP/IP would be able to communicate even if they were based on different hardware and software platforms. Data sent from one computer to the other would pass downward through all five layers, starting with the application layer of the sending computer and passing through the physical net. After the data reached the recipient host computer, they would travel up the layers. The TCP level would assemble the data into a format the receiving host computer could use. If the receiving computer found a damaged packet, it would ask the sending computer to retransmit it. This process would be reversed when the receiving computer responded.

The **Open Systems Interconnect (OSI)** model is an alternative model developed by the International Standards Organization for linking different types of computers and networks. It was designed to support global networks with large volumes of transaction processing. Like TCP/IP, OSI enables a computer connected to a network to communicate with any other computer on the same network or a different network, regardless of the manufacturer, by establishing communication rules that permit the exchange of information between dissimilar systems. OSI divides the telecommunications process into seven layers.

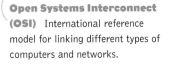
Open Systems Interconnect (OSI) International reference model for linking different types of computers and networks.

Other connectivity-promoting standards have been developed for graphical user interfaces, electronic mail, packet switching, and electronic data interchange (see the next section). Any manager wishing to achieve some measure of connectivity in his or her organization should try to use these standards when designing networks, purchasing hardware and software, or developing information system applications.

9.4 Electronic Commerce and Electronic Business Technologies

Baxter International, described in Chapter 2, realized the strategic significance of telecommunications. The company placed its own computer terminals in hospital supply rooms. Customers could dial up a local VAN and send their orders directly to the company. Other companies also are achieving strategic benefits by developing electronic commerce and electronic business applications based on telecommunications technology.

Facilitating Applications

Electronic mail (e-mail), voice mail, facsimile machines (fax), digital information services, teleconferencing, dataconferencing, videoconferencing, groupware, and electronic data interchange are key applications for electronic commerce and electronic business because they provide network-based capabilities for communication, coordination, and speeding the flow of purchase and sale transactions.

Electronic Mail

We already have described the capabilities of electronic mail, or e-mail, in Chapter 7. E-mail eliminates telephone tag and costly long-distance telephone charges, expediting communication between different parts of an organization. Nestlé SA, the Swiss-based multinational food corporation, installed an electronic-mail system to connect its 60,000 employees in 80 countries. Nestlé's European units can use the electronic-mail system to share information about production schedules and inventory levels to ship excess products from one country to another.

Many organizations operate their own internal electronic-mail systems, but communications companies such as GTE, MCI, and AT&T offer these services, as do commercial on-line information services such as America Online and Prodigy and public networks on the Internet (see Chapter 10).

The Window on Management looks at the privacy of e-mail messages from a different perspective, examining whether monitoring employees using e-mail, the Internet, and other network facilities is ethical.

Window on Management

Monitoring Employees on Networks: Unethical or Good Business?

Should managers monitor employees using networks? Is it unethical? Or is it just good business? Although many view monitoring employee e-mail as unethical and even an illegal invasion of privacy, many companies consider it to be legitimate. They claim they need to know that the business facilities they own are being used to further their business goals. Some also argue that they need to be able to search electronic-mail messages for evidence of illegal activities, racial discrimination, or sexual harassment. Others argue that the company needs access to business information stored in e-mail files the same as if it were stored in paper file cabinets.

E-mail privacy within a company is not covered by U.S. federal law. The Electronic Communications Privacy Act of 1986 only prohibits interception or disclosure of e-mail messages by parties outside the company where the messages were sent without a proper warrant. Lawsuits so far have failed to limit the right of companies to monitor e-mail. For example, when Alana Shoars, a former e-mail administrator at Epson America Inc., discovered that her supervisor was copying and reading employees' e-mail, she sued in the Los Angeles, California, courts, alleging invasion of privacy. Later she filed a class action suit in the name of 700 Epson employees and 1800 outsiders also charging privacy invasion. Both cases were dismissed on the grounds that e-mail does not fall within the state's wiretapping laws.

Despite the lack of legal restrictions, many observers see electronic-mail privacy as serious. Michael Godwin, legal adviser for the Electronic Frontier Foundation, recommends that employers who intend to monitor e-mail establish a stated policy to that effect. Some companies have such policies, including Nordstom, Eastman Kodak, and Federal Express, all of which claim the right to intercept and read employee e-mail. General Motors and Hallmark Cards have policies that grant employees greater privacy.

The Internet presents different issues—the use of company facilities not only for nonbusiness purposes but also for illegal uses such as retrieving pornography. Management can use new Web monitoring tools to monitor what employees are doing on the Internet. This software can track what Web sites users visit, the files they download, and even the categories of information they search. Some of these tools can block access to Web sites that employers consider inappropriate. Companies may use these tools to ensure that their employees are not wasting company time surfing the Web or that valuable network resources are not being wasted on nonbusiness activities.

For many firms, such as Miltope Inc. in Hope Hull, Alabama, the most essential step in employee Web-monitoring is not deploying the technology but establishing an appropriate Web usage policy. Miltope, which customizes computer equipment for military use, wanted to ensure that its 500 employees used the Internet strictly for business purposes. Its management decided to assign each employee to one of ten access categories, each providing access to different types of Web sites and to use SurfWatch Professional as its employee monitoring tool. When each Miltope employee clicks for a Web page, SurfWatch checks the user's identity against what is allowed for that employee's access category. The software then determines whether to load the requested page or notify the user that the request has been denied. SurfWatch logs requests for unauthorized Web pages so that they can be reviewed later by managers.

To Think About: Do you believe management should have the right to monitor employee e-mail and Internet usage? Why or why not? Describe the problems such monitoring might present to management.

Sources: Peter Cassidy, "Beaching Surfers," CIO Web Business Magazine, February 1, 1999; and Lawrence Magid, "Little Brother Is Watching," Information Week, February 16, 1998.

Voice Mail

voice mail A system for digitizing a spoken message and transmitting it over a network.

A **voice mail** system digitizes the spoken message of the sender, transmits it over a network, and stores the message on disk for later retrieval. When the recipient is ready to listen, the messages are reconverted to audio form. Various store-and-forward capabilities notify recipients that messages are waiting. Recipients have the option of saving these messages for future use, deleting them, or routing them to other parties.

Facsimile Machines (fax)

facsimile (fax) A machine that digitizes and transmits documents with both text and graphics over telephone lines.

Facsimile (fax) machines can transmit documents containing both text and graphics over ordinary telephone lines. A sending fax machine scans and digitizes the document image. The digitized document is transmitted over a network and reproduced in hard copy form by a receiving fax machine. The process results in a duplicate, or facsimile, of the original.

Table 9.3 Commercial Digital Information Services

Provider	Type of Service
America Online	General interest/business information
Prodigy	General interest/business information
Microsoft Network	General interest/business information
Dow Jones News Retrieval	Business/financial information
Dialog	Business/scientific/technical information
Lexis	Legal research
Nexis	News/business information

Digital Information Services

Powerful and far-reaching digital electronic services enable networked PC and workstation users to obtain information from outside the firm instantly without leaving their desks. Stock prices, periodicals, competitor data, industrial supplies catalogs, legal research, news articles, reference works, and weather forecasts are some of the information that can be accessed on-line. Many of these services provide capabilities for electronic mail, electronic bulletin boards, on-line discussion groups, shopping, and travel reservations as well as Internet access. Table 9.3 describes the leading commercial digital information services. The following chapter describes how organizations can access even more information resources by using the Internet.

Teleconferencing, Dataconferencing, and Videoconferencing

People can meet electronically, even though they are hundreds or thousands of miles apart, by using teleconferencing, dataconferencing, or videoconferencing. **Teleconferencing** allows a group of people to confer simultaneously via telephone or via electronic-mail group communication software. Teleconferencing that includes the ability of two or more people at distant locations to work on the same document or data simultaneously is called **dataconferencing.** With dataconferencing, users at distant locations are able to edit and modify data (text, such as word processing documents; numeric, such as spreadsheets; and graphic) files. Teleconferencing in which participants see each other over video screens is termed *video teleconferencing,* or **videoconferencing.**

teleconferencing The ability to confer with a group of people simultaneously using the telephone or electronic-mail group communication software.

dataconferencing
Teleconferencing in which two or more users are able to edit and modify data files simultaneously.

videoconferencing
Teleconferencing in which participants see each other over video screens.

America Online gives subscribers access to extensive information, including news reports, travel, weather, education, financial services, and information from the World Wide Web. Companies and individuals can use such digital information services to obtain information instantly from their desktops.

Netscape Communicator includes e-mail functions such as attaching files, displaying messages, and providing a log of all incoming messages. E-mail has become an important tool for facilitating organizational communication.

These forms of electronic conferencing are growing in popularity because they save travel time and cost. Legal firms might use videoconferencing to take depositions and to convene meetings between lawyers in different branch offices. Videoconferencing can help companies promote remote collaboration from different locations or fill in personnel expertise gaps. Electronic conferencing is useful for supporting telecommuting, enabling home workers to meet with or collaborate with their counterparts working in the office or elsewhere.

Videoconferencing usually has required special video conference rooms and videocameras, microphones, television monitors, and a computer equipped with a codec device that converts video images and analog sound waves into digital signals and compresses them for transfer over communications channels. Another codec on the receiving end reconverts the digital signals back into analog for display on the receiving monitor. PC-based, desktop videoconferencing systems in which users can see each other and simultaneously work on the same document are reducing videoconferencing costs so that more organizations can benefit from this technology.

Desktop videoconferencing systems typically provide a local window, in which you can see yourself, and a remote window to display the individual with whom you are communicating. Most desktop systems provide audio capabilities for two-way, real-time conversations and a whiteboard. The whiteboard is a shared drawing program that lets multiple users collaborate on projects by modifying images and text on-line. Software is available for desktop videoconferencing over the Internet, as described in the Window on Technology.

With PC desktop videoconferencing systems, users can see each other and simultaneously work on the same document. Organizations are using videoconferencing technology to improve coordination and to save travel time and costs.

Videoconferencing on the Internet

The Internet has opened many new ways for people to communicate, and videoconferencing is one of the most exciting. For the cost of a local telephone call, you can have a conference or work collaboratively on a whiteboard with anyone in the world.

MCI, the Washington, D.C.-based provider of telecommunications services, has over 550 intranet sites, which are used to save the company an estimated $112 million annually in printing, distribution, and travel costs. One use for MCI's intranets is to stage virtual conferences and "desktop events," such as internal meetings, product launches, contract announcements, and directors' roundtables. For example, more than 1200 employees participated in a company Web forum on Internet issues and application development trends. The technology for the "forum" included Compaq Pentium II PCs equipped with MultiMedia Access's Osprey-1000 video capture cards and Canon VC-C1 Communication Cameras. RealNetworks' Real System was used for driving streaming audio and video signals. (Streaming technology lets a user view and hear digitized content, such as video, sound, and animation, as it is being downloaded.) Employees could view the multicast events through Microsoft Internet Explorer or Netscape Navigator Web browser software enhanced by RealNetworks' RealPlayer plug-in and a Java-based plug-in for chat capabilities. Forum participants could chat interactively with the conference presenters during the live audio and video feed.

Other companies can use low-cost alternatives for Internet videoconferencing, such as Microsoft NetMeeting (a feature of the Windows 98 operating system) and CU-SeeMe.

CU-SeeMe was developed by Cornell University. A pared-down version is available as free shareware, but many businesses prefer Enhanced CU-SeeMe, a full-function version marketed by White Pine Software. These products are inexpensive to purchase and require little extra equipment. Those with a Windows PC system who need to be an active part of a meeting would need a videocamera, a video capture board (if not bundled with their camera), a sound card, and a microphone (if one is not bundled with their computer system). These tools are well suited for "talking head" applications, in which people are sitting at their desks and not giving elaborate presentations. For example, American Contractors Exchange, a national network of plumbing and HVAC contractors, uses the White Pine commercial version of CU-SeeMe to provide technical and business training to its members. Although the video images that CU-SeeMe produces are not as high quality as more expensive systems, the low cost and chat features provide interactive capabilities for delivering instruction that is easily accessible. ACE also uses CU-SeeMe for videoconferences where contractors meet monthly on-line to discuss issues affecting their business.

To Think About: What business processes can be streamlined through videoconferencing? What management, organization, and technology factors would you consider to decide whether to use Internet-based videoconferencing?

Sources: Kevin Bunden, "Coming into Focus," **Computerworld**, January 11, 1999; Mary Ryan Garcia, "Tools for Tracking the Web," **Beyond Computing**, October 1998; and Chris Devoney, "Go for the Bandwidth," **Computerworld**, April 13, 1998.

Groupware

Chapter 7 described the capabilities of groupware for supporting collaborative work. Individuals, teams, and work groups at different locations in the organization can use groupware to participate in discussion forums and work on shared documents and projects. More details on the use of groupware for collaborative work can be found in Chapter 14.

Electronic Data Interchange and Electronic Commerce

Electronic data interchange (EDI) is a key technology for electronic commerce because it allows the computer-to-computer exchange between two organizations of standard transaction documents such as invoices, bills of lading, or purchase orders. EDI lowers transaction costs because transactions can be automatically transmitted from one information system to another through a telecommunications network, eliminating the printing and handling of paper at one end and the inputting of data at the other. EDI also may provide strategic benefits by helping a firm lock in customers, making it easier for customers or distributors to order from them rather than from competitors. Chapter 2 also shows how EDI can curb inventory costs by minimizing the amount of time components are in inventory.

EDI differs from electronic mail in that it transmits an actual structured transaction (with distinct fields such as the transaction date, transaction amount, sender's name, and recipient's name) as opposed to an unstructured text message such as a letter. Figure 9-12 illustrates how EDI works.

electronic data interchange (EDI) The direct computer-to-computer exchange between two organizations of standard business transaction documents.

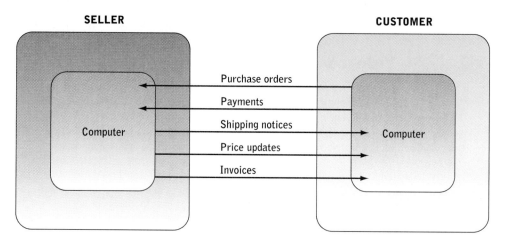

Figure 9-12 Electronic data interchange (EDI). Companies can use EDI to automate electronic commerce transactions. Purchase orders and payments can be transmitted directly from the customer's computer to the seller's computer. The seller can transmit shipping notices, price changes, and invoices electronically back to the customer.

Organizations can most fully benefit from EDI when they integrate the data supplied by EDI with applications such as accounts payable, inventory control, shipping, and production planning (Premkumar, Ramamurthy, and Nilakanta, 1994), and when they have carefully planned for the organizational changes surrounding new business processes. Management support and training in the new technology are essential (Raymond and Bergeron, 1996). Companies also must standardize the form of the transactions they use with other firms and comply with legal requirements for verifying that the transactions are authentic. Many organizations prefer to use private networks for EDI transactions, but use of the Internet is growing for this purpose (see Chapter 10).

9.5 Management Issues and Decisions

Telecommunications technology and networking are so deeply embedded in the core processes of businesses today that they require careful management and planning.

The Challenge of Managing Enterprise Networking

Implementing enterprise networking has created problems as well as opportunities for organizations. Managers need to address these problems as they design and build networks for their organizations.

Problems Posed by Enterprise Networking

The rapid, often unplanned, development of networks and distributed computing has created some of the problems. We already have described the connectivity problems created by incompatible network components and standards. Four additional problems stand out: loss of management control over information systems, the need for organizational change, the hidden costs of client/server computing, and the difficulty of ensuring network reliability and security (see Table 9.4).

Loss of Management Control

Managing information systems technology and corporate data are proving much more difficult in a distributed environment because of the lack of a single, central point where needed management can occur. Client/server computing and networks have empowered end users to become independent sources of computing power capable of collecting, storing, and dissemi-

Table 9.4 Problems Posed by Enterprise Networking

Connectivity problems

Loss of management control over systems

Organizational change requirements

Hidden costs of client/server computing

Network reliability and security

nating data and software. Data and software no longer are confined to the mainframe and under the management of the traditional information systems department.

Under enterprise networking, it becomes increasingly difficult to determine where data are located and to ensure that the same piece of information, such as a product number, is used consistently throughout the organization (see Chapter 8). User-developed applications may combine incompatible pieces of hardware or software. However, observers worry that excess centralization and management of information resources will stifle the independence and creativity of end users and reduce their ability to define their own information needs. The dilemma posed by enterprise networking is one of central-management control versus end-user creativity and productivity.

Organizational Change Requirements

Decentralization also results in changes in corporate culture and organizational structure. Enterprise-wide computing is an opportunity to reengineer the organization into a more effective unit, but it will only create problems or chaos if the underlying organizational issues are not fully addressed (Duchessi and Chengalur-Smith, 1998).

Hidden Costs of Client/Server Computing

Many companies have found that the savings they expected from client/server computing did not materialize because of unexpected costs. Hardware-acquisition savings resulting from significantly lower costs of MIPS on PCs often are offset by high annual operating costs for additional labor and time required for network and system management. Table 9.5 lists the major cost components of client/server systems.

The most difficult to evaluate and control are the hidden costs that accompany a decentralized client/server system. Considerable time must be spent on tasks such as network maintenance, data backup, technical problem solving, and hardware, software, and software-update installations. The largest cost component for client/server systems is operations staff.

Network Reliability and Security

Network technology is still immature and highly complex. The networks themselves have dense layers of interacting technology and the applications, too, are often intricately layered. Enterprise networking is highly sensitive to different versions of operating systems and network management software, with some applications requiring specific versions of each. It is difficult to make all of the components of large, heterogeneous networks work together as smoothly as management envisions. **Downtime**—periods of time in which the system is not operational— remains much more frequent in client/server systems than in established mainframe systems and should be considered carefully before taking essential applications off a mainframe.

Security is of paramount importance in organizations where information systems make extensive use of networks. Networks present end users, hackers, and thieves with many points of access and opportunities to steal or modify data in networks. Systems linked to the Internet are even more vulnerable because the Internet was designed to be open to everyone. We discuss these issues in greater detail in Chapter 16.

downtime Periods of time in which an information system is not operational.

Some Solutions

Organizations can counteract problems created by enterprise networking by planning for and managing the business and organizational changes, increasing end-user training, asserting data administration disciplines, and considering connectivity and cost controls when planning their information architecture.

Table 9.5   **Cost Breakdowns for Client/Server Systems**

Operations and support

Application development

Hardware, software, network installation, and maintenance

Education and training

Managing the change To gain the full benefit of any new technology, organizations must carefully plan for and manage the change. Business processes may need to be reengineered to ensure that the organization fully benefits from the new technology (see Chapter 11). The company's information architecture must be redrawn to shape the new client/server environment. Management must address the organizational issues that arise from shifts in staffing, function, power, and organizational culture.

Education and training A well-developed training program can help end users overcome problems resulting from the lack of management support and understanding of desktop computing (Westin et al., 1985; Bikson et al., 1985). Technical specialists will need training in client/server development and network support methods.

Data administration disciplines The role of data administration (see Chapter 8) becomes even more important when networks link many different applications and business areas. Organizations must systematically identify where their data are located, which group is responsible for maintaining each piece of data, and which individuals and groups are allowed to access and use that data. They need to develop specific policies and procedures to ensure that their data are accurate, available only to authorized users, and properly backed up.

Planning for connectivity Senior management must take a long-term view of the firm's information architecture and must make sure that its systems have the right degree of connectivity for its current and future information needs. It is usually too expensive to achieve complete connectivity in most organizations. It is far more sensible to identify classes of connectivity problems and specific application groups (such as critical electronic commerce and electronic business applications) that can be enhanced through increased connectivity.

A long-term strategy recognizes that incompatible systems cannot be eliminated overnight and focuses on achieving connectivity for future applications. New systems should then be developed only if (1) they support the firm's connectivity standards and (2) they build on existing networks and user applications in a seamless fashion. Management can establish policies to keep networks as homogeneous as possible, limiting the number of hardware, software, and network operating systems from different vendors.

The Telecommunications Plan

A telecommunications plan is more likely to succeed if it advances the key business goals of the company. During the planning process, managers can investigate ways of using telecommunications technology to enhance the firm's competitive position. Managers need to ask how telecommunications can reduce agency costs by increasing the scale and scope of operations without additional management. They need to determine if telecommunications technology can help them differentiate products and services, or if it can improve the firm's cost structure by eliminating intermediaries such as distributors or by accelerating business processes.

There are three steps to implementing a strategic telecommunications plan. First, start with an audit of the communications functions in your firm. What are your voice, data, video, equipment, staffing, and management capabilities? Identify priorities for improvement.

Second, you must know the long-range business plans of your firm. Your plan should include an analysis of how telecommunications will contribute to the specific five-year goals of the firm and to its longer range strategies (e.g., cost reduction, distribution enhancement).

Third, identify critical areas where telecommunications currently does or can have the potential to make a large difference in performance. In insurance, these may be systems that give field representatives quick access to policy and rate information; in retailing, inventory control and market penetration; and in industrial products, rapid, efficient distribution and transportation.

Implementing the Plan

Once an organization has developed a telecommunications plan, it must determine the initial scope of the telecommunications project. Managers should take eight factors into account when choosing a telecommunications network.

The first and most important factor is distance. If communication will be largely local and entirely internal to the organization's buildings and social networks, there is little or no need for VANs, leased lines, or long-distance communications.

Along with distance, one must consider the range of services the network must support, such as electronic mail, EDI, internally generated transactions, voice mail, videoconferencing, or imaging, and whether these services must be integrated in the same network.

A third factor to consider is security. The most secure means of long-distance communications is through lines that are owned by the organization. The next secure form of telecommunications is through dedicated leased lines. VANs and ordinary telephone lines are less secure.

A fourth factor to consider is whether multiple access is required throughout the organization or whether it can be limited to one or two nodes within the organization. A multiple-access system requirement suggests that there will be perhaps several thousand users throughout the corporation; therefore, a commonly available technology such as installed telephone wire is recommended. However, if access is restricted to fewer than 100 high-intensity users, a more advanced technology such as a high-bandwidth LAN may be recommended.

A fifth and most difficult factor to judge is utilization. There are two aspects of utilization that must be considered when developing a telecommunications network: the frequency and the volume of communications. Together, these two factors determine the total load on the telecommunications system. On the one hand, high-frequency, high-volume communications suggest the need for high-speed LANs for local communication and leased lines for long-distance communication. On the other hand, low-frequency, low-volume communications suggest dial-up, voice-grade telephone circuits operating through a traditional modem.

A sixth factor is cost. How much does each option cost? Total costs should include development, operations, maintenance, expansion, and overhead. Which cost components are fixed? Which are variable? Are there any hidden costs to anticipate? It is wise to recall the thruway effect. The easier it is to use a communications path, the more people will want to use it. Most telecommunications planners estimate future needs on the high side yet still often underestimate the actual need. Underestimating the cost of telecommunications projects or uncontrollable telecommunications costs are principal causes of network failure.

Seventh, managers must consider the difficulties of installing the telecommunications system. Are the organization's buildings properly constructed to install fiber optics? In some instances, buildings have inadequate wiring channels underneath the floors, which makes installation of fiber-optic cable extremely difficult.

Eighth, management must consider how much connectivity would be required to make all of the components in a network communicate with each other or to tie together multiple networks. We already have described some of the major connectivity standards. Internet technology could be used for this purpose. Table 9.6 summarizes these implementation factors.

Table 9.6	**Implementation Factors in Telecommunications Systems**

Distance

Range of services

Security

Multiple access

Utilization

Cost

Installation

Connectivity

Management

Managers need to be continuously involved in telecommunications decisions because many important business processes today are based on telecommunications and networks. Management should identify the business opportunities linked to telecommunications technology and establish the business criteria for selecting the firm's telecommunications platform. Planning should carefully consider network costs, the costs and benefits of client/server computing, and connectivity issues. Some measure of management control should be maintained as computing power is distributed throughout the organization.

Organization

Telecommunications technology enables organizations to reduce transaction and coordination costs, promoting electronic commerce and electronic business. The organization's telecommunications infrastructure should support its business processes and business strategy.

Technology

Telecommunications technology is intertwined with all the other information technologies and deeply embedded in contemporary information systems. Networks are becoming more pervasive and powerful, with capabilities to transmit voice, data, and video over long distances. Key technology decisions should consider network reliability, security, bandwidth, and connectivity.

For Discussion

1. Network design is a key business decision as well as a technology decision. Why?

2. If you were an international company with global operations, what criteria would you use to determine whether to use a value-added network (VAN) service or a private wide area network (WAN)?

Summary

1. Describe the basic components of a telecommunications system. A telecommunications system is a set of compatible devices that are used to develop a network for communication from one location to another by electronic means. The essential components of a telecommunications system are computers, terminals, other input/output devices, communications channels, communications processors (such as modems, multiplexers, controllers, and front-end processors), and telecommunications software. Different components of a telecommunications network can communicate with each other with a common set of rules termed *protocols*. Data are transmitted throughout a telecommunications network using either analog signals or digital signals. A modem is a device that translates analog to digital and vice versa.

2. Calculate the capacity of telecommunications channels and evaluate transmission media. The capacity of a telecommunications channel is determined by the range of frequencies it can accommodate. The higher the range of frequencies, called *bandwidth,* the higher the capacity (measured in bits per second). The principal transmission media are twisted copper telephone wire, coaxial copper cable, fiber-optic cable, and wireless transmission utilizing microwave, satellite, low-frequency radio waves, or infrared waves.

3. Compare the various types of telecommunications networks and network services. Networks can be classified by their shape or configuration or by their geographic scope and type of services provided. The three common network topologies are the star network, the bus network, and the ring network. In a star network, all communications must pass through a central computer. The bus network links a number of devices to a single channel and broadcasts all of the signals to the entire network, with special software to identify which components receive each message. In a ring network, each computer in the network can communicate directly with any other computer but the channel is a closed loop. Data are passed along the ring from one computer to another.

Local area networks (LANs) and private branch exchanges (PBXs) are used to link offices and buildings in close proximity. Wide area networks (WANs) span a broad geographical distance, ranging from several miles to continents and are private networks that are independently managed. Value-added networks (VANs) also encompass a wide geographic area but are managed by a third party, which sells the services of the network to other companies. Important network services include packet switching, frame relay, asynchronous transfer mode (ATM), ISDN, DSL, cable modem, and T1 lines.

4. Describe important connectivity standards for enterprise networking. Connectivity is a measure of how well computers and computer-based devices can communicate with one another and "share" information in a meaningful way without human intervention. It is essential in enterprise networking, in which different hardware, software, and network components must work together to transfer information seamlessly from one part of the organization to another. TCP/IP and OSI are important reference models for achieving connectivity in networks. Each divides the communications process into layers. UNIX is an operating system standard that can be used to create open systems as can the Linux operating system. Connectivity also can be achieved by using Internet technology and Java.

5. Identify the principal telecommunications applications for supporting electronic commerce and electronic business. The principal telecommunications applications for electronic commerce and electronic business are electronic mail, voice mail, fax, digital information services, teleconferencing, dataconferencing, videoconferencing, electronic data interchange (EDI), and groupware. Electronic data interchange is the computer-to-computer exchange between two organizations of standard transaction documents such as invoices, bills of lading, and purchase orders.

6. Analyze the management problems raised by enterprise networking and suggest solutions. Problems posed by enterprise networking include loss of management control over systems, the need to carefully manage organizational change, connectivity issues, difficulty of ensuring network reliability and security, and controlling the hidden costs of client/server computing.

Solutions include planning for and managing the business and organizational changes associated with enterprise-wide computing, increasing end-user training, asserting data administration disciplines, and considering connectivity and cost controls when planning their information architecture. A connectivity audit identifies existing capabilities and future needs. Although many corporations have assumed connectivity as a strategic goal, a more reasonable strategy would be to move incrementally toward greater connectivity while not giving up the vision of connectivity. Firms should develop strategic telecommunications plans to ensure that their telecommunications systems serve business objectives and operations. Important factors to consider are distance, range of services,

Key Terms

Analog signal, 263	Downtime, 283	Network operating system (NOS), 271	Smart phone, 267
Asynchronous transfer mode (ATM), 272	Electronic data interchange (EDI), 281	Open systems, 276	Star network, 268
Backbone, 264	Enterprise networking, 274	Open Systems Interconnect (OSI), 277	Switched lines, 271
Bandwidth, 267	Facsimile (fax), 278	Packet switching, 272	T1 line, 273
Baud, 267	Fiber-optic cable, 264	Paging system, 265	Telecommunications, 260
Bus network, 269	Frame relay, 272	Peer-to-peer, 271	Telecommunications system, 261
Cable modem, 273	Front-end processor, 267	Personal communication services (PCS), 266	Teleconferencing, 279
Cellular telephone, 266	Gateway, 270	Personal digital assistants (PDA), 266	Topology, 268
Channels, 263	Information superhighway, 261	Private branch exchange (PBX), 270	Transmission Control Protocol/Internet Protocol (TCP/IP), 276
Coaxial cable, 263	Integrated Services Digital Network (ISDN), 273	Protocol, 262	Twisted wire, 263
Concentrator, 267	Internetworking, 275	Ring network, 269	Value-added network (VAN), 272
Connectivity, 276	Local area network (LAN), 270	Router, 270	Videoconferencing, 279
Controller, 268	Microwave, 265	Satellite, 265	Voice mail, 278
Dataconferencing, 279	Mobile data networks, 266		Wide area network (WAN), 271
Dedicated lines, 271	Modem, 263		
Digital signal, 263	Multiplexer, 268		
Digital subscriber line (DSL), 273			

Review Questions

1. What is the significance of telecommunications deregulation for managers and organizations?

2. What is a telecommunications system? What are the principal functions of all telecommunications systems?

3. Name and briefly describe each of the components of a telecommunications system.

4. Distinguish between an analog and a digital signal.

5. Name the different types of telecommunications transmission media and compare them in terms of speed and cost.

6. What is the relationship between bandwidth and the transmission capacity of a channel?

7. Name and briefly describe the different kinds of communications processors.

8. Name and briefly describe the three principal network topologies.

9. Distinguish between a PBX and a LAN.

10. List and describe the various network services.

11. Define the following: modem, baud, wide area network (WAN), value-added network (VAN), and open systems.

12. What is enterprise networking? Why does it require connectivity?

13. Name and describe the telecommunications applications that can support electronic commerce and electronic business.

14. Give four examples of problems posed by enterprise networking.

15. What are some solutions to enterprise networking problems?

16. What are the principal factors to consider when developing a telecommunications plan?

Group Project

With a group of two or three of your fellow students, describe in detail the ways that telecommunications technology can provide a firm with competitive advantage. Use the companies described in Chapter 2 or other chapters you have read so far to il-lustrate the points you make, or select examples of other companies using telecommunications from business or computer magazines. Present your findings to the class.

Tools for Interactive Learning

○ Internet

The Internet Connection for this chapter will take you to the Rosenbluth Travel Web site where you can complete an exercise to analyze how Rosenbluth International uses the Web and communications technology in its daily operations. You can use the interactive software at the Goodyear Web site in an Electronic Commerce project to assist customers in making tire purchases. You can also use the Interactive Study Guide to test your knowledge of the topics in the chapter and get instant feedback where you need more practice.

○ CD-ROM

If you purchase and use the Multimedia Edition CD-ROM with this chapter, you can perform an interactive exercise to select an appropriate network topology for a series of business scenarios and identify the main issue your selection presents to management. You also can find a video demonstrating the capabilities of personal communication services, an audio overview of the major themes of this chapter, and bullet text summarizing the key points of the chapter.

Case Study   State Street Banks on Networks to Stay Competitive

What does a two-hundred-year-old bank have to do with telecommunications technology? Everything, actually, if you happen to be Nancy Gadberry, administrator of more than $20 billion in employee pension trust and health care funds for Atlanta's BellSouth Corp. Gadberry originally selected State Street to service BellSouth's accounts because it met her

two requirements: First, State Street had in place leading-edge technology that gave her the service and information she needed when and where she needed it. Second, but equally important to her, State Street was willing to establish a true partnership with BellSouth rather than working in the more traditional manner of the vendor–client relationship.

Ten years ago State Street was a re-spected bank with a history almost as old as the United States itself, having been founded in 1792. Then the bank began to remake itself, changing its whole business by sharpening its focus on servicing assets and managing money. The bank closed al-most all of its retail branches, sold its credit card business, ended all consumer lending, and focused on its commercial lending operations. Management apparently understood the growing demands of the financial industry for sophisticated information systems support. State Street management wanted to be part of the growing globalization of the financial ndustry.

Thus, in the late 1980s State Street began to build Global Horizon, its worldwide network-based security processing system, spending $100 million on it during the 1990s. Global Horizon put State Street years ahead of its competition, and today, the bank is a financial services giant, with revenues of $644 million as of March 31, 1998. Its 16,500 employees have custody of $4.4 trillion in assets. Moreover, State Street now has a record of more than 20 consecutive years of revenue and earnings growth.

How does State Street earn its revenue? The bank focuses on institutional investors rather than individual consumers, and it has developed clients throughout the world. A few years ago the company's strength was in back office support for the financial industry—settling trades, valuing portfolios, and receiving cash and securities from or sending them to its customers. The bank also stored and made available information on a customer's holdings. Today, however, their business has become very different. Although the back office functions are still an absolutely essential part of their business, fund managers are demanding much more and State Street is delivering. Fund managers now require instant access to information on their accounts instead of monthly statements on paper. And they want tools to analyze the data in order to make crucial investment decisions. State Street has given its customers just that. It has enhanced Global Horizon by adding the latest analytical tools so that, for example, at any time managers are able to perform risk analysis or measure fund and stock performance using real-time information.

Global Horizon is the key to the technical side of State Street's operations. The system is a global network based on the TCP/IP protocol. It processes more than 2 million securities-related transactions per month and transmits more than 100 million messages per day (up from 5 million daily only a couple of years earlier). The company has operations in 21 countries that are servicing its customers in 80 countries worldwide. One key is the global standardization of the system. According to State Street's CIO, James MacDonald, the same systems service all of the firm's operating areas around the globe and all of its clients. If you were to walk into any of State Street's operating areas in the United States, Europe, or Asia-Pacific you would see the same system being used.

Customers are able to access their accounts from virtually anywhere in the world, regardless of the type of computers they are using. The system can be accessed through dedicated lines or via the Internet. Its messaging architecture had to be infinitely scalable so that messages could be transferred between mainframes and client/server systems. According to MacDonald, they have been able to meet the astounding growth in daily message traffic by increasing the system's capacity without redesigning it. To achieve such a flexible system, its programming functions and features needed to be generic. For example, State Street first had to create and test a generic customer account object. Once that was completed, that object could then be enhanced to include specific functionalities needed for specific customers, markets, or locales.

A critical function is calculating the daily net asset values (NAVs) of mutual funds. There is only a narrow window of time to do this because the New York markets close at 4:00 P.M. The NASDAQ Stock Market gives providers until 5:40 P.M. to submit the day's NAVs before distributing them to the newspapers to be printed for the next morning's edition. Multimillions of mathematical calculations must be performed in a few minutes. (The NAV is calculated by multiplying the price of each financial instrument by the number of shares owned.) State Street's ability to send NAVs to the press on time is legendary. When other providers missed the NAV deadlines because of high market trading volumes or telecommunications outages, State Street usually came through.

By being able to process vast quantities of information on a single system, State Street can achieve economies of scale that can't yet be fully matched by its competitors, which include Citibank, The Chase Manhattan Bank, and Mellon Bank Corp. The number of firms capable of servicing institutional investors has been shrinking because many companies could not keep up with systems that could handle the huge transaction volume required to be profitable.

To stay ahead of competition and to meet customer needs, State Street has had to develop and integrate the latest new technologies, and the cost of this has been expensive. Over the past five years the bank has spent 20 percent of its total annual operating expenses on information technology. Eight percent of its revenues are devoted to development of new products and services. Such high information technology spending has been planned because the latest telecommunications and financial services technology are central to State Street's success.

Sources: Craig McGuire, "The Next Level of Proprietary Protection," **Wall Street and Technology,** January 1999; Lauren Gibbons Paul, "One World, One System," and "All Together Now," **CIO Magazine,** August 15, 1998; and www.statestreet.com.

CASE STUDY QUESTIONS

1. Analyze State Street using the competitive forces and value chain models.

2. What changing conditions caused State Street to abandon much of its traditional banking business in the 1980s? What competitive strategy did the company follow to address these changing conditions?

3. What role did telecommunications technology play in the bank's new strategy?

4. What management, organization, and technology issues did State Street have to address in changing its competitive strategy and building Global Horizon?

Chapter 10

The Internet: Electronic ## Commerce ## and Electronic Business

Learning Objectives

After completing this chapter, you will be able to:

1. Describe how the Internet works and its major capabilities.

2. Identify the benefits the Internet offers organizations.

3. Demonstrate how the Internet can be used for electronic commerce.

4. Demonstrate how Internet technology can be used to create private intraorganizational and interorganizational networks and the use of these networks for electronic business.

5. Examine the challenges posed by the Internet to businesses and society.

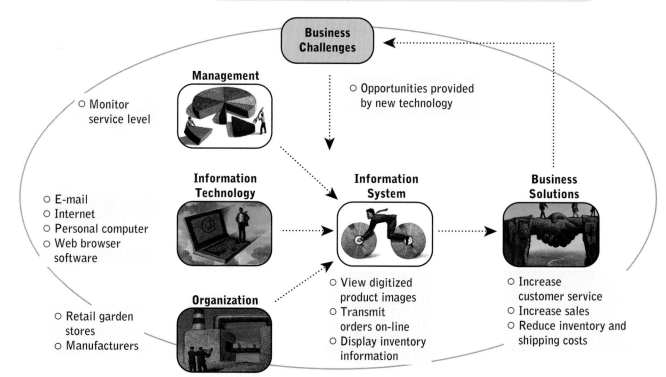

Business Challenges

Management
○ Monitor service level
○ Opportunities provided by new technology

Information Technology
○ E-mail
○ Internet
○ Personal computer
○ Web browser software

Information System
○ View digitized product images
○ Transmit orders on-line
○ Display inventory information

Business Solutions
○ Increase customer service
○ Increase sales
○ Reduce inventory and shipping costs

Organization
○ Retail garden stores
○ Manufacturers

Tiny Firms Become International
Giants on the Internet

New England Pottery Co. is a growing company with 100 employees that sells flower pots to thousands of small garden centers in the United States, Mexico, and Canada, as well as to large retail chains such as Wal-Mart, Home Depot, and Kmart. It has become the largest global vendor in the garden pottery industry, increasing sales at a rate of 20 percent per year.

One source of New England Pottery's rapid growth is its ability to respond quickly to changing market demands. Using the Internet, New England Pottery can communicate information simultaneously between its manufacturing partners in Europe and Asia and its retail customers. The company uses e-mail to send digitized images of its products so that clients can view the items with-

out having to wait for physical samples to be shipped from manufacturers overseas. New England Pottery's clients in turn can use this information to help them customize their orders to take advantage of sales trends they have identified.

New England Pottery also uses the Internet to send customer requests and orders to its overseas manufacturing parties, thus expediting the product procurement process. The company is in the process of developing an electronic clearinghouse service that lets clients access information about excess inventory from pottery manufacturers around the world.

Emerging companies like New England Pottery may not be global giants, but thanks to the Internet, they can become serious contenders in global marketplaces. Many small businesses are starting to use Internet technology to reach customers overseas, communicate with suppliers, speed the flow of sales and orders, improve customer service, and make their internal operations more efficient. More than 80 percent of today's small business owners are counting on the Internet to help their companies grow.

Sources: Natalie Engler, "Small but Nimble," *Information Week*, January 18, 1999; and "Industry Spotlight: Small Business Gets the Net," *The Industry Standard*, January 25, 1999.

chapter outline

Like New England Pottery, many companies are starting to use the Internet to communicate with both their customers and suppliers, creating new digital electronic commerce networks that bypass traditional distribution channels. They are using Internet technology to streamline their internal business processes as well. The Internet, the Web, and intranets can help companies achieve new levels of competitiveness and efficiency, but they raise the following management challenges:

1. Internet computing requires a complete change of mindset. To implement Internet technology for electronic commerce and electronic business successfully, companies may need to make organizational changes. They must examine and perhaps redesign an entire business process rather than throw new technology at existing business practices. Companies must consider a different organizational structure, changes in organizational culture, a different support structure for information systems, and different procedures for managing employees and networked processing functions.

2. Finding a successful Internet business model. Companies are racing to put up Web sites in the hope of increasing earnings through electronic commerce. However, many electronic commerce sites have yet to turn a profit or to make a tangible difference in firms' sales and marketing efforts. Cost savings or access to new markets promised by the Web may not materialize. Companies need to think carefully about whether they can create a genuinely workable business model on the Internet and how the Internet relates to their overall business strategy.

The Internet has opened up many exciting possibilities for organizing and running a business that are transforming organizations and the use of information systems in everyday life. It is creating a universal platform for buying and selling goods and for driving important business processes inside the firm. Along with bringing many new benefits and opportunities, the Internet has created a new set of management challenges. We describe these challenges so that organizations can understand the management, organization, and technology issues that must be addressed to benefit from the Internet, electronic commerce, and electronic business.

10.1 The Internet

The Internet is perhaps the most well-known, and the largest, implementation of internetworking, linking hundreds of thousands of individual networks all over the world. The Internet has a range of capabilities that organizations are using to exchange information internally or to communicate externally with other organizations. This giant network of networks has become a major catalyst for both electronic commerce and electronic business.

What Is the Internet?

The Internet began as a U.S. Department of Defense network to link scientists and university professors around the world. Even today individuals cannot connect directly to the Net, although anyone with a computer, a modem, and the willingness to pay a small monthly usage fee can access it through an Internet Service Provider. An **Internet Service Provider (ISP)** is a commercial organization with a permanent connection to the Internet that sells temporary connections to subscribers. Individuals also can access the Internet through such popular online services as Prodigy and America Online and through networks established by such giants as Microsoft and AT&T.

Internet Service Provider (ISP) A commercial organization with a permanent connection to the Internet that sells temporary connections to subscribers.

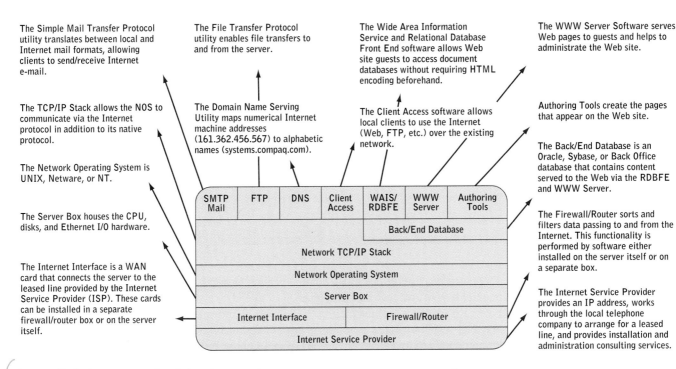

The Simple Mail Transfer Protocol utility translates between local and Internet mail formats, allowing clients to send/receive Internet e-mail.

The TCP/IP Stack allows the NOS to communicate via the Internet protocol in addition to its native protocol.

The Network Operating System is UNIX, Netware, or NT.

The Server Box houses the CPU, disks, and Ethernet I/O hardware.

The Internet Interface is a WAN card that connects the server to the leased line provided by the Internet Service Provider (ISP). These cards can be installed in a separate firewall/router box or on the server itself.

The File Transfer Protocol utility enables file transfers to and from the server.

The Domain Name Serving Utility maps numerical Internet machine addresses (161.362.456.567) to alphabetic names (systems.compaq.com).

The Wide Area Information Service and Relational Database Front End software allows Web site guests to access document databases without requiring HTML encoding beforehand.

The Client Access software allows local clients to use the Internet (Web, FTP, etc.) over the existing network.

The WWW Server Software serves Web pages to guests and helps to administrate the Web site.

Authoring Tools create the pages that appear on the Web site.

The Back/End Database is an Oracle, Sybase, or Back Office database that contains content served to the Web via the RDBFE and WWW Server.

The Firewall/Router sorts and filters data passing to and from the Internet. This functionality is performed by software either installed on the server itself or on a separate box.

The Internet Service Provider provides an IP address, works through the local telephone company to arrange for a leased line, and provides installation and administration consulting services.

Figure 10-1 Components of an Internet server. **Source:** © Copyright 1994, 1995, 1996, 1997 Compaq Computer Corporation.

One of the most puzzling aspects of the Internet is that no one owns it and it has no formal management organization. As a creation of the Defense Department for sharing research data, this lack of centralization was purposeful, to make it less vulnerable to wartime or terrorist attacks. To join the Internet, an existing network needs only to pay a small registration fee and agree to certain standards based on the TCP/IP (Transmission Control Protocol/Internet Protocol) reference model, which we described in Chapter 9. Costs are low because the Internet owns nothing and so has no costs to offset. Each organization, of course, pays for its own networks and its own telephone bills, but those costs usually exist independent of the Internet. Regional Internet companies have been established to which member networks forward all transmissions. These Internet companies route and forward all traffic, and the cost is still only that of a local telephone call. The result is that the costs of e-mail and other Internet connections tend to be far lower than equivalent voice, postal, or overnight delivery, making the Net a very inexpensive communications medium. It is also a very fast method of communication, with messages arriving anywhere in the world in a matter of seconds or a minute or two at most. We will now briefly describe the most important Internet capabilities.

Internet Technology and Capabilities

The Internet is based on client/server technology. Individuals using the Net control what they do through client applications, using graphical user interfaces or character-based products that control all functions. All the data, including e-mail messages, databases, and Web sites, are stored on servers. Servers dedicated to the Internet or even to specific Internet functions are the heart of the information on the Net (see Figure 10-1).

The most important Internet capabilities for business include e-mail, Usenet newsgroups, LISTSERVs, chatting, Telnet, FTP, gophers, and the World Wide Web. They can be used to retrieve and offer information. Table 10.1 lists these capabilities and describes the functions they support.

Internet Tools for Communication

Electronic Mail (E-Mail). The Net has become the most important e-mail system in the world because it connects so many people worldwide, creating a productivity gain that observers have compared to Gutenberg's development of movable type in the fifteenth century.

Table 10.1	Major Internet Capabilities
Capability	**Functions Supported**
E-mail	Person-to-person messaging; document sharing
Usenet newsgroups	Discussion groups on electronic bulletin boards
LISTSERVs	Discussion groups using e-mail mailing list servers
Chatting	Interactive conversations
Telnet	Log on to one computer system and do work on another
FTP	Transfer files from computer to computer
Gophers	Locate information using a hierarchy of menus
World Wide Web	Retrieve, format, and display information (including text, audio, graphics, and video) using hypertext links

Organizations use it to facilitate communication between employees and offices, and to communicate with customers and suppliers.

Researchers use this facility to share ideas, information, even documents. E-mail over the Net also has made possible many collaborative research and writing projects, even though the participants are thousands of miles apart. With proper software, the user will find it easy to attach documents and multimedia files when sending a message to someone or to broadcast a message to a predefined group. Figure 10-2 illustrates the components of an Internet e-mail address.

The portion of the address to the left of the @ symbol in Net e-mail addresses is the name or identifier of the specific individual or organization. To the right of the @ symbol is the domain name. The **domain name** is the unique name of a collection of computers connected to the Internet. The domain contains subdomains separated by a period. The domain that is farthest to the right is the top level domain, and each domain to the left helps further define the domain by network, department, and even specific computer. The top level domain name may be either a country indicator or a function indicator, such as *com* for a commercial organization or *gov* for a government institution. All e-mail addresses end with a country indicator except those in the United States, which ordinarily does not use one. In Figure 10-2, *it,* the top level domain, is a country indicator, indicating that the address is in Italy. *Edu* indicates that the address is an educational institution; *univpisa* (in this case, University of Pisa) indicates the specific location of the host computer.

Usenet Newsgroups (Forums). **Usenet** newsgroups are worldwide discussion groups in which people share information and ideas on a defined topic such as radiology or rock bands. Discussion takes place in large electronic bulletin boards where anyone can post messages for others to read. Almost 20,000 groups exist discussing almost all conceivable topics. Each Usenet site is financed and administered independently.

LISTSERV. A second type of public forum, **LISTSERV,** allows discussions to be conducted through predefined groups but uses e-mail mailing list servers instead of bulletin boards for

domain name The unique name of a collection of computers connected to the Internet.

Usenet Forums in which people share information and ideas on a defined topic through large electronic bulletin boards where anyone can post messages on the topic for others to see and respond to.

LISTSERV On-line discussion groups using e-mail broadcast from mailing list servers.

Figure 10-2 Analysis of an Internet address. In English, the e-mail address of physicist and astronomer Galileo Galilei would be translated as 'G. Galileo @ University of Pisa, educational institution, Italy'. The domain name to the right of the @ symbol contains a country indicator, a function indicator, and the location of the host computer.

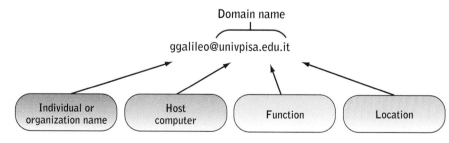

communications. If you find a LISTSERV topic you are interested in, you may subscribe. From then on, through your e-mail, you will receive all messages sent by others concerning that topic. You can, in turn, send a message to your LISTSERV and it will automatically be broadcast to the other subscribers. Tens of thousands of LISTSERV groups exist.

Chatting. **Chatting** allows two or more people who are simultaneously connected to the Internet to hold live, interactive conversations. Internet Relay Chat (IRC) is a general chat program for the Internet. Chat groups are divided into channels, and each is assigned its own topic of conversation. Most chat tools today are for written conversations in which participants type their remarks using their keyboard and read responses on their computer screen. However, systems featuring voice chat capabilities, such as those offered by Tribal Voice and by Mpath at its HearMe.com Web site are becoming available. Chatting can be an effective business tool if people who can benefit from interactive conversations set an appointed time to "meet" and "talk" on a particular topic. Many on-line retailers are enhancing their Web sites with chat services to attract visitors, to encourage repeat purchases, and to improve customer service.

> **chatting** Live, interactive conversations over a public network.

Telnet. **Telnet** allows someone to be on one computer system while doing work on another. Telnet is the protocol that establishes an error-free, rapid link between the two computers, allowing you, for example, to log on to your business computer from a remote computer when you are on the road or working from your home. You can also log in and use third-party computers that have been made accessible to the public, such as using the catalog of the U.S. Library of Congress. Telnet will use the computer address you supply to locate the computer you want to reach and connect you to it.

> **Telnet** Network tool that allows someone to log on to one computer system while doing work on another.

Information Retrieval on the Internet

Information retrieval is a second basic Internet function. Many hundreds of library catalogs are on-line through the Internet, including those of such giants as the Library of Congress, the University of California, and Harvard University. In addition, users are able to search many thousands of databases that have been opened to the public by corporations, governments, and nonprofit organizations. Individuals can gather information on almost any conceivable topic stored in these databases and libraries. Many use the Internet to locate and download some of the free, quality computer software that has been made available by developers on computers all over the world.

The Internet is a voluntary, decentralized effort with no central listing of participants or sites, much less a listing of the data located at those sites, so a major problem is finding what you need from among the storehouses of data found in databases and libraries. Here we introduce two major methods of accessing computers and locating files. We discuss additional information-retrieval methods in our section on the World Wide Web.

FTP. **File transfer protocol (FTP)** is used to access a remote computer and retrieve files from it. FTP is a quick and easy method if you know the remote computer site where the file is stored. After you have logged on to the remote computer, you can move around directories that have been made accessible for FTP to search for the file(s) you want to retrieve. Once located, FTP makes transfer of the file to your own computer very easy.

> **file transfer protocol (FTP)** Tool for retrieving and transferring files from a remote computer.

Gophers. Most files and digital information that are accessible through FTP also are available through gophers. A **gopher** is a computer client tool that enables the user to locate information stored on Internet gopher servers through a series of easy-to-use, hierarchical menus. The Internet has thousands of gopher server sites throughout the world. Each gopher site contains its own system of menus listing subject-matter topics, local files, and other relevant gopher sites. One gopher site might have as many as several thousand listings within its menus. When you use gopher software to search a specific topic and select a related item from a menu, the server will automatically transfer you to the appropriate file on that server or to the selected server wherever it is located. Once on that server, the process continues; you are presented with more menus of files and other gopher site servers that might interest you. You can move from

> **gopher** A tool that enables the user to locate information stored on Internet servers through a series of easy-to-use, hierarchical menus.

site to site, narrowing your search as you go, locating information anywhere in the world. With descriptive menu listings linked to other gopher sites, you do not need to know in advance where relevant files are stored or the exact FTP address of a specific computer.

The World Wide Web

The World Wide Web (the Web) is at the heart of the explosion in the business use of the Net. The Web is a system with universally accepted standards for storing, retrieving, formatting, and displaying information using a client/server architecture. It was developed to allow collaborators in remote sites to share their ideas on all aspects of a common project. If the Web was used for two independent projects and later relationships were found between the projects, information could flow smoothly between the projects without making major changes (Berners-Lee et al., 1994).

The Web combines text, hypermedia, graphics, and sound. It can handle all types of digital communication while making it easy to link resources that are half-a-world apart. The Web uses graphical user interfaces for easy viewing. It is based on a standard hypertext language called Hypertext Markup Language (HTML), which formats documents and incorporates dynamic links to other documents and pictures stored in the same or remote computers. (We have described HTML in Chapter 7.) Using these links, the user need only point at a highlighted key word or graphic, click on it, and immediately be transported to another document, probably on another computer somewhere else in the world. Users are free to jump from place to place following their own logic and interest.

Web browser software is programmed according to HTML standards (see Chapter 7). The standard is universally accepted, so anyone using a browser can access any of the millions of Web sites. Browsers use hypertext's point-and-click ability to navigate or *surf*—move from site to site on the Web—to another desired site. The browser also includes an arrow or back button to enable the user to retrace his or her steps, navigating back, site by site.

home page A World Wide Web text and graphical screen display that welcomes the user and explains the organization that has established the page.

Webmaster The person in charge of an organization's Web site.

uniform resource locator (URL) The address of a specific resource on the Internet.

hypertext transport protocol The communications standard used to transfer pages on the Web. Defines how messages are formatted and transmitted.

Those who offer information through the Web must establish a **home page**—a text and graphical screen display that usually welcomes the user and explains the organization that has established the page. For most organizations, the home page will lead the user to other pages, with all the pages of a company being known as a *Web site.* For a corporation to establish a presence on the Web, therefore, it must set up a Web site of one or more pages. Most Web pages offer a way to contact the organization or individual. The person in charge of an organization's Web site is called a **Webmaster.**

To access a Web site, the user must specify a **uniform resource locator (URL),** which points to the address of a specific resource on the Web. For instance, the URL for Prentice Hall, the publisher of this text, is

http://www.prenhall.com

Http stands for **hypertext transport protocol,** which is the communications standard used to transfer pages on the Web. HTTP defines how messages are formatted and transmitted and what actions Web servers and browsers should take in response to various commands. *Www.prenhall.com* is the domain name identifying the Web server storing the Web pages.

Searching for Information on the Web

Locating information on the Web is a critical function given the tens of millions of Web sites in existence and growth estimated at 300,000 pages per week. No comprehensive catalog of Web sites exists. The principal methods of locating information on the Web are Web site directories, search engines, and broadcast or "push" technology.

Several companies have created directories of Web sites and their addresses, providing search tools for finding information. Yahoo! is an example. People or organizations submit sites of interest, which then are classified. To search the directory, you enter one or more keywords and will see displayed a list of categories and sites with those key words in the title (see Figure 10-3).

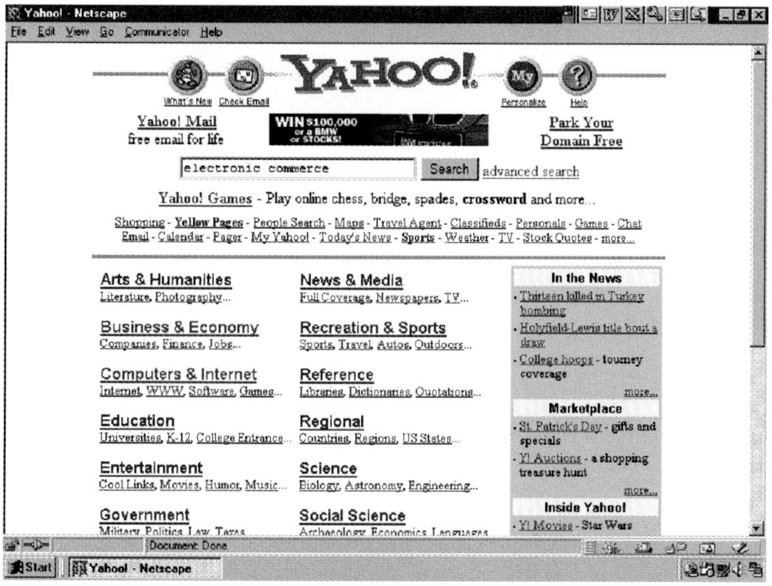

Figure 10-3 Yahoo! provides a directory of Web sites classified into categories and is a major Internet portal. Users can search for sites of interest by entering keywords or exploring the categories.

Other search tools do not require Web sites to be preclassified and will search Web pages on their own automatically. Such tools, called **search engines,** can find Web sites that may be little known. They contain software that looks for Web pages containing one or more of the search terms; then it displays matches ranked by a method that usually involves the location and frequency of the search terms. These search engines do not display information about every site on the Web, but they create indexes of the Web pages they visit. The search engine software then locates Web pages of interest by searching through these indexes. Alta Vista, Lycos, and Infoseek are examples of these search engines. Some are more comprehensive or current than others, depending on how their components are tuned. Some also classify Web sites by subject categories. Specialized search tools are also available to help users locate specific types of information easily. For example, Google is tuned to find the home pages of companies and organizations.

Some Web sites for search engines such as Yahoo! and Lycos have become so popular and easy to use that they also serve as *portals* for the Internet. A **portal** is a Web site or other service providing an initial point of entry to the Web. Portals typically offer a broad array of resources or services such as e-mail, on-line shopping, discussion forums, and tools for locating information.

search engine A tool for locating specific sites or information on the Internet.

portal Web site or service providing an initial point of entry to the Web; also offers other services and resources.

Broadcast and "Push" Technology

Instead of spending hours surfing the Web, users can have the information they are interested in delivered automatically to their desktops through **"push" technology.** A computer broadcasts information of interest directly to the user, rather than having the user "pull" content from Web sites.

"Push" comes from *server push,* a term used to describe the streaming of Web page contents from a Web server to a Web browser. Special client software allows the user to specify the categories of information he or she wants to receive, such as news, sports, financial data, and so forth, and how often this information should be updated. The software runs in the background of the user's computer while the computer performs other tasks. When they find the kind of information requested, push programs serve it to the push client, notifying him or her by sending e-mail, playing a sound, displaying an icon on the desktop, sending full articles or Web pages, or displaying headlines on a screen saver. The streams of information distributed through push technology are also known as *channels* and can include private intranet channels and extranet channels, as well as channels from the public Internet (see Figure 10-4). Microsoft's Internet Explorer and Netscape Communicator include push tools that automatically

"push" technology Method of obtaining relevant information on networks by having a computer broadcast information directly to the user based on prespecified interests.

Figure 10-4 Delivering information through "push" technology. In this Sales Infocenter, the BackWeb push delivery service was used to create channels that automatically deliver information of interest to sales representatives, such as industry news, updates on competitors, market presentations, and files of new sales leads.

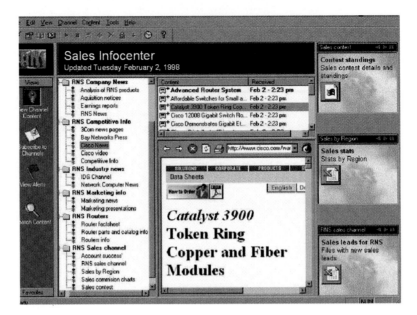

multicasting Transmission of data to a selected group of recipients.

download Web pages, inform the user of updated content, and create channels of user-specified sites. The use of push technology to transmit information to a select group of individuals is one example of **multicasting.** (LISTSERVs sending e-mail to members of specific mailing lists is another.)

The audience for push technology is not limited to individual users. Companies are using push technology to set up their own channels to broadcast important internal information via corporate intranets or extranets. For example, Fruit of the Loom is using Pointcast push technology to alert managers to updated inventory information stored on its IBM AS/400 intranet Web server. The company has long production schedules and a compressed selling season. When production of an item is behind schedule, warnings can be pushed to sales planners so they can contact customers or adjust promotions (Kador, 1998). Lufthansa is using the BackWeb push delivery service to alert consumers to fare discounts.

Intranets and Extranets

Organizations can use Internet networking standards and Web technology to create private networks called intranets. We introduced intranets in Chapter 1, explaining that an intranet is an internal organizational network that can provide access to data across the enterprise. It uses the existing company network infrastructure along with Internet connectivity standards and software developed for the World Wide Web. Intranets can create networked applications that can run on many different kinds of computers throughout the organization.

Intranet Technology

firewall Hardware and software placed between an organization's internal network and an external network to prevent outsiders from invading private networks.

The principal difference between the Web and an intranet is that whereas the Web is open to anyone, the intranet is private and is protected from public visits by **firewalls**—security systems with specialized software to prevent outsiders from invading private networks. The firewall consists of hardware and software placed between an organization's internal network and an external network, including the Internet. The firewall is programmed to intercept each message packet passing between the two networks, examine its characteristics, and reject unauthorized messages or access attempts. We provide more detail on firewalls in Chapter 16.

Intranets require no special hardware and can run over any existing network infrastructure. Intranet software technology is the same as that of the World Wide Web. Intranets use HTML to program Web pages and to establish dynamic, point-and-click hypertext links to other sites. The Web browser and Web server software used for intranets are the same as those on the Web. A simple intranet can be created by linking a client computer with a Web browser to a computer with Web server software via a TCP/IP network. A firewall keeps unwanted visitors out.

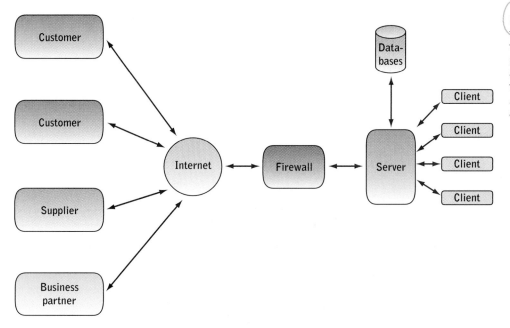

Figure 10-5 Model of an extranet. In this model of an extranet, selected customers, suppliers, and business partners can access a company's private intranet from the public Internet. A firewall allows access only to authorized outsiders.

Extranets

Some firms are allowing people and organizations outside the firm to have limited access to their internal intranets. Private intranets that are extended to authorized users outside the company are called **extranets.** For example, authorized buyers could link to a portion of a company's intranet from the public Internet to obtain information about the cost and features of its products. The company can use firewalls to ensure that access to its internal data is limited and remains secure; firewalls can also authenticate users, making sure that only authorized people can access the site.

extranet Private intranet that is accessible to select outsiders.

Extranets are especially useful for linking organizations with customers or business partners. They often are used for providing product-availability, pricing, and shipment data, and electronic data interchange (EDI), or for collaborating with other companies on joint development or training efforts. Figure 10-5 illustrates one way that an extranet might be set up.

Internet Benefits to Organizations

The Internet, intranets, and extranets are becoming the principal platforms for electronic commerce and electronic business because this technology provides so many benefits. The Internet's global connectivity, ease of use, low cost, and multimedia capabilities can be used to create interactive applications, services, and products. By using Internet technology, organizations can reduce communication and transaction costs, enhance coordination and collaboration, and accelerate the distribution of knowledge. Table 10.2 summarizes these benefits.

Connectivity and Global Reach

The value of the Internet lies in its ability to easily and inexpensively connect so many people from so many places all over the globe. Anyone who has an Internet address can log on to a computer and reach any other computer on the network, regardless of location, computer type, or operating system.

The Internet's global connectivity and ease of use can provide companies with access to businesses or individuals who normally would be outside their reach. Companies can link directly to suppliers, business partners, or individual customers at the same low cost, even if they are halfway around the globe. Businesses can find new outlets for their products and services abroad because the Internet facilitates cross-border transactions and information flows (Quelch and Klein, 1996). The Internet provides a low-cost medium for forming global

Table 10.2 **Internet Benefits to Organizations**

Connectivity and global reach

Reduced communication costs

Lower transaction costs

Reduced agency costs

Interactivity, flexibility, and customization

Accelerated distribution of knowledge

---

alliances and virtual organizations. The Web provides a standard interface and inexpensive global access, which can be used to create interorganizational systems among almost any organizations (Isakowitz, Bieber, and Vitali, 1998).

The Internet has made it easier and less expensive for companies to coordinate their staffs when opening new markets or working in isolated places because they do not have to build their own networks. Small companies who normally would find the cost of operating or selling abroad too expensive will find the Internet especially valuable.

Reduced Communication Costs

Before the Net, organizations had to build their own wide area networks or subscribe to a value-added network service. Employing the Internet, although far from cost-free, is certainly more cost-effective for many organizations than building one's own network or paying VAN subscription fees. One estimate is that a direct mailing or faxing to 1200 customers within the United States will cost $1200 to $1600, whereas the same coverage through the Net will cost only about $9. Adding 600 more recipients who are spread through six other countries would increase the cost only another $9. Thus, the Internet can help organizations reduce operational costs or minimize operational expenses while extending their activities.

Schlumberger Ltd., the New York and Paris oil-drilling equipment and electronics producer, operates in 85 countries, and in most of them employees are in remote locations. To install its own network for so few people at each remote location would have been prohibitively expensive. Using the Net, Schlumberger engineers in Dubai (on the Persian Gulf) can check e-mail and stay in close contact with management at a very low cost. The field staff also are able to follow research projects as well as personnel within the United States.

Schlumberger has found that since it converted to the Net from its own network, overall communications costs are down in spite of a major increase in network and IT infrastructure spending. The main reason for these savings is the dramatic drop in voice traffic and in overnight-delivery service charges (they attach complete documents to their e-mail messages).

Internet telephony The use of the Internet for telephone voice service.

Hardware and software have been developed for **Internet telephony,** allowing companies to use the Internet for telephone voice transmission. (Internet telephony products sometimes are called IP telephony products.) For example, Universal Sewing Supply, which provides sewing services to firms such as Fruit of the Loom and Levi Strauss, added an IP telephony gateway supplied by VocalTec Communications Ltd. to its private network in the fall of 1997. The monthly telephone bill for communications between its St. Louis corporate office and its factories in the Dominican Republic, which ranged from $4000 to $7000, plummeted by 80 percent. Although Internet telephony can help firms reduce their high charges for international calls, the Internet is currently not well suited to this purpose, having been designed for data communications, in which there are delays as data are downloaded. Most companies will not use Internet telephony services until the quality of telephone service improves (Korzeniowski, 1998).

Internet technology can also reduce communication costs by allowing companies to create virtual private networks as low-cost alternatives to private WANs. A **virtual private network (VPN)** is a secure connection between two points across the Internet and is available through Internet Service Providers (ISPs). The VPN provides many features of a private network at much lower cost than using private leased telephone lines or frame-relay connections. Companies are starting to use VPNs to reduce their wide area networking expenses. We describe the benefits of VPNs for companies operating internationally in Chapter 17.

Lower Transaction Costs

Businesses have found that conducting transactions electronically can be done at a fraction of the cost of paper-based processes. For instance, the paper and human cost of producing and processing a purchase order might total $45, compared with $1.25 if processed electronically over the Internet. The average retail banking transaction costs $1.50, compared with 15 to 25 cents for an electronic version. Using Internet technology reduces these transaction costs even further. Here are some examples:

- BeamScope Canada Inc. of Richmond Hill, Ontario, finds it can process Web orders for about 80 cents versus $5 to $15 for live orders. Customers appreciate the convenience of on-line shopping as well.

- Each time Federal Express clients use FedEx's Web site to track the status of their packages instead of inquiring by telephone, FedEx saves $8, amounting to a $2 million savings in operating costs each year.

- Pharmaceuticals manufacturer Merck and Co. Inc. found that having a human resources representative handle a transaction personally cost $16.96, and tracking down and fixing a mistake amounted to $128. Employee self-service over an intranet only cost $2.32 per transaction, with almost no cost to correct mistakes (Row, 1996).

Reduced Agency Costs

As organizations expand and globalization continues, the need to coordinate activities in far-flung locations is becoming more critical. The Internet reduces agency costs—the cost of managing employees and coordinating their work—by providing low-cost networks and inexpensive communication and collaboration tools that can be used on a global scale.

Schlumberger uses the Net for this purpose, as does Cygnus Support, a software developer with only 125 employees with offices in Mountain View, California, and Somerville, Massachusetts. Cygnus originally turned to the Internet to link its offices inexpensively via e-mail. It later developed an intranet to keep employees informed about company developments and to help manage the large number of telecommuters who work for the company.

By enabling scientists, physicians, and other professionals to exchange information and ideas instantaneously, the Internet is accelerating the pace of scientific collaboration and the spread of knowledge.

Interactivity, Flexibility, and Customization

Internet tools can create interactive applications that can be customized for multiple purposes and audiences. Web pages have capabilities for interacting with viewers that cannot be found in traditional print media. Visitors attracted by alluring displays of text, graphics, video, and sound also can click on hot buttons to make selections, take actions, or pursue additional information. Companies can use e-mail, chat rooms, and electronic discussion groups to create ongoing dialogues with their customers, using the information they have gathered to tailor communication precisely to fit the needs of each individual. Internet applications can be scaled up or down as the size of their audience changes because the technology works with the firm's existing network infrastructure.

Accelerated Distribution of Knowledge

In today's information economy, rapid access to knowledge is critical to the success of many companies. The Internet helps with this problem. Organizations are using e-mail and access to databases to gain immediate access to information resources in key areas such as business, science, law, and government. With blinding speed, the Internet can link a lone researcher sitting at a computer screen to mountains of data (including graphics) all over the world, which would be otherwise too expensive and too difficult to tap. For example, scientists can obtain photographs taken by NASA space probes within an hour of the picture being taken. It has become easy and inexpensive for corporations to obtain the latest U.S. Department of Commerce statistics, current weather data, and laws of legal entities worldwide.

In addition to accessing public knowledge resources on the Internet and the Web, companies can create internal Web sites as repositories of their own organizational knowledge. Multimedia Web pages can organize this knowledge, giving employees easier access to information and expertise. Web browser software provides a universal interface for accessing information resources from internal corporate databases as well as external information sources.

10.2 The Internet and Electronic Commerce

In earlier chapters, we described an array of information technologies that are transforming the way products are produced, marketed, shipped, and sold. Companies have been using their own WANs, VANs, electronic data interchange (EDI), e-mail, shared databases, digital image processing, bar coding, and interactive software to replace telephone calls and paper-based procedures for product design, marketing, ordering, delivery, payment, and customer support. Trading partners can directly communicate with each other, bypassing middlemen and inefficient multilayered procedures. The Internet provides a public and universally available set of technologies for these purposes.

The Internet is rapidly becoming the technology of choice for electronic commerce because it offers businesses an even easier way to link with other businesses and individuals at a very low cost. Web sites are available to consumers 24 hours a day. New marketing and sales channels can be created. Handling transactions electronically can reduce transaction costs and delivery time for some goods, especially those that are purely digital (such as software, text products, images, or videos). It is estimated that over $300 billion in goods and services will be exchanged over the Internet by 2002 (Hof et al., 1998).

Internet Business Models

Companies large and small are using the Internet to make product information, ordering, and customer support immediately available and to help buyers and sellers make contact. Some of these Internet electronic commerce initiatives represent automation of traditional paper-based business processes, while others are new business models. For example, Gardener's Eden uses the Web to advertise its traditional print catalog. Orders still must be placed by fax or telephone using the print catalog. But Amazon.com represents a new type of business, as does Virtual

1996 Eric Ross Winery Old Vine Zinfandel, Russian River Valley

Summary: A delicious, bona fide old vines Zin that deftly balances power and finesse. 700 cases produced. **$22.00**

ADD TO SHOPPING CART

FIND WINES BY:

- Category
- Varietal
- Price
- Origin
- Style
- Peter Says ...
- Producer

HINT - You can use one or more boxes.

FIND

Search Tips

▶ 1996 Sonora TC Vineyard "Old Vine" Zinfandel, Sierra Foothills $16.00 Classic Sierra Foothills Zinfandel from a 90-year-old vineyard. 900 cases made.

PETER'S TASTING CHART

PERCEPTION OF...

Intensity	Delicate · · · · · · · · ← · · · · Powerful
Dry Or Sweet	Bone Dry · · ← · · · · · · · · · · Dessert
Body	Light Body · · · · · · · · · ← · · Very Full Body
Acidity	Soft, Gentle · · · · · · · ← · · · · · Very Crisp
Tannin	None · · · · · · · ← · · · · · Heavy Tannins
Oak	None · · · · ← · · · · · · · · Heavy Oak
Complexity	Direct · · · · · · · · · ← · · · · Very Complex

ERIC ROSS

"Old vines" is one of the more enigmatic phrases now gracing many wine labels, especially those of Zinfandels. "Old compared to what?" one might ask. Is this the latest form of meaningless label-speak ("reserve" is my favorite)? Truth be told, the credibility

Peter's Tasting Chart on the Virtual Vineyards Web site provides evaluations of wines according to dimensions of taste to help visitors make informed wine selections. By providing this information along with the ability to purchase wine on-line, Virtual Vineyards has created a successful new business model for wine retailing.

Vineyards. Both are on-line storefronts that sell only over the Web. Another new business is Security First Network Bank, the virtual bank described in Chapter 2.

New business models have been created using the rich communication capabilities of the Internet. eBay is an on-line auction forum, using e-mail and other interactive features of the Web. People can make on-line bids for items such as computer equipment, antiques and collectibles, wine, jewelry, rock-concert tickets, and electronics that are posted by sellers from around the world. The system accepts bids for items entered on the Internet, evaluates the bids, and notifies the highest bidder. eBay collects a small commission on each listing and sale. Bid.com in Toronto, which started out hosting consumer cyberauctions, now has Web-based auction services for business-to-business sales of items such as agricultural equipment. The chapter ending case study describes OnSale, another Internet auction site and the challenges posed by its business model.

The Internet has created on-line communities, where people with similar interests can exchange ideas from many different locations. Some of these virtual communities are providing the foundation for new businesses. Electric Minds, a cyberspace community for people interested in technology and culture, generates revenue from advertisers who place banners on its Web site. In exchange, the sponsors have access to pockets of potential customers. Tripod attracts college students and young college graduates by providing "tools for life"—practical information about careers, health, personal finance, and travel, a resume-distribution service, and a facility to maintain a personal Web page. Members can participate in on-line discussion groups on women's issues, work and money, or the arts. Tripod's revenue comes from providing ways for corporate clients to target customers in the 18- to 30-year-old age group. In addition to selling electronic advertising space, Tripod allows corporate customers to sell products on the Web site and receives a percentage of each transaction (Eckerson, 1996). Even traditional retailing businesses are enhancing their Web sites with chat, message boards, and community building features as a means of encouraging customers to spend more time, return more frequently, and hopefully make more purchases on-line. For example, Gardner.com, which allows visitors to chat on-line about plants and flowers, found that registered members who chat are twice as likely to purchase at its Web site (Rafter, 1999).

Table 10.3 compares some of these Internet-based business models, which also are described at the Laudon Web site. Some replace internal organizational processes, some replace existing businesses, and some represent completely new kinds of businesses. All in one way or another add *value:* They provide the customer with a new product or service; they provide additional information or service along with a traditional product or service; or they provide a product or service at much lower cost than traditional means.

Tripod is an Internet business based on an on-line community for college students and young college graduates, with "pods" for specific interests such as health and fitness. The company generates revenue from advertising banners on its Web pages and from providing ways for corporate clients to target customers who are aged 18 to 30.

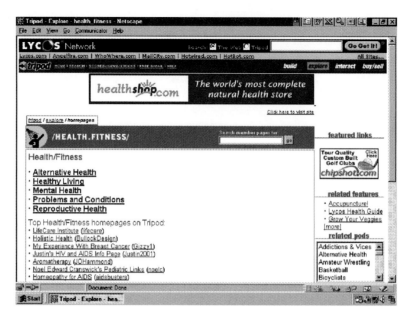

Table 10.3

Internet Business Models

Category	Description	Examples
Virtual Storefront	Sells physical goods or services on-line instead of through a physical storefront or retail outlet. Delivery of nondigital goods and services takes place through traditional means.	Amazon.com Virtual Vineyards Security First Network Bank
Marketplace Concentrator	Concentrates information about products and services from multiple providers at one central point. Purchasers can search, comparison-shop, and sometimes complete the sales transaction.	Internet Mall DealerNet Industrial Marketplace InsureMarket
Information Brokers	Provide product, pricing, and availability information. Some facilitate transactions, but their main value is the information they provide.	PartNet Travelocity Auto-by-Tel
Transaction Brokers	Buyers can view rates and terms, but the primary business activity is to complete the transaction.	E*Trade Ameritrade
Electronic Clearinghouses	Provide auction-like settings for products where price and availability are constantly changing, sometimes in response to customer actions.	Bid.com OnSale
Reverse Auction	Consumers submit a bid to multiple sellers to buy goods or services at a buyer-specified price.	Priceline.com
Digital Product Delivery	Sells and delivers software, multimedia, and other digital products over the Internet.	Build-a-Card PhotoDisc SonicNet
Content Provider	Creates revenue by providing content. The customer may pay to access the content, or revenue may be generated by selling advertising space or by having advertisers pay for placement in an organized listing in a searchable database.	Wall Street Journal Interactive Quote.com Tripod
On-line Service Provider	Provides service and support for hardware and software users.	Cyber Media Tune Up.com

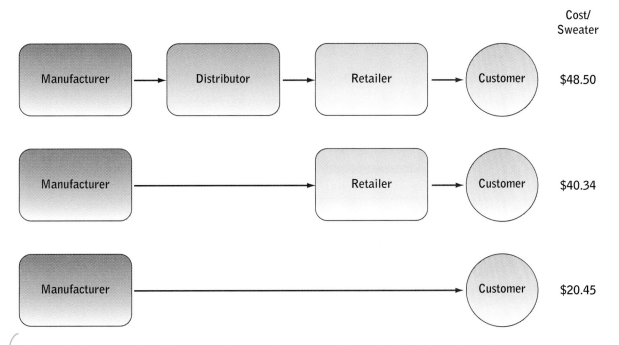

Cost/
Sweater

$48.50

$40.34

$20.45

Figure 10-6 The benefits of disintermediation to the consumer. The typical distribution channel has several intermediary layers, each of which adds to the final cost of a product, such as a sweater. Removing layers lowers the final cost to the consumer.

Customer-Centered Retailing

The Internet provides companies with new channels of communication and interaction that can create closer yet more cost-effective relationships with customers in sales, marketing, and customer support.

Direct Sales over the Web

Manufacturers can sell their products and services directly to retail customers, bypassing intermediaries such as distributors or retail outlets. Eliminating middlemen in the distribution channel can significantly lower purchase transaction costs. Operators of virtual storefronts such as the Amazon.com on-line bookstore or Virtual Vineyards do not have expenditures for rent, sales staff, and the other operations associated with a traditional retail store. Airlines can sell tickets directly to passengers through their own Web sites or through travel sites such as Travelocity without paying commissions to travel agents.

To pay for all the steps in a traditional distribution channel, a product may have to be priced as high as 135 percent of its original cost to manufacture (Mougayar, 1998). Figure 10-6 illustrates how much savings can result from eliminating each of these layers in the distribution process. By selling directly to consumers or reducing the number of intermediaries, companies can achieve higher profits while charging lower prices. The removal of organizations or business process layers responsible for intermediary steps in a value chain is called **disintermediation.**

The Internet is accelerating disintermediation in some industries and creating opportunities for new types of intermediaries in others. In certain industries, distributors with warehouses of goods, or middlemen such as real estate agents may be replaced by new intermediaries specializing in helping Internet users efficiently obtain product and price information, locate on-line sources of goods and services, or manage or maximize the value of the information captured about them in electronic commerce transactions (Hagel III and Singer, 1999). The information brokers listed in Table 10.3 are examples. In businesses impacted by the Internet, middlemen will have to adjust their services to fit the new business model or create new services based on the model.

disintermediation The removal of organizations or business process layers responsible for certain intermediary steps in a value chain.

Reebok International uses its Web site to maintain an ongoing dialogue with customers and learn more about their tastes and interests. Visitors to the Web site can obtain profiles of athletes, customized workout tips, and other information by filling out an on-line profile form.

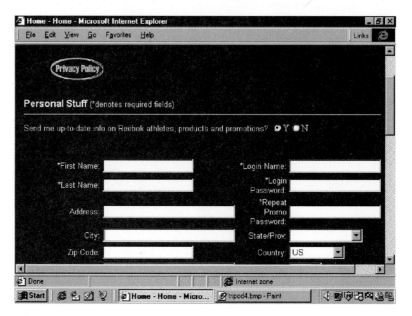

hit An entry into the log file of a Web server generated by each request to the server for a file.

Interactive Marketing

Marketers can use the interactive features of Web pages to hold consumers' attention or to capture information about their tastes and interests. Some of this information may be obtained by asking visitors to "register" on-line and provide information about themselves. Companies also can use special Web site auditing software capable of tracking the number of hits to their Web sites and the Web pages of greatest interest to visitors after they have entered the sites. (A **hit** is an entry into the log file of a Web server generated by each request to the server for a file.) They can analyze this information to develop more precise profiles of their customers. For instance, TravelWeb, a Web site offering electronic information on more than 16,000 hotels in 138 countries and an on-line reservation capability, tracks the origin of each user and the screens and hypertext links he or she uses to learn about customer preferences. The Hyatt hotel chain found that Japanese users are most interested in the golf facilities of a resort, valuable information in shaping market strategies and for developing hospitality-related products.

Companies can even use the Web and Internet capabilities such as electronic discussion groups, mailing lists, and e-mail to create ongoing dialogues with their customers. Communications and product offerings can be tailored precisely to individual customers (Bakos, 1998). For example, visitors to the Web site for Reebok International Ltd. can obtain profiles of athletes and training tips from coaches in fitness categories of their preference. If they fill out profile forms that ask them to list their favorite sports, they also will receive customized workout tips, news updates about their sports, and other information on future visits. By becoming site "members," they can send e-mail "postcards" to their favorite athletes. Reebok further enhanced its Web site with e-mail, discussion-group, and bulletin-board capabilities to create a community of users (Cole-Gomolski, 1998).

The cost of customer surveys and focus groups is very high. Learning how customers feel or what they think about one's products or services through electronic visits to Web sites is much cheaper. Web sites providing product information also lower costs by shortening the sales cycle and reducing the amount of time sales staff must spend in customer education (Sterne, 1995). The Web shifts more marketing and selling activities to the customer, as customers fill out their own on-line order forms (Hoffman, Novak, and Chatterjee, 1995).

Customer Self-Service

The Web and other network technologies are inspiring new approaches to customer service and support. Many companies are using their Web sites and e-mail to answer customer questions or to provide customers with helpful information. The Window on Technology describes the experiences of companies using chat rooms and Web-linked call centers for this purpose.

Interacting with the Customer

Internet chat rooms have had a somewhat unsavory reputation as havens for teenagers, misfits, and virtual pickup scenes, but companies have found that the interactive qualities of this technology can be harnessed in many valuable ways, especially in customer service and support. Pop-up messaging with instant responses can help companies communicate with customers even better than using e-mail or traditional telephone service.

Software maker Symantec, which deals with about 24,000 user queries per week, employs about 500 people to handle phone calls at its customer service center in Eugene, Oregon. The company has been encouraging people to solve their own problems by using a self-help database on its Web site because such support costs 40 percent to 60 percent less than telephone-based support. The database contains product information and discussion groups where customers can post questions. However, the average response time to questions submitted this way is 24 hours. To address this problem, Symantec recently added chat to its Web site to provide customers with more immediate feedback. Software from Business Evolution allows customers to click on a button on Symantec's Web site and enter a "room" to chat one-on-one with a customer service representative.

Other companies are experimenting with chat as a way to interact more closely with customers on the Internet. After visitors to the furniture.com Web site enter their style preferences, they are presented with a personalized showroom. A live company representative is available to discuss colors, fabrics, or prices using Web chat or Net phone. Egghead Software's Web site lets customers chat with a "sales egg" as they shop in its on-line store or chat with other customers in a "virtual lounge."

If customers still need to speak with a human representative, Web sites can be enhanced to connect them to corporate call centers. New software products such as WebAgent from Aspect Telecommunications Inc. in San Jose, California, allow Web sites to be browsed simultaneously by customers and customer service agents. They can talk to each other over a separate telephone line or an Internet connection to compare products or discuss their features. WebAgent synchronizes Web screens viewed by both parties as they talk and even lets each draw circles around words or pictures for both to see. This feature is useful for explaining how a complex device, such as a router, works while a diagram is viewed on-screen.

Such benefits prompted Logistix Inc., a Fremont, California, logistics technology company, to use WebAgent in conjunction with its 120-person call center. Logistix and other companies like the fact that the technology can turn the call center into a central point for customer contact where agents can answer customer inquiries from a number of sources—telephone, fax, e-mail, or the Web site.

To Think About: How does the Internet change business relationships with customers and the customer support process?

Sources: Marcia Stepanek, "You Wanna Hold Their Hands," *Business Week E-Biz*, March 22, 1999; Gary McWilliams, "Internet Firm Refocuses on Call Center Software," *The Wall Street Journal*, January 28, 1999; Matt Hamblen, "Call Centers and Web Sites Cozy Up," *Computerworld*, March 2, 1998; and Gordon Arnaut, "No Frills, Just Service with a Screen," *The New York Times*, January 26, 1998.

The Web provides a medium through which customers can interact with the company, at their convenience, and find information on their own that previously required a human customer-support expert. Some companies are realizing substantial cost savings from Web-based customer self-service applications. American, Northwest, and other major airlines have created Web sites where customers can review flight departure and arrival times, seating charts, and airport logistics, check frequent-flyer miles, and purchase tickets on-line.

These Web sites allow companies to engage in ongoing dialogues with their customers that can provide information for other purposes. For example, Dell Computer has established a Dell newsgroup on the Net and other on-line services to receive and handle customer complaints and questions. They answer about 90 percent of the questions within 24 hours. Dell also does market research for free through these newsgroups rather than paying a professional for the same information.

Business-to-Business Electronic Commerce: New Efficiencies and Relationships

Many believe that the most promising area of electronic commerce is not retailing to individuals but the automation of purchase and sale transactions from business to business. For a number of years, companies have used proprietary electronic data interchange (EDI) systems for

The Marshall Industries Web site supports a "virtual" distribution environment that automates the entire process of placing and receiving an order. Customers can use the Web site to review pricing information and product descriptions, input orders, and obtain customized information about their accounts and the status of their shipments with United Parcel Service. Marshall's Web site provides additional service and value by allowing visitors to test and run their designs over the Internet, obtain training, and access industry news.

this purpose; now they are turning to the Web and extranets. Cisco Systems, a leading manufacturer of networking equipment, conducts 40 percent of its sales electronically, with more than $1 billion in sales per year through its Web site. Order-taking, credit checking, production scheduling, technical support, and routine customer-support activities are handled on-line.

Marshall Industries' Virtual Distribution System

Marshall Industries, the world's fourth-largest distributor of industrial electronic components and production supplies, created a "virtual" distribution environment in which almost all of the processes it performed physically have been converted to a digital service on the Net.

Marshall's customers and suppliers can access its intranet to obtain customized information. For example, high-tech suppliers can see information about their own accounts, such as sales reports, inventory levels, and design data. They also can accept or reject price quotes or order training materials. A personal knowledge-assistant process called Plugged-In allows customers to specify the product categories they are interested in. They only receive information specific to their interests.

Visitors can view more than 100,000 pages of data sheets, up-to-date pricing, and inventory information from 150 major suppliers, and information on 170,000 parts' numbers. They can quickly locate products in Marshall's on-line catalog using a sophisticated search engine. The site links to the United Parcel Service (UPS), where customers can track the status of their shipments. Sales representatives have secure intranet access so they can check sales and activity status only in their territory.

When a customer places an order, the system verifies price and quantity and initiates a real-time credit authorization and approval. As soon as the order is approved, the system sends an automated request to the warehouse for scheduling. The system then sends the customer an order acknowledgment accompanied by relevant shipping and logistics information from UPS. Messages about order status are automatically "pushed" to the customer. The system thus integrates the entire process of placing and receiving an order.

Other features of Marshall's Web site provide additional service and value. Visitors can access a free "Electronic Design Center" to test and run their designs over the Internet. For example, an engineer might use Marshall's Web site to test Texas Instruments' (TI) digital signal processors (DSPs) for the design of a new piece of multimedia hardware. (DSP chips improve the performance of high-tech products such as computer hard disks, headphones, and power steering in cars.) At the site, the engineer can find technical specifications and even simulate designs using TI chips. The engineer would download sample code, modify the code

Table 10.4 Examples of Business-to-Business Electronic Commerce

Business	Electronic Commerce Applications
U.S. General Services Administration	The procurement arm of the U.S. federal government created an ordering system called GSA Advantage, which allows federal agencies to buy everything through its Web site. The Web site lists 220,000 products and accounts for annual sales of $12 million. By using the Web, agencies can see all of their purchasing options and make choices based on price and delivery.
AMP Inc.	By placing its 400 catalogs on the Web, this electrical-components manufacturer hopes to reduce and eventually eliminate $8 million to $10 million per year in printing and shipping costs while offering catalogs that are always up-to-date. AMP created a new division called AMPeMerce Internet Solutions to help manufacturers and other companies develop Internet-based product catalogs and selling mechanisms.
General Electric Information Services	Operates a Trading Process Network (TPN) where GE and other subscribing companies can solicit and accept bids from selected suppliers over the Internet. TPN is a secure Web site developed for internal GE use that now is available to other companies for customized bidding and automated purchasing. GE earns revenue by charging subscribers for the service and by collecting a fee from the seller if a transaction is completed.

to suit the product being built, test it on a "virtual chip" attached to the Web, and analyze its performance. If the engineer liked the results, Marshall could download his or her code, burn it into physical chips, and send back samples for designing prototypes. The entire process would take minutes.

Marshall's Web site provides after-sale training so that engineers do not have to attend special training classes or meetings in faraway locations. Marshall links to NetSeminar, a Web site where Marshall's customers can register for and receive educational programs developed for them by their suppliers using video, audio, and real-time chat capabilities.

For business-to-business electronic commerce, companies can use their own Web sites, like Cisco Systems and Marshall Industries, or they can conduct sales through Web sites set up as on-line marketplaces. (Marketplace concentrators are among the new Internet business models we introduced earlier in this chapter.) Industrial malls such as Industrial Marketplace bring together a large number of suppliers in one place, providing search tools so that buyers can quickly locate what they need. They make money by collecting fees from their "tenant" vendors. Companies also can sell to other companies through Web sites that run cyberauctions for electronic parts and industrial and scientific equipment. The auctions' operations are similar to those described earlier in this section (Deutsch, 1998).

Corporate purchasing traditionally has been based on long-term relationships with one or two suppliers. The Internet makes information about alternative suppliers more accessible so that companies can find the best deal from a wide range of sources, including those overseas. For example, Mike Maiorano, the purchasing manager for XLNT Designs Inc., a manufacturer of networking technologies, consults the Web when he is asked to buy from an unfamiliar supplier or locate a new type of part. It is not surprising that identifying and researching potential trading partners is the most common procurement activity on the Internet (Buchanan, 1997). Suppliers themselves can use the Web to research competitors' prices on-line.

Organizations also can use the Web to solicit bids from suppliers by advertising requests for proposals (RFPs) on-line. Government organizations, especially military agencies and state governments, have been quick to adopt this model. Table 10.4 describes other examples of business-to-business electronic commerce.

Table 10.5 **Examples of Electronic Commerce Servers**

Product	Description	Vendor
Icat Electronic Commerce Suite	Provides on-line catalog shopping and order placement for sophisticated Web sites; Icat Commerce on-line version available for small business storefronts	Icat
Net.Commerce	Lower priced START version has a store creation wizard for catalog pricing, shipping, taxing, and secure payment processing with business-to-consumer and business-to-business capability; high-end PRO version for more advanced Web site with intelligent catalog capability and tools to integrate the Web site with legacy systems and middleware	IBM
Netscape MerchantXpert	Supports high-end business-to-consumer site with catalog search tools, order management, tax, payment, and logistics modules and tools to integrate the site with legacy systems	Netscape
Open Market Transact	Commerce services include on-line customer authentication, order and payment processing, tax calculations, and customer service with multiple language capabilities	Open Market
Oracle Internet Commerce Server	Business-to-consumer commerce application that integrates with other Oracle applications for orders, inventory, customer service, call centers, and payment authorizations via third-party payment technology vendors	Oracle

Electronic Commerce Support Systems

A business interested in setting up a system to support electronic commerce has three options: (1) using a Web server with a toolkit to build its own system, (2) purchasing a packaged electronic commerce server system, or (3) outsourcing the system to an e-commerce service provider. A number of Internet commerce or merchant server systems are available. They typically provide a Web storefront, usually with some type of on-line catalog support, and a means for taking orders. Some of these systems link to financial networks to complete payment processing. Table 10.5 describes some of these products.

For companies that are not ready to operate their own electronic commerce sites, companies such as AT&T, MCI, Best Internet Communications, and BBN Planet offer Web hosting services that process electronic commerce transactions for other organizations. A **Web hosting service** maintains a large Web server or series of servers and provides fee-paying subscribers with space to maintain their Web sites. The subscribing companies may create their own Web pages or have the hosting service or a Web design firm create them. Web hosting services offer solutions to small companies that do not have the resources to operate their own commerce servers or companies that still are experimenting with electronic commerce.

Integrating all of the processes associated with electronic commerce requires additional software and tools, such as software providing interfaces between Web servers and the company's core-transaction databases and electronic payment systems. **Electronic payment systems** use technologies such as electronic funds transfer, credit cards, smart cards and debit cards, and new Internet-based payment systems to pay for products and services electronically. Software to track and monitor Web site usage for marketing analysis also is desirable.

The process of paying for products and services purchased on the Internet is complex and merits additional discussion. Many security issues are involved, and there are a large number of payment systems. We discuss secure electronic payment systems in detail in Chapter 16. Figure 10-7 provides an overview of the key information flows in electronic commerce.

Web hosting service Company maintaining large Web servers to maintain the Web sites of fee-paying subscribers.

electronic payment system The use of digital technologies such as electronic funds transfer, credit cards, smart cards and debit cards, and Internet-based payment systems to pay for products and services electronically.

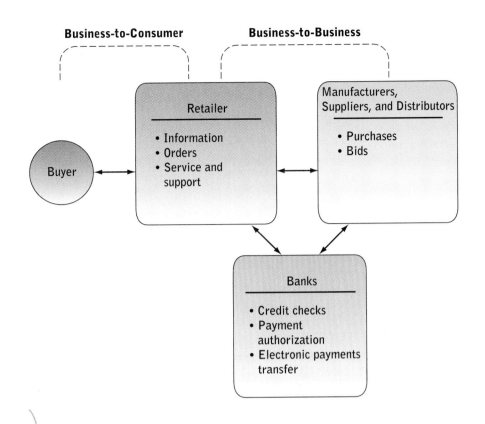

Business-to-Consumer   **Business-to-Business**

Buyer

Retailer
- Information
- Orders
- Service and support

Manufacturers, Suppliers, and Distributors
- Purchases
- Bids

Banks
- Credit checks
- Payment authorization
- Electronic payments transfer

Figure 10-7 Electronic commerce information flows. Individuals can purchase goods and services electronically from online retailers, who in turn can use electronic commerce technologies to link directly to their suppliers or distributers. Electronic payment systems are used in both business-to-consumer and business-to-business electronic commerce.

10.3 Intranets and Electronic Business

Businesses are finding some of the greatest benefits of Internet technology come from applications that lower agency and coordination costs. Although companies have used internal networks for many years to manage and coordinate internal business processes, intranets quickly are becoming the technology of choice for electronic business.

How Intranets Support Electronic Business

Intranets are inexpensive, scalable to expand or contract as needs change, and accessible from most computing platforms. Whereas most companies, particularly the larger ones, must support a multiplicity of computer platforms that cannot communicate with each other, intranets provide instant connectivity, uniting all computers into a single, virtually seamless, network system. Web software presents a uniform interface, which can be used to integrate many different processes and systems throughout the company. Companies can connect their intranet to company databases just as with the Web, enabling employees to take actions central to a company's operations. For instance, customer service representatives for U.S. West can access mainframe databases through the corporate intranet to turn on services such as call waiting or to check installation dates for new phone lines, all while the customer is on the telephone.

Intranets can help organizations create a richer, more responsive information environment. Internal corporate applications based on the Web page model can be made interactive using a variety of media, text, audio, and video. A principal use of intranets has been to create on-line repositories of information that can be updated as often as required. Product catalogs, employee handbooks, telephone directories, or benefits information can be revised immediately as changes occur. This "event-driven" publishing allows organizations to respond more rapidly to changing conditions than traditional paper-based publishing, which requires a rigid production schedule. Made available via intranets, documents always can be up-to-date, eliminating paper, printing, and distribution costs. Some estimates put the cost of using the paper-based model of distributing information as high as $15 per employee. An organization with 100,000 employees might save $1.5 million by converting a single application, such as an employee policy and benefits manual, to electronic form on an intranet (Levitt, 1996).

Table 10.6 Organizational Benefits of Intranets

Connectivity: Accessible from most computing platforms

Can be tied to legacy systems and core transaction databases

Can create interactive applications with text, audio, and video

Scalable to larger or smaller computing platforms as requirements change

Easy to use, universal Web browser interface

Low start-up costs

Richer, more responsive information environment

Reduced information distribution costs

Intranets have provided cost savings in other application areas as well. For instance, U.S. West saves $300,000 per year with an intranet application that automatically notifies service representatives of expiring service contracts. The intranet only cost $17,000 to build (Jahnke, 1998). KeyCorp's knowledge-bank intranet for distributing job postings, information on best practices, marketing material, and newsletters saves $1.8 million in annual cost versus an initial development cost of $300,000 (*Computerworld,* 1997). Conservative studies of returns on investment (ROIs) from intranets show ROIs of 23 percent to 85 percent, and some companies have reported ROIs of more than 1000 percent. More detail on the business value of intranets can be found in Chapter 11.

For companies with an installed network infrastructure, intranets are very inexpensive to build and run. Programming Web pages is quick and easy with Web page authoring tools; employees can create Web pages on their own. The intranet provides a universal e-mail system, remote access, group collaboration tools, electronic library, application-sharing system, and company communications network. Some companies are using their intranets for virtual conferencing. Intranets are simple, cost-effective communication tools. Table 10.6 summarizes the organizational benefits of using intranets.

Intranets and Group Collaboration

Intranets and other network technologies provide a rich set of tools for creating collaborative environments in which members of an organization can exchange ideas, share information, and work together on common projects and assignments regardless of their physical location. These tools include e-mail, fax, voice mail, teleconferencing, videoconferencing, dataconferencing, groupware, chat systems, newsgroups, and teamware. We already have described the capabilities of most of these tools.

teamware Group collaboration software that is customized for teamwork.

Teamware consists of intranet-based applications for building a work team, sharing ideas and documents, brainstorming, scheduling, and archiving decisions made or rejected by a project for future use. It is similar to groupware, but more customized for team work, and some teamware tools such as In Tandem from IntraACTIVE do not require an elaborate enterprise-wide infrastructure to be installed. Teamware and groupware frequently are used as support tools for the short-lived projects staffed by knowledge workers. Chapter 14 provides a detailed description of groupware and intranets for managing and distributing organizational knowledge resources.

Some companies are using intranets to create enterprise collaboration environments linking diverse groups, projects, and activities throughout the organization. The U.S. West Global Village intranet is a prominent example. Here are just a few of its capabilities:

○ A sales consultant in Chicago can check events throughout the company. He pulls up News of the Day, an internal newsletter.

○ A project manager can click on the lab page to inspect software being developed for a new service. He can test the software from his own computer.

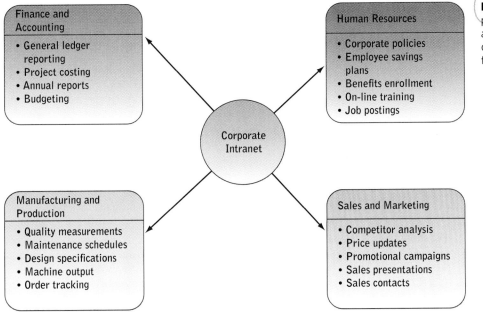

Figure 10-8 Functional applications of intranets. Intranet applications have been developed for each of the major functional areas of the business.

Finance and Accounting

- General ledger reporting
- Project costing
- Annual reports
- Budgeting

Human Resources

- Corporate policies
- Employee savings plans
- Benefits enrollment
- On-line training
- Job postings

Corporate Intranet

Manufacturing and Production

- Quality measurements
- Maintenance schedules
- Design specifications
- Machine output
- Order tracking

Sales and Marketing

- Competitor analysis
- Price updates
- Promotional campaigns
- Sales presentations
- Sales contacts

○ Repair technicians can share a map showing damage to phone lines caused by ice storms and explore a strategy for repairing them.

○ An executive can log onto the intranet from her home after dinner to catch up with e-mail and check out the next day's schedule for her project team.

○ An engineer researching the design of a new network component can link to the public Internet via a gateway built into the Global Village home page. She surfs the Web to locate possible suppliers, then returns to the company intranet to inform her colleagues via e-mail about what she has found.

These intranet applications have enabled U.S. West to improve communications and streamline business processes, saving the company millions of dollars each year.

Intranet Applications for Electronic Business

Intranets are springing up in all the major functional areas of the business, allowing them to manage more of their business processes electronically. Figure 10-8 illustrates some of the intranet applications that have been developed for finance and accounting, human resources, sales and marketing, and manufacturing and production.

Finance and Accounting

Many organizations have extensive TPS that collect operational data on financial activities, but their traditional management reporting systems, such as general ledger systems and spreadsheets, often cannot bring this detailed information together for decision making and performance measurement. Intranets can be very valuable for finance and accounting because they can provide an integrated view of financial and accounting information on-line in an easy-to-use format. Table 10.7 provides some examples.

Human Resources

One of the principal responsibilities of human resources departments is to keep employees informed of company issues as well as to provide information about their personnel records and employee benefits. Human resources can use intranets for on-line publishing of corporate policy manuals, job postings and internal job transfers, company telephone directories, and training classes. Employees can use an intranet to enroll in healthcare, employee savings, and other

Table 10.7 Intranets in Finance and Accounting

Organization	Intranet Application
Charles Schwab	SMART reporting and analysis application provides managers with a comprehensive view of Schwab financial activities, including a risk-evaluation template that helps managers assess nine categories of risk. Schwab's intranet also delivers the FinWeb General Ledger reporting system on-line in easy-to-digest format.
Jeffries & Co.	Intranet-based data marts consolidate data from different legacy systems to provide a unified view of customer accounts. Sales staff and executives can access data marts that consolidate trading and financial data using Netscape Web browsers to view summary-level reports or drill down for further detail. The data marts help support the investment bank's expansion into new markets such as corporate finance and research.
Pacific Northwest National Laboratory	Intranet Web Reporting System provides financial statistics for laboratory activities, including current costs charged to each project, the number of hours spent on each project by individual employees, and how actual costs compare to projected costs. Lab employees can use Web browsers to perform ad hoc queries on financial data.

benefit plans if it is linked to the firm's human resources or benefits database or to take on-line competency tests. Human resource departments can rapidly deliver information about upcoming events or company developments to employees using newsgroups or e-mail broadcasts. Table 10.8 lists examples of how intranets are used in the area of human resources.

Sales and Marketing

Earlier we described how the Internet and the Web can be used for selling to individual customers and to other businesses. Internet technology also can be applied to the internal management of the sales and marketing function. One of the most popular applications for corporate intranets is to oversee and coordinate the activities of the sales force. Sales staff can dial in for updates on pricing, promotions, rebates, or customers or obtain information about competitors. They can access presentations and sales documents and customize them for customers.

Wang Software created an intranet called Knowledge Exchange, which includes information about the work-flow products Wang sells, sales contacts, corporate strategies of existing and potential customers, case studies of current Wang customers, and troubleshooting tips

Table 10.8 Intranets in Human Resources

Organization	Intranet Application
Genentech	An on-line employee handbook provides company announcements and an employee directory along with information on research seminars, commuting options, benefits, child care, obtaining business cards, and safety equipment.
Public Service & Gas Co. of New Jersey	Employees can use an intranet to access information on company savings plans, track historical performance, and reallocate funds in their 401K savings plans, taking advantage of asset-allocation models to make decisions. They also can use the intranet to choose a health plan, reviewing reports on HMO providers to guide their selection, and even select their physicians.
TRW Inc.	Employees can view job postings on-line through an intranet.
Documentum Inc.	System engineers and consultants in the United States and Europe can receive on-line training on how to use the company's document management software products.

Table 10.9 Intranets in Manufacturing and Production

Organization	Intranet Application
Nortel Technologies	Intranet publishes 3-D models and animations for faster exploration of ideas, better feedback, and shorter development cycles. The application reduces miscommunication between process engineers and the shop floor because animations show how to fit different pieces together.
Sony Corporation	Intranet delivers financial information to manufacturing personnel so that workers can monitor the profit-and-loss performance of the production line and adapt performance accordingly. The intranet also provides data on quality measurements, such as defects and rejects, as well as maintenance and training schedules.
Duke Power	Intranet provides on-line access to a computer-aided engineering tool for retrieving equipment designs and operating specifications that allows employees to view every important system in the plant at various levels of detail. Different subsets of systems can be formatted together to create a view of all the equipment in a particular room. Maintenance technicians, plant engineers, and operations personnel can use this tool with minimal training.
Rockwell International	Intranet improves process and quality of manufactured circuit boards and controllers by establishing home pages for its Milwaukee plant's computer-controlled machine tools that are updated every 60 seconds. Quality control managers can check the status of a machine by calling up its home page to learn how many pieces the machine output that day, what percentage of an order that output represents, and to what tolerances the machine is adhering.

for software implementations. The intranet includes discussion groups, which are scanned by help desk staff for information of interest to sales representatives. The help desk documents telephone transactions with representatives and feeds solutions back to a database where they can be used to help others. Representatives can use the site's search engine to pull up Power-Point electronic presentations, documents, or spreadsheets based on specified keywords (Dahle, 1997).

Case Corp., a Racine, Wisconsin, manufacturer of earth-moving and farming equipment, supports its sales and marketing teams with intranet collaboration tools for contact management, discussion forums, document management, and calendars. Marketsmarter LLC develops customized intranet applications for marketing and sales personnel based on a proprietary process called PRAISE. (PRAISE stands for Purpose, Research, Analyze, Implement, Strategize, and Evaluate.) PRAISE applications facilitate sharing of information on competitors, potential product-development products, and research tasks and include time-sensitive accountability to measure results (Sterne, 1998).

Manufacturing and Production

In manufacturing, information-management issues are highly complex, involving massive inventories, capturing and integrating real-time production data flows, changing relationships with suppliers, and volatile costs. The manufacturing function typically uses multiple types of data, including graphics as well as text, which are scattered in many disparate systems. Manufacturing information is often very time-sensitive and difficult to retrieve because files must be continuously updated. Developing intranets that integrate manufacturing data under a uniform user interface is more complicated than in other functional areas.

Despite these difficulties, companies are launching intranet applications for manufacturing. Intranets coordinating the flow of information between lathes, controllers, inventory systems, and other components of a production system can make manufacturing information more accessible to different parts of the organization, increasing precision and lowering costs. Table 10.9 describes some of these uses.

Coordination and Supply Chain Management

Intranets and extranets also can be used to simplify and integrate business processes spanning more than one functional area. These cross-functional processes can be coordinated electronically, increasing organizational efficiency and responsiveness. One area of great interest to companies is the use of intranets and extranets to facilitate supply chain management.

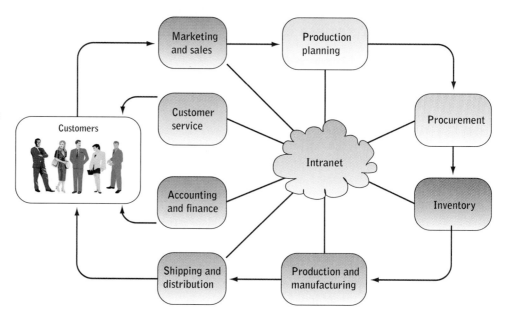

Figure 10-9 Intranet linking supply chain functions. Intranets can be used to integrate information from isolated business processes so that they can be coordinated for supply chain management. **Source:** Kalakota and Whinston, **Electronic Commerce: A Manager's Guide.** © 1997 by Addison-Wesley Publishing Company. Reprinted by permission of Addison Wesley Longman (p. 293).

Chapter 2 introduced the concept of supply chain management, which integrates procurement, production, and logistics processes to supply goods and services from their source to final delivery to the customer. The supply chain can be thought of as an "extended enterprise" linking material suppliers, distributors, retailers, and customers, as well as manufacturing facilities.

In the pre-Internet environment, supply chain coordination was hampered by the difficulties of making information flow smoothly between many different kinds of systems servicing different parts of the supply chain, such as purchasing, materials management, manufacturing, and distribution. Internet technology provides the connectivity to overcome these barriers. Firms can use intranets to improve coordination among their internal supply chain processes, and they can use extranets to coordinate supply chain processes shared with their business partners (see Figure 10-9). Marshall Industries' extranet, described earlier, has many powerful supply chain management capabilities, as does the extranet for supply chain management developed by Chrysler Corporation.

Chrysler's Supplier Partner Information Network (SPIN) allows 3500 of Chrysler's 12,000 suppliers selective access to portions of its intranet, where they can access the most current data on design changes, parts shortages, packaging information, and invoice tracking. Chrysler believes that by streamlining product delivery and shortening the time to communicate process or design changes, SPIN has reduced the time to complete various business processes by 25 percent to 50 percent. Chrysler can use the information from SPIN to manage employees more efficiently. A critical parts tracking application permits reassignment of workers so that shortages do not hold up assembly lines. Chrysler added invoice tracking to SPIN so that staff spends less time fielding phone calls from suppliers inquiring about payments. SPIN has been revised to incorporate Chrysler's proprietary EDI system and push technology. SPIN can automatically notify suppliers of critical parts shortages.

Not all Internet-based supply chain applications are as ambitious as those of Chrysler or Marshall Industries, but they are changing the way businesses work internally and with each other (Kalakota and Whinston, 1996). In addition to reducing costs, these supply chain management systems provide more responsive customer service, allowing the workings of the business to be driven more by customer demand. Earlier supply chain management systems were driven by production master schedules based on forecasts or best guesses of demand for products. With new flows of information made possible by intranets and extranets, supply chain management can follow a demand-driven model.

Some companies are starting to use the Internet for supply chain management on a global scale, as described in the Window on Organizations.

Window on Organizations

The Supply Chain Goes Global

Managing one's supply chain has been difficult enough in the past. But now, growing business globalization finds many companies obtaining supplies from all over the world. One might think that this would make the task of managing one's global supply chain impossible. Not so. The Internet is proving to be a tool that not only makes management of a global supply chain possible, but actually may even improve it.

What does the Internet offer the supply chain management function? Benefits begin with cost savings. Private networks are very expensive. For many companies, the cost of private networks makes obtaining supplies globally prohibitive. However, the Net is ubiquitous and only requires a Web browser to be able to use it. Neither seller nor buyer need build an expensive infrastructure. Suppliers and customers everywhere can easily afford to use it in their drive to participate in the global market. But cost savings is only one benefit of using the Net. The Net is fast, often dramatically cutting cycle times for sourcing, production, and delivery. Faster cycle times mean companies can be more responsive to the market while lowering inventory costs and errors. Let's look at a few examples of how it is working.

Adaptec Inc. is a Silicon Valley–based computer chip and board maker that obtains many of its products from East Asia. It is using the Internet to make available to its suppliers purchase orders and factory-status updates. The company says using the Net has cut the manufacturing cycle from 12 weeks to 8, making it a more responsive organization. At the same time, it claims savings of $10 million in inventory costs in only 4 months because of the Net. As Adaptec Electronic Commerce Manager Steve Robinson explains it, "It means data getting to the right people much faster, all in support of our No. 1 business driver—reducing cycle times."

Seven large retailers, including Lowe's hardware and PetSmart pet supply chains from the United States and French retailers Promodes and Carrefour, are using IBM's QCS.net to purchase from 5000 suppliers over the Internet. QCS.net provides catalog and transaction services, including purchase order, invoicing, and reordering capabilities along with work-flow templates to help retailers communicate and negotiate with suppliers. Retailers can track the status of their shipments on-line. By using the Internet, these companies can collaborate more easily with their suppliers in the United States, Europe, and Asia, eliminating buying errors and improving the quality of items that are shipped.

The combined automobile industry presents an unusually ambitious example. The automotive supply chain already is global, and in response to this, the industry has created the Automotive Network Exchange (ANX), a private network using Internet technology, which began operating in the summer of 1998. This partnership ultimately could enable as many as 40,000 automobile producers, parts suppliers, dealerships, and financial services companies to communicate worldwide. Auto industry experts estimate that, by using this network, costs will be cut by $1 billion annually, or about $70 per vehicle produced. Jim Lloyd, vice president of network and information resources at UT Automotive in Dearborn, Michigan, explains that ANX will help save money on basic telecommunications costs because companies do not have to build the telecommunications infrastructure. Other expected benefits include rapid response to changes in production and delivery schedules, a more rapid model development cycle, improved accuracy, and even higher product quality.

To Think About: Suggest other ways the Internet can be used to improve supply chain management. What problems do you see in using the Internet in this way?

Sources: Clinton Wilder, "Retailers Collaborate," **Information Week**, January 11, 1999; Bob Wallace, "Automakers Eye Global VPN," **Computerworld**, September 7, 1998; and Clinton Wilder, Gregory Dalton, and Beth Davis, "Global Links," **Information Week**, March 25, 1998.

10.4 Management Challenges and Opportunities

Although the Internet offers a wealth of new opportunities for electronic commerce and electronic business, it also presents managers with a series of challenges. These challenges largely stem from the fact that Internet technology and its business functions are relatively new.

Unproven Business Models

Not all companies make money on the Web. We can point to a number of Web sites that have closed because they failed to return benefits that could justify the outlay of hundreds of thousands and even millions of dollars. Industry.net, the comprehensive industrial mall run by IBM and Nets.Inc, no longer is in business. As of the writing of this chapter, such widely heralded sites as Amazon.com and Travelocity had yet to turn a profit. Business models built around the Internet are new and largely unproven. At the moment, the greatest benefit of Internet technology for many firms may be the use of intranets to reduce internal operating costs.

Business Process Change Requirements

Electronic commerce and electronic business require careful orchestration of the firm's divisions, production sites, and sales offices, as well as close relationships with customers, suppliers, banks, and other trading partners. Essential business processes must be redesigned and more closely integrated, especially those for supply chain management.

Channel Conflicts

Using the Web for on-line sales and marketing may create **channel conflict** with the firm's traditional channels, especially for less information-intensive products that require physical intermediaries to reach buyers (Palmer and Griffith, 1998). Its sales force and distributors may fear that their revenues will drop as customers make purchases directly from the Web or that they will be displaced by this new channel. The use of alternative channels created by the Internet requires very careful planning and management. The Window on Management describes how several companies are dealing with this problem.

Technology Hurdles

To make extensive use of the Internet, some companies need more expensive telecommunications connections, workstations, or high-speed computers that can handle transmission of bandwidth-hungry graphics and perhaps special computers dedicated as Web servers. Individuals and organizations in less-developed countries with poor telephone lines, limited hardware and software capacity, or government controls on communications will not be able to take full advantage of Internet resources (Goodman, Press, Ruth, and Rutkowski, 1994).

Bandwidth is another major technology issue. With the success of the Web, sound, graphics, and full-motion video are now important aspects of network computing. However, these all require immense quantities of data, greatly slowing down transmission and the downloading of screens. Some Web servers become overloaded with servicing requests and may be impossible to access during busy periods. The existing telecommunications infrastructure was not set up to handle large numbers of people using its services for hours at a time. (Current telephone systems were designed and priced under the assumption that 10 percent of all phones would be in use at any time and the average voice call lasted 3 to 4 minutes. The average Internet session lasts for 22 minutes, with many people connected for hours.) During peak periods of usage, Internet traffic slows to a crawl, and Internet Service

Avon sells its beauty products through its Web site as well as through its sales force. The company found that the Web site primarily attracts new customers and does not compete with its traditional sales channel of using door-to-door representatives.

Avoiding Channel Conflict

Gibson Musical Instruments of Nashville, Tennessee, struck a sour chord with its distributors when it opened a Web site to sell its electric guitars. Why sell on the Web? Well, for starters, selling via the Web is less costly. Gibson decided to offer its guitars through the Web at a 10 percent discount. The problem was that it did this without consulting Gibson dealers. Not surprisingly, the dealers were irate. Gibson was so dependent on them that it eliminated on-line sales within a month.

Selling on-line can be tricky for established companies. After all, they were selling their products before the Web site, and retailers, distributors, and sales representatives were making a living that way. Few if any existing companies can expect to replace their current sales chain with the Web any time soon. Gibson could not hope to replace its sales chain with only Web sales at any time in the foreseeable future. In fact, Gibson only hoped to reach new customers through the Web. They did not expect a Web site to threaten their current distributors, so they never asked, and, as it turned out, their distributors had a very different view.

It is not uncommon for companies like Gibson to act hastily by putting up a Web site without thinking through their Web strategy properly and without consulting their sales partners. However, other companies have turned to a Web site after proper planning and found the move to be a positive one. One company that successfully followed the Gibson approach was Avon, the New York City–based producer of beauty products. Avon did not have the problem of a sales staff or of retail stores because it works primarily through more than 2.3 million independent sales representatives selling door-to-door. Company management did not expect the Web site to compete with door-to-door sales. Nonetheless, to be sure, they undertook a lot of research that showed the Web site would not persuade existing customers to leave their personal sales representatives. Instead, research indicated that the site would attract new customers. Only then did they put up a Web site.

Computer-game producer Sega of America, Inc. followed a different strategy. They decided to sell from their Web site, but only after intensive consultations with their sales department. To allay fears from their sales staff and their retailers, products sold via the Web will not be discounted.

Sega also will charge a sales-and-handling fee for on-line sales, making the products more expensive when purchased via the Web. Sega did reserve the right to offer special promotions over the Web as long as those promotions do not revolve around price discounts. For example, they e-mailed 15,000 customers, offering them a package of games that includes a T-shirt not for sale elsewhere. About 25 percent of those customers purchased the special offer.

Channel conflict is an especially troublesome issue in business-to-business electronic commerce, where customers buy directly from manufacturers via the Web instead of through their geographic sales representatives. Milacron Inc. operates one of heavy industry's most extensive Web sites for selling machine tools to contract manufacturers. It is also benefiting from the customer information it collects on-line, which is forwarded to its research and development engineers. Milacron can use information on product improvements sought by customers to make better R&D decisions. To minimize negative repercussions from channel conflict, Milacron is paying full commissions to its reps for on-line sales made in their territory, even if they had not done any work on the sale or met the buyer. By not penalizing sales representatives for on-line sales that bypass them, this policy also creates a single face for the customer.

Gibson eventually came up with a Web strategy that it believes will boost sales without alienating dealers. It put its parts catalog on the Web, using the Web only to sell strings, accessories, and items such as chrome- or nickel-plated screws that were previously available only to dealers and repairers. The company finds that the Web site is an excellent way to service customers who cannot find these items at their dealers. Dealers also benefit because they can use the Web to order parts at a discount.

To Think About: What management, organization, and technology issues should be addressed when considering whether to use the Web for direct sales to consumers?

Sources: Clinton Wilder, "Tapping the Pipeline," **Information Week**, March 15, 1999 and "E-Commerce—Old Line Moves On-line," **Information Week**, January 11, 1999; and Sari Kalin, "Conflict Resolution," **CIO Magazine**, February 1, 1998.

Providers (ISPs) cannot keep up with the demand. Higher bandwidth alternatives are under development, but the public Internet in its current form is not reliable enough for many business-critical applications.

Web-based systems themselves are too slow for high-speed transaction processing. They can provide a useful interface, however, to core-transaction processing systems, such as order processing. Making this integration requires special software to link these systems and special technical expertise. Integrating data from multiple systems on an intranet can be a complex undertaking.

Legal Issues

Laws governing electronic commerce are mostly nonexistent or just being written. Legislatures, courts, and international agreements will have to settle such open questions as the legality and force of e-mail contracts including the role of electronic signatures and the application of copyright laws to electronically copied documents. Moreover, the Internet is global, and is used by individuals and organizations in hundreds of different countries. If a product were offered for sale in Thailand via a server in Singapore and the purchaser lived in Hungary, whose law would apply? Until greater clarity brings stability to these and other critical legal questions, doing business on the Internet will bring a level of unreliability that some will find unacceptable.

Security and Privacy

We already have described some of the potential security and privacy problems created by networked computing in previous chapters. Internet-based systems are even more vulnerable than those in private networks because the Internet was designed to be open to everyone. Many people have the skill and technology to intercept and spy on streams of electronic information as they flow through the Internet and all other open networks. Any information, including e-mail, passes through many computer systems on the Net before it reaches its destination. It can be monitored, captured, and stored at any of these points along the route. Valuable data that might be intercepted include credit card numbers and names, private personnel data, marketing plans, sales contracts, product development and pricing data, negotiations between companies, and other data that might be of value to competition. Concern over the security of electronic payments is one reason that electronic commerce has not grown more rapidly on the Net. We explore Internet security and the state of technology for secure electronic payments in greater detail in Chapter 16.

Chapter 5 described some of the ways that hackers, vandals, and computer criminals have exploited Internet weaknesses to break into computer systems. Stealing passwords, obtaining sensitive information, electronic eavesdropping, or "jamming" corporate Web servers to make them inaccessible can cause serious disruptions and harm.

Chapter 5 also described some of the threats to individual privacy raised by the Internet. Through the use of "cookies" and Web-site monitoring software, companies can gather information about individuals without their knowledge. In other instances, Web site visitors knowingly supply personal information such as their name, address, e-mail address, and special interests in exchange for access to the site without realizing how the organization owning the Web site may be using the information.

Effective use of the Internet, intranets, and extranets requires careful management planning. Table 10.10 lists what we believe are the top questions managers should ask when exploring the use of the Internet for electronic commerce and electronic business.

Table 10.10   Using the Internet in Business: Top Questions for Managers

1. What value will the Internet and intranets provide the business? Will the benefits outweigh the costs? How can we measure success?

2. How will business processes have to be changed to use this technology for electronic commerce or electronic business? How much process integration is required?

3. What technical skills and employee training will be required to use Internet technology?

4. Do we have the appropriate information technology infrastructure and bandwidth for using the Internet and intranets?

5. How can we integrate Internet applications with existing applications and data?

6. How can we make sure our intranet is secure from entry by outsiders? How secure is the electronic payment system we are using for electronic commerce?

7. Are we doing enough to protect the privacy of customers we reach electronically?

To obtain meaningful benefits from the Internet, managers need to determine how its technologies can support their business goals. Planning should carefully consider network costs, the costs and benefits of Internet computing, and new personnel requirements. Managers also should anticipate making organizational changes to take advantage of these technologies and plan to maintain some measure of management control over the process.

Management

The Internet can dramatically reduce transaction and agency costs and is fueling new business models. By using the Internet and other networks for electronic commerce, organizations can exchange purchase and sale transactions directly with customers and suppliers, eliminating inefficient middlemen. Organizational processes can be streamlined by using the Internet and intranets to make communication and coordination more efficient. To take advantage of these opportunities, organizational processes must be redesigned.

Organization

The Internet is creating a universal computing platform by using the TCP/IP network reference model and other standards for storing, retrieving, formatting, and displaying information. Web-based applications integrating voice, data, video, and audio are providing new products, services, and tools for communicating with employees and customers. Organizations can create intranets, internal networks based on Internet and Web technology, to reduce network costs and overcome connectivity problems. Key technology decisions should consider network reliability, security, bandwidth, and relationships to legacy systems, as well as the capabilities of Internet and other networking technologies.

Technology

For Discussion

1. The Internet is creating a business revolution and transforming the role of information systems in organizations. Do you agree? Why or why not?

2. What management, organization, and technology factors would you consider when deciding whether to build an intranet for your company?

Summary

1. Describe how the Internet works and its major capabilities. The Internet is a worldwide network of networks that uses the client/server model of computing and the TCP/IP network reference model. Using the Net, any computer can communicate with any other computer connected to the Net throughout the world. The Internet has no central management. The Internet is used for communications, including e-mail, public forums on thousands of topics, and live, interactive conversations. It also is used for information retrieval from hundreds of libraries and thousands of library, corporate, government, and nonprofit databases. It has developed into an effective way for individuals and organizations to offer information and products through a Web of graphical user interfaces and easy-to-use links worldwide. Major Internet capabilities include e-mail, Usenet, LIST-SERV, chatting, Telnet, FTP, gophers, and the World Wide Web.
2. Identify the benefits the Internet offers organizations. Many organizations use the Net to reduce communications costs when they coordinate organizational activities and communicate with employees. Researchers and knowledge workers are finding the Internet a quick, low-cost way to gather and disperse

knowledge. The global connectivity and low cost of the Internet helps organizations lower transaction and agency costs, allowing them to link directly to suppliers, customers, and business partners and to coordinate activities on a global scale with limited resources. The Web provides interactive multimedia capabilities that can be used to create new products and services and closer relationships with customers. Communication can be customized to specific audiences.

3. Demonstrate how the Internet can be used for electronic commerce. The Internet provides a universally available set of technologies for electronic commerce that can be used to create new channels for marketing, sales, and customer support and to eliminate intermediaries in buy and sell transactions. There are many different business models for electronic commerce on the Internet, including virtual storefronts, marketplace concentrators, information brokers, content providers, digital content delivery, and electronic clearinghouses. Interactive capabilities such as the Web, e-mail, and discussion groups can be used to build closer relationships with customers in marketing and customer support.

4. Explain how Internet technology can be used to create private intraorganizational and interorganizational networks and the use of these networks for electronic business. Private, internal corporate networks called intranets can be created using Internet connectivity standards, Web browsers, and Web servers. Extranets are private intranets that are extended to selected organizations or individuals outside the firm. Intranets and extranets are forming the underpinnings of electronic business by providing a low-cost technology that can run on almost any computing platform. Organizations can use intranets to create collaboration environments for coordinating work and information sharing, and they can use intranets to make information flow between different functional areas of the firm. Extranets are used in business-to-business electronic commerce, joint development projects between organizations, and supply chain management.

5. Examine the challenges posed by the Internet to businesses and society. Use of the Internet for electronic commerce and electronic business is in its infancy. Some of the new business models based on the Internet have not yet found proven ways to generate profits or reduce costs. Organizational change, including redesign of business processes and new roles for employees, is often required; channel conflicts may erupt as the firm turns to the Internet as an alternative outlet for sales. Security, privacy, legal issues, network reliability, bandwidth, and integration of Internet-based applications with the firm's legacy systems pose additional challenges to Internet computing.

Key Terms

Channel conflict, 318	Firewall, 298	Internet telephony, 300	Uniform resource locator
Chatting, 295	Gopher, 295	LISTSERV, 294	(URL), 296
Disintermediation, 305	Hit, 306	Multicasting, 298	Usenet, 294
Domain name, 294	Home page, 296	Portal, 297	Virtual private network
Electronic payment system, 310	Hypertext transport	"Push" technology, 297	(VPN), 301
Extranet, 299	protocol, 296	Search engine, 297	Web hosting service, 310
File transfer protocol	Internet Service Provider	Teamware, 312	Webmaster, 296
(FTP), 295	(ISP), 292	Telnet, 295	

Review Questions

1. What is the Internet? List and describe its principal capabilities.
2. Why is the World Wide Web so useful for individuals and businesses?
3. Describe the ways of locating information on the Web.
4. What are intranets and extranets? How do they differ from the Web?
5. Describe the benefits of the Internet to organizations.
6. How can the Internet facilitate electronic commerce and electronic business?
7. Describe six Internet business models for electronic commerce.
8. How can the Internet support sales and marketing to individual customers?
9. How can the Internet help provide customer service?
10. How can Internet technology support business-to-business electronic commerce?
11. Why are intranets so useful for electronic business?
12. How can intranets support organizational collaboration?
13. Describe the uses of intranets for electronic business in sales and marketing, human resources, finance and accounting, and manufacturing.
14. How can companies use extranets and Internet technology for supply-chain management?
15. Describe the management challenges posed by electronic commerce and electronic business on the Internet.
16. What is channel conflict? Why is it becoming a growing problem in electronic commerce?

Group Project

Form a group with three or four of your classmates. Select two businesses that are competitors in the same industry and using their Web sites for electronic commerce. Visit their Web sites. You might compare, for example, the Web sites for virtual banking created by Citibank and Wells Fargo Bank, or the Internet trading Web sites of E*Trade and Ameritrade. Prepare an evaluation of each business's Web site in terms of its functions, user-friendliness, and how well it supports the company's business strategy. Which Web site does a better job? Why? Can you make some recommendations to improve these Web sites?

Tools for Interactive Learning

○ Internet

You can take a virtual tour of Electronic Commerce sites illustrating each of the Internet business models described in this chapter. Once you have finished the tour, you can start the comprehensive Electronic Commerce project in which you will select an Internet business model and develop an Internet strategy for a new business. The Internet Connection for this chapter will take you to Virtual Vineyards and other Web sites where you can complete an exercise to evaluate virtual storefronts. You can also use the Interactive Study Guide to test your knowledge of the topics in this chap-

ter and get instant feedback where you need more practice.

○ CD-ROM

If you purchase and use the Multimedia Edition CD-ROM with this chapter, you can complete an interactive exercise that requires you to select the appropriate Internet service for a series of problems. You can also find a video demonstrating the Internet services provided by Apple Computer, an audio overview of the major themes of this chapter, and bullet text summarizing the key points of the chapter.

Case Study   Bidding the Profits of Web Companies Lower

How low can retail prices go on the Internet? OnSale Inc. of Menlo Park, California, is testing that very question with its new strategy of selling goods at cost. OnSale began as a Web site for auctioning overstock, closeout, and used computers and related products. Its offerings came from such computer leaders as IBM, Compaq, Dell, Hewlett-Packard (HP), and Sun. The company began by auctioning laptops, desktops, and digital cameras. It then expanded into auctioning vacation time-shares, frozen steaks, and many other items, although the noncomputer products accounted for only about 20 percent of sales.

OnSale's strategy was fairly straightforward. The used equipment was refurbished and then tested thoroughly, according to Lisa Jensen, worldwide strategic business planner in HP's equipment management and remarketing division. OnSale offered a 30-day warranty, after which the equipment reverted to any remaining time on the original warranty. Many of the used computers were coming off leases. In many cases, the computers had been on a two-to-four-year lease although some of the equipment was newer because lessees had upgraded before their leases were up to obtain more up-to-date technology.

New equipment was available for auction because retailers and producers needed to liquidate excess inventory and outdated equipment. Much of the equip-

ment offered was overstock. A lot of overstock existed because producers and retailers had difficulty anticipating consumer demand and produced or purchased too much. Closeouts consisted of old models that were outdated because of the rapidity of computer technology improvements. Manufacturers almost inevitably produced too much because they did not want to risk running out of stock and losing sales. The manufacturers were unable to predict with precision the speed of change in the new technology or the fickleness of purchasers.

Why were their customers willing to purchase used and outdated computers? The answer was price. These computers were always much cheaper, making them affordable when budget was an issue. Carl Godsoe, the manager of materials and support services at PMC Telecommunications in Anchorage, Alaska, explains that "We made the decision to go with HP equipment earlier this year and bought three of the workstations locally at retail price. Then I found a company called OnSale on the Internet and found the exact computer I bought retail at one-third the price." In many cases the purchaser did not need the power and technology of the newest models. Therefore, they were pleased not to have to pay high prices for technology they did not need.

The OnSale site was very successful for several years. The company had more than 650,000 registered bidders at the end of 1998, its third year in business. Signifi-

cantly, 75 percent of its sales went to repeat customers. In that year it registered $250 million in sales according to S. Jerrold (Jerry) Kaplan, founder and CEO of OnSale. For a while sales were rising at 50 percent a month, and, claimed Kaplan, there were days when they moved more than 100 computers. Of course, many potential customers were very cautious at first and would make only small purchases. Godsoe, for example, bought only one HP workstation the first time. However, he was so pleased with the quality of the equipment that he bought many more.

A fundamental part of OnSale's strategy was to use a number of techniques to stimulate interest in the bidding. Kaplan believed in constantly updating the Web site to keep it very attractive and competitive with other sites that function more like television or video games. Kaplan attempted regularly to change the offerings of the site, depending on what people seemed interested in. He also used Internet technology to stimulate more bidding. For example, OnSale used an automated e-mail system to notify the highest bidders when their bids were topped. The message also reminded the recipient of the deadline for a new bid. In addition, Kaplan used a push service to broadcast the bids to other potential bidders so they could keep up with the price and increase their bid if they desired. "This is really the stock market applied to bidding," explained Alan Fisher, OnSale's chief technology officer. "We would like to engage our customers by having them participate in auctions all day long."

Despite this well-thought-out strategy, OnSale ran into serious problems in 1998. One key issue OnSale found was that it was having increasing difficulty making money selling excess and refurbished computers. Margins kept falling on the products the company was selling, explained Charles Finney, a securities analyst at San Francisco brokerage firm Volpe, Brown. One reason was the increasing competition. New sites, such as Surplus Direct, owned by Egghead.com, offered the same products. In addition, OnSale was forced to cut its shipping rates to meet those of its Web-based competitors. Another problem that emerged involved parts for older equipment that were often too difficult to obtain. In addition, OnSale found that it had only 5 percent to 10 percent of what people wanted because no machines were being produced to meet their customers' specific demands.

The biggest problem OnSale faced, however, was the declining availability of excess and refurbished computers. Growing competition meant that OnSale had to split the limited supply with these other companies, leaving less for OnSale. In addition, supplies shrank because computer producers increasingly became more skilled in planning how much inventory they need, thereby reducing the number of leftovers. However, the most important reason for the shrinking supplies may have been the very success of OnSale.

From the perspective of the manufacturers, two strategies exist for getting rid of used and overstock equipment: (1) selling or auctioning by third parties such as OnSale and (2) selling or auctioning themselves. Traditionally, by selling outdated equipment through third parties, hardware and software vendors found they were recovering less than 10 cents on the dollar. Watching OnSale and others, the manufacturers realized they could recover closer to 50 percent if they were to auction or sell the items themselves. As a result, many manufacturers, including Compaq Computer and HP, began selling their own excess computers on their own Web sites, causing the supply to shrink further. To add insult to injury, OnSale said that the growing supply constraints caused prices to rise, thus further reducing their profit margins.

OnSale had no choice but to develop a new strategy. On January 19, 1999, On-Sale announced that new strategy. Without abandoning auctioning altogether, the company announced that it would now revert to selling new equipment. The centerpiece of its strategy is for OnSale to sell new products at its own cost. By selling at cost, the company's prices will be very low and thus very competitive. For example, OnSale would sell 3Com Corp's Palm II handheld computer for $269.47, whereas the same item sold for $369 on the 3Com Web site. OnSale's new service was named atCost, with its auction business being named atAuction.

By selling at cost, OnSale raises two obvious questions: How will the company cover its operating costs, and what will be the source of their profits? First, they claim they will not quite sell the computers and accessories at cost. Instead, they will add a small fee of $10 per product rather than marking up products the customary 20 percent to 50 percent. In addition, OnSale will add the normal processing and shipping charges. They will also add a 2.6 percent charge for all billing by credit card. The profit will be tiny on each sale, Kaplan claims, but he believes OnSale will be very profitable because of high volume.

Another issue is cost control. The company plans to keep its cost very low by not retaining any inventory. Tech Data Corp. of Clearwater, Florida, will manufacture the computers for them. Tech Data will also ship the computers directly to the customers from one of its four warehouses. Although Tech Data is not a commonly known company, it is actually the second-largest distributor of PCs in the world, with 1998 revenues reaching $12 billion. The company is not known because it has never sold directly to the public, and under its contract with OnSale that will not change. This strategy will save OnSale as much as 10 percent over other on-line resellers and 30 percent over resellers selling through stores.

OnSale expects revenue from advertising on its site as well. With consistently low prices, OnSale expects to draw a large number of regular customers, including many small businesses. The company believes that by having a large number of regular customers, it will be able to sell Web site advertising at favorable rates. To develop customer's trust in its pricing policy, all customers will have access to a breakdown of costs before they make a purchase. The breakdown will show the wholesale costs of items, the small add-on fee, and the shipping and handling fees. In addition, OnSale has hired Pricewaterhouse Coopers to certify the validity of its at-cost pricing policy.

Will the strategy work? Kaplan is optimistic. He points out that now customers will always be able to find the computers they want, a great improvement over their past strategy. He sees his business as filling a specific market niche, and he points out that "We're not going to put stores out of business." However, he also believes that he will remain the low-price seller. He says that no one can consistently undercut his prices. Such a policy "won't be sustainable," he claims. "No one can stake a business on negative margins." Kaplan expects that atCost will add $100 million to sales revenue in 1999 without having a significant impact on operating costs. Kaplan adds that "If we didn't do this, someone else would, so we decided to get there first and lead the market."

Noninsiders see many problems with the strategy. A key issue is that OnSale is entering a very competitive business. Many companies already sell computers at high discounts. Other critics point out that with this strategy, Kaplan's company won't always be offering the lowest price, even at cost. Some on-line companies are actually already selling some of their products below cost, as the following discussion of Buy.com clarifies. Other observers fear the strategy will also cut into OnSale's auction sales. In addition some observers predict this policy will further drive product prices down, resulting in a decline in margins.

The biggest criticism from analysts, however, is that it will be difficult for OnSale to make a profit with this strategy. "Anybody can sell products at cost and make a lot of revenue," explains Finney. "The question is how to make it profitable revenue. I could be selling $1 bills for 85 cents," he adds. The questions about the atCost strategy are obviously widely shared—on the day it announced its new strategy, OnSale's stock fell 14 percent.

One of OnSale's competitors, now that it is in the business of selling new computers, is Buy.com, a privately held company founded in November 1997, in Aliso Viejo, California. Initially, the company was only in the business of selling computers and computer-related products over the Web, but it has now expanded into selling books, music, and videos via the Web, all at close to wholesale prices. Buy.com guarantees its customers the best price on its products, and as a result, its sales price is occasionally even below cost.

To maintain the lowest price, Buy.com is using up-to-date Internet technology to check automatically and constantly the prices of its competitors. If the company finds that one of its prices is not lower than competitors', it immediately lowers its price to regain the lead position. For example, as of this writing, Buy.com was selling a 17-inch Sony color monitor at $306.95 whereas OnSale.com was selling it at cost for $331.79.

Buy.com has succeeded in generating high sales during its first year. Scott Blum, founder and CEO of Buy.com, believes his company has broken Conner Peripherals' first year sales record of $113 million set in 1987.

As a result of its success, Buy.com has started to expand from a company selling only computer products to one selling many, many products. In November 1998 Blum changed the company's name from Buy-Comp.com to Buy.com, an overarching name. It retains its BuyComp.com site for sales in the computer field. It also bought more than 2000 Internet domain names starting with the word "buy." This enabled the company to expand into many markets using a related name. The first to be launched starting early in 1999 were Buy-Books.com, BuyGames.com, BuySoft.com, BuyVideos.com, and BuyMusic.com. To support this expansion, Blum bought Speed-Serve Inc., a unit of Ingram Entertainment, which is the largest distributor of videos and video games in the United States.

To keep its costs down, Buy.com is committed to simplified Web sites that are less expensive to develop and operate. For example, BuyBooks.com will not offer book reviews or a chat facility, as does Amazon.com. "We are going for someone who knows what they want and wants it at the best price," says Blum. "We're trying to keep our site simple, effective, and easy to use." Blum expects that buyers will browse sites like Amazon.com and then go to BuyBooks.com to purchase the same products at a lower price.

To support this enormous expansion, Buy.com began a massive mainstream advertising campaign with **Monday Night Football** (ABC). It plans to spend $25 million in advertising in 1999. Blum has set Amazon.com as his target. He wants to "leap-frog" that company and become the biggest book seller on the Net.

To finance this expansion, Blum has received a lot of investments. In August 1998, Softbank Technology Ventures bought a 10 percent stake in Buy.com for $20 million. Two months later they were willing to pay twice the price for more shares, investing $40 million more for another 10 percent.

How can Buy.com profit from this strategy? Like OnSale, Buy.com also carries no inventory. In the computer area, for instance, Ingram Micro of Santa Ana, California, manufactures its product. Ingram fills Buy.com's orders the same day the order is taken. However, the key to the company's strategy is its ability to sell a lot of advertising on its Web sites. Like OnSale, Buy.com expects its advertising rates to be driven by the fact that the company's low prices do bring a lot of people to the site. At the end of 1998, Buy.com's home page had 12 ads, each selling for $3000 per month. Their strategy differs from OnSale in that Buy.com plans to have many sites, each carrying its share of advertising.

Some analysts are raising questions about Buy.com's strategy. "The first principle of Internet marketing is limited brand imprinting," explains Vern Keenan, an analyst with the e-commerce research firm Keenan Vision Inc. Amazon.com has built up enough trust to be a mainstream merchandiser, and it's very hard for a new brand to challenge that. Jeffrey P. Bezos, CEO of Amazon.com says that "Customers want selection, ease of use, and a low price—in that order," implying that Buy.com won't be a real threat to his company.

Sources: Suzanne Galante and Cory Johnson, "Caught in a Squeeze," **The Industry Standard,** January 1, 1999; George Anders, "Web Seller Asks: How Low Can PC Prices Go?" **The Wall Street Journal,** January 4, 1999; Tom Diederich, "PC Vendor Promises to Get It for You Wholesale," **Computerworld,** January 19, 1999; Eric Auchard, "OnSale to Sell PCs at Cost, Make Money on Ads," Infoseek.go.com, January 20, 1999; Eric C. Fleming, "OnSale to Sell PCs at Cost," **PCWeek** (Online), January 19, 1999; "E-Tailing's Future Lies in Auctions," www.cyberatlas.com, January 26, 1999; Larry Armstrong, "Anything You Can Sell, I Can Sell Cheaper," **Business Week,** December 14, 1998; "OnSale.Inc," Infoseek.go.com, January 25, 1999; Kevin Jones, "Two B-to-B Auction Models Emerge," **Inter@ctive Week,** March 23, 1998; Karen D. Schwartz, "Good Deals on Used Systems," **Information Week,** August 31, 1998; M. Duvall, "Buy.com Declares War on Competitor," **Inter@ctive Week,** November 19, 1998; and Stan Hibbard, Bruce Caldwell, and Clinton Wilder, "Season for Online Shopping Creates Retail Competition," **Information Week,** November 23, 1998.

CASE STUDY QUESTIONS

1. Analyze both OnSale and Buy.com using the value chain and competitive forces models. Compare their positions based on those analyses.

2. Based on their plans to sell only through the Web, what are the special or unique problems these companies face in developing a business strategy?

3. Visit the two Web sites and evaluate each in terms of how successfully you believe it meets its business objectives. Suggest ways the sites might be improved.

4. What management, organization, and technology problems do you think these companies faced in establishing their original and newer services?

5. With the existence of such companies as OnSale and Buy.com, what do you think will be the long-term effects of electronic commerce on prices, profits, and distribution? Do you think companies such as these two can continue to sell at or near cost? Why or why not? How viable are OnSale and Buy.com's business models? Explain.

Amazon.com versus Barnes & Noble:
The Battle of the Bookstores

 The recent romantic comedy **You've Got Mail** pits scrappy independent bookseller Meg Ryan against megastore operator Tom Hanks, using the characters' commercial rivalry as a backdrop for their blossoming affection. But in the real world, the joke may be on both of them: Internet-based commerce, which requires no physical retail outlets of any size, is changing the shape of the bookselling industry.

People around the world spent $82 billion on books in 1998, and Amazon.com and Barnes & Noble compete fiercely for shares of that pie. Amazon.com, founded by CEO Jeff Bezos in 1994 in his Seattle garage, has never owned a single retail store; all its sales from day 1 have taken place from its Internet storefront, and they totaled more than $500 million annually by 1998. Barnes & Noble was a century-old storefront on New York's Fifth Avenue until entrepreneur Leonard Riggio bought it in 1971; today it's a retail giant with more than 1000 stores, plans to open 500 more stores in the next decade, had 1997 sales of $2.8 billion—and a new Internet arm of its own, barnesandnoble.com.

Two completely different business models, each with advantages and disadvantages, are going head-to-head for the same consumer dollars. Will one prevail? Can both survive?

Amazon.com is widely regarded as the first significantly successful enterprise to sell traditional consumer goods over the Internet. Customers shop by visiting www.Amazon.com, a World Wide Web site where they can search among more than 3 million book titles and purchase ones they like by entering a shipping address, credit card number, and other information. After the first purchase, the customer's shipping and credit card information are stored securely in Amazon.com's information system. The next time, it only takes a single mouse click to complete an order. Amazon.com makes it very easy to buy a book on-line.

Making the customer's on-line experience warm and pleasant is a key Amazon.com strategy. The site retains information on each customer and even uses an information technology called collaborative filtering to recommend books based on the past purchases of buyers with similar histories. In addition to the personalization afforded each shopper, the site allows readers to post their own reviews of books, offers profiles of authors, and includes staff recommendations on lists such as "What We're Reading" and "Destined for Greatness." The result has been a perception among customers that they share a relationship with the company—one they value so highly that in February, 1999, when it was revealed Amazon.com accepted payment from publishers to have books placed on recommended lists, widespread protests led the company to include disclaimers on the site and to broaden its merchandise return policy.

Not only does Amazon.com lack a physical bookstore; it almost lacks books. Only a fraction of the titles available on its Web site are actually on shelves in one of its two warehouses. Most of the time, Amazon.com doesn't order a particular book from a distributor until after a consumer has ordered it from Amazon.com. One advantage to this structure is that Amazon.com avoids the overhead and carrying charges associated with a large inventory; the company turns its inventory over about 26 times a year. But a more important advantage lies in the way this arrangement affects Amazon.com's cash flow. Amazon.com charges a customer's credit card as soon as it ships that customer's book, and the credit card companies usually pay Amazon.com within a day. Amazon.com, however, takes an average of a month and a half to pay the book distributor for the book. Whereas most companies have to pay to finance sales, Amazon.com's negative operating cycle lets it profit from the use of its customers' money. Amazon.com earns about $25 million each year from the float, enough to cover many of its operating expenses.

Physical bookstores such as Barnes & Noble, in contrast, must stock up to 160 days of inventory to provide enough selection to satisfy customers. The bookseller must pay distributors and publishers 45 to 90 days after it purchases the books, carrying the costs of those books for up to four months.

However, because Amazon.com has no stores for people to walk into, it has to invest large sums in advertising in order to generate virtual foot traffic, or visits to its Web site. In 1998 Amazon.com spent $50 million on advertising, more than a quarter of that year's total revenue. One way Amazon.com works to attract visitors is through links from other Web sites, a technique that traditional brick-and-mortar outlets cannot duplicate. Soon after its launch, Amazon.com introduced a standing offer: Any Web site that gave Amazon.com a link (a button on its site that would connect users directly to Amazon.com) so customers could shop for books related to the site's subject matter would receive up to 15 percent of the sales that resulted from use of the link. Today this Associates Program boasts more than 140,000 participants. Still, Amazon.com has to pay for advertising space on more popular sites such as America Online (AOL), Yahoo, and Excite ($50 million in 1998 alone), and it jockeys with its competition to forge exclusive arrangements with some of those sites. One Barnes & Noble executive compared Amazon.com's marketing costs to the premium a brick-and-mortar store pays for a good location that will generate foot traffic.

Amazon.com's operation would be impossible without sophisticated information systems, many of which have been created in-house. (Wal-Mart sued the bookseller in October 1998, claiming that it had raided Wal-Mart's executives to steal its computerized distribution secrets.) In addition to the collaborative filtering system that enables Amazon.com to make individualized recommendations to its customers and the database that supports it, the company relies on sophisticated inventory, shipping, and billing systems. Although information technology has been Amazon.com's strength, it has also given the company a weakness that brick-and-mortar stores don't face: Twice in 1998, inadequate backup systems put Amazon.com out of action for as long as nine hours at a time.

Technology needs have fueled a new facet of Amazon.com's operation: buying other companies. In August, 1998, it spent $270 million to buy two firms, Junglee Corp. and PlanetAll. Junglee produces comparison-shopping technologies, which Amazon.com will use to connect customers to other products that it doesn't sell itself. PlanetAll is a global address book and daytimer site in which Ama-

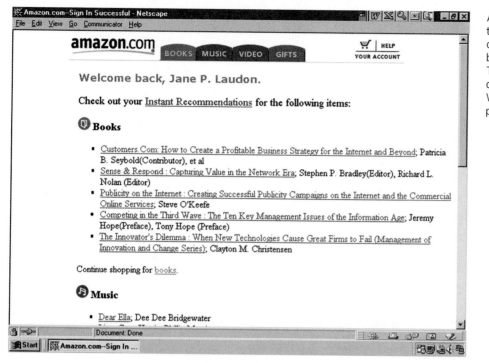

Amazon.com's collaborative filtering technology can make recommendations to customers based on their past purchases. The personalization and sense of community created by this Web site have drawn many repeat customers.

zon.com sees a new utility; people who use the site to track friends' birthdays, for example, might receive timely e-mail reminders complete with gift suggestions.

Having made a name for itself in the book business, Amazon.com is exploring other product categories. Already it has added music and videos to its lineup; in the first three months of selling CDs, Amazon.com's sales total of $14.4 million surpassed established on-line music seller Cdnow.com's performance during the same period. Amazon.com's video sales, launched in November, 1998, give it access to a $16 billion market worldwide. Both product categories offer tie-in possibilities with Amazon.com's established book business and with each other; both, however, operate on very low profit margins and may require Amazon.com to keep a larger inventory on hand, which would erode the advantage of its on-line structure. To bolster its video sales, Amazon.com acquired the Internet Movie Database, a popular site that lets users research films. The company is currently experimenting with selling consumer electronics, games, and toys, and in the future it may look into areas such as magazine subscriptions and travel packages.

In late January, 1999, Amazon.com bought 46 percent of Drugstore.com, a Web site selling prescription drugs as well as over-the-counter health and beauty products. The $150 billion U.S. pharmacy market is almost six times larger than the book market, making this an alluring area for expansion. In late March 1999, Amazon began offering on-line auctions to compete with eBay, a popular on-line auction house.

In addition to retail sales, Amazon.com generates revenue from its customer base by selling publishers and others preferred access to its customers and by earning a commission for directing its customers to other on-line retailers through the Shop the Web capability on its Web site.

Amazon.com's rise as the best-known Internet retailer has made it a target. Other, smaller e-sellers are forming alliances with each other in order to take on the market leader. In November, 1998, nine Internet retailers including Cdnow, eToys, computer merchant Cyberian Outpost, and video retailer Reel.com banded together to form a network called ShopperConnection. Each participating site advertises the network on its pages, allowing shoppers to jump from one member retailer to another. In the future, the network will add a frequent-shopper points program to reward patronage. As Amazon.com expands into new product categories and other retailers form groups to combat it, the goal line appears to be the potential creation of a Wal-Mart of the Web that would squeeze out competitors. Because

on-line shoppers can "travel" from one retailer to another with the click of a mouse and even use on-line comparison-shopping search engines, profit margins on the Internet promise to remain razor thin, and there may not be a prize for second place.

In large part because of its marketing expenses, Amazon.com has never shown a profit; industry analysts predict that it will continue to operate in the red until 2001. Its stock, however, has skyrocketed to the point that Wall Street analysts are questioning whether traditional methods of valuation apply to it. In late 1998, Amazon.com's stock price was $214 a share, which, with more than 50 million shares outstanding, gave it a paper value of more than $10 billion—all for a company that had never earned a cent or paid a dividend. Long-term investors say they are betting on Amazon.com's future growth; short-term investors see with their own eyes that the stock keeps rising, whether or not there's any real value behind what the ticker says. One analyst, however, calculated that in order to justify its market price, Amazon.com would have to post annual revenue growth on the order of 60 percent for the next 10 years—years during which competitors are likely to at least dull its initial market advantage.

Amazon.com founder Bezos says he is able to tolerate the company's severely low ledger because he views the conditions behind it as temporary. His chief operating principle has been to get big fast—to establish market dominance quickly, even at a high cost, to set up the company for long-term success. "Our advantage is that we know more about e-commerce than anybody else," Bezos said. "We've been doing it longer, and we've already leveled the playing field."

And despite the cost, the approach seems to be working. "When you think of Web shopping, you think of Amazon.com first," analyst Lauren Cooks Levitan says. In fact, a survey by the Intelliquest Information Group found that 50 percent of Internet users recognized the name Amazon.com without prompting, versus only 37 percent for long-established Barnes & Noble.

Like Amazon.com, Barnes & Noble prides itself on offering customers a pleasant shopping experience. Under the direction of the iconoclastic Riggio, the chain's superstores have become "modern village greens" where people are encouraged to spend time, peruse a book over some coffee, or attend a reading or children's storytime. Cathedral ceilings and hand-lettered signs are calculated to soften the feel of visiting a bookstore, which Riggio says has traditionally been "elitist and stand-offish."

Despite innovations in presentation, Barnes & Noble still faces the challenges that any physical store must overcome—and that Amazon.com avoids. It must carry huge inventories, and it uses information systems to track sales of individual titles so that nonperforming ones can be removed from shelves in as little as 120 days. Its array of more than 1000 stores requires an army of personnel, more than 27,000 employees. Amazon.com employs only about 1600. Barnes & Noble averages $100,000 in annual revenue per employee; Amazon.com averages $375,000. The physical plant of each Barnes & Noble store represents an expense as well.

Barnes & Noble's size shapes the way it does business—enabling it to command discounts from book distributors and offer them to customers—and the way it is perceived. The chain's hallmark, the stand-alone superstore with as many as 10 times more titles than at a traditional bookstore, was introduced in 1991, but controversy over Barnes & Noble's influence did not begin there. When the chain bought B. Dalton in 1996 to become the nation's largest bookseller, critics in the literary world feared that too great a concentration of the retail book market in one company's hands would spur a focus on best-sellers at the expense of small publishers and their often obscure titles. "The day I bought B. Dalton is the day I became a common enemy," Riggio said. He later added the Scribner and Doubleday & Co. mall chains to Barnes & Noble, only fueling complaints about his hold on the nation's book market. "Leonard Riggio wields immense power over the long-term health of our culture," Todd Gitlin, culture professor of New York University, said recently.

However, best-sellers made up only 3 percent of Barnes & Noble's total sales in 1997, which is similar to the figures reported by other bookstores, and some small publishers have acknowledged that Barnes & Noble's huge shelf space (typically 150,000 titles) leaves room for more diversity than at smaller stores. Still, membership in the American Booksellers' Association (ABA) stood at 5132 when Riggio began rolling out superstores in 1991, and it fell to just over 4000 by the end of 1998. Barnes & Noble's share of the U.S. book market has grown to about 25 percent, more than double its 1991 share, and only 35 buyers choose books to be sold in the chain's stores. The ABA sued Barnes & Noble and competitor Borders in April, 1998, claiming that the chains illegally coerced distributors to give them secret discounts and other advantages.

In mid-1997, with Amazon.com already three years out of the gate, Barnes & Noble joined the Internet fray with the launch of barnesandnoble.com. The imprimatur of the nation's largest traditional bookseller and the parent company's deep pockets were unquestionable assets, but the coming battle would be on Amazon.com's turf. "Amazon.com stole its major market position by acting faster, and now Barnes & Noble is playing catch-up ball," consultant John Hyland of McFarland Dewey & Co. said. And Renaissance IPO Fund analyst Linda Killian said the venerable book giant was entering the e-market from a position of weakness, not strength: "Barnes & Noble has a mindset of a bricks-and-mortar bookseller, and in some ways that's retarded their development." By December, 1998, barnesandnoble.com's customer base was still less than a quarter of Amazon.com's, and Amazon.com remained far ahead in its number of links with other Internet sites.

However, Barnes & Noble has made some powerful alliances in its bid to catch up. In December, 1998, it teamed up with Microsoft to become the exclusive bookseller for users who click the book shopping category on the MSN network. (By previous arrangements, Amazon.com's paid ad/links will still appear on some Microsoft pages, and Amazon.com has a similar deal with Microsoft to remain its exclusive music seller.)

More significant, though less visible to the consumer, is barnesandnoble.com's October, 1998, sale of a 50 percent stake to the German publishing giant Bertelsmann AG—right after Amazon.com's Bezos had spurned Bertelsmann's offer of a similar partnership with him. "This venture has one purpose—to compete with Amazon.com in the U.S.," said Bertelsmann CEO Thomas Middelhof. Barnesandnoble.com had been planning an initial public offering since August, but cancelled it in the wake of the Bertelsmann deal.

Bertelsmann owns Random House and other publishers, which may enable barnesandnoble.com to offer price-war discounts on titles from those houses. On November 6, 1998, Barnes & Noble also bought Ingram Book Group, a leading distributor that supplies 60 percent of Amazon.com's books. While Barnes & Noble promises that it will run Ingram impartially, Amazon.com will undoubtedly be forced to find other sources for books at higher costs. Clearly, Barnes & Noble hopes to use its weight and power over the supply of books to offset its disadvantages in Internet marketing; it also expects its partnership with Bertelsmann to help it expand into European markets. Barnes & Noble is also hoping that as Amazon.com expands into more areas of retailing it will leave key sections of the book market open to a more specialized company.

Judging whether Amazon.com or Barnes & Noble is winning the war for America's book market is difficult. On one hand, Amazon.com's revenues for the first half of 1998 were more than nine times barnesandnoble.com's over a similar period; on the other hand, Amazon.com's 1997 sales were one-nineteenth the 1997 sales of Barnes & Noble as a whole. Amazon.com stock is more than twice as valuable as Barnes & Noble stock and saw a 1998 price increase of 298 percent to Barnes & Noble's 35.6 percent, but Amazon.com has never made a profit whereas Barnes & Noble is solidly profitable.

Retailing is a business with very thin profit margins, leading some analysts to question whether Amazon.com will ever be profitable. If Amazon.com keeps moving into new markets, costs will continue to escalate. Analysts estimate that Amazon.com will spend nearly $200 million in marketing in 1999, 50 percent more than a year earlier.

Barnes & Noble, a traditional bookseller, launched its own on-line Web site, barnesandnoble.com, to compete with other on-line booksellers.

On average on-line retailers spent $26 per sale in advertising and marketing, whereas their physical counterparts spent only $2.50. Until Amazon.com and other retailers figure out a way to attract and retain customers without such enormous outlays, they will have a hard time making any money. As Merrill Lynch analyst Jonathan Cohen put it, Amazon.com has shown that "it can sell lots of books for less without making money and now it has shown that it can sell lots of music for less without making money."

Moreover, as Amazon.com moves into new markets, it will face traditional retailers that are starting to sell on the Web, many quite successfully. In other areas besides books and entertainment products, Amazon.com may have trouble creating meaningful brand recognition.

However, if Amazon.com and other Internet retailers have enough customers and sales to pay off their marketing and technology investments, any additional revenue will register as profits, and those could be enormous. It is this hope that Amazon.com's business model will eventually win big that has fueled its skyrocketing stock price.

The battle between these two booksellers is not taking place in a vacuum. Another major player in the market is Bor-ders, the second-biggest brick-and-mortar chain in the United States, which touts sales figures well below Barnes & Noble's but comparable with Amazon.com's at about half a billion dollars annually. Wary of the Internet, Borders is instead going global the old-fashioned way, opening stores in Britain, Australia, and Singapore. Some investors have welcomed the chain's embrace of terra firma, although others accuse it of missing the e-commerce boat, and its stock price was down in 1998 after a volatile year.

If, as Bezos claims, his upstart Amazon.com has "leveled the playing field" against the mighty Barnes & Noble, the battle is likely to boil down to Amazon.com's superior grasp of Internet commerce versus Barnes & Noble's superior purchasing power. However, a key characteristic of electronic commerce is the ephemeral nature of any advantage. Unless the balance shifts decisively because of some unforeseen innovation or a change in alliances, razor-thin margins will make it difficult for both sides to sustain the pitched battle indefinitely.

Sources: James Ledbetter, "Book Values," **The Industry Standard**, March 15, 1999; Peter de Jonge, "Riding the Wild, Perilous Waters of Amazon.com," **The New York Times Magazine**, March 14, 1999; Patrick M. Reilly, "In the Age of the Web, a Book Chain Flounders," **The Wall Street Journal**, February 22, 1999; Saul Hansell, "Amazon.com Moving into Drug and Cosmetic Retailing," **The New York Times**, February 25, 1999; and "The Next Trick for Amazon. comm: Auctions," **The Wall Street Journal**, March 30, 1999; Robert D. Hof with Ellen Neuborne and Heather Green, "Amazon.com: The Wild World of E-Commerce," **Business Week**, December 14, 1998; Cynthia Mayer, "Does Amazon = 2 Barnes & Nobles?" **The New York Times**, July 19, 1998; "Is Competition Closing in on Amazon.com?" **Fortune**, November 9, 1998; and I. Jeanne Dugan, "The Baron of Books," **Business Week**, June 29, 1998.

CASE STUDY QUESTIONS

1. Analyze both Amazon.com and Barnes & Noble using the value chain and competitive forces models.

2. Compare and evaluate the business models used by Amazon.com and Barnes & Noble. What are their core competencies? What role does the Internet play in each of these business models?

3. How viable is each business model? Explain your answer.

4. Which company will dominate the book retailing industry? Explain your answer.

Chapter 11

Redesigning the Organization with Information Systems

Learning Objectives

After completing this chapter, you will be able to:

1. Demonstrate how building new systems can produce organizational change.

2. Compare the role of information systems in total quality management (TQM) and business process reengineering (BPR).

3. Explain how the organization can develop information systems that fit its business plan.

4. Identify the core activities in the systems development process.

5. Evaluate models for determining the business value of information systems.

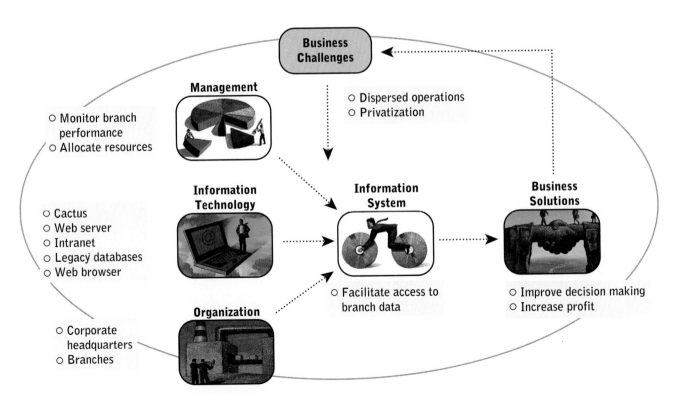

Business Challenges

Management
○ Monitor branch performance
○ Allocate resources

○ Dispersed operations
○ Privatization

Information Technology
○ Cactus
○ Web server
○ Intranet
○ Legacy databases
○ Web browser

Information System
○ Facilitate access to branch data

Business Solutions
○ Improve decision making
○ Increase profit

Organization
○ Corporate headquarters
○ Branches

Grupo Financiero Bital Moves
to Private Banking Systems

Grupo Financiero Bital controls assets of about $9 billion, making it one of the largest financial holding companies in Mexico. Bital is also a full-service retail bank with almost 1200 branches serving more than 3 million customers. The company was formed when Grupo Financiero Privado Mexicano acquired Banco Internacional from the Mexican government during the Mexican banking reprivatization in 1992. It is known for providing high-quality customer service along with comprehensive financial services all under one roof. Servicing Bital's customer base requires intensive use of information systems, and that task grew larger after privatization. The business is so dispersed that Bital had trouble maintaining its technology infrastructure.

New technology upgrades were installed manually by technicians who visited the widely scattered branch offices. This meant that some branches might have a new version of software running within a week, but others might not have the software installed and running for a month or more.

The situation grew more serious when the bank was privatized. Bital's information architecture was more appropriate for a government agency than for a profit-driven business. Branch managers could query Bital's massive databases for information, but the result might be a 500-page deluge of statistics rather than the exact information requested. Bital's information systems group was charged with making its systems more stable and adding the functionality required to support profit-driven banking.

Bital's information systems staff decided that the easiest way to solve these problems was to implement an intranet. The intranet would provide a Web-based application for querying the database that could generate compact reports on an individual branch without altering Bital's underlying, centralized database for existing systems. The information was arranged so that a branch manager could examine information for his or her branch and make intelligent branch-level decisions concerning resources, time, and money. By being able to look at each branch as a separate business, the branch manager could take the necessary measures to make the branch more profitable, benefiting the entire bank.

A team of information systems specialists led by Jorge Sosa, director of Bital's branch systems development, used the Cactus application development workbench from Information Builders to implement a system that accesses data from Bital's

chapter outline

legacy databases. The data are extracted from the database and stored on the company's Web server. Branch managers use their Web browsers to build queries against the extracted data.

Sosa's group created a special Web page called the "tablero" to help top management get a handle on the business. The tablero allows executives to examine aspects of Bital's business as well as the performance of bank branches. Bital's management can use this information to balance resources and make decisions about which branches to shrink and which to expand. Bital is also using Internet technology to improve customer service and created a Web home banking application linked to its legacy systems.

Sources: Geoffrey James, "Intranets Give New Life to BPR," *Datamation,* March 1998; Karyl Scott, "Information Builders Intros Pure Java Server," *Information Week,* July 24, 1998; and *www.bital.com.mx/visitors.*

Management Challenges

Grupo Financiero Bital's new intranet reporting system illustrates the many factors at work in the development of a new information system. Building the new system entailed analyzing the company's problems with existing information systems, assessing people's information needs, selecting appropriate technology, and redesigning procedures and jobs. Management had to monitor the system-building effort and to evaluate its benefits and costs. The new information system represented a process of planned organizational change.

However, building information systems, especially those on a large scale, presents many challenges. Here are some challenges to consider:

1. Major risks and uncertainties in systems development. Information systems development has major risks and uncertainties that make it difficult for the systems to achieve their goals. One problem is the difficulty of establishing information requirements, both for individual end users and for the organization as a whole. The requirements may be too complex or subject to change. Another problem is that the time and cost factors to develop an information system are very difficult to determine, especially in large projects. A third problem is the difficulty of managing the organizational change associated with a new system. Although building a new information system is a process of planned organizational change, this does not mean that change can always be planned or controlled. Although Chapter 13 describes some ways of dealing with these risks and uncertainties, the issues remain major management challenges.

2. Determining benefits of a system when they are largely intangible. As the sophistication of systems grows, they produce fewer tangible and more intangible benefits. By definition, there is no solid method for pricing intangible benefits. Organizations could lose important opportunities if they only use strict financial criteria for determining information systems benefits. However, organizations could make very poor investment decisions if they overestimate intangible benefits.

How a Call Center Changed a Company

When companies adopt new computer technology, they do not always reduce their workforces. What often happens is that employees acquire new roles and job skills.

Jacobs' Golf Group in Scottsdale, Arizona, which specializes in golf instruction, golf vacation packages, and golf-course management, has never had a bad year since starting out in 1971. But the number of customers in its market remains stagnant, and new competitors are constantly cropping up.

Company management realized that customers who waited too long for their telephone calls to be answered would call the next golf school on their list. So Jacobs' Golf installed an automated call distribution system in January 1997 to expedite reservation taking and to analyze telephone traffic. The system automatically answers calls, queues and routes incoming calls, and provides analytic reports on callers' activities. Gordon Petrie, the company president, is especially interested in call center statistics showing the number of calls received and the number of reservations made because they are indicators of how busy the company will be in four or five months. (Customers typically book several months in advance.) Jacobs' Golf can track the number of calls taken to the number of reservations booked. Within one year of installation, bookings increased 15 percent, largely thanks to the increased efficiency of the call center.

Before the new call center and automated reservation system was installed, staff taking telephone reservations would have to run over to the general booking ledger and then enter the information. As business grew, the pile of ledger sheets grew higher. Now five customer-service repre-

sentatives take the calls and instantly enter the reservations into the system from their desktops.

The system's capabilities for tracking call center activity in great detail allowed Jacobs' Golf to fine-tune its staffing levels. Management initially increased the number of telephone service representatives from five to eight, hoping to reduce the amount of time callers were put on hold. Later, reservations manager Marlene Pierce learned from the monitoring software that reps became unavailable to answer the phones because they were engaged in follow-up activities, such as mailing out confirmations. The company then decided to make the follow-up responsibilities a separate job, adding two administrative positions and reducing the number of telephone agents from eight to six. The call center is easily handling two to three times more calls than it did a year ago and without the two telephone reps.

The new system prompted Jacobs' Golf to change the call center's hours of operation. Monday mornings are still peak calling time, but system reports showed 180 calls coming in on a weekend day. Management added Saturday hours and is working on having the center available on Sundays as well.

To Think About: How did the new automated call distribution system change the way Jacobs' Golf Group ran its business?

Sources: Stanley Reed, "Wired-Collar Workers," **Business Week**, February 1, 1999; Alessandra Bianchi, "Lines of Fire," **Inc. Technology**, June 16, 1998; and Jim Champy, "Direct Sales or Electronic Channels? Give the Customer a Choice," **Computerworld**, November 23, 1998.

This chapter describes how new information systems are conceived, built, and installed, with special attention to organizational design issues and business reengineering. It describes systems analysis and design and other core activities that must be performed to build any information system. The chapter explains how to establish the business value of information systems and how to ensure that new systems are linked to the organization's business plan and information requirements.

11.1 Systems as Planned Organizational Change

This text has emphasized that an information system is a sociotechnical entity, an arrangement of both technical and social elements. The introduction of a new information system involves much more than new hardware and software. It also includes changes in jobs, skills, management, and organization. In the sociotechnical philosophy, one cannot install new technology without considering the people who must work with it (Bostrom and Heinen, 1977). When we design a new information system, we are redesigning the organization.

One important thing to know about building a new information system is that this process is one kind of planned organizational change. Frequently, new systems mean new ways of doing business and working together (see the Window on Organizations). The nature of tasks, the speed with which they must be completed, the nature of supervision (its frequency and intensity), and who has what information about whom will all be decided in the process of building an information system. This is especially true in contemporary systems, which deeply affect many parts of the organization. System builders must understand how a system will affect the organization as a whole, focusing particularly on organizational conflicts and changes in the locus of decision making. Builders must also consider how the nature of work groups will change under the impact of the new system. Builders determine how much change is needed.

Systems can be technical successes but organizational failures because of a failure in the social and political process of building the system. Analysts and designers are responsible for ensuring that key members of the organization participate in the design process and are permitted to influence the ultimate shape of the system. Information system builders (see Chapter 13) must carefully orchestrate this activity. As it turns out, managing the systems development process is exceedingly complex and requires very close monitoring by managers to ensure success (or avoid disaster) (Kirsch, 1996).

Linking Information Systems to the Business Plan

Deciding what new systems to build should be an essential component of the organizational planning process. Organizations need to develop an information systems plan that supports their overall business plan and that incorporates strategic systems into top-level planning (Grover, Teng, and Fedler, 1998). Once specific projects have been selected within the overall context of a strategic plan for the business and the systems area, an **information systems plan** can be developed. The plan serves as a road map indicating the direction of systems development, the rationale, the current situation, the management strategy, the implementation plan, and the budget (see Table 11.1).

The plan contains a statement of corporate goals and specifies how information technology supports the attainment of those goals. The plan shows how general goals will be achieved by specific systems projects. It lays out specific target dates and milestones that can be used later to judge the progress of the plan in terms of how many objectives were actually attained in the time frame specified in the plan. The plan indicates key management decisions concerning hardware acquisition; telecommunications; centralization/decentralization of authority, data, and hardware; and required organizational change. Although planning for global information systems is essentially the same as domestic systems, special legal, cultural, and organizational requirements—such as 24-hour availability—must be considered (Tractinsky and Jarvenpaa, 1995). Organizational changes are usually described in the plan, including management and employee training requirements; recruiting efforts; and changes in authority, structure, or management practice.

Establishing Organizational Information Requirements

To develop an effective information systems plan, the organization must have a clear understanding of both its long- and short-term information requirements. Two principal methodologies for establishing the essential information requirements of the organization as a whole are enterprise analysis and critical success factors.

Enterprise Analysis (Business Systems Planning)

Enterprise analysis (also called *business systems planning*) argues that the information requirements of a firm can only be understood by looking at the entire organization in terms of organizational units, functions, processes, and data elements. Enterprise analysis can help identify the key entities and attributes of the organization's data. This method starts with the notion that the information requirements of a firm or a division can be specified only with a thorough understanding of the entire organization. This method was developed by IBM in the 1960s explicitly for establishing the relationship among large system development projects (Zachman, 1982).

information systems plan A road map indicating the direction of systems development, the rationale, the current situation, the management strategy, the implementation plan, and the budget.

enterprise analysis An analysis of organization-wide information requirements by looking at the entire organization in terms of organizational units, functions, processes, and data elements; helps identify the key entities and attributes in the organization's data.

Table 11.1 Information Systems Plan

1. Purpose of the Plan
   Overview of plan contents
   Changes in firm's current situation
   Firm's strategic plan
   Current business organization
   Management strategy

2. Strategic Business Plan
   Current situation
   Current business organization
   Changing environments
   Major goals of the business plan

3. Current Systems
   Major systems supporting business functions
   Major current capabilities
      Hardware
      Software
      Database
      Telecommunications
   Difficulties meeting business requirements
   Anticipated future demands

4. New Developments
   New system projects
      Project descriptions
      Business rationale

   New capabilities required
      Hardware
      Software
      Database
      Telecommunications

5. Management Strategy
   Acquisition plans
   Milestones and timing
   Organizational realignment
   Internal reorganization
   Management controls
   Major training initiatives
   Personnel strategy

6. Implementation Plan
   Anticipated difficulties in implementation
   Progress reports

7. Budget Requirements
   Requirements
   Potential savings
   Financing
   Acquisition cycle

The central method used in the enterprise analysis approach is to take a large sample of managers and ask them how they use information, where they get the information, what their environment is like, what their objectives are, how they make decisions, and what their data needs are.

The results of this large survey of managers are aggregated into subunits, functions, processes, and data matrices (see Figure 11-1). Figure 11-1 is an output of enterprise analysis conducted by the Social Security Administration as part of a very-large-scale systems redevelopment effort.

Figure 11-1 shows a process/data class matrix depicting what information is required to support a particular process, which process creates the data, and which uses it. (*C* in an intersection stands for "creators of data"; *U* stands for "users of data.")

The shaded boxes in Figure 11-1 indicate a *logical application group*—a group of data elements that supports a related set of organizational processes. In this case, actuarial estimates, agency plans, and budget data are created in the planning process suggesting that an information system focused on those elements should be built to support planning.

One strength of enterprise analysis is that it gives a comprehensive view of the organization and of systems/data uses and gaps. Enterprise analysis was used to develop a comprehensive view of how the Social Security Administration has used information in its attempt to bring about long-term strategic changes in information processing.

The weakness of enterprise analysis is that it produces an enormous amount of data that are expensive to collect and difficult to analyze. Most of the interviews are conducted with senior or middle managers, with little effort to collect information from clerical workers and

LOGICAL APPLICATION GROUPS

DATA CLASSES — columns; **PROCESSES** — rows

Group	Process	Actuarial estimates	Agency plans	Budget	Program regs./policy	Admin. regs./policy	Labor agreements	Data standards	Procedures	Automated systems documentation	Educational media	Public agreements	Intergovernmental agreements	Grants	External	Exchange control	Administrative accounts	Program expenditures	Audit reports	Organization/position	Employee identification	Recruitment/placement	Complaints/grievances	Training resources	Security	Equipment utilization	Space utilization	Supplies utilization	Workload schedules	Work measurement	Enumeration I.D.	Enumeration control	Earnings	Employer I.D.	Earnings control	Claims characteristics	Claims control	Decisions	Payment	Collection/waiver	Notice	Inquiries control	Quality appraisal
PLANNING	Develop agency plans	C	C	C	U	U									U																												
PLANNING	Administer agency budget	C	C	C	U	U					U	U	U	U	U	U	U	U		U	U					U	U	U		U		U		U		U			U		U	U	
PLANNING	Formulate program policies	U	U		C				U						U			U				U														U							U
PLANNING	Formulate admin. policies		U		U	C	C		U						U					U	U	U																					
PLANNING	Formulate data policies		U	U		U		C	U	U																					U	U	U	U									
PLANNING	Design work processes		U		U	U			C	C		U	U							U																					U		U
GENERAL MANAGEMENT	Manage public affairs		U		U	U			U		C	C	C																														
GENERAL MANAGEMENT	Manage intrgovt. affairs	U	U		U	U			U		U	C	C	C									U	U		U	U			U		U											
GENERAL MANAGEMENT	Exchange data				U				U		U	U	U	U	C	U	U													U													
GENERAL MANAGEMENT	Maintain admin. accounts		U		U				U			U	U			C		U								U	U	U								U		U					
GENERAL MANAGEMENT	Maintain prog. accounts		U		U				U			U	U				C			U													U			U		U	U	U	U	U	
GENERAL MANAGEMENT	Conduct audits		U		U				U					U	U	C				U									U														U
GENERAL MANAGEMENT	Establish organizations		U		U				U											C	U								U	U													U
GENERAL MANAGEMENT	Manage human resources		U		U	U			U											C	C	C	C	C																			
GENERAL MANAGEMENT	Provide security		U		U		U	U	U																C	C	C	C		U													
GENERAL MANAGEMENT	Manage equipment		U		U		U	U	U																C	C	C	C															
GENERAL MANAGEMENT	Manage facilities		U		U				U																U	U	C																
GENERAL MANAGEMENT	Manage supplies		U		U				U																C	U	U	C															
GENERAL MANAGEMENT	Manage workloads	U	U		U	U			U						U										U	U	U	U	C	C		U		U		U						U	U
PROGRAM ADMIN.	Issue social security nos.								U			U		U																	C	C											
PROGRAM ADMIN.	Maintain earnings								U			U	U	U																	U		C	C	C	C	U						
PROGRAM ADMIN.	Collect claims information				U	U			U					U																	U	U				C	C	U	U	U			
PROGRAM ADMIN.	Determine elig./entlmt.								U																						U	U	U			U		C	U	U			
PROGRAM ADMIN.	Compute payments				U				U									U													U		U			U		U	C	C			
PROGRAM ADMIN.	Administer debt mgmt.				U				U									U																						U	C		
SUPPORT	Generate notices								U					U																	U		U			U			U	U	U	C	
SUPPORT	Respond to prog. inquiries				U				U	U																					U		U	U		U			U	U	U	U	C
SUPPORT	Provide quality assessment				U	U			U	U																					U		U			U			U			U	C

KEY
C = creators of data   U = users of data

Figure 11-1   Process/data class matrix. This chart depicts what data classes are required to support particular organizational processes and which processes are the creators and users of data.

supervisory managers. Moreover, the questions frequently focus not on the critical objectives of management and where information is needed, but rather on what existing information is used. The result is a tendency to automate whatever exists. In this manner, manual systems are automated. But in many instances, entirely new approaches to how business is conducted are needed, and these needs are not addressed.

Strategic Analysis: Critical Success Factors

The strategic analysis or critical success factor approach argues that the information requirements of an organization are determined by a small number of **critical success factors (CSFs)** of managers. CSFs are operational goals. If these goals can be attained, the success of the firm or organization is ensured (Rockart, 1979; Rockart and Treacy, 1982).

The industry, the firm, the manager, and the broader environment shape CSFs. This broader focus, in comparison with that of previous methods, accounts for the description of this technique as strategic. An important premise of the strategic analysis approach is that there are a small number of objectives that managers can easily identify and on which information systems can focus.

critical success factors (CSFs) A small number of easily identifiable operational goals shaped by the industry, the firm, the manager, and the broader environment that are believed to ensure the success of an organization. Used to determine the information requirements of an organization.

Table 11.2 **Critical Success Factors and Organizational Goals**

Example	Goals	CSF

Profit concern	Earnings/share
	Return on investment
	Market share
	New product
		Automotive industry
		  Styling
		  Quality dealer system
		  Cost control
		  Energy standards

Nonprofit	Excellent healthcare Meeting government regulations Future health needs	Regional integration with other hospitals Efficient use of resources Improved monitoring of regulations

Source: Rockart (1979).

The principal method used in CSF analysis is personal interviews—three or four—with a number of top managers to identify their goals and the resulting CSFs. These personal CSFs are aggregated to develop a picture of the firm's CSFs. Then systems are built to deliver information on these CSFs. (See Table 11.2 for examples of CSFs. For the method of developing CSFs in an organization, see Figure 11-2.)

The strength of the CSF method is that it produces a smaller data set to analyze than enterprise analysis. Only top managers are interviewed, and the questions focus on a small

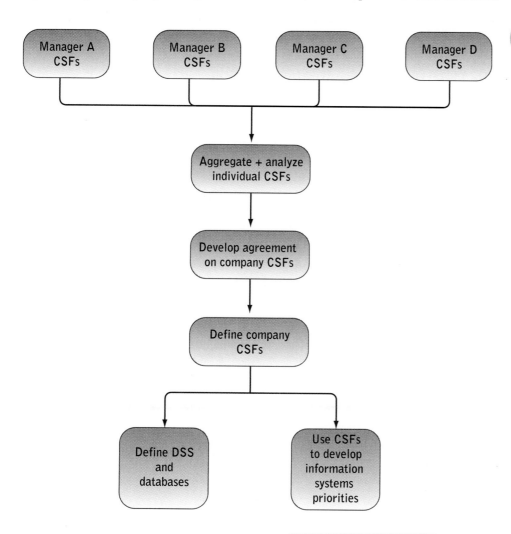

Figure II-2 Using CSFs to develop systems. The CSF approach relies on interviews with key managers to identify their CSFs. Individual CSFs are aggregated to develop CSFs for the entire firm. Systems can then be built to deliver information on these CSFs.

number of CSFs rather than a broad inquiry into what information is used or needed. This method can be tailored to the structure of each industry, with different competitive strategies producing different information systems. The CSF method also depends on the industry position and even the geographical location. Therefore, this method produces systems that are more custom tailored to an organization.

A unique strength of the CSF method is that it takes into account the changing environment with which organizations and managers must deal. This method explicitly asks managers to look at the environment and consider how their analysis of it shapes their information needs. It is especially suitable for top management and for the development of DSS and ESS. Unlike enterprise analysis, the CSF method focuses organizational attention on how information should be handled.

The weakness of this method is first that the aggregation process and the analysis of the data are art forms. There is no particularly rigorous way in which individual CSFs can be aggregated into a clear company pattern. Second, there is often confusion between individual and organizational CSFs. They are not necessarily the same. What can be critical to a manager may not be important for the organization. Moreover, this method is clearly biased toward top managers because they are the ones (generally the only ones) interviewed. Last, it should be noted that this method does not necessarily overcome the impact of a changing environment or changes in managers. Environments and managers change rapidly, and information systems must adjust accordingly. The use of CSFs to develop a system does not mitigate these factors.

11.2 Systems Development and Organizational Change

New information systems can be powerful instruments for organizational change, enabling organizations to redesign their structure, scope, power relationships, work flows, products, and services. Table 11.3 describes some of the ways that information technology is being used to transform organizations.

The Spectrum of Organizational Change

Information technology can promote various degrees of organizational change, ranging from incremental to far-reaching. Figure 11-3 shows four kinds of structural organizational change that are enabled by information technology: (1) automation, (2) rationalization, (3) reengineering, and (4) paradigm shifts. Each carries different rewards and risks.

Table 11.3 How Information Technology Can Transform Organizations

Information Technology	Organizational Change
Global networks	International division of labor: The operations of a firm are no longer determined by location; the global reach of firms is extended; costs of global coordination decline. Transaction costs decline.
Enterprise networks	Collaborative work and teamwork: The organization of work can now be coordinated across divisional boundaries; a customer and product orientation emerges; widely dispersed task forces become the dominant work group. The costs of management (agency costs) decline. Business processes are changed.
Distributed computing	Empowerment: Individuals and work groups now have the information and knowledge to act. Business processes are redesigned, streamlined. Management costs decline. Hierarchy and centralization decline.
Portable computing	Virtual organizations: Work is no longer tied to geographic location. Knowledge and information can be delivered anywhere they are needed, anytime. Work becomes portable. Organizational costs decline as real estate is less essential for business.
Graphical user interfaces	Accessibility: Everyone in the organization—even senior executives—can access information and knowledge; work flows can be automated; all can contribute from remote locations. Organizational costs decline as work flows move from paper to digital image, documents, and voice.

The most common form of IT-enabled organizational change is **automation.** The first applications of information technology involved assisting employees to perform their tasks more efficiently and effectively. Calculating paychecks and payroll registers, giving bank tellers instant access to customer deposit records, and developing a nationwide network of airline reservation terminals for airline reservation agents are all examples of early automation.

A deeper form of organizational change—one that follows quickly from early automation—is rationalization of procedures. Automation frequently reveals unseen bottlenecks in production and makes the existing arrangement of procedures and structures painfully cumbersome. **Rationalization of procedures** is the streamlining of standard operating procedures and eliminating of obvious bottlenecks so that automation can make operating procedures more efficient. For example, Grupo Financiero Bital's banking system is effective not just because it utilizes state-of-the-art computer technology but also because its design allows its bank to operate more efficiently. The procedures of Bital, or of any organization, must be rationally structured to achieve this result. Before Bital could automate its banking system, it had to have identification numbers for all accounts and standard rules for calculating interest and account balances. Without a certain amount of rationalization in Grupo Bital's organization, its computer technology would have been useless.

A more powerful type of organizational change is business reengineering, in which business processes are analyzed, simplified, and redesigned. Reengineering involves radically rethinking the flow of work and the business processes used to produce products and services with a mind to radically reduce the costs of business. Using information technology, organizations can rethink and streamline their business processes to improve speed, service, and quality. **Business reengineering** reorganizes work flows, combining steps to cut waste and eliminating repetitive, paper-intensive tasks (sometimes the new design eliminates jobs as well). It is much more ambitious than rationalization of procedures, requiring a new vision of how the process is to be organized.

A widely cited example of business reengineering is Ford Motor Company's invoiceless processing. Ford employed more than 500 people in its North American accounts payable organization. The accounts payable clerks spent most of their time resolving discrepancies between purchase orders, receiving documents, and invoices. Ford reengineered its accounts payable process, instituting a system wherein the purchasing department enters

automation Using the computer to speed up the performance of existing tasks.

rationalization of procedures The streamlining of standard operating procedures, eliminating obvious bottlenecks, so that automation makes operating procedures more efficient.

business reengineering The radical redesign of business processes, combining steps to cut waste and eliminating repetitive, paper-intensive tasks to improve cost, quality, and service and to maximize the benefits of information technology.

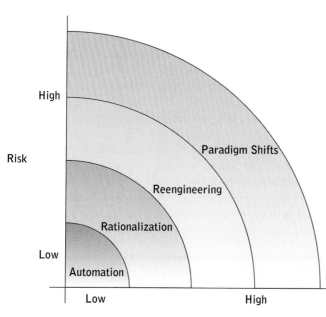

Figure 11-3 Organizational change carries risks and rewards. The most common forms of organizational change are automation and rationalization. These relatively slow-moving and slow-changing strategies present modest returns but little risk. Faster and more comprehensive change—such as reengineering and paradigm shifts—carry high rewards but offer a substantial chance of failure.

Table 11.4 — IT Capabilities and Their Organizational Impacts

Capability	Organizational Impact/Benefit
Transactional	IT can transform unstructured processes into routinized transactions.
Geographical	IT can transfer information with rapidity and ease across large distances, making processes independent of geography.
Automational	IT can replace or reduce human labor in a process.
Analytical	IT can bring complex analytical methods to bear on a process.
Informational	IT can bring vast amounts of detailed information into a process.
Sequential	IT can enable changes in the sequence of tasks in a process, often allowing multiple tasks to be worked on simultaneously.
Knowledge management	IT allows the capture and dissemination of knowledge and expertise to improve the process.
Tracking	IT allows the detailed tracking of task status, inputs, and outputs.
Disintermediation	IT can be used to connect two parties within a process who would otherwise communicate through an intermediary (internal or external).

Source: Adapted from Thomas H. Davenport and James E. Short, "The New Industrial Engineering: Information Technology and Business Process Redesign," *Sloan Management Review*, 11, Summer 1990.

a purchase order into an on-line database that can be checked by the receiving department when the ordered items arrive. If the received goods match the purchase order, the system automatically generates a check for accounts payable to send to the vendor. There is no need for vendors to send invoices. After reengineering, Ford was able to reduce headcount in accounts payable by 75 percent and produce more accurate financial information (Hammer and Champy, 1993).

Rationalizing procedures and redesigning business processes are limited to specific parts of a business. New information systems can ultimately affect the design of the entire organization by transforming how the organization carries out its business or even the nature of the business itself. For instance, Schneider National (described in Chapter 3) used new information systems to create a competitive on-demand shipping service and to develop a new business managing the logistics for other companies. Baxter International's stockless inventory system (described in Chapter 2) transformed Baxter into a working partner with hospitals and into a manager of its customers' supplies. This more radical form of business change is called a **paradigm shift.** A paradigm shift involves rethinking the nature of the business and the nature of the organization itself.

The Window on Technology illustrates how Internet technology can be used for making these organizational changes.

Paradigm shifts and reengineering often fail because extensive organizational change is so difficult to orchestrate (see Chapter 13). Why then do so many corporations entertain such radical change? Because the rewards are equally high (see Figure 11-3). In many instances firms seeking paradigm shifts and pursuing reengineering strategies achieve stunning, order-of-magnitude increases in their returns on investment (or productivity). Some of these success stories, and some failure stories, are included throughout this book.

Business Process Reengineering

Many companies today are focusing on building new information systems where they can redesign business processes. Table 11.4 describes ways that information technology can streamline and consolidate business processes. If the business process is redesigned before

paradigm shift Radical reconceptualization of the nature of the business and the nature of the organization.

Redesigning with the Internet

It has been said that Internet and Web technology provides so much flexibility that organizations can reengineer their business processes without modifying their legacy systems or switching to new technology platforms. Web browsers run on many types of computers and operating systems, so an organization can develop a Web application that runs on a mix of operating environments. Applications can be developed to facilitate business process reengineering using Web pages and interfaces to the organization's legacy systems on the Web server without changing the underlying systems themselves. Here are two examples.

Baylor Healthcare System is a north Texas-based, non-profit network of hospitals, acute-care facilities, and family health care centers. The organization has grown through a series of mergers and associations, and some of its problems were based on the legacy systems it inherited as it grew. Each organization brought to Baylor its own systems that supported a unique way of operating. For example, each constituent organization negotiated its own contract with pharmaceutical vendors, so Baylor was unable to take advantage of large discounts it could receive if the orders were consolidated. Looking at the potential cost savings, Baylor tried to pool the orders but found it required many meetings and numerous hours of costly manual time because of the incompatible systems.

To solve the problem inexpensively, management determined that the pharmaceutical-purchase process needed to be reengineered, placing much of the process on an intranet. The intranet portion of the new system was divided into three parts. The contract database made every contract available to anyone who needed to see it. A high-level exec-utive summary of every contract was stored in the system, including the price and quantity of each drug. It also contained either the full text or a scanned image of the contract. The work flow system was placed on the intranet to help keep the process moving. Every proposed purchase contract was put on-line where it was reviewed by medical analysts and others in the approval process. Thus review and approval could be achieved without delay. Finally, the intranet included a discussion forum where Baylor health providers could discuss appropriate drugs and resolve conflicts on what to order. The system has been a success. According to project manager Marylynn Henry, "The new system has had a substantial impact on Baylor's cost control." She adds that by making accurate information immediately available, the system is "making it easier for employees to do their jobs."

CIGNA Corporate Insurance, an arm of Hartford, Connecticut-based CIGNA, sells life insurance, primarily to corporations, insuring their highly paid employees. These policies are sold by independent insurance brokers. Problems emerge each year when the life insurance policies come up for renewal. Records on each policy must be updated, and the broker and the CIGNA employee each have part of the information needed. The updating process in the past was done through communications between the brokers and CIGNA staff, and it was labor-intensive, time-consuming, and costly. However, when the process was completed, much of the policy data remained out-of-date.

To enable the policies to be fully and accurately updated in a more efficient and less costly manner, CIGNA built an intranet and an extranet. Brokers use the extranet to retrieve information they need on CIGNA policy and investment offerings and to input required data for each policy sold. CIGNA case managers use the intranet to obtain the information they need on individual policies. This use, too, has been a success. According to Diana Rolny, a CIGNA business analyst, "Not only are we saving hundreds of thousands of dollars, but we're positioning ourselves to service the brokers and the customers more effectively."

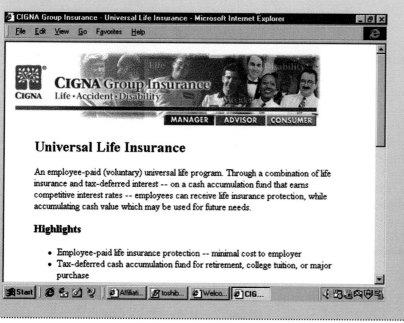

To Think About: How are these companies using the Internet for organizational design? What types of organizational change are taking place?

Sources: Jeff Sweat, "The Front Line," *Information Week*, February 22, 1999; and Geoffrey James, "Baylor Pulls It Together" and "CIGNA Saves a Bundle," *Datamation*, March 1, 1998.

computing power is applied, organizations can potentially obtain very large payoffs from their investments in information technology.

The home mortgage industry is a leading example in the United States of how major corporations have implemented business reengineering. The application process for a home mortgage currently takes about 6 to 8 weeks and costs about $3000. The goal of many mortgage banks is to lower that cost to $1000 and to reduce the time to obtain a mortgage to about 1 week. Leading mortgage banks such as BancBoston, Countrywide Funding Corporation, and Banc One Corporation have redesigned the mortgage application process.

The mortgage application process is divided into three stages: origination, servicing, and secondary marketing. Figure 11-4 illustrates how business process redesign has been used in each of these stages.

In the past, a mortgage applicant filled out a paper loan application. The bank entered the application into its computer system. Specialists, such as credit analysts and underwriters, from perhaps eight different departments accessed and evaluated the application individually. If the loan application was approved, the closing was scheduled. After the closing, bank specialists dealing with insurance or funds in escrow serviced the loan. This "desk to desk" assembly-line approach might take up to 17 days.

Leading banks have replaced the sequential desk-to-desk approach with a speedier "work cell" or team approach. Now, loan originators in the field enter the mortgage application directly into laptop computers. Software checks the application transaction to make sure that all of the information is correct and complete. The loan originators transmit the loan applications using a dial-up network to regional production centers. Instead of working on the application individually, the credit analysts, loan underwriters, and other specialists convene electronically, working as a team, to approve the mortgage. Some banks provide customers with a nearly instant credit lock-in of a guaranteed mortgage so they can find a house that meets their budget immediately. Such preapproval of a credit line is truly a radical reengineering of the traditional business process.

After closing, another team of specialists sets up the loan for servicing. The entire loan application process can take as little as two days. Loan information is easier to access than before, when the loan application could be in eight or nine different departments. Loan originators also can dial into the bank's network to obtain information on mortgage loan costs or to check the status of a loan for the customer.

By redesigning their approach to mortgage processing, mortgage banks have achieved remarkable efficiencies. They have not focused on redesigning a single business process, but, instead, they have reexamined the entire set of logically connected processes required to obtain a mortgage. Instead of automating the previous method of mortgage processing, the banks have completely rethought the entire mortgage application process.

Work Flow Management

To streamline the paperwork in the mortgage application process, banks have turned to workflow and document management software. By using this software to store and process documents electronically, organizations can redesign their work flow so that documents can be worked on simultaneously or moved more easily and efficiently from one location to another. The process of streamlining business procedures so that documents can be moved easily and efficiently is called **work flow management.** Work flow and document management software automates processes such as routing documents to different locations, securing approvals, scheduling, and generating reports. Two or more people can work simultaneously on the same document allowing much quicker completion time. Work need not be delayed because a file is out or a document is in transit. And with a properly designed indexing system, users will be able to retrieve files in many different ways, based on the content of the document. Chapter 2 describes how the United Services Automobile Association (USAA) developed a document imaging system to obtain such benefits.

work flow management The process of streamlining business procedures so that documents can be moved easily and efficiently from one location to another.

Steps in Effective Reengineering

To reengineer effectively, senior management needs to develop a broad strategic vision that calls for redesigned business processes. For example, Mitsubishi Heavy Industries management looked for breakthroughs to lower costs and accelerate product development that would enable

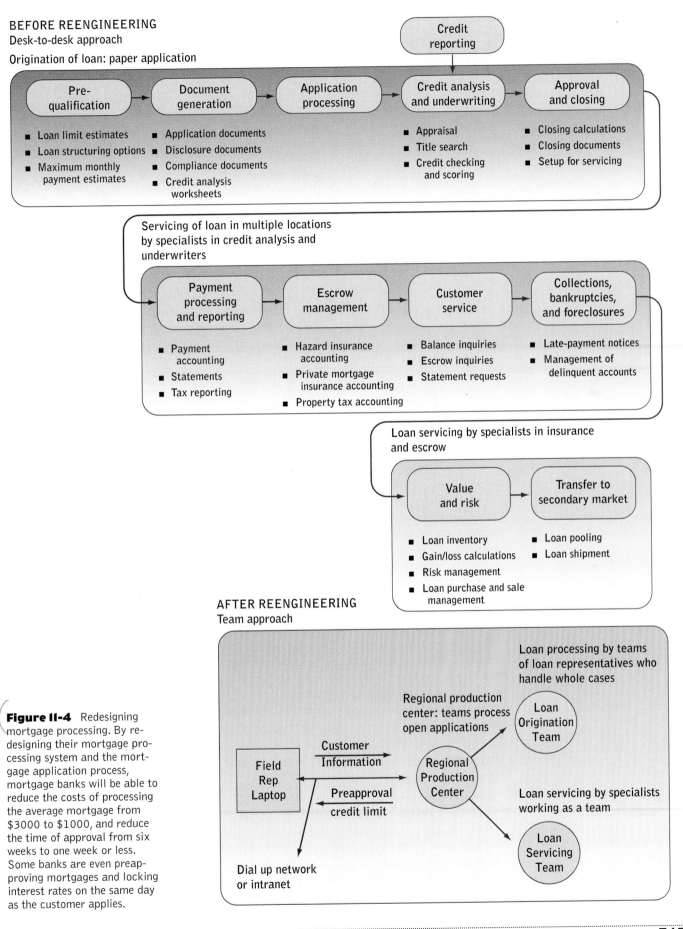

BEFORE REENGINEERING
Desk-to-desk approach

Origination of loan: paper application

Credit reporting

Pre-qualification
- Loan limit estimates
- Loan structuring options
- Maximum monthly payment estimates

Document generation
- Application documents
- Disclosure documents
- Compliance documents
- Credit analysis worksheets

Application processing

Credit analysis and underwriting
- Appraisal
- Title search
- Credit checking and scoring

Approval and closing
- Closing calculations
- Closing documents
- Setup for servicing

Servicing of loan in multiple locations by specialists in credit analysis and underwriters

Payment processing and reporting
- Payment accounting
- Statements
- Tax reporting

Escrow management
- Hazard insurance accounting
- Private mortgage insurance accounting
- Property tax accounting

Customer service
- Balance inquiries
- Escrow inquiries
- Statement requests

Collections, bankruptcies, and foreclosures
- Late-payment notices
- Management of delinquent accounts

Loan servicing by specialists in insurance and escrow

Value and risk
- Loan inventory
- Gain/loss calculations
- Risk management
- Loan purchase and sale management

Transfer to secondary market
- Loan pooling
- Loan shipment

AFTER REENGINEERING
Team approach

Loan processing by teams of loan representatives who handle whole cases

Regional production center: teams process open applications

Field Rep Laptop

Customer Information

Preapproval credit limit

Regional Production Center

Loan Origination Team

Loan servicing by specialists working as a team

Loan Servicing Team

Dial up network or intranet

Figure 11-4 Redesigning mortgage processing. By redesigning their mortgage processing system and the mortgage application process, mortgage banks will be able to reduce the costs of processing the average mortgage from $3000 to $1000, and reduce the time of approval from six weeks to one week or less. Some banks are even preapproving mortgages and locking interest rates on the same day as the customer applies.

Table 11.5 New Process Design Options with Information Technology

Assumption	Technology	Option	Examples
Field personnel need offices to receive, store, and transmit information.	Wireless communications	Personnel can send and receive information wherever they are.	Manitoba Insurance Price Waterhouse
Information can appear only in one place at one time.	Shared databases	People can collaborate on the same project from scattered locations; information can be used simultaneously wherever it is needed.	U.S. West Banc One
People are needed to ascertain where things are located.	Automatic identification and tracking technology	Things can tell people where they are.	United Parcel Service Schneider National
Businesses need reserve inventory to prevent stockouts.	Communications networks and EDI	Just-in-time delivery and stockless supply.	Wal-Mart Baxter International

the firm to regain market leadership in shipbuilding. The company redesigned its entire production process to use robotic machines and computer-aided design tools to replace expensive labor-intensive tasks. Companies should identify a few core business processes to be redesigned and focus on those with the greatest potential payback (Davenport and Short, 1990).

Management must understand and measure the performance of existing processes as a baseline. If, for example, the objective of process redesign is to reduce time and cost in developing a new product or filling an order, the organization needs to measure the time and cost consumed by the unchanged process. For example, before reengineering, it cost C.R. England & Sons Inc. $5.10 to send an invoice; after processes were reengineered the cost per invoice dropped to $.15 (Davidson, 1993).

The conventional method of designing systems establishes the information requirements of a business function or process and then determines how they can be supported by information technology. However, information technology can create new design options for various processes because it can be used to challenge longstanding assumptions about work arrangements that used to inhibit organizations. Table 11.5 provides examples of innovations that have overcome these assumptions using companies discussed in the text. Information technology should be allowed to influence process design from the start.

Following these steps does not automatically guarantee that reengineering will always be successful. In point of fact, the majority of reengineering projects do not achieve breakthrough gains in business performance; reengineering failure rates are estimated as high as 70 percent (Hammer and Stanton, 1995; King, 1994; Moad, 1993). Problems with reengineering are part of the larger problem of orchestrating organizational change, a problem that attends the introduction of all new innovations, including information systems. Managing change is neither simple nor intuitive. A reengineered business process or a new information system inevitably affects jobs, skill requirements, work flows, and reporting relationships (Teng, Jeong, and Grover, 1998). Fear of these changes breeds resistance, confusion, and even conscious efforts to undermine the change effort. We examine these organizational change issues more carefully in Chapter 13.

Process Improvement and Total Quality Management (TQM)

In addition to increasing organizational efficiency, companies are also changing their business processes to improve the quality in their products, services, and operations. Many are using the concept of **total quality management (TQM)** to make quality the responsibility of all people and functions within an organization. TQM holds that the achievement of quality control is an end in itself. Everyone is expected to contribute to the overall improvement of quality— the engineer who avoids design errors, the production worker who spots defects, the sales representative who presents the product properly to potential customers, and even the secretary who avoids typing mistakes. TQM derives from quality management concepts developed by

total quality management (TQM) A concept that makes quality control a responsibility to be shared by all people in an organization.

By simplifying the order-taking process, 1-800-FLOWERS could provide higher-quality customer service and floral products. Florists can obtain order information instantly by using 1-800-FLOWERS' Web site.

American quality experts such as W. Edwards Deming and Joseph Juran, but it was popularized by the Japanese. Studies have repeatedly shown that the earlier in the business cycle a problem is eliminated, the less it costs the company. Thus quality improvements can not only raise the level of product and service quality, but they can also lower costs.

How Information Systems Contribute to Total Quality Management

TQM is considered to be more incremental than business process reengineering (BPR) because its efforts often focus on making a series of continuous improvements rather than dramatic bursts of change. Sometimes, however, processes may have to be fully reengineered to achieve a specified level of quality. Information systems can help firms achieve their quality goals by helping them simplify products or processes, meet benchmarking standards, make improvements based on customer demands, reduce cycle time, and increase the quality and precision of design and production.

Simplifying the product or the production process. The fewer steps in a process, the less time and opportunity for an error to occur. Ten years ago, 1-800-FLOWERS, a multimillion-dollar telephone and Web-based floral service with a global reach, was a much smaller company that spent too much on advertising because it could not retain its customers. It had poor service, inconsistent quality, and a cumbersome manual order-taking process. Telephone representatives had to write the order, obtain credit card approval, determine which participating florist was closest to the delivery location, select a floral arrangement, and forward the order to the florist. Each step in the manual process increased the chance of human error, and the whole process took at least a half hour. Owners Jim and Chris McCann installed a new computer system that downloads orders taken at telecenters into a central computer and electronically transmits them to local florists. Orders are more accurate and arrive at the florist within one to two minutes (Gill, 1998).

Benchmarking. Many companies have been effective in achieving quality by setting strict standards for products, services, and other activities, and then measuring performance against those standards. This procedure is called **benchmarking.** Companies may use external industry standards, standards set by other companies, internally developed high standards, or some combination of the three. L.L. Bean, Inc., the Freeport, Maine, outdoor catalogue company, used benchmarking to achieve an order shipping accuracy of 99.9 percent. Its old batch order fulfillment system could not handle the surging volume and variety of items to be shipped. After studying German and Scandinavian companies with leading-edge order fulfillment operations, L.L. Bean carefully redesigned its order fulfillment process and information systems so that orders could be processed as soon as they were received and shipped out within 24

benchmarking Setting strict standards for products, services, or activities and measuring organizational performance against those standards.

hours. With a built-in Federal Express station, Bean's new automated $38 million Order Fulfillment Center provides high levels of customer service, productivity, and flexibility, and is considered a critical source of competitive advantage (Kane, 1997).

Use customer demands as a guide to improving products and services. Improving customer service, making customer service the number one priority, will improve the quality of the product itself. Facing falling profits, Pizza Hut decided to shift its business strategy from minimizing costs to keeping its customers happy. It launched a customer satisfaction measurement system that monitors customer satisfaction on a weekly basis. The system tracks the buying patterns of more than 2.5 million delivery customers using point-of-sale data captured when a customer buys a pizza. Each week, the system identifies 50,000 customers, who are telephoned and asked about their impressions of Pizza Hut's food and service. The results are analyzed by management to help identify and correct problems. Systems that provide information on service levels from competitors' customers and the firm's own employees are also useful in helping firms improve their service quality (Berry and Parasuraman, 1997).

Reduce cycle time. Reducing the amount of time from the beginning of a process to its end (cycle time) usually results in fewer steps. Shorter cycles mean that errors are often caught earlier in production (or logistics or design or whatever the function), often before the process is complete, eliminating many hidden costs. Iomega Corporation in Roy, Utah, a manufacturer of disk drives, was spending $20 million a year to fix defective drives at the end of its 28-day production cycle. Reengineering the production process allowed the firm to reduce cycle time to a day and a half, eliminating this problem and winning the prestigious Shingo Prize for Excellence in American Manufacturing.

Improve the quality and precision of the design. Computer-aided design (CAD) software has made dramatic quality improvements possible in a wide range of businesses from aircraft manufacturing to production of razor blades. Alan R. Burns, head of the Airboss Company in Perth, Australia, used CAD to invent and design a new modular tire made up of a series of replaceable modules or segments so that if one segment were damaged, only that segment, not the whole tire, would need replacing. Burns established quality performance measurements for such key tire characteristics as load, temperature, speed, wear life, and traction. He entered these data into a CAD software package, which he used to design the modules. Using the software he was able iteratively to design and test until he was satisfied with the results. He did not need to develop an actual working model until the iterative design process was almost complete. Because of the speed and accuracy of the CAD software, the product he produced was of much higher quality than would have been possible through manual design and testing.

Increase the precision of production. For many products, one key way to achieve quality is to tighten production tolerances. CAD software often includes a facility to translate design specifications into specifications both for production tooling and for the production process itself. Once his tire segment design was completed, Burns used the CAD software to design his manufacturing process. He was able to design a shorter production cycle, with more precise specifications, improving quality while increasing his ability to meet customer demand more quickly.

GE Medical Systems performed a rigorous quality analysis to improve the reliability and durability of its Lightspeed diagnostic scanner. It broke the processes of designing and producing the scanner into many distinct steps and established optimum specifications for each component part. By understanding these processes precisely, engineers learned that a few simple changes would significantly improve the product's reliability and durability (Deutsch, 1998).

11.3 Overview of Systems Development

Whatever their scope and objectives, new information systems are an outgrowth of a process of organizational problem solving. A new information system is built as a solution to some type of problem or set of problems the organization perceives it is facing. The problem may be one in which managers and employees realize that the organization is not performing as well as ex-

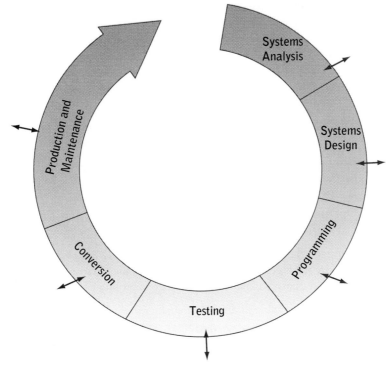

Figure II-5 The systems development process. Each of the core systems development activities entails interaction with the organization.

Organization

pected, or it may come from the realization that the organization should take advantage of new opportunities to perform more successfully.

Review the diagrams at the beginning of each chapter of this text. They show an information system that is a solution to a particular set of business challenges or problems. The resulting information system is an outgrowth of a series of events called systems development. **Systems development** refers to all the activities that go into producing an information systems solution to an organizational problem or opportunity. Systems development is a structured kind of problem solving with distinct activities. These activities consist of systems analysis, systems design, programming, testing, conversion, and production and maintenance.

Figure 11-5 illustrates the systems development process. The systems development activities depicted here usually take place in sequential order. But some of the activities may need to be repeated or some may be taking place simultaneously, depending on the approach to system building that is being employed (see Chapter 12). Note also that each activity involves interaction with the organization. Members of the organization participate in these activities, and the systems development process creates organizational changes. Chapter 13 describes the challenge of managing these organizational changes surrounding system building.

Systems Analysis

Systems analysis is the analysis of the problem that the organization will try to solve with an information system. It consists of defining the problem, identifying its causes, specifying the solution, and identifying the information requirements that must be met by a system solution. Systems analysis can also be used to identify new opportunities for using information technology.

The systems analyst creates a road map of the existing organization and systems, identifying the primary owners and users of data in the organization. These stakeholders have a direct interest in the information affected by the new system. In addition to these organizational aspects, the analyst also briefly describes the existing hardware and software that serve the organization.

From this organizational analysis, the systems analyst details the problems or limitations of existing systems. By examining documents, work papers, and procedures; observing system operations; and interviewing key users of the systems, the analyst can identify the problem areas

systems development The activities that go into producing an information systems solution to an organizational problem or opportunity.

systems analysis The analysis of a problem that the organization will try to solve with an information system.

and objectives to be achieved by a solution. Often the solution requires building a new information system or improving an existing one.

Feasibility

feasibility study As part of the systems analysis process, the way to determine whether the solution is achievable, given the organization's resources and constraints.

In addition to suggesting a solution, systems analysis involves a **feasibility study** to determine whether that solution is feasible, or achievable, given the organization's resources and constraints. Three major areas of feasibility must be addressed:

technical feasibility Determines whether a proposed solution can be implemented with the available hardware, software, and technical resources.

1. **Technical feasibility:** whether the proposed solution can be implemented with the available hardware, software, and technical resources.

2. **Economic feasibility:** whether the benefits of the proposed solution outweigh the costs. We explore this topic in greater detail in Section 11.4, Understanding the Business Value of Information Systems.

economic feasibility Determines whether the benefits of a proposed solution outweigh the costs.

3. **Operational feasibility:** whether the proposed solution is desirable within the existing managerial and organizational framework.

operational feasibility Determines whether a proposed solution is desirable within the existing managerial and organizational framework.

Normally the systems analysis process will identify several alternative solutions that can be pursued by the organization. The process will then assess the feasibility of each. Three basic solution alternatives exist for every systems problem:

1. To do nothing, leaving the existing situation unchanged

2. To modify or enhance existing systems

3. To develop a new system

There may be several solution design options within the second and third solution alternatives. A written systems proposal report will describe the costs, benefits, advantages, and disadvantages of each alternative. It is then up to management to determine which mix of costs, benefits, technical features, and organizational impacts represents the most desirable alternative.

Establishing Information Requirements

Perhaps the most difficult task of the systems analyst is to define the specific information requirements that must be met by the system solution selected. This is the area where many large system efforts go wrong and the one that poses the greatest difficulty for the analyst. At the most basic level, the **information requirements** of a new system involve identifying who needs what information, where, when, and how. Requirements analysis carefully defines the objectives of the new or modified system and develops a detailed description of the functions that the new system must perform. Requirements must consider economic, technical, and time constraints, as well as the goals, procedures, and decision processes of the organization. Faulty requirements analysis is a leading cause of systems failure and high systems development costs (see Chapter 13). A system designed around the wrong set of requirements either will have to be discarded because of poor performance or will need to be heavily revised. Therefore, the importance of requirements analysis must not be underestimated.

information requirements A detailed statement of the information needs that a new system must satisfy; identifies who needs what information, and when, where, and how the information is needed.

Developing requirements specifications may involve considerable research and revision. To derive information systems requirements, analysts may be forced to work and rework requirements statements in cooperation with users. Although this process is laborious, it is far superior to and less costly than redoing and undoing an entire system. There are also alternative approaches to eliciting requirements that help minimize these problems (see Chapter 12).

In many instances, building a new system creates an opportunity to redefine how the organization conducts its daily business. Some problems do not require an information system solution, but instead need an adjustment in management, additional training, or refinement of existing organizational procedures. If the problem is information related, systems analysis may still be required to diagnose the problem and arrive at the proper solution.

Systems Design

systems design Details how a system will meet the information requirements as determined by the systems analysis.

Whereas systems analysis describes what a system should do to meet information requirements, **systems design** shows how the system will fulfill this objective. The design

of an information system is the overall plan or model for that system. Like the blueprint of a building or house, it consists of all specifications that give the system its form and structure.

The systems designer details the system specifications that will deliver the functions identified during systems analysis. These specifications should address all the managerial, organizational, and technological components of the system solution. Table 11.6 lists the types of specifications that would be produced during systems design.

Logical and Physical Design

The design for an information system can be broken down into logical and physical design specifications. **Logical design** lays out the components of the system and their relationship to each other as they would appear to users. It shows what the system solution will do as opposed to how it is actually implemented physically. It describes inputs and outputs, processing functions to be performed, business procedures, data models, and controls. (Controls specify standards for acceptable performance and methods for measuring actual performance in relation to these standards. They are described in detail in Chapter 16.)

Physical design is the process of translating the abstract logical model into the specific technical design for the new system. It produces the actual specifications for hardware, software, physical databases, input/output media, manual procedures, and specific controls.

logical design Lays out the components of the information system and their relationship to each other as they would appear to users.

physical design The process of translating the abstract logical model into the specific technical design for the new system.

Table 11.6 Design Specifications

Output	**Controls**
Medium	Input controls (characters, limit, reasonableness)
Content	Processing controls (consistency, record counts)
Timing	Output controls (totals, samples of output)
	Procedural controls (passwords, special forms)
Input	
Origins	**Security**
Flow	Access controls
Data entry	Catastrophe plans
	Audit trails
User interface	
Simplicity	**Documentation**
Efficiency	Operations documentation
Logic	Systems documents
Feedback	User documentation
Errors	
	Conversion
Database design	Transfer files
Logical data relations	Initiate new procedures
Volume and speed requirements	Select testing method
File organization and design	Cut over to new system
Record specifications	
	Training
Processing	Select training techniques
Computations	Develop training modules
Program modules	Identify training facilities
Required reports	
Timing of outputs	**Organizational changes**
	Task redesign
Manual procedures	Job design
What activities	Process design
Who performs them	Office and organization structure design
When	Reporting relationships
How	
Where	

Physical design provides the remaining specifications that transform the abstract logical design plan into a functioning system of people and machines.

Like houses or buildings, information systems may have many possible designs. They may be centralized or distributed, on-line or batch, partially manual or heavily automated. Each design represents a unique blend of all the technical and organizational factors that shape an information system. What makes one design superior to others is the ease and efficiency with which it fulfills user requirements within a specific set of technical, organizational, financial, and time constraints.

The Role of End Users

User information requirements drive the entire systems-building effort. Users must have sufficient control over the design process to ensure that the system reflects their business priorities and information needs, not the biases of the technical staff (Hunton and Beeler, 1997).

Working on design increases users' understanding and acceptance of the system and reduces problems caused by power transfers, intergroup conflict, and unfamiliarity with new system functions and procedures. As Chapter 13 points out, insufficient user involvement in the design effort is a major cause of system failure.

The nature and level of user participation in design vary from system to system. There is less need for user involvement in systems with simple or straightforward requirements than in those with requirements that are elaborate, complex, or vaguely defined. Less-structured systems need more user participation to define requirements and may necessitate many versions of design before specifications can be finalized.

Different levels of user involvement in design are reflected in different systems development methods. Chapter 12 describes how user involvement varies with each development approach.

Completing the Systems Development Process

The remaining steps in the systems development process translate the solution specifications established during systems analysis and design into a fully operational information system. These concluding steps consist of programming, testing, conversion, and production and maintenance.

Programming

The process of translating design specifications into software for the computer constitutes a smaller portion of the systems development cycle than design and, perhaps, the testing activities. During the **programming** stage, system specifications that were prepared during the design stage are translated into program code. On the basis of detailed design documents for files, transaction and report layouts, and other design details, specifications for each program in the system are prepared.

programming The process of translating the system specifications prepared during the design stage into program code.

Testing

Exhaustive and thorough **testing** must be conducted to ascertain whether the system produces the right results. Testing answers the question, "Will the system produce the desired results under known conditions?"

The amount of time needed to answer this question has been traditionally underrated in systems project planning (see Chapter 16). As much as 50 percent of the entire software development budget can be expended in testing. Test data must be carefully prepared, results reviewed, and corrections made in the system. In some instances, parts of the system may have to be redesigned. Yet the risks of glossing over this step are enormous. Testing an information system can be divided into three types of activities:

testing The exhaustive and thorough process that determines whether the system produces the desired results under known conditions.

Unit testing, or program testing, consists of testing each program separately in the system. Although it is widely believed that the purpose of such testing is to guarantee that programs are error free, this goal is realistically impossible. Testing should be viewed instead as a means of locating errors in programs, focusing on finding all the ways to make a program fail. Once pinpointed, problems can be corrected.

unit testing The process of testing each program separately in the system. Sometimes called **program testing.**

System testing tests the functioning of the information system as a whole. It tries to determine if discrete modules will function together as planned and whether discrepancies exist between the way the system actually works and the way it was conceived. Among the areas examined are performance time, capacity for file storage and handling peak loads, recovery and restart capabilities, and manual procedures.

system testing Tests the functioning of the information system as a whole to determine if discrete modules will function together as planned.

Acceptance testing provides the final certification that the system is ready to be used in a production setting. Systems tests are evaluated by users and technical staff and reviewed by management. When all parties are satisfied that the new system meets their standards, the system is formally accepted for installation.

acceptance testing Provides the final certification that the system is ready to be used in a production setting.

It is essential that all aspects of testing be carefully considered and that they be as comprehensive as possible. To ensure this, the development team works with users to devise a systematic test plan. The **test plan** includes the preparations for the series of tests previously described.

Figure 11-6 shows an example of a test plan. The general condition being tested here is a record change. The documentation consists of a series of test-plan screens maintained on a database (perhaps a PC database) that is ideally suited to this kind of application.

test plan Prepared by the development team in conjunction with the users, it includes the preparations for the series of tests to be performed on the system.

Conversion

Conversion is the process of changing from the old system to the new system. It answers the question, "Will the new system work under real conditions?" Four main conversion strategies can be employed: the parallel strategy, the direct cutover strategy, the pilot study strategy, and the phased approach strategy.

conversion The process of changing from the old system to the new system.

Figure 11-6 A sample test plan to test a record change. When developing a test plan, it is imperative to include the various conditions to be tested, the requirements for each condition tested, and the expected results. Test plans require input from both end users and information system specialists.

Procedure	Address and Maintenance "Record Change Series"		Test Series 2		
Prepared By:		Date:	Version:		
Test Ref.	Condition Tested	Special Requirements	Expected Results	Output On	Next Screen
2	Change records				
2.1	Change existing record	Key field	Not allowed		
2.2	Change nonexistent record	Other fields	"Invalid key" message		
2.3	Change deleted record	Deleted record must be available	"Deleted" message		
2.4	Make second record	Change 2.1 above	OK if valid	Transaction file	V45
2.5	Insert record		OK if valid	Transaction file	V45
2.6	Abort during change	Abort 2.5	No change	Transaction file	V45

parallel strategy A safe and conservative conversion approach in which both the old system and its potential replacement are run together for a time until everyone is assured that the new system functions correctly.

direct cutover strategy A risky conversion approach in which the new system completely replaces the old one on an appointed day.

pilot study strategy A strategy to introduce the new system to a limited area of the organization until it is proven to be fully functional; only then can the conversion to the new system across the entire organization take place.

phased approach strategy Introduces the new system in stages either by functions or by organizational units.

conversion plan Provides a schedule of all activities required to install a new system.

documentation Descriptions of how an information system works from both a technical and end-user standpoint.

In a **parallel strategy,** both the old system and its potential replacement are run together for a time until everyone is assured that the new one functions correctly. This is the safest conversion approach, because in the event of errors or processing disruptions, the old system can still be used as a backup. However, this approach is very expensive, and additional staff or resources may be required to run the extra system.

The **direct cutover strategy** replaces the old system entirely with the new system on an appointed day. At first glance, this strategy seems less costly than the parallel conversion strategy. However, it is a very risky approach that can potentially be more costly than parallel activities if serious problems with the new system are found. There is no other system to fall back on. Dislocations, disruptions, and the cost of corrections may be enormous.

The **pilot study strategy** introduces the new system only to a limited area of the organization, such as a single department or operating unit. When this pilot version is complete and working smoothly, it is installed throughout the rest of the organization, either simultaneously or in stages.

The **phased approach strategy** introduces the new system in stages, either by functions or by organizational units. If, for example, the system is introduced by functions, a new payroll system might begin with hourly workers who are paid weekly, followed six months later by adding salaried employees who are paid monthly to the system. If organizational units introduce the system, corporate headquarters might be converted first, followed by outlying operating units four months later.

A formal **conversion plan** provides a schedule of all the activities required to install the new system. The most time-consuming activity in many cases is the conversion of data. Data from the old system must be transferred to the new system, either manually or through special conversion software programs. The converted data then must be carefully verified for accuracy and completeness.

Moving from an old system to a new one requires that end users be trained to use the new system. Detailed **documentation** showing how the system works from both a technical and end-user standpoint is finalized during conversion time for use in training and everyday operations. Lack of proper training and documentation because of time and cost constraints contributes to system failure (see Chapter 13) so this portion of the systems development process is very important.

Table 11.7 Systems Development

Core Activity	Description
Systems analysis	Identify problem(s) and opportunities Specify solution Establish information requirements
Systems design	Create logical design specifications Create physical design specifications Manage technical realization of system
Programming	Translate design specifications into program code
Testing	Unit test Systems test Acceptance test
Conversion	Plan conversion Prepare documentation Train users and technical staff
Production and maintenance	Operate the system Evaluate the system Modify the system

Production and Maintenance

After the new system is installed and conversion is complete, the system is said to be in **production.** During this stage, the system will be periodically reviewed by both users and technical specialists to determine how well it has met its original objectives and to decide whether any revisions or modifications are in order. Changes in hardware, software, documentation, or procedures to a production system to correct errors, meet new requirements, or improve processing efficiency are termed **maintenance.**

Studies of maintenance have examined the amount of time required for various maintenance tasks (Lientz and Swanson, 1980). Approximately 20 percent of the time is devoted to debugging or correcting emergency production problems; another 20 percent is concerned with changes in data, files, reports, hardware, or system software. But 60 percent of all maintenance work consists of making user enhancements, improving documentation, and recoding system components for greater processing efficiency. The amount of work in the third category of maintenance problems could be reduced significantly through better systems analysis and design practices. Table 11.7 summarizes the systems development activities.

Systems differ in terms of their size, technological complexity, and the organizational problems they are meant to solve. Because there are different kinds of systems and situations in which each is conceived or built, a number of methods have been developed to build systems. We describe these various methods in the next chapter.

production The stage after the new system is installed and the conversion is complete; during this time the system is reviewed by users and technical specialists to determine how well it has met its original goals.

maintenance Changes in hardware, software, documentation, or procedures to a production system to correct errors, meet new requirements, or improve processing efficiency.

11.4 Understanding the Business Value of Information Systems

Information systems can have several different values for business firms. A consistently strong information technology infrastructure can, over the longer term, play an important strategic role in the life of the firm. Looked at less grandly, information systems can permit firms simply to survive.

It is important also to realize that systems can have value but that the firm may not capture all or even some of the value. Although system projects can result in firm benefits such as profitability and productivity, some or all of the benefit can go directly to the consumer in the form of lower prices or more reliable services and products (Hitt and Brynjolfsson, 1996).

Society can reward firms that enhance consumer surplus by allowing them to survive or by rewarding them with increases in business revenues. Competitors who fail to enrich consumers will not survive. But from a management point of view, the challenge is to retain as much of the benefit of systems investments as is feasible in current market conditions.

Strategy cannot be pursued when a firm is financially unsound. The worth of systems from a financial perspective essentially revolves around the question of return on invested capital. The value of systems from a financial view comes down to one question: Does a particular IS investment produce sufficient returns to justify its costs? There are many problems with this approach, not the least of which is how to estimate benefits and count the costs.

Capital Budgeting Models

capital budgeting The process of analyzing and selecting various proposals for capital expenditures.

Capital budgeting models are one of several techniques used to measure the value of investing in long-term capital investment projects. The process of analyzing and selecting various proposals for capital expenditures is called **capital budgeting.** Firms invest in capital projects to expand production to meet anticipated demand or to modernize production equipment to reduce costs. Firms also invest in capital projects for many noneconomic reasons, such as to install pollution control equipment or to convert to a human resources database to meet some government regulations or to satisfy nonmarket public demands. Information systems are considered long-term capital investment projects.

Six capital budgeting models are used to evaluate capital projects:

The payback method

The accounting rate of return on investment (ROI)

The cost-benefit ratio

The net present value

The profitability index

The internal rate of return (IRR)

Cash Flows

All capital budgeting methods rely on measures of cash flows into and out of the firm. Capital projects generate cash flows into and out of the firm. The investment cost is an immediate cash outflow caused by the purchase of the capital equipment. In subsequent years, the investment may cause additional cash outflows that will be balanced by cash inflows resulting from the investment. Cash inflows take the form of increased sales of more products (for reasons including new products, higher quality, or increasing market share), or reduction in costs of production and operation. The difference between cash outflows and cash inflows is used for calculating the financial worth of an investment. Once the cash flows have been established, several alternative methods are available for comparison among different projects and decision making about the investment.

Limitations of Financial Models

Financial models are used in many situations: to justify new systems, to explain old systems post hoc, and to develop quantitative support for a political position. Political decisions made for organizational reasons have nothing to do with the cost and benefits of a system.

Financial models assume that all relevant alternatives have been examined, that all costs and benefits are known, and that these costs and benefits can be expressed in a common metric, specifically, money. When one has to choose among many complex alternatives, these assumptions are rarely met in the real world, although they may be approximated. Table 11.8 lists some of the more common costs and benefits of systems. **Tangible benefits** can be quantified and assigned a monetary value. **Intangible benefits,** such as more efficient customer service or enhanced decision making, cannot be immediately quantified but may lead to quantifiable gains in the long run.

tangible benefits Benefits that can be quantified and assigned monetary value; they include lower operational costs and increased cash flows.

intangible benefits Benefits that are not easily quantified; they include more efficient customer service or enhanced decision making.

Information Systems as a Capital Project

Many well-known problems emerge when financial analysis is applied to information systems (Dos Santos, 1991). Financial models do not express the risks and uncertainty of their

Table 11.8 Costs and Benefits of Information Systems

Costs	Benefits
Hardware	**Tangible**
	Cost savings
Telecommunications	Increased productivity
	Low operational costs
Software	Reduced workforce
	Lower computer expenses
Services	Lower outside vendor costs
	Lower clerical and professional costs
Personnel	Reduced rate of growth in expenses
	Reduced facility costs
	Intangible
	Improved asset utilization
	Improved resource control
	Improved organizational planning
	Improved organizational flexibility
	More timely information
	More information
	Increased organizational learning
	Legal requirements attained
	Enhanced employee goodwill
	Increased job satisfaction
	Improved decision making
	Improved operations
	Higher client satisfaction
	Better corporate image

own cost and benefits estimates. Costs and benefits do not occur in the same time frame—costs tend to be upfront and tangible, whereas benefits tend to be back loaded and intangible. Inflation may affect costs and benefits differently. Technology—especially information technology—can change during the course of the project, causing estimates to vary greatly. Intangible benefits are difficult to quantify. These factors play havoc with financial models.

The difficulties of measuring intangible benefits give financial models an application bias: Transaction and clerical systems that displace labor and save space always produce more measurable, tangible benefits than management information systems, decision-support systems, or computer-supported collaborative work systems (see Chapter 14).

There is some reason to believe that investment in information technology requires special consideration in financial modeling. Capital budgeting historically concerned itself with manufacturing equipment and other long-term investments such as electrical generating facilities and telephone networks. These investments had expected lives of more than one year and up to 25 years. Computer-based information systems are similar to other capital investments in that they produce an immediate investment cost, and are expected to produce cash benefits over a term greater than one year.

Information systems differ from manufacturing systems in that their expected life is shorter. The very high rate of technological change in computer-based information systems means that most systems are seriously out of date in five to eight years. The high rate of technological obsolescence in budgeting for systems means simply that the payback period must be shorter and the rates of return higher than typical capital projects with much longer useful lives.

The bottom line with financial models is to use them cautiously and to put the results into a broader context of business analysis. Let us look at an example to see how these problems arise and can be handled. The following case study is based on a real-world scenario, but the names have been changed.

Case Example: Primrose, Mendelson, and Hansen

Primrose, Mendelson, and Hansen is a 250-person law partnership on Manhattan's West Side. Founded in 1923, Primrose has excelled in corporate, taxation, environmental, and health law. Its litigation department is also well known.

The Problem

Spread out over three floors of a new building, each of the hundred partners has a secretary. Many partners still have five-year-old PCs on their desktops but rarely use them except to read the e-mail. Virtually all business is conducted face-to-face in the office, or when partners meet directly with clients on the clients' premises. Most of the law business involves marking up (editing), creating, filing, storing, and sending documents. In addition, the tax, pension, and real estate groups do a considerable amount of spreadsheet work.

With overall business off 10 percent since 1997, the chairman, Edward W. Hansen III, is hoping to use information systems to cut costs, enhance service to clients, and bring partner profits back up.

First, the firm's income depends on billable hours, and every lawyer is supposed to keep a diary of his or her work for specific clients in 30-minute intervals. Generally, senior lawyers at this firm charge about $500 an hour for their time. Unfortunately, lawyers often forget what they have been working on, and must go back to reconstruct their time diaries. The firm hopes that there will be some automated way of tracking billable hours.

Second, much time is spent communicating with clients around the world, with other law firms both in the United States and overseas, and especially with Primrose's branches in Los Angeles, Tokyo, London, and Paris. The fax machine has become the communication medium of choice, generating huge bills and developing lengthy queues. The firm looks forward to using some sort of secure e-mail, perhaps Lotus Notes or even the Internet. Law firms are wary of breaches in the security of confidential client information.

Third, Primrose has no client database! A law firm is a collection of fiefdoms—each lawyer has his or her own clients and keeps the information about them private. This, however, makes it impossible for management to find out who is a client of the firm, who is working on a deal with whom, and so forth. The firm maintains a billing system, but the information is too difficult to search. What Primrose needs is an integrated client management system that would take care of billing, hourly charges, and making client information available to others in the firm. Even overseas offices want to have information on who is taking care of a particular client in the United States.

Fourth, there is no system to track costs. The head of the firm and the department heads who compose the executive committee cannot identify what the costs are, where the money is being spent, who is spending it, and how the firm's resources are being allocated. A decent accounting system that could identify the cash flows and the costs a bit more clearly than the existing journal would be a big help.

The Solution

Information systems could obviously have some survival value and perhaps could grant a strategic advantage to Primrose if a system were correctly built and implemented. We will not go through a detailed systems analysis and design here. Instead, we will sketch the solution that in fact was adopted, showing the detailed costs and estimated benefits.

The technical solution adopted was to create a local area network composed of 100 fully configured Pentium III multimedia desktop PCs, three Windows 2000 servers, and an Ethernet 10 MBS (megabit per second) local area network on a coaxial cable. Multimedia computers are required because lawyers access a fair amount of information stored on CD-ROM. The network connects all the lawyers and their secretaries into a single integrated system yet permits each lawyer to configure his or her desktop with specialized software and hardware. The older machines were given away to charity.

All desktop machines were configured with Windows 98 and Office 2000 application software, while the servers ran Windows 2000. A networked relational database was installed to handle client accounting and mailing functions. Lotus Notes was chosen as the internal mail system because it provided an easy-to-use interface and secure links to external networks (including the Internet) and mail systems. The Internet was rejected as an e-mail technology because of its uncer-

Information systems can provide attorneys and legal researchers with legal data to expedite their research and recording processes.

tain security. The Primrose local area network is linked to external networks so that the firm can obtain information on-line from Lexis (a legal database) and several financial database services.

The new system required Primrose to hire a chief information officer and director of systems—a new position for most law firms. Four systems personnel were required to operate the system and train lawyers. Outside trainers were also hired for a short period.

Figure 11-7 shows the estimated costs and benefits of the system. The system had an actual investment cost of $1,210,500 in the first year (Year 0) and total cost over six years of $3,683,000. The estimated benefits total $6,075,000 after six years. Was the investment worthwhile? If so, in what sense? There are financial and nonfinancial answers to these questions. Let us look at the financial models first. They are depicted in Figure 11-8.

The Payback Method

The **payback method** is quite simple: It is a measure of the time required to pay back the initial investment of a project. The payback period is computed as

$$\frac{\text{Original investment}}{\text{Annual net cash inflow}} = \text{Number of years to pay back}$$

payback method A measure of the time required to pay back the initial investment of a project.

In the case of Primrose, it will take about 2.3 years to pay back the initial investment. (Since cash flows are uneven, annual cash inflows are summed until they equal the original investment in order to arrive at this number.) The payback method is a popular method because of its simplicity and power as an initial screening method. It is especially good for high-risk projects in which the useful life of a project is difficult to determine. If a project pays for itself in two years, then it matters less how long after two years the system lasts.

The weakness of this measure is its virtues: The method ignores the time value of money, the amount of cash flow after the payback period, the disposal value (usually zero with computer systems), and the profitability of the investment.

Accounting Rate of Return on Investment (ROI)

Firms make capital investments to earn a satisfactory rate of return. Determining a satisfactory rate of return depends on the cost of borrowing money, but other factors can enter into the equation. Such factors include the historic rates of return expected by the firm. In the long run, the desired rate of return must equal or exceed the cost of capital in the marketplace. Otherwise, no one will lend the firm money.

The **accounting rate of return on investment (ROI)** calculates the rate of return from an investment by adjusting the cash inflows produced by the investment for depreciation. It gives an approximation of the accounting income earned by the project.

To find the ROI, first calculate the average net benefit. The formula for the average net benefit is as follows:

$$\frac{(\text{Total benefits} - \text{Total cost} - \text{Depreciation})}{\text{Useful life}} = \text{Net benefit}$$

accounting rate of return on investment (ROI) Calculation of the rate of return from an investment by adjusting cash inflows produced by the investment for depreciation. Approximates the accounting income earned by the investment.

Primrose, Mendelson, and Hansen
Legal Information System
Estimated Costs and Benefits 1999–2004

Year:		0 1999	1 2000	2 2001	3 2002	4 2003	5 2004	Total
Costs								
Hardware								
File servers	3@20000	$ 60,000.00	$ 10,000.00	$ 10,000.00	$ 10,000.00	$ 10,000.00	$ 10,000.00	
PCs	100@3000	$ 300,000.00	$ 10,000.00	$ 10,000.00	$ 10,000.00	$ 10,000.00	$ 10,000.00	
Network cards	100@100	$ 10,000.00	$ -	$ -	$ -	$ -	$ -	
Scanners	6@500	$ 3,000.00	$ 500.00	$ 500.00	$ 500.00	$ 500.00	$ 500.00	
Telecommunications								
Gateways	3@5000	$ 15,000.00	$ 1,000.00	$ 1,000.00	$ 1,000.00	$ 1,000.00	$ 1,000.00	
Cabling	150000	$ 150,000.00	$ -	$ -	$ -	$ -	$ -	
Telephone connect costs	50000	$ 50,000.00	$ 50,000.00	$ 50,000.00	$ 50,000.00	$ 50,000.00	$ 50,000.00	
Software								
Database	15000	$ 15,000.00	$ 15,000.00	$ 15,000.00	$ 15,000.00	$ 15,000.00	$ 15,000.00	
Network	10000	$ 10,000.00	$ 2,000.00	$ 2,000.00	$ 2,000.00	$ 2,000.00	$ 2,000.00	
Groupware	100@500	$ 50,000.00	$ 3,000.00	$ 3,000.00	$ 3,000.00	$ 3,000.00	$ 3,000.00	
Windows OS 98	100@150	$ 15,000.00	$ -	$ -	$ 15,000.00	$ -	$ -	
Services								
Lexis	50000	$ 50,000.00	$ 50,000.00	$ 50,000.00	$ 50,000.00	$ 50,000.00	$ 50,000.00	
Training	300hrs@75/hr	$ 22,500.00	$ 10,000.00	$ 10,000.00	$ 10,000.00	$ 10,000.00	$ 10,000.00	
CIO	100000	$ 100,000.00	$ 100,000.00	$ 100,000.00	$ 100,000.00	$ 100,000.00	$ 100,000.00	
Systems personnel	4@60000	$ 240,000.00	$ 240,000.00	$ 240,000.00	$ 240,000.00	$ 240,000.00	$ 240,000.00	
Trainers	2@60000	$ 120,000.00	$ -	$ -	$ -	$ -	$ -	
Total Costs		$1,210,500.00	$491,500.00	$491,500.00	$506,500.00	$491,500.00	$491,500.00	$3,683,000.00
Benefits								
1. Billing enhancements		$ 350,000.00	$ 400,000.00	$ 500,000.00	$ 500,000.00	$ 500,000.00	$ 500,000.00	
2. Reduced paralegals		$ 50,000.00	$ 100,000.00	$ 150,000.00	$ 150,000.00	$ 150,000.00	$ 150,000.00	
3. Reduced clerical		$ 50,000.00	$ 100,000.00	$ 100,000.00	$ 100,000.00	$ 100,000.00	$ 100,000.00	
4. Reduced messenger		$ 15,000.00	$ 30,000.00	$ 30,000.00	$ 30,000.00	$ 30,000.00	$ 30,000.00	
5. Reduced telecommunications		$ 10,000.00	$ 10,000.00	$ 10,000.00	$ 10,000.00	$ 10,000.00	$ 10,000.00	
6. Lawyer efficiencies		$ 120,000.00	$ 240,000.00	$ 360,000.00	$ 360,000.00	$ 360,000.00	$ 360,000.00	
Total Benefits		$ 595,000.00	$ 880,000.00	$1,150,000.00	$1,150,000.00	$1,150,000.00	$1,150,000.00	$6,075,000.00

Figure 11-7 Costs and benefits of the Legal Information System. This spreadsheet analyzes the basic costs and benefits of implementing an information system for the law firm. The costs for hardware, telecommunications, software, services, and personnel are analyzed over a six-year period.

Year:	0	1	2	3	4	5
Net Cash Flow	$ (615,500.00)	$ 388,500.00	$ 658,500.00	$ 643,500.00	$ 658,500.00	$ 658,500.00

(1) Payback Period= 3 years
Initial investment $ 1,210,500.00

Cumulative Cash Flow

Year 1	$ 388,500.00	$ 388,500.00	
Year 2	$ 658,500.00	$ 1,047,000.00	
Year 3	$ 643,500.00	$ 1,690,500.00	
Year 4	$ 658,500.00	$ 2,349,000.00	
Year 5	$ 658,500.00	$ 3,007,500.00	

(2) Accounting Rate of Return

(Total benefits − Total costs − Depreciation)/Useful life

Total initial investment

Total benefits	$ 6,075,000.00
Total costs	$ 3,683,000.00
Depreciation	$ 1,210,500.00
	$ 1,181,500.00
Life	6 years
Initial investment	$ 1,210,500.00

$$ROI = \frac{1,181,500/6}{1,210,500} = 16.27\%$$

(3) Cost–Benefit Ratio $\dfrac{\text{Total benefits}}{\text{Total costs}} = \dfrac{\$6,075,000.00}{\$3,683,000} = 1.65$

(4) Net Present Value
@NPV(0.05,D46:I46) $ 1,871,771.00
Net present value 1,871,771 − 1,210,500 $ 661,271.00

(5) Profitability Index
NPV/Investment $1,871,771/$1,210,500   1.55

(6) Internal Rate of Return (IRR)
@IRR(B17D46:146)+B49   82%

Figure 11-8 Financial models. To determine the financial basis for a project, a series of financial models helps determine the return on invested capital. These calculations include the payback period, the accounting rate of return (ROI), the cost–benefit ratio, the net present value, the profitability index, and the internal rate of return (IRR).

This net benefit is divided by the total initial investment to arrive at ROI (rate of return on investment). The formula is

$$\frac{\text{Net benefit}}{\text{Total initial investment}} = \text{ROI}$$

In the case of Primrose, the average rate of return on the investment is 16.27 percent. The cost of capital (the prime rate) has been hovering around 8 to 10 percent, and returns on invested capital in corporate bonds are at about 10 percent. On the surface, this investment returns more than other financial investments. However, 16.27 percent would be too low to pass the hurdle rate at many firms because they seek more than 25 percent returns for internal projects.

The weakness of ROI is that it can ignore the time value of money. Future savings are simply not worth as much in today's dollars as are current savings. However, ROI can be modified (and usually is) so that future benefits and costs are calculated in today's dollars. (The present value function on most spreadsheets will perform this conversion.)

Net Present Value

Evaluating a capital project requires that the cost of an investment (a cash outflow usually in year 0) be compared with the net cash inflows that occur many years later. But these two kinds of inflows are not directly comparable because of the time value of money. Money you have been promised to receive three, four, and five years from now is not worth as much as money received today. Money received in the future has to be discounted by some appropriate percentage rate—usually the prevailing interest rate, or sometimes the cost of capital. **Present value** is the value in current dollars of a payment or stream of payments to be received in the future. It can be calculated by using the following formula:

$$\text{Payment} \times \frac{1 - (1 + \text{interest})^{-n}}{\text{Interest}} = \text{Present value}$$

> **present value** The value, in current dollars, of a payment or stream of payments to be received in the future.

Thus, to compare the investment (made in today's dollars) with future savings or earnings, you need to discount the earnings to their present value and then calculate the net present value of the investment. The **net present value** is the amount of money an investment is worth, taking into account its cost, earnings, and the time value of money. The formula for net present value is

$$\text{Present value of expected cash flows} - \text{Initial investment cost} = \text{Net present value}$$

> **net present value** The amount of money an investment is worth, taking into account its cost, earnings, and the time value of money.

In the case of Primrose, the present value of the stream of benefits is $1,871,771 and the cost (in today's dollars) is $1,210,500, giving a net present value of $661,271. In other words, the net present value of the investment is $661,271 over a six-year period. For a $1.2 million investment today, the firm will receive more than $600,000. This is a good rate of return on an investment.

Cost–Benefit Ratio

A simple method for calculating the returns from a capital expenditure is to calculate the **cost–benefit ratio,** which is the ratio of benefits to costs. The formula is

$$\frac{\text{Total benefits}}{\text{Total costs}} = \text{Cost–benefit ratio}$$

> **cost–benefit ratio** A method for calculating the returns from a capital expenditure by dividing total benefits by total costs.

In the case of Primrose, the cost–benefit ratio is 1.65, meaning that the benefits are 1.65 times greater than the costs. The cost–benefit ratio can be used to rank several projects for comparison. Some firms establish a minimum cost–benefit ratio that must be attained by capital projects. The cost–benefit ratio can of course be calculated using present values to account for the time value of money.

Profitability Index

One limitation of net present value is that it provides no measure of profitability. Neither does it provide a way to rank order different possible investments. One simple solution is provided by the profitability index. The **profitability index** is calculated by dividing the present value of the total cash inflow from an investment by the initial cost of the investment. The result can be used to compare the profitability of alternative investments.

$$\frac{\text{Present value of cash inflows}}{\text{Investment}} = \text{Profitability index}$$

> **profitability index** Used to compare the profitability of alternative investments; it is calculated by dividing the present value of the total cash inflow from an investment by the initial cost of the investment.

In the case of Primrose, the profitability index is 1.55. The project returns substantially more than its cost. Projects can be rank ordered on this index, permitting firms to focus on only the most profitable projects.

Internal Rate of Return (IRR)

Internal rate of return (IRR) is a variation of the net present value method. It takes into account the time value of money. **Internal rate of return (IRR)** is defined as the rate of return or profit that an investment is expected to earn. IRR is the discount (interest) rate that will equate the present value of the project's future cash flows to the initial cost of the project (defined here as a negative cash flow in year 0 of $615,500). In other words, the value of R (discount rate) is such that Present value − Initial cost = 0. In the case of Primrose, the IRR is 82 percent. This seems to be a healthy rate of return.

> **internal rate of return (IRR)** The rate of return or profit that an investment is expected to earn.

Results of the Capital Budgeting Analysis

Using methods that take into account the time value of money, the Primrose project is cash-flow positive over the time period and returns more benefits than it costs. Against this analysis, one might ask what other investments would be better from an efficiency and effectiveness

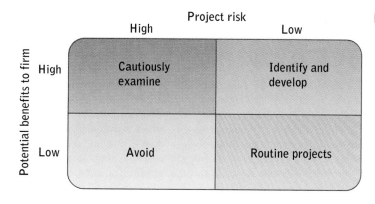

Project risk

	High	Low
High (Potential benefits to firm)	Cautiously examine	Identify and develop
Low	Avoid	Routine projects

Figure 11-9 A system portfolio. Companies should examine their portfolio of projects in terms of potential benefits and likely risks. Certain kinds of projects should be avoided altogether and others developed rapidly. There is no ideal mix. Companies in different industries have different profiles.

standpoint? Also, one must ask if all the benefits have been calculated. It may be that this investment is necessary for the survival of the firm, or necessary to provide a level of service demanded by its clients. What are other competitors doing? In other words, there may be other intangible and strategic business factors to take into account.

Nonfinancial and Strategic Considerations

Other methods of selecting and evaluating information system investments involve nonfinancial and strategic considerations. When the firm has several alternative investments from which to select, it can employ portfolio analysis and scoring models. Several of these methods can be used in combination.

Portfolio Analysis

Rather than using capital budgeting, a second way of selecting among alternative projects is to consider the firm as having a portfolio of potential applications. Each application carries risks and benefits. The portfolio can be described as having a certain profile of risk and benefit to the firm (see Figure 11-9). Although there is no ideal profile for all firms, information-intensive industries (e.g., finance) should have a few high-risk, high-benefit projects to ensure that they stay current with technology. Firms in noninformation-intensive industries should focus on high-benefit, low-risk projects.

The general risks are as follows:

- Benefits may not be obtained.
- Costs of implementation may exceed budgets.
- Implementation time frames are exceeded.
- Technical performance is less than expected.
- The system is incompatible with existing software or hardware.

Risks are not necessarily bad. They are tolerable as long as the benefits are commensurate. In general, there are three factors that increase the risks of a project: project size, organizational experience, and project task complexity (Ein-Dor and Segev, 1978; McFarlan, 1981; Laudon, 1989). These are described in Chapter 13.

Once strategic analyses have determined the overall direction of systems development, a **portfolio analysis** can be used to select alternatives. Obviously, one can begin by focusing on systems of high benefit and low risk. These promise early returns and low risks. Second, high-benefit, high-risk systems should be examined; low-benefit, high-risk systems should be totally avoided; and low-benefit, low-risk systems should be reexamined for the possibility of rebuilding and replacing them with more desirable systems having higher benefits.

portfolio analysis An analysis of the portfolio of potential applications within a firm to determine the risks and benefits and select among alternatives for information systems.

Scoring Models

A quick and sometimes compelling method for arriving at a decision on alternative systems is a **scoring model.** Scoring models give alternative systems a single score based on the extent to which they meet selected objectives (Matlin, 1989; Buss, 1983).

scoring model A quick method for deciding among alternative systems based on a system of ratings for selected objectives.

Extranet ROIs: Figuring the Payback

Many businesses are building extranets to link to customers and suppliers because they are inexpensive to build and use while providing efficiencies in inventory management, order processing, and distributing information. Steven Bell, an analyst at Forrester Research Inc. in Cambridge, Massachusetts, found that extranets linking companies with suppliers usually pay for themselves in one to four years. But as extranet projects grow in scope, companies expect their management to justify the development costs.

The problem is, measuring the payoff from extranets is more art than science. Since benefits are spread across multiple departments and companies, the return on investment must be measured not only within the company but also throughout business processes that span corporate boundaries. Most managers are not experienced in analyzing tasks involving outsiders.

One way to clarify the process of measuring extranet ROIs is to establish a few well-defined targets. Entex Information Services Inc., a $2.5 billion computer systems integrator based in Rye Brook, New York, started by identifying the business processes that were supposed to be improved by installing the extranet. Entex based its extranet ROI analysis on a study conducted by the consulting firm of KPMG Peat Marwick LLP that analyzed Entex's selling and distribution costs. Rob Laudadio, Entex's director of collaborative computing, first established baseline measurements for twelve activities highlighted in the consultant's report, including quote generation, order entry, and cash collection. He then planned an extranet that would increase productivity in those areas by eliminating manual or redundant tasks.

The KPMG analysis showed that 18 percent of the cost of Entex's sales organization was spent on writing up price quotes for simple computer packages. Laudadio specified that the extranet was to include capabilities for quickly calling up frequently ordered configurations. After the extranet was completed, Entex measured a 13 percent reduction across the organization in the cost of generating a quote. Entex expects a 161 percent ROI on extranet investments in the next two years.

To convince its customers to switch to extranet-based ordering, Laudadio prepared an analysis comparing the cost of executing a typical order, figuring it would cost $12 to look up prices of components and another $10 to create an order spreadsheet to submit to Entex. He then calculated the costs of performing the same activities using the extranet. Price lookups would cost around $1 and order spreadsheets would be generated automatically on the extranet. The customer's average cost of placing an order would drop to $126 from $196 if they used the Entex extranet.

Experts also point out that extranets bring many business benefits such as improved customer service or reductions in the customer payment cycle that can't be easily quantified using traditional ROI accounting methods, and many companies build extranets because of these broader business benefits.

To Think About: To what extent is ROI a useful way to measure investments on extranets?

Sources: Andy Raskin, "The ROIght Stuff," CIO Web Business Magazine, February 1, 1999; and Jeff Sweat, "What's Your ROI?" Information Week, August 24, 1998.

In Table 11.9 the firm must decide among three alternative office automation systems: (1) an IBM AS/400 client/server system with proprietary software, (2) a UNIX-based client/server system using an Oracle database, and (3) a Windows NT/2000 client/server system using Windows and Lotus Notes. Column 1 lists the criteria that decision makers may apply to the systems. These criteria are usually the result of lengthy discussions among the decision-making group. Often the most important outcome of a scoring model is not the score but simply agreement on the criteria used to judge a system (Ginzberg, 1979; Nolan, 1982). Column 2 lists the weights that decision makers attach to the decision criterion. The scoring model helps to bring about agreement among participants concerning the rank of the criteria. Columns 3 to 5 use a 1-to-5 scale (lowest to highest) to express the judgments of participants on the relative merits of each system. For example, concerning the percentage of user needs that each system meets, a score of 1 for a system argues that this system when compared with others being considered will be low in meeting user needs.

As with all objective techniques, there are many qualitative judgments involved in using the scoring model. This model requires experts who understand the issues and the technology. It is appropriate to cycle through the scoring model several times, changing the criteria and weights, to see how sensitive the outcome is to reasonable changes in criteria. Scoring models are used most commonly to confirm, to rationalize, and to support decisions, rather than as the final arbiters of system selection.

Table 11.9 Scoring Model Used to Choose Among Alternative Office Automation Systems*

Criterion	Weight	AS/400		UNIX		Windows NT/2000	
Percentage of user needs met	0.40	2	0.8	3	1.2	4	1.6
Cost of the initial purchase	0.20	1	0.2	3	0.6	4	0.8
Financing	0.10	1	0.1	3	0.3	4	0.4
Ease of maintenance	0.10	2	0.2	3	0.3	4	0.4
Chances of success	0.20	3	0.6	4	0.8	4	0.8
Final score			1.9		3.2		4.0

Scale: 1 = low, 5 = high

*One of the major uses of scoring models is in identifying the criteria of selection and their relative weights. In this instance, an office automation system based on Windows NT/2000 appears preferable.

If Primrose had other alternative systems projects to select from, it could have used the portfolio and scoring models as well as financial models to establish the business value of its systems solution.

Primrose did not have a portfolio of applications that could be used to compare the proposed system. Senior lawyers felt the project was low in risk using well-understood technology. They felt the rewards were even higher than the financial models stated. In particular they believed the financial models focused too much on cost savings, and not enough on new business creation. For instance, the ability to communicate with other law firms, with clients, and with the international staff of lawyers in remote locations was not even considered in the financial analysis.

The Window on Management explores the issue of returns on investment from corporate extranets.

Management Wrap-Up

Managers must link any systems development to the strategy of the firm, and identify precisely which systems should be changed to achieve large-scale improvements in results for the corporation as a whole. In other words, understanding what process to improve from the firm perspective is more important than blindly reengineering whatever business process happens to need fixing or happens to yield a huge ROI. There are many projects that have huge ROIs but in the scheme of things don't amount to much for the business as a whole.

Management

In corporate-wide systems-building, the leading organizational issue is how to balance local interests with corporate interests, and how to ensure that the overall strategy of the business dominates the system-building direction of local units. Many organizations have developed multitiered business processes to control the systems-building process as well as to permit local interests a significant voice in the development of a centralized infrastructure. Unfortunately, these firmwide control structures can become unwieldy, bureaucratic, and political and stifle local initiatives.

Organization

The key technological issues in system building involve how to use new technologies to enhance the system-building process and the selection of the right technology for the system solution. Some new technologies help the actual organizational process of design, whereas other new technologies have only limited impacts on technical design. Selecting a technology that fits the constraints of the problem to be solved and the organization's overall information technology infrastructure is a key decision.

Technology

For Discussion

1. It has been said that information systems design cannot be directed by technical specialists alone. Do you agree? Why or why not?

2. Information systems often have to be redesigned after testing. Why?

Summary

1. **Demonstrate how building new systems can produce organizational change.** Building a new information system is a form of planned organizational change that involves many different people in the organization. Because information systems are sociotechnical entities, a change in information systems involves changes in work, management, and the organization. The four levels of change that can result from the introduction of information technology are automation, rationalization of procedures, business process redesign (business reengineering), and paradigm shift. Business reengineering has the potential to dramatically improve productivity by streamlining work flows and redundant processes.

2. **Compare the role of information systems in total quality management (TQM) and business process reengineering (BPR).** Information systems can contribute to total quality management (TQM) by supporting improvements in business processes. Such process improvements include simplifying products and production processes, meeting benchmarking standards, improving customer service, reducing production cycle time, and improving the quality and precision of design and production. Information systems can also support business process reengineering (BPR) by helping organizations streamline work flows, eliminate redundant processes, and design new business processes that achieve radical breakthroughs in productivity. TQM efforts often focus on making a series of continuous improvements, whereas BPR focuses on dramatic bursts of change.

3. **Explain how the organization can develop information systems that fit its business plan.** Organizations should develop an information systems plan that describes how information technology supports the attainment of their business goals. The plan indicates the direction of systems development, the rationale, implementation strategy, and budget. Enterprise analysis and critical success factors (CSFs) can be used to elicit organization-wide information requirements that must be addressed by the plan.

4. **Identify the core activities in the systems development process.** The core activities in systems development are systems analysis, systems design, programming, testing, conversion, and production and maintenance. Systems analysis is the study and analysis of problems of existing systems and the identification of requirements for their solution. Systems design provides the specifications for an information system solution, showing how its technical and organizational components fit together.

5. **Evaluate models for determining the business value of information systems.** Capital budgeting models such as the payback method, accounting rate of return on investment (ROI), cost–benefit ratio, net present value, profitability index, and internal rate of return (IRR) are the primary financial models for determining the business value of information systems. Portfolio analysis and scoring models include nonfinancial considerations and can be used to evaluate alternative information systems projects.

Key Terms

Acceptance testing, 351	Documentation, 352	Paradigm shift, 340	Scoring model, 361
Accounting rate of return on investment (ROI), 357	Economic feasibility, 348	Parallel strategy, 352	System testing, 351
	Enterprise analysis, 334	Payback method, 357	Systems analysis, 347
Automation, 339	Feasibility study, 348	Phased approach strategy, 352	Systems design, 348
Benchmarking, 345	Information requirements, 348	Physical design, 349	Systems development, 347
Business reengineering, 339	Information systems plan, 334	Pilot study strategy, 352	Tangible benefits, 354
Capital budgeting, 354	Intangible benefits, 354	Portfolio analysis, 361	Technical feasibility, 348
Conversion, 351	Internal rate of return (IRR), 360	Present value, 360	Test plan, 351
Conversion plan, 352		Production, 353	Testing, 351
Cost–benefit ratio, 360	Logical design, 349	Profitability index, 360	Total quality management (TQM), 344
Critical success factors (CSFs), 336	Maintenance, 353	Programming, 351	Unit testing, 351
Direct cutover strategy, 352	Net present value, 360	Rationalization of procedures, 339	Work-flow management, 342
	Operational feasibility, 348		

Review Questions

1. Why can a new information system be considered planned organizational change?

2. What are the major categories of an information systems plan?

3. How can enterprise analysis and critical success factors be used to establish organization-wide information system requirements?

4. Describe four kinds of organizational change that can be promoted by information technology.

5. What is business reengineering? What steps are required to make it effective?

6. What is total quality management (TQM)? How can business processes be improved to support TQM?

7. What is the difference between systems analysis and systems design?

8. What is feasibility? Name and describe each of the three major areas of feasibility for information systems.

9. What are information requirements? Why are they difficult to determine correctly?

10. What is the difference between the logical design and the physical design of an information system?

11. Why is the testing stage of systems development so important? Name and describe the three stages of testing for an information system.

12. What is conversion? Why is it important to have a detailed conversion plan?

13. What roles do programming, production, and maintenance play in systems development?

14. Name and describe the capital budgeting methods used to evaluate information systems projects.

15. What are the limitations of financial models for establishing the value of information systems?

16. Describe how portfolio analysis and scoring models can be used to establish the worth of systems.

17. Why should corporate intranet projects—or certain other projects—be excluded from traditional and rigorous financial analysis?

Group Project

With three or four of your classmates, select a description of another system in this text. Examples might be the Envirofacts system in Chapter 8, the OnSale system in Chapter 10, and the GMER system in Chapter 3. Prepare a report describing (on the basis of the information provided) some of the design specifications that might be appropriate for the system you select. Present your findings to the class.

Tools for Interactive Learning

○ Internet

The Internet Connection for this chapter will direct you to a series of Web sites where you can complete an exercise to analyze the capabilities of various tools for work flow management and business process reengineering. You can visit the TravelWeb site to explore its capabilities and complete an Electronic Commerce project for sales planning. You can also use the Interactive Study Guide to test your knowledge of the topics in this chapter and get instant feedback where you need more practice.

○ CD-ROM

If you purchase and use the Multimedia Edition CD-ROM with this chapter, you can complete two interactive exercises. The first asks you to select the appropriate information technology solution to improve a series of business processes. The second requires you to perform a systems analysis for a multidivisional corporation experiencing revenue slowdown. You can also find a video clip on Andersen Consulting's Smart Store and Retail Place illustrating the innovative use of technology to rethink the delivery of goods and services, an audio overview of the major themes of this chapter, and bullet text summarizing the key points of the chapter.

How many times does an organization need to build an information system? In the case of Mobil Oil's lubricants division, the answer was to do it until they got it right. Mobil, the Fairfax, Virginia, corporation, had 1997 revenues of about $60 billion, making it the second largest U.S. oil company. It ranks number 8 in the Fortune 500 list. Mobil is the largest marketer of finished lubricants in the United States. The lubricants division's major products include bulk industrial oils and greases, motor oils, and waxes. These products are essential to the functioning of virtually all machinery because the lubricants can withstand the intense heat and pressure generated by combustion engines, allowing machines to operate at high speeds while virtually eliminating friction.

The lubricants division distributes 60 to 70 percent of its product through about 300 small regional oil distributors. The division actually has two types of sales: Direct purchases are ordinary purchases by the distributors using purchase orders, and buybacks occur when a distributor delivers products from its own inventory to a Mobil national account holder. In the case of buybacks, once the delivery has been made, the distributor requests that Mobil "buy back" the inventory it has delivered; the distributor is paid its cost plus a commission. Distributors submit 12 times as many buyback orders as purchase orders.

Prior to 1995, the division processed all purchase and buyback orders manually. The manual system was based on telephone, fax, and mail-in orders. All were paper based and involved a great deal of handling and filing. The process was very slow and extremely costly. The costs of the manual approach arose from paper, printing, mailing, order entry, telephone charges, and a customer telephone staff and its support.

In 1995 the division abandoned the purely manual process and converted to a DOS-based electronic data interchange (EDI) system. It wanted to input data electronically to facilitate operations. As with other EDI systems, Mobil's new system was used to order products, submit invoices, and exchange other business documents.

Although the system was an improvement, it still had problems. From the viewpoint of Mobil, perhaps the key issue was that too few distributors used it. In fact,

most new orders were not entered through this system. Another major concern was that the cost for processing each order was way too high. The EDI system was based on the use of a VAN (value-added network), and for Mobil that cost alone was more than $100,000 per year. The system also required a great deal of staff manual support, partially because so many orders were still submitted the old way. According to an estimate by Forrester Research, under the EDI system the total cost to Mobil per order was $45.

Mobil staff had another major reason to dislike the EDI system—it put lubricants into the software business. Because its 300 distributors were small, Mobil had to maintain the EDI software for them—distributing the correct versions, ensuring that all are using the correct version, and providing technical support for upgrades.

The distributors were also unhappy with the system. They had to pay a fee for each workstation, and then they paid dial-up costs for each usage. They also had to pay their own VAN charges. However, the primary reason so many avoided the system was because they found it difficult to use. One major problem was that many orders were rejected by the system for failure to meet Mobil's complex business rules. These rules are important, but the system had no way to build in the business rules for each order. For example, one rule sets the maximum weight for shipment on a single truck, another establishes a minimum quantity for an order, and several enforce intricate requirements for product pallets. An order rejection often meant a 24-hour delay because of Mobil's four-hour turn-around time for reviewing orders. This problem was particularly acute for distributers in the west (Mobil's time zone is in the east). For both Mobil and its customers, rejections meant not only time delays but also duplicate work preparing, entering, and processing orders.

The lubricants' staff recognized very quickly that the DOS EDI system was a failure, and so in 1996 they moved to a Windows-based EDI system. The specific goals of the new project were to simplify the ordering process, to reduce the number of order rejections, and to cut costs. Using Windows, Mobil was able to program its business rules into the software. The new system would reject orders that did not

meet Mobil's business rules before the distributor even submitted them to Mobil. According to Forrester estimates, the new system dramatically cut costs, reducing Mobil's cost per order to $2.50 (1/18 of the DOS version cost).

However, after 18 months Mobil had been able to implement the system at only 38 distributors. Most were still using the old methods, including EDI, telephone, and fax. Those distributors did not want to use computers, and in fact, many did not even own a computer because the purchase of a computer seemed a high cost for using the system. In addition, each company had to pay the cost of a software licensing agreement for each seat and often distributors needed more than one seat for product ordering and buybacks. The companies restructured their organizations, establishing separate units that combined purchases and buybacks. Thus, Mobil's software was now driving the organizational structure of many of its customers.

Mobil had other problems with the system. It found itself still in the burdensome business of distributing, maintaining, and supporting the EDI software for its customers. The new system also resulted in many data entry errors because Mobil was still using legacy systems to process and store the information. These systems required redundant data entry. Also, the new system did not support invoicing. In addition, Mobil's inventory data were updated only weekly so that both Mobil and the distributors lacked real-time inventory information. In the end, the new Windows EDI system did not increase the percentage of new orders entered through EDI.

Late in 1996, Mobil made its third try in three years to fix its problems. Lubricants had several goals in moving to yet another system. It wanted orders to be processed as they arrived and errors corrected at once without much intervention. The system had to be extremely easy to use so that distributors would be willing to adopt it. It also had to be easy to distribute in order to retire Mobil from the software support business for its 300 distributors. Further, the new system had to reduce costs for both Mobil and the distributors. This time they turned to a whole new concept (for Mobil): a Web-based extranet. The new system was dubbed Pegmost. ("Peg" is short for Mobil's Pegasus logo, and "most" is the acronym for Mobil Online Subscriber Toolbox.)

The new system was based on a Mobil Web server that both Mobil and distributor employees could access using Web browsers as front ends, which meant that Mobil need not support its distributors' software. Mobil also took advantage of its Web server to embed its business rules into its programs using Java applets so that when business rules change, Mobil need only reprogram them in one place. Security was addressed by point-to-point encryption software sitting on both Mobil and customer Web servers. In addition all Mobil systems are protected by a network firewall (see Chapter 16).

The company decided temporarily to retain its back-end EDI system. Orders via Pegmost are processed through the EDI system and then data are stored in legacy mainframe COBOL IMS database applications. Customer data are stored in an Oracle database customer system. This system contains records of both past and present customer orders and includes invoices. Mobil retained its EDI system because it was in the process of installing software to replace its back-end systems with a SAP ERP (enterprise resource planning) system. It wanted to complete that project first, eliminating the need to build an interim back-end solution. Mobil was in a rush because the SAP system would solve Mobil's Y2K problems. Once the SAP system is in and running, Mobil will replace the legacy systems, using the SAP software to both process and store its order data.

Development of Pegmost began when lubricants built a prototype at the end of 1996. The testing of the prototype involved all Mobil units that might have a stake in the system, which helped the developers avoid some of the problems that occurred in the first two attempts. The system was also actually tested with some distributors, resulting in modifications. Early in January 1997, after the tests were completed, the staff began four months of development. Then the rollout began. Proxicom, a Reston, Virginia, Internet consulting and development firm, developed the system.

Mobil mandated that all purchase and buyback orders were to be submitted through Pegmost after a given date. To facilitate this, Mobil arranged training classes to make certain that all distributors had the skills to use the system. The one-day classes offered training on Windows 95, on browsing the Internet in general, and on Mobil's Pegmost system.

To build enthusiasm for the new system, the trainers also spent time demonstrating to the distributors other valuable aspects of the Web, such as Federal Express's package tracking facility. Rollout to all 300 distributors was completed within a year.

At the beginning there was some distributor resistance. Many distributors were unwilling to change the way they worked. For instance, some were not committed to paperless offices and demanded the ability to batch-print orders in the old way. In some cases management expressed concerns that employees might waste valuable company time using the Web for personal reasons or entertainment.

However, on the whole, distributor reaction to the new system was very positive. First, it reduced their costs by eliminating both VAN and seat charges. Some small distributors, those who only placed orders a few times a year, were able to avoid even computer and ISP expenses by using their public libraries to access the Web. Distributors could enter partial orders and then place them on hold, saving time and reducing errors.

Second, some welcomed the Web interface because it was familiar to them. Moreover, because the Internet is based on open systems, individual distributors could use whatever hardware they wished, as long as it could run Windows 95 and a Web browser. Under the new system, orders are approved in real-time, thanks to the Java programming. Also, distributors are able to see the status of their accounts, including their current and past orders. The system includes on-line access to Mobil lubricant inventories. Given their ability to enter orders quickly, easily, and without rejection, distributors are finding they are able to avoid entering rush orders for which Mobil adds a large special charge.

Third, distributor organizations were affected positively by Pegmost. Several people are able to access the system simultaneously, enabling companies to revert to their previous organizational structures wherein separate people or departments are assigned to handle purchases and buybacks. Using the Web also contributes to worker freedom, enabling some employees to work from home. At least one distributor is now spending part of each day working from home.

Distributors also like the ability to work at night from home if needed.

One other benefit is that distributors are all now connected to e-mail and able to communicate with each other. An informal distributors communication network has developed with exchanges on shared problems, marketing ideas, and strategic ideas.

For Mobil, the benefits are obvious. The company is no longer in the software business. In addition, most order processing is now automated. Even more basic, because Mobil made Pegmost mandatory, distributors are no longer using telephones and faxes to enter orders. As for the bottom line, the new system has further reduced the processing cost per order by half again. Forrester estimates that the cost is now $1.25 per order, 1/36 of the manual process cost of just three years earlier. Proxicom's analysis showed that Mobil can expect a return on investment (ROI) of 194 percent in five years.

Sources: Lori Piquet, "Slick Business" and Patty Ames, "Distributors Switch Gears," **Internet Business**, November 1998; and Joe Mullich, "Mobil Is Moving EDI to an Intranet," **PC Week**, April 11, 1997.

CASE STUDY QUESTIONS

1. Why did the order entry process become a problem for Mobil lubricants? Analyze the strategic impact of the problem. Was the order entry process a problem for Mobil's distributors? Explain your answers.

2. Prepare a report analyzing the problems with Mobil's first two systems. Describe the problems and their causes. What management, organization, and technology factors were responsible?

3. If you were a systems analyst for Mobil, list five questions you would ask during interviews to elicit the information you needed for your systems analysis report.

4. What management, technology, and organization issues did Mobil have to face with the Pegmost project?

5. Was the Pegmost system a good solution for Mobil? Why or why not?

6. How did the Pegmost system change the way Mobil and its distributors conducted their business?

Chapter 12

Approaches to Systems-Building

Learning Objectives

After completing this chapter, you will be able to:

1. Appraise system-building alternatives: the traditional systems lifecycle, prototyping, application software packages, end-user development, and outsourcing.

2. Compare the strengths and limitations of each approach.

3. Assess the solutions to the management problems created by these approaches.

4. Describe the principal tools and methodologies used for systems development.

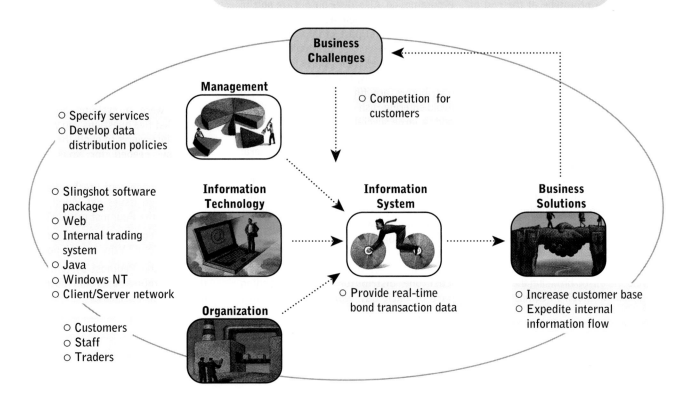

Business Challenges

Management
- Specify services
- Develop data distribution policies

- Competition for customers

Information Technology
- Slingshot software package
- Web
- Internal trading system
- Java
- Windows NT
- Client/Server network

Information System
- Provide real-time bond transaction data

Business Solutions
- Increase customer base
- Expedite internal information flow

Organization
- Customers
- Staff
- Traders

Euro Brokers Lures New Clients on the Net

Euro Brokers Investment Corporation, a fixed-income interdealer broker based in New York City, wanted to find a way to attract new customers using the Web. It decided to expand its real-time services and make them available to selected prospective customers. It implemented CSK Software's Slingshot real-time data-publishing software package to provide prospective customers with access to up-to-the-minute, emerging-markets transaction information, which previously only was available to company insiders. CSK Software provides customized financial systems to investment banks, commercial banks, and securities companies.

Data generated by traders on Euro Brokers' internal trading system are processed by Slingshot and fed onto a public Web site, where prospective customers provided with passwords can take a look at the data. Euro Brokers considered building its own system to accomplish this function, but realized it lacked the in-house expertise and resources to do so. The Slingshot software package provided a solution.

Euro Brokers also is using Slingshot to distribute its real-time, emerging-markets bonds transaction data internally. Staff members access the data by clicking on icons on their computers. This action opens up Java clients linked to Slingshot's mechanism for collecting and distributing the data from the firm's internal trading system. Users can view the data via the Internet or through proprietary networks. Slingshot runs only on NT servers.

Although only a handful of people at Euro Brokers currently use the system, the firm plans to use Slingshot to publish all of its real-time securities transaction information on the intranet and on the Internet.

Sources: Sarah Stirland, "Euro Brokers Shoots for Clients with Slingshot," *Wall Street and Technology Product Review,* Spring 1998; and CSK Software, "Pacemetrics Brings Four-Way Expertise to Focus on Bank's Most Urgent Problem," February 9, 1999.

chapter outline

Like Euro Brokers, many organizations are examining alternative methods of building new information systems. Although they are designing and building some applications on their own, they also are turning to software packages, rapid application development tools, external consultants, and other strategies to reduce time, cost, and inefficiency. They also are experimenting with alternative tools to document, analyze, design, and implement systems. The availability of alternative systems-building approaches raises the following management challenges:

1. **Controlling information systems development outside the information systems department.** There may not be a way to establish standards and controls for systems development that is not managed by the information systems department, such as end-user development or outsourcing. Standards and controls that are too restrictive may not only generate user resistance but also may stifle end-user innovation. If controls are too weak, the firm may encounter serious problems with data integrity and connectivity. It is not always possible to find the right balance.

2. **Enforcing a standard methodology.** Although structured methodologies have been available for over 25 years, very few organizations have been able to enforce them. It is impossible to use CASE or object-oriented methods effectively unless all participants in system-building adopt a common development methodology as well as common development tools. Methodologies are organizational disciplines.

This chapter examines the use of prototyping, application software packages, end-user development, and outsourcing as systems-building alternatives to the traditional systems lifecycle method of building an entire information system from scratch. It also looks at various systems development methodologies and tools. There is no one approach that can be used for all situations and types of systems. Each of these approaches has advantages and disadvantages, and each provides managers with a range of choices. We describe and compare the system-building approaches and methodologies so that managers know how to choose among them.

12.1 The Traditional Systems Lifecycle

systems lifecycle A traditional methodology for developing an information system that partitions the systems development process into formal stages that must be completed sequentially with a very formal division of labor between end users and information systems specialists.

The **systems lifecycle** is the oldest method for building information systems and is still used today for medium or large complex systems projects. This methodology assumes that an information system has a lifecycle similar to that of any living organism, with a beginning, middle, and end. The lifecycle for an information system has six stages: (1) project definition, (2) systems study, (3) design, (4) programming, (5) installation, and (6) post-implementation. Figure 12-1 illustrates these stages. Each stage consists of basic activities that must be performed before the next stage can begin.

The lifecycle methodology has a very formal division of labor between end users and information systems specialists. Technical specialists such as systems analysts and programmers are responsible for much of the systems analysis, design, and implementation work; end users are limited to providing information requirements and reviewing the work of the technical staff. Formal sign-offs or agreements between end users and technical specialists are required as each stage is completed. Figure 12-1 also shows the product or output of each stage of the lifecycle that is the basis for such sign-offs. We now describe the stages of the lifecycle in detail.

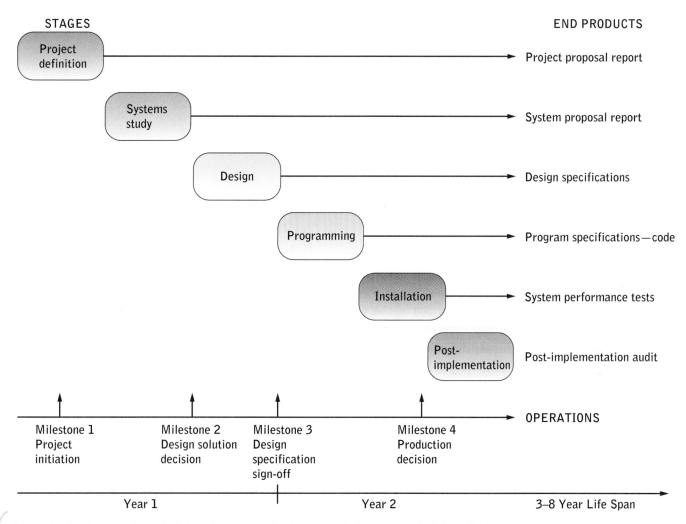

Figure 12-1 The lifecycle methodology for systems development. The lifecycle methodology divides systems development into six formal stages with specifics for milestones and end products at each stage. A typical medium-size development project requires two years to deliver and has an expected life span of three to eight years.

Stages of the Systems Lifecycle

The **project definition** stage tries to answer the questions, "Why do we need a new system project?" and "What do we want to accomplish?" This stage determines whether the organization has a problem and whether that problem can be solved by building a new information system or by modifying an existing one. If a system project is called for, this stage identifies its general objectives, specifies the scope of the project, and develops a project plan that can be shown to management.

The **systems study** stage analyzes the problems of existing systems (manual or automated) in detail, identifies objectives to be attained by a solution to these problems, and describes alternative solutions. The systems study stage examines the feasibility of each solution alternative for review by management.

Systems study requires extensive information gathering and research; sifting through documents, reports, and work papers produced by existing systems; observing how these systems work; polling users with questionnaires; and conducting interviews. All of the information gathered during the systems study phase will be used to determine information system requirements. Finally, the systems study stage describes in detail the remaining lifecycle activities and the tasks for each phase.

project definition A stage in the systems lifecycle that determines whether the organization has a problem and whether the problem can be solved by launching a system project.

systems study A stage in the systems lifecycle that analyzes the problems of existing systems, defines the objectives to be attained by a solution, and evaluates various solution alternatives.

design A stage in the systems lifecycle that produces the logical and physical design specifications for the system solution.

The **design** stage produces the logical and physical design specifications for the solution. The lifecycle emphasizes formal specifications and paperwork, so many of the design and documentation tools described in Section 12.3, such as data flow diagrams, program structure charts, or system flowcharts, are likely to be utilized.

The **programming** stage translates the design specifications produced during the design stage into software program code. Systems analysts work with programmers to prepare specifications for each program in the system. Programmers write customized program code, typically using a conventional third-generation programming language such as COBOL or FORTRAN or a high-productivity fourth-generation language. Large systems have many programs with hundreds of thousands of lines of program code, and entire teams of programmers may be required.

The **installation** stage consists of the final steps to put the new or modified system into operation: testing, training, and conversion. The software is tested to make sure it performs properly from both a technical and a functional business standpoint. (More detail on testing can be found in Chapter 11.) Business and technical specialists are trained to use the new system. A formal conversion plan provides a detailed schedule of all of the activities required to install the new system, and the old system is converted to the new one.

The **post-implementation** stage consists of using and evaluating the system after it is installed and is in production. Users and technical specialists will go through a formal post-implementation audit that determines how well the new system has met its original objectives and whether any revisions or modifications are required. After the system has been fine-tuned it will need to be maintained while it is in production to correct errors, meet requirements, or improve processing efficiency. Over time, the system may require so much maintenance to remain efficient and meet user objectives that it will come to the end of its useful life span. Once the system's lifecycle comes to an end, a completely new system is called for and the cycle may begin again.

Limitations of the Lifecycle Approach

The systems lifecycle is still used for building large transaction processing systems (TPS) and management information systems (MIS) where requirements are highly structured and well defined (Ahituv and Neumann, 1984). It will also remain appropriate for complex technical systems such as space launches, air traffic control, and refinery operations. Such applications need a rigorous and formal requirements analysis, predefined specifications, and tight controls over the systems-building process.

However, the systems lifecycle approach is costly, time-consuming, and inflexible. Volumes of new documents must be generated and steps repeated if requirements and specifications need to be revised. The lifecycle approach is inflexible and discourages change. Because of the time and cost to repeat the sequence of lifecycle activities, the methodology encourages freezing of specifications early in the development process. The lifecycle method is ill-suited to decision-oriented applications. Decision makers may need to experiment with concrete systems to clarify the kinds of decisions they wish to make. Formal specification of requirements may inhibit system-builders from exploring and discovering the problem structure (Fraser et al., 1994). Likewise, the lifecycle approach is not suitable for many small desktop systems, which tend to be less structured and more individualized.

12.2 Alternative System-Building Approaches

Some of the problems of the traditional systems lifecycle can be solved by alternative system-building approaches. These approaches include prototyping, application software packages, end-user development, and outsourcing.

Prototyping

Prototyping consists of building an experimental system rapidly and inexpensively for end users to evaluate. By interacting with the prototype, users can get a better idea of their information requirements. The prototype endorsed by the users can be used as a template to create the final system.

The **prototype** is a working version of an information system or part of the system, but it is meant to be only a preliminary model. Once operational, the prototype will be further refined until it conforms precisely to users' requirements. Once the design has been finalized, the prototype can be converted to a polished production system.

The process of building a preliminary design, trying it out, refining it, and trying again has been called an **iterative** process of systems development because the steps required to build a system can be repeated over and over again. Prototyping is more explicitly iterative than the conventional lifecycle, and it actively promotes system design changes. It has been said that prototyping replaces unplanned rework with planned iteration, with each version more accurately reflecting users' requirements.

iterative A process of repeating over and over again the steps to build a system.

Steps in Prototyping

Figure 12-2 shows a four-step model of the prototyping process, which consists of the following:

Step 1: *Identify the user's basic requirements.* The system designer (usually an information systems specialist) works with the user only long enough to capture his or her basic information needs.

Step 2: *Develop an initial prototype.* The system designer creates a working prototype quickly, most likely using the fourth-generation software tools described in Chapter 7 that speed application development. Some features of computer-aided software engineering (CASE) tools described later in this chapter can be used for prototyping as can multimedia software tools that present users with interactive storyboards that sketch out the tasks of the proposed system for evaluation and modification (Madsen and Aiken, 1993).

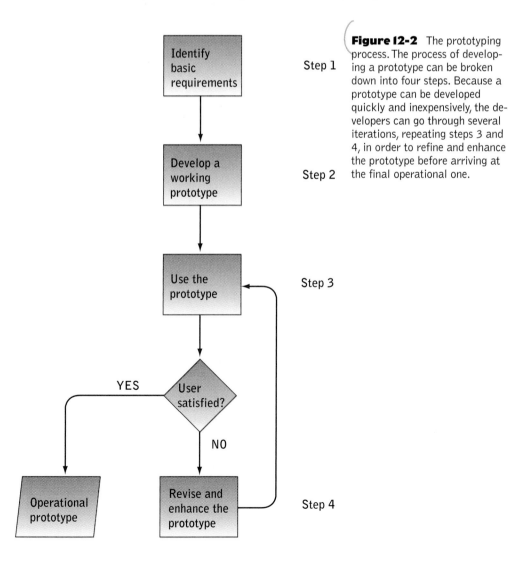

Figure 12-2 The prototyping process. The process of developing a prototype can be broken down into four steps. Because a prototype can be developed quickly and inexpensively, the developers can go through several iterations, repeating steps 3 and 4, in order to refine and enhance the prototype before arriving at the final operational one.

Step 3: *Use the prototype.* The user is encouraged to work with the system in order to determine how well the prototype meets his or her needs and to make suggestions for improving the prototype.

Step 4: *Revise and enhance the prototype.* The system builder notes all changes requested by the user and refines the prototype accordingly. After the prototype has been revised, the cycle returns to step 3. Steps 3 and 4 are repeated until the user is satisfied.

When no more iterations are required, the approved prototype then becomes an operational prototype that furnishes the final specifications for the application. Sometimes the prototype itself is adopted as the production version of the system.

Advantages and Disadvantages of Prototyping

Prototyping is most useful when there is some uncertainty about requirements or design solutions. For example, a major securities firm requests consolidated information to analyze the performance of its account executives. But what should the measures of performance be? Can the information be extracted from the personnel system alone, or must data from client billings be incorporated as well? What items should be compared on reports? Users may not be initially able to see how the system will work.

Prototyping is especially valuable for the design of the **end-user interface** of an information system (the part of the system that end users interact with, such as on-line display and data-entry screens, reports, or Web pages). The prototype enables users to react immediately to the parts of the system with which they will be dealing. Figure 12-3 illustrates the prototyping process for an on-line calendar for retail securities brokers. The first version of the screen was built according to user-supplied specifications for a calendar to track appointments and activities. But when users actually worked with the calendar screen, they suggested adding labels for month and year to the screen and a box to indicate whether the appointment had been met or an activity completed. The brokers also found that they wanted to access information that was maintained in the system about clients with whom they had appointments. The system designer added a link enabling brokers to move directly from the calendar screen to client records.

Prototyping encourages intense end-user involvement throughout the systems development lifecycle (Cerveny et al., 1986). Prototyping is more likely to produce systems that fulfill user requirements. For instance, when the DuPont Company used prototyping to build its systems, it produced more than 400 new programs with no failures (Arthur, 1992).

Prototyping is better suited for smaller applications. Large systems would have to be subdivided so that prototypes could be built one part at a time (Alavi, 1984), which may not be possible without a thorough requirements analysis using the conventional approach.

Rapid prototyping can gloss over essential steps in systems development. Once finished, if the prototype works reasonably well, management may not see the need for reprogramming, redesign, or full documentation and testing. Some of these hastily constructed systems may not easily accommodate large quantities of data or a large number of users in a production environment. Successful prototyping requires management and mechanisms for defining expectations, assigning resources, signaling problems, and measuring progress (Baskerville and Stage, 1996).

Application Software Packages

Another alternative strategy is to develop an information system by purchasing an application software package. As introduced in Chapter 7, an **application software package** is a set of prewritten, precoded application software programs that are commercially available for sale or lease. Application software packages may range from a simple task (e.g., printing address labels from a database on a PC) to more than 400 program modules with 500,000 lines of code for a complex mainframe system.

end-user interface The part of an information system through which the end user interacts with the system, such as on-line screens and commands.

application software package A set of prewritten, precoded application software programs that are commercially available for sale or lease.

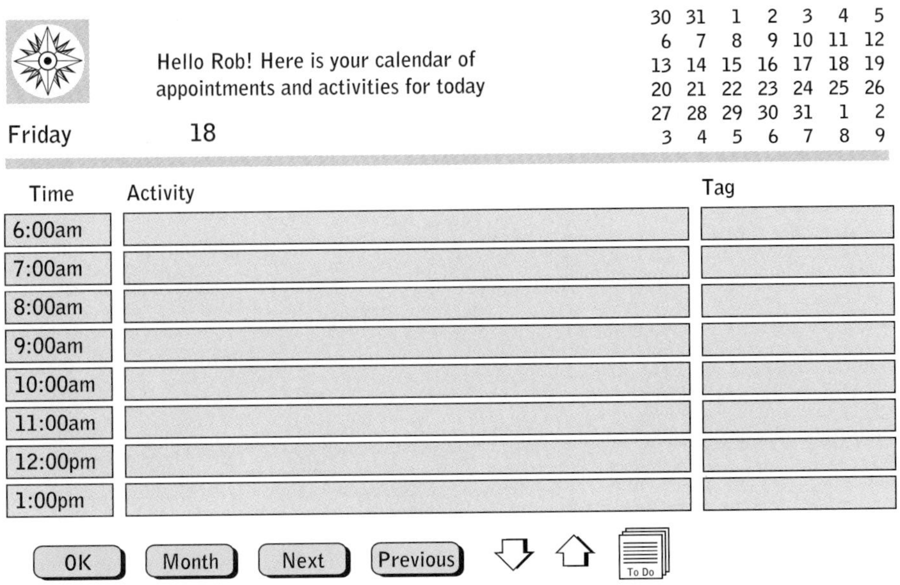

Figure 12-3 Prototyping a portfolio management application. This figure illustrates the process of prototyping one screen for the Financial Manager, a client and portfolio management application for securities brokers. Figure 12-3a shows an early version of the on-line appointment screen. Based on the special needs of a client, Figure 12-3b has two enhancements: a **done** indicator to show whether the task has been completed and a link to reference information maintained by the system on the client with whom the broker has an appointment.

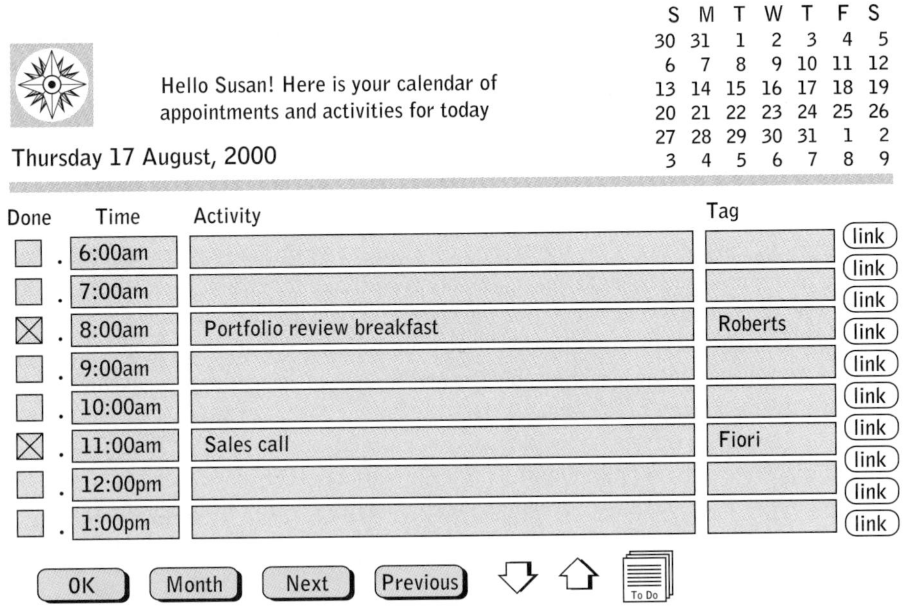

Packages have flourished because there are many applications that are common to all business organizations—for example, payroll, accounts receivable, general ledger, or inventory control. For such universal functions with standard procedures, a generalized system will fulfill the requirements of many organizations. Table 12.1 provides examples of applications for which packages are commercially available.

When an appropriate software package is available, it is often not necessary for a company to write its own programs; the prewritten, predesigned, pretested software package can fulfill most of the requirements and can be substituted instead. The package vendor has already done most of the design, programming, and testing, so the time frame and costs for developing a new system should be considerably reduced.

Table 12.1 Examples of Application Software Packages

Accounts receivable	Job costing
Bond and stock management	Library systems
Computer-aided design (CAD)	Life insurance
Document imaging	Mailing labels
E-mail	Mathematical/statistical modeling
Enterprise resource planning (ERP)	Order processing
Groupware	Payroll
Healthcare	Process control
Hotel management	Tax accounting
Internet telephone	Web browser
Inventory control	Word processing

Advantages and Disadvantages of Software Packages

Using other development strategies, design activities may easily consume up to 50 percent or more of the development effort. However, with packages, most of the design work has been accomplished in advance. Software package programs are pretested before they are marketed so that purchaser testing can be accomplished in a relatively short period. Vendors supply much of the ongoing maintenance and support for the system, supplying enhancements to keep the system in line with ongoing technical and business developments.

Package disadvantages can be considerable with a complex system. To maximize market appeal, packages are geared to the most common requirements of all organizations. What happens if an organization has unique requirements that the package does not address? To varying degrees, package software developers anticipate this problem by providing features for customization that do not alter the basic software. **Customization** features allow a software package to be modified to meet an organization's unique requirements without destroying the integrity of the package software. For instance, the package may allocate parts of its files or databases to maintain an organization's own unique pieces of data. Some packages have a modular design that allows clients to select only the software functions with the processing they need from an array of options.

An alternative way of satisfying organizational information requirements unmet by a software package is to supplement the package with another piece of software. The Window on Technology describes how problems can result from trying to integrate the data from the two systems, requiring the organization to use special software called middleware to act as a bridge between the two systems.

Ultimately, required customization and additional programming may become so expensive and time-consuming that they eliminate many of the advantages of software packages. Figure 12-4 shows how package costs in relation to total implementation costs rise with the degree of customization. The initial purchase price of the package can be deceptive because of these hidden implementation costs.

Selecting Software Packages

Application software packages must be thoroughly evaluated before they can be used as the foundation of a new information system. The most important evaluation criteria are the functions provided by the package, flexibility, user-friendliness, hardware and software resources, database requirements, installation and maintenance effort, documentation, vendor quality, and cost. The package evaluation process often is based on a **Request for Proposal (RFP),** which is a detailed list of questions submitted to vendors of packaged software.

When a system is developed using an application software package, systems analysis will include a package evaluation effort. Design activities will focus on matching requirements

---

customization The modification of a software package to meet an organization's unique requirements without destroying the integrity of the package software.

Request for Proposal (RFP)

A detailed list of questions submitted to vendors of software or other services to determine how well the vendor's product can meet the organization's specific requirements.

Window on Technology

Enterprise Resource Planning Systems: Benefits and Headaches

Enterprise resource planning (ERP) systems are increasingly the software of choice for organizations that are both large and complex (see Chapters 1 and 18). They help companies integrate all facets of the business, including planning, manufacturing, sales, and marketing. ERP software systems, such as SAP's R/3 (described in the chapter ending case study), integrate modules for such differing functions as production, factory automation, finance, sales, purchasing, and personnel. However, many companies who swear by ERP systems find they are not robust or flexible enough to deliver the special budgeting, international consolidation, or other financial features that their managements expect. The predominant solution has been to install a separate, purchased financial system that meets the company's requirements to run alongside the ERP system. That solution, however, creates another problem.

Companies try to choose what they consider to be the best available ERP and financial software systems. They rarely select both systems because they fit well together. Unfortunately, making two such systems work together can be a difficult task because they usually present major difficulties arising from differing data structures. The way that data are represented in vendor files, for example, may not correspond to the way that data are represented in customer files. It may be difficult, if not impossible, to integrate financial, statistical, and operational information. The cost in money and time to integrate the two systems can be daunting. The effort can easily cost between $200,000 and $2 million and take up to six months. Even then, the job is not done. Each time the producer of either the ERP or the financial system releases a new version of their product, extensive work must be done to reintegrate the two systems, so addressing the lack in financial reporting only leads to other problems.

One approach to the data integration problem is a software interface—middleware—installed between the two systems. Commercial middleware software is available, but here, a similar problem exists—getting the middleware to work well with the ERP and financial systems that have been chosen. Some companies choose to build their own middleware. When completed, the middleware system will pass the data between the ERP and financial systems, enabling the organization to use the ERP system it needs to integrate its many functions, and allowing management to obtain the data it desires.

Motorola Corp. used this approach and did improve its reporting cycle, reducing the time to produce management reports from 48 hours to 29 hours. The company's messaging product division created a UNIX-based middleware system that funnels data extracted monthly from 20 general ledger systems worldwide into Walker financial-reporting and consolidation software, which then is used to generate management reports.

When Fujitsu Microelectronics, Inc., faced this integration problem with its SAP R/3 system installed in 1995, it used Microsoft Corp.'s Excel spreadsheets to analyze budget information, but users found the system inadequate. Analyzing data to compare, for example, a ratio of line-item expenses with revenue, could take weeks. Then Fujitsu found that Hyperion, a vendor of financial software that would meet its needs, also offered an accompanying set of tools to help create the interface between its system and R/3. The Hyperion utilities enabled Fujitsu to build a middleware system within four days. When completed, it transferred data between SAP's R/3 and Hyperion's Enterprise. Fujitsu now has switched from a monthly reporting system to a weekly system, enabling the company to react much faster to market changes.

To Think About: What management, organization, and technology issues are raised by installing ERP package software systems in large, complex organizations?

Sources: Thomas Hoffman, "Extending ERP's Reach," **Computerworld**, February 9, 1998; and Debra O'Donnell, "Bridging the Application Divide," **Software Magazine**, September 1998.

---

to package features. Instead of tailoring the system design specifications directly to user requirements, the design effort will consist of trying to mold user requirements to conform to the features of the package.

When a software package solution is selected, the organization no longer has total control over the system design process. At best, packages can meet only 70 percent of most organizations' requirements. If the package cannot adapt to the organization, the organization will have to adapt to the package and change its procedures.

End-User Development

In many organizations end users are developing a growing percentage of information systems with little or no formal assistance from technical specialists. This phenomenon is called **end-user development.** End-user development has been made possible by the special fourth-generation software tools introduced in Chapter 7. With fourth-generation languages, graphics languages,

end-user development The development of information systems by end users with little or no formal assistance from technical specialists.

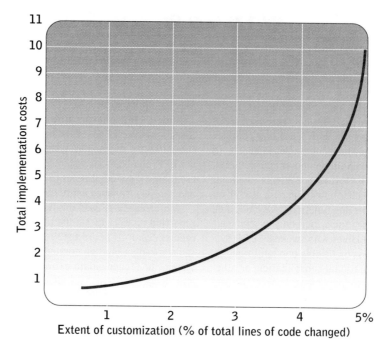

Figure 12-4 The effects of customizing a software package on total implementation costs. As the modifications to a software package rise, so does the cost of implementing the package. Sometimes the savings promised by the package are whittled away by excessive changes. As the number of lines of program code changed approaches 5 percent of the total lines in the package, the costs of implementation rise fivefold.

Total implementation costs (y-axis: 1–11)

Extent of customization (% of total lines of code changed) (x-axis: 1, 2, 3, 4, 5%)

and PC software tools, end users can access data, create reports, and develop entire information systems on their own, with little or no help from professional systems analysts or programmers. Many of these end-user developed systems can be created much more rapidly than with the traditional systems lifecycle. Figure 12-5 illustrates the concept of end-user development.

End-User Computing Tools: Strengths and Limitations

Many organizations have reported gains in application development productivity by using fourth-generation tools. Productivity enhancements based on conventional programming languages, such as structured programming (see Section 12.3), have resulted in a maximum productivity improvement of only 25 percent (Jones, 1979) and often only modest advantages. In contrast, some studies of organizations developing applications with fourth-generation tools have reported more substantial productivity gains that in a few cases reached 300 to 500 percent, although the benefits are highly variable (Glass, 1999; Green, 1984–85; Harel, 1985). Fourth-generation tools have new capabilities, such as graphics, spreadsheets, modeling, and ad hoc information retrieval, that meet important business needs.

Unfortunately, fourth-generation tools still cannot replace conventional tools for some business applications because their capabilities remain limited. Fourth-generation processing

SAP's R/3 software package runs in a client/server environment and can be customized to accommodate different languages, currencies, tax laws, and accounting practices.

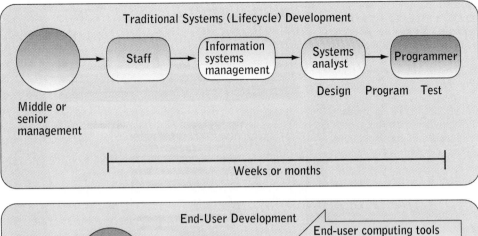

Figure 12-5 End-user versus systems lifecycle development. End users can access computerized information directly or develop information systems with little or no formal technical assistance. On the whole, end-user developed systems can be completed more rapidly than those developed through the conventional systems lifecycle. From **Application Development without Programmers,** by James Martin, © 1982. Reprinted by permission of Prentice-Hall, Inc., Upper Saddle River, NJ.

is relatively inefficient, processing individual transactions too slowly and at too high a cost to make these systems suitable for very large transaction processing systems. Slow response time and computer performance degradation often result when very large files are used.

Most fourth-generation tools are more nonprocedural than conventional programming languages. They cannot easily handle applications with extensive procedural logic and updating requirements, such as systems used for optimal production scheduling or tracking daily trades of stocks, bonds, and other securities that require complex processing and often the matching of multiple files. Fourth-generation tools make their greatest contribution to the programming and detail-design aspects of the systems development process but have little impact on other system-building activities.

Management Benefits and Problems

Without question, end-user development provides many benefits to organizations. These include the following:

○ *Improved requirements determination* as users specify their own business needs.

○ *Increased user involvement and satisfaction.* As users develop their systems themselves and control the system development process, they are more likely to use the system.

○ *Reduced application backlog* when users are no longer totally reliant on overburdened professional information systems specialists.

At the same time, end-user computing poses organizational risks because it occurs outside of traditional mechanisms for information system management and control. Most organizations have not yet developed strategies to ensure that end-user-developed applications meet organizational objectives or meet quality assurance standards appropriate to their function. When systems are created rapidly, without a formal development methodology, testing and documentation may be inadequate.

Control over data can be lost in systems outside the traditional information systems department. When users create their own applications and files, it becomes increasingly

Emboss Technologies, which provides outsourcing services, leading-edge software products, and consulting for employee benefits and executive compensation programs, developed an early version of an executive compensation system using PowerBuilder as a fourth-generation software tool. This screen lists individual participants in a deferred compensation plan.

difficult to determine where data are located and to ensure that the same piece of information (such as product number or annual earnings) is used consistently throughout the organization (see Chapters 8 and 9).

Managing End-User Development

How can organizations maximize the benefits of end-user applications development while keeping it under management control? A number of strategies have been suggested.

One way to facilitate and manage end-user application development is to set up an information center. The **information center** is a special facility that provides training and support for end-user computing. Information centers feature hardware, software, and technical specialists that supply end users with tools, training, and expert advice so they can create information system applications on their own. With information center tools, users can create their own computer reports, spreadsheets, or graphics, or extract data for decision making and analysis with minimal technical assistance. Information center consultants are available to instruct users and to assist in the development of more complex applications.

information center A special facility within an organization that provides training and support for end-user computing.

Staff receive training in this computer management class. An important function of information centers is to make end users feel proficient with computers.

Information centers provide many management benefits. They can help end users find tools and applications that will make them more productive. They prevent the creation of redundant applications. They promote data-sharing and minimize integrity problems (see Chapter 8). They ensure that the applications developed by end users meet audit, data quality, and security standards. They can help establish and enforce standards for hardware and software so that end users do not introduce many disparate and incompatible technologies into the firm (Fuller and Swanson, 1992; see Chapter 9). The information center will assist users with only hardware and software that have been approved by management.

In addition to using information centers, managers can pursue other strategies to ensure that end-user computing serves larger organizational goals (see Alavi, Nelson, and Weiss, 1987–88; Rockart and Flannery, 1983). Management should control the development of end-user applications by incorporating them into its strategic systems plans. Training and support should consider individual users' attitudes toward computers, educational levels, cognitive styles, and receptiveness to change (Harrison and Rainer, 1992). Management should also develop controls on critical end-user development, such as insisting on cost justification of end-user information system projects and establishing hardware, software, and quality standards for user-developed applications.

Outsourcing

If a firm does not want to use its internal resources to build or operate information systems, it can hire an external organization that specializes in providing these services to do the work. The process of turning over an organization's computer center operations, telecommunications networks, or applications development to external vendors is called **outsourcing.** In firms where the cost of the information systems function has risen rapidly, managers are turning to outsourcing to control these costs.

outsourcing The practice of contracting computer center operations, telecommunications networks, or applications development to external vendors.

Outsourcing has become popular because some organizations perceive it as a cost-effective measure that eliminates the need for maintaining their own computer center and information systems staff. The provider of outsourcing services benefits from economies of scale (the same knowledge, skills, and capacity can be shared with many different customers) and is likely to charge competitive prices for information systems services. Outsourcing allows a company with fluctuating needs for computer processing to pay for only what it uses rather than to build its own computer center, which would be underutilized when there is no peak load.

Some firms outsource because their internal information systems staff cannot keep pace with technological change or innovative business practices or because they want to free up scarce and costly talent for activities with higher payback. By outsourcing, companies hope to exploit the benefits of information technology in key business processes and improve the productivity of their information system resources (see the Window on Management).

When to Use Outsourcing

Not all organizations benefit from outsourcing, and the disadvantages of outsourcing can create serious problems for organizations if they are not well understood and managed (Earl, 1996). When a firm allocates the responsibility for developing and operating its information systems to another organization, it can lose control over its information systems function. Outsourcing can be advantageous to the vendor because the client has to accept whatever the vendor does and pay whatever fees the vendor charges. If the organization lacks the expertise to negotiate a sound contract, this dependency eventually could result in high costs or loss of control over technological direction (Lacity, Willcocks, and Feeny, 1996). Trade secrets or proprietary information may leak out to competitors when a firm's information systems are run or developed by outsiders. This could be harmful if a firm allows an outsourcer to develop or to operate applications that give it some type of competitive advantage.

Despite such drawbacks, there are a number of circumstances in which outsourcing application development to an external vendor is advantageous.

○ *To reduce costs or offload some of the work of the information systems department.* Applications such as payroll, for which the firm obtains little competitive advantage from excellence, or travel expense processing, where the predictability of uninterrupted

Window on Management

VISA's Outsourcing Triumph

When information systems management awards a multimillion-dollar outsourcing contract for a highly visible strategic project, and the winner has been underbid by several other companies, management must have good reasons. And the project must prove to be a success. That was precisely the situation when VISA International, Inc. offered a large and critical development project to DMR Consulting of Montreal, Canada.

VISA International's commercial card division, which is based in San Francisco, California, decided it needed to offer VISA's large corporate customers worldwide a way for them to produce reports related to their VISA expenditures. The goal was to enable the customers to easily summarize and analyze all VISA charges through a report that each corporation could customize. A project was established to develop the customizable software system so that it could be distributed to customers. This extra service could be a strategic advantage for VISA.

According to Ronald Prather, vice president of information services at VISA's commercial card division, the company originally planned to develop the system itself. Although VISA's 1000-person IS staff did not have the necessary skills, the intent was for them to learn the technology so they could support the new system after it was in use. However, after the project began, according to Prather, VISA found "We didn't have enough resources to do everything we wanted." Ultimately he decided to outsource the whole project, despite the fact that quality and on-time delivery were critical, because the final product was to be distributed to customers.

Outsourcing was a risky alternative. This was a large, mission-critical project, the kind that most companies want to develop themselves. In addition, studies have shown that almost 25 percent of outsourcing projects are canceled due to high costs and/or poor quality. Nonetheless, Prather proceeded and in the end received about 10 bids on the project. DMR was selected despite the fact that several bids were lower. What were the keys to DMR's successful bid submission? First, DMR's proposal included a complete development project methodology. Prather was informed as to how the project would proceed, how he and his staff would relate to the project, and what kinds of reports would be submitted. In addition, whereas many bids answered request-for-proposal questions with a simple "yes," DMR added a full explanation of how it would accomplish the task. Prather felt comfortable knowing exactly what he was buying and how it would be done. The DMR responses gave him confidence in the quality of its work and in the likelihood of a positive outcome. Also, all the programming was to be done in Quebec City, which saved VISA the expense of supplying DMR's 40 staffers office space. Prather also was pleased to find that the project would have two managers, one each from VISA and DMR. Thus, Prather (who became the VISA project manager) always would know what was happening and be able to ensure a quality product.

The project was a success. VISA maintained control over the project, being able, for example, to review designs before they were implemented. DMR met its schedule, and the project ended on time and within budget. More than 300 large corporations now are using the system. Ultimately, VISA awarded DMR a long-term contract to maintain the system.

To Think About: Do you consider Prather's decision to outsource and his choice to award the project to DMR to have been risky? Do you think you would have done the same in his position? Explain your responses.

Sources: Julia King, "VISA Expands Outsourcing Deal," **Computerworld**, January 26, 1998; and Rochelle Garver, "Strategic Outsourcing: It's Your Move," **Datamation**, February 1998.

---

information systems service is not very important, are strong candidates for outsourcing if the company's objective is to reduce costs or save internal information system resources for more important work. Firms should be more cautious about using outsiders to develop applications such as airline reservations or catalog shopping systems that represent critical business processes. Should these systems fail to operate for a few days or even a few hours, they could close down the business (see Chapter 2).

○ *When the firm's existing information system capabilities are limited, ineffective, or technically inferior.* Some organizations use outsourcers as an easy way to revamp their information systems technology. For instance, they might use an outsourcer to help them make the transition from traditional mainframe-based computing to a distributed client/server computing environment or to acquire expertise in newer technologies such as object-oriented programming, Java, or Web site creation.

○ *To improve the contribution of information technology to business performance.* Organizations are starting to turn more to external vendors to help them develop critical or innovative business applications because these vendors have more expertise in technology, management, and business process reengineering. For instance, Rolls Royce

Aerospace Group uses Electronic Data Systems (EDS) as consultants for systems integration and for business transformation projects relating to time-to-market, customer service, supply chain management, and manufacturing and engineering operations.

○ *To create new sources of revenue and profit.* Companies are starting to enlist external vendors to help them leverage technology-related assets, including information systems applications, infrastructure, operations, and expertise, in the commercial marketplace. External vendors provide the know-how to help companies create, develop, and market new technology-based products and services that can be licensed or sold to other companies. For instance, Swiss Bank Corporation contracted with Perot Systems to help with its infrastructure transformation. Perot created a new division to provide state-of-the-art systems and network services to SBC and other global financial service companies (DiRomualdo and Gurbaxani, 1998).

Organizations need to manage the outsourcer as they would manage their own internal information systems department by setting priorities and guaranteeing that information systems are running smoothly. They should establish criteria for evaluating the outsourcing vendor. Firms should design outsourcing contracts carefully so that the outsourcing services can be adjusted if the nature of the business changes. The firm's relationship with the vendor specified in the outsourcing contract, decision rights, performance measures, and assessment of risks and rewards should be aligned with the strategic intent for outsourcing. The most successful outsourcing projects are ones where a climate of trust exists between both parties, and the outsourcing relationship should be structured to balance good feelings with proper controls (Sabherwal, 1999).

Solution Centers

Outsourcing vendors are adding to their range of services by setting up **solution centers** where teams of experts provide reusable or repeatable processes, models, and architecture solutions to address problems in areas such as Year 2000 remediation or enterprise resource planning (ERP). The centers may be oriented toward a specific industry or technology. For example, Andersen Consulting operates a network of 42 solution centers in 12 countries, which provide expertise in electronic commerce and supply chain management technologies for industries such as utilities and financial services (Violino, 1999).

Table 12.2 compares the advantages and disadvantages of each of the system-building alternatives described in this chapter.

solution center Facility operated by a commercial information technology vendor which provides clients with repeatable or reusable processes, models, and architectures for solving common information system problems.

12.3 System-Building Methodologies and Tools

Various tools and development methodologies have been employed to help system builders document, analyze, design, and implement information systems. A **development methodology** is a collection of methods, one or more for every activity within every phase of a systems development project. Some development methodologies are suited to specific technologies, whereas others reflect different philosophies of systems development. The most widely used methodologies and tools include the traditional structured methodologies, object-oriented software development, computer-aided software engineering (CASE), and software reengineering.

development methodology A collection of methods, one or more for every activity within every phase of a development project.

Structured Methodologies

Structured methodologies have been used to document, analyze, and design information systems since the 1970s and remain an important methodological approach. **Structured** refers to the fact that the techniques are step-by-step, with each step building on the previous one. Structured methodologies are top-down, progressing from the highest, most abstract level to the lowest level of detail—from the general to the specific. For example, the highest level of a top-down description of a human resources system would show the main human resources functions: personnel, benefits, compensation, and Equal Employment Opportunity (EEO). Each of these would be broken down into the next layer. Benefits, for instance, might include pension, employee savings, healthcare, and insurance. Each of these layers in turn would be broken down until the lowest level of detail could be depicted.

structured Refers to the fact that techniques are carefully drawn up, often step-by-step, with each step building on a previous one.

Table 12.2   Comparison of Systems-Development Approaches

Approach	Features	Advantages	Disadvantages
Systems lifecycle	Sequential step-by-step formal process Written specification and approvals Limited role of users	Necessary for large complex systems and projects	Slow and expensive Discourages changes Massive paperwork to manage
Prototyping	Requirements specified dynamically with experimental system Rapid, informal, and iterative process Users continually interact with the prototype	Rapid and inexpensive Useful when requirements uncertain or when end-user interface is very important Promotes user participation	Inappropriate for large, complex systems Can gloss over steps in analysis, documentation, and testing
Application software package	Commercial software eliminates need for internally developed software programs	Design, programming, installation, and maintenance work reduced Can save time and cost when developing common business applications Reduces need for internal information systems resources	May not meet organization's unique requirements May not perform many business functions well Extensive customization raises development costs
End-user development	Systems created by end users using fourth-generation software tools Rapid and informal Minimal role of information systems specialists	Users control systems-building Saves development time and cost Reduces application backlog	Can lead to proliferation of uncontrolled information systems and data Systems do not always meet quality assurance standards
Outsourcing	Systems built and sometimes operated by external vendor	Can reduce or control costs Can produce systems when internal resources not available or technically deficient	Loss of control over the information systems function Dependence on the technical direction and prosperity of external vendors

The traditional structured methodologies are process-oriented rather than data-oriented. Although data descriptions are part of the methods, the methodologies focus on how the data are transformed rather than on the data themselves. These methodologies are largely linear; each phase must be completed before the next one can begin. Structured methodologies include structured analysis, structured design, and the use of flowcharts.

Structured Analysis

Structured analysis is widely used to define system inputs, processes, and outputs. It offers a logical graphic model of information flow, partitioning a system into modules that show manageable levels of detail. It rigorously specifies the processes or transformations that occur within each module and the interfaces that exist between them. Its primary tool is the **data flow diagram (DFD),** a graphic representation of a system's component processes and the interfaces (flow of data) between them.

Figure 12-6 shows a simple data flow diagram for a mail-in university course registration system. The rounded boxes represent processes, which portray the transformation of data. The square box represents an external entity, which is an originator or receiver of information located outside the boundaries of the system being modeled. The open rectangles represent data stores, which are either manual or automated inventories of data. The arrows represent data flows, which show the movement between processes, external entities, and data stores. They always contain packets of data with the name or content of each data flow listed beside the arrow.

structured analysis A method for defining system inputs, processes, and outputs and for partitioning systems into subsystems or modules that show a logical graphic model of information flow.

data flow diagram (DFD) A primary tool in structured analysis that graphically illustrates the system's component processes and the flow of data between them.

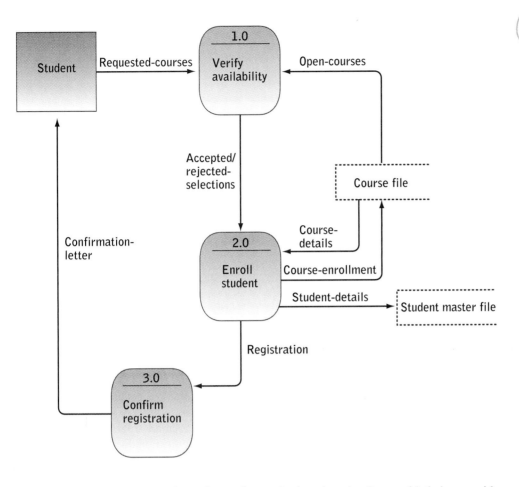

Figure 12-6 Data flow diagram for mail-in university registration system. The system has three processes: Verify availability (1.0), Enroll student (2.0), and Confirm registration (3.0). The name and content of each of the data flows appear adjacent to each arrow. There is one external entity in this system: the student. There are two data stores: the student master file and the course file.

This data flow diagram shows that students submit registration forms with their name, identification number, and the numbers of the courses they wish to take. In process 1.0 the system verifies that each course selected is still open by referencing the university's course file. The file distinguishes courses that are open from those that have been canceled or filled. Process 1.0 then determines which of the student's selections can be accepted or rejected. Process 2.0 enrolls the student in the courses for which he or she has been accepted. It updates the university's course file with the student's name and identification number and recalculates the class size. If maximum enrollment has been reached, the course number is flagged as closed. Process 2.0 also updates the university's student master file with information about new students or changes in address. Process 3.0 then sends each student applicant a confirmation-of-registration letter listing the courses for which he or she is registered and noting the course selections that could not be fulfilled.

The diagrams can be used to depict higher level processes as well as lower level details. Through leveled data flow diagrams, a complex process can be broken down into successive levels of detail. An entire system can be divided into subsystems with a high-level data flow diagram. Each subsystem, in turn, can be divided into additional subsystems with second-level data flow diagrams, and the lower level subsystems can be broken down again until the lowest level of detail has been reached.

Another tool for structured analysis is a data dictionary, which contains information about individual pieces of data and data groupings within a system (see Chapter 8). The data dictionary defines the contents of data flows and data stores so that system builders understand exactly what pieces of data they contain. **Process specifications** describe the transformation occurring within the lowest level of the data flow diagrams. They express the logic for each process.

process specifications Describes the logic of the processes occurring within the lowest levels of the data flow diagrams.

Structured Design

Structured design encompasses a set of design rules and techniques that promotes program clarity and simplicity, thereby reducing the time and effort required for coding, debugging, and maintenance. The main principle of structured design is that a system should be designed from

structured design Software design discipline, encompassing a set of design rules and techniques for designing a system from the top down in a hierarchical fashion.

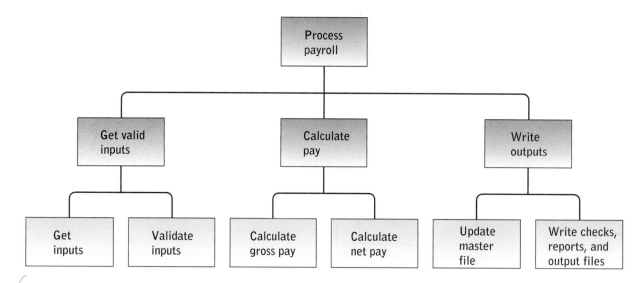

Figure 12-7 High-level structure chart for a payroll system. This structure chart shows the highest or most abstract level of design for a payroll system, providing an overview of the entire system.

the top down in hierarchical fashion and refined to greater levels of detail. The design should first consider the main function of a program or system, then break this function into subfunctions and decompose each subfunction until the lowest level of detail has been reached. The lowest level modules describe the actual processing that will occur. In this manner all high-level logic and the design model are developed before detailed program code is written. If structured analysis has been performed, the structured specification document can serve as input to the design process. Our earlier human resources top-down description provides a good overview example of structured design.

As the design is formulated, it is documented in a structure chart. The **structure chart** is a top-down chart, showing each level of design, its relationship to other levels, and its place in the overall design structure. Figure 12-7 shows a high level structure chart for a payroll system. If a design has too many levels to fit onto one structure chart, it can be broken down further on more detailed structure charts. A structure chart may document one program, one system (a set of programs), or part of one program.

Structured Programming

Structured programming extends the principles governing structured design to the writing of programs to make software programs easier to understand and modify. It is based on the principle of modularization, which follows from top-down analysis and design. Each of the boxes in the structure chart represents a component **module** that is usually directly related to a bottom-level design module. It constitutes a logical unit that performs one or several functions. Ideally, modules should be independent of each other and should have only one entry to and exit from their parent modules. They should share data with as few other modules as possible. Each module should be kept to a manageable size. An individual should be able to read and understand the program code for the module and easily keep track of its functions.

Proponents of structured programming have shown that any program can be written using three basic control constructs, or instruction patterns: (1) simple sequence, (2) selection, and (3) iteration. These control constructs are illustrated in Figure 12-8.

The **sequence construct** executes statements in the order in which they appear, with control passing unconditionally from one statement to the next. The program will execute statement A and then statement B.

The **selection construct** tests a condition and executes one of two alternative instructions based on the results of the test. Condition R is tested. If R is true, statement C is executed. If R is false, statement D is executed. Control then passes to the next statement.

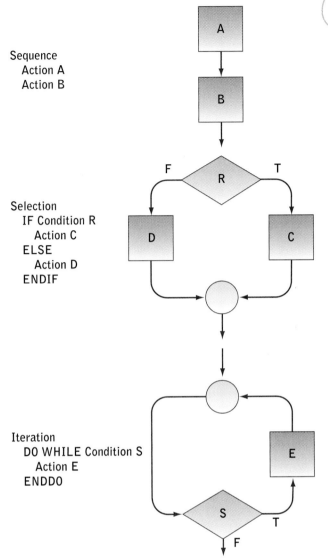

Sequence
   Action A
   Action B

Selection
   IF Condition R
      Action C
   ELSE
      Action D
   ENDIF

Iteration
   DO WHILE Condition S
      Action E
   ENDDO

Figure 12-8 Basic control constructs. The three basic control constructs used in structured programming are sequence, selection, and iteration.

The **iteration construct** repeats a segment of code as long as a conditional test remains true. Condition S is tested. If S is true, statement E is executed and control returns to the test of S. If S is false, E is skipped and control passes to the next statement.

Flowcharts

Flowcharting is an old design tool that is still in use. **System flowcharts** detail the flow of data throughout an entire information system. Program flowcharts describe the processes taking place within an individual program in the system and the sequence in which they must be executed. Flowcharting is no longer recommended for program design because it does not provide top-down modular structure as effectively as other techniques. However, system flowcharts still may be used to document physical design specifications because they can show all inputs, major files, processing, and outputs for a system, and they can document manual procedures.

Using specialized symbols and flow lines, the system flowchart traces the flow of information and work in a system, the sequence of processing steps, and the physical media on which data are input, output, and stored. Figure 12-9 shows some of the basic symbols for system flowcharting. The plain rectangle is a general symbol. Flow lines show the

iteration construct The logic pattern in programming where certain actions are repeated while a specified condition occurs or until a certain condition is met.

system flowchart A graphic design tool that depicts the physical media and sequence of processing steps used in an entire information system.

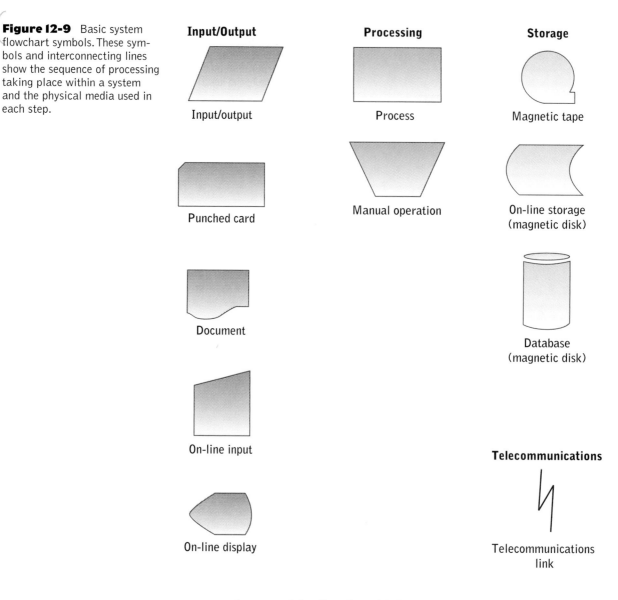

Figure 12-9 Basic system flowchart symbols. These symbols and interconnecting lines show the sequence of processing taking place within a system and the physical media used in each step.

Input/Output

Input/output

Punched card

Document

On-line input

On-line display

Processing

Process

Manual operation

Storage

Magnetic tape

On-line storage (magnetic disk)

Database (magnetic disk)

Telecommunications

Telecommunications link

sequence of steps and the direction of information flow. Arrows are employed to show direction if it is not apparent in the diagram. Figure 12-10 illustrates a high-level system flowchart for a payroll system.

Limitations of Traditional Methods

Although traditional methods are valuable, they can be inflexible and time-consuming. Completion of structured analysis is required before design can begin, and programming must await the completed deliverables from design. A change in specifications requires that first the analysis documents and then the design documents must be modified before the programs can be changed to reflect the new requirement. Structured methodologies are function-oriented, focusing on the processes that transform the data. Yet business management has come to understand that most information systems must be data-oriented. Consequently, system builders are turning to object-oriented software development, computer-aided software engineering (CASE), and software reengineering to deal with these issues.

Object-Oriented Software Development

In Chapter 7 we explained that object-oriented programming combines data and the specific procedures that operate on those data into one object. Object-oriented programming is part of a larger approach to systems development called *object-oriented software development.*

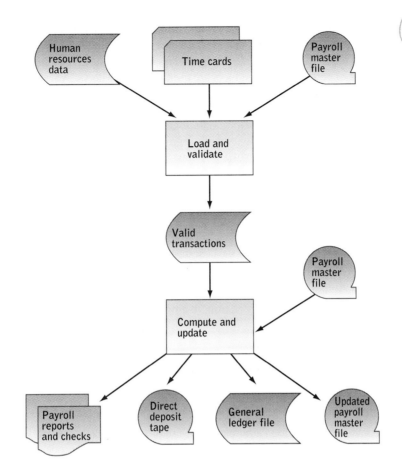

Figure 12-10 System flow-chart for a payroll system. This is a high-level system flowchart for a batch payroll system. Only the most important processes and files are illustrated. Data are input from two sources: time cards and payroll-related data (such as salary increases) passed from the human resources system. The data are first edited and validated against the existing payroll master file before the payroll master is updated. The update process produces an updated payroll master file, various payroll reports (such as the payroll register and hours register), checks, a direct deposit tape, and a file of payment data that must be passed to the organization's general ledger system. The direct deposit tape is sent to the automated clearinghouse that serves the banks offering direct deposit services to employees.

Object-oriented software development differs from traditional methodologies by shifting the focus from separately modeling business processes and data to combining data and procedures into unified objects. The system is viewed as a collection of classes and objects and includes the relationships among them. The objects are defined, programmed, documented, and saved as building blocks for future applications.

Objects are easily reusable, so object-oriented software development directly addresses the issue of reusability and is expected to reduce the time and cost of writing software. Of course, no organization will see savings from reusability until it builds up a library of objects to draw on and understands which objects have broad use (Pancake, 1995). In theory, design and programming can begin as soon as requirements are completed through the use of iterations of rapid prototyping. Object-oriented frameworks have been developed to provide reusable semicomplete applications that can be further customized by the organization into finished applications (Fayad and Schmidt, 1997).

Although the demand for training in object-oriented techniques and programming tools is exploding, object-oriented software development is still in its infancy (Fayad and Tsai, 1995). No agreed-on object-oriented development methodology exists. Information systems specialists must learn a completely new way of modeling a system. Conversion to an object-oriented approach may require large-scale organizational investments, which management must balance against the anticipated payoffs.

Computer-Aided Software Engineering (CASE)

Computer-aided software engineering (CASE)—sometimes called *computer-aided systems engineering*—is the automation of step-by-step methodologies for software and systems development to reduce the amount of repetitive work the developer needs to do. Its adoption can free the developer for more creative problem-solving tasks. CASE tools also facilitate the creation of clear documentation and the coordination of team development efforts. Team members can

object-oriented software development An approach to software development that deemphasizes procedures and shifts the focus from modeling business processes and data to combining data and procedures to create objects.

computer-aided software engineering (CASE) The automation of step-by-step methodologies for software and systems development to reduce the amount of repetitive work the developer needs to do.

share their work easily by accessing each other's files to review or modify what has been done. Some studies have found that systems developed with CASE and the newer methodologies are more reliable, and they require repairs less often (Dekleva, 1992). Modest productivity benefits can also be achieved if the tools are used properly. Many CASE tools are PC-based, with powerful graphical capabilities.

CASE tools provide automated graphics facilities for producing charts and diagrams, screen and report generators, data dictionaries, extensive reporting facilities, analysis and checking tools, code generators, and documentation generators. Most CASE tools are based on one or more of the popular structured methodologies. Some are starting to support object-oriented development. In general, CASE tools try to increase productivity and quality by doing the following:

- Enforce a standard development methodology and design discipline.
- Improve communication between users and technical specialists.
- Organize and correlate design components and provide rapid access to them via a design repository.
- Automate tedious and error-prone portions of analysis and design.
- Automate code generation, testing, and control rollout.

CASE Tools

Many CASE tools have been classified in terms of whether they support activities at the front end or the back end of the systems development process. Front-end CASE tools focus on capturing analysis and design information in the early stages of systems development, whereas back-end CASE tools address coding, testing, and maintenance activities. Back-end tools help convert specifications automatically into program code.

CASE tools automatically tie data elements to the processes where they are used. If a data flow diagram is changed from one process to another, the elements in the data dictionary would be altered automatically to reflect the change in the diagram. CASE tools also contain features for validating design diagrams and specifications. CASE tools thus support iterative design by automating revisions and changes and providing prototyping facilities.

A CASE information repository stores all the information defined by the analysts during the project. The repository includes data flow diagrams, structure charts, entity-relationship diagrams, data definitions, process specifications, screen and report formats, notes and comments, and test results.

CASE tools now have features to support client/server applications, object-oriented programming, and business process redesign. Methodologies and tool sets are being created to leverage organizational knowledge of business process reengineering (Nissen, 1998). Figure 12-11 illustrates the use of Scitor's Process 98, a flowcharting and process-analysis tool that lets developers diagram business processes with information such as resource requirements, costs, efficiencies, and delays. Developers can use this tool to visualize how processes are affected by internal and external factors.

The Challenge of Using CASE

To be used effectively, CASE tools require organizational discipline. Every member of a development project must adhere to a common set of naming conventions, standards, and development methodology. The best CASE tools enforce common methods and standards, which may discourage their use in situations where organizational discipline is lacking.

CASE is not a magic cure-all. It does not enable systems to be designed automatically or ensure that business requirements are met. Systems designers still have to understand what a firm's business needs are and how the business works. Systems analysis and design still depend on the analytical skills of the analyst/designer.

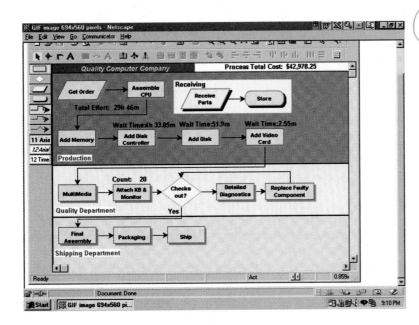

Figure 12-11 Scitor's Process 98 provides tools to map out business processes and to simulate the processes in real-time. The process models include time and cost information.

Rapid Application Development (RAD)

Using CASE tools, reusable software, object-oriented software tools, prototyping, and fourth-generation tools is helping system builders create working systems much more rapidly than they could using traditional structured approaches. The term **rapid application development (RAD)** is used to describe this process of creating workable systems in a very short period of time. RAD can include the use of visual programming and other tools for building graphical user interfaces, iterative prototyping of key system elements, the automation of program code generation, and close teamwork among end users and information systems specialists. Simple systems often can be assembled from prebuilt components. The process does not have to be sequential, and key parts of development can occur simultaneously.

The Window on Organizations shows some of the benefits of using rapid application development. In this instance, Gulf Canada Resources was able to use an object-oriented application development tool to create a budgeting system in only a few months.

Sometimes a technique called **JAD (joint application design)** is used to accelerate the generation of information requirements and to develop the initial systems design. JAD brings end users and information systems specialists together in an interactive session to discuss the design of the system. Properly prepared and facilitated, JAD sessions can significantly speed the design phase while involving users at an intense level.

Software Reengineering

Software reengineering is a methodology that addresses the problem of aging software. A great deal of the software that organizations use was written without the benefit of a methodology such as structured analysis, design, and programming. Such software is difficult to maintain or update. However, the software serves the organization well enough to continue to be used, if only it could be more easily maintained. The purpose of software reengineering is to salvage such software by upgrading it so that users can avoid a long and expensive replacement project. In essence, developers use reengineering to extract design and programming intelligence from existing systems, thereby creating new systems without starting from scratch. Reengineering involves three steps: (1) reverse engineering, (2) revision of design and program specifications, and (3) forward engineering.

rapid application development (RAD) Process for developing systems in a very short time period by using prototyping, fourth-generation tools, and close teamwork among users and systems specialists.

joint application design (JAD) Process to accelerate the generation of information requirements by having end users and information systems specialists work together in intensive interactive design sessions.

software reengineering A methodology that addresses the problem of aging software by salvaging and upgrading it so that the users can avoid a long and expensive replacement project.

Gulf Canada Refines Budgeting with Object-Oriented Software

How can a company control its cash flow when its estimates differ greatly from its actual expenditures? If that company is Gulf Canada Resources Ltd., it solves the problem by building an object-oriented budgeting system known as Odin, to be run over its corporate intranet.

Gulf Canada is a $4.48 billion oil and natural gas drilling and refining company that is headquartered in Calgary, Alberta. It has a few thousand active drilling sites scattered throughout the vast regions of northwestern Alberta. Traditionally the field foremen managing these sites have compiled and submitted budget forecasts for each site annually. But the foremen were stationed in such remote locations that it was difficult for them to submit their estimates directly. Instead, they sent their estimates to their managers to be passed on to the corporate accountants. Their managers customarily "adjusted" the numbers to conform with their own views. Problems arose because history indicated that the estimates from the foremen, who were at the drilling sites, were much more accurate than the revisions made by managers. Corporate management decided that the site foremen needed a way to submit their estimates directly, a decision that resulted in Gulf Canada's new intranet-based budgeting system.

The timing of the decision to build a new budgeting system created a development problem because there were only three months remaining in the 1997 fiscal year. Management wanted the system ready for the 1998 fiscal year, so IT had to develop it on a crash basis. IT decided to bypass the traditional request-for-proposal process used to purchase a package and chose to develop its own system. The project staff used Cactus object-oriented development tools from Information Builders, Inc. The system uses a Sun Microsystems SPARC3000 server running an Oracle database.

Cactus is an application-development environment useful for business applications that can combine transaction processing, decision support, and batch processing. It provides visual object-based development tools that can create highly reusable components for distributed client/server or Web environments.

Gulf Canada met the deadline, and according to Kevin Rasmussen, applications coordinator, the company now has "an application that allows us to assemble all our corporate production and cost forecasts within our system." Outfitted with Web browsers, the company's field force can forecast costs on a well-by-well basis.

With the existence of the new system, the company no longer needs to rely on an annual cost estimate to compare to annual expenditures. Instead, the new plan is to use the system on a rolling 12-month basis, enabling appropriate staffers regularly to check field-level production figures against cost forecasts. Now, according to Rasmussen, the company can react to expense variances more effectively, adding or removing capital from projects where needed. In addition to the field foremen, employees from the accounting, corporate services, IT, legal, and financial departments are also using the new system. Rasmussen claims that before the system, "The budget cycle was a hellish time, because we had to add everything up from scratch. Now, we're able to run scenarios in a matter of minutes."

To Think About: Why do you think the choice of an object-oriented development tool was critical to this project? What are the technology, organization, and management implications of the move to this new system?

Sources: Hakhi Alakhun El, "Content by Committee," *Information Week*, January 12, 1998; and Thomas Hoffman, "Gulf Canada Refines Budgeting," *Computerworld*, January 12, 1998.

---

reverse engineering The process of converting existing programs, files, and database descriptions into corresponding design-level components that can then be used to create new applications.

forward engineering The final step in reengineering when the revised specifications are used to generate new, structured program code for a structured and maintainable system.

Reverse engineering entails extracting the underlying business specifications from existing systems. Older, nonstructured systems do not have structured documentation of the business functions the system is intended to support. Nor do they have adequate documentation of either the system design or the programs. Reverse engineering tools read and analyze the program's existing code, file, and database descriptions and produce structured documentation of the system. The output shows design-level components, such as entities, attributes, and processes. With structured documentation to work from, the project team can then revise the design and specifications to meet current business requirements. In the final step, **forward engineering,** the revised specifications are used to generate new, structured code for a structured, and now maintainable, system. In Figure 12-12, you can follow the reengineering process.

Although software reengineering can reduce system development and maintenance costs, it is a very complex undertaking. Additional research and analysis are usually required to determine all of the business rules and data requirements for the new system (Aiken, Muntz, and Richards, 1994).

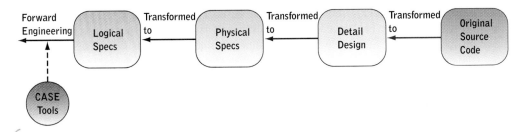

Figure 12-12 The reverse engineering process. Reverse engineering captures an existing system's functional capabilities and processing logic in a simplified form that can be revised and updated as the basis of a new replacement system. CASE tools can be used during forward engineering.

Management Wrap-Up

Selection of a systems-building approach can have a large impact on the time, cost, and end product of systems development. Managers should be aware of the strengths and weaknesses of each systems-building approach and the types of problems for which each is best suited.

Management

Organizational needs should drive the selection of a systems-building approach. The impact of application software packages and of outsourcing should be carefully evaluated before they are selected because these approaches give organizations less control over the systems-building process.

Organization

Various tools and methodologies are available to support the systems-building process. Key technology decisions should be based on the organization's familiarity with the methodology or technology and its compatibility with the organization's information requirements and information architecture. Organizational discipline is required to use these technologies effectively.

Technology

For Discussion

1. Why is selecting a systems development approach an important business decision? Who should participate in the selection process?

2. Some have said that the best way to reduce system development costs is to use application software packages or fourth-generation tools. Do you agree? Why or why not?

Summary

1. Appraise system-building alternatives: the traditional systems lifecycle, prototyping, application software packages, end-user development, and outsourcing. The traditional systems lifecycle—the oldest method for building systems—breaks the development of an information system into six formal stages: (1) project definition, (2) systems study, (3) design, (4) programming, (5) installation, and (6) post-implementation. The stages must proceed sequentially and have defined outputs; each requires formal approval before the next stage can commence.

Prototyping consists of building an experimental system rapidly and inexpensively for end users to interact with and evaluate. The prototype is refined and enhanced until users are

satisfied that it includes all of their requirements and can be used as a template to create the final system.

Developing an information system using an application software package eliminates the need for writing software programs when developing an information system. Using a software package cuts down on the amount of design, testing, installation, and maintenance work required to build a system.

End-user development is the development of information systems by end users, either alone or with minimal assistance from information systems specialists. End-user-developed systems can be created rapidly and informally using fourth-generation software tools.

Outsourcing consists of using an external vendor to build (or operate) a firm's information systems. The system may be custom-built or may use a software package. In either case, the work is done by the vendor rather than by the organization's internal information systems staff.

2. Compare the strengths and limitations of each approach. The traditional system lifecycle is still useful for large projects that need formal specifications and tight management control over each stage of system-building. However, the traditional method is very rigid and costly for developing a system and is not well suited for unstructured, decision-oriented applications where requirements cannot be immediately visualized.

Prototyping encourages end-user involvement in systems development and iteration of design until specifications are captured accurately. The rapid creation of prototypes can result in systems that have not been completely tested or documented or that are technically inadequate for a production environment.

Application software packages are helpful if a firm does not have the internal information systems staff or financial resources to custom-develop a system. To meet an organization's unique requirements, packages may require extensive modifications that can substantially raise development costs. A package may not be a feasible solution if implementation necessitates extensive customization and changes in the organization's procedures.

The primary benefits of end-user development are improved requirements determination, reduced application backlog, and increased end-user participation in, and control of, the systems development process. However, end-user development, in conjunction with distributed computing, has introduced new organizational risks by propagating information systems and data resources that do not necessarily meet quality assurance standards and that are not easily controlled by traditional means.

Outsourcing can save application development costs or allow firms to develop applications without an internal information systems staff; however, firms risk losing control over their information systems and becoming too dependent on external vendors.

3. Assess the solutions to the management problems created by these approaches. Organizations can overcome some of the limitations of using software packages by performing a thorough requirements analysis and using rigorous package selection procedures to determine the extent to which a package will satisfy their requirements. The organization can customize the package or modify its procedures to ensure a better fit with the package.

Information centers help promote and control end-user development. They provide end users with appropriate hardware, software, and technical expertise to create their own applications and encourage adherence to application development standards. Organizations can also develop new policies and procedures concerning system development standards, training, data administration, and controls to manage end-user computing effectively.

Organizations can benefit from outsourcing by only outsourcing part of their information systems, by thoroughly understanding which information systems functions are appropriate to outsource, by designing outsourcing contracts carefully, and by trying to build a working partnership with the outsourcing vendor.

4. Describe the principal tools and methodologies used for systems development. Structured analysis highlights the flow of data and the processes through which data are transformed. Its principal tool is the data flow diagram. Structured design and programming are software design disciplines that produce reliable, well-documented software with a simple, clear structure that is easy for others to understand and maintain. System flowcharts are useful for documenting the physical aspects of system design.

Computer-aided software engineering (CASE) automates methodologies for systems development. It promotes standards and improves coordination and consistency during systems development. CASE tools help system builders build a better model of a system and facilitate revision of design specifications to correct errors. Object-oriented software development is expected to reduce the time and cost of writing software and of making maintenance changes because it models a system as a series of reusable objects that combine both data and procedures. Software reengineering helps system builders reconfigure aging software to conform to structured design principles, making it easier to maintain.

Key Terms

Application software package, 374

Computer-aided software engineering (CASE), 389

Customization, 376

Data flow diagram (DFD), 384

Design, 371

Development methodology, 383

End-user development, 377

End-user interface, 374

Forward engineering, 392

Information center, 380

Installation, 372

Iteration construct, 387

Iterative, 373

Joint application design (JAD), 391

Module, 386

Object-oriented software development, 389

Outsourcing, 381

Post-implementation, 372

Process specifications, 385

Programming, 372

Project definition, 371

Prototype, 372

Prototyping, 372

Rapid application development (RAD), 391

Request for Proposal (RFP), 376

Reverse engineering, 392

Selection construct, 386

Sequence construct, 386

Software reengineering, 391

Solution center, 383

Structure chart, 386

Structured, 383

Structured analysis, 384

Structured design, 385

Structured programming, 386

System flowchart, 387

Systems lifecycle, 370

Systems study, 371

Review Questions

1. What is the traditional systems lifecycle? Describe each of its steps.

2. What are the advantages and disadvantages of building an information system using the traditional systems lifecycle?

3. What do we mean by information system prototyping? What are its benefits and limitations?

4. List and describe the steps in the prototyping process.

5. What is an application software package? What are the advantages and disadvantages of developing information systems based on software packages?

6. What do we mean by end-user development? What are its advantages and disadvantages?

7. What is an information center? How can information centers solve some of the management problems created by end-user development?

8. Name some policies and procedures for managing end-user development.

9. What is outsourcing? Under what circumstances should it be used for building information systems?

10. What is structured analysis? What is the role of the data flow diagram in structured analysis?

11. What are the principles of structured design? How is it related to structured programming?

12. Describe the use of system flowcharts.

13. What is the difference between object-oriented software development and traditional structured methodologies?

14. What is CASE? How can it help system builders?

15. What is rapid application development (RAD)? What system-building tools and methods can be used in RAD?

16. What are software reengineering and reverse engineering? How can they help system builders?

Group Project

With a group of your classmates, obtain product information for two similar PC application software packages. You might compare Dac/Easy Accounting/Payroll and QuickBooks for small business accounting or Quicken and Microsoft Money for personal finance. You can obtain some of this information from the Web and perhaps find demonstration versions of the packages on the vendor Web sites. Evaluate the strengths and limitations of the packages you select. Present your findings to the class.

Tools for Interactive Learning

○ Internet

The Internet Connection for this chapter will direct you to the SAP Web site where you can complete an exercise to evaluate the capabilities of this major multinational software package and learn more about enterprise resource planning. You can also use the Interactive Study Guide to test your knowledge of the topics in this chapter and get instant feedback where you need more practice.

○ CD-ROM

If you purchase and use the Multimedia Edition CD-ROM with this chapter, you can complete two interactive exercises. The first asks you to construct a data flow diagram, and the second asks you to select an appropriate systems development approach for various business scenarios. You can also find a video clip illustrating the use of Lotus Notes as an application development platform, an audio overview of the major themes of this chapter, and bullet text summarizing the key points of the chapter.

SAP A.G., based in Walldorf, Germany, is Europe's largest vendor of software running on IBM mainframe computers and the world's leading enterprise resource planning (ERP) software vendor, commanding 36 percent of this market. Among its clients are E.I. du Pont de Nemours & Company, Chevron Corporation, Apple Computer, IBM, Intel, and the Exxon Corporation.

SAP's R/3 software package for client/server environments automates a wide range of business processes in human resources, plant management, and manufacturing. The software modules are integrated so they can automatically share data between them, and they have their own database-management system. The programs come in 12 different languages. Specific versions are tailored to accommodate different currencies, tax laws, and accounting practices. Managers can generate reports in their own local languages and currencies and have the same reports generated in the language and currency that are used as the corporate standard by top management.

Businesses appreciate the multinational flavor of the software, especially its ability to overcome language and currency barriers and to connect divisions and operating units spread around the world. Marion Merrel Dow Inc. is using SAP software for its financial and sales-and-service departments because it believes that no other available packages can handle its global business needs.

Despite being a standard software package, SAP software can be customized approximately 10 percent to handle multinational currencies and accounting practices. The company has also developed modules of R/3 applications that are further customized for specific industries. An example would be its Apparel Footwear Solution (AFS) for the footware industry which has many variables, such as style, size, and color, that must be integrated into production and distribution processes. SAP makes this flexibility one of its key selling points. As another selling point, SAP promotes the package as a platform for business reengineering and integration of business processes.

R/3 is an integrated, client/server, distributed system with a graphical user interface. It can operate on a wide range of mainframes, minicomputers, and servers and many different operating systems. The R/3 package includes integrated financial accounting, production planning, sales and distribution, cost-center accounting, order-costing, materials management, human resources, quality assurance, fixed assets management, plant maintenance, and project planning applications. Users do not have to shut down one application to move to another; they can click on a menu choice. R/3 also provides word processing, filing systems, e-mail, and other office support functions.

R/3 can be configured to run on a single hardware platform, or it can be partitioned to run on separate machines (in whatever combination users choose) in order to minimize network traffic and place data where users need them the most. For instance, a firm could put the data used most frequently by its accounting department on a server located close to the accounting department to minimize network traffic. A central data dictionary keeps track of data and their location to maintain the integrity of distributed data. SAP will sell clients a blueprint of R/3's information, data, and function models and software tools to facilitate custom development and integration of existing applications into R/3.

SAP has been touted as a software solution that will enable companies to reach new levels of efficiency by integrating all facets of their business. By adopting the system design offered by the package, companies can evaluate and streamline their business processes. The promise of reengineering was what attracted the Eastman Kodak Company to SAP software. Kodak initially installed SAP programs to redefine the job of order taking. The SAP package lets order takers make immediate decisions about granting customers credit and lets them access production data on-line so that they can tell customers exactly when their orders will be available for shipment. The project resulted in a 70 percent reduction in the amount of time it took to deliver products;

response time to customers also was cut in half. These results prompted Kodak to use SAP software as the global architecture for all of its core systems.

The intricate and sophisticated features of SAP software deeply affect the infrastructure of a corporation. Installing SAP's fully integrated suite of software modules with all the business alterations required is a complex process with many interdependent options, which can overwhelm smaller firms lacking the resources of top-tier large corporations. Forrester Research, in Cambridge, Massachusetts, estimated that for every dollar spent on SAP R/3 software, five more must be spent on training and systems integration.

Owens-Corning Fiberglass Corporation adopted R/3 as an engine for broad company overhaul. Until recently, customers had to call an Owens-Corning shingles plant for a load of shingles and place additional calls to order insulation or siding. Each plant had its own product lines, pricing schedules, and trucking carriers. Factories limped along with antiquated PCs. The company operated like a collection of autonomous fiefdoms.

R/3 demanded that the corporation adopt a single product list and a single price list. Staff members initially resisted. The company grossly underestimated the cost of installing the system and of training employees to use the new system. (Actual training costs were expected to reach 13 percent, compared with initial estimates of 6 percent.) For example, when the system was installed, order-entry transactions took ten times longer to process than they had before. It took several weeks of research and the use of a special software tool to track transactions through a network to diagnose and fix the problem.

On the other hand, Owens-Corning expected R/3 to save the company $18 million in 1997 and $50 million in 1998 by streamlining business processes and eliminating jobs. Factory-floor employees would be able to use R/3 to confirm shipments of insulation or roofing shingles as the products left the plant. The shipping information would automatically update the general ledger. But if someone made a mistake and did not catch it right away,

R/3's internal logic would force the company's finance staff to hunt for that transaction to balance the books.

SAP has a large internal staff to support its software packages, but it also uses legions of consultants from large consulting firms such as Andersen Consulting, EDS Corporation, and Pricewaterhouse Coopers, as well as smaller consulting firms. These external consultants work with SAP clients to install the SAP packages. SAP is growing so fast that there is a worldwide shortage of SAP experts with experience implementing R/3.

One reason for the shortage of consultants is that it can take years for even experienced technologists to understand all of the complexities and methodologies of SAP software. It takes about three years, or two or three installations of the package, before a consultant becomes an expert in the software. (R/3 was built with SAP's own internally developed programming language called Abap. Users must work with Abap to modify or extend the SAP software package.) SAP pairs one or more of its seasoned eight- to ten-year German veterans with less-experienced U.S. consultants at each installation. However, the SAP experts tend to be troubleshooters or product experts, rather than business consultants, so clients do not necessarily get the best advice on how to integrate the software into their business operations efficiently and painlessly. The perception remains among some U.S. companies that even an on-site SAP expert who knows the financial accounting module cannot correct a problem in the sales and distribution module.

It may take years and millions of dollars to install SAP, making the package more appropriate for very large corporations than for smaller companies. Competing ERP packages such as those offered by PeopleSoft and Baan are considered more flexible and user-friendly, with installations that might cost half the price of SAP per 1000 users. SAP's package also lacks strong capabilities to link the enterprise to external customers and suppliers, leading companies to turn to packages from Manugistics and i2 Technologies for supply-chain management functions.

SAP's lack of flexibility and complexity have created serious problems for some companies. FoxMeyer Health Corporation filed a $500 million lawsuit against SAP in the summer of 1998, claiming that the software was totally inappropriate for the wholesale distribution business and could not handle the transaction load and high level of warehouse automation required by its business. Dell Computer found that the system was incompatible with its new decentralized management model. Companies such as Applied Materials and Mobil Europe have also cancelled their SAP implementations midstream after running into difficulties.

SAP recently introduced Accelerated SAP (ASAP), a program that promises to cut implementation time by as much as half. ASAP provides tools, templates, and questionnaires for companies to create a step-by-step road map that lets users clearly define each task. The templates incorporate "best practices" that show how things are done and help users figure out where to begin. To make installations easier, SAP has broken down the R/3 system into independent modules that can be installed one at a time and it has created a more user-friendly interface for the software.

Sources: Stephan Herrera, "Paradise Lost," **Forbes**, February 8, 1999; Deborah Ashbrand, "Peering Across the Abyss: Clothing and Shoe Companies Cross the ERP Chasm," **Datamation**, January 1999; Randy Weston, "Users Gravitate to 'Broken' Software," **Computerworld**, February 23, 1998; "This German Software Is Complex, Expensive—and Wildly Popular," **The Wall Street Journal**, March 4, 1997; and Tom Stein, "Fast Deployment," **InformationWeek**, February 3, 1997.

CASE STUDY QUESTIONS

1. What advantages and disadvantages of application software packages are illustrated by SAP?

2. Analyze the specific strengths and weaknesses of the SAP software package.

3. If you were the manager of a corporation looking for enterprise application software, would you choose SAP? Would you choose another package? Why or why not? What management, organization, and technology factors would you consider?

Chapter 13

System Success and Failure: Implementation

Learning Objectives

After completing this chapter, you will be able to:

1. Identify major problem areas in information systems.

2. Assess whether a system is successful.

3. Analyze the principal causes of information system failure.

4. Analyze the relationship between the implementation process and system outcome.

5. Select appropriate strategies to manage the implementation process.

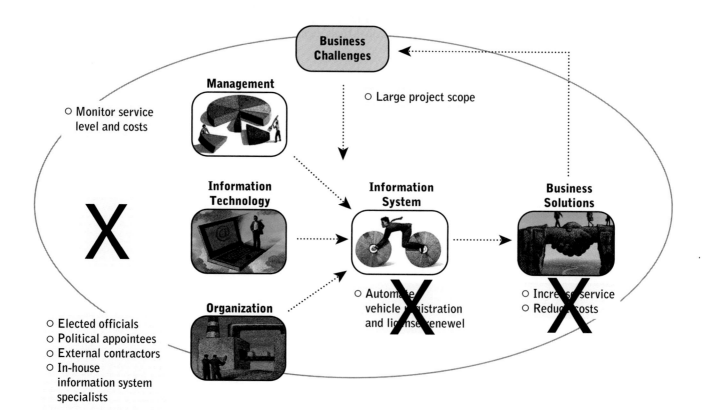

Lights Go Out for Washington State's LAMP Project

In 1990, the Washington State Department of Licensing launched a License Application Mitigation Project (LAMP) budgeted at $41.8 million to automate the state's vehicle registration and license renewal processes. The department's in-house information systems specialists and a private contractor were in charge of the system design, and a group of elected officials and political appointees provided oversight.

From its inception, the project suffered from poor coordination, conflicting agendas, and numerous delays. The system builders' work was poorly coordinated. Legislators passed new licensing and registration laws, diverted funds allocated to LAMP to the construction of an off-ramp at a racetrack, and changed

the scope of the project, causing additional delays. Three years later, projected costs had swelled to $51 million. State legislators eventually learned that when completed, the new system would cost $4.2 million more per year to operate than existing systems and would be too big and obsolete. In 1997, after seven years and $40 million had been wasted, they cancelled the entire effort.

The Washington State Department of Licensing is not alone. Although management of software projects is improving, it is estimated that cost overruns and project failures amounted to nearly $100 billion in 1998 alone. Large, complex projects such as LAMP are more likely to fail than smaller, simpler projects. The Standish Group in Dennis, Massachusetts, found that 49 percent of very large projects costing over $10 million were cancelled before completion, and 51 percent were completed but were over budget, behind schedule, and unable to deliver all of the features and functions that were originally planned.

Sources: Tom Field, "Lights Out on LAMP," *CIO Magazine,* December 1, 1998; and Rick Whiting, "Development in Disarray," *Software Magazine,* September 1998.

chapter outline

There is a very high failure rate among information systems projects. In nearly every organization, information systems projects take much more time and money to implement than originally anticipated, or the completed system does not work properly. Some of these problems are caused by information system technology, but many can be attributed to managerial and organizational factors. Implementing an information system is a process of organizational change, and you should be aware of the following management challenges:

1. **Dealing with the complexity of large-scale systems projects.** Large-scale systems that affect large numbers of organizational units and staff members and that have extensive information requirements are difficult to oversee, coordinate, and plan for. Implementing such systems, which have multiyear development periods, is especially problem-ridden because the systems are so complex.

2. **Estimating the time and cost to implement a successful large information system.** There are few reliable techniques for estimating the time and cost to develop medium- to large-scale information systems. Few projects take into account the long-term maintenance costs of systems. Guidelines presented in this chapter are helpful but cannot guarantee that a large information system project can be precisely planned with accurate cost figures.

When information systems fail to work properly or cost too much to develop, companies may not realize any benefits from their information system investment, and the system may not be able to solve the problems for which it was intended. Because so many information systems are trouble-ridden, designers, builders, and users of information systems should understand how and why they succeed or fail. This chapter explores the managerial, organizational, and technological factors responsible for information system success and failure and examines the process of system implementation.

13.1 Information System Failure

As many as 75 percent of all large systems may be considered to be operating failures. Although these systems are in production, they take so much extra time and money to implement or are so functionally deficient that businesses can't reap the expected benefits. A recent study by Standish Group International Inc. found that 28 percent of all corporate software development projects are canceled before completion and 46 percent are behind schedule or over budget (Whiting, 1998).

system failure An information system that either does not perform as expected, is not operational at a specified time, or cannot be used in the way it was intended.

Many information **system "failures"** are not necessarily falling apart, but either they clearly are not used in the way they were intended, or they are not used at all. Users often have to develop parallel manual procedures to make these systems work properly.

In some systems, nearly all reports put out for management are never read. They are considered worthless and full of figures of no consequence for decision making or analysis. For instance, managers in a prominent commercial bank with branches throughout the United States and Europe found its batch loan account system virtually useless. Pages of reports were filled with zeros, making it practically impossible to assess the status of a client's loan. The amount of the loan, the outstanding balance, and the repayment schedule had to be tracked manually.

Other automated systems go untouched because they are either too difficult to use or because their data cannot be trusted. Users continue to maintain their records manually. For

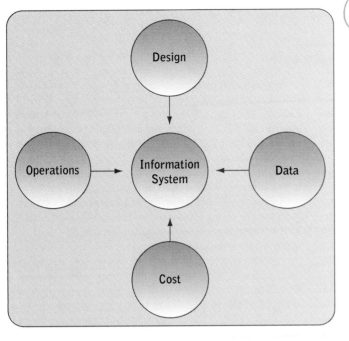

Figure 13-1 Information system problem areas. Problems with an information system's design, data, cost, or operations can be evidence of a system failure.

example, the employee benefits department of a multiunit manufacturing concern continues to maintain all the benefits data for the company's 20,000 employees manually, despite the presence of an automated, on-line system for pension and life insurance benefits. Users complain that the data in the system are unreliable because they do not capture the prior benefits plan data for employees from acquisitions and because payroll earnings figures are out of date. All pension calculations, preretirement estimates, and benefits analysis must be handled manually.

Still other systems flounder because of processing delays, excessive operational costs, or chronic production problems. For instance, the batch accounts receivable system of a medium-size consumer products manufacturer was constantly breaking down. Production runs were aborting several times a month, and major month-end runs were close to three weeks behind schedule. Because of excessive reruns, schedule delays, and time devoted to fixing antiquated programs, the information systems staff had no time to work out long-term solutions or convert to an on-line system.

In all of these cases, the information systems in question must be judged failures. Why do system failures occur?

Information System Problem Areas

The problems causing information system failure fall into multiple categories, as illustrated by Figure 13-1. The major problem areas are design, data, cost, and operations. These problems can be attributed not only to technical features of information systems but to nontechnical sources as well. In fact, most of these problems and risks of system failure stem from organizational factors (Keil, Cule, Lyytinen, and Schmidt, 1998).

Design
The actual design of the system fails to capture essential business requirements or improve organizational performance. Information may not be provided quickly enough to be helpful; it may be in a format that is impossible to digest and use; or it may represent the wrong pieces of data.

The way in which nontechnical business users must interact with the system may be excessively complicated and discouraging (see the Window on Organizations). A system may be designed with a poor **user interface.** The user interface is the part of the system with which end users interact. For example, an input form or an on-line screen may be so poorly arranged that no one wants to submit data. The procedures to request on-line information retrieval may

user interface The part of the information system through which the end user interacts with the system; type of hardware and the series of on-screen commands and responses required for a user to work with the system.

Facing Up to ERP Software

Enterprise resource planning (ERP) systems are a natural winner for many organizations. After all, they bring important benefits, such as corporate-wide data integration, improved tracking of key business data, and in some cases, year 2000 (Y2K) compliance. So why are many companies complaining? In addition to the technical complexity and massive large-scale organizational change requirements of ERP systems, one must also look at their user interfaces.

Dental equipment maker A-dec, of Newberg, Oregon, found that when it installed Baan Co.'s ERP software, calls to its help desk jumped by 64 percent. "That tells you right there that it's not an intuitive application," explains A-dec's CIO, Keith Gearden. Even worse, company workers discovered the system was including inventory that had already been shipped. The problem turned out to be that after entering the inventory shipment data, warehouse employees needed to go to another screen to confirm the shipment. Incredibly, the software did not prompt them to do that.

When Miami-based Hydro Agri's Canadian fertilizer stores switched to SAP's very popular R/3, order entry time jumped from approximately 20 seconds per order to about 90 seconds, an increase of 450 percent. At 45,000 orders every six weeks, company workers were spending an extra 150 hours each week just to enter the current number of orders. The company had to assign extra staff-power to the task during high-volume times. In addition, company loading dock workers at its warehouses, who had to enter the quantities of products being received or shipped out, found the user interface confusing. The company delayed installing the same software in their U.S. retail outlets.

Eric Schaffer, president of Human Factors International, Inc. of Fairfield, Iowa, believes that the developers of ERP packages have approached things from a system or a management point of view, not from a user point of view. The main objective of the system is to help managers and planners, not the people who are entering the data. To work with the system and input data, users may have to switch back and forth from screen to screen, window to window, wasting many hours.

Solutions are difficult and slow in coming. As with any purchased software, companies are finding they must modify their business procedures to adjust to the new ERP system, which is a time-consuming process that often requires extensive worker retraining. Education on the new software sometimes begins as early as four months prior to its going into production. In many cases, such as at Hydro Agri, companies are writing their own interfaces to simplify data entry.

Happily, some ERP software manufacturers are beginning to address the issue—SAP, PeopleSoft, and Baan have simplified their user interfaces. The new SAP interface for its R/3 ERP applications can be personalized so that each individual, such as a salesperson, only sees those screens most relevant to his or her job. Instead of drilling through four screens to complete a transaction, users can complete their work on a single screen.

To Think About: Given the problems poorly designed user interfaces can cause, discuss whether or not such systems are worth installing. What steps might companies take to reduce these problems early in a development project?

Sources: Tom Stein, "SAP Puts New Face on R/3 Apps," *Information Week,* March 22, 1999; Craig Stedman, "ERP User Interfaces Drive Workers Nuts," *Computerworld,* November 2, 1998; http://www2.baan.com/cgi-bin/bvisapi.dll; and http://www.peoplesoft.com/.

A well-designed user interface can make a system easy to use, whereas one that is cluttered will add to users' frustrations. American Airlines redesigned its Web pages to make its Web site more inviting.

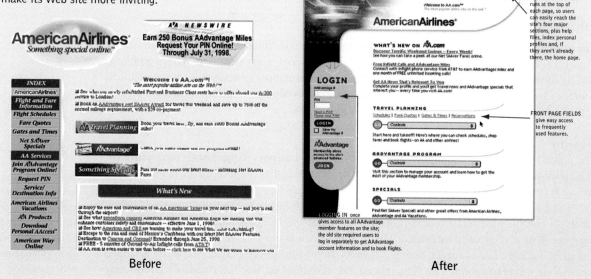

Before   After

be so unintelligible that users are too frustrated to make requests. A graphical user interface that is supposed to be intuitively easy to learn may discourage use because display screens are cluttered and poorly arranged or because users don't understand the meaning and function of the icons.

An information system will be judged a failure if its design is not compatible with the structure, culture, and goals of the organization as a whole. Historically, information system design has been preoccupied with technical issues at the expense of organizational concerns. The result has often been information systems that are technically excellent but incompatible with their organization's structure, culture, and goals. Without a close organizational fit, such systems have created tensions, instability, and conflict.

Data

The data in the system have a high level of inaccuracy or inconsistency. The information in certain fields may be erroneous or ambiguous; or they may not be broken out properly for business purposes. Information required for a specific business function may be inaccessible because the data are incomplete.

Cost

Some systems operate quite smoothly, but their cost to implement and run on a production basis is way over budget. Other systems may be too costly to compete. In both cases, the excessive expenditures cannot be justified by the demonstrated business value of the information they provide.

Operations

The system does not run well. Information is not provided in a timely and efficient manner because the computer operations that handle information processing break down. Jobs that abort too often lead to excessive reruns and delayed or missed schedules for delivery of information. An on-line system may be operationally inadequate because the response time is too long.

Measuring System Success

How can we tell whether a system is successful? This is not always an easy question to answer. Not everyone may agree about the value or effectiveness of a particular information system. Individuals with different decision-making styles or ways of approaching a problem may have totally different opinions about the same system. To further complicate the picture, what users say they like or want in a new information system may not necessarily produce any meaningful improvements in organizational performance (Markus and Keil, 1994).

Nevertheless, MIS researchers have looked for a formal set of measures for rating systems. Various criteria have been developed, but the following measures of system success, illustrated in Figure 13-2, are considered the most important.

1. *High levels of system use,* as measured by polling users, employing questionnaires, or monitoring parameters such as the volume of on-line transactions.

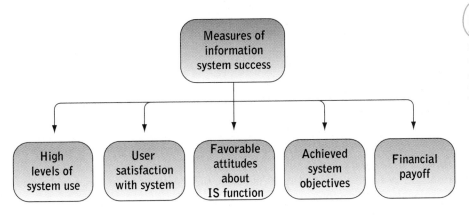

Figure 13-2 Measures of information system success. MIS researchers have different criteria for measuring the success of an information system. They consider the five measures in the figure to be the most important.

2. *User satisfaction with the system,* as measured by questionnaires or interviews. This might include users' opinions on the accuracy, timeliness, and relevance of information; on the quality of service; and perhaps on the schedule of operations. Especially critical are managers' attitudes on how well their information needs were satisfied (Davis, 1989; Ives et al., 1983; Westcott, 1985) and users' opinions about how well the system enhanced their job performance.

3. *Favorable attitudes* of users about information systems and the information systems staff.

4. *Achieved objectives,* the extent to which the system meets its specified goals, as reflected by improved organizational performance and decision making resulting from use of the system.

5. *Financial payoff* to the organization, either by reducing costs or by increasing sales or profits.

The fifth measure is considered to be of limited value even though cost-benefit analysis may have figured heavily in the decision to build a particular system. The benefits of an information system may not be totally quantifiable. Moreover, tangible benefits cannot be easily demonstrated for the more advanced decision-support system applications. And even though cost-benefit methodology has been rigorously pursued, the history of many systems development projects has shown that realistic estimates have always been difficult to formulate. MIS researchers have preferred to concentrate instead on the human and organizational measures of system success such as information quality, system quality, and the impact of systems on organizational performance (Lucas, 1981; DeLone and McLean, 1992).

13.2 Causes of Information System Success and Failure

As described in Chapter 3, systems are developed in the first place because of powerful external environmental forces and equally powerful internal or institutional forces. Many systems fail because of the opposition of either the environment or the internal setting.

As many MIS researchers have pointed out, the introduction or alteration of an information system has a powerful behavioral and organizational impact. It transforms the way various individuals and groups perform and interact. Changes in the way information is defined, accessed, and used to manage the resources of the organization often lead to new distributions of authority and power (Lucas, 1975). This internal organizational change breeds resistance and opposition and can lead to the demise of an otherwise good system. An important characteristic of most information systems is that individuals are asked or required to change their behavior to make the system function.

But there are other reasons why a system may fail. Several studies have found that in organizations with similar environments and institutional features, the same innovation will be successful in some organizations but fail in others (Robey and Sahay, 1996). Why? One explanation focuses on different patterns of implementation.

The Concept of Implementation

implementation All organizational activities working toward the adoption, management, and routinization of an innovation.

Implementation refers to all organizational activities working toward the adoption, management, and routinization of an innovation. Figure 13-3 illustrates the major stages of implementation described in research literature and the major approaches to the subject (see also Tornatsky et al., 1983).

Some of the implementation research focuses on actors and roles. The belief is that organizations should select actors with appropriate social characteristics and systematically develop organizational roles, such as "product champions," to innovate successfully (see Figure 13-4). Generally, this literature focuses on early adoption and management of innovations.

A second school of thought in the implementation literature focuses on strategies of innovation. The two extremes are top-down innovation and grassroot innovation. There are many examples of organizations in which the absence of senior management support for innovation dooms the project from the start. At the same time, without strong grass roots, end-user participation and information system projects can also fail.

APPROACHES	IMPLEMENTATION STAGES		
	Adoption	Management	Routinization
Actors' roles	XXXX	XXXX	
Strategy		XXXX	
Organizational factors		XXXX	XXXX

Figure 13-3 Approaches and implementation stages in the implementation literature. The Xs indicate the stages of implementation on which the different approaches tend to focus. For instance, literature that uses an actor/role approach to implementation tends to focus on the early stages of adoption and management.

A third approach to implementation focuses on general organizational change factors as being decisive to the long-term routinization of innovations. Table 13.1 illustrates some key organizational actions required for long-term, successful implementation, and indicators of success (Yin, 1981). Actions to increase organizational learning and overcome barriers to acquiring new knowledge and practices are also useful (Attewell, 1992).

In the context of implementation, the systems analyst is a **change agent.** The analyst not only develops technical solutions but also redefines the configurations, interactions, job activities, and power relationships of various organizational groups. The analyst is the catalyst for the entire change process and is responsible for ensuring that the changes created by a new system are accepted by all parties involved. The change agent communicates with users, mediates between competing interest groups, and ensures that the organizational adjustment to such changes is complete.

One model of the implementation process is the Kolb/Frohman model of organizational change. This model divides the process of organizational change into a seven-stage relationship between an organizational *consultant* and his or her *client.* (The consultant corresponds to the information system designer and the client to the user.) The success of the change effort is determined by how well the consultant and client deal with the key issues at each stage (Kolb and Frohman, 1970). Other models of implementation describe the relationship as one

change agent In the context of implementation, the individual acting as the catalyst during the change process to ensure successful organizational adaptation to a new system or innovation.

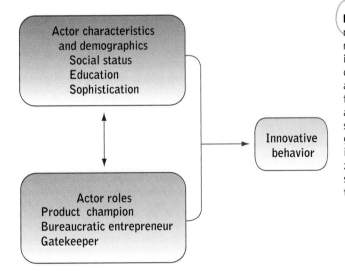

Figure 13-4 Actors in the innovation process. During implementation, the roles of actors include being product champions, bureaucratic entrepreneurs, and gatekeepers. To be successful in their roles as innovators and sponsors of change, actors should have certain demographic characteristics including social status in the organization, higher education, and social, technical, and organizational sophistication.

Table 13.1	**Actions and Indicators for Successful System Implementation**
	Support by local funds
	New organizational arrangements
	Stable supply and maintenance
	New personnel classifications
	Changes in organizational authority
	Internalization of the training program
	Continual updating of the system
	Promotion of key personnel
	Survival of the system after turnover of its originators
	Attainment of widespread use

Source: Yin (1981).

between designers, clients, and decision makers, who are responsible for managing the implementation effort to bridge the gap between design and utilization (Swanson, 1988). Recent work on implementation stresses the need for flexibility and improvisation with organizational actors not limited to rigid prescribed roles (Markus and Benjamin, 1997; Orlikowski and Hofman, 1997).

Causes of Implementation Success and Failure

Implementation research to date has found no single explanation for system success or failure. Nor does it suggest a single formula for system success. However, it has found that implementation outcome can be largely determined by the following factors:

- The role of users in the implementation process
- The degree of management support for the implementation effort
- The level of complexity and risk of the implementation project
- The quality of management of the implementation process

These are largely behavioral and organizational issues and are illustrated in Figure 13-5.

User Involvement and Influence

User involvement in the design and operation of information systems has several positive results. First, if users are heavily involved in systems design, they have more opportunities to mold the system according to their priorities and business requirements and more opportunities to control the outcome. Second, they are more likely to react positively to the completed system because they have been active participants in the change process itself. It is often difficult to get users involved in a development project if they are pressed for time. Even when such involvement is limited, hands-on experience with the system helps users appreciate its benefits and provides useful suggestions for improvement (De and Ferrat, 1998).

Incorporating the user's knowledge and expertise leads to better solutions. However, users often take a very narrow and limited view of the problem to be solved and may overlook important opportunities for improving business processes or innovative ways to apply information technology. The skills and vision of professional system designers are still required much in the same way that the services of an architect are required when building a new house. The outcome would most likely be inferior if people tried to design their houses entirely on their own (Markus and Keil, 1994). The Window on Management shows how the nature of user involvement affected the outcome of a series of system projects.

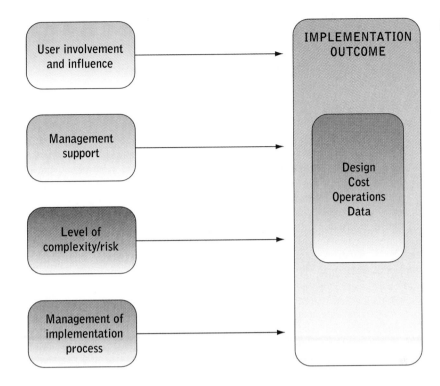

Figure 13-5 Factors in information system success or failure. The implementation outcome can be largely determined by the role of users; the degree of management support; the level of risk and complexity in the implementation project; and the quality of management of the implementation process. Evidence of success or failure can be found in the areas of design, cost, operations, or data of the information system.

The user–designer communications gap The relationship between consultant and client has traditionally been a problem area for information system implementation efforts. Users and information systems specialists tend to have different backgrounds, interests, and priorities. This is referred to as the **user–designer communications gap.** These differences lead to divergent organizational loyalties, approaches to problem solving, and vocabularies. Information systems specialists, for example, often have a highly technical, or machine, orientation to problem solving. They look for elegant and sophisticated technical solutions in which hardware and software efficiency is optimized at the expense of ease of use or organizational effectiveness. Users prefer systems that are oriented to solving business problems or facilitating organizational tasks. Often the orientations of both groups are so at odds that they appear to speak in different tongues. These differences are illustrated in Table 13.2, which depicts the typical concerns of end users and technical specialists (information system designers) regarding the development of a new information system. Communication problems between end users and designers are a major reason why user requirements are not properly incorporated into information systems and why users are driven out of the implementation process.

Systems development projects run a very high risk of failure when there is a pronounced gap between users and technicians and when these groups continue to pursue different goals. Under such conditions, users are often driven out of the implementation process. Participation in the implementation effort is extremely time consuming and takes them away from their daily activities and responsibilities. Because they cannot comprehend what the technicians are saying, the users conclude that the entire project is best left in the hands of the information specialists alone. With so many implementation efforts guided by purely technical considerations, it is no wonder that many systems fail to serve organizational needs.

user–designer communications gap The difference in backgrounds, interests, and priorities that impede communication and problem solving among end users and information systems specialists.

Management Support and Commitment

If an information systems project has the backing and commitment of management at various levels, it is more likely to be perceived positively by both users and the technical information services staff. Both groups will believe that their participation in the development process will receive higher level attention and priority. They will be recognized and rewarded for the time and effort they devote to implementation. Management backing also ensures that a systems project will receive sufficient funding and resources to be successful. Furthermore, all the

Window on Management

Are the Users Involved In Your Project?

How important is user involvement in system development projects to the success of such a project? Some believe that their importance cannot be overstated. Let us examine the role of users in several development projects.

Federal Express Corp. recently decided to install a new pilot scheduling system from Ad Opt Technologies of Montreal. The system had received rave reviews from such airlines as Sabena, Air Canada, Northwest, and Delta, so FedEx purchased it and had it in production within three months. Loud pilot protests began immediately. The system did schedule all the routes efficiently, and the pilots were back at their home base at the end. But the pilots had two complaints. The schedules were strange and inconvenient, and the pilots found them difficult to follow. And just as important, pilots had lost the ability to make schedule requests—the old system built the pilots' schedules from such pilot requests.

The problems arose because the speed of installation left no time to consider the pilots or to adapt the system to FedEx's specific needs. The pilots were never consulted before the system was implemented. TWA, however, had tested its system for a year before putting it into production, and had involved their pilot union reps from the beginning, according to Ad Opt's CEO, Tom Ivaskiv. At last report the FedEx problems were being solved slowly, taking many months. One negative effect according to management was the way the system unified the pilots just as they were negotiating a new contract with FedEx. The company and union found they had another difficult bargaining issue to settle.

U.S. Automobile Association (USAA) is the fifth-largest auto insurer in the United States. Recently its Property and Casualty Division in San Antonio developed a new needs-based sales and services application. Cindy Colunga, division manager of the cross-functional, performance-centered design team, stated that the users worked closely with the information systems staff from the project's beginning. For example, users helped design the graphical user interface screens that were to be used by 4000 people. "By involving users up-front," reports Colunga, "we work most of the kinks out." Reportedly, user involvement resulted in a better designed system that was easy to navigate. As a result, Colunga estimated, user-training time was cut by 60 percent. User involvement also solved a major unforeseen critical problem. Nearly 70 percent of the testers complained of wrist pain, the result of key stroke combinations that were awkward for their wrists. Information systems specialists solved the problem by developing hot key sequences that greatly reduced the number of key strokes. The company estimates that solving the problem in advance of any injury saved the company $1 million.

Meijer Inc., a Grand Rapids, Michigan, retail chain, undertook a project to replace its mainframe e-mail system with an e-mail system based on its 16,000 desktops. The project took 18 months, cost $3 million, and the users hated it. The old system had been very fast and was highly reliable, whereas the new system was slower and less reliable. Ultimately the technology team was forced to replace all the existing hardware with faster hardware, at a great cost. System builders had not paid attention to the organization's culture and users' needs.

To Think About: With so many problems arising from lack of adequate user involvement, why do you think the problems arise so often? If you were in charge of implementing a new system, how would you prevent such problems?

Sources: Sharon Gaudin, "Migration Plans? Remember to Talk to End Users Up Front," Computerworld, October 26, 1998; and Julia King, "Ergonomics Helps the Bottom Line," Computerworld, April 27, 1998.

---

changes in work habits and procedures and any organizational realignments associated with a new system depend on management backing to be enforced effectively. If a manager considers a new system to be a priority, the system will more likely be treated that way by his or her subordinates (Doll, 1985; Ein-Dor and Segev, 1978).

However, management support can backfire sometimes. Sometimes management becomes overcommitted to a project, pouring excessive resources into a systems development effort that is failing or that should never have been undertaken in the first place (Newman and Sabherwal, 1996).

Management support may be somewhat less essential for small businesses that do not have the resources or highly developed bureaucracies of large organizations. Technical and methodological expertise from external sources such as consultants or information technology vendors may play a larger role in successful implementations because small businesses do not have large, internal information systems staff from whom to draw (Thong, Yap, and Raman, 1996).

Table 13.2 The User–Designer Communications Gap

User Concerns	Designer Concerns
Will the system deliver the information I need for my work?	How much disk storage space will the master file consume?
How quickly can I access the data?	How many lines of program code will it take to perform this function?
How easily can I retrieve the data?	How can we cut down on CPU time when we run the system?
How much clerical support will I need to enter data into the system?	What is the most efficient way of storing this piece of data?
How will the operation of the system fit into my daily business schedule?	What database management system should we use?

Level of Complexity and Risk

Systems differ dramatically in their size, scope, level of complexity, and organizational and technical components. Some systems development projects, such as the project described in the Window on Technology, are more likely to fail or suffer delays because they carry a much higher level of risk than others.

Researchers have identified three key dimensions that influence the level of project risk (McFarlan, 1981). These include project size, project structure, and the level of technical experience of the information systems staff and project team.

Project size The larger the project—as indicated by the dollars spent, the size of the implementation staff, the time allocated to implementation, and the number of organizational units affected—the greater the risk. Therefore, a $5 million project lasting for four years and affecting five departments in 20 operating units and 120 users will be much riskier than a $30,000 project for two users that can be completed in two months. Another risk factor is the company's experience with projects of given sizes. If a company is accustomed to implementing large, costly systems, the risk of implementing the $5 million project will be lowered. The risk may even be lower than that of another concern attempting a $200,000 project when the firm's average project cost has been around $50,000.

Project structure Some projects are more highly structured than others. Their requirements are clear and straightforward so the outputs and processes can be easily defined. Users know exactly what they want and what the system should do; there is almost no possibility of them changing their minds. Such projects run a much lower risk than those whose requirements are relatively undefined, fluid, and constantly changing; where outputs cannot be easily fixed because they are subject to users' changing ideas; or because users cannot agree on what they want.

Experience with technology The project risk will rise if the project team and the information system staff lack the required technical expertise. If the team is unfamiliar with the hardware, system software, application software, or database management system proposed for the project, it is highly likely that the project will experience technical problems or take more time to complete because of the need to master new skills.

These dimensions of project risk will be present in different combinations for each implementation effort. Table 13.3 shows that eight different combinations are possible, each with a different degree of risk. The higher the level of risk, the more likely it is that the implementation effort will fail.

Boston Tunnel's Data Gridlock

Chronic congestion and gridlock have made downtown Boston a traffic nightmare. Boston's Central Artery/Tunnel project (CA/T) is being built to relieve the problem with a series of elevated highways, tunnels, and bridges through the heart of the city. CA/T is the largest and most technically challenging public infrastructure project the United States has ever experienced, requiring more than 100 contractors, 36 simultaneous field offices, and 109 separate construction contracts ranging in cost from $40 million to $400 million each. Two giant, international construction engineering firms, Bechtel and Parsons Brinckerhoff (together called B/PB) were selected to jointly manage the project.

When project design began in 1986, no information technology planning occurred for data integration or data storage because no one foresaw the need for them. Also, because far fewer computer systems were networked together at that time, no one understood the need to standardize software requirements. Each contractor used whatever software he or she wanted.

Project managers and engineers who were doing or supervising the design work used different CAD (computer-aided design) systems to exchange design plans and drawings. Bechtel used GDS CAD, a very powerful tool for those days, but most contractors used less-expensive packages, the most popular being AutoCAD. The data formats of the two CAD packages were incompatible. People worked overtime to translate between the two systems, creating backlogs, and much of the detail of the drawings was lost.

CA/T contractors were required to use Primavera Project Planner (P3) for project management, but only as part of CA/T's master schedule. Yet each unit of the project kept its own progress-tracking and expenditures records, some using project-management software tools, many using spreadsheets, others only using pencil and paper. Even data that were exchanged between the project management partners, Bechtel and Parsons Brinckerhoff, created problems because each used different spreadsheets to manage their project data.

Integrating these data manually was an extremely slow process, but even worse, project management reports contradicted reports from the contractors. The ultimate result of this lack of adequate electronic data-sharing was near gridlock. Finally, in 1992, Bechtel decided it needed to build a new system, which it called the Construction Information System (CIS). The main goal of this system was to produce standardized reports using SQL (Structured Query Language—see Chapter 8) and Oracle database management software.

The Oracle system helped standardize the reports so that all the organizations participating in the project were able to share their information. However, the CIS project failed to build interfaces for the various systems used in the field, and so field data were not automatically fed into the Oracle system. Instead, Oracle programmers had to enter the data manually, thus reducing their availability for development work while creating new bottlenecks.

In addition, project management kept its records on Oracle whereas the contractors used their own systems for work progress and cost estimates. In essence, CA/T had an expensive, redundant duplicate-entry system. To keep the data up-to-date and accurate, project management validated cost and progress data every two weeks with the contractors. This was a very labor-intensive, wasteful process. On a typical large job the field office and the contractor exchange at least 10,000 documents. Given this circumstance, the current project was in danger of drowning in paperwork, and the Oracle system did not address this problem.

By early 1998, many problems had been addressed. Legacy files still were being converted to Oracle, but the project required that all new development be done as part of CIS using Windows 95 or NT. An application was built that enabled contractors to query B/PB engineers through Oracle. One Oracle application tracked deficient materials. Daily engineering data were entered directly into the Oracle system, and all 12,000 daily engineers' reports were issued via Oracle.

An IT integration plan for the project called the IT Enable Office project requires that all software be compatible not only with the Oracle database, but also with certain applications that some contractors already are using. Now, rather than sending documents back and forth, the relevant data are entered directly into Oracle by the contractors.

To Think About: What management, organization, and technology factors were responsible for CA/T's problems?

Sources: Ann Harrison, "Unsnarling Information for the Real Superhighway," *Software Magazine,* March 1998; and "Facts and Figures: Details Behind the CA/T," www.bigdig.com.

Table 13.3 Dimensions of Project Risk

Project Structure	Project Technology Level	Project Size	Degree of Risk
High	Low	Large	Low
High	Low	Small	Very low
High	High	Large	Medium
High	High	Small	Medium-low
Low	Low	Large	Low
Low	Low	Small	Very low
Low	High	Large	Very high
Low	High	Small	High

Management of the Implementation Process

The development of a new system must be carefully managed and orchestrated. Each project involves research and development. Requirements are hard to define at the level of detail for automation. The same piece of information may be interpreted and defined differently by different individuals. Multiple users have different sets of requirements and needs. Costs, benefits, and project schedules must be assessed. The final design may not be easy to visualize. Because complex information systems involve so many interest groups, actors, and details, it is sometimes uncertain whether the initial plans for a system are truly feasible.

Often basic elements of success are forgotten. Training to ensure that end users are comfortable with the new system and fully understand its potential uses is often sacrificed or forgotten in systems development projects. If the budget is strained at the very beginning, toward the end of a project there will likely be insufficient funds for training (Bikson et al., 1985).

The conflicts and uncertainties inherent in any implementation effort will be magnified when an implementation project is poorly managed and organized. As illustrated in Figure 13-6, a systems development project without proper management will most likely suffer these consequences:

- Cost overruns that vastly exceed budgets
- Unexpected time slippage
- Technical shortfalls resulting in performance that is significantly below the estimated level
- Failure to obtain anticipated benefits

How badly are projects managed? On average, private sector projects are underestimated by one-half in terms of budget and time required to deliver the complete system promised in the system plan. A very large number of projects are delivered with missing functionality (promised for delivery in later versions). Government projects suffer about the same failure level, perhaps worse (Laudon, 1989; Helms and Weiss, 1986).

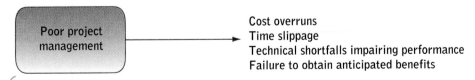

Figure 13-6 Consequences of poor project management. Without proper management, a systems development project will take longer to complete and most often will exceed the budgeted cost. The resulting information system will most likely be technically inferior and may not be able to demonstrate any benefits to the organization.

Why are projects managed so poorly and what can be done about it? Here we discuss some possibilities.

Ignorance and optimism The techniques for estimating the length of time required to analyze and design systems are poorly developed. Most applications are "first time" (i.e., there is no prior experience in the application area). Academics generally do not study large-scale commercial systems but instead focus on small-scale, easily taught or learned software projects. The larger the scale of systems, the greater the role of ignorance and optimism. Very-large-scale systems (VLSS)—sometimes called *grand design systems*—suffer extraordinary rates of failure (Laudon, 1989; United States General Services Administration, 1988). The net result of these factors is that estimates tend to be optimistic, "best case," and wrong. It is assumed that all will go well when in fact it rarely does.

man-month The traditional unit of measurement used by systems designers to estimate the length of time to complete a project. Refers to the amount of work a person can be expected to complete in a month.

The mythical man-month The traditional unit of measurement used by systems designers to project costs is the **man-month.** Projects are estimated in terms of how many man-months will be required. However, while costs may vary as a product of people and months, the progress of the project does not, as pointed out by Frederick P. Brooks (Brooks, 1974). As it turns out, people and months are not interchangeable in the short run on systems projects. In other words, adding more workers to projects does not necessarily reduce the elapsed time needed to complete a systems project.

Unlike cotton picking—when tasks can be rigidly partitioned, communication between participants is not required, and training is unnecessary—systems analysis and design involves *tasks that are sequentially linked, cannot be performed in isolation, and require extensive communications and training.* Software development is inherently a group effort, and hence communication costs rise exponentially as the number of participants increases.

Given these characteristics, adding labor to projects can often slow down delivery as the communication, learning, and coordination costs rise very fast and detract from the output of participants. For comparison, imagine what would happen if five amateur spectators were added to one team in a championship professional basketball game. Chances are quite good that the team composed of five professional basketball players would do much better in the short run than the team with five professionals and five amateurs.

Falling behind: bad news travels slowly upward Slippage in projects, failure, and doubts are often not reported to senior management until it is too late. To some extent, this is characteristic of projects in all fields. The CONFIRM project, a very-large-scale information systems project to integrate hotel, airline, and rental car reservations, is a classic example. It was sponsored by the Hilton Hotels, Budget Rent-A-Car, and Marriott Corporations and developed by AMR Information Services, Inc., a subsidiary of American Airlines Corporation. The project was very ambitious and technically complex, employing a staff of 500. Members of the CONFIRM project management team did not immediately come forward with accurate information when the project started encountering problems coordinating various transaction processing activities. Clients continued to invest in a project that was faltering because they were not informed of its problems with database, decision-support, and integration technologies (Oz, 1994).

The Challenge of Business Process Reengineering (BPR) and Enterprise Resource Planning (ERP)

Given the challenges of innovation and implementation, it is not surprising to find a very high failure rate among business process reengineering (BPR) and enterprise resource planning (ERP) projects, which typically require extensive organizational change. A number of studies have indicated that 70 percent of all business processing reengineering projects fail to deliver promised benefits. Likewise, 70 percent of all enterprise resource planning projects fail to be fully implemented or to meet the goals of their users even after three years of work (Gillooly, 1998). Both BPR and ERP problems are part of the larger problem of organizational implementation and change management.

Many reengineering projects have been undermined by poor implementation and change management practices that failed to address employees' concerns about change. Dealing with fear and anxiety throughout the organization; overcoming resistance by key managers; changing job functions, career paths, and recruitment practices; and training posed greater threats to reengineering than the difficulties companies faced visualizing and designing breakthrough changes to business processes (Maglitta, 1994).

Enterprise resource planning creates myriad interconnections among various business processes and data flows to ensure that information in one part of the business can be obtained by any other unit, to help people eliminate redundant activities, and to make better management decisions. Massive organizational changes are required to make this happen (see Chapter 18). Information that was previously maintained by different systems and different departments or functional areas must be integrated and made available to the company as a whole. Business processes must be tightly integrated, jobs must be redefined, and new procedures must be created throughout the company. Employees are often unprepared for new procedures and roles (Davenport, 1998).

The Implementation Process: What Can Go Wrong

The following problems are considered typical for each stage of systems development when the implementation process is poorly managed.

Analysis

○ Time, money, and resources have not been allocated to researching the problem. The problem remains poorly defined. Objectives of the implementation project will be vague and ambiguous; benefits will be difficult to measure.

○ Little or no time is spent in preliminary planning. There are no standards to use in estimating preliminary costs or the duration of the project.

○ The project team is not properly staffed. Personnel are assigned on an "as available" basis and cannot dedicate themselves to the project. User groups to be served by the system are not represented on the team.

○ The information services staff promises results that are impossible to deliver.

○ Requirements are derived from inadequate documentation of existing systems or incomplete findings from systems study activities.

○ Users refuse to spend any time helping the project team gather the requisite information.

○ Project analysts cannot interview users properly. They do not know how to ask the right questions. They cannot carry on extended conversations with users because they lack good communication skills.

Design

○ Users have no responsibility for or input to design activities. The design, therefore, reflects the biases of the technical staff. It does not mesh well with the structure, activities, and culture of the organization or the priorities of management.

○ The system is designed only to serve current needs. No flexibility has been built in to anticipate the future needs of the organization.

○ Drastic changes in clerical procedures or staffing are planned without any organizational impact analysis.

○ Functional specifications are inadequately documented.

Programming

○ The amount of time and money required for software development is underestimated.

○ Programmers are supplied with incomplete specifications.

- Not enough time is devoted to the development of program logic; too much time is wasted on writing code.
- Programmers do not take full advantage of structured design or object-oriented techniques. They write programs that are difficult to modify and maintain.
- Programs are not adequately documented.
- Requisite resources (such as computer time) are not scheduled.

Testing

- The amount of time and money required for proper testing is underestimated.
- The project team does not develop an organized test plan.
- Users are not sufficiently involved in testing. They do not help to create sample test data or review test results. They refuse to devote much time to the testing effort.
- The implementation team does not develop appropriate acceptance tests for management review. Management does not review and sign off on test results.

Conversion

- Insufficient time and money are budgeted for conversion activities, especially for data conversion.
- Not all the individuals who will use the system are involved until conversion begins. Training begins only when the system is about to be installed.
- To compensate for cost overruns and delays, the system is made operational before it is fully ready.
- System and user documentation is inadequate.
- Performance evaluations are not conducted. No performance standards are established, and the results of the system are not weighed against the original objectives.
- Provisions for system maintenance are inadequate. Insufficient information systems personnel are trained to support the system and to make maintenance changes.

13.3 Managing Implementation

Not all aspects of the implementation process can be easily controlled or planned (Alter and Ginzberg, 1978). However, the chances for system success can be increased by anticipating potential implementation problems and applying appropriate corrective strategies. Various project management, requirements gathering, and planning methodologies have been developed for specific categories of problems. Strategies have also been devised for ensuring that users play an appropriate role throughout the implementation period and for managing the organizational change process.

Controlling Risk Factors

One way implementation can be improved is by adjusting the project management strategy to the level of risk inherent in each project. If a systems development project is placed in the proper risk category, levels of risk can be predicted in advance and strategies developed to counteract high-risk factors (McFarlan, 1981).

Implementers must adopt a contingency approach to project management, handling each project with the tools, project management methodologies, and organizational linkages geared to its level of risk. There are four basic project management techniques:

1. External integration tools link the work of the implementation team to that of users at all organizational levels.

2. Internal integration tools ensure that the implementation team operates as a cohesive unit.

Table 13.4 Strategies to Manage Projects by Controlling Risks

Project Structure	Project Technology Level	Project Size	Degree of Risk	Project Management Tool
1. High	Low	Large	Low	High use of formal planning High use of formal control
2. High	Low	Small	Very low	High use of formal control Medium use of formal planning
3. High	High	Large	Medium	Medium use of formal control Medium use of formal planning
4. High	High	Small	Medium-low	High internal integration
5. Low	Low	Large	Low	High external integration High use of formal planning High use of formal control
6. Low	Low	Small	Very low	High external integration High use of formal control
7. Low	High	Large	Very high	High external integration High internal integration
8. Low	High	Small	High	High external integration High internal integration

3. Formal planning tools structure and sequence tasks, providing advance estimates of the time, money, and technical resources required to execute them.

4. Formal control tools help monitor the progress toward goals.

The risk profile of each project will determine the appropriate project management technique to apply, as illustrated in Table 13.4.

External Integration Tools

Projects with relatively *little structure* must involve users fully at all stages. Users must be mobilized to support one of many possible design options and to remain committed to a single design. Therefore, **external integration tools** must be applied.

> **external integration tools**
> Project management technique that links the work of the implementation team to that of users at all organizational levels.

- ◯ Users can be selected as project leaders or as the second-in-command on a project team.
- ◯ User steering committees can be created to evaluate the system's design.
- ◯ Users can become active members of the project team.
- ◯ The project can require formal user review and approval of specifications.
- ◯ Minutes of all key design meetings can be distributed widely among users.
- ◯ Users can prepare the status reports for higher management.
- ◯ Users can be put in charge of training and installation.
- ◯ Users can be responsible for change control, putting a brake on all nonessential changes to the system once final design specifications have been completed.

Internal Integration Tools

Projects with *high levels of technology* benefit from **internal integration tools.** The success of such projects depends on how well their technical complexity can be managed. Project leaders need both heavy technical and administrative experience. They must be able to anticipate problems and develop smooth working relationships among a predominantly technical team.

> **internal integration tools**
> Project management technique that ensures that the implementation team operates as a cohesive unit.

- ◯ Team members should be highly experienced.
- ◯ The team should be under the leadership of a manager with a strong technical and project management background.

This project team of professionals is using computing tools to enhance communication, analysis, and decision making.

○ Team meetings should take place frequently, with routine distribution of meeting minutes concerning key design decisions.

○ The team should hold regular technical status reviews.

○ A high percentage of the team should have a history of good working relationships with each other.

○ Team members should participate in setting goals and establishing target dates.

○ Essential technical skills or expertise not available internally should be secured from outside the organization.

Formal Planning and Control Tools

formal planning tools Project management technique that structures and sequences tasks, budgeting time, money, and technical resources required to complete the tasks.

formal control tools Project management technique that helps monitor the progress toward completion of a task and fulfillment of goals.

Projects with *high structure* and *low technology* present the lowest risk. The design is fixed and stable and the project does not pose any technical challenges. If such projects are large, they can be successfully managed by **formal planning** and **formal control tools.** With project management techniques, such as PERT (Program Evaluation and Review Technique) or Gantt charts, a detailed plan can be developed. (PERT lists the specific activities that make up a project, their duration, and the activities that must be completed before a specific activity can start. A Gantt chart such as that illustrated in Figure 13-7 visually represents the sequence and timing of different tasks in a development project as well as their resource requirements.) Tasks can be defined and resources budgeted. These project management techniques can help managers identify bottlenecks and determine the impact that problems will have on project completion times. They can also help system developers partition implementation into smaller, more manageable segments with defined, measurable business results (Fichman and Moses, 1999).

○ Milestone phases can be selected.

○ Specifications can be developed from the feasibility study.

○ Specification standards can be established.

○ Processes for project approval can be developed.

Standard control techniques will successfully chart the progress of the project against budgets and target dates, so that the implementation team can make adjustments to meet their original schedule.

○ Disciplines to control or freeze the design can be maintained.

○ Deviations from the plan can be spotted.

○ Periodic formal status reports against the plan will show the extent of progress.

HRIS COMBINED PLAN-HR

Task	Da	Who
DATA ADMINISTRATION SECURITY		
QMF security review/setup	20	EF TP
Security orientation	2	EF JV
QMF security maintenance	35	TP GL
Data entry sec. profiles	4	EF TP
Data entry sec. views est.	12	EF TP
Data entry security profiles	65	EF TP
DATA DICTIONARY		
Orientation sessions	1	EF
Data dictionary design	32	EF WV
DD prod. coordn-query	20	GL
DD prod. coordn-live	40	EF GL
Data dictionary cleanup	35	EF GL
Data dictionary maint.	35	EF GL
PROCEDURES REVISION DESIGN PREP		
Work flows (old)	10	PK JL
Payroll data flows	31	JL PK
HRIS P/R model	11	PK JL
P/R interface orient. mtg.	6	PK JL
P/R interface coordn. I	15	PK
P/R interface coordn.	8	PK
Benefits interfaces (old)	5	JL
Ben. interfaces new flow	8	JL
Ben. communication strategy	3	PK JL
New work flow model	15	PK JL
Posn. data entry flows	14	WV JL

RESOURCE SUMMARY

Name		Who	1999 Oct	Nov	Dec	2000 Jan	Feb	Mar	Apr	May	Jun	Jul	Aug	Sep	Oct	Nov	Dec	2000 Jan	Feb	Mar
Edith Farrell	5.0	EF	2	21	24	24	23	22	22	27	34	34	29	26	28	19	14			
Woody Holand	5.0	WH	5	17	20	19	12	10	14	10	2							4	3	
Charles Pierce	5.0	CP		5	11	20	13	9	10	7	6	8	4	4	4	4	4			
Ted Leurs	5.0	TL		12	17	17	19	17	14	12	15	16	2	1	1	1	1			
Toni Cox	5.0	TC	1	11	10	11	11	12	19	19	21	21	21	17	17	12	9			
Patricia Clark	5.0	PC	7	23	30	34	27	25	15	24	25	16	11	13	17	10	3	3	2	
Jane Lawton	5.0	JL	1	9	16	21	19	21	21	20	17	15	14	12	14	8	5			
David Holloway	5.0	DH	4	4	5	5	5	2	7	5	4	16	2							
Diane O'Neill	5.0	DO	6	14	17	16	13	11	9	4										
Joan Albert	5.0	JA	5	6			7	6	2	1				5	5	1				
Marie Marcus	5.0	MM	15	7	2	1	1													
Don Stevens	5.0	DS	4	4	5	4	5	1												
Casual	5.0	CASL		3	4	3			4	7	9	5	3	2						
Kathy Manley	5.0	KM		1	5	16	20	19	22	19	20	18	20	11	2					
Anna Borden	5.0	AB					9	10	16	15	11	12	19	10	7	1				
Gail Loring	5.0	GL		3	6	5	9	10	17	18	17	10	13	10	10	7	17			
UNASSIGNED	0.0	X										9			236	225	230	14	13	3
Co-op	5.0	CO		6	4				2	3	4	4	2	4	16			216	178	9
Casual	5.0	CAUL							3	3	3									
TOTAL DAYS			49	147	176	196	194	174	193	195	190	181	140	125	358	288	284	237	196	12

Figure 13-7 Formal planning and control tools help to manage information systems projects successfully. The Gantt chart in this figure was produced by a commercially available project management software package. It shows the task, person-days, and initials of each responsible person, as well as the start and finish dates for each task. The resource summary provides a good manager with the total person-days for each month and for each person working on the project to successfully manage the project. The project described here is a data administration project.

Overcoming User Resistance

In addition to fine-tuning project management strategies, implementation risks can be reduced by securing management and user support of the implementation effort. Section 13.2 has shown how user participation in the design process builds commitment to the system. The final product is more likely to reflect users' requirements. Users are more likely to feel that they control and own the system. Users are also more likely to feel satisfied with an information system if they have been trained to use it properly (Cronan and Douglas, 1990).

However, MIS researchers have also noted that systems development is not an entirely rational process. Users leading design activities have used their position to further private interests and to gain power rather than to promote organizational objectives (Franz and Robey, 1984). Users may not always be involved in systems projects in a productive way.

Participation in implementation activities may not be enough to overcome the problem of user resistance. The implementation process demands organizational change. Such change may be resisted because different users may be affected by the system in different ways. Whereas some users may welcome a new system because it brings changes they perceive as beneficial to them, others may resist these changes because they believe the shifts are detrimental to their interests (Joshi, 1991).

If the use of a system is voluntary, users may choose to avoid it; if use is mandatory, resistance will take the form of increased error rates, disruptions, turnover, and even sabotage. Therefore, the implementation strategy must not only encourage user participation and involvement, it must also address the issue of counterimplementation (Keen, 1981). **Counterimplementation** is a deliberate strategy to thwart the implementation of an information system or an innovation in an organization.

Researchers have explained user resistance with one of three theories (Markus, 1983; Davis and Olson, 1985):

1. **People-oriented theory.** Factors internal to users as individuals or as a group produce resistance. For instance, users may resist a new system or any change at all because they are fearful or do not wish to learn new ways of doing things.

2. **System-oriented theory.** Factors inherent in the design create user resistance to a system. For instance, users may resist a system because its user interface is confusing and they have trouble learning how to make the system work.

3. **Interaction theory.** Resistance is caused by the interaction of people and systems factors. For instance, the system may be well designed and welcomed by some users but resisted by others who fear it will take away some of their power or stature in the organization or even their jobs.

Strategies have been suggested to overcome each form of user resistance:

People oriented:	User education (training)
	Coercion (edicts, policies)
	Persuasion
	User participation (to elicit commitment)
System oriented:	User education
	Improve human factors (user/system interface)
	User participation (for improved design)
	Package modification to conform to organization when appropriate
Interaction:	Solve organizational problems before introducing new systems
	Restructure incentives for users
	Restructure the user–designer relationship
	Promote user participation when appropriate

Strategies appropriate for the interaction theory incorporate elements of people-oriented and system-oriented strategies. There may be situations in which user participation is not appropriate. For example, some users may react negatively to a new design even though its overall benefits outweigh its drawbacks. Some individuals may stand to lose power as a result of design decisions (Robey and Markus, 1984). In this instance, participation in design may actually exacerbate resentment and resistance.

Designing for the Organization

The entire systems development process can be viewed as planned organizational change because the purpose of a new system is to improve the organization's performance. Therefore, the development process must explicitly address the ways in which the organization will change when the new system is installed, including installation of intranets, extranets, and

---

counterimplementation A deliberate strategy to thwart the implementation of an information system or an innovation in an organization.

people-oriented theory User-resistance theory focusing on factors internal to users.

system-oriented theory User-resistance theory focusing on factors inherent in the design of the system.

interaction theory User-resistance theory stating that resistance is caused by the interaction of people and systems factors.

Table 13.5	Organizational Factors in Systems Planning and Implementation

Employee participation and involvement

Job design

Standards and performance monitoring

Ergonomics (including equipment, user interfaces, and the work environment)

Employee grievance resolution procedures

Health and safety

Government regulatory compliance

Internet applications. In addition to procedural changes, transformations in job functions, organizational structure, power relationships, and behavior will all have to be carefully planned. When technology-induced changes produce unforeseen consequences, the organization can benefit by improvising to take advantage of new opportunities. Information systems specialists, managers, and users should remain open-minded about their roles in the change management process and not adhere to rigid narrow perceptions (Orlikowski and Hofman, 1997; Markus and Benjamin, 1997). Table 13.5 lists the organizational dimensions that would need to be addressed for planning and implementing many systems.

Although systems analysis and design activities are supposed to include an organizational impact analysis, this area has traditionally been neglected. An **organizational impact analysis** explains how a proposed system will affect organizational structure, attitudes, decision making, and operations. To integrate information systems successfully with the organization, thorough and fully documented organizational impact assessments must be given more attention in the development effort.

organizational impact analysis Study of the way a proposed system will affect organizational structure, attitudes, decision making, and operations.

Allowing for the Human Factor

The quality of information systems should be evaluated in terms of user criteria rather than the criteria of the information systems staff. In addition to targets such as memory size, access rates, and calculation times, systems objectives should include standards for user performance. For example, an objective might be that data entry clerks learn the procedures and codes for four new on-line data entry screens in a half-day training session.

Areas where users interface with the system should be carefully designed, with sensitivity to ergonomic issues. **Ergonomics** refers to the interaction of people and machines in the work environment. It considers the design of jobs, health issues, and the end-user interface of information systems. The impact of the application system on the work environment and job dimensions must be carefully assessed. One noteworthy study of 620 Social Security Administration claims representatives showed that the representatives with on-line access to claims data experienced greater stress than those with serial access to the data via teletype. Even though the on-line interface was more rapid and direct than teletype, it created much more frustration. Representatives with on-line access could interface with a larger number of clients per day. This changed the dimensions of the job for claims representatives. The restructuring of work—involving tasks, quality of working life, and performance—had a more profound impact than the nature of the technology itself (Turner, 1984).

ergonomics The interaction of people and machines in the work environment, including the design of jobs, health issues, and the end-user interface of information systems.

Sociotechnical Design

Most contemporary systems-building approaches tend to treat end users as essential to the systems-building process but play a largely passive role relative to other forces shaping the system such as the specialist system designers and management. A different tradition rooted in the European social democratic labor movement assigns users a more active role, one that empowers them to codetermine the role of information systems in their workplace (Clement and Van den Besselaar, 1993).

sociotechnical design Design to produce information systems that blend technical efficiency with sensitivity to organizational and human needs.

This tradition of participatory design emphasizes participation by the individuals most affected by the new system. It is closely associated with the concept of sociotechnical design. A **sociotechnical design** plan establishes human objectives for the system that lead to increased job satisfaction. Designers set forth separate sets of technical and social design solutions. The social design plans explore different work group structures, allocation of tasks, and the design of individual jobs. The proposed technical solutions are compared with the proposed social solutions. Social and technical solutions that can be combined are proposed as sociotechnical solutions. The alternative that best meets both social and technical objectives is selected for the final design. The resulting sociotechnical design is expected to produce an information system that blends technical efficiency with sensitivity to organizational and human needs, leading to high job satisfaction (Mumford and Weir, 1979). Systems with compatible technical and organizational elements are expected to raise productivity without sacrificing human and social goals.

Management Wrap-Up

Management

Two principal reasons for system failure are inadequate management support and poor management of the implementation process. Managers should fully understand the level of complexity and risk in new systems projects and provide realistic levels of support and resources.

Organization

The reason why most information systems fail is that system builders ignore organizational behavior problems, especially organizational inertia and resistance to change. Eliciting user support and maintaining an appropriate level of user involvement at all stages of system building are essential.

Technology

Systems sometimes fail because the technology is too complex or sophisticated to be easily implemented or because system builders lack the requisite skills or experience to work with it. Managers and systems builders should be fully aware of the risks and rewards of various technologies as they make their technology selections.

For Discussion

1. If you were a member of your corporation's management committee to oversee and approve systems development projects, what criteria would you use in evaluating new project proposals? What would you look for to determine whether the project was proceeding successfully?

2. It has been said that most systems fail because system builders ignore organizational behavior problems. Why?

Summary

1. Identify major problem areas in information systems. A high percentage of systems are considered failures because they are not used in the way they were intended. Some are not used at all. System failure is evidenced by problems with design, data, cost, or operations. The sources of system success or failure are primarily behavioral and organizational.

2. Assess whether a system is successful. Criteria for evaluating the success of an information system include (1) level of system use, (2) user satisfaction, (3) favorable user attitudes

about the information system and its staff, (4) achieved objectives, and (5) financial payoff to the organization.

3. Analyze the principal causes of information system failure. The principal causes of information system failure are (1) insufficient or improper user participation in the systems development process, (2) lack of management support, (3) high levels of complexity and risk in the systems development process, and (4) poor management of the implementation process. There is a very high failure rate among business process reengineering and enterprise resource planning projects because they require extensive organizational change.

4. Analyze the relationship between the implementation process and system outcome. Implementation is the entire process of organizational change surrounding the introduction of a new information system. One can better understand system success and failure by examining different patterns of implementation. Especially important is the relationship between participants in the implementation process, notably the interactions between system designers and users. Conflicts between the technical orientation of system designers and the business orientation of end users must be resolved. The success of organizational change can be determined by how well information systems specialists, end users, and decision makers deal with key issues at various stages in implementation.

5. Select appropriate strategies to manage the implementation process. Management support and control of the implementation process are essential, as are mechanisms for dealing with the level of risk in each new systems project. Some companies experience organizational resistance to change. Project risk factors can be brought under some control by a contingency approach to project management. The level of risk in a systems development project is determined by three key dimensions: (1) project size, (2) project structure, and (3) experience with technology. The risk level of each project will determine the appropriate mix of external integration tools, internal integration tools, formal planning tools, and formal control tools to be applied.

Appropriate strategies can be applied to ensure the correct level of user participation in the systems development process and to minimize user resistance. Information system design and the entire implementation process should be managed as planned organizational change. Participatory design emphasizes the participation of the individuals most affected by a new system. Sociotechnical design aims for an optimal blend of social and technical design solutions.

Key Terms

Change agent, 405	Formal planning tools, 416	Organizational impact analysis, 419	System-oriented theory, 418
Counterimplementation, 418	Implementation, 404		User–designer communications gap, 407
Ergonomics, 419	Interaction theory, 418	People-oriented theory, 418	
External integration tools, 415	Internal integration tools, 415	Sociotechnical design, 420	User interface, 401
Formal control tools, 416	Man-month, 412	System failure, 400	

Review Questions

1. What do we mean by information system failure?
2. What kinds of problems are evidence of information system failure?
3. How can we measure system success? Which measures of system success are the most important?
4. Define implementation. What are the major approaches to implementation?
5. Why is it necessary to understand the concept of implementation when examining system success and failure?
6. What are the major causes of implementation success or failure? How are they related to the failure of enterprise resource planning (ERP) and business process reengineering (BPR) projects?
7. What is the user–designer communications gap? What kinds of implementation problems can it create?
8. List some of the implementation problems that might occur at each stage of the systems development process.
9. What dimensions influence the level of risk in each systems development project?
10. What project management techniques can be used to control project risk?
11. What strategies can be used to overcome user resistance to systems development projects?
12. What organizational considerations should be addressed by information system design?

Group Project

Form a group with two or three other students. Write a description of the implementation problems you might expect to encounter for the information system you designed for the business process redesign project in Appendix A. Write an analysis of the steps you would take to solve or prevent these problems.

Alternatively, you could describe the implementation problems that might be expected for one of the systems described in the Window boxes or chapter ending cases in this text. Present your findings to the class.

Tools for Interactive Learning

○ Internet

The Internet Connection for this chapter will direct you to a series of Web sites where you can complete an exercise to evaluate user interfaces and user-system interactions. You can also use the Interactive Study Guide to test your knowledge of the topics in this chapter and get instant feedback when you need more practice.

○ CD-ROM

If you purchase and use the Multimedia Edition CD-ROM with this chapter, you can complete an interactive exercise to analyze the sources of a series of system problems and to identify the implementation stage when they occurred. You can also find an audio overview of the major themes of this chapter, and bullet text summarizing the key points of the chapter.

Case Study — Healtheon's Healthcare System Struggle

Over $1 trillion is spent on healthcare annually in the United States, with one-fifth of that ($200 billion) being spent on record keeping. If a company could find a way to cut record keeping costs by only 5 percent, it would save the country $10 billion per year. In addition, if the cost cuts came through streamlining the support operations of doctors' offices, hospitals, and other health providers, health care providers would flock to it, generating immense profits. The health care industry is clearly ready to spend a lot to solve its cost problems. According to J. D. Kleinke, a health economist from Denver, the industry spent $15 billion in 1997 alone for new information systems.

Healtheon, a young Silicon Valley company, is one of the numerous companies that sprang up to develop information system solutions to these problems. James Clark, a co-founder of both Silicon Graphics Inc. and Netscape Communications Corp., helped establish Healtheon in 1996 and became its chairman.

The problem of medical record keeping is immense and extremely complex, and the current system is often chaotic. Let us look at two of the most crucial elements that need to be addressed. First, most patients' medical records are scattered among a number of doctors' offices, hospitals, pharmacies, and various specialized labs. Such records are only available at the specific health care provider where each originated. Each piece of the total record can take a long time to locate—it may even be stored in a carton in a storage area somewhere

else. Moreover, these records are often difficult to read and interpret. Finding and reading all these records is an expensive and time-consuming task. Assembling these records into a single computer record for each patient has been difficult because the records come in many forms, such as paper, X rays, test results, electrocardiograms, sonograms, and on and on. And if they are computerized, security becomes a difficult issue because patients have a clear right to keep their medical records private.

Second, and an even more expensive problem for most health care providers, is that of collecting medical fees from patients and insurance companies. Individual doctors often have one or more staff members devoted wholly to this issue, and offices of three or four doctors may even have ten or more staff persons working exclusively on insurance-related issues.

The computer and medical industries, including such giants as EDS and Eli Lilly, have been working hard on using technology to ease these record keeping problems. While many of these efforts ended in failure (including Eli Lilly's), the founders of Healtheon took on the same problem, only with a twist. While other companies were basing their systems primarily on private networks, which are secure but expensive, Healtheon is offering a system that is Internet based. If it is successful, such a system should be far less expensive for a client to set up and to operate. However, it would not be as secure.

Bringing together and computerizing various pieces of an individual's health record, while expensive, has recently become technically feasible and is now being done. By using object-oriented technology, various types of patient records can all be stored in a single computerized patient record (CPR). A CPR stores patient statistical information, including name, address, and date of birth, and also contains patient medical information, such as illnesses, prescriptions, treatments history, family history, and even health care insurance coverage. The technology also enables the CPR to store data, graphics, video, and even voice records, such as lab tests, X rays, magnetic resonance imaging (MRI) tests, and the doctor's oral notes. Placed on a network, all components of the record can be viewed by appropriate medical providers wherever they are. Not only does such a system make the patient's medical records easily available, but it also enables several health care providers to have access to the same record simultaneously.

The CPR should also help health care providers collect their fees because the patient's up-to-date insurance information is stored in that record. However, Healtheon has a much broader vision of how to streamline the collection of fees. According to this vision, medical office staffs will be able to use the Internet to access insurance company databases to verify patient insurance eligibility and even to submit claims. The company sees other uses for the Internet as well, including ways to reduce the complexity and speed up the record keeping work of health care providers. For example, according to Healtheon, using their system, doctors would be able to use the Internet to process specialist referrals, write prescriptions, check lab results, and accomplish many other tasks.

One obvious problem is that Healtheon created too many false expectations. Pediatrician William Solomon of San Francisco, feeling his office was "drowning in paper," agreed to purchase the promised system. It was supposed to be installed in August, 1998, and yet had not been delivered as of this writing.

Another Healtheon error, one that is common to the software industry, was the company's poor choice in hiring technical specialists. The company hired top-notch computer specialists from such technology leaders as Microsoft Corp. and Silicon Graphics, but few had any prior experience working on health care projects. Yet healthcare, like many other specialized areas, has its own characteristics and problems. Perhaps the most fundamental problems in this field are cultural. Doctors are notoriously independent. They insist on doing things their own way, whereas software packages require users to make a lot of adjustments. Moreover, if doctors don't trust a system, they will just refuse to use it. For a project the size of Healtheon's, the technical staff must include many with subject matter experience.

Data created many problems for the project. Because health care records are so numerous, scattered, and varied, any CPR project faces major problems in gathering together all these data. To make matters worse, the collection of data must be done customer-by-customer. The data on the Internet presented even more difficult problems. For example, although Healtheon had assumed that an office manager could retrieve a patient's insurance status within five seconds, in many cases the data were simply unreliable. Secretaries found that patients' names and addresses were often garbled or wrong. Internet records were not up-to-date, so that, for example, newborns often had not

been added. Correcting and updating these data at each step resulted in many weeks of extra work, work that does not correct future data problems. Some companies, such as PacifiCare Health Systems Corp., refused to put patient data on the Internet because they do not believe private patient data will be kept confidential. In fact, only one insurer, Blue Shield of California, agreed to cooperate with Healtheon.

Automating doctor referrals also proved to be a very difficult issue. When Healtheon demonstrated its system, it showed a primary care doctor simply typing a note on the computer, including the name of the referred doctor. The demonstration system then automatically took care of scheduling, billing, and clinical feedback. However, in the real system, any referral required insurance company approvals, which in turn required an expert system rule base. The rule base had to be different for each insurance company, and in addition, different referrals required different rules. For instance, a referral for treatment for a broken bone might have very different insurance rules than would a referral for treatment for depression. Healtheon had to write a 72-part rule engine from scratch.

Healtheon ran into many other complications as well. For example, the 1250 San Francisco physicians who joined together as Brown & Toland demanded that their new system be installed under its existing system (which used software from IDX Systems Corporation of Burlington, Vermont, dating as far back as 1986) rather than replacing it. The purpose? To make the transition to the new system easier for the doctors. The task proved exceedingly difficult, and Healtheon's information systems specialists spent months learning about the idiosyncrasies of the IDX software.

Healtheon's clients wanted airtight security to protect confidential patient data as they flowed through the Internet. Healtheon's technical staff built in data encryption and passwords for every user so that, for example, a receptionist could not see clinical data that should only be available to a physician. But the security system

was so elaborate and complex that first-time users found it very difficult to learn.

Healtheon leadership has also been called into question. Clark, the company's chairman, has been out of the country for about a week every month, spending some of that time visiting a boatyard in Holland that was building a yacht for him. When he is at home, he spends only two to three days per week at Healtheon.

Healtheon accumulated losses of $73 million during its first three and one-half years (through mid-1998). About 98 percent of its 1998 revenues came from only four clients, and most of that amount was for fees for non-Internet work, such as managing clients' existing information systems. Yet eventually Healtheon may succeed, and if it does, the prize is gigantic. In the meantime, how should Healtheon be judged? What went wrong? What problems has Healtheon faced that have caused many to judge the company a failure?

Sources: Todd Woody, "Health Risks," **The Industry Standard,** February 15, 1999; George Anders, "Healtheon Struggles in Efforts to Remedy Doctors' Paper Plague," **The Wall Street Journal,** October 2, 1998; Gregory Dalton, "Health Pros Turn to the Web," **Information Week,** March 2, 1998; "Healtheon to Acquire ActaMed," **Information Week,** February 25, 1998; and "Medicine's New Weapon: Data," **Business Week,** March 27, 1995.

CASE STUDY QUESTIONS

1. Analyze Healtheon from the viewpoint of the competitive forces and value chain models.

2. What management, organization, and technology problems did the company face in attempting to develop and build its new product?

3. Describe the role of data and the data problems encountered in developing its system.

4. Evaluate the management, organization, and technology problems within Healtheon, indicating how each contributed to the project's failure.

System Modernization at the Social Security Administration

The Social Security Administration (SSA) consists of approximately 65,000 employees located in 1300 field offices, 10 regional offices, 7 processing centers, 4 data operations centers, and the Baltimore headquarters. SSA administers the major social insurance programs in the United States, delivering benefits to more than 50 million people each month.

In order to administer these programs, SSA maintains 260 million names in its account number file (enumeration file), 240 million earnings records, and 50 million names on its master beneficiary file. In addition to keeping these files current, SSA annually issues 10 million new Social Security cards, pays out $170 billion, posts 380 million wage items reported by employers, receives 7.5 million new claims, recomputes (because of changes in beneficiary status) 19 million accounts, and handles 120 million bills and queries from private health insurance companies, carriers, and intermediaries. SSA processes more than 25 million transactions per day. Virtually every living American has some relationship with SSA.

In the early 1980s, the long-term funding for Social Security payments in the United States was in serious jeopardy, and SSA's computerized administrative systems were nearing collapse. This was an unusual state of affairs for SSA. As the flagship institution of the New Deal, SSA had developed broad bipartisan support, and there was never any serious question about its long-term financial viability until the late 1970s. In addition, since its inception in 1935, SSA had been one of the leading innovators and implementors of advanced information technology in the United States.

In 1982, SSA announced its Systems Modernization Plan (SMP), which turned into a $1 billion, ten-year effort to completely rebuild its information systems and administrative processes. The SMP was one of the largest civilian information system rebuilding efforts in history. Ten years later, SSA embarked on another ambitious round of technology modernization as it tried to create an information architecture for the twenty-first century.

SSA illustrates many central problems of management, information technology, and organization faced by private and public organizations in a period of rapid technical and social change. Although SSA operates in a unique federal government environment, many large private organizations have exhibited similar problems during this time period. The problems and solutions illustrated in this case are generic.

The case is organized into three sections. Section I describes the overall situation at SSA in the period before SMP, roughly 1972 to 1982. Section II describes the experience of SMP. Section III considers the long-term prospects of SSA.

SECTION I: ORGANIZATION, MANAGEMENT, AND SYSTEMS, 1972–1982

The overall system environment at SSA in 1982 could best be described as a hodgepodge of software programs developed over a 20-year period in four different machine environments. In the history of the agency, no one had ever conducted an information system requirements study to understand the overall requirements of the agency or the specific requirements of its subunits. There had been no planning of the information systems function for more than 20 years. Instead, as in many private organizations, systems drifted along from year to year, with only incremental changes.

Software

SSA software resulted from decades of programming techniques. The enumeration system, which supports the issuance of Social Security numbers, was designed in the late 1950s and had never been changed. The earning system was designed in 1975, the claims processing system was unchanged from the early 1960s, and other systems were also inherited from the late 1960s and 1970s. The software was a product of unplanned patchwork, with no regard given to its deterioration over time.

From the 1950s to the 1980s, there were four major equipment transitions. However, the software was not improved or redesigned at any of these transitions. All of SSA's files and programs were maintained on more than 500,000 reels of magnetic tape, which were susceptible to aging, cracking, and deterioration. Because tape was the storage medium, all data processing was batch sequential.

In summary, there were 76 different software systems making up SSA's basic computer operations. There were more than 1300 computer programs encompassing more than 12 million lines of COBOL and other code. Most of the 12 million lines of code were undocumented. They worked, but few people in the organization knew how or why, which made maintenance extremely complex. In the 1960s and 1970s, Congress and the president made continual changes in the benefit formulas, each of which required extensive maintenance and changes in the underlying software. A change in cost-of-living rates, for instance, required sorting through several large interwoven programs, which took months of work.

Because of the labor-intensive work needed to change undocumented software and the growing operations crisis, software development staff were commonly shifted to manage the operations crisis. The result was little development of new programs.

It did not help matters that few people in Congress, the Office of the President, the Office of Management and Budget, or other responsible parties understood the deleterious impact of program changes on SSA systems capabilities. Unfortunately, SSA did not inform Congress of its own limitation.

Even by the late 1970s, SSA had not begun to make the transition to newer storage technology, file management and database technology, or more modern software techniques. In this respect, SSA was about five years behind private industry in making important technological transitions.

Hardware

By 1982, SSA was operating outdated, unreliable, and inadequate hardware, given its mission. Many of the computers had not been manufactured or marketed for 10 years or more. Eleven IBM 360/65 systems were no longer manufactured or supported. Although more modern equipment might have required $1 million annually for maintenance and operations expenses, SSA was spending more than $4 million to keep these antiquated machines in service.

Because of frequent breakdowns, more than 25 percent of the production jobs ended before completion (abended jobs), and 30 percent of the available computer processing power was idle. As a result of hardware deficiencies, a number of specific program impacts became apparent in 1982:

○ Earnings enforcement operations, which help detect overpayments, were more than three years behind schedule.

○ The computation of benefit amounts to give credit for additional earnings after retirement was three years behind schedule.

○ Supplemental Security Income (SSI) claims and posteligibility redeterminations could be processed only three times a week rather than five times a week. This meant delays of several days or weeks for SSI beneficiaries.

○ To process cost-of-living increases in 1982 for 42 million individuals, SSA had to suspend all other data processing for one week.

SSA estimated that its gross computing capacity was deficient by more than 2000 CPU hours per month. SSA estimated that it needed 5000 central processing hours per month, but its capacity was only 3000 CPU hours per month.

Telecommunications

SSA depends heavily on telecommunications to perform its mission. Its 1300 field offices need timely access to data stored at the central computer facility in Baltimore. In 1982, however, SSA's telecommunications was the result of an evolving system dating back to 1966. The primary telecommunications system was called the Social Security Administration Data Acquisition and Response System (SSADARS), and it was designed to handle 100,000 transactions per day. One year after it was built in 1975, the system was totally saturated. Each year teleprocessing grew by 100 percent. By 1982 the SSADARS network was frequently breaking down and was obsolete and highly inefficient.

By 1982, there was little remaining CPU telecommunications capacity in the off-peak periods to handle the normal growth of current workloads. Entire streams of communications were frequently lost. At peak times, when most people wanted to use the system, it was simply unavailable. The result was telecommunications backlogs ranging from 10,000 to 100,000 messages at a time.

Database

The word **database** can be used only in a very loose sense to refer to SSA's 500,000 reels of magnetic tape on which it stored information on clients in major program areas. Each month SSA performed 30,000 production jobs, requiring more than 150,000 tapes to be loaded onto and off of machines. The tapes themselves were disintegrating, and errors in the tapes, along with their physical breakdown, caused very high error rates and forced a number of reruns. More than one-third of the operations staff (200 people) was required simply to handle the tapes.

As in many private organizations, data were organized at SSA by programs, and many of the data elements were repeated from one program to the next. SSA estimated that there were more than 1300 separate programs, each with its own data set. Because there was no data administration function, it was difficult to determine the total number of data elements, or the level of redundancy within the agency as a whole or even within program areas.

Management Information Systems

In 1982, SSA had a woefully inadequate capability in the MIS area. Because the data were stored on magnetic tape and were generally not available to end-user managers throughout the organization, all requests for reports had to be funneled through the information systems operations area.

But there was a crisis in operations, and this meant delays of up to several years in the production of reports crucial for management decision making. As long as all data were stored in a format that required professional computer and information systems experts to gain access to them, general management always had to deal with the information systems department. This group had a stranglehold on the organization. Their attitude, as one commentator noted, was summed up in the statement, "Don't bother us or the checks won't go out."

How Could This Happen?

There are two explanations for SSA's fall from a leading-edge systems position to near collapse in the early 1980s. First, there were internal institutional factors involving middle and senior management. Second, a sometimes hostile and rapidly changing environment in the 1970s added to SSA's woes.

In the 1970s, Congress had made more than 15 major changes in the Retirement and Survivors Insurance (RSI) program alone. These changes increasingly taxed SSA's systems to the point that systems personnel were working on weekends to make required program changes.

In 1972 Congress passed the Supplemental Security Income (SSI) program, which converted certain state-funded and -administered income maintenance programs into federal programs. SSA suddenly found itself in the welfare arena, which was far removed from that of a social insurance agency. Other programs, such as Medicaid and changes in disability insurance, as well as cost-of-living (COLA) escalators, all severely taxed SSA's systems and personnel capacity. The 1978 COLA required changes in more than 800 SSA computer programs.

The number of clients served by SSA doubled in the 1970s. But because of a growing economic crisis combining low growth and high inflation (stagflation), Congress was unwilling to expand SSA's workforce to meet the demands of new programs. There was growing public and political resistance to expanding federal government employment at the very time when new programs were coming on-line and expectations of service were rising.

SSA management at this time consistently overstated its administrative capacity to Congress and failed to communicate the nature of the growing systems crisis. SSA pleas for additional personnel were consistently turned down or reduced by Congress and the White House. Workloads of employees dramatically increased, and morale and job satisfaction declined. Training was reduced, especially in the systems area, as all resources were diverted to the operations crisis.

Toward the end of the 1970s, the growing conservative movement among Republicans and Democrats interested in reducing the size of all federal programs led to increasing pressure on SSA to reduce employment levels. In the long actuarial funding debate at the beginning of the 1980s, there was talk about "privatizing" Social Security and abolishing the agency altogether.

Complicating SSA's environment was the Brooks Act of 1965, which mandated competitive procurement of computing equipment and services. Until 1965, SSA had had a long-standing and beneficial relationship with IBM. Virtually all of SSA's equipment was manufactured by IBM and purchased on a noncompetitive basis. IBM provided planning, technical support, software support, and consulting services to SSA as part of this relationship.

By the 1970s this close relationship had ended. IBM shifted its support and marketing efforts away from the federal arena because of the Brooks Act. SSA found itself in a new competitive environment, forced to do all of its own planning, development, and procurement work. As the workload rapidly expanded at SSA in the 1970s, the agency needed a well-planned, closely managed transition to new computing equipment and software. This transition never occurred.

A challenging environment might have been overcome by a focused and dedicated management group. Perhaps the most critical weakness of all in SSA's operation in the 1970s was its inability to gain management control over the information systems function and over the information resource on which the organization itself was based.

Senior management turnover was a critical problem. In its first 38 years, SSA had six commissioners with an average tenure of 6.5 years. Two men led the agency for 27 of its 38 years. But from 1971 to 1981, SSA had seven commissioners or acting commissioners with an average tenure of 1.1 years. None of these commissioners had any experience at SSA. The senior staff of the agency was also repeatedly shaken up in this period. Compared with earlier senior managers, those of the 1970s failed to realize the critical importance of information systems to SSA's operation. Long-range planning of the agency or systems became impossible.

With new senior management came four major reorganizations of the agency. Major SSA programs were broken down into functional parts and redistributed to new functional divisions. Program coherence was lost. Performance measures and management control disappeared as managers and employees struggled to adapt to their new functions.

Efforts at Reform

SSA made several efforts in this period to regain control and direction in the systems area on which its entire operation critically depended. In 1975, SSA created the Office of Advanced Systems (OAS) within the Office of the Commissioner. SSA hoped that this advanced, high-level planning group with direct access to senior management would develop a strategy for change. Unfortunately, this effort failed to

reform SSA's manual and batch processes and was opposed by systems operations management and the union. There was no White House support for it and no suggestion from Congress or the White House that needed funding would be forthcoming. In 1979 the OAS was abolished by a new management team.

A second effort at reform began in 1979. This time the idea originated with new senior management. Called partitioning, the new reform effort sought to break SSA's internal operations into major program lines—similar to product lines—so that each program could develop its own systems. This plan was quickly rejected by the White House, Congress, and outside professionals.

A third reform effort also began in 1979. Here SSA sought to replace the aging SSADARS telecommunications network with new, high-speed communications terminals in the district offices and new telecommunications computers in the Baltimore headquarters. After a competitive procurement process, SSA contracted with the Paradyne Corporation for 2000 such terminals. Unfortunately, the first 16 systems failed all operational tests on delivery in 1981. Investigations produced charges of bidding fraud (selling systems to SSA that did not exist, "black boxes with blinking lights"), securities fraud, bribery, bid rigging, perjury, and an inadequate SSA systems requirements definition. By 1983 SSA took delivery of all the terminals, and they did perform for their expected life of eight years. But the procurement scandal further reduced SSA's credibility in Congress and the White House.

Senior management turnover, lack of concern, and failed efforts at reform took a severe toll in the systems area. Planning of information systems was either not done or was done at such a low operational level that no major changes in operations could be accomplished.

SECTION II: THE SYSTEMS MODERNIZATION PLAN

As the crisis at SSA became increasingly apparent to Congress, the General Accounting Office, and the President's Office, pressure was placed on SSA to develop a new strategy. In 1981 a new commissioner, John Svahn, a recently appointed former insurance executive with systems experience, began work on a strategic plan to try to move SSA data processing from collapse to a modern system. The result was a five-year plan called the Systems Modernization Plan

(SMP). SMP was intended to bring about long-range, tightly integrated changes in software, hardware, telecommunications, and management systems. At $500 million, the original cost estimate in 1982, the SMP was one of the single most expensive information systems projects in history.

SMP Strategy

As a bold effort to secure a total change at SSA, the SMP adopted a conservative strategy. This strategy called for SSA to do the following:

- ○ Achieve modernization through incremental, evolutionary change, given the unacceptable risks of failure.
- ○ Build on the existing systems, selecting short-term, feasible approaches that minimize risks.
- ○ Separate the modernization program from the operations and maintenance programs.
- ○ Use an external system integration contractor to provide continuity to the five-year project.
- ○ Use industry-proven, state-of-the-art systems engineering technology.
- ○ Establish a single organizational body to plan, manage, and control SMP.
- ○ Elevate systems development and operations to the highest levels of the agency.

SMP Implementation

The original plan foresaw a five-year effort broken into three stages: survival, transition, and state of the art. In the survival stage (18 months), SSA would focus on new hardware acquisition to solve immediate problems of capacity shortage. In the transition stage (18 months), SSA would begin rebuilding software, data files, and telecommunications systems. In the final state-of-the-art stage, SSA would finalize and integrate projects to achieve a contemporary level of systems. The SMP involved six interrelated programs.

Capacity Upgrade Program (CUP).

CUP was developed to reconfigure and consolidate the physical computing sites around central headquarters in Baltimore, to acquire much higher capacity and more modern computers, to eliminate sequentially organized magnetic tape files and switch to direct access devices, and to develop a local computing network for high-speed data transfers.

System Operation and Management Program (SOMP). SOMP was intended to provide modern automated tools and procedures for managing and controlling SSA's main computer center operations in Baltimore. Included were automated job scheduling tools, job station monitoring and submission systems, operational job procedures, training, and a central integrated control facility to ensure that SSA would make a smooth transition to a modern data center environment.

Data Communications Utility Program (DCUP). DCUP was designed to reengineer SSA's major telecommunications system (SSADARS). What SSA wanted was a transparent conduit for the transmission of data between and among processing units of different manufacture using a single integrated network. More than 40,000 on-line terminals were to be used in the 1300 field offices.

Software Engineering Program (SEP). SEP was designed to upgrade the existing software and retain as much of it as possible so that entirely new code did not have to be written. A critical part of the SEP was a top-down, functional analysis (using the enterprise system planning method) of the Social Security process—all of the business and organizational functions of SSA. Hopefully, this top-down planning effort would provide the framework for the redesign of SSA's total system by establishing the requirements for improvements in existing software. A second key aspect of the software engineering effort was the implementation of new software engineering technology. This involved developing and enforcing programming standards, developing quality controls, and using modern computer-aided software development tools. Special emphasis was placed on the development of modern program documentation, standardization of programs, and conversion to higher level languages when possible.

Database Integration. The database integration project involved four objectives. As a survival tactic, SSA wanted to reduce the current labor-intensive, error-prone magnetic tape operation by converting all records to high-speed disk, direct access storage devices (DASD). A second goal was to establish a data administration function to control the definition of data elements and files. A third goal was to eliminate the data errors by establishing data controls, validating files, and developing modern storage disk technology. A fourth objective was to integrate the variety of databases, making communication among them transparent.

Administrative Management Information Engineering Program (AMIEP). SSA was fundamentally dependent on manual activities to conduct most of its administration. Requests for personnel actions, purchase requisitions, telephone service, travel orders, building modifications, training requests—all these administrative matters—were processed manually. The AMIEP program was designed to integrate MIS with other programmatic modernization activities: to automate and modernize labor-intensive administrative processes and to develop management MIS to improve the planning and administrative process.

The End of SMP: Success and Failure

SMP had become increasingly controversial: Critics claimed failure whereas the agency's leaders claimed success. By 1988 Dorcas Hardy, the new SSA commissioner, quietly ended SMP and announced a new plan called "2000: A Strategic Plan." What had the SMP accomplished in five years?

For much of the early years of SMP the environment was supportive of and sympathetic to the modernization program. By 1986, however, criticism was beginning to develop over the rising costs and seemingly endless time frame. In large part the critics drew strength from the fact that the SMP project had been extended by SSA for an additional five years (to 1992) and had doubled in expected cost to $1 billion; no major software breakthroughs were apparent to the public or Congress; and the effort to modernize SSA's "backend" or database appeared to stall.

The White House increasingly pressed SSA to make plans for reducing its staff by one-quarter, or 20,000 positions. By the end of 1988, the SSA staff had been reduced by 17,000 workers, from 83,000 to 66,000, mostly by attrition. These reductions were made in anticipation of sharp increases in productivity brought about by the SMP modernization efforts. There was little systematic effort to examine this hope.

The General Accounting Office (GAO), responding to requests from the House Government Operations Committee (Rep. Jack Brooks, Democrat of Texas, chairman), issued many highly critical reports of SSA's procurement policies. In one report issued in 1986, GAO charged that SSA failed to redevelop software or to develop a true database architecture. In another 1987 report, GAO claimed that SSA's new Claims Modernization Software would handle only 2 percent of the workload (merely initial applications for retirement and not the application processing or postentitlement changes)! The report chided SSA for dropping modernization of the postentitlement process, which accounts for 94 percent of daily SSA transactions. SSA management heatedly denied GAO's allegations, but the backsliding in software became a major weapon of SMP opponents. GAO called for a halt in procurements. Hardy refused and began purchasing 40,000 full-color desktop terminals.

A review of SMP by the Office of Technology Assessment (OTA), a congressional research agency, concluded that the White House, Congress, and SSA were all to blame for SSA's failure. The White House was blamed for prematurely seeking huge workforce reductions before the new systems were in place. It was also blamed for continuing political interference in the agency and for failure to support senior management. Congress was blamed for failing to understand the complexity of SSA programs and the long-term nature of total systems change. In addition, OTA blamed new procurement laws for slowing down and complicating the purchase of new hardware.

OTA pointed to a number of faults at SSA. From the very beginning of SMP, SSA failed to rethink its method of doing business. SMP basically sought to automate an organizational structure and a way of doing business established in the 1930s. SSA failed, for instance, to question the role of 1300 field offices—are they really needed in a day of wide area networks and desktop PCs? Should SSA's major data files be centralized in Baltimore? SSA failed to rethink its basic architecture of a centralized mainframe operation in Baltimore serving the entire country. Why not a more decentralized structure? Why not minicomputers in every district office? OTA also pointed to SSA's failure to develop new software on a timely basis and a new database architecture. It was felt these shortcomings, especially in software and database, would ultimately come to haunt SSA thereafter.

In general, SMP lacked a vision for the future around which it could build a powerful new information architecture.[1]

GAO, OTA, and labor critics believed that whatever increases in productivity occurred from 1982 to 1988 resulted largely from workforce reduction, deterioration in service, and asking the remaining employees to work harder, rather than any result of technology per se. Although public surveys published by SSA showed the general public thought SSA did a fine job, surveys of field office employees and managers with direct knowledge of the situation showed declining service quality, employee performance, and morale.

As employee levels dropped, managers complained in interviews that the "work load is oppressive," recalling days in the 1960s when lines of clients surrounded SSA offices. Although managers praised the new claims modernization software, teleservice centers, and preinterviewing techniques that permit clericals to answer questions of clients using on-line queries, the overall reduction in labor force put a "crushing load on District Office personnel." Employees and managers reported many of the most capable managers and claims representatives were leaving SSA for the private sector or other government jobs as working conditions deteriorated.[2]

For the critics, SSA had made some improvements in service and processing, but these resulted early in the SMP plan and were largely the result of hardware purchases and running the old software faster. Whatever progress in productivity occurred did so at the expense of employees and service to clients.

By 1988, SSA management conceded that SMP had indeed doubled in size to a projected $1 billion, but by 1988 the SMP plan had actually spent slightly less ($444 million) than the original estimate of $500 million. Management conceded that the time required to reach state-of-the-art processing had been extended to 1992; that there was an excessive emphasis on hardware, that software development was slow, and that the agency carried over large balances of unbudgeted funds from year to year (indicating difficulty in managing projects and allocated funds).[3] In fact, software development was four years behind schedule, and the database redesign (the so-called "back-end" of the system) was still being considered after five years. Nevertheless, SSA had documented steady improvements in a number of measures of services

to beneficiaries, many of which are due to the SMP:

○ A 25 percent decrease in RSI claims processing time.

○ A small decrease in disability insurance (DI) claims processing time (2.2 days).

○ A high and improving rate of RSI claims accuracy (95.7 to 97.2 percent).

○ A 41 percent decrease in SSI processing time.

○ A 7 percent decrease in SSI blind/disabled processing time.

○ A 47 percent decrease in retired survivors disability insurance (RSDI) status processing time.

○ Stable administrative costs in RSI since 1980 (1.1 percent of benefits).

Management pointed to the following key changes brought about by the SMP: Management claimed that overall SMP brought about a 25 percent increase in productivity. The agency was doing slightly more work in 1988 than it was in 1982 but with 17,000 fewer employees. SSA created a new deputy commissioner for systems development and raised the status of systems in the organization to the senior management level. Management noted that SMP had made great progress in its specific program areas.

Hardware Capacity Upgrade

Between 1982 and 1988 SSA increased processing capacity twentyfold, from 20 MIPS to a total of 400 MIPS, replacing outdated computers purchased without competitive bids with hardware supplied by three manufacturers on a competitive basis.

System Operation and Management Program (SOMP)

The central processing facility in Baltimore developed efficient job scheduling standards and procedures for handling tapes and documents so that 95 percent of its processing is completed on time.

Data Communications Utility Program (DCUP)

Under SMP a network of more than 50,000 devices was installed nationwide, with the objective of putting a terminal on every claims representative's desktop. Network capacity increased from 1200 characters per second in 1982 to 7000 characters per second in 1988.

Software Engineering

SSA made major progress redesigning the software for the retirement program. Now millions of retired persons can initiate the claims process or inquire about their accounts using an 800-number teleservice or have a claims representative initiate the claim on-line from a district office. In 1982 this capability was not even imagined. Developing such interactive systems to deliver services required entirely new code; the old software could not be salvaged.

Database Integration

SSA converted 500,000 reels of tape to more modern DASDs. All master files were converted to disk, making it possible to handle more than 2 million inquiries per day directly on-line. SSA developed its own in-house data management system called the Master Data Access Method (MADAM) to handle all on-line and batch access to SSA master files. However, the data are still organized according to major program areas. SSA has yet to develop an integrated database for all or even some of its major programs that could provide a "whole person" view of SSA clients. A major difficulty is deciding on an overall database architecture that could integrate information from the major program areas.

SECTION III: SSA'S STRATEGIC PLAN AND INFORMATION SYSTEMS PLAN

SSA issued a new Agency Strategic Plan (ASP) in 1988. The plan was updated in 1991 to incorporate a wider vision of the agency's future. The new ASP strategic priorities called for improvements in client access to SSA, the appeals process, and the disability process; movement toward a paperless agency; and establishment of a decentralized data processing structure.

In August 1990 Renato A. DiPentima took over as deputy commissioner of systems. DiPentima initiated a seven-year Information Systems Plan (ISP) in September 1991 to support the ASP. The ISP was updated in 1992 and late 1993.

The ISP is SSA's long-range plan for managing information systems as the agency moves into the 1990s and beyond. Its primary goal is to support the ASP by building a systems environment that improves service to the public and SSA users. Long-term strategic priorities include improving the disability process, the appeals process, and the public's access to SSA by turning SSA into a paperless agency with electronic claims folders, and establishing a cooperative processing architecture. The ISP was designed to be a continuous plan that could always be upgraded.

Both plans address the challenges faced by SSA as it moves into the twenty-first century. SSA's total workload is expected to increase by 26 percent between 1990 and 2005. There will be limited funding for new initiatives, coupled with increased demands for higher levels of service to the public. In the past, most SSA clients preferred to visit SSA field offices. Today, they prefer to conduct their business over the telephone, and they expect the same fast, efficient service they receive in the private sector. SSA must enhance systems to handle increasing workloads without hiring more employees and keep costs low because of scarce budgetary resources. The number of field and operational employees has already decreased substantially since the 1980s and the remaining employees require new technologies to handle the increased workload.

The ISP calls for moving SSA toward a distributed architecture, ending its total reliance on centralized mainframe computers for its programmatic applications that deliver services to SSA clients. Selected business functions are being distributed between headquarters and local processors. Most SSA employees will use LAN-based intelligent workstations with multiple levels of software running on platforms ranging from mainframes to PCs. Databases are being distributed. Greater efficiency will result from having processing close to the data source and information user.

The SSA's technology modernization calls for an IWS/LAN (intelligent workstation and local area network) Technology Program. IWS/LAN is intended to move SSA to a more decentralized computing environment by replacing SSA's "dumb terminals" with 60,000 PCs arranged in token ring LANs. The LANs give SSA field staff more autonomous computing power and the ability to perform word processing, to share data, and to exchange e-mail messages. They are being linked to the agency's main network, SSANet. By early 1999, SSA had converted 80 applications to Windows NT servers.

By distributing processing and storing data at the level where the work is done, the number of data accesses and the volume of network traffic should be minimized, decreasing the response time for many workloads. For example, access time for important records has been reduced from several minutes to 30 seconds. This arrangement allows the automation of many functions that are presently not cost effective to do on a mainframe or practical to do on a PC.

The SSA's computer center in Baltimore will continue to supply mainframe processing power for programs such as retirement and supplemental security. But as applications are rewritten, the PCs will perform more of the processing and the mainframe will gradually evolve into a database server role. SSA has argued that implementation of IWS/LAN is essential to provide an infrastructure for future electronic delivery and reengineering initiatives and to avoid problems and expenditures resulting from breakdowns in existing dumb terminals.

SSA replaced many batch applications with on-line interactive systems, starting with the Title II claims process, then the Title XVI, disability, and Title II postentitlement processes. By the year 2000, SSA expects to convert most of its major systems to an interactive environment using an appearance-of-update technique, which from the user's perspective appears to update master records on-line. Expert systems, such as an application to provide answers to telephone inquiries, will help reduce manual processing.

Although databases will be distributed over SSA's multilevel telecommunications system, commercial DBMS are still not capable of handling SSA's specific requirements under a distributed processing environment. SSA plans to monitor the performance improvements of commercial DBMS as they mature for future consideration. The decision to distribute SSA's large databases will be based on cost/benefit and service improvement considerations.

SSA is reducing transmission costs by using telephone switching systems to integrate network access when possible. It will provide a common connection to be shared by voice services, video teleconferencing, fax, LAN interconnections, and SSANet. SSA communications planning will use OSI standards, specifying appropriate protocols, interfaces, and network technologies to obtain required intercommunication and interoperability.

SSA points to many service improvements that resulted from these systems initiatives. An 800 phone number now receives more than 64 million calls annually. Customers can use this 800 number to file retirement or survivor claims immediately. Seventy percent of babies in the United States are enumerated at birth, eliminating the need to make separate applications for Social Security numbers.

Is Distributed Technology Enough?

In the spring of 1994, the OTA released a report stating that the SSA's $1.1 billion five-year migration from mainframe to client/server computing was technically sound but ahead of the agency's understanding of how to use intelligent workstations and LANs to improve service delivery. The OTA report reiterated concerns raised by the GAO that SSA was unlikely to realize significant benefits because it had not linked its proposed technology strategy to specific service delivery improvements. GAO questioned SSA's plans to implement IWS/LAN before determining the service delivery improvements that could result from this technology. OTA noted that SSA had made a good-faith effort to restructure its service delivery but that the agency had "prioritized . . . installation according to current SSA operational and service delivery needs—essentially automating marginal improvements in the status quo." OTA believed that SSA needed to include its clients, labor representatives, and individuals with experience in electronic service delivery into its planning process, and it needed to reengineer its business processes to dramatically improve service. OTA also believed SSA had not done enough analysis of the costs and benefits of automation, including IWS/LAN, and of the impact of automation against specific performance goals.

OTA pointed out that SSA's ever-increasing workload, coupled with staff reductions from further government downsizing, could again threaten SSA's ability to deliver the level of service expected by Congress and the public. OTA also questioned the feasibility of managing a massive distributed computing environment from a single facility in Baltimore. Deputy Commissioner DiPentima responded by noting that it was a big challenge to maintain such a large network and monitor it centrally. If SSA were to monitor the network locally, it would require 2000 LAN managers. The centrally managed network has been able to process 20 million transactions per day with 99.9 percent uptime.

OTA recommended that SSA receive funding for reengineering and service delivery planning and that the agency

Taxpayers can use the Social Security Administration Web site to request personal earnings and benefits estimate statements. SSA is trying to use the Web and other information technology to improve its service to the public while keeping down costs.

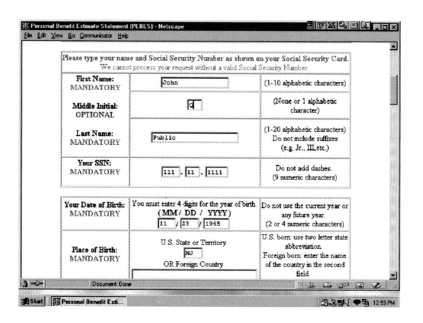

participate in government-wide electronic delivery pilots and projects such as the following:

- ○ Electronic data interchange (EDI) for filing earnings reports by business.
- ○ Direct electronic deposit of benefits payments.
- ○ Electronic bulletin boards and networks to provide the public with information about SSA.
- ○ Multiprogram electronic benefits delivery in which a single card could be used to obtain payment for Social Security benefits, Medicaid, and food stamps.
- ○ Integrated electronic records for SSA recipients, providing a single electronic folder instead of separate electronic and paper files.
- ○ Automated disability determination to streamline determination of initial and ongoing medical qualifications for disability insurance benefits.

Determining eligibility for disability benefits is considered the most troubled SSA service. SSA must continually ensure that recipients are eligible based on their medical and financial condition. Candidates for disability benefits are currently evaluated by state Disability Determination Service (DDS) offices, which are funded by SSA but are run by the states. Initial disability determinations can take up to several months, with a backlog of 750,000 cases. The backlog of continuing

reviews is even larger. The error rate for disability insurance, resulting in overpayments to eligible recipients, payments to ineligible recipients, or denial of benefits to qualified people, is estimated to be about 3.5 percent, which is similar to the error rate for SSI programs. SSA-sponsored studies have suggested that automation will play a small role in improving the disability process in comparison to radically changing the organization and the flow of disability work. SSA set up a reengineering task force in mid-1993, with the full support of top management, to focus on ways to radically improve the disability benefit determination process. Its findings served as the basis of a blueprint for streamlining the disability process.

In its drive toward paperless processing, SSA developed capabilities for small businesses to submit wage reports electronically using a PC or high-speed data transmission lines. In 1998, wage reports for nearly 14 million employees were submitted this way. The electronic filing effort could replace the 62 million paper forms SSA receives annually from small businesses and reduce the workload at SSA's Wilkes Barre data operations center. (Companies with more than 250 employees already file electronically.)

Most requests for benefits estimates are made on paper forms that cost SSA about $5.23 each to process. Congress has ordered the agency to provide annual benefits estimates for every worker over age 25, amounting to 123 million people, by the year 2000. SSA enhanced its Web

site to allow visitors to request benefits estimates on-line, but it has backed away from delivering their estimates over the Web because of concerns about security and protection of individual privacy. Taxpayers must still receive their benefits estimates and history of reported earnings by mail.

Reengineering services is starting to pay off. SSA is being described as the federal agency providing the best service to its customers, winning praise from Vice President Al Gore and business reengineering expert Michael Hammer. SSA was one of the first government agencies to tackle date problems, having made date changes part of its regular maintenance since 1989. The agency expects to be year 2000-ready well in advance. SSA prints about 45 million checks per month, representing $300 billion to $400 billion flowing yearly into the U.S. economy. But even if all SSA programs are year 2000-compliant, SSA could still experience millennium problems because it has so many interrelated ties to other government agencies. For example, SSA feeds and accepts data from the Veterans Administration and the Treasury Department. So SSA's year 2000 problem won't be solved until all related systems from other federal agencies are fixed.

Much has been learned by SSA about the difficulties of building systems that can meet ever-changing business needs. Management has learned that deploying new information technology does not automatically translate into fewer employees, especially when transaction volumes are increasing. Can SSA continue to decentralize? Will SSA's information systems maintain the level of service the public and Congress expect? These are just some of the difficult questions facing SSA as it moves into the twenty-first century.

Sources: Edward Cone, "Social Security Gets It Right," **Information Week Online,** January 12, 1998; Matt Hamblen, "Are U.S. Agencies Ready for Year 2000?" **Computerworld,** January 11, 1999; Richard W. Stevenson, "Social Security: Divergent Paths," **The New York Times,** March 24, 1999; "Social Security Unit to Close a Web Site for Security Review," **The Wall Street Journal,** April 10, 1997; Sharon Machlis, "Web Apps May Cut Costs at Social Security," **Computerworld,** April 7, 1997; Dale Buss, "Social Security Going Paperless," **Home-Office Computing,** February 1997; David Bank, "Social Security Plans to Test W2 Forms Filed on the Internet," **The Wall Street Journal,** October 25, 1996; Martha T. Moore, "Social Security Reengineers: Agency Puts Focus on Its Customers," **USA Today,** August 30, 1995; Social Security Administration, "Information Systems Plan," Baltimore, MD: Department of Health and Human Services (September 1994); Office of Technology Assessment, "The Social Security Administration's Decentralized Computer Strategy," Washington, D.C.: U.S. Government Printing Office (April 1994); and Office of Technology Assessment, "The Social Security Administration and Information Technology: A Case Study," Washington, D.C.: U.S. Congress (1986).

CASE STUDY QUESTIONS

1. What were the major factors in SSA's past that made it a leading innovator in information systems technology? How did these supportive factors change in the 1970s?

2. Describe briefly the problems with SSA's hardware, software, data storage, and telecommunications systems prior to SMP.

3. What were the major environmental and institutional factors that created the crisis at SSA?

4. Why did SSA's reform efforts in the late 1970s fail?

5. What were the major elements of SSA's implementation strategy for SMP? Describe its major projects.

6. What successful changes in management and organizational structure have been brought about by SMP? How secure are these changes (what environmental factors could destroy them)?

7. In what areas has SMP had the greatest success? In what areas has SMP not succeeded? Why?

8. Evaluate SSA's IWS/LAN technology program in light of SSA's history of information systems projects.

9. How successful has SSA been in creating an appropriate information system architecture for the year 2000? Justify your explanation.

[1]Office of Technology Assessment, "The Social Security Administration and Information Technology, A Case Study," Washington, D.C.: U.S. Congress (1986).

[2]Based on interviews in northeastern U.S. metropolitan area district offices by the authors and Alan F. Westin.

[3]Social Security Administration, "Report on Social Security Administration Computer Modernization and Related Expenditures," prepared for the Senate Appropriations Committee, February 1989, p. ii.

Chapter 14

Managing
Knowledge

Learning Objectives

After completing this chapter, you will be able to:

1. Explain the importance of knowledge management in contemporary organizations.

2. Describe the applications that are most useful for distributing, creating, and sharing knowledge in the firm.

3. Evaluate the role of artificial intelligence in knowledge management.

4. Demonstrate how organizations can use expert systems and case-based reasoning to capture knowledge.

5. Demonstrate how organizations can use neural networks and other intelligent techniques to improve their knowledge base.

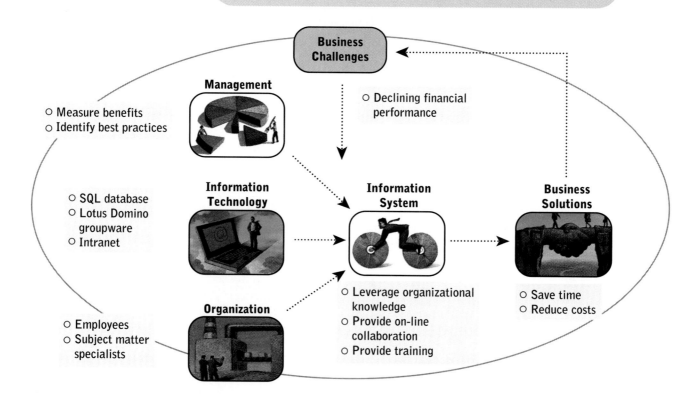

Business Challenges

Management
- Measure benefits
- Identify best practices

- Declining financial performance

Information Technology
- SQL database
- Lotus Domino groupware
- Intranet

Information System
- Leverage organizational knowledge
- Provide on-line collaboration
- Provide training

Business Solutions
- Save time
- Reduce costs

Organization
- Employees
- Subject matter specialists

Shell Wakes Up with Knowledge Management

In 1991, Shell Oil Co. reported the worst financial results in its history. That news became a wake-up call to make some serious changes in the way it ran its business. One solution was to put more emphasis on making better use of the knowledge and experience of its employees. If Shell's entire work force of 21,000 could learn about the "best practice" of a single person, the company might reap enormous savings in time and effort and perhaps use these ideas to innovate further.

Shell used information systems to create a communications and collaboration environment that would act as a "knowledge multiplier." Ten subject-matter specialists scoured Shell sources and external sources such as universities, consultants, other companies, and research literature for leading-edge practices

and ideas to populate a Knowledge Management System (KMS). The KMS contains knowledge in three areas: business models, leadership, and engagement, or human interactions. Its repository contains 1000 documents and 50 "best practices," such as a model developed by a university professor to help an organization meet its goals. The model was adopted by all of Shell's four major operating units. Other groups at Shell, such as geologists, use similar knowledge management systems.

The Knowledge Management System was developed by Shell and a systems integrator and became operational in September 1997. Its knowledge repository uses an SQL database. A Lotus Domino groupware application allows employees to carry on dialogues through the company intranet. The author of a best practice in the repository might use this tool to talk with colleagues about his or her experiences.

Sandi Fitch, a senior executive at Shell Services International, uses the KMS to mentor technical subordinates in business leadership. By using the KMS, she can walk through a business model, review concepts, do some exercises with her team, and then examine the best practices of others.

According to Teltech Resource Network Corporation, a Minneapolis research and knowledge services company, firms that leverage their best practices can realize widespread benefits. Shell management will initially measure benefits in terms of usage and the number of best practices posted to the database. Later it will track the ideas from the system that actually are put into practice.

Sources: Carol Hildebrand, "Making KM Pay Off," *CIO Enterprise Magazine*, February 15, 1999; and Gary H. Anthes, "Learning How to Share," *Computerworld*, February 23, 1998.

Shell Oil Co.'s use of its Knowledge Management System is one example of how systems can be used to leverage organizational knowledge by making it more easily available. Collaborating and communicating with practitioners and experts and sharing ideas and information have become essential requirements in business, science, and government. In an information economy, capturing and distributing intelligence and knowledge and enhancing group collaboration have become vital to organizational innovation and survival. Special systems can be used for managing organizational knowledge, but they raise the following management challenges:

1. **Designing information systems that genuinely enhance the productivity of knowledge workers.** Information systems that truly enhance the productivity of knowledge workers may be difficult to build because the manner in which information technology can enhance higher level tasks such as those performed by managers and professionals (i.e., scientists or engineers) is not always clearly understood (Sheng et al., 1989/90). Some aspects of organizational knowledge cannot be captured easily or codified, or the information that organizations finally manage to capture may become outdated as environments change (Malhotra, 1998). High-level knowledge workers may resist the introduction of any new technology, or they may resist knowledge work systems because such systems diminish personal control and creativity.

2. **Creating robust expert systems.** Expert systems must be changed every time there is a change in the organizational environment. Each time there is a change in the rules used by experts, they must be reprogrammed. It is difficult to provide expert systems with the flexibility of human experts. Many thousands of businesses have undertaken experimental projects in expert systems, but only a small percentage have created expert systems that actually can be used on a production basis.

This chapter examines information system applications specifically designed to help organizations create, capture, and distribute knowledge and information. First, we examine information systems for supporting information and knowledge work. Then we look at the ways that organizations can use artificial intelligence technologies for capturing and storing knowledge and expertise.

14.1 Knowledge Management in the Organization

Chapter 1 described the emergence of the information economy, in which the major source of wealth and prosperity is the production and distribution of information and knowledge. For example, 55 percent of the U.S. labor force consists of knowledge and information workers, and 60 percent of the gross domestic product of the United States comes from the knowledge and information sectors, such as finance and publishing. Knowledge-intensive technology is vital to these information-intense sectors, but it also plays a major role in traditional industrial sectors such as the automobile and mining industries.

In an information economy, knowledge and core competencies—the two or three things that an organization does best—are key organizational assets. Producing unique products or services or producing them at a lower cost than competitors is based on superior knowledge of the production process and superior design. Knowing how to do things effectively and efficiently in ways that other organizations cannot duplicate is a primary source of profit. Some management theorists believe that these knowledge assets are as important, if not more important, than physical and financial assets in ensuring the competitiveness and survival of the firm. Management of organizational knowledge may be especially important in flattened or network organizations where layers of management have been eliminated to help members of teams and task forces maintain ties to other specialists in their field (Favela, 1997).

As knowledge becomes a central productive and strategic asset, the success of the organization increasingly depends on its ability to gather, produce, maintain, and disseminate knowledge. Developing procedures and routines to optimize the creation, flow, learning, protection, and sharing of knowledge and information in the firm becomes a central management responsibility. The process of systematically and actively managing and leveraging the stores of knowledge in an organization is called **knowledge management.** Information systems can play a valuable role in knowledge management, helping the organization optimize its flow of information and capture its knowledge base.

Companies cannot take advantage of their knowledge resources if they have inefficient processes for capturing and distributing knowledge, or if they fail to appreciate the value of the knowledge they possess. Some corporations, such as Shell Oil Company described in the chapter opening vignette and others discussed in this chapter, have created explicit knowledge management programs for protecting and distributing knowledge resources that they have identified and for discovering new sources of knowledge. These programs are often headed by a **chief knowledge officer (CKO).** The chief knowledge officer is a senior executive who is responsible for the firm's knowledge management program. The CKO helps design programs and systems to find new sources of knowledge or to make better use of existing knowledge in organizational and management processes (Earl and Scott, 1999).

Information Systems and Knowledge Management

All the major types of information systems described so far facilitate the flow of information and have organizational knowledge embedded in them. However, office automation systems (OAS), knowledge work systems (KWS), group collaboration systems, and artificial intelligence applications are especially useful for knowledge management because they focus on supporting information and knowledge work and on defining and capturing the organization's knowledge base. This knowledge base may include (1) structured internal knowledge, such as product manuals or research reports; (2) external knowledge, such as competitive intelligence; and (3) informal internal knowledge, often called **tacit knowledge,** which resides in the minds of individual employees but has not been documented in structured form (Davenport, DeLong, and Beers, 1998).

Figure 14-1 illustrates the array of information systems specifically designed to support knowledge management. Office automation systems (OAS) help disseminate and coordinate the flow of information in the organization. Knowledge work systems (KWS) support the activities of highly skilled knowledge workers and professionals as they create new knowledge and try to integrate it into the firm. Group collaboration and support systems support the creation and sharing of knowledge among people working in groups. Artificial intelligence systems provide organizations and managers with codified knowledge that can be reused by others in the organization.

Knowledge Work and Productivity

In information economies, organizational productivity depends on increasing the productivity of information and knowledge workers. Consequently, companies have made massive investments in technology to support information work. Information technology now accounts for 41 percent of total business expenditures on capital equipment in the United States (Roach, 1996). Much of that information technology investment has poured into offices and the service sector. Office automation and professional work systems are among the fastest-growing information system applications.

Although information technology has increased productivity in manufacturing, the extent to which computers have enhanced the productivity of information workers is under debate. Some studies show that investment in information technology has not led to any appreciable growth in productivity among office workers. The average white-collar productivity gain from 1980 to 1990 was only 0.28 percent each year. Corporate downsizings and cost-reduction measures have increased worker efficiency but have not yet led to sustained enhancements signifying genuine productivity gains (Roach, 1988 and 1996). Other studies

knowledge management The process of systematically and actively managing and leveraging the stores of knowledge in an organization.

chief knowledge officer (CKO) Senior executive in charge of the organization's knowledge management program.

tacit knowledge Expertise and experience of organizational members that has not been formally documented.

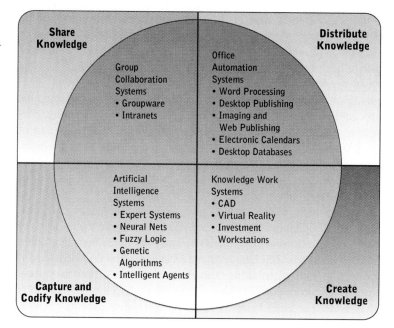

Figure 14-1 A number of contemporary information systems are designed to give close-in support to information workers at many levels in the organization.

suggest that information technology investments are starting to generate a productivity payback. Brynjolfsson and Hitt's examination of information systems spending at 380 large firms during a five-year period found that return on investment (ROI) averaged more than 50 percent per year for computers of all sizes (Brynjolfsson and Hitt, 1993). It is too early to tell whether these gains are short-term or represent a genuine turnaround in service-sector productivity.

Productivity changes among information workers are difficult to measure because of the problems of identifying suitable units of output for information work (Panko, 1991). How does one measure the output of a law office? Should one measure productivity by examining the number of forms completed per employee (a measure of physical unit productivity) or by examining the amount of revenue produced per employee (a measure of financial unit productivity) in an information- and knowledge-intense industry? In addition, different types of organizations derive different levels of productivity benefit from information technology (Brynjolfsson and Hitt, 1998).

In addition to reducing costs, computers may increase the quality of products and services for consumers. These intangible benefits are difficult to measure and consequently are not addressed by conventional productivity measures. Moreover, because of competition, the value created by computers may primarily flow to customers rather than to the company making the investments (Brynjolfsson, 1996).

Introduction of information technology does not automatically guarantee productivity. Desktop computers, e-mail, and fax applications actually can generate more drafts, memos, spreadsheets, and messages—increasing bureaucratic red tape and paperwork. Firms are more likely to produce high returns on information technology investments if they rethink their procedures, processes, and business goals.

14.2 Information and Knowledge Work Systems

Information work is work that consists primarily of creating or processing information. It is carried out by information workers who usually are divided into two subcategories: **data workers,** who primarily process and disseminate information; and **knowledge workers,** who primarily create knowledge and information.

Examples of data workers include secretaries, sales personnel, accountants, and draftsmen. Researchers, designers, architects, writers, and judges are examples of knowledge workers. Data workers usually can be distinguished from knowledge workers because knowledge workers usually have higher levels of education and memberships in professional organizations. In addition,

information work Work that primarily consists of creating or processing information.

data workers People such as secretaries or bookkeepers who process and disseminate the organization's information and paperwork.

knowledge workers People such as engineers, scientists, or architects who design products or services or create knowledge for the organization.

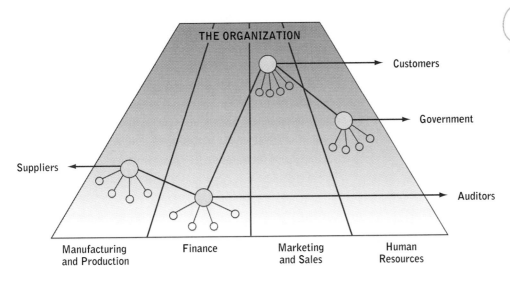

Figure 14-2 The three major roles of offices. Offices perform three major roles. (1) They coordinate the work of local professionals and information workers. (2) They coordinate work in the organization across levels and functions. (3) They couple the organization to the external environment.

knowledge workers exercise independent judgment as a routine aspect of their work. Data and knowledge workers have different information requirements and different systems to support them.

Distributing Knowledge: Office and Document Management Systems

Most data work and a great deal of knowledge work takes place in offices, including most of the work done by managers. The office plays a major role in coordinating the flow of information throughout the entire organization. The office has three basic functions (see Figure 14-2):

- Managing and coordinating the work of data and knowledge workers
- Connecting the work of the local information workers with all levels and functions of the organization
- Connecting the organization to the external world, including customers, suppliers, government regulators, and external auditors.

Office workers span a very broad range: professionals, managers, sales, and clerical workers working alone or in groups. Their major activities include the following:

- Managing documents, including document creation, storage, retrieval, and dissemination
- Scheduling for individuals and groups
- Communicating, including initiating, receiving, and managing voice, digital, and document-based communications for individuals and groups
- Managing data, such as on employees, customers, and vendors.

These activities can be supported by office automation systems (see Table 14.1). **Office automation systems (OAS)** can be defined as any application of information technology that intends to increase productivity of information workers in the office. Fifteen years ago, office automation meant only the creation, processing, and management of documents. Today professional knowledge and information work remains highly document-centered. However, digital image processing—words and documents—is also at the core of systems, as are high-speed digital communications services. Because office work involves many people jointly engaged in projects, contemporary office automation systems have powerful group assistance tools like networked digital calendars. An ideal office environment would be based on a seamless network of digital machines linking professional, clerical, and managerial work groups and running a variety of types of software.

Although word processing and desktop publishing address the creation and presentation of documents, they only exacerbate the existing paper avalanche problem. Work-flow problems arising from paper handling are enormous. It has been estimated that up to 85 percent of corporate information is stored on paper. Locating and updating information in that format is a great source of organizational inefficiency.

office automation systems (OAS) Computer systems, such as word processing, voice mail, and imaging, that are designed to increase the productivity of information workers in the office.

Table 14.1	Typical Office Automation Systems	

Office Activity	Technology
Managing documents	Word processing; desktop publishing; document imaging; Web publishing; work flow managers
Scheduling	Electronic calendars; groupware, intranets
Communicating	E-mail; voice mail; digital answering systems; groupware; intranets
Managing data	Desktop databases; spreadsheets; user-friendly interfaces to mainframe databases

document imaging systems
Systems that convert documents and images into digital form so they can be stored and accessed by the computer.

jukebox A device for storing and retrieving many optical disks.

index server In imaging systems, a device that stores the indexes that allow a user to identify and retrieve a specific document.

One way to reduce problems stemming from paper work-flow is to employ document imaging systems. **Document imaging systems** are systems that convert documents and images into digital form so they can be stored and accessed by a computer. Such systems store, retrieve, and manipulate a digitized image of a document, allowing the document itself to be discarded. The system must contain a scanner that converts the document image into a bit-mapped image, storing that image as a graphic. If the document is not in active use, it usually is stored on an optical disk system. Optical disks, kept on-line in a **jukebox** (a device for storing and retrieving many optical disks), require up to a minute to retrieve the document automatically.

An imaging system also requires an **index server** to contain the indexes that will allow users to identify and retrieve a document when needed. Index data are entered so that a document can be retrieved in a variety of ways, depending upon the application. For example, the index may contain the document scan date, the customer name and number, the document type, and some subject information. Finally, the system must include retrieval equipment, primarily workstations capable of handling graphics, although printers usually are included. USAA's imaging system in Chapter 2 illustrates the kinds of benefits imaging technology can provide.

Traditional document-management systems can be expensive, requiring proprietary client/server networks, special client software, and storage capabilities. Intranets provide a low-cost and universally available platform for basic document publishing, and many companies are using them for this purpose. Employees can publish information using Web-page authoring tools and post it to an intranet Web server where it can be shared and accessed throughout the company with standard Web browsers. These Weblike "documents" can be multimedia objects combining text, graphics, audio, and video along with hyperlinks. After a document has been posted to the server, it can be linked to other documents (see Figure 14-3).

For more sophisticated document-management functions, such as controlling changes to documents, maintaining histories of activity and changes in the managed documents, and the ability to search documents on either content or index terms, commercial Web-based systems such as those from IntraNet Solutions or Open Text are available. Vendors such as FileNet and Documentum have enhanced their traditional document-management systems with Web capabilities.

The Window on Management describes the benefits of the Web-based system from BidCom, Inc. for work flow management, document control, and project management in the architectural, engineering, and construction industries.

Figure 14-3 Web publishing and document management. An author can post information on an intranet Web server, where it can be accessed through a variety of mechanisms.

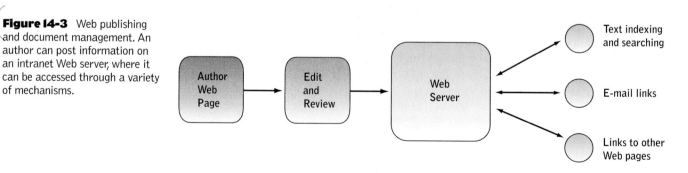

Managing Building Projects with the Internet

Many people think that the most widely used tool on a large construction site is a hammer, but it's probably a fax machine. A complex construction project, such as the Boston Artery Tunnel described in Chapter 13, requires the coordination of many different groups and hundreds of thousands of blueprints and other design documents. Many different CAD/CAM and document management systems have been developed to deal with this problem. Now such tools are available on the Web, allowing project managers to exchange documents and work on-line wherever they are working using Web browser software.

BidCom, a San Francisco–based firm founded in 1995, is hoping to revolutionize the architecture and construction industry by allowing managers to coordinate project workflow and documents from a Web-based system called in-Site. Architects, project owners, or general contractors can purchase time and space on the BidCom system, paying for setup and monthly fees, which are based on the number of system users and level of service required by the project. The project owner or general contractor creates a specific profile for each user based on his or her role in the project, which determines what documents and portions of the system the user can access and update.

Users can post CAD drawings of project plans and even use a "markup layer" to redline drawings of the subsystems for which they are responsible. They can also post budgets, contracts, schedules, material safety data sheets, design descriptions, announcements, forms, field reports, daily diaries, and government safety regulations, as well as project team directories and proceedings of project meetings or construction permits. All of these documents can be tracked easily individually or by type of document. The system can identify different versions of each document.

BidCom uses the Oracle8 database management system, running on Windows NT Web servers at various locations. Oracle Application Server serves the Web pages built by the database, which can be accessed and read by users equipped with Netscape or Internet Explorer Web browsers over the Internet. In-Site also uses the Oracle8: Lite database management system, which runs on small wireless devices. Construction foremen can input data into the system using wireless personal digital assistants, or engineers can be contacted through the system using pagers. Recently in-Site has been enhanced with capabilities for a photo gallery, local weather reports from AccuWeather, and global project management.

Swinerton and Walberg Builders, an old San Francisco construction management and general contracting firm, used in-Site in a project to renovate the headquarters of discount broker Charles Schwab & Co. in downtown San Francisco to house Schwab's Information Technology Department and 2000 people. Swinerton and Walberg were in charge of coordinating 100 people and 30 vendors responsible for air-handling, communication, and electrical systems. In-Site helped manage the paper flow between the vendors, saving money and clerical time. A document such as meeting minutes could be posted to the system, categorized, and made available for everyone to view and download.

Swinerton and Walberg are using the system in other projects as well. According to Swinerton's senior vice president and northern California division manager Charlie Kuffner, if the company can shave a week or two off a project using BidCom, it could save a big customer $50,000 in rental fees.

To Think About: What are the management benefits of using Web-based document and project management systems? Are there any drawbacks?

Sources: Michael Miley, "Hard Hats and Laptops," **Oracle Magazine**, January/February 1999; and Adam Feuerstein, "BidCom Builds Business on Construction Management," **San Francisco Business Times**, November 23, 1998.

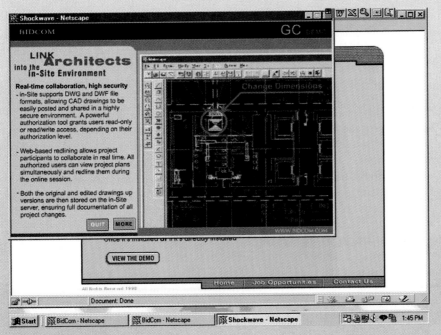

To achieve the large productivity gains promised by imaging technology, organizations must redesign their work flow. In the past, the existence of only one copy of a document largely shaped work flow. Work had to be performed serially; two people could not work on the same document at the same time. Significant staff time was devoted to filing and retrieving documents. After a document has been stored electronically, work flow management can change the traditional methods of working with documents (see Chapter 11).

Creating Knowledge: Knowledge Work Systems

Knowledge work is that portion of information work that creates new knowledge and information. For example, knowledge workers create new products or find ways to improve existing ones. Knowledge work is segmented into many highly specialized fields, and each field has a different collection of **knowledge work systems (KWS)** that are specialized to support workers in that field. Knowledge workers perform three key roles that are critical to the organization and to the managers who work within the organization:

- ○ Keeping the organization up-to-date in knowledge as it develops in the external world—in technology, science, social thought, and the arts
- ○ Serving as internal consultants regarding the areas of their knowledge, the changes taking place, and the opportunities
- ○ Acting as change agents evaluating, initiating, and promoting change projects.

Knowledge workers and data workers have somewhat different information systems support needs. Most knowledge workers rely on office automation systems such as word processors, voice mail, and calendars, but they also require more specialized knowledge work systems. Knowledge work systems are specifically designed to promote the creation of knowledge and to ensure that new knowledge and technical expertise are properly integrated into the business.

Requirements of Knowledge Work Systems

Knowledge work systems have characteristics that reflect the special needs of knowledge workers. First, knowledge work systems must give knowledge workers the specialized tools they need, such as powerful graphics, analytical tools, and communications and document-management tools. These systems require great computing power in order to handle rapidly the sophisticated graphics or complex calculations necessary to such knowledge workers as scientific researchers, product designers, and financial analysts. Because knowledge workers are so focused on knowledge in the external world, these systems also must give the worker quick and easy access to external databases.

A user-friendly interface is very important to a knowledge worker's system. User-friendly interfaces save time by allowing the user to perform needed tasks and get to required information without having to spend a lot of time learning how to use the computer. Saving time is more important for knowledge workers than for most other employees because knowledge workers are highly paid—wasting a knowledge worker's time is simply too expensive. Figure 14-4 summarizes the requirements of knowledge work systems.

Knowledge workstations often are designed and optimized for the specific tasks to be performed, so a design engineer will require a different workstation than a lawyer. Design engineers need graphics with enough power to handle 3-D computer-aided design (CAD) systems. However, financial analysts are more interested in having access to a myriad of external databases and in optical disk technology so they can access massive amounts of financial data very quickly.

Examples of Knowledge Work Systems

Major knowledge work applications include computer-aided design (CAD) systems, virtual reality systems for simulation and modeling, and financial workstations. **Computer-aided design (CAD)** automates the creation and revision of designs, using computers and sophisticated graphics software. Using a more traditional physical design methodology, each design modification requires a mold to be made and a prototype to be physically tested. That process must be repeated many times, which is a very expensive and time-consuming process. Using a CAD workstation, the designer only needs to make a physical prototype toward the end of the design process because the design can be easily tested and changed on the computer. The ability of

knowledge work systems (KWS) Information systems that aid knowledge workers in the creation and integration of new knowledge in the organization.

computer-aided design (CAD) Information system that automates the creation and revision of designs using sophisticated graphics software.

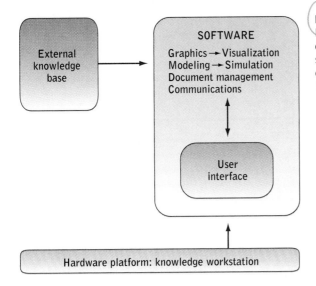

Figure 14-4 Requirements of knowledge work systems. Knowledge work systems require strong links to external knowledge bases in addition to specialized hardware and software.

CAD software to provide design specifications for the tooling and the manufacturing process also saves a great deal of time and money while producing a manufacturing process with far fewer problems. For example, The Maddox Design Group of Atlanta, Georgia, uses MicroArchitect CAD software from IdeaGraphix for architectural design. Designers can quickly put the architectural background in, popping in doors and windows, and then do the engineering layout. The software can generate door and window schedules, time accounting reports, and projected costs. Additional descriptions of CAD systems can be found in Chapters 2 and 11.

Virtual reality systems have visualization, rendering, and simulation capabilities that go far beyond those of conventional CAD systems. They use interactive graphics software to create computer-generated simulations that are so close to reality that users almost believe they are participating in a real-world situation. In many virtual reality systems, the user dons special clothing, headgear, and equipment, depending on the application. The clothing contains sensors that record the user's movements and immediately transmit that information back to the computer. For instance, to walk through a virtual reality simulation of a house, you would need garb that monitors the movement of your feet, hands, and head. You also would need goggles that contain video screens and sometimes audio attachments and feeling gloves so that you can be immersed in the computer feedback.

Virtual reality is just starting to provide benefits in educational, scientific, and business work. AB Volvo, the Swedish automobile and truck manufacturer, allows prospective buyers of its latest models of garbage trucks to "test drive" them in virtual reality. Burger King used a virtual reality version of a futuristic restaurant to show franchisees new store and equipment designs (Adhikari, 1996).

Surgeons at Boston's Brigham and Women's Hospital are using a virtual reality system in which a 3-D representation of the brain using CT and MRI scans is superimposed on live video. With this version of X-ray vision, surgeons can pinpoint the location of a tumor in the brain with 0.5 millimeter accuracy (Ditlea, 1998).

Virtual reality applications are being developed for the Web using a standard called **Virtual Reality Modeling Language (VRML).** VRML is a set of specifications for interactive, 3-D modeling on the World Wide Web that can organize multiple media types, including animation, images, and audio to put users in a simulated real-world environment. VRML is platform-independent, operates over a desktop computer, and requires little bandwidth. Users can download a 3-D virtual world designed using VRML from a server over the Internet using their Web browser. (Recent versions of Netscape Navigator and Microsoft Internet Explorer are VRML-compliant.)

Lockheed Martin Missile & Space is using VRML in a 3-D training environment to show employees how to operate large pieces of machinery. DuPont, the Wilmington, Delaware, chemical company, created a VRML application called HyperPlant, which allows users to access 3-D data

virtual reality systems Interactive graphics software and hardware that create computer-generated simulations that provide sensations that emulate real-world activities.

Virtual Reality Modeling Language (VRML) A set of specifications for interactive 3-D modeling on the World Wide Web.

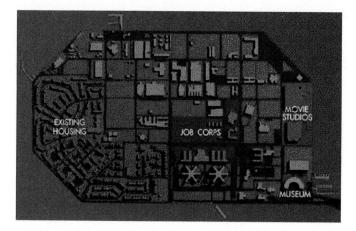 

Planet 9 Studios, which specializes in providing 3-D content on the Internet, used Virtual Reality Modeling Language (VRML) to model Treasure Island for KMD San Francisco's bid at master planning for the island. Planet 9 produced flyover animation, plan graphics, and dissolves between existing aerial photos and the animated project.

Investment workstation Powerful desktop computer for financial specialists, which is optimized to access and manipulate massive amounts of financial data.

over the Internet with Netscape Web browsers. Engineers can go through 3-D models as if they were physically walking through a plant, viewing objects at eye level. This level of detail reduces the number of mistakes they make during construction of oil rigs, oil plants, and other structures.

Tower Records in West Sacramento, California, is using VRML to build a virtual store to serve buyers over the Internet. Sales clerks will be figure representations with the real clerk's face, and buyers will be able to hear the clerk's voice in real time over the Net (Adhikari, 1997).

The financial industry is using specialized **investment workstations** to leverage the knowledge and time of its brokers, traders, and portfolio managers. Firms such as Merrill Lynch and Paine Webber have installed investment workstations that integrate a wide range of data from both internal and external sources, including contact management data, real-time and historical market data, and research reports (Stirland, 1998). Previously, financial professionals had to spend considerable time accessing data from separate systems and piecing together the information they needed. By providing one-stop information faster and with fewer errors, the workstations streamline the entire investment process from stock selection to updating client records.

Table 14.2 summarizes the major types of knowledge work systems.

Sharing Knowledge: Group Collaboration Systems and Intranet Knowledge Environments

Although many knowledge and information work applications have been designed for individuals working alone, organizations have an increasing need to support people working in groups. Chapters 9 and 10 introduced key technologies that can be used for group coordina-

Table 14.2   Examples of Knowledge Work Systems

Knowledge Work System	Function in Organization
CAD/CAM (Computer-aided design/ computer-aided manufacturing)	Provides engineers, designers, and factory managers with precise control over industrial design and manufacturing
Virtual reality systems	Provide drug designers, architects, engineers, and medical workers with precise, photorealistic simulations of objects
Investment workstations	High-end PCs used in financial sector to analyze trading situations instantaneously and facilitate portfolio management

tion and collaboration: e-mail, teleconferencing, dataconferencing, videoconferencing, groupware, and intranets. Groupware and intranets are especially valuable for this purpose.

Groupware

Until recently, **groupware** (which we introduced in Chapter 7) was the primary tool for creating collaborative work environments. Groupware is built around three key principles: communication, collaboration, and coordination. It allows groups to work together on documents, schedule meetings, route electronic forms, access shared folders, develop shared databases, and send e-mail. Table 14.3 lists the capabilities of major commercial groupware products that make them such powerful platforms for capturing information and experiences, coordinating common tasks, and distributing work through time and place.

Information-intensive companies such as consulting firms and law firms have found groupware a valuable tool for leveraging their knowledge assets. For example, Ernst & Young, one of the Big Five accounting firms, used Lotus Notes to create a worldwide collaboration environment to help staff work together on projects that required teams assembled from different locations. Its offices in the United States, United Kingdom, Canada, the Netherlands, and Australia linked Lotus Notes to Oracle relational databases, eliminating the need for multiple copies of files. Employees can share a diary, access a common prospect-and-client database, and work on projects requiring regional and international teamwork (Black, 1995).

> **groupware** Software that recognizes the significance of groups in offices by providing functions and services that support the collaborative activities of work groups.

Intranet Knowledge Environments

Chapter 10 described how some organizations are using intranets and Internet technologies for group collaboration, including e-mail, discussion groups, and multimedia Web documents. Some of these intranets are providing the foundation for knowledge environments in which information from a variety of sources and media, including text, sound, video, and even digital slides, can be shared, displayed, and accessed across an enterprise through a simple common interface. Shell Oil Company's Knowledge Management System (see the chapter opening vignette) is one example. Another is the enterprise-wide knowledge environment developed by Ford Motor Company.

Ford's intranet connects 95,000 professional employees worldwide. It was built as one way to shorten the product-development cycle for automobiles. The intranet delivers a wealth of information that previously would have required several telephone calls or a library visit. On the enterprise home page, called the Ford Hub, is a directory of categories, including News, People, Processes, Products, and Competition. Also on-line are training registration forms, maps, the company telephone directory, building layouts, human resource information, a PointCast "push" channel with automatic news and stock updates, and text feeds from the Ford

Table 14.3 **Knowledge Management Capabilities of Groupware**

Capability	Description
Publishing	Posting documents as well as simultaneous work on the same document by multiple users along with a mechanism to track changes to these documents
Replication	Maintaining and updating identical data on multiple PCs and servers
Discussion tracking	Organizing discussions by many users on different topics
Document management	Storing information from various types of software in a database
Work-flow management	Moving and tracking documents created by groups
Security	Preventing unauthorized access to data
Portability	Availability of the software for mobile use to access the corporate network from the road
Application development	Developing custom software applications with the software

Communications Network, an internal closed-circuit telephone network. Employees can access on-line libraries and a Web Center of Excellence with information on best practices, standards, and recommendations. Ford believes it can shave weeks off design processes because engineers can access images on an intranet from wherever they are in the world instead of waiting for project documentation to arrive by mail. Ford says this comprehensive network transformed decades-old processes, allowing people to disseminate information, share best practices, communicate, conduct research, and collaborate in ways that were never before possible (Stuart, 1997).

These features of intranets, combined with their low cost, have made them attractive alternatives to proprietary groupware for collaborative work, especially among small and medium-size businesses. For simple tasks such as sharing documents or document publishing, an intranet generally is less expensive to build and maintain than applications based on commercial products such as Lotus Notes, which requires proprietary software and client/server networks.

However, for applications requiring extensive coordination and management, groupware software such as Notes has important capabilities that intranets cannot yet provide. Notes is more flexible when documents must be changed, updated, or edited on the fly. It can track revisions to a document as it moves through a collaborative editing process. Internal Notes-based networks are more secure than intranets. Web sites are more likely to crash or to have their servers overloaded when there are many requests for data. Notes is thus more appropriate for applications requiring production and publication of documents by many authors, frequent updating and document tracking, and high security and replication.

Intranet technology works best as a central repository with a small number of authors and relatively static information that does not require frequent updating, although intranet tools for group collaboration are improving. Netscape Communications' Communicator software bundles a Web browser with messaging and collaboration tools, including e-mail, newsgroup discussions, a group scheduling and calendaring tool, and point-to-point conferencing. Web technology is most useful for publishing information across multiple types of computer platforms and for displaying knowledge as multimedia objects linked to other knowledge objects in hyperlinks.

At the same time, Notes and other groupware products are being enhanced so they can be integrated with the Internet or private intranets. Recent versions of Domino, a server version of Notes, allow Notes to act as a Web server, providing an easy route for companies to take their document-based data to the Internet or an intranet. Notes clients can act as Web browsers to access information on the World Wide Web. Notes servers and data can be accessed by Web browsers as well as by Notes clients; Notes databases can contain HTML pages as well as Notes documents.

Collaborative work and organizational learning also can be enhanced by using intranets and other multimedia platforms for employee training and knowledge acquisition. The Window on Organizations describes some of these interactive multimedia training systems.

Group collaboration technologies alone cannot promote information-sharing if team members do not feel it is in their interest to share, especially in organizations that encourage competition among employees. This technology can best enhance the work of a group if the applications are properly designed to fit the organization's needs and work practices and if management encourages a collaborative atmosphere (Alavi, 1999).

14.3 Artificial Intelligence

Organizations are using artificial intelligence technology to capture individual and collective knowledge and to codify and extend their knowledge base.

What Is Artificial Intelligence?

artificial intelligence (AI)
The effort to develop computer-based systems that can behave like humans, with the ability to learn languages, accomplish physical tasks, use a perceptual apparatus, and emulate human expertise and decision making.

Artificial intelligence (AI) can be defined as the effort to develop computer-based systems (both hardware and software) that behave as humans. Such systems would be able to learn natural languages, accomplish coordinated physical tasks (robotics), use a perceptual apparatus that informs their physical behavior and language (visual and oral perception systems), and emulate human expertise and decision making (expert systems). Such systems also would exhibit

Window on Organizations

Multimedia Education for Learning Organizations

Should companies scrap human instructors for computers to train their employees? Many think so, because they are experiencing a shortage of skilled workers and searching for ways to provide employees with the expertise that they need. For example, in the information-technology field alone, 346,000 positions were unfilled due to a lack of qualified candidates, according to a 1998 study done by the Information Technology Association of Arlington, Virginia. In addition, the emergence of multimedia and Web technology along with new educational approaches, such as collaborative training, have improved the quality of computer-based learning.

General Motors has established an electronic performance support system (EPSS) that captures knowledge that is created when employees are working while learning. The targets of this system are mechanics who need training as they work. The system relies heavily upon the latest voice-recognition technology. It runs on notebook-sized PCs, which are worn on the mechanics' belts. The system delivers learning materials directly to the user based upon the difficulty of the problem and the knowledge level of the learner. When users of this system complete their repair work, they verbally describe the procedure they followed into the computer, including any undocumented problems or solutions they discovered. The computer converts the words into text that eventually reaches technicians at GM headquarters. If students discover any new knowledge that the headquarter's technicians deem as widely useful, they can change service procedures and training materials. According to Jim Roach, the program manager of GM's service technology group, this system will not only change the way mechanics learn, but also will change the way they work. Mechanics will be able to work on a wider variety of vehicles than in the past because the knowledge they need will be built into the training equipment they use.

Eli Lilly & Co., the $8.5 billion pharmaceuticals company, has developed Spin (Scientific Performance Improvement Network), a network-based system embedding collaborative education in work processes. Spin is designed for Lilly's research scientists who access the system either through a Lilly network or through the Web. Spin differs from most on-line education systems in that it not only aims to deliver current knowledge to the scientist/student but also to create new knowledge through interaction with other scientists. Each Spin course is linked to a discussion database so scientists can discuss what they are learning with each other, with teachers, and with other scientists. In addition, every course requires that all students carry out a project that will apply the concepts learned in the course. The students have access to an index of relevant Web sites, including proprietary databases stored in Eli Lilly's own databases. Students are able to customize their own Spin interface to include links to commonly used Web sites and databases. They also can make their own links available to other Spin students.

Using the Web for training has helped companies such as Lilly reduce their training costs by as much as 75 percent, but experts caution that Web delivery requires a different approach to course development. For instance, instructor-led classes may last an entire day, but most students can't handle more than a few hours of Web-based training at one time. Not all companies have the bandwidth to deliver pictures and sounds rapidly to the desktop. Some firms continue to supplement their Web courses with teacher-led sessions or CD-ROMs. For instance, Convergys Corporation, a Cincinnati customer-service outsourcing firm, first used CD-ROMs and instructor-led sessions to help telephone representatives learn new enterprise software from SAP AG. Only after the trainees learned basic navigation of the software did the company roll out more detailed Web-based training.

To Think About: How do the systems described here enhance organizational knowledge? How do they make the organization more effective? What drawbacks do you see for multimedia and Web-based learning systems?

Sources: Barb Cole-Gomolski, "Web Training Requires Different Educational Approach," **Computerworld**, February 22, 1999; and Justin Hibbard, "The Learning Revolution," **Information Week**, March 9, 1998.

---

logic, reasoning, intuition, and the just-plain-common-sense qualities that we associate with human beings. Figure 14-5 illustrates the elements of the artificial intelligence family. Another important element is intelligent machines, the physical hardware that performs these tasks.

Successful artificial intelligence systems are based on human expertise, knowledge, and selected reasoning patterns, but they do not exhibit the intelligence of human beings. Existing artificial intelligence systems do not come up with new and novel solutions to problems. Existing systems extend the powers of experts but in no way substitute for them or capture much of their intelligence. Briefly, existing systems lack the common sense and generality of naturally intelligent human beings.

Human intelligence is vastly complex and much broader than computer intelligence. A key factor that distinguishes human beings from other animals is their ability to develop associations and to use metaphors and analogies such as *like* and *as*. Using metaphor and analogy,

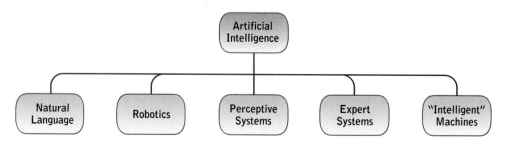

Figure 14-5 The artificial intelligence family. The field of AI currently includes many initiatives: natural language, robotics, perceptive systems, expert systems, and intelligent machines.

humans create new rules, apply old rules to new situations, and at times act intuitively and/or instinctively without rules. Much of what we call common sense or generality in humans resides in the ability to create metaphor and analogy.

Human intelligence also includes a unique ability to impose a conceptual apparatus on the surrounding world. Meta-concepts such as cause-and-effect and time, and concepts of a lower order such as breakfast, dinner, and lunch, are all imposed by human beings on the world around them. Thinking in terms of these concepts and acting on them are central characteristics of intelligent human behavior.

Why Business Is Interested in Artificial Intelligence

Although artificial intelligence applications are much more limited than human intelligence, they are of great interest to business for the following reasons:

○ To preserve expertise that might be lost through the retirement, resignation, or death of an acknowledged expert

○ To store information in an active form—to create an organizational knowledge base—that many employees can examine, much like an electronic textbook or manual, so that others may learn rules of thumb not found in textbooks

○ To create a mechanism that is not subject to human feelings such as fatigue and worry. This may be especially useful when jobs may be environmentally, physically, or mentally dangerous to humans. These systems also may be useful advisers in times of crisis.

○ To eliminate routine and unsatisfying jobs held by people

○ To enhance the organization's knowledge base by suggesting solutions to specific problems that are too massive and complex to be analyzed by human beings in a short period of time.

Capturing Knowledge: Expert Systems

In limited areas of expertise, such as diagnosing a car's ignition system or classifying biological specimens, the rules of thumb used by real-world experts can be understood, codified, and placed in a machine. Information systems that solve problems by capturing knowledge for a very specific and limited domain of human expertise are called **expert systems.** An expert system can assist decision making by asking relevant questions and explaining the reasons for adopting certain actions.

expert system Knowledge-intensive computer program that captures the expertise of a human in limited domains of knowledge.

Expert systems lack the breadth of knowledge and the understanding of fundamental principles of a human expert. They are quite narrow, shallow, and brittle. They typically perform very limited tasks that can be performed by professionals in a few minutes or hours. Problems that cannot be solved by human experts in the same short period of time are far too difficult for an expert system. However, by capturing human expertise in limited areas, expert systems can provide benefits, helping organizations make high-quality decisions with fewer people.

How Expert Systems Work

knowledge base Model of human knowledge that is used by expert systems.

Human knowledge must be modeled or represented in a way that a computer can process. The model of human knowledge used by expert systems is called the **knowledge base.** Two ways of representing human knowledge and expertise are rules and knowledge frames.

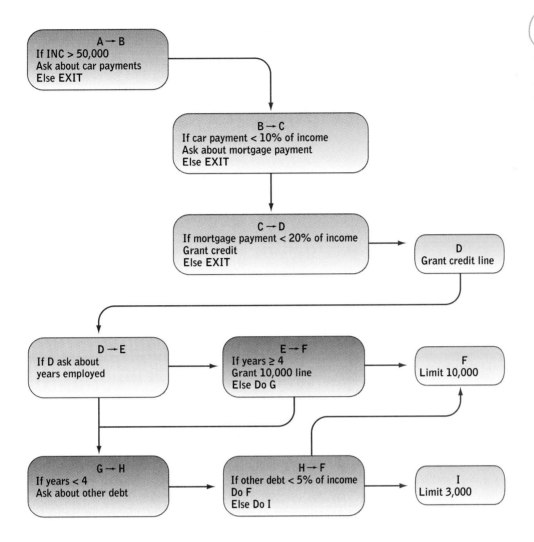

Figure 14-6 Rules in an AI program. An expert system contains a number of rules to be followed when utilized. The rules themselves are interconnected; the number of outcomes is known in advance and is limited; there are multiple paths to the same outcome; and the system can consider multiple rules at a single time. The rules illustrated are for simple credit-granting expert systems.

A standard structured programming construct (see Chapter 12) is the IF–THEN construct, in which a condition is evaluated. If the condition is true, an action is taken. For instance,

IF INCOME > $45,000 (condition)

THEN PRINT NAME AND ADDRESS (action)

A series of these rules can be a knowledge base. Any reader who has written computer programs knows that virtually all traditional computer programs contain IF–THEN statements. The difference between a traditional program and a **rule-based expert system** program is one of degree and magnitude. AI programs can easily have 200 to 10,000 rules, far more than traditional programs, which may have 50 to 100 IF–THEN statements. Moreover, in an AI program the rules tend to be interconnected and nested to a far greater degree than in traditional programs, as shown in Figure 14-6. Hence the complexity of the rules in a rule-based expert system is considerable.

Could you represent the knowledge in the Encyclopedia Britannica this way? Probably not, because the **rule base** would be too large, and not all the knowledge in the encyclopedia can be represented in the form of IF–THEN rules. In general, expert systems can be efficiently used only in those situations in which the domain of knowledge is highly restricted (such as in granting credit) and involves no more than a few thousand rules.

Knowledge frames can be used to represent knowledge by organizing information into chunks of interrelated characteristics. The relationships are based on shared characteristics rather than a hierarchy. This approach is grounded in the belief that humans use frames, or

rule-based expert system An AI program that has a large number of interconnected and nested IF–THEN statements, or rules, that are the basis for the knowledge in the system.

rule base The collection of knowledge in an AI system that is represented in the form of IF–THEN rules.

knowledge frames A method of organizing expert system knowledge into chunks; the relationships are based on shared characteristics determined by the user.

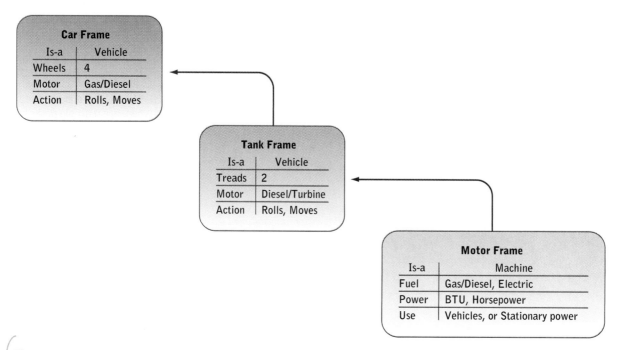

Figure 14-7 Frames to model knowledge. Knowledge and information can be organized into frames. Frames capture the relevant characteristics of the objects of interest. This approach is based on the belief that humans use "frames" or concepts to narrow the range of possibilities when scanning incoming information to make rapid sense out of perceptions.

AI shell The programming environment of an expert system.

inference engine The strategy used to search through the rule base in an expert system; can be forward or backward chaining.

forward chaining A strategy for searching the rule base in an expert system that begins with the information entered by the user and searches the rule base to arrive at a conclusion.

backward chaining A strategy for searching the rule base in an expert system that acts like a problem solver by beginning with a hypothesis and seeking out more information until the hypothesis is either proved or disproved.

concepts, to make rapid sense out of perceptions. For instance, when a person is told, "Look for a tank and shoot when you see one," experts believe that humans invoke a concept, or frame, of what a tank should look like. Anything that does not fit this concept of a tank is ignored. In a similar fashion, AI researchers can organize a vast array of information into frames. The computer then is instructed to search the database of frames and list connections to other frames of interest. The user can follow the pathways pointed to by the system.

Figure 14-7 shows a part of a knowledge base organized by frames. A "CAR" is defined by characteristics or slots in a frame as a vehicle, with four wheels, a gas or diesel motor, and an action such as rolling or moving. This frame could be related to almost any other object in the database that shares any of these characteristics, such as the tank frame.

The **AI shell** is the programming environment of an expert system. In the early years of expert systems, computer scientists used specialized programming languages such as LISP or Prolog that could process lists of rules efficiently. Today a growing number of expert systems use AI shells that are user-friendly development environments. AI shells can quickly generate user-interface screens, capture the knowledge base, and manage the strategies for searching the rule base.

The strategy used to search through the rule base is called the **inference engine.** Two strategies are commonly used: forward chaining and backward chaining (see Figure 14-8).

In **forward chaining** the inference engine begins with the information entered by the user and searches the rule base to arrive at a conclusion. The strategy is to fire, or carry out, the action of the rule when a condition is true. In Figure 14-8, beginning on the left, if the user enters a client with income greater than $100,000, the engine will fire all rules in sequence from left to right. If the user then enters information indicating that the same client owns real estate, another pass of the rule base will occur and more rules will fire. Processing continues until no more rules can be fired.

In **backward chaining** the strategy for searching the rule base starts with a hypothesis and proceeds by asking the user questions about selected facts until the hypothesis is either confirmed or disproved. In our example, in Figure 14-8, ask the question, "Should we add this

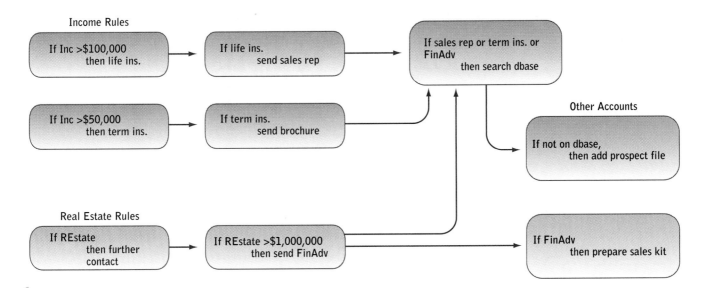

Figure 14-8 Inference engines in expert systems. An inference engine works by searching through the rules and "firing" those rules that are triggered by facts gathered and entered by the user. Basically, a collection of rules is similar to a series of nested "IF" statements in a traditional software program; however, the magnitude of the statements and degree of nesting are much greater in an expert system.

person to the prospect database?" Begin on the right of the diagram and work toward the left. You can see that the person should be added to the database if a sales representative is sent, term insurance is granted, or a financial advisor visits the client.

Building an Expert System

Building an expert system is similar to building other information systems, although building expert systems is an iterative process with each phase possibly requiring several iterations before a full system is developed. Typically the environment in which an expert system operates is continually changing so that the expert system must also continually change. Some expert systems, especially large ones, are so complex that in a few years the maintenance costs will equal the development costs.

An AI development team is composed of one or more experts, who have a thorough command of the knowledge base, and one or more knowledge engineers, who can translate the knowledge (as described by the expert) into a set of rules or frames. A **knowledge engineer** is similar to a traditional systems analyst but has special expertise in eliciting information and expertise from other professionals.

The team members must select a problem appropriate for an expert system. The project will balance potential savings from the proposed system against the cost. The team members will develop a prototype system to test assumptions about how to encode the knowledge of experts. Next, they will develop a full-scale system, focusing mainly on the addition of a very large number of rules. The complexity of the entire system grows with the number of rules, so the comprehensibility of the system may be threatened. Generally the system will be pruned to achieve simplicity and power. The system is tested by a range of experts within the organization against the performance criteria established earlier. Once tested, the system will be integrated into the data flow and work patterns of the organization.

Examples of Successful Expert Systems

There is no accepted definition of a successful expert system. What is successful to an academic ("It works!") may not be successful to a corporation ("It costs a million dollars!"). The following are examples of expert systems that provide organizations with an array of benefits, including reduced errors, reduced cost, reduced training time, improved decisions, and improved quality and service.

knowledge engineer A specialist who elicits information and expertise from other professionals and translates it into a set of rules or frames for an expert system.

Countrywide Funding Corporation developed an expert system called CLUES to evaluate the creditworthiness of loan applicants. Countrywide is using the rules in this system to answer inquiries from visitors to its Web site who want to know if they can qualify for a loan.

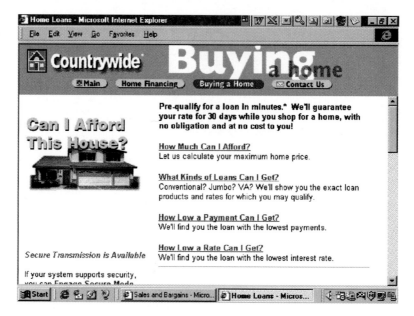

Countrywide Funding Corp. in Pasadena, California, is a loan-underwriting firm with about 400 underwriters in 150 offices around the country. The company developed a PC-based expert system in 1992 to make preliminary creditworthiness decisions on loan requests. The company had experienced rapid, continuing growth and wanted the system to help ensure consistent, high-quality loan decisions. CLUES (Countrywide's Loan Underwriting Expert System) has about 400 rules. Countrywide tested the system by sending every loan application handled by a human underwriter to CLUES as well. The system was refined until it agreed with the underwriter in 95 percent of the cases.

Countrywide will not rely on CLUES to reject loans, because the expert system cannot be programmed to handle exceptional situations such as those involving a self-employed person or complex financial schemes. An underwriter will review all rejected loans and will make the final decision. CLUES has other benefits. Traditionally, an underwriter could handle six or seven applications a day. Using CLUES, the same underwriter can evaluate at least 16 per day (Nash, 1993). Countrywide now is using the rules in its expert system to answer e-mail inquiries from visitors to its Web site who want to know if they qualify for a loan (Cole-Gomolski, 1998).

The Digital Equipment Corporation (DEC) and Carnegie-Mellon University developed XCON in the late 1970s to configure VAX computers on a daily basis. The system configured customer orders and guided the assembly of those orders at the customer site. XCON was used for major functions such as sales and marketing, manufacturing and production, and field service, and played a strategic role at DEC (Sviokla, June 1990; Barker and O'Conner, 1989). It is estimated that XCON and related systems saved DEC approximately $40 million per year. XCON started out with 250 rules but expanded to about 10,000.

Whirlpool uses the Consumer Appliance Diagnostic System (CADS) to help its customer-service representatives handle its 3 million annual telephone inquiries. The system expedites customer service by directing customers to a single source of help without delay. Previously, customers who had a problem or question about Whirlpool products might have been put on hold or directed to two or three different customer representatives before their questions could be answered. Whirlpool developed CADS using Aion's Development System for OS/2 as its expert system shell. Two knowledge engineers worked with one programmer and three of the company's customer-service experts to capture 1000 rules for 12 product lines. By 1999, Whirlpool expects to use CADS to respond to 9 million calls annually.

Problems with Expert Systems

Although expert systems lack the robust and general intelligence of human beings, they can provide benefits to organizations if their limitations are well understood. Only certain classes of problems can be solved using expert systems. Virtually all successful expert systems deal with problems of classification in which there are relatively few alternative outcomes and in which these possible outcomes are all known in advance. Many expert systems require large, lengthy, and expensive development efforts. Hiring or training more experts may be less expensive than building an expert system.

The knowledge base of expert systems is fragile and brittle; they cannot learn or change over time. In fast-moving fields such as medicine or the computer sciences, keeping the knowledge base up to date is a critical problem. Digital Equipment Corporation stopped using XCON because its product line was constantly changing and it was too difficult to keep updating the system to capture these changes.

Expert systems can only represent limited forms of knowledge. IF–THEN knowledge exists primarily in textbooks. There are no adequate representations for deep causal models or temporal trends. No expert system, for instance, can write a textbook on information systems or engage in other creative activities not explicitly foreseen by system designers. Many experts cannot express their knowledge using an IF–THEN format. Expert systems cannot yet replicate knowledge that is intuitive, based on analogy and on a sense of things.

Contrary to early promises, expert systems are most effective in automating lower level clerical functions. They can provide electronic checklists for lower level employees in service bureaucracies such as banking, insurance, sales, and welfare agencies. The applicability of expert systems to managerial problems is very limited. Managerial problems generally involve drawing facts and interpretations from divergent sources, evaluating the facts, and comparing one interpretation of the facts with another, and are not limited to simple classification. Expert systems based on the prior knowledge of a few known alternatives are unsuitable to the problems managers face on a daily basis.

Organizational Intelligence: Case-Based Reasoning

Expert systems primarily capture the knowledge of individual experts, but organizations also have collective knowledge and expertise that they have built up over the years. This organizational knowledge can be captured and stored using case-based reasoning. In **case-based reasoning (CBR),** descriptions of past experiences of human specialists, represented as cases, are stored in a database for later retrieval when the user encounters a new case with similar parameters. The system searches for stored cases with problem characteristics similar to the new one, finds the closest fit, and applies the solutions of the old case to the new case. Successful solutions are tagged to the new case and both are stored together with the other cases in the knowledge base. Unsuccessful solutions also are appended to the case database along with explanations as to why the solutions did not work (see Figure 14-9).

Expert systems work by applying a set of IF–THEN–ELSE rules against a knowledge base, both of which are extracted from human experts. Case-based reasoning, in contrast, represents knowledge as a series of cases, and this knowledge base is continuously expanded and refined by users.

For example, let us examine Compaq Computer of Houston, Texas, a company that operates in a highly competitive, customer service-oriented business environment and is daily flooded with customer phone calls crying for help. Keeping those customers satisfied requires Compaq to spend millions of dollars annually to maintain large, technically skilled, customer-support staffs. When customers call with problems, they must describe the problems to the customer-service staff and then wait on hold while customer service transfers the calls to appropriate technicians. The customers then describe the problem all over again while the technicians try to come up with answers—all in all, a most frustrating experience. To improve customer service and rein in costs, Compaq began giving away expensive case-based reasoning software to customers purchasing their Pagemarq printer.

case-based reasoning (CBR)
Artificial intelligence technology that represents knowledge as a database of cases and solutions.

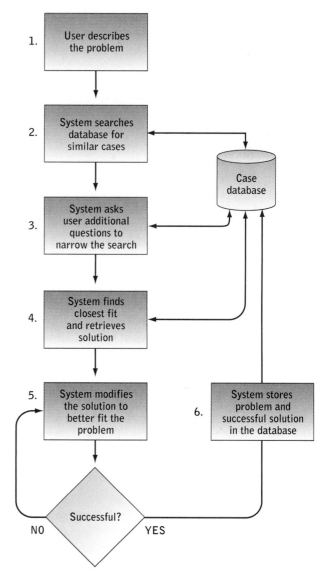

Figure 14-9 How case-based reasoning works. Case-based reasoning represents knowledge as a database of past cases and their solutions. The system uses a six-step process to generate solutions to new problems encountered by the user.

The software knowledge base is a series of several hundred actual cases of Pagemarq printer problems—actual war stories about smudged copies, printer memory problems, jammed printers—all the typical problems people face with laser printers. Trained CBR staff entered case descriptions in textual format into the CBR system. They entered key words necessary to categorize the problem, such as smudge, smear, lines, streaks, and paper jam. They also entered a series of questions that might be needed to allow the software to further narrow the problem. Finally, solutions also were attached to each case.

With the Compaq-supplied CBR system running on their computer, owners no longer need to call Compaq's service department. Instead they run the software and describe the problem to the software. The system swiftly searches actual cases, discarding unrelated ones, selecting related ones. If necessary to further narrow the search results, the software will ask the user for more information. In the end, one or more cases relevant to the specific problem are displayed, along with their solutions. Now, customers can solve most of their own problems quickly without a telephone call, and Compaq saves $10 million to $20 million annually in customer-support costs.

New commercial software products, such as Inference's CasePoint WebServer, allow customers to access a case database through the Web. Using case-based reasoning, the server

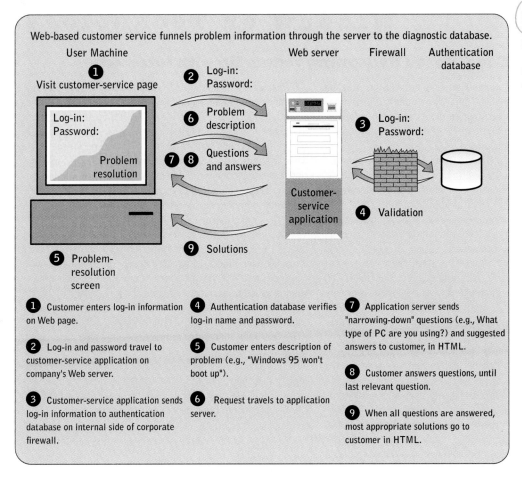

Web-based customer service funnels problem information through the server to the diagnostic database.

① Customer enters log-in information on Web page.

② Log-in and password travel to customer-service application on company's Web server.

③ Customer-service application sends log-in information to authentication database on internal side of corporate firewall.

④ Authentication database verifies log-in name and password.

⑤ Customer enters description of problem (e.g., "Windows 95 won't boot up").

⑥ Request travels to application server.

⑦ Application server sends "narrowing-down" questions (e.g., What type of PC are you using?) and suggested answers to customer, in HTML.

⑧ Customer answers questions, until last relevant question.

⑨ When all questions are answered, most appropriate solutions go to customer in HTML.

Figure 14-10 Typical Web-based customer-service system.
Source: Anne Bilodeau Zeiger, "Help Desks Make the Web Connection," Byte, April 1998. Used by permission of CMPnet.

asks customers to answer a series of questions to narrow down the problems. CasePoint then extracts solutions from the database and passes them on to customers. Audio-product manufacturer Kenwood USA used this tool to put its manuals and technical-support solutions on the Web. Figure 14-10 illustrates how a Web-based customer-service system with case-based reasoning might work.

The Window on Technology describes another case-based reasoning application for an intranet.

14.4 Other Intelligent Techniques

Organizations are using other intelligent computing techniques to extend their knowledge base by providing solutions to problems that are too massive or complex to be handled by people with limited resources. Neural networks, fuzzy logic, genetic algorithms, and intelligent agents are developing into promising business applications.

Neural Networks

There has been an exciting resurgence of interest in bottom-up approaches to artificial intelligence in which machines are designed to imitate the physical thought process of the biological brain. Figure 14-11 shows two neurons from a leech's brain. The soma, or nerve cell at the center, acts like a switch, stimulating other neurons and being stimulated in turn. Emanating from the neuron is an axon, which is an electrically active link to the dendrites of other neurons. Axons and dendrites are the "wires" that electrically connect neurons to one another. The junction of the two is called a synapse. This simple biological model is the metaphor for the

Case-Based Reasoning Teams Up with Intranets

Information and knowledge may be pivotal, but what does an organization do when it has so much information that it cannot make use of it? One company faced with immense information-overload problems is based in Kansas City, Missouri: Cerner Corp. Cerner provides services and software to the health care industry throughout the world. The company fields a software development, consulting, and support staff of approximately 2000 people worldwide. One technology that is proving particularly useful is a case-based reasoning system that is simply called CKR (pronounced "seeker"), which stands for Cerner Knowledge Reference. CKR uses case-based reasoning software from Inference Corp., Microsoft Office, and an intranet. The system was designed primarily to help those staffing Cerner's two help desks, one that supports Cerner's internal users and one that supports Cerner's clients.

Although the system is new, it already has a knowledge base of 13,000 cases. When a caller contacts a help desk, the person at the desk types a simple, English-text question into CKR. CKR responds with its own questions until it has enough information to offer solutions that come from similar problems stored in the database. The technology makes everyone smarter. As knowledge-management team leader Rhonda Dalzell explains, "You can get an answer without a deep knowledge about similar situations." One of the exciting features of this system is the ease with which new cases can be added to the database. All the user must do is click on a "feedback" button and then type in his or her experiences concerning the problem. The information is automatically sent to the case author for consideration. The case author examines the new input and, if it is deemed appropriate, adds the new case with appropriate questions.

This system has benefits beyond the fact that knowledge is easily stored in an organized way so that it is quickly accessed. It also is useful to the organization because it solves the problem faced in earlier times when support staffs in different locations had to reinvent the same wheel. Now, when a solution to a specific problem is found in one location, the knowledge is quickly made available at all other locations through CKR. For instance, one group can study how best to implement Windows NT and immediately share what they have learned with others. The system helps staff in different locations to specialize because management knows the knowledge gained at each location will be easy for staff everywhere to access. Groups of employees with common problems have formed "communities of interest" similar to Internet newsgroups on the intranet.

One unexpected benefit is that Cerner is finding that incoming staff can be trained in half the time. Dalzell claims that, whereas it took six months to train new employees in the past, using CKR enables them to be trained in three months. In addition, that training now concentrates on understanding concepts rather than on memorizing details, making the employees more effective in their work. Cerner has grown very rapidly and CKR is one way to bring new employees up to speed.

To Think About: What were the business benefits of using a case-based reasoning system? How did using this system change the way Cerner ran its business? What other types of problems do you think case-based reasoning can be used to solve?

Sources: "Cerner Consulting Meets Healthcare System Need for Expert Services," Cerner Corporation, February 22, 1999; and Gary H. Anthes, "Learning How to Share," **Computerworld**, February 23, 1998.

---

neural network Hardware or software that attempts to emulate the processing patterns of the biological brain.

development of neural networks. A **neural network** consists of hardware or software that attempts to emulate the processing patterns of the biological brain.

The human brain has about 100 billion (10^{11}) neurons, each having about 1000 dendrites, which form 100,000 billion (10^{14}) synapses. The brain's neurons operate in parallel, and the human brain can accomplish about 10^{16}, or ten million billion, interconnections per second. This far exceeds the capacity of any known machine or any machine planned or ever likely to be built with current technology.

However, complex networks of neurons have been simulated on computers. Figure 14-12 shows an artificial neural network with two neurons. The resistors in the circuits are variable and can be used to teach the network. When the network makes a mistake (i.e., chooses the wrong pathway through the network and arrives at a false conclusion), resistance can be raised on some circuits, forcing other neurons to fire. If this learning process continues for thousands of cycles, the machine learns the correct response. The neurons are highly interconnected and operate in parallel.

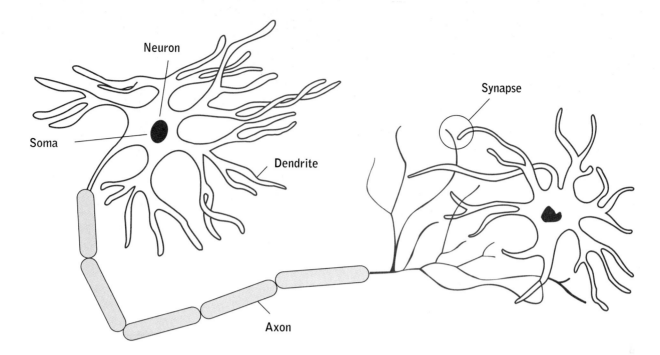

Figure 14-11 Biological neurons of a leech. Simple biological models, like the neurons of a leech, have influenced the development of artificial or computational neural networks in which the biological cells are replaced by transistors or entire processors. **Source:** Defense Advance Research Projects Agency (DARPA), 1988. Unclassified.

A neural net has a large number of sensing and processing nodes that continuously interact with each other. Figure 14-13 represents a neural network comprising an input layer, an output layer, and a hidden processing layer. The network is fed a training set of data for which the inputs produce a known set of outputs or conclusions. This helps the computer learn the correct solution by example. As the computer is fed more data, each case is compared with the known outcome. If it differs, a correction is calculated and applied to the nodes in the hidden processing layer. These steps are repeated until a condition, such as corrections being less than a certain amount, is reached. The neural network in Figure 14-13 has "learned" how to identify a good credit risk.

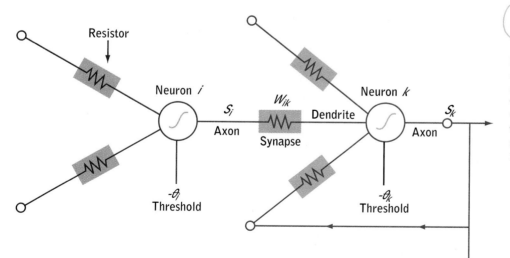

Figure 14-12 Artificial neural network with two neurons. In artificial neurons, the biological neurons become processing elements (switches), the axons and dendrites become wires, and the synapses become variable resistors that carry weighted inputs (currents) that represent data. **Source:** DARPA, 1988. Unclassified.

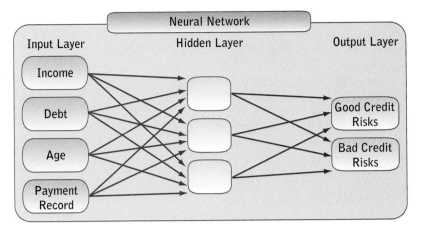

Figure 14-13 A neural network uses rules it "learns" from patterns in data to construct a hidden layer of logic. The hidden layer then processes inputs, classifying them based on the experience of the model. **Source:** Herb Edelstein, "Technology How-To: Mining Data Warehouses," InformationWeek, January 8, 1996. Copyright © 1996 CMP Media, Inc., 600 Community Drive, Manhasset, NY 11030. Reprinted with permission.

The Difference Between Neural Networks and Expert Systems

What is different about neural networks? Expert systems seek to emulate or model a human expert's way of solving problems, but neural network builders claim that they do not model human intelligence, do not program solutions, and do not aim to solve specific problems per se. Instead, neural network designers seek to put intelligence into the hardware in the form of a generalized capability to learn. In contrast, the expert system is highly specific to a given problem and cannot be easily retrained.

Take a simple problem like identifying a cat. An expert system approach would interview hundreds of people to understand how humans recognize cats, resulting in a large set of rules, or frames, programmed into an expert system. In contrast, a trainable neural network would be brought to a test site, connected to a television, and started on the process of learning. Every time a cat was not correctly perceived, the system's interconnections would be adjusted. When cats were correctly perceived, the system would be left alone and another object scanned.

Neural network applications are emerging in medicine, science, and business to address problems in pattern classification, prediction and financial analysis, and control and optimization. Papnet is a neural net-based system that distinguishes between normal and abnormal cells when examining Pap smears for cervical cancer that has far greater accuracy than visual examinations by technicians. The computer is not able to make a final decision, so a technician will review any selected abnormal cells. Using Papnet a technician requires one-fifth the time to review a smear while attaining perhaps ten times the accuracy of the existing manual method.

Neural networks are being used by the financial industry to discern patterns in vast pools of data that might help investment firms predict the performance of equities, corporate bond ratings, or corporate bankruptcies. Japanese firms are using neural networks for predicting securities ratings, timing stock buying and selling, determining future yields of securities, inspecting flaws in steel plates, classifying welding defects, analyzing sound, and identifying parts on a lens production line (Asakawa and Takagi, 1994). VISA International Inc. is using a neural network to help detect credit card fraud by monitoring all VISA transactions for sudden changes in the buying patterns of cardholders (Fryer, 1996).

Unlike expert systems, which typically provide explanations for their solutions, neural networks cannot always explain why they arrived at a particular solution. Moreover, they cannot always guarantee a completely certain solution, arrive at the same solution again with the same input data, or always guarantee the best solution (Trippi and Turban, 1989–1990). They are very sensitive and may not perform well if their training covers too little or too much data. In most current applications, neural networks are best used as aids to human decision makers instead of substitutes for them.

Fuzzy Logic

Traditional computer programs require precision: on–off, yes–no, right–wrong. However, we human beings do not experience the world this way. We might all agree that +120 degrees is hot and −40 degrees is cold; but is 75 degrees hot, warm, comfortable, or cool? The answer depends on many factors: the wind, the humidity, the individual experiencing the temperature, one's clothing, and one's expectations. Many of our activities also are inexact. Tractor-trailer drivers would find it nearly impossible to back their rig into a space precisely specified to less than an inch on all sides.

Fuzzy logic, a relatively new, rule-based development in AI, tolerates imprecision and even uses it to solve problems we could not have solved before. Fuzzy logic consists of a variety of concepts and techniques for representing and inferring knowledge that is imprecise, uncertain, or unreliable. Fuzzy logic can create rules that use approximate or subjective values and incomplete or ambiguous data. By expressing logic with some carefully defined imprecision, fuzzy logic is closer to the way people actually think than traditional IF–THEN rules.

Ford Motor Co. developed a fuzzy logic application that backs a simulated tractor-trailer into a parking space. The application uses the following three rules:

> IF the truck is *near* jackknifing, THEN *reduce* the steering angle.
> IF the truck is *far away* from the dock, THEN steer *toward* the dock.
> IF the truck is *near* the dock, THEN point the trailer *directly* at the dock.

This logic makes sense to us as human beings, for it represents how we think as we back that truck into its berth.

How does the computer make sense of this programming? The answer is relatively simple. The terms (known as *membership functions*) are imprecisely defined so that, for example, in Figure 14-14, cool is between 50 degrees and 70 degrees, although the temperature is most clearly cool between about 60 degrees and 67 degrees. Note that *cool* is overlapped by *cold* or *norm*. To control the room environment using this logic, the programmer would develop similarly imprecise definitions for humidity and other factors such as outdoor wind and temperature. The rules might include one that says: "*If the temperature is cool or cold and the humidity is low while the outdoor wind is high and the outdoor temperature is low, raise the heat and humidity in the room.*" The computer would combine the membership function readings in a weighted manner and, using all the rules, raise and lower the temperature and humidity.

Fuzzy logic is widely used in Japan and is gaining popularity in the United States. Its popularity has occurred partially because managers find they can use it to reduce costs and shorten development time. Fuzzy logic code requires fewer IF–THEN rules, making it simpler than traditional code. The rules required in the previous trucking example, plus its term definitions, might require hundreds of IF–THEN statements to implement in traditional logic. Compact code requires less computer capacity, allowing Sanyo Fisher USA to implement camcorder controls without adding expensive memory to their product.

fuzzy logic Rule-based AI that tolerates imprecision by using non-specific terms called **membership functions** to solve problems.

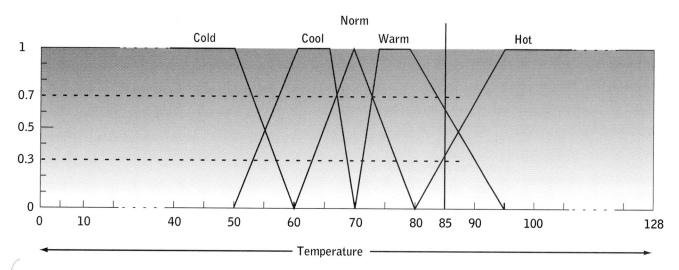

Figure 14-14 Implementing fuzzy logic rules in hardware. The membership functions for the input called **temperature** are in the logic of the thermostat to control the room temperature. Membership functions help translate linguistic expressions such as "warm" into numbers that can be manipulated by the computer. **Source:** James M. Sibigtroth, "Implementing Fuzzy Expert Rules in Hardware," **AI Expert,** April 1992. © 1992 Miller Freeman, Inc. Reprinted with permission.

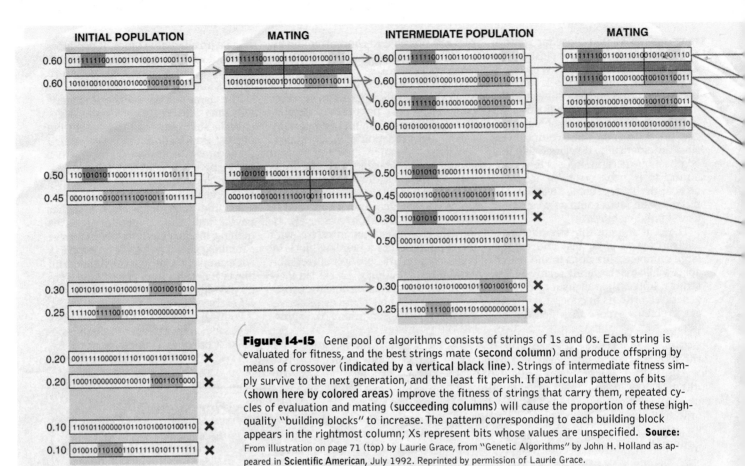

Figure 14-15 Gene pool of algorithms consists of strings of 1s and 0s. Each string is evaluated for fitness, and the best strings mate (**second column**) and produce offspring by means of crossover (**indicated by a vertical black line**). Strings of intermediate fitness simply survive to the next generation, and the least fit perish. If particular patterns of bits (**shown here by colored areas**) improve the fitness of strings that carry them, repeated cycles of evaluation and mating (**succeeding columns**) will cause the proportion of these high-quality "building blocks" to increase. The pattern corresponding to each building block appears in the rightmost column; Xs represent bits whose values are unspecified. **Source:** From illustration on page 71 (top) by Laurie Grace, from "Genetic Algorithms" by John H. Holland as appeared in **Scientific American**, July 1992. Reprinted by permission of Laurie Grace.

Fuzzy logic also allows us to solve problems not previously solvable, thus improving product quality. In Japan, Sendai's subway system uses fuzzy logic controls to accelerate so smoothly that standing passengers need not hold on. Mitsubishi Heavy Industries in Tokyo has been able to reduce the power consumption of its air conditioners by 20 percent through implementing control programs in fuzzy logic. The auto-focus device in our cameras is only possible because of fuzzy logic. Williams-Sonoma sells an "intelligent" steamer made in Japan that uses fuzzy logic. A variable heat setting detects the amount of grain, cooks it at the preferred temperature, and keeps food warm up to 12 hours.

Management also has found fuzzy logic useful for decision making and organizational control. A Wall Street firm had a system developed that selects companies for potential acquisition, using the language stock traders understand. Recently a system has been developed to detect possible fraud in medical claims submitted by health care providers anywhere in the United States.

Genetic Algorithms

genetic algorithms Problem-solving methods that promote the evolution of solutions to specified problems using the model of living organisms adapting to their environment.

Genetic algorithms (also referred to as *adaptive computation*) refer to a variety of problem-solving techniques that are conceptually based on the method that living organisms use to adapt to their environment—the process of evolution. They are programmed to work the way populations solve problems—by changing and reorganizing their component parts using processes such as reproduction, mutation, and natural selection. Thus, genetic algorithms promote the evolution of solutions to particular problems, controlling the generation, variation, adaptation, and selection of possible solutions using genetically based processes. As solutions alter and combine, the worst ones are discarded and the better ones survive to go on to produce even better solutions. Genetic algorithms breed programs that solve problems even when no person can fully understand their structure (Holland, 1992).

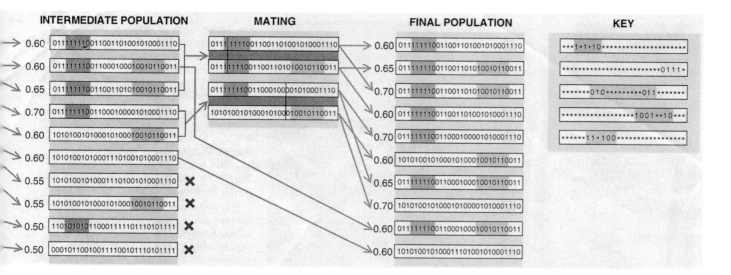

Genetic algorithms originated in the work of John H. Holland, a professor of psychology and computer science at the University of Michigan, who devised a genetic code of binary digits that could be used to represent any type of computer program with a 1 representing true and a 0 representing false. With a long enough string of digits, any object can be represented by the right combination of digits. The genetic algorithm provides methods of searching all possible combinations of digits to identify the right string representing the best possible structure for the problem.

In one method, the programmer first randomly generates a population of strings consisting of combinations of binary digits. Each string corresponds to one of the variables in the problem. One applies a test for fitness, ranking the strings in the population according to their level of desirability as possible solutions. After the initial population is evaluated for fitness, the algorithm then produces the next generation of strings, consisting of strings that survived the fitness test plus offspring strings produced from mating pairs of strings, and tests their fitness. The process continues until a solution is reached (see Figure 14-15).

Like neural networks, genetic algorithms are ideal applications for massively parallel computers. Each processor can be assigned a single string. Thus, the entire population of a genetic algorithm can be processed in parallel, offering growing potential for solving problems of enormous complexity.

Solutions to certain types of problems in areas of optimization, product design, and the monitoring of industrial systems are especially appropriate for genetic algorithms. Many business problems require optimization because they deal with issues such as minimization of costs, maximization of profits, efficient scheduling, and use of resources. If these situations are very dynamic and complex, involving hundreds of variables or hundreds of formulas, genetic algorithms are suitable for solving them because they can attack a solution from many directions at once.

Commercial applications of genetic algorithms are emerging. Engineers at General Electric used a genetic algorithm to help them design jet turbine aircraft engines, which was a complex problem involving about 100 variables and 50 constraint equations. The engineers evaluated design changes on a workstation that ran a simulation of the engine in operation. Because each design change required a new simulation to test its effectiveness, the designers could spend weeks on solutions that might not be optimal. Using an expert system reduced the time to produce a satisfactory design from several weeks to several days, but it would produce solutions only up to a point. Further improvements required simultaneous changes in large numbers of variables. At that point GE introduced a genetic algorithm that took the initial population of designs produced by the expert system and generated a design that contained three times the number of improvements over the best previous version in a period of only two days. Other organizations using genetic algorithms include the Coors Brewing Company, which uses genetic algorithms for scheduling the fulfillment and shipment of orders, and the U.S. Navy, which uses genetic algorithms for scheduling F-16 tryouts (Burtka, 1993).

Excite's Product Finder uses Jango intelligent agent technology to search virtual retailers for price and availability of products specified by the user. Displayed here are the results of a search for sources of Kenya regular coffee.

Excite Product Finder powered by Jango

Coffee - Products

New Coffee Search

Your Search: Description = "Kenya", Type = "Regular"

Instructions: Click a column title to sort results by the information in that column. For more details on a particular coffee, click on a link in the Description column.

Search Results: 19 results have been returned from 16 of 17 Web sites searched. Your search is still running.

Description	Type	Quantity	Store	Price	
Kenya AA	Regular	1 lb.	Ahrre's Coffee Roastery	$9.00	Buy!
Kenya AA	Regular	1 lb	Armeno Coffee Roasters, LTD.	$11.25	Buy!
Kenya AA	Regular	1/2 lb	Armeno Coffee Roasters, LTD.	$5.75	Buy!
Kenya AA	Regular	1 lb	Aroma Borealis	$12.40	Buy!
KENYA AA	Regular	1 lb	The Coffee Bean of Leesburg, Ltd.	$10.45	Buy!

hybrid AI systems Integration of multiple AI technologies into a single application to take advantage of the best features of these technologies.

intelligent agent Software program that uses a built-in or learned knowledge base to carry out specific, repetitive, and predictable tasks for an individual user, business process, or software application.

Hybrid AI Systems

GE's system for jet engine design achieved impressive results by combining genetic algorithm and expert system technology. Genetic algorithms, fuzzy logic, neural networks, and expert systems can be integrated into a single application to take advantage of the best features of these technologies. Such systems are called **hybrid AI systems.** Hybrid applications in business are growing. In Japan, Hitachi, Mitsubishi, Ricoh, Sanyo, and others are starting to incorporate hybrid AI in products such as home appliances, factory machinery, and office equipment. Matsushita has developed a "neurofuzzy" washing machine that combines fuzzy logic with neural networks. Nikko Securities has been working on a neurofuzzy system to forecast convertible-bond ratings.

Intelligent Agents

Intelligent agents are software programs that work in the background to carry out specific, repetitive, and predictable tasks for an individual user, business process, or software application. The agent uses a built-in or learned knowledge base to accomplish tasks or make decisions on behalf of the user. Intelligent agents can be programmed to make decisions based on the user's personal preferences—for example, to delete junk e-mail, schedule appointments, or travel over interconnected networks to find the cheapest airfare to California. The agent can be likened to a personal digital assistant collaborating with the user in the same work environment. It can help the user by performing tasks on the user's behalf, training or teaching the user, hiding the complexity of difficult tasks, helping the user collaborate with other users, or monitoring events and procedures (Maes, 1994).

There are many intelligent agent applications today in operating systems, application software, e-mail systems, mobile computing software, and network tools. For example, the Wizards found in Microsoft Office software tools have built-in capabilities to show users how to accomplish various tasks, such as formatting documents or creating graphs, and to anticipate when users need assistance. (Most search engines for locating information on the World Wide Web do not actually qualify as agents even though they sometimes are classified as such. These engines do not search the Internet for a query. They simply sort through a massive database of Web pages that the search engine has gathered.)

Of special interest to business are intelligent agents used to cruise networks, including the Internet, in search of information. They are being used in electronic commerce applications to help consumers find products they want and assist them in comparing prices and other features. Because these mobile agents are personalized, semiautonomous, and continuously running, they can help automate several of the most time-consuming stages of the buying process and thus reduce transaction costs. Agents can help people interested in making a purchase filter and retrieve information

Table 14.4 Examples of Intelligent Agents for Electronic Commerce

Agent Product	Description	Vendor
Firefly	Helps users find music or films of interest. Users send critiques of movies and music to the Firefly Web site. When they want to select a new movie to see or a CD to buy, they supply data on their personal favorites, and Firefly will produce a list of similar items based on the critiques. The service is being extended to books, restaurants, and mutual funds.	Agents Inc.
BargainFinder and LifestyleFinder	BargainFinder does real-time comparison shopping among on-line participating CD music stores and returns the names of vendors that offer the lowest price. LifestyleFinder recommends Web sites to users based on information they provide about their lifestyles.	Andersen Consulting
Jango	Automatically consults Web sites and prepares reports to users on prices and other features of products such as books, clothing, wine, and PCs.	Excite
Smart NewsReader	Windows application that provides access to Usenet newsgroups based on interests specified by the user. It can read through an article and score each thread of conversation based on the user's past interests.	Intel
AuctionBot	Allows sellers to set up their own auctions where buyers and sellers can place bids according to the protocols and parameters that have been established for the auction.	University of Michigan

about products of interest, evaluate competing products according to criteria they have established, and negotiate with vendors for price and delivery terms (Maes, Guttman, and Moukas, 1999).

Agents can also help buyers identify items they might need to buy, including repetitive purchases such as out-of-stock supplies or purchases that can be predicted based on earlier purchasing habits. For example, "Eyes" is an automated personal-notification service from the Amazon.com on-line bookstore that performs agent functions by automatically sending e-mail notices to users concerning new books that might be of interest to them. After the user provides information on his or her specific interests, "Eyes" tracks every newly released book pertaining to those interests, automatically alerting the user to new arrivals.

Yahoo! and Excite, two of the major Web search services, now offer "shopping agents" for a few merchandise categories, such as music, books, electronics, and toys. To use these agents, the consumer enters the desired product into an on-line shopping form. Using this information, the shopping agent searches the Web for product pricing and availability. It returns a list of sites that sell the item along with pricing information and a purchase link.

Firefly identifies products of interest to consumers, but instead of filtering products based on features, this agent system recommends products using an automated "word of mouth" recommendation mechanism called "collaborative filtering." Firefly first compares a shopper's product ratings with those of other shoppers, identifying users with similar taste. It then recommends products based on recommendations of like-minded people. Buyers can use Firefly to find music, restaurants, Web pages, and mutual funds.

Tete-à-Tete and AuctionBot have systems to help buyers and sellers settle on price or other terms of the transaction. Using AuctionBot, sellers create auctions by selecting the type of auction and parameters (such as clearing time or number of sellers) they wish to use. AuctionBot then manages the buyer bidding according to the specified parameters. Tete-à-Tete features shopping agents for consumers and sales agents for merchants which cooperatively negotiate multiple terms of a transaction, including warranties, delivery times, and loan options as well as sale price. Table 14.4 compares the various types of electronic commerce agents.

Agent-based electronic commerce will become even more widespread as agent and Web technology become more powerful and flexible. Software agents have difficulty obtaining information from Web pages coded in HTML because they are format-oriented, static, and meant for human eyes. Increased use of XML (extensible markup language), Java, and distributed objects (see Chapter 7) will allow software agents and other automated processes to access and interact with Web-based information more easily (Glushko, Tenenbaum, and Meltzer, 1999; Wong, Paciorek, and Moore, 1999).

Management Wrap-Up

Management

Leveraging and managing organizational knowledge have become core management responsibilities. Managers need to identify the knowledge assets of their organizations and make sure that appropriate systems and processes are in place to maximize their utilization.

Organization

Systems for knowledge and information work and artificial intelligence can enhance organizational processes in a number of ways. They can facilitate communication, collaboration, and coordination, bring more analytical power to bear in the development of solutions, or reduce the amount of human intervention in organizational processes.

Technology

An array of technologies is available to support knowledge management, including artificial intelligence technologies and tools for knowledge and information work and group collaboration. Managers should understand the costs, benefits, and capabilities of each technology and the knowledge management problem for which each is best suited.

For Discussion

1. Discuss some of the ways that knowledge management provides organizations with strategic advantage. How strategic are knowledge management systems?

2. How much can the use of artificial intelligence change the management process?

Summary

1. Explain the importance of knowledge management in contemporary organizations. Knowledge management is the process of systematically and actively managing and leveraging the stores of knowledge in an organization. Knowledge is a central productive and strategic asset in an information economy. Information systems can play a valuable role in knowledge management, helping the organization optimize its flow of information and capture its knowledge base. Office automation systems (OAS), knowledge work systems (KWS), group collaboration systems, and artificial intelligence applications are especially useful for knowledge management because they focus on supporting information and knowledge work and on defining and codifying the organization's knowledge base.

2. Describe the applications that are most useful for distributing, creating, and sharing knowledge in the firm. Offices coordinate information work in the organization, link the work of diverse groups in the organization, and couple the organization to its external environment. Office automation systems (OAS) support these functions by automating document management, communications, scheduling, and data management. Word processing, desktop publishing, Web publishing, and digital imaging systems support document management activities. Electronic-mail systems and groupware support communications activities. Electronic calendar applications and groupware support scheduling activities. Desktop data-management systems support data management activities.

Knowledge work systems (KWS) support the creation of knowledge and its integration into the organization. KWS require easy access to an external knowledge base; powerful computer hardware that can support software with intensive graphics, analysis, document management, and communications capabilities; and a friendly user interface. Knowledge work systems often run on workstations that are customized for the work they must perform. Computer-aided design (CAD) systems and virtual reality systems, which create interactive simulations that behave like the real world, require graphics and powerful modeling capabilities. Knowledge work systems for financial professionals provide access to external databases and the ability to analyze massive amounts of financial data very quickly.

Groupware is special software to support information-intensive activities in which people work collaboratively in groups. Intranets can perform many group collaboration and support functions and allow organizations to use Web publishing capabilities for document management.

3. Evaluate the role of artificial intelligence in knowledge management. Artificial intelligence is the development of computer-based systems that behave like humans. There are five members of the artificial intelligence family tree: natural language, robotics, perceptive systems, expert systems, and intelligent machines. Artificial intelligence lacks the flexibility, breadth, and generality of human intelligence, but it can be used to capture and codify organizational knowledge.

4. Explain how organizations can use expert systems and case-based reasoning to capture knowledge. Expert systems are knowledge-intensive computer programs that solve problems that heretofore required human expertise. The systems capture a limited domain of human knowledge using rules or frames. The strategy to search through the knowledge base, called the *inference engine,* can use either forward or backward chaining. Expert systems are most useful for problems of classification or diagnosis. Case-based reasoning represents organizational knowledge as a database of cases that can be continually expanded and refined. When the user encounters a new case, the system searches for similar cases, finds the closest fit, and applies the solutions of the old case to the new case. The new case is stored with successful solutions in the case database.

5. Explain how organizations can use neural networks and other intelligent techniques to improve their knowledge base. Neural networks consist of hardware and software that attempt to mimic the thought processes of the human brain. Neural networks are notable for their ability to learn without programming and to recognize patterns that cannot be easily described by humans. They are being used in science, medicine, and business primarily to discriminate patterns in massive amounts of data.

Fuzzy logic is a software technology that expresses logic with some carefully defined imprecision so that it is closer to the way people actually think than traditional IF–THEN rules. Fuzzy logic has been used for controlling physical devices and is starting to be used for limited decision-making applications.

Genetic algorithms develop solutions to particular problems using genetically based processes such as fitness, crossover, and mutation to breed solutions. Genetic algorithms are beginning to be applied to problems involving optimization, product design, and monitoring industrial systems.

Intelligent agents are software programs with built-in or learned knowledge bases that carry out specific, repetitive, and predictable tasks for an individual user, business process, or software application. Intelligent agents can be programmed to search for information or conduct transactions on networks, including the Internet.

Key Terms

AI shell, 448	Data workers, 436	Inference engine, 448	Knowledge workers, 436
Artificial intelligence, 444	Document imaging systems, 438	Information work, 436	Knowledge work systems
Backward chaining, 448	Expert system, 446	Intelligent agent, 460	(KWS), 440
Case-based reasoning (CBR), 451	Forward chaining, 448	Investment workstation, 442	Neural network, 454
	Fuzzy logic, 457	Jukebox, 438	Office automation systems
Chief knowledge officer	Genetic algorithms, 458	Knowledge base, 446	(OAS), 437
(CKO), 435	Groupware, 443	Knowledge engineer, 449	Rule base, 447
Computer-aided design	Hybrid AI systems, 460	Knowledge frames, 447	Rule-based expert system, 447
(CAD), 440	Index server, 438	Knowledge management, 435	

Review Questions

1. What is knowledge management? List and briefly describe the information systems that support it.

2. What is the relationship between information work and productivity in contemporary organizations?

3. Describe the roles of the office in organizations. What are the major activities that take place in offices?

4. What are the principal types of information systems that support information worker activities in the office?

5. What are the generic requirements of knowledge work systems? Why?

6. Describe how the following systems support knowledge work: computer-aided design (CAD), virtual reality, investment workstations.

7. How does groupware support information work? Describe its capabilities and Internet and intranet capabilities for collaborative work.

8. What is artificial intelligence? Why is it of interest to business?

9. What is the difference between artificial intelligence and natural or human intelligence?

10. Define an expert system and describe how it can help organizations use their knowledge assets.

11. Define and describe the role of the following in expert systems: rule base, frames, inference engine.

12. What is case-based reasoning? How does it differ from an expert system?

13. Describe three problems of expert systems.

14. Describe a neural network. With what kinds of tasks would a neural network excel?

15. Define and describe fuzzy logic. For what kinds of applications is it suited?

16. What are genetic algorithms? How can they help organizations solve problems? For what kinds of problems are they suited?

17. What are intelligent agents? How can they be used to benefit businesses?

Group Project

With a group of classmates, select two Web sites that provide intelligent agent technologies for electronic commerce and compare their capabilities; you can find lists of intelligent agent software by using Yahoo! to search for "intelligent software agents." Or compare two of the intelligent agent products described in this chapter. Present your findings to the class.

Tools for Interactive Learning

○ Internet

The Internet Connection for this chapter will take you to the National Aeronautics and Space Administration (NASA) Web site, where you can complete an exercise showing how this Web site can be used by knowledge workers. You can also use the Interactive Study Guide to test your knowledge of the topics in this chapter and get instant feedback where you need more practice.

○ CD-ROM

If you purchase and use the Multimedia Edition CD-ROM with this chapter, you will find two interactive exercises. The first asks you to choose the proper software tools for solving a series of knowledge management problems. The second asks you to select an appropriate AI technology to solve another series of problems. You can also find a video clip illustrating how the Papnet neural network is used for medical testing, an audio overview of the major themes of this chapter, and bullet text summarizing the key points of the chapter.

Case Study — Booz, Allen's Quest for Knowledge Management

Booz, Allen & Hamilton, founded in 1914, is an international management and technology consulting firm serving both government agencies and private corporations. It offers specialized consulting services in areas such as financial services; computers, communications, and electronics; marketing and media; engineering and manufacturing; energy, chemicals, and pharmaceuticals; operations management; and information technology.

During the past decade, Booz, Allen has experienced tremendous growth. Revenues nearly doubled from $500 million in 1990 to $950 million in 1994. The staff has nearly doubled as well, from about 3500 in 1988 to 7000 today in 100 offices around the globe. However, the company faces stiff competition from rival consulting firms such as Andersen Consulting, McKinsey & Co. Inc., and KPMG Peat Marwick. Several years ago these companies seemed to be moving ahead of Booz, Allen because of their sophisticated use of information technology.

Clients depend on the members of a Booz, Allen consulting team to provide the best knowledge and skills to them from the firm as a whole. Fifty years ago, the company consisted of a small group of local consultants who understood each other's experience and skills. By the 1990s, geographic distance, lack of personal knowledge of individual consultants, and the sheer volume of employees made locating knowledge and information a formidable challenge.

Booz, Allen consultants were using a variety of technologies—e-mail, video conferencing, phone calls, and face-to-face meetings—to locate the knowledge they needed. But the company had no central store for its information, and consultants had to rely on informal networks and personal contacts to locate specific documents or employees with the knowledge and expertise they needed. For instance, to assemble a team for a specific project, a Booz, Allen officer had to manually review resumes, areas of expertise, and previous assignments of potential team members who were either already known or recommended by co-workers. Productivity was obviously diminished, but the impact was magnified because Booz, Allen's expansion made it especially difficult for newly hired consultants to reach peak effectiveness. Booz, Allen's competitors were reaping benefits from on-line knowledge management systems they had already developed. Clients were asking Booz, Allen to help them implement knowledge management capabilities, but the company had no expertise of its own.

Recognizing the critical role played by knowledge and ideas in the consulting business, Booz, Allen management initiated an ambitious program to facilitate the creation and sharing of knowledge throughout the firm. The company created a senior position for a chief knowledge officer (CKO) who would be responsible for managing research, development, and organizational processes that would enhance knowledge creation and sharing and would also be responsible for the construction of an appropriate technological and human resources infrastructure for this purpose.

In early 1995 the company created its first knowledge management system consisting of a simple bulletin board application for Apple Macintosh computers. Although the system saved time and money, its technology was too restrictive. Users could only post and categorize documents using folders, which took a long time to search.

Booz, Allen then decided to rebuild the system to take advantage of the low cost, connectivity, and simplicity of intranet technology as well as the powerful information management capabilities of Oracle's relational database management system. The new system, called Knowledge Online 2.0 (KOL), is a dynamic, interactive repository of consultants' knowledge and experience, which can be accessed by staff members all over the world using a Web browser. The company mandated that any new system that enhanced business capability should utilize 80 percent of existing technology and that KOL use the company's existing infrastructure.

KOL 2.0 consists of a main Web page that provides access to areas of information that can be used for knowledge and information sharing throughout the firm. These areas include a searchable knowledge database organized around Booz, Allen specialties and best practices; links to job histories and resumes; intellectual capital, including documents, research reports, presentations, graphs, and images; interactive training materials; links to home pages for local offices; and a listing of calendar items, business news, and human resource information.

The information in any of these six areas is no more than three mouse clicks away. Each employee's use of KOL is based on the person's position in the firm. For example, only officers and principals have access to client and financial information. The Oracle database contains all of the business processes and rules needed to create each individual's Web pages dynamically.

When a project is completed, information experts called knowledge managers evaluate its output to identify lessons that might benefit the company. The knowledge managers assess how the knowledge fits into existing knowledge categories in the repository or whether the new knowledge changes those categorizations. They also determine how to extract the essential information from a specific document yet protect client confidentiality. Another set of specialists abstracts and cleanses the information before adding it to KOL.

The knowledge base is housed in an Oracle relational database, which can be searched with a text-search and retrieval engine called PLS Search from Personal Library Software Corporation in Rockville, Maryland. KOL also has a capability called KOLaborate, which allows project teams to work together on-line using shared work areas, discussion groups, bulletin boards, and e-mail provided by Livelink, an intranet groupware product from Open Text Corporation in Toronto. The work groups can draw directly on the knowledge base for collaborative information. "Innovation teams" of consultants in many different locations assigned to build knowledge assets in specific areas, such as business process reengineering, also use these collaborative tools.

Booz, Allen's budget for technical upgrades and support for KOL was $250,000, but managing the content cost three times as much. Creating the content cost even more, an amount the company has been reluctant to quantify, because its consultants, who are paid up to $750 per hour, produce

hundreds of documents for KOL's knowledge base. Over time the focus of KOL content has changed. Initially, Booz, Allen allocated half of the content of KOL to advanced thinking developed by leading experts in various fields. After studying KOL usage patterns, management learned that the heaviest users of the system were new employees trying to learn the basics. The system was changed to provide more training tools to help new employees learn company practices and standard frameworks for solving problems. Management also realized that the expert knowledge in the database could not be substituted for human experts. Leading-edge material was removed from the repository, and content was refocused on defining each employee's areas of expertise. With the major thrust of the knowledge program to encourage more collaboration, the new design encourages people to reach for the expert instead of the material.

KOL is often used to "jump-start" a team at the beginning of a new project by allowing members to examine similar activities from the past for a particular client or task. Other popular uses include locating expertise within the company by searching KOL for similar projects or knowledge created on a specified subject, or searching resumes for certain skills. By learning about similar projects, teams can anticipate what issues are likely to cause problems and develop solutions in advance.

In the highly competitive world of consulting, giving one's knowledge to others or admitting that someone else's knowledge or skills may be better than one's own, has not been rewarded. Booz, Allen's culture did not promote knowledge sharing; it rewarded individual achievement over collaboration. Management tried to address this problem by structuring KOL to showcase the accomplishments of contributors. One-third of consultants' performance appraisals is based on knowledge creation and contributions that help the firm increase client business. The system was designed to make content submission easy. Although Booz, Allen's culture has become more collaborative recently, employees note that it still has a large measure of individual entrepreneurship.

Assignments for Booz, Allen's commercial clients—who tend to be Fortune 200 multinationals—are staffed with "virtual teams" of consultants drawn from offices and practices all over the world. These teams come together for an assignment based on their expertise and may never work together

again. So, the ability to become knowledgeable about one another's specific areas of expertise is key. By researching one another's contributions to the knowledge program a team can "know" what every team member knows—even before the first meeting at the client's site. This allows teams to bond quickly and get the engagement off to a good start.

Booz, Allen believes that KOL, along with the company's knowledge program, has provided both quantitative and qualitative benefits. Booz, Allen is able to leverage and use its best thinking for all clients on every assignment. Since the implementation of KOL, the firm has doubled its publication output. KOL has saved time compared to previous manual methods of information transfer, enabling the firm to deliver results faster and more effectively to clients. Clients who have seen KOL have requested that Booz, Allen create similar applications for them.

To calculate its return on investment for KOL, management surveyed a cross section of Booz, Allen consultants in order to understand the amount of actual time saved by using KOL to share and retrieve knowledge. This average was then reduced by a correction factor to account for the inefficient transfer of time. To place a value on this time, the composite billing rate of an average Booz, Allen & Hamilton consultant was used as a fair indicator of the additional billable hours that were created by using KOL.

Sources: Philip J. Gill, "Knowledge and Experience Online," **Oracle Magazine**, May/June 1998; Claire Tristram, "Common Knowledge," **CIO Magazine**, September 1, 1998; and Ian Campbell, "The Intranet: Slashing the Cost of Doing Business," International Data Corporation, http://home.netscape.com/comprod/announce/roi.html

CASE STUDY QUESTIONS

1. Analyze Booz, Allen & Hamilton using the competitive forces and value chain models.

2. How significant a strategic advantage does Knowledge Online provide for Booz, Allen? Does it differentiate the company's service from competitors?

3. What management, organization, and technology issues had to be addressed when building KOL? How successful was KOL as a solution?

4. How did Knowledge Online change Booz, Allen's business processes?

Chapter 15

Enhancing Management Decision Making

Learning Objectives

After completing this chapter, you will be able to:

1. Differentiate a decision-support system (DSS) and a group decision-support system (GDSS).

2. Describe the components of decision-support systems and group decision-support systems.

3. Demonstrate how decision-support systems and group decision-support systems can enhance decision making.

4. Describe the capabilities of executive support systems (ESS).

5. Assess the benefits of executive support systems.

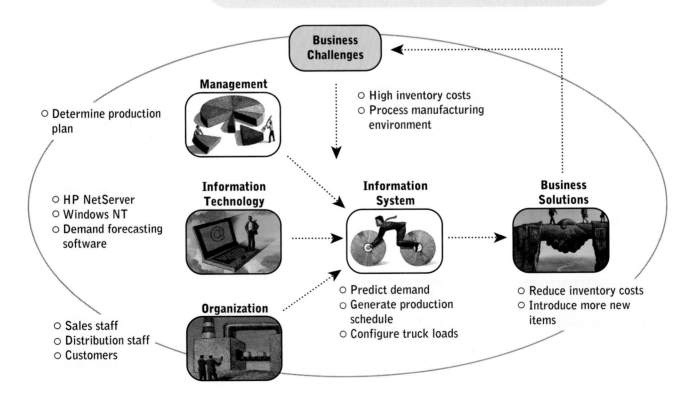

Business Challenges

Management
- Determine production plan

○ High inventory costs
○ Process manufacturing environment

Information Technology
- HP NetServer
- Windows NT
- Demand forecasting software

Information System
○ Predict demand
○ Generate production schedule
○ Configure truck loads

Business Solutions
○ Reduce inventory costs
○ Introduce more new items

Organization
- Sales staff
- Distribution staff
- Customers

Foiling Bad Forecasts
with a DSS

For the Reynolds Metal Company, aluminum sitting on the warehouse shelf is lost revenue. The company's foodservice division wanted to find a way to keep aluminum foil and plastic wrap moving more efficiently from the production line to restaurants and schools worldwide. Like most process manufacturers who make goods from raw materials, Reynolds must base its production on the demand it forecasts rather than the orders it receives. Dave Seibert, the foodservice division's director of marketing, likened this process to "a roll of the dice." When Reynolds puts the product in a box, it is hoping the customers will buy it.

About 99 percent of the foodservice division's manufacturing plan is based on these forecasts, so accuracy is paramount. Reynolds had been using demand-forecasting software to help its production planning, but the software was more than 20 years old and ran on an IBM 9672 mainframe. It limited the company's ability to introduce items because the system only could be updated once a month. Error rates hovered in the mid-teens.

Reynolds decided to install a new demand-forecasting system that would provide a higher degree of precision when predicting customer needs. The new system runs on a Hewlett-Packard NetServer LS 100 running Microsoft's Windows NT operating system. The system can be updated daily if required.

Information such as sales history is entered into the system and used to make a preliminary prediction of the month's demand. The initial forecast is passed on to a distribution-planning module and combined with inventory and customer order projections. The system then generates requirements for when and where to ship a projected order. The distribution staff uses this information to help them configure the loads for the trucks. Managers in the manufacturing plants use the information to see what needs to be produced and where. The system has helped Reynolds reduce forecasting errors by 1 percent to 2 percent, and each percentage point translates into about 500,000 pounds of inventory that does not have to be maintained. Reynolds could thus lower costs at a time when sales revenue had weakened because of dropping aluminum prices.

Sources: "Reynolds Metals Company Provides Outlook for Full Year 1999 and First Quarter," March 3, 1999 and "Reynolds Foils Forecasting Errors," *Computerworld*, February 23, 1998.

Reynolds' demand-forecasting system is an example of a decision-support system (DSS). Such systems have powerful analytic capabilities to support managers during the process of arriving at a decision. Other systems in this category are group decision-support systems (GDSS), which support decision making in groups, and executive support systems (ESS), which provide information for making strategic-level decisions. These systems can enhance organizational performance, but they raise the following management challenges:

1. **Building information systems that can actually fulfill executive information requirements.** Even with the use of critical success factors and other information requirements determination methods, it may still be difficult to establish information requirements for ESS and DSS serving senior management. Chapter 4 has already described why certain aspects of senior management decision making cannot be supported by information systems because the decisions are too unstructured and fluid. Even if a problem can be addressed by an information system, senior management may not fully understand its actual information needs. For instance, senior managers may not agree on the firm's critical success factors, or the critical success factors they describe may be inappropriate or outdated if the firm is confronting a crisis requiring a major strategic change.

2. **Integrating DSS and ESS with existing systems in the business.** Even if system builders do know the information requirements for DSS or ESS, it may not be possible to fulfill them using data from the firm's existing information systems. Various MIS or TPS may define important pieces of data, such as the time period covered by the fiscal year, in different ways. It may not be possible to reconcile data from incompatible internal systems for analysis by managers even through data cleansing and data warehousing. A significant amount of organizational change may be required before the firm can build and install effective DSS and ESS.

M ost information systems described throughout this text help people make decisions in one way or another, but DSS, GDSS, and ESS are part of a special category of information systems that are explicitly designed to enhance managerial decision making. This chapter describes the characteristics of each of these types of information systems and shows how each enhances the managerial decision-making process.

DSS, GDSS, and ESS can support decision making in a number of ways. They can automate certain decision procedures (for example, determining the highest price that can be charged for a product to maintain market share). They can provide information about different aspects of the decision situation and the decision process, such as what opportunities or problems triggered the decision process, what solution alternatives were generated or explored, and how the decision was reached. Finally, they can stimulate innovation in decision making by helping managers question existing decision procedures or explore different solution designs (Dutta, Wierenga, and Dalebout, 1997).

15.1 Decision-Support Systems (DSS)

decision-support system (DSS)
Computer system at the management level of an organization that combines data, analytical tools, and models to support semistructured and unstructured decision making.

As noted in Chapter 2, a **decision-support system (DSS)** assists management decision making by combining data, sophisticated analytical models and tools, and user-friendly software into a single powerful system that can support semistructured or unstructured decision making. A DSS provides users with a flexible set of tools and capabilities for analyzing important blocks of data.

DSS and MIS

DSS are more targeted than MIS. An MIS provides managers with reports based on routine flows of data and assists in the general control of the organization. In contrast, a DSS is tightly focused on a specific decision or classes of decisions such as routing, queueing, evaluating, predicting, and so forth. In philosophy, a DSS promises end-user control of data, tools, and sessions. An MIS focuses on structured information flows, whereas a DSS emphasizes change, flexibility, and a quick response. With a DSS there is less of an effort to link users to structured information flows and a correspondingly greater emphasis on models, assumptions, ad hoc queries, and display graphics. Both the DSS and MIS rely on professional analysis and design. However, whereas an MIS usually follows a traditional systems development methodology, freezing information requirements before design and throughout the lifecycle, a DSS is consciously iterative and never frozen.

Chapter 4 introduced the distinction between structured, semistructured, and unstructured decisions. Structured problems are repetitive and routine, for which known algorithms provide solutions. Unstructured problems are novel and nonroutine, for which there are no algorithms for solutions. One can discuss, decide, and ruminate about unstructured problems, but they are not solved in the sense that one finds an answer to an equation (Henderson and Schilling, 1985). Semistructured problems fall between structured and unstructured problems. A DSS is designed to support semistructured and unstructured problem analysis.

Chapter 4 also introduced Simon's description of decision making, which consists of four stages: intelligence, design, choice, and implementation. Decision-support systems are intended to help design and evaluate alternatives and monitor the adoption or implementation process.

Types of Decision-Support Systems

The earliest DSS tended to draw on small subsets of corporate data and were heavily model driven. Recent advances in computer processing and database technology have expanded the definition of a DSS to include systems that can support decision making by analyzing vast quantities of data.

Today there are two basic types of decision-support systems, model driven and data driven (Dhar and Stein, 1997). Early DSS developed in the late 1970s and 1980s were model driven. **Model-driven DSS** were primarily stand-alone systems isolated from major organizational information systems that used some type of model to perform "what-if" and other kinds of analyses. Such systems were often developed by end-user divisions or groups not under central IS control. Their analysis capabilities were based on a strong theory or model combined with a good user interface that made the model easy to use. The voyage-estimating DSS described in Chapter 2 is an example of a model-driven DSS.

model-driven DSS Primarily stand-alone system that uses some type of model to perform "what-if" and other kinds of analyses.

The second type of DSS is a **data-driven DSS.** These systems analyze large pools of data found in major organizational systems. They support decision making by allowing users to extract useful information that previously was buried in large quantities of data. Often data from transaction processing systems (TPS) are collected in data warehouses for this purpose. On-line analytical processing (OLAP) and datamining can then be used to analyze the data. Companies are starting to build data-driven DSS to mine customer data gathered from their Web sites as well (Wilder, 1999).

data-driven DSS A system that supports decision making by allowing users to extract and analyze useful information that was previously buried in large databases.

Traditional database queries answer such questions as, "How many units of product number 403 were shipped in November 1999?" OLAP, or multidimensional analysis, supports much more complex requests for information, such as, "Compare sales of product 403 relative to plan by quarter and sales region for the past two years." We described OLAP and multidimensional data analysis in Chapter 8. With OLAP and query-oriented data analysis, users need to have a good idea about the information for which they are looking.

Datamining is more discovery driven. **Datamining** provides insights into corporate data that cannot be obtained with OLAP by finding hidden patterns and relationships in large databases and inferring rules from them to predict future behavior. The patterns and rules then can

datamining Technology for finding hidden patterns and relationships in large databases and inferring rules from them to predict future behavior.

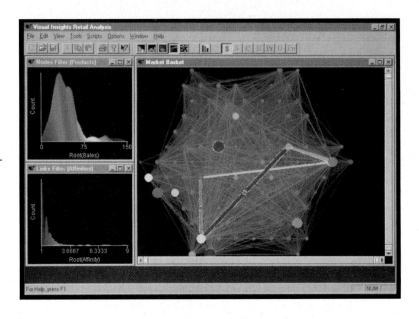

Lucent Technologies Visual Insights software can help businesses detect patterns in their data. Each dot in this example represents items purchased at one supermarket, with lines drawn between the purchases of individual shoppers. The software shows links between different purchase items, such as cookies and milk.

be used to guide decision making and forecast the effect of those decisions. The types of information that can be yielded from datamining include associations, sequences, classifications, clusters, and forecasts (Edelstein, 1996).

Associations are occurrences linked to a single event. For instance, a study of supermarket purchasing patterns might reveal that when corn chips are purchased, a cola drink is purchased 65 percent of the time, but when there is a promotion, cola is purchased 85 percent of the time. With this information, managers can make better decisions because they have learned the profitability of a promotion.

In *sequences,* events are linked over time. One might find, for example, that if a house is purchased, then a new refrigerator will be purchased within two weeks 65 percent of the time, and an oven will be bought within one month of the home purchase 45 percent of the time.

Classification recognizes patterns that describe the group to which an item belongs by examining existing items that have been classified and by inferring a set of rules. For example, businesses such as credit card or telephone companies worry about the loss of steady customers. Classification can help discover the characteristics of customers who are likely to leave and can provide a model to help managers predict who they are so that they can devise special campaigns to retain such customers.

Clustering works in a manner similar to classification when no groups have yet been defined. A datamining tool will discover different groupings within data, such as finding affinity groups for bank cards or partitioning a database into groups of customers based on demographics and types of personal investments.

Although these applications involve predictions, *forecasting* uses predictions in a different way. It uses a series of existing values to forecast what other values will be. For example, forecasting might find patterns in data to help managers estimate the future value of continuous variables such as sales figures.

Datamining uses statistical analysis tools as well as neural networks, fuzzy logic, genetic algorithms, or rule-based and other intelligent techniques (described in Chapter 14).

As noted in Chapter 4, it is a mistake to think that decisions are made only by individuals in large organizations. In fact, most decisions are made collectively. Chapter 4 describes the rational, bureaucratic, political, and "garbage can" models of organizational decision making. Frequently, decisions must be coordinated with several groups before being finalized. In large organizations, decision making is inherently a group process, and a DSS can be designed to facilitate group decision making. Section 15.2 deals with this issue.

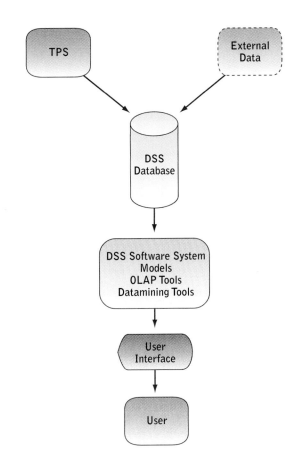

Figure 15-1 Overview of a decision-support system (DSS). The main components of the DSS are the DSS database, the DSS software system, and the user interface. The DSS database may be a small database residing on a PC or a massive data warehouse.

Components of DSS

Figure 15-1 illustrates the components of a DSS. They include a database of data used for query and analysis, a software system with models, datamining, and other analytical tools and a user interface.

The **DSS database** is a collection of current or historical data from a number of applications or groups. It may be a small database residing on a PC that contains a subset of corporate data that has been downloaded and possibly combined with external data. Alternatively, the DSS database may be a massive data warehouse that is continuously updated by major organizational TPS. The data in DSS databases are generally extracts or copies of production databases so that using the DSS does not interfere with critical operational systems.

The **DSS software system** contains the software tools that are used for data analysis. It may contain various OLAP tools, datamining tools, or a collection of mathematical and analytical models that easily can be made accessible to the DSS user. A **model** is an abstract representation that illustrates the components or relationships of a phenomenon. A model can be a physical model (such as a model airplane), a mathematical model (such as an equation), or a verbal model (such as a description of a procedure for writing an order). Each decision-support system is built for a specific set of purposes and will make different collections of models available depending on those purposes.

Perhaps the most common models are libraries of statistical models. Such libraries usually contain the full range of expected statistical functions including means, medians, deviations, and scatter plots. The software has the ability to project future outcomes by analyzing a series of data. Statistical modeling software can be used to help establish relationships, such as relating product sales to differences in age, income, or other factors between communities. Optimization models, often using linear programming, determine optimal resource allocation

DSS database A collection of current or historical data from a number of applications or groups. Can be a small PC database or a massive data warehouse.

DSS software system Collection of software tools that are used for data analysis, such as OLAP tools, datamining tools, or a collection of mathematical and analytical models.

model An abstract representation that illustrates the components or relationships of a phenomenon.

Figure 15-2 Sensitivity analysis. This table displays the results of a sensitivity analysis of the effect of changing the sales price of a necktie and the cost per unit on the product's breakeven point. It answers the question "What happens to the breakeven point if the sales price and the cost to make each unit increase or decrease?"

Total fixed costs	19000
Variable cost per unit:	3
Average sales price	17
Contribution margin	14
Breakeven point	1357

			Variable Cost per Unit			
Sales	1357	2	3	4	5	6
Price	14	1583	1727	1900	2111	2375
	15	1462	1583	1727	1900	2111
	16	1357	1462	1583	1727	1900
	17	1267	1357	1462	1583	1727
	18	1188	1267	1357	1462	1583

to maximize or minimize specified variables such as cost or time. The Advanced Planning System (discussed in the next section) uses such software to determine the effect that filling a new order will have on meeting target dates for existing orders. A classic use of optimization models is to determine the proper mix of products within a given market to maximize profits.

Forecasting models often are used to forecast sales. The user of this type of model might supply a range of historical data to project future conditions and the sales that might result from those conditions. The decision-maker could vary those future conditions (entering, for example, a rise in raw materials costs or the entry of a new, low-priced competitor in the market) to determine how these new conditions might affect sales. Companies often use this software to attempt to predict the actions of competitors. Model libraries exist for specific functions, such as financial and risk analysis models.

sensitivity analysis Models that ask "what-if" questions repeatedly to determine the impact of changes in one or more factors on outcomes.

Among the most widely used models are **sensitivity analysis** models that ask "what-if" questions repeatedly to determine the impact of changes in one or more factors on outcomes. "What-if" analysis—working forward from known or assumed conditions—allows the user to vary certain values to test results in order to better predict outcomes if changes occur in those values. "What happens if" we raise the price by 5 percent or increase the advertising budget by $100,000? What happens if we keep the price and advertising budget the same? Desktop spreadsheet software, such as Lotus 1-2-3 or Microsoft Excel, often is used for this purpose (see Figure 15-2). Backward sensitivity analysis software is used for goal seeking: If I want to sell one million product units next year, how much must I reduce the price of the product?

The DSS user interface permits easy interaction between users of the system and the DSS software tools. A graphic, easy-to-use, flexible user interface supports the dialogue between the user and the DSS. The DSS users are usually corporate executives or managers, persons with well-developed working styles and individual preferences. Often they have little or no computer experience and no patience for learning to use a complex tool, so the interface must be relatively intuitive. In addition, what works for one may not work for another. Many executives, offered only one way of working (a way not to their liking), simply will not use the system. To mimic a typical way of working, a good user interface should allow the manager to move back and forth between activities at will. Building successful DSS requires a high level of user participation and, often, the use of prototyping to ensure these requirements are met.

Examples of DSS Applications

There are many ways in which DSS can be used to support decision making. Table 15.1 lists examples of DSS in well-known organizations. To illustrate the range of capabilities of a DSS, we describe some successful DSS applications. Pioneer Natural Resources' business simulation system, the Advanced Planning System, and Reynolds' demand-forecasting system (de-

Table 15.1   Examples of Decision-Support Systems

Organization	DSS Application
American Airlines	Price and route selection
Equico Capital Corporation	Investment evaluation
General Accident Insurance	Customer buying patterns and fraud detection
Bank of America	Customer profiles
Frito-Lay, Inc.	Price, advertising, and promotion selection
Burlington Coat Factory	Store location and inventory mix
National Gypsum	Corporate planning and forecasting
Southern Railway	Train dispatching and routing
Texas Oil and Gas Corporation	Evaluation of potential drilling sites
United Airlines	Flight scheduling
U.S. Department of Defense	Defense contract analysis

scribed in the chapter opening vignette) are examples of model-driven DSS. Southern California Gas Company, ShopKo Stores, and Barclays' Group Portfolio Management System are examples of data-driven DSS. We will also examine some applications of geographic information systems (GIS), a special category of DSS for visualizing data geographically.

Pioneer Natural Resources

In the oil and gas industry, there are many variables associated with running an energy company, including development and production costs and the ratio of gas and oil in a field. The number and complex relationship among these variables makes it difficult for managers to determine the cost-effectiveness of their business decisions. Pioneer Natural Resources (PNR) in Las Colinas, Texas, decided to create a DSS that could provide more precise information for those decisions.

In 1995, PNR executives started identifying all of the management variables and diagrammed all of the business processes in their company to create a model that could show the impact on the business when one or more of those variables changed. The company built a prototype DSS using Powersim, a simulation development tool from Powersim Corporation in Herndon, Virginia. PNR executives first tested the prototype to simulate PNR's volatile Gulf Coast division, which had very long production time lines.

The company primarily uses Powersim to create a model for scenario planning and what-if analyses. For example, by modeling different scenarios with Powersim, PNR management can determine how much more to pay a service company to put a well into production earlier yet still earn a profit. Powersim runs on a Windows-based PC and uses Microsoft Excel spreadsheet software and Access database software for the input and output of business variables.

The company believes that each of its five divisions could potentially raise revenues by 25 to 40 percent using Powersim to model scenarios and adjust business variables. In addition, the simulation technology provides management with more control by helping managers determine the specific actions necessary to arrive at a desired business result or model the result of each business decision under consideration (Baldwin, 1998).

The Advanced Planning System—A Manufacturing DSS

To support most kinds of manufacturing, companies use a type of software known as manufacturing resources planning (MRPII). The typical MRPII system includes such applications as master production scheduling, purchasing, material requirements planning, and even general ledger. Many MRPII systems are too large and slow to be used for "what-if" simulations and too procedural to be modified into decision-support software. A Canadian company, Carp

Systems International of Kanata, Ontario, sells the Advanced Planning System (APS) to give the user DSS functionality using the data from existing MRPII systems.

APS allows a range of "what-if" processing by pulling the relevant data from the manufacturing software and performing calculations based on user-defined variables. After Hurricane Andrew hit south Florida in 1992, Trane's Unitary Productions division in Fort Smith, Arkansas, was asked to quickly ship 114 five-ton air conditioning systems to small businesses in the affected area. Using APS, within minutes Trane could determine not only how long it would take to build the units but also how the added production would affect its existing customer commitments. The company found that it was able to fit the added production in without disrupting existing orders. It delivered the units weeks before the competition did.

Pitney Bowes, the $3.3 billion business equipment manufacturer, uses the software to simulate supply changes. Pitney Bowes carries enough manufacturing inventory to satisfy demand for 30 days. Using APS, the firm asked to see the impact if it would reduce the inventory to 15 days. APS responded with an answer within five minutes, including an estimate of what Pitney Bowes would save.

Southern California Gas Company

Southern California Gas Company needed to be more competitive in a recently deregulated industry. It created a marketing department and used datamining to focus the company's marketing efforts. Southern California Gas created a data mart—a departmental data warehouse consisting of billing records combined with credit data from Equifax and U.S. census records. Using datamining techniques, the marketing department was able to identify a segment of customers most likely to sign up for a level payment plan.

Southern California Gas also used the system to decrease churn by identifying customers who were most likely to leave. Marketers learned that small, heating-only commercial customers were more sensitive to price increases than had been imagined. If the company were to raise its rates, this group of customers would switch to electric heating (mostly through space heaters). The company then performed a cost-benefit analysis to find out how much it cost to have such customers leave. Management decided that the company was not losing enough money from churn from this group of customers to warrant spending much money to keep them. It did, however, change its marketing approach to this group. These customers receive different literature that addresses the issue (Varney, 1996).

ShopKo Stores

ShopKo Stores, a $2 billion regional discounter, based in Green Bay, Wisconsin, competes head-to-head with Wal-Mart. The company started using datamining in about 1994 to discover cause-and-effect relationships between store items and customer buying habits. By using IBM's Intelligent Miner software across its advertising and merchandising departments, it discovered that customers who come in to purchase one product often buy another associated product, but that many associations are one-way streets. For example, a camera sale often triggers a film sale, but a film sale usually doesn't cause a camera sale.

ShopKo also learned that sales increased when merchandise was arranged in the store to match the way items were advertised in local circulars. Sometimes, however, the company ignores the results of datamining to maintain a high level of customer service. For example, ShopKo did increase sales by displaying baby formula next to baby clothes, but customers reported that they felt manipulated by that layout. ShopKo returned baby formula to its original location (Gerber, 1996).

The Window on Technology describes a data-driven decision-support system used in the financial industry.

Geographic Information Systems (GIS)

Geographic information systems (GIS) are a special category of DSS that can analyze and display data for planning and decision making using digitized maps. The software can assemble, store, manipulate, and display geographically referenced information, tying data to

Window on Technology

Utilizing Barclays' Bulging Data Warehouse

Data warehousing has become so successful that corporations often find they have more data than they can profitably use with their existing technology. The data warehouse of Barclays, the United Kingdom banking giant, was bulging, but they could not get the data they needed from all of it without new software. For example, they urgently needed to better manage their credit risk. They estimated that slicing just a few basis points from their average loan-default rate would result in millions of dollars more in profits each year, but to accomplish this they would need to examine huge quantities of data. Although it was possible to do, the time required to analyze the data was unacceptably slow. One model they wanted to use required 72 hours to run. Moreover, the model required that all the data be read from the warehouse database and loaded into the computer's memory before they could be processed. This would require that their hardware have immense amounts of very expensive computer memory.

Barclays was able to solve this problem by taking advantage of new features of on-line analytical processing (OLAP) software. This software was designed to enable the computer to dig deeply into the data warehouse, extracting large quantities of data at the very bottom of the data hierarchy. For example, in the past, for certain applications Barclays only could analyze its data at the regional level. With new software, they would be able to drill down to approximately 2000 branches and even beyond that to individual accounts.

To meet its needs, Barclays joined forces with White-Light Systems, an emerging software company based in Palo Alto, California. They knew about WhiteLight because Barclays had been looking for ways to solve its problems for several years and had briefly used an earlier WhiteLight product. This time, however, they allied with WhiteLight to complete development of the company's newest, most powerful version. Initial tests of the new software showed that processing time for the model described here was cut to about one hour, an amazing reduction of 96 percent. Barclays' new data-driven decision-support system, called the Group Portfolio Management System (GPMS) used a Teradata database, an NCR 4300 quad processor, a Pentium Pro 200 server with 1 gigabyte of memory, and client computers using Pentium 200s with 128 megabytes of memory. With this less expensive hardware arrangement, using the model became feasible.

A bonus feature of the new software was that it supplied a highly detailed audit trail of the processing. With this audit trail, the bank staff was able to understand precisely how the calculations were being performed. In this way they could better understand the meaning of the information produced by WhiteLight. Barclays could begin the process of analyzing its giant quantity of data to find ways to reduce the risk of loan defaults.

To Think About: Suggest ways the success of this new technology at Barclays might affect the company's business strategy, technology commitment, and organization.

Sources: Andy Webb, "Slice & Dice Massive Data Sets," **Wall Street and Technology,** Spring 1998 Edition and "Barclays' Bank Selects WhiteLight for Portfolio Analysis," WhiteLight Systems, 1998.

---

points, lines, and areas on a map. GIS can thus be used to support decisions that require knowledge about the geographic distribution of people or other resources in scientific research, resource management, and development planning. For example, GIS might be used to help state and local governments calculate emergency response times to natural disasters or to help banks identify the best locations for installing new branches or ATM terminals. GIS tools have become affordable even for small businesses and some can be used on the Web.

GIS have modeling capabilities, allowing managers to change data and automatically revise business scenarios to find better solutions. Johanna Dairies of Union, New Jersey, used GIS software to display its customers on a map and then design the most efficient delivery routes, saving the company $100,000 annually for each route that was eliminated. Sonny's Bar-B-Q, the Gainesville, Florida-based restaurant chain, used GIS with federal and local census data on median age, household income, total population, and population distribution to help management decide where to open new restaurants. The company's growth plan specifies that it will only expand into regions where barbecue food is very popular but where the number of barbecue restaurants is very small. Sonny's restaurants must be at least seven miles away from each other. Quaker Oats has used GIS to display and analyze sales and customer data by store locations. This information helps the company determine the best product mix for each retail store that carries Quaker Oats products and design advertising campaigns targeted specifically to each store's customers.

Geographic information systems (GIS) software presents and analyzes data geographically, tying business data to points, lines, and areas on a map. This map can help decision makers with market analysis, using pie charts and color variation of territories to display potential market share and income breakdown in the target market.

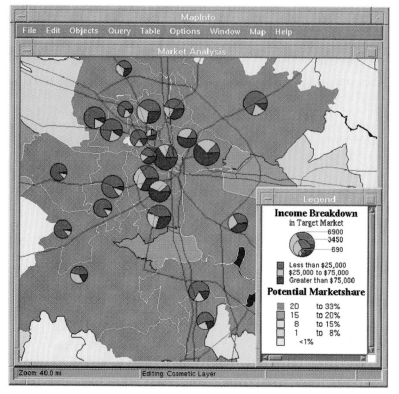

Web-Based DSS

DSS based on the Web and the Internet are being developed to support decision making, providing on-line access to various databases and information pools along with software for data analysis. Some of these DSS are targeted toward management, but some have been developed to attract customers by providing information and tools to assist their decision making as they select products and services. Companies are finding that deciding which products and services to purchase has become increasingly information-intensive. People use more information from multiple sources to make purchasing decisions (such as purchasing a car or computer) before they interact with the product or sales staff. **Customer decision-support systems (CDSS)** support the decision-making process of an existing or potential customer.

Figure 15-3 illustrates generic Internet facilities for a customer DSS. People interested in purchasing a product or service can use Internet search engines, intelligent agents, on-line catalogs, Web directories, newsgroup discussions, e-mail, and other tools to help them locate the information they need to help with their decision. Information brokers, such as Auto-by-Tel, described in Chapter 10, are also sources of summarized, structured information for specific products or industries and may provide models for evaluating the information.

Companies also have developed specific customer Web sites where all the information, models, or other analytical tools for evaluating alternatives are concentrated in one location. Some examples would be General Electric Plastics, Fidelity Investment's On-line Investor Center, and Pedestal Capital's Bond Network.

General Electric Plastics' DSS on the Web

General Electric Plastics (GEP) makes raw plastics that are packaged for specific uses such as bathroom sealants or that are used in the manufacture of other products. One of its ongoing problems is the need to constantly update product-specification information, which is vital to engineers using plastics in product design. GEP decided to use its Web site to provide a searchable repository of product-specification information that could be updated weekly. When launched,

customer decision-support system (CDSS) System to support the decision-making process of an existing or potential customer.

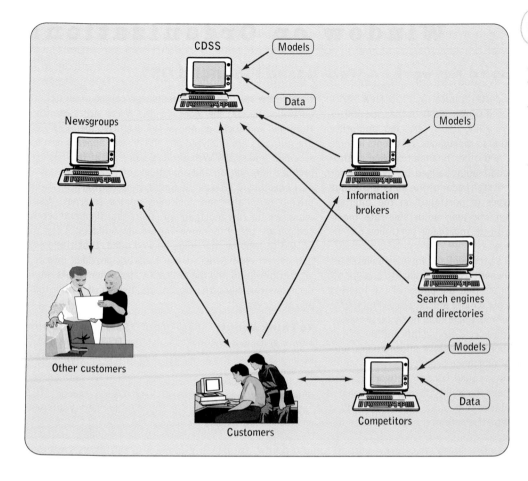

Figure 15-3 Customer decision support on the Internet. The Internet provides many sources of information and tools to assist customer purchasing decisions, including Web sites customized for this purpose. **Source:** Robert M. O'Keefe and Tim McEachern, "Web-Based Customer Decision Support Systems," **Communications of the ACM,** 41, No. 3 (March 1998). Reprinted by permission.

the site contained more than 15,000 pages of technical information. An e-mail capability allows visitors to forward technical questions to engineers, who then contact the customer.

Much of the data in the technical specifications are generated by continuous-simulation models. For example, a simulation model would be used to find out how a particular plastic might behave at very high temperatures. GEP's Web site was enhanced to make these simulation models available to customers so they could perform their own analysis. The Web site could dynamically generate graphs and diagrams in response to customer inputs (O'Keefe and McEachern, 1998).

Bond Network is a Web-based financial DSS that visitors can use to evaluate alternative investments in mortgage portfolios. DSS based on the Web can provide information from multiple sources and analytical tools to help potential customers select products and services.

Information Systems Security and Control

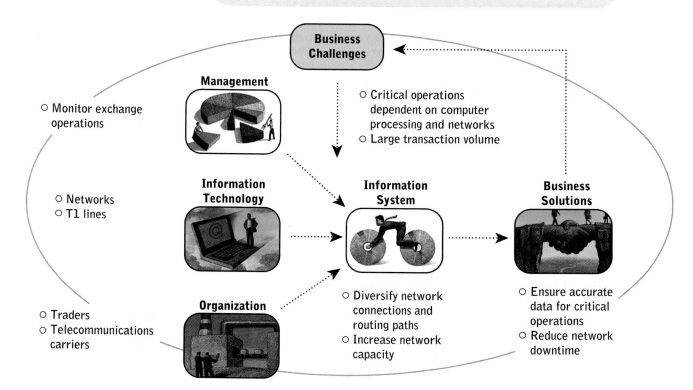

Learning Objectives

After completing this chapter, you will be able to:

1. Demonstrate why information systems are so vulnerable to destruction, error, abuse, and system quality problems.

2. Compare general controls and application controls for information systems, including controls to safeguard use of the Internet.

3. Select the factors that must be considered when developing the controls for information systems.

4. Describe the most important software quality assurance techniques.

5. Demonstrate the importance of auditing information systems and safeguarding data quality.

Business Challenges

Management

○ Monitor exchange operations

○ Critical operations dependent on computer processing and networks
○ Large transaction volume

Information Technology

○ Networks
○ T1 lines

Information System

○ Diversify network connections and routing paths
○ Increase network capacity

Business Solutions

○ Ensure accurate data for critical operations
○ Reduce network downtime

Organization

○ Traders
○ Telecommunications carriers

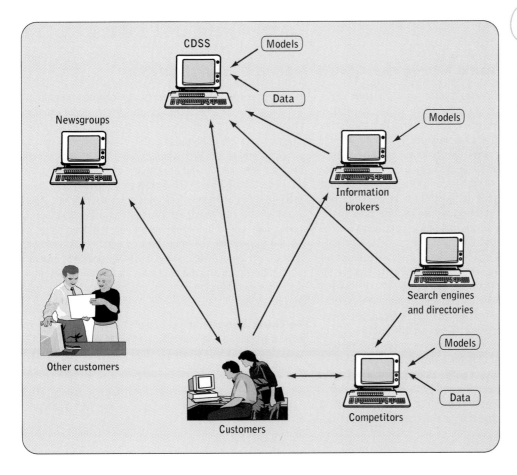

Figure 15-3 Customer decision support on the Internet. The Internet provides many sources of information and tools to assist customer purchasing decisions, including Web sites customized for this purpose. **Source:** Robert M. O'Keefe and Tim McEachern, "Web-Based Customer Decision Support Systems," **Communications of the ACM,** 41, No. 3 (March 1998). Reprinted by permission.

the site contained more than 15,000 pages of technical information. An e-mail capability allows visitors to forward technical questions to engineers, who then contact the customer.

Much of the data in the technical specifications are generated by continuous-simulation models. For example, a simulation model would be used to find out how a particular plastic might behave at very high temperatures. GEP's Web site was enhanced to make these simulation models available to customers so they could perform their own analysis. The Web site could dynamically generate graphs and diagrams in response to customer inputs (O'Keefe and McEachern, 1998).

Bond Network is a Web-based financial DSS that visitors can use to evaluate alternative investments in mortgage portfolios. DSS based on the Web can provide information from multiple sources and analytical tools to help potential customers select products and services.

Bond Network: A Web-Based Financial DSS

Pedestal Capital Inc. is a New York–based brokerage firm that specializes in reselling loans, servicing, and other financial products related to mortgages. Its clients include banks, broker/dealers, and other financial service institutions. Web sites for bond trading lagged behind those for stock trading, and Pedestal became the first brokerage firm to offer these types of portfolios on the Internet. Products ranging from one-year, adjustable-rate mortgages to 30-year, fixed-rate mortgage portfolios can be bought and sold this way.

Yung Lim, Pedestal's president and founder, believes his company's clients can benefit from the ability to analyze offerings on-line. He realizes that the power of the Internet can be harnessed to create a more efficient marketplace for the purchase and sale of mortgage-loan financial products. By providing clients with access to its staff and the use of its Web site, Pedestal hopes to improve information transfer and the valuation of mortgage products.

Pedestal's Web site, called Bond Network (www.bondnetwork.com), offers the ability to perform in a few minutes a number of tasks that often take hours with a spreadsheet. For instance, if a potential buyer wants to de-termine the level of prepayments that can be expected of a portfolio, he or she goes to the Web, accesses Bond Network, and clicks on one of the displayed menu options. The numbers are analyzed and the answer appears in a few seconds. Pedestal's Web servers store all of the required product information and analytical software tools.

Pedestal's DSS was the first system to offer live on-line pricing of whole loan portfolios on the Internet. Whole loans are the raw mortgage products that financial service companies offer to home buyers or builders. They are pooled to become mortgage-backed bonds that trade very actively on Wall Street. Bond Network provides investors with information and the analysis to help them make smart decisions regarding the buying and selling of whole loans and servicing.

To Think About: What kind of DSS is illustrated here? How can using a Web-based customer DSS help promote a company's business strategy? Suggest other applications for Web-based DSS.

Sources: Jim Frederick, "What About Bonds?" **Money**, March 1999; and Alex Knight, "Whole Loans on the Net," **Wall Street and Technology**, January 1998.

Web-Based Financial DSS: Fidelity Investments and Pedestal Capital

Fidelity Investments' Web site features an on-line, interactive decision-support application to help clients make decisions about investment savings plans and investment portfolio allocations. The application allows visitors to experiment with numerous "what-if" scenarios to design investment savings plans for retirement or a child's college education. If the user enters information about his or her finances, time horizon, and tolerance for risk, the system will suggest appropriate portfolios of mutual funds. The application performs the required number-crunching and displays the changing return on investment as the user alters these assumptions.

The Window on Organizations describes another Web-based customer DSS for financial services. Bond Network is a Web site providing data on potential investments and financial models that visitors can use to evaluate alternative investments in mortgage portfolios.

15.2 Group Decision-Support Systems (GDSS)

Early DSS focused largely on supporting individual decision making. However, because so much work is accomplished in groups within organizations, system developers and scholars began to focus on how computers can support group and organizational decision making. A new category of systems developed known as group decision-support systems (GDSS).

What Is a GDSS?

group decision-support system (GDSS) An interactive computer-based system to facilitate the solution to unstructured problems by a set of decision makers working together as a group.

A **group decision-support system (GDSS)** is an interactive computer-based system to facilitate the solution of unstructured problems by a set of decision makers working together as a group (DeSanctis and Gallupe, 1987).

Groupware and Web-based tools for videoconferencing and electronic meetings described earlier in this text can support some group decision processes, but their focus is primarily on communication. This section focuses on the tools and technologies geared explicitly toward group decision making. GDSS were developed in response to a growing concern over the quality and effectiveness of meetings. The underlying problems in group decision making have been the explosion of decision-maker meetings, the growing length of those meetings, and the increased number of attendees. Estimates on the amount of a manager's time spent in meetings range from 35 percent to 70 percent.

Meeting facilitators, organizational development professionals, and information systems scholars have been focusing on this issue and have identified a number of discrete meeting elements that need to be addressed (Grobowski et al., 1990; Kraemer and King, 1988; Nunamaker et al., 1991). Among these elements are the following:

1. *Improved preplanning,* to make meetings more effective and efficient.

2. *Increased participation,* so that all attendees will be able to contribute fully even if the number of attendees is large. Free riding (attending the meeting but not contributing) must also be addressed.

3. *Open, collaborative meeting atmosphere,* in which attendees from various organizational levels feel able to contribute freely. The lower level attendees must be able to participate without fear of being judged by their management; higher status participants must be able to participate without having their presence or ideas dominate the meeting and result in unwanted conformity.

4. *Criticism-free idea generation,* enabling attendees to contribute without undue fear of feeling personally criticized.

5. *Evaluation objectivity,* creating an atmosphere in which an idea will be evaluated on its merits rather than on the basis of the source of the idea.

6. *Idea organization and evaluation,* which require keeping the focus on the meeting objectives, finding efficient ways to organize the many ideas that can be generated in a brainstorming session, and evaluating those ideas not only on their merits but also within appropriate time constraints.

7. *Setting priorities and making decisions,* which require finding ways to encompass the thinking of all the attendees in making these judgments.

8. *Documentation of meetings,* so that attendees will have as complete and organized a record of the meeting as may be needed to continue the work of the project.

9. *Access to external information,* which will allow significant, factual disagreements to be settled in a timely fashion, thus enabling the meeting to continue and be productive.

10. *Preservation of "organizational memory,"* so that those who do not attend the meeting can also work on the project. Often a project will include teams at different locations who will need to understand the content of a meeting at only one of the affected sites.

One response to the problems of group decision making has been the adoption of new methods of organizing and running meetings. Techniques such as facilitated meetings, brainstorming, and criticism-free idea generation have become popular and are now accepted as standard. Another response has been the application of technology to the problems resulting in the emergence of group decision-support systems.

Characteristics of GDSS

How can information technology help groups arrive at decisions? Scholars have identified at least three basic elements of a GDSS: hardware, software tools, and people. *Hardware* refers to the conference facility itself, including the room, the tables, and the chairs. Such a facility must be physically laid out in a manner that supports group collaboration. It also must include some electronic hardware, such as electronic display boards, as well as audiovisual, computer, and networking equipment.

A wide range of *software tools,* including tools for organizing ideas, gathering information, ranking and setting priorities, and other aspects of collaborative work are being used to support decision-making meetings. We describe these tools in the next section. *People* refers not only to the participants but also to a trained facilitator and often to a staff that supports the hardware and software. Together these elements have led to the creation of a range of different kinds of GDSS, from simple electronic boardrooms to elaborate collaboration

Figure 15-4 Illustration of the Gjensidige Insurance collaborative meeting room. There is one microphone for every two seats and a speaker system on the wall. This equipment is used for same-time meetings between Gjensidige's offices in Oslo and Trondheim.

laboratories. In a collaboration laboratory, individuals work on their own desktop PCs or workstations. Their input is integrated on a file server and is viewable on a common screen at the front of the room; in most systems the integrated input is also viewable on the individual participant's screen. See Figure 15-4 for an illustration of an actual GDSS collaborative meeting room.

GDSS Software Tools

Some features of groupware tools for collaborative work described in Chapters 7 and 14 can be used to support group decision making. There also are specific GDSS software tools for supporting group meetings. These tools were originally developed for meetings in which all participants are in the same room, but they also can be used for networked meetings in which participants are in different locations. Specific GDSS software tools include the following:

○ *Electronic questionnaires* aid the organizers in premeeting planning by identifying issues of concern and by helping to ensure that key planning information is not overlooked.

○ *Electronic brainstorming tools* allow individuals simultaneously and anonymously to contribute ideas on the topics of the meeting.

○ *Idea organizers* facilitate the organized integration and synthesis of ideas generated during brainstorming.

○ *Questionnaire tools* support the facilitators and group leaders as they gather information before and during the process of setting priorities.

○ *Tools for voting or setting priorities* make available a range of methods from simple voting, to ranking in order, to a range of weighted techniques for setting priorities or voting (see Figure 15-5).

○ *Stakeholder identification and analysis tools* use structured approaches to evaluate the impact of an emerging proposal on the organization and to identify stakeholders and evaluate the potential impact of those stakeholders on the proposed project.

○ *Policy formation tools* provide structured support for developing agreement on the wording of policy statements.

○ *Group dictionaries* document group agreement on definitions of words and terms central to the project.

Additional tools are available, such as group outlining and writing tools, software that stores and reads project files, and software that allows the attendees to view internal operational data stored by the organization's production computer systems.

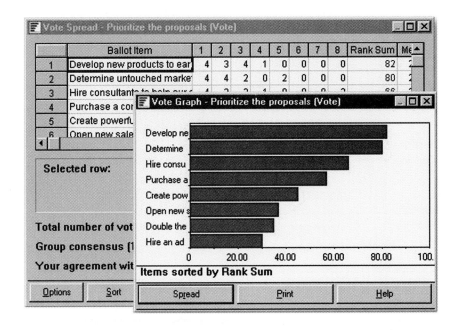

Figure 15-5 GDSS software tools. The Ventana Corporation's Group Systems electronic meeting software helps people create, share, record, organize, and evaluate ideas in meetings, between offices, or around the world.

Overview of a GDSS Meeting

An **electronic meeting system (EMS)** is a type of collaborative GDSS that uses information technology to make group meetings more productive by facilitating communication as well as decision making. It supports any activity in which people come together, whether at the same place at the same time or in different places at different times (Dennis et al., 1988; Nunamaker et al., 1991). IBM has a number of EMSs installed at various sites. Each attendee has a workstation. The workstations are networked and are connected to the facilitator's console, which serves as both the facilitator's workstation and control panel and the meeting's file server. All data that the attendees forward from their workstations to the group are collected and saved on the file server. The facilitator is able to project computer images onto the projection screen at the front center of the room. The facilitator also has an overhead projector available. Whiteboards are visible on either side of the projection screen. Many electronic meeting rooms are arranged in a semicircle and are tiered in legislative style to accommodate a large number of attendees.

The facilitator controls the use of tools during the meeting, often selecting from a large tool box that is part of the organization's GDSS. Tool selection is part of the premeeting planning process. Which tools are selected depends on the subject matter, the goals of the meeting, and the facilitation methodology the facilitator will use.

Attendees have full control over their own desktop computers. An attendee is able to view the agenda (and other planning documents), look at the integrated screen (or screens as the session progresses), use ordinary desktop PC tools (such as a word processor or a spreadsheet), tap into production data that have been made available, or work on the screen associated with the current meeting step and tool (such as a brainstorming screen). However, no one can view anyone else's screens so participants' work is confidential until it is released to the file server for integration with the work of others. All input to the file server is anonymous—at each step everyone's input to the file server (brainstorming ideas, idea evaluation and criticism, comments, voting, etc.) can be seen by all attendees on the integrated screens, but no information is available to identify the source of specific inputs. Attendees enter their data simultaneously rather than in round-robin fashion as is done in meetings that have little or no electronic systems support.

Figure 15-6 shows the sequence of activities at a typical EMS meeting. For each activity it also indicates the type of tools used and the output of those tools. During the meeting all input to the integrated screens is saved on the file server. As a result, when the meeting is completed, a full record of the meeting (both raw material and resultant output) is available to the attendees and can be made available to anyone else with a need for access.

electronic meeting system (EMS) A collaborative GDSS that uses information technology to make group meetings more productive by facilitating communication as well as decision making. Supports meetings at the same place and time or at different places and times.

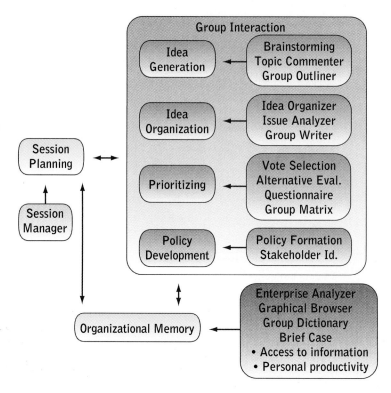

Figure 15-6 Group system tools. The sequence of activities and collaborative support tools used in an electronic meeting system (EMS) facilitates communication among attendees and generates a full record of the meeting. **Source:** From Nunamaker et al., "Electronic Meeting Systems to Support Group Work" in **Communications of the ACM,** July 1991. Reprinted by permission.

How GDSS Can Enhance Group Decision Making

GDSS are being used more widely, so we are able to understand some of their benefits and evaluate some of the tools. We look again at how a GDSS affects the 10 group meeting issues raised earlier.

1. *Improved preplanning.* Electronic questionnaires, supplemented by word processors, outlining software, and other desktop PC software, can structure planning, thereby improving it. The availability of the planning information at the actual meeting also can serve to enhance the quality of the meeting. Experts seem to feel that these tools add significance and emphasis to meeting preplanning.

2. *Increased participation.* Studies show that in traditional decision-making meetings without GDSS support the optimal meeting size is three to five attendees. Beyond that size, the meeting process begins to break down. Using GDSS software, studies show the meeting size can increase while productivity also increases. One reason for this is that attendees contribute simultaneously rather than one at a time, which makes more efficient use of the meeting time. Interviews of GDSS meeting attendees indicate that the quality of participation is higher than in traditional meetings.

3. *Open, collaborative meeting atmosphere.* A GDSS contributes to a more collaborative atmosphere in several ways. First, anonymity of input is essentially guaranteed. Individuals need not be afraid of being judged by their boss for contributing a possibly offbeat idea. Second, anonymity reduces or eliminates the deadening effect that often occurs when high-status individuals contribute. And third, the numbing pressures of social cues are reduced or eliminated.

4. *Criticism-free idea generation.* Anonymity ensures that attendees can contribute without fear of personally being criticized or of having their ideas rejected because of the identity of the contributor. Several studies show that interactive GDSS meetings generate more ideas and more satisfaction with those ideas than verbally interactive meetings (Nunamaker et al., 1991). GDSS can help reduce unproductive interpersonal conflict (Miranda and Bostrum, 1993–1994).

5. *Evaluation objectivity.* Anonymity prevents criticism of the source of ideas, thus supporting an atmosphere in which attendees focus on evaluating the ideas themselves. The same anonymity allows participants to detach from their own ideas so they are able to view them from a critical perspective. Evidence suggests that evaluation in an anonymous atmosphere increases the free flow of critical feedback and even stimulates the generation of new ideas during the evaluation process.

6. *Idea organization and evaluation.* GDSS software tools used for this purpose are structured and are based on methodology. They usually allow individuals to organize and then submit their results to the group (still anonymously). The group then iteratively modifies and develops the organized ideas until a document is completed. Attendees generally have viewed this approach as productive.

7. *Setting priorities and making decisions.* Anonymity helps lower level participants have their positions taken into consideration along with the higher level attendees.

8. *Documentation of meetings.* Evidence at IBM indicates that postmeeting use of the data is crucial. Attendees use the data to continue their dialogues after the meetings, to discuss the ideas with those who did not attend, and even to make presentations (Grobowski et al., 1990). Some tools enable the user to zoom in to more details on specific information.

9. *Access to external information.* Often a great deal of meeting time is devoted to factual disagreements. More experience with GDSS will indicate whether GDSS technology reduces this problem.

10. *Preservation of "organizational memory."* Specific tools have been developed to facilitate access to the data generated during a GDSS meeting, allowing nonattendees to locate needed information after the meeting. The documentation of a meeting by one group at one site has also successfully been used as input to another meeting on the same project at another site.

Studies to date suggest that GDSS meetings can be more productive, make more efficient use of time, and produce the desired results in fewer meetings, although these results are not dramatically better than face-to-face meetings. GDSS seem most useful for tasks involving idea generation, complex problems, and large groups (Fjermestad and Hiltz, 1998–1999). One problem with understanding the value of GDSS is their complexity. A GDSS can be configured in an almost infinite variety of ways. In addition, the effectiveness of the tools will partially depend on the effectiveness of the facilitator, the quality of the planning, the cooperation of the attendees, and the appropriateness of tools selected for different types of meetings. GDSS can enable groups to exchange more information, but can't always help participants process the information effectively or reach better decisions (Dennis, 1996).

Researchers have noted that the design of an electronic meeting system and its technology is only one of a number of contingencies that affect the outcome of group meetings. Other factors, including the nature of the group, the task, the manner in which the problem is presented to the group, and the organizational context (including the organization's culture and environment) also affect the process of group meetings and meeting outcomes (Dennis et al., 1999; Fjermestad, 1998; Caouette and O'Connor, 1998; Dennis et al., 1988 and 1996; Nunamaker et al., 1991; Watson, Ho, and Raman, 1994). New types of group support systems with easy-to-use Web-based interfaces and multimedia capabilities may provide additional benefits.

15.3 Executive Support Systems (ESS)

We have described how DSS and GDSS help managers make unstructured and semistructured decisions. **Executive support systems (ESS)** also help managers with unstructured problems, focusing on the information needs of senior management. Combining data from internal and external sources, ESS create a generalized computing and communications environment that can be focused and applied to a changing array of problems. ESS help senior executives monitor organizational performance, track activities of competitors, spot problems, identify opportunities, and forecast trends.

executive support system (ESS) Information system at the strategic level of an organization designed to address unstructured decision making through advanced graphics and communications.

The Role of ESS in the Organization

Before ESS, it was common for executives to receive numerous fixed-format reports, often hundreds of pages every month (or even every week). By the late 1980s, analysts found ways to bring together data from throughout the organization and allow the manager to select, access, and tailor them easily as needed. Today, an ESS is apt to include a range of easy-to-use desktop analytical tools and on-line data displays. Use of the systems has migrated down several organizational levels so that the executive and any subordinates are able to look at the same data in the same way.

Today's systems try to avoid the problem of data overload so common in paper reports because the data can be filtered or viewed in graphic format (if the user so chooses). Systems have the ability to **drill down,** moving from a piece of summary data to lower and lower levels of detail.

One limitation in an ESS is that it uses data from systems designed for very different purposes. Often data that are critical to the senior executive are simply not there. For example, sales data coming from an order-entry transaction processing system are not linked to marketing information, a linkage the executive would find useful. External data now are much more available in many ESS systems. Executives need a wide range of external data from current stock market news to competitor information, industry trends, and even projected legislative action. Through their ESS, many managers have access to news services, financial market databases, economic information, and whatever other public data they may require. Managers can also use the Internet for this purpose, as described in the Window on Management.

ESS today include tools for modeling and analysis. For example, many ESS use Excel or other spreadsheets as the heart of their analytical tool base. With only a minimum of experience, most managers find they can use these common software packages to create graphic comparisons of data by time, region, product, price range, and so on. Costlier systems include more sophisticated specialty analytical software. (Whereas DSS use such tools primarily for modeling and analysis in a fairly narrow range of decision situations, ESS use them primarily to provide status information about organizational performance.) Some ESS are being developed for use with the Web.

Developing ESS

ESS are executive systems, and executives create special systems development problems (we introduced this topic in Chapter 4). Because executives' needs change so rapidly, most executive support systems are developed through prototyping. A major difficulty for developers is that high-level executives expect success the first time. Developers must be certain that the system will work before they demonstrate it to the user. In addition, the initial system prototype must be one that the executive can learn very rapidly. Finally, if executives find that the ESS offers no added value, they will reject it.

One area that merits special attention is the determination of executive information requirements. ESS need to have some facility for environmental scanning. A key information requirement of managers at the strategic level is the capability to detect signals of problems in the organizational environment that indicate strategic threats and opportunities (Walls et al., 1992). The ESS needs to be designed so that both external and internal sources of information can be used for environmental scanning purposes. The Critical Success Factor methodology for determining information requirements (see Chapter 11) is recommended for this purpose.

ESS potentially could give top executives the capability of examining other managers' work without their knowledge, so there may be some resistance to ESS at lower levels of the organization. Implementation of ESS should be carefully managed to neutralize such opposition (see Chapter 13).

Cost justification presents a different type of problem with an ESS. Because much of an executive's work is unstructured, how does one quantify benefits for a system that primarily supports such unstructured work? An ESS often is justified in advance by the intuitive feeling that it will pay for itself (Watson et al., 1991). If ESS benefits can ever be quantified, it is only after the system is operational.

drill down The ability to move from summary data down to lower and lower levels of detail.

Netting Information on Your Competition

Keeping track of the competition is probably as old as business itself. Companies are always anxious to learn anything they can about a change in strategy, the release of new products, a change in management, or anything else that will help get the jump on them. In the past, gathering competitive intelligence involved lots of legwork and reams of paper. Today, managers can find an astonishing amount of competitive intelligence without leaving their desktops—much of it for free—by using the Internet.

The Internet is quick to use, easy to search, and offers a breathtaking array of information. Many companies have Web sites, enabling you to monitor them regularly. Companies often place more on their Web sites than they release publicly in any other way, making the sites a potentially rich source of information or at least providing clues to what is happening. Organization charts, customer lists, and news releases can be analyzed for clues to strategies, new products, and possible mergers. Net search engines allow the researcher to locate a great deal of information on corporate executives, often including some of their speeches and articles. Government sites on the Web provide public documents, such as patent applications, financial filings, and documents filed with information from regulatory agencies, that may be of value. Push delivery services can also be customized to deliver competitive intelligence.

Usenet discussion groups often become a gold mine in the search for meaningful data. Usenet groups are specialized, allowing researchers to focus on specific issues of interest to the target companies. Participating in or just monitoring them might tell you much about your competition, and they are fully public. They even make available names and e-mail addresses to anyone interested. The search tool Deja News allows individuals to search news groups by e-mail address, enabling researchers to determine which news groups the target person reads and all postings of that person to those groups. Thus, researchers can target an area of interest, locate individuals from companies about which they are interested, and trace all discussions of those people. Usenet groups also can lead researchers to individuals who have similar interests as themselves and so can be of help.

Staff at Fuld & Co., a Cambridge, Massachusetts, firm specializing in competitive intelligence issues, once noticed that a high-technology hardware producer was searching via Usenet for software engineers to hire. Fuld was able to conclude that the hardware company was making a strategic shift in its product line.

Many companies also keep up with customers and even business partners via the Net. Proper research can enable you to be knowledgeable about the issues your customers are facing. BellSouth Corporation's Leadership Institute started a market dynamics program that teaches executives how to study customers using the Internet before calling them.

One warning about the process, however. Collecting data is only the beginning. The data usually will come in bits and pieces that require a major analytical effort. In addition, gathering data this way does have its problems. The information gathered on the Net is often stale, incomplete, tainted, or from questionable sources. Moreover, the huge quantities of data found on the Net, most of it irrelevant, can make the task of gathering useful information daunting and tedious. In addition, companies conducting this research under their corporate Internet account can be identified. The way around this last problem is to not use a corporate Net account but rather an account from a commercial service provider and use an e-mail address that cannot be linked to the firm.

To Think About: How important do you think competitive intelligence is to senior management and why? How does it support decision making? What are the management benefits of using the Web for this purpose?

Sources: Jeff Sweat, "Vendors Push Forward," **Information Week**, February 15, 1999; Sreenath Sreeinvasan, "Corporate Intelligence: A Cloakhold on the Web," **The New York Times**, March 2, 1998; and Leonard M. Fuld, "Spyer Beware," **CIO Web Business Magazine**, August 1998.

Benefits of ESS

How do executive support systems benefit managers? As we stated earlier, it is difficult at best to cost-justify an executive support system. Nonetheless, interest in these systems is growing, so it is essential to examine some of the potential benefits scholars have identified.

Much of the value of ESS is found in their flexibility. These systems put data and tools in the hands of executives without addressing specific problems or imposing solutions. Executives are free to shape the problems as necessary, using the system as an extension of their own thinking processes. These are not decision-making systems; they are tools to aid executives in making decisions.

The most visible benefit of ESS is their ability to analyze, compare, and highlight trends. The easy use of graphics allows the user to look at more data in less time with greater clarity and insight than paper-based systems can provide. In the past, executives obtained the

Platinum Technology's Forest & Trees enables organizations to create quickly executive information system (EIS) and decision-support system (DSS) applications that let users slice and dice business data any way they want and present the data in a format that is easy to view and understand. These intuitive applications can alert managers graphically to business problems and pinpoint details that require action.

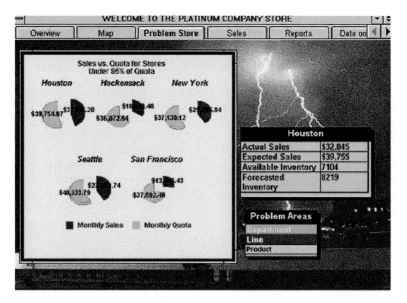

same information by taking up days and weeks of their staffs' valuable time. By using ESS, those staffs and the executives themselves are freed up for the more creative analysis and decision making in their jobs. ESS capabilities for drilling down and highlighting trends also may enhance the quality of such analysis and can speed up decision making (Leidner and Elam, 1993–1994).

Executives are using ESS to monitor performance more successfully in their own areas of responsibility. Some are using these systems to monitor key performance indicators. The timeliness and availability of the data result in needed actions being identified and taken earlier. Problems can be handled before they become too damaging; opportunities also can be identified earlier.

Executive support systems can and do change the workings of organizations. Immediate access to so much data allows executives to better monitor activities of lower units reporting to them. That very monitoring ability often allows decision making to be decentralized and to take place at lower operating levels. Executives are often willing to push decision making further down into the organization as long as they can be assured that all is going well. ESS can enable them to get that assurance. A well-designed ESS could dramatically improve management performance and increase upper management's span of control.

Examples of ESS

To illustrate the ways in which an ESS can enhance management decision making, we now describe three executive support systems, two for private industry and one for the public sector. These systems were developed for very different reasons and serve their organizations in different ways.

Sutter Home Winery: ESS for Business Intelligence

Unlike other businesses, Sutter Home Winery cannot analyze its sales data to determine consumer buying patterns. The Twenty-first Amendment to the U.S. Constitution ended Prohibition, but it also created laws forbidding producers of alcoholic beverages from selling directly to retailers. Because of this restriction, Sutter can only find out how much and what types of products its distributors sell, and such information is often a month old. Sutter needs more data about who buys its wines and who buys its competitors' wines. In order to comply with the law, this $200 million producer of wine and food products must collect information in other ways.

Sutter's management compensates by using information systems to combine business intelligence from external sources, including data from the Internet and point-of-sale data about consumer purchasing from market data-collection firms such as A.C. Nielsen or Information Resources, with the company's internal sales data. A variety of tools and technologies transform a motley collection of information into valuable insights that can be used to guide long-term planning and forecasting by senior management.

Sutter's salespeople who work with distributors and retailers provide information about what products are selling best and why, along with competitors' activities in pricing and promotional campaigns. They enter this information into a Lotus Notes database that can be accessed by sales managers and by management at corporate headquarters, including the company president. Occasionally the company adds data from focus groups and market research, especially when it is launching a new product. The data are organized and analyzed using AS/400 and PC databases, spreadsheets, groupware, and OLAP decision-support tools such as Cognos' PowerPlay. Sutter executives use this information for short- and long-term sales forecasts, marketing campaigns, and capital investment plans.

Sutter has assigned an employee to monitor Web sites that are industry-specific or related to the company's products and distribute reports two or three times a week to winery staff and senior managers. Business intelligence from the Internet has proven a useful and timely source of industry news (Wreden, 1997).

Royal Bank of Canada

Royal Bank of Canada, headquartered in Toronto, is one of the five largest lending institutions in North America, with assets of over $146 billion (U.S.). Its Risk Management division is responsible for analysis and control of the risk exposure of the bank's global credit portfolio. Its financial managers need information about the level of risk it is exposed to by clients, countries, or sectors. Obtaining this information used to be a cumbersome process, requiring programmers to create and run special batch reports on the mainframe that might take two days or more to produce.

Royal Bank used rapid application development tools from Information Builders to create a PC-based executive information system called the Portfolio Query System (PQS) that presents credit risk information directly to managers in a graphical format. The system uses data from Royal Bank's mainframe database but provides an intuitive interface with easy-to-use drill down, navigation, sorting, reporting, and printing capabilities.

PQS is widely used in many Royal Bank locations. Managers can view and analyze credit portfolio data using many different criteria, including market segment, line of business, management responsibility, assigned risk ratings, customer residency, and industry. The data can be presented as either graphical or tabular displays that allow for more than 15 criteria (Information Builders, 1998).

The U.S. General Services Administration

The General Services Administration (GSA) manages the vast real estate holdings of the U.S. government. In a period of tight federal budget restraints and as part of Vice President Al Gore's "reinventing government" initiatives, the organization needed to find ways to optimize the use of the government's multibillion-dollar inventory of 16,000 properties worldwide. Yet GSA managers facing this challenge had no system that would support them by making easily available to them the four gigabytes of data stored in their computers. The data were available only in old-fashioned printed reports and through slow, expensive custom programming. Analysis of the data was nearly impossible. GSA's response was GAMIS (Glenn Asset Management Information System), an executive support system based primarily on Lotus Notes that puts the needed data and analysis at the fingertips of the GSA's nontechnical managers.

The main purpose of the system was to give management quick and easy views of the organization's assets. Managers now can easily use ad hoc queries and perform "what-if" analysis, receiving the results on screen, in graphics format when desired. After indicating a specific office building, for example, the user will be offered 13 choices of data on that building, such as who occupies it, its financials, information on the congressional district it is in (if it is in the United States), and even a scanned photograph of the building. The data can be accessed via geographic information system (GIS) software from MapInfo Corp. Through this software interface, the user begins with a national map and drills down into regional and city maps that show detail on location and type of property. With another click of the mouse, the user will pull up all the data on that piece of property. Users can limit the data at the outset, specifying, for example, that they want to look only at Justice Department properties with more than 50,000 square feet of floor space. All data are available to about 100 GSA employees in Washington, and about 50 employees in each of the 10 regions have access to all data for their own region. Washington employees also have available a database of commercial properties with rental space available.

With GAMIS, nontechnical managers can access and analyze gigabytes of information that were formerly available only via printouts and custom programming. The system has received high marks from many officials, including John Glenn, then Democratic senator from Ohio and long a vocal critic of the GSA's antiquated computer system. When Glenn saw the system demonstrated, he was reported to have been so impressed that the GSA named the system after him. Observers have also praised the system because it was built from off-the-shelf software, making it quick and inexpensive to develop, providing high returns with minimum investments (Anthes, 1994).

Management Wrap-Up

Management

Management is responsible for detemining where management support systems can make their greatest contribution to organizational performance and for allocating the resources to build them. At the same time, management needs to work closely with system builders to make sure that these systems effectively capture their information requirements and decision processes.

Organization

Management support systems can improve organizational performance by speeding up decision making or improving the quality of management decisions themselves. However, some of these decision processes may not be clearly understood. A management support system will be most effective when system builders have a clear idea of its objectives, the nature of the decisions to be supported, and how the system will actually support decision making.

Technology

Systems to support management decision making can be developed with a range of technologies, including the use of large databases, modeling tools, graphics tools, datamining and analysis tools, and electronic meeting technology. Identifying the right technology for the decision or decision process to be supported is a key technology decision.

For Discussion

1. As a manager or user of information systems, what would you need to know to participate in the design and use of a DSS or an ESS? Why?

2. If businesses used DSS, GDSS, and ESS more widely, would they make better decisions? Explain.

Summary

1. Differentiate a decision-support system (DSS) and a group decision-support system (GDSS). A decision-support system (DSS) is an interactive system under user control that combines data, sophisticated analytical models and tools, and user-friendly software into a single powerful system that can support semistructured or unstructured decision making. There are two kinds of DSS: model-driven DSS and data-driven DSS. DSS targeted toward customers as well as managers are becoming available on the Web. A group decision-support system (GDSS) is an interactive computer-based system to facilitate the solution of unstructured problems by a set of decision makers working together as a group rather than individually.

2. Describe the components of decision-support systems and group decision-support systems. The components of a DSS are the DSS database, the DSS software system, and the user interface. The DSS database is a collection of current or historical data from a number of applications or groups that can be used for analysis. The DSS software system consists of OLAP and datamining tools or mathematical and analytical models that are used for analyzing the data in the database. The user interface allows users to interact with the DSS software tools directly.

Group decision-support systems (GDSS) have hardware, software, and people components. Hardware components consist of the conference room facilities, including seating arrangements and computer and other electronic hardware. Software components include tools for organizing ideas, gathering information, ranking and setting priorities, and documenting meeting sessions. People components include participants, a trained facilitator, and staff to support the hardware and software.

3. Explain how decision-support systems and group decision-support systems can enhance decision making. Both DSS and GDSS support steps in the process of arriving at decisions. A DSS provides results of model-based or data-driven analysis that help managers design and evaluate alternatives and monitor the progress of the solution that was adopted. A GDSS helps decision makers meeting together to arrive at a decision more efficiently and is especially useful for increasing the productivity of meetings larger than four or five people. However, the effectiveness of GDSS is contingent on the nature of the group, the task, and the context of the meeting.

4. Describe the capabilities of executive support systems (ESS). Executive support systems help managers with unstructured problems that occur at the strategic level of management. ESS provide data from both internal and external sources and provide a generalized computing and communications environment that can be focused and applied to a changing array of problems. ESS help senior executives spot problems, identify opportunities, and forecast trends. These systems can filter out extraneous details for high-level overviews, or they can drill down to provide senior managers with detailed transaction data if required.

5. Assess the benefits of executive support systems. ESS help senior managers analyze, compare, and highlight trends so that they more easily may monitor organizational performance or identify strategic problems and opportunities. ESS may increase the span of control of senior management and allow decision making to be decentralized and to take place at lower operating levels.

Key Terms

Customer decision-support system (CDSS), 476

Data-driven DSS, 469

Datamining, 469

Decision-support system (DSS), 468

Drill down, 484

DSS database, 471

DSS software system, 471

Electronic meeting system (EMS), 481

Executive support system (ESS), 483

Geographic information system (GIS), 474

Group decision-support system (GDSS), 478

Model, 471

Model-driven DSS, 469

Sensitivity analysis, 472

Review Questions

1. What is a decision-support system (DSS)? How does it differ from a management information system (MIS)?

2. How can a DSS support unstructured or semistructured decision making?

3. What is the difference between a data-driven DSS and a model-driven DSS? Give examples.

4. What are the three basic components of a DSS? Briefly describe each.

5. What is a customer decision-support system? How can the Internet be used for this purpose?

6. What is a group decision-support system (GDSS)? How does it differ from a DSS?

7. What are the three underlying problems in group decision making that have led to the development of GDSS?

8. Describe the three elements of a GDSS.

9. Name five GDSS software tools.

10. What is an electronic meeting system (EMS)? Describe its capabilities.

11. For each of the three underlying problems in group decision making referred to in question 7, describe one or two ways GDSS can contribute to a solution.

12. Define and describe the capabilities of an executive support system.

13. How can the Internet be used to enhance executive support systems?

14. In what ways is building executive support systems different from building traditional MIS systems?

15. What are the benefits of ESS? How do these systems enhance managerial decision making?

Group Project

With three or four of your classmates, identify several groups in your university that could benefit from a GDSS. Design a GDSS for one of those groups, describing its hardware, software, and people elements. Present your findings to the class.

Tools for Interactive Learning

○ Internet

The Internet Connection for this chapter will take you to a series of Web sites where you can complete an exercise using Web-based DSS for buying or financing a home. You can use the interactive software at the Fidelity Investments Web site in an Electronic Commerce project using a Web-based DSS for investment portfolio analysis. You can also use the Interactive Study Guide to test your knowledge of the topics in this chapter and get instant feedback where you need more practice.

○ CD-ROM

If you purchase and use the Multimedia Edition CD-ROM with this chapter, you can complete an interactive exercise asking you to design a group decision-support system (GDSS). You can also find a video clip illustrating the use of Intel videoconferencing technology, an audio overview of the major themes of this chapter, and bullet text summarizing the key points of the chapter.

Case Study — Premier Inc. Learns to Make Healthier Decisions

Premier Inc. is the largest hospital alliance in the United States. It has offices in Chicago, San Diego, Washington, D.C., and Charlotte, North Carolina. Premier Inc. was created in January 1996 from the merger of American Healthcare Systems, SunHealth Alliance, and Premier Health Alliance. Premier is owned by approximately 215 healthcare and hospital organizations and has affiliations with an additional 900 hospitals. Premier's owners and affiliates operate approximately 1800 hospitals and healthcare facilities. The alliance allows participating hospitals and health systems to obtain economies of scale in making group purchases of supplies and services.

Healthcare reform initiatives have placed mounting pressures on Premier and other healthcare providers to reduce costs while improving the quality of patient care. To better analyze efficiency and find areas for cost savings, healthcare managers require an even more precise understanding of their business and the activities of competitors. Such data often require weeks to integrate and analyze if they are stored in a number of incompatible databases.

Premier had a DSS business unit that was considered a leader in its field. It was providing competitive information on pricing, efficiency, quality of care and service, pricing, and market to member hospitals and affiliates. However, the information was on paper reports, and it consisted primarily of summary-level data. Premier's customers wanted more detailed access to market data that they could slice and dice quickly on their own. For example, hospitals felt they could make valuable analyses if they could directly access the 25 million patient entries and 200 million rows of data on the Medicare roster. They wanted some of the data stored at their own locations and access to larger pools of data using a dial-up network and a Web browser. The DSS group determined that a new system would have to provide an identical interface for all users yet provide data tailored to the needs of each hospital, coupled with a rapid response time.

Scott Palmer, Premier's director of business development and marketing, worked with the DSS group to research various data warehouse and on-line analytical processing (OLAP) tools. He and Stephanie Alexander, general manager of the DSS unit, decided to base the warehouse design on the decision-support tools that were appropriate for the company. The conventional approach to data warehousing is that the database is much more important than query tools. Premier took the opposite approach, designing a DSS that it knew its member organizations could use. The data warehouse also had to be populated with data of extraordinary depth and breadth because Premier's member organizations already had access to high-level market data from other organizations.

Premier selected MicroStrategy's relational OLAP tools because this solution was the only one that would work in its users' multiple environments. Users could access data using either MicroStrategy's DSS Agent or DSS Web tools. MicroStrategy could also optimize SQL (Structured Query Language—see Chapter 8) for all of the major relational DBMS. This decision gave Premier more flexibility in the selection of its data warehouse technology.

Premier was also favorably impressed with the data warehouse package from

Red Brick Software. Premier brought in consultants from both MicroStrategy and Red Brick to review its database design. During a three-month period, the project experimented with several prototype designs until a final design was selected and implemented. Premier's 140 gigabyte Red Brick data warehouse runs on a Digital Alpha server with Digital UNIX and a Clarion disk array. Project members continuously tested the reporting capabilities of the system while it was under development to make sure the data it provided would be useful.

Premier's new data warehouse-based DSS is called Market Vantage and uses data from the National Database of all Medicare Discharges and All-Payor Data from 28 states. It provides an intuitive interface for hospitals to obtain instant access to detailed healthcare data. Users can analyze market share, hospital efficiency, quality of care, patient demographics, and physician profiles. A hospital interested in knowing how its market share varies by physician or which providers handle the most cardiac surgeries with the best outcomes can now use the system to find an answer. Hospitals can also use the system to compare their charges and costs with their competitors for Medicare and other

patients. Premier plans to add capabilities so that users can access the data warehouse from the Web.

The system is being used by Premier's decision-support and consulting departments as well as Premier's member hospitals. Peter Bird, Premier's director of sales and product management, believes that the system provides a depth and breadth of data analysis that can't be matched by competitors. Users can immediately find out which areas of practice they need to focus on to improve outcomes or reduce costs.

For example, one Premier member used Market Vantage to determine in which areas it could reduce costs without sacrificing quality of care, examining benchmarks of costs and best practices in hospitals around the nation. The organization applied what it learned from Market Vantage to redesign its systems and business processes, and it anticipates cost reductions of $2 million as a result.

Another member hospital learned that most of the patients living in its surrounding county were traveling to another county or a competing hospital for vascular surgery because the member hospital did not provide that service. Using Market Vantage, the hospital learned that a vascular surgery center could generate over $9 million in revenue

per year and is developing a surgery service line to capture more business.

The total cost of the warehouse effort was close to $2 million, including hardware, software, and salaries. Premier estimates that by allowing staff to focus on and develop other products, it is saving as much as $450,000 each year in employment costs and expenses. Bird believes that systems such as Market Vantage can actually help promote healthcare reform by showing hospitals how to operate more efficiently.

Sources: "Keeping Hospitals Healthy," The Data Warehouse Institute and MicroStrategy Inc., May 1998, and **www.premierinc.com**.

CASE STUDY QUESTIONS

1. What problems did Premier face in trying to make good decisions?

2. What was Premier's business strategy and how was decision making related to its business strategy?

3. What kind of decision-support system did Premier develop? What kinds of decisions did the DSS support?

4. What management, organization, and technology issues had to be addressed when building the new system?

Can Boeing Fly High Again?

The Boeing Company of Seattle is the single largest exporter in the United States and the number one commercial aircraft producer in the world, with at least 55 to 60 percent of the world market since the 1970s. Recently, it acquired new muscle in military and defense production when it purchased its longtime archrival, the McDonnell Douglas Corporation, and the aerospace and defense operations of Rockwell International. A few years ago, company profits started to nosedive, but it responded with two efforts. This case looks at the role played by information systems in both those efforts: the design process for the 777 line of commercial aircraft; and Boeing's attempt to modernize its aircraft production.

For years, Boeing had no serious competitors. Then Airbus Industrie entered the commercial airplane market, and by 1994 it commanded 28 percent of the market. The competition has become fierce. Boeing and Airbus agree that air traffic will triple over the next 20 years, and Airbus has made jumbo jets the main focus of its current and future strategy. Airbus management believes that jumbo jets are a key to the future because they will be needed to fly the increased mass of passengers. They project that few new airports will be built over the next several decades, despite the expected explosion in air traffic. Moreover, they foresee increasingly stringent environmental restrictions that will require fewer planes. In addition Airbus believes that operational costs are key and that a newly designed jumbo jet will greatly reduce those costs. Therefore the company's strategy has been to develop its new jumbo A3XX-100. While the Boeing 747-400 jumbo has a seating capacity of 420, a range of 8300 miles, and a length of 231 feet, Airbus's A3XX-100 will be virtually the same length, 232 feet, and will fly 8400 miles. However its seating capacity is 550 or more. Moreover, Airbus expects that its operation costs will be nearly 20 percent less than those of the 747-400.

Boeing has a very different vision. Its management concludes that the passenger expansion will require smaller, longer-range planes. Boeing believes most travelers prefer to fly from their own city directly to their destination, for example,

Detroit-to-Shanghai rather than Detroit-to-Tokyo-to-Shanghai. Such flights do not need jumbo jets. Quite the contrary, Boeing management believes passengers do not want to fly in planes with more than 400 passengers due to the long waits for boarding, deplaning, and customs processing. The company's strategy is to continue building smaller, long-range planes like its new 777, discussed below. Who is correct? Even the major airlines cannot agree. United Airlines prefers jumbo jets but American Airlines owns no 747s.

Boeing management committed itself to holding Airbus to no more than 40 percent of the market, which Airbus achieved in the mid-1990s. The two companies operate under very different conditions, and those conditions have favored Airbus in recent years. Production costs at Airbus are lower than at Boeing. As important, Airbus is government-subsidized. The company is actually a consortium of state-run European aerospace companies, and it has been treated as a vehicle to generate European jobs and prestige rather than for profit. In the past Boeing's innovation and quality gave it a crucial advantage. However, aircraft are now viewed more like commodities—the airlines no longer feel they must turn to Boeing for the best and most advanced.

Unfortunately for Boeing, its production process has been very inefficient. By competing on price, Boeing's profit margins have been cut very sharply. Its problems became most visible when Airbus's market share reached 45 percent in 1997.

Boeing began to address its problems early in the 1990s when orders for new planes had dropped. Boeing reduced its workforce by one-third while also moving to make design changes so that new planes would be significantly cheaper to purchase and operate than older ones. Management established a goal of reducing production costs by 25 percent and defects by 50 percent by 1998. They also set a goal to radically reduce the time needed to build a plane, for example, lowering the production time of 747s and 767s from 18 months in 1992 down to 8 months in 1996.

Why was Boeing so inefficient? Mainly because it has been making airplanes with the same World War II—era production process used to produce its famous B-17 and B-29 bombers. Over the following decades,

Boeing had no competition and met no pressure requiring it to become more efficient. The Pentagon, a major customer, put no price pressure on Boeing because it had unlimited budgets due to the Cold War. The United States airline industry had been regulated for decades and their profits were protected, so they too put no price pressure on Boeing. All of this changed in the early 1990s with the end of the Cold War, airline deregulation, and the emergence of Airbus.

The WWII system worked well when Boeing was building 10,000 identical bombers, but it became a major headache when airlines wanted different configurations for each of their new aircraft. Today, every order for a plane or group of planes is customized according to the customer's requirement. So, for example, the seating arrangements and the electronic equipment will differ from order to order. In fact customers are given literally thousands of choices on each aircraft. Some are meaningful, such as the choice of engines, but others are meaningless, such as the location of emergency flashlight holders. Boeing offered far too many choices of colors, including 109 shades of white alone.

Boeing's production process was paper-intensive, with a final design of the Boeing 747 consisting of approximately 75,000 paper engineering drawings. Boeing designers long ago realized they would save much production time if they reused existing designs rather than designing each aircraft from scratch. However, the process of design customization was manual and took more than 1000 engineers a year of full-time work to complete. For every customization choice on every airplane built, hundreds of pages of detailed drawings needed to be drawn manually. To reuse old paper-aircraft configurations and parts designs, the engineers first needed to search through an immense number of paper drawings to find appropriate designs to reuse for the specific configuration. They then laboriously copied the old designs to use for the new plane. Inevitably, errors crept into the new designs—large numbers of errors, given the large numbers of design sheets—because of unavoidable copying mistakes.

For example, the bulkhead configuration affects the placement of 2550 parts, and 990 pages of manual drawings. Each drawing had to be manually tabbed for every configuration used. To make the problem worse, the alphanumeric code used on the tabs is so mysterious that it took an employee two years to learn. Thirty percent of these engineering drawings have been found to have coding errors and must be redrawn. And yet these drawings are used by the procurement department to know which parts to order and by manufacturing to determine how to assemble the parts. If a customer wanted to change the cockpit thrust-reverse lever from aluminum to titanium, Boeing employees would need to spend 200 hours on design changes and another 480 hours retabbing the drawings with customer identification codes. Planes were built in fits and starts, filling warehouses with piles of paper and years' worth of wasted byproducts. The process was so complex that Robert Hammer, Boeing's vice president in charge of production process reform, exclaimed: "You know the Baldrige prize for the best manufacturing processes? Well, if there was a prize for the opposite, this system would win it hands down."

Production did include the use of computers. However, it took 800 computers to manage the coordination of engineering and manufacturing and many of these did not communicate directly with each other. The list of parts produced by engineering for a given airplane was configured differently from the lists used by manufacturing and customer service. Ultimately the parts list had to be broken down, converted, and recomputed up to 13 times during the production of a single plane.

Another problem with manual design was that the staff needed to create life-size mock-ups in plywood and plastic to ensure that everything fit and that the pipes and wires that run through the plane are placed properly and do not interfere with other necessary equipment. They were also needed to verify the accuracy of part specifications. Building mock-ups was a slow, expensive, laborious process. At production time, errors would again occur when part numbers of specifications were manually copied and at times miscopied onto order sheets, resulting in many wrong or mis-sized parts arriving.

Engineers worked in separate fiefdoms based on their field of specialization. Some engineers designed the plane's parts, others assembled them, and others designed the parts' packing crates. They rarely compared notes. If production engineers discovered a part that didn't fit, they sent a complaint back to the designers located in another plant. The designers then pulled out their drawings, reconfigured the part to

make it match drawings of the surrounding parts, and sent the new design back to the plant. Warehouses were filled with paper.

Boeing also had a massive supply chain problem. Five-to-six million parts are required for its large twin-aisle airplanes alone. Inventory of these parts has been handled manually, and the production sites became infamous for the large piles of parts not being used. Not surprisingly, Boeing inventory turned over only two to three times per year compared to 12 times a year in an efficient manufacturing operation. Needed parts often arrived late. Boeing had to assign about 300 materials planners in different plants just to find needed parts on the shop floor.

Boeing's first action to cut costs and make planes cheaper to fly was a decision early in the 1990s to computerize the design and production of its planned new Boeing 777. This new aircraft line was meant to dominate the twin-engine wide-body long-distance market that was just opening. The 777 aircraft carries 300 to 440 passengers. It is designed to fly with only two pilots, thus reducing operating costs. Also, using only two engines saves on fuel, maintenance, and spare parts. Among other new technology, the planes use a new electronic method of controlling elevators, rudder ailerons, and flaps which is easier to construct, weighs less, and requires fewer spare parts and less maintenance. With lighter materials and fewer engines, a 777 weighs 500,000 pounds, about 38 percent less than a 747. With other savings designed into the 777, Boeing claimed that it could reduce operational costs by 25 percent compared to other Boeing models. In addition the 777 was designed to please passengers. Ceilings are higher, coach seats are the widest available, and aisles are broader.

To develop the 777 faster and at a lower cost, Boeing management decided to move to paperless design by using a CAD system. The system also supported a team approach. The system is gigantic, employing nine IBM mainframes, a Cray supercomputer, and 2200 workstations. It stores 3500 billion bits of information. The system enables engineers to call up any of the 777's millions of parts, modify them, fit them into the surrounding structure, and put them back into the plane's "electronic box" so that other engineers can make their own adjustments. Boeing assembled a single parts list that can be used by every division without modification and without tab-

bing. In addition management established design–production teams that brought together designers and fabricators from a range of specialties throughout the whole process. In this way changes needed for production were being made during design, thus saving time and money.

Ultimately the airplane was designed entirely on the computer screen and was initially assembled without expensive mock-ups. The CAD system proved to be more accurate than could have been done by hand. Moreover, the company reports that it exceeded its goal of cutting overall engineering design errors by 50 percent while designing and building a 777 in 10 months. Total cost to design and bring the 777 to production was $4 billion. Boeing made its first delivery of 777s on time to United Airlines on May 15, 1995, and the 777 commenced commercial service the following month.

Although computerizing the design of new aircraft proved a success, it did not solve all of Boeing's problems. Analysts agree that Boeing will not be designing other new airplanes for a long time so they will not have the opportunity to repeat the process. Production of other Boeing aircraft remained painfully inefficient. What Boeing needed was more efficient ways to manufacture its 737s, 747s, and other existing aircraft. The problem became a crisis when, after a commercial airline profit slump ended in the mid-1990s, demand for new aircraft jumped. Boeing took all orders it could to prevent them from going to Airbus, even though Boeing's production capabilities were insufficient for fulfilling the orders. The company determined it had to increase its passenger aircraft production from 18.5 planes per month in 1996 to 43 per month in 1997, more than doubling output in one year.

In 1994 Boeing had initiated a process improvement program known as Define and Control Airplane Configuration/ Manufacturing Resource Management (DCAC/MRM) to streamline and simplify the processes of configuring and producing airplanes. Management quickly decided to limit customer configuration choices to a finite number of options packages. Special requests would be fulfilled, but only at an additional price. In addition they realized they were using 400 software production programs, each with its own independent database, to support production. The management team decided to replace these 400 programs with four interconnected, off-the-shelf software packages, one each for configuration, manufacturing, purchasing, and inventory control. This would enable everyone to work from the same database, offering data integrity and coordination. Each airplane was assigned its own unique identification number that could be used to identify all the parts required by that plane. Each airplane would have only one parts list, and it would be updated electronically during the production cycle. Management estimated that the project would cost $1 billion and would require more than 1000 employees but would pay for itself within two years. The project was implemented in stages to be fully operational by the year 2000.

Boeing decided to purchase enterprise resource processing (ERP) software. The team selected the Baan IV finance, manufacturing, and distribution modules from the Baan Co., of Putten, Netherlands. They selected Baan because it could be used to control the flow of parts, because it was based upon client/server architecture, and because it was considered particularly well suited for companies with multi-site hybrid manufacturing processes such as Boeing. The software also includes EDI links with external suppliers and database links for internal suppliers. "As soon as our ERP system determines we don't have enough of a certain part in the assembly line to satisfy an airplane," explained one production manager, "we can identify which supplier we need and where that supplier's part needs to be delivered." Boeing's goal was that 45,000 persons would use the system at 70 plants to coordinate commercial airplane manufacturing around the Baan system. Rollout completion was targeted for the end of 1997.

In addition to Baan's software, Boeing selected forecasting software from i2 Technologies, factory floor process planning software from CimLinc, product data management software from Structural Dynamics Research, and a product configuration system from Trilogy.

The biggest challenge for the project was selling process changes to the lines of business. Therefore, the project started with an emphasis upon training. Boeing offered an eight-week knowledge transfer course on the new systems. Due to the past culture of independence and isolation of each department, the company also offered cross-functional training. The goals were to reduce the isolation of each of the various areas such as finance and engineering, and to help each understand the

impact of any change made by one department on the other departments. On the assembly line, the goal was to change to lean manufacturing. Employees attended five-day "accelerated improvement workshops" where they brainstormed on ways to do their jobs more efficiently. Job changes included transforming the materials expediters into buyers who order raw materials from suppliers, letting the parts tracking be done by the new system.

The overall project was complex and sweeping, and so it should not be a surprise that the results have been mixed. One key question has been the viability of the ERP system. Baan was a relatively small company, with 1996 sales of $388 million compared to sales of $2.39 billion for SAP, the ERP leader. Baan set itself a goal of catching up with SAP. To modernize the software, the company migrated its software to Windows NT and linked its applications to the Internet. However, analysts generally believe the company was trying to do too much too fast.

Boeing's project also ran into internal problems. Due to the jump in demand of the mid-1990s, it hired 38,000 workers from late 1995 through the end of 1997. Such a large new staff required much training due to the complex nature of the airplanes being built. Speeding up the intricate production process with so many new workers triggered many mistakes, causing delays. At the end of 1997, Boeing announced it would reduce its workforce by 12,000 during the second half of 1998, once its assembly lines were running more smoothly.

Although new orders were rising, many observers believe management was not focused on production. CEO Philip Condit's goal for Boeing was to transform it from the largest producer of commercial jet aircraft to the world's biggest aerospace company, forcing management to focus on swallowing McDonnell Douglas and Rockwell. "This company is trying to do so much at the same time—increase production, make its manufacturing lean, and deal with mergers," states Gordon Bethune, the CEO of Continental Airlines and a former Boeing executive and a supporter of Condit. In addition, according to Boeing's new CFO, Deborah Hopkins, senior management didn't understand the profit margins in selling jetliners. She has recently begun educating them on this and other key financial issues.

In 1997 Boeing was hit by the Asian economic crisis just as it was expanding its production and trying to reform its production process. Close to one-third of Boe-

ing's backlog was from Asian customers, and most Asian airlines reported significantly reduced profits or losses. The crisis had a particularly negative effect on wide-body orders. The Asian economic crisis proved to be much deeper and more prolonged than Boeing had first estimated.

The seriousness of the problems became public when Boeing announced its first loss in 50 years in 1997 as a result of production problems. In October the company halted production on two major assembly lines for a month. The main cause was late shipment of parts, preventing workers from installing components in the correct order. To catch up, extra work was required causing a huge increase in overtime and a jump of up to 30 percent in labor costs. In late 1997, Boeing also warned that production problems would reduce its 1998 earnings by $1 billion. By the spring of 1998 Boeing's backlog of 737s was 850 aircraft.

Production problems also affected Boeing customers. For example Gary Kelly, Southwest Airlines' CFO, told reporters in April 1998 that some of Southwest Air's expansion plans had to be postponed due to delayed delivery. Boeing had to compensate Southwest with millions of dollars for the delayed delivery.

In 1998 Boeing delivered 560 jetliners—a record. However, on December 1, 1998, Boeing announced a new round of production cutbacks extending into late 2000. Cutbacks were also announced for 757, 767, and 777 production. Job cutbacks at Boeing were increased to 48,000 for 1999. A staff cut of 10,000 was also announced for 2000. Boeing has also indicated it is having transition problems. "Right now, part of the company is in the new system, and part is in the old," explained Hammer. "So we constantly have to translate data from one to the other. We're in the worst of all worlds."

Nonetheless, Boeing management believes progress can be seen. By the end of 1998, the new ERP software was already running in four plants with 5000 users. By the end of 1998 CimLinc was rolled out to 19 parts plants. Plans call for rolling it out to engineering and sales employees by summer 1999. Production machines were changed and new tools were designed. In addition the whole company is now working from a single source for product data. A factory that builds wings for 737s and 747s has reduced production time from 56 to 28 days while eliminating unnecessary inventory. Another plant has shown an 80 percent reduction in cycle time for part flow. One machine fabrication plant in Auburn, Washington, reports it has reduced costs by 25 percent (its target), and 85 to 90 percent of the time it is delivering sales orders ahead of schedule (up from 65–75 percent under old methods). Alan Mulally, the president of Boeing's Commercial Airplane Group, in late 1998 said, "We delivered our planned 62 airplanes in November and we are on target to deliver 550 airplanes in 1998."

All of this demonstrates how Boeing has been whipsawed—expensive ramping up production to record levels due to great increases in orders, followed by sudden cutbacks due to world economic problems. It is interesting to note that Airbus has indicated it is not being affected by the Asian crisis and expects to maintain its planned 30 percent increase in production. Airbus is expanding its A320 production (rival to the 737), and observers note that the two expansions will result in a glut of this type of plane in a few years.

Sources: Lawrence Zuckerman, "Boeing Weighs Tough Steps to Increase Profits," **The New York Times,** February 25, 1999 and "Super-Jumbo or Super-Dumbo?" **The New York Times,** January 6, 1998; Frederic M. Biddle and John Helyar, "Boeing May Be Hurt Up to 5 Years by Asia," **The Wall Street Journal,** December 3, 1998 and "Behind Boeing's Woes: Clunky Assembly Line, Price War with Airbus," **The Wall Street Journal,** April 24, 1998; David Orenstein, "IT Integration Buoys Boeing," **Computerworld,** October 26, 1998; Adam Bryant, "Boeing Has Its Feet on the Ground," **The New York Times,** July 22, 1997; Jeff Cole, "Rivalry Between Boeing, Airbus Takes New Direction," **The Wall Street Journal,** April 30, 1997 and "Onslaught of Orders Has Boeing Scrambling to Build Jets Faster," **The Wall Street Journal,** July 24, 1996; Alex Taylor III, "Boeing: Sleepy in Seattle," **Fortune,** August 7, 1995; John Holusha, "Can Boeing's New Baby Fly Financially?" **The New York Times,** March 27, 1994; Shawn Tully, "Why to Go for Stretch Targets," **Fortune,** November 4, 1994; and www.boeing.com.

CASE STUDY QUESTIONS

1. Analyze Boeing's competitive position using the competitive forces and value chain models.

2. What management, organization, and technology problems did Boeing have? How did they prevent Boeing from executing its business strategy?

3. How did Boeing redesign its airplane production process and information systems to support its strategy? How helpful were information systems in helping Boeing pursue this strategy?

4. What role does knowledge work systems play in Boeing's business strategy? Evaluate the significance of that role.

5. What management, organization, and technology problems do you think Boeing encountered in building the 777 and redesigning its production process? What steps do you think they did take, or should have taken, to deal with these problems?

6. How successful has Boeing been in pursuing its strategy? In what ways do you consider its strategy sound? Risky?

Information Systems [Security] and Control

After completing this chapter, you will be able to:

1. Demonstrate why information systems are so vulnerable to destruction, error, abuse, and system quality problems.

2. Compare general controls and application controls for information systems, including controls to safeguard use of the Internet.

3. Select the factors that must be considered when developing the controls for information systems.

4. Describe the most important software quality assurance techniques.

5. Demonstrate the importance of auditing information systems and safeguarding data quality.

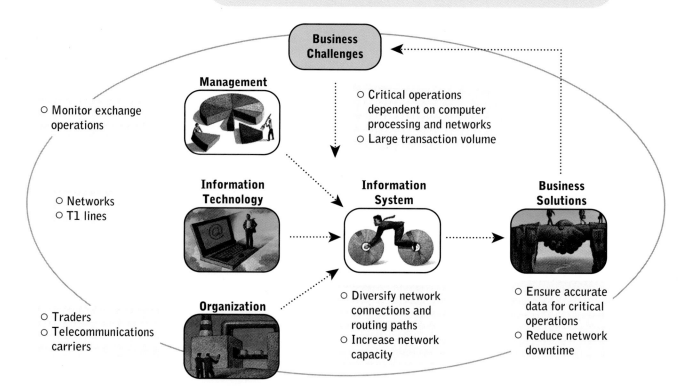

Business Challenges

Management
- Monitor exchange operations

- Critical operations dependent on computer processing and networks
- Large transaction volume

Information Technology
- Networks
- T1 lines

Information System
- Diversify network connections and routing paths
- Increase network capacity

Business Solutions
- Ensure accurate data for critical operations
- Reduce network downtime

Organization
- Traders
- Telecommunications carriers

The Pacific Exchange Invests in Uptime

On July 16, 1997, construction workers at Barstow, California, inadvertently cut a major fiber-optic backbone, severing two of the Pacific Exchange's T1 links to New York and California. (T1s are dedicated, high-capacity phone lines supporting transmission rates of 1.544 megabits per second.) The backbone was quickly repaired. Then on July 17, construction near Baltimore cut the exchange's other T1 line. This too was repaired. Then on July 18, construction in Barstow again severed the fiber trunk that carried all of the exchange's trading information between California and New York.

One would think that there would be minimal impact on the stock exchange's network because each of its T1 lines had been bought from different telecommunications carriers. Presumably their fiber cables had different locations; however, all of the exchange's New York–San Francisco traffic wound up on the same line. This meant that the third-largest stock exchange in the United States was handling all of its business on a single cable.

Dave Eisenlohr, the Exchange's vice president for data center operations, observed that "downtime is not an option." The Exchange's profitability is directly related to the reliability of its systems and networks. A network outage of only 30 to 60 minutes could cost millions in lost trades.

The Exchange had diversified its network connections so that no single point of failure was permitted; instead of using a single large link, it used multiple T1 lines from different carriers. Network administrators from the exchange personally inspected the links and routes for its communications traffic. What they failed to investigate was how their carriers handled spare bandwidth. It turned out that these carriers leased spare capacity on their backbones to other carriers. Several of these carriers rerouted their lines through the same concentration points. In Baltimore, lines from Cable & Wireless and Sprint converged, and fiber from WilTel and Cable & Wireless ran through Barstow. There were no alternative routing paths when the lines got cut.

The Exchange concluded that the carriers were not sufficiently coordinated to guarantee diverse routing paths. Management ordered the Exchange to install additional capacity—four times the amount needed. It also demanded that carriers guarantee they could ensure route diversity to keep the Exchange's business.

Sources: Laura DiDio, "An Investment in Uptime," *Computerworld,* February 23, 1998; and Clinton Wilder, Gregory Dalton, and Jeff Sweat, "Changing the Rules," *Information Week,* August 24, 1998.

The experience of the Pacific Exchange illustrates one of many problems that organizations relying on computer-based information systems may face. Hardware and software failures, communication disruptions, natural disasters, employee errors, and use by unauthorized people may prevent information systems from running properly or running at all. As you read this chapter, you should be aware of the following management challenges.

1. **Designing systems that are neither overcontrolled nor undercontrolled.** The biggest threat to information systems is posed by authorized users, not outside intruders. Most security breaches and damage to information systems come from organizational insiders. If a system requires too many passwords and authorizations to access information, the system will go unused. However, there is a growing need to create secure systems based on distributed multiuser networks and the Internet. Controls that are effective but that do not prevent authorized individuals from using a system are difficult to design.

2. **Applying quality assurance standards in large systems projects.** This chapter explains why the goal of zero defects in large, complex pieces of software is impossible to achieve. If the seriousness of remaining bugs cannot be ascertained, what constitutes acceptable—if not perfect—software performance? And even if meticulous design and exhaustive testing could eliminate all defects, software projects have time and budget constraints that often prevent management from devoting as much time to thoroughly testing as it should. Under such circumstances it will be difficult for managers to define a standard for software quality and to enforce it.

C omputer systems play such a critical role in business, government, and daily life that organizations must take special steps to protect their information systems and to ensure that they are accurate and reliable. This chapter describes how information systems can be *controlled* and made secure so that they serve the purposes for which they are intended.

16.1 System Vulnerability and Abuse

Before computer automation, data about individuals or organizations were maintained and secured as paper records dispersed in separate business or organizational units. Information systems concentrate data in computer files that potentially can be accessed more easily by large numbers of people and by groups outside the organization. Consequently, automated data are more susceptible to destruction, fraud, error, and misuse.

When computer systems fail to run or work as required, firms that depend heavily on computers experience a serious loss of business function. For example, it costs brokerage firms more than $6 million for every hour their computer systems are not working. The longer computer systems are down, the more serious the consequences for the firm. Some firms relying on computers to process their critical business transactions might experience a total loss of business function if they lose computer capability for more than a few days.

Why Systems Are Vulnerable

When large amounts of data are stored in electronic form they are vulnerable to many more kinds of threats than when they exist in manual form. Table 16.1 lists the most common threats against computerized information systems. They can stem from technical, organizational, and environmental factors compounded by poor management decisions.

Table 16.1	**Threats to Computerized Information Systems**
Hardware failure	Fire
Software failure	Electrical problems
Personnel actions	User errors
Terminal access penetration	Program changes
Theft of data, services, equipment	Telecommunications problems

Computerized systems are especially vulnerable to such threats for the following reasons:

○ A complex information system cannot be replicated manually.

○ Computerized procedures appear to be invisible and are not easily understood or audited.

○ Although the chances of disaster in automated systems are no greater than in manual systems, the effect of a disaster can be much more extensive. In some cases all of a system's records can be destroyed and lost forever.

○ On-line information systems are directly accessible by many individuals. Legitimate users may gain easy access to portions of computer data that they are not authorized to view. Unauthorized individuals can also gain access to such systems.

Advances in telecommunications and computer software have magnified these vulnerabilities. Through telecommunications networks, information systems in different locations can be interconnected. The potential for unauthorized access, abuse, or fraud is not limited to a single location but can occur at any access point in the network.

Additionally, more complex and diverse hardware, software, organizational, and personnel arrangements are required for telecommunications networks, creating new areas and opportunities for penetration and manipulation. Wireless networks using radio-based technology are even more vulnerable to penetration because radio frequency bands are easy to scan. The Internet poses special problems because it was explicitly designed to be accessed easily by people on different computer systems. The vulnerabilities of telecommunications networks are illustrated in Figure 16-1.

Hackers and Computer Viruses

The efforts of hackers to penetrate computer networks have been widely publicized. A **hacker** is a person who gains unauthorized access to a computer network for profit, criminal mischief, or personal pleasure. The potential damage from intruders is frightening. The Window on Organizations describes problems created by hackers for organizations that use the Internet.

Most recently, alarm has risen over hackers propagating **computer viruses,** rogue software programs that spread rampantly from system to system, clogging computer memory or destroying programs or data. Many thousands of viruses are known to exist, with 200 or more new viruses created each month. Table 16.2 describes the characteristics of the most common viruses. Many newer viruses are "macro" viruses, which exist inside executable programs, also called macros, that provide functions within programs such as Microsoft Word.

In addition to spreading via computer networks, viruses can invade computerized information systems from "infected" diskettes from an outside source, through infected machines, from files of software downloaded via the Internet, or from files attached to e-mail transmissions. The potential for massive damage and loss from future computer viruses remains.

Organizations can use antivirus software and screening procedures to reduce the chances of infection. **Antivirus software** is special software designed to check computer systems and disks for the presence of various computer viruses. Often the software can eliminate the virus from the infected area. However, most antivirus software is only effective against viruses already known when the software is written—to protect their systems, management must continually update their antivirus software.

hacker A person who gains unauthorized access to a computer network for profit, criminal mischief, or personal pleasure.

computer virus Rogue software programs that are difficult to detect that spread rapidly through computer systems, destroying data or disrupting processing and memory systems.

antivirus software Software designed to detect, and often eliminate, computer viruses from an information system.

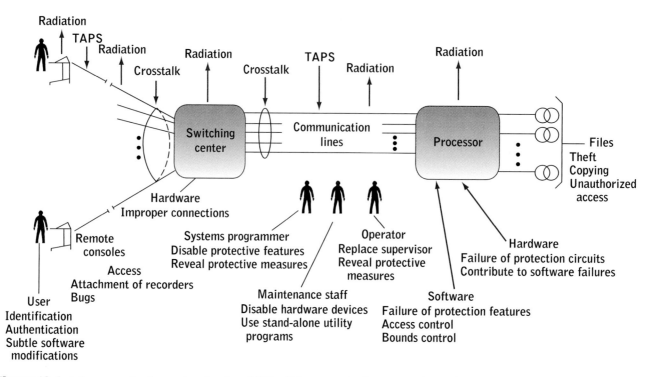

Figure 16-1 Telecommunications network vulnerabilities. Telecommunications networks are highly vulnerable to natural failure of hardware and software and to misuse by programmers, computer operators, maintenance staff, and end users. It is possible to tap communications lines and illegally intercept data. High-speed transmission over twisted wire communications channels causes interference called **crosstalk.** Radiation can disrupt a network at various points as well.

Concerns for System Builders and Users

The heightened vulnerability of automated data has created special concerns for the builders and users of information systems. These concerns include disaster, security, and administrative error.

Disaster

Computer hardware, programs, data files, and other equipment can be destroyed by fires, power failures, or other disasters. It may take many years and millions of dollars to reconstruct destroyed data files and computer programs and some may not be able to be replaced. If an organization needs them to function on a day-to-day basis, it will no longer be able to operate. This is why companies such as VISA USA Inc. and National Trust employ elaborate emergency backup facilities. VISA USA Inc. has duplicate mainframes, duplicate network pathways, duplicate terminals, and duplicate power supplies. VISA even uses a duplicate data center in McLean, Virginia, to handle half of its transactions and to serve as an emergency backup to its primary data center in San Mateo, California. National Trust, a large bank in Ontario, Canada, uses uninterruptable power supply technology provided by International Power Machines (IPM) because electrical power at its Mississauga location fluctuates frequently.

Fault-tolerant computer systems contain extra hardware, software, and power supply components that can back the system up and keep it running to prevent system failure. Fault-tolerant computers contain extra memory chips, processors, and disk storage devices. They can use special software routines or self-checking logic built into their circuitry to detect hardware failures and automatically switch to a backup device. Parts from these computers can be removed and repaired without disruption to the computer system.

Fault-tolerant technology is used by firms for critical applications with heavy on-line transaction processing requirements. In **on-line transaction processing,** transactions entered on-line are immediately processed by the computer. Multitudinous changes to databases, reporting, or requests for information occur each instant.

fault-tolerant computer systems Systems that contain extra hardware, software, and power supply components that can back a system up and keep it running to prevent system failure.

on-line transaction processing Transaction processing mode in which transactions entered on-line are immediately processed by the computer.

Window on Organizations

Internet Hackers on the Rise

Both business and personal use of the Internet and electronic commerce have been growing rapidly. Reports of Internet security breaches are rising. The main concern comes from unwanted intruders, or hackers, who use the latest technology and their skills to break into supposedly secure computers or to disable them.

U.S. military security analysts have been uncovering and deterring computer hackers who continually find new ways to attack open Pentagon networks on the Internet. These open networks contain unclassified material and pose no national security concern. For instance, a military computer server near San Antonio was probed for two days from foreign Web sites. The probes only reached the open military networks connected to the Internet. It is unclear whether the probes actually originated overseas or were merely routed through the overseas Web sites as a way of covering the hackers' tracks.

In a closed-door hearing before Congress in late February, 1999, a Pentagon spokesperson reported that there have been hundreds of attempts to break into Pentagon computers every week. The Pentagon has estimated that 99.95 percent of computer hackers fail to penetrate beyond the open networks, and thus pose no national security threat. Each U.S. armed service's division has installed new programs to detect hackers and to protect sensitive material.

Although there may be cachet in breaking into a military system, many more hackers are focusing on corporate targets where the payoffs are much bigger. In its fourth annual survey, the Computer Security Institute (CSI) in San Francisco reported that businesses, banks, and government agencies faced a growing threat from computer crime and other information security breaches. The Institute's survey of 521 information security managers found that security breaches from outside the organization increased for the third year in a row, with 57 percent of the respondents reporting assaults on their Internet connections. In the past, nearly 80 percent of documented security breaches came from within organizations. It now appears that the number of attacks from outside hackers is catching up with the number of breaches from insiders.

There are many ways that hacker break-ins can harm businesses. Some malicious intruders have planted logic bombs, Trojan horses, and other software that can hide in a system or network until executing at a specified time. In denial of service attacks, hackers flood a network server or Web server with requests for information or other data in order to crash the network.

Don Erwin, an information security strategy specialist at Dow Chemical Company in Midland, Michigan, noted that many companies have opened themselves up to attack by installing firewalls without allocating the resources to manage them effectively. Firewalls must be managed professionally and audited regularly, and effective security requires training, management support, and an adequate budget. Marcus Ranum, a security tools developer who is known as the "father of the firewall," observed that many companies don't update their firewall software to guard against known vulnerabilities. Richard Power, CSI's editorial director, said security management accounts for less than 3 percent of information technology budgets, with an average of only 1 security staff member assigned for every 1000 users.

To Think About: How can break-ins from the Internet harm organizations? What management, organization, and technology issues should be considered when developing an Internet security plan?

Sources: Ann Harrison, "Cyberattacks on the Rise," **Computerworld**, March 8, 1999; and Elisabeth Becker, "Computer Hackers Are Stopped; Pentagon Networks Were Victim," **The New York Times**, March 5, 1999.

Table 16.2 Common Computer Viruses

Virus Name	Description
Concept	Macro virus that attaches itself to Microsoft Word documents and can be spread when Word documents are attached to e-mail. Can copy itself from one document to another and delete files.
Form	Makes a clicking sound with each keystroke but only on the eighteenth day of the month. May corrupt data on the floppy disks it infects.
One_Half	Encrypts the hard disk so that only the virus can read the data there, flashing "One_Half" on the computer screen when its activity is half-completed. Very destructive because it can mutate, making it difficult to identify and eliminate.
Monkey	Makes the hard disk look like it has failed because Windows will not run.
Junkie	A "multipartite" virus that can infect files as well as the boot sector of the hard drive (the section of a PC hard drive that the PC first reads when it boots up). May cause memory conflicts.
Ripper (or Jack the Ripper)	Corrupts data written to a PC's hard disk about one time in every thousand.

Window on Management

Disaster Recovery in the Information Age

Thinking about protecting your data from a disaster? In the information age, data are the key to continued operation. The cost to a company without a disaster system can be high, even calamitous. The problem management faces is that backup and recovery are becoming ever more complex, reflecting the rapidly growing complexity of information systems technology. Finding the right approach can be challenging.

When Landstar Corp.'s roof collapsed from heavy rain, flooding its data center, the Florida transportation company was able to recover within four days because of its disaster recovery system. The company had backed up its data onto tape every night and then moved the tapes to a fireproof vault 26 miles away. This is the approach followed by many corporations. But is four days fast enough anymore? According to a recent report from Gartner Group Inc., in our current competitive environment, customers are no longer satisfied with their suppliers or service partners being down for four days. Competitive companies will need to be able to recover within 24 hours by the year 2003, the report concludes.

Faster recovery from disaster is available. Comdisco Corp., a specialist in backup and recovery, offers a system that promises recovery within four hours. It includes a preconfigured disk drive stored at one of Comdisco's recovery sites along with the backed-up data. When a customer experiences a disaster, the programs and data can be quickly loaded onto the already prepared drive, and the customer is back in business. Comdisco even offers access to the data via its virtual private networks (VPN). As with other recovery sites, customers can also use Comdisco's computers until their own are back in operation. The problem with this approach is it is very expensive and time consuming. Management will have to be convinced that such a high cost is necessary.

Another problem, faced by more and more companies, is that much of their valuable data is on notebook computers that travel around with employees. Vital customer and contract data, spreadsheets, and even crucial e-mail are stored

on these notebooks. Many on-the-move employees do not reliably back up their data, and even if they do, the backup is not available to the organization. Ways must be found to back up these data regularly, reliably, and in a way that the data are available to the corporation. For this purpose, Connected Corp. offers Online Backup for remote users. When the employee calls in, the system automatically backs up the data. Moreover, the system even enables employees to do their own recovery quickly and easily when needed.

Yet another crucial problem is that various critical applications run on different platforms and use different operating systems. This is particularly true in companies that have multiple locations (most companies, these days). The problem management faces is the ability to back up all their companies' applications easily. Computer Associates offers ArcServe and Unicenter TNG, which are capable of backing up from many platforms. The software uses one interface for all platforms, making it easy to learn and to use. In addition, the system enables the organization to manage its backups from one central location. When data problems occur, the administrator is even able to restore data remotely.

The dilemma for management is that no one system offers all of these functions. Moreover, many needed functions are rather expensive. The ideal backup and recovery system must offer a wide range of capabilities while being inexpensive, reliable, and fast. Although such systems do not exist, observers believe they may become available within the next few years.

To Think About: What are the management benefits of a disaster recovery plan? The costs? What management, organization, and technology issues should be addressed in a disaster recovery plan?

Sources: Jennifer Mateyaschuk, "Backup Plans Become Critical," *Information Week*, January 11, 1999; Brian Walsh, "RFP: Heading for Disaster?" *TechSearch*, January 11, 1999; and Jenny C. McCune, "Why You Need a Business Recovery Plan," *Beyond Computing*, March, 1999.

Rather than build their own backup facilities, many firms contract with disaster recovery firms, such as Comdisco Disaster Recovery Services in Rosemont, Illinois, and Sungard Recovery Services headquartered in Wayne, Pennsylvania. These disaster recovery firms provide *hot sites* housing spare computers at locations around the country where subscribing firms can run their critical applications in an emergency. Disaster recovery services offer backup for client/server systems as well as traditional mainframe applications. The Window on Management explores some of the issues that need to be addressed by organizations as they create disaster recovery plans.

Security

security Policies, procedures, and technical measures used to prevent unauthorized access, alteration, theft, or physical damage to information systems.

Security refers to the policies, procedures, and technical measures used to prevent unauthorized access or alteration, theft, and physical damage to information systems. Security can be promoted with an array of techniques and tools to safeguard computer hardware, software, communications networks, and data. We already have discussed disaster protection measures. Other tools and techniques for promoting security will be discussed in subsequent sections.

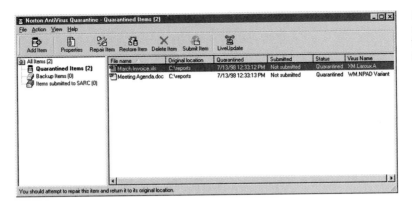

Companies can detect and eliminate many computer viruses in their systems by using antivirus software regularly.

Errors

Computers also can serve as instruments of error, severely disrupting or destroying an organization's record keeping and operations. For instance, on February 25, 1991, during Operation Desert Storm, a Patriot missile defense system operating at Dharan, Saudi Arabia, failed to track and intercept an incoming Scud missile because of a software error in the system's weapons control computer. The Scud hit an army barracks, killing 28 Americans. Errors in automated systems can occur at many points in the processing cycle: through data entry, program error, computer operations, and hardware. Figure 16-2 illustrates all of the points in a typical processing cycle where errors can occur.

System Quality Problems: Software and Data

In addition to disasters, viruses, and security breaches, defective software and data pose a constant threat to information systems, causing untold losses in productivity. An undiscovered error in a company's credit software or erroneous financial data can result in millions of dollars of losses. Several years ago, a hidden software problem in AT&T's long distance system brought down that system, bringing the New York–based financial exchanges to a halt and interfering with billions of dollars of business around the country for a number of hours. Modern passenger and commercial vehicles are increasingly dependent on computer programs for critical functions. A hidden software defect in a braking system could result in the loss of lives.

Bugs and Defects

A major problem with software is the presence of hidden **bugs** or program code defects. Studies have shown that it is virtually impossible to eliminate all bugs from large programs. The main source of bugs is the complexity of decision-making code. Even a relatively small program of several hundred lines will contain tens of decisions leading to hundreds or even thousands of different paths. Important programs within most corporations are usually much larger, containing tens of thousands or even millions of lines of code, each with many times the choices and paths of the smaller programs. Such complexity is difficult to document and design—designers document some reactions wrongly or fail to consider some possibilities. Studies show that about 60 percent of errors discovered during testing are a result of specifications in the design documentation that were missing, ambiguous, in error, or in conflict.

bugs Program code defects or errors.

Zero defects, a goal of the total quality management movement, cannot be achieved in larger programs. Complete testing simply is not possible. Fully testing programs that contain thousands of choices and millions of paths would require thousands of years. Eliminating software bugs is an exercise in diminishing returns, because it would take proportionately longer testing to detect and eliminate obscure residual bugs (Littlewood and Strigini, 1993). Even with rigorous testing, one could not know for sure that a piece of software was dependable until the product proved itself after much operational use. The message? We cannot eliminate all bugs, and we cannot know with certainty the seriousness of the bugs that do remain.

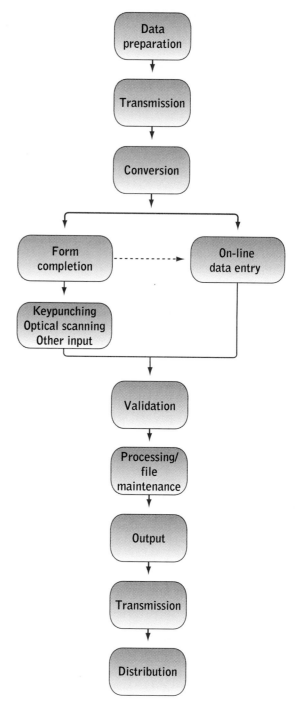

Figure 16-2 Points in the processing cycle where errors can occur. Each of the points illustrated in this figure represents a control point where special automated and/or manual procedures should be established to reduce the risk of errors during processing.

The Maintenance Nightmare

Another reason that systems are unreliable is that computer software traditionally has been a nightmare to maintain. Maintenance, the process of modifying a system in production use, is the most expensive phase of the systems development process. In most organizations nearly half of information systems staff time is spent in the maintenance of existing systems.

Why are maintenance costs so high? One major reason is organizational change. The firm may experience large internal changes in structure or leadership, or change may come from its surrounding environment. These organizational changes affect information requirements. Another reason appears to be software complexity, as measured by the number and

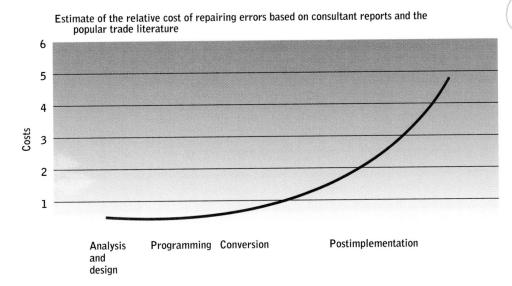

Estimate of the relative cost of repairing errors based on consultant reports and the popular trade literature

Costs

6
5
4
3
2
1

Analysis and design   Programming   Conversion   Postimplementation

Figure 16-3 The cost of errors over the systems development cycle. The most common, most severe, and most expensive system errors develop in the early design stages. They involve faulty requirements analysis. Errors in program logic or syntax are much less common, less severe, and less costly to repair than design errors. **Source:** Alberts, 1976.

size of interrelated software programs and subprograms and the complexity of the flow of program logic between them (Banker, Datar, Kemerer, and Zweig, 1993). A third common cause of long-term maintenance problems is faulty systems analysis and design, especially information requirements analysis. Some studies of large TPS systems by TRW, Inc., have found that a majority of system errors—64 percent—result from early analysis errors (Mazzucchelli, 1985).

Figure 16-3 illustrates the cost of correcting errors based on the experience of consultants reported in the literature.

If errors are detected early, during analysis and design, the cost to the systems development effort is small. But if they are not discovered until after programming, testing, or conversion has been completed, the costs can soar astronomically. A minor logic error, for example, that could take 1 hour to correct during the analysis and design stage could take 10, 40, and 90 times as long to correct during programming, conversion, and postimplementation, respectively.

Data Quality Problems

Chapter 5 has pointed out that the most common source of information system failure is poor data quality. Data that are inaccurate, untimely, or inconsistent with other sources of information can create serious operational and financial problems for businesses. When bad data go unnoticed, they can lead to bad decisions, product recalls, and even financial losses (Redman, 1998).

Data quality problems plague the public sector as well. A study of the FBI's computerized criminal record systems found a total of 54.1 percent of the records in the National Crime Information Center System to be inaccurate, ambiguous, or incomplete, and 74.3 percent of the records in the FBI's semiautomated Identification Division system exhibited significant quality problems. A summary analysis of the FBI's automated Wanted-Persons File also found that 11.2 percent of the warrants were invalid. A study by the FBI itself found that 6 percent of the warrants in state files were invalid and that 12,000 invalid warrants are sent out nationally each day.

The FBI has taken some steps to correct these problems, but low levels of data quality in these systems have disturbing implications. In addition to their use in law enforcement, computerized criminal history records are increasingly being used to screen employees in both the public and private sectors. Many of these records are incomplete and show arrests but no court disposition; that is, they show charges without proof of conviction or guilt. Many individuals may be denied employment unjustifiably because these records overstate their criminality. These criminal record systems are not limited to violent felons. They contain the records of 36 million people, about one-third of the labor force. Inaccurate and potentially damaging information is being maintained on many law-abiding citizens. The level of data quality in these systems threatens citizens' constitutional rights to due process and impairs the efficiency and effectiveness of any law enforcement programs in which these records are used (Laudon, 1986a).

Poor data quality may stem from errors during data input or faulty information system and database design (Wand and Wang, 1996; Strong, Lee, and Wang, 1997). In the following sections we examine how organizations can deal with data and software quality problems as well as other threats to information systems.

16.2 Creating a Control Environment

To minimize errors, disaster, computer crime, and breaches of security, special policies and procedures must be incorporated into the design and implementation of information systems. The combination of manual and automated measures that safeguard information systems and ensure that they perform according to management standards is termed *controls*. **Controls** consist of all the methods, policies, and organizational procedures that ensure the safety of the organization's assets, the accuracy and reliability of its accounting records, and operational adherence to management standards.

In the past, the control of information systems was treated as an afterthought, addressed only toward the end of implementation, just before the system was installed. Today, however, organizations are so critically dependent on information systems that vulnerabilities and control issues must be identified as early as possible. The control of an information system must be an integral part of its design. Users and builders of systems must pay close attention to controls throughout the system's life span.

Computer systems are controlled by a combination of general controls and application controls.

General controls are those that control the design, security, and use of computer programs and the security of data files in general throughout the organization. On the whole, general controls apply to all computerized applications and consist of a combination of system software and manual procedures that create an overall control environment.

Application controls are specific controls unique to each computerized application, such as payroll, accounts receivable, and order processing. They consist of controls applied from the user functional area of a particular system and from programmed procedures.

General Controls

General controls are overall controls that ensure the effective operation of programmed procedures. They apply to all application areas. General controls include the following:

- ○ Controls over the system implementation process
- ○ Software controls
- ○ Physical hardware controls
- ○ Computer operations controls
- ○ Data security controls
- ○ Administrative disciplines, standards, and procedures

Implementation Controls

Implementation controls audit the systems development process at various points to ensure that the process is properly controlled and managed. The systems development audit should look for the presence of formal review points at various stages of development that enable users and management to approve or disapprove the implementation.

The systems development audit also should examine the level of user involvement at each stage of implementation and check for the use of a formal cost/benefit methodology in establishing system feasibility. The audit should look for the use of controls and quality assurance techniques for program development, conversion, and testing and for complete and thorough system, user, and operations documentation.

---

controls All of the methods, policies, and procedures that ensure protection of the organization's assets, accuracy and reliability of its records, and operational adherence to management standards.

general controls Overall controls that establish a framework for controlling the design, security, and use of computer programs throughout an organization.

application controls Specific controls unique to each computerized application.

implementation controls The audit of the systems development process at various points to make sure that it is properly controlled and managed.

Software Controls

Controls are essential for the various categories of software used in computer systems. **Software controls** monitor the use of system software and prevent unauthorized access of software programs, system software, and computer programs. System software is an important control area because it performs overall control functions for the programs that directly process data and data files.

Hardware Controls

Hardware controls ensure that computer hardware is physically secure, and they check for equipment malfunction. Computer hardware should be physically secured so that it can be accessed only by authorized individuals. Computer equipment should be specially protected against fires and extremes of temperature and humidity. Organizations that are critically dependent on their computers also must make provisions for emergency backup in case of power failure.

Many kinds of computer hardware contain mechanisms that check for equipment malfunction. Parity checks detect equipment malfunctions responsible for altering bits within bytes during processing. Validity checks monitor the structure of on–off bits within bytes to make sure that it is valid for the character set of a particular computer machine. Echo checks verify that a hardware device is performance ready. Chapter 6 discussed computer hardware in detail.

Computer Operations Controls

Computer operations controls apply to the work of the computer department and help ensure that programmed procedures are consistently and correctly applied to the storage and processing of data. They include controls over the setup of computer processing jobs, operations software, and computer operations, and backup and recovery procedures for processing that ends abnormally.

Instructions for running computer jobs should be fully documented, reviewed, and approved by a responsible official. Controls over operations software include manual procedures designed to both prevent and detect error. Specific instructions for backup and recovery can be developed so that in the event of a hardware or software failure, the recovery process for production programs, system software, and data files does not create erroneous changes in the system.

Data Security Controls

Data security controls ensure that valuable business data files on either disk or tape are not subject to unauthorized access, change, or destruction. Such controls are required for data files when they are in use and when they are being held for storage.

When data can be input on-line through a terminal, entry of unauthorized input must be prevented. For example, a credit note could be altered to match a sales invoice on file. In such situations, security can be developed on several levels:

○ Terminals can be physically restricted so that they are available only to authorized individuals.

○ System software can include the use of passwords assigned only to authorized individuals. No one can log on to the system without a valid password.

○ Additional sets of passwords and security restrictions can be developed for specific systems and applications. For example, data security software can limit access to specific files, such as the files for the accounts receivable system. It can restrict the type of access so that only individuals authorized to update these specific files will have the ability to do so. All others will only be able to read the files or will be denied access altogether.

Many systems that allow on-line inquiry and reporting must have data files secured. Figure 16-4 illustrates the security allowed for two sets of users of an on-line personnel database with sensitive information such as employees' salaries, benefits, and medical histories. One set of users consists of all employees who perform clerical functions such as inputting employee data into the system. All individuals with this type of profile can update the system but can neither read nor update sensitive fields such as salary, medical history, or earnings

SECURITY PROFILE 1

User: Personnel Dept. Clerk

Location: Division 1

Employee Identification
Codes with This Profile: 00753, 27834, 37665, 44116

Data Field Restrictions	Type of Access
All employee data for Division 1 only	Read and Update
• Medical history data	None
• Salary	None
• Pensionable earnings	None

SECURITY PROFILE 2

User: Divisional Personnel Manager

Location: Division 1

Employee Identification
Codes with This Profile: 27321

Data Field Restrictions	Type of Access
All employee data for Division 1 only	Read Only

data. Another profile applies to a divisional manager, who cannot update the system but who can read all employee data fields for his or her division, including medical history and salary. These profiles would be established and maintained by a data security system. The data security system illustrated in Figure 16-4 provides very fine-grained security restrictions, such as allowing authorized personnel users to inquire about all employee information except in confidential fields such as salary or medical history.

Administrative Controls

administrative controls Formalized standards, rules, procedures, and disciplines to ensure that the organization's controls are properly executed and enforced.

segregation of functions The principle of internal control to divide responsibilities and assign tasks among people so that job functions do not overlap, to minimize the risk of errors and fraudulent manipulation of the organization's assets.

Administrative controls are formalized standards, rules, procedures, and control disciplines to ensure that the organization's general and application controls are properly executed and enforced. The most important administrative controls are (1) segregation of functions, (2) written policies and procedures, and (3) supervision.

Segregation of functions means that job functions should be designed to minimize the risk of errors or fraudulent manipulation of the organization's assets. The individuals responsible for operating systems should not be the same ones who can initiate transactions that change the assets held in these systems. A typical arrangement is to have the organization's information systems department responsible for data and program files and end users responsible for initiating transactions such as payments or checks.

Written policies and procedures establish formal standards for controlling information system operations. Procedures must be formalized in writing and authorized by the appropriate level of management. Accountabilities and responsibilities must be clearly specified.

Supervision of personnel involved in control procedures ensures that the controls for an information system are performing as intended. Without adequate supervision, the best-designed set of controls may be bypassed, short-circuited, or neglected.

Table 16.3 Effect of Weakness in General Controls

Weakness	Impact
Implementation controls	New systems or systems that have been modified will have errors or fail to function as required.
Software controls (program security)	Unauthorized changes can be made in processing. The organization may not be sure of which programs or systems have been changed.
Software controls (system software)	These controls may not have a direct effect on individual applications. Other general controls depend heavily on system software, so a weakness in this area impairs the other general controls.
Physical hardware controls	Hardware may have serious malfunctions or may break down altogether, introducing numerous errors or destroying computerized records.
Computer operations controls	Random errors may occur in a system. (Most processing will be correct, but occasionally it may not be.)
Data file security controls	Unauthorized changes can be made in data stored in computer systems or unauthorized individuals can access sensitive information.
Administrative controls	All of the other controls may not be properly executed or enforced.

Weakness in each of these general controls can have a widespread effect on programmed procedures and data throughout the organization. Table 16.3 summarizes the effect of weaknesses in major general control areas.

Application Controls

Application controls are specific controls within each separate computer application, such as payroll or order processing. They include automated and manual procedures that ensure that only authorized data are completely and accurately processed by that application. The controls for each application should encompass the whole sequence of processing.

Not all of the application controls discussed here are used in every information system. Some systems require more of these controls than others, depending on the importance of the data and the nature of the application.

Application controls can be classified as (1) input controls, (2) processing controls, and (3) output controls.

Input Controls

Input controls check data for accuracy and completeness when they enter the system. There are specific input controls for input authorization, data conversion, data editing, and error handling.

input controls The procedures to check data for accuracy and completeness when they enter the system.

Input must be properly authorized, recorded, and monitored as source documents flow to the computer. For example, formal procedures can be set up to authorize only selected members of the sales department to prepare sales transactions for an order entry system.

Input must be properly converted into computer transactions, with no errors as it is transcribed from one form to another. Transcription errors can be eliminated or reduced by keying input transactions directly into computer terminals or by using some form of source data automation.

Table 16.4 Important Edit Techniques

Edit Technique	Description	Example
Reasonableness checks	To be accepted, data must fall within certain limits set in advance, or they will be rejected.	If an order transaction is for 20,000 units and the largest order on record was 50 units, the transaction will be rejected.
Format checks	Characteristics of the contents (letter/digit), length, and sign of individual data fields are checked by the system.	A nine-position Social Security number should not contain any alphabetic characters.
Existence checks	The computer compares input reference data to tables or master files to make sure that valid codes are being used.	An employee can have a Fair Labor Standards Act code of only 1, 2, 3, 4, or 5. All other values for this field will be rejected.
Dependency checks	The computer checks whether a *logical* relationship is maintained between data for the *same* transaction. When it is not, the transaction is rejected.	A car loan initiation transaction should show a logical relationship between the size of the loan, the number of loan repayments, and the size of each installment.

control totals A type of input control that requires counting transactions or quantity fields prior to processing for comparison and reconciliation after processing.

edit checks Routines performed to verify input data and correct errors prior to processing.

processing controls The routines for establishing that data are complete and accurate during updating.

run control totals The procedures for controlling completeness of computer updating by generating control totals that reconcile totals before and after processing.

computer matching The processing control that matches input data to information held on master files.

output controls Measures that ensure that the results of computer processing are accurate, complete, and properly distributed.

Control totals can be established beforehand for input transactions. These totals can range from a simple document count to totals for quantity fields such as total sales amount (for a batch of transactions). Computer programs count the totals from transactions input.

Edit checks include various programmed routines that can be performed to edit input data for errors before they are processed. Transactions that do not meet edit criteria will be rejected. The edit routines can produce lists of errors to be corrected later. Important types of edit techniques are summarized in Table 16.4.

Processing Controls

Processing controls establish that data are complete and accurate during updating. The major processing controls are run control totals, computer matching, and programmed edit checks.

Run control totals reconcile the input control totals with the totals of items that have updated the file. Updating can be controlled by generating control totals during processing. The totals, such as total transactions processed or totals for critical quantities, can be compared manually or by computer. Discrepancies are noted for investigation.

Computer matching matches the input data with information held on master or suspense files, with unmatched items noted for investigation. Most matching occurs during input, but under some circumstances it may be required to ensure completeness of updating. For example, a matching program might match employee time cards with a payroll master file and report missing or duplicate time cards.

Most edit checking occurs at the time data are input. However, certain applications require some type of reasonableness or dependency check during updating. For example, consistency checks might be used by a utility company to compare a customer's electric bill with previous bills. If the bill was 500 percent higher this month compared to last month, the bill would not be processed until the meter was rechecked.

Output Controls

Output controls ensure that the results of computer processing are accurate, complete, and properly distributed. Typical output controls include the following:

NetGuard's Guardian firewall software provides a simple, user-friendly graphical interface for defining security rules. Guardian provides tools to monitor and control Internet access to private corporate networks.

○ Balancing output totals with input and processing totals

○ Reviews of the computer processing logs to determine that all of the correct computer jobs executed properly for processing

○ Formal procedures and documentation specifying authorized recipients of output reports, checks, or other critical documents

Security and the Internet

Linking to the Internet or transmitting information via intranets and extranets require special security measures. Large public networks, including the Internet, are more vulnerable because they are virtually open to anyone and because they are so huge that when abuses do occur, they can have an enormously widespread impact. When the Internet becomes part of the corporate network, the organization's information systems can be vulnerable to actions from outsiders. Chapter 10 described the use of *firewalls* to prevent unauthorized users from accessing private networks. As growing numbers of businesses expose their networks to Internet traffic, firewalls are becoming a necessity.

A firewall is generally placed between internal LANs and WANs and external networks such as the Internet. The firewall controls access to the organization's internal networks by acting like a "Checkpoint Charlie" that examines each user's credentials before they can access the network. The firewall identifies names, Internet Protocol (IP) addresses, applications, and other characteristics of incoming traffic. It checks this information against the access rules that have been programmed into the system by the network administrator. The firewall prevents unauthorized communication into and out of the network, allowing the organization to enforce a security policy on traffic flowing between its network and the Internet (Oppliger, 1997).

There are essentially two major types of firewall technologies: proxies and stateful inspection. *Proxies* stop data originating outside the organization at the firewall, inspect them, and pass a proxy to the other side of the firewall. If a user outside the company wants to communicate with a user inside the organization, the outside user first "talks" to the proxy application and the proxy application communicates with the firm's internal computer. Likewise a computer user inside the organization goes through the proxy to "talk" to computers on the outside. Because the actual message doesn't pass through the firewall, proxies are considered more secure than stateful inspection. However, they have to do a lot of work and can consume system resources, degrading network performance. The Raptor Firewall product is primarily a proxy-based firewall.

In *stateful inspection,* the firewall scans each packet of incoming data, checking its source, destination addresses, or services. It sets up state tables to track information over multiple packets. User-defined access rules must identify every type of packet that the organization does not want to admit. Although stateful inspection consumes fewer network resources than proxies, it is theoretically not as secure because some data pass through the firewall. Cisco Systems' firewall product is an example of a stateful inspection firewall. Hybrid firewall products are being developed. For instance, Check Point is primarily a stateful inspection product but it has incorporated some proxy capabilities for communication.

To create a good firewall, someone must write and maintain the internal rules identifying the people, applications, or addresses that are allowed or rejected in very fine detail. Firewalls can deter, but not completely prevent, network penetration from outsiders and should be viewed as one element in an overall security plan. In order to deal effectively with Internet security, broader corporate policies and procedures, user responsibilities, and security awareness training may be required (Segev, Porra, and Roldan, 1998).

Security and Electronic Commerce

Security of electronic communications is a major control issue for companies engaged in electronic commerce. It is essential that commerce-related data of buyers and sellers be kept private when they are transmitted electronically. The data being transmitted also must be protected against being purposefully altered by someone other than the sender, so that, for example, stock market execution orders or product orders accurately represent the wishes of the buyer and seller.

encryption The coding and scrambling of messages to prevent their being read or accessed without authorization.

Many organizations rely on encryption to protect sensitive information transmitted over networks. **Encryption** is the coding and scrambling of messages to prevent unauthorized access to or understanding of the data being transmitted. A message can be encrypted by applying a secret numerical code called an encryption key so that it is transmitted as a scrambled set of characters. (The key consists of a large group of letters, numbers, and symbols.) In order to be read, the message must be decrypted (unscrambled) with a matching key. A number of encryption standards exist, including Data Encryption Standard (DES), which is used by the U.S. government, RSA (by RSA Data Security), SSL (Secure Sockets Layer), and S-HTTP (Secure Hypertext Transport Protocol). SSL and S-HTTP are used for Web-based traffic.

There are several alternative methods of encryption, but "public key" encryption is becoming popular. Public key encryption, illustrated in Figure 16-5, uses two different keys, one private and one public. The keys are mathematically related so that data encrypted with one key only can be decrypted using the other key. To send and receive messages, communicators first create separate pairs of private and public keys. The public key is kept in a directory and the private key must be kept secret. The sender encrypts a message with the recipient's public key. On receiving the message, the recipient uses his or her private key to decrypt it.

Figure 16-5 Public key encryption. A public key encryption system can be viewed as a series of public and private keys that lock data when they are transmitted and unlock the data when they are received. The sender locates the recipient's public key in a directory and uses it to encrypt a message. The message is sent in encrypted form over the Internet or a private network. When the encrypted message arrives, the recipient uses his or her private key to decrypt the data and read the message.

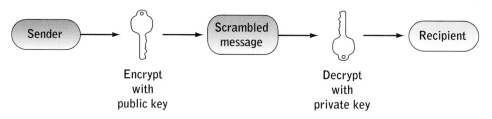

Encryption is especially useful to shield messages on the Internet and other public networks because they are less secure than private networks. Encryption helps protect transmission of payment data, such as credit card information, and addresses problems of authentication and message integrity. **Authentication** refers to the ability of each party to know that the other parties are who they claim to be. In the nonelectronic world, we use our signatures. Bank-by-mail systems avoid the need for signatures on checks they issue for their customers by using well-protected private networks where the source of the request for payment is recorded and can be proven. **Message integrity** is the ability to be certain that the message that is sent arrives without being copied or changed.

Experts are working on methods that involve encryption for creating agreed-on certified digital signatures. A **digital signature** is a digital code attached to an electronically transmitted message that is used to verify the origins and contents of a message. It provides a way to associate a message with the sender, performing a function similar to a written signature. A recipient of data can use the digital signature to verify who sent the data and that the data were not altered after being "signed."

Authentication can be further reinforced by attaching a **digital certificate** to an electronic message. A digital certificate system uses a trusted third party known as a certificate authority (CA) to verify a user's identity. The CA system can be run as a function inside an organization or by an outside company such as VeriSign Inc. in Mountain View, California. The CA verifies a digital certificate user's identity off-line by telephone, postal mail, or in person. This information is put into a CA server, which generates an encrypted digital certificate containing owner identification information and a copy of the owner's public key. The certificate authenticates that the public key belongs to the designated owner. The CA makes its own public key available publicly either in print or perhaps on the Internet. The recipient of an encrypted message uses the CA's public key to decode the digital certificate attached to the message, verifies it was issued by the CA, and then obtains the sender's public key and identification information contained in the certificate. Using this information, the recipient can send an encrypted reply. The digital certificate system would enable, for example, a credit card user and merchant to validate that their digital certificates were issued by an authorized and trusted third party before they exchange data.

Much on-line commerce continues to be handled through private EDI networks usually run over VANs. VANs (value-added networks) are relatively secure and reliable. However, because they have to be privately maintained and run on high-speed private lines, VANs are expensive, easily costing a company $100,000 per month. They also are inflexible, being connected only to a limited number of sites and companies. As a result, the Internet is emerging as the network technology of choice. EDI transactions on the Internet run from one-half to one-tenth the cost of VAN-based transactions (Knowles, 1997).

Special electronic payment systems have been developed for the Internet. VISA International, MasterCard International, American Express, and other major credit card companies and banks have adopted the **Secure Electronic Transaction (SET)** protocol for encrypting credit card payment data over the Internet and other open networks. A user acquires a digital certificate and digital wallet from his or her bank, which acts like a middleman in an e-commerce transaction. The wallet and certificate specify the identity of the user and the credit card being used. When the user shops at a Web site and selects the SET payment method, the merchant's servers send a signal over the Internet that invokes the user's SET wallet. The digital wallet encrypts the payment information and sends it to the merchant. The merchant verifies that the information is a SET packet and adds its digital certificate to the message. The merchant then encrypts this information and passes it on to the clearinghouse and certificate authority, which verifies the transaction. The clearinghouse approves or denies the transaction based on credit standing and passes that information over the Internet to the merchant and back to the user's wallet. The transaction is sent to the merchant's bank, which arranges for the fund transfer from user to merchant. Figure 16-6 illustrates how SET works.

CyberCash/Checkfree Wallet gives away client software that encrypts and forwards transaction and credit card information to a Web-based merchant. The merchant in turn forwards the information to a CyberCash server. The server takes the information behind a firewall, decrypts it, and sends it to the merchant's bank. The merchant's bank then forwards an

authentication The ability of each party in a transaction to ascertain the identity of the other party.

message integrity The ability to ascertain that a transmitted message has not been copied or altered.

digital signature A digital code that can be attached to an electronically transmitted message to uniquely identify its contents and the sender.

digital certificate An attachment to an electronic message to verify the identity of the sender and to provide the receiver with the means to encode a reply.

Secure Electronic Transaction (SET) A standard for securing credit card transactions over the Internet and other networks.

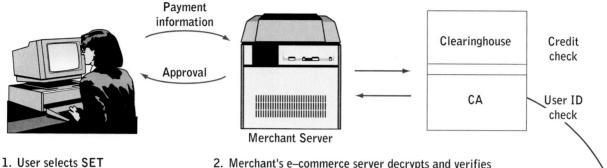

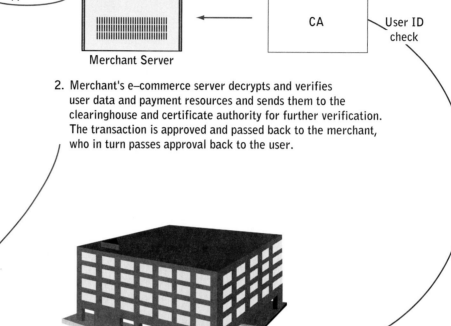

Payment information

Approval

Merchant Server

Clearinghouse

CA

Credit check

User ID check

1. User selects SET to pay for on-line purchase. Encryption payment information is sent from the user to the merchant's electronic commerce system.

2. Merchant's e–commerce server decrypts and verifies user data and payment resources and sends them to the clearinghouse and certificate authority for further verification. The transaction is approved and passed back to the merchant, who in turn passes approval back to the user.

USER

4. The merchant sends the user the purchase.

3. The transaction record is sent to the merchant's bank, which arranges for funds to be debited from the user's account and credited to the merchant's account.

Figure 16-6 How SET (Secure Electronic Transaction proto col) works. The SET standard for secure credit card transactions supports both sellers and buyers.

electronic cash (e-cash) Currency represented in electronic form that moves outside the normal network of money, preserving the anonymity of its users.

authorization request to the bank that issued the credit card. After verifying the information, the bank issuing the card forwards either an approval or denial of payment to CyberCash. CyberCash transmits this information back to the merchant, who notifies the customer. The chance of a security breach is lessened because the merchant on the Web never sees or stores a credit card number.

DigiCash uses "**e-cash,**" or **electronic cash,** for anonymous on-line purchasing. Electronic cash is currency represented in electronic form that is moving outside the normal network of money (paper currency, coins, checks, credit cards) and for now is not under the purview of the Federal Reserve within the United States. Users are supplied with client software and can exchange money with another e-cash user over the Internet. When customers make an on-line purchase, the e-cash software creates a "coin" in an amount specified by the user and sends it to the bank wrapped in a virtual envelope. The bank withdraws the amount requested from the user's account, puts a validating stamp on the envelope to validate the coin's value, and returns it to the user. When the user receives the envelope back, he or she can spend the coin.

First Virtual Internet Payment System takes a different approach than the others. Instead of devising a secure way to transmit information over the Internet, they avoid it entirely. Prospective customers must apply for a unique alphanumeric personal identification number called a VirtualPIN that can be used at any participating site. The VirtualPIN is

Window on Technology

Building a Security Infrastructure for Electronic Commerce

Electronic commerce poses a security paradox, requiring companies to be more open yet more closed at the same time. To benefit from electronic commerce and the Internet, companies need to be open to outsiders, such as customers and trading partners, yet they must be closed to hackers and other intruders. Businesses are trying to create a security culture and infrastructure that allows them to straddle this fine line.

First Union Corporation, the sixth-largest bank in the United States, is rapidly moving into on-line banking. Customers can open and close accounts, transfer funds, and apply for loans and mortgages on-line. It is one of the first banks to introduce an on-line stock trading service. Security is so important that First Union's IT security chief is on the same level as its chief information officer (CIO) on the company organization chart, and its budget for information systems security alone is more than $5 million. When First Union considers mergers or acquisitions, it first reviews the security measures at the other company even before examining the other company's finances.

First Union uses a wide array of security tools to protect its information assets. Multiple internal and external firewalls protect the bank's networks and Internet connections from both external and internal intruders. Secure virtual private networks (VPNs) connect the bank to its business partners. The bank is trying to use encryption for virtually all external communication, including e-mail. To provide additional security for its Internet offerings and funds transfer services, First Union is using authentication tokens from Vasco Data Security International, which generates one-time passwords.

First Union built security-compliance software tools for all of its hardware and software platforms. These tools evaluate the level of security of specified systems or network components against a company standard so that security personnel can determine if systems are meeting First Union's compliance goals. The bank's security programs take into account the level of risk of a system. For example,

a system supporting funds transfer would have a high risk level and, therefore, require a high level of security.

First Union provides ongoing security training for employees through videos, manuals, and the Web. The bank posts security updates on its intranet, and information systems managers and administrators can download security standards for specific computing platforms from its Web site. Managers must attend information systems security training sessions several times a year.

Libbey Inc., a glass manufacturer and china and tableware distributor based in Toledo, Ohio, became concerned about its security exposure with its growing presence on the Web. Libbey has about 300 users authorized for Web access and wanted to isolate its internal network from external Internet users except for a few well-defined points. Phil Reed, Libbey's network administrator, had helped install the company's network for its 1100 employees in 1996. When he began testing for new vulnerabilities, he found numerous security holes. Reed immediately started searching for a firewall and installed FireWall-1 from CheckPoint Software Technologies. Reed found CheckPoint's user interface for defining access rules easy to use. Reed could also pick and choose the products from CheckPoint's suite that best fit his security plan.

Initially, Libbey's firewall ran on a 166 MegaHertz Pentium computer running the Windows NT operating system. Reed observed that the firewall was starting to require more resources than could be provided by its computer hardware platform. Libbey's firewall has to handle 85,000 to 100,000 accesses per day, most of which are from internal company users surfing the Web for business reasons.

To Think About: What management, organization, and technology issues should be considered when developing a security infrastructure for electronic commerce?

Sources: Bob Violino and Amy K. Larsen, "Security: An E-Biz Asset," **Information Week**, February 15, 1999; and Gerald Lazar, "A Net for the Net," **Datamation**, January 1999.

---

stored with the user's credit card number off-line on a secure computer. Only First Virtual has access to sensitive data. Merchants using this system must obtain a Seller's VirtualPIN and set up an account. When a customer makes a purchase over the Internet, all that travels on the Internet is the customer's VirtualPIN. To process a payment, the merchant submits its Seller's VirtualPIN along with the shopper's VirtualPIN to First Virtual. First Virtual then e-mails the customer to confirm the purchase. If the customer approves the transaction, First Virtual processes the transaction, sending confirmation to the seller. The seller then ships the purchased item to the buyer.

Payment systems, such as NetCheck, that use electronic checks are also available. These checks are encrypted with a signature that can be verified and can be used for payments in electronic commerce.

The Window on Technology describes how companies are using encryption, firewalls, and other technologies to create secure infrastructures for electronic commerce.

On-Line Order Processing Risk Assessment

Exposure	Probability of Occurrence (%)	Loss Range/ Average ($)	Expected Annual Loss ($)
Power failure	30	5000–200,000 (102,500)	30,750
Embezzlement	5	1000–50,000 (25,500)	1275
User error	98	200–40,000 (20,100)	19,698

This chart shows the results of a risk assessment of three selected areas of an on-line order processing system. The likelihood of each exposure occurring over a one-year period is expressed as a percentage. The next column shows the highest and lowest possible loss that could be expected each time the exposure occurred and an average loss calculated by adding the highest and lowest figures together and dividing by 2. The expected annual loss for each exposure can be determined by multiplying the average loss by its probability of occurrence.

Developing a Control Structure: Costs and Benefits

Information systems can make exhaustive use of all the control mechanisms previously discussed. But they may be so expensive to build and so complicated to use that the system is economically or operationally unfeasible. Some cost/benefit analysis must be performed to determine which control mechanisms provide the most effective safeguards without sacrificing operational efficiency or cost.

One of the criteria that determines how much control is built into a system is the *importance of its data.* Major financial and accounting systems, for example, such as a payroll system or one that tracks purchases and sales on the stock exchange, must have higher standards of control than a *tickler* system to track dental patients and remind them that their six-month checkup is due. For instance, Swissair invested in additional hardware and software to increase its network reliability because it was running critical reservation and ticketing applications.

The cost-effectiveness of controls also will be influenced by the efficiency, complexity, and expense of each control technique. For example, complete one-for-one checking may be time consuming and operationally impossible for a system that processes hundreds of thousands of utilities payments daily. But it might be possible to use this technique to verify only critical data such as dollar amounts and account numbers, while ignoring names and addresses.

A third consideration is the *level of risk* if a specific activity or process is not properly controlled. System builders can undertake a **risk assessment**, determining the likely frequency of a problem and the potential damage if it were to occur. For example, if an event is likely to occur no more than once a year, with a maximum of $1000 loss to the organization, it would not be feasible to spend $20,000 on the design and maintenance of a control to protect against that event. However, if that same event could occur at least once a day, with a potential loss of more than $300,000 a year, $100,000 spent on a control might be entirely appropriate.

Table 16.5 illustrates sample results of a risk assessment for an on-line order processing system that processes 30,000 orders per day. The probability of a power failure occurring in a one-year period is 30 percent. Loss of order transactions while power is down could range from $5000 to $200,000 for each occurrence, depending on how long processing was halted. The probability of embezzlement occurring over a yearly period is about 5 percent, with potential losses ranging from $1000 to $50,000 for each occurrence. User errors have a 98 percent chance of occurring over a yearly period, with losses ranging from $200 to $40,000 for each occurrence. The average loss for each event can be weighted by multiplying it by the probability of its occurrence annually to determine the expected annual loss. Once the risks have been assessed, system builders can concentrate on the control points with the greatest vulner-

risk assessment Determining the potential frequency of the occurrence of a problem and the potential damage if the problem were to occur. Used to determine the cost/benefit of a control.

| Function: Personal Loans _____ | Prepared by: _____ J. Ericson _____ | Received by: _____ T. Barrow _____ |
| Location: Peoria, Ill. _____ | Preparation date: __ June 16, 1999 _____ | Review date: _____ June 28, 1999 _____ |

Nature of Weakness and Impact	Chance for Substantial Error		Effect on Audit Procedures	Notification to Management	
	Yes/No	Justification	Required Amendment	Date of Report	Management Response
Loan repayment records are not reconciled to borrower's records during processing.	Yes	Without a detection control, errors in individual client balances may remain undetected.	Confirm a sample of loans.	5/10/99	Interest Rate Compare Report provides this control.
There are no regular audits of computer-generated data (interest charges).	Yes	Without a regular audit or reasonableness check, widespread miscalculations could result before errors are detected.		5/10/99	Periodic audits of loans will be instituted.
Programs can be put into production libraries to meet target deadlines without final approval from the Standards and Controls group.	No	All programs require management authorization. The Standards and Controls group controls access to all production systems, and assigns such cases to a temporary production status.			

Figure 16-7 Sample auditor's list of control weaknesses. This chart is a sample page from a list of control weaknesses that an auditor might find in a loan system in a local commercial bank. This form helps auditors record and evaluate control weaknesses and shows the results of discussing those weaknesses with management, as well as any corrective actions taken by management.

ability and potential loss. In this case, controls should focus on ways to minimize the risk of power failures and user errors. Increasing management awareness of the full range of actions they can take to reduce risks can substantially reduce system losses (Straub and Welke, 1998).

In some situations, organizations may not know the precise probability of threats occurring to their information systems, and they may not be able to quantify the impact of such events. In these instances, management may choose to describe risks and their likely impact in a qualitative manner (Rainer, Snyder, and Carr, 1991).

To decide which controls to use, information system builders must examine various control techniques in relation to each other and to their relative cost-effectiveness. A control weakness at one point may be offset by a strong control at another. It may not be cost-effective to build tight controls at every point in the processing cycle if the areas of greatest risk are secure or if compensating controls exist elsewhere. The combination of all of the controls developed for a particular application will determine its overall control structure.

The Role of Auditing in the Control Process

How does management know that information systems controls are effective? To answer this question, organizations must conduct comprehensive and systematic *audits*. An **MIS audit** identifies all of the controls that govern individual information systems and assesses their effectiveness. To accomplish this, the auditor must acquire a thorough understanding of operations, physical facilities, telecommunications, control systems, data security objectives, organizational structure, personnel, manual procedures, and individual applications.

The auditor usually interviews key individuals who use and operate a specific information system concerning their activities and procedures. Application controls, overall integrity controls, and control disciplines are examined. The auditor should trace the flow of sample transactions through the system and perform tests, using, if appropriate, automated audit software.

The audit lists and ranks all control weaknesses and estimates the probability of their occurrence. It then assesses the financial and organizational impact of each threat. Figure 16-7 is

MIS audit Identifies all the controls that govern individual information systems and assesses their effectiveness.

a sample auditor's listing of control weaknesses for a loan system. It includes a section for notifying management of such weaknesses and for management's response. Management is expected to devise a plan for countering significant weaknesses in controls.

16.3 Ensuring System Quality

Organizations can improve system quality by using software quality assurance techniques and by improving the quality of their data.

Software Quality Assurance

Solutions to software quality problems include using an appropriate systems development methodology, proper resource allocation during systems development, the use of metrics, attention to testing, and the use of quality tools.

Methodologies

Chapter 12 has already described widely used systems development methodologies. The primary function of a development methodology is to provide discipline to the entire development process. A good development methodology establishes organization-wide standards for requirements gathering, design, programming, and testing. To produce quality software, organizations must select an appropriate methodology and then enforce its use. The methodology should call for systems requirement and specification documents that are complete, detailed, accurate, and documented in a format the user community can understand before they approve it. Specifications also must include agreed on measures of system quality so that the system can be evaluated objectively while it is being developed and once it is completed.

Resource Allocation during Systems Development

resource allocation The determination of how costs, time, and personnel are assigned to different phases of a systems development project.

Views on **resource allocation** during systems development have changed significantly over the years. Resource allocation determines the way the costs, time, and personnel are assigned to different phases of the project. In earlier times, developers focused on programming, with only about 1 percent of the time and costs of a project being devoted to systems analysis (determining specifications). More time should be spent in specifications and systems analysis, decreasing the proportion of programming time and reducing the need for so much maintenance time. Documenting requirements so that they can be understood from their origin through development, specification, and continuing use can also reduce errors as well as time and costs (Domges and Pohl, 1998). Current literature suggests that about one-quarter of a project's time and cost should be expended in specifications and analysis, with perhaps 50 percent of its resources being allocated to design and programming. Installation and postimplementation ideally should require only one-quarter of the project's resources. Investments in software quality initiatives early in a project are likely to provide the greatest payback (Slaughter, Harter, and Krishnan, 1998).

Software Metrics

software metrics The objective assessments of the software used in a system in the form of quantified measurements.

Software metrics can play a vital role in increasing system quality. **Software metrics** are objective assessments of the system in the form of quantified measurements. Ongoing use of metrics allows the IS department and the user jointly to measure the performance of the system and identify problems as they occur. Examples of software metrics include the number of transactions that can be processed in a specified unit of time, on-line response time, the number of payroll checks printed per hour, and the number of known bugs per hundred lines of code. Unfortunately, most manifestations of quality are not so easy to define in metric terms. In those cases developers must find indirect measurements. For example, an objective measurement of a system's ease of use might be the number of calls for help the IS staff receives per month from system users.

For metrics to be successful, they must be carefully designed, formal, and objective. They must measure significant aspects of the system. In addition, metrics are of no value unless they are used consistently and users agree to the measurements in advance.

Testing

Early, regular, and thorough testing will contribute significantly to system quality. In general, software testing is often misunderstood. Many view testing as a way to prove the correctness of work they have done. In fact, we know that all sizable software is riddled with errors, and we must test to uncover these errors.

Testing begins at the design phase. Because no coding yet exists, the test normally used is a **walkthrough**—a review of a specification or design document by a small group of people carefully selected based on the skills needed for the particular objectives being tested. Once coding begins, coding walkthroughs also can be used to review program code. However, code must be tested by computer runs. When errors are discovered, the source is found and eliminated through a process called **debugging.**

Chapter 11 described the stages of testing required to put an information system in operation—program testing, system testing, and acceptance testing. Testing will be successful only if planned properly.

Quality Tools

Finally, system quality can be significantly enhanced by the use of quality tools. Many tools have been developed to address every aspect of the systems development process. Information systems professionals are using project management software to manage their projects. Products exist to document specifications and system design in text and graphic forms. Programming tools include data dictionaries, libraries to manage program modules, and tools that actually produce program code (see Chapters 7 and 12). Many types of tools exist to aid in the debugging process. The most recent set of tools automates much of the preparation for comprehensive testing.

Data Quality Audits

Information system quality also can be improved by identifying and correcting faulty data, making error detection a more explicit organizational goal (Klein, Goodhue, and Davis, 1997). The analysis of data quality often begins with a **data quality audit,** which is a structured survey of the accuracy and level of completeness of the data in an information system. Data quality audits are accomplished by the following methods:

- ○ Surveying end users for their perceptions of data quality
- ○ Surveying entire data files
- ○ Surveying samples from data files

walkthrough A review of a specification or design document by a small group of people carefully selected based on the skills needed for the particular objectives being tested.

debugging The process of discovering and eliminating the errors and defects—the bugs—in program code.

data quality audit A survey of files and samples of files for accuracy and completeness of data in an information system.

Auditors can analyze the quality of data in a system by conducting a survey of data files for accuracy.

Unless regular data quality audits are undertaken, organizations have no way of knowing to what extent their information systems contain inaccurate, incomplete, or ambiguous information. Unfortunately, many organizations are not giving data quality the priority it deserves (Tayi and Ballou, 1998). Some organizations, such as the Social Security Administration, have established data quality audit procedures. These procedures control payment and process quality by auditing a 20,000-case sample of beneficiary records each month. The FBI, however, did not conduct a comprehensive audit of its record systems until 1984. With few data quality controls, the FBI criminal record systems were found to have serious problems.

Management Wrap-Up

Management

Management is responsible for developing the control structure and quality standards for the organization. Key management decisions include establishing standards for systems accuracy and reliability, determining an appropriate level of control for organizational functions, and establishing a disaster recovery plan.

Organization

The characteristics of the organization play a large role in determining its approach to quality assurance and control issues. Some organizations are more quality and control conscious than others. Their cultures and business processes support high standards of quality and performance. Creating high levels of security and quality in information systems can be a process of lengthy organizational change.

Technology

A number of technologies and methodologies are available for promoting system quality and security. Technologies such as antivirus and data security software, firewalls, and programmed procedures can be used to create a control environment, whereas software metrics, systems development methodologies, and automated tools for systems development can be used to improve software quality. Organizational discipline is required to use these technologies effectively.

For Discussion

1. It has been said that controls and security should be one of the first areas to be addressed in the design of an information system. Do you agree? Why or why not?

2. How much software testing is "enough"? What management, organization, and technology issues should you consider in answering this question?

Summary

1. Demonstrate why information systems are so vulnerable to destruction, error, abuse, and system quality problems. With data concentrated into electronic form and many procedures invisible through automation, computerized information systems are vulnerable to destruction, misuse, error, fraud, and hardware or software failures. The effect of disaster in a computerized system can be greater than in manual systems because all of the records for a particular function or organization can be destroyed or lost. On-line systems and those utilizing the Internet are especially vulnerable because data and files can be immediately and directly accessed through computer terminals or at many points in the network. Computer viruses can spread rampantly from system to system, clogging computer memory

or destroying programs and data. Software presents problems because of the high costs of correcting errors and because software bugs may be impossible to eliminate. Data quality can also severely impact system quality and performance.

2. Compare general controls and application controls for information systems, including controls to safeguard use of the Internet. Controls consist of all the methods, policies, and organizational procedures that ensure the safety of the organization's assets, the accuracy and reliability of its accounting records, and adherence to management standards. There are two main categories of controls: general controls and application controls.

General controls handle the overall design, security, and use of computer programs and files for the organization as a whole. They include physical hardware controls, system software controls, data file security controls, computer operations controls, controls over the system implementation process, and administrative disciplines. Firewalls help safeguard private networks from unauthorized access when organizations use intranets or link to the Internet. Encryption is a widely used technology for securing electronic payment systems.

Application controls are those unique to specific computerized applications. They focus on the completeness and accuracy of input, updating and maintenance, and the validity of the information in the system. Application controls consist of (1) input controls, (2) processing controls, and (3) output controls.

3. Select the factors that must be considered when developing the controls for information systems. To determine which controls are required, designers and users of systems must identify all of the control points and control weaknesses and perform risk assessment. They must also perform a cost/benefit analysis of controls and design controls that can effectively safeguard systems without making them unusable.

4. Describe the most important software quality assurance techniques. The quality and reliability of software can be improved by using a standard development methodology, software metrics, thorough testing procedures, quality tools, and by reallocating resources to put more emphasis on the analysis and design stages of systems development.

5. Demonstrate the importance of auditing information systems and safeguarding data quality. Comprehensive and systematic MIS auditing can help organizations to determine the effectiveness of the controls in their information systems. Regular data quality audits should be conducted to help organizations ensure a high level of completeness and accuracy of the data stored in their systems.

Key Terms

Administrative controls, 508	Data quality audit, 519	Hacker, 499	Resource allocation, 518
Antivirus software, 499	Data security controls, 507	Hardware controls, 507	Risk assessment, 516
Application controls, 506	Debugging, 519	Implementation controls, 506	Run control totals, 510
Authentication, 513	Digital certificate, 513	Input controls, 509	Secure Electronic Transaction
Bugs, 503	Digital signature, 513	Message integrity, 513	(SET), 513
Computer matching, 510	Edit checks, 510	MIS audit, 517	Security, 500
Computer operations controls, 507	Electronic cash (e-cash), 514	On-line transaction processing, 500	Segregation of functions, 508
Computer virus, 499	Encryption, 512	Output controls, 510	Software controls, 507
Control totals, 510	Fault-tolerant computer system, 500	Processing controls, 510	Software metrics, 518
Controls, 506	General controls, 506		Walkthrough, 519

Review Questions

1. Why are computer systems more vulnerable than manual systems to destruction, fraud, error, and misuse? Name some of the key areas where systems are most vulnerable.

2. Name some features of on-line information systems that make them difficult to control.

3. What are *fault-tolerant computer systems?* When should they be used?

4. How can bad software and data quality affect system performance and reliability? Describe two software quality problems.

5. What are *controls?* Distinguish between *general controls* and *application controls.*

6. Name and describe the principal general controls for computerized systems.

7. List and describe the principal application controls.

8. How does MIS auditing enhance the control process?

9. What is the function of risk assessment?

10. Name and describe four software quality assurance techniques.

11. Why are data quality audits essential?

12. What is security? List and describe controls that promote security for computer hardware, computer networks, computer software, and computerized data.

13. What special security measures must be taken by organizations linking to the Internet?

14. Describe the role of firewalls and encryption systems in promoting security.

Group Project

Form a group with two or three other students. Select a system described in one of the chapter ending cases. Write a description of the system, its functions, and its value to the organization. Then write a description of both the general and application controls that should be used to protect the organization. Present your findings to the class.

Tools for Interactive Learning

○ Internet

The Internet Connection for this chapter will take you to a series of Web sites where you can complete an exercise to evaluate various secure electronic payment systems for the Internet. You can also use the Interactive Study Guide to test your knowledge of the topics in this chapter and get instant feedback where you need more practice.

○ CD-ROM

If you purchase and use the Multimedia Edition CD-ROM with this chapter, you can complete an interactive exercise asking you to identify the security and control problems faced by a company and select appropriate solutions. You can also find a video clip illustrating the Comdisco disaster recovery service, an audio overview of the major themes of this chapter, and bullet text summarizing the key points of the chapter.

Case Study — Did the FAA Fly Off Course?

The Federal Aviation Administration (FAA), through its air traffic controllers, controls all commercial planes in the air in the United States. With many thousands of flights daily, the airspace of the United States is very crowded, and without the air traffic controllers, airplane crashes would probably occur daily. The controllers give permission for landings and taking offs, they approve flight paths, and they monitor all airplanes in flight. The air traffic controllers have a simple goal—flight safety. With so many airplanes, computer systems are vital to the success of the controllers. The issue in the minds of most observers and many travelers is how well does the FAA manage its computer systems?

The FAA has over 250 separate computer systems to manage. Before a flight, pilots file their flight plans, which are then entered into a computer. Once in the air, each plane continually transmits data to computers, including its flight number, location, and altitude. The computers also continually receive data from radar stations around the country and data from

weather computers. The system keeps track of all planes in U.S. airspace, displaying their locations on a screen. These systems also have specialty functions, such as issuing warnings when two planes are coming too close or are flying too low. In today's world, controllers could not manage airplane traffic without these computers.

Controller applications are divided into two major types of systems. The airport control systems, at all commercial airports, control all aircraft when they are within 20–30 miles of the airport. The others, the Air Route Traffic Control (enroute) systems, operate at 20 centers around the country and control the high-altitude planes that are flying between their point-of-origin and their destination.

What is the condition of current FAA computer systems? Many of their computers are very old, particularly those used at the Air Route Traffic Control centers. Some even go back to the 1950s and are still using vacuum tubes. Most of the "newer" ones are from the 1960s and 1970s. Of the 20 en-route control

sites, only New York, Chicago, Washington, Fort Worth, and Cleveland have modern ES/9121 mainframes. All the other 15 sites have IBM 3083 large computers that are at least 15 years old and haven't even been produced or sold by IBM for 10 years. In fact, according to IBM, fewer than 100 of the 3083s are still in operation. "This is old equipment," explains Craig Lowder, IBM spokesperson, "and it is well past its natural life cycle."

These old computers present many problems. Despite their huge size, these mainframes have less power than today's desktops. Spare parts are getting harder to obtain. IBM no longer makes many replacement parts for 3083s. One such part, the thermal conduction module, is necessary to keep the computers from overheating. As of February 1998 only seven spares existed in the world. Another problem is that fewer and fewer technicians are available to keep these computers running. Being so old, these computers suffer many breakdowns. For example, from September 1994 to September 1995, 11 major breakdowns occurred. Small outages occur nearly every day at one site or another. To make matters worse, the FAA employs 5000 fewer computer technicians today than seven or eight years ago, despite the growing number of failures as the equipment ages. In addition to the age of the hardware, much of the software is 30 years old. Outdated software often cannot be updated due to the computers' age. Newer, more sophisticated software could make air travel much safer.

Backup systems do exist, but they do not have many of the more sophisticated functions, such as the warnings when airplanes are too close or too low. Also, many are just as old as the front-line systems. In addition, the controllers' training in these systems is very limited. When the backups also fail, the controllers switch to working with pilots, using slips of paper to keep track of each flight, an impossible task given the number of flights. At those times, many flights are not allowed to take off at the affected airports, and flights due into those airports must be put into a holding pattern or diverted to other airports. This situation costs airlines hundreds of millions of dollars yearly, and it costs passengers major delays and inconvenience.

Air traffic controllers suffer major stress under the best of circumstances. Many feel that the workload on controllers is too heavy, partially due to all the manual processing the old systems require. However, when systems fail, "It's total chaos," says Chicago controller Ken Kluge. "The minute the computer flops, our heart jumps into overdrive," he adds. "There's an extreme sense of helplessness," explains Mike Seko, a Fremont, California, air traffic controller, because "your tools have been taken away." Peter Neumann, a specialist in computer reliability and safety, described it this way: "Controllers are under enormous pressure, and anything that goes slightly wrong makes their job inordinately harder."

The FAA, recognizing it had potential problems, began planning for upgrading in 1983. The project, labeled AAS (Advanced Automation System), called for a complete overhaul of its computers, software, radar units, and communications network. Its original goals were to lower operating costs, to improve systems reliability and efficiency, and to make flying safer. In 1988 the AAS contract was awarded to IBM. The projected was budgeted at $4.8 billion, and completion was targeted for 1994.

The project did not go well. In December 1990, IBM announced that the project was 19 months behind schedule. By late 1992, IBM announced that the project was now 33 months late, and it estimated that the cost had risen to $5.1 billion. The project was scaled back. In December 1993, the estimated cost of the now smaller project rose to $5.9 billion. In April 1994 an independent study commissioned by the FAA concluded that the project design has "a high risk of failure."

In June 1994, the FAA announced further major changes. The contract was shifted from IBM to Lockheed Martin Corp. In addition major parts of the project were dropped, including: a project to combine the two major controller systems; and another to replace the hardware and software that controls aircraft near the airports. The plan to replace control tower equipment at the 150 largest airports was downsized to include only the 70 largest airports. The estimated cost of the slimmed-down project was $6 billion and the planned completion date was postponed to the year 2000.

Evaluations of the new project were mixed. An analyst for a congressional aviation oversight committee summarized the new system as "basically just a replacement of the radar screen for air traffic controllers." On the other hand, Frederico Peña, the U.S. Secretary of Transportation, stated the project "is now back on track and will deliver important safety improvements that will carry aviation into the next century."

Meanwhile, signs of system aging were multiplying. For example, in June 1995 a computer outage at Washington Air Route Traffic Control Center lasted 41 hours, while one in Chicago a year later lasted 122 hours. In August 1998 the Nashua, New Hampshire, center, which is responsible for all of New England and part of New York, went down for 37 minutes. Even before this outage, there were many complaints of frozen radar screens and minor outages. For instance, in October 1996, there was a minor outage in Phoenix in which the power-conditioning system triggered an electrical surge that brought the terminal's radar control system down. Its effects lasted several minutes longer while the computer recaptured the flight-path data. According to Ben Phelps, a national safety coordinator for the National Air Traffic Controllers Association (NATCA), "We have outages daily that are significant [and] do affect safety."

In 1996 the National Transportation Safety Board (NTSB) issued a report that referred to the many FAA computer failures in recent months that had resulted in reliance upon the backup system. The report listed a series of problems, including the special features not found in the backup control systems. It cited frequent hardware failures due to reliance on mainframes that are so old.

In September 1996 a new project, the Standard Terminal Automation Replacement System (STARS), was announced. This announcement marked the end of AAS. Estimates of the cost of AAS range from $7.6 billion to $23 billion, and yet it failed to improve much of the FAA's IT infrastructure. STARS is planned to bring together flight-plan data, air-traffic automation systems, terminal-control facilities, and radar systems around the United States. The prime contractor this time is Raytheon Co., of Lexington, Massachusetts.

STARS is targeted to replace the 20-year-old systems used by air traffic controllers to control flights near the airports. Its goals are to improve safety and reduce flight delays. It is to be installed at 317 airports and military bases, with installation beginning at Boston's Logan Airport in 1998. The project, scheduled to be completed in 2007, is estimated to cost about $11 billion through 2003. The new system will have four computers at each site: one primary, one backup, and a second pair that mirrors the first (redundancy).

Like all other organizations, the FAA has had to pay attention to the Year 2000 (Y2K) problem. The FAA started much too late addressing this issue. The FAA had promised an assessment of the Y2K problem by January 1998, but a major report from the Government Accounting Office (GAO), dated February 1998, indicated that the FAA assessment was not yet completed. The report warned that the air traffic controller systems would fail if they were not Y2K-compliant.

During February 1998 IBM announced that it would not make its 3083s Y2K-compliant. In response, the FAA quickly announced that it would reprogram its 3083s at a cost of $91 million. On July 23, 1998 the FAA announced that its 3083 computers had been tested for three months and will function after the year 2000 begins. This announcement has been met with serious doubt. In late October 1998 in a letter from IBM to Lockheed Martin Air Traffic Management, the contractor for these FAA systems, IBM stated that "The appropriate skills and tools do not exist to conduct a complete Year 2000 test assessment" of the 3083 computers. It added, "IBM believes it is imperative that the FAA replace the equipment" before year 2000. In January 1999 Paul Takemoto, an FAA spokesperson stated, "We believe we have both the tools and the people to certify [the 3083s] as Y2K-compliant."

To be doubly sure its computers would work properly, the FAA also announced in February 1998 that it would simultaneously work to replace its 3083s before January 1, 2000, at a cost of about $100 million. An FAA spokesperson stated that "We'll know in 90 to 120 days if we can move this [3083 replacement] up." While replacement of the 40 computers may be a possible solution, as of the beginning of 1999 the FAA had budgeted no money for replacement although the cost was recently estimated as high as $200 million. Even the FAA official in charge of the en-route systems stated in early January 1999 that "it would be an extraordinary feat" to replace approximately forty 3083s by the year 2000.

Why is the FAA having so many problems upgrading its computers and addressing the Y2K problem? One specific issue is the lack of an FAA systems architecture. The FAA did develop a logical architecture, titled the National Airspace System (NAS). This architecture document describes FAA's services and functions and then outlines the systems needed for both air traffic management and navigation systems. It even includes a systems plan through the year 2015. Thus, it gives a high-level overview of the business functions and the systems needed to serve them, including the interconnection between the various systems. However, the FAA did not then go on to translate this plan into the required physical or technical architecture. The FAA's air traffic control development work is assigned to one of 10 teams, and the lack of a technical architecture has left all 10 teams to determine their own specific standards for developing the

software, hardware, communications, data management, security, and performance characteristics.

Let's look at the results of the lack of standards. Of the 10 development teams, seven have no technical architecture at all. The other three developed their own architectures, and they are not the same. One result is the systems that feed the main computers use several different communications protocols and data formats. Of the three teams with standards, one architecture specifies Ethernet while another specifies Fiber Distributed Data Interface (the two are incompatible). Two of the architectures specify writing programs in C and C++ whereas the third one specifies Ada. Altogether the 10 teams developed 54 air traffic control system applications using 53 different languages. Incompatibility is one result. Staffs are forced to spend time (and money) creating complex interfaces which also then must be supported. These translation programs also increase the possibility of data errors. Moreover, the use of multiple standards greatly increases staff training costs. The February 1998 GAO report said that the result of the lack of an FAA uniform architecture is that "the FAA permits and perpetuates" inconsistency and incompatibilities. It stresses that any organization must implement a technical architecture before it replaces an old computer system.

The FAA agreed that the report reflected a problem, but they pointed out that the FAA does have an informal architecture control system in place. "We don't envision having a complete document of technical specifications that we would publish," stated Steven Zaidman, FAA's director of system architecture. He added, "We're light-years ahead of where we were. We have learned from our past failures."

Congressional observers have severely criticized the culture of the FAA, characterizing its employees as being unwilling to face up to its problems. Rona B. Stillman, the GAO's chief scientist for computers, stated that the "FAA has a culture . . . that is averse to change and has entrenched autonomous organizations that tend not to respond to change." David Schaefer, the counsel to the U.S. House Aviation Sub-

committee, said, "The FAA will say they've worked out their problems, but it turns out it's not enough."

One issue appears to be the organization of the information systems function within the agency. As described, with 10 independent development organizations, the FAA lacks needed central control. Regionalized management appears not to work well. According to the GAO, "The FAA certainly could use stronger central direction to ride herd over the regions to ensure technological consistency." The 1997 GAO report concluded, "No FAA organizational entity is responsible for developing and maintaining the technical Air Traffic Control architecture." In its opinion, this leaves the agency "at risk of making ill-informed decisions on critical multimillion-dollar, even billion-dollar, air-traffic-control systems." The same report, in referring to the failure of the AAS project, determined that the "FAA did not recognize the technical complexity of the effort, realistically estimate the resources required, adequately oversee its contractors' activities, or effectively control system requirements."

The IT Management Reform Act of 1996, known also as the Clinger-Cohen Act, mandates major information technology (IT) reforms in government agencies, including a requirement that federal agencies have CIOs. The reason that the FAA has no such centralized management is that the agency successfully lobbied to have itself exempted from the act.

One other problem, cited by several labor representatives of the controllers' union, is the communications gap between the FAA management and the users of the traffic control systems. That the gap exists perhaps is no surprise. Problems developed between management and controllers in the 1970s and became a disaster when the controllers went out on strike in 1981 (the Patco union strike). Ultimately, President Reagan dismissed more than 11,000 controllers. The current communications gap is seen when management claims positive results on the STARS project while the controllers apparently disagree. Controllers have often spoken out in meetings, saying that STARS is cumbersome, that the controls are complex, and the terminal displays are unclear.

Sources: Patrick Thibodeau, "IBM Says FAA Air Traffic Computers Should Be Retired," **Computerworld**, January 15, 1999 and "Air Traffic Controllers Say Old Computers Hobble, FAA," **Computerworld**, June 22, 1998; Matthew L. Wald, "Warning Issued on Air Traffic Computers," **The New York Times**, January 12, 1999; Thomas Hoffman, "On a Wing and a Prayer...," **Computerworld**, February 2, 1999 and "Feds Slam FAA for Millennium Mess," **Computerworld**, February 9, 1998; Matt Hamblen, "IBM, Others Question FAA's 2000 Progress," **Computerworld**, July 24, 1998, "FAA: Systems Are a Go for 2000," **Computerworld**, July 24, 1998, and "FAA's IT Management Slammed," **Computerworld**, February 10, 1997; Jeff Cole, "FAA, Air Groups Agree on Traffic Plan," **The Wall Street Journal**, April 23, 1998; Edward Cone, z January 12, 1998; Mary Mosquera, "FAA Faces Year 2000 Emergency, Report Says," **TechWeb**, February 4, 1998; Jeff Sweat, "FAA: We're Y2K OK," **Information Week**, October 5, 1998; Bruce D. Nordwall, "FAA Structural Problems Impede ATC Upgrades," **Aviation Week and Space Technology**, February 10, 1997; Gary Anthes, "Ancient Systems Put Scare in Air," and "Revamp Flies Off Course," **Computerworld**, August 5, 1996; "$1B Award to Fix Air Traffic System," **Computerworld**, September 23, 1996; and George Leopold, "FAA Sets Massive Systems Overhaul, But Will It Fly?" **TechWeb News**, October 28, 1996.

CASE STUDY QUESTIONS

1. List and explain the control weaknesses in the FAA and its air traffic control systems.

2. What management, organization, and technology factors were responsible for the FAA's control weaknesses?

3. How effectively did FAA deal with its control weaknesses? Evaluate the importance of the AAS and STARS projects for the FAA, for the air traffic controllers, and for the flying public.

4. Design a complete set of controls for the FAA to deal effectively with its control problems and the management of the FAA's information systems projects.

Chapter 17

Managing International Information Systems

Learning Objectives

After completing this chapter, you will be able to:

1. Identify the major factors behind the growing internationalization of business.

2. Compare global strategies for developing business.

3. Demonstrate how information systems support different global strategies.

4. Plan the development of international information systems.

5. Evaluate the main technical alternatives in developing global systems.

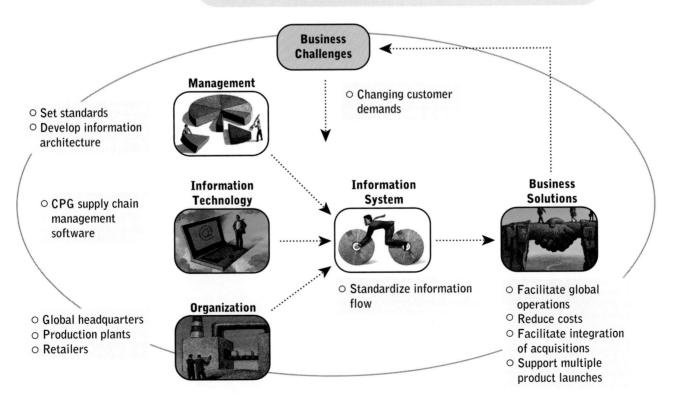

Business Challenges

Management
- Set standards
- Develop information architecture

○ Changing customer demands

Information Technology
- CPG supply chain management software

Information System
○ Standardize information flow

Business Solutions
- Facilitate global operations
- Reduce costs
- Facilitate integration of acquisitions
- Support multiple product launches

Organization
- Global headquarters
- Production plants
- Retailers

Kellogg Seeks
Global Coordination

Kellogg Co., the maker of Corn Flakes, Rice Krispies, and Pop Tarts, practically owns breakfast, holding more than 40 percent of the breakfast-food market. To keep sales high, Kellogg wants to meet the demands of customers such as Wal-Mart as they expand outside the United States. To accomplish this goal, the company will need new business processes and new information systems.

Kellogg is investing millions in new information systems to support global operations. Wal-Mart and other sophisticated retailers and grocery chains are setting up shop in every corner of the globe. These companies want their key suppliers, such as Kellogg, to provide them with the same level of service that they provide domestically. According to Doug Wegner, Kellogg's global program director, Kellogg will need globally integrated

systems where data can be entered at one place and flow seamlessly to another. The company would like to take an order anywhere, make the product anywhere, and ship it from any place in the world.

Kellogg selected Oracle Corporation's Consumer Packaged Goods (CPG) software, which allows it to distribute systems while standardizing on one product. CPG includes Oracle's financial and manufacturing management software bundled with software from niche vendors such as Manugistics, Inc., from Rockville, Maryland; IndustriMatematik International Corporation in Tarrytown, New York; Indus International Inc. in San Francisco; and Information Resources Inc. in Chicago. The components are separate software products, so CPG is not as tightly integrated as Kellogg would wish, but the company hopes that future versions will allow data to flow effortlessly through the system.

Kellogg plans to implement the system region by region in North America, Latin America, Europe, and Asia-Pacific. Each region will implement the same software but make its own decisions about the priority of each component. Kellogg is not insisting on central control. Jay Schreiner, Kellogg's chief information officer in Battle Creek, Michigan, distinguishes between central and global systems. Global systems give people in various areas "the tools to make the right decisions for Kellogg's. Headquarters needs access to certain information, but we do not believe in running the worldwide supply chain explicitly from Battle Creek."

Kellogg sees several benefits from implementing a global supply chain system, including improved inventory management, support for multiple product launches, and easier integration of acquisitions into the system.

Sources: Dara Canedy and Reed Abelson, "Can Kellogg Break Out of the Box?" *The New York Times,* January 24, 1999; Randy Weston, "Software to Tame Supply Chain Tiger," *Computerworld,* February 16, 1998.

Management Challenges

Kellogg Co. is one of many business firms moving toward global forms of organization that transcend national boundaries. Kellogg could not make this move unless it reorganized its information systems and standardized some of its information systems so that the same information could be used by disparate business units in different countries. Such changes are not always easy to make, and they raise the following management challenges:

1. **Lines of business and global strategy.** Firms must decide whether some or all of their lines of business should be managed on a global basis. There are some lines of business in which locale variations are slight, and the possibility exists to reap large rewards by organizing globally. PCs and power tools may fit this pattern, as well as industrial raw materials. Other consumer goods may be quite different by country or region. It is likely that firms with many lines of business will have to maintain a very mixed organizational structure.

2. **The difficulties of managing change in a multicultural firm.** Although engineering change in a single corporation in a single nation can be difficult, costly, and long term, bringing about significant change in very-large-scale global corporations can be daunting. Both the agreement on "core business processes" in a transnational context and the decision on common systems require either extraordinary insight, a lengthy process of consensus building, or the exercise of sheer power.

The changes Kellogg seeks are some of the changes in international information systems infrastructure—the basic systems needed to coordinate worldwide trade and other activities—that organizations need to consider if they want to operate across the globe. This chapter explores how to organize, manage, and control the development of international information systems.

17.1 The Growth of International Information Systems

We already have described two powerful worldwide changes driven by advances in information technology that have transformed the business environment and posed new challenges for management. One is the transformation of industrial economies and societies into knowledge- and information-based economies. The other is the emergence of a global economy and global world order.

The new world order will sweep away many national corporations, national industries, and national economies controlled by domestic politicians. Much of the Fortune 500—the 500 largest U.S. corporations—will disappear in the next 50 years, mirroring past behavior of large firms since 1900. Many firms will be replaced by fast-moving networked corporations that transcend national boundaries. The growth of international trade has radically altered domestic economies around the globe. About $1 trillion worth of goods, services, and financial instruments—one-fifth of the annual U.S. gross national product—changes hands each day in global trade.

Consider a laptop computer as an example: The CPU is likely to have been designed and built in the United States; the DRAM (or dynamic random access memory, which makes up the majority of primary storage in a computer) was designed in the United States but built in Malaysia; the screen was designed and assembled in Japan, using American patents; the keyboard is from Taiwan; and it was all assembled in Japan, where the case also was made. Management of the project, located in Silicon Valley, California, along with marketing, sales, and finance, coordinated all the activities from financing and production to shipping and sales efforts. None of this would be possible without powerful international information and telecommunication systems, an international information systems infrastructure.

To be effective, managers need a global perspective on business and an understanding of the support systems needed to conduct business on an international scale.

Developing the International Information Systems Infrastructure

This chapter describes how to go about building an international information systems infrastructure suitable for your international strategy. An infrastructure is the constellation of facilities and services, such as highways or telecommunications networks, required for organizations to function and prosper. An **international information systems infrastructure** consists of the basic information systems required by organizations to coordinate worldwide trade and other activities. Figure 17-1 illustrates the reasoning we will follow throughout the chapter and depicts the major dimensions of an international information systems infrastructure.

The basic strategy to follow when building an international system is to understand the global environment in which your firm is operating. This means understanding the overall market forces, or business drivers, that are pushing your industry toward global competition. A **business driver** is a force in the environment to which businesses must respond and that influences the direction of the business. Likewise, examine carefully the inhibitors or negative factors that create *management challenges*—factors that could scuttle the development of a global business. Once you have examined the global environment, you will need to consider a corporate strategy for competing in that environment. How will your firm respond? You could ignore the global market and focus on domestic competition only, sell to the globe from a domestic base, or organize production and distribution around the globe. There are many in-between choices.

After you have developed a strategy, it is time to consider how to structure your organization so it can pursue the strategy. How will you accomplish a division of labor across a global environment? Where will production, administration, accounting, marketing, and human resource functions be located? Who will handle the systems function?

Next, you must consider the management issues in implementing your strategy and making the organization design come alive. Key here will be the design of business procedures. How can you discover and manage user requirements? How can you induce change in local units to conform to international requirements? How can you reengineer on a global scale, and how can you coordinate systems development?

The last issue to consider is the technology platform. Although changing technology is a key driving factor leading toward global markets, you need to have a corporate strategy and structure before you can rationally choose the right technology.

After you have completed this process of reasoning, you will be well on your way toward an appropriate international information systems infrastructure capable of achieving your corporate goals. Let us begin by looking at the overall global environment.

international information systems infrastructure The basic information systems required by organizations to coordinate worldwide trade and other activities.

business driver A force in the environment to which businesses must respond and that influences the direction of business.

Figure 17-1 International information systems infrastructure. The major dimensions for developing an international information systems infrastructure are the global environment, the corporate global strategies, the structure of the organization, the management and business procedures, and the technology platform.

Global Environment:
Business Drivers and Challenges

Corporate Global Strategies

Organization Structure

Management and Business Procedures

Technology Platform

International Information Systems Infrastructure

The Global Environment: Business Drivers and Challenges

Table 17.1 illustrates the business drivers in the global environment that are leading all industries toward global markets and competition.

The global business drivers can be divided into two groups: general cultural factors and specific business factors. There are easily recognized general cultural factors driving internationalization since World War II. Information, communication, and transportation technologies have created a *global village* in which communication (by telephone, television, radio, or computer network) around the globe is no more difficult and not much more expensive than

Businesses need an international information systems infrastructure to coordinate the activities of their sales, manufacturing, and warehouse units worldwide.

Table 17.1 The Global Business Drivers

General Cultural Factors

Global communication and transportation technologies

Development of global culture

Emergence of global social norms

Political stability

Global knowledge base

Specific Business Factors

Global markets

Global production and operations

Global coordination

Global workforce

Global economies of scale

communication down the block. Moving goods and services to and from geographically dispersed locations has fallen dramatically in cost.

The development of global communications has created a global village in a second sense: There is now a **global culture** created by television and other globally shared media such as movies that permits different cultures and peoples to develop common expectations about right and wrong, desirable and undesirable, heroic and cowardly. The collapse of the Eastern bloc has speeded up the growth of a world culture enormously, increased support for capitalism and business, and reduced the level of cultural conflict considerably.

A last factor to consider is the growth of a global knowledge base. At the end of World War II, knowledge, education, science, and industrial skills were highly concentrated in North America, Europe, and Japan, with the rest of the world euphemistically called the *Third World*. This is no longer true. Latin America, China, Southern Asia, and Eastern Europe have developed powerful educational, industrial, and scientific centers, resulting in a much more democratically and widely dispersed knowledge base.

These general cultural factors leading toward internationalization result in specific business globalization factors that affect most industries. The growth of powerful communications technologies and the emergence of world cultures create the condition for *global markets*— global consumers interested in consuming similar products that are culturally approved. Coca-Cola, American sneakers (made in Korea but designed in Los Angeles), and CNN News (a television show) can now be sold in Latin America, Africa, and Asia.

Responding to this demand, global production and operations have emerged with precise on-line coordination between far-flung production facilities and central headquarters thousands of miles away. At Sealand Transportation, a major global shipping company based in Newark, New Jersey, shipping managers in Newark can watch the loading of ships in Rotterdam on-line, check trim and ballast, and trace packages to specific ship locations as the activity proceeds. This is all possible through an international satellite link.

The new global markets and pressure toward global production and operation have called forth whole new capabilities for global coordination of all factors of production. Not only production but also accounting, marketing and sales, human resources, and systems development (all the major business functions) can be coordinated on a global scale. Frito Lay, for instance, can develop a marketing sales force automation system in the United States and, once provided, may try the same techniques and technologies in Spain. Micromarketing—marketing to very small geographic and social units—no longer means marketing to neighborhoods in the United States, but to neighborhoods throughout the world! These new levels of global coordination permit for the first time in history the location of business activity according to comparative advantage. Design should be located where it is best accomplished, as should marketing, production, and finance.

global culture The development of common expectations, shared artifacts, and social norms among different cultures and peoples.

Table 17.2	**Challenges and Obstacles to Global Business Systems**

General

Cultural particularism: regionalism, nationalism

Social expectations: brand-name expectations; work hours

Political laws: transborder data and privacy laws

Specific

Standards: different EDI, e-mail, telecommunications standards

Reliability: phone networks not reliable

Speed: data transfer speeds differ, slower than United States

Personnel: shortages of skilled consultants

Finally, global markets, production, and administration create the conditions for powerful, sustained global economies of scale. Production driven by worldwide global demand can be concentrated where it can be best accomplished, fixed resources can be allocated over larger production runs, and production runs in larger plants can be scheduled more efficiently and precisely estimated. Lower cost factors of production can be exploited wherever they emerge. The result is a powerful strategic advantage to firms that can organize globally. These general and specific business drivers have greatly enlarged world trade and commerce.

Not all industries are similarly affected by these trends. Clearly, manufacturing has been much more affected than services that still tend to be domestic and highly inefficient. However, the localism of services is breaking down in telecommunications, entertainment, transportation, financial services, and general business services including law. Clearly those firms within an industry that can understand the internationalization of the industry and respond appropriately will reap enormous gains in productivity and stability.

Business Challenges

Although the possibilities of globalization for business success are significant, fundamental forces are operating to inhibit a global economy and to disrupt international business. Table 17.2 lists the most common and powerful challenges to the development of global systems.

At a cultural level, **particularism,** making judgments and taking action on the basis of narrow or personal characteristics, in all its forms (religious, nationalistic, ethnic, regionalism, geopolitical position) rejects the very concept of a shared global culture and rejects the penetration of domestic markets by foreign goods and services. Differences among cultures produce differences in social expectations, politics, and ultimately legal rules. In certain countries, such as the United States, consumers expect domestic name-brand products to be built domestically and are disappointed to learn that much of what they thought of as domestically produced is in fact foreign made.

Different cultures produce different political regimes. Among the many different countries of the world there are different laws governing the movement of information, information privacy of their citizens, origins of software and hardware in systems, and radio and satellite telecommunications. Even the hours of business and the terms of business trade vary greatly across political cultures. These different legal regimes complicate global business and must be considered when building global systems.

For instance, European countries have very strict laws concerning transborder data flow and privacy. **Transborder data flow** is defined as the movement of information across international boundaries in any form. Some European countries prohibit the processing of

particularism Making judgments and taking actions on the basis of narrow or personal characteristics.

transborder data flow The movement of information across international boundaries in any form.

Marine Power Europe's Extranet Challenge

Building an extranet overseas can be rewarding, but it poses challenges for companies at all phases of globalization. Boat engine company Marine Power Europe learned this lesson when it decided to implement a multilingual extranet in about a dozen European countries. Marine Power Europe is a subsidiary of Brunswick Corp.

The extranet cost $500,000 to build. It allows the company's independent dealers to check prices and then submit and track orders. Mercury Marine, the company's U.S. counterpart, had much less difficulty implementing a similar extranet because it was based on one language and one set of business rules. The European extranet, in contrast, had to operate with eight different languages and account for local differences such as an oil tax in Italy and a horsepower tax in Norway. Marine Power Europe's Managing Director Randy Gray warns that a global extranet will take three times as long and cost three times as much as comparable projects in the United States because of such regulatory and cultural complexities. "It requires very intricate local knowledge," he asserts.

Marine Power's extranet runs on IBM AS/400 servers with Web server software provided by Click Interactive Inc., a Chicago-based company. The extranet is supported by a 14-person information systems development and logistics staff at the company's regional headquarters in Brussels.

Marine Power believes that its extranet effort was helped by users' experience with France's Minitel system. Minitel is a government information service dating back to the early 1980s. Consumers use dumb terminals to look up telephone numbers, send personal ads, and conduct other on-line transactions from their homes. About 85 percent of Marine Power's French customers use Minitel to place orders, making them comfortable conducting business on-line.

Although the Internet provided a common set of technical standards, Marine Power Europe still had to grapple with an array of differences in the 11 countries where it sells engines. For example, information systems problems were fixed quickly in Belgium, but in Italy it could take an entire month to repair a broken printer. European countries have different levels of technological acceptance. In Italy, where PCs are not widely used by small businesses, Marine Power had relatively greater difficulty getting dealers to invest in information technology. In contrast, 90 percent of Marine Power's dealers already owned PCs in Scandinavian countries. Unlike the United States, European Internet service providers (ISPs) charge for Internet usage by the minute.

As a result, Marine Power decided not to impose the extranet on its small dealers. Instead of putting its catalogues on the Web, it offered them on CD-ROMs that dealers could use without network connections. Only price lists are on Marine Power's Web site for now.

To Think About: What management, organization, and technology issues did Marine Power Europe have to address in implementing its extranet?

Sources: Gregory Dalton, "Ready to Go Global?" **Information Week,** February 9, 1998, and "Integrating OLTP and Legacy Systems," **Business News,** June 11, 1998.

---

financial information outside their boundaries or the movement of personal information to foreign countries. The European Union Data Protection Directive, which went into effect in October 1998, restricts the flow of any information to countries (such as the United States) that do not meet strict European information laws on personal information. Financial services, travel, and health care companies could be directly affected. For example, information on an airline passenger's food preferences collected in one of the European Union countries might not be able to be forwarded to the United States, given its privacy laws. In response, most multinational firms develop information systems within each European country to avoid the cost and uncertainty of moving information across national boundaries.

Cultural and political differences profoundly affect organizations' standard operating procedures. A host of specific barriers arise from the general cultural differences, everything from different reliability of phone networks to the shortage of skilled consultants (see Steinbart and Nath, 1992). The Window on Organizations illustrates how such differences can affect efforts to implement an extranet globally.

National laws and traditions have created disparate accounting practices in various countries, which impact the ways profits and losses are analyzed. German companies generally do not recognize the profit from a venture until the project is completely finished and they have been paid. Conversely, British firms begin posting profits before a project is completed, when they are reasonably certain they will get the money.

These accounting practices are tightly intertwined with each country's legal system, business philosophy, and tax code. British, U.S., and Dutch firms share a predominantly Anglo-Saxon outlook that separates tax calculations from reports to shareholders to focus on showing shareholders how fast profits are growing. Continental European accounting practices are less oriented toward impressing investors, focusing rather on demonstrating compliance with strict rules and minimizing tax liabilities. These diverging accounting practices make it difficult for large international companies with units in different countries to evaluate their performance.

Cultural differences can also affect the way organizations use information technology. For example, Japanese firms fax extensively but have been reluctant to take advantage of the capabilities of e-mail. One explanation is that the Japanese view e-mail as poorly suited for much intragroup communication and for depiction of the complex symbols used in the Japanese written language (Straub, 1994).

Language remains a significant barrier. Although English has become a kind of standard business language, this is truer at higher levels of companies and not throughout the middle and lower ranks. Software may have to be built with local language interfaces before a new information system can be successfully implemented.

Currency fluctuations can play havoc with planning models and projections. A product that appears profitable in Mexico or Japan may actually produce a loss due to changes in foreign exchange rates. Some of these problems will diminish as the euro becomes more widely used.

These inhibiting factors must be taken into account when you are designing and building an international infrastructure for your business. For example, companies trying to implement "lean production" systems spanning national boundaries typically underestimate the time, expense, and logistical difficulties of making goods and information flow freely across different countries (Levy, 1997).

State of the Art

One might think, given the opportunities for achieving competitive advantages as outlined previously and the interest in future applications, that most international companies have rationally developed marvelous international systems architectures. Nothing could be further from the truth. Most companies have inherited patchwork international systems from the distant past, often based on concepts of information processing developed in the 1960s—batch-oriented reporting from independent foreign divisions to corporate headquarters, with little on-line control and communication. Corporations in this situation increasingly will face powerful competitive challenges in the marketplace from firms that have rationally designed truly international systems. Still other companies have recently built technology platforms for an international infrastructure but have nowhere to go because they lack global strategy.

As it turns out, there are significant difficulties in building appropriate international infrastructures. The difficulties involve planning a system appropriate to the firm's global strategy, structuring the organization of systems and business units, solving implementation issues, and choosing the right technical platform. Let us examine these problems in greater detail.

17.2 Organizing International Information Systems

There are three organizational issues facing corporations seeking a global position: choosing a strategy, organizing the business, and organizing the systems management area. The first two are closely connected, so we will discuss them together.

Global Strategies and Business Organization

Four main global strategies form the basis for global firms' organizational structure. These are domestic exporter, multinational, franchiser, and transnational. Each of these strategies is pursued with a specific business organizational structure (see Table 17.3). For simplicity's sake,

Table 17.3 Global Business Strategy and Structure

Business Function	Strategy			
	Domestic Exporter	Multinational	Franchiser	Transnational
Production	Centralized	Dispersed	Coordinated	Coordinated
Finance/Accounting	Centralized	Centralized	Centralized	Coordinated
Sales/Marketing	Mixed	Dispersed	Coordinated	Coordinated
Human Resources	Centralized	Centralized	Coordinated	Coordinated
Strategic Management	Centralized	Centralized	Centralized	Coordinated

we describe three kinds of organizational structure or governance: centralized (in the home country), decentralized (to local foreign units), and coordinated (all units participate as equals). There are other types of governance patterns observed in specific companies (e.g., authoritarian dominance by one unit, a confederacy of equals, a federal structure balancing power among strategic units, and so forth; see Keen, 1991).

The **domestic exporter** strategy is characterized by heavy centralization of corporate activities in the home country of origin. Nearly all international companies begin this way, and some move on to other forms. Production, finance/accounting, sales/marketing, human resources, and strategic management are set up to optimize resources in the home country. International sales are sometimes dispersed using agency agreements or subsidiaries, but even here foreign marketing is totally reliant on the domestic home base for marketing themes and strategies. Caterpillar Corporation and other heavy capital-equipment manufacturers fall into this category of firm.

The **multinational** strategy concentrates financial management and control out of a central home base while decentralizing production, sales, and marketing operations to units in other countries. The products and services on sale in different countries are adapted to suit local market conditions. The organization becomes a far-flung confederation of production and marketing facilities in different countries. Many financial service firms, along with a host of manufacturers such as General Motors, Chrysler, and Intel, fit this pattern.

Franchisers are an interesting mix of old and new. On the one hand, the product is created, designed, financed, and initially produced in the home country, but for product-specific reasons must rely heavily on foreign personnel for further production, marketing, and human resources. Food franchisers such as McDonald's, Mrs. Fields Cookies, and Kentucky Fried Chicken fit this pattern. McDonald's created a new form of fast-food chain in the United States and continues to rely largely on the United States for inspiration of new products, strategic management, and financing. Nevertheless, because the product must be produced locally—it is perishable—extensive coordination and dispersal of production, local marketing, and local recruitment of personnel are required. Generally, foreign franchisees are clones of the mother country units, but fully coordinated worldwide production that could optimize factors of production is not possible. For instance, potatoes and beef can generally not be bought where they are cheapest on world markets but must be produced reasonably close to the area of consumption.

Transnational firms are the stateless, truly globally managed firms that may represent a larger part of international business in the future. Transnational firms have no single national headquarters but instead have many regional headquarters and perhaps a world headquarters. In a **transnational** strategy, nearly all the value-adding activities are managed from a global perspective without reference to national borders, optimizing sources of supply and demand wherever they appear, and taking advantage of any local competitive advantages. Transnational firms take the globe, not the home country, as their management frame of reference. The governance of these firms has been likened to a federal structure in which there is a strong central management core of decision making, but considerable dispersal of power and financial

domestic exporter A strategy characterized by heavy centralization of corporate activities in the home country of origin.

multinational A global strategy that concentrates financial management and control out of a central home base while decentralizing production, sales, and marketing operations to units in other countries.

franchiser A firm where a product is created, designed, financed, and initially produced in the home country, but for product-specific reasons must rely heavily on foreign personnel for further production, marketing, and human resources.

transnational Truly globally managed firms that have no national headquarters; value-added activities are managed from a global perspective without reference to national borders, optimizing sources of supply and demand and taking advantage of any local competitive advantage.

muscle throughout the global divisions. Few companies have actually attained transnational status, but Citicorp, Sony, Ford, and others are attempting this transition.

Information technology and improvements in global telecommunications are giving international firms more flexibility to shape their global strategies. Protectionism and a need to serve local markets better encourage companies to disperse production facilities and at least become multinational. At the same time, the drive to achieve economies of scale and take advantage of short-term local advantage moves transnationals toward a global management perspective and a concentration of power and authority. Hence, there are forces of decentralization and dispersal, as well as forces of centralization and global coordination (Ives and Jarvenpaa, 1991).

Global Systems to Fit the Strategy

The configuration, management, and development of systems tend to follow the global strategy chosen (Roche, 1992; Ives and Jarvenpaa, 1991). Figure 17-2 depicts the typical arrangements. By *systems* we mean the full range of activities involved in building information systems: conception and alignment with the strategic business plan, systems development, and ongoing operation. For the sake of simplicity, we consider four types of systems configuration. *Centralized systems* are those in which systems development and operation occur totally at the domestic home base. *Duplicated systems* are those in which development occurs at the home base but operations are handed over to autonomous units in foreign locations. *Decentralized systems* are those in which each foreign unit designs its own unique solutions and systems. *Networked systems* are those in which systems development and operations occur in an integrated and coordinated fashion across all units. As can be seen in Figure 17-2, domestic exporters tend to have highly centralized systems in which a single domestic systems development staff develops worldwide applications. Multinationals offer a direct and striking contrast: Here foreign units devise their own systems solutions based on local needs with few if any applications in common with headquarters (the exceptions being financial reporting and some telecommunications applications). Franchisers have the simplest systems structure: Like the products they sell, franchisers develop a single system usually at the home base and then replicate it around the world. Each unit, no matter where it is located, has identical applications. Last, the most ambitious form of systems development is found in the transnational: Networked systems are those in which there is a solid, singular global environment for developing and operat-

Figure 17-2 Global strategy and systems configurations. The large X's show the dominant patterns, and the small x's show the emerging patterns. For instance, domestic exporters rely predominantly on centralized systems, but there is continual pressure and some development of decentralized systems in local marketing regions.

SYSTEM CONFIGURATION	STRATEGY			
	Domestic Exporter	Multinational	Franchiser	Transnational
Centralized	X			
Duplicated			X	
Decentralized	x	X	x	
Networked		x		X

ing systems. This usually presupposes a powerful telecommunications backbone, a culture of shared applications development, and a shared management culture that crosses cultural barriers. The networked systems structure is the most visible in financial services where the homogeneity of the product—money and money instruments—seems to overcome cultural barriers.

Reorganizing the Business

How should a firm organize itself for doing business on an international scale? To develop a global company and an information systems support structure, a firm needs to follow these principles:

1. Organize value-adding activities along lines of comparative advantage. For instance, marketing/sales functions should be located where they can best be performed, for least cost and maximum impact; likewise with production, finance, human resources, and information systems.

2. Develop and operate systems units at each level of corporate activity—regional, national, and international. To serve local needs, there should be *host country systems units* of some magnitude. *Regional systems units* should handle telecommunications and systems development across national boundaries that take place within major geographic regions (European, Asian, American). *Transnational systems units* should be established to create the linkages across major regional areas and coordinate the development and operation of international telecommunications and systems development (Roche, 1992).

3. Establish at world headquarters a single office responsible for development of international systems, a global chief information officer (CIO) position.

Many successful companies have devised organizational systems structures along these principles. The success of these companies relies not only on the proper organization of activities, but also on a key ingredient—a management team that can understand the risks and benefits of international systems and that can devise strategies for overcoming the risks. We turn to these management topics next.

17.3 Managing Global Systems

Table 17.4 lists the principal management problems posed by developing international systems. It is interesting to note that these problems are the chief difficulties managers experience in developing ordinary domestic systems as well! But these are enormously complicated in the international environment.

A Typical Scenario: Disorganization on a Global Scale

Let us look at a common scenario. A traditional multinational consumer-goods company based in the United States and operating in Europe would like to expand into Asian markets and knows that it must develop a transnational strategy and a supportive information

---

Table 17.4 Management Challenges in Developing Global Systems

Agreeing on common user requirements

Introducing changes in business procedures

Coordinating applications development

Coordinating software releases

Encouraging local users to support global systems

systems structure. Like most multinationals it has dispersed production and marketing to regional and national centers while maintaining a world headquarters and strategic management in the United States. Historically, it has allowed each of the subsidiary foreign divisions to develop its own systems. The only centrally coordinated system is financial controls and reporting. The central systems group in the United States focuses only on domestic functions and production. The result is a hodgepodge of hardware, software, and telecommunications. The e-mail systems between Europe and the United States are incompatible. Each production facility uses a different manufacturing resources planning system (or a different version with local variations), and different marketing, sales, and human resource systems. The technology platforms are wildly different: Europe is using mostly UNIX-based file servers and IBM PC clones on desktops. Communications between different sites are poor, given the high cost and low quality of European intercountry communications. The U.S. group is moving from an IBM mainframe environment centralized at headquarters to a highly distributed network architecture based on a national value-added network, with local sites developing their own local area networks. The central systems group at headquarters recently was decimated and dispersed to the U.S. local sites in the hope of serving local needs better and reducing costs.

What do you recommend to the senior management leaders of this company, who now want to pursue a transnational strategy and develop an information systems infrastructure to support a highly coordinated global systems environment? Consider the problems you face by reexamining Table 17.4. The foreign divisions will resist efforts to agree on common user requirements; they have never thought about much other than their own units' needs. The systems groups in American local sites, which have been enlarged recently and told to focus on local needs, will not easily accept guidance from anyone recommending a transnational strategy. It will be difficult to convince local managers anywhere in the world that they should change their business procedures to align with other units in the world, especially if this might interfere with their local performance. After all, local managers are rewarded in this company for meeting local objectives of their division or plant. Finally, it will be difficult to coordinate development of projects around the world in the absence of a powerful telecommunications network and, therefore, difficult to encourage local users to take on ownership in the systems developed.

Strategy: Divide, Conquer, Appease

Figure 17-3 lays out the main dimensions of a solution. First, consider that not all systems should be coordinated on a transnational basis; only some core systems are truly worth sharing from a cost and feasibility point of view. **Core systems** are systems that support functions that are absolutely critical to the organization. Other systems should be partially coordinated because they share key elements, but they do not have to be totally common across national boundaries. For such systems, a good deal of local variation is possible and desirable. A final group of systems are peripheral, truly provincial, and are needed to suit local requirements only.

core systems Systems that support functions that are absolutely critical to the organization.

Define the Core Business Processes

How do you identify *core systems?* The first step is to define a short list of critical core business processes. Business processes were defined in Chapter 3, which you should review. Briefly, business processes are sets of logically related tasks such as shipping out correct orders to customers or delivering innovative products to the market. Each business process typically involves many functional areas, communicating and coordinating work, information, and knowledge.

The way to identify these core business processes is to conduct a work-flow analysis. How are customer orders taken, what happens to them once they are taken, who fills the orders, how are they shipped to the customers? What about suppliers? Do they have access to manufacturing resource planning systems so that supply is automatic? You should be able to identify and set priorities in a short list of 10 business processes that are absolutely critical for the firm.

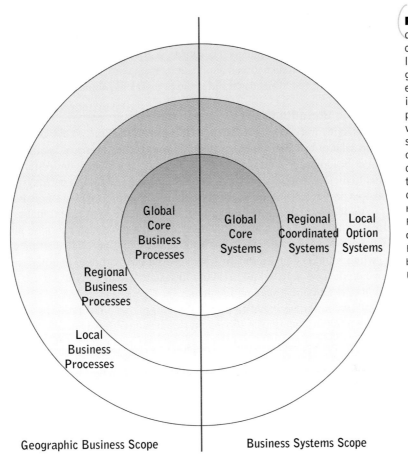

Global
Core
Business
Processes

Regional
Business
Processes

Local
Business
Processes

Global
Core
Systems

Regional
Coordinated
Systems

Local
Option
Systems

Geographic Business Scope | Business Systems Scope

Figure 17-3 Agency and other coordination costs increase as the firm moves from local option systems toward regional and global systems. However, transaction costs of participating in global markets probably decrease as firms develop global systems. A sensible strategy is to reduce agency costs by developing only a few core global systems that are vital for global operations, leaving other systems in the hands of regional and local units. **Source:** From Managing Information Technology in Multinational Corporations by Edward M. Roche, © 1993. Adapted by permission of Prentice-Hall, Inc., Upper Saddle River, NJ.

Next, can you identify centers of excellence for these processes? Is the customer order fulfillment superior in the United States, manufacturing process control superior in Germany, and human resources superior in Asia? You should be able to identify some areas of the company, for some lines of business, where a division or unit stands out in the performance of one or several business functions.

When you understand the business processes of a firm, you can rank-order them. You then can decide which processes should be core applications, centrally coordinated, designed, and implemented around the globe, and which should be regional and local. At the same time, by identifying the critical business processes, the really important ones, you have gone a long way to defining a vision of the future that you should be working toward.

Identify the Core Systems to Coordinate Centrally

By identifying the critical core business processes, you begin to see opportunities for transnational systems. The second strategic step is to conquer the core systems and define these systems as truly transnational. The financial and political costs of defining and implementing transnational systems are extremely high. Therefore, keep the list to an absolute minimum, letting experience be the guide and erring on the side of minimalism. By dividing off a small group of systems as absolutely critical, you divide opposition to a transnational strategy. At the same time, you can appease those who oppose the central worldwide coordination implied by transnational systems by permitting peripheral systems development to progress unabated, with the exception of some technical platform requirements.

Choose an Approach: Incremental, Grand Design, Evolutionary

A third step is to choose an approach. Avoid piecemeal approaches. These surely will fail for lack of visibility, opposition from all who stand to lose from transnational development, and lack of power to convince senior management that the transnational systems are worth it. Likewise, avoid grand design approaches that try to do everything at once. These also tend to fail, due to an inability to focus resources. Nothing gets done properly, and opposition to organizational change is needlessly strengthened because the effort requires huge resources. An alternative approach is to evolve transnational applications from existing applications with a precise and clear vision of the transnational capabilities the organization should have in five years.

Make the Benefits Clear

What is in it for the company? One of the worst situations to avoid is to build global systems for the sake of building global systems. From the beginning, it is crucial that senior management at headquarters and foreign division managers clearly understand the benefits that will come to the company as well as to individual units. Although each system offers unique benefits to a particular budget, the overall contribution of global systems lies in four areas.

Global systems—truly integrated, distributed, and transnational systems—contribute to superior management and coordination. A simple price tag cannot be put on the value of this contribution, and the benefit will not show up in any capital budgeting model. It is the ability to switch suppliers on a moment's notice from one region to another in a crisis, the ability to move production in response to natural disasters, and the ability to use excess capacity in one region to meet raging demand in another.

A second major contribution is vast improvement in production, operation, and supply and distribution. Imagine a global value chain, with global suppliers and a global distribution network. For the first time, senior managers can locate value-adding activities in regions where they are most economically performed.

Third, global systems mean global customers and global marketing. Fixed costs around the world can be amortized over a much larger customer base. This will unleash new economies of scale at production facilities.

Last, global systems mean the ability to optimize the use of corporate funds over a much larger capital base. This means, for instance, that capital in a surplus region can be moved efficiently to expand production of capital-starved regions; that cash can be managed more effectively within the company and put to use more effectively.

These strategies will not by themselves create global systems. You will have to implement what you strategize and this is a whole new challenge.

Implementation Tactics: Cooptation

The overall tactic for dealing with resistant local units in a transnational company is cooptation. **Cooptation** is defined as bringing the opposition into the process of designing and implementing the solution without giving up control over the direction and nature of the change. As much as possible, raw power should be avoided. Minimally, however, local units must agree on a short list of transnational systems, and raw power may be required to solidify the idea that transnational systems of some sort are truly required.

How should cooptation proceed? Several alternatives are possible. One alternative is to permit each country unit the opportunity to develop one transnational application first in its home territory, and then throughout the world. In this manner, each major country systems group is given a piece of the action in developing a transnational system, and local units feel a sense of ownership in the transnational effort. On the downside, this assumes the ability to develop high-quality systems is widely distributed, and that, say, the German team can successfully implement systems in France and Italy. This will not always be the case. Also, the transnational effort will have low visibility.

A second tactic is to develop new transnational centers of excellence, or a single center of excellence. There may be several centers around the globe that focus on specific business processes. These centers draw heavily from local national units, are based on multinational teams, and must report to worldwide management—their first line of responsibility is to the core applications. Centers of excellence perform the initial identification and specification of the business process, define the information requirements, perform the business and systems analysis, and accomplish all design and testing. Implementation, however, and pilot testing occur in World Pilot Regions where new applications are installed and tested first. Later, they are

cooptation Bringing the opposition into the process of designing and implementing the solution without giving up control over the direction and nature of the change.

rolled out to other parts of the globe. This phased rollout strategy is precisely how national applications are successfully developed.

The Management Solution

We now can reconsider how to handle the most vexing problems facing managers developing the transnational information system infrastructures that were described in Table 17.4.

○ *Agreeing on common user requirements:* Establishing a short list of the core business processes and core support systems will begin a process of rational comparison across the many divisions of the company, develop a common language for discussing the business, and naturally lead to an understanding of common elements (as well as the unique qualities that must remain local).

○ *Introducing changes in business procedures:* Your success as a change agent will depend on your legitimacy, your actual raw power, and your ability to involve users in the change design process. **Legitimacy** is defined as the extent to which your authority is accepted on grounds of competence, vision, or other qualities. The selection of a viable change strategy, which we have defined as evolutionary but with a vision, should assist you in convincing others that change is feasible and desirable. Involving people in change, assuring them that change is in the best interests of the company and their local units, is a key tactic.

○ *Coordinating applications development:* Choice of change strategy is critical for this problem. At the global level there is far too much complexity to attempt a grand design strategy of change. It is far easier to coordinate change by making small incremental steps toward a larger vision. Imagine a five-year plan of action rather than a two-year plan of action, and reduce the set of transnational systems to a bare minimum to reduce coordination costs.

○ *Coordinating software releases:* Firms can institute procedures to ensure that all operating units convert to new software updates at the same time so that everyone's software is compatible.

○ *Encouraging local users to support global systems:* The key to this problem is to involve users in the creation of the design without giving up control over the development of the project to parochial interests. Recruiting a wide range of local individuals to transnational centers of excellence helps send the message that all significant groups are involved in the design and will have an influence.

Even with the proper organizational structure and appropriate management choices, it is still possible to stumble over technological issues. Choices of technology, platforms, networks, hardware, and software are the final elements in building transnational information system infrastructures.

legitimacy The extent to which one's authority is accepted on grounds of competence, vision, or other qualities.

17.4 Technology Issues and Opportunities

Information technology is itself a powerful business driver for encouraging the development of global systems, but it creates significant challenges for managers. Global systems presuppose that business firms develop a solid technical foundation and are willing to continually upgrade facilities.

Main Technical Issues

Hardware, software, and telecommunications pose special technical challenges in an international setting. The major hardware challenge is finding some way to standardize the firm's computer hardware platform when there is so much variation from operating unit to operating unit and from country to country. Managers need to think carefully about where to locate the firm's computer centers and how to select hardware suppliers. The major global software challenge is finding applications that are user friendly and that truly enhance the productivity of international work teams. The major telecommunications challenge is making data flow seamlessly across networks shaped by disparate national standards. Overcoming these challenges requires systems integration and connectivity on a global basis.

Hardware and Systems Integration

The development of transnational information system infrastructures based on the concept of core systems raises questions about how the new core systems will fit in with the existing suite of applications developed around the globe by different divisions, different people, and for different kinds of computing hardware. The goal is to develop global, distributed, and integrated systems. Briefly, these are the same problems faced by any large, domestic, systems development effort. However, the problems are more complex because of the international environment. For instance, in the United States, IBM operating systems have played the predominant role in building core systems for large organizations, whereas in Europe, UNIX was much more commonly used for large systems. How can the two be integrated in a common transnational system?

The correct solution often will depend on the history of the company's systems and the extent of commitment to proprietary systems. For instance, finance and insurance firms typically have relied almost exclusively on IBM proprietary equipment and architectures, and it would be extremely difficult and cost ineffective to abandon that equipment and software. Newer firms and manufacturing firms generally find it much easier to adopt open UNIX systems for international systems. As pointed out in previous chapters, open UNIX-based systems are far more cost effective in the long run, provide more power at a cheaper price, and preserve options for future expansion.

After a hardware platform is chosen, the question of standards must be addressed. Just because all sites use the same hardware does not guarantee common, integrated systems. Some central authority in the firm must establish data, as well as other technical standards, with which sites are to comply. For instance, technical accounting terms such as the beginning and end of the fiscal year must be standardized (review our earlier discussion of the cultural challenges to building global businesses), as well as the acceptable interfaces between systems, communication speeds and architectures, and network software.

Connectivity

The heart of the international systems problem is telecommunications—linking together the systems and people of a global firm into a single integrated network just like the phone system but capable of voice, data, and image transmissions. However, integrated global networks are extremely difficult to create (see Table 17.5). For example, many countries cannot fulfill basic business telecommunications needs such as obtaining reliable circuits, coordinating among different carriers and the regional telecommunications authority, obtaining bills in a common currency standard, and obtaining standard agreements for the level of telecommunications service provided.

Table 17.5 Problems of International Networks

Costs and tariffs

Network management

Installation delays

Poor quality of international service

Regulatory constraints

Changing user requirements

Disparate standards

Network capacity

Despite moves toward economic unity, Europe remains a hodgepodge of disparate national technical standards and service levels. The problem is especially critical for banks or airlines that must move massive volumes of data around the world. Although most circuits leased by multinational corporations are fault-free more than 99.8 percent of the time, line quality and service vary widely from the north to the south of Europe. Network service is much more unreliable in southern Europe.

Existing European standards for networking and EDI (electronic data interchange) are very industry specific and country specific. Most European banks use the SWIFT (Society for Worldwide Interbank Financial Telecommunications) protocol for international funds transfer, whereas automobile companies and food producers often use industry-specific or country-specific versions of standard protocols for EDI. Complicating matters further, the United States standard for EDI is ANSI (American National Standards Institute) X.12. The Open Systems Interconnect (OSI) reference model for linking networks is more popular in Europe than it is in the United States. Various industry groups have standardized on other networking architectures, such as Transmission Control Protocol/Internet Protocol (TCP/IP) or IBM's proprietary Systems Network Architecture (SNA). Even standards such as ISDN (Integrated Services Digital Network) vary from country to country.

Firms have several options for providing international connectivity: build their own international private network, rely on a network service based on the public switched networks throughout the world, or use the Internet and intranets.

One possibility is for the firm to put together its own private network based on leased lines from each country's PTT (post, telegraph, and telephone authorities). Each country, however, has different restrictions on data exchange, technical standards, and acceptable vendors of equipment. These problems magnify in certain parts of the world. Despite such limitations, in Europe and the United States, reliance on PTTs still makes sense while these public networks expand services to compete with private providers.

The second major alternative to building one's own network is to use one of several expanding network services. With deregulation of telecommunications around the globe, private providers have sprung up to service business customers' data needs, along with some voice and image communication.

Already common in the United States, IVANs (International Value-Added Network Services) are expanding in Europe and Asia. These private firms offer value-added telecommunications capacity, usually rented from local PTTs or international satellite authorities, and then resell it to corporate users. IVANs add value by providing protocol conversion, operating mail-

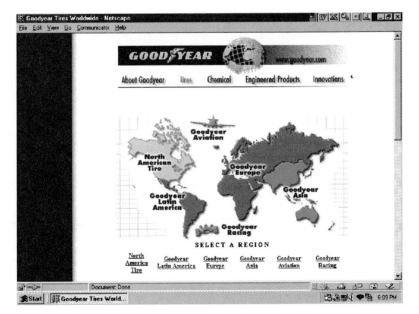

Goodyear Tire and Rubber Company provides country-specific information on its Web site using corporate guidelines for technology and interfaces. Companies need to consider these issues as well as Internet availability when designing an international Web strategy.

Developing an International Web Strategy

The Internet now links over 200 countries but is it ready to be a world tool for conducting business? Managers trying to develop a Web strategy to reach customers, suppliers, and distributors need to think about certain realities. Only half of the households throughout the globe have a telephone, let alone a personal computer. It is estimated that only 1.5 percent to 2.5 percent of the world's 6 billion people can access the Internet, and most of them live in wealthy industrial nations. Even there, the level of Internet access varies widely. For example, Germany has no flat rate for local telephone calls, so 20 hours of off-peak Internet access could amount to $75 per month with an additional $40 for telephone charges. Countries with more advanced telecommunications infrastructures such as Finland generally have faster and more reliable Internet access than countries such as Greece.

Internet use should grow and prices should drop as European telecommunications deregulation continues and governments promote Internet use in schools and workplaces. But it is very important for businesses to understand the variable Internet presence in different countries when they target their Web efforts. Germany and northern Europe would be more lucrative Web targets at present, with continental Europe becoming more attractive a few years from now. In Asia, Hong Kong, Singapore, and Malaysia have very rich technology and international business infrastructures, and Japan, Korea, and Taiwan are also active in global business. Among Latin American countries, telecommunications services are growing most rapidly in Brazil.

Internet access in the countries served by Avis Europe PLC was sufficient for the company to develop an extranet to allow licensees in 35 countries in Asia, Africa, and Central Europe to connect to its mainframe Wizard car rental reservation system. In the past, small licensees in countries such as Russia and Kenya had to communicate with Avis Europe's headquarters in England using fax or telex because they did not conduct enough business to warrant the cost of linking to the corporate wide-area network. Now licensees can use their PC Web browser and a dial-up Internet service from a local provider for this communication.

In addition to Internet access, global Web strategies need to consider timing and coordination issues. Dell Computer Corporation coordinates its Web priorities with its business priorities, rolling out new country-specific Web stores at the same time that it launches manufacturing and marketing operations in a particular area. Most of Dell's on-line business is in the United States, but about one-fifth of Dell's Web sales now come from other countries.

Goodyear Tire & Rubber's public Web site first had country-specific information for five Latin-American countries, but had to wait some months before posting similar information for Europe. The company wanted to make sure that its non-U.S. Web content matched corporate Web standards for look and feel as well as technology. For example, the Web site put up by its German units had to be modified to look like the corporate site.

To Think About: What management, organization, and technology issues should be addressed when developing a global Web strategy?

Sources: Sari Kalin, "The Worldlier Wider Web," CIO Web Business Magazine, March 1, 1999; and John Tagliabue, "Foie Gras and Chips, Anyone?" The New York Times, March 27, 1999.

---

boxes and mail systems, and by offering integrated billing that permits a firm to track its data communications costs. Currently these systems are limited to data transmissions, but in the future they will expand to voice and image.

The third alternative, which is becoming increasingly attractive, is to create global intranets to use the Internet for international communication. However, the Internet is not yet a worldwide tool because many countries lack the communications infrastructure for extensive Internet use. Countries face high costs, government control, or government monitoring.

Western Europe faces both high transmission costs and lack of common technology because it is not politically unified and because European telecommunications systems are still in the process of shedding their government monopolies. The lack of an infrastructure and the high costs of installing one is even more widespread in the rest of the world. In South Africa only 10 percent of the population has telephone lines, and Internet users must pay for each minute they spend on-line (Manson, 1998). Low penetration of PCs and widespread illiteracy limit demand for Internet service in India (Burkhardt, Goodman, Mehta, and Press, 1999). Where an infrastructure exists, as in China and Pakistan, it is often outdated, lacks digital circuits, and has very noisy lines.

The Window on Management explores the question of Internet availability in greater detail as an important issue for managers developing an international Web strategy.

Software interfaces may have to be translated to accommodate users in East Asia or other parts of the world.

Many countries monitor transmissions. The governments in China and Singapore monitor Internet traffic and block access to Web sites considered morally or politically offensive (Blanning, 1999). Corporations may be discouraged from using this medium. Companies planning international operations through the Internet still will have many hurdles.

Software

Compatible hardware and communications provide a platform but not the total solution. Also critical to global core infrastructure is software. The development of core systems poses unique challenges for software: How will the old systems interface with the new? Entirely new interfaces must be built and tested if old systems are kept in local areas (which is common). These interfaces can be costly and messy to build. If new software must be created, another challenge is to build software that can be realistically used by multiple business units from different countries given these business units are accustomed to their unique procedures and definitions of data.

Aside from integrating the new with the old systems, there are problems of human interface design and functionality of systems. For instance, to be truly useful for enhancing productivity of a global workforce, software interfaces must be easily understood and mastered quickly. Graphical user interfaces are ideal for this but presuppose a common language—often English. When international systems involve knowledge workers only, English may be the assumed international standard. But as international systems penetrate deeper into management and clerical groups, a common language may not be assumed and human interfaces must be built to accommodate different languages and even conventions.

What are the most important software applications? Although most international systems focus on basic transaction and MIS systems, there is an increasing emphasis on international collaborative work groups. EDI—electronic data interchange—is a common global transaction processing application used by manufacturing and distribution firms to connect units of the same company, as well as customers and suppliers on a global basis. Groupware systems such as electronic mail, videoconferencing, Lotus Notes, and other products supporting shared data files, notes, and electronic mail are much more important to knowledge- and data-based firms such as advertising firms, research-based firms in medicine and engineering, and graphics and publishing firms. The Internet will be increasingly employed for such purposes.

Virtual Private Networks to the Rescue

What do you do when your company needs global networking capability but the costs of a private WAN are very high? One solution that has emerged is to build a virtual private network (VPN) based on Internet technology.

Instead of using private or leased lines like traditional networks such as frame-relay systems, VPNs use the worldwide Internet infrastructure to communicate with distant computers. Internet service providers (ISPs) assign subscribing companies a slice of their backbone bandwidth to use as a VPN. Companies requiring wide area networking pay their ISPs for the amount of bandwidth required. The company saves the cost of a private network and the staff needed to install and support it. To connect to another company thousands of miles away, users need only make a local telephone call to the nearest access point of the ISP. Companies using VPNs can cut their networking expenses by 50 percent or more.

Another advantage of VPNs is the ease with which they can be set up and accessed. It can take months to install a leased line in certain parts of the world; extra users or offices can be added to a VPN within a day. Mobile workers can tap into the VPNs using dial-up software (included in Windows 95 and 98), VPN software, and an Internet account with an ISP. Both large and small companies can benefit.

Decker Outdoor Sandal Corporation, which makes sandals, shoes, and boots, uses a VPN to link its 20-person office in Hoek Van Holland with staff in Goleta, California, so that both groups can collaborate on product development. To increase security Decker installed NetFortress VPN1, a software package from Fortress Technologies Inc. in Tampa, Florida. The software automatically changes encryption keys every 24 hours. The VPN saves Decker $10,000 per month compared to its previous frame-relay connection.

The Forum Corporation, a Boston-based global training and consulting firm, is using a VPN to network with both external and internal users. To help its 350 staff members share knowledge, the company established a VPN linking its Boston, Hong Kong, and Toronto offices in early 1997, adding a link to its London office a year later. The VPN supports all of Forum's applications and communications between the United States and international sites other than telephone and fax, including e-mail, intranet and file access, order processing, financial tracking, technical support, real-time collaboration, videoconferencing, and on-line learning. The VPN costs $6000 less per month than the cost of leased lines for linking Forum's Hong Kong office alone, compared to using ISDN. In Forum's busy London office, which requires more networking capacity, the VPN provided four times the bandwidth for an added cost of only $1000 per month. Forum expects to standardize all of its networking on the VPN, allowing users worldwide to connect directly to headquarters via the Internet wherever they are located.

To Think About: What are the management, organization, and technology implications of switching to a VPN? If VPNs prove their value in the next few years, what might be their impact on the networking industry and on world trade?

Sources: Polly Schneider, "The Bargain Hunter's Guide to Global Networking," CIO Magazine, April 1, 1999; and Bob Wallace, "Remote Users to Make Gains with New Network," Computerworld, February 2, 1998.

Asian Sources Online assists companies that would like to do business with companies in Asia. It offers services such as links to trade shows and travel information, and a search capability for visitors to locate producers of items that interest them.

New Technical Opportunities and the Internet

Technical advances described in Chapter 9, such as ISDN and Digital Subscriber Line (DSL) services, should continue to fall in price and gain in power, facilitating the creation and operation of global networks. *Communicate and compute any time, anywhere* networks based on satellite systems, digital cellular phones, and personal communications services will make it even easier to coordinate work and information in many parts of the globe that cannot be reached by existing ground-based systems. Thus a salesperson in China could send an order-confirmation request to the home office in London effortlessly and expect an instant reply.

Companies are using Internet technology to construct virtual private networks (VPNs) to reduce wide area networking costs and staffing requirements. Instead of using private, leased telephone lines or frame-relay connections, the company outsources the VPN to an Internet service provider. The VPN comprises WAN links, security products, and routers, providing a secure and encrypted connection between two points across the Internet to transmit corporate data. These VPNs from Internet service providers can provide many features of a private network to firms operating internationally (see the Window on Technology). Figure 17-4 illustrates how a virtual private network (VPN) works.

However, VPNs may not provide the same level of quick and predictable response as private networks, especially during times of the day when Internet traffic is very congested. VPNs may not be able to support large numbers of remote users.

Throughout this text we have shown how the Internet facilitates global coordination, communication, and electronic business. As Internet technology becomes more widespread outside the United States, it will expand opportunities for electronic commerce and international trade. The global connectivity and low cost of Internet technology will further remove obstacles of geography and time zones for companies seeking to expand operations and sell their wares abroad. Small companies may especially benefit (Quelch and Klein, 1996).

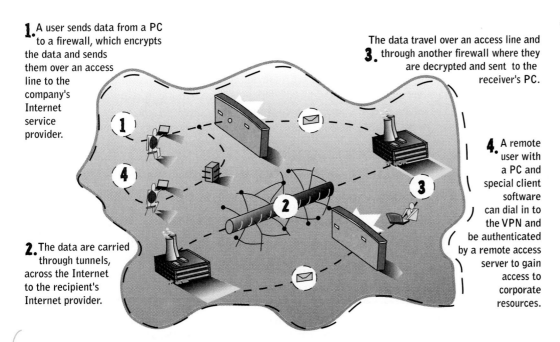

1. A user sends data from a PC to a firewall, which encrypts the data and sends them over an access line to the company's Internet service provider.

2. The data are carried through tunnels, across the Internet to the recipient's Internet provider.

3. The data travel over an access line and through another firewall where they are decrypted and sent to the receiver's PC.

4. A remote user with a PC and special client software can dial in to the VPN and be authenticated by a remote access server to gain access to corporate resources.

Figure 17-4 How a virtual private network (VPN) works. **Source:** "How It Works," Computerworld, February 2, 1998, p. 28. Copyright © 1998 by COMPUTERWORLD, Inc. Reprinted by permission.

Management Wrap-Up

Management

Managers are responsible for devising an appropriate organizational and technology infrastructure for international business. Choosing a global business strategy, identifying core business processes, organizing the firm to conduct business on an international scale, and selecting an international information systems infrastructure are key management decisions.

Organization

Cultural, political, and language diversity magnifies differences in organizational culture and standard operating procedures when companies operate internationally in various countries. These differences create barriers to the development of global information systems that transcend national boundaries.

Technology

The main technology decision in building international systems is finding a set of workable standards in hardware, software, and networking for the firm's international information systems infrastructure. The Internet and intranets will increasingly be used to provide global connectivity and to serve as a foundation for global systems, but many companies will still need proprietary systems for certain functions, and therefore international standards.

For Discussion

1. If you were a manager in a company that operates in many countries, what criteria would you use to determine whether an application should be developed as a global application or as a local application?

2. Describe ways the Internet can be used in international information systems.

Summary

1. Identify the major factors behind the growing internationalization of business. There are general cultural factors and specific business factors to consider. The growth of cheap international communication and transportation has created a world culture with stable expectations or norms. Political stability and a growing global knowledge base that is widely shared contribute also to the world culture. These general factors create the conditions for global markets, global production, coordination, distribution, and global economies of scale.

2. Compare global strategies for developing business. There are four basic international strategies: domestic exporter, multinational, franchiser, and transnational. In a transnational strategy, all factors of production are coordinated on a global scale. However, the choice of strategy is a function of the type of business and product.

3. Demonstrate how information systems support different global strategies. There is a connection between firm strategy and information systems design. Transnational firms must develop networked system configurations and permit considerable decentralization of development and operations. Franchisers almost always duplicate systems across many countries and use

centralized financial controls. Multinationals typically rely on decentralized independence among foreign units with some movement toward development of networks. Domestic exporters typically are centralized in domestic headquarters with some decentralized operations permitted.

4. Plan the development of international information systems. Implementing a global system requires an implementation strategy. Typically, global systems have evolved without a conscious plan. The remedy is to define a small subset of core business processes and focus on building systems that could support these processes. Tactically, you will have to coopt widely dispersed foreign units to participate in the development and operation of these systems, being careful to maintain overall control.

5. Evaluate the main technical alternatives in developing global systems. The main hardware and telecommunications issues are systems integration and connectivity. The choices for integration are to go either with a proprietary architecture or with an open systems technology such as UNIX. Global networks are extremely difficult to build and operate. Some measure of connectivity may be achieved by relying on local

PTT authorities to provide connections, building a system oneself, relying on private providers to supply communications capacity, or using the Internet and intranets. Companies can use Internet services to create virtual private networks (VPNs) as low-cost alternatives to global private networks. The main software issue concerns building interfaces to existing systems and providing much needed group support software.

Key Terms

Business driver, 529	Franchiser, 535	Legitimacy, 541	Transborder data flow, 532
Cooptation, 540	Global culture, 531	Multinational, 535	Transnational, 535
Core systems, 538	International information	Particularism, 532	
Domestic exporter, 535	systems infrastructure, 529		

Review Questions

1. What are the five major factors to consider when building an international information systems infrastructure?
2. Describe the five general cultural factors leading toward growth in global business and the four specific business factors. Describe the interconnection among these factors.
3. What is meant by a *global culture?*
4. What are the major challenges to the development of global systems?
5. Why have firms not planned for the development of international systems?
6. Describe the four main strategies for global business and organizational structure.
7. Describe the four different system configurations that can be used to support different global strategies.
8. What are the major management issues in developing international systems?
9. What are three principles to follow when organizing the firm for global business?
10. What are three steps of a management strategy for developing and implementing global systems?
11. What is meant by *cooptation,* and how can it be used in building global systems?
12. Describe the main technical issues facing global systems.
13. Describe three new technologies that can help firms develop global systems.

Group Project

With a group of students, identify an area of emerging information technology and explore how this technology might be useful for supporting global business strategies. For instance, you might choose an area such as digital telecommunications (e.g., electronic mail, wireless communications, value-added networks) or collaborative work group software or new standards in operating systems, EDI, or the Internet. It will be necessary to choose a business scenario to discuss the technology. You might choose, for instance, an automobile parts franchise or a clothing franchise such as the Limited Express as example businesses. What applications would you make global, what core business processes would you choose, and how would the technology be helpful?

Tools for Interactive Learning

○ Internet

The Internet Connection for this chapter will take you to a series of Web sites where you can complete an exercise to evaluate the capabilities of various global package tracking and delivery services. You can use the interactive software at a series of Web sites to complete an Electronic Commerce project for international marketing and pricing. You can also use the Interactive Study Guide to test your knowledge of the topics in this chapter and get instant feedback where you need more practice.

○ CD-ROM

If you purchase and use the Multimedia Edition CD-ROM with this chapter, you can complete an interactive exercise asking you to design a global network for a multinational corporation. You can also find a video clip illustrating the United Parcel Service International Shipping and Processing System (ISPS), an audio overview of the major themes of this chapter, and bullet text summarizing the key points of the chapter.

Although the global economy presents great opportunities for many companies, those heavily involved with it often are buffeted by its global ups and downs. The Pirelli Group, an international tire manufacturer headquartered in Milan, Italy, was forced to face the erratic nature of the global economy in the early 1990s. Automobile sales fell worldwide in those years, resulting in a concurrent drop in tire sales. Coincidentally, sales in Pirelli's second major product line, electronic cables, suffered the same fate when worldwide spending on telecommunications and energy also dropped sharply. To make matters worse, competition was intensifying as global markets developed and evolved.

Pirelli's management team had to find ways to return the company to its accustomed level of profitability and do so rapidly. The plan the team developed was not unusual in these circumstances: Focus on core products, cut costs, improve competitiveness by developing new technologies, and improve response to customer demands. The plan stressed the central role of information, including the need to access it and react to it very rapidly. Of necessity, the information technology (IT) group was vital to these changes.

In 1991, when these problems emerged, Pirelli had 102 plants in 14 countries and employed more than 51,000 people. The company also had a marketing and sales presence in many other countries. The information systems within all these countries were developed locally with no guidance from the corporate office because Pirelli had not established international standards for either hardware or software. The resulting lack of integration made data-sharing across national borders difficult and left Pirelli as something less than a genuine global company despite its presence in so many countries. Arrigo Andreoni, Pirelli's corporate director of information, concluded that to respond to the new management plan, Pirelli's worldwide IT infrastructure needed to be redesigned and standardized. "The more standardization there is," he explained, "the easier it is to implement new ideas and respond to new opportunities." Key to his approach was his belief that IT "must be in tune with the overall business strategy."

One fundamental element of Andreoni's strategy was the establishment of a full-fledged global network. Each national unit is to be linked to the Milan headquarters by the year 2000 so that corporate management will have immediate and complete access to the information it needs to carry out its executive and planning functions. The infrastructure will be built on open systems so that data can be moved from site to site with ease. The strategy also has a companywide groupware platform that includes office automation, personal computing, e-mail, and work-flow software. All of this is aimed at providing employees with the tools they need while instituting standardization that enables communication from person to person regardless of the location of the employee.

The centerpiece of the new infrastructure is Andreoni's goal of installing the same comprehensive, integrated software at all Pirelli sites throughout the world. He selected SAP's R/3 as that software. R/3 is a client-server–based ERP system that includes integrated modules for production, factory automation, finance, sales, purchasing, and personnel (see the Chapter 12 case study and Chapter 18). Andreoni hoped R/3 could act as a catalyst for companywide reengineering. However, finding and selecting the best software package was actually the easy part. Implementing R/3 in Pirelli's multinational environment of local control was the more challenging problem and is the stage at which many such projects flounder.

The most conspicuous problems to be faced were the different languages, currencies, legal systems, and tax laws in each of the locations. However, corporate culture presented an even more formidable hurdle because the local units were used to making their own decisions and building their own systems to meet their specific local needs. Andreoni decided that before he proceeded with the project, he had to travel to Pirelli sites throughout the world, visiting and meeting with local Pirelli organizations. He needed not only to sell his approach, but also to gather information on the local systems and the stages of development at each site.

To implement his strategy, Andreoni developed an approach he calls "democratic governance." His goal was to achieve standardization in each of the core areas while leaving each local unit to maintain its local culture and projects. In this way, for example, the local unit would be able to address its own language, currency, and legal needs. He also did not want to impose an overly rapid companywide implementation of the new system in the core areas. He believes in moving ahead with small steps, explaining, "If a CEO of a particular unit does not view SAP as a real competitive weapon, we don't want to insist. We wait until the CEO is open to the idea, then we explain what the technology does and offer to implement the changeover." He adds, however, "We in information technology must be ready at the crucial time when the culture is changing." Pirelli companies are allowed to implement SAP in tune with their local requirements, but Andreoni encourages them to avoid unnecessary customizations. They must justify local differences in the system by demands in the local market.

Andreoni also believes in moving ahead at a carefully measured pace after a local unit is ready to make the changeover. His approach is to begin with a pilot project for one specific function within a specified Pirelli national unit. He is careful to select a function with a strong likelihood of success. In Spain, tire distribution was selected as the pilot project. In Scandinavia, because electronic commerce already is widely accepted, the pilot project was the use of the Internet for transacting business. After the pilot is successful, staff support will grow for the overall project, and the pilot becomes a prototype for the implementation of the rest of the system.

Pirelli units had to maintain their old systems as they made the changeover to R/3. In each country, they relied on outsourcing to handle both the new and old systems. Selection of outsourcing vendors was based on local conditions. In Italy, for example, IBM Global Services helped Pirelli with its legacy mainframe applications. Pirelli staff were trained by working alongside the outsourcing consultants.

Pirelli is developing a full-fledged global network by linking a UNIX server in each country with the company's global headquarters in Milan. By the year 2000, this network will provide company management with complete and immediate access to information from its worldwide operations. Local units with appropriate management approval in turn will have total access to company information. This open systems environment, along with the integration in operations provided by R/3, will allow all information to move from and through fully integrated platforms. One platform is for queries, corporate reporting, data modeling, navigation, and financial systems. A groupware platform will feature office automation, personal computing, e-mail, multimedia, image processing, and work-flow management. A research and development platform will include CAD/CAM, simulations, and test data systems.

What has been the effect of this global IT program? The Pirelli IT department itself has been reduced from 700 personnel to 562, a drop of nearly 20 percent, and it is scheduled to fall to 490 (30 percent) by the year 2000. The decline in IT staff is a direct result of the growing standardization; software and hardware support are much less labor-intensive. For example, before standardization, Scandinavia,

France, Switzerland, Austria, and the Benelux countries each had an independent, full-service, back-office operation to support its sales function. Today, they share one back-office operation located in Basel, Switzerland. However, the local front-end systems that were used to deal directly with customers were left intact. Today, Pirelli does rely more on information technology despite the drop in IT staff, as is clear from the fact that IT expenditures have grown from 1.5 percent of Pirelli revenues in 1993 to 1.64 percent in 1997. The IT effort has supported other changes within the company as Pirelli has reduced the number of plant facilities from 102 to 74. At the same time, Pirelli's staff has fallen by nearly 30 percent, from 51,572 to 36,534.

All of this has shown up on the bottom line. Company debt fell 56 percent between 1991 and 1995. Net income in 1996 was up 43 percent from the previous year. This is so despite the fact that the project was not yet fully implemented. As for Andreoni, he says that he spends a majority of his time interacting with top Pirelli management and with the CEOs in

the various countries. His task, he says, is "explaining our proposals and the reasons for them. In short, I market IT's ideas to the rest of the company."

Sources: Dr. Edward Wakin, "Global Strategies Drive Pirelli," **Beyond Computing**, January–February 1998; and Robert L. Scheier, "IT Budgets Dodge Global Downturn," **Computerworld**, October 26, 1998.

CASE STUDY QUESTIONS

1. What kind of global business strategy is Pirelli pursuing?

2. Analyze Pirelli's problems using the competitive forces and value chain models. How well did Pirelli's information systems support its business strategy?

3. What problems did Pirelli's systems have? What management, organization, and technology factors were responsible for these problems?

4. Analyze Pirelli's strategy for dealing with these problems in relation to its global business strategy. Do you agree with this strategy?

Chapter 18

Managing Firm Infrastructure and Enterprise Systems

Learning Objectives

After completing this chapter, you will be able to:

1. Describe the features of enterprise computing and industrial networks.

2. Explain the business and technology drivers behind enterprise computing and industrial networks.

3. Identify the elements and key decisions in building an information technology (IT) infrastructure.

4. Compare the basic vision of enterprise systems and industrial networks with the management reality.

5. Plan the development of enterprise systems and industrial networks.

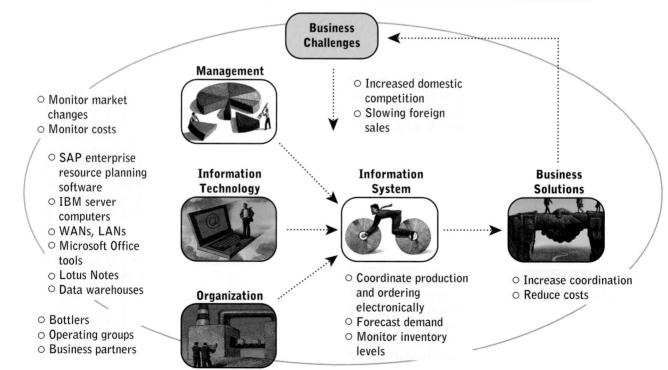

Business Challenges

Management
- Monitor market changes
- Monitor costs

- Increased domestic competition
- Slowing foreign sales

Information Technology
- SAP enterprise resource planning software
- IBM server computers
- WANs, LANs
- Microsoft Office tools
- Lotus Notes
- Data warehouses

- Bottlers
- Operating groups
- Business partners

Organization

Information System
- Coordinate production and ordering electronically
- Forecast demand
- Monitor inventory levels

Business Solutions
- Increase coordination
- Reduce costs

Coca-Cola Creates
an Extended Enterprise

Coca-Cola is one of the most recognized companies on Earth; its soft drink empire reaches nearly 200 countries. Although it dominates most world markets, the company faces very tough business challenges. Coca-Cola today derives 63 percent of its revenue from countries outside North America. Sales growth has slowed in Russia, Asia, and Latin America because of their weakened economies, and Coke faces competition domestically from new products such as bottled waters and health drinks. PepsiCo Inc., the company's main rival, recently restructured its North American business to take away some of Coke's market share.

Coke is counting on a major information systems initiative to stay competitive. It is implementing SAP enterprise resource planning (ERP) software

within its own organization and extending this system to other companies, such as its major bottling partners. The new system will link Coke and its partners together into an extended enterprise where they can pool resources, share best practices, and leverage their combined size to obtain lower raw material costs. Another goal is to share sales information and increase communication with partners in order to react rapidly to market changes and deploy products efficiently to the places where they are most likely to sell.

Creating an interconnected enterprise requires a standard information architecture that allows all participants to share data and that provides a standard view of the business in terms of brands, customers, and packages. Once completed, Coca-Cola should be able to answer questions such as what bottling plant and what channel were used to sell Coca-Cola in a 500 milliliter plastic bottle in a Singapore supermarket, and Coke should also achieve better control over its supply chain. Improved forecasting and production planning also will help Coca-Cola and its partners reduce the costs of making and shipping products.

The enterprise system is being implemented in stages, with financial, purchasing, human resource, and project management modules rolled out first, followed by modules for production and materials management, plant maintenance, and sales and distribution. Coke and its partners will be able to exchange electronic purchase orders and key inventory information. Expanded data warehouses for each of Coke's five major operating groups in North America, Europe, the Middle East, and Asia will capture more detailed sales and promotional data and link to the SAP enterprise resource planning system modules to integrate this information with details from manufacturing, finance, and procurement. Coke and its partners should emerge with a very clear picture of market demand and trends that will help them deliver products more efficiently.

The enterprise system requires a common information architecture to make data flow seamlessly. The architecture includes standards for desktop and server software, hardware (IBM Netfinity servers running Windows NT and RS/6000 servers running the AIX version of UNIX), network services (frame relay running on all WANs and the Windows NT operating system for all LANs), document technology, security, and applications. Desktops use Microsoft Office productivity tools, Internet Explorer, and Windows 95, along with Lotus Notes as a common e-mail system.

Coca-Cola's bottlers are independent companies, locally owned and operated, which are authorized to package and sell Coca-Cola soft drinks using centrally established quality and uniformity standards. Coke had to make special efforts to convince them to participate in the ERP system. All of the company's 11 anchor bottlers (major partners in which Coke has a controlling stake) are rolling out the ERP applications at their own pace. Coke hopes that many more of the 1000 other bottlers it uses around the world will eventually switch to the new system as well.

Coke is now working on establishing electronic links to customers such as Burger King, McDonald's, and Wal-Mart and other business partners such as Alcoa, Reynolds Metals, and Archer Daniels Midland. Coke's electronic integration both internally and with other companies should prove to be a powerful weapon.

Sources: Bob Violino, "Extended Enterprise," *Information Week,* March 22, 1999; Constance L. Hays, "Pulp Friction," *The New York Times,* May 19, 1999; and www.coca-cola.com.

Management Challenges

The opening vignette presents the potential rewards to firms with well-conceived systems linking the entire enterprise and organizations within the same industry. Coca-Cola and its bottlers and business partners would not be able to succeed at this task without a significant amount of organizational and management change. Moreover, to be successful in developing industry-wide enterprise systems, organizations have to work together for a common goal. These changes are generally very difficult to make, especially over a long period of time. Enterprise systems, and the related phenomenon of industrial networks, raise the following management challenges:

1. **Enlarging the scope of management thinking.** Most managers are trained to manage a product line, a division, or an office. They are rarely trained to optimize the performance of the organization as a whole, and often are not given the means to do so. But enterprise systems and industrial networks required managers to take a much larger view of their own behavior, to include other products, divisions, departments, and even outside business firms.

Investments in enterprise systems are huge, they must be developed over long periods of time, and they must be guided by a shared vision of the objectives. For many firms, it is very difficult to develop a shared, enterprise-wide vision of the firm to guide system investments.

2. **Technological complexity.** Enterprise systems and industrial networks are built on powerful new technologies that require very different skill sets than do legacy, mainframe systems. Most large or-

ganizations still require the use of large-scale, mainframe, legacy systems. Managers are finding it very challenging to manage the technological complexity of different platforms and to harness the technological power of new enterprise technology.

18.1 Managing IT Infrastructure and Architecture: Enterprise Computing

This chapter is concerned with the creation of new information flows across entire organizations and industries through enterprise-wide computing and computer-based industrial networks. Until the past decade, very few firms had developed a firmwide view of their own information systems. They had simply built systems incrementally with piecemeal solutions to specific problems. Firms invested in information technology based on the specific needs of specific applications. We can call this pattern an **application specific view** of a firm's systems. In general, CEOs and financial planners in firms measured the success of IT investments one system at a time, using standard return-on-investment methods.

The application specific view allows organizations with limited resources to concentrate on solving their most immediate problems. However, the applications approach to information system investments in most firms has led to highly uncoordinated information system capabilities, very poor communication between systems built at different times, a limited ability of managers to control or even understand the overall organization (as opposed to specific segments), and little understanding by senior management of precisely how the IT investment supported the overall strategic goals of the corporation. More importantly, there is no overall plan for the evolution of computing in such firms.

In this traditional organizational setting, the key elements of the value chain have been controlled by separate and disparate information systems that could not communicate with each other. Not only did firms not take an integrated view of their own business processes, they had an equally dim understanding of how their systems related to the systems of their suppliers, competitors, support organizations, distributors, and customers. (See Figure 18-1.)

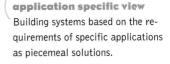

application specific view
Building systems based on the requirements of specific applications as piecemeal solutions.

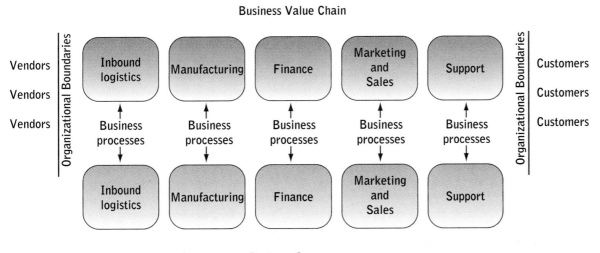

Figure 18-1 Traditional view of systems. In the traditional organization—which includes most of today's organizations—separate systems built over a long period of time support discrete business processes and discrete segments of the business value chain. Vendors and customers are rarely considered a part of an organization's systems. Firm boundaries tend to be impermeable, tightly controlled, and a part of the hierarchy.

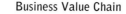

Business Value Chain

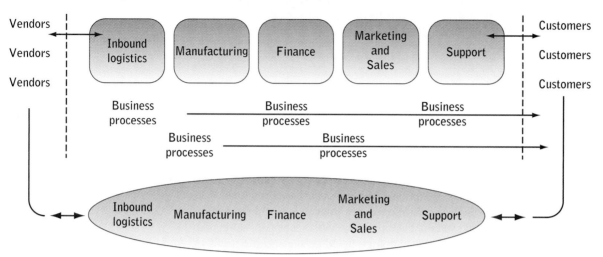

Enterprise Business Systems

Figure 18-2 Enterprise view of systems. Enterprise systems potentially can integrate the key business processes of an entire firm into a single software and hardware system. Customers and vendors are consciously included in business process and business systems operation and even development. Organizational boundaries become permeable but are still manageable and controllable.

In this traditional environment, simple but important business questions could not be answered. For instance, sales personnel could not tell at the time of order entry what was in inventory; customers could not track their orders; manufacturing could not communicate easily with finance to plan for new production. And often manufacturing did not know what was in its own warehouse because that was a separate system.

But in recent years there has been a revolution in systems planning and design. In this new view, managers take an integrated firmwide view of their IT investments and choices, and consider how to design and build firmwide system solutions that integrate the key business processes within a firm, and even integrate business processes across an entire industry. This revolution in the planning and design of systems is called **enterprise computing** (see Figure 18-2). Until recently, this feat was technically impossible. Today it is technically possible but organizationally difficult.

This chapter describes how to develop an enterprise-wide view of your firm and how to implement enterprise systems in your firm, and across an entire industry. We begin by defining some basic terms: IT investment portfolio, firm infrastructure and architecture, and enterprise systems. Then we examine the main business drivers that are causing firms to develop enterprise- and industry-wide system architectures. We then examine more closely the dynamics of enterprise systems and industry networks. We conclude with a discussion of the steps you need to take in order to develop firmwide and industry-wide architectures.

enterprise computing

Firmwide information systems that integrate key business processes within the firm or business processes shared by multiple firms.

Basic Concepts of Enterprise Computing

There are four management concepts that are required for understanding enterprise computing. These concepts include the information technology (IT) investment portfolio, information technology (IT) infrastructure, business logic, and information architecture; they are summarized in Table 18.1. We have introduced some of these concepts in earlier chapters.

Firms invest capital in information technology and purchase a portfolio of information technology investments. For some firms—in retail and financial services—the IT investment is the largest part of capital spending. For the U.S. economy as a whole, IT investment represents about 25 percent of all capital investment. Like any other capital investment, the key

Table 18.1 Basic Concepts of Enterprise Computing

Concept	Measure	Key Questions
IT investment portfolio	Benchmark competitors' expenditures	Are we spending too much, or too little on IT? Are we receiving a good return on investment?
IT infrastructure	Lists of technical capabilities	Do we have the technical capability to achieve our strategic objectives?
Business logic	Descriptions of business model and processes	How do we plan to make money and what business activities and processes should we emphasize?
IT architecture	Descriptions of systems that support business model and processes	Do we have the right systems environment and applications to implement the business logic?

question here is whether or not the firm is receiving a good return on its investment in information technology. And, when compared with competitors, are we spending too much or too little? Notice that this is not the same question as "does this particular system show a sizable return on our investment?" Instead, the key question from the firmwide or enterprise-wide view is whether or not the entire **information technology (IT) investment portfolio** is returning an acceptable benefit to the firm given the competitive circumstances. The nature of the benefits may be financial returns in the short term, or long-term strategic positioning, or market share. There are many challenges in addressing this issue, one of which includes using reasonable numbers to determine the financial aspect of the question. A second and altogether different challenge is understanding precisely how the firm's strategic position is affected by the firmwide IT investment. Many firms recognize that it may be necessary to accept a low financial return on investment for a few years in order to establish a market-dominating strategic position.

The investment in information technology results in the purchase of IT equipment, software, and human resources required to operate the equipment. Broadly speaking, this is the firm's *information technology (IT) infrastructure*. The IT infrastructure, a concept we introduced in Chapter 1, is essentially a bill of materials that can be described in terms of a list of hardware, software, and employees. In turn, this bill of materials has certain technical capabilities such as total processing power, average transaction throughput, and telecommunications bandwidth. Like any other infrastructural system (electrical, telephone, plumbing, etc.), key questions are, "Has our firm made the right choices in the purchase of processor hardware, telecommunications, software, and human resources in the various supply markets?" and "More important, do we have the technical capability to achieve the business's strategic objectives?" Obviously, if poor choices are made, there will be a very low return on the IT portfolio. Right choices generally mean being reliable, cost efficient, extensible, and supportable. But right choices also suggest that the infrastructure must support the strategic business interests of the firm. The challenge in addressing these issues is that there are no simple quantitative measures of right choices.

The third ingredient in enterprise computing is the **business logic.** Put simply, business logic involves an assessment of how your firm plans to make money, and what specific business processes need to be defined to make money. If you're an Internet company, your business logic might be, "We're going to give away free on-line services and draw a huge international audience. Then we will charge advertisers for space on our Web site. In order to do this, we need to develop a very attractive site and build a database of knowledge for users to visit, a chat capability, and a customer database that tracks their use of our site. We believe the advertising revenues of the site will far exceed its operational costs."

Last, in order for the IT infrastructure to be useful in supporting the business logic, managers have to design real-world applications, systems, and networks that explicitly support the

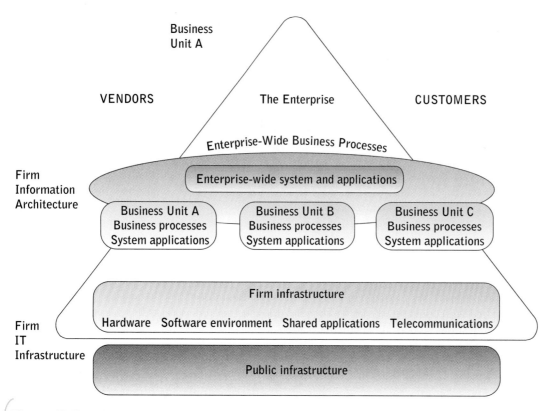

Figure 18-3 Enterprise computing concepts. Enterprise computing is based on an organization-wide view of the firm's business processes, information architecture, and information technology (IT) infrastructure, including the organization's use of public infrastructure, such as the Internet.

key business processes. The resulting set of applications, and their relationship to the firm's business logic, is a firm's *information architecture* or overall IT form and shape. Information architecture, which we first described in Chapter 1, is where the hardware meets the business.

Information architecture generally cannot be portrayed simply as a list of applications but, just like an understanding of a house architecture, requires instead a graphic plan and descriptions that systematically relate business processes and IT form. The key questions of information architecture are: Have we used the infrastructure so as to optimize the business processes? Have we made the correct design and implementation decisions? How well have we converted the IT investment into meaningful business value?

Of all the questions in enterprise computing, the architecture questions are perhaps the most difficult to answer. Nevertheless, clearly some firms get more business value out of the same financial investments, and the same infrastructures, than do other firms. By benchmarking your firm's performance on key IT investments, infrastructures, and architectures, you can begin to determine whether your firm has made the correct choices, or where you have made mistakes.

Figure 18-3 illustrates the relationship among the key concepts in enterprise computing.

Industrial Networks and Trans-enterprise Systems

It's a short step from enterprise systems to industrial networks of systems. Instead of thinking about the systems in a firm, think about the systems of all the firms in an entire industry. Now ask, "What would happen if we connected the major enterprise systems of firms in an entire industry?" Computer-based industrial networks are logical extensions of enterprise systems at the industry level. (See Figure 18-4.)

industrial networks Networks linking the systems of multiple firms in an industry. Also called extended enterprises.

Industrial networks, which are sometimes called *extended enterprises,* link together the enterprise systems of multiple firms in an industry. For instance, Procter & Gamble, the world's largest consumer goods company, developed an integrated industry-wide system that

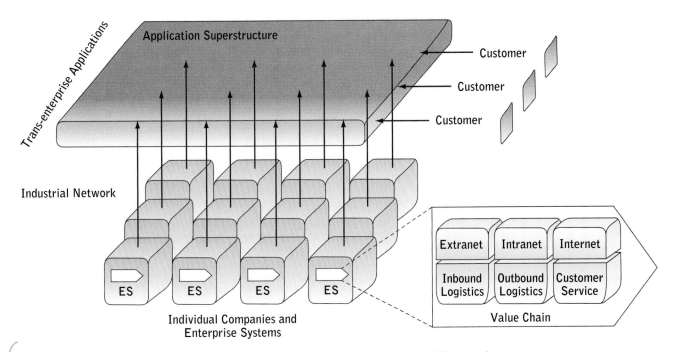

Figure 18-4 Industrial networks. Industrial networks link the enterprise systems of firms in the same industry. The application superstructure serve the entire network. © 1998 The Concours Group and Edward M. Roche. All rights reserved. Used with permission.

coordinated grocery store point-of-sale systems with grocery store warehouses and shippers, and its own manufacturing facilities and suppliers of raw materials. This single industry spanning system effectively allowed P&G to monitor the movement of all its products from raw materials to customer purchase.

In the next decade, the emergence of industrial networks will change greatly how products are produced and distributed, which will change the economics and alter the competitive forces of entire industries. We discuss these changes and the issues raised by industrial networks in a later section.

Business Drivers: The Changing Business Environment

The development of enterprise systems within single firms and the emergence of industrial networks or trans-enterprise systems both represent a fundamental change in thinking about firms and industries. Table 18.2 lists a number of factors in today's business environment that are driving the development of enterprise systems and industrial networks.

Enterprise planning and systems have become necessary for corporate survival and success today because of a number of changes in the environments of business.

Markets

The globalization of markets has greatly increased competition in traditional industries and squeezed margins. This affects traditional industries the most because knowing how to produce these products has spread throughout the world. An explosion of information technologies from e-commerce and the Internet to digital product registries and exchanges has further intensified price competition in traditional industries. Suppliers, customers, and distributors now have more information than before on price and availability. Insofar as profit margins are based in part on asymmetries in the distribution of information, IT has lowered margins. Certain nontraditional industries have not yet felt these impacts because what they do is not yet known globally, and local or regional geographical factors are still important sources of information and knowledge asymmetry. Both of these factors—globalization and information intensity—cause firms to seek out cost reduction, margin strengthening strategies, and systems like enterprise systems.

Table 18.2	**Business Drivers of Enterprise Systems: Changing Environments**

Business Driver	Impact
Market change	Globalization and increasing information intensity reduce margins in traditional industries.
Industry change	Mergers, acquisitions, and consolidations in traditional industries increase scale economies and intensify industry competition.
Firm-level change	Business process redesign efforts of the 1990s in traditional industries force jettisoning legacy systems and highlight the need for enterprise-wide systems to support the newly defined business processes.
Product change	The growth of information, knowledge, and high-tech-based products shortens product cycle times; increasing information intensity of traditional products and services shortens cycle times.
Management process thinking	From discrete business process focus toward a view of the firm as an integrated set of processes; from neoclassical competition firm-based views toward industry-based views of cooperation and alliance.
Management strategy	Growing belief that information architecture investments could lead to unique knowledge that could not be purchased on input factor markets.

Industries

In many traditional industries the nature of competition has shifted from product innovation to scale economies. This has spurred a recent wave of mergers, acquisitions, and consolidations, especially in the United States, as firms seek out these scale economies through acquisitions. The merging of firms frequently is the occasion for a careful examination of systems; often the new scale of operations simply cannot be supported by traditional legacy systems. Enterprise systems promise some of the benefits of acquisitions. Industry networks promise to deliver scale economies without experiencing the costs of merging and acquiring.

Firms and Organizations

In the 1990s managers tried to reinvent their firms using business process redesign. They discovered that they did not have the systems in place to support the newly invented business processes, and that the trick was not to optimize discrete businesses in isolation from one another but instead to optimize the full set of processes that constitute the business.

The widespread acceptance and understanding of business process thinking that requires firms to develop horizontal links among otherwise separate divisions and departments inherently raises the visibility of poorly performing legacy systems that cannot support the new business processes. It suggests firms take an enterprise-wide view of systems. Enterprise systems promise to optimize the firm as a whole. Industry networks promise to optimize both the firm and industry performance resulting in greater consumer welfare and firm profits.

Products and Services

Information technology–based products and services have grown to a larger percentage of gross domestic product (GDP) than before, while the production and distribution of traditional products has become increasingly information-intense. The unique feature of information and knowledge-based products and services is the speed with which they change because of the rapid change in underlying information technology. Reduced new product lifecycle times,

Table 18.3 Technology Drivers of Enterprise Systems and Industrial Networks

Technology Driver	Nature of Change
Relational database technology	Relational technology approaches hierarchical database speeds but with greatly enhanced flexibility.
Reductions in storage costs	Storage devices double in capacity every six months.
Expanded public network infrastructure	Open Internet networking technologies cause network costs to plunge; digital communication costs drop by a factor of $1000\times$ in the 1990s; public switched network and dedicated Internet trunk lines displace proprietary networks and make transcompany information transfers commonplace; development of common protocols—XML, HTTP, TCP/IP.
Deployment of client/server	Client/server becomes the dominant mode of computing causing major drops in information storage, processing, and distribution costs in the 1990s.
Evolution of desktop computing	Desktop computing becomes the dominant mode of information distribution and 60 percent of the labor force comes online at work, greatly increasing the role of information in the firm.
Enterprise software and crossware	Enterprise software emerges with standardized applications in an integrated environment that greatly reduces the costs of enterprise systems.

faster required market response times, and increased manufacturing flexibility requirements force managers to devise ways to speed up product innovation, speed up response to market conditions, and increase microcontrol over manufacturing. Enterprise systems promise to deliver solutions to these problems by enhancing management controls over purchase, manufacturing, finance, and sales. Industrial networks promise to increase greatly production and distribution efficiencies and to enhance the ability of firms to know about and respond to industry and market conditions.

Management Process Thinking

A keen understanding among managers of the interconnectedness of businesses and industries and economies is another important driver of enterprise systems. Prior to the 1990s, the dominant paradigm of business rested on neoclassical economics and emphasized the individual firm in a competitive environment. Inevitably this led to focusing on optimizing the value chain in each firm. But in the emerging networked environment of the late 1990s, managers began to understand that the efficiency of their individual firms—and ultimately the cost and quality of goods delivered to the consumer—depended in part on optimizing the value chain of the entire organization and the entire industry. Both enterprise systems and industry networks promise to deliver these efficiencies.

Management Strategic Thinking

There has been a growing awareness among managers and academics that firms could compete on the basis of their systems architecture and infrastructure. The nature of this strategic advantage seemed to lie in two areas: (1) superior self-knowledge of their own costs, operations, and customers and (2) a keen awareness of market conditions (e.g., price, delivery, and quality). These advantages could not be purchased in external markets (like so many other technical advances); they could only be attained through the difficult and costly path of building powerful infrastructures and appropriate architectures. Once they were successfully built,

Figure 18-5 An ideal model for planning enterprise systems. Ideally, in order to optimize the return on IT investments, management decisions about firm infrastructure should be driven by business strategy, business models, business processes, and information architecture decisions.

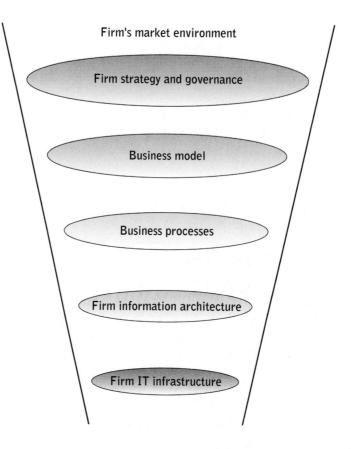

Firm's market environment

Firm strategy and governance

Business model

Business processes

Firm information architecture

Firm IT infrastructure

it would take competitors years to build competing infrastructures, and there was always the possibility the competitors would stumble in the process. Enterprise systems and industry networks are among the tools capable of fulfilling these strategic ambitions.

Technology Drivers: The New Networked Environment

Table 18.3 lists six technology drivers behind the new networked environment: evolution of relational database technology, radical reductions in storage costs, greatly expanded public network infrastructure, the rapid deployment of client/server architecture, the evolution of desktop computing, and the emergence of enterprise software packages and crossware.

These technological advances show that for the first time in history there are information technologies capable of tightly coupling and coordinating the microdecisions of entire firms and industries. Networks are so powerful that much of the coordination economies heretofore achieved through vertical and horizontal integration (mergers and acquisitions) can be achieved through networks (see Chapters 2 and 3). By keeping firm size relatively small (rather than getting bigger and bigger), *agency costs* can be kept to a minimum. Coordinating industry networks also permits lowering *transaction costs* when compared to pure market situations. Industry networks are so valuable that it is possible in some instances to move from a competitive strategy to a cooperative strategy in an industry in order to maximize firm profits.

Potentially, firms that adopt enterprise systems, and participate in the development of industry networks, should be able to compete more effectively through lower agency costs, lower transaction costs, greater reach and range, and greater agility.

An Ideal Model of Enterprise Computing

Ideally there should be a connection between business environments, business strategy, and the IT portfolio of investments, infrastructure, architecture, and business processes. Moreover, in the ideal world, the business environment and strategy should be the main driving force behind decisions about IT infrastructure and information architecture. Figure 18-5 depicts this ideal world.

In order to optimize the return on investment in IT infrastructure four conditions must be present. First, just enough infrastructure should be purchased to adequately support the firm's business processes and overall strategy. Second, there should be a close coupling between the architecture (the design of the IT) and the business processes it is intended to support. Third, the firm must possess an adequate strategy to cope with a rapidly shifting environment and competitive pressures. Last, the firm must have an adequate governance model that permits the rational alignment of IT infrastructure to business strategy. Put in colloquial terms, the senior managers of the firm must first decide "who we are and where we want to be in five years" before they can answer the question of how to get there. The Window on Technology describes the experience of one company that revamped its infrastructure to better support its business strategy.

Of course the real world is quite different from the ideal world. Realistically, CIOs and CEOs inherit a collection of infrastructural capabilities that had evolved over decades, generally in response to crises. Typically, the firm's legacy information architecture does not support newly designed business processes; the new, reengineered business processes in turn are themselves islands in a sea of inherited legacy business practices from long ago. And senior management often does not sufficiently understand the identity of the firm to establish a clear-cut five-year objective.

The challenge then for managers as we describe in this chapter is to bridge the gap between the ideal world described in Figure 18-5 and the typical reality faced by senior managers.

18.2 Managing the New IT Infrastructure

A new IT infrastructure is essential for enabling day-to-day operations based on the smooth flow of information from the environment to the organization and within the organization itself. It serves as the platform for executing business strategy, coping with environmental change, and providing a new set of skills and processes for its management (see Figure 18-6).

Elements of the New IT Infrastructure

Four major system infrastructures exist: legacy systems, client/server, Internet/intranets, and wireless/cellular communications. A large amount of corporate computing is still based on client/server architecture to the desktop, backed up by legacy system mainframe applications and databases. This traditional infrastructure must now be integrated with the public Internet, and corporate intranets and extranets. In addition, a new mobile workforce is now using portable PC and PDA (personal digital assistants) devices that must have nearly equal access to corporate data. Complicating matters even more, each firm often has to interact with the systems of other firms.

The old legacy infrastructure was comparatively simple: It involved mainframe computers, controlled by a single IS department, using well-integrated and defined software and telecommunications (often from the same vendor as the computer). The new infrastructure environment has changed significantly. The new environment has four major features described in the following sections.

Reliance on Networked Desktop and Personal Device Computing

Today's firms rely extensively on networked desktop computers supported by many vendors, communications firms, and software companies. The desktop itself has been extended to a larger workspace that includes mobile personal information devices from PalmPilots to programmable mobile phones and pagers. Coordinating and integrating these new devices into a single coherent corporate architecture is a major management challenge.

Rise of the Internet

In just a few years the Internet and related technologies have become central components of the firm's IT infrastructure. The Internet, and corporate intranets and extranets, are becoming a major communication channel with customers, employees, vendors, and distributors.

Growing Significance of Public Infrastructure

In the past there was a boundary between public and private infrastructures, such as the telephone system and corporate computing. Today the boundaries between public and private infrastructures are blurring as more organizations incorporate the Internet into their IT infrastructure or use

Harley-Davidson Fights Back with Its IT Infrastructure

Harley-Davidson is on a roll. Its logo is a popular tattoo and customers are willing to wait up to two years for its legendary motorcycles to be delivered. Yet, 15 years ago, it was on the brink of bankruptcy. A new management team has been implementing an ambitious plan to restore Harley as an American icon and world-class competitor. Product sales have soared from $757 million in 1988 to $1.8 billion in 1998.

Information technology is a key ingredient in the company's plans for growth and for staving off a new wave of competition at home and from Japan. New technology investments will increase production from 150,000 motorcycles per year in 1998 to a capacity of more than 200,000 annually by 2003 and they will also reduce production and inventory costs by $40 million. Accomplishing these goals requires upgrading Harley-Davidson's information technology (IT) infrastructure.

In the past, IT played a minor role at the company. Harley's IT budget was only 1.3 percent of its revenue in 1994, merely enough to "tread water," according to Cory Mason, Harley's director of IS for production. The information systems organization was functionally oriented, with a hierarchical structure that did not work well with the company's decentralized management. Three standing committees known as "circles of leadership" for (1) customers, (2) production, and (3) corporate support manage the company and report directly to CEO Jeffrey Bleustein. Harley had an antiquated parts distribution system with information systems that were much too paper intensive. Orders were printed out and handed to employees who would walk over and pick supplies off warehouse shelves. Filling parts orders took up to 12 days, compared to 3 days or less among Harley's competitors.

Harley reorganized the information systems department around the "circles of leadership," doubled IT staff to 180 employees, and invested in new hardware, software, and applications that would make its spending and supplier relationships more efficient and capable of handling future production growth. The company has installed Manugistics' supply-chain software to run on Windows NT computers, supported by an Oracle database. Harley acquired Parametric's Pro-E computer-aided design and manufacturing software to support more than 5000 users internally and among its motorcycle component suppliers. Metaphase product-data management tools were employed to create a custom Web browser interface for 400 UNIX workstations used by purchasing, inspection, manufacturing, and dealer support at eight locations. Through this interface, users can search current and historical parts drawings stored in a special data vault repository running on an Oracle database. In the past, new drawings had to be shipped overnight throughout the company, and users were never sure they had the latest version of a drawing. Harley's parts suppliers will be given security clearance to access the drawings so that the suppliers can collaborate more closely with Harley staffers, eventually saving the company $40 million in product development and manufacturing costs.

Harley built a new 250,000-square-foot distribution center in Franklin, Wisconsin, close to its corporate headquarters and installed a new warehouse management and shipping system on IBM AS/400 minicomputers. Productivity doubled, and order-fulfillment time dropped to only two days. Harley uses an AS/400 electronic data interchange (EDI) system running on a value-added network to communicate inventory needs to its suppliers. Harley uses American Software Inc.'s AS/400 manufacturing suite at all of its manufacturing facilities.

Harley is working on a data warehouse system that will initially support a customer relationship management application and later financial and warranty applications. Other IT infrastructure improvements include a new human resources management system based on PeopleSoft's application package, an intranet, and upgrades to 3000 desktops for new versions of Microsoft Office productivity tools and the Windows operating system.

To Think About: How is Harley-Davidson's IT infrastructure related to its business strategy? What management, organization, and technology issues had to be addressed when rebuilding this infrastructure?

Sources: Nick Wreden, "Connecting Suppliers to an Electronic Highway," *Beyond Computing,* March 1999; and Bruce Caldwell, "Harley Shifts into Higher Gear," *Information Week,* November 30, 1998.

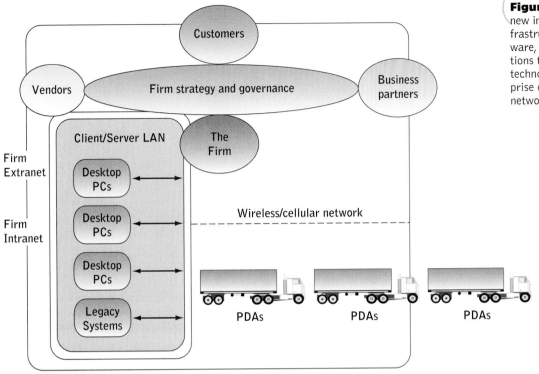

public network services and electronic devices in their systems. In making infrastructure decisions today, a firm has to consider existing and emerging public infrastructures.

Reliance on Third Parties

In the past, firms generally built their own software and developed their own IT/IS facilities. Today this is far less true. In most large firms today, the IS department is increasingly a manager of packages purchased from third-party vendors than it is a developer of entire systems. Today firms outsource a significant part of their transaction processing to third parties.

Key Infrastructure Decisions

As we pointed out in Chapter 1, information technologies enable key business processes and business models (business logic). Therefore, the choice of technology must be guided by a keen understanding of the current and future business model. The overarching question is "What business capabilities are we seeking?"

There are four key infrastructure decisions involving shared facilities: processor family, software environment, shared applications, and telecommunications (see Table 18.4). The central issues in processor or hardware families involve scale, leverage, and future trajectory. Processor families firmwide should be chosen only if they can scale up in the future to meet firm needs, and only if they can leverage existing IT assets. This generally means that new processor families, for example, Windows-based Intel processor workstations, must be able to work with existing legacy systems (usually through the development of middleware that translates legacy mainframe data into a form usable by these machines). In addition, the future direction of the technology must be understood so as to avoid building new legacy systems that cannot change to meet future requirements. For instance, firms should avoid processor families that may be at the end of their useful life spans, or hold an uncertain future. Two major client/server platforms to decide between are UNIX (including AS/400) and Windows 2000/NT.

The key issues in firmwide software environments involve whether to build your own environment; buy a packaged application-oriented, enterprise environment like SAP; or rely

Table 18.4 Key Infrastructure Decisions

Technology	Typical Choices	Criteria
Processors	S/390, UNIX, AS/400, WINTEL	Scale, leverage, technology trajectory
Software environment	Custom/SAP/PeopleSoft/Baan/Oracle/DB2	Scale, leverage, technology trajectory
Shared applications	Enterprise (Global)/Regional/SBU/Local	Business logic, governance
Telecommunications	Global and local, public/private/firm	Business model and strategy

on an external general-purpose database vendor like Oracle or IBM's DB2. Building your own software environment generally means hiring a large staff of application developers and relying on "crossware" or middleware to integrate new applications into existing legacy systems. This involves great complexity but assures a customized software solution. However, most firms today are moving away from self-developed environments and toward either enterprise packages or database environments that come with entire development tool sets that reduce the complexity of having hundreds of incompatible development tools and crossware products (see Figure 18-7). These moves toward enterprise-wide solutions are also fraught with risks and rapid and deep organizational changes. They require entire new skill sets than those that exist in most organizations. We discuss these difficulties in the next section.

Infrastructure software applications also involve questions of the location of software development. There are four options: enterprise-wide, regional, product of business unit, and local. A number of business factors are pushing organizations toward enterprise-wide software solutions—globalization, customer demand for a single "organizational face," and cost pressures. For instance, enterprise-wide order entry, cash flow, and capital budgeting are typical global applications where a single system might make sense. Yet clearly certain kinds of applications—payroll for instance—are best done locally.

The central questions in telecommunications infrastructure involve the choice between global and local solutions, and private versus public solutions. In general, as manufacturing and distribution become more global, local telecommunications solutions are expensive and

Figure 18-7 Migration toward integration of software applications. Firms are slowly moving toward more integrated software environments that can provide firm-wide solutions to business problems. © 1998 The Concours Group and Edward M. Roche. All rights reserved. Used with permission.

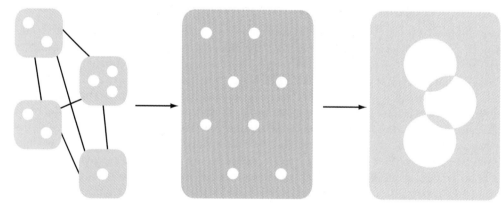

Disparate processes, systems, and infrastructure are linked

Disparate processes, systems, common infrastructure, some shared services

Common processes, systems, infrastructure

inadequate. Local telecommunications providers are typically oligopolists operating under government protection, whereas global communications providers—satellite and long distance phone companies—are much more competitive. Building your own private communications network is often advisable to maintain security and achieve very high reliability objectives. However, public switched infrastructures and the Internet are orders of magnitude less expensive and have become very reliable. Firms today are moving telecommunications applications toward public infrastructure, including value-added networks (VANs) and virtual private networks (VPNs) based on the Internet, using private leased lines only for high-security communications where cost is less important.

Infrastructure decisions have both technical and business components. The technical issues involve questions of reliability, scalability, and the future of innovation. But the business drivers behind infrastructure decisions involve fundamental business capabilities:

- How much access do employees, customers, and business partners need to your systems?
- How much connectivity is required among corporate locations?
- What information must be held in common or shared, and what information can remain local?
- How fast is the product lifecycle changing and how can systems cope with this change?
- Can an existing infrastructure respond to rapidly changing market conditions?
- Can the existing infrastructure support new business models and new business logic?

Answers to these questions provide managers with a set of *business outcomes* that should drive infrastructure decisions.

Connecting Infrastructure to Strategy: Governance

Correct infrastructure decisions are most likely to occur when those decisions are related clearly to the strategies of the firm. In the past, the traditional legacy infrastructure and architecture grew haphazardly and were locally optimized like weeds in a garden. With the new infrastructure, firms need a model of governance in which senior executives can influence infrastructure decisions and understand how infrastructure shapes business capabilities. Figure 18-8 illustrates the connection between infrastructure and governance.

Infrastructure decision making should occur at four levels. The highest level involves the CEO and CIO and the firm's strategic council, including members of the board. This group needs to determine who the firm is, where it wants to be, and what kinds of business capabilities are required. The second level is an operational group that can translate general strategic considerations into a set of functional specifications and establish the budget for the infrastructure investment. The third level directly involves the business units and regional units around the globe. This council of business unit presidents and IS managers must decide how to allocate funds to specific IT infrastructure projects and other projects needed for the business units. The fourth level of firm governance involves specific business functions, such as finance, manufacturing, marketing, and human resources. These functional groups both devise plans for infrastructure to support new business processes and implement infrastructure decisions made at higher levels.

Dealing with Mergers and Acquisitions

Mergers and acquisitions are a major growth engine for businesses. In 1998 the value of global mergers and acquisitions was approximately $1.9 trillion (compared to $400 billion in 1992). The reasons behind mergers and acquisitions are economies of scale, scope, knowledge, and time. Potentially firms can cut costs significantly by merging with competitors, reduce their capital risks and business cycle risk by expanding into different industries (e.g., conglomerating), and create a larger pool of competitive knowledge and expertise by joining forces with other players. There are also economies of time: A firm can sometimes gain market share and expertise very quickly through acquisition rather than building over the long term. Some firms—like

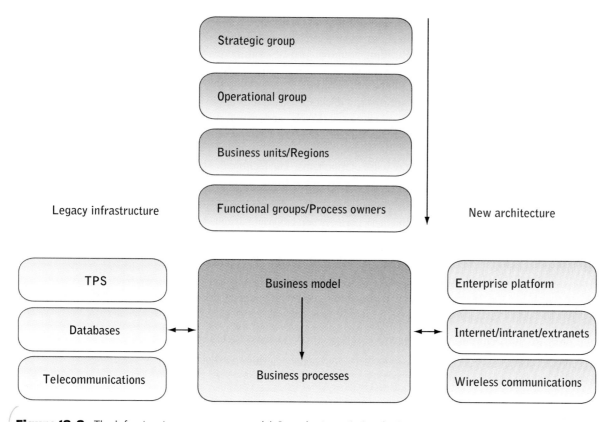

Figure 18-8 The infrastructure governance model. In order to optimize the investment in IT infrastructure, a firm-wide governance structure is needed to ensure that legacy investments are properly amortized, and that the new infrastructure supports the strategy of the firm. At each level of strategic planning the proper conversations have to occur.

General Electric—are quite successful in carrying out mergers and acquisitions. But in general, research has found that more than 70 percent of all M&As result in a decline in shareholder value and often lead to divestiture at a later time (Braxton Associates, 1997; *Economist,* 1997).

One reason that mergers and acquisitions fail is the difficulty of integrating the systems of different companies. (This problem is described in the Window on Management.) Without a successful systems integration, the intended economies cannot be realized, or, worse, the merged entity cannot execute its business processes and loses customers. Unfortunately, systems integration problems often wreak havoc on well-laid plans for corporate infrastructure development. In failed M&A situations, firms become a hodgepodge of inherited legacy systems built by aggregating the systems of one firm after another, with little time or resources devoted to integrating systems, or shedding complexity. Often in these failed firms, IT management was never consulted before or during the acquisition process.

The question for managers is how can information systems play a helpful role in the merger and acquisition process? One way to think about this is to divide the merger and acquisition process into stages and examine the role of information technology (IT) management in each stage (see Table 18.5).

Mergers and acquisitions typically go through four stages: strategic exploration, valuation, purchase, and transition. In the strategic exploration stage IT management should be directly involved with the CEO in identifying candidate firms who may offer unusual system assets, knowledge bases, or economies of scale. IT managers can help CEOs avoid system nightmares that can occur when the target company's systems are themselves problematic and require—postacquisition—major investments.

In the valuation stage, when a target company has been identified, IT managers need to identify the realistic costs of integration, and the estimated benefits of economies in operation,

Bank Mergers: More Than Meets the Eye

When two companies join, what does it take for them to live happily ever after? Some say that the real marriage takes place in their information systems. Companies in the banking and financial services industries are starting to find this out.

For a time, merger mania swept Canadian banks as well as the banking industry in the United States. In January 1998, Royal Bank, which held the most assets of any Canadian bank at that time, announced it would merge with Bank of Montreal, Canada's third-largest bank. The merged unit would have more than Canadian $475 billion, making it one of the top 10 banks in North America. Shortly thereafter, Toronto–Dominion Bank and Canadian Imperial Bank of Canada (CIBC) announced a similar merger to create a combined unit with more than Canadian $460 billion in assets.

Banks and other organizations around the world are pursuing such mergers in the hope that they can become more competitive through economies of scale. Every bank typically has demand deposit and money transfer systems. When two banks merge, these systems can be consolidated. The cost savings resulting from these new efficiencies can be applied to new systems for increasing revenue, such as on-line banking and electronic commerce.

The giant Canadian banks attempting to merge never had a chance to explore this scenario. In December 1998, their merger plans were blocked by the Canadian Ministry of Finance on the grounds that they would not benefit consumer welfare. But had these banks been given a green light to go ahead, they would probably have found that merging was more difficult and costly than they had originally thought.

Both the Royal Bank–Bank of Montreal merger and the Toronto–Dominion–CIBC merger anticipated heavy investments in technology for new information support systems, products and services that would offer customers better service and better value. Royal Bank–Bank of Montreal expected to spend Canadian $1.4 billion over a five-year period for this purpose.

Banks and other financial service firms typically expect these massive investments to pay for themselves quickly by generating more profitable services for new and existing customers. Bank CEOs typically anticipate 30 to 40 percent reductions in information technology (IT) costs, hoping they can economize by laying off all the application development staff at one bank. The reality is often the opposite. According to Octavio Marenzi, research director at Meridien Research Inc., integrating the systems of two different banks is so difficult and risky that the banks often have to hire extra contractors to do the work, and costs actually go up. Overlapping deposit systems and other redundant applications can take years to consolidate and are expensive to maintain.

Helen Sinclair, head of BankWorks Trading, Inc., a Toronto company that advises banks on technology, observed that the bank mergers involve "knitting together two organizations that have a lot of different technology platforms." In addition to IBM systems, the Canadian banks were also using UNIX and Windows NT platforms, creating a hodgepodge systems environment. The core systems of the large Canadian banks are more than 25 years old and have had numerous enhancements done to them during that time. According to Ed Nazarko, a consultant for the banking, finance, and securities industry group at IBM, the challenge for these banks would have been determining which system survived.

Analysts predicted that the Canadian banks would have seen a significant rise in IT expenditures as they grappled with combining different systems. Most of these expenditures would have been allocated for solutions and development work including additional consultants, rather than hardware.

To Think About: What management, organization, and technology issues are posed by merging two companies' information systems?

Sources: Thomas Hoffman and Julia King, "Banks Spare IT as Layoffs Pile Up," **Computerworld**, March 1, 1999; and Jim Middlemiss, "Canadian Mergers Claim Massive Customer Base," **Wall Street and Technology,** 16, no. 7, July 1998.

---

scope, knowledge, and time. IT managers will have to critically examine the target's systems environment and estimate any likely costs required to upgrade IT infrastructure or major system improvements. In the purchase phase the CIO should develop a small, core *systems integration team* to validate the costs and benefits of systems integration. In addition, the CIO should develop a new *business process team* (to critically examine the target's business model and processes) and an *IT infrastructure team* (to examine the target firm's infrastructure).

In the transition phase IT managers need to identify the "best of breed" systems in the combined company, eliminate systems no longer needed, and attempt to rationalize the inherited structure by integrating the target company's systems into the firm.

But how should CIOs prepare for future acquisitions? Here are some suggestions. First, CIOs should develop robust systems with standardized interfaces that can easily be scaled up in operations. This argues for enterprise-wide packages rather than homegrown custom software. Second, CIOs should maintain a sufficiently robust infrastructure to sustain a 30 to 50

Table 18.5	The Role of Information Technology (IT) in the Merger and Acquisition Process

Stage	Role of IT Management
Strategic exploration	Identify firms with strong IT assets and systems, and/or knowledge bases; work with CEO to identify acquisitions where rapid system integration is possible.
Valuation	Identify the specific integration costs of target corporations; explore with target company the key dimensions of their systems operation; identify and estimate economies of scale, scope, knowledge, and time.
Purchase	Postclosing establish transition team; validate costs and benefits; establish business process integration and IT infrastructure teams.
Transition	Develop transition team into systems coordinating group; search for best of breed systems; rationalize IT infrastructure by eliminating redundancies. Prepare for next acquisition.

percent increase in transaction volume. Although this might make good business sense in any event, in industries where M&A activity is strong, such as pharmaceuticals, it is absolutely necessary. Third, CIOs should maintain a transition superstructure or a team that can act quickly during the typically fast-paced M&A process. Acquisitions are not a one-time event but instead happen routinely. Being prepared with appropriate intrastructure plans and skilled management personnel is important.

18.3 Enterprise Systems

Enterprise systems are an effort on the part of firms to develop coherent, integrated systems and information environments. In that sense, they are grand designs that require sweeping changes in both systems technology and the organization. Grand design approaches to solving organizational challenges are based on long-term fundamental assumptions about the organizational environment, and a planned systematic effort to solve a number of related problems over a long time. Here some powerful knowledge and strong assumptions about the environment are needed; as one grand design is chosen, experimentation with other designs will be limited, and a significant resource commitment will have to be made over a long period of time. The grand design approach is inherently nonadaptive and depends on a faithful execution of all its elements to work properly (Laudon, 1989).

The grand design approach stands in contrast to problem-solving through *incremental design*—breaking problems into smaller, more manageable pieces that can be resolved individually as each emerges. Results are quick (both failures and successes), and solutions can evolve in small chunks through trial and error. A great deal of system building has followed this pattern.

Enterprise Systems: The Vision

Enterprise systems promise to integrate the diverse business processes of a firm into a single integrated information architecture (review the previous Figure 18-3). Enterprise computing, as promoted by the major vendors (SAP, BAAN, PeopleSoft, and others) promises to solve a wide variety of business challenges at once, or at least to lay the foundation for a systemic, long-term, and planned trajectory of change. Enterprise systems promise to greatly change four dimensions of business: firm structure, management process, technology platform, and business capability.

Firm Structure and Organization: One Organization

Enterprise thinking promises to eliminate the duchies and baronies that make up many modern business organizations and replace them with a more rational, single, integrated view of the firm. It promises to do this by installing an enterprise-wide technical platform serving all processes and levels. Islands of automation are connected in business-wide systems that serve all functions. There is a single culture, focused on overall business performance, measured on organization-wide performance standards like return on assets, stock price, growth, or market share.

Management: Firmwide Knowledge-based Management Processes

The enterprise view promises—based on the firmwide technical information platform—to give general managers a firmwide understanding of value creation, a firmwide understanding of cost structure, and nearly unlimited abilities to change business processes based on this new information and knowledge. No longer will general managers be stuck without any hard data on firm performance, or old data, or data that applies only to their own immediate department. Because the knowledge created by a firm's enterprise systems cannot be purchased by competitor firms, managers are promised by ES vendors a sustainable competitive advantage.

Technology: "Total Unified Information System"

Enterprise systems promise to provide firms with a single, unified, and all-encompassing information system platform and environment. Enterprise systems promise to create a single, integrated corporate database environment that gathers data on all the key business processes. Because of their modular design, and contemporary rapid development software tools, enterprise systems are promised to be robust—capable of adapting to mergers and acquisitions, business process change, and new technologies.

Business: Customer-driven Business Processes

Perhaps the most important business promise of ES is to create for the first time a customer-driven or demand organization, to replace the old production-driven, supply organization. A number of new business capabilities are promised: integration of the discrete business processes like sales–production–finance–logistics into a single business process; the ability to understand and serve the customer's value chain; the ability to understand and fit into the firm's vendors' business processes and systems; and finally the ability to forecast new products, and build and deliver them as demand appears. Enterprise systems—because they capture unit cost and quality data as never before—promise to give firms value leadership: the best products for less. Enterprise systems, in other words, promise to give businesses the ability to serve customers better, and thereby gain market advantage.

The promise of enterprise systems is to deliver a whole new set of business capabilities to the firm and its managers. Firms would be able to truly optimize their current business based on real knowledge of the firm's operation; enter new businesses before their competitors; exit less profitable lines and products before their competitors; and destabilize the existing competitive environment by changing the rules of competition, offering the highest quality products for prices below the competition selling inferior products.

Enterprise Systems: The Reality

While the vision and possibilities of enterprise systems and industry networks are worthwhile, getting there, surviving there, and prospering there are the real challenges. Enterprise systems raise five important issues for firms: a daunting implementation process, surviving a cost/benefit analysis, achieving robustness, attaining interoperability, and realizing strategic value.

Daunting Implementation

Enterprise systems purport to replace legacy systems based on outdated mainframe technology and function-specific COBOL-coded software. But the legacy systems that must be replaced are the primary control systems of the corporation, the vital cybernetic nervous system of the company. Typical legacy systems contain millions of lines of code in thousands of computer programs. Thousands of employees use and rely on these systems everyday, as well as customers and vendors. The prospect of successfully and rapidly transforming the corporate nervous system, retraining thousands of workers, and redesigning the fundamental business processes, all at once, while carrying on business as usual is remote. The older legacy systems were never designed at a single time; rather, they evolved over decades in a manner similar to the growth of a weed patch field, responding to various corporate needs. The prospect of replacing these evolved systems with a single new one, and getting it right on the first try, is extremely small.

Because of the centrality and size of existing legacy systems, one implementation path for enterprise systems is to work around and with existing legacy systems. Enterprise systems can be implemented one piece at a time. For instance, human resource modules can be installed first, then finance, then accounting, and then production. This building block approach usually leaves existing legacy systems intact, or worked around, and disruptions to corporate life can be localized. Although this building block approach enhances the success rate and survivability of enterprise system efforts, it can also lead to disconnected islands of automation, a patchwork of enterprise-like systems, and increases in the cost and use of crossware and middleware programs that connect the enterprise packages to the legacy systems. It simply delays the day when a fully connected enterprise system emerges. Implementation problems with enterprise systems are so pervasive that we have devoted the chapter ending case study to this topic.

Surviving a Cost/Benefit Analysis

The costs of enterprise systems are large, upfront, highly visible, and politically charged. Although the costs to build the system are obvious, the benefits are elusive to describe in concrete terms at the beginning of an enterprise project. One reason is that the benefits often accrue from employees using the system after it is completed and gaining the knowledge of business operations heretofore impossible to learn.

One solution to this challenge is to benchmark to the experience of other firms in the same or different industries. Quite often one's competitors will not willingly give up such benchmarking information, but it is possible to learn from firms in other industries about the cost benefits of enterprise systems in specific areas like finance, human resources, and logistics. Most of the enterprise package provider firms have large collections of success stories based on their customers' experiences (but are reluctant to publicize their failures). However, the accuracy of these benchmarking comparisons depends on the validity of assumptions about your manager's ability to use the enterprise system correctly and to learn from the experience. The value of the enterprise system comes from the learning and knowledge about your specific firm. The very uniqueness of firms makes this kind of comparison difficult.

Achieving Robustness and Avoiding Digital Concrete

The programming and development environments of enterprise packages and crossware software are complex, difficult to master, hard to communicate, and lack the support (because of their newness) expected of older technologies. Moreover, the enterprise systems built with these tools involve software programs that can be just as difficult to understand, complex, poorly documented, and yet intertwined with corporate business processes as the legacy systems they will replace. There is the prospect that the new enterprise systems will be as brittle and hard to change as old legacy systems—a new kind of digital concrete that will bind firms to outdated business processes and systems rather than introduce them to a new age of business capability.

If we have learned anything in the past decade, surely one lesson is that business environments will change. This means that business processes also must change and that business process design is a continuous activity. Therefore, enterprise systems must be robust in the sense of being quickly adaptable to new environments and new designs of business processes. It is not clear this is the case with contemporary ES. Instead, the new enterprise software could easily become a new kind of digital concrete.

Attaining Interoperability

One of the difficulties of older legacy environments was achieving interoperability among the thousands of software programs in the corporate library. Enterprise software promises to deliver a more rational environment where every program written in the new system is at least compatible with other programs written in the new environment. And the new software also achieves fairly good integration with common desktop computing environments and programs. But this still leaves the question of how the new enterprise systems exchange data with the older legacy systems, which may still be required at least temporarily. In many instances, building these interfaces to existing software has proven to be very costly.

Realizing Strategic Value

Perhaps the most significant issue facing enterprise systems is learning how to realize strategic value from the investment. Because so much of technology can be purchased by all competitors, technology per se, including ES, will not produce a sustainable strategic advantage.

However, using ES to achieve a better understanding of your business operations and customers is a totally unique asset that cannot be duplicated easily by your competitors. The only strategic assets in the end are knowledge and information unavailable to your competitors. The challenge posed by ES is how to teach managers to use the new information available to them. Companies may also fail to achieve strategic benefits from enterprise systems if integrating business processes using the generic models provided by standard ERP software packages prevents the firm from using unique business processes that had been sources of competitive advantage. Some companies do not need the level of integration provided by enterprise systems (Davenport, 1998).

18.4 Industrial Networks and Extended Enterprise Systems

Industrial networks link together in a single industry-wide system the enterprise systems of firms who are participants in a single industry. Industries have both vertical and horizontal dimensions (see Figure 18-9). Vertically organized industrial networks, such as Coca-Cola's extended enterprise described in the chapter opening vignette, integrate the operations of a firm, such as a manufacturer, and its suppliers. Horizontally organized industrial networks link firms across an entire industry, such as the OASIS network of utility industry firms. Most industrial networks today are vertical and do not link together competitors in the same industry. The Window on Organizations describes some examples.

In the past, many firms, such as General Motors, described in the Part 1 case study, vertically integrated by acquiring their suppliers and building their own transportation and logistics operations in order to reduce their *transaction costs* of purchasing these services. Some of these firms also merged with direct competitors along the horizontal dimension to reduce their *agency costs* (and achieve economies of scale and scope). Chapter 2 has shown that industrial networks make it possible to avoid acquisition as a vertical strategy by enabling the coordination of business processes across an entire industry. Industrial networks are also beginning to enable the coordination of seemingly competitive firms through strategic alliances. For example, Yamaha Europe, Honda, Aprilia, and Piaggio, competing manufacturers of motor scooters, are now working together to share suppliers. They hope to ultimately reduce the number of suppliers, which will boost the production efficiency in the remaining group, and they all expect to benefit from the savings from this change (Abramson, 1999). Perhaps one of the best examples of an emerging industrial network is provided by Procter & Gamble's efforts over many years to build an industry-wide system for the coordination of independent firms in the consumer packaged goods market (see Figure 18-10).

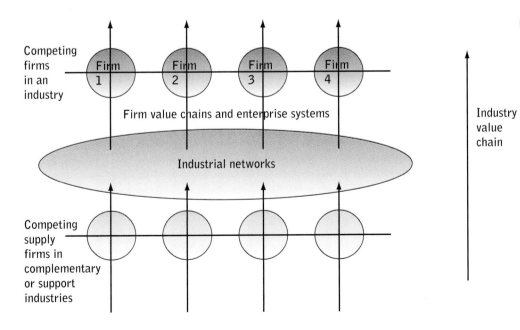

Figure 18-9 Vertical and horizontal dimensions of industry and industrial networks. Generally industrial networks link together the vertical elements in the industry value chain although they may in the future link together competing firms.

Extending the Supply Chain

In the past, corporate strategy and value chain analysis looked primarily inside each company, searching for ways that a company's internal operations could provide competitive advantage. Today the focus is shifting outside corporate walls. Companies are looking for increased efficiencies in their links with suppliers, partners, and customers as new sources of competitive advantage. The Internet, electronic data interchange (EDI), transportation and warehouse management software, and other related technologies are allowing companies to create electronic networks with suppliers and manufacturers where they can manage inventory that you can't see and don't own. A study conducted by the Performance Measurement Group found that companies that integrated their supply chains reported a 16 to 28 percent improvement in delivery performance, a 25 to 60 percent reduction in inventories, and a 30 to 50 percent improvement in fulfillment cycle time, as well as a 10 to 16 percent increase in productivity.

Airbus Industrie, the European aerospace consortium, outsources the production of parts and the development of components to external suppliers. Airbus is building a standard communication and collaboration platform for its four member companies (DA Airbus, British Aerospace, Aerospatiale, and the Spanish CASA) and their thousands of suppliers. The system will be used to support the development of its new 555-seat jetliner and is expected to reduce both production time and recurrent costs by 30 percent. Airbus is using Parametric Technology Corporation's product information automation system to store all data, including product geometry and parts of the bills of materials.

Office Depot has prospered by offering a wider range of stationery and office supplies at lower cost than small retailers through just-in-time replenishment and tight inventory control systems. It uses information from a sophisticated demand forecasting system and point-of-sale data to replenish its inventory, placing 95 percent of its purchase orders directly to suppliers through EDI. Vendors who participate in the company's EDI program are supplied with weekly data about the sales performance of their products. Using these electronic links to Office Depot, most vendors can replenish inventory within one to two weeks, and often within a few days. Many suppliers use the EDI system to post advance shipment notifications to alert Office Depot that goods are about to be dispatched.

Instead of leaving the job of transporting goods to individual vendors, Office Depot hired a third-party freight optimizing service provider to consolidate deliveries and reduce transport costs. The service provider receives a copy of every purchase order Office Depot places with vendors and identifies opportunities to group inbound shipments together. If, instead of three trucks heading to Office Depot from Omaha, only one is required, Office Depot can realize additional savings. According to Bill Seltzer, Office Depot's chief information officer and executive vice president, improvements such as the inventory replenishment system have cut the company's distribution costs to 1 percent of total sales, down from 2 percent five years earlier.

Safeway, the third-largest supermarket chain in the United Kingdom, is using new supply chain management systems to speed the process of getting products from suppliers such as Birds Eye Wall's to customers. Safeway uses an IBM 4690 point-of-sale system to capture 800,000 consumer transactions daily, which are stored in a massive data warehouse running on an IBM ES/9000 mainframe. It developed its own software for making accurate and timely decisions about inventory replenishment, promotions, and production. Safeway shares this information about forecasts, inventory, and available shelf space electronically with its suppliers so that they can track demand for their products, adjust production, and calculate the size and timing of deliveries accordingly. Suppliers can also download the information into their enterprise resource planning (ERP) or production planning systems. The system also provides suppliers with news flashes about unanticipated demand and information on key contacts and contract terms. Suppliers in turn can use the system to send Safeway information about product availability, production capacity, inventory levels, and promotional proposals.

To Think About: What are the organizational benefits of using information systems to improve links with suppliers?

Sources: Gregory Dalton, "Global Gravity," *Information Week*, January 18, 1999; Nick Wredon, "Connecting Suppliers to an Electronic Highway," **Beyond Computing**, March 1999; and Malcom Wheatley, "Retail: The Next Wave," **CIO Magazine**, April 15, 1998.

Industrial Networks: The Vision

Industrial networks promise significant change along four dimensions: industry structure, management process, technology platform, and business capability.

Industry Structure: From Marketspace to "Value Web"

Industrial networks promise to replace distant marketplace relationships among complementary firms in an industry with a more cohesive, integrated industry value chain and to better coordinate the flow of information among competitors. For instance, until the discovery of industrial networks, flower growers, transporters like FedEx and UPS, flower wholesalers, and

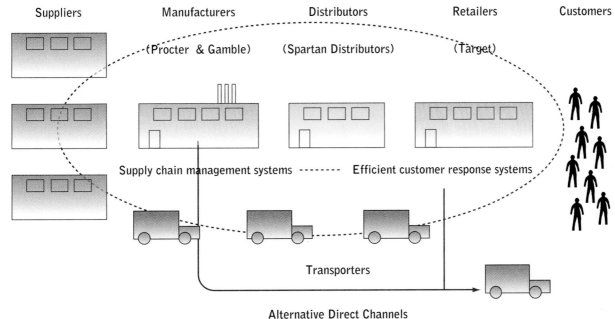

Suppliers   Manufacturers   Distributors   Retailers   Customers

(Procter & Gamble)   (Spartan Distributors)   (Target)

Supply chain management systems ------- Efficient customer response systems

Transporters

Alternative Direct Channels
e.g. The Web, QVC

Figure 18-10 Procter & Gamble's emerging industrial network. Industrial networks potentially can coordinate the behavior of independent, complementary (noncompeting) firms into a single industry value web.

retailers all acted alone without coordination. It took the vision of entrepreneurs at Calyx and Carolla, and later Internet entrepreneurs PCFlowers, to systematically connect the separate computer systems of growers, transporters, and distributors. In so doing these entrepreneurs created a "value web"—a collection of firms acting together in an industrial value chain coordinated by networks.

Management Process: Industry-wide Knowledge-based Management

Industrial networks promise a revolution in management thinking. Instead of thinking only about their isolated firm, managers will now be encouraged to think about their industry as a whole and they will be enabled to adjust their firm's behavior to the requirements of industry-wide growth. Managers will recognize that they may be in competition with other industries for the customer dollar, and that if their industry does poorly in this competition, their firm will surely suffer.

Technology: Industry-wide Platforms

Prior to enterprise systems, IT was usually thought of as an application designed to solve a specific problem, and not a firmwide asset or infrastructure. The same mind-set prevailed for industrial networks. Industrial networks force managers to think about industry-wide platforms. They must examine not only how well their IT choices solve firm problems but also how their IT choices should be guided by industry requirements. The goal of industrial networks is a tightly coupled set of technologies that can be developed once and used by all industry participants, including competitors.

Business Capability

The vision of industrial networks is then to create entirely new firm and industry capabilities to serve customers. By linking together the unique resources of individual firms in an industry, the entire industry can collectively serve customers better than any single firm. At the same time, by strengthening the industry, firms contribute to their own business acumen and success. The goal is to create a "value web" of industry participants—including even former

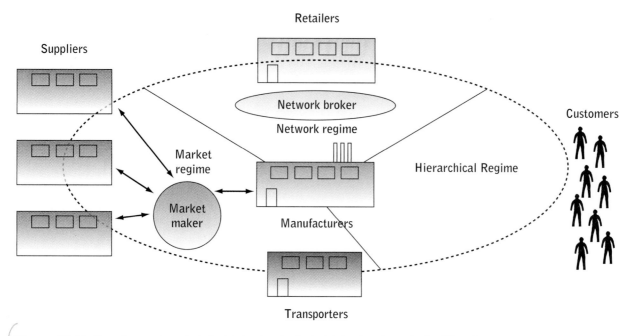

Retailers

Suppliers

Network broker

Network regime

Market regime

Customers

Market maker

Hierarchical Regime

Manufacturers

Transporters

Figure 18-11 Boundary regimes in industrial networks. Industrial networks make traditional organizational boundaries permeable and can be threatening to the firm's ability to control its information environment.

competitors—so as to fend off competition from competing industries and the industrial networks in other global markets.

One example of an emerging industrial network is the recently announced agreement between Dell and IBM to coordinate the development of computer components. Here we have two huge firms in competition with one another in the PC marketplace who will necessarily have to closely integrate their existing enterprise-wide systems into a shared industrial network that can coordinate IBM's production schedule with Dell's daily demand for built-to-order PCs.

Industrial Networks: The Reality

Industrial networks raise three major issues for firms: controlling the boundary exchange of information, retaining the benefits of industrial networks while distributing the costs fairly across the industry, and increased vulnerability and dependence.

Choosing the Boundary Regime

Industry networks make the traditional boundaries of a firm permeable to outsiders. Important corporate information will be going out, and critical corporate information will be inbound (see Figure 18-11). How will this critical juncture be controlled?

There are three options. One is to use *hierarchy* to control the industry network interface. In this regime, one powerful corporation owns the network facility and tightly controls the exchange of information with channel partners and suppliers. Although it protects corporate control, this option raises issues of whose standards will be maintained and also issues of political trust and legitimacy. A second option is a *market interface* in which the facility is owned by a market-maker. All market participants are equals, and they enter and leave the market at will seeking the best possible prices. This option presumes there are enough participants to make the market efficient and that enforceable market rules will be developed. A third option is a *network interface* in which key participants work with a network broker or establish an organizing committee controlled by the participants. Although it achieves good corporate control and offers the prospect of moderate legitimacy, this option risks the prospect of dominance by large players (similar to standard-setting committees), less than perfect firm control over the network, and uncertain destination of information. Regardless of which option is chosen, some option must be chosen and each option has risks and rewards.

Sharing Costs, Retaining Benefits

Like other complex systems, the costs of industry networks are palpable and up front, while the benefits can be diffuse and back end. Researchers have found that investment in IT by firms results in large benefits to consumers but much smaller benefits to firms in terms of increased profitability, market share, or share price (Brynjolfsson, 1996). It is unclear with industry networks just how the gains to firms and to consumers will be allocated and each firm in each industry will have to estimate how the gains of industrial networks will be distributed.

A related issue is sharing the cost of industry networks. In hierarchical networks the cost will be borne by the firm owning the facility (control has its costs), but in market and network interfaces the costs are borne by all participants. If an industry network will benefit suppliers, trucking and transportation firms, warehousing firms, distributors, and ultimately consumers, what should each participant's contribution be on the cost side?

Vulnerability and Dependence

Advances in information technology and building a firm around these technologies inevitably means that firms become dependent on information systems. In the case of industry networks, these problems of dependence and vulnerability are compounded by the fact that many different organizations are involved. Even temporary network outages could be as expensive as temporary enterprise system outages.

Dealing with vulnerability has costs. The general strategy is to build security into the system and add redundancy. Emergency backup plans and systems are required. All of these measures add cost.

Steps to Building and Managing Enterprise Systems and Industrial Networks

In order to build useful enterprise systems and create industrial networks, the top managers of a firm need to go through a series of steps that question the fundamental nature of their business. Here are some useful starting points for what will be a long journey.

1. **Know where you are relative to the technology and other firms.** Before starting on a trip, you need to know where you are and where you want to go, indeed, where it is possible to go. Table 18.6 provides a matrix that can help your firm discover where it is and where it might be able to go.

   Once you locate your firm and your competitors on the ES matrix, you should be able to identify a migration trajectory to the future. Key elements of this process will be to identify what is needed to get to the next stage, what are the mechanisms available to effect the required changes, and what are the barriers to change.

2. **Know who you are and where you want to be.** The path your firm takes will—or should—result from a series of conversations among senior managers and the board concerning the identity of the firm today, and what it would like to be in the future. For example, your firm may be the leading regional distributor of a certain category of industrial products, but in five years it may want to be a player in the global markets for these products. If so, then global enterprise systems will need to be built during the next five years to support the new business. The senior management of a firm needs to develop a business vision of the future and then build systems to support that vision (King, 1995).

3. **Devise a long-term plan (five years) for achieving the strategic plan, but do not redesign everything at once.** Keep the best of both incrementalism and grand design by building systems needed today, keeping in mind the planned infrastructure, and systems that fit into a long-term grand vision of where the firm should be in five years. Without the grand vision, you will end up with a collection of islands of excellence in a sea of corporate confusion.

4. **Recognize that to achieve the enterprise system and industrial network visions will require significant cultural and managerial process change.** Industrial networks inherently cause organizations to develop a more industry-wide cultural orientation, and enterprise systems inherently involve a shift from divisional, product, and

Table 18.6 **The ES Matrix**

Dimensions	Level 1 Initial stage: legacy paradigm	Level 2 Preparing for change	Level 3 New technical capabilities	Level 4 New business capabilities	Level 5 Arrival: new business/IT paradigm
Technology platform and ES capability	Traditional legacy environment; highly interfaced systems	Partial ES components installed in "islands of excellence." Moving toward a more coherent IT architecture	Islands of excellence grow to encompass more aspects of information processing; reliable integrated IT environment, but highly challenged by complexities of introducing new capabilities; fragmented capabilities	Established IT infrastructure and architecture to connect anyone, anytime, anywhere to the resources required to effect their business initiative	Flexible, component-based, fast to change, no barriers; technical infrastructure anticipates business change
IS role and capability	Service organization with little leadership role and limited contact with senior management	IS attempting to assume new role as business consultants, but credibility still limited	Value of integrated business model is recognized; journey toward IT and business integration is explicit; IS being transformed to deliver higher business value; beginnings of industrial network systems	IS transformed and delivering value on key fronts; resource allocation based on value added; business owns the business model and IT governance; functional industrial networks in place with key suppliers and distributors	Business/IS relationship seamless; IT vision all-pervasive; IT managed as an inter-enterprise resource; firm IT closely integrated with industry IT
Organization	Internally focused, "stovepiped" functional organization; limited process management	Predominantly traditional, but gaining appreciation of potential to leverage processes across organizational divisions and departments	Process mindset established across functions/organizations; intra- and interorganizational relationships and processes developing; development of industrial network partners	Performance measurement and process focus flourishing; beginning to extend the reach and range of external relationships; beginning to move to a virtual organization	Visionary senior management team continually rebuilding organization to meet new market opportunities and challenges
Business management	Fragmented, hierarchical, and departmental	Managing the business traditionally, operating with more integrated information to assist local decision making	Leveraging information and technology for competitive advantage; moving to managing the business "outside-in" from the customer to production; precise understanding of costs	Leveraging ES-related technologies and new business competencies to transform and innovate the business; ability to anticipate market change	Destabilizing the competitive environment; changing the rules of competition
Business capability	Allows traditional business to operate	Provides capabilities to improve business efficiencies	Leverages integrated information and process to dramatically reduce costs and cycle times. Moving to greater interconnectedness with customers and suppliers	Leverage the business operating model to create new business opportunities and competitive advantage	Capable of entirely new types of business; sustainable marketplace advantage

department loyalties to a firmwide loyalty. Managers will be required to manage across the firm, and not just to manage their division or function.

5. **The new business capabilities will not be achieved without retraining your managers and employees.** You will need to teach managers how to manage with information and knowledge as opposed to management by whim, by historical precedent, or by instinct. Develop simulations and have managers practice with the new data available. The real promise of enterprise systems is not merely a more efficient business process, but a new management capability to use fine-grained data about daily operations to manage the firm.

6. **Develop incentive systems to support the new information environments.** Reward managers for using enterprise systems, and reward managers for managing across organizational boundaries to improve industry performance. This is far more difficult than it sounds simply because the sources of industry performance can be difficult to measure.

Management Wrap-Up

Enterprise systems and industrial networks require management to take a firmwide and industry-wide view of business processes and information flows. Managers need to determine which business processes should be integrated, the short-term and strategic benefits of this integration, and the appropriate level of financial and organizational resources to support enterprise and industry-wide computing.

Management

Enterprise systems and industrial networks require extensive organizational change. Diverse business processes must be coordinated and redesigned, impacting organizational structure, culture, job design, and procedures. Many enterprise efforts fail because the organizational change requirements are too extensive or complex to execute.

Organization

Enterprise systems and industrial networks require major technology investments and planning. Firms must have an information technology (IT) infrastructure that can support organization or industry-wide computing and they should be proficient in the technologies used in enterprise system software and tools. Linking enterprise systems to older legacy systems adds to the technical complexity of such projects.

Technology

For Discussion

1. Can all organizations benefit from enterprise systems?

2. Why are enterprise systems and industrial networks difficult to implement successfully?

Summary

1. Describe the features of enterprise computing and industrial networks. Enterprise computing takes an integrated firmwide view of information systems. It integrates the key business processes of a firm into a single software system so that information can flow seamlessly throughout the organization, improving coordination, efficiency, and decision making. It takes a firmwide view of technology, business processes, and strategy. Industrial networks link other organizations in the same industry in a single industry-wide system. Vertical industrial networks consist of an organization and its suppliers, whereas horizontal networks consist of competitors in the same industry.

2. Explain the business and technology drivers behind enterprise computing and industrial networks. Both business and technology factors are driving the growth of enterprise systems and industrial networks. The globalization of markets has increased competition, causing firms to seek out solutions that will reduce costs, optimize business processes, and even merge with other organizations to achieve economies of scale. Radical reduction in data storage costs, expanded public network infrastructure, the rise of client/server and desktop computing, and the availability of enterprise software packages have been technology drivers for enterprise computing and industrial networks.

3. Identify the elements and key decisions in building an information technology (IT) infrastructure. Changes in information technology (IT) infrastructure are usually required to make information flow smoothly among different business processes and parts of the organization. Legacy mainframe systems and traditional client/server systems must be integrated with the public Internet, corporate intranets and extranets, and various wireless and mobile computing devices. Public infrastructures and service providers and third-party software vendors are also important elements. Key infrastructure decisions include selection of hardware processor families, custom software development versus software packages or toolsets from commercial vendors, organization-wide versus local software applications, and choosing among global or local telecommunications services from either public or private providers. These infrastructure decisions should be made by an appropriate governance structure.

4. Compare the basic vision of enterprise systems and industrial networks with the management reality. Enterprise systems promise to integrate the diverse business processes of the firm into a single information architecture, whereas industrial networks promise to link together the enterprise systems of firms into a single industry-wide system.

These comprehensive, integrated systems promise efficiencies from better coordination of both internal and external business processes. The reality is that firm- and industry-wide systems are very difficult to implement successfully. They require extensive organizational change, use complicated technologies, require integration with older legacy systems, and require large up-front costs for long-term benefits that are difficult to quantify. Management vision and foresight is required to take a firm- and industry-wide view of problems and to find solutions that realize strategic value from the investment.

5. Plan the development of enterprise systems and industrial networks. Planning successful enterprise systems and industrial networks is a multistep process. Firms need to set five-year goals and objectives, devise a long-term plan for achieving these goals, prepare for significant managerial and process change as well as extensive retraining of managers and employees, and create incentive systems to support the new information environment.

Key Terms

Application specific view, 555	Enterprise computing, 556	Information technology (IT)
Business logic, 557	Industrial network, 558	investment portfolio, 557

Review Questions

1. What is enterprise computing? How does it differ from the application specific view of information systems in organizations?

2. What are industrial networks? How are they related to enterprise systems?

3. List and describe the business drivers behind the growth of enterprise systems.

4. List and describe the technology drivers behind the growth of enterprise systems.

5. Describe the information technology (IT) infrastructure required for enterprise computing.

6. List and describe the types of technology decisions managers must make when creating a platform for enterprise computing.

7. What groups in the organization should make the key IT infrastructure decisions?

8. How do information systems affect organizational mergers and acquisitions?

9. Describe the impact of enterprise systems on firm structure, management processes, technology platform, and business capabilities.

10. Why are enterprise systems difficult to implement and use effectively?

11. Describe the difference between industrial networks organized along vertical lines and industrial networks organized along horizontal lines.

12. How could industrial networks change industry structure, management processes, technology platforms, and business capability?

13. What challenges do industrial networks pose for businesses? Describe each of them.

14. List and describe the steps that managers should follow when building and managing enterprise systems and industrial networks.

Group Project

With a group of three or four other students, select a business using an industrial network for supply chain management. Use the Web, newspapers, journals, and computer or business magazines to find out more about that organization and its use of information technology to provide links to other organizations. Present your findings to the class.

Tools for Interactive Learning

○ Internet

The Internet Connection for this chapter will take you to a series of Web sites used in business-to-business electronic commerce where you can complete an exercise to evaluate the use of the Web in supply chain management. You can also use the Interactive Study Guide to test your knowledge of the topics in this chapter and get instant feedback when you need more practice.

○ CD-ROM

If you purchase and use the Multimedia Edition CD-ROM with this chapter, you can complete an interactive exercise to analyze an enterprise system implementation. You can also find an audio overview of the major themes of this chapter and bullet text summarizing the key points of the chapter.

Case Study   Using a Shoehorn to Fit in an ERP System

AeroGroup International, the Edison, New Jersey, producer of Aerosoles shoes, has had a remarkable history. The company began in 1987 when Jules Schneider purchased the $7 million junior footwear division of Kenneth Cole Productions, a $225 million fashion shoe company in New York City. Schneider, who had been president of the division he purchased, had an idea. The traditional shoe culture in the 1980s was split into fashion shoes and athletic footwear. The athletic footwear featured casual, rugged shoes such as those made by Bass and Timberland. During that time, interest in sneakers was exploding, led by such companies as Reebok and Nike. Fashion shoes were a separate industry and included many competing producers. Schneider wanted to produce and sell shoes that were both stylish and athletic, including loafers, sandals, and pumps. And he wanted to sell them for as low as $40 a pair!

Behind Schneider's concept was a new technology. Schneider and a partner in Italy had discovered a way to construct shoes using the soft, flexible method central to slipper manufacturing while giving them the durability of a shoe. Using this technology he quickly began selling his Aerosoles shoes in high-class department stores such as Nordstrom's and Bloomingdales, as well as in footwear specialty stores. The shoes were manufactured abroad in such countries as Italy, Portugal, Sri Lanka, Brazil, and China. With Schneider as its CEO, AeroGroup's sales climbed to $150 million in 1998, an annual growth of more than 30 percent during its 11-year history. That the company's growth was continuing was shown when 1997 sales of $120 million grew by 24 percent to reach its 1998 level. The corporate plan is to grow sales to $500 million by the year 2003, and Schneider also plans to take

the company public with an initial public offering (IPO) in the near future. Schneider was named Man of the Year by the footwear industry weekly journal, **Footwear News.**

In 1997 Aerosoles was facing many problems. The immediate issue was the flattening of growth in the footwear market, which had grown only 1 percent from 1995 to 1996 (the slowdown continued at least through 1998). For Aerosoles to meet its growth objectives, it would have to find new ways to increase its sales. In addition, other companies had begun selling knock-offs that copy Aerosoles' patented shoe bottoms. Aerosoles did sue for trademark and patent infringement, but lost most of the suit in May 1997. Aerosoles' response to these changing conditions was to begin spending about 5 percent of its sales on TV advertising.

The company was also facing serious management problems. In 1997, despite its rapid growth, Schneider remained the only senior executive in the company. Even worse, he was central to all decisions. For example, every pending order entered into Aerosoles' computer system had to be printed for Schneider to review so that he personally could decide which to fill. Deciding which customer received which product was critical. And the seasonality of footwear required getting the right product to the right customer at the right time. Schneider also had to sign off personally on all wholesale returns.

Schneider decided he needed to hire a new management team, something that would be essential to taking the company public. In 1997 he hired Richard Morris as executive vice president. Morris was to supervise administration, information technology, the legal department, and shipping. He had been the chief financial officer of

Handleman Company, a $1.2 billion distributor of music, videos, books, and software. Morris found that the company's financial reports were unreliable and so would be unacceptable to investment bankers who were central to the process of taking the company public. Morris began making many changes, including implementing discipline in budgeting and planning. Later, in December 1997, Morris and Schneider hired Jeffery Zonenshine as vice president and chief information officer (CIO).

In 1998 AeroGroup's computer system, Footworks, was 10 years old, having been developed when the company was very much smaller. Aside from the installation of an e-mail system, its operational systems hadn't changed in five years. Because the sales force was only able to call in sales data nightly, sales information was always one day behind. The warehouse system was more modern. The warehouse receives 25,000 cases of shoes monthly, usually arriving in three to four deliveries per day. AeroGroup also bought an EDI system a number of years earlier and wrote its own code to add its own functions. The company added a bar code system in 1995. Each case arrived with a bar code label that was applied at the factory. The warehouse staff used radio-frequency-scanning guns to transmit the data to a warehouse computer, which was connected directly to Footworks.

By 1997 AeroGroup's computer could no longer handle the data from the vastly increased sales. The company not only needed to modernize the computers to handle its current business, but it also needed to increase resources so the company would be ready if the sales were to expand according to the plan and projections. A new system would have "many bells and whistles that we don't need today," explained Schneider, "but that we'll need in five years. That's something that excites us and also makes us nervous." Schneider went on to say that "Last year [1997] was as tough as anything," referring to the many mishandled orders and inventory mismatches that resulted from the existing computer. Schneider also felt the system was too dependent on him.

In addition, the data from Aerosoles' systems were incomplete. Both the sales force and the factory complained about the lack of sales histories and projections. Footworks was also isolated from key systems. Although it stored order and pricing data, it had no connection to the inventory and manufacturing systems. Often Footworks numbers differed from the numbers in the accounting systems, and Morris had no way to reconcile or verify the various sets of numbers. "And we were basing decisions on that information," exclaimed Schneider (who was trained as an accountant). "It was very scary stuff." At the end of 1997, when Zonenshine, Schneider, and Morris assessed Footworks, they concluded that they should not apply any more fixes to Footworks. Instead they decided to investigate enterprise resource planning (ERP). A new ERP system would integrate finance, sales, and marketing; and inventory modules to give the company control and produce reliable reports. Implementation of an ERP system also would offer the company a good opportunity to make major operational changes, and would remove Schneider from responsibility for many of the day-to-day details.

The project became real on March 30, 1998, when AeroGroup sent out a request for proposal (RFP) for an ERP system. Zonenshine had hired a New York City consulting firm, Transaction Information Systems, to document AeroGroup's requirements and to help the company prepare the RFP. Rather than send the proposal to software companies, the 154-page document went to consulting firms that would help with the installation of the software. Included in the RFP was a request for profiles of the project manager and the other staff to be assigned to the Aerosoles project. Zonenshine wanted to be able to screen the staffs for SAP experience in the footwear and similar industries. In addition he wanted to avoid the common consulting firm practice of using highly qualified people for sales and then assigning less experienced personnel on the actual project.

When the Aerosoles staff received responses to its RFP, they undertook a function-by-function comparison with the

various possible systems. However, according to Zonenshine, "The decision [was] based less on functions than on architecture and the future of our company." With projections of very rapid growth for Aerosoles over the next few years, Zonenshine understood that the company would be making many changes in its systems in the near future, and so he wanted an open architecture. Ultimately Aerosoles selected R/3 from SAP AG as the ERP software.

R/3 is very open in that it can be run under many different operating systems using many different databases. In addition the system offers flexibility in functions because hundreds of specialty application add-ons are available. By adopting R/3, AeroGroup will have the ability to add specific functions easily. Aerosoles was also impressed with SAP's experience in the apparel and footwear fields. SAP offered a suite of R/3 applications specifically developed for the footwear industry, called Apparel Footwear Solution (AFS). Developing modules directed at specific industries has long been part of R/3's marketing plan.

Zonenshine also liked the fact that SAP had an implementation methodology called Accelerated SAP (ASAP), which had been developed in 1996. ASAP combines a specific methodology for implementing R/3, including the tools needed for the project. It was designed for smaller companies with revenues under $500 million, thus fitting AeroGroup. SAP claimed ASAP cuts the time of implementation in half. A study by AMR Research, Boston, was not quite that optimistic but still claimed a time saving of 25 to 50 percent. SAP also claimed that 34 percent of the organizations successfully installing R/3 had revenues under $200 million, again a good fit for AeroGroup. However, AMR Research did point out that most of these organizations were in Europe, not the United States, where conditions are quite different.

Before the final decision was made, Aerosoles held a demonstration of R/3 on April 7. It was attended by Aerosoles' department heads as well as representatives from several other companies that had responded to Aerosoles' RFP and were still in the running. It was a very-high-level demonstration with few details, according to Schneider, Morris, and Zonenshine. Schneider characterized it as "a fiasco." Aerosoles insisted that R/3 be demonstrated again with more details.

The second demonstration took place a week later, and the reaction at Aerosoles was even worse. Morris claimed that it was

simply a high-level sales pitch, that the group making the presentation still did not understand or address Aerosoles' business. On April 16 several people from Aerosoles met with Jeff Singer, business development manager of the Apparel Footwear Solution component of the R/3 package, to discuss the demonstration problems. Zonenshine also asked to speak with another Apparel Footwear Solution (AFS) user. Singer worked to put together a better team for a third demonstration, and the meeting was carefully planned. The demonstration was held on May 8 and was considered a success by Aerosoles. The reason, according to Zonenshine and Morris, was improved communications between the parties.

R/3 had a main contender, JBA software, but it was designed to run only on IBM's AS/400 minicomputer and therefore did not offer Aerosoles the flexibility it wanted. When Aerosoles decided to adopt R/3, the company also selected Richard A. Eisner & Co. of New York City as the consulting firm on the project.

The installation of an ERP system entailed serious risks. ERP projects had a reputation of draining corporate resources and funds. Moreover, ERP implementation is so complex that it has proven to be too difficult for many organizations. R/3 implementation had been abandoned by many organizations in the previous 18 months, including Alcoa, Dell Computer, and NEC Technologies.

Part of the issue is that ERP systems can bring massive organizational change. These systems consist of many functional modules that can span the whole organization and yet share a common database. Because departments are part of larger organizations, they are forced to share systems and act not as independent units but as part of a larger organization, requiring a whole new understanding of their work. Decisions must be for the betterment of the company, not for the betterment of individual units. All of this forces greater cooperation and teamwork. Ultimately, ERP implementation is not just a software project but an organizational change project and must be treated that way. Cooperation, teamwork, and planning for organizational change are difficult to do when senior management is too busy to give the project adequate attention.

The project began in the summer of 1998, and the team set February 1999 as the date to go live. The project was the largest capital project in the history of the company. The project budget was set at $3.2 million: $750,000 for software, $250,000 for hardware, and a $2 million fixed fee for

Eisner's consulting. The price also included $200,000 that Aerosoles set aside for employee incentive bonuses.

"I wouldn't have expected [the consulting fee] to be that high," remarked Morris. Sam Wee, a partner in Benchmarking Partners, a Cambridge, Massachusetts, consulting firm, pointed out that the ratio of consulting-to-hardware costs is more normally two or three to one. In the Aerosoles project it is eight to one. However, it is common for small companies like Aerosoles to pay for much more outside help, according to Wee, because they do not have the expertise on the computer or software technology, and they are too busy on their regular jobs to work nearly full-time on a development project. In the case of Aerosoles both factors apply. Aerosoles executives and departmental managers who took on major responsibility for the project had to continue their ongoing business responsibilities as well, and this was during a time of growth and challenges for the company. Aerosoles actually had a small staff for a $150 million company. Zonenshine had only four direct reports—a very small staff. Eisner assigned five of its staff for the project, and 11 Aerosoles employees were assigned.

The project began several weeks behind as a result of the three R/3 presentations. This put Aerosoles under very heavy time pressures. A full project team meeting was held on July 21. Such meetings were clearly going to be almost impossible in the future due to the travel schedule of many of Aerosoles' team. Much of the work would have to be done on the road, with distributions often taking place via e-mail. The material distributed at the meeting included detailed questionnaires, but "We didn't tailor the questionnaires as ASAP would have you do," Lake said, "because we didn't have time before the meeting." The project team was broken into six subteams, focusing on specific functions such as warehousing and production. Each subteam set its own meeting schedules. Wee expressed concern that with the division into subteams, whole-team meetings would not occur, fragmenting the project. Resulting problems might include not identifying conflicts and interdependencies, and not being able to see opportunities for positive functional and organizational change.

Problems occurred with AFS. It contained much new programming code that had never been used in actual production environments. Moreover, AFS was particularly difficult to develop because of the uniqueness and complexities of the footwear business.

"Some of the most complex design problems in any manufacturing sector are in footwear," explained Nick Brown, a partner with Comprehensive Computer Services Inc. (CCSI), which had produced Footworks.

In fact SAP had not decided to develop AFS itself. Rather it did so at the request of Peter Burrows, Reebok's chief technology officer. Key to the request was that SAP clothing and shoe customers, not SAP, would pay for development costs. The clothing and shoe industries "appeared messy and hard to deal with," explained Burrows, "and [SAP] said, 'Why should we be in it?'" The shoe and clothing production industries must keep track of thousands of items daily, many of which have a very short (months or only weeks) shelf life due to rapid changes in fashion. In addition many products are produced in small, technologically unsophisticated production facilities abroad, making the supply chain very complex and difficult to manage and control. In order to persuade SAP to agree to develop AFS, a consortium was formed by Reebok and VF Corp., the largest apparel company in the United States, producing such brands as Vanity Fair, Lee, and Wrangler. The consortium agreed to underwrite the development costs and would be the source of the system's requirements. Later, Sara Lee Hosiery, Kurt Salmon Associates of Atlanta, and other companies, hearing about the consortium, agreed to join it as associate members without the ability to add functionality to the software. The enthusiasm for the project "caught SAP by surprise," explained Burrows. "I think SAP underestimated how desperate the industry was for a good solution."

Ultimately the consortium unraveled. Reebok and VF are subject to rapidly changing fashion demands, and they needed software that would manage a manufacturing process that underwent frequent changes. Sara Lee, conversely, was not subject to rapid fashion changes. It was able to produce only one product line for a whole year—a repetitive manufacturing process. When SAP deleted repetitive manufacturing from the AFS production-planning module, Sara Lee withdrew from the project. Other smaller companies also could not get their needs met.

The big companies developed other problems. During 1998, soft sales in clothing and shoe industries caused the stocks of a number of companies to fall. Many customers, including Florsheim, Warnaco, and even Reebok, withdrew their interest in the project. Eventually, during 1998, the consortium died of its own weight.

Despite the problems with the consortium, AFS was introduced in April 1998. Some companies did not trust it. Harry Kubetz, senior vice president of operations for Kenneth Cole, said, "Although SAP had a product, it wasn't evident to us that it was available." Cole chose the JBA product instead. Only two companies were using it by the beginning of 1999. One was the Greg Norman division of Reebok International. That division had $100 million in sales within a company with $3.6 billion in revenues—not a vote of confidence from Reebok. The other user was Justin Industries, a $440 million conglomerate, which used it at its Fort Worth, Texas, footwear unit. However, Justin predicted that problems with the software would have a significant negative impact on its revenues.

Aerosoles also had difficulties with ASAP and, like some other companies, stopped using it. Compounding that problem for Aerosoles, Zonenshine claimed that the Eisner staff was not familiar with AFS despite their ample experience with R/3.

By early January 1999, the project had run into many problems. AeroGroup abandoned AFS and R/3 and instead signed a contract to purchase the JBA package. Morris and Zonenshine said they abandoned AFS because it was incomplete and too costly to be used to address Aerosoles' problems. The question is, what had actually gone wrong?

Sources: Larry Marion, "Autopsy of a Debacle," **Datamation**, February 1999; Deborah Ashbrand, "Peering across the Abyss," **Datamation**, January 1999, "Riskier Business! The High Cost of ERP Implementations," **Datamation**, September 1998, and "Risky Business: Bold R/3 Effort by Aerosoles," **Datamation**, July 1998; Michael Hammer, "Out of the Box," **Information Week**, February 8, 1999; and Tom Stein, "SAP Feels the Pinch," **Information Week**, January 11, 1999.

CASE STUDY QUESTIONS

1. Analyze Aerosoles using the value chain and competitive forces models.

2. Describe the problems facing Aerosoles that caused it to turn to ERP. Do you think ERP was an appropriate response to these problems? Explain your response.

3. Do you think Aerosoles originally should have adopted R/3 and AFS? Explain your answer.

4. Describe the management, organizational, and technology problems faced by Aerosoles in the R/3 project.

5. Evaluate the responsibility for each of the parties involved in the failed project: Aerosoles, Eisner, and SAP.

When Two Titans Merge: Management, Organization, and Technology Challenges at Citigroup

The financial world was shaken on April 5, 1998, when Citibank Corp. (Citicorp) and the Travelers Group announced they would merge. The size of the merger is stunning. It is the largest in history, with a market value of over $83 billion on the day it was announced. In addition, the merger is historic; it directly challenges United States laws that have governed the American financial industries since the days of the Great Depression by keeping the banking and insurance businesses separated. The new company, named Citigroup, Inc., is being characterized as a financial supermarket. The chief executives of the two companies are co-chairmen and co-chief executive officers of Citigroup. The merger was approved and went into effect in October 1998.

The Citigroup merger reflects a late 1990s desire to increase market share through merging. The two companies bring very different financial businesses to Citigroup. It thus is strong in traditional banking, consumer finance (including home mortgages), credit cards, savings and IRA plans, investment banking, securities brokerage, asset management, and property, casualty and life insurance. A financial company embracing such a broad business spectrum is common in other parts of the world but had not existed in the United States due to regulatory restrictions dating from the 1932 Glass-Steagall Act. By combining the two companies, Citigroup has a dramatically enlarged client base and extensive domestic and international distribution channels.

The new company is massive. In 1997 Citicorp and Travelers had combined assets of $700 billion, net revenues of nearly $50 billion, a combined equity of more than $44 billion, and an operating income of approximately $7.5 billion. Citigroup is starting with about 150,000 employees and over 100 million customers. It is the largest financial services company in the world.

THE MERGING COMPANIES: CITICORP AND TRAVELERS

Citicorp is one of the largest banks in the world and is the world's largest issuer of bankcards with over 60 million active cards in 1998. In addition it has a major global reach, with more than 1000 bank locations in over 40 countries around the world, plus banking services in about 60 other countries. The bank also specializes in transaction and funding services both for global corporations and for growth companies in emerging market areas.

Citicorp's CEO, John S. Reed, combines a thorough understanding of business with a broad knowledge of information technology. Reed was involved with the development of Citibank's highly successful ATM machines and was responsible for pushing Citibank into the credit card business. As a result, in 1984, at age 45, he became Citibank's CEO. In 1991, when Citibank stock price fell to single digits, Reed was almost unable to hold on to his job. It was during this crisis that he made the decision to change Citibank's focus from large corporate customers to individual customers in order to achieve more growth.

The Travelers Group is best known as an insurance company, but it is much more. Among its subsidiaries is Salomon Smith Barney, a major Wall Street brokerage firm. It is also the parent of Salomon Smith Barney Asset Management, Travelers Life & Annuity, Primerica Financial Services, and Travelers Property Casualty Corp. The Travelers Group specializes in investment services, asset management, consumer lending, life insurance, and property casualty insurance.

The Travelers we know in the 1990s is actually the creation of its current CEO: Sanford I. Weill. He has an extensive and very successful brokerage industry background. In 1993 Weill bought the ailing Travelers Insurance Company, and through new management and severe cost cutting, turned it around. He then bought various companies including Shearson Lehman and Smith Barney, the stock brokerage firms. In 1997 he bought Salomon Bros., merging them all. Today Travelers is a huge and very successful company.

A Study in Contrasts

Citicorp and Travelers have two fundamental principles in common: First, both have a core commitment to customer service; and second, in this age of globalization both companies have a desire for a major global reach. However, their differences are numerous.

○ **Global reach:** Citibank is a leader in electronic commerce, using it as a basic underpinning of its strategy to offer round-the-clock service all over the globe. As Ed Horowitz, Citibank executive vice president, explains it, "In essence, our goal is to be within one click, one call, one mile from our customers, no matter where they are around the world." On the other hand, Travelers has only a relatively limited reach globally.

○ **Domestic reach:** Despite Citicorp's great international product and service distribution systems, within the United States, Citicorp is just another important bank that falls far short of achieving nationwide coverage. Travelers, on the other hand, has 80,000 people selling its products in homes and offices throughout the United States.

○ **Customer base:** Citibank has a younger, less affluent customer base, while Travelers' customer base is older and more affluent.

○ **Sales channels:** Citibank is strong at mail, telephone, bankcards, and branches, while Travelers' strength is in personal, often home, sales staff selling.

○ **Product offerings:** While both corporations are part of the financial industry, they offer very different products, with little overlap, as you can see in the previous section describing the two companies.

○ **Customer asset management:** Although Citicorp is a bank, it is weak in asset management, while Travelers is a major asset manager, with more than $200 billion in mutual funds.

○ **Technology:** Citicorp stresses the development and use of advanced, innovative technology and is a leader in electronic banking services. Travelers, on the other hand, has a decided preference for low-cost no-frills systems. For example, Travelers forced Smith Barney to abandon its technologically advanced trading systems and instead use Travelers' older, simpler systems inherited from Shearson Lehman.

○ **Centralization and standardization:** Finally, while both companies are working toward centralized information systems, Travelers, particu-

By combining the banking services of Citicorp and the investment and insurance services of the Travelers Group, Citigroup plans to become a one-stop source of financial services.

larly Salomon Smith Barney, is much more advanced in standardizing and integrating its systems than is Citicorp.

Why the Merger?

The basic concept driving Citigroup is that it is to be a financial one-stop supermarket. That is, it will be a customer-centered organization that offers a wide variety of product lines that can be cross-marketed and cross-sold to its customers. At a congressional hearing on the proposed merger, Charles O. Prince, General Counsel of the Travelers Group, and John J. Roche, Citicorp General Counsel, jointly declared that "The ultimate test for our new company will be simple: Will we provide a high level of value and convenience to our customers?" They stressed the cross-selling synergies that are created by the merger, and emphasized their belief that Citigroup will succeed due both to the quality and to the breadth of their joint products. They also stressed their greatly expanded and innovative distribution channels that will include branch office locations in over one hundred countries around the world, individualized in-home service, and the Internet. The complementary nature of the two companies' outreach strengths is the key.

A major reason both companies became interested in this merger is that most people purchase different financial services from different companies. A person will bank with one company, buy life insurance elsewhere, handle her investments with a third company, and

may even have her home mortgage with a fourth company. Once the two firms have become more integrated, Travelers agents will be able to offer a whole set of Citicorp products to their current customers, and Citicorp employees likewise will have a new set of Travelers products to offer. For example, Travelers agents could sell mutual funds, and auto and life insurance to Citicorp customers, while Citicorp could sell home equity loans and bankcards to Travelers customers. Reed offered this comment: "The revenue has to come from enhancing each other's businesses. I know how Salomon Smith Barney can enhance our banking business: It will greatly enhance our ability to service customers around the world in an area where we were relatively weak—capital markets."

Combining the market strengths of these two firms is another reason for the merger—Travelers gains globalization while Citibank secures an expanded presence in the United States. With such worldwide coverage, the two CEOs believe the merger will give them cross-selling opportunities throughout the world. In addition both CEOs are concerned about competition from foreign companies who do not face the United States legal restrictions against combining banking with insurance. "U.S. financial services companies must be able to offer customers the same array of products and services that their international competitors are now free to provide," they stated.

The two companies see other advantages as well. For example, Weill stresses

the reduced risk that comes with greater diversity, saying, "Our company will be so diversified and in so many different areas that we will be able to withstand these storms [future market collapses]." Both companies believe that as a single company, they will be able dramatically to expand their customer base. In April 1998 Citibank executive vice-president, Edward Horowitz, announced a goal of one billion customers worldwide for Citigroup by 2010, a ten-fold increase. They will rely heavily upon electronic connections such as home banking and electronic commerce.

Management also sees opportunities for cost savings through improved and more efficient customer service, and reduced overhead and distribution costs. Citibank claims its Asia-Pacific credit and bankcard costs per transaction have fallen dramatically through centralized backroom processing. Some also see vast savings by standardizing and integrating their information technology. Diogo Teixeira, president of Tower Group, estimates that the combined organizations can save about $700 million annually in IT costs. He believes the one-time cost of the IT merger will be about $100 million, thus leaving vast funds available for new IT investment.

Will Cross-Selling Be a Successful Business Strategy?

Many observers have raised questions about the theory behind the merger. They point to repeated past cross-selling failures, including attempts in the 1980s by Sears and American Express. Studies indicate that only about 20 percent of all financial services customers bundle their services with one provider. They cite an interesting statistic, that 80 percent of life insurance agents have never even sold an auto insurance policy. According to Paul Newsome, CIBC Oppenheimer analyst who follows Travelers, "The basic risk is that they put these [consumer operations] together and nothing happens. Something will happen there, but it could be very small."

Today the conditions for cross-selling may be worse than ever before because customer choices have multiplied. The Internet is now making comparison shopping for financial services quick and easy. Potential customers shop on-line from the comfort of home, comparing services and costs, making decisions, and even entering transactions. On-line banks are beginning to appear, and brokerage houses with on-line facilities, such as Charles Schwab and E*Trade, are taking business from traditional brokerage houses. In addition, computer financial packages such as Intuit's Quicken offer similar services that customers can also use with relative ease. The question analysts ask is, why would most people buy their financial products from one place when they can easily do better by selecting the best products for themselves?

Merging Two Cultures

The process of merging two such large organizations is fraught with dangers. Cultural differences are fundamental and must be addressed if the merger is to succeed. Citibank and Travelers concepts and practices regarding pay structure are quite different. Citicorp compensates its bank officers and executives much as other banks do. It has about 1100 corporate calling officers of whom only three earned more than $1 million in 1997. Citicorp uses grants of restricted Citicorp stock to reward and hold onto its high-level people, although once the employees have purchased their shares, Citicorp imposes no general requirement that they hold on to those shares. In addition, Citicorp does not require its officers and board members to be significant shareholders. As a result the officers and directors combined owned less than one-half of one percent of the company's stock, giving them only a minimal financial stake in the future success of the company. Travelers views compensation very differently. First, Salomon Smith Barney, its brokerage and investment banking company, has about

1000 investment bankers of whom about 150 were paid over $1 million in 1997. In addition, Travelers offers bountiful stock option grants and binds its executives' fortunes tightly to that of the company by including stringent restrictions on their right to sell their stock. Weill personally owned 1.3 percent of Travelers' shares, and the other officers and directors combined owned another 1.1 percent.

The two companies also differ on compensation for back-office operations. Back-office pay traditionally is high in investment banking firms like Salomon because the staff works on sophisticated, highly speculative derivative products. At Citicorp the back-office pay is much lower because they work on much less intricate products such as check processing.

Many analysts fear that such different pay structures will destroy the morale of many employees, and so they believe it is essential to achieve a unified approach. But this may not be possible. Citicorp vice-president Robert McCormack defends the bank's compensation policy, arguing that Citicorp's corporate banking business "is the most profitable corporate banking business on earth. We don't do that under-paying people." Yet Travelers can hardly cut its investment banking salaries and still compete in hiring and retaining top employees. Executives at Travelers believe that its stock options policy has resulted in a very strong sense of teamwork. As they see it, executive compensation has been heavily tied to Travelers stock price, which reflects the profitability of the entire company, not just one's own area. Yet Reed argues that stock options are not appropriate for a global organization with many foreign senior managers because options are strange to most foreigners. Interestingly, Citicorp's culture is reputed to be much more "go-it-alone" than is Travelers', and even Reed says he would like to see more teamwork at Citicorp.

Risk-taking is another area of sharp cultural contrast. Citicorp has been much more risk-averse than Travelers. Citicorp trades stocks, bonds, and currencies for its clients but not for its own account while Salomon takes large trading positions for its own account.

Other Nontechnical Merger Problems

Still other problems exist. History at both companies shows that their business units have been unwilling to share proprietary cus-

tomer data for cross-selling even within their own companies. This has made integration of its own units very difficult. For instance, while Travelers acquired Shearson Lehman Brothers in 1993 and Salomon Brothers in 1997, the two units continue to operate separately. Citicorp also "has struggled for years," according to Larry Tabb, to integrate its disparate financial systems in order to develop cross-selling opportunities. (Tabb, an analyst at The Tower Group, Newton, Mass., was the head of back-office operations at Citicorp's U.S. government securities unit during the mid-1980s.) In addition, bankers on both sides of the merger appear concerned about sharing customers in case the merger does not work out.

Another possible roadblock is the need to alter the legal environment. The 1932 Glass-Steagall Act separated commercial banking (Citibank) from investment banking (Salomon). It also bars commercial banks from engaging in most forms of insurance underwriting, a major Travelers business. The Bank Holding Company Act, 1976 does allow a nonbank company such as Travelers to own a bank for two years as a bank holding company while it is bringing itself into compliance with Glass-Steagall. At the end of that period, the Federal Reserve could grant three one-year extensions before the company must bring itself into compliance. However, after that, Glass-Steagall will rule and the company will have to be broken apart again unless the law is changed. The Federal Reserve has now given its approval, and in essence the merger is now a giant bet that Congress will radically change or repeal the Glass-Steagall Act by October 2003.

Power sharing at the top is yet another minefield that Citigroup will have to navigate. Weill and Reed are known for their strong personalities and egos, and any differences between the two might be difficult to solve. Commentators believe the merger would not have happened if either had insisted on being the boss in the new company, given their strong egos. The co-CEO arrangement will have to last several years while the two parts of the company are welded together; Reed and Weill have agreed that neither will retire until the two companies are genuinely merged.

Integrating Information Technology Infrastructure

It is clear that IT also is critical to the success of the merger. Some analysts even say that success or failure of the financial services supermarket will depend upon how well the two companies' information technology infrastructures and information architectures can be integrated. Creating a financial services supermarket requires integrating information systems, customer databases, product lines, and multiple transaction types. Yet both Citibank and Travelers have very different information architectures, with applications, databases, and processes that are based on very different business models.

Over the years, Citicorp built up a very decentralized information architecture by allowing its business units to have a great deal of local autonomy. Many of its information systems are very fragmented, with traders and their offices worldwide allowed to use different servers and applications. Citicorp's information technology infrastructure has about 20,000 different pieces of technology and it is spread throughout many locations throughout the world. Salomon Smith Barney's systems are somewhat more integrated and centrally managed, although they are smaller and locally based.

Experts point out two ways of handling the information technology issues associated with the merger. One is to emulate Morgan Stanley and Dean Witter, which did not integrate their businesses and services when they merged, keeping two primary dealers, sales forces, and trading desks. The other alternative is to integrate both companies as tightly as possible. The question is whether Citigroup could cross-sell products and become a financial supermarket without this full IT integration.

All financial service organizations are very information-dependent because they generate and store immense quantities of data that have been described as "the jewels of the company." Such data are vital not only for customer sharing, but also for datamining to create tailored marketing and sales efforts. By pooling customer data from all of its business units, Citigroup could target banking customers, who for example, might be interested in insurance or investment services.

In 1997, combined Travelers and Citicorp IT spending amounted to $6.8 billion, an enormous expense. The payoffs from integration could be significant. For instance, once the systems are merged, future development costs for Internet-based marketing and transaction systems or other capabilities would be shared. In addition to product-related systems, it is

likely the two companies could combine other systems, such as accounting and billing systems, marketing and sales, in order to achieve even greater savings. In addition, both Citicorp and Travelers have been experiencing a growing reliance on wide area networks, an essential factor in the success of any globalized business that is centrally controlled and managed. Some experts also claim that bank regulations require that their balance sheets, credit risk assessments, and settlement procedures be integrated.

Citicorp has been trying to centralize many of its systems for years and only now is achieving some success. For example, the bank has only recently succeeded in centralizing the processing of bankcards in Asia-Pacific after many years of effort. (International Case Study 4 explores this topic.) Citicorp has also spent years trying to reduce its wide area networks (WANs), down to the current 11 regional networks. To finally unite them into one centrally managed network, Citicorp recently had to resort to outside help, signing a five-year $750 million contract with AT&T to outsource its networking in 98 countries worldwide. Travelers is further along with integrating its systems, although key systems of Salomon Brothers and Smith Barney will not be integrated until well into 1999.

Citigroup could opt for total systems integration, creating a common hardware and software platform, servers, risk management software, and back-office operations. But building a standard information technology infrastructure serving all of its organizations would require both massive expenditures and organizational changes. Alternatively, it could keep separate information technology infrastructures but create a data warehouse for customer information that could be used for cross-selling. (Citicorp already has a project in process to create a data warehouse to store data on its largest customers.) The expanded data warehouse would be populated with customer data from both Travelers and Citicorp units, but both organizations could continue with their own systems and business processes. The data warehouse approach is more expedient and less disruptive to the organization, but analysts suggest that complete system integration would be required to realize the full range of benefits of a financial supermarket and efficient management of risk.

Merging trading floor technology poses difficult technical questions. The two com-

panies use technologically disparate trading systems. Citicorp uses Reuters' Triarch 2000 whereas Salomon Smith Barney relies primarily upon TIB (Tibco Finance) systems (also owned by Reuters but operated independently). Salomon also makes some use of Triarch as well as FS Partner, a mixture that is the result of the 1997 Salomon Smith Barney merger. Triarch and TIB are both important systems in the industry, but they are fundamentally different. TIB is highly configurable—"a tinkerer's paradise," according to Ed Miller, the president of MarketNet, a New York company specializing in trading room technology support. It is easily customized for individual users. On the other hand, Miller calls Triarch "highly resilient, bullet-proof, shrink-wrapped, easy to maintain." However, the price of this resiliency is its lack of ability to be customized. The technology issue is confused in other ways as well. Salomon Bros. has a huge investment in UNIX and Sun Microsystems' UNIX-based servers and workstations, while Smith Barney uses both UNIX and Windows-based IBM-PCs. Citicorp uses Windows NT on PCs as well as UNIX-based Sun and Digital Equipment Corp. servers and workstations. Rationalizing all of this will be difficult and costly. Questions being asked include: Do the various units have the short-run will to move to a single technology in order to bring about major long-run cost savings? If so, how much money are the two companies willing to spend on the transition? And perhaps more difficult, how much valuable trading room equipment and software that has not yet been depreciated are they willing to write off in order to achieve integration? And, of course, can they overcome cultural differences relating to centralization and the use of cutting-edge technology?

The federal and state regulatory environment is another key issue because banks and insurance companies are regulated differently. Citibank has been under much stricter regulations that was Travelers because of its need to meet regulatory banking standards. The surviving Citigroup may now come under some of those regulations, forcing changes in Travelers' IT systems.

Since the merger was announced, Citigroup's information system efforts have focused primarily on solving Year 2000 problems and modifying systems to handle Euro currency conversion (see Chapters 3 and 7). If the two companies do move to standardize their systems, power struggles and personnel problems will surely emerge. The dynamic between the IT department's desire to standardize and the desire of the business groups to customize is complex and difficult to deal with. IT personnel problems also are a real possibility due to a fear of layoffs. As pointed out by Bob Harman, bank technology consultant for Deloitte & Touche, "When you rationalize the merger [i.e., integrate strategies and systems], you know that somebody's team wins, someone's loses." Both companies announced massive layoffs just a month prior to their legal merger and more are being planned.

Many are wondering whether an IT merger can or should ever take place. Bill Burnham, senior analyst at Piper Jaffray Cos., of Minneapolis, believes Citigroup would "have to stop the business for three years" to effectively merge the databases and systems of the two companies. Other analysts conclude that the risks of a full IT merger outweigh any possible benefits. Larry Cone, a banking analyst with the Ryan Beck & Co. investment bank, says he "can't imagine why they would merge them. That is a very low order of business."

Sources: Tara Siegel, "Citigroup Is Ready to Realize Benefits of Cross-Selling," **The Wall Street Journal**, March 15, 1999; Paul Beckett, "Citigroup Revamps Derivatives Business," **The Wall Street Journal**, January 21, 1999 and "Citigroup Unit of Bankers Begins to Meld," **The Wall Street Journal**, January 11, 1999; Thomas Hoffman, "Citigroup Cuts to Pinch IT Support Staff," **Computerworld**, December 21, 1998; Erik Helland, "Can Citigroup Reign in Citicorp's Decentralized Strategy," **Wall Street & Technology**, July 1998; Robert Sales, "A Battle Brews on Citigroup Trading Floor," **Wall Street & Technology**, July 1998; Ivy Schmerken, "The Big Gamble: Mergers & Technology," **Wall Street & Technology**, July 1998; Saul Hansell, "Clash of Technologies in Merger," **The New York Times**, April 13, 1998 and "Citibank Sets New On-Line Bank System," **The New York Times**, October 5, 1998; Michael Schrage, "IT and the Citigroup Gamble," **Computerworld**, April 27, 1998; Thomas Hoffman and Kim S. Nash, "Titanic Tangle," **Computerworld**, April 13, 1998; Jennifer Bresnahan, "Someone to Watch Over IT," **Enterprise Magazine**, May 15, 1998; Bruce Caldwell, "Citibank Outsources Data Networks to AT&T in $750 Million Deal," **InformationWeek**, March 10, 1998; Charles Pelton, "Redefining Scalability," **InformationWeek**, April 20, 1998; Lawrence Quinn, "If the Systems Fit, So Must the Corporate Cultures," **Wall Street & Technology**, July 1998; "Citicorp and Travelers Group to Merge, Creating Citigroup: The Global Leader in Financial Services," Citicorp press release, April 6, 1998; Beth Davis and Rich Levin, "Bank Shot," **InformationWeek**, April 20, 1998; Stephen E. Frank, Anita Raghavan, and Matt Murray, "Travelers and Citicorp Agree to Join Forces in $83 Billion Merger," **The Wall Street Journal**, April 7, 1998; Mary Kelleher, "Citigroup Faces Cross-selling Hurdle," Pathfinder [http://www. pathfinder.com/money/] July 2, 1998; Mark Landler, "Bold Step for Citigroup on Shaky Asian Ground," **The New York Times**, April 9, 1998; Carol J. Loomis, James Aley, and Lixandra Urresta, "One Helluva Candy Store," **Fortune**, May 11, 1998; Kim S. Nash, "Reed Shifts from Programmer to CEO," **Computerworld**, April 13, 1998; Anita Raghavan and Rick Brooks, "Citigroup, BankAmerica's Goals Differ," **The Wall Street Journal**, April 14, 1998; Anita Raghavan and Stephen E. Frank, "Making Oil and Water (Citicorp, Travelers Group) Mix," **The Wall Street Journal**, April 17, 1998; Leslie Scism, Anita Raghavan, and Stephen E. Frank, "If Weill, Reed Merge Their Firms, Can They Also Merge Their Egos?" **The Wall Street Journal**, April 7, 1998; Richard W. Stevenson, "In Largest Deal Ever, Citicorp Plans Merger with Travelers Group," **The New York Times**, April 7, 1998; Patrick Thibodeau, "AT&T Snags $750M Citibank Outsourcing Job," **Computerworld**, March 10, 1998; Peter Truell, "Travelers Deal with Nikko Expected Today," **The Wall Street Journal**, July 1, 1998 and "Travelers and Citicorp Plan to Cut Jobs," **The New York Times**, September 18, 1998.

CASE STUDY QUESTIONS

1. What will be the business strategy of Citigroup? How is the merger of Citicorp and Travelers related to this business strategy?

2. How is information technology vital to the success of Citigroup's strategy?

3. What options does Citigroup have in building an information technology infrastructure to support its strategy? What management, organization, and technology issues must be addressed by each option?

4. List each of the factors that will be key to a successful integration of Citicorp and Travelers. Explain why each is so important.

5. Develop a strategy for integrating the IT systems of the two companies. Be certain that your strategy handles all the key factors you listed in question three.

Business Process Redesign Project

Healthlite Yogurt Company

Healthlite Yogurt Company is a market leader in the expanding U.S. market for yogurt and related health products. Healthlite is experiencing some sharp growing pains. With the growing interest in low-fat, low-cholesterol health foods, spurred on by the aging of the baby boomers, Healthlite's sales have tripled over the past five years. At the same time, however, new local competitors, offering fast delivery from local production centers and lower prices, are challenging Healthlite for retail shelf space with a bevy of new products. Without shelf space, products cannot be retailed in the United States, and new products are needed to expand shelf space. Healthlite needs to justify its share of shelf space to grocers and is seeking additional shelf space for its new yogurt-based products such as frozen desserts and low-fat salad dressings.

Healthlite's biggest challenge, however, has not been competitors but the sweep of the second hand. Yogurt has a very short shelf life. With a shelf life measured in days, yogurt must be moved very quickly.

Healthlite maintains its U.S. corporate headquarters in Danbury, Connecticut. Corporate headquarters has a central mainframe computer that maintains most of the major business databases. All production takes place in processing plants that are located in New Jersey, Massachusetts, Tennessee, Illinois, Colorado, Washington, and California. Each processing plant has its own minicomputer, which is connected to the corporate mainframe. Customer credit verification is maintained at corporate headquarters, where customer master files are maintained and order verification or rejection is determined. Once processed centrally, order data are then fed to the appropriate local processing plant minicomputer.

Healthlite has 20 sales regions, each with approximately 30 sales representatives and a regional sales manager. Healthlite has a 12-person marketing group at corporate headquarters and a corporate director of sales and marketing. Each salesperson is able to store and retrieve data for assigned customer accounts using a terminal in the regional office linked to the corporate mainframe. Reports for individual salespeople (printouts of orders, rejection notices, customer account inquiries, etc.) and for sales offices are printed in the regional offices and mailed to them.

Sometimes, the only way to obtain up-to-date sales data is for managers to make telephone calls to subordinates and then piece the information together. Data about sales and advertising expenses and customer shelf space devoted to Healthlite products are maintained manually at the regional offices. Each regional office maintains its own manual records of customer shelf space and promotional campaigns. The central computer contains only consolidated, companywide files for customer account data and order and billing data. The aging mainframe runs programs built back in the early 1980s.

The existing order processing system requires sales representatives to write up hardcopy tickets to place orders through the mail or by fax. Each ticket lists the amount and kind of product ordered by the customer account. Approximately one hundred workers at Healthlite corporate headquarters open, sort, keypunch, and process 500,000 order tickets per week. Frequently orders are delayed when the fax machines break down. This order information is transmitted every evening from the mainframe to a minicomputer at each of Healthlite's processing sites. This daily order specifies the total yogurt and yogurt product demand for each processing center. The processing center then produces the amount and type of yogurt and yogurt-related products ordered and then ships the orders out. Shipping managers at the processing centers assign the shipments to various transportation carriers, who deliver the product to receiving warehouses located in the regions.

Rapid growth, fueled by Healthlite's "health" image and its branching into new yogurt-based products, has put pressures on Healthlite's existing information systems. By mid-1999, growth in new products and sales had reached a point where Healthlite was printing new tickets for the sales force every week. The firm was choking on paper. For each order, a salesperson filled out at least two forms per account. Some sales representatives have more than 80 customers.

As it became bogged down in paper, Healthlite saw increased delays in the processing of its orders. Since yogurt is a fresh food product, it could not be held long in inventory. Yet Healthlite had trouble shipping the right goods to the right places in time. It was taking between four and fourteen days to process and ship out an order, depending on mail delivery rates. Healthlite also found accounting discrepancies of $1.5 million annually between the sales force and headquarters.

Communication between sales managers and sales representatives has been primarily through the mail or by telephone. For example, regional sales managers have to send representatives letters with announcements of promotional campaigns or pricing discounts. Sales representatives have to write up their monthly reports of sales calls and then mail this information to regional headquarters.

Healthlite is considering new information system solutions. First of all, the firm would like to solve the current order entry crisis and develop immediately a new order processing system. Management would also like to make better use of information systems to support sales and marketing activities and to take advantage of new Web-based information technologies. In particular, management wants a sales-oriented Web site to help market the products but is unsure how this will fit into the sales effort. Management wants to know how these new technologies can assist the local groceries and large chains who sell the product to the actual consumer.

Senior management is prepared to make a considerable investment in a plan for rescuing the company's systems and business operations. However, management is looking for a modest reduction in sales force head count as new, more effective systems come on-line and to help pay for the systems investment. While senior management wants the company to deploy contemporary systems, they do not want to experiment with new technologies and are only comfortable using technology that has proven itself in real-world applications.

Sales and Marketing Information Systems: Background

Sales and marketing are vital to the operation of any business. Orders must be processed and related to production and inventory. Sales of products in existing markets must be monitored and new products developed for new markets. The firm must be able to respond to rapidly changing market demands, proliferation of new products and competing firms, shortened product life spans, changing consumer tastes, and new government regulations.

Firms need sales and marketing information in order to do product planning, make pricing decisions, devise advertising and other promotional campaigns, forecast market potential for new and existing products, and determine channels of distribution. They must also monitor the efficiency of the distribution of their products and services.

The sales function of a typical business captures and processes customer orders and produces invoices for customers and data for inventory and production. A typical invoice is illustrated here.

```
┌─────────────────────────────────────────────────────────────────┐
│                    Healthlite Yogurt, Inc.                        │
│ Customer:                                                         │
│ Highview Supermarket                                              │
│ 223 Highland Avenue                                               │
│ Ossining, New York 10562                                          │
│                                                                   │
│ Order Number:          679940                                     │
│ Customer Number:       #00395                                     │
│ Date:                  04/15/99                                   │
│                                                                   │
│ Quantity    SKU#       Description       Unit Price      Amount   │
│ 100         V3392      8 oz Vanilla      .44             44.00    │
│ 50          S4456      8 oz Strawberry   .44             22.00    │
│ 65          L4492      8 oz Lemon        .44             28.60    │
│                                                                   │
│ Shipping:                                                10.00    │
│ Total Invoice:                                           104.60   │
└─────────────────────────────────────────────────────────────────┘
```

Data from order entry are also used by a firm's accounts receivable system and by the firm's inventory and production systems. The production planning system, for instance, builds its daily production plans based on the prior day's sales. The number and type of product sold will determine how many units to produce and when.

Sales managers need information to plan and monitor the performance of the sales force. Management also needs information on the performance of specific products, product lines, or brands. Price, revenue, cost, and growth information can be used for pricing decisions, for evaluating the performance of current products, and for predicting the performance of future products.

From basic sales and invoice data, a firm can produce a variety of reports with valuable information to guide sales and marketing work. For weekly, monthly, or annual time periods, information can be gathered on which outlets order the most, on what the average order amount is, on which products move slowest and fastest, on which salespersons sell the most and least, on which geographic areas purchase the most of a given product, and on how current sales of a product compare to last year's product.

The Assignment

Either alone, or with a group of three or four of your classmates, develop a proposal for re-designing Healthlite's business processes for sales, marketing, and order processing that would make the company more competitive. Your report should include the following:

○ An overview of the organization—its structure, products, and major business processes for sales, marketing, and order processing.

○ An analysis of Healthlite's problems: What are Healthlite's problems? How are these problems related to existing business processes and systems? What management, organization, and technology factors contributed to these problems?

○ An overall management plan for improving Healthlite's business and system situation. This would include a list of objectives, a time-frame, major milestones, and an assessment of the costs and benefits of implementing this plan.

○ Identification of the major changes in business processes required to achieve your plan.

○ Identification of the major new technology components of your plan that are required to support the new business processes. If your solution requires a new system or set of systems, describe the functions of these systems, what pieces of information these systems should contain, and how this information should be captured, organized, and stored.

○ A sample data entry screen or report for one of the new systems, if proposed.

○ A description of the steps you would take as a manager to handle the conversion from the old system to the new.

○ Quality assurance measures.

Your report should also describe the organizational impact of your solution. Consider human interface issues, the impact on jobs and interest groups, and any risks associated with implementing your solution. How will you implement your solution to take these issues into account?

It is important to establish the scope of the system. It should be limited to order processing and related sales and marketing activities. You do not have to redesign Healthlite's manufacturing, accounts receivable, distribution, or inventory control systems for this exercise.

CASE STUDY 1: Geelong & District Water Board to Barwon Water: An Integrated IT Infrastructure[1]

Joel B. Barolsky and Peter Weill, University of Melbourne (Australia)

Joe Adamski, the Geelong and District Water Board's (GDWB) executive manager of information systems, clicked his mouse on the phone messages menu option. Two messages had been left. The first was from an IT manager from a large Sydney-based insurance company confirming an appointment to "visit the GDWB and to assess what the insurance company could learn from the GDWB's IT experience." The second was from the general manager of another large water board asking whether Adamski and his team could assist, on a consultancy basis, in their IT strategy formulation and implementation.

The site visit from the insurance company was the thirty-fifth such request the Board had received since the completion of the first stage of their IT infrastructure investment strategy in January 1992. These requests were a pleasant diversion but the major focus of the GDWB's IT staff was to nurture and satisfy the increasing demands from the operational areas for building applications utilizing the newly installed IT infrastructure. The Water Board also faced the problem of balancing further in-house developments with external requests for consulting and demands from the GDWB's IT staff for new challenges and additional rewards.

ORGANIZATION BACKGROUND

The GDWB was constituted as a public utility of the Australian State of Victoria in July 1984 following an amalgamation of the Geelong Waterworks and Sewerage Trust and a number of other smaller regional water boards. The Board has the responsibility for the collection and distribution of water and the treatment and disposal of wastewater within a 1600-square-mile region in the southwest part of the state. In 1991, the permanent population serviced by the Board exceeded 200,000 people, this number growing significantly in the holiday periods with an influx of tourists.

The GDWB financed all its capital expenditure and operational expenditure through revenue received from its customers and through additional loan borrowings. Any profits generated were reinvested in the organization or used to pay off long-term debt. For the financial year 1990–91 the Board invested over $35.3 million in capital works and spent over $25 million in operating expenditures. Operating profit for the year 1990–91 exceeded $62.4 million on total assets of $292.5 million.

In 1992, the GDWB was headed by a governing board with a state government-appointed chairperson and eight members, elected by the residents of the community, who each sat for a three-year term. Managerial and administrative responsibilities were delegated to the GDWB's Executive Group which consists of the CEO and executive managers from each of the five operating divisions, namely information systems, finance, corporate services, engineering development, and engineering operations. From 1981 to 1992, the number of GDWB employees across all divisions rose from 304 to 454.

The GDWB's head office, situated in the regional capital city of Geelong, housed most of the Board's customer service, administrative, engineering, IT, and other managerial staff. Complementing these activities, the GDWB operated five regional offices and a specialized 24-hour emergency contact service.

Commenting on the Board's competitive environment at the time, the GDWB's CEO, Geoff Vines, stated, "Although the organization operated in a monopolistic situation there still were considerable pressures on us to perform efficiently. Firstly, and most importantly, our objective was to be self-funding—our customers wouldn't tolerate indiscriminate rate increases as a result of our inefficiencies and we could not go cap in hand to the state government. Secondly, the amalgamation trend of water boards was continuing and the stronger the Board was the less likely it would be a target of a takeover. And thirdly, we did in a sense compare ourselves with private sector organizations and in some ways with other water boards. We had limited resources and we have to make the most of them."

KEY PROBLEM AREAS

Relating the situation up until the mid-1980s, Vines said that the Board faced a major problem in collectively identifying its largest assets—the underground pipes, drains, pumps, sewers, and other facilities. He explained that most of these facilities were installed at least two or three meters below the surface and therefore it was almost impossible to gain immediate physical access to them. The exact specifications of each particular asset could only be ascertained through a thorough analysis of the original installation documentation and other geophysical surveys and maps of the area.

The limitations on identifying these underground facilities impacted operational performance in a number of key areas:

○ Most of the maintenance work conducted by the Board was based on reactive responses to leaks and other faults in the systems. It was difficult to introduce a coordinated preventative maintenance program because it was not possible to accurately predict when a particular pipe or piece of equipment was nearing the end of its expected life span.

○ Only a limited number of hard copies of this facility information could be kept. This significantly reduced the productivity of the engineering and operations staff, especially in remote areas where they had to request this information from the central record-keeping systems. Backlogs and inaccuracies in filing also impacted efforts to repair, upgrade, or install new piping, pumps, and other equipment. On numerous occasions changes would be made to one set of plans without the same changes being recorded on the other copies of the same plans. Engineers designing improvements to existing facilities were often confronted with the problem of not being sure whether they were using the most up-to-date information of the facilities currently installed in the area concerned.

○ The Board could not place realistic replacement values and depreciation charges on these underground assets.

With over 100,000 rateable properties in its area of responsibility, the GDWB maintained a centralized paper filing system containing more than a billion pages of related property information. The documents, most of which were of different sizes, quality, and age, were divided into 95,000 different files and sorted chronologically within each file. Access to the documents was made difficult as larger documents were cumbersome to copy and older documents were beginning to disintegrate. Having only one physical storage area significantly increased the potential exposure to fire and other risks and limited the wider distribution and sharing of the information. In the early 1980s, it was commonplace for a customer request for a statement of encumbrances placed at one of the GDWB's regional offices to take in excess of four weeks. The delays usually centered on finding the appropriate documents at the Property Services' central files, making the necessary copies, and transferring the documents back to the regional offices.

THE INFORMATION SYSTEMS DIVISION

In 1985, PA Consulting was commissioned to conduct a comprehensive review of the Board's strategy, management, operations structures, and systems. One recommendation made by the consultants was that the Board should institute a more systematic approach to strategic planning. A major outcome of the planning process that followed was to create a new division for computing services and to recruit a new manager for this new area who reported directly to the CEO. The EDP Division was created with the objectives of "satisfying the Board's Information System needs through the provision of integrated and secure corporate computer systems and communication network." Vines said that the Board needed a stand-alone information services group that could be used as a resource center for all users and that could add value to the work conducted by each functional group within the Board.

In April 1987, Joe Adamski was employed to fill the new position of EDP manager (later changed to executive manager of information systems). At the time of his arrival, only a small part of the GDWB's work systems were computerized, the main components of which included:

❍ a "low-end" IBM System 38, primarily to run financial and other accounting software and some word processing applications. The system ran an in-house-developed rate collection system which kept basic information on ratepayers including property details and consumption records;
❍ 19 "dumb" terminals—none of the Board's regional offices had terminal access to the central computer systems;

❍ a terminal link to the local university's DEC 20 computer to support the technical and laboratory services; and
❍ four stand-alone PCs, running some individual word processing packages as well as spreadsheet (Lotus 1-2-3), basic CAD, and database applications.

Computer maintenance, support, and development was allocated to the finance division and delegated to an EDP supervisor (and three staff) who reported to the finance manager. Adamski noted, "The computer set-up when I joined was pretty outdated and inefficient. For example, the secretarial staff at the Head Office were using the System 38's word processing facility and had to collect their dot matrix printouts from the computer room situated on the ground floor of the five-story building. In the technical area, some water supply network analysis data was available through the use of the DEC 20 system; however, hard copy output had to be collected from the University which was over five kilometers away. Most of the design engineers were using old drafting tables with rulers, erasers, and pencils as their only drafting tools."

Recognizing that some users required immediate solutions to problems they were facing, the Board purchased additional terminals, peripherals, and stand-alone microcomputers for the various areas thought to be in greatest need. Adamski said that these additional purchases further compounded some of the Board's computer-related problems. "We had a situation where we had at least four different CAD packages in use in different departments and we couldn't transfer data between them. There was a duplication of peripheral equipment with no sharing of printers, plotters, and other output devices. In addition, various managers began to complain that system expertise was too localized and that there was little compatibility between the various applications."

PLANNING THE NEW ROLE FOR IT

In July 1988, Adamski initiated a long-term computing strategy planning process with the establishment of a special planning project team with both IT and user representatives. The team embarked on a major program of interviews and discussion with all user areas within the Board. They investigated other similar public utilities across Australia to assess their IT strategies and infrastructures and made contact with various computer hardware and software ven-

dors to determine the latest available technologies and indicative costs.

The Project Team developed a comprehensive corporate computing strategy that would provide, as Adamski put it, the "quantum leap forward in the Board's IT portfolio." Adamski said that central to the devised computing strategy was that there should be as much integration and flexibility as possible in all the Board's technical and administrative systems. "Linked to this strategy was the notion that we should strive for an 'open systems' approach with all our applications. This meant that each system had to have publicly specifiable interfaces or 'hooks' so that each system could talk to each other. From the users' perspective an open systems approach meant that all the different applications looked pretty much the same and it was simple and easy to cross over from one to the other. It also meant that if we weren't happy with one particular product within the portfolio or we wanted to add a new one we could do it without too much disruption to the whole system."

He continued, "A key decision was made that we should build on our existing IT investments. With this in mind we had to make sure that the new systems were able to use the data and communicate with the System 38. We wanted only one hardware platform using only one operating system and only one relational database management system [RDBMS]. We also wanted only one homogenous network that was able to cater to a number of protocols and interfaces such as the network system for the microcomputers, workstations, and the Internet connection. There also had to be a high degree of compatibility and interaction with all the data files and applications that were proposed. In view of this, we chose a UNIX platform with a client/server architecture."

In addition to specifying the software components of the system, the Project Team outlined the hardware that was necessary to run the new systems and the additional staff that needed to be hired. To achieve the stated computing strategies and benefits, the Team also recommended that implementation take place over three key stages, with a formal progress review instituted at the end of each stage.

APPROVAL

In February 1989, the corporate computing strategy planning process was completed and Adamski presented the key recommendations to the governing Board. In his presentation, Adamski stated that the infrastructure cost of implementing the strategy

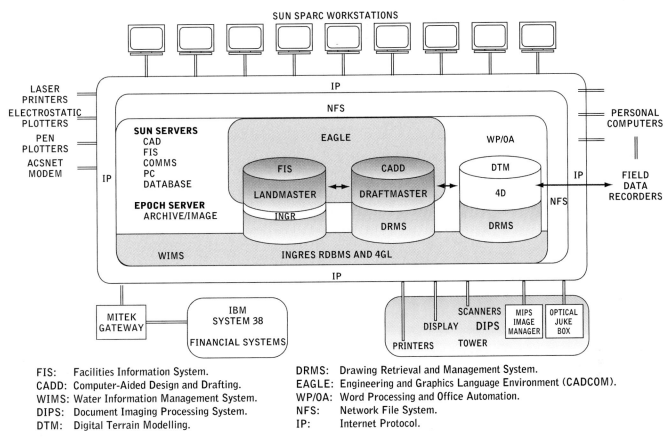

SUN SPARC WORKSTATIONS

LASER PRINTERS
ELECTROSTATIC PLOTTERS
PEN PLOTTERS
ACSNET MODEM

IP

NFS

SUN SERVERS
CAD
FIS
COMMS
PC
DATABASE

EPOCH SERVER
ARCHIVE/IMAGE

EAGLE

WP/OA

FIS
LANDMASTER
INGR

CADD
DRAFTMASTER

DTM
4D
DRMS

DRMS

WIMS

INGRES RDBMS AND 4GL

IP

PERSONAL COMPUTERS

IP   FIELD DATA RECORDERS

NFS

MITEK GATEWAY

IBM SYSTEM 38
FINANCIAL SYSTEMS

PRINTERS   DISPLAY

SCANNERS   DIPS
TOWER

MIPS IMAGE MANAGER

OPTICAL JUKE BOX

FIS: Facilities Information System.
CADD: Computer-Aided Design and Drafting.
WIMS: Water Information Management System.
DIPS: Document Imaging Processing System.
DTM: Digital Terrain Modelling.

DRMS: Drawing Retrieval and Management System.
EAGLE: Engineering and Graphics Language Environment (CADCOM).
WP/OA: Word Processing and Office Automation.
NFS: Network File System.
IP: Internet Protocol.

Figure 1 GDWB corporate computing system.

was estimated to be about $5 million for the entire project (excluding data capture costs) and that the project would take up to the end of 1995 for full commissioning.

Vines stated, "From my perspective, the proposed IT strategy took into account the critical functions in the organization that needed to be supported, such as customer services, asset management, and asset creation. These were fundamental components of the Board's corporate objectives, and the computer strategy provided a means to realize these objectives and provide both short- and long-term benefits. There were some immediate short-term benefits, such as securing property services data that had no backup, and productivity gains in design and electronic mail. From a long-term perspective, I believe you can never really do an accurate rate-of-return calculation and base your decision solely on that. If you did you probably would never make such a large capital investment in IT. We did try to cost-justify all the new systems as best we could but we stressed that implementing IT strategy should be seen as providing long-term benefits for the entire organization that were not immediately measurable and would come to fruition many years later. Until all

the information was captured and loaded on the IT facilities from the manual systems, the full benefits could not be realized."

Following an extensive and rigorous tendering process, it was decided that the Board should follow a multivendor solution as no one vendor could provide a total solution. Sun Microsystems was selected as the major hardware vendor and was asked to act as "prime contractors" in implementation. As prime contractors Sun was paid one project fee and then negotiated separate contracts with all other suppliers.

IMPLEMENTATION

In April 1990, the implementation of the IT strategy commenced with the delivery of the Sun file servers and workstations and installation of a homogenous network throughout the Board. Adamski said that the implementation stage went surprisingly smoothly. "We didn't fire anybody as a direct result of the new systems, but jobs were changed. There was some resistance to the new technology—most of it was born out of unfamiliarity and fear of not having the appropriate skills. Some people were very committed in doing things 'their way.' When some of these people started to

perceive tangible productivity benefits, their perspectives started to change. We tried to counsel people as best we could and encourage them to experiment with the new systems. Most people eventually converted but there were still some objectors."

Adamski added that while they were implementing the new systems it was important for the IS Division not to lose sight of its key objectives and role within the organization. "We had to make sure that we didn't get carried away with the new whiz-bang technology and reduce our support and maintenance of the older, more conventional systems. For example, the Board went onto a new tariff system and we had to make significant changes to our rating system to accommodate this. Having an application generator in place significantly improved the systems upgrade time."

In May 1992, the Board's computer facilities included 4 Sun file servers, 80 Sun workstations, 100 microcomputers, 40 terminals, and the IBM System 38 Model 700. By this time, the IS Division had implemented the following components of the systems (see Figure 1 for a schematic of the systems):

Figure 2 Example of a building plan kept for each rateable property.

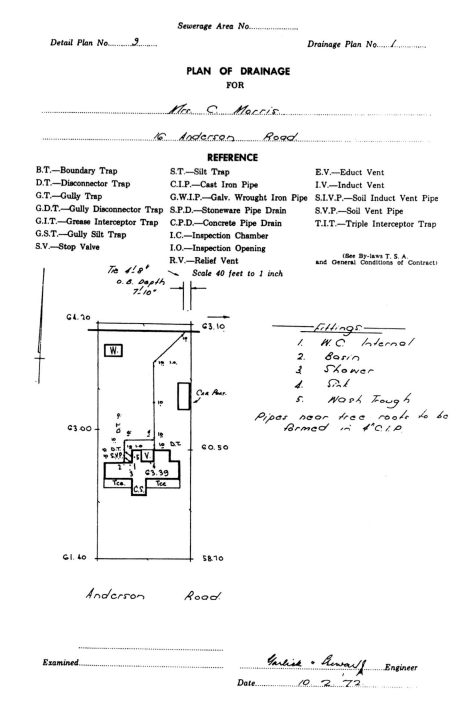

TORQUAY SEWERAGE AUTHORITY

Sewerage Area No.....................

Detail Plan No..........*9*.......   Drainage Plan No......*1*..........

PLAN OF DRAINAGE
FOR

.... *Mrs. C. Morris* ....

.... *16 Anderson Road* ....

REFERENCE

B.T.—Boundary Trap	S.T.—Silt Trap	E.V.—Educt Vent
D.T.—Disconnector Trap	C.I.P.—Cast Iron Pipe	I.V.—Induct Vent
G.T.—Gully Trap	G.W.I.P.—Galv. Wrought Iron Pipe	S.I.V.P.—Soil Induct Vent Pipe
G.D.T.—Gully Disconnector Trap	S.P.D.—Stoneware Pipe Drain	S.V.P.—Soil Vent Pipe
G.I.T.—Grease Interceptor Trap	C.P.D.—Concrete Pipe Drain	T.I.T.—Triple Interceptor Trap
G.S.T.—Gully Silt Trap	I.C.—Inspection Chamber	
S.V.—Stop Valve	I.O.—Inspection Opening	
	R.V.—Relief Vent	(See By-laws T. S. A. and General Conditions of Contract)

Scale 40 feet to 1 inch

Examined..

Garlick & Stewart Engineer

Date............*10. 2. '72*................

1. A **Document Imaging Processing System (DIPS)** used for scanning, storing, and managing all documents on each property within the GDWB region which were being kept in the 95,000 separate paper files. This system was also used for the storage, backup, and retrieval of 25,000 engineering plans and drawings. DIPS gave designated Head Office departments and regional offices real-time access to all property documentation and allowed them to print out scanned images when required. The system had a sophisticated indexing system that facilitated easy retrieval of stored images by users and access by other programs. Figure 2 presents a copy of a scanned property plan from DIPS.

2. A digital mapping **Facilities Information System (FIS)** that provided for the storage, management, and ongoing maintenance of all graphic (map related) and nongraphic information relating to water and wastewater services, property information, property boundaries, and easements throughout the Board's region. The FIS provided a computerized

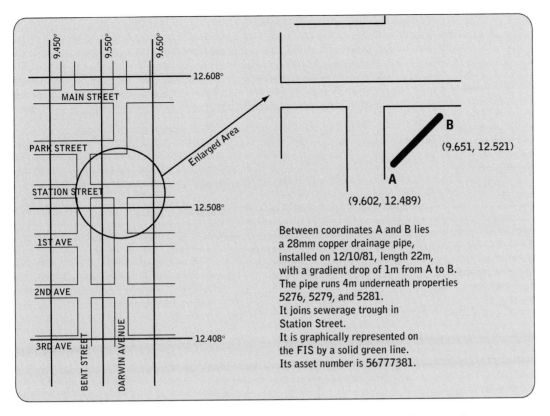

Figure 3 Illustration of the type of information available on the Facilities Information System.

"seamless" geographic map covering the entire GDWB region. The system encompassed the storing of all maps in digital form and attaching map coordinates to each digital point. Every point on a digital map was linked to a unique X and Y coordinate, based on the standard Australian Mapping Grid system, and had a specific address linked to it. Once each point on a map was precisely addressed and identified, specific attributes were attached to it. These attributes were then used as methods of recording information or used as indexes for access to or by other programs, for example, sewer pipe details, property details, water consumption, and vertical heights above sea level. The selected map area with all the related attributes and information was then displayed graphically in full color on a high-resolution workstation monitor (see Figure 3).

The FIS allowed cross-referencing to financial, rating, and consumption data (through indexing) held on the System 38. It also enabled each underground facility to be numbered, catalogued, and identified as an asset with its associated data being integrated into other asset management systems. The FIS enabled data stored on a particular map to be "layered," with water pipes at one layer, sewer pipes at another, property boundaries at a third, future plans at another, and so on. This gave users the ability to recall maps in layers and to select the level and amount of detail they required. The system was centered around a mouse-driven graphic interface where the user zoomed in and out and/or panned around particular areas—at the broadest level, showing the whole of southern Victoria, and at the most detailed, the individual plumbing and drainage plan of one particular property (through cross-referencing to the DIPS).

3. A **Computer-Aided Design and Drafting (CADD)** system that provided an integrated programmable 3-D environment for a range of civil, mechanical, electrical, surveying, and general engineering design and drafting applications. It offered the following features:

   ○ display manipulation, including multiple angle views, zooms, and pans;
   ○ geometric analysis, including automatic calculation of areas, perimeters, moments of inertia, and centroids; and
   ○ various customization features such as user-defined menus and prompts and a user-friendly macro language.

4. **Word Processing and Office Automation (WP/OA)** systems providing users the ability to prepare quality documentation integrating graphics, spreadsheets, mail merge, and databases, as well as other utilities such as electronic mail and phone message handling.

5. A **Relational Database Management System (RDBMS)** and a **Fourth-Generation Language** as a base foundation for the development of new applications. Some of the RDBMS applications included:

   ○ a Drawing and Retrieval Management System (DRMS) to control the development, release, and revision of all CADD projects and files; and
   ○ a Water Information Management System (WIMS) used for the storage and management of hydrographic engineering and laboratory data, both current and historical.

OUTCOMES

Vines said that one of the most important strategic outcomes of the changes introduced had been the way in which decision making at all levels within the organization had been enhanced. "This improvement is largely due to the fact that people have now got ready access to information they have never had before. This information is especially useful in enhancing our ability to forward plan. The flow and reporting of financial information has also speeded up and we now complete our final accounts up to two months earlier than we used to. In the areas that have come on-line there has been a definite improvement in productivity and in customer service. The CADD system, for example, is greatly enhancing our ability to design and plan new facilities. The turn-around time, the accuracy of the plans, and the creativity of the designers has been improved dramatically. In many departments there has been a change in work practices—some of the mundane activities are handled by the computer, allowing more productive work to be carried out, like spending more time with customers. Our asset management and control also started to improve. There was greater integrity in the information kept, and having just one central shared record meant that updating with new data or changes to existing data was far more efficient."

Adamski added that the initial reaction by Board staff to the whole corporate computing strategy "ranged from skepticism to outright hostility." He continued, "By the end of 1991, I would say that there had been a general reversal in attitude. Managers started to queue outside my office asking if we could develop specific business applications for them. They had begun to appreciate what the technology could do and most often they suddenly perceived a whole range of opportunities and different ways in which they could operate. One manager asked me, for example, if we could use document imaging technology to eliminate the need for any physical paper flows within his office. Technically this was possible but it was not really cost justifiable and the corporate culture would not really have supported it. Putting together the IS Division budget is now a difficult balancing act with a whole range of options and demands from users. I now ask the users to justify the benefits to be derived from new application proposals and I help out with the cost side. Cost-benefit justification usually drives the decisions as well as the

'fit' with the existing IT and other corporate objectives. What also must be considered is that these objectives are not written in stone. They are flexible and can and should adjust to changes in both the internal and external environment."

A number of GDWB staff indicated that the new systems had enhanced their ability to fulfill their work responsibilities:

○ A customer-service officer at one of the Board's regional offices stated that the DIPS had enabled her to respond to customer requests for encumbrance statements within a matter of minutes instead of weeks. She added that a number of customers had sent letters to their office complimenting them on the improvements in the service they received. She said that new DIPS had "flow on" benefits that weren't fully recognized. She cited the case in which local architects were able to charge their clients less because they had more ready access to information from the GDWB.

○ A maintenance manager declared that the FIS had enabled his department to predict when pipes and drains should be replaced before they actually ruptured or broke down, by examining their installation dates and the types of materials used. He said this process over time started to shift the emphasis of his department's maintenance work from being reactive to being more preventative. He added that the system also enabled him to easily identify and contact the residents that would be affected by the work that the Board was going to do in a particular area. He said that the FIS enabled him to plot out with his mouse a particular area of a map on his screen. It would then "pick up" all the relevant properties in the area and identify the names and addresses of the current ratepayers residing in those properties.

○ A secretary to a senior head office manager said that despite being a little daunted at first by the new word processing system, she felt the system had helped her considerably. She said that besides the obvious benefits in being able to prepare and edit documents on a WYSIWYG screen, she also had the ability of viewing as well as integrating scanned property plans, correspondence, and other documents from the DIPS.

Adamski said that one of the flow-on benefits from the FIS in particular was that

the Board had the potential of selling the information stored on the system to authorities such as municipal councils and other public utilities such as Telecom, the State Electricity Commission, and the Gas and Fuel Corporation. He added that they had also considered marketing the information to private organizations such as building managers, architects, and property developers, and that the return from these sales could significantly reduce the overall costs in developing the FIS.

THE FUTURE

Commenting on the future prospects for the Board's IS Division, Adamski said, "There are some very complex applications that we are developing but we now have the skills, the tools, and the infrastructure to develop them cost effectively and to ensure that they deliver results. I think one of the main reasons why we are in this fortuitous position is that we chose a UNIX platform with client/server processing and a strong networking backbone. It gives us the flexibility and integration that we set out to achieve and we will need in the future to realize both our long- and short-term objectives. It's a lot easier now to cost-justify requests for new applications. The challenges ahead lie in three areas. Firstly, it's going to be difficult to consistently satisfy all our users' needs in that their expectations will be increasing all the time and they will become more demanding. We have to recognize these demands and at the same time keep investing in and maintaining our infrastructure. Secondly, we still have some way to go in developing a total corporate management information system. There are still some 'islands of data' floating around and the challenge is to get it all integrated. And thirdly, as the most senior IT manager at the Board I have to make sure that we retain our key IT staff and we compensate them adequately, both monetarily and in providing them stimulating and demanding work."

The Geelong and District Water Board changed its name to Barwon Water in February 1994. The name change reflected the change in the organization's governance structure with the appointment by the state government of a professional, "skills-based" governing board to replace the community-elected members. This initiative was part of a broader government strategy to commercialize state-owned utilities and to strive for greater efficiencies and productivity across the whole public service.

Four months after the name change, Geoff Vines retired and was replaced by Dennis Brockenshire as Barwon Water's chief executive. Brockenshire, formerly a senior manager with the State Electricity Commission, had considerable business and engineering experience relating to large-scale supply systems serving a large customer base. Commenting on Barwon Water's information technology (IT) infrastructure, Brockenshire stated, "Barwon Water has made and continues to make a significant investment in IT. The organization has spent something in the region of $7 to $10 million in building its IT infrastructure and has recurrent costs of 3 percent of total expenditure. I want to make sure we get an appropriate return for this investment. It is critical that IT delivers real business benefits. Since I've come into this role, I have insisted that my line managers justify any new IT investment on the grounds of the business value it will create."

From the period 1992 to 1995, Barwon Water's information systems (IS) department had focused most of its efforts in capturing all the relevant mapping, customer, and facilities data for its key systems. Significant resources were allocated to utilize the existing IT infrastructure to improve customer service and to streamline work-flows. Improvements in security were also a major priority given the confidential and private nature of information stored on the various databases and the listing of Barwon Water's home page on the World Wide Web. In terms of hardware and software, the IBM System 38 was replaced by a Sun Sparcstation server running the Prophecy accounting package in a UNIX operating environment. The IS department had commenced work on an executive information system to assist with cost and performance measurement, particularly at the business unit level. This system would provide the core information to support a major benchmarking exercise in which Barwon Water compared its performance on key processes with other organizations, both within and external to the water industry.

Business processes were mapped and examined where steps could be eliminated or substituted by new IT applications. An interesting example of this was the introduction of a paperless, encumbrance certificating system. In this system a solicitor handling a property matter could interact with Barwon Water via the fax machine without the need to actually visit an office.

All documents sent to and from Barwon Water and those transferred within the organization were accomplished entirely on the system with no need to print a hard copy. Processing times for these applications were reduced from an average of 10 days to a few hours.

A number of other efficiency gains were realized with the utilization of the IT infrastructure. The productivity of the engineering design staff increased by 20 to 50 percent for most drawings and by 90 percent for redrawings. The systems' distributed computing design also reduced design cycles by enabling staff to share files and work on a common file to avoid duplicated effort. Overall staff numbers with Barwon Water had dropped to 400 by July 1995. Adamski said that although the total reduction in staff numbers could not be directly attributed to the new systems, there were several areas where staff had been made redundant or redeployed. He said that in many cases the systems "freed-up" front-line service personnel to spend more time listening and being responsive to customer concerns.

Barwon Water continued to receive acclaim for its innovative IT systems. In 1994 it was awarded the Geelong Business Excellence Award in the Innovation Systems/Development of Technology category. It also received a nomination for the award for innovation by the Washington-based Smithsonian Institute.[2]

A major organizational restructure in early 1995 saw Joe Adamski take over the responsibility for strategic planning as well as information systems. Adamski said that this restructure ensured that IT developments would be closely aligned with broader business objectives and strategies. He added that having the senior IT executive responsible for business planning symbolized how essential IT had become to the organization's operations and its management and control systems. As part of the restructure, new business units were formed with the managers of these units made accountable for both revenue and cost items.

Commenting on future challenges, Adamski outlined his vision for Barwon Water as the computing center for the Greater Geelong region. "Geelong and district covers 4000 square kilometers. Within this region, there has recently been an amalgamation of councils into two super-councils—the City of Greater Geelong and the Surf Coast Council. These two organizations, serve the same customers as ourselves. We have articulated what we see as benefits of using common databases, mapping, and other information to serve these customers. Suggested benefits include a service shopfront where customers could pay rates, water tariffs, and apply for property approvals at the same place. These systems we now have in place at Barwon Water would be a good starting point in building this regional concept. Data is our most valuable asset and there is no point in duplicating it."[3]

Source: Copyright © by Joel B. Barolsky and Peter Weill. Funding for this research was provided by IBM Consulting (USA). Reprinted by permission of Joel B. Barolsky and Peter Weill.

CASE STUDY QUESTIONS

1. Describe the Geelong and District Water Board and the environment in which it operates. What problems did GDWB have before 1988? What were the management, organization, and technology factors that contributed to those problems?

2. Describe the role of information systems at GDWB and the GDWB's information system portfolio before July 1988.

3. Describe and critique the process of upgrading GDWB's information systems portfolio.

4. How did the Water Board justify its investments in new information system technology? What were the benefits?

[1]This case was prepared by Joel B. Barolsky and Professor Peter Weill as part of the Infrastructure Study funded by **IBM Consulting Group (International)**. It should be read in conjunction with the **Geelong and District Water Board Information Technology Management** (CL298-1992) case. Both of these cases were written as the basis of discussion rather than to illustrate either effective or ineffective handling of a managerial situation. Copyright © 1995 Joel B. Barolsky and Peter Weill, Melbourne Business School Limited, The University of Melbourne.

[2]The original case study written by Barolsky and Weill on Geelong and District Water Board was awarded the Australian Computer Society Prize for best IT Case Study in 1993.

[3]"IT Manager Leads Corporate Plan to Water," **MIS**, April 1994, 41–46.

Len Fertuck, University of Toronto (Canada)

Ginormous Life is an insurance company with a long tradition. The company has four divisions that each operate their own computers. The IS group provides analysis, design, and programming services to all of the divisions. The divisions are actuarial, marketing, operations, and investment. All divisions are located at the corporate headquarters building. Marketing also has field offices in 20 cities across the country.

○ **The Actuarial Division** is responsible for the design and pricing of new kinds of policies. They use purchased industry data and weekly summaries of data obtained from the Operations Division. They have their own DEC VAX minicomputer, running the UNIX operating system, to store data files. They do most of their analysis on PCs and Sun workstations, either on spreadsheets or with a specialized interactive language called APL.

○ **The Marketing Division** is responsible for selling policies to new customers and for follow-up of existing customers in case they need changes to their current insurance. All sales orders are sent to the Operations Division for data entry and billing. They use purchased external data for market research and weekly copies of data from operations for follow-ups. They have their own IBM AS/400 minicomputer with dumb terminals for clerks to enter sales data. There are also many PCs used to analyze market data using statistical packages like SAS.

○ **The Operations Division** is responsible for processing all mission-critical financial transactions including payroll. They record all new policies, send regular bills to customers, evaluate and pay all claims, and cancel lapsed policies. They have all their data and programs on two IBM ES/9000 mainframes running under the OS/390 operating system. The programs are often large and complex because they must service not only the 15 products currently being sold but also the 75 old kinds of policies that are no longer being sold but still have exist-

ing policy holders. Clerks use dumb terminals to enter and update data. Applications written in the last five years have used an SQL relational database to store data, but most programs are still written in COBOL. The average age of the transaction processing programs is about ten years.

○ **The Investment Division** is responsible for investing premiums until they are needed to pay claims. Their data consist primarily of internal portfolio data and research data obtained by direct links to data services. They have a DEC minicomputer to store their data. The internal data are received by a weekly download of cash flows from the Operations Division. External data are obtained as needed. They use PCs to analyze data obtained either from the mini or from commercial data services.

A controlling interest in Ginormous Life has recently been purchased by Financial Behemoth Corp. The management of Financial Behemoth has decided that the firm's efficiency and profitability must be improved. Their first move has been to put Dan D. Mann, a hotshot information systems specialist from Financial Behemoth, in charge of the Information Systems Division. He has been given the objective of modernizing and streamlining the computer facilities without any increase in budget.

In the first week on the job, Dan discovered that only seven junior members of the staff of 200 information systems specialists know anything about CASE tools, End-User Computing, or LANs. They have no experience in implementing PC systems. There is no evidence of any formal decision-support systems or executive information systems in the organization. New applications in the last five years have been implemented in COBOL on DB2, a relational database product purchased from IBM. Over two-thirds of applications are still based on COBOL flat files. One of the benefits of using DB2 is that it is now possible to deliver reports quickly based on ad hoc queries. This is creating a snowballing demand for conversion of more systems to a relational data-

base so that other managers can get similar service.

There have been some problems with the older systems. Maintenance is difficult and costly because almost every change to the data structure of applications in operations requires corresponding changes to applications in the other divisions. There has been a growing demand in other divisions for faster access to operations data. For instance the Investment Division claims that they could make more profitable investments if they had continuous access to the cash position in operations. Marketing complains that they get calls from clients about claims and cannot answer them because they do not have current access to the status of the claim. Management wants current access to a wide variety of data in summary form so they can get a better understanding of the business. The IS group says that it would be difficult to provide access to data in operations because of security considerations. It is difficult to ensure that users do not make unauthorized changes to the COBOL files.

The IS group complains that they cannot deliver all the applications that users want because they are short-staffed. They spend 90 percent of their time maintaining the existing systems. The programmers are mostly old and experienced and employee turnover is unusually low, so there is not likely to be much room for improvement by further training in programming. Employees often remark that the company is a very pleasant and benevolent place to work. At least they did until rumors of deregulation and foreign competition started to sweep the industry.

Dan foresees that there will be an increasing need for computer capacity as more and more applications are converted to on-line transaction processing and more users begin to make ad hoc queries. Dan is also wondering if intranets or the Internet should become part of any new software.

Dan began to look for ways to solve the many problems of the Information Systems Division. He solicited proposals from various vendors and consultants in the computer industry. After a preliminary review of the proposals, Dan was left with three broad options suggested by IBM, Oracle Corp., and

Datamotion, a local consulting firm. The proposals are briefly described below.

IBM proposes an integrated solution using IBM hardware and software. The main elements of the proposal are:

○ **Data and applications will remain on a mainframe.** The IBM ES/9000 series of hardware running their OS/390 operating system will provide mainframe services. Mainframe hardware capacity will have to be approximately doubled by adding two more ES/9000 series machines. The four machines will run under OS/390 with Parallel Sysplex clustering technology that allows for future growth. The Parallel Sysplex system can be scaled by connecting up to 32 servers to work in parallel and be treated as a single system for scheduling and system management. The OS/390 operating system can also run UNIX applications.

○ **AS/400 minicomputers running under the OS/400 operating system** will replace DEC minicomputers.

○ **RS/6000 workstations running AIX**—a flavor of the UNIX operating system—can be used for actuarial computations. All hardware will be interconnected with IBM's proprietary SNA network architecture. PCs will run under the OS/2 operating system and the IBM LAN Server to support both Microsoft Windows applications and locally designed applications that communicate with mainframe databases.

○ **A DB2 relational database will store all data on-line.** Users will be able to access any data they need through their terminals or through PCs that communicate with the mainframe.

○ **Legacy systems will be converted using reengineering tools,** like Design Recovery and Maintenance Workbench from Intersolv, Inc. These will have the advantage that they will continue to use the COBOL code that the existing programmers are familiar with. New work will be done using CASE tools with code generators that produce COBOL code.

○ **Proven technology.** The IBM systems are widely used by many customers and vendors. Many mission-critical application programs are available on the market that address a wide variety of business needs.

Oracle Corp. proposed that all systems be converted to use their Oracle database product and its associated screen and report generators. They said that such a conversion would have the following advantages:

○ **Over 90 hardware platforms are supported.** This means that the company is no longer bound to stay with a single hardware vendor. Oracle databases and application programs can be easily moved from one manufacturer's machine to another manufacturer's machine by a relatively simple export and import operation as long as applications are created with Oracle tools. Thus the most economical hardware platform can be used for the application. Oracle will also access data stored in an IBM DB2 database.

○ **Integrated CASE tools and application generators.** Oracle has its own design and development tools called Designer/2000 and Developer/2000. Applications designed with Designer/2000 can be automatically created for a wide variety of terminals or for the World Wide Web. The same design can be implemented in Windows, on a Macintosh, or on X-Windows in UNIX. Applications are created using graphic tools that eliminate the need for a language like COBOL. The designer works entirely with visual prototyping specifications.

○ **Vertically integrated applications.** Oracle sells a number of common applications, like accounting programs, that can be used as building blocks in developing a complete system. These applications could eliminate the need to redevelop some applications.

○ **Distributed network support.** A wide variety of common network protocols like SNA, DecNet, Novell, and TCP/IP are supported. Different parts of the database can be distributed to different machines on the network and accessed or updated by any application. All data are stored on-line for instant access. The data can be stored on one machine and the applications can be run on a different machine, including a PC or workstation, to provide a client/server environment. The ability to distribute a database allows a large database on an expensive mainframe to be distributed to a number of cheaper minicomputers.

Datamotion proposed a data warehouse approach using software tools from Information Builders Inc. Existing applications would be linked using EDA, a middleware data warehouse server that acts as a bridge between the existing data files

and the users performing enquiries. New applications would be developed using an application tool called Cactus. The advantages of this approach are:

○ **Data Location Transparency** EDA Hub Server provides a single connection point from which applications can access multiple data sources anywhere in the enterprise. In addition, users can join data between any supported EDA databases—locally, cross-server, or cross-platform. Users can easily access remote data sources for enhanced decision-making capabilities.

○ **The EDA server can reach most nonrelational databases** and file systems through its SQL translation engine. EDA also supports 3GL, 4GL, static SQL, CICS, IMS/TM, and proprietary database stored procedure processing.

○ **Extensive network and operating system support.** EDA supports 14 major network protocols and provides protocol translation between dissimilar networks. EDA also runs on 35 different processing platforms. EDA servers support optimized SQL against any RDBMS. And the EDA server can automatically generate the dialect of SQL optimal for the targeted data source. It is available on Windows 3.x, Windows 95/98, Windows NT, OS/2, MVS, UNIX, CICS, VM, OpenVMS, Tandem, and AS/400.

○ **Comprehensive Internet Support.** With EDA's Internet services, users can issue requests from a standard Web browser to any EDA-supported data source and receive answer sets formatted as HTML pages.

○ **Cactus promotes modern development methods.** Cactus allows the developer to partition an application, keeping presentation logic, business logic, and data access logic separate. This partitioning of functionality can occur across a large number of enterprise platforms to allow greater flexibility in achieving scalability, performance, and maintenance. Cactus provides all the tools needed to deal with every aspect of developing, testing, packaging, and deploying client/server traditional applications or Web-based applications.

Dan is not sure which approach to take for the future of Ginormous Life. Whichever route he follows, the technology will have an enormous impact on the kinds of applications his staff will be able to produce in the future and the way in which they will produce them. While industry trends toward downsizing and distribution of systems may eventually prove to be more efficient, Dan's staff does not have much experience with the new technologies that would be required. He is uncertain about whether there will be a sufficient payoff to justify the organizational turmoil that will result from a major change in direction. Ideally he would like to move quickly to a modern client/server system with minimal disturbance to existing staff and development methods, but he fears that both of these are not simultaneously possible.

Source: Reprinted by permission of Len Fertuck, University of Toronto, Canada.

CASE STUDY QUESTIONS

Dan must prepare a strategy for the renewal of the Information Systems Division over the next three years. As his assistant, prepare an outline, in point form, containing the following items:

1. A list of factors or issues that must be considered in selecting a technology platform for the firm.
2. Weights for each factor obtained by dividing up 100 points among the factors in proportion to their importance.
3. A score from 0 to 10 of how each of the three proposals performs on each factor.
4. A grand score for each proposal obtained by summing the product of the proposal score times the factor weight for each proposal.
5. The technology that you would recommend that Dan adopt and the reason for choosing the particular technology that you recommend.
6. The order in which each component of the technology should be introduced and the reason for selecting the order.

International Case Study

CASE STUDY 3: Analysis to Interface Design—The Example of Cuparla

Gerhard Schwabe, Stephan Wilczek, and Helmut Krcmar
University of Hohenheim (Germany)

Like in other towns, members of the Stuttgart City Council have a large workload: In addition to their primary professions (e.g., an engineer at Daimler Benz) they devote more than 40 hours a week to local politics. This extra work has to be done under fairly unfavorable conditions. Only council sessions and party meetings take place in the city hall; the deputies of the local council do not have an office in the city hall to prepare or coordinate their work. This means, for example, that they must read and file all official documents at home. In a city with more than 500,000 inhabitants, they receive a very large number of documents. Furthermore, council members believe they could be better informed by the administration and make better use of their time. Therefore Hohenheim University and partners launched the Cuparla project to improve the information access and collaboration of council members.[1]

A detailed analysis of their work revealed the following characteristics of council work:

○ Council members need support available to them any time and in any place as they are very mobile.
○ Council members collaborate and behave differently in different contexts:

While they act informally and rather open in the context of their own party, they behave more controlled and formal in official council sessions.

○ A closer investigation of council work reveals a low degree of process structure. Every council member has the right of initiative and can inform and involve other members and members of the administration in any order.
○ Council members rarely are power computer users. Computer support for them has to be straightforward and intuitive to use.

When designing computer support we initially had to decide on the basic orientation of our software. We soon abandoned a work-flow model as there are merely a few steps and little order in the collaboration of local politicians. Imposing a new structure into this situation would have been too restrictive for the council members. We then turned to pure document orientation, imposing absolutely no structure on the council members' work. We created a single, large database with all the documents the city council ever needs. However, working with this database turned out to be too complex for the council members. In addition, they need to control the access to certain documents at all stages of the decision-

making process. For example, a party may not want to reveal its proposals to other parties before it has officially been brought up in the city council. Controlling access to each document individually and changing the access control list were not feasible.

Therefore, the working context was chosen as a basis of our design. Each working context of a council member can be symbolized by a "room." A private office corresponds to the council member working at home; there is a party room, in which the member collaborates with party colleagues, and a committee room symbolizes the place for committee meetings. In addition, there is a room for working groups, a private post office, and a library for filed information. All rooms hence have an electronic equivalent in the Cuparla software. When opening the Cuparla software, a council member sees all the rooms from the entrance hall (see Figure 1).

The council member creates a document in one room (e.g., a private office) and then shares it with other council members in other rooms. If the member moves a document into the room of his party, the member shares it with his party colleagues; if he hands it on to the administration, he shares it with the mayors, administration officials, all council members, and so forth.

The interface of the electronic rooms resembles the setup of the original rooms.

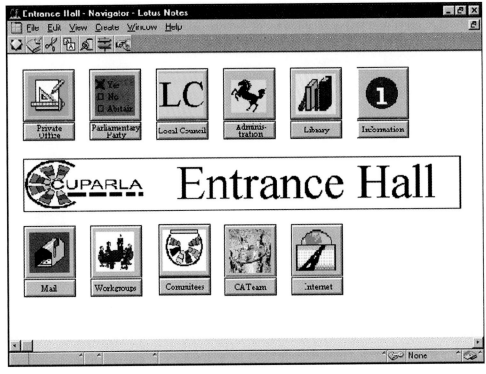

FIGURE I Entrance hall.

Figure 2 shows the example of the room for a parliamentary party. On the left side of the screen are document locations, and on the right side are the documents of the selected location. Documents that are currently worked on are displayed on the "desk." These documents have the connotation that they need to be worked on without an additional outside trigger. If a document is in the files, it belongs to a topic that is still on the political agenda; however, a trigger is necessary to move it out of the shelf. If a topic is no longer on the political agenda, all documents belonging to it are moved to the archive.

The other locations support the collaboration within the party. The conference desk contains all documents for the next (weekly) party meeting. Any council member of the party can put documents there. When preparing for the meeting, the council member simply has to check the conference desk for relevant information. The mailbox for the chairman contains all documents about which the chairman needs to decide. In contrast to the e-mail account, all members have access to the mailbox. Duplicate work is avoided as every council member is aware of the chairman's agenda. The mailbox of the assistant contains tasks for the party assistants—the mailbox for the secretary, assignments for the secretary (e.g., a draft for a letter). The inbox contains documents that have been moved from other rooms into this room.

Thus, in the electronic room all locations correspond to the current manual situation. Council members do not have to relearn their work. Instead, they collaborate in the shared environment to which they are accustomed, with shared expectations on the other people's behavior. Feedback from the pilot users indicates that this approach is appropriate.

Some specific design features make the software easy to use. The software purposely does not have a fancy 3-D interface that has the same look as a real room. Buttons (in the entrance hall) and lists (in the rooms) are much easier to use and do not distract the user from the essential parts. Each location (e.g., the desk) has a small arrow. If a user clicks on this arrow, a document is moved to the location. This operation is much easier for a beginner than proceeding by "drag and drop."

Furthermore, software design is not restricted to building an electronic equivalent of a manual situation. If a user wants to truly benefit from the opportunities of electronic collaboration support systems, one has to include new tools that are not possible in the manual setting. For example, additional cross-location and room search features are needed to make it easy for the council member to retrieve information.

The challenge of interface design is to give the user a starting point that is similar to a familiar situation. A next step is to provide users with options to improve and adjust their working behaviors to the opportunities offered by the use of a computer.

Source: Reprinted by permission of Gerhard Schwabe, Stephan Wilczek, and Helmut Krcmar, University of Hohenheim (Germany).

CASE STUDY QUESTIONS

1. Analyze the management, organization, and technology issues that had to be addressed by the Cuparla project.
2. Analyze the interface and design of the Cuparla system. How easy is it to use? What problems does it solve? What organizational processes does the system support? How effective is it? Would you make any changes? If so, what would they be?
3. Could the Cuparla software be used for other applications in business? Why or why not? What modifications would be required?

[1] The project partners are Hohenheim University (Coordinator), Datenzentrale Baden-Wüttemberg, and Group Vision Softwaresysteme GmbH. The project is funded as part of its R&D program by DeTeBerkom GmbH, a 100 percent subsidiary of German Telekom.

FIGURE 2 Parliamentary party room.

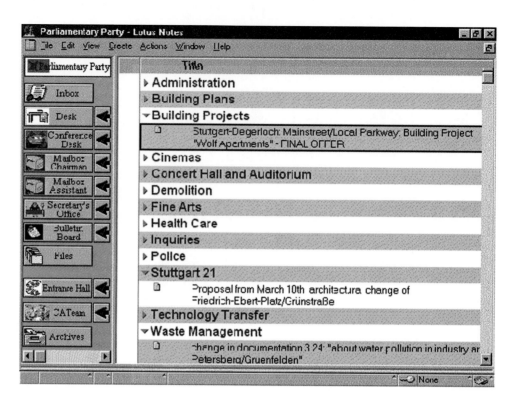

International Case Study

CASE STUDY 4: Citibank Asia-Pacific: Rearchitecting Information Technology Infrastructure for the Twenty-First Century

Boon Siong Neo and Christina Soh
Information Management Research Center (IMARC), Nanyang Business School
Nanyang Technological University (Singapore)

I. CITICORP

Citicorp in 1991 recorded a net loss of $457 million,[1] suspended the dividend on its common stock, and saw the price of that stock fall to a long-time low before rebounding after year end. Nevertheless, and despite the magnitude of our problems, 1991 for Citicorp was in key respects a transitional, turnaround year.

John Reed, Citicorp's chairman, acknowledged Citicorp's problems in his letter to stockholders in the 1991 annual report. The bank had been struggling with a large Third-World loan portfolio, as well as significant problems with its commercial property loans, and with its financing of highly leveraged transactions in the United States. The bank needed more equity but Third-World debt costs prevented Citicorp from increasing its equity through retention of earnings.

The severe storms to which Citicorp had been subjected prompted significant changes. To combat the slowdown in revenue growth and the rise in consumer and credit write-offs, Citicorp aggressively reduced expenses to improve the operating margin, and issued stock to improve their capital ratio. Structural changes were aimed at providing more focused direction to the business. John Reed articulated three requirements for being a "great bank in the 1990s"—meeting customer needs, having financial strength, and "marshalling human and **technological** resources . . . **more imaginatively and cost-effectively** than one's competitors."

In the midst of this organizational turbulence, one of Citicorp's undisputed strengths was its global presence. It is unrivaled in its network of banks in more than 90 countries. Its overseas consumer banking operations in particular were showing healthy growth. Global consumer banking includes mortgage and insurance business and non-U.S. credit card business. Citicorp only entered the field of consumer banking in the mid-1970s. John Reed's vision was to pursue growth in the consumer banking area, and to pursue it through global expansion and leveraging IT.

The primary vision in consumer banking is "Citibanking"—combining relationship banking with technology that enables Citibank to serve its customers anywhere anytime with the same high standard of service that they receive in their home countries. Some examples of the manner in which technology enables the Citibanking vision include having a one-stop account opening, paperless transactions, instant card and check issuance, and instant account availability; having a customer relationship

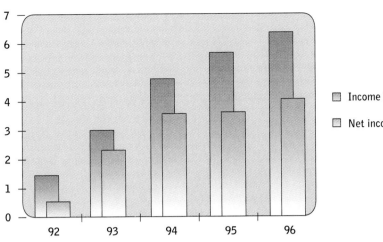

FIGURE I Income in billions. Source: Citicorp Annual Report, 1996.

☐ Income before taxes

☐ Net income

database that supports cross-product relationships, creation of hybrid products and customized products, and relationship pricing that more closely matches the value to the customer. The Citicard is the key to Citibanking services such as checking, money market, and bankcard accounts. Consumer banking products are distributed through bank branches, Citicard centers, and Citiphone banking, which gives 24-hour, 7-day-a-week service. The global services available to customers were augmented in 1991 when Citibank joined the CIRRUS ATM network, allowing Citicard holders access to cash around the world.

The results of operating and structural changes, as well as the impact of the growing Asian consumer market, contributed to a turnaround at Citicorp, where the 1992 net earning was $772 million. This earned it an A-minus credit rating from **Standard and Poor**, which also upgraded the bank's outlook from negative to stable. Their performance continued to improve each year (see Figure 1). In early 1994, the bank was also given permission by the U.S. regulatory agency to resume issuing dividends. These improvements were reflected in Citicorp's share price, which moved up to $36.88 during 1993, from a low of $23 in 1990. By 1997, the stock price was 10 times its low in 1990.[2]

II. CITIBANK IN ASIA-PACIFIC

Even in 1991, the profit that Citicorp made on its Asian business was a healthy $400m, if one excludes the loan write-offs for Australia and New Zealand, and their slow progress in the difficult Japanese retail banking market. This compares well with the $894m loss in the United States, and the $132m profit in Europe, Africa, and the

Middle East.[3] The Asian market also had a high growth potential. Asian consumer deposits grew six-fold to $13.6 billion between 1983 and 1992, while loans grew seventeen-fold to $10.8 billion over the same period.[4] This growth is a reflection of the region's high gross savings rate (about 35 percent) and high GNP growth.

Citicorp has been in Asia since 1902 when it set up finance houses in a number of Asian ports, such as Shanghai and Singapore. It has built up an understanding of these local markets. Today, consumer banking in the Asia-Pacific is organized into three regions—North Asia (Korea, Taiwan, Hong Kong, and the Philippines), South Asia (Thailand, Malaysia, Singapore, Indonesia, and Australia), and Central Europe/Middle Eastern Asia (India, Pakistan, Saudi Arabia, United Arab Emirates, and Eastern Europe). The regional directors report to New York–based Executive Vice President De Sousa, who also heads the Private Bank. Besides the country managers, functions reporting to the regional directors include financial control, marketing and business development, technology and operations, treasury, credit, human resources, and service quality. Citicorp's major competitors in terms of established presence throughout Asia are Hong Kong Bank and Standard Chartered Bank, but neither has the global reach that Citicorp offers.

Citibank began pursuing consumer banking in Asia in earnest in 1986, and since then Asian accounts have increased from 1 million to 6 million in 1997 and are expected to reach 13 million by the year 2000. Critics suggest that Citicorp may run into credit problems because Asians have little experience with personal debt. Nonetheless, Citicorp continues to pioneer

the concept of consumer credit in Asia— besides the usual mortgage and auto loans, Citicorp offers round-the-clock phone banking and automated teller cards that can be used in Singapore as well as New York.[5] Interestingly, some innovations such as phone banking were motivated by local regulations that severely restricted the number of branches that it may operate. To compete with the local banks, Citibank has had to be very focused in its customer base.

Citibank has made significant innovations in packaging financial services for the relatively rich customer and has managed to corner the market. Part of the underlying philosophy is that its market position requires continual research into local customer needs—what one senior Citibank officer called the "let a hundred flowers bloom" approach. That approach has resulted in each country having its own IT infrastructure and unique applications. Although it has worked adequately in the past, the local markets approach does not allow Citibank to integrate its products, services, and information to serve its highly sophisticated, mobile, and increasingly demanding global customers. Further, there were substantial economies of scale that may be gained from standardizing and consolidating bank products and processing across the diverse countries of the Asia-Pacific region. The key to achieving these goals lies in rearchitecting the technology infrastructure that enables the consumer banking business.

III. TECHNOLOGY INFRASTRUCTURE IN CITIBANK ASIA-PACIFIC

In the early 1990s, each of Citibank's Asia-Pacific countries belonged to one of three automation platforms—MVS,

AS/400, or UNIX—and had one of two consumer banking applications—COSMOS or CORE. COSMOS was an earlier set of applications and was fairly typical of most U.S. banks' off-shore banking applications. It was written in COBOL to provide flexibility in complying with varying regulatory reporting formats, and it provided back-office support for standard areas such as current accounts, general ledger, and some loans processing. Subsequently, Citibank began to replace COSMOS with CORE, which was to provide a comprehensive system to run on AS/400s. CORE was used in a number of countries with smaller operations, such as Indonesia. It was not suitable for countries, such as India, where IBM did not have a presence, and in countries with high volumes, such as Hong Kong. Both COSMOS and CORE were subject to many country-specific modifications over time, as each country operation responded to varying regulatory and business requirements. The result was significant differences in each country's basic banking software.

A two-pronged strategy was adopted: First, rearchitect the IT infrastructure by standardizing and centralizing all back-office banking functions; and second, develop centers of excellence by encouraging individual countries to take the lead in developing products and processes where they have significant leadership and competitive advantages in the marketplace. The only rule in the latter strategy is that the lead country should develop products and processes that meet the requirements for all countries in the region and must provide ongoing support for the systems in which such products and processes are embedded.

IV. REGIONAL CARD CENTER AS PROTOTYPE OF THE NEW STRATEGY

A significant piece of Citibank's Asia-Pacific IT infrastructure that provided the prototype for further subsequent consolidation in consumer banking is the Regional Card Center (RCC). The RCC was set up in Singapore in 1989 to support start-up credit card businesses in Southeast Asia. Country managers whose credit card data processing were to be centralized demanded exacting performance standards from the center because of its direct impact on their operating performance. Ajit Kanagasundram, who used to run the data center for Citibank Singapore, was given the mandate to set up and run the center:

The purpose of the RCC was to jump-start the credit card businesses in Citibank countries in Southeast Asia. Setting up the processing infrastructure before offering credit card services in each country would take too long and be too costly for start-up businesses. According to the sentiment at that time, we had planned the RCC for the initial three years, and then put processors in each country after that. The time constraint to make the RCC operational also dictated our approach, which was to get the operational software requirements from a couple of lead businesses, in this case, Citibank Hong Kong and Singapore. Trying to get requirements from all countries would be too time consuming and result in missed market opportunities. Further, 80 percent of credit card operational requirements are stipulated by the card associations and were common across countries. We recruited a few staff experienced in credit card operations, used our own production experience, plus on-site consultants to modify the software, and got the RCC operational in eight months.

By 1990, we had reduced the processing cost per credit card by 45 percent and we were given the mandate to extend our operations to cover the Middle East and North Asia, excluding Hong Kong. In 1991, credit card software that had been developed by Citicorp in London and that was scheduled for implementation in Thailand was scrapped in favor of CARDPAC, the package used by the RCC. By 1994, in the midst of heightened cost consciousness because of corporate financial troubles, our cost per card was down to 32 percent of the 1989 cost. None of the country managers asked for decentralization of the credit card operations—who wants cost per card to triple overnight? We are now processing cards for 15 countries and the number of cards processed have increased from 230,000 in 1990 to 5 million in 1996. We have also decreased the time it took to launch a new business from 14 months to 3 months.

In 1993, Citibank beat out other regional rivals to become the issuer of affinity Visa and MasterCard for Passages, a joint frequent-flyer program of 15 Asian airlines. Citibank credits its ability to launch and support the cards regionally, enabled by the RCC, as being a key factor for being selected. By the end of 1996, the RCC was processing credit cards for 5 million customers in 15 countries from Japan in the north to New Zealand in the south, and from Turkey in the west to Guam in the east. The cost economies offered by the RCC made it obvious for countries to join it rather than go on their own. Citibank projects that, by 1999, its cost per card would drop by a further one-third from the current levels, the benefits of which would be reflected in each country's bottom line.

The RCC concept combines both centralization and decentralization ideas to meet specific local business needs and low costs of processing at the same time. The business strategy, marketing, credit evaluation, and customer service for credit cards continue to be decentralized in each country to cater to local market conditions and needs. The front-end data capture and printing of customer statements are also decentralized to each country. What is centralized is the back-end transaction processing and data repository. The control and active management of credit card businesses continue to be with country managers, and the business gains are reflected in the financial performance of each country. The RCC provides the technology infrastructure for lowering operational costs, diffusing best practices, and attracting the needed technical talent. RCC's accumulated experience and infrastructure also enable Citibank to launch the card business in new countries within four months.

The strategic architecture of the RCC is shown in Figure 2. An IBM ES/9000 Model 821 designed for high-volume, on-line, and batch transaction processing formed the main platform for the system. Input/output operations performed at Citibank branches, ATMs, and other electronic systems include new account opening, collections, authorizations, printing of reports and monthly statements, and customer service. These input/output operations at individual countries are linked via leased lines of different capacities (2.4 kbps to 64 kbps). The databases and transaction history are stored centrally at the RCC.

The decreasing costs of telecommunications and the cost savings from standardizing

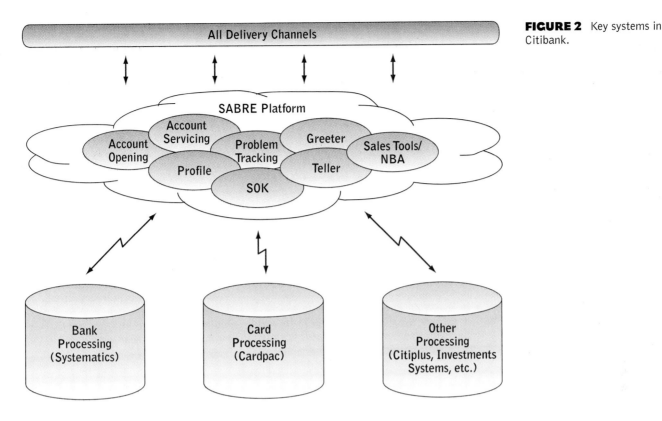

FIGURE 2 Key systems in Citibank.

hardware, software, and procedures enable RCC to reap ever-increasing economies of scale as each new country joins its fold, and as businesses of member countries grow. The centralization of credit card operations in the RCC provided other benefits as well:

○ It could devote the necessary resources to ensure superior service levels around the clock (100 percent availability and four-second terminal response time 99 percent of the time).

○ It could recruit and retain talent from the best in the region because of the size of its operations; its 60 professional staff have developed in-depth knowledge and expertise in credit card operations and operations of the IBM S/390 platform.

The major concern of the RCC is that of telecommunication costs. Although the RCC has employed advanced data compression techniques, the current costs of leased land/sea circuits are significantly higher than equivalent lines in the United States. Although costs are expected to come down when fiber-optic submarine cables are put in place, the RCC's heavy reliance on telecommunications makes it vulnerable to corporate pressure to locate network processing in areas that minimize its total operating costs. The RCC experience provided the ex-

periential base for subsequent rearchitecting of the technology of the consumer bank. The experience and expertise that RCC had built up would be repositioned to serve the processing requirements of the Asia-Pacific Consumer Bank.

V. REARCHITECTING THE IT INFRASTRUCTURE

The fundamental changes in IT infrastructure were motivated by the need to enable the Citibanking vision. The appointment of George DiNardo as the new chief technology officer in 1993 signaled the bank's strategic intent to develop a new technology infrastructure for capitalizing the opportunities from rapid economic growth in Asian countries which is expected to continue well into the twenty-first century. Recipient of **Information Week's** CIO of the Year Award for 1988, DiNardo had been with Mellon Bank in Pittsburgh from 1969 to 1991, and was its executive vice president of information systems function from 1985 to 1991. Prior to joining Citicorp, he was a consulting partner for Coopers and Lybrand and a professor of information systems at a leading U.S. university. DiNardo's plan for IT in Citibank is to enable Citibanking, through standardization of the IT platform, to significantly reduce processing costs per trans-

action through economies of scale, to reduce product to market times by 50 percent, and to increase systems reliability. He crisply summed up his job portfolio at Citibank:

> My job is to introduce the most advanced technology possible in Asia and I spent 35 years doing that for other banks, Bankers Trust and Mellon Bank. I am truly a bank businessman and a technologist. The vision requires that a customer going anywhere in the world be able to transact the same way wherever he goes. It is moving to [the concept of] Citibank recognizes you, and relationship manages you. If you have $100,000 with Citibank, you have certain services free, and it will be the same wherever you go. It's the ability to use the ATM wherever you are.

Moving toward this level of global banking requires that a Citibank branch anywhere in the world will have access to the customer's addresses, customary services, and relationships anywhere else in the world. It would have been costly to achieve this with the then decentralized computing structure, where each country in the Asia-Pacific has its own host computer and where each country has a different technology platform. It would also be difficult to ensure simultaneous rollout across countries of new products. Hence, the foundational changes to computing at Citibank Asia-Pacific began with the centralization of processing and a uniform back-office platform. The bank standardized on an IBM MVS platform. DiNardo explained the logic of centralization for Citibank Asia:

> The old days of having the computer center next to you are gone. Where should your computer center be—remote! Now, with fiber, put your console, command center in your main office, and your big box is remote. Our command center is here in Singapore. . . . The telecommunications are improving enough that we can centralize. The economies of large IBMs are important to banking. I have promised that if we regionalize on a new single system, we will get savings. It will cost $50m to do this, but we will break even in year two. We will put the largest IBM box we can get in a center in Singapore. I have promised a 10 to 20 percent computing reduction every year. How am I going to do that? You buy the biggest building, so you can pull any computer in any time, backup for 100 percent up-time, 99.9 percent on-time completion of batch jobs. Then you don't need backup all over Asia. You put in all the other countries' account processing, and transmit all the rest.

Initially, the major saving will come from avoiding the need to build a computer center in Hong Kong. Savings arise also from having all processing in one site, with only one other hot backup site, as compared with having processing distributed in 14 countries, and with each country having its own backup. Citibank will be leveraging off the networks that are already in place as a result of the regional card center. Another significant source of savings comes from the centralization of software development.

Citibank is aiming for uniformity in its back-room processing software. Previously, each country controlled its own systems development efforts, so that while each country started out with the same basic software, over time the plethora of systems development efforts resulted in significantly different systems. The advent of PCs and client/server computing com-

pounded the rate of change. Citibank replaced individual country systems that have evolved over time with a $20-million integrated back-office banking applications package from Systematics.

The strength of the Systematics package is that it has evolved significantly through its sale to more than 400 banks, and therefore offers many functions and features. It uses a traditional design based on the MVS/CICS/COBOL platform and has been proved capable of supporting high volumes. According to DiNardo, the idea is to not reinvent the wheel by writing yet another in-house back-office processing system, but to take this package and "turn the 2000 Citibank systems professionals loose on innovation . . . it's delivery and panache that counts . . . to create reusable modules to be called in through Systematics user exits. Systematics have promised to keep the exits constant through time." The plan also calls for eventual conversion of all other programs to the Systematics format, for example, using the same approach to data modeling, COBOL programming, and naming conventions.

A new Asia-Pacific data center running an IBM ES/9000 model 821 mainframe was set up in Singapore's Science Park on the western part of the island in October 1994. The hot-site backup running an IBM ES/9000 model 500 was located in Singapore's Chai Chee Industrial Park on the eastern part of the island. The intent is to relocate the backup site to another country to mitigate against country risks once the conversion is complete and the systems are running smoothly. Investments are also made to increase programmer productivity at development centers in Singapore, India, and the Philippines. Citibank is planning to spend $5 million on tools that will increase programmer productivity by 5 to 10 percent each year. Programmers in the centers will do remote TSO development using terminals with channel connects in all countries. Citibank is also considering putting in hyper channels if necessary.

By the first quarter of 1997, six countries had been converted to the Systematics platform—Australia, Singapore, Turkey, Guam, the Philippines, and Malaysia. The other countries were expected to be converted by 1998. By 1999 when the data center consolidation and regionalization are complete, Citibank expects to save about $17.6 million and reduce its staff by about 96 people. Its unit cost for banking transactions is expected to drop by 44 percent from 1996 levels.

VI. BUILDING COMMON FRONT-END SYSTEMS

Peter Mills, director for business improvement, is a 26-year Citibank veteran who has worked in most of the Citibank Asian divisions in his career and has oversight responsibilities for developing common processes for all Asia-Pacific businesses.

> Citibanking is our business vision. We have consolidated on a common platform for efficient back-room processing. My role is to create common business processes that may result in common front-end systems that are compatible with our backend platforms. As part of the rearchitecting of Citibank's technology infrastructure, we initiated several process reengineering projects to develop new process templates for the Asia-Pacific. It is thus crucial that we manage our key reengineering projects very carefully.

A common thread that has emerged from both the reengineering and infrastructural change efforts is the idea of incorporating best practice—what Citibank calls "centers of excellence." In the area of software development, the emphasis on adopting best practice among the Citibank countries is a guard against the common trap of settling for the lowest common denominator in the process of standardization. The commitment to develop a reengineering template incorporating the best redesigned processes from each country, for use in developing common systems, is another embodiment of this idea. DiNardo explains what is being practiced in Citibank Asia-Pacific:

> The purchase of the Systematics package provides the bank with increased functionality and standardized processing without significant systems development effort. In-house development effort will be focused on strategic products such as those for currency trading, Citiplus, and the SABRE front-end teller and platform systems. The approach to future systems development will no longer be one of letting "a hundred flowers bloom." There will no longer be systems development or enhancement only for individual countries. Any country requiring any change needs to convince at least two other countries to support it. Any changes made would then be made for all Citibank countries in Asia. Several countries have now been identified

as likely centers of excellence for front-end software development: Taiwan for auto loans processing, Australia for mortgage products, Hong Kong for personal finance products, India, the Philippines, and Singapore will become centers for application software development, design, and the generation of high-quality code at competitive cost.

The reengineering of business processes in Singapore provides a glimpse of how Citibank intends to introduce best practices in banking products and service delivery, which would be built into common front-end systems. Citibank has been in Singapore for more than 90 years. It started out as a wholesale bank. The consumer bank business was started later in the 1960s. Being a foreign bank, it is allowed to set up only three branches in Singapore. Nonetheless, Citibank has done very well in Singapore. Customer accounts have more than tripled since 1989, largely due to the successful introduction of Citibank's Visa card business. There has been an accompanying ten-fold increase in profit in the same period.

Citibank's retail customers in Singapore represent the more affluent segment of the population. The bank's fees and rates are not the lowest, but they feel that they are able to offer a higher level of service and more innovative banking products. This image of innovation and customer service is reinforced through a series of advertisements in print and on television. Innovative products include ready credit and Citiphone banking. The Citiphone service is Citibank Singapore's attempt to provide a high level of customer service despite the regulations that limit its number of branches to three. The vice president in charge of customer service, and the person responsible for implementing Citiphone, calls it their branch in the sky. This is a 24-hour, 7-day-a-week service that is manned by accredited Citibank officers, who are empowered to make decisions on the spot.

The increase in account volume, however, has been accomplished without any major increase in staff or changes in processes. Staff, processes, and infrastructure that were originally designed to support about 50,000 accounts, were strained when they had to support an account volume of about 250,000. This has contributed to a drop in customers' perception of service levels. Annual surveys indicated that customer satisfaction has dropped from a high of 90 percent in 1987 to a low of 65 percent in 1993. Some departments

are experiencing high overtime and employee turnover. A cultural assessment study conducted by consultants confirmed that some employees did not feel valued and trusted. Front-line operations were also paper intensive and perceived to have significant opportunities for improvements. In addition, there was the need to achieve the vision of Citibanking, which required cross-product integration as a basis for relationship banking.

The project was carried out in three phases: (1) building the case for action, (2) design, and (3) implementation. In the first two phases, the consultants worked closely with four Citibankers who were assigned full time to the reengineering project. After six months, the team completed phase two and composed a list of 28 recommended process changes. Three core processes were identified for change—delivery of services to the customer, marketing, and transaction processing. The delivery process included account opening and servicing, credit, and customer problem resolution. The team found that it was encumbered with many hand-offs, a "maker-checker" mindset where transactions had to be checked by someone other than the originating employee, and unclear accountability for problem resolution. The transaction processing process was basically the back-end processing for the transactions originating in the branches. The major observation here was that the processing was fragmented by product or system. The marketing processes were currently also product focused, and there was limited understanding of customer segments and individual customers.

The vision which the team presented included a streamlined front-end delivery process with clear accountability and quick turnaround on customer problem resolution, a unified approach to transaction processing, and segment-focused, cross-product marketing. They felt that the most radical change required would be that of the organizational culture. One aspect of culture manifested in the "maker-checker" was a legacy of the days when the bank was a wholesale bank, and each transaction value was very high while volume was relatively low. In the retail bank business, the high volume and low individual value of transactions required a different mindset. Other aspects of Citibank culture that would need to change include the emphasis and the incentive system that rewarded product innovation and individuality. The process changes required a culture

that focused more on relationships with customers and on team efforts.

The team also set detailed targets for each of the core processes. Among the many targets set for the delivery process, a rise in the percentage of customers who were highly satisfied from 64 to 80 percent, an increase in percentage of customers served within five minutes from 71 to 80 percent, and an improvement in transactions processing accuracy from 2 errors per 5000 transactions to 1 error per 5000 transactions. Detailed targets for productivity and cost improvements were also set. These targets that were in effect also listed measures that would be used to evaluate each process on a recurring basis.

Phase three involved the formation of three implementation teams—service delivery, operations, and product development and marketing—and many more employees. Each team was headed by the vice president in charge of the function. The role of the consultants in phase three was scaled back and they resisted some recommended changes. George Di-Nardo and Peter Mills addressed the problem of resistance by having discussions with key stakeholders of the processes to be reengineered, and by focusing on a number of projects. Before the end of the first year, the consultants had been phased out. The Citibank implementation teams were driving their own implementation.

A major part of implementation was to develop and implement the information systems needed to support the reengineered processes. Figure 3 is a representation of the key front-end systems within Citibank. One resulting new system is Strategic Asia-Pacific Branch Retail Environment (SABRE). SABRE consists of two complementary subsystems: SABRE I is at the teller level and provides automated support for signature verification, paperless teller transactions, and Citicard transactions. SABRE II includes the phone banking systems, together with facilities for telemarketing and cross-product marketing at the branches. The bank is developing the SABRE system in-house, because it considers this to be a strategic product.

The process change efforts, in tandem with the ongoing changes to the IT systems, have resulted in measurable improvements. Citibank tracks performance indicators before and after process changes (see Table 1) to assess the extent of the improvements.

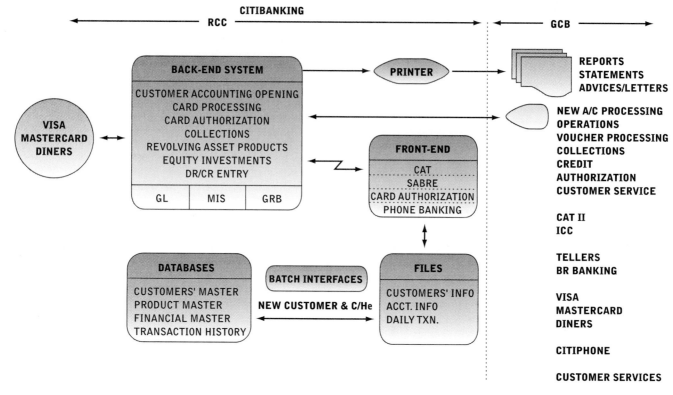

Figure 3 Strategic architecture.

VII. MANAGING IMPLEMENTATION AND CHANGE

It is evident that the structure of computing in Citibank is undergoing significant change. The changes are not trivial and will have "strategic impacts on the future business of the bank." The credibility and experience of George DiNardo were crucial in convincing senior officers of the bank in corporate headquarters and in Asia of the need for drastic change to the IT infrastructure. He has the backing of Citibank's top management and since taking the job, has already brought a different perspective to technology management. He starts from the premise that the IT infrastructure will be standardized to obtain the maximum benefit for the bank. Countries wanting to be different will have to justify it, quite a change from the days when country managers decide the types of technology they want for each country. The IT management team is charging ahead at great speed. When asked for the planned sequence of change activities, DiNardo replied that his approach was "to get all changes bubbling along at the same time . . . get a few good people who know what they are doing."

The RCC experience provides a useful model for the current consumer bank consolidation. The in-depth technical expertise gained from running a regional data center would be directly relevant to the new infrastructure that Citibank is putting in place for consumer banking. Not surprisingly, Ajit now directs and runs the data center for the new Asia-Pacific Consumer Bank technology infrastructure. However, the new infrastructure is more than just scaling up to process more transactions. The business of Citibanking in Global Consumer Banking is more diverse and complex than cards and requires the internalization of many business parameters in developing software to support back-end banking operations. Correspondingly, the business impact is also far greater. Citibank, as an American bank operating in Asia, is subjected to restrictions in the number of branches allowed in each country. The reliance on an electronic interface with customers and for an electronic channel for delivery of banking services is significantly higher than many local banks. Citibank sees the new technological infrastructure as a key enabler for flexibility and integration in its product and service offerings throughout Asia at a competitive cost.

The conversion approach is to first bring the bank's internal processes into conformity with the Systematics process flow. Reengineering principles were applied to streamline and standardize these processes. The Systematics package also has a customer information systems module that will be used by the bank to support its relationship banking strategy. The conversion to a new technology infrastructure at Citibank Asia-Pacific spells some loss of control over computing for the Citibank country managers. Surprisingly, there has not been serious opposition to the changes, although country managers are understandably "nervous" about the sweeping changes. DiNardo offered a few reasons:

> It's an idea whose time has come. The Asia Pacific high profit margin must be maintained! They all know this. They know the value of what we're doing. Computer costs will be down for them, it will affect their bottom line. There is no longer any desire for the sophisticated manager to have his/her own mainframe computer. They know that I have done it 700 times already. No one objects to the logic of the idea. We will insist on a postimplementation audit. The country managers in Asia

Table 1   Results of Citicard Benchmarking Program

	Cycle Time		No. of Hand-offs		Paperless	
	Before	After	Before	After	Before	After
Statement rendition	41 hrs	24 hrs	2	1	—	—
Duplicate charges	6 days	24 hrs	3	1	no	yes
Card not received charges	6 days	24 hrs	3	1	no	yes
Address change	24 hrs	instant	2	none	no	yes
Payment status inquiry	1–3 days	instant	3	none	no	yes
Account cancellation	24 hrs	instant	2	none	no	yes
Application status inquiry	1–2 days	instant	3	none	no	yes
Expired card charges	2 days	instant	2	1	—	—

did see that to survive the next 10 years something like this is necessary. It's all about customer service.

However, it is the level of service and support from the center that country managers are concerned about. The standardization and centralization strategy obviously restricted some flexibility in individual country operations. The strategy was adopted consciously and the gain in integrated customer service and economies of scale is substantial. From experience in other areas of business activities, there is a tendency for most centralized operations to develop a life of their own that over time makes it less responsive to the needs of the end users. Will the Citibank Asia-Pacific data center go the same way eventually? Citibank is putting in place processes to ensure that country needs are not neglected. "Through the conversion and development, we know their needs very well. For example, we will even help them get support from the two other countries needed to justify enhancements," DiNardo explained. The issue of responsiveness to local needs is unlikely to go away despite such assurances. There is also a related concern about how priorities for enhancements will be handled if there are not enough resources and capacity to meet requests in a timely manner.

A number of factors may impede the progress of the plans. First is the risk that the Systematics conversion may surface unexpected technical problems, as Citibank experienced in converting operations in the Philippines. "We are learning as we go," commented one member of the technical staff. The conversion and implementation schedule may need to be stretched and the expected payback delayed. The Asia-Pacific conversion that was originally supposed to be completed by 1997 was pushed to 1998. Part of the reason is the shortage of technical personnel in the region. Further,

those who have "cut their teeth" doing the technical implementation are being lured away by other international banks beginning to embark on similar strategies.

Second, the Asian technical staff, although skilled and highly motivated, are, in DiNardo's opinion, conservative. This makes it more difficult to push for the adoption of certain technologies that are perceived to be new in the region. "They tend to be too conservative in planning change—they are not aggressive in their time and payoff targets." DiNardo's experience and confidence have provided the needed leadership to his technical staff in setting the pace and standards for change. The question is whether the pace of change will continue at the same rate after DiNardo retires.

Third, the standardization and consolidation of technologies and systems have created a sophisticated but highly complex operation at Citibank's Asia-Pacific headquarters. For example, the Asia-Pacific data center has to deal with the integration of various operating systems such as MVS, Stratus, and UNIX. DiNardo admitted that "there are very few people able to run such massive data centers in the region." The high level of operational complexity presents challenges in maintaining consistently high availability, reliability, and quick response times.

Characteristically, DiNardo considers these minor problems that will not affect the overall success of the planned change. Although the implementation is still in progress, the plans have been well received by top management at Citicorp, and it is making plans for similar technology regionalization strategies for Europe, the United States, and Latin America. The Asia-Pacific Consumer Bank is setting the pace and direction for Citicorp in its technology strategy. The Citiplus multicurrency time deposits and Systematics product processes have now been adopted as standards for

Citicorp worldwide. One important unanticipated gain accruing to Citibank as a result of the massive infrastructural change is that it has finessed its Year 2000 problems in the process. Once the 15 Asia-Pacific countries are converted by 1998, there will be no legacy systems and no Year 2000 problems to worry about, saving Citibank an estimated $60 million. The new architecture has also eliminated the need to find programmers with very rare operating system skills needed by the old systems. The successful implementation of the changes will reduce the cost of IT services and increase the ability of IT to support product innovation and integration. Today, Citibank services primarily the high net worth customers in Asia. IT may enable the bank to also offer its brand of services to the growing middle class.

Source: From Boon Siong Neo and Christina Soh, Information Management Research Center (IMARC), Nanyang Business School, Nanyang Technological University, Singapore. Reprinted by permission.

CASE STUDY QUESTIONS

1. What business strategy is Citicorp pursuing in Asia?
2. Evaluate Citibank's Asia-Pacific information systems in light of this strategy. How well do they support it?
3. Evaluate Citibank's strategy for managing its Asia-Pacific information systems infrastructure.

[1] All financial figures are in U.S. $ unless otherwise stated.
[2] "Citicorp Credit Card Chief to Retire," **Business Times**, April 21, 1997.
[3] "Citicorp in Asia: Eastward Look," **The Economist**, October 24, 1992, p. 90.
[4] "Thinking Globally, Acting Locally," **China Business Review**, May–June, 1993, pp. 23–25.
[5] "For Citibank, There's No Place Like Asia," **Business Week**, March 30, 1992, pp. 66–69.

International Case Study

CASE STUDY 5: Heineken Netherlands B.V.: Reengineering IS/IT to Enable Customer-Oriented Supply Chain Management

Donald A. Marchand, Thomas E. Vollmann, and Kimberly A. Bechler, International Institute for Management Development (Switzerland)

In June 1993, Jan Janssen, financial manager of Heineken Netherlands B.V. and the person responsible for Information Systems (IS) and Information Technology (IT), and his IS manager, Rob Pietersen, faced the challenge of developing an IS/IT configuration that would add value to the business and support the ongoing transformation of Heineken's supply chain management system. This system was extensive, not only supplying the Dutch home market, but also providing a significant part of the supply to more than 100 export countries served by the Heineken Group. Supply chain management was central to enterprise-wide transformation.

Management was committed to a process-driven organization, customer-service partnerships, 24-hour delivery lead time, major innovations in the transport system, and resulting changes in the way people worked. And Janssen knew that all of these—and more—required fundamental changes in the way this new work was to be supported by information systems and technology.

Janssen was convinced that the effective management of information as well as a more appropriate IT infrastructure were critical to achieving Heineken's goals of increased flexibility, greater coordination, and a sharper focus on customer needs.

In his mind, the change program initiated in 1990 in the IS/IT area had just been the beginning. Now, he and Pietersen needed to design an information systems and technology backbone that would be flexible enough to evolve with the changing business needs and adapt to continuous changes in technology.

HEINEKEN NETHERLANDS B.V.

Heineken Netherlands B.V. was the principal operating company responsible for operations in Heineken's home market. It also accounted for a significant part of Heineken N.V.'s worldwide exports. Of the 60.4 million hectoliters[1] of beer produced worldwide under the supervision of the Heineken Group in 1994, a significant portion was produced in the company's two Dutch breweries—Zoeterwoude and 's-Hertogenbosch (Den Bosch). Likewise, 11 percent of the Heineken Group's sales took place in the domestic market, and more than 5400 employees worked for Heineken Netherlands.

Supply Chain Management

The supply chain at Heineken Netherlands began with the receipt of the raw materials that went into the brewing process, and continued through packaging, distribution, and delivery. Brewing took six weeks; it began with the malt mixture of barley and ended with the filtering of the beer after fermentation. Depending on the distribution channel, the beer was then packaged in "one-way" or returnable bottles or cans of different sizes and labels, put in kegs, or delivered in bulk.

The variety of outlets meant that the company had to manage differences in response time (beer for the domestic market was produced to stock, while exported beer was produced to order) and three distinct distribution channels. While each channel consisted mainly of the same steps from the receipt of raw materials through brewing, they differed greatly in packaging and distribution. Beer could be distributed to either on-premise outlets (hotels, restaurants, and cafes, where it was delivered in kegs or poured directly into cellar beer tanks), off-premise outlets (supermarkets, grocery and liquor stores, where it was sold in a variety of bottle and package sizes for home consumption), or to export markets (export deliveries were made to order).

Ongoing Transformation

With key customers requesting faster response times, the development of a process-driven view of Heineken's supply chain activities became critical. The company started the transformation of its supply chain management system by creating customer-service partnerships with its largest domestic customers. The overall objective was to improve the logistics chain dramatically for these customers. In response, delivery lead times were reduced and the transport system was changed. However, the supply chain transformation was seen as a never-ending process.

New Customer-Service Partnerships

In these new service partnerships, Heineken was requested to reduce the time from the placement of the product order to the actual delivery. Before, this delivery lead time had been three days, but the supermarket chains wanted Heineken to supply their warehouses in the Netherlands in 24 hours. Each of the warehouses carried only 8 hours of stock at any time, so the supermarket chains depended on quick and flexible delivery to maintain low inventories and fast response times.

To further enhance its close cooperation with customers, Heineken had embarked on a pilot test of a new logistics improvement called "Comakership" with Albert Heijn, the largest supermarket chain in the Netherlands. Comakership was part of Albert Heijn's Efficient Customer Response project, "Today for Tomorrow." The Albert Heijn retail stores sent their sales information as scanning data to the computer in their central head office. There, the data for Heineken products were scanned out and separated. The beer sales information was then relayed via a standard EDI system (provided by a value-added network operator) from the central office of Albert Heijn directly to Heineken's Zoeterwoude brewery. Heineken was usually able to deliver within 18 hours. Although the pilot had been initiated in only one of Albert Heijn's distribution centers (and the set of stores it served), it had already resulted in lower lead times, decreased costs, and less complexity in the distribution system.

Moving to a 24-Hour Delivery Lead Time

As a result of these successes, top management concluded that delivery lead time could be cut to 24 hours for most domestic customers. However, it would require major shifts in the company's stock levels, distribution centers, work organization, transport system, organizational structure, and information systems.

The 24-hour lead time allowed for greater stock turnover and for lower stock levels in the customer distribution centers. There was, however, more interdepot traffic and higher stocks of packaging material ("returnables") on the brewery premises (which had been located elsewhere along the supply chain). But management believed that as less total inventory was held in the system, these packaging material stocks might be reduced over time.

New Transport System

Until 1991, Heineken Netherlands had contracted out the transportation of its products from the two breweries to about 50 transporters. All of them used a lorry-trailer system with "dedicated" drivers—a driver and his "truck" could make an average of 2.1 deliveries per day. To meet the 24-hour lead time, Heineken had to completely change the fleet used for transport and reduce the number of transporters from 50 to 10. Heineken then contracted 4 cabin trucks from each transporter (40 cabin trucks in total) and paid them for the use of the trailers. The ability of the driver to move from one trailer to another without waiting for unloading meant that he could make an average of 2.4 deliveries per day (a cost reduction of approximately G1.5 million).[2]

New Information Management (IM) Needs

Heineken's customer-service partnership with Albert Heijn and the other changes Heineken had implemented in its supply chain activities brought new information requirements to support the more stringent delivery dictates. With the pilot testing of the Comakership logistics improvement, Heineken needed to implement systems which could manage this new transfer of information, and make appropriate modifications in work activities and organizational structure. Furthermore, the new IS/IT infrastructure needed to be flexible enough to handle and reflect individual retailer and customer beer purchasing patterns.

In the context of these changes in supply chain activities, Janssen reflected on the beginnings of the transformation of IS/IT:

The transformation of IS/IT and the shifts occurring in our supply chain activities were concurrent without causality. That is very strange, but it just happened that way. I can't say to you that it is a "chicken and egg" kind of story. Of course, there was a link but not an explicit one. Somewhere in our minds, when you do one you do the other, too.

Janssen knew that the relationship between information management, information systems, and information technology had to be clearly defined to have optimum support for the new approaches to value creation. Information management focused on supporting customers and creating new "bundles of goods and services." Information systems focused on developing applications software, managing data, and supporting the new business processes. Finally, information technology related primarily to data and text services, and the underlying operating systems, interfaces, hardware, and networks.

PHASE 1: RECOGNIZING THE NEED FOR CHANGE

In July 1989, at the beginning of all the changes at Heineken, Janssen (then at headquarters and responsible for IS/IT worldwide) received a request for a second mainframe at Heineken Netherlands, costing G6 million (with another G6 million required in three to four years); Janssen brought in the consulting firm Nolan, Norton, Inc. to evaluate the IS/IT infrastructure, first at the corporate level and then at the operating company level for Heineken Netherlands:

A proposal to purchase a second mainframe focused everybody on our IS/IT infrastructure. You have to have some kind of crisis to get people thinking.

IS/IT Benchmarking

Nolan, Norton, Inc. benchmarked Heineken's IS/IT cost structure against the beverage industry IS/IT average and it was clear that Heineken was indeed not competitive—the company was spending twice the money for half the functionality. "The Nolan, Norton report confirmed what a very wide group of the users thought," Janssen commented. In response, management recommended decentralizing the data center and having each business area manage its own computing resources.

At the same time, Janssen asked Heineken Netherlands, the largest operating company, to develop a new IS/IT plan based on new computer technology, "which meant looking for mid-range platforms, decentralized computing, and standard software packages, rather than developing customized programs for every new application—previously the standard practice." Before determining an appropriate IS/IT plan, Janssen made sure that information management scans were conducted in every functional area. Managers were asked, "What do you need and how can that

support our business?" The results were used to create information plans. Working with KPMG Management Consultants and Nolan, Norton, Inc., Janssen developed a list of priorities for IS/IT and selected a new IT platform (IBM AS/400)—both were accepted in July 1990:

The AS/400 became the core of our new IT platform for two reasons: first, we had been a client with IBM for roughly 40 years, and it was not their fault that we used their mainframes in the wrong way; second, we already knew that huge masses of application software were being written for the AS/400, as a quick scan easily confirmed. Furthermore, we were starting to think about an appropriate IT architecture and we were considering the possibility of using personal computers as peripherals linked together through local area and wide area networks.

Implementation of the New IS/IT Plan

Before the end of 1990, Janssen was appointed financial manager. He became the person responsible for IS/IT at Heineken Netherlands and was to oversee the implementation of the new IS/IT plan. Janssen concluded that outsourcing would play a critical role in this process:

The decision to outsource was part of the plan. When we came to the conclusion that a major change was necessary, that we should look for mid-range computers, that we should go for standard software, that we should not go for dumb terminals but for personal computers as peripherals, it became clear to us that this was a big operation and we could not evolve to it. We could not manage just to keep the old systems in the air with all the problems and have enough management attention for building up the new systems. So we told the organization, "Gentlemen, we are going to outsourcers, and we are going to freeze the applications to free up management time."

PHASE 2: OUTSOURCING TO DEVELOP THE NEW IS/IT INFRASTRUCTURE

Outsourcing enabled the IS group to keep the "old" mainframe applications running while it developed a new IT approach—focusing on the development of its client/server distributed processing

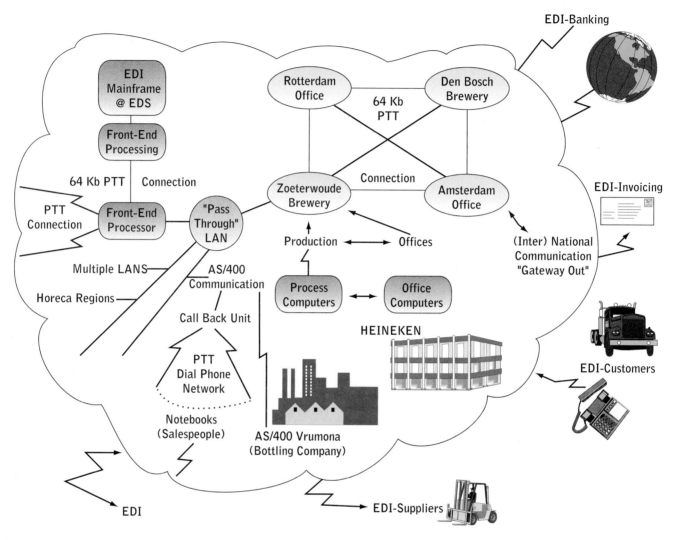

Figure 1 Heineken network era WAN/LAN.

infrastructure, the appropriate new IT architecture, and the IS people and skills to achieve these new objectives.

Outsourcing

In 1991, after scanning the outsourcers' market, Janssen chose Electronic Data Systems (EDS), the largest provider of computer services in the United States. EDS provided the **expertise** and **infrastructure** required to meet Heineken's information systems and technology needs, and **career possibilities** for Heineken's mainframe personnel, both vital to the successful transformation of its IS/IT infrastructure. Finally, the five-year contract (with declining involvement each year) provided "guaranteed continuity" while Heineken maintained control. The plan indicated that the last mainframe program would be replaced in 1996 and the contract with EDS would end.

Development of the New IT Architecture

The development of the new IT architecture took place almost concurrently:

> We moved in two directions—one, to outsource our operational concerns, and two, to focus on our new architecture development, eventually replacing everything which was on the mainframe with standard packages on AS/400s.

With the decision to downsize—to move off the mainframe platform—and to decentralize the information management and systems, Janssen chose a comprehensive client/server strategy using a combination of workstations, local and wide area networks, mid-range systems such as AS/400s, and local area servers to complete the technology architecture. (Refer to

Figure 1 for Heineken's IT architecture.) "Personal computers" became "Heineken workstations" to eliminate the confusion and "mess" of having 2000 "personal" workstations—in this way, every workstation had the same setup. Furthermore, the sales force began using "Notebooks" for customer sensing and information sharing.

Changing Over to Standard Packages and Developing Greater Flexibility to Serve the Business

In 1993, Rob Pietersen became IS manager at Heineken Netherlands. He believed that the decentralized IS/IT operations gave more "computer power to the people," and enabled the "user" to become the process owner. Old mainframe programs were replaced with new standard

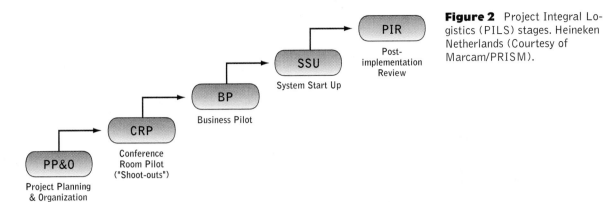

Figure 2 Project Integral Logistics (PILS) stages. Heineken Netherlands (Courtesy of Marcam/PRISM).

application packages that covered all the functions in the supply chain. Heineken started this "changeover" by focusing on the software applications dealing with clients: order entry, delivery, transport, invoicing, and accounts receivable.

Selecting Standard Software Packages

To increase flexibility and customer responsiveness, Pietersen knew that Heineken had to shift from the "waterfall approach" to the development of standard software packages:

> At that time in the mainframe world, we were developing software applications using a methodology often referred to as the "waterfall." You started with a requirements definition from the users, developed a design and the code to implement that design (getting signoffs at each point along the way). You put the code in production, tested the code, released the code into operation and then you maintained it. When you adopted the code, you went back to the users and asked them if this was what they wanted, and often they said "What?" This waterfall process took 18 to 36 months or more, and by the time it was completed, the users' requirements often had changed.

Pietersen began using the PILS (Project Integral Logistics)—named after the successful approach developed to select appropriate logistics software—to test and select standard software packages (refer to Figure 2). The PILS approach involved:

○ identifying appropriate software packages;
○ setting the top two package vendors against one another in a "shoot-out"—as in the American "Wild West"—where the specific elements of each software package were compared and contrasted;

○ creating a business pilot;
○ implementing it;
○ evaluating its performance.

For IS people, this meant moving from COBOL programming to developing a thorough knowledge of the business.

Pietersen chose PRISM for the logistics area and JD Edwards for the financial area. Pietersen found that the new systems and policies better fit the information needs of the company:

> We needed more flexibility, more power, and less cost. Our current systems have scored high in each of those areas. Computer power is now where it belongs: not with the IT people, but in the hands of the people who need it.

IS Group Reconfiguration

Outsourcing the mainframe and mainframe applications to EDS led to a change in the configuration of the IS group as well. Contracts with employees from software houses were stopped, and many of the individuals working on the mainframe went with the mainframe systems to EDS while other staff shifted to other areas of the IS group, such as systems management.

Pietersen was convinced that the competencies and capabilities of the IS group had to be expanded to align the use of IT with the evolving supply chain, rather than simply promoting IT solutions as "answers" to the company's information management "problems." Pietersen understood that this change in approach for the IS group required not only a deeper knowledge of business processes and strategy, but also an understanding of how people used the information.

Pietersen therefore transformed the IS department from units for application development, customer support, and operations (a functional structure) to teams

servicing production, commercial, distribution, and customer-service areas—the "process owners" (a team-oriented business approach). (Refer to Figures 3 and 4 for the IS organization before and after 1993.) The information management needs of the business areas were thus defined by people from both the business areas and IS. These **account teams** helped select standard application packages and, afterwards, adapt the business process to the software package **or** adapt the software package to the business process. These teams thus developed and implemented systems that gave the required support for the respective business processes and delivered information to enable a better control of the supply chain. Shrinking from 130 to 40 people, the IS group was now "doing what they had been doing differently."

Pietersen and Janssen believed that increasing overall access to information would support management's efforts to enhance the employees' empowerment. Client/server systems also fostered teamwork and horizontal decision making. They were fast, flexible, and permitted greater communication with customers and suppliers, which resulted in improved customer service. And they promoted the development of a "process view" (focusing on total processes rather than on discrete tasks). Furthermore, the new configuration of the IS group, with its more team-oriented business approach, also promoted a spirit of greater cooperation and communication. Pietersen commented, "If we still had the mainframe, all this would not be possible."

Evaluating IS Performance

In 1995, Pietersen and Janssen were still trying to determine how to measure the performance of the IS/IT department. They agreed that IS/IT needed to serve the business, and different service level

Figure 3 IS organization before 1993. Heineken Netherlands.

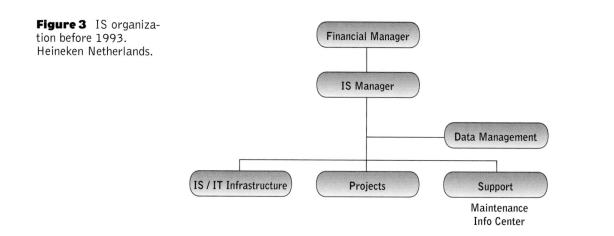

agreements were to be negotiated with the different functional areas (as shown in Figure 5):

> What is our business? Is it information technology? No, our business is brewing and selling premium beer of high quality. We changed our IT policy to make it clear that IT **supports** the business, but doesn't **drive** the business. We started to focus on having a beautiful bottom line rather than beautiful IT applications.

IS performance then became based on the timely and successful completion of projects. The most important **measure** was the improvement of the business process for which a system or service was meant. In the future, Pietersen and Janssen would be trying to develop criteria to measure the impact of an IS project on improving **overall business performance.**

PHASE 3: LEVERAGING INFORMATION ASSETS IN THE BUSINESS

Executive Information Systems (EIS)

By 1995, Heineken's operational supply chain system—from supplier to end customer—was in its final phase, and the company had begun to add the decision-support element. Decision-support or executive information systems would make it possible for managers to express their information requirements directly. Pietersen hoped that their ease of use would encourage managers to analyze past performance in greater depth and enable them to simulate the possible consequences of proposed actions more accurately. When it came to selecting the appropriate software, Pietersen had chosen EIS Express:

I call it the technical infrastructure; the basic logical infrastructure of all these systems is in place, and now we come to enabling real improvement, not just the EDI links we have with our retailers, but also such things as installing executive information systems (EIS) to give our management team the control instruments they need to navigate us through the more turbulent business environments we will face in the coming years. The executive information systems gather their data from the data warehouses of the different business systems in all areas and can show this easily through different (graphical) viewpoints.

One of Janssen and Pietersen's goals for the use of executive information systems was to have unity in the data. Janssen explained:

Figure 4 IS organization after 1993. Heineken Netherlands.

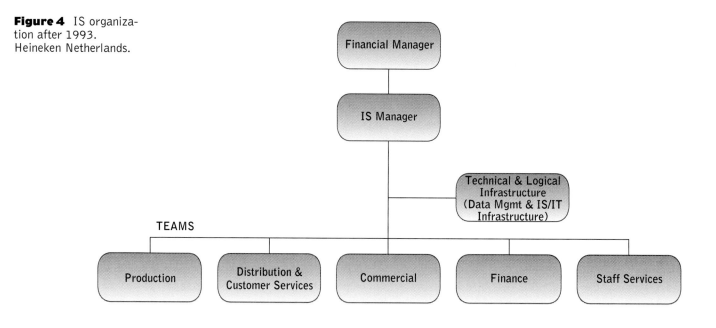

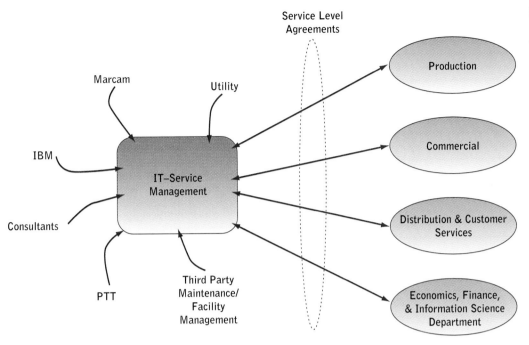

Figure 5 What is service management? "To assemble and offer." Heineken Netherlands (Courtesy of Pink Elephant).

Having unity in our data is crucial. Only a few years ago we discovered some departments were using different unit volumes than we were. And that just should not happen in any organization.

Better Planning Tools

A key part of the IS/IT strategy was to develop an integrated set of systems to plan and control the overall supply chain, both in the short run (bottle-line scheduling and daily operations) and over a longer horizon (sales forecasts and long-term operations research). The aim was faster and more flexible control of supply chain activities. Jan Janssen elaborated:

What we are working toward is a coherent and consistent set of planning and scheduling tools which are more or less compatible and interconnectible so that you can build up or build down the basic data. Our goal is to be able to model business processes and to have the data, like sales forecasts, to support our decisions about capacity, bottling lines, and stocks. We want to be in a position where, if you have to make a decision, you can run simulations based on actual data.

The concept of supply chain management ultimately served as the driver for better planning tools. Management understood that an overall planning function

with multiple time horizons was essential to optimize the supply chain activities as well as to ensure better information management. (Refer to Figure 6 for Heineken's information systems.)

Janssen and Pietersen had put in place information systems to collect and integrate information on Heineken's "on-premise" customer activity. Information on each hotel, restaurant, and cafe/pub that Heineken Netherlands had contact with (as owner, financing agent, or product supplier) was included in these systems. In this way, Heineken Netherlands was able to provide the relevant sales force with an integrated view of their customers (large or small) as well as with information on competitors catering to the same establishments, beer sold, and contract terms. Janssen elaborated:

We are thinking about what the "next stage of the rocket" will be. We have defined the baseline and are looking at workflow, EDI and planning information systems—how should these planning systems interrelate? We are in the process of defining the next phase of the vision for Heineken as a business in the Netherlands and for the IS/IT fit to that. The current debate is just how far to go.

This case is a condensed version of Heineken Netherlands B.V. A&B. It was prepared by Research Associate Kimberly A. Bechler under the supervision of Professors Donald A. Marchand

and Thomas E. Vollmann, as a basis for class discussion rather than to illustrate either effective or ineffective handling of a business situation. The names of the Heineken managers involved have been disguised. It was developed within the research scope of Manufacturing 2000, a research and development project conducted with global manufacturing enterprises. The authors wish to acknowledge the generous assistance of Heineken management, especially IS manager Gert Bolderman. Copyright © 1996 by IMD–International Institute for Management Development, Lausanne, Switzerland. Not to be used or reproduced without written permission directly from IMD.

CASE STUDY QUESTIONS

1. Analyze Heineken Netherlands using the value chain and competitive forces models. Why did the company feel it needed to transform its supply chain?

2. Analyze all the elements of the new IT infrastructure that Heineken selected for its new business processes. Were Heineken's technology choices appropriate? Why or why not?

3. What management, organization, and technology issues had to be addressed when Heineken Netherlands reengineered its supply chain?

[1]Hectolitre = 22 Imperial gallons = 26.418 U.S. gallons; Heineken 1994 Annual Report.
[2]1000 Guilders (G) = approximately £368 = U.S.$575 (at December 31, 1994); Heineken 1994 Annual Report.

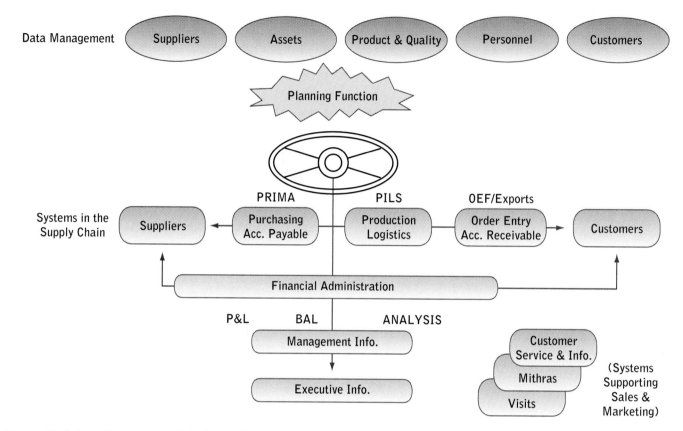

Figure 6 Information systems. Heineken Netherlands.

References

CHAPTER 1

Ackoff, R. L. "Management Misinformation System." *Management Science* 14, no. 4 (December 1967), B140–B116.

Alavi, Maryam, and **Patricia Carlson.** "A Review of MIS Research and Disciplinary Development." *Journal of Management Information Systems* 8, no. 4 (Spring 1992).

Allen, Brandt R., and **Andrew C. Boynton.** "Information Architecture: In Search of Efficient Flexibility." *MIS Quarterly* 15, no. 4 (December 1991).

Anthony, R. N. *Planning and Control Systems: A Framework for Analysis.* Cambridge, MA: Harvard University Press (1965).

Applegate, Lynda, and **Janice Gogan.** "Electronic Commerce: Trends and Opportunities." Harvard Business School, 9-196-006 (October 6, 1995).

Applegate, Lynda M., Clyde W. Holsapple, Ravi Kalakota, Franz J. Radermacher, and **Andrew B. Whinston.** "Electronic Commerce: Building Blocks of New Business Opportunity." *Journal of Organizational Computing and Electronic Commerce* 6, no. 1 (1996).

Armstrong, Arthur, and **John Hagel, III.** "The Real Value of On-line Communities." *Harvard Business Review* (May–June 1996).

Bakos, J. Yannis. "A Strategic Analysis of Electronic Marketplaces." *MIS Quarterly* 15, no. 3 (September 1991).

Barrett, Stephanie S. "Strategic Alternatives and Interorganizational System Implementations: An Overview." *Journal of Management Information Systems* (Winter 1986–1987).

Benjamin, Robert, and **Rolf Wigand.** "Electronic Markets and Virtual Value Chains on the Information Superhighway." *Sloan Management Review* (Winter 1995).

Brown, Carol V., and **Sharon L. Magill.** "Alignment of the IS Functions with the Enterprise: Toward a Model of Antecedents." *MIS Quarterly* 18, no. 4 (December 1994).

Brynjolfsson, E. T., T. W. Malone, V. Gurbaxani, and **A. Kambil.** "Does Information Technology Lead to Smaller Firms?" *Management Science* 40, no. 12 (1994).

Cash, James I., F. Warren McFarlan, James L. McKenney, and **Lynda M. Applegate.** *Corporate Information Systems Management,* 4th ed. Homewood, IL: Irwin (1996).

Clark, Thomas D., Jr. "Corporate Systems Management: An Overview and Research Perspective." *Communications of the ACM* 35, no. 2 (February 1992).

Davis, Gordon B., and **Margrethe H. Olson.** *Management Information Systems: Conceptual Foundations, Structure, and Development,* 2nd ed. New York: McGraw-Hill (1985).

Deans, Candace P., and **Michael J. Kane.** *International Dimensions of Information Systems and Technology.* Boston, MA: PWS-Kent (1992).

Engler, Natalie. "Small but Nimble." *Information Week* (January 18, 1999).

Fedorowicz, Jane, and **Benn Konsynski.** "Organization Support Systems: Bridging Business and Decision Processes." *Journal of Management Information Systems* 8, no. 4 (Spring 1992).

Feeny, David E., and **Leslie P. Willcocks.** "Core IS Capabilities for Exploiting Information Technology." *Sloan Management Review* 39, no. 3 (Spring 1998).

Feitzinger, Edward, and **Hau L. Lee.** "Mass Customization at Hewlett-Packard: The Power of Postponement." *Harvard Business Review* (January–February 1997).

Garud, Raghu, and **Henry C. Lucas, Jr.** "Welcome to the Virtual Organization." *Stern Business* (Summer 1998).

Gilmore, James H., and **B. Joseph Pine, II.** "The Four Faces of Mass Customization." *Harvard Business Review* (January–February 1997).

Gorry, G. A., and **M. S. Scott Morton.** "A Framework for Management Information Systems." *Sloan Management Review* 13, no. 1 (1971).

Hardwick, Martin, and **Richard Bolton.** "The Industrial Virtual Enterprise." *Communications of the ACM* 40, no. 9 (September 1997).

Johnston, Russell, and **Michael J. Vitale.** "Creating Competitive Advantage with Interorganizational Information Systems." *MIS Quarterly* 12, no. 2 (June 1988).

Keen, Peter G. W. *Shaping the Future: Business Design Through Information Technology.* Cambridge, MA: Harvard Business School Press (1991).

King, John. "Centralized vs. Decentralized Computing: Organizational Considerations and Management Options." *Computing Surveys* (October 1984).

Kling, Rob, and **William H. Dutton.** "The Computer Package: Dynamic Complexity." In *Computers and Politics,* edited by James Danziger, William H. Dutton, Rob Kling, and Kenneth Kraemer. New York: Columbia University Press (1982).

Laudon, Kenneth C. "A General Model for Understanding the Relationship Between Information Technology and Organizations." Working paper, Center for Research on Information Systems, New York University (1989).

Leonard-Barton, Dorothy. *Wellsprings of Knowledge.* Boston, MA: Harvard Business School Press (1995).

Liker, Jeffrey K., David B. Roitman, and **Ethel Roskies.** "Changing Everything All at Once: Work Life and Technological Change." *Sloan Management Review* (Summer 1987).

Lucas, Henry C., Jr., and **Jack Baroudi.** "The Role of Information Technology in Organization Design." *Journal of Management Information Systems* 10, no. 4 (Spring 1994).

Malone, T. W., and **J. F. Rockart.** "Computers, Networks and the Corporation." *Scientific American* 265, no. 3 (September 1991).

Malone, Thomas W., **JoAnne Yates,** and **Robert I. Benjamin.** "Electronic Markets and Electronic Hierarchies." *Communications of the ACM* (June 1987).

———. "The Logic of Electronic Markets." *Harvard Business Review* (May–June 1989).

McFarlan, F. Warren, **James L. McKenney,** and **Philip Pyburn.** "The Information Archipelago—Plotting a Course." *Harvard Business Review* (January–February 1983).

———. "Governing the New World." *Harvard Business Review* (July–August 1983).

McKenney, James L., and **F. Warren McFarlan.** "The Information Archipelago—Maps and Bridges." *Harvard Business Review* (September–October 1982).

Niederman, Fred, **James C. Brancheau,** and **James C. Wetherbe.** "Information Systems Management Issues for the 1990s." *MIS Quarterly* 15, no. 4 (December 1991).

Orlikowski, Wanda J., and **Jack J. Baroudi.** "Studying Information Technology in Organizations: Research Approaches and Assumptions." *Information Systems Research* 2, no. 1 (March 1991).

Rayport, J. F., and **J. J. Sviokla.** "Managing in the Marketspace." *Harvard Business Review* (November–December 1994).

Roach, Stephen S. "Technology and the Services Sector: The Hidden Competitive Challenge." *Technological Forecasting and Social Change* 34 (1988).

———. "Services Under Siege—The Restructuring Imperative." *Harvard Business Review* (September–October 1991).

Roche, Edward M. "Planning for Competitive Use of Information Technology in Multinational Corporations." AIB UK Region, Brighton Polytechnic, Brighton, UK, Conference Paper (March 1992). Edward M. Roche, W. Paul Stillman School of Business, Seton Hall University.

Rockart, John F. "The Line Takes the Leadership—IS Management in a Wired Society." *Sloan Management Review* 29, no. 4 (Summer 1988).

Rockart, John F., and **James E. Short.** "IT in the 1990s: Managing Organizational Interdependence." *Sloan Management Review* 30, no. 2 (Winter 1989).

Scott Morton, Michael, ed. *The Corporation in the 1990s.* New York: Oxford University Press (1991).

Strassman, Paul. *The Information Payoff—The Transformation of Work in the Electronic Age.* New York: Free Press (1985).

Tornatsky, Louis G., **J. D. Eveland, Myles G. Boylan, W. A. Hertzner, E. C. Johnson, D. Roitman,** and **J. Schneider.** "The Process of Technological Innovation: Reviewing the Literature." Washington, DC: National Science Foundation (1983).

Upton, David M., and **Andrew McAfee.** "The Real Virtual Factory." *Harvard Business Review* (July–August 1996).

Warson, Albert. "Tool Time." *Forbes ASAP* (October 7, 1996).

Weill, Peter, and **Marianne Broadbent.** *Leveraging the New Infrastructure.* Cambridge, MA: Harvard Business School Press (1998).

———. "Management by Maxim: How Business and IT Managers Can Create IT Infrastructures," *Sloan Management Review* (Spring 1997).

Winter, Susan J., and **S. Lynne Taylor.** "The Role of IT in the Transformation of Work: A Comparison of Post-Industrial, Industrial, and Proto-Industrial Organization." *Information Systems Research* 7, no. 1 (March 1996).

CHAPTER 2

Allen, Brandt R., and **Andrew C. Boynton.** "Information Architecture: In Search of Efficient Flexibility." *MIS Quarterly* 15, no. 4 (December 1991).

Anthony, R. N. *Planning and Control Systems: A Framework for Analysis.* Cambridge, MA: Harvard University Press (1965).

Bakos, J. Yannis, and **Michael E. Treacy.** "Information Technology and Corporate Strategy: A Research Perspective." *MIS Quarterly* (June 1986).

Barua, Anitesh, **Charles H. Kriebel,** and **Tridas Mukhopadhyay.** "An Economic Analysis of Strategic Information Technology Investments." *MIS Quarterly* 15, no. 5 (September 1991).

Beath, Cynthia Mathis, and **Blake Ives.** "Competitive Information Systems in Support of Pricing." *MIS Quarterly* (March 1986).

Berry, Leonard L., and **A. Parasuraman.** "Listening to the Customer—the Concept of a Service-Quality Information System." *Sloan Management Review* (Spring 1997).

Bower, Joseph L., and **Thomas M. Hout.** "Fast-Cycle Capability for Competitive Power." *Harvard Business Review* (November–December 1988).

Caldwell, Bruce. "A Cure for Hospital Woes." *Information Week* (September 9, 1991).

Cash, J. I., and **Benn R. Konsynski.** "IS Redraws Competitive Boundaries." *Harvard Business Review* (March–April 1985).

Cash, J. I., and **P. L. McLeod.** "Introducing IS Technology in Strategically Dependent Companies." *Journal of Management Information Systems* (Spring 1985).

Chan, Yolande E., **Sid L. Huff, Donald W. Barclay,** and **Duncan G. Copeland.** "Business Strategic Orientation, Information Systems Strategic Orientation, and Strategic Alignment." *Information Systems Research* 8, no. 2 (June 1997).

Clemons, Eric K. "Evaluation of Strategic Investments in Information Technology." *Communications of the ACM* (January 1991).

Clemons, Eric K., and **Bruce W. Weber.** "Segmentation, Differentiation, and Flexible Pricing: Experience with Information Technology and Segment-Tailored Strategies." *Journal of Management Information Systems* 11, no. 2 (Fall 1994).

Clemons, Eric K., and **Michael Row.** "McKesson Drug Co.: Case Study of a Strategic Information System." *Journal of Management Information Systems* (Summer 1988).

———. "Sustaining IT Advantage: The Role of Structural Differences." *MIS Quarterly* 15, no. 3 (September 1991).

———. "Limits to Interfirm Coordination through IT." *Journal of Management Information Systems* 10, no. 1 (Summer 1993).

Copeland, Duncan G., and **James L. McKenney.** "Airline Reservations Systems: Lessons from History." *MIS Quarterly* 12, no. 3 (September 1988).

Culnan, Mary J. "Transaction Processing Applications as Organizational Message Systems: Implications for the Intelligent Organization." Working paper no. 88-10, Twenty-second Hawaii International Conference on Systems Sciences (January 1989).

Dhar, Vasant, and **Roger Stein.** *Intelligent Decision Support Methods.* Upper Saddle River, NJ: Prentice Hall (1997).

Eardley, Alan, David Avison, and Philip Powell. "Developing Information Systems to Support Flexible Strategy." *Journal of Organizational Computing and Electronic Commerce* 7, no. 1 (1997).

Evans, Philip P., and Thomas S. Wurster. "Strategy and the New Economics of Information." *Harvard Business Review* (September–October 1997).

Fabris, Peter. "Going South." *Webmaster* (April 1997).

Feeny, David E., and Blake Ives. "In Search of Sustainability: Reaping Long-Term Advantage from Investments in Information Technology." *Journal of Management Information Systems* (Summer 1990).

Fisher, Marshall L. "What Is the Right Supply Chain for Your Product?" *Harvard Business Review* (March–April 1997).

Henderson, John C., and John J. Sifonis. "The Value of Strategic IS Planning: Understanding Consistency, Validity, and IS Markets." *MIS Quarterly* 12, no. 2 (June 1988).

Hopper, Max. "Rattling SABRE-New Ways to Compete on Information." *Harvard Business Review* (May–June 1990).

Houdeshel, George, and Hugh J. Watson. "The Management Information and Decision Support (MIDS) System at Lockheed Georgia." *MIS Quarterly* 11, no. 1 (March 1987).

Huber, George P. "Organizational Information Systems: Determinants of Their Performance and Behavior." *Management Science* 28, no. 2 (1984).

Ives, Blake, and Gerald P. Learmonth. "The Information System as a Competitive Weapon." *Communications of the ACM* (December 1984).

Ives, Blake, and Michael R. Vitale. "After the Sale: Leveraging Maintenance with Information Technology." *MIS Quarterly* (March 1986).

Johnston, H. Russell, and Shelley R. Carrico. "Developing Capabilities to Use Information Strategically." *MIS Quarterly* 12, no. 1 (March 1988).

Johnston, Russell, and Michael R. Vitale. "Creating Competitive Advantage with Interorganizational Information Systems." *MIS Quarterly* 12, no. 2 (June 1988).

Johnston, Russell, and Paul R. Lawrence. "Beyond Vertical Integration—The Rise of the Value-Adding Partnership." *Harvard Business Review* (July–August 1988).

Kambil, Ajit, and James E. Short. "Electronic Integration and Business Network Redesign: A Roles-Linkage Perspective." *Journal of Management Information Systems* 10, no. 4 (Spring 1994).

Keen, Peter G. W. *Competing in Time: Using Telecommunications for Competitive Advantage.* Cambridge, MA: Ballinger Publishing Company (1986).

———. *Shaping the Future: Business Design Through Information Technology.* Cambridge, MA: Harvard Business School Press (1991).

Keen, Peter G. W., and M. S. Morton. *Decision Support Systems: An Organizational Perspective.* Reading, MA: Addison-Wesley (1978).

Kettinger, William J., Varun Grover, Subashish Guhan, and Albert H. Segors. "Strategic Information Systems Revisited: A Study in Sustainability and Performance." *MIS Quarterly* 18, no. 1 (March 1994).

King, John. "Centralized vs. Decentralized Computing: Organizational Considerations and Management Options." *Computing Surveys* (October 1984).

"Komag Chooses MES for Production Control." *Datamation* (September 15, 1994).

Konsynski, Benn R., and F. Warren McFarlan. "Information Partnerships—Shared Data, Shared Scale." *Harvard Business Review* (September–October 1990).

Korzeniowski, Paul. "Boosting Bandwidth." *Beyond Computing* (September 1997).

Lasher, Donald R., Blake Ives, and Sirkka L. Jarvenpaa. "USAA-IBM Partnerships in Information Technology: Managing the Image Project." *MIS Quarterly* 15, no. 4 (December 1991).

Lederer, Albert L., Dinesh A. Mirchandani, and Kenneth Sims. "The Link Between Information Strategy and Electronic Commerce." *Journal of Organizational Computing and Electronic Commerce* 7, no. 1 (1997).

Lee, Hau, L., V. Padmanabhan, and Seugin Whang. "The Bullwhip Effect in Supply Chains." *Sloan Management Review* (Spring 1997).

Levy, David. "Lean Production in an International Supply Chain." *Sloan Management Review* (Winter 1997).

McFarlan, F. Warren. "Information Technology Changes the Way You Compete." *Harvard Business Review* (May–June 1984).

Main, Thomas J., and James E. Short. "Managing the Merger: Building Partnership Through IT Planning at the New Baxter." *MIS Quarterly* 13, no. 4 (December 1989).

Mata, Franciso J., William L. Fuerst, and Jay B. Barney. "Information Technology and Sustained Competitive Advantage: A Resource-Based Analysis." *MIS Quarterly* 19, no. 4 (December 1995).

Porter, Michael. *Competitive Strategy.* New York: Free Press (1980).

———. *Competitive Advantage.* New York: Free Press (1985).

———. "How Information Can Help You Compete." *Harvard Business Review* (August–September 1985a).

Rackoff, Nick, Charles Wiseman, and Walter A. Ullrich. "Information Systems for Competitive Advantage: Implementation of a Planning Process." *MIS Quarterly* (December 1985).

Rangan, V. Kasturi, and Marie Bell. "Dell Online." Harvard Business School Case 9-598-116 (1998).

Rebello, Joseph. "State Street Boston's Allure for Investors Starts to Fade" *The Wall Street Journal* (January 4, 1995).

Rockart, John F., and Michael E. Treacy. "The CEO Goes On-line." *Harvard Business Review* (January–February 1982).

Shapiro, Carl, and Hal R. Varian. *Information Rules.* Boston, MA: Harvard Business School Press (1999).

Short, James E., and N. Venkatraman. "Beyond Business Process Redesign: Redefining Baxter's Business Network." *Sloan Management Review* (Fall 1992).

Sprague, Ralph H., Jr., and Eric D. Carlson. *Building Effective Decision Support Systems.* Englewood Cliffs, NJ: Prentice Hall (1982).

"USAA Insuring Progress." *Information Week* (May 25, 1992).

Vitale, Michael R. "The Growing Risks of Information System Success." *MIS Quarterly* (December 1986).

Wiseman, Charles. *Strategic Information Systems.* Homewood, IL: Richard D. Irwin (1988).

CHAPTER 3

Alter, Steven, and Michael Ginzberg. "Managing Uncertainty in MIS Implementation." *Sloan Management Review* 20, no. 1 (Fall 1978).

Jessup, Leonard M., Terry Connolly, and Jolene Galegher. "The Effects of Anonymity on GDSS Group Process with an Idea-Generating Task." *MIS Quarterly* 14, no. 3 (September 1990).

Kanter, Rosabeth Moss. "The New Managerial Work." *Harvard Business Review* (November–December 1989).

Kotter, John T. "What Effective General Managers Really Do." *Harvard Business Review* (November–December 1982).

Laudon, Kenneth C. *Computers and Bureaucratic Reform.* New York: Wiley (1974).

———. *Dossier Society: Value Choices in the Design of National Information Systems.* New York: Columbia University Press (1986).

Leonard-Barton, Dorothy. *Wellsprings of Knowledge: Building and Sustaining the Sources of Innovation.* Boston: Harvard Business School Press (1995).

Lindblom, C. E. "The Science of Muddling Through." *Public Administration Review* 19 (1959).

Machlup, Fritz. *The Production and Distribution of Knowledge in the United States.* Princeton, NJ: Princeton University Press (1962).

McKenney, James L., and Peter G. W. Keen. "How Managers' Minds Work." *Harvard Business Review* (May–June 1974).

Malcolm, Andrew H. "How the Oil Spilled and Spread: Delay and Confusion Off Alaska." *The New York Times* (April 16, 1989).

March, James G., and G. Sevon. "Gossip, Information, and Decision Making." In *Advances in Information Processing in Organizations,* edited by Lee S. Sproull and J. P. Crecine. vol. 1. Hillsdale, NJ: Erlbaum (1984).

March, James G., and Herbert A. Simon. *Organizations.* New York: Wiley (1958).

Markus, M. L. "Power, Politics, and MIS Implementation." *Communications of the ACM* 26, no. 6 (June 1983).

Mintzberg, Henry. "Managerial Work: Analysis from Observation." *Management Science* 18 (October 1971).

———. *The Nature of Managerial Work.* New York: Harper & Row (1973).

Orlikowski, Wanda J. "The Duality of Technology: Rethinking the Concept of Technology in Organizations." *Organization Science* 3, no. 3 (August 1992).

Orlikowski, Wanda J., and Daniel Robey. "Information Technology and the Structuring of Organizations." *Information Systems Research* 2, no. 2 (June 1991).

Prahalad, C. K., and Gary Hamel. "The Core Competence of the Corporation," *Harvard Business Review* (May–June 1990).

Quinn, James B. *Intelligent Enterprise: A Knowledge and Service Based Paradigm for Industry.* New York: Free Press (1992).

Schwenk, C. R. "Cognitive Simplification Processes in Strategic Decision Making." *Strategic Management Journal,* 5 (1984).

Simon, H. A. *The New Science of Management Decision.* New York: Harper & Row (1960).

Starbuck, William H. "Organizations as Action Generators." *American Sociological Review* 48 (1983).

Starbuck, William H., and Frances J. Milliken. "Executives' Perceptual Filters: What They Notice and How They Make Sense." In *The Executive Effect: Concepts and Methods for Studying Top Managers,* edited by D. C. Hambrick. Greenwich, CT: JAI Press (1988).

Tversky, A., and D. Kahneman. "The Framing of Decisions and the Psychology of Choice." *Science* 211 (January 1981).

Wrapp, H. Edward. "Good Managers Don't Make Policy Decisions." *Harvard Business Review* (July–August 1984).

CHAPTER 5

Anderson, Ronald E., Deborah G. Johnson, Donald Gotterbarn, and Judith Perrolle. "Using the New ACM Code of Ethics in Decision Making." *Communications of the ACM* 36, no. 2 (February 1993).

Andrews, Edmund L. "AT&T Will Cut 15,000 Jobs to Reduce Costs." *The New York Times* (February 11, 1994).

Association of Computing Machinery. "ACM's Code of Ethics and Professional Conduct." *Communications of the ACM* 36, no. 12 (December 1993).

Baig, Edward C., Marcia Stepanek, and Neill Gross. "Privacy." *Business Week* (April 5, 1999).

Barlow, John Perry. "Electronic Frontier: Private Life in Cyberspace." *Communications of the ACM* 34, no. 8 (August 1991).

Bjerklie, David. "Does E-Mail Mean Everyone's Mail?" *Information Week* (January 3, 1994).

Brod, Craig. *Techno Stress—The Human Cost of the Computer Revolution.* Reading MA: Addison-Wesley (1982).

Brown Bag Software vs. Symantec Corp. 960 F2D 1465 (Ninth Circuit, 1992).

Carvajal, Dorren. "Book Publishers Worry about Threat of Internet." *The New York Times* (March 18, 1996).

Cavazos, Edward A. "The Legal Risks of Setting up Shop in Cyberspace." *Journal of Organizational Computing* 6, no. 1 (1996).

Chabrow, Eric R. "The Internet: Copyrights." *Information Week* (March 25, 1996).

Chen, David W. "Man Charged with Sabotage of Computers." *The New York Times* (February 18, 1998).

Cheng, Hsing K., Ronald R. Sims, and Hildy Teegen. "To Purchase or to Pirate Software: An Empirical Study." *Journal of Management Information Systems* 13, no. 4 (Spring 1997).

Clarke, Roger. "Internet Privacy Concerns Confirm the Case for Intervention." *Communications of the ACM* 42, no. 2 (February 1999).

Collins, W. Robert, Keith W. Miller, Bethany J. Spielman, and Phillip Wherry. "How Good Is Good Enough? An Ethical Analysis of Software Construction and Use." *Communications of the ACM* 37, no. 1 (January 1994).

Computer Systems Policy Project. "Perspectives on the National Information Infrastructure." (January 12, 1993).

Couger, J. Daniel. "Preparing IS Students to Deal with Ethical Issues." *MIS Quarterly* 13, no. 2 (June 1989).

Cranor, Lorrie Faith, and Brian A. LaMacchia. "Spam!" *Communications of the ACM* 41, no. 8 (August 1998).

Dejoie, Roy, George Fowler, and David Paradice, eds. *Ethical Issues in Information Systems.* Boston: Boyd & Fraser (1991).

Denning, Dorothy E., et al., "To Tap or Not to Tap." *Communications of the ACM* 36, no. 3 (March 1993).

Diamond, Edwin, and Stephen Bates. "Law and Order Comes to Cyberspace." *Technology Review* (October 1995).

Furger, Roberta. "In Search of Relief for Tired, Aching Eyes." *PC World* (February 1993).

Gabriel, Trip. "Reprogramming a Convicted Hacker." *The New York Times* (January 14, 1995).

Gopal, Ram D., and G. Lawrence Sanders. "Preventive and Deterrent Controls for Software Piracy." *Journal of Management Information Systems* 13, no. 4 (Spring 1997).

Graham, Robert L. "The Legal Protection of Computer Software." *Communications of the ACM* (May 1984).

Leavitt, Harold J., and **Thomas L. Whisler.** "Management in the 1980s." *Harvard Business Review* (November–December 1958).

Lee, Ho-Geun. "Do Electronic Marketplaces Lower the Price of Goods?" *Communications of the ACM* 41, no. 1 (January 1998).

Leifer, Richard. "Matching Computer-Based Information Systems with Organizational Structures." *MIS Quarterly* 12, no. 1 (March 1988).

Maier, Jerry L., R. Kelly Rainer, Jr., and **Charles A. Snyder.** "Environmental Scanning for Information Technology: An Empirical Investigation." *Journal of Management Information Systems* 14, no. 2 (Fall 1997).

Malone, Thomas W. "Is Empowerment Just a Fad? Control, Decision-Making, and IT." *Sloan Management Review* (Winter 1997).

March, James G., and **Herbert A. Simon.** *Organizations.* New York: Wiley (1958).

Markus, M. L. "Power, Politics, and MIS Implementation." *Communications of the ACM* 26, no. 6 (June 1983).

Mendelson, Haim, and **Ravindra R. Pillai.** "Clock Speed and Informational Response: Evidence from the Information Technology Industry." *Information Systems Research* 9, no. 4 (December 1998).

Michels, Robert. *Political Parties.* New York: Free Press (1962; original publication, 1915).

Millman, Zeeva, and **Jon Hartwick.** "The Impact of Automated Office Systems on Middle Managers and Their Work." *MIS Quarterly* 11, no. 4 (December 1987).

Mintzberg, Henry. *The Structuring of Organizations.* Englewood Cliffs, NJ: Prentice Hall (1979).

Parsons, Talcott. *Structure and Process in Modern Societies.* New York: Free Press (1960).

Pindyck, Robert S., and **Daniel L. Rubinfield.** *Microeconomics.* Upper Saddle River, NJ: Prentice Hall (1997).

Porat, Marc. *The Information Economy: Definition and Measurement.* Washington, DC: U.S. Department of Commerce, Office of Telecommunications (May 1977).

Robey, Daniel, and **Sundeep Sahay.** "Transforming Work through Information Technology: A Comparative Case Study of Geographic Information Systems in County Government." *Information Systems Research* 7, no. 1 (March 1996).

Schein, Edgar H. *Organizational Culture and Leadership.* San Francisco: Jossey-Bass (1985).

Scott Morton, Michael S., ed. *The Corporation of the 1990s.* New York: Oxford University Press (1991).

Shore, Edwin B. "Reshaping the IS Organization." *MIS Quarterly* (December 1983).

Simon, H. A. *The New Science of Management Decision.* New York: Harper & Row (1960).

Simon, Herbert A. "Applying Information Technology to Organization Design." *Public Administration Review* (May–June 1973).

Starbuck, William H. "Organizations as Action Generators." *American Sociological Review* 48 (1983).

Straub, Detmar, and **James C. Wetherbe.** "Information Technologies for the 1990s: An Organizational Impact Perspective." *Communications of the ACM* 32, no. 11 (November 1989).

Turner, Jon A. "Computer Mediated Work: The Interplay Between Technology and Structured Jobs." *Communications of the ACM* 27, no. 12 (December 1984).

Turner, Jon A., and **Robert A. Karasek, Jr.** "Software Ergonomics: Effects of Computer Application Design Parameters on Operator Task Performance and Health." *Ergonomics* 27, no. 6 (1984).

Tushman, Michael L., and **Philip Anderson.** "Technological Discontinuities and Organizational Environments." *Administrative Science Quarterly* 31 (September 1986).

Tushman, Michael L., William H. Newman, and **Elaine Romanelli.** "Convergence and Upheaval: Managing the Unsteady Pace of Organizational Evolution." *California Management Review* 29, no. 1 (1986).

Weber, Max. *The Theory of Social and Economic Organization.* Translated by Talcott Parsons. New York: Free Press (1947).

Williamson, Oliver E. *The Economic Institutions of Capitalism.* New York: Free Press, (1985).

CHAPTER 4

Adams, Carl. R., and **Jae Hyon Song.** "Integrating Decision Technologies: Implications for Management Curriculum." *MIS Quarterly* 13, no. 2 (June 1989).

Allison, Graham T. *Essence of Decision—Explaining the Cuban Missile Crisis.* Boston: Little, Brown (1971).

Anthony, R. N. "Planning and Control Systems: A Framework for Analysis." Harvard University Graduate School of Business Administration (1965).

Arrow, Kenneth J. *Information and Economic Behavior.* Stockholm: Federation of Swedish Industries (1972).

Badaracco, Joseph. *The Knowledge Link: How Firms Compete Through Strategic Alliances.* Boston: Harvard Business School Press (1991).

Boulding, Kenneth. "The Economics of Knowledge and the Knowledge of Economics." *American Economic Review* (May 1966).

Cohen, Michael, James March, and **Johan Olsen.** "A Garbage Can Model of Organizational Choice." *Administrative Science Quarterly* 17 (1972).

George, Joey. "Organizational Decision Support Systems." *Journal of Management Information Systems* 8, no. 3 (Winter 1991–1992).

Gorry, G. Anthony, and **Michael S. Scott-Morton.** "A Framework for Management Information Systems." *Sloan Management Review* 13, no. 1 (Fall 1971).

Grobowski, Ron, Chris McGoff, Doug Vogel, Ben Martz, and **Jay Nunamaker.** "Implementing Electronic Meeting Systems at IBM: Lessons Learned and Success Factors." *MIS Quarterly* 14, no. 4 (December 1990).

Huber, George. "Organizational Learning: The Contributing Processes and Literature." *Organization Science,* 2 (1991), pp. 88–115.

Huber, George P. "Cognitive Style as a Basis for MIS and DSS Designs: Much Ado About Nothing?" *Management Science* 29 (May 1983).

Isenberg, Daniel J. "How Senior Managers Think." *Harvard Business Review* (November–December 1984).

Ives, Blake, and **Margrethe H. Olson.** "Manager or Technician? The Nature of the Information Systems Manager's Job." *MIS Quarterly* (December 1981).

Jensen, M. C., and **W. H. Meckling.** "Specific and General Knowledge and Organizational Science." In *Contract Economics,* edited by L. Wetin and J. Wijkander. Oxford: Basil Blackwell (1992).

Jessup, Leonard M., Terry Connolly, and Jolene Galegher. "The Effects of Anonymity on GDSS Group Process with an Idea-Generating Task." *MIS Quarterly* 14, no. 3 (September 1990).

Kanter, Rosabeth Moss. "The New Managerial Work." *Harvard Business Review* (November–December 1989).

Kotter, John T. "What Effective General Managers Really Do." *Harvard Business Review* (November–December 1982).

Laudon, Kenneth C. *Computers and Bureaucratic Reform.* New York: Wiley (1974).

———. *Dossier Society: Value Choices in the Design of National Information Systems.* New York: Columbia University Press (1986).

Leonard-Barton, Dorothy. *Wellsprings of Knowledge: Building and Sustaining the Sources of Innovation.* Boston: Harvard Business School Press (1995).

Lindblom, C. E. "The Science of Muddling Through." *Public Administration Review* 19 (1959).

Machlup, Fritz. *The Production and Distribution of Knowledge in the United States.* Princeton, NJ: Princeton University Press (1962).

McKenney, James L., and Peter G. W. Keen. "How Managers' Minds Work." *Harvard Business Review* (May–June 1974).

Malcolm, Andrew H. "How the Oil Spilled and Spread: Delay and Confusion Off Alaska." *The New York Times* (April 16, 1989).

March, James G., and G. Sevon. "Gossip, Information, and Decision Making." In *Advances in Information Processing in Organizations,* edited by Lee S. Sproull and J. P. Crecine. vol. 1. Hillsdale, NJ: Erlbaum (1984).

March, James G., and Herbert A. Simon. *Organizations.* New York: Wiley (1958).

Markus, M. L. "Power, Politics, and MIS Implementation." *Communications of the ACM* 26, no. 6 (June 1983).

Mintzberg, Henry. "Managerial Work: Analysis from Observation." *Management Science* 18 (October 1971).

———. *The Nature of Managerial Work.* New York: Harper & Row (1973).

Orlikowski, Wanda J. "The Duality of Technology: Rethinking the Concept of Technology in Organizations." *Organization Science* 3, no. 3 (August 1992).

Orlikowski, Wanda J., and Daniel Robey. "Information Technology and the Structuring of Organizations." *Information Systems Research* 2, no. 2 (June 1991).

Prahalad, C. K., and Gary Hamel. "The Core Competence of the Corporation," *Harvard Business Review* (May–June 1990).

Quinn, James B. *Intelligent Enterprise: A Knowledge and Service Based Paradigm for Industry.* New York: Free Press (1992).

Schwenk, C. R. "Cognitive Simplification Processes in Strategic Decision Making." *Strategic Management Journal,* 5 (1984).

Simon, H. A. *The New Science of Management Decision.* New York: Harper & Row (1960).

Starbuck, William H. "Organizations as Action Generators." *American Sociological Review* 48 (1983).

Starbuck, William H., and Frances J. Milliken. "Executives' Perceptual Filters: What They Notice and How They Make Sense." In *The Executive Effect: Concepts and Methods for Studying Top Managers,* edited by D. C. Hambrick. Greenwich, CT: JAI Press (1988).

Tversky, A., and D. Kahneman. "The Framing of Decisions and the Psychology of Choice." *Science* 211 (January 1981).

Wrapp, H. Edward. "Good Managers Don't Make Policy Decisions." *Harvard Business Review* (July–August 1984).

CHAPTER 5

Anderson, Ronald E., Deborah G. Johnson, Donald Gotterbarn, and Judith Perrolle. "Using the New ACM Code of Ethics in Decision Making." *Communications of the ACM* 36, no. 2 (February 1993).

Andrews, Edmund L. "AT&T Will Cut 15,000 Jobs to Reduce Costs." *The New York Times* (February 11, 1994).

Association of Computing Machinery. "ACM's Code of Ethics and Professional Conduct." *Communications of the ACM* 36, no. 12 (December 1993).

Baig, Edward C., Marcia Stepanek, and Neill Gross. "Privacy." *Business Week* (April 5, 1999).

Barlow, John Perry. "Electronic Frontier: Private Life in Cyberspace." *Communications of the ACM* 34, no. 8 (August 1991).

Bjerklie, David. "Does E-Mail Mean Everyone's Mail?" *Information Week* (January 3, 1994).

Brod, Craig. *Techno Stress—The Human Cost of the Computer Revolution.* Reading MA: Addison-Wesley (1982).

Brown Bag Software vs. Symantec Corp. 960 F2D 1465 (Ninth Circuit, 1992).

Carvajal, Dorren. "Book Publishers Worry about Threat of Internet." *The New York Times* (March 18, 1996).

Cavazos, Edward A. "The Legal Risks of Setting up Shop in Cyberspace." *Journal of Organizational Computing* 6, no. 1 (1996).

Chabrow, Eric R. "The Internet: Copyrights." *Information Week* (March 25, 1996).

Chen, David W. "Man Charged with Sabotage of Computers." *The New York Times* (February 18, 1998).

Cheng, Hsing K., Ronald R. Sims, and Hildy Teegen. "To Purchase or to Pirate Software: An Empirical Study." *Journal of Management Information Systems* 13, no. 4 (Spring 1997).

Clarke, Roger. "Internet Privacy Concerns Confirm the Case for Intervention." *Communications of the ACM* 42, no. 2 (February 1999).

Collins, W. Robert, Keith W. Miller, Bethany J. Spielman, and Phillip Wherry. "How Good Is Good Enough? An Ethical Analysis of Software Construction and Use." *Communications of the ACM* 37, no. 1 (January 1994).

Computer Systems Policy Project. "Perspectives on the National Information Infrastructure." (January 12, 1993).

Couger, J. Daniel. "Preparing IS Students to Deal with Ethical Issues." *MIS Quarterly* 13, no. 2 (June 1989).

Cranor, Lorrie Faith, and Brian A. LaMacchia. "Spam!" *Communications of the ACM* 41, no. 8 (August 1998).

Dejoie, Roy, George Fowler, and David Paradice, eds. *Ethical Issues in Information Systems.* Boston: Boyd & Fraser (1991).

Denning, Dorothy E., et al., "To Tap or Not to Tap." *Communications of the ACM* 36, no. 3 (March 1993).

Diamond, Edwin, and Stephen Bates. "Law and Order Comes to Cyberspace." *Technology Review* (October 1995).

Furger, Roberta. "In Search of Relief for Tired, Aching Eyes." *PC World* (February 1993).

Gabriel, Trip. "Reprogramming a Convicted Hacker." *The New York Times* (January 14, 1995).

Gopal, Ram D., and G. Lawrence Sanders. "Preventive and Deterrent Controls for Software Piracy." *Journal of Management Information Systems* 13, no. 4 (Spring 1997).

Graham, Robert L. "The Legal Protection of Computer Software." *Communications of the ACM* (May 1984).

Green, R. H. *The Ethical Manager.* New York: Macmillan (1994).

Harrington, Susan J. "The Effect of Codes of Ethics and Personal Denial of Responsibility on Computer Abuse Judgments and Intentions." *MIS Quarterly* 20, no. 2 (September 1996).

Huff, Chuck, and C. Dianne Martin. "Computing Consequences: A Framework for Teaching Ethical Computing." *Communications of the ACM* 38, no. 12 (December 1995).

Joes, Kathryn. "EDS Set to Restore Cash-Machine Network." *The New York Times* (March 26, 1993).

Johnson, Deborah G. "Ethics Online." *Communications of the ACM* 40, no. 1 (January 1997).

Johnson, Deborah G., and John M. Mulvey. "Accountability and Computer Decision Systems." *Communications of the ACM* 38, no. 12 (December 1995).

King, Julia. "It's CYA Time." *Computerworld* (March 30, 1992).

Kling, Rob. "When Organizations Are Perpetrators: The Conditions of Computer Abuse and Computer Crime." In *Computerization & Controversy: Value Conflicts & Social Choices,* edited by Charles Dunlop and Rob Kling. New York: Academic Press (1991).

Laudon, Kenneth C. "Ethical Concepts and Information Technology." *Communications of the ACM* 38, no. 12 (December 1995).

Levinson, Marc. "Thanks. You're Fired." *Newsweek* (May 23, 1994).

Lohr, Steve. "A Nation Ponders Its Growing Digital Divide." *The New York Times* (October 21, 1996).

McPartlin, John P. "A Question of Complicity." *Information Week* (June 22, 1992).

———. "The Terrors of Technostress." *Information Week* (July 30, 1990).

Markoff, John. "Growing Compatibility Issue: Computers and User Privacy." *The New York Times* (March 3, 1999).

———. "In the Data Storage Race, Disks Are Outpacing Chips." *The New York Times* (February 23, 1998).

Mason, Richard O. "Applying Ethics to Information Technology Issues." *Communications of the ACM* 38, no. 12 (December 1995).

Mason, Richard O. "Four Ethical Issues in the Information Age." *MIS Quarterly* 10, no. 1 (March 1986).

Memon, Nasir, and Ping Wah Wong. "Protecting Digital Media Content." *Communications of the ACM* 41, no. 7 (July 1998).

Milberg, Sandra J., Sandra J. Burke, H. Jeff Smith, and Ernest A. Kallman. "Values, Personal Information Privacy, and Regulatory Approaches." *Communications of the ACM* 38, no. 12 (December 1995).

Mykytyn, Kathleen, Peter P. Mykytyn, Jr., and Craig W. Slinkman. "Expert Systems: A Question of Liability." *MIS Quarterly* 14, no. 1 (March 1990).

Neumann, Peter G. "Inside RISKS: Computers, Ethics and Values." *Communications of the ACM* 34, no. 7 (July 1991).

———. "Inside RISKS: Fraud by Computer." *Communications of the ACM* 35, no. 8 (August 1992).

Nissenbaum, Helen. "Computing and Accountability." *Communications of the ACM* 37, no. 1 (January 1994).

Okerson, Ann. "Who Owns Digital Works?" *Scientific American* (July 1996).

Oz, Effy. "Ethical Standards for Information Systems Professionals," *MIS Quarterly* 16, no. 4 (December 1992).

———. *Ethics for the Information Age.* Dubuque, Iowa: W. C. Brown (1994).

Pollack, Andrew. "San Francisco Law on VDTs Is Struck Down." *The New York Times* (February 14, 1992).

Ramirez, Anthony. "AT&T to Eliminate Many Operator Jobs." *The New York Times* (March 4, 1992).

Reagle, Joseph, and Lorrie Faith Cranor. "The Platform for Privacy Preferences." *Communications of the ACM* 42, no. 2 (February 1999).

Redman, Thomas C. "The Impact of Poor Data Quality on the Typical Enterprise." *Communications of the ACM* 41, no. 2 (February 1998).

Rifkin, Glenn. "The Ethics Gap." *Computerworld* (October 14, 1991).

Rifkin, Jeremy. "Watch Out for Trickle-Down Technology." *The New York Times* (March 16, 1993).

Rigdon, Joan E. "Frequent Glitches in New Software Bug Users." *The Wall Street Journal* (January 18, 1995).

Rotenberg, Marc. "Communications Privacy: Implications for Network Design." *Communications of the ACM* 36, no. 8 (August 1993).

———. "Inside RISKS: Protecting Privacy." *Communications of the ACM* 35, no. 4 (April 1992).

Samuelson, Pamela. "Computer Programs and Copyright's Fair Use Doctrine." *Communications of the ACM* 36, no. 9 (September 1993).

———. "Copyright's Fair Use Doctrine and Digital Data." *Communications of the ACM* 37, no. 1 (January 1994).

———. "Digital Media and the Law." *Communications of the ACM* 34, no. 10 (October 1991).

———. "First Amendment Rights for Information Providers?" *Communications of the ACM* 34, no. 6 (June 1991).

———. "Liability for Defective Electronic Information." *Communications of the ACM* 36, no. 1 (January 1993).

———. "Self Plagiarism or Fair Use?" *Communications of the ACM* 37, no. 8 (August 1994).

———. "The Ups and Downs of Look and Feel." *Communications of the ACM* 36, no. 4 (April 1993).

———. "Updating the Copyright Look and Feel Lawsuits." *Communications of the ACM* 35, no. 9 (September 1992).

Schnorr, Teresa M. "Miscarriage and VDT Exposure." *New England Journal of Medicine* (March 1991).

Sipior, Janice C., and Burke T. Ward. "The Ethical and Legal Quandary of E-mail Privacy." *Communications of the ACM* 38, no. 12 (December 1995).

Smith, H. Jeff. "Privacy Policies and Practices: Inside the Organizational Maze." *Communications of the ACM* 36, no. 12, (December 1993).

Smith, H. Jeff, and John Hasnas. "Ethics and Information Systems: The Corporate Domain." *MIS Quarterly* 23, no. 1 (March 1999).

Smith, H. Jeff, Sandra J. Milberg, and Sandra J. Burke. "Information Privacy: Measuring Individuals' Concerns about Organizational Practices." *MIS Quarterly* 20, no. 2 (June 1996).

Stevens, William K. "Major U.S. Study Finds No Miscarriage Risk from Video Terminals." *The New York Times* (March 14, 1991).

Straub, Detmar W., Jr., and Rosann Webb Collins. "Key Information Liability Issues Facing Managers: Software Piracy, Proprietary Databases, and Individual Rights to Privacy." *MIS Quarterly* 14, no. 2 (June 1990).

Straub, Detmar W., Jr., and William D. Nance. "Discovering and Disciplining Computer Abuse in Organizations: A Field Study." *MIS Quarterly* 14, no. 1 (March 1990).

Tabor, Mary W., with **Anthony Ramirez**. "Computer Savy, with an Attitude." *The New York Times* (July 23, 1992).

The Telecommunications Policy Roundtable. "Renewing the Commitment to a Public Interest Telecommunications Policy." *Communications of the ACM* 37, no. 1 (January 1994).

Thong, James Y. L., and **Chee-Sing Yap**. "Testing an Ethical Decision-Making Theory." *Journal of Management Information Systems* 15, no. 1 (Summer 1998).

Turner, Jon. "Will Telecommuting Ever Get Off the Ground?" *Stern Business* (Summer 1998).

Tuttle, Brad, **Adrian Harrell**, and **Paul Harrison**. "Moral Hazard, Ethical Considerations, and the Decision to Implement an Information System." *Journal of Management Information Systems* 13, no. 4 (Spring 1997).

United States Department of Health, Education, and Welfare. *Records, Computers, and the Rights of Citizens.* Cambridge: MIT Press (1973).

Wang, Huaiqing, Matthew K. O. Lee, and **Chen Wang.** "Consumer Privacy Concerns about Internet Marketing." *Communications of the ACM* 41, no. 3 (March 1998).

Weisband, Suzanne P., and **Bruce A. Reinig.** "Managing User Perceptions of E-mail Privacy." *Communications of the ACM* 38, no. 12 (December 1995).

Wilder, Clinton. "Feds Allege Internet Scam." *Information Week* (June 10, 1996).

Wilson, Linda. "Devil in Your Data." *Information Week* (August 31, 1992).

Wolinsky, Carol, and **James Sylvester.** "Privacy in the Telecommunications Age." *Communications of the ACM* 35, no. 2 (February 1992).

CHAPTER 6

Anthes, Gary. "The Long Arm of Moore's Law." *Computerworld* (October 5, 1998).

Bell, Gordon. "Ultracomputers: A Teraflop Before Its Time." *Communications of the ACM* 35, no. 8 (August 1992).

Bulkeley, William. "Peering Ahead, Thinking about Tomorrow." *The Wall Street Journal* (November 16, 1998).

Camp, W. J., S. J. Plimpton, B. A. Hendrickson, and **R. W. Leland.** "Massively Parallel Methods for Engineering and Science Problems." *Communications of the ACM* 37, no. 4 (April 1994).

Feder, Barnaby J. "For Amber Waves of Data." *The New York Times* (May 4, 1998).

Fitzmaurice, George W. "Situated Information Spaces and Spatially Aware Palmtop Computers." *Communications of the ACM* 36, no. 7 (July 1993).

Freeman, Eva. "No More Gold-Plated MIPS: Mainframes and Distributed Systems Converge." *Datamation* (March 1998).

Halfhill, Tom R. "Cheaper Computing." *Byte* (April 1997).

Hardaway, Don, and **Richard P. Will.** "Digital Multimedia Offers Key to Educational Reform." *Communications of the ACM* 40, no. 4 (April 1997).

Jacobs, April. "The Network Computer: Where It's Going." *Computerworld* (December 23, 1997/January 2, 1998).

Kay, Emily. "Hello Mr. Chips! Multimedia in the Classroom." *Technology Training* (June 1997).

Lambert, Craig. "The Electronic Tutor." *Harvard Magazine* (November–December 1990).

Lieberman, Henry. "Intelligent Graphics." *Communications of the ACM* 39, no. 8 (August 1996).

Lohr, Steve. "The Network Computer as the PC's Evil Twin," *The New York Times* (November 4, 1996).

Markoff, John. "Inside Intel, the Future Is Riding on a New Chip." *The New York Times* (April 5, 1998).

Messina, Paul, David Culler, Wayne Pfeiffer, William Martin, **J. Tinsley Oden,** and **Gary Smith.** "Architecture." *Communications of the ACM* 41, no. 11 (November 1998).

Peleg, Alex, Sam Wilkie, and **Uri Weiser.** "Intel MMX for Multimedia PCs." *Communications of the ACM* 40, no. 1 (January 1997).

Press, Larry. "Compuvision or Teleputer?" *Communications of the ACM* 33, no. 3 (September 1990).

———. "Personal Computing: Dynabook Revisited—Portable Computers Past, Present, and Future." *Communications of the ACM* 35 no. 3 (March 1992).

Selker, Ted. "New Paradigms for Using Computers." *Communications of the ACM* 39, no. 8 (August 1996).

Smarr, Larry, and **Charles E. Catlett,** "Metacomputing." *Communications of the ACM* 35, no. 6 (June 1992).

Strassman, Paul. "40 Years of IT History." *Datamation* (October 1997).

Thomborson, Clark D. "Does Your Workstation Computation Belong to a Vector Supercomputer?" *Communications of the ACM* 36, no. 11 (November 1993).

Vaughan-Nichols, Steven J. "To NC or Not to NC?" *NetWorker* 1, no. 1 (March/April 1997).

Weiser, Mark. "Some Computer Science Issues in Ubiquitous Computing." *Communications of the ACM* 36, no. 7 (July 1993).

CHAPTER 7

Barrett, Jim, Kevin Knight, Inderject Man, and **Elaine Rich.** "Knowledge and Natural Language Processing." *Communications of the ACM* 33, no. 8 (August 1990).

Bochenski, Barbara. "GUI Builders Pay Price for User Productivity." *Software Magazine* (April 1992).

Clark, Don. "Sun Microsystems Still Has a Legion of Believers." *The Wall Street Journal* (March 23, 1998).

Fayad, Mohamed, and **Marshall P. Cline.** "Aspects of Software Adaptability." *Communications of the ACM* 39, no. 10 (October 1996).

Flynn, Jim, and **Bill Clarke.** "How Java Makes Network-Centric Computing Real." *Datamation* (March 1, 1996).

Gowan, J. Arthur, Chris Jesse, and **Richard G. Mathieu.** "Y2K Compliance and the Distributed Enterprise." *Communications of the ACM* 42, no. 2 (February 1999).

Greenbaum, Joshua. "The Evolution Revolution." *Information Week* (March 14, 1994).

Haavind, Robert. "Software's New Object Lesson," *Technology Review* (February–March 1992).

Jalics, Paul J. "Cobol on a PC: A New Perspective on a Language and Its Performance." *Communications of the ACM* 30, no. 2 (February 1987).

Johnson, Ralph E. "Frameworks = (Components + Patterns)." *Communications of the ACM* 40, no. 10 (October 1997).

Kappelman, Leon A., Darla Fent, Kellie B. Keeling, and **Victor Prybutok.** "Calculating the Cost of Year 2000 Compliance." *Communications of the ACM* 41, no. 2 (February 1998).

Kim, Yongbeom, and **Edward A. Stohr.** "Software Reuse." *Journal of Management Information Systems* 14, no. 4 (Spring 1998).

Korson, Tim, and John D. McGregor. "Understanding Object-Oriented: A Unifying Paradigm." *Communications of the ACM* 33, no. 9 (September 1990).

Korson, Timothy D., and Vijay K. Vaishnavi. "Managing Emerging Software Technologies: A Technology Transfer Framework." *Communications of the ACM* 35, no. 9 (September 1992).

Layer, D. Kevin, and Chris Richardson. "LISP Systems in the 1990s." *Communications of the ACM* 34, no. 9 (September 1991).

Littlewood, Bev, and Lorenzo Strigini. "The Risks of Software." *Scientific American* 267, no. 5 (November 1992).

Mandelkern, David. "Graphical User Interfaces: The Next Generation." *Communications of the ACM* 36, no. 4 (April 1993).

Meyer, Marc H., and Robert Seliger, "Product Platforms in Software Development." *Sloan Management Review* 40, no. 1 (Fall 1998).

Monarchi, David E., and Gretchen I. Puhr. "A Research Typology for Object-Oriented Analysis and Design." *Communications of the ACM* 35, no. 9 (September 1992).

Morse, Alan, and George Reynolds. "Overcoming Current Growth Limits in UI Development." *Communications of the ACM* 36, no. 4 (April 1993).

Mukhopadhyay, Tridas, Stephen S. Vicinanza, and Michael J. Prietula. "Examining the Feasibility of a Case-Based Reasoning Model for Software Effort Estimation." *MIS Quarterly* 16, no. 2 (June 1992).

Nielsen, Jakob. "Noncommand User Interfaces." *Communications of the ACM* 36, no. 4 (April 1993).

Nilsen, Kelvin. "Adding Real-Time Capabilities to Java." *Communications of the ACM* 41, no. 6 (June 1998).

Noffsinger, W. B., Robert Niedbalski, Michael Blanks, and Niall Emmart. "Legacy Object Modeling Speeds Software Integration." *Communications of the ACM* 41, no. 12 (December 1998).

Purao, Sandeep, Hemant Jain, and Derek Nazareth. "Effective Distribution of Object-Oriented Applications." *Communications of the ACM* 41, no. 8 (August 1998).

Satzinger, John W., and Lorne Olfman. "User Interface Consistency Across Applications." *Journal of Management Infomation Systems* 14, no. 4 (Spring 1998).

Schonberg, Edmond, Mark Gerhardt, and Charlene Hayden. "A Technical Tour of Ada,." *Communications of the ACM* 35, no. 11 (November 1992).

Semich, Bill, and David Fisco. "Java: Internet Toy or Enterprise Tool?" *Datamation* (March 1, 1996).

Sheetz, Steven D., Gretchen Irwin, David P. Tegarden, H. James Nelson, and David E. Monarchi. "Exploring the Difficulties of Learning Object-Oriented Techniques." *Journal of Management Information Systems* 14, no. 2 (Fall 1997).

Tyma, Paul. "Why Are We Using Java Again?" *Communications of the ACM* 41, no. 6 (June 1998).

Vassiliou, Yannis. "On the Interactive Use of Databases: Query Languages." *Journal of Management Information Systems* 1 (Winter 1984–1985).

White, George M. "Natural Language Understanding and Speech." *Communications of the ACM* 33, no. 8 (August 1990).

Wiederhold, Gio, Peter Wegner, and Stefano Ceri. "Toward Megaprogramming." *Communications of the ACM* 35, no. 11 (November 1992).

Wilkes, Maurice V. "The Long-Term Future of Operating Systems." *Communications of the ACM* 35, no. 11 (November 1992).

CHAPTER 8

Belkin, Nicholas J., and W. Bruce Croft. "Information Filtering and Information Retrieval: Two Sides of the Same Coin?" *Communications of the ACM* 35, no. 12 (November 1992).

Butterworth, Paul, Allen Otis, and Jacob Stein, "The GemStone Object Database Management System." *Communications of the ACM* 34, no. 10 (October 1991).

Carmel, Erran, William K. McHenry, and Yeshayahu Cohen. "Building Large, Dynamic Hypertexts: How Do We Link Intelligently?" *Journal of Management Information Systems* 6, no. 2 (Fall 1989).

Chang, Shih-Fu, John R. Amith, Mandis Beigi, and Ana Benitez. "Visual Information Retrieval from Large Distributed On-line Repositories." *Communications of the ACM* 40, no. 12 (December 1997).

Clifford, James, Albert Croker, and Alex Tuzhilin. "On Data Representation and Use in a Temporal Relational DBMS." *Information Systems Research* 7, no. 3 (September 1996).

Date, C. J. *An Introduction to Database Systems,* 6th ed. Reading, MA: Addison-Wesley (1995).

Everest, G. C. *Database Management: Objectives, System Functions, and Administration.* New York: McGraw-Hill (1985).

Fiori, Rich. "The Information Warehouse." *Relational Database Journal* (January–February 1995).

Francett, Barbara. "Data Warehousing Is the Sum of Its Marts." *Software Magazine* (February 1997).

Gardner, Stephen R. "Building the Data Warehouse." *Communications of the ACM* 41, no. 9 (September 1998).

Garvey, Martin J. "A New Face on Legacy Data," *Information Week* (July 28, 1997).

Goldberg, Michael, and Jaikumar Vijayan. "Data 'Wearhouse' Gains." *Computerworld* (April 8, 1996).

Goldstein, R. C., and J. B. McCririck. "What Do Data Administrators Really Do?" *Datamation* 26 (August 1980).

Goodhue, Dale L., Judith A. Quillard, and John F. Rockart. "Managing the Data Resource: A Contingency Perspective." *MIS Quarterly* (September 1988).

Goodhue, Dale L., Laurie J. Kirsch, Judith A. Quillard, and Michael D. Wybo. "Strategic Data Planning: Lessons from the Field." *MIS Quarterly* 16, no. 1 (March 1992).

Goodhue, Dale L., Michael D. Wybo, and Laurie J. Kirsch. "The Impact of Data Integration on the Costs and Benefits of Information Systems." *MIS Quarterly* 16, no. 3 (September 1992).

Greengard, Samuel. "Assembling a Hybrid Data Warehouse." *Beyond Computing* (March 1999).

Grosky, William I. "Managing Multimedia Information in Database Systems." *Communications of the ACM* 40, no. 12 (December 1997).

Grover, Varun, and James Teng. "How Effective Is Data Resource Management?" *Journal of Information Systems Management* (Summer 1991).

Gupta, Amarnath, and Ranesh Jain. "Visual Information Retrieval." *Communications of the ACM* 40, no. 5 (May 1997).

Hoffman, Thomas. "Improved Analytics Drive Office Depot Sales." *Computerworld* (February 9, 1998).

Inman, W. H. "The Data Warehouse and Data Mining." *Communications of the ACM* 39, no. 11 (November 1996).

Kahn, Beverly K. "Some Realities of Data Administration." *Communications of the ACM* 26 (October 1983).

Kahn, Beverly, and Linda Garceau. "The Database Administration Function." *Journal of Management Information Systems* 1 (Spring 1985).

Kent, William. "A Simple Guide to Five Normal Forms in Relational Database Theory." *Communications of the ACM* 26, no. 2 (February 1983).

King, John L., and Kenneth Kraemer. "Information Resource Management Cannot Work." *Information and Management* (1988).

Kroenke, David. *Database Processing: Fundamentals, Design, and Implementation,* 6th ed. Upper Saddle River, NJ: Prentice Hall (1997).

Lange, Danny B. "An Object-Oriented Design Approach for Developing Hypermedia Information Systems." *Journal of Organizational Computing and Electronic Commerce* 6, no. 2 (1996).

Madnick, Stuart E., and Richard Y. Wang. "Evolution Towards Strategic Application of Databases through Composite Information Systems." *Journal of Management Information Systems* 5, no. 3 (Winter 1988–1989).

March, Salvatore T., and Young-Gul Kim. "Information Resource Management: A Metadata Perspective." *Journal of Management Information Systems* 5, no. 3 (Winter 1988–1989).

Qing, Li, and Frederic H. Lochovsky, "Advanced Database Support Facilities for CSCW Systems." *Journal of Organizational Computing and Electronic Commerce* 6, no. 2 (1996).

Ricciuti, Mike. "Winning the Competitive Game." *Datamation* (February 15, 1994).

Silberschatz, Avi, Michael Stonebraker, and Jeff Ullman, eds. "Database Systems: Achievements and Opportunities." *Communications of the ACM* 34, no. 10 (October 1991).

Smith, John B., and Stephen F. Weiss. "Hypertext." *Communications of the ACM* 31, no. 7 (July 1988).

Watson, Hugh J., and Barbara J. Haley. "Managerial Considerations." *Communications of the ACM* 41, no. 9 (September 1998).

Watterson, Karen. "When It Comes to Choosing a Database, the Object Is Value." *Datamation* (December–January 1998).

CHAPTER 9

Bikson, Tora K., Cathleen Stasz, and Donald A. Monkin. "Computer-Mediated Work: Individual and Organizational Impact on One Corporate Headquarters." Rand Corporation (1985).

Brandel, Mary. "Videoconferencing Slowly Goes Desktop." *Computerworld* (February 20, 1995).

Chatterjee, Samir. "Requirements for Success in Gigabit Networking." *Communications of the ACM* 40, no. 7 (July 1997).

Dertouzos, Michael. "Building the Information Marketplace." *Technology Review* (January 1991).

Donovan, John J. "Beyond Chief Information Officer to Network Manager." *Harvard Business Review* (September–October 1988).

Duchessi, Peter, and InduShobha Chengalur-Smith. "Client/Server Benefits, Problems, Best Practices." *Communications of the ACM* 41, no. 5 (May 1998).

Fisher, Sharon. "TCP/IP." *Computerworld* (October 7, 1991).

Gefen, David, and Detmar W. Straub. "Gender Differences in the Perception and Use of E-Mail: An Extension to the Technology Acceptance Model." *MIS Quarterly* 21, no. 4 (December 1997).

Gilder, George. "Into the Telecosm." *Harvard Business Review* (March–April 1991).

Grover, Varun, and Martin D. Goslar. "Initiation, Adoption, and Implementation of Telecommunications Technologies in U.S. Organizations." *Journal of Management Information Systems* 10, no. 1 (Summer 1993).

Hall, Wayne A., and Robert E. McCauley. "Planning and Managing a Corporate Network Utility." *MIS Quarterly* (December 1987).

Hammer, Michael, and Glenn Mangurian. "The Changing Value of Communications Technology." *Sloan Management Review* (Winter 1987).

Hansen, James V., and Ned C. Hill. "Control and Audit of Electronic Data Interchange." *MIS Quarterly* 13, no. 4 (December 1989).

Hart, Paul J., and Carol Stoak Saunders. "Emerging Electronic Partnerships: Antecedents and Dimensions of EDI Use from the Supplier's Perspective." *Journal of Management Information Systems* 14, no. 4 (Spring 1998).

Huff, Sid, Malcolm C. Munro, and Barbara H. Martin. "Growth Stages of End User Computing." *Communications of the ACM* (May 1988).

Imielinski, Tomasz, and B. R. Badrinath. "Mobile Wireless Computing: Challenges in Data Management." *Communications of the ACM* 37, no. 10 (October 1994).

Keen, Peter G. W. *Competing in Time.* Cambridge, MA: Ballinger Publishing Company (1986).

Keen, Peter G. W., and J. Michael Cummins. *Networks in Action: Business Choices and Telecommunications Decisions.* Belmont, CA: Wadsworth Publishing Company (1994).

Kim, B. G., and P. Wang. "ATM Network: Goals and Challenges." *Communications of the ACM* 38, no. 2 (February 1995).

Laudon, Kenneth C. "From PCs to Managerial Workstations." In Matthias Jarke, *Managers, Micros, and Mainframes.* New York: John Wiley (1986).

Lee, Sunro, and Richard P. Leifer. "A Framework for Linking the Structure of Information Systems with Organizational Requirements for Information Sharing." *Journal of Management Information Systems* 8, no. 4 (Spring 1992).

Massetti, Brenda, and Robert W. Zmud. "Measuring the Extent of EDI Usage in Complex Organizations. Strategies and Illustrative Examples." *MIS Quarterly* 20, no. 3 (September 1996).

Mueller, Milton. "Universal Service and the Telecommunications Act: Myth Made Law." *Communications of the ACM* 40, no. 3 (March 1997).

Nakamura, Kiyoh, Toshihiro Ide, and Yukio Kiyokane. "Roles of Multimedia Technology in Telework." *Journal of Organizational Computing and Electronic Commerce* 6, no. 4 (1996).

Ngwenyama, Ojelanki, and Allen S. Lee. "Communication Richness in Electronic Mail: Critical Social Theory and the Contextuality of Meaning." *MIS Quarterly* 21, no. 2 (June 1997).

"Plans and Policies for Client/Server Technology." *I/S Analyzer* 30, no. 4 (April 1992).

Premkumar, G., K. Ramamurthy, and Sree Nilakanta. "Implementation of Electronic Data Interchange: An Innovation Diffusion Perspective." *Journal of Management Information Systems* 11, no. 2 (Fall 1994).

Railing, Larry, and Tom Housel. "A Network Infrastructure to Contain Costs and Enable Fast Response." *MIS Quarterly* 14, no. 4 (December 1990).

Raymond, Louis, and Francois Bergeron. "EDI Success in Small- and Medium-sized Enterprises: A Field Study." *Journal of Organizational Computing and Electronic Commerce* 6, no. 2 (1996).

Richardson, Gary L., Brad M. Jackson, and Gary W. Dickson. "A Principles-Based Enterprise Architecture: Lessons from Texaco and Star Enterprise." *MIS Quarterly* 14, no. 4 (December 1990).

Roche, Edward M. *Telecommunications and Business Strategy.* Chicago: The Dryden Press (1991).

Sharda, Nalin. "Multimedia Networks: Fundamentals and Future Directions." *Communications of the Association for Information Systems* (February 1999).

Sinha, Alok. "Client-Server Computing." *Communications of the ACM* 35, no. 7 (July 1992).

Teo, Hock-Hai, Bernard C. Y. Tan, and Kwok-Kee Wei. "Organizational Transformation Using Electronic Data Interchange: The Case of TradeNet in Singapore." *Journal of Management Information Systems* 13, no. 4 (Spring 1997).

Thompson, Marjorie Sarbough, and Martha S. Feldman. "Electronic Mail and Organizational Communication." *Organization Science* 9, no. 6 (November–December 1998).

Torkzadeh, Gholamreza, and Weidong Xia. "Managing Telecommunications Strategy by Steering Committee." *MIS Quarterly* 16, no. 2 (June 1992).

Varshney, Upkar. "Networking Support for Mobile Computing." *Communications of the Association for Information Systems* 1 (January 1999).

Vetter, Ronald J. "ATM Concepts, Architectures, and Protocols." *Communications of the ACM* 38, no. 2 (February 1995).

Westin, Alan F., Heather A. Schweder, Michael A. Baker, and Sheila Lehman. *The Changing Workplace.* New York: Knowledge Industries (1995).

CHAPTER 10

Applegate, Lynda, and Janice Gogan. "Paving the Information Superhighway: Introduction to the Internet," *Harvard Business School* 9-195-202 (August 1995).

Bakos, Yannis. "The Emerging Role of Electronic Marketplaces and the Internet." *Communications of the ACM* 41, no. 8 (August 1998).

Barua, Anitesh, Sury Ravindran, and Andrew B. Whinston. "Efficient Selection of Suppliers over the Internet." *Journal of Management Information Systems* 13, no. 4 (Spring 1997).

Berners-Lee, Tim, Robert Cailliau, Ari Luotonen, Henrik Frystyk Nielsen, and Arthur Secret. "The World-Wide Web." *Communications of the ACM* 37, no. 8 (August 1994).

Bowman, C. Mic, Peter B. Danzig, Udi Manger, and Michael F. Schwartz. "Scalable Internet Resource Discovery: Research Problems and Approaches." *Communications of the ACM* 37, no. 8 (August 1994).

Buchanan, Lee. "Procurative Powers." *Webmaster* (May 1997).

Caldwell, Bruce. "Can It Be Saved?" *Information Week* (April 8, 1996).

Chabrow, Eric R. "On-line Employment," *Information Week* (January 23, 1995).

Choi, Soon-Yong, Dale O. Stahl, and Andrew B. Whinston. *The Economics of Electronic Commerce.* Indianapolis, IN: Macmillan Technical Publishing (1997).

Cole-Gomolski, Barbara. "Groupware Gives Lift to Reebok Site." *Computerworld* (January 19, 1998).

Cortese, Amy. "Here Comes the Intranet." *Business Week* (February 26, 1996).

Crede, Andreas. "Electronic Commerce and the Banking Industry: The Requirement and Opportunities for New Payment Systems Using the Internet." *JCMC* 1, no. 3 (December 1995).

Cronin, Mary. *The Internet Strategy Handbook.* Boston, MA: Harvard Business School Press (1996).

Dahle, Cheryl. "Sellular Chemistry." *Webmaster* (January 1997).

Darling, Michael. "The Internet: Hot or Just Cool?" *Stern Business* (Spring 1996).

Dearth, Jeffrey, and Arnold King. "Negotiating the Internet," *Information Week* (January 9, 1995).

Deutsch, Claudia. "Businesses Explore Cyberauctions." *The New York Times* (June 1, 1998).

Downes, Larry, and Chunka Mui. *Unleashing the Killer App: Digital Strategies for Market Dominance.* Boston, MA: Harvard Business School Press (1998).

Eckerson, Wayne. "Doing Business on the Web." Patrica Seybold Group's Notes on Information Technology (April 1996).

Elofson, Greg, and William N. Robinson. "Creating a Custom Mass Production Channel on the Internet." *Communications of the ACM* 41, no. 3 (March 1998).

Ghosh, Shikhar. "Making Business Sense of the Internet." *Harvard Business Review* (March–April 1998).

Goodman, S. E., L. I. Press, S. R. Ruth, and A. M. Rutkowski. "The Global Diffusion of the Internet: Patterns and Problems." *Communications of the ACM* 37, no. 8 (August 1994.)

Hagel, John III, and Marc Singer. *Net Worth.* Boston, MA: Harvard Business School Press (1999).

———. "Unbundling the Corporation." *Harvard Business Review* (March–April 1999).

Halper, Mark. "Meet the New Middlemen." *Computerworld Emmerce* (May 5, 1997).

Hardman, Vicky, Martina Angela Sasse, and Isidor Kouvelas. "Successful Multiparty Audio Communication over the Internet." *Communications of the ACM* 41, no. 5 (May 1998).

Hof, Robert D., Gary McWilliams, and Gabrielle Saveri. "The 'Click Here', Economy." *Business Week* (June 22, 1998).

Hoffman, Donna L., Thomas P. Novak, and Patrali Chatterjee. "Commercial Scenarios for the Web: Opportunities and Challenges." *JCMC* 1, no. 3 (December 1995).

Hoffman, Donna L., William D. Kalsbeek, and Thomas P. Novak. "Internet and Web Use in the U.S." *Communications of the ACM* 39, no. 12 (December 1996).

Horwitt, Elisabeth. "Intranet Intricacies." *Computerworld Client/Server Journal* (February 1996).

"How to Use Intranets to Support Business Applications." *I/S Analyzer Case Studies* 35, no. 5 (May 1996).

Isakowitz, Tomas, Michael Bieber, and Fabio Vitali. "Web Information Systems." *Communications of the ACM* 41, no. 7 (July 1998).

Jahnke, Art. "It Takes a Village." *CIO WebBusiness* (February 1, 1998).

Kalakota, Ravi, and Andrew B. Whinston. *Electronic Commerce: A Manager's Guide.* Reading MA: Addison-Wesley (1997).

———. *Frontiers of Electronic Commerce.* Reading, MA: Addison-Wesley (1996).

Kanan, P. K., Ai-Mei Chang, and Andrew B. Whinston. "Marketing Information on the I-Way." *Communications of the ACM* 41, no. 3 (March 1998).

Kautz, Henry, Bart Selman, and Mehul Shah. "ReferralWeb: Combining Social Networks and Collaborative Filtering." *Communications of the ACM* 40, no. 3 (March 1997).

Kendall, Kenneth E., and Julie E. Kendall. "Information Delivery Systems: An Exploration of Web Push and Pull Technologies." *Communications of the Association for Information Systems* 1 (April 1999).

Korzeniowski, Paul. "IP Telephony: Ready for Prime Time?" *Datamation* (April 1998).

Kuo, Geng-Sheng and Jing-Pei Lin. "New Design Concepts for an Intelligent Internet." *Communications of the ACM* 41, no. 11 (November 1998).

Lee, Ho Geun. "Do Electronic Marketplaces Lower the Price of Goods?" *Communications of the ACM* 41, no. 1 (January 1998).

Lee, Ho Geun, and Theodore H. Clark. "Market Process Reengineering through Electronic Market Systems: Opportunities and Challenges." *Journal of Management Information Systems* 13, no. 3 (Winter 1997).

Leiner, Barry M. "Internet Technology," *Communications of the ACM* 37, no. 8 (August 1994).

Levitt, Lee. "Intranets: Internet Technologies Deployed Behind the Firewall for Corporate Productivity." Process Software Corporation (1996).

Lohr, Steve. "Business to Business in the Internet." *The New York Times* (April 28, 1997).

Lohse, Gerald L., and Peter Spiller. "Electronic Shopping." *Communications of the ACM* 41, no. 7 (July 1998).

Maddox, Kate. "On-line Data Push." *Information Week* (February 24, 1997).

Markoff, John. "Commerce Comes to the Internet," *The New York Times* (April 13, 1994).

Meeker, Mary, and Chris DePuy. "The Internet Report." New York: Morgan Stanley & Co. (1996).

Mougayar, Walid. *Opening Digital Markets,* 2nd ed. New York: McGraw-Hill (1998).

Nouwens, John, and Harry Bouwman. "Living Apart Together in Electronic Commerce: The Use of Information and Communication Technology to Create Network Organizations." *JCMC* 1, no. 3 (December 1995).

O'Leary, Daniel E., Daniel Koukka, and Robert Plant. "Artificial Intelligence and Virtual Organizations." *Communications of the ACM* 40, no. 1 (January 1997).

Palmer, Jonathan W., and David A. Griffith. "An Emerging Model of Web Site Design for Marketing." *Communications of the ACM* 41, no. 3 (March 1998).

Price Waterhouse. "Technology Forecast: 1996." Menlo Park, CA: Price Waterhouse World Technology Centre (1995).

Quelch, John A., and Lisa R. Klein. "The Internet and International Marketing." *Sloan Management Review* (Spring 1996).

Rafter, Michelle V. "Can We Talk?" *The Industry Standard* (February 15, 1999).

Richard, Eric. "Anatomy of the World-Wide Web." *Internet World* (April 1995).

Row, Heath. "Personnel Best." *Webmaster* (September 1996).

Sarkar, Mitra Barun, Brian Butler, and Charles Steinfield. "Intermediaries and Cybermediaries: A Continuing Role for Mediating Players in the Electronic Marketplace." *JCMC* 1, no. 3 (December 1995).

Semich, J. William. "The World Wide Web: Internet Boomtown?" *Datamation* (January 15, 1995).

Smarr, Larry, and Charles E. Catlett. "Metacomputing." *Communications of the ACM* 35, no. 6 (June 1992).

Sprout, Alison L. "The Internet Inside Your Company." *Fortune* (November 27, 1995).

Steinfield, Charles. "The Impact of Electronic Commerce on Buyer-Seller Relationships." *JCMC* 1, no. 3 (December 1995).

Sterne, Jim. "Customer Interface." *CIO WebBusiness* (February 1, 1998).

———. *World Wide Web Marketing.* New York: John Wiley (1995).

———. "The Premier 100: On Track to Internet Success." *Computerworld* (February 24, 1997).

Ubois, Jeffrey. "CFOs in Cyberspace." *CFO* (February, 1995).

Verity, John W., with Robert D. Hof. "The Internet: How It Will Change the Way You Do Business." *Business Week* (November 14, 1994).

Wigand, Rolf T., and Robert Benjamin. "Electronic Commerce: Effects on Electronic Markets." *JCMC* 1, no. 3 (December 1995).

Withers, Suzanne. "The Trader and the Internet." *Technical Analysis of Stocks & Commodities* (March 1995).

CHAPTER 11

Bacon, C. James. "The Uses of Decision Criteria in Selecting Information Systems/Technology Investments." *MIS Quarterly* 16, no. 3 (September 1992).

Barua, Anitesh, Sophie C. H. Lee, and Andrew B. Whinston. "The Calculus of Reengineering." *Information Systems Research* 7, no. 4 (December 1996).

Beath, Cynthia Mathis, and Wanda J. Orlikowski. "The Contradictory Structure of Systems Development Methodologies: Deconstructing the IS-User Relationship in Information Engineering." *Information Systems Research* 5, no. 4 (December 1994).

Bostrom, R. P., and J. S. Heinen. "MIS Problems and Failures: A Socio-Technical Perspective. Part I: The Causes." *MIS Quarterly* 1 (September 1977); "Part II: The Application of Socio-Technical Theory." *MIS Quarterly* 1 (December 1977).

Brier, Tom, Jerry Luftman, and Raymond Papp. " Enablers and Inhibitors of Business—IT Alignment." *Communications of the Association for Information Systems* 1 (March 1999).

Bullen, Christine, and John F. Rockart. "A Primer on Critical Success Factors." Cambridge, MA: Center for Information Systems Research, Sloan School of Management (1981).

Buss, Martin D. J. "How to Rank Computer Projects." *Harvard Business Review* (January 1983).

Cerveny, Robert P., Edward J. Garrity, and G. Lawrence Sanders. "A Problem-Solving Perspective on Systems Development." *Journal of Management Information Systems* 6, no. 4 (Spring 1990).

Davenport, Thomas H., and James E. Short. "The New Industrial Engineering: Information Technology and Business Process Redesign." *Sloan Management Review* 31, no. 4 (Summer 1990).

Davidson, W. H. "Beyond Engineering: The Three Phases of Business Transformation." *IBM Systems Journal* 32, no. 1 (1993).

Davis, Fred R. "Perceived Usefulness, Ease of Use, and User Acceptance of Information Technology." *MIS Quarterly* 13, no. 3 (September 1989).

Davis, Gordon B. "Determining Management Information Needs: A Comparison of Methods." *MIS Quarterly* 1 (June 1977).

———. "Information Analysis for Information System Development." In *Systems Analysis and Design: A Foundation for the 1980's,* edited by W. W. Cotterman, J. D. Cougar, N. L. Enger, and F. Harold. New York: Wiley (1981).

———. "Strategies for Information Requirements Determination." *IBM Systems Journal* 1 (1982).

Dennis, Alan R., Robert M. Daniels, Jr., Glenda Hayes, and Jay F. Nunamaker, Jr. "Methodology-Driven Use of Automated Support in Business Process Reengineering." *Journal of Management Information Systems* 10, no. 3 (Winter 1993–1994).

Desmarais, Michel C., Richard Leclair, Jean-Yves Fiset, and Hichem Talbi. "Cost-Justifying Electronic Performance Support Systems." *Communications of the ACM* 40, no. 7 (July 1997).

Deutsch, Claudia. "Six Sigma Enlightenment." *The New York Times* (December 7, 1998).

Dos Santos, Brian. "Justifying Investments in New Information Technologies." *Journal of Management Information Systems* 7, no. 4 (Spring 1991).

Ein-Dor, Philip, and Eli Segev. "Strategic Planning for Management Information Systems." *Management Science* 24, no. 15 (1978).

El Sawy, Omar, and Burt Nanus. "Toward the Design of Robust Information Systems." *Journal of Management Information Systems* 5, no. 4 (Spring 1989).

Emery, James C. "Cost/Benefit Analysis of Information Systems." Chicago: Society for Management Information Systems Workshop Report No. 1 (1971).

Franz, Charles, and Daniel Robey. "An Investigation of User-Led System Design: Rational and Political Perspectives." *Communications of the ACM* 27 (December 1984).

Gerlach, James H., and Feng-Yang Kuo. "Understanding Human-Computer Interaction for Information Systems Design." *MIS Quarterly* 15, no. 4 (December 1991).

Gill, Philip. "Flower Power." *Oracle Profit Magazine* (August 1998).

Gould, John D., and Clayton Lewis. "Designing for Usability: Key Principles and What Designers Think." *Communications of the ACM* 28 (March 1985).

Grudnitski, Gary. "Eliciting Decision Makers' Information Requirements." *Journal of Management Information Systems* (Summer 1984).

Grover, Varun. "IS Investment Priorities in Contemporary Organizations." *Communications of the ACM* 41, no. 2 (February 1998).

Hammer, Michael. "Reengineering Work: Don't Automate, Obliterate." *Harvard Business Review* (July–August 1990).

Hammer, Michael, and James Champy. *Reengineering the Corporation.* New York: HarperCollins Publishers (1993).

Hammer, Michael, and Steven A. Stanton. *The Reengineering Revolution.* New York: HarperCollins (1995).

Helms, Glenn L., and Ira R. Weiss. "The Cost of Internally Developed Applications: Analysis of Problems and Cost Control Methods." *Journal of Management Information Systems* (Fall 1986).

Huizing, Ard, Esther Koster, and Wim Bouman. "Balance in Business Process Reengineering: An Empirical Study of Fit and Performance." *Journal of Management Information Systems* 14, no. 1 (Summer 1997).

Hunton, James E., and Beeler, Jesse D., "Effects of User Participation in Systems Development: A Longitudinal Field Study." *MIS Quarterly* 21, no. 4 (December 1997).

Janz, Brian D., James C. Wetherbe, Gordon B. Davis, and Raymond A. Noe. "Reengineering the Systems Development Process: The Link between Autonomous Teams and Business Process Outcomes." *Journal of Management Information Systems* 14, no. 1 (Summer 1997).

Jesser, Ryan, Rodney Smith, Mark Stupeck, and William F. Wright. "Information Technology Process Reengineering and Performance Measurement." *Communications of the Association for Information Systems* 1 (February 1999).

Kane, Karen. "L. L. Bean Delivers the Goods." *Fast Company* (August/September 1997).

Karat, John. "Evolving the Scope of User-Centered Design." *Communications of the ACM* 40, no. 7 (July 1997).

Keen, Peter W. "Information Systems and Organizational Change." *Communications of the ACM* 24 (January 1981).

Kendall, Kenneth E., and Julie E. Kendall. *Systems Analysis and Design,* 4th ed. Upper Saddle River, NJ: Prentice Hall (1998).

King, Julia. "Reengineering Slammed." *Computerworld* (June 13, 1994).

King, William R. "Alternative Designs in Information System Development." *MIS Quarterly* (December 1982).

Lederer, Albert, and Jayesh Prasad. "Nine Management Guidelines for Better Cost Estimating." *Communications of the ACM* 35, no. 2 (February 1992).

Lederer, Albert L., Rajesh Mirani, Boon Siong Neo, Carol Pollard, Jayesh Prasad, and K. Ramamurthy. "Information System Cost Estimating: A Management Perspective." *MIS Quarterly* 14, no. 2 (June 1990).

Lientz, Bennett P., and E. Burton Swanson. *Software Maintenance Management.* Reading, MA: Addison-Wesley (1980).

Mahmood, Mo Adam, and Gary J. Mann. "Measuring the Organizational Impact of Information Technology Investment." *Journal of Management Information Systems* 10, no. 1 (Summer 1993).

Matlin, Gerald. "What Is the Value of Investment in Information Systems?" *MIS Quarterly* 13, no. 3 (September 1989).

McFarlan, F. Warren. "Portfolio Approach to Information Systems." *Harvard Business Review* (September–October 1981).

McKeen, James D., and Tor Guimaraes. "Successful Strategies for User Participation in Systems Development." *Journal of Management Information Systems* 14, no. 2 (Fall 1997).

Moad, Jeff. "Does Reengineering Really Work?" *Datamation* (August 1993).

Nolan, Richard L. "Managing Information Systems by Committee." *Harvard Business Review* (July–August 1982).

Parker, M. M. "Enterprise Information Analysis: Cost-Benefit Analysis and the Data-Managed System." *IBM Systems Journal* 21 (1982).

Premkumar, G., and William R. King. "Organizational Characteristics and Information Systems Planning: An

Empirical Study." *Information Systems Research* 5, no. 2 (June 1994).

Raghunathan, Bhanu, and **T. S. Raghunathan.** "Adaptation of a Planning System Success Model to Information Systems Planning." *Information Systems Research* 5, no. 3 (September 1994).

Rai, Arun, Ravi Patnayakuni, and **Nainika Patnayakuni.** "Technology Investment and Business Performance." *Communications of the ACM* 40, no. 7 (July 1997).

Robey, Daniel, and **M. Lynne Markus.** "Rituals in Information System Design." *MIS Quarterly* (March 1984).

Rockart, John F. "Chief Executives Define Their Own Data Needs." *Harvard Business Review* (March–April 1979).

Rockart, John F., and **Michael E. Treacy.** "The CEO Goes On-Line." *Harvard Business Review* (January–February 1982).

Shank, Michael E., Andrew C. Boynton, and **Robert W. Zmud.** "Critical Success Factor Analysis as a Methodology for MIS Planning." *MIS Quarterly* (June 1985).

Sia, Siew Kien, and **Boon Siong Neo.** "Reengineering Effectiveness and the Redesign of Organizational Control: A Case Study of the Inland Revenue Authority in Singapore." *Journal of Management Information Systems* 14, no. 1 (Summer 1997).

Teng, James T. C., Seung Ryul Jeong, and **Varun Grover.** "Profiling Successful Reengineering Projects." *Communications of the ACM* 41, no. 6 (June 1998).

Thompson, Sian Hin Teo, and **William R. King.** "Integration between Business Planning and Information Systems Planning: An Evolutionary-Contingency Approach." *Journal of Management Information Systems* 14, no. 1 (Summer 1997).

Venkatraman, N. "Beyond Outsourcing: Managing IT Resources as a Value Center." *Sloan Management Review* (Spring 1997).

Vessey, Iris, and **Sue Conger.** "Learning to Specify Information Requirements: The Relationship between Application and Methodology." *Journal of Management Information Systems* 10, no. 2 (Fall 1993).

Vitalari, Nicholas P. "Knowledge as a Basis for Expertise in Systems Analysis: Empirical Study." *MIS Quarterly* (September 1985).

Zachman, J. A. "Business Systems Planning and Business Information Control Study: A Comparison." *IBM Systems Journal* 21 (1982).

Zmud, Robert W., William P. Anthony, and **Ralph M. Stair, Jr.** "The Use of Mental Imagery to Facilitate Information Identification in Requirements Analysis." *Journal of Management Information Systems* 9, no. 4 (Spring 1993).

CHAPTER 12

Ahituv, Niv, and **Seev Neumann.** "A Flexible Approach to Information System Development." *MIS Quarterly* (June 1984).

Aiken, Peter, Alice Muntz, and **Russ Richards.** "DOD Legacy Systems: Reverse Engineering Data Requirements." *Communications of the ACM* 37, no. 5 (May 1994).

Alavi, Maryam. "An Assessment of the Prototyping Approach to Information System Development." *Communications of the ACM* 27 (June 1984).

Alavi, Maryam, R. Ryan Nelson, and **Ira R. Weiss.** "Strategies for End-User Computing: An Integrative Framework." *Journal of Management Information Systems* 4, no. 3 (Winter 1987–1988).

Anderson, Evan A. "Choice Models for the Evaluation and Selection of Software Packages." *Journal of Management Information Systems* 6, no. 4 (Spring 1990).

Arthur, Lowell Jay. "Quick and Dirty." *Computerworld* (December 14, 1992).

Baskerville, Richard L., and **Jan Stage.** "Controlling Prototype Development through Risk Analysis." *MIS Quarterly* 20, no. 4 (December 1996).

Martin, J., and **C. McClure.** "Buying Software Off the Rack." *Harvard Business Review* (November–December 1983).

Martin, James. *Application Development without Programmers.* Englewood Cliffs, NJ: Prentice Hall (1982).

Martin, James, and **Carma McClure.** *Structured Techniques: The Basis of CASE.* Englewood Cliffs, NJ: Prentice Hall (1988).

Mason, R. E. A., and **T. T. Carey.** "Prototyping Interactive Information Systems." *Communications of the ACM* 26 (May 1983).

Matos, Victor M., and **Paul J. Jalics.** "An Experimental Analysis of the Performance of Fourth-Generation Tools on PCs." *Communications of the ACM* 32, no. 11 (November 1989).

Mazzucchelli, Louis. "Structured Analysis Can Streamline Software Design." *Computerworld* (December 9, 1985).

McIntyre, Scott C., and **Lexis F. Higgins.** "Object-Oriented Analysis and Design: Methodology and Application." *Journal of Management Information Systems* 5, no. 1 (Summer 1988).

McMullen, John. "Developing a Role for End Users." *Information Week* (June 15, 1992).

Moran, Robert. "The Case Against CASE." *Information Week* (February 17, 1992).

Nerson, Jean-Marc. "Applying Object-Oriented Analysis and Design." *Communications of the ACM* 35, no. 9 (September 1992).

Nissen, Mark E. "Redesigning Reengineering through Measurement-Driven Inference," *MIS Quarterly* 22, no. 4 (December 1998).

Norman, Ronald J., and **Jay F. Nunamaker, Jr.** "CASE Productivity: Perceptions of Software Engineering Professionals." *Communications of the ACM* 32, no. 9 (September 1989).

Pancake, Cherri M. "The Promise and the Cost of Object Technology: A Five-Year Forecast." *Communications of the ACM* 38, no. 10 (October 1995).

Rivard, Suzanne, and **Sid L. Huff.** "Factors of Success for End-User Computing." *Communications of the ACM* 31, no. 5 (May 1988).

Roche, Edward M. *Managing Information Technology in Multinational Corporations.* New York: Macmillan Publishing Company (1992).

Rockart, John F., and **Lauren S. Flannery.** "The Management of End-User Computing." *Communications of the ACM* 26, no. 10 (October 1983).

Sabherwahl, Rajiv. "The Role of Trust in IS Outsourcing Development Projects." *Communications of the ACM* 42, no. 2 (February 1999).

Schmidt, Douglas C., and **Mohamed E. Fayad.** "Lessons Learned Building Reusable OO Frameworks for Distributed Software." *Communications of the ACM* 40, no. 10 (October 1997).

Timmreck, Eric M. "Performance Measurement: Vendor Specifications and Benchmarks." In *The Information Systems Handbook,* edited by F. Warren McFarlan and Richard C. Nolan. Homewood, IL: Dow-Jones-Richard D. Irwin (1975).

Trauth, Eileen M., and Elliot Cole. "The Organizational Interface: A Method for Supporting End Users of Packaged Software." *MIS Quarterly* 16, no. 1 (March 1992).

Vessey, Iris, and Sue A. Conger. "Requirements Specification: Learning Object, Process, and Data Methodologies." *Communications of the ACM* 37, no. 5 (May 1994).

Violino, Bob. "Outside Help Wanted." *Information Week* (January 4, 1999).

White, Clinton E., and David P. Christy. "The Information Center Concept: A Normative Model and a Study of Six Installations." *MIS Quarterly* (December 1987).

Willis, T. Hillman, and Debbie B. Tesch. "An Assessment of Systems Development Methodologies." *Journal of Information Technology Management* 2, no. 2 (1991).

Yourdon, Edward, and L. L. Constantine. *Structured Design.* New York: Yourdon Press (1978).

Zahniser, Richard A. "Design by Walking Around." *Communications of the ACM* 36, no. 10 (October 1993).

CHAPTER 13

Alter, Steven, and Michael Ginzberg. "Managing Uncertainty in MIS Implementation." *Sloan Management Review* 20 (Fall 1978).

Attewell, Paul. "Technology Diffusion and Organizational Learning: The Case of Business Computing." *Organization Science,* no. 3 (1992).

Barki, Henri, and Jon Hartwick. "Rethinking the Concept of User Involvement." *MIS Quarterly* 13, no. 1 (March 1989).

Baroudi, Jack, Margrethe H. Olson, and Blake Ives. "An Empirical Study of the Impact of User Involvement on System Usage and Information Satisfaction." *Communications of the ACM* 29, no. 3 (March 1986).

Baroudi, Jack, and Wanda Orlikowski. "A Short Form Measure of User Information Satisfaction: A Psychometric Evaluation and Notes on Use." *Journal of Management Information Systems* 4, no. 4 (Spring 1988).

Batiste, John L. "The Application Profile." *MIS Quarterly* (September 1986).

Best, James D. "The MIS Executive as Change Agent." *Journal of Information Systems Management* (Fall 1985).

Bikson, Tora K., Cathleen Stasz, and D. A. Mankin. "Computer Mediated Work. Individual and Organizational Impact in One Corporate Headquarters." Santa Monica, CA: Rand Corporation (1985).

Brooks, Frederick P. "The Mythical Man-Month." *Datamation* (December 1974).

Bulkeley, William. "Programmers Need to Keep It Simple." *Wall Street Journal* (June 30, 1992).

Bulkeley, William. "When Things Go Wrong." *Wall Street Journal* (November 18, 1996).

Cafasso, Rosemary. "Few IS Projects Come in on Time, on Budget." *Computerworld* (September 12, 1994).

Caldwell, Bruce. "Missteps, Miscues." *Information Week* (June 20, 1994).

Christiansen, Lars Chr., Tore R. Christiansen, Yan Jin and Raymond E. Levitt. "Modeling and Simulation Coordination in Projects." *Journal of Organizational Computing and Electronic Commerce* 9, no. 1 (1999).

Clement, Andrew, and Peter Van den Besselaar. "A Retrospective Look at PD Projects." *Communications of the ACM* 36, no. 4 (June 1993).

Cooper, Randolph B., and Robert W. Zmud. "Information Technology Implementation Research: A Technological Diffusion Approach." *Management Science* 36, no. 2 (February 1990).

Corbato, Fernando J. "On Building Systems That Will Fail." *Communications of the ACM* 34, no. 9 (September 1991).

Cronan, Timothy Paul, and David E. Douglas. "End-user Training and Computing Effectiveness in Public Agencies: An Empirical Study." *Journal of Management Information Systems* 6, no. 4 (Spring 1990).

Davenport, Tom. "Putting the Enterprise into Enterprise Systems." *Harvard Business Review* (July–August 1998).

Davis, Fred R., "Perceived Usefulness, Ease of Use, and User Acceptance of Information Technology." *MIS Quarterly* 13, no. 3 (September 1989).

Davis, Gordon B., and Margrethe H. Olson. *Management Information Systems,* 2nd ed. New York: McGraw-Hill (1985).

De, Prabudda, and Thomas W. Ferrat. "An Information System Involving Competing Organizations." *Communications of the ACM* 41, 12 (December 12, 1998).

DeLone, William H., and Ephrain R. McLean. "Information System Success: The Quest for the Dependent Variable." *Information Systems Research* 3, no. 1 (March 1992).

Delong, William H. "Determinants of Success for Computer Usage in Small Business." *MIS Quarterly* (March 1988).

De Michelis, Giorgio, Eric Dubois, Mathias Janke, Florian Mathes, John Mylopoulos, Joachin W. Schmidt, Carson Woo, and Eric Yu. "A Three-Faceted View of Information Systems." *Communications of the ACM* 41, 12 (December 1998).

Doll, William J. "Avenues for Top Management Involvement in Successful MIS Development." *MIS Quarterly* (March 1985).

Ein-Dor, Philip, and Eli Segev. "Organizational Context and the Success of Management Information Systems." *Management Science* 24 (June 1978).

Fichman, Robert G., and Scott A. Moses. "An Incremental Process for Software Implementation." *Sloan Management Review* 40, no. 2 (Winter 1999).

Franz, Charles, and Daniel Robey. "An Investigation of User-Led System Design: Rational and Political Perspectives." *Communications of the ACM* 27 (December 1984).

Ginzberg, Michael J. "Early Diagnosis of MIS Implementation Failure: Promising Results and Unanswered Questions." *Management Science* 27 (April 1981).

Gogan, Janis L., Jane Fedorowicz, and Ashok Rao. "Assessing Risks in Two Projects: A Strategic Opportunity and a Necessary Evil." *Communications of the Association for Information Systems* 1 (May 1999).

Gould, John D., and Clayton Lewis. "Designing for Usability: Key Principles and What Designers Think." *Communications of the ACM* 28 (March 1985).

Gullo, Karen. "Stopping Runaways in Their Tracks." *Information Week* (November 13, 1989).

Hammer, Michael, and Steven A. Stanton. *The Reengineering Revolution.* New York: HarperCollins (1995).

Helms, Glenn L., and Ira R. Weiss. "The Cost of Internally Developed Applications: Analysis of Problems and Cost Control Methods." *Journal of Management Information Systems* (Fall 1986).

Hirscheim, R. A. "User Experience with and Assessment of Participative Systems Design." *MIS Quarterly* (December 1985).

Ives, Blake, Margrethe H. Olson, and Jack J. Baroudi. "The Measurement of User Information Satisfaction." *Communications of the ACM* 26 (October 1983).

Joshi, Kailash. "A Model of Users' Perspective on Change: The Case of Information Systems Technology Implementation." *MIS Quarterly* 15, no. 2 (June 1991).

Keen, Peter W. "Information Systems and Organizational Change." *Communications of the ACM* 24 (January 1981).

Keil, Mark, Paul E. Cule, Kalle Lyytinen, and Roy C. Schmidt. "A Framework for Identifying Software Project Risks." *Communications of the ACM* 41, 11 (November 1998).

Keil, Mark, Richard Mixon, Timo Saarinen, and Virpi Tuunainen. "Understanding Runaway IT Projects." *Journal of Management Information Systems* 11, no. 3 (Winter 1994–95).

Kolb, D. A., and A. L. Frohman. "An Organization Development Approach to Consulting." *Sloan Management Review* 12 (Fall 1970).

Laudon, Kenneth C. "CIOs Beware: Very Large Scale Systems." Center for Research on Information Systems, New York University Stern School of Business, working paper (1989).

Lederer, Albert, and Jayesh Prasad. "Nine Management Guidelines for Better Cost Estimating." *Communications of the ACM* 35, no. 2 (February 1992).

Lederer, Albert L., Rajesh Mirani, Boon Siong Neo, Carol Pollard, Jayesh Prasad, and K. Ramamurthy. "Information System Cost Estimating: A Management Perspective." *MIS Quarterly* 14, no. 2 (June 1990).

Lucas, Henry C., Jr. *Toward Creative Systems Design.* New York: Columbia University Press (1974).

Lucas, Henry C., Jr. *Why Information Systems Fail.* New York: Columbia University Press (1975).

Lucas, Henry C., Jr. *Implementation: The Key to Successful Information Systems.* New York: Columbia University Press (1981).

McFarlan, F. Warren. "Portfolio Approach to Information Systems." *Harvard Business Review* (September–October 1981).

McPartlin, John P. "Uncle Sam Calls in the Reserves." *Information Week* (April 27, 1992).

Maglitta, Joseph. "Rocks in the Gears." *Computerworld* (October 3, 1994).

Marcus, Aaron. "Human Communication Issues in Advanced UIS." *Communications of the ACM* 36, no. 4 (April 1993).

Markus, M. L. "Power, Politics and MIS Implementation." *Communications of the ACM* 26 (June 1983).

Markus, M. Lynne, and Mark Keil. "If We Build It, They Will Come: Designing Information Systems That People Want to Use." *Sloan Management Review* (Summer 1994).

Markus, M. Lynne, and Robert I. Benjamin. "Change Agentry—The Next IS Frontier." *MIS Quarterly* 20, no. 4 (December 1996).

Markus, M. Lynne, and Robert I. Benjamin. "The Magic Bullet Theory of IT-Enabled Transformation." *Sloan Management Review* (Winter 1997).

Miller, Steven E. "From System Design to Democracy." *Communications of the ACM* 36, no. 4 (June 1993).

Moore, Gary C., and Izak Benbasat. "Development of an Instrument to Measure the Perceptions of Adopting an Information Technology Innovation." *Information Systems Research* 2, no. 3 (September 1991).

Mumford, Enid, and Mary Weir. *Computer Systems in Work Design: The ETHICS Method.* New York: John Wiley (1979).

Newman, Michael, and Rajiv Sabherwal. "Determinants of Commitment to Information Systems Development: A Longitudinal Investigation." *MIS Quarterly* 20, no. 1 (March 1996).

Nidumolu, Sarma R., Seymour E. Goodman, Douglas R. Vogel, and Ann K. Danowitz. "Information Technology for Local Administration Support: The Governorates Project in Egypt." *MIS Quarterly* 20, no. 2 (June 1996).

Orlikowski, Wanda J., and J. Debra Hofman. "An Improvisational Change Model for Change Management: The Case of Groupware Technologies." *Sloan Management Review* (Winter 1997).

Oz, Effy. "When Professional Standards Are Lax: The CONFIRM Failure and Its Lessons." *Communications of the ACM* 37, no. 10 (October 1994).

Raymond, Louis. "Organizational Context and Information System Success: A Contingency Approach." *Journal of Management Information Systems* 6, no. 4 (Spring 1990).

Robey, Daniel, and M. Lynne Markus. "Rituals in Information System Design." *MIS Quarterly* (March 1984).

Robey, Daniel, and Sundeep Sahay. "Transforming Work Through Information Technology: A Comparative Case Study of Geographic Information Systems." *Information Systems Research* 7, no. 1 (March 1996).

Singleton, John P., Ephraim R. McLean, and Edward N. Altman. "Measuring Information Systems Performance." *MIS Quarterly* 12, no. 2 (June 1988).

Swanson, E. Burton. *Information System Implementation.* Homewood, IL: Richard D. Irwin (1988).

Tait, Peter, and Iris Vessey. "The Effect of User Involvement on System Success: A Contingency Approach." *MIS Quarterly* 12, no. 1 (March 1988).

Thong, James Y. L., Chee-Sing Yap, and K. S. Raman. "Top Management Support, External Expertise, and Information Systems Implementation in Small Business." *Information Systems Research* 7, no. 2 (June 1996).

Tornatsky, Louis G., J. D. Eveland, M. G. Boylan, W. A. Hetzner, E. C. Johnson, D. Roitman, and J. Schneider. *The Process of Technological Innovation: Reviewing the Literature.* Washington, DC: National Science Foundation (1983).

Turner, Jon A. "Computer Mediated Work: The Interplay Between Technology and Structured Jobs." *Communications of the ACM* 27 (December 1984).

United States General Services Administration. "An Evaluation of the Grand Design Approach to Developing Computer-Based Application Systems." Washington, DC: General Services Administration (September 1988).

Westcott, Russ. "Client Satisfaction: The Yardstick for Measuring MIS Success." *Journal of Information Systems Management* (Fall 1985).

Westin, Alan F., Heather A. Schweder, Michael A. Baker, and Sheila Lehman. *The Changing Workplace.* White Plains, NY, and London: Knowledge Industry Publications, Inc. (1985).

White, Kathy Brittain, and Richard Leifer. "Information Systems Development Success: Perspectives from Project Team Participants." *MIS Quarterly* (September 1986).

Whiting, Rick. "Development in Disarray." *Software Magazine* (September 1998).

Yin, Robert K. "Life Histories of Innovations: How New Practices Become Routinized." *Public Administration Review* (January–February 1981).

CHAPTER 14

Adhikari, Richard. "Virtually Superior." *Information Week* (November 3, 1997).

Alavi, Maryam, and **Dorothy Leidner.** "Knowledge Management Systems: Issues, Challenges, and Benefits." *Communications of the Association for Information Systems* 1 (February 1999).

Allen, Bradley P. "CASE-Based Reasoning: Business Applications." *Communications of the ACM* 37, no. 3 (March 1994).

Amaravadi, Chandra S., Olivia R. Liu Sheng, Joey F. George, and **Jay F. Nunamaker, Jr.** "AEI: A Knowledge-Based Approach to Integrated Office Systems." *Journal of Management Information Systems* 9, no. 1 (Summer 1992).

Applegate, Linda. "Technology Support for Cooperative Work: A Framework for Studying Introduction and Assimilation in Organizations." *Journal of Organizational Computing* 1, no. 1 (January–March 1991).

Asakawa, Kazuo, and **Hideyuki Takagi.** "Neural Networks in Japan." *Communications of the ACM* 37, no. 3 (March 1994).

Bair, James H. "A Layered Model of Organizations: Communication Processes and Performance." *Journal of Organizational Computing* 1, no. 2 (April–June 1991).

Balasubramanian, V., and **Alf Bashian.** "Document Management and Web Technologies: Alice Marries the Mad Hatter." *Communications of the ACM* 41, no. 7 (July 1998).

Bansal, Arun, Robert J. Kauffman, and **Rob R. Weitz.** "The Modeling Performance of Regression and Neural Networks." *Journal of Management Information Systems* 10, no. 1 (Summer 1993).

Barker, Virginia E., and **Dennis E. O'Connor.** "Expert Systems for Configuration at Digital: XCON and Beyond." *Communications of the ACM* (March 1989).

Beer, Randall D., Roger D. Quinn, Hillel J. Chiel, and **Roy E. Ritzman.** "Biologically Inspired Approaches to Robots." *Communications of the ACM* 40, no. 3 (March 1997).

Bikson, Tora K., J. D. Eveland, and **Barbara A. Gutek.** "Flexible Interactive Technologies for Multi-Person Tasks: Current Problems and Future Prospects." Rand Corporation (December 1988).

Black, George. "Taking Notes, Big Sixer Aims for Head of the Class." *Software Magazine* (March 1995).

Blanning, Robert W., David R. King, James R. Marsden, and **Ann C. Seror.** "Intelligent Models of Human Organizations: The State of the Art." *Journal of Organizational Computing* 2, no. 2 (1992).

Bobrow, D. G., S. Mittal, and **M. J. Stefik.** "Expert Systems: Perils and Promise." *Communications of the ACM* 29 (September 1986).

Bohn, Roger E. "Measuring and Managing Technological Knowledge." *Sloan Management Review* (Fall 1994).

Braden, Barbara, Jerome Kanter, and **David Kopcso.** "Developing an Expert Systems Strategy." *MIS Quarterly* 13, no. 4 (December 1989).

Brutzman, Don. "The Virtual Reality Modeling Language and Java." *Communications of the ACM* 41, no. 6 (June 1998).

Brynjolfsson, Erik. "The Contribution of Information Technology to Consumer Welfare." *Information Systems Research* 7, no. 3 (September 1996).

———. "The Productivity Paradox of Information Technology." *Communications of the ACM* 36, no. 12 (December 1993).

Brynjolfsson, Erik, and **Lorin M. Hitt.** "Information Technology and Organizational Design: Evidence from Micro Data." (January 1998).

Brynjolfsson, Erik, and **Lorin M. Hitt.** "Beyond the Productivity Paradox." *Communications of the ACM* 41, no. 8 (August 1998).

———. "New Evidence on the Returns to Information Systems." MIT Sloan School of Management (October 1993).

Burtka, Michael. "Generic Algorithms." *The Stern Information Systems Review* 1, no. 1 (Spring 1993).

Busch, Elizabeth, Matti Hamalainen, Clyde W. Holsapple, Yongmoo Suh, and **Andrew B. Whinston.** "Issues and Obstacles in the Development of Team Support Systems." *Journal of Organizational Computing* 1, no. 2 (April–June 1991).

Byrd, Terry Anthony. "Implementation and Use of Expert Systems in Organizations: Perceptions of Knowledge Engineers." *Journal of Management Information Systems* 8, no. 4 (Spring 1992).

Carlson, David A., and **Sudha Ram.** "A Knowledge Representation for Modeling Organizational Productivity." *Journal of Organizational Computing* 2, no. 2 (1992).

Churchland, Paul M., and **Patricia Smith Churchland.** "Could a Machine Think?" *Scientific American* (January 1990).

Clifford, James, Henry C. Lucas, Jr., and **Rajan Srikanth.** "Integrating Mathematical and Symbolic Models through AESOP: An Expert for Stock Options Pricing." *Information Systems Research* 3, no. 4 (December 1992).

Cole, Kevin, Olivier Fischer, and **Phyllis Saltzman.** "Just-in-Time Knowledge Delivery." *Communications of the ACM* 40, no. 7 (July 1997).

Cole-Gomolski, Barbara. "Customer Service with a :-)" *Computerworld* (March 30, 1998).

Creecy, Robert H., Brij M. Masand, Stephen J. Smith, and **Davis L. Waltz.** "Trading MIPS and Memory for Knowledge Engineering." *Communications of the ACM* 35, no. 8 (August 1992).

Davenport, Thomas H., David W. DeLong, and **Michael C. Beers.** "Successful Knowledge Management Projects." *Sloan Management Review* 39, no. 2 (Winter 1998).

Davenport, Thomas H., and **Lawrence Prusak.** *Working Knowledge: How Organizations Manage What They Know.* Boston, MA: Harvard Business School Press (1997).

Dhar, Vasant. "Plausibility and Scope of Expert Systems in Management." *Journal of Management Information Systems* (Summer 1987).

Dhar, Vasant, and **Roger Stein.** *Intelligent Decision Support Methods: The Science of Knowledge Work.* Upper Saddle River, NJ: Prentice Hall (1997).

Earl, Michael J., and **Ian A. Scott.** "What Is a Chief Knowledge Officer?" *Sloan Management Review* 40, no. 2 (Winter 1999).

El Najdawi, M. K., and **Anthony C. Stylianou.** "Expert Support Systems: Integrating AI Technologies." *Communications of the ACM* 36, no. 12 (December 1993).

Etzioni, Oren, and **Daniel Weld.** "A Softbot-Based Interface to the Internet." *Communications of the ACM* 37, no. 7 (July 1994).

Favela, Jesus. "Capture and Dissemination of Specialized Knowledge in Network Organizations." *Journal of Organizational Computing and Electronic Commerce* 7, nos. 2 and 3 (1997).

Feigenbaum, Edward A. "The Art of Artificial Intelligence: Themes and Case Studies in Knowledge Engineering." *Proceedings of the IJCAI* (1977).

Fryer, Bronwyn. "Visa Cracks Down on Fraud." *Information Week* (August 26, 1996).

Gelernter, David. "The Metamorphosis of Information Management." *Scientific American* (August 1989).

Gill, Philip J. "A False Rivalry Revealed." *Information Week* (May 20, 1996).

Giuliao, Vincent E. "The Mechanization of Office Work." *Scientific American* (September 1982).

Glushko, Robert J., Jay M. Tenenbaum, and **Bart Meltzer.** "An XML Framework for Agent-Based E-Commerce." *Communications of the ACM* 42, no. 3 (March 1999).

Goldberg, David E. "Genetic and Evolutionary Algorithms Come of Age." *Communications of the ACM* 37, no. 3 (March 1994).

Grant, Robert M. "Prospering in Dynamically-Competitive Environments: Organizational Capability as Knowledge Integration." *Organization Science* 7, no. 4 (July–August 1996).

Grief, Irene. "Desktop Agents in Group-Enabled Projects." *Communications of the ACM* 37, no. 7 (July 1994).

Griggs, Kenneth. "Visual Aids that Model Organizations." *Journal of Organizational Computing* 2, no. 2 (1992).

Hansen, Morton T., Nitin Nohria, and **Thomas Tierney.** "What's Your Strategy for Knowledge Management?" *Harvard Business Review* (March–April 1999).

Hayes-Roth, Frederick. "Knowledge-Based Expert Systems." *Spectrum IEEE* (October 1987).

Hayes-Roth, Frederick, and **Neil Jacobstein.** "The State of Knowledge-Based Systems." *Communications of the ACM* 37, no. 3 (March 1994).

Hibbard, Justin. "Knowing What We Know." *Information Week* (October 20, 1997).

Hinton, Gregory. "How Neural Networks Learn from Experience." *Scientific American* (September 1992).

Holland, John H. "Genetic Algorithms." *Scientific American* (July 1992).

"How Organizations Use Groupware to Improve a Wide Range of Business Processes." *I/S Analyzer* 35, no. 2 (February 1996).

Jacobs, Paul S., and **Lisa F. Rau.** "SCISOR: Extracting Information from On-line News." *Communications of the ACM* 33, no. 11 (November 1990).

Johansen, Robert. "Groupware: Future Directions and Wild Cards." *Journal of Organizational Computing* 1, no. 2 (April–June 1991).

Kanade, Takeo, Michael L. Reed, and **Lee E. Weiss.** "New Technologies and Applications in Robotics." *Communications of the ACM* 37, no. 3 (March 1994).

Kock, Ned, and **Robert J. McQueen.** "An Action Research Study of Effects of Asynchronous Groupware Support on Productivity and Outcome Quality in Process Redesign Groups." *Journal of Organizational Computing and Electronic Commerce* 8, no. 2 (1998).

Lee, Soonchul. "The Impact of Office Information Systems on Power and Influence." *Journal of Management Information Systems* 8, no. 2 (Fall 1991).

Leonard-Barton, Dorothy, and **John J. Sviokla.** "Putting Expert Systems to Work." *Harvard Business Review* (March–April 1988).

Lieberman, Henry. "Intelligent Graphics." *Communications of the ACM* 39, no. 8 (August 1996).

Liker, Jeffrey K., Mitchell Fleischer, Mitsuo Nagamachi, and **Michael S. Zonnevylle.** "Designers and Their Machines: CAD Use and Support in the U.S. and Japan." *Communications of the ACM* 35, no. 2 (February 1992).

Lin, Frank C., and **Mei Lin.** "Neural Networks in the Financial Industry." *AI Expert* (February 1993).

Lou, Hao, and **Richard W. Scannell.** "Acceptance of Groupware: The Relationships Among Use, Satisfaction, and Outcomes." *Journal of Organizational Computing and Electronic Commerce* 6, no. 2 (1996).

Maes, Patti. "Agents that Reduce Work and Information Overload." *Communications of the ACM* 38, no. 7 (July 1994).

Maes, Patti, Robert H. Guttman, and **Alexandros G. Moukas.** "Agents that Buy and Sell." *Communications of the ACM* 42, no. 3 (March 1999).

Malhotra, Yogesh. "Toward a Knowledge Ecology for Organizational White-Waters." Keynote Presentations for the Knowledge Ecology Fair '98 (1998).

Mann, Marina M., Richard L. Rudman, Thomas A. Jenckes, and **Barbara C. McNurlin.** "EPRINET: Leveraging Knowledge in the Electronic Industry." *MIS Quarterly* 15, no. 3 (September 1991).

Marsden, James R., David E. Pingry, and **Ming-Chian Ken Wang.** "Intelligent Information and Organization Structures: An Integrated Design Approach." *Journal of Organizational Computing* 2, no. 2 (1992).

McCarthy, John. "Generality in Artificial Intelligence." *Communications of the ACM* (December 1987).

McCune, Jenny C. "All Together Now." *Beyond Computing* (May 1996).

Meyer, Marc H., and **Kathleen Foley Curley.** "An Applied Framework for Classifying the Complexity of Knowledge-Based Systems." *MIS Quarterly* 15, no. 4 (December 1991).

Motiwalla, Luvai, and **Jay F. Nunamaker, Jr.** "Mail-Man: A Knowledge-Based Mail Assistant for Managers." *Journal of Organizational Computing* 2, no. 2 (1992).

Munakata, Toshinori, and **Yashvant Jani.** "Fuzzy Systems: An Overview." *Communications of the ACM* 37, no. 3 (March 1994).

Mykytyn, Kathleen, Peter P. Mykytyn, Jr., and **Craig W. Stinkman.** "Expert Systems: A Question of Liability." *MIS Quarterly* 14, no. 1 (March 1990).

Naj, Amal Kumar. "Virtual Reality Isn't a Fantasy for Surgeons." *The Wall Street Journal* (March 3, 1993).

Nash, Jim. "State of the Market, Art, Union, and 'Technology." *AI Expert* (January 1993).

Newquist, Harvey P. "AI at American Express." *AI Expert* (January 1993).

O'Leary, Daniel, Daniel Kuokka, and **Robert Plant.** "Artificial Intelligence and Virtual Organizations." *Communications of the ACM* 40, no. 1 (January 1997).

Orlikowski, Wanda J. "Learning from Notes: Organizational Issues in Groupware Implementation." Sloan Working Paper, no. 3428. Cambridge, MA: Sloan School of Management, Massachusetts Institute of Technology.

Panko, Raymond R. "Is Office Productivity Stagnant?" *MIS Quarterly* 15, no. 2 (June 1991).

Porat, Marc. "The Information Economy: Definition and Measurement." Washington, DC: U.S. Department of Commerce, Office of Telecommunications (May 1977).

Press, Lawrence. "Lotus Notes (Groupware) in Context." *Journal of Organizational Computing* 2, nos. 3 and 4 (1992b).

Roach, Stephen S. "Industrialization of the Information Economy." New York: Morgan Stanley and Co. (1984).

———. "Making Technology Work." New York: Morgan Stanley and Co. (1993).

———. "Services Under Siege—The Restructuring Imperative." *Harvard Business Review* (September–October 1991).

———. "Technology and the Service Sector." *Technological Forecasting and Social Change* 34, no. 4 (December 1988).

———. "The Hollow Ring of the Productivity Revival." *Harvard Business Review* (November–December 1996).

Ruhleder, Karen, and John Leslie King. "Computer Support for Work Across Space, Time, and Social Worlds." *Journal of Organizational Computing* 1, no. 4 (1991).

Rumelhart, David E., Bernard Widrow, and Michael A. Lehr. "The Basic Ideas in Neural Networks." *Communications of the ACM* 37, no. 3 (March 1994).

Schatz, Bruce R. "Building an Electronic Community System." *Journal of Management Information Systems* 8, no. 3 (Winter 1991–1992).

Schultze, Ulrike, and Betty Vandenbosch. "Information Overload in a Groupware Environment: Now You See It, Now You Don't." *Journal of Organizational Computing and Electronic Commerce* 8, no. 2 (1998).

Searle, John R. "Is the Brain's Mind a Computer Program?" *Scientific American* (January 1990).

Self, Kevin. "Designing with Fuzzy Logic." *Spectrum IEEE* (November 1990).

Selker, Ted. "Coach: A Teaching Agent that Learns." *Communications of the ACM* 37, no. 7 (July 1994).

Sheng, Olivia R. Liu, Luvai F. Motiwalla, Jay F. Nunamaker, Jr., and Douglas R. Vogel. "A Framework to Support Managerial Activities Using Office Information Systems." *Journal of Management Information Systems* 6, no. 3 (Winter 1989–1990).

Sibigtroth, James M. "Implementing Fuzzy Expert Rules in Hardware." *AI Expert* (April 1992).

Simon, H. A., and A. Newell. "Heuristic Problem Solving: The Next Advance in Operations Research." *Operations Research* 6 (January–February 1958).

Sproull, Lee, and Sara Kiesler. *Connections: New Ways of Working in the Networked Organization.* Cambridge, MA: MIT Press (1992).

Starbuck, William H. "Learning by Knowledge-Intensive Firms." *Journal of Management Studies* 29, no. 6 (November 1992).

Stein, Eric W. "A Method to Identify Candidates for Knowledge Acquisition." *Journal of Management Information Systems* 9, no. 2 (Fall 1992).

Stirland, Sarah. "Armed with Insight." *Wall Street and Technology* 16, no. 8 (August 1998).

Storey, Veda C., and Robert C. Goldstein. "Knowledge-Based Approaches to Database Design," *MIS Quarterly* 17, no. 1 (March 1993).

Stuart, Anne. "Under the Hood at Ford." *WebMaster* (June 1997).

Stylianou, Anthony C., Gregory R. Madey, and Robert D. Smith. "Selection Criteria for Expert System Shells: A Socio-Technical Framework." *Communications of the ACM* 35, no. 10 (October 1992).

Sviokla, John J. "An Examination of the Impact of Expert Systems on the Firm: The Case of XCON." *MIS Quarterly* 14, no. 5 (June 1990).

———. "Expert Systems and Their Impact on the Firm: The Effects of PlanPower Use on the Information Processing Capacity of the Financial Collaborative." *Journal of Management Information Systems* 6, no. 3 (Winter 1989–1990).

Tam, Kar Yan. "Automated Construction of Knowledge-Bases from Examples." *Information Systems Research* 1, no. 2 (June 1990).

Tank, David W., and John J. Hopfield. "Collective Computation in Neuronlike Circuits." *Scientific American* (October 1987).

Trippi, Robert, and Efraim Turban. "The Impact of Parallel and Neural Computing on Managerial Decision Making." *Journal of Management Information Systems* 6, no. 3 (Winter 1989–1990).

Turban, Efraim, and Paul R. Watkins. "Integrating Expert Systems and Decision Support Systems." *MIS Quarterly* (June 1986).

Wallich, Paul. "Silicon Babies." *Scientific American* (December 1991).

Waltz, David L. "Artificial Intelligence." *Scientific American* (December 1982).

Weitzel, John R., and Larry Kerschberg. "Developing Knowledge Based Systems: Reorganizing the System Development Life Cycle." *Communications of the ACM* (April 1989).

Weizenbaum, Joseph. *Computer Power and Human Reason—From Judgment to Calculation.* San Francisco: Freeman (1976).

White, George M. "Natural Language Understanding and Speech Recognition." *Communications of the ACM* 33, no. 8 (August 1990).

Wijnhoven, Fons. "Designing Organizational Memories: Concept and Method." *Journal of Organizational Computing and Electronic Commerce* 8, no. 1 (1998).

Widrow, Bernard, David E. Rumelhart, and Michael A. Lehr. "Neural Networks: Applications in Industry, Business, and Science." *Communications of the ACM* 37, no. 3 (March 1994).

Wong, David, Noemi Paciorek, and Dana Moore. "Java-Based Mobile Agents." *Communications of the ACM* 42, no. 3 (March 1999).

Zadeh, Lotfi A. "The Calculus of Fuzzy If/Then Rules." *AI Expert* (March 1992).

Zadeh, Lotfi A. "Fuzzy Logic, Neural Networks, and Soft Computing." *Communications of the ACM* 37, no. 3 (March 1994).

CHAPTER 15

Alavi, Maryam, and Erich A. Joachimsthaler. "Revisiting DSS Implementation Research: A Meta-Analysis of the Literature and Suggestions for Researchers." *MIS Quarterly* 16, no. 1 (March 1992).

Anthes, Gary H. "Notes System Sends Federal Property Data Nationwide." *Computerworld* (August 8, 1994).

Bonczek, R. H., C. W. Holsapple, and A. B. Whinston. "Representing Modeling Knowledge with First Order Predicate Calculus." *Operations Research* 1 (1982).

Brachman, Ronald J., Tom Khabaza, Willi Kloesgen, Gregory Piatetsky-Shapiro, and Evangelos Simoudis. "Mining Business Databases." *Communications of the ACM* 39, no. 11 (November 1996).

Briggs, Robert O., Mark Adkins, Daniel Mittelman, John Kruse, Scot Miller, and Jay F. Nuramaker, Jr. "A Technology Transition Model Derived from Field Investigation of GSS Use Aboard the USS Coronado." *Journal of Management Information Systems* 15, no. 3 (Winter 1998–1999).

Caouette, Margarette J., and Bridget N. O'Connor. "The Impact of Group Support Systems on Corporate Teams' Stages of Development." *Journal of Organizational Computing and Electronic Commerce* 8, no. 1 (1998).

Chidambaram, Laku. "Relational Development in Computer-Supported Groups." *MIS Quarterly* 20, no. 2 (June 1996).

Chidambaram, Laku, Robert P. Bostrom, and Bayard E. Wynne. "A Longitudinal Study of the Impact of Group Decision Support Systems on Group Development." *Journal of Management Information Systems* 7, no. 3 (Winter 1990–1991).

Dennis, Alan R. "Information Exchange and Use in Group Decision Making: You Can Lead a Group to Information, but You Can't Make It Think." *MIS Quarterly* 20, no. 4 (December 1996).

Dennis, Alan R., Craig K. Tyran, Douglas R. Vogel, and Jay Nunamaker, Jr. "Group Support Systems for Strategic Planning." *Journal of Management Information Systems* 14, no. 1 (Summer 1997).

Dennis, Alan R., Jay E. Aronson, William G. Henriger, and Edward D. Walker III. "Structuring Time and Task in Electronic Brainstorming." *MIS Quarterly* 23, no. 1 (March 1999).

Dennis, Alan R., Jay F. Nunamaker, Jr., and Douglas R. Vogel. "A Comparison of Laboratory and Field Research in the Study of Electronic Meeting Systems." *Journal of Management Information Systems* 7, no. 3 (Winter 1990–1991).

Dennis, Alan R., Joey F. George, Len M. Jessup, Jay F. Nunamaker, and Douglas R. Vogel. "Information Technology to Support Electronic Meetings." *MIS Quarterly* 12, no. 4 (December 1988).

Dennis, Alan R., Sridar K. Pootheri, and Vijaya L. Natarajan. "Lessons from Early Adopters of Web Groupware." *Journal of Management Information Systems* 14, no. 4 (Spring 1998).

DeSanctis, Geraldine, Marshall Scott Poole, Howard Lewis, and George Desharnias. "Computing in Quality Team Meetings." *Journal of Management Information Systems* 8, no. 3 (Winter 1991–1992).

DeSanctis, Geraldine, and R. Brent Gallupe. "A Foundation for the Study of Group Decision Support Systems." *Management Science* 33, no. 5 (May 1987).

Dhar, Vasant, and Roger Stein. *Intelligent Decision Support Methods: The Science of Knowledge Work.* Upper Saddle River, NJ: Prentice Hall (1997).

Dutta, Soumitra, Berend Wierenga, and Arco Dalebout. "Designing Management Support Systems Using an Integrative Perspective." *Communications of the ACM* 40, no. 6 (June 1997).

Easton, George K., Joey F. George, Jay F. Nunamaker, Jr., and Mark O. Pendergast. "Two Different Electronic Meeting Systems." *Journal of Management Information Systems* 7, no. 3 (Winter 1990–1991).

Edelstein, Herb. "Technology How To: Mining Data Warehouses." *Information Week* (January 8, 1996).

El Sawy, Omar. "Personal Information Systems for Strategic Scanning in Turbulent Environments." *MIS Quarterly* 9, no. 1 (March 1985).

El Sherif, Hisham, and Omar A. El Sawy. "Issue-Based Decision Support Systems for the Egyptian Cabinet." *MIS Quarterly* 12, no. 4 (December 1988).

Etzioni, Oren. "The World-Wide Web: Quagmire or Gold Mine?" *Communications of the ACM* 39, no. 11 (November 1996).

Fayyad, Usama, Gregory Piatetsky-Shapiro, and Padhraic Smyth. "The KDD Process for Extracting Useful Knowledge from Volumes of Data." *Communications of the ACM* 39, no. 11 (November 1996).

Fjermestad, Jerry. "An Integrated Framework for Group Support Systems." *Journal of Organizational Computing and Electronic Commerce* 8, no. 2 (1998).

Fjermestad, Jerry, and Starr Roxanne Hiltz. "An Assessment of Group Support Systems Experimental Research: Methodology, and Results." *Journal of Management Information Systems* 15, no. 3 (Winter, 1998–1999).

Gallupe, R. Brent, Geraldine DeSanctis, and Gary W. Dickson. "Computer-Based Support for Group Problem-Finding: An Experimental Investigation." *MIS Quarterly* 12, no. 2 (June 1988).

Gerber, Cheryl. "Excavate Your Data." *Datamation* (May 1, 1996).

Ginzberg, Michael J., W. R. Reitman, and E. A. Stohr, eds. *Decision Support Systems.* New York: North Holland Publishing Co. (1982).

Gopal, Abhijit, Robert P. Bostrum, and Wynne W. Chin. "Applying Adaptive Structuration Theory to Investigate the Process of Group Support Systems Use." *Journal of Management Information Systems* 9, no. 3 (Winter 1992–1993).

Grobowski, Ron, Chris McGoff, Doug Vogel, Ben Martz, and Jay Nunamaker. "Implementing Electronic Meeting Systems at IBM: Lessons Learned and Success Factors." *MIS Quarterly* 14, no. 4 (December 1990).

Henderson, John C., and David A. Schilling. "Design and Implementation of Decision Support Systems in the Public Sector." *MIS Quarterly* (June 1985).

Hiltz, Starr Roxanne, Kenneth Johnson, and Murray Turoff. "Group Decision Support: Designated Human Leaders and Statistical Feedback." *Journal of Management Information Systems* 8, no. 2 (Fall 1991).

Ho, T. H., and K. S. Raman. "The Effect of GDSS on Small Group Meetings." *Journal of Management Information Systems* 8, no. 2 (Fall 1991).

Hogue, Jack T. "Decision Support Systems and the Traditional Computer Information System Function: An Examination of Relationships During DSS Application Development." *Journal of Management Information Systems* (Summer 1985).

Hogue, Jack T. "A Framework for the Examination of Management Involvement in Decision Support Systems." *Journal of Management Information Systems* 4, no. 1 (Summer 1987).

Houdeshel, George, and Hugh J. Watson. "The Management Information and Decision Support (MIDS) System at Lockheed, Georgia." *MIS Quarterly* 11, no. 2 (March 1987).

Imielinski, Tomasz, and Heikki Mannila. "A Database Perspective on Knowledge Discovery." *Communications of the ACM* 39, no. 11 (November 1996).

Jessup, Leonard M., Terry Connolly, and Jolene Galegher. "The Effects of Anonymity on GDSS Group Process with an Idea-Generating Task." *MIS Quarterly* 14, no. 3 (September 1990).

Jones, Jack William, Carol Saunders, and Raymond McLeod, Jr., "Media Usage and Velocity in Executive Information Acquisition: An Exploratory Study." *European Journal of Information Systems* 2 (1993).

Kalakota, Ravi, Jan Stallaert, and Andrew B. Whinston. "Worldwide Real-Time Decision Support Systems for Electronic Commerce Applications." *Journal of Organizational Computing and Electronic Commerce* 6, no. 1 (1996).

Kasper, George M. "A Theory of Decision Support System Design for User Calibration." *Information Systems Research* 7, no. 2 (June 1996).

Keen, Peter G. W., and M. S. Scott Morton. *Decision Support Systems: An Organizational Perspective.* Reading, MA: Addison-Wesley (1982).

King, John. "Successful Implementation of Large Scale Decision Support Systems: Computerized Models in U.S. Economic Policy Making." *Systems Objectives Solutions* (November 1983).

Kraemer, Kenneth L., and John Leslie King. "Computer-Based Systems for Cooperative Work and Group Decision Making." *ACM Computing Surveys* 20, no. 2 (June 1988).

Laudon, Kenneth C. *Communications Technology and Democratic Participation.* New York: Praeger (1977).

Le Blanc, Louis A., and Kenneth A. Kozar. "An Empirical Investigation of the Relationship Between DSS Usage and System Performance." *MIS Quarterly* 14, no. 3 (September 1990).

Leidner, Dorothy E., and Joyce Elam. "Executive Information Systems: Their Impact on Executive Decision Making." *Journal of Management Information Systems* (Winter 1993–1994).

Leidner, Dorothy E., and Joyce Elam. "The Impact of Executive Information Systems on Organizational Design, Intelligence, and Decision Making." *Organization Science* 6, no. 6 (November–December 1995).

Lewe, Henrik, and Helmut Krcmar. "A Computer-Supported Cooperative Work Research Laboratory." *Journal of Management Information Systems* 8, no. 3 (Winter 1991–1992).

Lou, Hao, and Richard W. Scannell. "Acceptance of Groupware: The Relationships among Use, Satisfaction, and Outcomes." *Journal of Organizational Computing and Electronic Commerce* 6, no. 2 (1996).

McLeod, Poppy Lauretta, and Jeffry R. Liker. "Electronic Meeting Systems: Evidence from a Low Structure Environment." *Information Systems Research* 3, no. 3 (September 1992).

Meador, Charles L., and Peter G. W. Keen. "Setting Priorities for DSS Development." *MIS Quarterly* (June 1984).

Miranda, Shaila M., and Robert P. Bostrum. "The Impact of Group Support Systems on Group Conflict and Conflict Management." *Journal of Management Information Systems* 10, no. 3 (Winter 1993–1994).

Mohan, Lakshmi, William K. Holstein, and Robert B. Adams. "EIS: It Can Work in the Public Sector." *MIS Quarterly* 14, no. 4 (December 1990).

Nidumolu, Sarma R., Seymour E. Goodman, Douglas R. Vogel, and Ann K. Danowitz. "Information Technology for Local Administration Support: The Governorates Project in Egypt." *MIS Quarterly* 20, no. 2 (June 1996).

Niederman, Fred, Catherine M. Beise, and Peggy M. Beranek. "Issues and Concerns about Computer-Supported Meetings: The Facilitator's Perspective." *MIS Quarterly* 20, no. 1 (March 1996).

Nunamaker, J. F., Alan R. Dennis, Joseph S. Valacich, Douglas R. Vogel, and Joey F. George. "Electronic Meeting Systems to Support Group Work." *Communications of the ACM* 34, no. 7 (July 1991).

Nunamaker, Jay, Robert O. Briggs, Daniel D. Mittleman, Douglas R. Vogel, and Pierre A. Balthazard. "Lessons from a Dozen Years of Group Support Systems Research: A Discussion of Lab and Field Findings." *Journal of Management Information Systems* 13, no. 3 (Winter 1997).

O'Keefe, Robert M., and Tim McEachern. "Web-based Customer Decision Support Systems." *Communications of the ACM* 41, no. 3 (March 1998).

Panko, Raymond R. "Managerial Communication Patterns." *Journal of Organizational Computing* 2, no. 1 (1992).

Post, Brad Quinn. "A Business Case Framework for Group Support Technology." *Journal of Management Information Systems* 9, no. 3 (Winter 1992–1993).

Rockart, John F., and David W. DeLong. "Executive Support Systems and the Nature of Work." Working Paper: Management in the 1990s. Sloan School of Management (April 1986).

Rockart, John F., and David W. DeLong. *Executive Support Systems: The Emergence of Top Management Computer Use.* Homewood, IL: Dow-Jones Irwin (1988).

Sambamurthy, V., and Marshall Scott Poole. "The Effects of Variations in Capabilities of GDSS Designs on Management of Cognitive Conflict in Groups." *Information Systems Research* 3, no. 3 (September 1992).

Sanders, G. Lawrence, and James F. Courtney. "A Field Study of Organizational Factors Influencing DSS Success." *MIS Quarterly* (March 1985).

Sharda, Ramesh, and David M. Steiger. "Inductive Model Analysis Systems: Enhancing Model Analysis in Decision Support Systems." *Information Systems Research* 7, no. 3 (September 1996).

Silver, Mark S. "Decision Support Systems: Directed and Nondirected Change." *Information Systems Research* 1, no. 1 (March 1990).

Sprague, R. H., and E. D. Carlson. *Building Effective Decision Support Systems.* Englewood Cliffs, NJ: Prentice Hall (1982).

Stefik, Mark, Gregg Foster, Daniel C. Bobrow, Kenneth Kahn, Stan Lanning, and Luch Suchman. "Beyond the Chalkboard: Computer Support for Collaboration and Problem Solving in Meetings." *Communications of the ACM* (January 1987).

"The New Role for 'Executive Information Systems.'" *I/S Analyzer* (January 1992).

Turban, Efraim and Jay E. Aronson. *Decision Support Systems and Intelligent Systems: Management Support Systems,* 5th ed. Upper Saddle River, NJ: Prentice Hall (1998).

Turoff, Murray. "Computer-Mediated Communication Requirements for Group Support." *Journal of Organizational Computing* 1, no. 1 (January–March 1991).

Tyran, Craig K., Alan R. Dennis, Douglas R. Vogel, and J. F. Nunamaker, Jr. "The Application of Electronic Meeting Technology to Support Senior Management." *MIS Quarterly* 16, no. 3 (September 1992).

Vandenbosch, Betty, and Michael J. Ginzberg. "Lotus Notes and Collaboration: Plus ca change . . ." *Journal of Management Information Systems* 13, no. 3 (Winter 1997).

Varney, Sarah E. "Database Marketing Predicts Customer Loyalty." *Datamation* (September 1996).

Vogel, Douglas R., Jay F. Nunamaker, William Benjamin Martz, Jr., Ronald Grobowski, and Christopher McGoff. "Electronic Meeting System Experience at IBM." *Journal of Management Information Systems* 6, no. 3 (Winter 1989–1990).

Volonino, Linda, and Hugh J. Watson. "The Strategic Business Objectives Method for EIS Development." *Journal of Management Information Systems* 7, no. 3 (Winter 1990–1991).

Walls, Joseph G., George R. Widmeyer, and Omar A. El Sawy. "Building an Information System Design Theory for Vigilant EIS." *Information Systems Research* 3, no. 1 (March 1992).

Watson, Hugh J., Astrid Lipp, Pamela Z. Jackson, Abdelhafid Dahmani, and William B. Fredenberger. "Organizational Support for Decision Support Systems." *Journal of Management Information Systems* 5, no. 4 (Spring 1989).

Watson, Hugh J., R. Kelly Rainer, Jr., and Chang E. Koh. "Executive Information Systems: A Framework for Development and a Survey of Current Practices." *MIS Quarterly* 15, no. 1 (March 1991).

Watson, Richard T., Geraldine DeSanctis, and Marshall Scott Poole. "Using a GDSS to Facilitate Group Consensus: Some Intended and Unintended Consequences." *MIS Quarterly* 12, no. 3 (September 1988).

Watson, Richard T., Teck-Hua Ho, and K. S. Raman. "Culture: A Fourth Dimension of Group Support Systems." *Communications of the ACM* 37, no. 10 (October 1994).

Wilder, Clinton. "Tapping the Pipeline." *Information Week* (March 15, 1999).

Wreden, Nick. "Business Intelligence: Turning on Success," *Beyond Computing* (September 1997).

Zigurs, Ilze, and Kenneth A. Kozar. "An Exploratory Study of Roles in Computer-Supported Groups." *MIS Quarterly* 18, no. 3 (September 1994).

CHAPTER 16

Abdel-Hamid, Tarek K. "The Economics of Software Quality Assurance: A Simulation-Based Case Study." *MIS Quarterly* (September 1988).

Alberts, David S. "The Economics of Software Quality Assurance." Washington, DC: National Computer Conference, 1976 Proceedings.

Anderson, Ross J. "Why Cryptosystems Fail." *Communications of the ACM* 37, no. 11 (November 1994).

Anthes, Gary H. "Viruses Continue to Wreak Havoc at Many U.S. Companies." *Computerworld* (June 28, 1993).

Banker, Rajiv D., Robert J. Kaufmann, and Rachna Kumar. "An Empirical Test of Object-Based Output Measurement Metrics in a Computer-Aided Software Engineering (CASE) Environment." *Journal of Management Information Systems* 8, no. 3 (Winter 1991–1992).

Banker, Rajiv D., Srikant M. Datar, Chris F. Kemerer, and Dani Zweig. "Software Complexity and Maintenance Costs." *Communications of the ACM* 36, no. 11 (November 1993).

Banker, Rajiv D., and Chris F. Kemerer. "Performance Evaluation Metrics in Information Systems Development: A Principal-Agent Model." *Information Systems Research* 3, no. 4 (December 1992).

Boehm, Barry W. "Understanding and Controlling Software Costs." *IEEE Transactions on Software Engineering* 14, no. 10 (October 1988).

Boockholdt, J. L. "Implementing Security and Integrity in Micro-Mainframe Networks." *MIS Quarterly* 13, no. 2 (June 1989).

Borning, Alan. "Computer System Reliability and Nuclear War." *Communications of the ACM* 30, no. 2 (February 1987).

Buss, Martin D. J., and Lynn M. Salerno. "Common Sense and Computer Security." *Harvard Business Review* (March–April 1984).

Chaum, David. "Security Without Identification: Transaction Systems to Make Big Brother Obsolete." *Communications of the ACM* 28 (October 1985).

Corbato, Fernando J. "On Building Systems that Will Fail." *Communications of the ACM* 34, no. 9 (September 1991).

Davis, Beth. "In Certificates We Trust." *Information Week,* (March 23, 1998).

Dekleva, Sasa M. "The Influence of Information Systems Development Approach on Maintenance." *MIS Quarterly* 16, no. 3 (September 1992).

DeMarco, Tom. *Structured Analysis and System Specification.* New York: Yourdon Press (1978).

Dijkstra, E. "Structured Programming." In *Classics in Software Engineering,* edited by Edward Nash Yourdon. New York: Yourdon Press (1979).

Domges, Rolf, and Klaus Pohl. "Adapting Traceability Environments to Project-Specific Needs." *Communications of the ACM* 41, no. 12 (December 1998).

Dutta, Soumitra, Luk N. Van Wassenhove, and Selvan Kulandaiswamy. "Benchmarking European Software Management Practices." *Communications of the ACM* 41, no. 6 (June 1998).

Fraser, Martin D., and Vijay K. Vaishnavi. "A Formal Specifications Maturity Model." *Communications of the ACM* 40, no. 12 (December 1997).

Forrest, Stephanie, Steven A. Hofmeyr, and Anil Somayaji. "Computer Immunology." *Communications of the ACM* 40, no. 10 (October 1997).

Gane, Chris, and Trish Sarson. *Structured Systems Analysis: Tools and Techniques.* Englewood Cliffs, NJ: Prentice Hall (1979).

Halper, Stanley D., Glenn C. Davis, Jarlath P. O'Neill-Dunne, and Pamela R. Pfau. *Handbook of EDP Auditing.* Boston: Warren, Gorham, and Lamont (1985).

Hoffman, Lance. *Rogue Programs.* New York: Van Nostrand Reinhold (1990).

Jarzabek, Stan, and Riri Huang. "The Case for User-Centered CASE Tools." *Communications of the ACM* 41, no. 8 (August 1998).

Johnson, Philip M. "Reengineering Inspection." *Communications of the ACM* 41, no. 2 (February 1998).

Kahane, Yehuda, Seev Neumann, and Charles S. Tapiero. "Computer Backup Pools, Disaster Recovery, and Default Risk." *Communications of the ACM* 31, no. 1 (January 1988).

Kaplan, David, Ramayya Krishnan, Rema Padman, and James Peters. "Assessing Data Quality in Accounting Information Systems." *Communications of the ACM* 41, no. 2 (February 1998).

Kemerer, Chris F. "Progress, Obstacles, and Opportunities in Software Engineering Economics." *Communications of the ACM* 41, no. 8 (August 1998).

Keyes, Jessica. "New Metrics Needed for New Generation." *Software Magazine* (May 1992).

King, Julia. "It's C.Y.A. Time." *Computerworld* (March 30, 1992).

Klein, Barbara D., Dale L. Goodhue, and Gordon B. Davis. "Can Humans Detect Errors in Data?" *MIS Quarterly* 21, no. 2 (June 1997).

Knowles, Ann. "EDI Experiments with the Net." *Software Magazine* (January 1997).

Laudon, Kenneth C. "Data Quality and Due Process in Large Interorganizational Record Systems." *Communications of the ACM* 29 (January 1986a).

———. *Dossier Society: Value Choices in the Design of National Information Systems.* New York: Columbia University Press (1986b).

Lientz, Bennett P., and E. Burton Swanson. *Software Maintenance Management.* Reading, MA: Addison-Wesley (1980).

Littlewood, Bev, and Lorenzo Strigini. "The Risks of Software." *Scientific American* 267, no. 5 (November 1992).

———. "Validation of Ultra-high Dependability for Software-based Systems." *Communications of the ACM* 36, no. 11 (November 1993).

Loch, Karen D., Houston H. Carr, and Merrill E. Warkentin. "Threats to Information Systems: Today's Reality, Yesterday's Understanding." *MIS Quarterly* 16, no. 2 (June 1992).

McPartlin, John P. "The True Cost of Downtime." *Information Week* (August 3, 1992).

Mazzucchelli, Louis. "Structured Analysis Can Streamline Software Design." *Computerworld* (December 9, 1985).

Needham, Roger M. "Denial of Service: An Example." *Communications of the ACM* 37, no. 11 (November 1994).

Nerson, Jean-Marc. "Applying Object-Oriented Analysis and Design." *Communications of the ACM* 35, no. 9 (September 1992).

Neumann, Peter G. "Risks Considered Global(ly)." *Communications of the ACM* 35, no. 1 (January 1993).

Oppliger, Rolf. "Internet Security, Firewalls, and Beyond." *Communications of the ACM* 40, no.7 (May 1997).

Orr, Kenneth. "Data Quality and Systems Theory." *Communications of the ACM* 41, no. 2 (February 1998).

Parsons, Jeffrey, and Yair Wand. "Using Objects for Systems Analysis." *Communications of the ACM* 40, no. 12 (December 1997).

Post, Gerald V., and J. David Diltz. "A Stochastic Dominance Approach to Risk Analysis of Computer Systems." *MIS Quarterly* (December 1986).

Putnam, L. H., and A. Fitzsimmons. "Estimating Software Costs." *Datamation* (September 1979, October 1979, and November 1979).

Rainer, Rex Kelley, Jr., Charles A. Snyder, and Houston H. Carr. "Risk Analysis for Information Technology." *Journal of Management Information Systems* 8, no. 1 (Summer 1991).

Redman, Thomas. "The Impact of Poor Data Quality on the Typical Enterprise." *Communications of the ACM* 41, no. 2 (February 1998).

Rettig, Marc. "Software Teams." *Communications of the ACM* 33, no. 10 (October 1990).

Segen, Arie, Janna Porra, and Malu Roldan. "Internet Security and the Case of Bank of America." *Communications of the ACM* 41, no. 10 (October 1998).

Slaughter, Sandra A., Donald E. Harter, and Mayuram S. Krishnan. "Evaluating the Cost of Software Quality." *Communications of the ACM* 41, no. 8 (August 1998).

Straub, Detmar W. "Controlling Computer Abuse: An Empirical Study of Effective Security Countermeasures." Curtis L. Carlson School of Management, University of Minnesota (July 20, 1987).

Straub, Detmar W., and Richard J. Welke. "Coping with Systems Risk: Security Planning Models for Management Decision Making." *MIS Quarterly* 22, no. 4 (December 1998).

Strong, Diane M., Yang W. Lee, and Richard Y. Wang. "Data Quality in Context." *Communications of the ACM* 40, no. 5 (May 1997).

Swanson, Kent, Dave McComb, Jill Smith, and Don McCubbrey. "The Application Software Factory: Applying Total Quality Techniques to Systems Development." *MIS Quarterly* 15, no. 4 (December 1991).

Tate, Paul. "Risk! The Third Factor." *Datamation* (April 15, 1988).

Tayi, Giri Kumar, and Donald P. Ballou. "Examining Data Quality." *Communications of the ACM* 41, no. 2 (February 1998).

Thyfault, Mary E., and Stephanie Stahl. "Weak Links." *Information Week* (August 10, 1992).

United States General Accounting Office. "Computer Security: Virus Highlights Needed for Improved Internet Management." GAO/IMTEC-89-57 (June 1989).

———. "Patriot Missile Defense: Software Problem Led to System Failure at Dharan, Saudi Arabia." GAO/IMTEC-92-26 (February 1992).

Wand, Yair, and Richard Y. Wang. "Anchoring Data Quality Dimensions in Ontological Foundations." *Communications of the ACM* 39, no. 11 (November 1996).

Wang, Richard. "A Product Perspective on Total Data Quality Management." *Communications of the ACM* 41, no. 2 (February 1998).

Wang, Richard Y., Yang W. Lee, Leo L. Pipino, and Diane M. Strong. "Manage Your Information as a Product." *Sloan Management Review* 39, no. 4 (Summer 1998).

Weber, Ron. *EDP Auditing: Conceptual Foundations and Practice,* 2nd ed. New York: McGraw-Hill (1988).

Wilson, Linda. "Devil in Your Data." *Information Week* (August 31, 1992).

Yourdon, Edward, and L. L. Constantine. *Structural Design.* New York: Yourdon Press (1978).

CHAPTER 17

Blanning, Robert W. "Establishing a Corporate Presence on the Internet in Singapore." *Journal of Organizational Computing and Electronic Commerce* 9, no. 1 (1999).

Burkhardt, Grey E., Seymour E. Goodman, Arun Mehta, and Larry Press. "The Internet in India: Better Times Ahead?" *Communications of the ACM* 41, no. 11 (November 1998).

Cash, James I., F. Warren McFarlan, James L. McKenney, and Lynda M. Applegate. *Corporate Information Systems Management,* 4th ed. Homewood, IL: Irwin (1996).

Chismar, William G., and Laku Chidambaram. "Telecommunications and the Structuring of U.S. Multinational Corporations." *International Information Systems* 1, no. 4 (October 1992).

Cox, Butler. *Globalization: The IT Challenge.* Sunnyvale, CA: Amdahl Executive Institute (1991).

Deans, Candace P., and Michael J. Kane. *International Dimensions of Information Systems and Technology.* Boston, MA: PWS-Kent (1992).

Deans, Candace P., Kirk R. Karwan, Martin D. Goslar, David A. Ricks, and Brian Toyne. "Key International Issues in U.S.-Based Multinational Corporations." *Journal of Management Information Systems* 7, no. 4 (Spring 1991).

Dutta, Amitava. "Telecommunications Infrastructure in Developing Nations." *International Information Systems* 1, no. 3 (July 1992).

Holland, Christopher, Geoff Lockett, and Ian Blackman. "Electronic Data Interchange Implementation: A Comparison of U.S. and European Cases." *International Information Systems* 1, no. 4 (October 1992).

Ives, Blake, and Sirkka Jarvenpaa. "Applications of Global Information Technology: Key Issues for Management." *MIS Quarterly* 15, no. 1 (March 1991).

———. "Global Business Drivers: Aligning Information Technology to Global Business Strategy. *IBM Systems Journal* 32, no. 1 (1993).

———. "Global Information Technology: Some Lessons from Practice." *International Information Systems* 1, no. 3 (July 1992).

Jarvenpaa, Sirkka L., Kathleen Knoll, and Dorothy Leidner. "Is Anybody Out There? Antecedents of Trust in Global Virtual Teams." *Journal of Management Information Systems* 14, no. 4 (Spring 1998).

Karin, Jahangir, and Benn R. Konsynski. "Globalization and Information Management Strategies." *Journal of Management Information Systems* 7 (Spring 1991).

Keen, Peter. *Shaping the Future.* Cambridge, MA: Harvard Business School Press (1991).

King, William R., and Vikram Sethi. "An Analysis of International Information Regimes." *International Information Systems* 1, no. 1 (January 1992).

Levy, David. "Lean Production in an International Supply Chain." *Sloan Management Review* (Winter 1997).

Mannheim, Marvin L. "Global Information Technology: Issues and Strategic Opportunities." *International Information Systems* 1, no. 1 (January 1992).

Manson, Herman. "Where Politics, Economics, and the Internet Meet." *Computerworld Emmerce* (May 18, 1998).

Nelson, R. Ryan, Ira R. Weiss, and Kazumi Yamazaki. "Information Resource Management within Multinational Corporations: A Cross-Cultural Comparison of the U.S. and Japan." *International Information Systems* 1, no. 4 (October 1992).

Neumann, Seev. "Issues and Opportunities in International Information Systems." *International Information Systems* 1, no. 4 (October 1992).

Palvia, Shailendra, Prashant Palvia, and Ronald Zigli, eds. *The Global Issues of Information Technology Management.* Harrisburg, PA: Idea Group Publishing (1992).

Quelch, John A., and Lisa R. Klein. "The Internet and International Marketing." *Sloan Management Review* (Spring 1996).

Roche, Edward M. *Managing Information Technology in Multinational Corporations.* New York: Macmillan (1992).

Sadowsky, George. "Network Connectivity for Developing Countries." *Communications of the ACM* 36, no. 8 (August 1993).

Stahl, Stephanie. "Global Networks: The Headache Continues." *Information Week* (October 12, 1992).

Steinbart, Paul John, and Ravinder Nath. "Problems and Issues in the Management of International Data Networks." *MIS Quarterly* 16, no. 1 (March 1992).

Straub, Detmar W. "The Effect of Culture on IT Diffusion: E-Mail and FAX in Japan and the U.S." *Information Systems Research* 5, no. 1 (March 1994).

Tan, Zixiang (Alex), Milton Mueller, and Will Foster. "China's New Internet Regulations: Two Steps Forward, One Step Backward." *Communications of the ACM* 40, no. 12 (December 1997).

Tractinsky, Noam, and Sirkka L. Jarvenpaa. "Information Systems Design Decisions in a Global Versus Domestic Context." *MIS Quarterly* 19, no. 4 (December 1995).

Walsham, Geoffrey, and Sundeys Sahay. "GIS and District Level Administration in India: Problems and Opportunities." *MIS Quarterly* 23, no. 1 (March 1999).

Watson, Richard T., Gigi G. Kelly, Robert D. Galliers, and James C. Brancheau. "Key Issues in Information Systems Management: An International Perspective." *Journal of Management Information Systems* 13, no. 4 (Spring 1997).

Wong, Poh-Kam. "Leveraging the Global Information Revolution for Economic Development: Singapore's Evolving Information Industry Strategy." *Information Systems Research* 9, no. 4 (December 1998).

CHAPTER 18

Abramson, Gary. "Cluster Power." *CIO Magazine* (August 15, 1998).

Adhikari, Richard. "The ERP-to-ERP Connection." *Information Week* (October 19, 1998).

Anderson, Erin, George S. Day, and V. Kasturi Rangan. "Strategic Channel Design." *Sloan Management Review* (Summer 1997).

Brancheau, James C., Brian D. Janz, and James C. Wetherbe. "Key Issues in Information Systems Management: 1994–1995 SIM Delphi Results." *MIS Quarterly* 20, no. 2 (June 1996).

Brynjolfsson, Erik. "The Contribution of Information Technology to Consumer Welfare." *Information Systems Research* 7, no. 3 (September, 1996).

Cecere, Marc. "Architecting Architecture." *CIO Magazine* (April 15, 1998).

Cone, Edward. "Cautious Automation." *Information Week* (October 19, 1998).

Davenport, Tom. "Living with ERP." *CIO Magazine* (December 1998).

Davenport, Tom. "Putting the Enterprise into Enterprise Systems." *Harvard Business Review* (July–August 1998).

Edwards, John. "Expanding the Boundaries of ERP." *CIO Magazine* (July 1, 1998).

Gillooly, Caryn. "Disillusionment." *Information Week* (February 16, 1998).

Hansell, Saul. "Is This the Factory of the Future?" *The New York Times* (July 26, 1998).

King, W. R. "Creating a Strategic Capabilities Architecture." *Information Systems Management* 12, no. 1 (Winter 1995).

Laudon, Kenneth C. "CIOs Beware: Very Large Scale Systems." Center for Research on Information Systems, New York University Stern School of Business, working paper (1989).

Laudon, Kenneth C. "The Promise and Potential of Enterprise Systems and Industrial Networks." Working paper, The Concours Group. Copyright Kenneth C. Laudon (1999).

Melymuka, Kathleen. "An Expanding Universe." *Computerworld* (September 14, 1998).

Schneider, Helmut, and Edward E. Watson, "Using ERP Systems in Education," *Communications of the Association for Information Systems* 1 (February 1999).

Slater, Derek. "The Hidden Costs of Enterprise Software." *CIO Magazine* (January 15, 1998).

Weill, Peter, and Marianne Broadbent. *Leveraging the New Infrastructure.* Cambridge, MA: Harvard Business School Press (1998).

Indexes

Name Index

Organization Index

International Organization Index

Heineken Netherlands B.V., ICS20-26
Hitachi, 452
Hohenheim University, ICS10
Honda Motor Company, 156, 573

IBM, ICS3
Imperial Oil Resources Ltd., 43
Ingram Micro Inc., 22
Intel, 535

Jigsaw Consortiums system, 59, 60

Kellogg Co., 527-28
Kentucky Fried Chicken, 535
Kimberly-Clark, 60
KPMG Management Consultants, ICS21

La Scala, 246
Lufthansa Airlines, 244

McDonald's, 535
Manitoba Public Insurance, 259, 260, 344t
Marine Power Europe, 533
Marks & Spencer, 97
Matsushita, 452
Mazda, 157
Merisel Inc., 22
Mitsubishi Heavy Industries, 342, 344, 450, 452
Mobil Europe, 397
Mobil Oil Canada Properties Ltd., 43
Mrs. Fields Cookies, 535

Navigation Canada, 161, 162
Nestlé SA, 277
Newsworld Online, 184
Nikko Securities, 452
Nissan, 157
Nolan, Norton, Inc., ICS21
Nova Scotia Resources Ltd., 43

Open Text Corporation, 312, 430, 457

PA Consulting, ICS2
Parsons Brinckerhoff, 410
Perot Systems, 383
Piaggio, 573
Pirelli Group, 550-51
Price Waterhouse, 177
Promodes, 317

Ricoh, 452
Rikshospitalet, 193, 194
Rolls Royce Aerospace Group, 382-83
Royal Bank of Canada, 487, 569
Royal Dutch Shell, 33

Sabena, 408
Sable Offshore Energy Project, 42, 43
Safeway, 574
Sanyo, 452
SAP AG, 378, 396-97, 402, 437, 570, 582, 583
Schlumberger Ltd., 300, 301
Sealand Transportation, 531
Sendai, 450
Shell Canada Ltd., 43
Sinanet.com, 18
Sony, 536
Spanish CASA, 574
Stone Rich Sight (SRS), 18
Sun Microsystems Corporation, ICS3
Swiss Bank Corporation, 383
Swissair, 516
Systematics, ICS16, ICS18

Toronto Dominion Bank, 24, 569
Toyota Motor Corporation, 155-56
TravelPlus, Inc., 176

Unilever, 60

Vienna University, 275
Volvo, AB, 433

Walden International Group, 18
Wal-Mart, 527

Yamaha Europe, 573

Subject Index

Accelerated SAP (ASAP), 397
Acceptance testing, 351
Access, 207f, 209, 211f, 239
Accountability. *See* Moral issues
Accounting, 11t
    information systems of, 37, 37f, 38, 39
    intranets for, 313, 313f, 313t, 314t
    transaction processing systems and, 40, 41f, 42
Accounting rate of return on investment (ROI), 354, 357, 359, 359f, 362
ActiveX, 215
Actor/role approach to implementation, 404, 405f, 406f
Ada, 206
Adaptive computation. *See* Genetic algorithms
Adhocracy, 76t
Administrative-bureaucratic school of management, 100, 100f
Administrative controls, 508-9, 509t
ADSL. *See* Asymmetric digital subscriber line
Advanced Planning System, 472, 473-74
Agency costs
    enterprise systems and, 338t, 562
    industrial networks and, 573
    Internet and, 301
Agency theory, 86-87, 87f, 88
Agents. *See* Intelligent agents
AI. *See* Artificial intelligence
AJ shell, 440
Allocation, operating system and, 196
Alpha microprocessor, 171t, 172
ALU. *See* Arithmetic-logic unit
AMD-K6 microprocessor, 173
American Society for Mechanical Engineers (ASME), 98-99
American Standard Code for Information Interchange. *See* ASCII
Analog signal, 263
ANSI (American National Standards Institute) X.12, 543
Antivirus software, 499, 503
APL, 207f
Applet programs, 201, 215
Application controls. *See* Controls
Application generators, 208
Application software, 195-217. *See also* Programming languages; Software tools
    systems building and, 374-77, 376t, 378f, 384t
Application specific view of systems, 555f, 555-56
Arithmetic-logic unit (ALU), 163f, 167f, 168
Artificial intelligence (AI), 187, 427, 428f, 436-54
    business interest in, 439
    case-based reasoning and, 443-45, 445f, 446
    definition of, 436-38, 438f
    expert systems and, 426, 436, 438-43, 439f
    fuzzy logic and, 448-50, 449f
    genetic algorithms and, 450f-51f, 450-52

hybrid AI systems, 452
    intelligent agents and, 452-53, 453t
    natural language and, 207
    neural networks and, 445-48, 447f, 448f
Artificial intelligence shell, 440
AS/400, 362, 363t, 565
ASCII (American Standard Code for Information Interchange), 163f, 164, 164t, 167
Assembler, 199
Assembly language, 199, 204, 204f, 205
Assignment, operating system and, 196
Associations, datamining and, 470
Asymmetric digital subscriber line (ADSL), 273
Asynchronous transfer mode (ATM), 272-73, 273t
ATM. *See* Asynchronous transfer mode
Attribute, in computer file, 230, 230f
AuctionBot, 453t
Audio output, 183
Audits
    control process and, 517f, 517-18
    data quality and, 519-20
    implementation controls and, 506, 509t
    management information systemsand, 517
Authentication, encryption and, 513
Automatic teller machines (ATMs), 51
Automation, organizational change and, 338, 339, 339f
Automobile industry, 6
AVP Sales/Use Tax, 207f

Backbone, in network, 264
Back-end CASE tools, 390
Backward chaining, 440-41, 441f
Backward sensitivity analysis software, 472
Bandwidth, 267, 318-19
Bank debit cards, 51
Banks, 51, 54
    business reengineering and, 342, 343f
    international, 543
    mergers and, 569
    virtual, 303
Bar codes, 181
BargainFinder, 453t
BASIC, 198, 204, 204f, 205-6
Basic Rate ISDN, 273, 273t
Batch processing, 182, 183f
Baud, 267
Baud rate, 267
Behavioral theories. *See also* Management
    on effect of information systems on organizations, 87-90, 89f
    on information systems, 13, 13f
    on organization, 72-73, 73f
Benchmarking, total quality management and, 345-46
Binary digits, 163-64, 164f
Bit mapping, 182
Bits, 163, 163f, 167, 229, 229f
Bits per second (PBS). *See* Baud rate
Bond Network, 477f, 478
Boundary regimes, in industrial networks, 576, 576f
Bounded rationality, decision making and, 113
BPS. *See* Bits per second
Brainstorming, group decision making support system software for, 480, 482
Brown Bag Software vs. Symantec Corp., 138
Bugs, system quality and, 503
Bureaucracy, 73-74
    decision making and, 115t, 115-16
Buses, 162, 163, 166
Business enterprise, transformation of, 7
Business-level strategy. *See* Strategic information systems
Business logic, 556, 557, 557t, 558f
Business models, Internet for, 302-4, 304t
Business plan, information systems plan and, 334, 335t

storage. *See also* primary storage; secondary storage, *above*
    trends, 184-87. *See also* Multimedia
Health issues, computer and, 148*t*, 148-49
Hertz, 267
Hierarchical data model, 237-38, 238*f*, 239-40, 241, 241*t*
Hierarchy, in industrial networks, 576, 576*f*
High-level language, 204
Hit, World Wide Web and, 306
Home page, for World Wide Web, 296
Host country systems, for globalization, 537
HTML. *See* Hypertext markup language
Human relations, 100*f*
Human resources, 11*t*, 429*f*
    information systems of, 37, 37*f*, 38, 39
    intranets for, 313*t*, 313-14, 314*t*
    privacy and, 132-33
    structured methodologies and, 383
    transaction processing systems and, 40, 41*f*
Hybrid AI systems, 452
Hybrid object-relational DBMS, 245, 247
Hypermedia, hypertext markup language and, 213, 217, 219*f*, 296
Hypermedia database, 245, 245*f*, 246
Hypertext markup language (HTML), 204*f*, 213, 217, 219*f*, 296
Hypertext transport protocol (http), 296

Icat Electronic Commerce Suite, 310*t*
Icons, 199-200
Idea organizers, group decision making and, 480, 483
Identification, automatic, 344
Implementation, 400, 404-18
    actors/role approach to, 404, 405*f*, 406*f*
    business reengineering and, 412-13
    change agent and, 405
    counterimplementation and, 418
    enterprise resource planning and, 412-13
    failure and, 401*f*, 401-3
    grassroot innovation and, 404
    Kolb/Frohman model and, 405
    management and, 414-18. *See also* risk/complexity levels and, *below*
    organizational change and, 405-6, 406*t*
    risk/complexity levels and, 414-18
    stages of, 404, 404*f*
    strategic approach to, 404
    success and failure of, 406-12. *See also* risk/complexity levels and, *above*
    top-down innovation and, 404
Implementation controls, 506, 509*t*
Implementation stage, of decision making, 111*t*, 112, 112*t*
IMS, 241
Incremental decision making, 114
Incremental design, 570
Index, to computer file, 231, 231*f*
Indexed sequential access method (ISAM), 230-31, 231*f*
Index server, 430
Individual models of decision making. *See* Decision making
Individuals, as level in organization, 80*t*
Industrial economies, transformation of, 5*t*, 5-6, 6*f*
Industrial networks, 558-59, 559*f*, 573-79
    building and managing, 577-78, 578*t*
    business capability of, 575-76
    costs of, 577
    industry structure and, 574-75
    management and, 575
    technology and, 575
    vertical and horizontal dimensions of, 573, 573*f*
    vulnerability and dependence and, 577
Industry-level strategy. *See* Strategic information systems

Inference engine, 440-41, 441*f*
Information, definition of, 7
Information architecture, 556, 557*t*, 557-58, 558*f*
    business goals supported by, 27-29
    definition of, 27, 28*f*
    development of, 82, 83*f*
Information brokers, as Internet business model, 304*t*
Information center, end-user development and, 380-81
Information economy, 5*t*, 5-6, 6*f*
Information partnerships, 58-59
Information policy, 251
Information requirements, systems analysis establishing, 348
Information rights. *See* Moral issues
Information roles of managers, 103, 103*t*, 104
Information superhighway, 261. *See also* Internet
Information systems
    business environment changes and, 4-7
    business perspective on, 10*f*, 10-12. *See also* Business value of information systems; Information technology; Management; Organizations
    contemporary approaches to, 12-14, 13*f*
    definition of, 7*f*, 7-8, 10*f*
    integration of, 36, 47-48, 48*f*
    kinds of. *See* Knowledge-level systems; Management-level systems; Operational-level systems; Strategic-level systems
    knowledge management and, 427, 428*f*
    reasons for, 4-12. *See also* business environment changes and; business perspective on, *above*
    role of, 82, 83*f*
Information systems department, 82, 84
Information systems function, 82, 84, 84 *f*. *See also* Hardware; Software
Information systems managers, 82, 84
Information systems plan, 334, 335*f*
Information systems specialists, 82
Information technology, management process changed by, 117-20, 119*t*
Information technology infrastructure, 28-29. *See also* Enterprise computing
    conditions necessary for, 563, 564
    decisions on, 565-67, 566*f*
    elements of, 563-65, 565*f*
    in enterprise computing, 557, 557*t*, 558*f*
    governance and, 567-70, 568*f*
    in international information systems, 529, 530, 530*f*
    mergers and acquisitions and, 567-70, 570*t*
    telecommunications and, 566*t*, 566-67
Information technology infrastructure team, 569
Information technology investment portfolio, 556-57, 557*t*, 558*f*
Information Technology Management Reform Act of 1996, 524
Information work, 428. *See also* Knowledge management
Information workers, 427, 428
Infrastructure. *See* Information technology infrastructure
Inheritance, object-oriented programming and, 214*f*, 214-15
Innovating, as management function, 119*t*. *See also* Implementation
Input, 8, 350*t*
Input controls, 509-10, 510*t*
Input devices. *See* Hardware
Installation, in systems lifecycle, 370, 370*f*, 372
Institutional factors, systems development and, 86, 86*f*
Instruction cycle, of machine cycle, 168, 169*f*
In Tandem, 312

Intangible benefits, of information systems, 354, 355, 355*t*
Integrated circuits, third-generation computers and, 166
Integrated Services Digital Network (ISDN), 273, 273*t*, 543, 547
Integrated software packages, 209-10
Integration of information systems, 36, 47-48, 48*f*
Integration team, 569
Intel 8088 chip, 172
Intellectual property, property rights and, 136-37. *See also* Privacy
Intelligence stage, of decision making, 110-11, 111*t*, 112*t*
Intelligent agents, 452-53, 453*t*
Intelligent computing techniques. *See* Artificial intelligence
Intelligent machines, artificial intelligence and, 438*f*
Interaction theory, of user resistance, 418
Interactivity, Internet and, 302
Interdepartmental committees, 80, 81*t*. *See also* Work groups
Internal integration tools, risk and, 414, 415-16
Internal rate of return (IRR), 354, 359*f*, 360
International information systems, 526-51
    benefits of, 540
    collaborative teamwork and, 20
    euro currency and, 85
    global environment and, 530-34
    growth of, 528-29
    implementation tactics and, 540-41
    infrastructure of, 529, 530, 530 *f*. *See also* global environment and, *above*
    Internet and, 18, 317, 544-45, 546-47, 547*f*
    management of, 537*t*, 537-41
    organization of, 534-37
    particularism and, 532
    privacy law and, 135
    state of art of, 534
    technological issues, 541-47
    transborder data flow and, 532-33
Internet, 16-18, 82, 261, 277, 292-302, 563. *See also* World Wide Web
    benefits of to organization, 299-302
    building projects managed with, 431
    business opportunities created with, 3-4
    business reengineering and, 340, 341
    capabilities of, 16-18, 17*t*, 293-97. *See also* Electronic mail
    client/server computing and, 173, 174, 174*f*, 282-83, 283*t*
    competition tracked with, 485
    competitive advantage and, 36
    crime and abuse and, 147, 147*t*. *See also* Computer crime and abuse
    decision-support systems based on, 476-78, 477*f*
    definition of, 16
    description of, 292-93, 293*f*
    electronic market and, 23-25. *See also* Electronic business; Electronic commerce
    extranets and, 299, 299*f*, 362, 363, 533
    flatter organizations and, 19
    groupware and, 212, 212*f*, 212*t*, 281, 312, 435, 435*t*
    high-capacity connections on, 273, 273*t*
    increased use of, 218-19
    information retrieval on, 295-96
    information technology infrastructure and, 563
    intellectual property protections and, 139
    international, 18, 317, 544-45, 546-47, 547*f*
    Internet telephony and, 300
    intranets and, 25, 298, 312-13, 435-36, 446, 563
    levels of business strategy supported by, 61, 61*t*
    organizations and, 90-91
    privacy and, 125-26, 132-33, 136, 278

Photo Credits
and Screen Shots

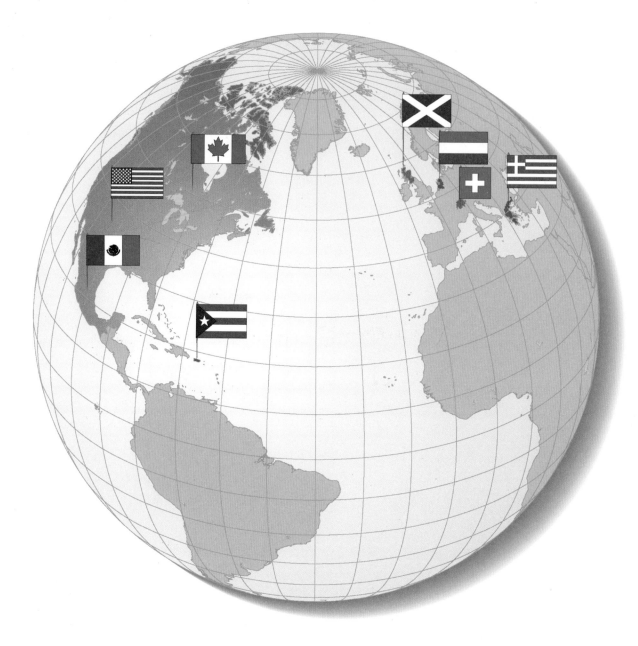

Contributors

 AUSTRALIA

Joel B. Barolsky, University of Melbourne
Peter Weill, University of Melbourne

 CANADA

Len Fertuck, University of Toronto

GERMANY

Helmut Krcmar, University of Hohenheim
Gerhard Schwabe, University of Hohenheim
Stephen Wilczek, University of Hohenheim

SINGAPORE

Boon Siong Neo, Nanyang Technological
  University
Christina Soh, Nanyang Technological
  University

✚ **SWITZERLAND**

Kimberly A. Bechler, International
  Institute for Management Development
Donald A. Marchand, International
  Institute for Management Development
Thomas E. Vollmann, International
  Institute for Management Development

Consultants

AUSTRALIA

Robert MacGregor, University of
  Wollongong
Alan Underwood, Queensland
  University of Technology
Peter Weill, University of Melbourne

CANADA

Wynne W. Chin, University of Calgary
Len Fertuck, University of Toronto
Robert C. Goldstein, University of
  British Columbia
Rebecca Grant, University of Victoria
Kevin Leonard, Wilfrid Laurier University
Anne B. Pidduck, University of Waterloo

GREECE

Anastasios V. Katos, University of
  Macedonia

HONG KONG

Enoch Tse, Hong Kong Baptist University

INDIA

Sanjiv D. Vaidya, Indian Institute of
  Management, Calcutta

ISRAEL

Phillip Ein-Dor, Tel-Aviv University
Peretz Shoval, Ben Gurion University

MEXICO

Noe Urzua Bustamante, Universidad
  Tecnológica de México

NETHERLANDS

E.O. de Brock, University of Groningen
Theo Thiadens, University of Twente
Charles Van Der Mast, Delft University
  of Technology

PUERTO RICO, Commonwealth
  of the United States

Brunilda Marrero, University of Puerto
  Rico

SWEDEN

Mats Daniels, Uppsala University

✚ **SWITZERLAND**

Andrew C. Boynton, International
  Institute for Management Development